RATS
ALLEY

Trench Nomenclature

Genius named them, as I live! What but genius could compress
In a title what man's humour said to man's supreme distress?
Jacob's Ladder ran reversed, from earth to a fiery pit extending
With not angels but poor Angles, those for the most part descending.
Thence *Brock's Benefit* commanded endless fireworks by two nations,
Yet some voices there were raised against the rival coruscations.
Picturedrome peeped out upon a dream, not Turner could surpass,
And presently the picture moved, and greyed with corpses and morass.
So down south; and if remembrance travel north, she marvels yet
At the sharp Shakespearean names, and with sad mirth her eyes are wet.
The Great Wall of China rose, a four-foot breastwork, fronting guns
That, when the word dropped, beat at once its silly ounces with brute tons;
Odd *Krab Krawl* on paper looks, and odd the foul-breathed alley twisted,
As one feared to twist there too, if Minnie, forward quean, insisted.
Where the Yser at *Dead End* floated on its bloody waters
Dead and rotten monstrous fish, note (east) *The Pike and Eel* headquarters.
Ah, such names and apparitions! Name on name! What's in a name?
From the fabled vase the genie in his cloud of horror came.

Edmund Blunden

RATS ALLEY

TRENCH NAMES OF THE WESTERN FRONT, 1914–1918

PETER CHASSEAUD

FOREWORD BY ALAN SILLITOE

Maps and photographs in the text are from the author's collection unless otherwise credited.

First published 2006

This revised and updated second edition first published 2017

The History Press
The Mill, Brimscombe Port
Stroud, Gloucestershire, GL5 2QG
www.thehistorypress.co.uk

© Peter Chasseaud 2006, 2017
Foreword © Alan Sillitoe 2006, 2017

The right of Peter Chasseaud to be identified as the Author
of this work has been asserted in accordance with the
Copyright, Designs and Patents Act 1988.

British Library Cataloguing in Publication Data.
A catalogue record for this book is available from the British
Library.

ISBN 978 0 7509 8055 5

Typesetting and origination by The History Press
Printed in Turkey

Trench Names

The column, like a snake, winds through the fields,
Scoring the grass with wheels, with heavy wheels
And hooves, and boots. The grass smiles in the sun,
Quite helpless. Orchard and copse are Paradise
Where flowers and fruits grow leisurely, and birds
Rise in the blue, and sing, and sink again
And rest. The woods are ancient. They have names—
Thiepval, deep vale, La Boisselle, Aubépines,
Named long ago by dead men. And their sons
Know trees and creatures, earth and sky, the same.

We gouge out tunnels in the sleeping fields.
We turn the clay and slice the turf, and make
A scheme of cross-roads, orderly and mad,
Under and through, like moles, like monstrous worms.
Dig out our dens, like cicatrices scored
Into the face of earth. And we give names
To our vast network in the roots, imposed,
Imperious, desperate to hide, to hurt.

The sunken roads were numbered at the start.
A chequer board. But men are poets, and names
Are Adam's heritage, and English men
Imposed a ghostly English map on French
Crushed ruined harvests and polluted streams.

So here run Piccadilly, Regent Street,
Oxford Street, Bond Street, Tothill Fields, Tower Bridge,
And Kentish places, Dover, Tunbridge Wells,
Entering wider hauntings, resonant,
The Boggart Hole, Bleak House, Deep Doom and Gloom.

Remembering boyhood, soldier poets recall
The desperate deeds of Lost Boys, Peter Pan,
Hook Copse, and Wendy Cottage. Horrors lurk
In Jekyll Copse and Hyde Copse. Nonsense smiles

As shells and flares disorder tiny lines
In Walrus, Gimble, Mimsy, Borogrove—
Which lead to Dum and Dee and to that Wood
Where fury lurked, and blackness, and that Crow.

There's Dead Man's Dump, Bone Trench and Carrion Trench,
Cemetery Alley, Skull Farm, Suicide Road,
Abuse Trench and Abyss Trench, Cesspool, Sticky Trench,
Slither Trench, Slimy Trench, Slum Trench, Bloody Farm.
Worm Trench, Louse Post, Bug Alley, Old Boot Street.
Gas Alley, Gangrene Alley, Gory Trench.
Dreary, Dredge, Dregs, Drench, Drizzle, Drivel, Bog.

Some frame the names of runs for frames of mind.
Tremble Copse, Wrath Copse, Anxious Crossroads, Howl,
Doleful and Crazy Trenches, Folly Lane,
Ominous Alley, Worry Trench, Mad Point,
Lunatic Sap, and then Unbearable
Trench, next to Fun Trench, Worry Trench, Hope Trench,
And Happy Alley.

How they swarm, the rats.
Fat beasts and frisking, yellow teeth and tails
Twitching and slippery. Here they are at home
As gaunt and haunted men are not. For rats
Grow plump in ratholes and are not afraid,
Resourceful little beggars, said Tom Thinn,
The day they ate his dinner, as he died.

Their names are legion. Rathole, Rat Farm, Rat Pit,
Rat Post, Fat Rat, Rats' Alley, Dead Rats' Drain,
Rat Heap, Flat Rat, the Better 'Ole, King Rat.
They will outlast us. This is their domain.

And when I die, my spirit will pass by
Through Sulphur Avenue and Devil's Wood
To Jacob's Ladder along Pilgrim's Way
To Eden Trench, through Orchard, through the gate
To Nameless Trench and Nameless Wood, and rest.

A.S. Byatt

CONTENTS

FOREWORD

The names of many people who came to inhabit my novels were taken, after happy, and minute examination, from the 1-inch sheets of the Ordnance Survey. The name of a river, farm or, more generally, village, was given to a character if the surrounding landscape and the sound of the word fitted his or her temperament, and mirrored in some way what their fate was going to be. In any case this seemed a sure method of making the name easy on the memory of the reader. Thus many Nottinghamshire villages, in name at least, have adorned – or otherwise – my books.

It gives me great pleasure to see Peter Chasseaud's erudite analysis on the subject of nomenclature with regard to the Western Front in the Great War. Trench names from that conflict have always fascinated me, so not only should the book be of much use to historians, but it will also be a gold mine to the intelligent and questing tourist and battlefield enthusiast who roams the areas with which it deals. Above all, it will delight the general reader who has any feeling for that war.

The author of this work is the most knowledgeable person I know on the landscape and cartography of that murderous campaign, as all his former works prove. The same subjects have always been of great interest to me, and I recall talks with Dr Chasseaud a few years ago, concerning the necessity of some treatment about the multifarious trench names of the Western Front. The topic seemed to us full of arcane but real value.

I am therefore delighted to see that he has now completed a book, with its scholarly introduction, whose contents will remain memorable in the mind of whoever reads it. Such a volume does indeed deserve to reach a wide audience, and I do not see how it can fail to do so.

Alan Sillitoe
2006

PRELIMINARY NOTES

ACKNOWLEDGEMENTS

I would like to thank the staff of The National Archives (formerly Public Record Office), the British Library Map Library, the Royal Geographical Society (RGS), the Imperial War Museum (IWM), the Mapping and Charting Establishment (Map Research and Library Group) Royal Engineers, Military Survey, the Defence Geographical and Intelligence Agency (DGIA), the Defence Surveyors Association (formerly the Field Survey Association), the Corps of Royal Engineers, The Royal Artillery Institution Library and Archives, the Ordnance Survey, the Royal United Services Institute, the Service Historique de l'Armeé de Terre (now part of the Service Historique de la Défense) (Vincennes), the Bundesarchiv-Militärarchiv (Freiburg-im-Breisgau), the *Militärgeschichtliches Forschungsamt* (Potsdam), and Francis Herbert of the RGS Map Room, Colonel (retd.) Phillip Robinson RE, Colonel (retd.) Mike Nolan RE, Christopher Hunt, Alan Jeffreys and Nigel Steel of the IWM, Andy Robertshaw of the National Army Museum Education Department, Martin Brown, Professor Peter Doyle, Peter Barton, Andy Gammon, Henry Daniels, Nicki Jackowska, John Page, George Craig, Sir John Tomlinson, Ian Passingham, Neil Howlett, Anne-Marie de Villèle, Claude Ponou, Peter Duffy and Berndt Nogli for their particular help. I would also like to thank Peter K. Clark, the late Dr Ian Mumford, Dr Yolande Hodson, Dr Tim Nicholson and Dr Roger Hellyer for their friendship, assistance and support over four decades of research into First World War survey and mapping, which formed an invaluable springboard for the writing of this book. Profuse thanks to the late Alan Sillitoe for contributing the foreword to the first edition, and to A.S. Byatt and Gabriel Josipovici for their kind permission to reproduce their works. I should particularly like to thank Christine McMorris, Commissioning Editor at The History Press, for her sympathetic and thorough attention and support during the production of this second edition. Finally I would like to pay particular tribute to my wife, Carolyn Trant, whose wonderful support, encyclopaedic knowledge and sound advice have underpinned the writing of this book.

'Trench Names' from *The Children's Book* by A.S. Byatt. Published by Chatto & Windus. Copyright © A.S. Byatt. Reproduced by kind permission of the author c/o Rogers, Coleridge & White Ltd., 20 Powis Mews, London W11 1JN.

'Trench Nomenclature' by Edmund Blunden from his *Undertones of War*, first published by Cobden-Sanderson in 1928.

Gabriel Josipovici for permission to quote from his book *The World and the Book, A Study of Modern Fiction*, first published by Stanford University Press in 1971.

THE SCOPE OF THIS BOOK

This book is aimed at general readers and military historians interested in the First World War, particularly those who would like to be able to locate particular trenches on the map – perhaps with a view to visiting the ground. It should also appeal to those with family connections – possibly even with letters or diaries that mention a particular trench – with the Western Front. On a rather different level, it might prove of some value to those of a more academic bent who are curious about the 'discourse' of the Western Front as represented by its trench and topographical nomenclature.

Part Two includes a large Gazetteer of trench names and names of other tactical features, containing more than 24,000 names, listed alphabetically and by 1:10,000 trench map sheet. This list includes map references, enabling a trench to be found on trench maps in The National Archives (Public Record Office), in the Imperial War Museum, British Library and other archival collections, in my trench map atlas *Topography of Armageddon* or on the various Imperial War Museum/National Archives/Naval & Military Press CD Roms and DVDs. It has been compiled from maps in my own and other collections, and from certain official, divisional and regimental histories, and checked against an original but very incomplete listing compiled many decades ago at the Imperial War Museum.

As it is impossible in a book of this size to include all the trench and topographical names within the whole of the British Army area on the Western Front, I have decided to focus on the area and map sheets covering what John Masefield called 'The Old Front Line' – essentially that held by the British Expeditionary Force up to the opening of the Battle of the Somme in July 1916, and the major battles of the Somme, Ancre, Arras, Messines, Third Ypres and Cambrai, and also the 1918 battles. It is not guaranteed that every trench name, and certainly not every place, associated with these battles will be included, as I have had to limit the length of the Gazetteer, but sufficient names have been included from the later battles to give a flavour of naming practice and policy. Not all trench names appeared on the maps, and even the secret editions showing British trenches do not give all the names, which appear and disappear over time, usually as trenches were newly constructed or left to fall into disrepair. Often the more ephemeral manuscript and duplicated map sheets, as well as war diaries, regimental and divisional histories and various documentary and literary sources, are an important quarry to be mined for trench names, some of which (though very few) are very difficult to pin down to a specific location within a 500 yard sub-square.

EXPLANATORY NOTE

By British trench names I mean those appearing on British Army trench maps produced – largely by lithographic processes – during the 1914–18 war, and used during operations and also, as far as can be ascertained, those names that were used but either not shown on the maps, or only shown on manuscript or duplicated sketch maps. These names were given to both British and German trenches, and some of the British trenches retained names bestowed earlier by French troops serving in sectors taken over by the British. Moreover, German names were often used by the British where these could be determined from captured maps; sometimes these names were replaced by new British ones, and sometimes not. The same goes for French names for trenches taken over by the British. Occasionally, therefore, but not simultaneously, a trench would have two names, and possibly even three – for example a French trench on the Vimy Ridge captured by the Germans and renamed by them, and later renamed by the British. It has not been possible to determine all these changes of name, but some have been indicated where they are known.

While a trench name is generally understood to refer to a specific trench, within clearly defined limits – for example a communication trench might begin by a road behind the lines, and finish where it met the front-line trench, crossing reserve and support lines on the way – this is often not the case. Long stretches of trench were frequently divided up into shorter stretches, each with its own name. Now the problem here is that these named lengths of trench were not always clearly defined, and their limits were neither marked on the ground nor on the map. To overcome this problem, pinpoint map references were used in orders as well as the trench name, and the British front-line trench was usually not named at all on the trench map, but was divided into clearly delimited sections, each lettered and numbered to provide a precise location for the staff and the artillery. Boards carrying these designations were often erected in the front trench, facing to the rear, for the use of artillery observers behind the front line. These were sometimes called artillery boards (not to be confused with artillery map boards, or battery boards, which were often described as artillery boards).

A further problem is name drift or migration. This is particularly apparent in 1917 and 1918, when British or German advances led to old trenches being abandoned and new ones being dug nearby. Many cases exist in the Lens and Fonquevillers–Hébuterne sectors where old trench names have been appropriated for new trenches in the same vicinity, or for trenches formerly known by a different name. In several cases, the old name has been used to cover part of the trench it formerly designated, and also part of a new trench or a former British or German trench previously known by another name. An example of a map that specifically shows such changes is 3rd Field Survey Company's *Hendecourt* special 1:20,000 sheet of November 1917, which states: '*Detail and Trenches revised to 25-9-17; New Work to 12-11-17 shown in Green.*' This shows some old trench names crossed out and new ones added. In several places in this sheet, the old name was retained for part of the original trench, together with its new extension, while the remainder of the old trench was given a new name.[1]

Spelling and punctuation of trench names also changed over time, and between map editions, often through some misreading or maladroitness on the part of a map draughtsman, an example being that of *Tara Redoubt*, east of Albert, which in edition 3A of the Ovillers sheet (trenches corrected to 1 September 1916) became *Tarn Redoubt*. Many names had a considerable history of cartographic use, with opportunities at each stage of transfer for errors. The name originally bestowed by a unit in the line might first be painted on a board, and entered on to a rough sketch map by that unit. It might then be transferred by a draughtsman of an RE Field Company, under the Divisional CRE, responsible for trench construction and maintenance, on to that Company's master manuscript map, using the topographical or trench map produced by the Army Topographical Section or, from February 1916, Field Survey Company (FSC), as a base map. Such drawings would then be used by the Topographical Section or FSC to compile the secret edition trench map showing the British trenches. In early 1917, when Corps Topographical Sections were formed, an additional intermediate stage of map production, and therefore a further source of error, was introduced. If drawings were sent home by the FSC to the Ordnance Survey at Southampton for fair drawing and printing, this created yet another possibility of error.

The dropping of an apostrophe was a common change, and in some cases it is very difficult to determine the original form of a name – for example *Rat's Alley*, *Rats' Alley* or *Rats Alley* – and in some cases alternative forms are given. The form given in this book should not therefore be considered definitive. The same goes for spelling, which was not always reliable or consistent on the maps. Names changed over the course of the war, the result being some curious distorted forms that only the study of successive map editions can elucidate. *Rudkin House* became *Birdkin House*, *Mule Track* became *Mole Track*, *Sully Trench* became *Scully Trench*. *Nairne Street* in the Thiepval Wood sector was also *Nairn Street* or *Naire Street* on other editions. *Tara Redoubt* (the correct name) on Tara Hill, east of Albert, appeared as *Tarn Redoubt* on an edition of September 1916.[2] There are many other cases. Where they have been identified, these are indicated in the Gazetteer. Where French or German trench names were adopted, accents were often omitted and spelling sometimes anglicised.

We should also remember that names of localities, given by the troops and often appearing in orders with a map reference, were not always printed on the trench maps. For example, *Tank Farm* in the Ypres Salient, or *Crucifix Corner* (Bazentin-le-Grand) and *Cosy Corner* (Montauban) on the Somme. This goes for certain trenches and trench junctions as well, such as *Trafalgar Square* at Fricourt (Bois Français) or *Leicester Square* at Cuinchy.

METHOD AND ACCURACY OF BRITISH 1914–18 MAP REFERENCES

The British did not use a theatre grid on the Western Front. British 1:10,000 regular series trench maps (see index maps) formed quarters of 1:20,000 sheets, which in turn formed quarters of the 1:40,000 sheets of the Belgian national survey, the sheetlines of which were extended by the British over northern France. An alphanumeric reference system was based on the 1:40,000 sheet, which was divided into twenty-four zones, each designated by a capital letter (A–X), containing thirty or thirty-six numbered squares, each of 1,000 yards side. Each of these 1,000 yard squares was subdivided into four 500 yard squares, lettered a–d. Thus a reference such as K.17.c would define an area 500 yards square on the map. This was clearly insufficient for the provision of accurate (pinpoint) references so, following French practice, a system of decimal coordinates, using the south-west corner of the 500 yard square as its origin and giving easting before northing, was soon introduced, with the added refinement that additional figures could be used to indicate hundredths rather than tenths. In this way, a reference could now appear as K.17.c.4.3 (accurate to 50 yards), or as K.17.c.45.37 (accurate to 5 yards). It should be noted that this square reference system, based on the map sheet, was completely independent of the survey system used by the Field Survey Companies/Battalions of the Royal Engineers and by the Royal Artillery for predicted fire.

On some British map sheets, particularly in the Neuve Chapelle–Loos area in 1915, the reference squares were out of position by some 300 yards in a north-south direction.[3] This means that positions given for trenches taken from 1915 sheets may well appear in a neighbouring square on 1916–18 sheets. Thus if a British 1915 trench cannot be found in square G 10 b on a 1917 Loos sheet, it might well appear in G 10 d. On the other hand it might not appear at all on the later sheet, even on a secret edition showing the British trench system, as many old trenches were allowed to become derelict, not being incorporated into the new defence scheme for that sector. The aim has been to give the general position of a trench within a 500 yard sub-square, and if the trench extends over several sub-squares to indicate its rough extent by giving all the sub-squares covering its extent. In the case of groups of German trenches named by the British, using a common name followed by the descriptive qualifier – e.g. *Caliban Trench*, *Caliban Support*, *Caliban Reserve*, *Caliban Drive*, *Caliban Avenue*, etc. – to save space only one entry has as a rule been given for the whole group, with its sub-square locator. Armed with this information, the researcher can then inspect the relevant squares of the map sheets in the National Archives (Public Record Office) at Kew or elsewhere. It may be necessary to look at several editions of the sheet, and particularly secret editions in the case of British trenches. A warning – in The National Archives catalogue, many of the secret editions of the 1:10,000 trench maps sheets are listed separately at the end of WO 297, in 'Supplement to 1:10,000 (British) Series I' (see opposite).

ARCHIVAL AND OTHER SOURCES

The most complete collection of trench maps, particularly for secret editions showing British trenches, is to be found in The National Archives (Public Record Office) at Kew (WO 153 and WO 297). The British Library, Bodleian Library (Oxford), Cambridge University Library, National Library of Scotland and other copyright libraries in the UK hold a certain number. The Imperial War Museum archive has reasonably good coverage. There are also significant holdings of trench maps in official archives in Australia, Canada and the United States.

The Imperial War Museum, in collaboration with Naval & Military Press, has produced a CD Rom of trench maps that provides an invaluable home-search tool. Naval & Military Press has also produced, in association with The National Archives, a set of DVDs of trench maps, including captured German maps. The Western Front Association has produced, in association with the Imperial War Museum, a series of DVDs covering its trench map collection.

In France, the most comprehensive archive of trench maps (*plans directeurs*) is to be found at the Service Historique de la Défense (Chateau de Vincennes, Paris), while in Germany the equivalent for *Stellungskarten* is the Bundesarchiv-Militärarchiv at Freiburg-im-Breisgau; the archives of some of the individual German states (Bavaria, Württemberg, etc.) also contain significant holdings.

TREATMENT OF TRENCH, MAP SHEET AND PLACE NAMES IN THE TEXT

In the text, trench and other names given to features and localities are given in italics, thus: *Idiot Trench*, while the names of trench map sheets are referred to thus: Ovillers sheet, or (Longueval) after a name or group of trench names. The location of map sheets can be found from the index maps provided. In the Gazetteer, British 1914–18 map square references, as used on the trench maps, are given, as well as sheet numbers and names.

The spelling of place names (towns, villages, localities) is that which was current during the war, which is to say that the names appear as used on the maps and in the orders used by the BEF. In the case of Belgium, these were the French rather than Flemish forms; the former had been officially adopted by the *Institut Cartographique Militaire* – the Belgian national survey organisation. Names of places in France are as spelled by the *Service Géographique de l'Armée*, the French national survey organisation. British military maps followed these usages, which is not to say that there was total consistency in the orthography.

GLOSSARY

ADS	Advanced Dressing Station
Alley/Avenue	British communication trench
BEF	British Expeditionary Force in France and Belgium
BFL	British Front Line
Boyau	French communication trench (alley; literally gut)
Breastwork	Parapet built up (with sandbags, etc.) above ground level in wet areas, in place of trench
Cadastrals	Large-scale land registration plans
Corons	Settlement of coal miners' cottages
CRE	Commander Royal Engineers
CT	Communication Trench (one linking front, support and reserve lines with the rear)
Defended Localities	Entrenched and wired areas behind keeps; part of sector defence scheme
DGOS	Director General of the Ordnance Survey
Feste	Redoubt (German)
Formation	Relatively permanent grouping of units or lower formations – e.g. brigade, division, corps, army
Fort	Strong-point, either permanent (e.g. concrete) or field work
Fortin	Small temporary field defence (French)
Fortress	Defended area comprising many forts, often around a town that itself is fortified – e.g. Verdun
Fosse	Pit (coal mine), and by association the adjoining slag heap
Front Line	Foremost infantry position; a traversed fire trench, from which saps went out into no man's land to listening posts, bombing posts, etc.
FSC/B	Field Survey Company/Battalion, Royal Engineers, responsible for mapping and artillery survey

GCTA	*Groupe de canevas de tir* (French field survey unit – equivalent of British Field Survey Company/Battalion and German *Vermessungs-Abteilung*)
GFL	German Front Line
GHQ	General Headquarters (British) at Saint-Omer, then at Montreuil
GHQ Line	Rear defence position, normally comprising front, support and reserve lines
GOC	General Officer Commanding
Graben	Trench [German]
GS	General Staff (of Army, Corps or Division)
GSGS	Geographical Section of the General Staff (London)
GS(I)	General Staff (Intelligence)
HQ	Headquarters
I	Intelligence
Keep	Small post close behind support trench, with garrison of up to one platoon
Line	Either a single trench line or a defence position comprising front, support and reserve lines, e.g. the Hindenburg Line was in fact a position (*Siegfried Stellung*)
MG	Machine Gun
No Man's Land	The killing zone between the opposing front lines; deserted by day (except for the occasional well-concealed sniper) but busy at night with patrols, wiring parties, etc.
Nose	A small salient formed by the trench lines of either side
OBOS	Overseas Branch of the Ordnance Survey
OP	Observation Post
OS	Ordnance Survey (Southampton)
Plan Directeur	French large-scale military survey
Position	Defence system, normally comprising front, support and reserve lines
Post	Forward position normally wired-in for all-round defence; in an attack usually refers to temporary advanced positions defending the main line of defence
RA	Royal Artillery
RAP	Regimental Aid Post
RE	Royal Engineers
Redan	Strongpoint comprising field work with two faces, forming salient angle

Redoubt	Strongpoint covering large area, square, polygonal or circular, organised for all-round defence; usually connected to main trench system by flanking trenches
Reserve	A reserve trench/reserve line was about 1,000–2,000m behind the support line
Retrenchment	Inner defence-line, or back-line
RFA	Royal Field Artillery
RFC	Royal Flying Corps
RGA	Royal Garrison Artillery (medium and heavy batteries)
RHA	Royal Horse Artillery
Riegel	German switch line or position, or retrenchment
Sally Port	Specially protected exit from breastwork into no man's land, for use of patrols, wiring parties, etc.
Sap	Short dead-end trench running out into no man's land, to provide a sentry, listening or sniper's post
SP	Strong-Point; Sniper's Post
Stellung	German defensive position, normally comprising front, support and reserve lines
Stellungskarte	German trench map
Strasse	German street
Street	Communication trench
Support	The support line was normally about 50m behind the front line, close enough for an immediate counter-attack to be made if the front trench was captured by the enemy
Supporting Point	Works or defended localities behind keeps; garrison from one company to one battalion
Switch	A trench obliquely linking a forward defensive position with one further back
TM	Trench Mortar
Topo	Topographical – as in Topographical Section, Topographical Survey
Trench	General word for variety of field works – e.g. traversed fire trench, communication trench, breastwork, etc. – providing protection from fire
Trig	Trigonometrical point
Unit	Self-contained tactical command – e.g. infantry battalion, RE field company, RA battery
VA	*Vermessungs-Abteilung* (German field survey unit), equivalent of French *Groupe de canevas de tir* and British Field Survey Company/Battalion

| WO | War Office (London) |
| Work | A small fort or redoubt, similar to the French *ouvrage* and German *Werk* |

Notes

1   3rd Field Survey Company *Hendecourt* special 1:20,000 sheet, Ed. 5: 'Detail and Trenches revised to 25-9-17. New Work to 12-11-17 shown in Green.' Author's collection.

2   Sheet *57dSE4 Ovillers, Edn. 3A, Trenches corrected to 1-9-16. Ordnance Survey 1916*. All trenches shown in red. Author's collection.

3   For an explanation of this, see Chasseaud, Peter, *Artillery's Astrologers – A History of British Survey and Mapping on the Western Front, 1914–1918*, Lewes: Mapbooks, 1999, Chapters 5, 7 and 10.

INTRODUCTION TO THE 2017 EDITION

The centenary years of the First World War are a most appropriate time for the publication by History Press of this revised, and greatly enlarged, edition. Its most significant feature is the doubling in size of the Gazetteer; it has grown from some 10,000 names and map references of trenches and topographical features to more than 24,000. Appearing in the 100th anniversary year of the Battles of Arras, Messines, Third Ypres (Passchendaele) and Cambrai, the enlarged Gazetteer commemorates the terrain nomenclature of these titanic engagements, a nomenclature that is for ever associated with human drama, heroism and tragedy.

With the development of new technology and wider marketing, digital versions of the trench maps themselves have become increasingly available on DVD and online. The original 'paper landscape' of the trench maps themselves can be inspected in the various archives noted above, and in the Gazetteer section (Part 2) of this book.

I am greatly indebted to A.S. Byatt for her kind permission to display her wonderful poem 'Trench Names' alongside Edmund Blunden's elegiac 'Trench Nomenclature', which formed the frontispiece to the original edition.

Peter Chasseaud
Lewes, Sussex
2017

INTRODUCTION TO THE 2006 EDITION
THE SIGNIFICANCE OF TRENCH NAMES

The poet and memoirist Edmund Blunden encapsulated much of the heroism, humour, magic and myth and tragedy of the Western Front in his poem 'Trench Nomenclature', which first appeared in his masterpiece of war autobiography *Undertones of War* (1928), and which is reproduced as the frontispiece to this book. He summed it up thus: 'Genius named them, as I live! What but genius could compress/In a title what man's humour said to man's supreme distress?' He clearly believed that trench names and other battlefield nomenclature were important markers not only of the 'topography of Golgotha', as Wilfred Owen powerfully described the battlefield landscape, but also of the human condition. That is to say, those trench nameboards stood out on the battlefield as cultural signifiers, as way-markers not only to the troops but also to succeeding generations in trying to decode the confused and opaque operations and experiences of the Great War. There were more than 10,000 miles of Allied and German trenches on the Western Front, and every stretch of trench bore a name, or in some cases a number.

Trench signboard from the Fonquevillers sector, facing Gommecourt, of the Somme battlefield, now in the Imperial War Museum, London.

Just as the network of trenches seamed the terrain and, intersecting the map grid, defined the coordinates and parameters of Armageddon, so their names equally provided a literary text which generated key cultural coordinates, as this study seeks to demonstrate. The patterns of naming created a cryptic cultural map that can be decoded.

Writers and philosophers have always been fascinated by names. Charles Lamb linked being and naming when describing a state '... before we have existence, and a name',[1] while Shakespeare in *A Midsummer Night's Dream* brilliantly described the imaginative process of naming, having Theseus speak of:

> The poets's eye, in a fine frenzy rolling
> Doth glance from heaven to earth, from earth to heaven;
> And, as imagination bodies forth
> The forms of things unknown, the poet's pen
> Turns them to shapes, and gives to airy nothing
> A local habitation and a name.

Shakespeare also linked the names of people and places in *Twelfth Night*, when Viola, replying to Olivia, announces her desire to 'Halloo your name to the reverberate hills'.[2] The landscape of the Western Front still reverberates to the names of 1914–18, and we are not faced with the problems acknowledged by Sir Thomas Browne when, in *The Garden of Cyrus*, he noted of the Garden of Eden that 'Of deeper doubt is its Topography and Local designation'.[3] But we might consider, in the context of the trench systems we are about to explore, the subtitle to his book: *The Quincuncial Lozenge, or Net-work Plantations of the Ancients, Artificially, Naturally, Mystically considered.*

Names are frequently powerfully evocative, and deal with repute; power is transferred by magical association, as the namers of boats, ships, racehorses, steam locomotives and express trains have always known. Millennia ago, that monument to ancestor worship that we know as the Old Testament, spoke of 'them that have left a name behind them'.[4] That names conjure up associations of grandeur or dread is a point made by many a writer. Samuel Johnson spoke of 'the name, at which the world grew pale',[5] while Dryden described 'A name to all succeeding ages curst'.[6] In my youth we were all familiar with the words of the song 'The British Grenadier', which invokes 'Hector and Lysander, and such great names as these',[7] and Lucan spoke not only of the heroes but also of the place names, when he described the Trojan Plain 'where so many heroes have died', and where those events ensured that now 'no stone is nameless', and observed that 'there stands the shadow of a glorious name'. In the same breath, he recorded that Julius Caesar 'walked around what had once been Troy, now only a name'.[8] Battlefield tourism is not therefore a modern phenomenon (we generally think of the Waterloo battlefield as the first to be the subject of large-scale tourism), and just across the Dardanelles from Troy lies the tragic 20th-century battlefield of Gallipoli, now visited by hundreds of thousands every year. Heroes, though, are distinctly unfashionable at present.

Shakespeare, that great philosopher who was not unfamiliar with trench and mine warfare, asked 'What's in a name?', with the implication that the name itself was irrelevant: '... that which we call a rose/By any other name would smell as sweet'.[9] But, inverting the olfactory sense of this, should we believe that the names of stinking trenches are unworthy of consideration? The names given to trenches, and to other topographical and tactical features of the battlefield by the general staff, troops and cartographers during the First World War reveal a great deal about their cultural attitudes and identity. The classic study of British soldiers' nomenclature, language and slang was *The Long Trail – What the British soldier sang and said in 1914–1918*, by John Brophy and Eric Partridge.[10] This in fact was the end result of three earlier editions of a publication by those authors (both of whom had fought in the infantry on the Western Front): *Songs and Slang of the British Soldier 1914–1918*, first published in 1930.[11] Of course, we are aware that degrees of censorship, and self-censorship, were applied to the various editions of this work, just as they were to the original war reporting, trench naming, letters home, and so on. That said, there are sufficient sources of cross-referencing, including many first-hand accounts, to enable us to take back-bearings to a great deal of the original thoughts and language.

For my generation – that of the Beatles – the crucial introduction to the same material was provided by reading Blunden, Jones, Sassoon, Graves, Rosenberg, Owen and others, and by Joan Littlewood's masterly but distorted musical *Oh! What a Lovely War* of 1963, soon transformed into a film. Unfortunately, this simplistic view of the Great War as a matter of butchers, bunglers, lions and donkeys has more recently been perpetuated by the BBC's *Blackadder*. Acting as a counterpoint, we did, however, have John Terraine's magisterial BBC series of 1964, commemorating the fiftieth anniversary of the outbreak of the war. War, as an integral part of the human condition, will always be with us, and its mysteries are perhaps more appropriately explored by Jones and Blunden (who fought) than by Littlewood, Curtis and Elton. That said, despite a historical attitude that annoys the current revisionists and post-revisionists (and post-revisionist synthesists?), there is clearly a great deal of real value – especially the irony and the humour – in both these later cultural manifestations of what Paul Fussell called *The Great War and Modern Memory*.[12] Attitudes ingrained during the 1930s, which resurfaced in the 1960s, have proved remarkably tenacious and, it must be said in the light of subsequent events up to and including the Second Gulf War and the associated 'War on Terror', with a lot of justification. However, whatever the cynical attitudes of politicians and, to a lesser extent, commanders, the P.B.I. (Poor Bloody Infantry), as David Jones was at pains to point out, have always had to make the best of things, and developed their language and discourse accordingly. This is recognisable in Shakespeare, and in earlier authors.

The soldiers of each warring nation went through very similar experiences; the mincing machine did not look very different from either side. Although there are clear parallels between the naming practices of the British, French and Germans, there are distinct areas in which the presence of national characteristics suggest themselves. There is certainly a strong case for arguing that the British are distinguished by their use of humour and irony, while the Germans display a seriousness more in keeping with the dominant professional military culture of the Prussian General Staff Mentality. What typifies the French? Military tradition certainly, especially the campaigns and battles of Napoleon – La Gloire – and also a pride in French cultural achievements and the desire to commemorate officers killed in action.

Speaking of glory, is a number a name? Richard Holmes, in Redcoat, quotes an amusing story of a British officer, Colonel Poole, who rebelled at the thought of the old regimental numbers, 'wreathed in glory', giving way to names: 'Damned names mean nothing. Since time immemorial regiments have been numbered according to their precedence in the Line.'[13] Since then, soldiers have become equally attached to regimental names. Clearly the number of the regiment, say the 23rd Foot, served the same function as the name The Royal Welch Fusiliers. In that sense the number and the name fulfilled the purpose of designation and establishing an identity and focus of loyalty. They were, to all intents and purposes, the same thing. New Yorkers may feel the same about their numbered streets.

It is important to pause briefly to consider what a name is, and what it does. Naming is a profound human urge, the origins of which are lost in pre-history. That huge volume, the misnamed Shorter Oxford English Dictionary, tells us that the Old English word nama has cognates in all the Indo–European languages, including Sanskrit, Greek and Latin, and clinically defines a name as the particular combination of vocal sounds employed as the individual designation of a single person, animal, place or thing.[14] That will do as a starting point, and immediately brings the realisation, as any walk around a district with a local inhabitant or glance at a map reminds us, that localities, places and topographical features are nearly always named. Geographers and cartographers call this toponymy.[15] We name stars and planets, oceans and seas, mountains and hills, canyons, valleys and nullahs, deserts and rivers, cities, towns and villages, forests, woods and copses, and so on down to roads and alleyways. The earliest and closest approaches to toponyms, although not site-specific, were *The Front*, a term that had been used in the Boer War (and in the song of that period, 'Goodbye Dolly Gray') and probably earlier, and *No Man's Land*. At various stages of the war, these had very specific geographical locations, but were so extensive that they could not be called proper names, whereas names of trenches or defensive positions were clearly associated with specific stretches of earthworks. As communication ditches joining up individual rifle pits and machine gun posts, it is not surprising that the names of trenches were usually related to streets, avenues, alleys and so forth. Further, the appellation 'trench' (less often 'road' or 'street', which were often used for communication trenches) usually meant a fire trench (front, support, reserve, often designated as such), while 'avenues' and 'alleys' (French *boyau* and German *Weg* or *Gasse*) were communication trenches.

We also love naming animals and our own homes and more mobile creations. Particularly imaginative names have been (and are) given to racehorses, and to sailing and steamships and steam locomotives, and indeed there was much cross-fertilisation in this respect. How we love the *Golden Hind*, the *Cutty Sark* and the *Marie Celeste*, with all their romance and magic. The Royal Navy dignified its ship of the line, Britain's 'wooden walls' (and, later, ironclads and steel vessels) with magnificent names – *Redoubtable*, *Indomitable*, *Indefatigable*, *Ajax*, *Achilles*, *Agamemnon*, *Dreadnought*, etc. Many of these drew on classical accounts (notably Homer's *Iliad*) and mythology. The Great Western Railway adopted many of these warship names for its locomotives, as did the London and North Western. An amusing account of locomotive naming, including the trawling of a classical dictionary and some unintentional howlers, was given in Volume I of MacDermot's *History of the Great Western Railway*.[16] Reverting to the question of names versus numbers, W.A. Tuplin, in his book *North Western Steam*, considered many names downright inappropriate, and concluded that if 'one believes that the main purpose of a name is to give an engine a sonorous title, one may doubt the value of adding a name to the number that is in any case essential'. To him, 'Eleven seventy three' sounds at least as euphonious as *The Auditor* and 'Fifteen ninety five' more dignified than *Wild Duck*.[17] One can't help feeling that he was missing something! Many (but not all!) of the racehorse names given by the London and North Eastern Railway to its express locomotives seemed to fit. And surely the North British Railway got it right with its engines named after Walter Scott's characters.

Military operations were also given names – sometimes as concealment devices (code-names) – e.g. BARBAROSSA, SEALION, NEPTUNE, OVERLORD – and more recently as ponderous political propaganda –

OPERATION ENDURING FREEDOM in the case of the invasion of Iraq. Names have a particular psychological significance to men in action; as Winston Churchill pointed out in the Second World War, servicemen should not be called upon to risk their lives in operations named MICKY MOUSE, but rather in ANVIL or OVERLORD. Similarly, soldiers were more likely to make a big effort to capture *Potsdam Trench* than a set of merely numbered points. The propaganda point is obvious. The French in particular were rather keen on using derogatory names for German trenches – for example the *Ouvrage de la Défaite* or the *Tranchée des Homosexuels* in the Champagne region.

So what is a name for, and what does it do? It operates simultaneously on many levels. It is in some way more real and easy to grasp than any other way of describing features on the terrain. It is a sign and a signifier; it designates and it identifies. It is also a code-word; it encapsulates. If it does not already have multiple meanings and associations, it soon acquires them. That icy grip around the heart and sinking feeling in the stomach on being told you are destined to hold, or attack, a certain trench happens because you know the history of that bloody place. As David Jones knew very well, quoting Malory, the Western Front landscape spoke 'with a grimly voice'.[18]

In the next war, Henry Reed wrote a wonderful poem (or rather Part I of his *Lessons of the War*) that he called *Naming of Parts*, in which he drew ironic parallels between the names, which soldiers had to learn by heart, of the parts of the deadly Lee–Enfield rifle and those of the life-creating sexualised ambience of the English springtime in which the men were being taught their lethal trade. The author remembers similar, less poetic but more forthright, instruction from regular NCOs regarding the problem of finding the lower cover on a Bren. Such names, in their specificity and the need to get them absolutely right, took on liturgical meaning, as David Jones rightly recognised.

Getting very close indeed to the phenomenon of trench naming, Gabriel Josipovici highlighted the 'naming of parts' of the Atlantic rock in William Golding's novel *Pincher Martin* as a crucial cultural activity dealing with:

> ... one man's struggle to retain his identity in the face of an alien nature. He is alone on a rock in the middle of the Atlantic, waiting to be rescued. It is vital for him to keep himself healthy and sane till rescue arrives, and the first thing he has to do if he is to achieve this is to humanise his rock, to 'tame' it and thus turn it into something he can control and understand. So he names its parts: Oxford Circus, Piccadilly, Leicester Square. To name is to master. Men give names to nature and make patterns which they superimpose on nature, whether it is simply by moving two stones to come into line with a third or building a city. This is culture, civilisation: the separation of oneself from nature.[19]

It is more than mere coincidence that Golding chooses these particular London street names; he was aware that they had already been utilised – as trench names – in not too dissimilar circumstances in wartime, when survival and sanity had also been key issues. So we need to control our environment, to render it comprehensible, to reduce its fearful dimensions closer to the human scale we can understand, and also, if possible, to make it familiar, homely and

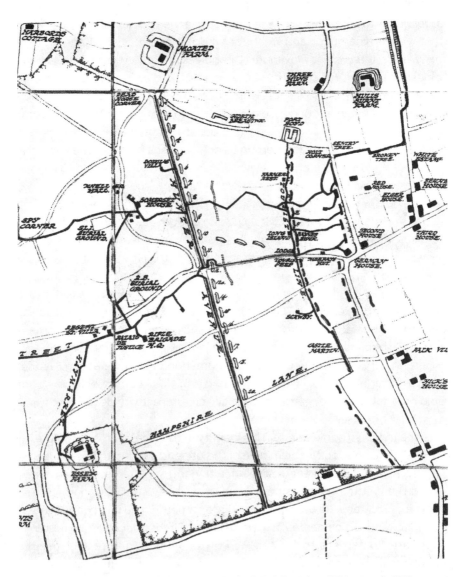

Detail of manuscript map of Ploegsteert Wood, Belgium, late 1914 or early 1915, showing named features, trenches, breastworks and duckboard or corduroy tracks.

comfortable. These are all survival strategies. Neither is it mere coincidence that Golding's rock turns out to be nothing more than the hollow of his tooth, felt by his tongue. Robert Graves told of a fellow officer, revisiting the Laventie sector after the war, using precisely the same metaphor to describe crawling over no man's land on a night patrol. Describing the peacetime appearance of this absurdly small area, as compared with its seemingly extensive wartime dimensions, he compared it to the real size of a hollow in one's tooth, as opposed to the great crater felt by one's tongue.[20]

In 1903 Jack London, in *The People of the Abyss*, described the East End of his namesake city in terms of 'solid walls of brick, the slimy pavements ... screaming streets',[21] while four years later, in a fascinating inversion of the usually accepted chronological relationship between trench names and city streets, Joseph Conrad, anticipating the First World War by seven years, described a London thoroughfare in his book *The Secret Agent* as a 'short and narrow street like a wet, narrow trench', and again as a 'slimy, deep trench'.[22] Doubtless the analogy had suggested itself to earlier authors. In late-1914 and in 1915, several trenches on the Western Front were lined with brick (archaeologists have recently uncovered two such, at St Yvon in Belgium and Auchonvillers on the Somme), thus turning the trope back on itself. We shall see later that London names feature prominently among trench names in France and Flanders, much more so than those of Paris or Berlin.

Following the introduction of trench names at the front at the very outset of trench warfare during the Battle of the Aisne (September 1914), new topographical and trench names moved into popular culture remarkably quickly. In a period when censorship was still relatively relaxed, *The Illustrated London News* for 4 September 1915 carried several drawings by an officer in the Ploegsteert Wood sector, showing various British military constructions and dugouts dating from the winter of 1914–15, with nameboards proclaiming *Somerset House*, *Hotel de Lockhart*, *Plugstreet Hall* and *Scawby*. The commentary claimed that the drawings of *Plug Street Hall* and other 'rustic residences' built by soldiers at the front 'in a style suggestive of Robinson Crusoe's hut, illustrated the British soldier's love of home and his capacity for making himself comfortable in the most adverse circumstances'. A correspondent of *The Times* wrote of Ploegsteert Wood that the Army knew it as *Plug Street*, and was proud of it, its defence being 'one of the best-remembered episodes along this battle-front'. In it, he continued:

> a forest town of comfortable dug-outs has been laid out, new roads have been constructed upon which the men can reach any portion of the wood dry-shod ... We passed up the 'Haymarket,' which in Plug Street, as in London, led us to 'Piccadilly Circus,' off which in some

geographical confusion branched not only 'Regent Street' but 'Fleet Street' as well. The Strand and Oxford Circus also have their counterpart here ... Spy Corner and Dead Horse Corner bring one back to the realities of Plug Street.

He also noted that in the spring of 1915 these routes were all deep in mud, and the men laid 'corduroy' tracks on top – primitive duckboard tracks and plank roads – comprising small branches laid across stouter parallel branches.[23]

The popular song of 1914 that saw the Regular Army marching off to war – 'It's a Long Way to Tipperary' – contained that still well-known refrain 'Goodbye Piccadilly, farewell Leicester Square'. But in fact the survivors of the first encounters carried those London thoroughfares with them, and planted them deep in the soil of France and Flanders. Archaeologists are still finding them; below the disturbed and ploughed surface, the old trenches, duckboards, bones, ammunition, grenades and other battlefield detritus survive, in varying states of decomposition and metamorphosis depending on the height of the water table and the chemical conditions of the terrain. For Dr Johnson, Virginia Woolf and many other Londoners, London was a celebration of life itself, but all too many of the optimists who named and inhabited the trenches failed to return to their mother city.

The names were also planted in journalistic accounts and literary works. Ian Hay, in his upbeat, fictionalised, autobiographical account of a Scottish unit in the first Kitchener Army in 1914–15, *The First Hundred Thousand*, published in 1916, chose to use real trench names from a part of the front – the Bois Grenier sector, south of Armentières – with which he was familiar and which, like those of the Ploegsteert Wood sector described above, were largely London names.[24] One result of this, as was the case with the earlier cartoon work of Bruce Bairnsfather, was that the public (and soldiers still in Britain) became extremely familiar with trench-naming practice. Elsewhere in his account Hay mentions dugouts named *Potsdam View* and *Maxim Villa*, a British trench called *Orchard Trench*, and an old German communication trench, *Unter den Linden*, while farther south in the Loos sector he speaks of *Fountain Alley*, *Scottish Trench*, *Central Boyau*, *Bart's Alley*, *Fosse Alley* and the *Hohenzollern Redoubt* with its attendant *Big Willie* and *Little Willie*, names forever associated with the battle of September–October 1915. Henry Williamson later conjured them up in the inter-war period when revisiting the battlefields he had fought over.

The classic literature of the Western Front immediately brings trench names to the attention of the reader. Robert Graves, Siegfried Sassoon, Edmund Blunden, David Jones, Isaac Rosenberg and many others make very deliberate use of them to set the scene and evoke associations. They were, of course, writing for an audience, many of whom had had a classical education, which was very familiar with the events and culture of the front – many of their readers had themselves served in France and Flanders – so these trench names provide crucial mental, historical and geographical reference points, and anchors to the terrain. When Graves wrote of the *Hohenzollern Redoubt*, *Brick Trench*, *Maison Rouge Alley*, *Mine Point*, the *Pope's Nose*, the *Brickstacks* and the *Duck's Bill*,[25] he was documenting precise locations and moments of the Battle of Loos, in which he participated, and also evoking events, memories and associations. All this is a kind of referencing. The name becomes the key to open the data-bank, the password to enter the archive.

A significant parallel is the practice by emigrants of attaching familiar names from home to the new, wild or hostile territory they are colonising. A good example of this is the naming of places by English and French settlers in the American Colonies, or indeed in any part of their empires. This process undoubtedly staked a claim, but also established continuity with the past, and a sense of familiarity and security. A new label was attached to a place; the old native label was usually (but not always) discarded in the process. After the immediate and violent colonising phase, map-makers were often keen to find out the old native names for places.

Wittgenstein noted that 'naming is something like attaching a label to a thing. One can say that this is preparatory to the use of a word. But *what* is it a preparation *for*?',[26] and also that '... a great deal of stage-setting in the language is presupposed if the mere act of naming is to make sense'.[27] This suggests that names are associated with a certain theatricality. Of course, we already speak of the 'theatre of war', so we should not be too surprised to find this scene-setting, especially for something the military actually call a 'set-piece' battle and for which they arrange a 'dress rehearsal'. The notion that the name is a preparation for something – an event – is something that our context of military operations immediately clarifies; it is a preparation for defence or attack, for those very operations that provide the context. It is the case, for example, that the British named the German trenches at Gommecourt and on the Somme front in 1916, immediately before attacking those very trenches. Wittgenstein's label metaphor is particularly apposite in the case of trenches and many other battlefield features, for they *were* indeed labelled. Each trench was signed with one or more name-boards which did exactly that.

Although Bertrand Russell came up with the odd idea that the referent of a name *was* its meaning, he sensibly commented that the point of names was that they referred. Roger Scruton, seizing on this observation, agreed that 'this must be the fundamental fact about the meaning of a name'.[28] And in military terms this is the crucial function of a trench name; it rigidly designates a military defence line, defended locality, attack objective or communication route, particularly for artillery bombardment fire ('artillery preparation', which is offensive, or 'counter-preparation', which is defensive) as a specific geographic location. As plotted on the map (with its name), a trench is defined in space by its three-dimensional cartesian coordinates – i.e. two dimensions (x and y) of planimetry, and one dimension (z) of height. It exists in this geodetic matrix as a fly does in amber. This mathematical placing is, as has been suggested, crucial for artillery work, for if the guns are also similarly located on our three-dimensional grid, the exact range, bearing and vertical angle-of-sight of the trench as a target (assuming it is correctly plotted on the map) can be calculated or found graphically on an artillery board and, assuming no ballistic and atmospheric errors, the shells will find their target.[29]

But as well as this primary function of a trench name, there are many others, and an attempt is made in this book to suggest what these might be. A model of the naming function might include:

Trench Name

Primary Function	Secondary Functions
(Tactical)	(Psychological/Cultural)
Important for commanders and staff	Important for front-line troops
Content: Precise geographical location	Content: Control of hostile environment
(pinpoint map refs)	Security, reassurance & mnemonic
	Homely associations
	Regimental or group associations
	Nostalgia
	Humour
	Irony, etc.

Thus in terms of the primary or tactical function, any name might do. However, when it comes to the secondary functions, any name clearly will not do. The name chosen, whether through a careful thought process or by a flash of humour or other inspiration, has to be 'right' – it has to fit the case, whatever the desiderata of the troops happen to be. While the primary function is purely tactical, the secondary functions are all clearly social and psychological in some way. Indeed, we might reverse the ranking; for the front-line infantry the social and psychological functions were primary, and the tactical function secondary. For them the important thing is the group. The great military thinker Clausewitz recognised the supreme importance of morale (as well as training and experience) in overcoming the danger, toil, chance, uncertainty and friction generated by war.[30]

Philosophers have, in recent years, considered the nature of proper names rather than common ones. Gottlob Frege[31] held that proper names have sense as well as reference, in contradistinction to John Stuart Mill's belief, currently supported by Saul Kripke,[32] that they only had a reference function. To Kripke, proper names are 'rigid designators', whose reference operates through an external causal chain linking one's use of a name to the original occasion on which the name was first assigned to that person or place, not through any 'sense' which one attaches to them. In this 'causal theory of reference', as the name is passed on from person to person, all that is necessary for the name to be used successfully to refer to the place originally named by it is that each subsequent user should intend to refer to the *same* place as the name was used to refer to by the person from whom he received the name. This does not answer all the questions, and Gareth Evans points out that it cannot cope with some of the ways in which names *change* their reference over time.[33]

Some philosophers have also been puzzled by the use of the names of fictional characters and places, considering that fictional characters and places do not exist; if they did, they would not be fictional.[34] Here we enter the intriguing territory of the fictional domain, and the possibility of crossover, or transference between the fictional (or magical) and the real world. To David Jones, Ploegsteert was Broceliande; the Ypres Salient became the enchanted forest of the grail legend. We have to accept that the storyteller and the artist operate on a metaphysical level, and that there is more than one reality. We only have to read Paul Fussell's stimulating book *The Great War in Modern Memory*, or Richard Holmes's comprehensive *Tommy*, to realise that the 'reality' of the Western Front was different to different people, and that our current conception of it is coloured by their different memories and agendas, as well as by their artistic and literary creations.

After he had been severely wounded on the Somme, Robert Graves included in a poem about the episode an amazing passage about being carried away on a stretcher past 'the door that Cerberus guards' and then, not the usual signboard – *To Dressing Station* – but 'an old Greek signpost' pointing *To Lethe*. His classically educated audience would understand exactly his references to death.[35]

A name encapsulates a shared understanding of location, properties and experience, as well as other levels of shared cultural associations. Thus if I speak to you of Glastonbury Tor, I am releasing in your mind everything you know about that place, including all its Arthurian associations – the name speaks volumes, and also conjures up visual images. It is thus a vital shorthand, a code-word, which enables us to communicate a mass of information in the briefest possible time, and avoids the use of clumsy map coordinates (which would normally be used in written orders in any case, to provide precision and avoid vagueness).

A map is, of course, a text of a sort, and we commonly speak of 'reading a map'. However, in a very literal way we read the names on a map, and they form a text that can be decoded in a cultural sense. This is not the place to enter into a discussion of late 20th-century literary or cultural 'Theory', but in a very real sense this book aims to decode the trench names found on the maps, and to reconstruct some of the cultural structures that informed them.

Being printed on the map next to the feature, the name creates mental links and associations between the ground, the map, the soldiers fighting over that terrain, the commanders planning operations in the rear, and the politicians, newspapers and public at home. Simplified maps appeared in the newspapers. If the communiqué spoke of heavy fighting at the *Hohenzollern Redoubt*, all were immediately connected by those two words of the name.

War artists recognised the iconic nature of battlefield name boards and signs. William Roberts, the vorticist, produced a pen and watercolour piece that he entitled: *In the Ypres Sector: an infantry duck-board track being shelled by the Germans*. By this track he featured prominently a sign proclaiming *Overland to KIT and KAT*, the names of two positions in enemy territory prior to the Third Battle of Ypres.[36]

That trench names were potent cultural signifiers was recognised in 1918 by Charlie Chaplin, who had trench name boards prominently featured at a trench junction for a publicity still for his 1918 film *Shoulder Arms*. The names in question were *Rotten Row* and *Broadway*,[37] both names of actual British trenches (and London streets), but carefully chosen for their London and New York associations signifying Allied solidarity. In a less striking vein, the 'mock trenches' that were dug in Kensington Gardens, at Blackpool, and other locations during the war, for both training and propaganda purposes, were adorned with nameboards to complete the illusion of reality. On Salisbury Plain, and also at Bovington and other training areas in the UK, systems of practice trenches were complete with the names of their German counterparts in France, including the *Hohenzollern Redoubt*.

Similarly, photographs and paintings reproduced in post-1918 books commonly included trench nameboards (and others); their iconic quality appealed to the authors and editors. Such books often also featured trench maps, another example of iconic imagery, on many of which the names of the trenches and other key points were printed. It is no accident that both the first edition of Graves's *Goodbye to All That* (1928) and the edition of Sassoon's *Memoirs of an Infantry Officer* illustrated by Barnett Freedman (1931) carried images of trench maps (photograph and graphic respectively) on their dust jackets (*Goodbye to All That* also included some reproductions of trench maps bound into the text), while the first edition of David Jones's *In Parenthesis* (1937) included a sketchy drawing by Jones of a trench map). One recent book contained six photographs of trench signboards, the signboards proclaiming: *Savoy Grill* (1915, Company HQ), *Marschstrasse 4/Seven Dials*, *Oblige Trench* (north-west of Wytschaete; with trench name deleted by the censor), *Field Dressing Station*, *Railway Alley* and *Gas Alert Off* (Cambrin), and *2nd F.A.* (Field Ambulance). The author noted: 'Seven Dials being in a part of London near the "Tipperary" places Piccadilly and Leicester Square, perhaps there was a subtext of nostalgia as well as wit in the choice of name.'[38] Tony Ashworth's book on trench warfare included a photograph of officers at a dugout entrance in early 1915, with a trench nameboard proclaiming *The Strand* clearly visible.[39] Another popular book included a photograph of the huge signboard the Germans erected in Péronne at the time of their retreat to the Hindenburg Line in 1917: *Nicht ärgern, nur wundern!* (Don't be angry, just be amazed!)[40] This sign still exists in the Péronne Historial de la Grande Guerre. In the current iconography of the First World War, trench nameboards are always an essential part of the classic image presented. Displays at the Imperial War Museum and the National Army Museum both include replicas of sections of trench, complete with nameboards (*Bully Alley* in the NAM), rats, dugouts, corrugated iron, trench periscope, sentry with rifle on the firestep, duckboards, grenade boxes, signal rockets, etc.

So far we have looked at wider cultural reasons for naming, but we should also look at the more narrow utilitarian functions of trench names. Above all, in strictly operational terms, a name is convenient and efficient; more efficient, in fact, than grid references alone. Staff officers soon learned that the too slavish use of grid references, or rather their 1914–18 square reference equivalents, was not only clumsy and time-consuming but also led to errors in orders. Much better to say that the 11th Royal Sussex will capture and consolidate *Stuff Trench*, than to order that battalion to attack the *trench between X.17.d.4.3 and X.24.c.5.6*. Provided, of course, that all concerned were issued with the appropriate map, on which the trenches and brigade and battalion boundaries were marked, the objective could be seen at a glance and the company and platoon boundaries and objectives easily assigned.

Apart from the purely practical value of easy identification of a specific section of defences – while map square references were essential for precise pinpointing and artillery work, the naming of features and trenches helped to make spatial and conceptual sense of the battlefield, names being easily associated and remembered, unlike numbers, and were particularly useful in emergencies when there was no time to recall or look up square references. A name commemorates, reminds and encourages. It also comforts, and helps combatants to make some sort of sense, or nonsense, of where they are and what is happening to them. Humour, irony, pathos and sentiment all play a part. Soldiers like to remind themselves of home.

A name also implies permanence of a sort, so it tells us something about the nature of trench, or position, warfare. A trench is a place for living in, and also a protected way of getting from one point to another – a route. The simultaneous familiarity and means of communication thus implied immediately suggests the domesticity and bustle of city life, so it is no surprise to find innumerable groups of trenches whose names reflect the familiar thoroughfares of urban living – the English, Scottish, Irish or Welsh street network metamorphosed into the shell-blasted French or Belgian rural landscape. This theme is developed in Chapter VII.

Names of places, woods and localities already existed of course, and were printed on the national maps. More local names were to be found on the larger-scale cadastral plans, kept by the mayor of each village. Some of the first names used by the troops arriving in a new sector were these pre-existing names; those they found too unfamiliar, or simply too much of a mouthful, they anglicised in a way long familiar in the Royal Navy in which HMS *Bellerophon* was english'd as *Billy Ruffian*; thus Ploegsteert became *Plugstreet*, Wytschaete became *White Sheet*, Goedevaeresvelde became *Gertie Wears Velvet*, and Auchonvillers became *Ocean Villas*, Delville Wood became *Devil's Wood*, Fonquevillers became *Funky Villas*, Leuze Wood became *Lousy Wood*, Gris Pot became *Grease Pot*, Monchy Breton became *Monkey Britain*, and so on.

The first headquarters buildings and those used as observation posts, before they were reduced by shelling to heaps of rubble, were named with affectionate irony after hotels, music halls or pubs – the *Ritz*, *Savoy*, *Maxims*, *Carlton Grill*, *Coliseum*, etc. *Maxims*, of course, when in the front line at Ploegsteert Wood, had a double meaning. While the main purpose of such names was easy identification, they served a secondary purpose in providing a measure of security. A name would act as a code-word; if overheard by the enemy in a telephone conversation (a common source of intelligence) it might not easily be identified. But it also introduced a comforting, if illusory, element of home and safety into a lethal, dirty and uncomfortable reality. Such pretence became a consistent feature of the battlefield.

We find names popping up on every front, and in every army. The 1915 Gallipoli campaign provides a rich harvest, as does the Salonica (Macedonia) front, Palestine, Mesopotamia, the Eastern Front; in fact everywhere. This phenomenon is only briefly examined here. The tradition continued in the next war, with its *Maginot Line*, *Siegfried Line*, its *Knightsbridge* and *Admin Box*. RAF bomber crews named the heavily defended Ruhr target area *Happy Valley*, with the same fine irony that served the same purpose so well in the previous war.

Names of trenches and localities were quick to seize the imagination of the war poets and memoir-writers (often the same people). Blunden was not the only poet or writer to recognise the particular ironic and mesmeric quality of trench names; David Jones built the trench and topographical names into the structure of his epic prose poem *In Parenthesis* (1937), in which he created 'a veritable litany' including Pecantin (or Picantin), Le Plantin, Cats Post and Dogs Post, Rags Post and Bones Post, Mole hole Keep, Croix Barbée, and Gorre, to whose shelter relieved troops returned from the isolated posts known as the Islands, or (with the twist of a Shakespearian reference to mine warfare in its tail) from the Duck's Bill, 'where his concavities is sufficient'.[41]

The names permeated the post-Great War popular and literary imagination. In that modernist milestone of post-war self-examination of the decadent state of Western civilisation, *The Waste Land* (1922), the American T.S. Eliot (who had spent the war in London) wrote, if not with the trenches in the forefront of his mind, then certainly with them seared in recent memory: 'I think we are in rats' alley/Where the dead men lost their bones.'[42]

Paul Fussell, in his influential book *The Great War and Modern Memory*,[43] developed this idea of a specific First World War vocabulary, and in particular of irony as its dominant mode. Not far removed from this is the mournful and gallows humour, so common in trench names. It is therefore vital to venture at least a little way up this 'sap of retrogression', as Blunden might have called it.

Irony

The horrors of trench warfare – indeed of any type of war – have been so thoroughly documented in an extensive literature that readers should need no reminding that it was not just out in no man's land, and in fighting through the enemy position, that soldiers were exposed to wounds, mutilation and death. The routine business of 'holding the line', even in so-called 'quiet sectors', was a lethal one. Skulls were split by snipers' bullets, shrapnel balls or shell splinters; men were blown apart by shells or trench mortar bombs; whole sections or platoons were disintegrated, pulped or entombed by mines exploded in galleries deep below them; lungs and mucous membranes were eroded by gas, men choking and drowning. Even without hostile action by the enemy, life was often hideous with the discomforts of dirt, smell and lice, and the painful or deadly hazards of exposure and trench feet. Irony was clearly one way of living with all this.

The ironic mode of trench naming is only one of several, and we should not be carried away by the ideas of literary commentators who, holding that irony was the supreme mode of soldierly poetic expression in the First World

War, intimate that we should view everything in ironic terms. Much trench naming was totally without irony – for example that which had the function of commemorating comrades killed in action or died of wounds, or appealed to a sense of regimental history. Nevertheless, a great deal *was* ironic in its intention, or *became* ironic as the war's cumulative horrors unfolded (one of the ways in which names change their meaning). The naming of trenches after the familiar streets of home towns and cities may originally have had a simple function that became overlain with irony. The original act of naming may not have been made with contrast in mind, but contrast there certainly was. Often the irony was in the ambiguity.

By irony we usually imply that meaning is expressed using language that, in normal usage, would express the opposite – we encounter here a binary opposition or inversion. There is a silent 'I don't think!' about many such names, which highlight the huge discrepancy between an expected (or desired) and an actual state of affairs – for example, *Rose Cottage*, or *Happy Valley*. This ironic spirit, conscious or not, and even if not the dominant mode, was widespread. Giving trenches pompous (high-status?) metropolitan names such as *Pall Mall*, *Piccadilly*, *Park Lane* or *Bond Street* may, or may not, immediately imply ironic intention, but it was impossible not to be aware of the stupefying contrast between the iconic original model and the stinking, muddy reality of the narrow ditch so named.

The names emphasise the contradictory or ill-timed outcome of events as if mocking the fitness of things. The ancient Greeks used tragic irony to reveal to the audience the tragic or fatal significance of a character's words or actions, while making it clear that the character is unaware of such significance. In the First World War, however, the players were only too well aware. And yet forms of irony persisted. In the Hill 60, Caterpillar and Battle Wood area south-east of Ypres, the British named a system of German trenches '*Immovable*' – *Immovable Trench*, *Immovable Support*, *Immovable Row*, *Immovable Avenue* – in the full knowledge that these very trenches were to be bombarded by heavy artillery and then blown sky-high by British deep mines at the opening of the Messines battle on 7 June 1917. As General 'Tim' Harrington, Second Army's Chief of Staff, told journalists on the eve of this battle: 'Gentlemen, I don't know whether we are going to make history tomorrow, but at any rate we shall change geography.'[44]

Ironic contrasts in terms of juxtaposition of names are also striking; in the Westroosebeke sheet we find *Wonderland* cheek by jowl with *Whitechapel*, as well as *Radio* and *Void Farms*, *Spider* and *Vindictive Cross Roads*. Here we cross the border between irony and serendipity.

Signboard, much perforated by shell splinters, from the Western Front, now in the Imperial War Museum, London.

Serendipity

Horace Walpole coined this word in 1754 from the old name of Ceylon, having in mind the fairy tale 'The Three Princes of Serendip', whose heroes 'were always making discoveries, by accidents or sagacity, of things they were not in quest of'. Our reaction to trench names is very much in this serendipitous realm of accidentally making happy and unexpected discoveries, not least in their juxtapositions. A glance at the Gazetteer that makes up Part Two of this book will confirm this, but much of the serendipity depends upon the way the names are sorted. As far as the intentions of the namers are concerned, the most important thing is to look at the original map for it is only by doing so in the map-and-landscape-space, a space at once geographical and conceptual, that the original juxtapositions are found. It is then that the intentions of the name-bestowers become clear.

Notes

1 Lamb, Charles, *Essays of Elia*: *Dream Children*.
2 Shakespeare, William, *Twelfth Night*, in: *The Complete Works* (ed. Peter Alexander), London & Glasgow: Collins, 1961.
3 Browne, Sir Thomas, *The Garden of Cyrus; or, The Quincuncial Lozenge, or Network Plantations of the Ancients, Artificially, Naturally, Mystically considered*. London, 1668, p. 34.
4 The Bible, *Old Testament*; *Apocrypha*, *Ecclesiasticus*.

5   Johnson, Dr Samuel, *Vanity of Human Wishes*, p. 219.

6   Dryden, John, *Absalom and Achitophel*.

7   Anonymous, *The British Grenadier*.

8   Lucan, *Pharsalia*.

9   Shakespeare, William, *Romeo and Juliet*, II.ii.43, in: *The Complete Works* (ed. Peter Alexander), London & Glasgow: Collins, 1961.

10 Brophy, J. & Partridge, E., *The Long Trail – What the British soldier sang and said in 1914–1918*, London: Andre Deutsch, 1965.

11 Brophy, J. & Partridge, E., *Songs and Slang of the British Soldier 1914–18*, London: Scholartis Press, 1930.

12 Fussell, Paul, *The Great War and Modern Memory*, London: Oxford University Press, 1975.

13 Weekes, Alan, *The Royal Hampshire Regiment*, London, 1969, p. 41; quoted in Holmes, Richard, *Redcoat, The British Soldier in the Age of Horse and Musket*, London: HarperCollins, 2002, p. 31.

14 *Shorter Oxford English Dictionary*, 3rd Edition, Revised with Addenda, corrections, etc, Oxford: The Clarendon Press, 1965, p. 1308.

15 Kadmon, N., *Toponymy – The Lore, Laws and language of Geographical Names*, New York: United Nations, 2000.

16 MacDermot, E.T, *History of the Great Western Railway*. Vol. I, 1833–1863, revised by C R Clinker, London: Ian Allan, 1964, pp. 417–9.

17 Tuplin, W A, *North Western Steam*, London: George Allen & Unwin, 1963, p. 151.

18 Jones, David, *In Parenthesis*, London: Faber & Faber, 1937, p. xi. The original Malory reference is to *Le Morte Darthur*, Book IV, Chapter 15.

19 Josipovici, Gabriel, *The World and the Book, A Study of Modern Fiction*, London: Macmillan, 1971, p. 243.

20 Graves, Robert, *Goodbye to All That*, London: Penguin Modern Classics edition, 1961, p. 110.

21 London, Jack, *The People of the Abyss*, New York: Macmillan, 1903.

22 Conrad, Joseph, *The Secret Agent*, London: Penguin Modern Classics edition, 1971, pp. 114 & 206.

23 *The Illustrated London News*, 4 Sept. 1915, London, p. 310. Drawings believed to be by Capt. J.E. Dixon-Spain, RFA.

24 Hay, Ian, *The First Hundred Thousand*, Edinburgh & London: Blackwood, 1916, pp. 203–5.

25 Graves, op. cit., pp. 122–33.

26 Wittgenstein, L. (trans. G.E.M. Anscombe), *Philosophical Investigations*, Oxford: Blackwell, 1953, I, §26.

27 Wittgenstein, op. cit., §257.

28 Scruton, Roger, *Modern Philosophy, A Survey*, London: Sinclair-Stevenson, 1994, p. 163.

29 For information about artillery survey and mapping, see Chasseaud, Peter, *Artillery's Astrologers – A History of British Survey and Mapping on the Western Front, 1914–1918*, Lewes: Mapbooks, 1999.

30 Clausewitz, General Karl Maria von, *Vom Kriege*, Vols. 1–7, Berlin: Ferdinand Dümmler, 1832–37.

31 Frege, Gottlob, 'On Sense and Meaning', in: P.T. Geach and Max Black (eds), *Translations from the Philosophical Writings of Gottlob Frege*, London: OUP, 1980.

32 Kripke, Saul A., *Naming and Necessity*, London & Oxford: OUP, 1980.

33 See also Moore, A.W. (ed.), *Meaning and Reference*, London: OUP, 1993, and Salmon, N., *Reference and Essence*, N.J.: Princeton, 1982.

34 Lewis, D., 'Truth in Fiction', *American Philosophical Quarterly*, 1978.

35 Graves, Robert, 'Escape', in *Fairies and Fusiliers*, London: Heinemann, 1917, p. 63.

36 IWM Dept of Art 5195.

37 Winter, J. & Baggett, B., *1914–18 – The Great War and the Shaping of the 20th Century*, London: BBC Books, 1996, p. 142.

38 Brown, Malcolm, *The Imperial War Museum Book of The Western Front*, London: BCA, 1993.

39 Ashworth, Tony, *Trench Warfare 1914–1918, The Live and Let Live System*, London: Pan Books, 2000 (Illustration 19 – 'British Troops in France', BBC Hulton Picture Library).

40 Winter, J. & Baggett, B., op. cit., p. 211.

41 Jones, op. cit., p. 116.

42 Eliot, T.S., *The Waste Land*, London: Faber & Faber, 1922, lines 115–6.

43 Fussell, op. cit.

44 Wolff, Leon, *In Flanders Fields, The Flanders Campaign of 1917*, London: Corgi, 1966, p. 114, quoting Lytton, Neville, *The Press and the General Staff*, London: Collins, 1920.

PART ONE

I

TRENCHES AND THE LANDSCAPE

The first part of this chapter looks at how the trench system developed and became part of the landscape, while the second part examines the way in which the battlefield landscape and the natural world were perceived and mythologised by the troops, and the impact this had on trench naming. The following chapters follow the development of naming along the front, and focus on specific naming themes.

The Development of Trenches and Trench Systems

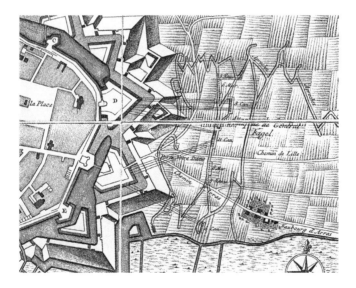

Early 18th-century plan of the siege of Béthune (1710), showing, on the right, the attacking trenches and batteries of the Duke of Marlborough's forces. The 'Aproches' zig-zagged between the successively advanced 'parallels' in a way that exactly prefigured First World War communication trenches (approaches or avenues). The batteries fired at Vauban's fortifications until a breach was made, and when this was deemed 'practicable' the infantry assault was launched.

Historical Overview

Trenches and field fortifications were not a new concept and have existed in various forms since pre-history. A principal feature of warfare in the medieval and renaissance periods (Leonardo da Vinci was a military engineer), they had assumed a new importance with the invention of gunpowder and firearms, and by the 17th century sieges had become intricate and scientific affairs with a vast trench vocabulary, much of which survived into the 20th century. Readers of Lawrence Sterne's *Tristram Shandy* (1757) will recognise, in Uncle Toby's development of sieges in miniature on his bowling green, the parallels (in more than one sense) between early 18th-century siege warfare and the Western Front in 1914–18, including the use of mortars. The Crimean and American Civil Wars of the 19th-century saw the widespread use of trenches and breastworks, while the Russo–Japanese War of 1904–5 and Balkan Wars of 1912–13 drove home the message that trench warfare was likely to be a significant feature of early 20th-century conflict, at least at certain stages of operations.

Permanent fortifications had always been named for identification, and earlier wars had seen names given to temporary field works for the same reason, for example the *La Bassée Lines* and Louis XIV's *Ne Plus Ultra Lines* of Marlborough's time, and Wellington's *Lines of Torres Vedras* in the Peninsula. In the Crimean War, the *Great Redoubt* and *Lesser Redoubt* crowned the heights of the Alma, the *Sandbag Redoubt* appeared, and the prolonged siege of Sebastopol was executed according to classic siege-war principles. Many features and works here were named accordingly: the *Great Redan*, *Little Redan* and *Malakoff* redoubts defending Sebastopol, the *Mamelon*, *McKenzie's Heights*, *Frenchman's Hill*, *Greenhill*, *Tryon's Trench*, the *Cochorn Battery*, *Lancaster Right* and *Left Batteries*, the Allied *Picquet House*, *Left*, *Right* and *New Boyaux* (approaches or communication trenches), *Victoria Redoubt* and the *1st* to *5th Parallels*, from the last of which the Allied assault was launched. Several of these names were to reappear on the Western Front in 1914–18.

The practice of naming defensive lines continued after the Crimean and American Civil Wars, with the *Bulair Lines* defending the Gallipoli Peninsula and the *Chataldja Lines* defending Constantinople in the Balkan Wars, and so forth. Most of the defence lines took their names from the local topography. On the Eastern Front in 1914, the Germans held back the invading Russians on the *Angerapp Line* in East Prussia. In the west, 1914 saw many permanent fortifications facing the German invader, and in key defensive zones such as Serré de Rivière's Verdun–Nancy–Belfort fortress belt defending France's eastern frontier there were many named forts, *ouvrages*, batteries and so forth. When these were augmented by temporary earthworks, it was natural that they should be similarly named. Thus another reason for trench naming was historical precedent – it had always been done, and had been picked up by regular soldiers and others from reading regimental and campaign histories.

1914 – The Start of Trench Warfare

The infantry soldiers of 1914 were trained in the first instance to dig individual scrapes and rifle pits with their 'grubbers' or entrenching tools, which they all carried, and with which they quickly dug in at Mons and Le Cateau. If no forward movement was possible or rearward movement intended, they were trained to link these up into fire trenches as soon as possible. Sections of fire-trench were then linked laterally to provide communication between sections, platoons, companies and then battalions, and also forward and backward to provide communication between firing line, supports and reserves, and with headquarters. All this was provided for in pre-war training manuals.

This pattern had developed on the Aisne in September 1914 within two weeks of movement coming to a halt, with Field Companies of the Royal Engineers helping to survey and construct defences. In open country, modern weapons made it quite impossible to move in daylight without such communications, and even at night heavy casualties could be expected in moonlight, or when the enemy were equipped with flares. In any case, even if illumination was lacking, the ground would be swept by rifles and machine guns firing on fixed lines. Brigadier General Hunter-Weston was proud of the trenches constructed by his 11th Brigade, and exhorted his battalion commanders to take the education of their officers in trench construction very seriously. On 30 September 1914 his brigade major sent the following message to each battalion (Hants, Rifle Brigade, Somersets, East Lancs):

> Brig-Gen is desirous that all the Officers of the battalions should profit by the experience of entrenching under active service conditions which is now afforded by our sections of defence. He is of opinion that most of the work [which] is now executed is admirable. He directs therefore that commanding officers will go round the whole section of defence with half the officers of their battalions today and with the other half tomorrow pointing out for instruction purposes the good and bad points of the various works.[1]

The troops again dug in during the encounter battles of La Bassée and First Ypres in October and November 1914, and at the end of these battles the trench system again solidified, as it had on the Aisne. Trenches, or in waterlogged terrain breastworks (as in parts of the Ypres Salient and long

British and German front breastworks in the low-lying Richebourg sector facing the Aubers Ridge, May 1915. The British front breastwork is two-thirds of the way up the photo, and beyond that lies no man's land and the German front breastwork. Further on again rises the Aubers Ridge.

stretches of the line southwards to Festubert and Givenchy) were essential for survival, and some form of primitive 'splinter-proofs' or dugouts had to be provided for protection from fire and the weather. In the winter of 1914–15, the infantry and engineers watched helplessly as trenches filled with water and sandbag breastworks spread and sank into the slime. The most that could be done in several low-lying parts of the front – notably the Lys Valley and parts of the Ypres Salient – was to construct short lengths of revetted breastwork ('grouse butts' or 'islands'), reached only by night by an overland route, which could be held by outlying pickets, most men of the front battalions remaining in 'keeps', ruins and villages behind the front line. Where possible, wire was strung out in front of these meagre defences to improve their security. Grim ground conditions were nothing new in warfare, or in Flanders. Uncle Toby, in *Tristram Shandy*, declared that 'Our armies swore terribly in Flanders'.

Trenches systems did not grow at random. Vital to their planning and siting were the experts in field works – the Divisional Royal Engineers, and the all-important 'defence scheme' for each sector that detailed the units and sub-units responsible for holding each trench or feature, their dispositions and 'stand-to' positions, and their deployment to meet an expected attack. The scheme included support and reserve positions, and routes to be used to reinforce and counter-attack. Over an extended period of time, the relationship between a defence scheme and trench system was symbiotic; the original defence scheme determined the trace of the trenches on the ground (though this was also partly inherited from the first scrapes and diggings of the initial encounter battles), and where brigadiers, divisional, corps and army commanders felt that there needed to be changes or developments these took concrete form in the shape of new trenches, dugouts and tunnels, machine gun and mortar emplacements, battery positions, etc. The pattern of trenches might also be changed in response to geological and terrain conditions – an old, waterlogged line would be abandoned and replaced by a new line on higher ground, or an exposed position on a forward slope would be replaced by a protected one (with a good field of fire) on a reverse slope, leaving only observation posts forward, with saps running back to the new line.

1915 – Trench Systems Develop

German policy for 1915 was to remain on the defensive in the west while attacking to finish off the Russians in the east. They therefore dug deep and well, constructing a practically impregnable position that included, wherever possible, deep dugouts in which their machine gunners could shelter during the preliminary bombardment. In the battles of the winter of 1914–15 in the Champagne, Joffre 'nibbled' at the German position, incurring high casualties in the process – a sort of attrition in reverse. This put the Germans even more on the defensive.

When the 27th Division took over trenches in the St Eloi sector from the French on 6 January 1915, they found them 'wide ditches mostly, very uncared for, ankle, knee and even waist deep in liquid mud'.[2] Despite the grim weather and dreadful ground conditions (in the winter of 1914–15 men had to be dug out of the mud, an exercise taking several hours), the trench systems developed slowly but remorselessly from the first encounter battles. At first there was little more than a single line of short sections of trench, as on the Aisne, and even in early 1915 there were still many disconnected sections of trench, particularly where the French, who relied for defence on their quick-firing 75mm field guns, were holding the line. The French learned very quickly to man the front trenches with only small pickets, keeping their main force farther back. The British took longer to learn from experience, and packed their forward trenches with troops, thus exposing them to vile conditions (and trench feet) and unnecessary casualties.

Behind the thin front line at this stage there were isolated strong points, but little else. On 3 January 1915 7th and 8th Divisions in the Neuve Chapelle–La Boutillerie area had started to construct twelve 'pivot points' lettered A

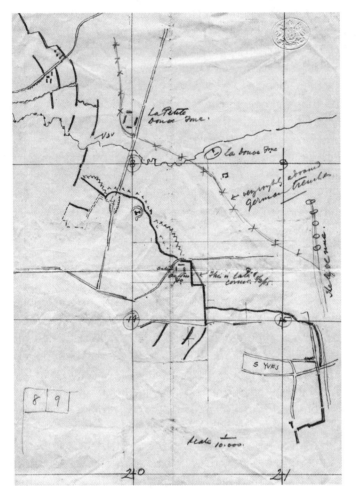

British manuscript sketch map of the St Yvon (St Yves) sector from early 1915, showing the British trenches and breastworks facing the German positions around La Petite Dove and La Douve Farms.

to M on a 1:10,000 map, 'in support of the existing line of entrenchments'.[3] These pivot points, organised for all-round defence, were soon called keeps on First Army Front. A IV Corps letter of 26 January ordered completion of these keeps all along the front of the 7th and 8th Divisions 'at the earliest possible moment'. The insecurity of the existing feeble defences was keenly felt, and the letter continued: 'With the exception of the two new works 1A and 1B in rear of "A" and "B" lines of the 8th Division, all these keeps will be fit for occupation and wired up all round by January 31st.' At the same time instructions were issued on how to draw up tracings of the British defence works on a lithographed 1:10,000 map base, including the use of a broad range of conventional signs; existing works and those under construction were to be in red, and proposed works in blue.[4] There was also a discontinuous 'GHQ

Line', to act as a fall-back position, and this was particularly important in key sectors such as the Ypres Salient.

As late as April 1915, a battalion new to the front, the 1/4th Duke of Wellington's (West Riding) Regiment, could report that 'movement to and from the front line, in the Fleurbaix Sector, was almost entirely across the open, communication trenches being practically non-existent'. One of the first tasks undertaken by this battalion was to begin a new communication trench, *Dead Dog Alley* (taking its name from the eponymous farm); this trench was still being completed two months later when the battalion left the sector.[5] This situation was the norm in the Lys valley, and indeed along many parts of the front. Where ground conditions were better, for example in the chalk of the Givenchy sector, faster progress was made. Even in the spring of 1916, Edmund Blunden found that that were no communication trenches in the marshy Festubert area out to the front-line posts in the *Islands*;[6] attempts had been made here in December 1915, as recorded by Siegfried Sassoon,[7] to build communication breastworks, but these had simply sunk into the soft ground.

To a great extent, the development of the trench system was dictated by geological conditions. In the early days, trenches and breastworks had to be revetted with locally obtained materials, and countrymen in the British battalions were particularly adept at making hurdles from the willows growing along every stream and ditch in Flanders. Many a dugout was at first a mere lean-to, propped against the side of the trench or breastwork. Farms and cottages close behind the front line were soon denuded of timber and doors for such constructions, as well as for firewood. Progress was speeded up by deliveries of specific trench stores – particularly sandbags, 'A-frames', dugout frames, corrugated-iron sheets, pit-props and trench boards (also known as grids or duckboards), which accelerated during 1915. Later, expanded metal was added to the list of revetting materials, and concrete was widely used for gunpits and strongpoints. Of course, all these had to be carried 'up the line' by infantry working parties – and installed by them ('under the direction of the RE'), the 'Poor Bloody Infantry' indeed. More progress was made as additional RE Field Companies were formed, equipped and sent to the front. The greater quantities of picks, shovels, pumps, bailing ladles and similar RE stores assisted this progress, and later in the war the RE Tunnelling Companies also helped with dugout construction for the infantry. It was only by the application of millions of laborious man-hours by successive battalions during 1915 that the trench system of 'The Old Front Line' gradually approached something like its final form.

In July, 27th Division was responsible for the *Bois Grenier Line*, a continuous rear breastwork position extending through that village (which was later organised for all-round defence). There were also numerous deep communication trenches. In the midsummer of 1915, after the limited success of the Neuve Chapelle attack in March, the German success at Ypres in April and May, and the failure of the Aubers Ridge, Festubert and Givenchy–Rue d'Ouvert attacks in May and June, pessimism about the prospects of an advance was rife, and on 22 July 1915 27th Division's Chief Engineer addressed a memorandum, entitled 'Preparations for Winter', to III Corps, recommending that 'New Communication Avenues should be made by erecting lanes of hurdles or other revetments, backed by earth, built on the surface of the ground', and also that a new breastwork support line should be built in rear of the existing support line, which was liable to waterlogging. In addition, 'rear defended localities' were also to be established.[8]

Gradually, the front line was augmented by support and reserve lines, all linked together by duckboard tracks and communication trenches, the whole forming the first position. The isolated posts, strongpoints and keeps behind the front and support lines were soon linked with this system by communication, switch and lateral trenches. Front trenches were invariably identified by their sector letter, and numbered, but there was infinite scope for naming communication, support and reserve trenches. The trace and strongpoints of the 'GHQ Line' provided an embryonic British second position. By the summer of 1915, after their experiences in the winter and spring battles in which the Allies were attacking, the Germans were also everywhere constructing a second position in the west. Their strategy was to defend in the west while attacking on the Eastern Front. During 1915 they constructed deep dugouts of the type that the British later claimed to be surprised to find when they attacked on the Somme in 1916. In fact the French had already encountered such deep dugouts in the chalk country of Artois (Lorette and Vimy), the Somme (Touvent Farm) and the Champagne, in May, June and September 1915, while the British found them in the captured German lines on the Loos battlefield in September 1915. There was, therefore, no such surprise. The Allies, always on the attack, were not so anxious to dig in, and concentrated on preparations for attack. Nevertheless, by the end of 1915 the Allies too had developed a defence in depth of a sort in most sectors.

1916 – Arras and the Somme

British units taking over new sectors from the French, on the Somme in 1915 and in Artois in 1915–16, often found well-developed trench systems in rolling chalk country. These systems were in various states of sanitation and repair – a common complaint among the British infantry was that the French paid too little attention to proper latrines and burial of corpses – while on the Vimy

Ridge, as a result of the French policy of holding the front with a minimum of infantry while relying on the rapid fire of their excellent 75mm field guns, it was found that the French trenches ('of the crudest description') were disconnected and in an extremely poor state, an effective truce with the enemy having to be observed while they were connected, deepened and put into repair. Even on the high, chalk terrain of the Vimy Ridge in March 1916, the ground was a quagmire, littered with unburied corpses from the battles of the previous year.[9] As we shall see in subsequent chapters, French trenches were found to be systematically named, and these names were, in most cases, soon changed by their new inhabitants.

The German offensive at Verdun in February 1916 found the French ill-prepared. The defence of this crucial fortress sector had been based on the rings of permanent brick, stone and concrete forts, with their retractable steel gun and machine gun turrets, and field fortifications had been neglected. This was only partially remedied by the construction by the French of trench lines on the left bank behind Verdun, and just before the German attack by a new intermediate defence line ordered by de Castelnau in front of Verdun on the right bank. As a result, the Germans almost broke through in the first few days, only being held at bay by a heroic defence in hastily dug trenches. The French commanders were forced to compensate for the lack of good defensive positions by piling up men upon men, to be pounded to pulp by the superior German artillery. In fact, even where trenches were dug, the artillery soon flattened them.

Battle of the Somme, July to November 1916

The Verdun and Somme battles of 1916, with their overwhelming and ground-pulverising bombardments by heavy artillery, were the first large-scale operations during which not only individual trenches but also whole trench systems disappeared. They were simply obliterated by the shelling, and the process of degradation of their remains was accelerated by periods of wet and frosty weather. In places the whole battlefield, like that of much of Third Ypres the following year, became a morass. The digging and maintenance of trenches became impossible in this flooded terrain, and men held shell-hole positions where they could, movement, in the absence of communication trenches, being possible only at night. Men, both wounded and unwounded, were known to drown in the mud; even when they were found alive, they could often not be extracted by their mates. However, much of the Somme battle was fought for the possession and consolidation of specific trench lines, and many new trenches were dug by both the Allies (British and French)

The war of the guns: A battery of British improvised 8-inch howitzers in position in Caterpillar Valley on the Somme battlefield, firing by the map and observation to bombard the German defences prior to an attack.

and the Germans in the summer, autumn and even winter of 1916. The lesson learned at Verdun was reinforced on the Somme in the summer and autumn of the same year, and led the Germans to adopt a new system of defence in depth, abandoning the rigid, continuous trench lines that, when accurately plotted from air photos on to the trench maps, provided such an obvious artillery target. This new defence system proved its worth on the Aisne and at Ypres the following year.

The 1917 Battles

Following the Battle of the Somme ('the muddy grave of the German field army'), heavy German losses caused by their defensive policy of continual counter-attack to regain lost ground within the context of continuous trench lines (which formed ideal targets for artillery bombardment) led to a reformulation of their defensive policy. Colonel von Lossberg of the General Staff developed a new system of defence-in-depth, based on the

A British II Corps sign, now in the Imperial War Museum, prepared for the assault on Vimy Ridge in April 1917, showing the direction to the Advanced Cage, Pulpit Crater. This was east of Neuville St Vaast. Advanced cages were temporary holding places, fenced with barbed wire, for prisoners captured during an advance.

interlocking fields of fire of numerous strongpoints distributed throughout the zone behind an outpost line. This new system was not adopted before the Hindenburg Line (*Siegfried Stellung*) was built, and in fact rendered the Hindenburg system obsolete. It was, however, influential in the layout of German dispositions during the Arras battle, and particularly during Third Ypres. During the latter battle, German defensive policy depended on heavily wired rear positions, covered by masses of pillboxes and shell-hole positions arranged in a chequer-board pattern behind them. These were intended to so thin out the attacking troops that they would fall easy prey to counter-attack divisions waiting out of British artillery range.

The German defences on the Arras battlefield were a hybrid in two senses. Firstly, in the northern part they were essentially the old defence system, augmented by new rear positions, notably the Drocourt–Quéant Line, while south of the Scarpe, starting at the immense redoubt known to the British as *The Harp*, the new *Siegfried Stellung* broke from the old main position towards the south-east, running past Saint-Quentin to join the old front system once more north of the Aisne. Secondly, the Germans had not completed their reorganisation in terms of a conversion to the tactics of defence-in-depth and counter-attack. Aspects of the Arras battle, notably the British plan to use predicted artillery fire for counter-battery work, based on increasingly efficient flash-spotting and sound-ranging techniques and air-photo interpretation, and compilation of these enemy-battery-location results using sophisticated statistical techniques, and fuller cooperation between tanks, cavalry, infantry, artillery and flying corps than had happened on the Somme, demonstrated that the British Army was becoming forward-looking and more scientific in its approach. However, it was not until the Battle of Cambrai in November 1917, and the Battles of the Hundred Days in 1918, that the new operational and tactical methods were fully exploited. In the meantime, trench warfare and semi-open warfare predominated.

During the course of the Messines and Third Ypres battles the German trenches in the area to be attacked were pulverised by shelling, and from the opening of the latter battle (31 July) their remains became uninhabitable through flooding caused by heavy rainfall and the impermeable nature of much of the soil. The British Army, through its prolonged artillery bombardment, created its own obstacle. Tanks, guns and infantry became bogged down during the August fighting, and again in October and November. In fact, ground conditions became so atrocious that the tanks were withdrawn from this sector; they found firm going on the unshelled chalk terrain at Cambrai. Partly as a result of the new German defensive tactics, the battlefield of Third Ypres displayed certain characteristics distinguishing it from those of earlier engagements, and a concomitant of this type of fighting (and terrain) was the lack of definite trenches and trench names. The attacking British, Canadian and Anzac forces found themselves fighting many small battles to capture individual German pillboxes, clusters of pillboxes, or concrete gun-pits often constructed in and among the ruins of old farm buildings. Thus trench fighting became the exception rather than the rule during Third Ypres, troops surviving in shell-hole positions and captured German pillboxes, various types of concrete structures built from 1915 as a protection against shellfire.

The Winter of 1917–18: Preparations for the German Offensive

Following the Russian revolutions of 1917, particularly the Bolshevik coup of October–November, their military effort was clearly at an end as far as fighting the Central Powers was concerned. The Germans could now concentrate on the Western Front in an attempt to knock out the British and French before massive American reinforcements could arrive. The British position in northern France and Flanders was perilous, as they had their backs to the Channel ports with not a great depth of country behind them; as actually happened in 1940, the great danger was that the Germans would drive through to Abbeville and divide the Allied forces, cutting the BEF in half. The British had always embraced defence-in-depth, but now they also adopted the German system of defensive zones. The certainty that Germany would transfer significant forces from the Eastern Front led to a sudden switch to a defensive stance; hitherto British operations had been primarily offensive, and this had led to the neglect of proper surveys and mapping of British trenches and defensive works.

Army commanders were asked for their views on defensive organisation, following which GHQ on 14 December 1917 issued instructions for the creation of three defensive zones, named *Forward*, *Battle* and *Rear*, all defended in depth on the German model.[10] Old trench systems, now in rear of the front line after the Allied attacks of 1915–17, were included in the schemes, and new maps were drawn up showing these. All armies pressed ahead with the construction of defences and the preparation of new maps showing all actual and proposed works. In January 1918 the previous misguided policy on secret editions was relaxed, and it was ruled that all 1:10,000 trench maps should show British trenches. A new secret edition of the 1:20,000 scale sheets was authorised at the same time for defence purposes. Colonel Jack, of 'Maps GHQ', noted that:

> Monthly defence schemes, reports on defence lines, etc., necessitated the production of large numbers of these secret 1/20,000 maps, which, owing to the absence of an official issue, had to be drawn by hand. This was recognised by the order of January, 1918, which permitted the production of a secret 1/20,000.[11]

Defence positions were not just a matter of trenches and strongpoints. On Third Army front south of Arras, VI Corps's defence scheme included maps showing the general organisation of the defences, distribution of defence garrison by battalions with HQs of formations and units, artillery positions, heavy and field artillery, SOS lines and OPs, corps and divisional boundaries, machine gun defence, administrative areas, light railways, tram lines and main dumps, dressing stations and tracks, road traffic routes and rendezvous and routes into the battle zone. There were also large-scale plans of the defences of the more important defended localities.[12]

On 10 January 1918 GHQ sent secret instructions to Rawlinson's Fourth Army to draw up plans for a retirement from the Passchendaele (actually most of the Ypres) Salient, in order to shorten the line so that divisions could be released for a general reserve.[13] Rawlinson envisaged withdrawal to the line Polygon Wood–St Julien, but he thought it might take four days to move the heavy artillery back over the terrible ground.[14] New defensive positions, including trenches wherever possible in the shattered and waterlogged ground, were prepared.

It had unfortunately been decided that Gough's Fifth Army, moving south from the Ypres battle at the end of 1917, should take over part of Third Army's right flank, but a new agreement with the French soon led it to extend the British line southwards, taking over the Saint-Quentin–La Fère front and eventually finding itself near Barisis, between Noyon and Laon. French maps taken over by Fifth Army did not show much in the way of rear defences, not even marking the *Rear Zone* as planned works (*projet*).[15] On 4 February, Lieut. Rothwell, of 'R' Sound Ranging Section,[16] saw much staff reconnaissance and digging of rear defence lines and strongpoints between 4,000 and 5,000 yards behind the front in his sector. Studying a secret defence map at Grand Seraucourt, he noted that the existing British front system was overprinted in blue as the *Forward Zone*, the new system being dug was shown in red as the *Battle Zone*, while a third unnamed zone marked in green farther to the rear was plotted along features that led themselves naturally to defence; this was known with desperate humour as the *God Help Us* line.[17]

Other armies printed similar rear defence positions showing the names given to these lines, which were in some cases continuous wired trenches and in others posts and isolated stretches of trench. In all cases, these lines, whether dug continuously or not, were wired, and posts or defended localities were wired all-round and organised for all-round defence.

The German Offensives of 1918 and Subsequent British Defence Lines

The German offensives of March and April did not, luckily for the Allies, succeed in capturing Amiens, reaching the Somme estuary and forcing the British forces thus isolated north of the Somme back on the Channel ports.

Early in 1918 when Fifth Army took over more front from the French as far south as Barisis, beyond La Fère, existing French trench names were adopted or the trenches renamed. The area was divided into *Forward*, *Battle* and *Rear Zones*, like the rest of the BEF front, but Fifth Army in particular was spread too thinly. Behind the front trench system was the area devastated by the Germans before their retirement to the Hindenburg Line in 1917, and behind this again was the destroyed terrain of the old Somme and Arras battlefields, with their shell holes, lengths of bombarded and eroded trenches, tangles of wire and other hazards. This was not good country for defence, offering many opportunities for infiltration. Behind this destroyed zone again were the *Outer* and *Inner Amiens Defence Lines*, protecting the crucial railway junctions at Amiens. Beyond that city lay Abbeville and the sea.

British troops occupied the southern sector only briefly, for in March the Germans attacked and Gough's Army was, together with the right of Third Army to its left, forced to retire on Amiens across the old battlefields of 1916–17. While a certain amount of trench renaming had occurred in previous years, the 1918 battles, sweeping backwards and forwards across old battlefields in which the trenches had been shelled to bits or fallen in through neglect, saw an unprecedented amount of renaming.

Following the retreat of Fifth and Third Armies, two special 1:20,000 map sheets of the area between Doullens and Amiens were hurriedly prepared by a Topographical Section to show a rear defence line, the *GHQ Line* in the Villers Bocage–St Sauveur–Argoeuves–Floxicourt area, and printed in April and May. The *GHQ Line* was shown as at 29 April and 9 May respectively, running in front of Villers Bocage, Bertangles and Vaux-en-Amienois, and then south-west through the Ailly-sur-Somme, Dreuil-les-Amiens and Bovelles area. The 3rd Field Survey Company printed regular sheet *57eSE* on 11 May with the trenches of the *Amiens Defence Line* as existing on the previous day.[18] The 5th Field Survey Company, soon back in operation after the retreat, overprinted the new back-area sheet *62aSE,* covering the area to the west of Amiens, with new defence lines that were being constructed, and three successive editions (trenches dated 22 May, 1 June and 2 July) recorded the development of these lines. Even if the Germans captured Amiens, they would face further resistance before reaching Abbeville and the sea.

In Flanders, MacLeod's 4th FSC carried out an extensive programme of 1:10,000 back-area mapping following the Lys battle in April. Regular series 1:20,000 sheets existed as far west as Saint-Omer, but these had been hastily plane-tabled by the 1st Ranging Section in early 1915, and needed revision and correction. All the new rear trench lines also had to be plotted, and this work was based on plane table survey and air photos. During the summer of 1918, 4th FSC/B conducted a three-month programme of mapping in the Hazebrouck area using this method, during which more than twenty 1:10,000 regular series sheets were produced. The area covered was about 5 square miles per man per month. The work of XV Corps Topographical Section, including assistance with back-area surveys, may be taken as typical of all Corps Topographical Sections at this time. It overprinted German and British defences and tactical information with the duplicator. British defence construction work was surveyed, and special maps were produced showing these back lines, with their names.

The Allied Counter-Offensives and the Final Advance

The battles of the 'hundred days', from 8 August to the Armistice, were fought over the old battlefields of the previous four years and few new trenches appeared. The principal new defensive positions encountered were the German rear positions, which are dealt with in Chapters IV and IX.

Trench Life and Routine

For most of the war, on most of the front, the trench systems had become veritable subterranean cities, in which the garrisons lived and worked according to a well-administered routine. The staff bureaucracy extended its tentacles forward from GHQ to Army Headquarters, and thence to corps, divisions, brigades and finally the battalions holding the reserve, support and front lines. Every battalion headquarters had its clerks, typewriters and telephonists, supervised by the adjutant, the right-hand man of the battalion commander, assisted by the signal officer. In 1916 each battalion appointed, in addition to its bombing officer, intelligence officer, gas officer and Lewis gun officer, many of whom were also platoon commanders, a 'field works officer', whose task it was to supervise the daily maintenance of the trenches. Hitherto this had been a task for the Royal Engineers ('sappers'), assisted by infantry working parties, but the RE could not cope with routine maintenance in addition to all their other duties.

There is a huge literature on trench warfare, and this is not the place to develop the theme. Most readers are familiar with at least some of the original war writers – Robert Graves, Siegfried Sassoon, etc. – and the reader who wants to find out more is referred to books such as Tony Ashworth's *Trench Warfare 1914–1918*,[19] and Paddy Griffith's *Battle Tactics of the Western Front*,[20] which themselves refer to an extensive bibliography. An even more revealing source of information is the whole range of unit and formation war diaries in Class WO 95 in The National Archives. Suffice it to say that trench life and routine was a rich source of trench nomenclature, and this theme is developed in the following chapters.

The Landscape and Trench Naming

As the writers and artists involved in the war realised, the landscape of the Western Front helped to create an iconography of the battlefield. Certain images became shorthand signs, immediately recognisable to soldiers and civilians as conveying some important part of the war experience. Many of these signs recurred as trench or topographical names, and some are explored below and in subsequent chapters. Perhaps the most potent visual landscape images appeared in the paintings, drawings and prints of Paul Nash, with their vorticist vocabulary of stark diagonals evoking shattered trees, traversed trenches, starshell light, cloud formations, zig-zag duckboard tracks, wire-pickets, shell-bursts, etc.

Among the war writers, while Edmund Blunden insisted on the ironic contrast of peacetime pastoral landscape with wartime lunacy and destruction, *et in arcadia ego* forming the keynote, the landscape for David Jones was rather a mythologised place, in which the present day soldiers of both sides were part of a historical and cultural continuum of experience. Some form of mixture of precise and local geographical identifications with the vague and semi-mythical, reminiscent of the 'geographical indications' of *The Nibelungenlied*, as described by A.H. Hatto,[21] recurs in accounts of the war. Indeed the Germans, when it came to naming their own trenches and defensive positions, made a great point of using names from Nordic mythology, particularly *The Nibelungenlied*, and incorporated by Wagner into his Ring Cycle; the German name for the Hindenburg Line was the *Siegfried Stellung*, and this was followed by the *Brunnhilde*, *Hunding*, *Wotan* and other rear positions. German naming is addressed in Chapter IX. The British (who may have taken it from French *plans directeurs*) gave the name *Siegfried Copse* to a feature south of the Somme (Vermandovillers). What was true of *The Nibelungenlied*, *The Iliad*, *The Battle of Maldon* and the *Morte d'Arthur* is also, in some sense, true of the First World War. It inhabited at the time, and has become, a sort of mythologised cultural and psychological space. The names tell us something about this and, as has been suggested, serve as keys to unlock some of these doors to a generation's Bluebeard's Castle.

The Enchanted and Mythical Landscape

David Jones was, as always, right and wrong when his artistic sensibility, escaping from south-east London streets, transformed the landscape of the Western Front into one of enchantment. To him, Ploegsteert Wood, and indeed the whole Ypres Salient, were the enchanted forest of Broceliande, and he painted a similar pagan and mythic picture of Mametz Wood, where he was wounded, on the Somme. Irony, of course, is inescapable in this vocabulary of enchantment, when we set the straight literary images against the vile reality of the foul, shell-shattered, stinking landscape. Even in the landscape of the

Passchendaele battlefield, we find *Pan Cotts*, *Peter Pan* and *Wonderland*, *Celtic*, *Cyclops* and *Puck Lodge*, which last, by some magical transposition by a Belgian draughtsman, had evolved out of the British name *Duck Lodge*. We would perhaps expect also to find here Oberon and Titania; but we do not.

The imagination of the field survey cartographers sometimes reinforces this picture; east of the Hindenburg Line, south of Saint-Quentin, they assigned the names *Mystery*, *Magician* and *Dream* to woods, yet were perhaps thinking in theatrical rather than metaphysical terms, as these were in company with *Stepmother*, *Wig*, *Thunder* and (glorious pun) *Ply Woods*. Nearby, west of the Sambre et Oise Canal, were *Saturn*, *Neptune* and *Uranus Woods*, while farther west, in the Itancourt and Berthenicourt sheets, were *Mars*, *Venus* (and *Milo!*), *Jupiter*, *Pegasus*, *Regulus*, *Arcturus*, *Andromeda*, *Orion*, *Castor* and *Pollux Woods*, and *Polaire*, *Pleides* and *Procyon Copses*. There was also *Sphinx* and *Dragon Woods*, and a *Haunted House*. East of the canal were woods named after every sign of the zodiac but for Libra. Also in a no man's land between the magical and the theatrical were: *Mannequin*, *Fairy* and *Charity* and *Juno Woods*, and *Elf* and *Daly's Copses* (Saint-Quentin area). East of Saint-Quentin were *Chariot Wood*, *Grail Copse* and *Cupidon* and *Ciros Copses*, *Diana's Hill* and *Wood*.

The prehistoric, Celtic and iron-age landscape of France and Belgium was remembered in several *Caesar's Camps*, *Druid's Camp* (Hébuterne), *Druid Trench*, *Druid Farm* (Wytschaete), *Woad Farm* (Merville), *Dolmen* (Noyelle-sous-Bellonne) east of Arras, and *Stone* (Ecoivres), which in fact referred to the more prominent of a pair of prehistoric *menhirs*, west of Mont St Eloi. There were many ancient earthworks and standing stones in northern France and Belgium, as archaeologists such as Mortimer Wheeler, serving with the artillery, and 'Ogs' Crawford (3rd Topographical Section, 3rd Field Survey Company and Royal Flying Corps) immediately recognised.

The enchanted landscape also encompassed *Fairy House* (Kemmel), *Pan Post* (Bois Grenier), *Pan Lane* (Bellicourt), *Pan Trench* (Wervicq), various apparitions from *A Midsummer Night's Dream* and related fairy tales: *Bottom Bridge*, *Goblin*, *Dwarf*, *Imp* and *Elfin Banks*, *Ogre Pit*, *Sun* and *Moon Quarries*, *Star Corner* (Vis-en-Artois), *Gargantua Alley* (Gricourt), *Puck Trench* (Bertincourt), *Centaur Copse* (near *Poet Woods*, and west of *Argosy Woods*, in the Athies sheet), and *Odin's Copse* (Vermand). *Unicorn Trench* and *Avenue* appeared at Bullecourt, and *Unicorn Trench* at Rouvroy.

The Hindenburg Line south-east of Arras was the location of a concentration of names from classical and Celtic mythology, many at the southern end given by the French. At the northern end was *Jove Trench* (Neuville Vitasse), and then, just north-west of Bullecourt, a series of German concrete pillboxes, part of the Hindenburg Line defences; *Alpha*, *Beta*, *Gamma*, *Zeta*, *Flora*,

Juno, *Minerva*, *Argus*, *Uranus*, *Mercury*, *Mars*, *Jove*, *Vulcan*, *Pluto*, *Neptune*, *Og*, *Gog* and *Magog* (the last two were sacred to London). On the Somme (Bouchavesnes), were *Jupiter Trench* and *Support*, *Bacchus Trench*, *Pallas Trench* and *Support*, and in the Combles area were *Mars Avenue* and *Prometheus* and *Furies Trenches*. Mars was a particularly appropriate deity, and reappeared in *Mars* (a German pillbox) and *Mars Lane* near Bullecourt. At Bailleul was *Pegasus Farm* and at Elverdinghe, near Ypres, were *Fantasia* and *Erebus Farms*. The Zonnebeke sheet contained a farm-cum-concrete gunpit or pillbox called *Cyclops*, perhaps featuring a single large aperture. *Vulcan* (pillbox) and *Vulcan Alley* appeared at Bullecourt, and a further *Vulcan Alley* at Itancourt. Blunden likened the clouds of an evening sky in Flanders to cherubim and seraphim, and this leads us on to that airy element.

Heavenly Bodies and Phenomena, and the Weather

It was inevitable, as Cyrano de Bergerac might have said, that those who lived in the mud (Napoleon's fifth element) should gaze at the stars. Indeed, a medical officer of the 36th (Ulster) Division on the Somme told his men to do just this.[22] The sky dominated the landscape of Flanders, Artois and Picardy, as the wonderful paintings of Paul and John Nash and other war artists demonstrate, and the outcome of battles often depended on the weather.

The developing science of meteorology has been welcomed at the front by the high command, the artillery and the Royal Flying Corps. The German gas attack at Ypres in April 1915 depended on the wind direction and speed for its success, while for the Loos battle in September 1915 General Haig appointed a meteorologist, Captain Gold, to his First Army staff to advise on the timing of the release of the chlorine gas; however sluggish air blew the wind back in the faces of the British attackers. The advent of British sound-ranging (very much affected by wind direction and strength), also in 1915, led to the proliferation of weather reports throughout the day and, in 1917, the setting up of special 'wind sections', one per army, to supply the sound-ranging sections with local data. The artillery depended on 'meteor' reports to calculate the 'error of the day' and even 'of the moment', while the Royal Flying Corps' operations were greatly influenced by the weather forecasts. Infantry attacks were frequently postponed because of adverse weather conditions, particularly if the supporting artillery forward observation officers could not see their targets.

The opening stage of the Battle of Arras in April 1917 was fought in a blizzard, while the opening and concluding phases of Third Ypres later in the year were washed out. The German offensive in March 1918 succeeded partly because of fog, and so on. Living very much in the open air, especially during operations when no dugouts were available or inhabitable, soldiers were exposed to all weather conditions, and sometimes succumbed to them. Even just holding the line, the condition of 'trench foot' was prevalent in flooded trenches. In the winter, frostbite was not unknown, and deaths from exposure occurred, as Wilfred Owen's poem, entitled *Exposure*, occasioned by his experience lying out in the snow with his company on the plateau facing Serre, witnessed.

Not only did the fate of battles depend on the weather, but the sky was also a place in which danger lurked and from which death plunged. David Jones, steeped in Celtic mythology, imagined the dogs of Annwn riding 'the trajectory zone',[23] while utilising the Wagnerian imagery favoured by the Germans in both World Wars, Thomas Pynchon, writing of the next war, spoke of German rockets hunting the sky 'like Wuotan and his mad army'.[24] It had to be regarded as a third dimension to the battlefield, and watched carefully. Gun and howitzer shells roared and screamed through it, some on trajectories as high as the patrolling artillery observation and photographing aircraft, which were sometimes smashed by them. The burning fuzes (the Royal Artillery's preferred spelling) of mortar bombs tumbling, and shrapnel shells spinning, through the air left trails of fire and sparks at night. The lethal hail of indirect fire of massed machine guns crackled down through the sky to create beaten zones of interdiction. Clouds of gas, depending on the wind direction, wafted across no man's land.

The dramatic events and lighting conditions of autumn and winter skies over the Somme battlefield inspired an array of atmospheric, meteorological and apocalyptic trench names in the Combles–Villers-au-Flos area, to the east of Flers, Gueudecourt and Morval, some of which were reminiscent of George Borrow while others might have come straight out of *King Lear*: *Autumn Support, Stormy Trench, Gusty Trench, Mild Alley, Cloudy Trench, Cirrus Trench, Mirage Trench, Misty Trench, Muggy Trench, Rainy Trench, Foggy Trench, Dewdrop Trench, Hazy Trench, Snow Trench, Slush Trench, Frosty Trench, Windy Trench, Hail Trench, Sleet Trench, Solar Lane, Sunray Trench, Moonray Trench, Beam Trench, Gleam Trench, Shine Trench, Rainbow Trench, Spectrum Trench, Spec Lane, Mercury Trench, Sun Trench, Moon Trench, Star Trench, Comet Trench, Planet Trench, Zenith Trench, Eclipse Trench, Meteor Trench, Atom Trench, Ozone Avenue, Ether Lane, Sulphur Avenue, Brimstone Trench, Molten Trench, Fire Trench, Thunder Trench, Bolt Alley, Lightning Trench, Orion Trench, Pollux Trench* and *The Nebula*.

Captain J.C. Dunn, of the Royal Welch Fusiliers, remarked of this group of 'weather' trenches in the Sailly–Saillisel area on 25 October 1916 that the so-called trenches were but figments of the imagination of the Staff, but that the names had what he called a 'colloquial' use in identifying the locations of the shell-hole positions that provided good concealment and defence for the Germans.[25] He rather implied that names such as *Misty Trench* and *Hazy Trench* were as much to do with the staff's difficulty in making positive identifications of enemy positions as with imaginative systems of nomenclature; such names certainly conjure up for us the realities of the Royal Flying Corp's difficulties in attempting to photograph the enemy trenches in appalling weather conditions. We will encounter this group of trenches again. *Foggy Trench* appeared not just at Combles, but also at Harnes, Vimy and Oppy, while near Fonquevillers appeared *Misty Trench* and *Blizzard Post*.

Townscape and Landscape (Spoke with a Grimly Voice)

The bucolic, pastoral and also industrial aspects of the French and Belgian landscape are well represented in the topographical and trench names. There were many rural industries – farms, lace factories, sugar beet refineries, breweries, coal mines, railway installations, etc., which were important topographical features. They were used as reference points, and some had tall chimneys or other structures that made excellent observation posts. At Armentières the many factory and textile mill chimneys were invaluable for observation, while at Richebourg a lace factory (at *Factory Corner*) housed an observation post known as *The Ritz*, which also gave its name to a nearby trench. In the Steenwerck sheet, the Flemish textile and lace industries were recalled by *Dimity*, *Spool* and *Twine Farms*. A group of textile names also appeared in the Villers-Guislain sheet: *Satin*, *Silk*, *Linen Trenches*. The Roeux Chemical Works east of Arras had many gable ends and chimneys that were invaluable as trig points and aiming points to 3rd Field Survey Company and to the artillery. In the Somme area were several sugar beet works (*sucreries* on the French maps). Quarries, chalkpits, sandpits (*sabliers*), brickworks and tileworks were also common. The names of all these appeared on the maps, and were often also used to identify nearby trenches – *Factory Trench*, etc.

There were many comparatively large urban areas close to the front, or actually in the front line. Ypres, Armentières, Arras, Albert, etc. were crucial bastions, and housed many military and associated activities. As the war went on, the increasingly damaged nature of buildings and landscape was reflected in the names of these features and their associated trenches – *Hull's Burnt Farm*, *Debris Farm*, *Decrepit Farm*, *Wobbly House*, and so on.

The coal mining area around Lens was particularly densely scattered with mining and related industrial manifestations. The pits were known as *puits* or *fosses* on the French maps. Pithead buildings, winding towers and slag heaps (*crassiers*) were everywhere in the Loos district. In Loos itself were *Tower Bridge* (*The Pylons*) and *Loos Crassier*, while nearby were *Puits 14 bis*, the *Double Crassier*, *The Dump* of *Fosse 8*, the similarly flat-topped dump of *Fosse 5*, and the conical slag heaps of *Fosse 3* and *Fosse 9* near Annequin. At Lens an old slag heap in the front line was known as the *Green Egg*. South of here, again in the front line, was the *Burning Bing*, a north British name (also the title of a folk song) given to a slowly burning slag heap.

High Places, Lumps and Bumps

The gently rolling landscape of Artois, Picardy and Cambresis afforded many ridges, hills and ridges, which formed vital observation posts, and the names of these soon found their way on to the maps – the *Lorette Spur* and *Vimy Ridge*, *Greenland Hill*, *Orange Hill*, *Observation Ridge*, *Infantry Hill* and *Artillery Hill* on the Arras battlefield, *Redan Ridge*, *Hawthorn Ridge*, *Thiepval Ridge*, *Usna* and *Tara Hills*, *Chapes Spur* and *High Wood* on the Somme, *Welsh Ridge*, *Highland Ridge* and *Fusilier Ridge* on the Cambrai battlefield, etc. Some of these hills had in the Napoleonic period been crowned by tall timber semaphore telegraph stations, these being commemorated in the names – *Telegraph Hill*, *Ginchy Telegraph*. By association, trenches in these localities were called *Telegraph Redoubt*, etc.

Flanders, while generally fairly flat, boasted some prominent eminences, notably the Monts des Flandres culminating in the *Scherpenberg* and *Kemmelberg*, or *Mount Kemmel*, overlooking the Messines–Wytschaete Ridge. Nearby was *The Mound*, sometimes known as *The Mound of Death* (the British soldier preferred to avoid such hyperbole) at St Eloi. The ridges of the Ypres battlefield – *Pilckem*, *Gravenstafel*, *Bellewaarde*, *Observatory* and *Westhoek Ridges* – and the *Gheluvelt Plateau* were gentle rises, but even a few metres height was sufficient to give commanding artillery observation, at *Crest Farm* and *Abraham Heights*.

There were many hills numbered by their height in metres, taken from the French or Belgian maps and their British derivatives – *Hill 60*, south-east of Ypres, was undoubtedly the most famous, but there were also *Hill 40* at Zonnebeke, *Hill 62* at Sanctuary Wood, *Hill 63* at Ploegsteert, *Hill 70* at Loos, and so forth.

Many lumps and bumps were artificial formations, some ancient, such as the *Butte de Warlencourt* (*Le Sars*), and others more modern – windmill mounds, or spoil heaps formed as the result of excavations for canals and railways, or by mine explosions, the most famous of the former probably being *The Dump*,

Hill 60 and *The Caterpillar* near Ypres. Others in the Zillebeke and Wytschaete areas were *The Bluff, Triangular Bluff, Spoil Bank* and *The Mound* at St Eloi. Some were poetically named: *Sheba's Breasts* (on Vimy Ridge, taken from Rider Haggard's book *King Solomon's Mines*), *The Mound* (east of Arras), *Marion Mound* (Oppy), *Pulpit Crater* (Roclincourt), *Jerusalem Hill* and *Crater, The Hog's Back* at the *Hohenzollern Redoubt, The Pimple* at the north end of the Vimy Ridge and another south of the *Butte de Warlencourt*.

Valleys

Valleys, gullies and ravines were of vital tactical importance for the concealment of troops, guns, dumps and communications, and were therefore shelled regularly. Many names for these features have entered history, as for example *Colne Valley* north of Ypres, *Dead Man's Bottom* east of Railway Wood, *The Ravine* south of Hill 60, *Zouave Valley* west of the Vimy Ridge, *Musketry Valley* and *Tramway Valley* north of the Scarpe on the Arras battlefield, *Happy Valley, Jigsaw Valley* and *Battery Valley* south of the Scarpe, *Battery Valley* south of Grandcourt, *Y Ravine* at Beaumont Hamel, *Sausage* and *Mash Valleys* at La Boisselle, and *Boom Ravine, Death Valley, Nab Valley, Usna* and *Tara Valleys, Avoca Valley, Caterpillar Valley, Happy Valley* and *Chimpanzee Valley* elsewhere on the Somme battlefield. The Cambrai battlefield contained a large group of ravines and valleys: *Grand Ravine, Banteux Ravine, Twenty Two Ravine, Flag Ravine, Pioneer Valley, Oxford Valley*, etc.

Rivers

The natural flow of rivers caused them to give their names to many communication trenches. A large number of these can be found in the Arras area, where German communication trenches north-east of the city were given river names – *Cam, Clyde, Tees, Trent, Tweed*, etc., and in Chapter VIII it will be seen that the Germans made good use of river names.

In the Ypres Salient, before Third Ypres, the British named several of the fortified farms and pillboxes in the German area after rivers (some of these being in turn the names of battles): *Aisne Farm, Fleet Cott., Marne, Nile, Rhine, Seine, Somme, Thames* and *Tiber*. No obvious reason for such naming comes to mind, unless it be that the Germans were using river-worn gravel from the Rhine (the cause of a diplomatic protest to neutral Holland) for the concrete used to construct their pillboxes.

The only example of a river being given a new name on the Western Front appears to be the Warnave River, a tributary of the Lys, south of Ploegsteert Wood, which was renamed McKenna by the Canadians. This name appears on a 1:10,000 map of the Ploegsteert Wood area dating from around April 1915.[26] There is no indication why it was renamed; the original name was shown on maps, and was hardly unpronounceable. The Canadians later named many railways and roads in the Lens–Vimy area (see Chapter V).

Shape

Many trench and woods names were derived from the accident of planimetry. The cartographer would look at the shape and, like the reaction to the later Rorschach ink blot, come up with an association. The plan view of a feature on the map or air photograph would suggest the name, or at least part of it. Pilots and observers of the Royal Flying Corps were especially grateful for these distinctive silhouettes, which enabled them to locate themselves when lost, and also to get their orientation. Thus we find along the front such names

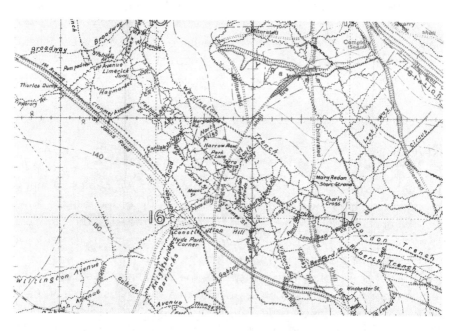

British early 1917 trench map of *Y Ravine*, so called from its plan view on the map, and the area to its south. This was between Beaumont Hamel and Hamel, just north of the River Ancre on the Somme battlefield. First assaulted on 1 July 1916, the German positions here (on the right of the map) were not captured until November.

as *Leg of Mutton* and *Needle Woods* (Bouchavesnes), *Tent Peg Copse* near Westroosebeke, *Norah's Arm*, *Clara's Fan* and *Irma's Elephant* near Aubers and Richebourg, *Elbow Wood*, *The Kink* near the *Hohenzollern Redoubt*, *The Lozenge*, *Calling Card Wood* north-east of Riencourt-lez-Cagnicourt, *Y Wood* west of Hooge, *Y Ravine* at Beaumont Hamel, the *Y Sap* at La Boisselle, *Bois en Hache* east of Notre Dame de Lorette, *Cigarette* and *Diamond Copses*, *Round Wood* and *Lozenge Wood* near Bécourt, *Square Wood* and *Triangular Wood* near St Eloi, *Starry Wood* near Vermandovillers, *Acid Drop Copse* and *Acid Drop Trench* west of Mametz Wood, *Sabot Copse* and *Flatiron Copse* near Mametz Wood, *Pendant Copse* (Serre), *The Harp* and *The String* (Neuville Vitasse), *Tadpole Copse* (Quéant), *Rudder Copse* north of Saint-Quentin, *The Quadrangle* near Mametz Wood, *Step Wood* and *The Ribbon* (Fonsommes), *Hindleg Wood* (Maricourt) and *Sword Wood* near Péronne. South of the Somme (Vaux sheet) were *Oval Wood* and *Triangular Wood*. Although the famous *Polygon Wood* was in the Ypres Salient (Zonnebeke), there was another on the Somme (Vermandovillers). Although there were several *Diagonals* and *Diagonal Trenches*, Harry Potter fans will be disappointed to find that there does not appear to have been a *Diagon Alley*.

The Natural World

Trees. The agricultural landscape of France and Flanders was, and is, punctuated at frequent intervals by forests, woods and copses, while many villages were surrounded by orchards. Apart from their associations with the enchanted forest of David Jones, and the outraged bucolic pastoral of Edmund Blunden (who pointed out that trees on the battlefield had been well-described by Dante), trees were highly significant features of the battlefield, serving as reference points for all arms, as artillery, trench mortar and machine gun aiming points, as orienting points for the infantry, and as trigonometrical points for survey and mapping. They also provided shelter from observation, cover from fire, raw material for trench and dugout construction and fuel for fires. Shattered trees on the battlefield provide some of the starkest images of the horrific effects of shellfire, and we see these captured in the paintings, drawing and prints of Paul and John Nash, in photographs taken by official photographers (on the Gillemont–Ginchy road on the Somme, and at Château Wood at Hooge and Garter Point in the Ypres salient). As Blunden pointed out, trees on the battlefield had been described centuries before by Dante in his *Inferno*.

Examples of the many prominent tree features were *Lone Tree* (many of these, the most famous being on the Loos battlefield), *The Danger Tree*,

Lone Pine (Gallipoli), *The Kaiser's Oak* (Gommecourt), *Ten Tree Alley*, *Snipers Tree*, *Broken Tree* (east of Ploegsteert Wood) and *Broken Tree House* (east of St Yvon). Important reference points on the Somme for the artillery and trig points for survey and mapping were the *Filiform Tree*, *Shamrock Tree*, *The Poodles* (Ovillers) and *Forked Tree*. Sometimes *Prominent Tree* was the only title, and there was a *Solitary Elm* west of Saint-Quentin. A group of communication trenches in the Bois Grenier sector was named in 1915 after trees: *Willow Avenue*, *Elm Street*, *Thorn Street*, *Oak Street*, *Ash Street*. *Oak Trench*, *Ash Trench* and *Walnut Trench* appeared in the Hébuterne sheet, and the last also appeared at Fampoux. In the Gouzeaucourt area were *Plane Trench*, *Beech Avenue*, *Fir Support*, *Poplar Trench* and *Chestnut Avenue* (Villers-Guislain). Many trees, shrubs and other growths appear south-east of Arras: *Bramble*, *Deal*, *Fern*, *Leaf*, *Chestnut*, *Cedar*, *Damson*, *Orange*, *Date*, *Alder*, *Box*, *Poplar*, *Withy* and *Moss Trenches*, and *Apple*, *Fir* and *Acorn Alleys*, *Tree*, *Twig*, *Oak* and *Deodar Lanes* (Neuville Vitasse). In the Hooglede sheet were the following: *Birch House*, *Willow Farm*, *Sallow Cross*, *Maple Farm*, *Privet Farm*, *Chestnut Farm*, *Cedar Farm*, *Spruce Farm*, *Hickory Farm*, *Mulberry Farm*, *Hawthorn Farm* and *Cherry Farm*.

The many rivers, streams and ditches of Flanders, Artois and Picardy, being significant tactical features, were always shown on the map, and often we find associated names: in the Ransart and Blairville sector were *The Osier Bed*, *Withy Patch*, *Hedge Street*, *Willows Street* and *Osier Street*, all named after local topographical features. *Yew Support* was near Villers-Guislain. Perhaps the most delightful tree name apart from *The Poodles* was *The Weary Willows* (Vimy).

The 1st Field Survey Company used a system of assonance to name its flash-spotting OPs after flowers and shrubs: *Lavender* (Laventie), *Birch* (Beuvry), *Forget-me-not* (Fosse 9), *Fir Tree* (Fosse 3), *Sycamore* (65 Metre Point), *Laurel* (Lorette), etc.

Orchards and their associated fruit trees were a feature of almost all villages in Artois and Picardy, and are reflected in the trench names in many areas. At Villers-Bretonneux, east of Amiens, were *Orchard* and *Peach Streets*, but these rapidly became more exotic, with *Pineapple* and *Banana Switches* nearby. Sassoon was struck by the pastoral names of a group of German trenches in the Fricourt–Mametz sector – *Apple Alley*, *Orchard Alley*, *Rose Trench* and *Willow Avenue* – which he identified with a 'topographical Arcadia'.[27] He might also have mentioned *Pear Trench* in the same locality.

Vegetables. These were represented by *Cabbage Patch Redoubt* (La Bassée; may possibly refer to The Cabbage Patch pub at Twickenham), *Turnip Alley* (Grugies/Itancourt), *Turnip Lane* (Bellicourt), *Wurzel Street* (Hébuterne),

Wurzel Trench (Fampoux), and many others. Apart from large flower and tree groups, the Hooglede sheet contains many plant and vegetable names; *Myrtle Farm*, *Worzel Farm*, *Cress Farm*, *Artichoke Farm*, *Shamrock Farm*, *Heather Copse*, *Swede Farm*, *Cabbage Farm*, *Potato Farm*, *Mint Copse*, *Parsley Farm*, *Stockweed Farm*, *Moss Farm*, *Barley Copse*, *Nettle Farm*, *Bullrush Farm* and *Dock Farm*. The French also achieved a large group of trenches named after vegetables (see Chapter VIII). The vegetable names remind us that these were also used in the next war for the ill-fated SOE agents and wireless operators in the Netherlands.

Flowers. We all associate poppies with the battlefield, and even during the war this association was being made, notably by John McCrae with his famous poem *In Flanders Fields*. The name does crop up in the trenches, but not in an overwhelming way: *Poppy Redoubt* (Givenchy), *Poppy Lane* (Wytschaete), *Poppy Post* (Villers-Guislain) and *Poppy Trench* (Longueval). The other signifier, this time associated with the Somme battlefield, was the rose. The sentimental song *Roses of Picardy* ensured its enduring place in the mythology of the war. There were a large number of rose names, by no means all in Picardy: *Rose Trench* appeared at Méaulte, Roclincourt, Westroosebeke, Villers-Guislain, Epéhy and Bellicourt, *Rose Alley* at Méaulte, *Rose Reserve* at Le Sars, *Rose Street* at La Bassée and Bixschoote/Westroosebeke, and *Rose Support* at Villers-Guislain.

There were plenty of other flower names, among others: *Tulip Trench* (Rouvroy), *Lilac Cott*, *Tulip Cotts* and *Primrose Cotts* (all Zonnebeke), *Lily Trench* (Bellicourt), and *Lily Road*, *Lily Lane*, *Laurel Lane*, *Lotus Lane* and *Leaf Lane* (Blaireville–Fonquevillers). In the Hooglede sheet, alongside the vegetables listed above, occur *Daisy Farm*, *Primrose Farm*, *Violet Farm*, *Bluebell Copse*, *Dandelion Farm*, *Cowslip Corner*, *Geranium Farm*, *Lobelia Farm*, *Primula Copse*, *Lilly Farm*, *Narcissus Farm*, *Tulip Farm*, *Saffron Farm* and *Pink Farm*. The last two overlap with yet another group relating to colour and pigments: *Black Farm*, *Cobalt Cross Roads*, *Purple Corner*, *Golden Farm*, *Blue Corner*, *Grey Corner*, *Pewter Corner*, *Yellow Corner* and *Indigo Corner*. The presence of composers' names in this sheet reminds us that Stanley Cursiter, 4th FSC's printing officer, was a musician as well as a painter familiar with the pigments obtained from an artists' colour man.

Beasts of the Fields and Fowls of the Air

The names of animals, birds and even insects also feature widely up and down the front. The first to be used were those unfortunate landmarks used as reference points by the troops – *Dead Cow*, *Dead Horse*, and so on. Later the need to name trenches in the enemy zone, well behind the front line, led to many natural names being used. There was, in fact, a proliferation of wildlife. At Richebourg were *Cats Post* and *Dogs Post*. West of Saint-Quentin were *Badger* and *Otter Copses* (Saint-Quentin), while east of the town were *Dog Hill* and *Dog Copse*, *Ferret Wood* (Homblières). In Flanders, the double meaning of *Pike House* led into *Arrow*, *Feather* and *Head Farms*, which were all contiguous in the south-eastern corner of the Wytschaete sheet. *Zoo Trench* appeared at Gouy and Neuville Vitasse.

When it came to naming the Hindenburg Line trenches animals also featured – a sector known as *The Ark* included *Mule*, *Rat*, *Cat*, *Dog* and *Horse Lanes* (Neuville Vitasse). Perhaps inspiration ran out, because the horse was swiftly dismembered into its constituent parts, or at least some of them: *Blaze*, *Ear*, *Eye*, *Head* and *Hoof Lanes*. A German redoubt called *The Zoo* by the British contained *Lion*, *Tiger*, *Leopard* and *Panther Lanes*. We also find *Ant Trench* (Hébuterne), *Antelope Alley* (Rouvroy) and *Antelope Trench* (Lens and Combles).

Animals and birds were particularly well represented in the Vis-en-Artois sheet, which drew heavily on both these categories and represents a veritable bestiary. Many of the animals were exotic, and they were located near *Jungle Alley* and *Spoor Lane*: *Shikar*, *Buck*, *Bison*, *Monkey*, *Tiger*, *Stag*, *Panther*, *Lion*, *Ape*, *Boar* and *Ibis Trenches*.

Perhaps it was no accident that these were found next to *Orient* and *Occident Lanes*, *Ophir* and *Olga Trenches*, and *Aden Mound*. Others were more prosaic, and even descended to the domestic and insectiferous: *Badger*, *Dog*, *Poodle*, *Puppy* and *Beetle Trenches*. In the Fampoux sheet, just to the north, was *Weasel Trench*, while *Wolves Alley* was near Vendeuil. There were also *Yak Post* (Epéhy), *Goat Redoubt* (Beaumont), *Goat Street* and *Post* (Ficheux), *Goat Trench* (La Bassée/Loos) and *Goat Lane* (Vis-en-Artois and Gouy). Finally, *Zebra Post* and *Trench* appeared near Epéhy and Itancourt respectively.

Many bird names occurred in the Hooglede sheet: *Crane Cross Roads*, *Grouse Corner*, *Partridge Corner*, *Swallow Farm*, *Mavis Farm*, *Blackbird Farm*, *Magpie Farm*, *Corncrake Cross Roads*, *Guinea Farm*, *Moorhen Farm* (by *Decoy Cross Roads*), *Wood-king Farm*, *Hawks Farm*, *Lark Corner*, *Rook Farm*, *Parrot Farm*, *Storknest Cross Roads*, *Dovecot Corner*, *Cygnet Farm*, *Owl Corner*, *Jay Copse*, *Wagtail Farm*, *Linnet Copse* and *Canary Farm*. In trench warfare, the canary was the tunneller's friend, as it gave warning of gas by toppling off its perch.

The bird names in the Vis-en-Artois area swirled around *The Nest* and *The Rookery*: *Albatross*, *Crow*, *Starling*, *Puffin*, *Cuckoo*, *Mallard*, *Robin*, *Bullfinch*,

Wren, *Eagle*, *Lark*, *Pelican*, *Swift*, *Buzzard*, *Swan*, *Falcon*, *Curlew*, *Gannet*, *Heron*, *Shawk*, *Kestrel*, *Egret*, *Thrush*, *Sparrow*, *Duck* and *Bat* Trenches (the last was classified as a bird in this context). The sole insects were *Moth Street*, and *Gnat*, the latter also appearing in the Gueudecourt sheet. East of Fonquevillers and Hébuterne appeared *Ostrich*, *Starling*, *Stork*, *Jay* and *Sparrow* Support Trenches. Near Gouzeaucourt, in the Villers-Guislain sheet, appeared *The Perch*, *Bird Post*, *Fly Catcher Post*, *Swallows Trench*, *Chaffinch Lane*, *Dove Lane*, *Eagle Trench*, and *Quail Lane*. A further group of bird names appears in the Hooglede sheet, near Ypres. In the Hébuterne sheet were *Duck*, *Swan*, *Owl* and *Hawk* Trenches. South of Saint-Quentin, between the Somme and Oise rivers, appear *Starling*, *Titmouse*, *Swallow*, *Guinea Fowl*, *Duck*, *Fowl*, *Robin*, *Warbler*, *Blackbird* and *Magpie Woods* (Essigny-le-Grand and Berthenicourt). *Wren Way* was near Wytschaete. Partly because of the number of French or Belgian hamlets named after the bird, there were many nightingales along the front, including *Rossignol Avenue* (Wytschaete) and *Rossignol* (Beaumont and Ploegsteert). Many writers, from John McCrae to Beech Thomas, noted the larks flying above the trenches, even singing, in the din of battle. This seems to be confirmed by the large number of lark names: *Lark Lane* (Vis-en-Artois/Bullecourt), *Lark Lane* and *Corner* (Wytschaete), *Lark Post* (Quéant and Epéhy), *Lark Spur* (Villers-Guislain) and *Lark Trench* (Epéhy). However, we should always remember the possibility of ambiguity; soldiers were not averse to larking about.

The British never achieved parity with the French in giving unpleasant names to German trenches, but we find *Fly*, *Midge*, *Wasp* and *Bee Farms* near Wytschaete, south of Ypres. In the Hébuterne sheet were *Wasp Trench* and *Support*, *Slug Street* and *Pig Trench*, the latter possibly a reference to the heavy trench mortar bomb known as the flying pig. There were also *Louse Post* (Quéant), *Beetle* Alley (Longueval and Maricourt), *Beetle Trench* (Vis-en-Artois), *Earwig Trench* (Roclincourt), *Ant Lane*, *Bee Lane*, *Bug Lane* and *Tick Lane* (Fonquevillers).

Fish of the Sea (and of Rivers)

Given the prevalence of flooded trenches, it is surprising that fish, and other river and sea creatures did not appear more often on the map sheets. References to Salmon have to be examined closely, as there was a survey officer of that name with 3rd Field Survey Company. In watery Flanders were *Trout*, *Eel*, *Salmon*, *Cod*, *Lake* and *Whale Farms*, and *Pike House* (Wytschaete), while a group of fishy names also appear in the Hooglede sheet: *Speckle Farm* and *Trout Fork*, and *Fillet*, *Cuttle*, *Herring*, *Eel*, *Prawn*, *Mull*, *Mussell* and

Turtle Farms. Farther south, we find *Salmon*, *Trout* and *Roach Trenches* in the Neuville Vitasse sheet, and another group appeared in the Hébuterne sheet: *Fish*, *Cod*, *Grilse*, *Salmon*, *Trout*, *Carp*, *Roach*, *Pike*, *Eel*, *Grayling*, *Bass* and *Herring*. There were also *Trout Copse* (Saint-Quentin), *Eel Copse* and *Trout Copse* (Fonsommes), *Narwal Trench* (Lens), *Whale Trench* (Oppy/Fampoux and Le Sars), and *Crayfish Trench* and *Newt Lane* (Hébuterne).

The next three chapters examine the origin and development of trench names, while Chapters V to VII further explore various significant themes in British trench naming.

Notes

1   11th Brigade War Diary, The National Archives (PRO) WO 95/1486.

2   27th Division General Staff War Diary, TNA(PRO) WO 95/2254.

3   7th Division General Staff War Diary, with sketch maps, TNA(PRO) WO 95/1627.

4   Ibid.

5   Bales, Capt. P.G., *The History of the 1/4th Battalion, Duke of Wellington's (West Riding) Regiment, 1914–1919*, London & Halifax: Edward Mortimer, 1920, p. 14.

6   Blunden, Edmund, *Undertones of War*, London: Cobden-Sanderson, 1928, pp. 9–10.

7   Sassoon, Siegfried, *Memoirs of a Fox-Hunting Man*, in *The Complete Memoirs of George Sherston*, London: Faber, 1972, p. 248.

8   27th Division General Staff War Diary, TNA(PRO) WO 95/2254.

9   Edmonds, J.E., *History of the Great War, Military Operations, France and Belgium, 1916*, Vol. I, London: Macmillan, 1932, pp. 211–12.

10 Edmonds, J.E., *History of the Great War, Military Operations, France and Belgium, 1918*, Vol.1, London: Macmillan, 1935, p. 41.

11 Jack, Col. E.M., *Report on Survey on the Western Front*, Geographical Section, General Staff, War Office, London: HMSO, 1920, p. 48.

12 Edmonds, 1935, op. cit., p. 121.

13 Ibid, p. 44.

14 Ibid, p. 100.

15 Ibid, p. 122.

16 Innes, J.R., *Flash Spotters and Sound Rangers*, London: George Allen & Unwin, 1935, p. 289–90.

17 Ibid.

18 1:20,000 sheet *57eSE*, *Edition 1A*, *3rd FSC (10562) 11-5-18*, showing trenches of *Amiens Defence Line 10-5-18*.

19 Ashworth, Tony, *Trench Warfare 1914–1918, The Live and Let Live System*, London: Pan Books, 2000.

20 Griffith, Paddy, *Battle Tactics of the Western Front, The British Army's Art of Attack 1916–18*, New Haven and London: Yale University Press, 1994.

21 Hatto, A.H. (transl.), *The Nibelungenlied*, London: Penguin Classics, 1975, pp. 396–9.

22 Orr, Philip, *The Road to the Somme, Men of the Ulster Division Tell Their Story*, Belfast: Blackstaff Press, 1987, p. 112.

23 Jones, David, *In Parenthesis*, London: Faber & Faber, 1937, p. 52.

24 Pynchon, Thomas, *Gravity's Rainbow*, London: Picador (Pan Books), 1975, p. 72.

25 Dunn, Capt. C.J., *The War the Infantry Knew*, London: Jane's, 1987, p. 268.

26 Map in *The London Rifle Brigade, 1859–1919*, Naval & Military Press reprint.

27 Sassoon, Siegfried, *Memoirs of an Infantry Officer*, in *The Complete Memoirs of George Sherston*, London: Faber, 1972, p. 322.

II

THE EARLY DEVELOPMENT OF TRENCH NAMING BY THE BRITISH, 1914–15

In the Introduction we briefly examined the phenomenon of naming. This and the following two chapters look at why trench names arose in 1914, and how they subsequently developed, while subsequent chapters deal with patterns of naming and compare British with French and German practice. Needless to say, it was not only the British who named trenches. All the warring nations did the same, and at the same time. As most British trench names in the

Coldstream Guards officer and runner at the junction of *Old Kent Road* and *Hertford Street*, Cuinchy Sector, south of the La Bassée Canal, April 1915. (IWM Q50589)

zone of the Old Front Line appeared during 1915, it is worth examining this period closely to see how the practice developed. We shall see that although a system (usually alphanumeric) was apparent from an early date in the designation of front-line or fire trenches, the naming of communication and other trenches developed in a very ad hoc way.

The British official account of 1914–18 survey and mapping – *Report on Survey on the Western Front*[1] – made no reference at all to trench names (or indeed any other sort of names) or naming policy or practice. Nor did it include any illustration of a trench map, as opposed to the topographical map that was used as a base for the former. By contrast, the French equivalent, the *Rapport de Guerre*,[2] contained several references to naming policy, and included many coloured extracts from trench maps of various scales, some of which included names. It is a mystery why British official sources were so reticent on this point, but it was clearly not considered to be a significant issue as it was in the French Army. Any British instructions that were issued were concerned with matters such as scale, reference systems and scales of issue, rarely with names. When names were mentioned in instructions or orders, it was on an army rather than a whole BEF basis. Similarly with censorship, which was applied on a discreet and local level. Second Army decreed in 1915 that coordinates should be used in preference to local names and, where names were used, forms offensive to the command – possibly because the generals feared the possible effect on morale – were adjusted accordingly; thus *Stink Post* became *Odour* (more properly *Oder*, one of many house and farm names in the Salient given river names by the British) *Houses*, *Shell Trap Farm* became *Mouse Trap Farm*. This early squeamishness was not widespread, and did not prevent certain appropriately gruesome, or merely realistic, names becoming established at an early date – for example, *Shellfire Corner*, *Shrapnel Corner* and *Suicide Corner* in the Ypres district.

The use of names was also a security risk, particularly if the enemy captured a trench map on which the names of Allied trenches were shown. Intercepted messages (the Germans regularly overheard British field telephone messages at the front, via their listening sets) or captured orders could immediately be located in space. There were further implications; as that master cryptanalyst Cyrus H. Gordon pointed out, in a higher-level context than that of simple tactical messages, that one of the most frequent errors made by cryptographers was to insert proper names in plain text. By the clues to the content thus provided, they supplied the enemy with an opening wedge for decipherment. It is no coincidence that proper names are the most frequent keys to the decipherment of ancient scripts.[3]

But the warning was equally valid for low-level battlefield messages, which were regularly deciphered by the Germans. Wireless was used from 1914 for artillery–air cooperation, and later in the war for intercommunication between formations down to brigade level. Even when messages were not sent *en claire*, which they frequently were in 1914, there were ample opportunities for interception and decryption. In the period of the Battle of Arras (April– May 1917), a warning was circulated that the Germans were breaking British Playfair codes.[4]

Large-scale topographical maps, usually squared for artillery use, were soon duplicator-printed and lithographed in the field, but at first did not feature the trenches – a peculiar omission. The reason was that trenches could only be plotted accurately from air photos. There were very few of these in the early months, and the techniques of plotting trenches from them on to a good base map were only beginning to develop. German trenches (rarely British) began to be shown on lithographed field-printed maps in the spring of 1915, but trench names rarely appeared on the first such productions. Even on the eve of the Second Battle of Ypres (April 1915), the trenches were not printed on the maps issued to British and Canadian divisions taking over from the French in the Ypres Salient; they had to be drawn on laboriously by hand. Luckily the divisions were able to benefit from excellent French 1:20,000 *plans directeurs*, on which the German trenches were printed in blue, though without names. The Allied trenches, however, still had to be added in manuscript.

We can therefore conclude that trench names were mostly bestowed in the first instance by the troops on the ground, initially nearly always reflecting regimental names and their geographical origins and associations, and also local features. It has always been an infantry drill to nominate reference points, for fire-control purposes and for use as rendezvous, etc. Thus appropriate graphic names were given at the same time to significant buildings and other features – *Dead Cow Farm*, *Rifle Farm*, *Thatched Cottage*, *Lone Tree*, and so on. Such trench and other names were not always used at a higher level; Second Army insisted that farms should be known only by their map references (names had sometimes been changed in a very confusing and dangerous way), and that front trenches should be numbered – *Trench 36*, etc. Corps within Second Army adopted their own numbering systems, but always numbering from the right – i.e. the southern end of their frontages – as was traditional military practice.

How Trench Names Arose – the Battle of the Aisne

The naming of British trenches and posts, begun, according to the Official Historian, in the British Expeditionary Force on the Aisne in September– October 1914 by Brigadier-General Hunter-Weston (GOC 11th Brigade,

4th Division), gradually became a general practice during the winter of 1914–15.[5] As usual, the truth is rather more complex. Names were first given by the rank and file and also, slightly later, by their commanders. The former tended to be informal, nostalgic, ironic and humorous, the latter more formal, commemorative, regimental and descriptive. These two strands – naming from below and naming from above – intertwined throughout the war.

At first trenches were referred to in messages and orders in terms of the regiments to which their battalions belonged, their companies, and company commanders, but these everyday appellations had not yet become formalised. An 11th Brigade sketch map of 16 September, only three days after the crossing of the Aisne, showed *SLI* [Somerset Light Infantry] *trench* and *RDF* [Royal Dublin Fusiliers] *trench* with a haystack (later to become *Yatman's Post*) centrally to their front. A message of 20 September referred to *Captain Coventry's Trench* ('in turnip field on E of our wood'). The 11th Brigade was certainly naming a few positions by 29 September, when *Pit Post* and *Captain Yatman's Haystack* (where Yatman had an observation post) were both mentioned in messages.[6] A message of 2 October referred to *Bottomley's Pit* (elsewhere referred to as *Bottomless Pit*) and *Yatman's Post*. A 1:20,000 sketch map of the same date, showing the *East Lancs Trenches*, designated *Somerset*, *A2*, *A1 E. Lancs.*, *A. Advanced Post*, *A3*, *A4*, *B*, *B Dummy*, *B Support*, *C1*, *Support* (behind *C1*), *D1*, *D2*, and *Zouave*. *Somerset* and *Zouave* referred to the regiments holding those trenches, while the letters presumably referred to the companies of the East Lancs holding these trenches.[7] A sketch map dated 13 October showed *S[outh] Stafford Trench*.[8] Specific lengths of trenches (mostly still isolated at this stage, but not for very long) had by this time received positive designations. The evidence suggests that most early trench (and feature) naming on the Aisne, and later in the Ypres–Ploegsteert–La Bassée area, was related to the regimental names, and officers' names, of the battalions holding those trenches. An exception on the Aisne was *Hyde Park Corner*, the name given by the Kings Liverpool Regiment to a feature east of the north-south canal cutting through the Chemin-des-Dames ridge.

In a post-war letter to the Official Historian, to clear up a query about the naming question, Hunter-Weston stated:

> my recollection that my 11th Infantry Brigade had names to their trenches even before the Ploegsteert days [October 1914 onwards]. In my training of my brigade at Colchester … before the war, I always laid stress on accuracy in the description of localities and advised my officers to give definite names to localities or posts they were constantly using, if no such name had already been given to these posts on the map.

Thus it was that in our very first trenches ... above the Aisne, the 11th Infantry Brigade gave definite names to their various posts and to the various parts of the trenches which they constructed above Bucy-le-Long ...[9]

In October (he says the 17th, but by then his brigade was in Flanders) Hunter-Weston wrote to his wife about the Aisne trenches, eulogising that:

My trenches are a dream, as made by my men. Officers of other brigades and officers also of the French Army, who are in touch with us, on my left, come round to see them as one of the sights. They are dry, roomy, comfortable, roofed, and in fact almost cosy. The men give their different posts and trenches definite names such as, 'Woodbine Villa', 'Wheatsheaf Inn', or such and such a trench. They are very proud of their work and very happy. The sick rate in these trenches north of Bucy was less than in our barracks at Colchester. I look after my men though I work them hard.[10]

These first names were clearly given from below, by the non-commissioned ranks.

Hunter-Weston was not the only person responsible for naming trenches and features on the Aisne, and his 11th Brigade not the only formation that made use of this practice. As we have seen, for all officers and NCOs, the naming of posts and reference points was part of their pre-war tactical training. The 1st Division's sketch maps on the Aisne from 2 October 1914 referred to *Lomax Hill* (west of Bois de Bourg, east of Courteconne), *Emergency Trenches*, *Zouave Trenches* and *Rifle Point* (west of Moussy). *Lomax Hill* had been named by Sir Douglas Haig, commander of I Corps, after Major-General S.H. Lomax, the commander of 1st Division, who had his headquarters there from 15 to 20 September.[11] Haig, later to become C-in-C, was thus one of the first figures to be instrumental in naming positions on the Western Front. Unfortunately, the name was thereafter forgotten, and did not appear on the British 1:20,000 trench maps of this area produced in May 1918. In fact, French *plans directeurs* of the Aisne area produced during the war bear no evidence at all of the British presence there in September–October 1914.

Naming Recommences – Flanders 1914

The move of the BEF from the Aisne to Flanders in the first half of October 1914 signalled a brief return to a war of movement, and trench naming was, for a short while, a thing of the past. However, after the encounter battles of La Bassée and First Ypres in October and early November, trench warfare (or rather stalemate) immediately developed once more. In the Ypres Salient, the close country with its scattering of woods, road and track junctions and unnamed farms lent itself to spontaneous naming in a situation in which military necessity demanded reference names. Where they were printed on the existing Belgian military maps used by the Allies, the names were immediately seized upon and used. One of the few exceptions was the Bois de Polygone, which of course became *Polygon Wood*. The Belgian farms were generally only known by their owners' names, which were not marked on the copies of the Belgian map, and it is remarkable how many of the woods were hitherto unnamed.

During and after First Ypres, therefore, British names were bestowed on features in the Salient that became significant landmarks in later battles – the *Menin Road*, *Greenjacket Ride*, *Northampton Farm*, *Sanctuary Wood*, *Shrewsbury Forest*, *Black Watch Corner*, *White House* (*White Chateau*), *Stirling Castle*, *Clapham Junction* and so on. Hill 60 east of Zillebeke was named after its metric height shown on the map. *FitzClarence Farm* was in fact misnamed on later maps; the Official Historian noted that during the preparation for reproduction of the British map in the winter of 1914, the name was shifted slightly, and the farm so designated throughout the war was in fact not the one used by Brigadier-General FitzClarence during First Ypres.[12] After First Ypres, the British handed the Salient over to the French, and did not reoccupy it until the early months of 1915. Maps showing these names were lithographed by the GHQ Printing Company RE during the winter of 1914–15. German salients and other easily identified strongpoints were the first enemy trenches to be named by the British. At Le Pelerin, just north of Le Gheer, east of Ploegsteert Wood, a wired group of buildings forming a strong German salient was soon called the *Bird Cage*, from the appearance of its surrounding entanglements on air photos, and was still known by this name at the time of the Messines battle of June 1917.[13]

As in the early days of stalemate on the Aisne, the first trenches in Flanders were short, disconnected lengths with no communication trenches. Local advances and retirements meant that the line did not stabilise for some weeks, but when it did greater efforts were made to consolidate the existing trenches into something like a proper defensive system, to dig communication trenches to the rear, and to construct breastworks where the high water table made the trenches flood. As the system became more permanent, trench names soon appeared once more on some of the, initially manuscript, sketchy and embryonic, trench maps which were first drawn at this time. On brigade sketch maps of the October–November period, the trenches were usually identified by the regimental names of the units holding them. However, many such sketch maps produced during the winter of 1914–15 still did not show the local trench names, if they existed.

In Flanders, Hunter-Weston's brigade was once more at the forefront of naming and, what is more, the Brigadier did not, at first, seem in the least to mind his affectionate 'figure-of-fun' nickname being used – he was known in the Brigade as 'Hunter-Bunter'. On 24 October his brigade headquarters was in the *Café Royal* at Ploegsteert.[14] It was here that 11th Brigade began naming trenches and other features in earnest. Hunter-Weston noted that:

> At Ploegsteert all the trenches of the 11th Infantry Brigade and all the communication paths through Ploegsteert Wood had their definite names. For instance, the two main communications up through Ploegsteert Wood were called respectively 'Strand' and 'Regent Street'. The first, second and third lines of defence were called respectively 'Tourist Line', 'Hunter Avenue' and 'Bunter Avenue'. 'Tourist Line', which was just inside the edge of the Wood was so called because it was into this line of trenches that we were able to bring Lord Balfour and the other distinguished folk who came to see our lines and to have a look at the German trenches which were within a few yards of Tourist Line.
>
> The Headquarters shelter of the Somerset Light Infantry was called 'Somerset House'. The Headquarters of another of my battalions was, I see, called the 'Carlton Restaurant' and the shelter for the immediate reserves was called 'Hunter's Town'.[15]

By the turn of the year, however, Hunter-Weston's sense of humour seems to have suffered, to the extent that *Bunter Avenue*[16] was renamed *Bunhill Row*, one of the many names apparently bestowed in this area by the London Rifle Brigade. During the winter of 1914–15, an impressive array of names, including many London ones, appeared in the Ploegsteert Wood area. Among them were many personal and regimental names, or those descriptive of local conditions, but there were also several flights of fancy: *Mud Lane, Hunter Avenue, Prowse Point, The Tabernacle, Long Island, Holt Corner, Fort Boyd, Three Huns Farm, Hulls Burnt Farm, Spy Corner, The Chateau, Sentry Tree, Broken Tree, Douglas Villa, Baynes Bunk Lodge, Murray's Hut, North Breastwork, Old Bread Street, Old Trench Line, Rough & Ready Villa, Anton's House, Picket House, The Birdcage, Belchiers Cottages, Farmers Rest, Kneller Hall, Dead Horse Corner, Castle Martin, Scawby, Tourist Line, The Tourists Peep, Plugstreet Hall* and *Hunterston North & South*. Among the London names were *The Strand, Bunhill Row, Tothill Fields, Regent Street, Piccadilly Circus, Haymarket, Oxford Circus, Fleet Street, Maximes* [sic] and *Tower Bridge*. Regimental names were *Somerset House*,

Hampshire Lane, *Rifle House* and *Essex Farm*. The Rifle Brigade Orderly Room was very appropriately called the *Palais de Justice*.[17]

On 4 November 1914 a 'Rough sketch of Defensive Position near Lindenhoek to be occupied by 2. S. LAN. R' (2nd Battalion, South Lancashire Regiment) showed short isolated sections of trench but no names.[18] In the same month, front trenches in the same sector were numbered 10–14.[19] In the Zwarteleen–Zillebeke sector in mid-November 1914, just after First Ypres, a 7th Brigade sketch map pinpointing the position of a German trench mortar showed *London Scots* and *Welch* trenches, while a sketch map of the position of the 2nd Battalion, King's Own Scottish Borderers, identifying the occupying companies, showed '*B Co*' and '*C Co*' trenches. In December in the Kemmel sector, 7th Brigade sketch maps only referred to their trenches by the regimental names of the battalions holding them, and to *Centre Trench, Left Trench*, etc. relative to the battalion sector,[20] while at Wulverghem, 5th Division trenches in sectors *A–D* were numbered *1–14*.[21] Clearly, while they may have been appearing unofficially, trench names were not being officially encouraged; in many commands, strict alphanumeric designation was the order of the day. In fact, this remained the case for front-line trenches throughout the war.

London in Germany

Although belonging to a Hamburg trading family with a long history, and himself living in Hamburg, the businessman L.W. Brandt had been born in England and thus had British nationality. One of his sons was Bill Brandt, later to become one of the most famous photographers of the 20th century. The father was one of 5,000 British men who, from 15 November 1914, were interned at Ruhleben racecourse at Spandau, near Berlin. Here, probably unaware of the similar naming taking place far to the west in Flanders, they transformed their prison camp into a 'little England', part of the process involving renaming their alleys Bond Street, Regent Street and Trafalgar Square.[22] The same process of reassurance, of creating a memory space of an environment of peace and security, through naming, was occurring independently and simultaneously in places geographically distant but psychologically similar.

First Army Area 1914–15

Naming also developed slowly along the line, in the areas of other formations. In what was later to become First Army Area, 7th Brigade referred on

Officer at the junction of *Bond Street* and *Conduit Street*, Cuinchy sector, south of the La Bassée Canal, in early 1915. (IWM Q52982M)

26 October 1914 to *the triangle* at Neuve Chapelle,[23] while a 2½-inch to the mile sketch map of the Neuve Chapelle sector on 28 October only identified the British trenches by the regimental names of the units holding them (*Royal West Kents, 9th Bhopal*, [20th & 21st Companies of the Indian] *Sappers & Miners, 47th Sikhs, Royal Fusiliers, Lincolns, 5th Fusiliers, Royal Scots*).[24] A road junction near *Picquet House* at Festubert was called *Hell Corner* in November.[25] In the La Boutillerie sector on 15 November 1914, a 1:20,000 scale sketch map of 'British Lines as existing and German Lines as believed to exist' produced by 7th Division showed British trenches in red and German in blue but indicated no names. Another sketch map of this area at about the same date showed the *GHQ Line* in green. By 18 December 1914, the British trenches in the La Boutillerie sector had received numbered sub-section designations: 'No. 5 Sub Section,' etc.[26]

A lithographed 1:20,000 map of 8th Division front, showing in blue manuscript the position of German trenches attacked on the night of 18–19 December, also showed the British front, communication and support trenches in red, divided (from the right) into sections A to F; these corresponded to the sections known as *A Lines, B Lines*, etc.[27] A 1:20,000 sketch map of the Fauquissart–Neuve Chapelle area, dated 20 December, identified *B Lines* south of Moated Farm (north of Neuve Chapelle), *C Lines* north of Moated Farm, and *D Lines* at Chapigny.[28] The Instruction of 8th Divisional Artillery for the action of the night 18–19 December stated that the 'Primary objective is the hostile trench P5 to J1', and that the 'Secondary objective is the hostile trench P5 to P20'. It went on to instruct '33rd F[ield] A[rtillery] Brigade to open fire at 4.15 p.m. on enemy's trench P5, J 21 C and D, P9 and P14', a confusing mix of arbitrary target numbers and map square references.[29] This shows that the system of arbitrary target numbers for artillery reference purposes was already in use at this early date, as well as the map square reference system.

A 1:8,000 spirit-duplicated map of the Fauquissart–Moulin du Pietre–Aubers area, produced in December, showed the British trenches in manuscript identified by Regimental names – *R Berks R*, *Rif Brig*, *Linc R* – and the German main and other trenches shown in blue and designated by the letters A and B. During December, the construction of 'Pivot Points' or 'Supporting Points' behind the front line had been started, and 8th Division ordered that these should be known as *A1a, A1b, B1, B2, C1, C2*, etc. up to *F5*. These designations corresponded to the lettered 'Sections' or 'Lines'.[30] By the end of the year, 7th and 8th Divisions in the Neuve Chapelle–La Boutillerie area had started to construct twelve 'Pivot Points' or 'Supporting Points' lettered *A–M* behind the front line, 'in support of the existing line of entrenchments.'[31] These points, organised for all-round defence, were soon called 'keeps' on First Army Front. Defence in depth developed fairly rapidly, and by the end of January 1915, the *G.H.Q. Line* behind the front system was supported by points numbered *GHQ 1–16*, while posts in the *Third Line* were named *Fort A, Fort B*, etc.[32]

On 23 January IV Corps issued a letter about the construction of new 'strong supporting points', each to be garrisoned by one or two companies, 'in rear of 2nd line of defence passing through Croix Barbée and Fleurbaix'. It ordained that these should be 'not redoubts or works of that nature but fortified houses, short lengths of fire trenches and Machine Gun emplacements, grouped together and entirely surrounded by an efficient wire entanglement'. Bridgehead positions were also to be constructed to defend various watercourse crossings in the areas of 7th and 8th Divisions.[33] Three days later, IV Corps issued a further letter stating that the fighting in the Givenchy–Cuinchy area on 25 January proved the value of 'points d'appuis' or keeps in rear of the front trenches at both places, and 'saved the situation'. Divisions were therefore instructed to push ahead rapidly with the construction of such keeps. The insecurity of the existing feeble defences was keenly felt, and the letter continued: 'With the exception of the two new works 1A and 1B in rear of "A" and "B" lines of the 8th Division, all these keeps will be fit for occupation and wired up all round by January 31st.'[34]

February 1915 saw the British defence system developing rapidly. As far as names were concerned, an 8th Division defence scheme of 4 February referred, among others, to the *Doll's House* on the La Bassée Road, *Foresters Lane*, *Port Arthur* and *Red Barn*.[35] On 16 February, IV Corps sent a letter to 8th Division trying to rationalise existing designations:

> In order to avoid confusion and admit of ready reference to individual works, the Lieutenant-General Commanding [Rawlinson] wishes the following system adopted in the nomenclature of redoubts and supporting points in the first, second and third lines.[36]

As far as the 1st Line was concerned, 7th Division was instructed to letter these points from the right, with the number of the Section prefixed to the letter, e.g. *1.A*, *3.G*, etc. The 8th Division had to number points from the right of each Section, with the Section letter prefixed to the number, e.g. *A.1*, *A.2*, *E.2*, *F.3*, etc. Points in the 2nd Line were to be numbered consecutively by the corps from right to left, while 3rd Line points were to be lettered consecutively from right to left.[37] Whether the outcome was to clarify or confuse the issue was not subsequently stated. A IV Corps letter of 18 February reported that the 'Port Arthur Salient [is] practically finished, and that the GOC proposed a new communication trench from A1 Post to No. 2 Section of "A" Lines, along which it might be possible to run a tram line.'[38]

Battle of Neuve Chapelle, March 1915

Very large-scale (1:5,000) trench maps were first printed in the field for the Neuve Chapelle attack of 12 March, but although these showed the German trenches in red (plotted from air photos, and unnamed) they did not show British trenches. British positions before the attack included *A–D Lines*, *Port Arthur* and *Crescent Redoubt*. Roads named by the British in this area included *Edgware Road*, *Signpost Lane*, *Chimney Crescent* and *Cameron Lane*. The German trenches were not named by the British (except for the *Quadrilateral* and the *Smith-Dorrien Trench*), but the maps were provided with lettered or numbered reference points for precise designation of targets and objectives. The war diary of 8th Division's CRA referred to the 'Neuve Chapelle 1:5,000 sheet' on 8 March, to trenches on it numbered *18*, *22*, *78* etc., and to *Clump 77*.[39] The Indian Corps also printed its own version of these Neuve Chapelle sheets.

Before the attack, new breastworks and trenches along the Rue Tilleloy and in the orchards behind 'B Lines' were constructed to provide cover for the attacking troops.[40] The *A–F* Section designations remained in use during the period of the battle, and more trench names were appearing. A 1:5,000 spirit-duplicated map of the Neuve Chapelle area, produced before the battle, entitled 'Diagram of Support Trenches "B" Lines', showed *Worcester Way*, *Tram Line*, *Rutland Row communication trench*, *High Street communication trench* and *Posts B1* and *B2*.[41] The pattern of naming in this sector was becoming clear; front trenches and posts retained their alphanumeric designations, but names were being used for communication and other trenches.

Manuscript additions made by 8th Division to the 1:5,000 trench maps printed for the assault showed that new appellations, notably for road junctions and crossroads, proliferated in and around Neuve Chapelle during and just after the battle: *Greybreeks Road*, *Church Road*, *Trivia Cross*, *Gahrwal* [sic] *Cross*, *Gahrwal* [sic] *Road*, *Gurkha Cross*, *Gurkha Road*, *Kukri Cross*, *Graham's Cross*, *Grange Cross*, *West Yorks Orchard*, *Lynedoch Cross*, *Irish*

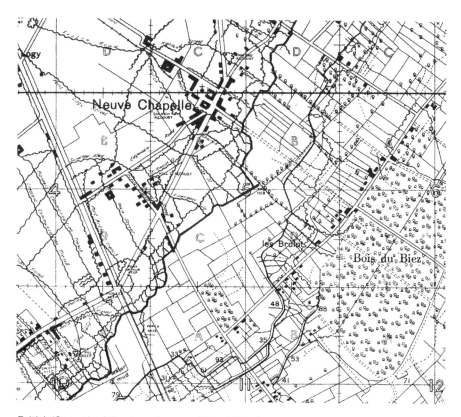

British 'Secret' edition trench map of late-1915, showing the British (left) and German (right) trench systems at Neuve Chapelle. The British First Army (Haig) captured the village in March 1915, and many of the trench names date from that period.

Cross, *Sherwood Cross*, etc.[42] The regimental names and associations, particularly those of the Indian Army, are worth noting.

Operation Order No. 21 of the Meerut Division for the battle echoed the system of alphanumeric designation of front trenches:

> The Dehra Dun Brigade will be in support and will be formed up in positions of readiness in Work A.1, works D.6 and D.7, and the breastwork connecting them, E.7 and E.8, and E.9 and 10, and work about cross roads at St. Vaast.[43]

However, it also instructed that the Garhwal Brigade 'will form for the assault in Port Arthur, Advanced Post No. 2, the trenches along the Estaires–La Bassée Road and in the two new lines of breastwork immediately in rear of them.'[44] Thus some positions were named, others were lettered and numbered, and the new breastworks do not appear to have received any official designation at all.

Between the Neuve Chapelle and Aubers Ridge Battles: March–May 1915

The capture of Neuve Chapelle meant that new trenches and breastworks had to be constructed to the east of the village, and trench names proliferated rapidly after the battle. First Army front was relatively quiet for a couple of months, but on 22 April Second Army experienced the dramatic gas attack heralding the Second Battle of Ypres. In April 1915 in the Richebourg Sector, just south of Neuve Chapelle, the Divisional Section was still designated *E*, with Subsections *E1*, *E2* and *E3*. Certain localities were named: *Orchard Redoubt*, the *Factory* (also known as the *Ritz*), *Cinder Track*, and small keeps at *Chocolat Menier Corner*, *Burlington Arcade* and the *Copse*. Near *Albert* and *Edward Roads* were the *D5* and *D6* works.[45]

The Richebourg–Festubert–Givenchy Sector

A 1:5,280 trace of trenches in 1st Division's area, *Sketch of Position from Rue de Bethune to Givenchy*, dated 28 November 1914, showed roads, fire trenches, communication and support trenches and German saps but no trench names. The front was divided into *Right*, *Centre* and *Left Sections*, and the British trenches were numbered from right to left, and also lettered. No trench names were shown, but reference points were given – *Red cart*, *Green* carts, *Haystacks*, *Lone Trees*, etc.[46] There were few trenches as yet, and it is clear that, at this stage, reference point designations and landmarks had not yet undergone the metamorphosis into formal names. Presumably trench names would have been included on such a sketch map had they existed.

East of Festubert, 4th (Guards) Brigade relieved units of the Indian Corps on 24 December, taking over various trenches including 'the *Dead Cow Trench*' (near *Dead Cow Farm*), a curiously tentative designation, while on 10 January 1915 the brigade was working on *Richebourg Redoubt*. Two days later it was working on the *Big Redoubt* at Richebourg St Vaast, probably the same set of defences, and two days after that it referred to the road junction named *First Aid Corner*.[47] The Guards Brigade remained some time in this sector, one of its roles being to train Territorial and New Army units in trench routine, and *Guards Trench*, east of the Rue du Bois at Richebourg, was a memento of their occupation. A support trench near here was called *Blackadder's*, a name again to be associated with the Western Front by a future generation in the form of the anti-hero of Rowan Atkinson's eponymous television series. This trench was probably (mis-)named after Brigadier-General C.G. Blackader, commanding the Garhwal Brigade of the Indian Corps. In this sector appeared the communication trenches *Mole*, *Pear*, *Peach*, *Plum*, *Hazard* and *Copse Streets*, the London names *Vine Street*, *Bond Street*, *Ritz* (by the *Cinder Track*), *Pall Mall*, *Cockspur Street* and *Embankment*, and *Factory Trench* leading to the observation post in the lace factory known as *The Ritz*.

In December 1914 names for special points or localities were becoming well-established all along the front. 3rd Division referred to several names in the Festubert area towards the end of December: *Tuning Fork*, *Willow Corner*, *Picquet House*, *Willow Hedge* (first line), and *Sap Head* of the South Wales Borderers.[48] *Brewery Corner* near Festubert had also been named by December. A drainage dyke north of La Quinque Rue, in the vicinity of *Dead Cow Farm*, was in April 1915 known as the *Grand Canal*. *Welsh Tree* was also in this area, while *House A* and *House B* were on either side of the Rue de Cailloux.[49]

Battles of Aubers Ridge and Festubert, May 1915

First Army's Aubers Ridge attacks of 9 May 1915 failed totally, but its Festubert attack of 15 May, and the days following gained a little ground. In this attack troops found First Army's maps of this flat, dyked region very confusing. Apart from *North* and *South Breastworks* and the *Quadrilateral*, no German trenches were named on the British maps. Confusion was introduced by showing objectives by small circles on the map, containing arbitrary target numbers, regardless of the nature of the feature to be identified. Most of them were in fact trench junctions. To confuse matters further, the Festubert trench map was full of inaccuracies, with positional errors as great as 450 yards. Worse, it was printed upside down.

On 25 May similar problems were encountered when working parties from the 2nd Brigade moved forward to consolidate the new line at point *L8*. They found it still in German hands; the attacking party, confused by the unreliable maps and the ground, which was 'trenched and retrenched in all directions', had occupied positions farther to the west. The historian of the

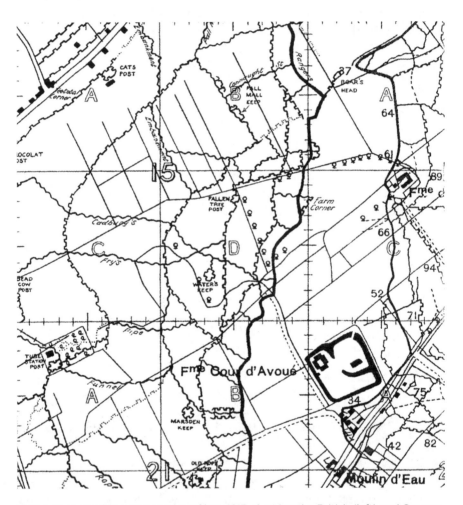

British 'Secret' edition trench map of late-1915, showing the British (left) and German (right) trench systems at Richebourg, south of Neuve Chapelle. The *Boar's Head* salient (German) is at the top, while this and the British communication trenches named *Cadbury's*, *Fry's* and *Pipe* feature in Edmund Blunden's *Undertones of War*.

Post Office Rifles stated that on 22 May they received orders to take over part of the captured trench system, defined on the recent issue of trench diagrams as the sector *K3–J1*, from the Canadians. These points represented junctions between main and communication trenches. A sketch map showing the layout of the sector – trenches and letter/number references for positions but nothing else – was issued to the company commanders.[50] On 23 May 140th Infantry Brigade referred in its *Operation Order No.6* to 'Trench Map 1/5,000', and arbitrary target numbers such as *K5* at Festubert.[51] There is no doubt that the use of trench names would have considerably improved the situation during these operations.

The captured German positions were consolidated and incorporated into the British system, and new communication breastworks were pushed forward. All these trenches were named except for the 'island' outposts closest to the Germans, which were numbered. The old British and German front lines and a German communication breastwork were now marked on the map as *Old German Line*, *Old British Line* and *Old German Breastwork*. The new German front line now pivoted on a rump of their old front position, and this was now named the *Boar's Head*, from its appearance on the map. *The Sally Port*, a concealed exit where the front breastwork crossed the main road south of *The Neb*, later gave its name to the stretch of German front line across no man's land, which became *Sally Trench*.

South of here, in the area east of Festubert, the new communication trenches, constructed over the next few months, were called *Connaught Street*, *Cadbury's*, *Fry's*, *Pipe*, *Funnel*, *Rope* and *Kinkroo* (named after the road La Quinque Rue); continuing south, regional and regimental names took over: *Shetland Road*, *Coleman Street*, *Richmond Terrace*, *Argyll Road*, *Pioneer Road*, *Orkney Road*, *Lothian Road*, *Stafford Road*, *Barnton Road*, *Stuart Road*, *Fife Road*, *Coldstream Road* and *Grenadier Road*. The apex of the new British line east of Festubert was at *Canadian Orchard*, reminding us of the Canadian part in this battle. The southern end of this bitten-off German area was just north of Givenchy at the feature called the *Duck's Bill* (the Germans knew it by the same name – *Enten Schnabel*) where a stretch of old trench in no man's land was named *Dead Man's* (or *Deadmans*) *Trench*.

From Givenchy to the La Bassée Canal

On 1st Division front (1st Brigade), between Givenchy and the La Bassée Canal, the following names had become established by 27 December 1914 (the numbers 1–11 refer to positions marked on a map):[52]

Trench/ Position No.	Name	Rifle Strength
1	French Farm	130 Scots Guards
2	Scottish Trench	100 L[ondon] Scottish
3	Second Trench	120 Cold[stream] Guards
4	South Trench	180 Camerons
5	Wagon Trench	80 Cold[stream] G[uar]ds
6	Road Reserve	120 Camerons
7	Bridge Guard	160 S[cots] Guards, 100 L[ondon] Scottish
8	Coldstreams	Rem. 35, London Scottish 195
9	Black Watch	800
10	Camerons	260
11	B[rigade] HQ	

In addition, *Windy Corner*, west of Givenchy, had been named, and most of the roads in the area had also been given names such as *Princes Road*, *Yellow Road* and *Willow Road*. The naming of *Chocolat Menier Corner* north of Festubert, from an advertising panel at that road junction, later by association led to the naming of two nearby communication trenches *Cadbury's* and *Fry's*.

By January 1915, and probably earlier, *Spoil Bank* and *The Embankment* on the La Bassée Canal, and *The Orchard* and *The Keep* at Givenchy had received their names. The last was an ancient word that had come back into use on First Army Front to denote a strongpoint, close behind the support trench, organised for all-round defence and usually garrisoned by a platoon. In areas with a high water table where the trenches were susceptible to flooding, as much of the Lys valley was, such strongpoints on slightly higher ground or in substantial buildings, provided the backbone of the defence scheme. The following additional names were in use at Givenchy in February: *Givenchy Keep*, *Village Trench* (or *the Village Trenches*), the famous *Duck's Bill* salient, the *Orchard*, *Mairie Redoubt* (at the town hall), *Old British Line*, *New Communicating Trench*, *Old* (water-filled) *Communicating Trench*, *Loop Trench* and *Glasgow Trench*.[53] By March, further British positions in the Givenchy area included *Welch Trench*, *Red House* and *White House*.[54] In that month the Guards Brigade took over trenches at Givenchy, the Brigadier reconnoitring *German Redoubt* from *New Cut Trench*, and *German Redoubt* and *German Trench E3* and *E4* from Le Plantin, on the 15th.[55]

Thus far naming in this area had been, with a few striking exceptions such as the *Duck's Bill*, largely prosaic – a mixture of topographical reference points and regimental associations. However, a new group of London street names soon appeared in the Givenchy sector as the trench system was rapidly

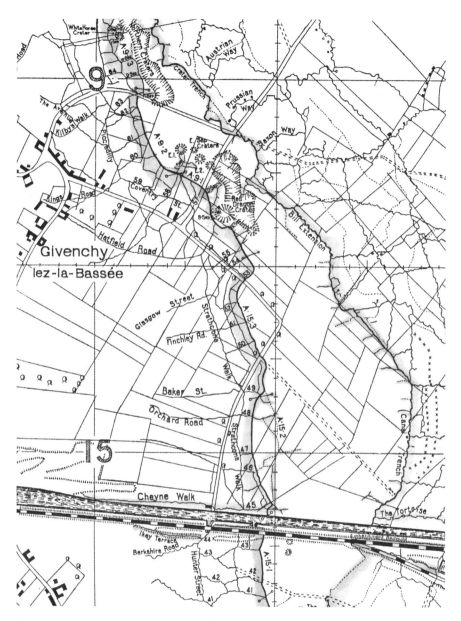

British 1916 trench map showing the British (left) and German (right) trench systems at Givenchy-lez-La Bassée (there was another similarly named village – Givenchy-en-Gohelle – near the Vimy Ridge) astride the La Bassée canal (near bottom), showing the mine craters, including *Red Dragon Crater*, north and east of Givenchy.

developed on and around the chalk knoll on which the village was situated, and the units of the Guards Brigade that held it were all commemorated here or south of the canal. The Givenchy defences at this time included: *Coldstream Road*, *Grenadier Road*, *Whitehall*, *Cambridge Terrace*, *Bayswater* (support line), *Caledonian Road*, *Cheyne Walk*, *Baker Street*, *Finchley Road*, *Shaftesbury* (Ave), *Regent Street*, *Bond Street*, *Oxford Street* (front line), *Curzon Street* (support line), *Piccadilly* (reserve line), *Berkeley Street*, *Clarges Street*, *Half Moon Street*, *Down Street* and *Kings Road*. There were also *Oxford Terrace* and *Cambridge Terrace* (both support line), *Gunners Siding*, *Orchard Street*, *Glasgow Street*, *Queens Road*, *Coldstream Lane*, *Lone Tree*, *Y Corner*, *Herts Road* and *Hitchin Road*. A regular battalion of The Hertfordshire Regiment (unofficially known as the 'Herts Guards') was part of the Guards Brigade at this time. In April the brigade also referred to *Canal Trench*, the *Grouse Butts* and a British digging at the *Duck's Bill* known as *Dead Man's Trench*. A British mine gallery was dug from *The Shrine*. While in this sector, 4th (Guards) Brigade issued an order on 28 April stating that: 'No signs or notice boards put up in the trenches are to be taken down except for renewal.'[56] On 20 June First Army, instructing lower formations to adapt the Givenchy trenches for offensive operations, referred to 'the trench now known as Piccadilly'.[57]

The German trenches in this sector were lettered and numbered by the British in the following fashion: *A1, A2; B1, B2; C1, C2; D1, D2; E1–E4*, etc. This system was soon abandoned in favour of arbitrary target numbers, or combinations of letters and numbers, indicating specific points rather than stretches of trench. This later system was in use by the Aubers Ridge and Festubert battles in May. Other German positions here in April were the *North Breastwork*, *South Breastwork*, *'K' Redoubt*, *'R' Redoubt* and *S Bend*.[58]

South of the La Bassée Canal

At Cambrin, south of the La Bassée Canal, between 10 and 29 January 1915, 1st Division referred to *Eastern* and *Western communication trenches*, *Embankment*, the *Keep*, *New Cuinchy Supporting Point*, *Sussex trench* and *Culvert post*.[59] At Cuinchy, a report of the 4th (Guards) Brigade on 26 January referred to *The Keep*, *Old Kent Road*, *High Street* (communication trench), *Suez Canal*, *Brick Heaps* (brickstacks), *The Triangle*, *Vine Cottage*, *Pudding Lane*, *Barossa Trench* (at the brickstacks), *The Embankment* and *The Bombing Trench*.[60] It can be seen that during this period names were in the process of becoming formalised; some were very tentative, being only temporary descriptions or reference points, others were semi-formalised, while yet others such as *Old Kent Road* were the subject of a very deliberate naming process.

In early February, in addition to the names given above, the Guards Brigade was using the names of the *Brickstacks*, *The Culvert*, *Culvert Position*, 'the *Culvert Road* communicating trench', the *Big Culvert*, the *Culvert Line*, *Brickfields*, *The Cockshy* (also known as *Cock Shie*) position at the *Brickstacks*, *The Mill*, *Railway Embankment*, *The Hollow*, *Machine Gun House*, *Distillery* (at Pont Fixe), *Hertford Street*, 'trench marked *ZZ*' and *Trench Z*, *The Quarries* (held at this time by the French), and the *Cinder Heap* (*Fosse 9*) at Annequin. In March the Guards Brigade was also using *Harley Street*, near Pont Fixe, *Park Lane*, *Praed Street*, *Hunter Street*, *Upper Lovers Walk* and *Glasgow Road*.[61]

Very soon, a plethora of new names appeared south of the Canal – *Grenadier Trench*, *Cabbage Patch Redoubt* and so on. In April, 6th Brigade were using *Ridley Walk*, *Judy's Passage*, *Stafford Redoubt*, *Leicester Square*, *Esperanto Street* (or *Terrace*), *Hanover Street* and *Coldstream Lane*.[62] Lieutenant Robert Graves of the Royal Welch Fusiliers first went into the Cambrin trenches, south of the La Bassée Canal, and then into the Brickstacks sector at Cuinchy, in May 1915. London trench names were well-established here, and he recorded *Petticoat Lane* and *Lowndes Square*.[63] At some stage there appeared across the La Bassée Canal *Battersea Bridge* and *Westminster Bridge*. Nearby were *Cheyne Walk* and *Addison Road*.

By June the number of trenches and therefore names had grown still further in Section *A*, south of the canal. This Section was divided into Sub-Sections *A1* (Vermelles–Auchy Road to the Tower), *A2* (the *Tower* to *Regent Street*) and *A3* (*Regent Street* to the Canal). As well as the trenches already given, and numbered 'saps' or '*boyaux*',[64] 6th Brigade Defence Schemes and sketch maps dated 21–26 June gave *First Line* positions as *Brickfield Terrace*, *Leicester Square*, *Upper Lovers Lane* and *Hunter Street*; in the *Second Line* were *Kingsway*, *Tower Reserve Trench*, *Esperanto Terrace* and *Banbury Cross*, while in the *Third Line* were *Maison Rouge*, *Braddell Point*, *Willow Line*, *Cambrin Support Point*, etc. There were also *Maison Rouge 'Dug-outs'*, *Seventh Street*, *Lovers Keep*, *Berkshire Road*, *Glasgow Road*, *Lewis Keep* and *Braddell*. 'Supporting points' were *Cuinchy Support*, *Cambrin Support* and *Maison Rouge*.[65]

In the Brickstacks sector south of the canal, as far south as the La Bassée Road, were shown *Railway Hollow*, *Worcester Lane*, *Davies Street*, *Hyde Park Corner*, *Loundes* [sic] *Square*, *Upper Lovers Walk*, *Leicester Square*, *Cock Shie* (or *Cockshie*) *Lane*, *Cock Shie Keep*, *German Lane*, *Ridley Walk*, *The Keep*, *Brigand Lane*, *Seymour Street* (front line), *Regent Street* (*New* and *Old*), *Oxford Street*, *Portland Street* (front line), *Hanover Street*, *Brickfield Terrace* (support line), *Old Kent Road*, *Morphia Street*, *Fairclough Road* (or *Lane*), *Lime Street*, *Schinpa* (or *Shipka*) *Pass* and *Coldstream Lane*. Then came *Straight Street*, *Conduit Street*, *Clive Road* (or *Street*), A2 Subsection

HQ at *Woburn Abbey*, *Praed Street*, *Chapel Street*, *Edgeware* [sic] *Road*, *Brook Street*, *Park Lane*, *Bond Street*, *Conduit Street* and *Waterloo Place*. The defence scheme of 21 June included for the Brickstacks sector a 'List of Dug-Outs in A3 [Sub-Section]', which included the following trenches apart from the above: *Front Trench*, *The Hollow*, *The Bulge*, *Hunter Street*, *Abingdon Road*, *Pudding Lane*, *Banbury Cross*, *Bath Road*, *Bakshae* [?] *Lane*, *Esperanto Terrace*, *Kings Cross*, *Petticoat Lane*, *Coldstream Lane*, *Leicester Square*, *Cabbage Patch*, *Pall Mall*, *Willow Lane*, *Sidings 8–13*, *Waterloo Place*, *Seymour Street*, *Marylebone Road* and *Stafford Road*.[66]

South of the La Bassée Road were more London names, punctuated by some exotic vulcanological examples where man-made mine craters had been named after their natural counterparts: *Holloway* (main trench), *The Parade* (front line), *High Street* (support line), *Back Street* (behind High Street), *Kingsway*, *The Lane*, *Tower Reserve Trench*, *Tower Street*, *Tunnel Trench* (or *Street*), *Short Cut*, *Tower Hamlets*, *Quarry Trench*, *Vesuvius Crater*, *Crater Trench* (opposite *Vesuvius*), *Etna Crater*, *Lava Trench* (or *Street*, behind *Crater Trench*), *Arthur's Keep*, *Russell's Keep* and *No 1 Keep*.[67] By September, yet more names had appeared for British and German positions: *The Tortoise* (from its shape), *Mine Point*, *German Lane*, *Sunken Road Trench*, *Gun Street*, *Canal Alley*, *Mill Alley*, *Chateau Alley*, *Les Briques Trench*, etc.[68]

Second Army Area 1914–15

Following the creation of First and Second Armies towards the end of December 1914, trench designation was systematised, but names already bestowed remained in use. Front trenches received numeric or alphanumeric designations, depending on the corps, but communication trenches were named. At the southern end of Second Army front, in II Corps area, in April 1915, the 1/4th Duke of Wellington's (West Riding) Regiment began a new communication trench, *Dead Dog Alley* (named after the nearby farm) in the Bois Grenier sector; this trench was still being completed two months later when the battalion left the sector.[69] Later in the year it was renamed *Dead Dog Avenue* in conformity with Army policy. Other named communication breastworks appeared in this period; a sketch diagram of the Le Bridoux sector dated 25 September 1915, showed *Boutillerie Avenue* and *Devon Avenue*.[70]

In the Armentières sector, on the Franco–Belgian border, names appeared, as elsewhere along the Old Front Line, as communication trenches (or breastworks) were established. As this was a particularly difficult area for digging, the ground being flat and the River Lys prone to flooding, breastworks were the norm, and during 1915 there appeared south of the Lys: *Plank Avenue, Buterne Avenue, Central Avenue, Lothian Avenue, Spain Avenue, London, Quebec, Australia, Porte Egal Avenue, Quality Street, Leith Walk, Headquarters Walk, Brick Sand Walk*, etc., as well as *Five Dugouts Post, Lille Post, Egal Post*. The moated *Ferme Grand Porte Egal* [sic] just behind the front line was made into a strong redoubt, while just south of this a small British salient was called the *Mushroom*. Other names appearing in this sector were *Miners Lane, Pear Tree Farm, Piggott Farm, Haystack Farm*, and *Subsidiary Line*.[71]

On 12 April 1915, Lieut. Roland Leighton (7th Worcester Regt.), writing to Vera Brittain, listed some of the names attached to 'passages' and dugouts in the watery Armentières sector: *The Pulpit, Le Château Germaine, Southend Pier*, the punning *Bridge of Size and Tiers*, and the inevitable London names: *Ludgate Hill, Marble Arch, Dean's Yard, Westminster Bridge, The Junior Carlton, Buckingham Palace*, etc.[72]

North of the Lys, the BEF was in Belgium, an area in which few farm names appeared on the maps of the national survey. There was therefore both a necessity and an opportunity for naming them. At Le Touquet, north-east of Armentières and east of the *A la ½ Lune Cabaret*, appeared a cluster of British names, mostly associated with buildings: *Carters Farm, Halfway House, Lukers Houses, Barkenham, Old Snipers House, Progress Row, German M.G. House, White House, Red House, Machine Gun House, Monmouth House, Essex Central Farm, Reserve Farm, Chelmsford Cottage, Warley Lodge, London Farm, Essex Farm, Gunner Farm, Salford Village, Pompadour Farm* and so on. The last is one of the few examples of a regimental nickname (The Essex Regiment) being used as a name for a locality on the battlefield (the name *Pompadour Trench* also appeared elsewhere).

Around Ploegsteert Wood (III Corps), front trenches were initially only numbered: *Trench 121, 122, 123*, etc. The names in use in and around Ploegsteert Wood have already been described. To the north of the Wood, and protecting its left flank, was Hill 63, which provided vital observation to the Wytschaete–Messines Ridge which was held by the Germans. On Hill 63 were *Crest House* and *Barrel House*, while on the north-east slope, east of the hamlet of Le Rossignol, was *Dead Cow Farm*. North of Le Rossignol were *Irish Farm, Five Haystacks, Stinking Farm, Boyle's Farm* and *Gabion Farm* and a steam traction engine was considered prominent enough to be named *Traction Engine* on the map as a reference point. In late 1914 and early 1915, these buildings were not yet completely destroyed, and as well as being used for supporting pickets, formed important shelters, observation posts, stores and cookhouses, and their names at this period were as important, perhaps even more important, than trench names. Crucially, they provided vital reference points on the terrain and pinpoint positions on the map, known to the yard by the artillery of both sides.

North of Wulverghem (where in July 1915 a dugout was named *The Nook*) appeared *Cable Farm, Elbow Farm, Burnt Farm, R.E. Farm, Shell Farm, Cooker Farm, Tea Farm, Pond Farm* and *Frenchman's Farm*. West of Spanbroekmolen were *Store Farm* and *Spy Farm*, the latter a reminder of the epidemic of spy scares in the BEF in 1914–15. Opposite Wytschaete appeared *Byron Farm, Parret Farm, Wiltshire House, Alston House* and *Irish House*, while the farm between Spanbroekmolen and Maedelstede Farm was named *Peckham*.[73]

In the Wytschaete and St Eloi sectors (II Corps), trenches were given letters for the sector, and numbers within that sector – thus we find in late 1914 and early 1915, from south to north, sectors *D, E, F, G, H, J, K, L, M, N* and *O* opposite Wytschaete, running up to *P, Q, R* and *T* at St Eloi and *V* at

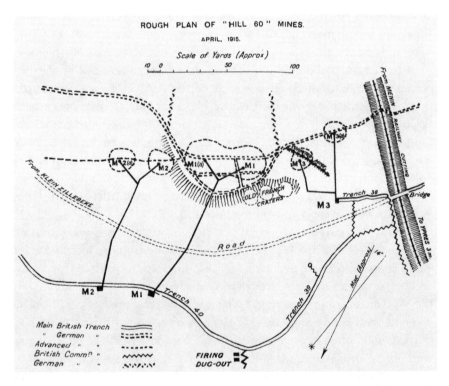

British plan of the mines laid and blown under the German position on Hill 60, south-east of Ypres, just before the Second Battle of Ypres in April 1915. The British front line (at bottom) is *Trenches 38, 39* and *40* (Second Army, and its constituent corps, lettered and numbered its trenches from right to left – the usual military practice), and the mine shafts, galleries and charge chambers are *M1, M2* and *M3*. (*Work of the Royal Engineers in the European War 1914–19: Military Mining*, Chatham, 1922)

Voormezeele, and within each of these lettered sectors were the numbered trenches – e.g. *H1, H2, H3, H4, H5* directly west of Wytschaete. The letter '*S*' was reserved for 'Support Redoubts' (strongpoints or keeps) along the whole Army front, and '*I*' was not used to avoid any confusion with the figure 1. However, '*I*' was used as one of the capital letters designating a square zone on the maps. Such lettering and numbering became the rule along the whole of the British front-line trenches, but names were used for most trenches behind the front line – support, reserve, switch, communication trenches. In the front line, a sentry would report to the officer on duty along the company front: 'C 4 trench, number 6 post, wind safe, all correct',[74] or not as the case may be. The reference to the wind direction was introduced after the German gas attack at Ypres in April 1915. Boards indicating the correct sector, trench and post designations were placed along the front line.

North of St Eloi, trenches were again only numbered – any sector letter was discarded. Key positions on the front taken over by 28th Division from the French in early 1915 included *The Bluff*, *Hill 60*, *The Caterpillar* and *The Dump*; all were artificial features, resulting from excavations for the canal and railway running south-east from Ypres. Before the attack on the strong German position of Hill 60 on 17 April 1915, we find *Trench 37* south of the railway cutting (on the *Caterpillar* side), and *38, 39, 40*, etc., to the north (on the Hill 60 side). *Trench 41* was a support trench and *Trench 42* was still farther back, astride the Zwarteleen–Zillebeke Road. *Trenches 43–45* formed a sharp salient jutting into the German-held village of Zwarteleen. The communication trenches up to the front line from Larch Wood (e.g. *Lovers Lane*) and points to the north do not appear, at this time, to have been named,[75] though it was often the case that names in use did not appear on the maps.

Trenches taken over by 27th Division from the French in early to mid-April, before the German gas attack, in the Sanctuary Wood–Hooge–Zonnebeke area, were again numbered from *1* (north-east of Zwarteleen) to *79* (Polygon Wood), and those along the south edge of Polygon Wood were lettered *A* to *C*.[76]

If any of these British trenches were named by the troops occupying them – e.g. *Hampshire Trench* at Ploegsteert Wood – these names were not generally shown on the crude trench maps of late 1914 and early 1915, on most of which the British trenches, and for that matter the German, were only shown in manuscript. The first large-scale maps showing British trenches were drawn up in manuscript form by the Divisional Field Companies of the Royal Engineers during the Battle of the Aisne and the trench stalemate that followed (September and early October 1914), and then in Flanders following the race to the sea in October and the Battles of La Bassée and First Ypres. In late 1914 and early 1915, the defences proliferated and many more names appeared at this stage.

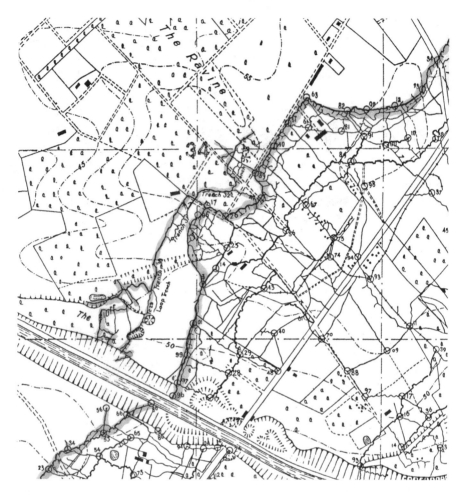

British trench map of *The Bluff* area. The British front line, on the left, including *Loop Trench*, and Trenches *29, 30, 31, 32* and *33*, and the German trench system (right), in the area between The Ravine and the Ypres–Comines canal. *The Bluff*, formed of earth excavated during the digging of the canal, and its mine craters were the scene of savage mine warfare in 1916.

In these early months of trench warfare, not all the British trenches were joined up into a single, connected system – there were many isolated sections of trench, particularly in the Ypres Salient where British and Canadian divisions were taking over from the French in March and April 1915. During and after Second Ypres, new trenches were dug closer to Ypres, becoming the British front-line system for the next two years. If trenches were not yet named on the maps, farms and other features (even if unnamed) certainly were. Some features had been at the time of First Ypres. British troops immediately gave their own names to hitherto unnamed farms, isolated buildings, copses and so forth.

By February and March 1915 we find west of St Eloi, in the Vierstraat–Voormezeele sector, buildings in the area behind the front line named *Moated Grange*, *Middle Farm*, *Dead Dog Farm*, *Redoubt Farm*, *Beggars Rest*, *Snipers Barn*, *Old Farms* and *Brasserie Farm*. At St Eloi, the following trench and place names were in use at the time: *RB* [Rifle Brigade] *Trench*, *KSLI* [King's Shropshire Light Infantry] *Trench*, *C9 Trench*, Trenches *1* to *23*, *German Parallel* (or *German fire trench*), *The Breastwork*, *New Support Trenches*, *Canadian Trenches*, *The Mound*, *Bus House* (named after a wrecked London omnibus), *Piccadilly Farm* and *White Horse Cellars* (possibly a Royal West Kents connection), *Shelley Farm* (reputedly named after the cause of its destruction rather than a person), *Ruined Farm*, *Square Wood* and *Triangular Wood*.[77] Many of these names had appeared months earlier. Roads also receiving names; north of Lock 7 on the Ypres–Comines Canal were *King's Way* and *Sandbag Track*, while east of Kemmel was the delightfully named *Milky Way*. In the same area were *Arundel* and *Norfolk Lodge*, *Chester Farm*, *Bedford House*, *Gunners Lodge*, *Hazelbury* and *Home Farm*. A prominent lock-keeper's house was known as *The Doll's House*. Spoil heaps by the side of the Canal, the result of excavation, were named *Spoil Bank* (on the south side) and *The Bluff* (on the northern).

Second Battle of Ypres, April–May 1915

Although the old Army had fought in the Ypres Salient in the autumn of 1914, it was unknown ground to many of the troops of 1915. We have seen that many names were given to features and localities in 1914, and several had already passed into history – the *Menin Road*, the *Menin Gate*, the *Cloth Hall*, the *Lille Gate*, *Sanctuary Wood*, *Hellfire Corner*, *Shrapnel Corner*, *Polygon Wood* and so on. Local designations and names were not known to units coming to Second Army for the first time, and much of the line in the Ypres Salient had only recently been taken over from the French. Probably for this reason, it was Second Army policy to identify features by coordinates within sub-squares, or merely by the sub-squares. A Second Army order of 15 April 1915 stated that 'references in reports to trenches will be by reference to map square and decimal system. Numbers of trenches and local names will not be used in reports to 2nd Army.'[78] Thus even though the troops preferred names to abstract map references, they were prohibited to avoid confusion.

On some Second Army 1:5,000 sheets of early 1915, the standard system of reference squares was used, as were arbitrary target numbers. The latter were not in circles as in the First Army (GS 'I') inverted maps, but under arcs, as it were, to suggest the '"épaulement" of the battery' position. When German trenches appeared, they were in blue, as were reference numbers in the German trenches, e.g. *A7*, *K13*, *C4A*, etc., and names such as *The Necklace* and *Railway Barricade* near Armentières.

As is always the case, locally given names were in use before they appeared on the maps; the regular series 1:40,000 and 1:20,000 sheets printed at the War Office or Ordnance Survey in late 1914 and early 1915 and issued to fighting units were squared, but did not carry locally given names; on the other hand the 1:10,000 sheets prepared by Second Army Intelligence and reproduced by the Royal Engineers' Printing Company at GHQ did carry some British names for local features. Such names were gradually added to Second Army's trench maps, and in the summer of 1915 they were transferred on to the new 1:10,000 regular series sheets (series *GSGS 3062*) photographically reproduced from the original Belgian drawings. The later Second Army demy sheets of August and September, intended as backgrounds for overprinting by the Army's Printing Section, were photographically reproduced from these regular sheets, and therefore also included the local names.

During the Second Battle of Ypres in April and May 1915, operation orders contained detailed square references as we have seen, partly because of the lack of names on the map in the area recently taken over from the French, partly to avoid confusing troops new to the area, and partly because of confusion between names. Most of the farms were named during or after the Second Battle of Ypres. *Shell Trap Farm* (shown as such on the 1:10,000 Second Army *Saint-Jean* demy sheet) was also known as *Canadian Farm*, but was simply *Chateau* on the Belgian map, and was renamed *Mouse Trap Farm* by the staff to prevent demoralisation. It had also been called *Chateau du Nord* by the French and Belgians, and *Wieltje Chateau* by the Germans. British orders simply referred to the square position – 'Farm in C.22.b'. Another farm nearby, later known as *Canadian Farm*, had earlier been called *Moated Farm* and also *Oblong Farm*. This last name was later used for yet another farm to the east. Altogether a baffling and dangerous situation.[79] *Von Kluck Farm* (so named in 1915) later became *Von Hugel Farm*.

The contemporary use of square references is illustrated by a typical order of the time, the 'Preparatory Order for Withdrawal from tip of Salient' issued by Plumer's Force on 29 April 1915:

The line to be finally occupied will be as follows:- From present trench line in I.30.b [in front of Armagh Wood] due north to Hooge Chateau, I.18.b., thence north-west to G.H.Q. line about C.29.a.c. [east of Wieltje] along G.H.Q. line to farm in C.22.b. [Mouse Trap Farm], and thence along present British and French trench lines. A tracing of this line, which has been reconstructed during the last few days, is attached.[80]

Yet another toponymic difficulty associated with British maps of the Ypres Salient arose with the naming of streams. The Official Historian noted that:

The various reaches and branches of the streams are sometimes differently named on British and German maps. On the British 1:40,000, below St Julien, the same watercourse is first called Steenbeek, then Haanebeek, then St. Jansbeek, and, finally, Martjevaart. Here [in the Official History] the Haanebeek means its lower course, marked Steenbeek on the maps accompanying this volume.[81]

In the spring and summer months following the Second Battle of Ypres, during which the Allied front at the tip of the Salient near Passchendaele and east of Polygon Wood was withdrawn under pressure to a new line much closer to Ypres, Second Army front again became settled and new front, support, reserve and communication trenches were dug and wired, and rear strongpoints constructed. After the severe fright of the German offensive, it was realised that the new British defensive system had to be considerably stronger than the old. It was clearly not Second Army policy at this or any other time to name fire trenches, and in fact this generally applies to the whole of the BEF. The new front trenches were therefore lettered and numbered from the right as before, but communication and other trenches were named throughout the Salient. There was a widespread use of London names – *Haymarket*, *Piccadilly*, etc. – in many parts of the front system in the Salient in mid-1915: around Cross Roads Farm, at Potijze, Railway Wood, Hooge, Sanctuary Wood, and opposite the Messines–Wytschaete Ridge. This London theme is explored further in Chapter VII.

In May and June 1915, Trenches *Q1* to *Q3*, and *R*, at St Eloi were overlooked by the German-held *Mound*, also occasionally known to the British as the *Mound of Death*, and other British positions in this area were named *Hyde Park Corner* and *Queen Victoria Street*, the latter possibly named by the Queen Victoria's Rifles who held the sector.[82]

The designations *Points Y1–Y11* were in use on 16 June to define German trenches in the attack of 9th (supported by 7th) Brigade on *Y Wood* in the Bellewaarde Ridge area. On the front between Hooge, Zouave Wood and Sanctuary Wood in June and July, British front trenches were designated *G1* to *G10*, forward posts were *The Sap* and *The Appendix*, communication and other trenches were called *Old* and *New Bond Street*, *Fleet Street*, *The Strand* and *Oxford Street*, while other positions near *Hooge Chateau* and

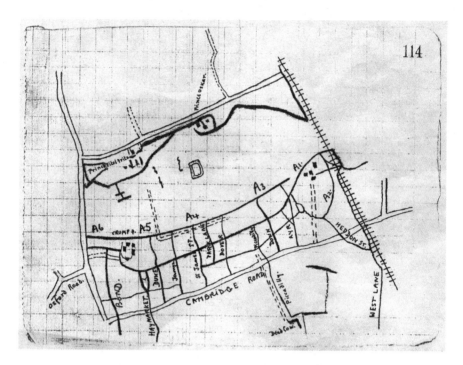

British sketch map of the 'Right Half of 'A' Sector' showing British trenches and
breastworks along the Cambridge Road in the Potijze sector, north of the Ypres–
Roulers railway, Ypres salient, August 1915. The British front line includes Trenches
A1 to *A6*, and a group of London street names – *Bond*, *Haymarket*, *Duke*, *Jermyn*,
Piccadilly, etc., is shown behind. The German front trenches are at the top, running
through Prince Eitel Fritz and Prince Oskar Farms. Edmund Blunden described this
sector in *Undertones of War*. (The late John Page)

The Stables were known as *Tunnel House, Island Posts* and *Bull Farm*. Certain
communication trenches were designated *S1, S2, S3*. The British blew and
captured Hooge Crater (under the chateau's stables) on 19 July. The Germans
successfully counter-attacked with liquid fire on 30–31 July, and the British in
turn counter-attacked on 9 August and recaptured Hooge, the crater being
reoccupied the following day. On 3 August Lieutenant G.W. Rogers reported
on the condition of the 'new (Sherwood) communication trench', while the
following day Lieutenant C.E. Pumphrey of the 10th Durham Light Infantry
reconnoitred some of the communication trenches, numbered *1–7* on his
sketch map, across the Menin Road at Hooge.[83]

In July communication trenches in the Hooge–Bellewaarde–Potijze sector
included *Castle Street, Union Street, Mud Lane, East Lane, West Lane,
Piccadilly, Haymarket, Bond Street*, etc.[84] Trenches in Railway Wood do
not appear to have been named for some time, but at some stage there

appeared *New Mud Lane*, *Wood Trench* and *Junction Trench*. On several maps they were only numbered. In September, British front trenches in the Hooge–Bellewaarde Lake area retained their designations *B4–B8* and *C1–C12*, clearly a continuation of the system used for the Sanctuary Wood trenches in July (see below).[85] Trench names mentioned in the 7th Brigade Operation Order issued for the diversionary attack at Hooge on 25 September were *Regent Street*, *Upper* and *Lower Grafton Street*, *Conduit Street*, *Savile Row*, *Regent Street*, *Union Street*, *Castle Street*, *Zillebeke Lake Promenade*, etc.[86] These names had come into use as and when they were dug during the early summer.

A trace of the Sanctuary Wood trenches issued by 138th Brigade on 4 July showed the British front trenches designated from the right: *50*, *1–12*, *B1–B8* (*B4* and *B5* were at a forward sap called *The Appendix*), while points in the German trenches were awarded the arbitrary target numbers *Y39*, *Y48*, *Y52*, *Y53*, etc. No names were in evidence on this trace, yet by this time they were certainly in use in the Salient, particularly for communication trenches.

Just north of the Ypres–Roulers railway running past Railway Wood was the Potijze sector. Here, as far north as Crump Farm, the new British front system after Second Ypres, in the Right Half of A Sector included *Bond Street*, *Duke Street*, *Jermyn Street*, *St James's Street*, *Park Lane*, *Dover Street*, *Down Street*, *Air Street*, *Haymarket*, *Piccadilly*, *Heddon Street*, *West Lane* and *East Lane*.[87] These were all communication trenches – the front and support lines in front of Cambridge Road being alphanumerically designated – the front trenches as *A1* to *A6*. The fire trenches were described as *Advance Line*, *Firing Line* and *Unmanned Fire Trench*.

Farther north, in B Sector around Cross Roads Farm and Buffs Road north of Wieltje, were the communication trenches *Mark Lane*, *Praed Street*, *Euston Road*, *Finch Street*, *Moorgate Street*, *Liverpool Street* and *Threadneedle Street*.[88] This system continued in the Hill Top Farm–Glimpse Cottage sector facing the Pilckem Ridge in June 1915, where British front trenches were numbered from right to left *D18–21*, *E22–29*, *F30*, and so on. Thus the numbering remained sequential, while the sector letters changed sequentially without disturbing the numbering. Communication trench names here at this time were *Bow Street* and *Argyll Street*, west and east respectively of Lancashire Farm.[89] The former was later renamed *Huddersfield Road*, while the latter seems later to have disappeared altogether.[90] In this northern section of the Salient, the trenches of the new front system broke away from the London paradigm; many were named by north-country troops of 4th Division, and of 49th Division, which subsequently relieved the French to the north and feinted against the Pilckem Ridge (*Caesar's Nose*) on 8 August. Unusually, some of the front trenches of the latter division were named –

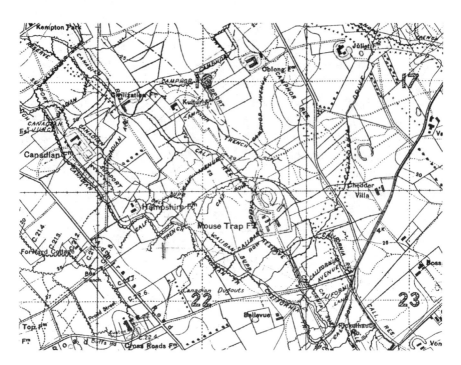

British 1917 trench map showing the British (bottom left) and German trench systems in the area facing the Pilckem Ridge, north-east of Ypres, showing *Canadian*, *Civilization* and *Mouse Trap* (formerly *Shell Trap*) Farms, and the names given by the British to their own and German trenches. The German trenches in this area were captured on the first day of Third Ypres – 31 July 1917.

Essex Trench, *Yorkshire Trench*, *White Trench* – and there were many other Yorkshire and Lancashire names.

Many farm and other names in this north-east section of the Ypres Salient commemorated the French contribution to its defence: *Algerian Cottage*, *Turco Farm*, *Spahi Farm*, *Joffre Farm*, *Foch Farm*, *La Belle Alliance*, etc., but the British and Canadian part in Second Ypres was already emphasised by *Canadian Farm*, *Fusilier Farm* and *Lancashire Farm*. The German presence on the Pilckem Ridge was marked by *Von Kluck Cottages*, *Hindenburg Farms*, *Mauser Cottage*, *Müller Cottage*, *Krupp Farm*, *Essen Farm*, *Von Spree Farm*, etc.[91]

This trench system, already well-established by mid-1915, was further elaborated and strengthened up to the Third Battle of Ypres, which began at the end of July 1917. The next chapter examines the development of trench naming from the period of the Battle of Loos to the end of the war.

Notes

1   Jack, Col. E.M., *Report on Survey on the Western Front*, Geographical Section, General Staff, War Office, London: HMSO, 1920.

2   *Rapport sur les Travaux Exécutés du 1er août 1914 au 31 décembre 1919 (Rapport de Guerre)* (1924 & 1936), Paris: Service Géographique de l'Armée.

3   Gordon, Professor Cyrus H., *Forgotten Scripts, The Story of their Decipherment*, London: Pelican, 1971, p. 24 (fn).

4   Third Army General Staff War Diary, TNA(PRO) WO 95/361.

5   Edmonds, Brig.-Gen. J.E. & Wynne, Capt. G.C., *History of The Great War, Military Operations, France and Belgium*, 1915, Vol. I, London: Macmillan, 1927, p. 5.

6   11th Brigade War Diary, TNA(PRO) WO 95/1486.

7   11th Brigade War Diary (Appendices), TNA(PRO) WO 95/1487.

8   3rd Division General Staff War Diary, TNA(PRO) WO 95/1274.

9   Hunter-Weston to Edmonds, 20 October 1926, in 11th Brigade War Diary, TNA(PRO) WO 95/1486.

10 Hunter-Weston to his wife, 17 October 1914, quoted in Hunter-Weston to Edmonds, 20 October 1926, in 11th Brigade War Diary, TNA(PRO) WO 95/1486.

11 Note on sketch map in 1st Division General Staff War Diary, TNA(PRO) WO 95/1227.

12 Edmonds, J.E. (1925), *History of the Great War, Military Operations, France and Belgium, 1914*, Vol. II, London: Macmillan, p. 426 & fn.

13 Ibid., p. 415.

14 11th Brigade War Diary, TNA(PRO) WO 95/1486.

15 Hunter-Weston to Edmonds, 20 October 1926, in 11th Brigade War Diary, TNA(PRO) WO 95/1486.

16 The name *Bunter Avenue* appears on the *Ploegsteert Wood* 1:10,000 sheet lithographed by the 1st Printing Company RE, GHQ, in or before December 1914.

17 1:5,000 and 1:10,000 manuscript trench maps of Ploegsteert Wood area, February and March 1915, private collection.

18 7th Brigade War Diary, TNA(PRO) WO 95/1413.

19 5th Division General Staff War Diary, TNA(PRO) WO 95/1510.

20 7th Brigade War Diary, TNA(PRO) WO 95/1413.

21 5th Division General Staff War Diary, TNA(PRO) WO 95/1510.

22 Delany, Paul, *Bill Brandt, A Life*, London: Jonathan Cape/Pimlico, 2004, p. 21.

23 7th Brigade War Diary, TNA(PRO) WO 95/1413.

24 Sketch map in II Corps General Staff War Diary, TNA(PRO) WO 95/629.

25 Hamilton, H.W.R., 'History of the 20th (Field) Company; Royal Bombay Sappers and Miners. Great War: 1914–1918', Part I, France, *Royal Engineers Journal*, December 1926, pp. 537–63.

26 7th Division General Staff War Diary, TNA(PRO) WO 95/1627.

27 8th Division General Staff War Diary, TNA(PRO) WO 95/1671.

28 Ibid.

29 Ibid.

30 Ibid.

31 7th Division General Staff War Diary, with sketch maps, TNA(PRO) WO 95/1627.

32 8th Division General Staff War Diary, TNA(PRO) WO 95/1671.

33 Ibid.

34 Ibid.

35 Ibid.

36 Ibid.

37 Ibid.

38 Ibid.

39 8th Division CRA War Diary, TNA(PRO) WO 95 1683.

40 8th Division General Staff War Diary, TNA(PRO) WO 95/1671.

41 Ibid.

42 Ibid.

43 Edmonds, 1927, op. cit, Appendix 13, p. 385.

44 Ibid.

45 2nd Brigade War Diary, TNA(PRO) WO 95/1267.

46 Sketch map on stout tracing paper in 1st Division General Staff War Diary, TNA(PRO) WO 95/1227.

47 4th (Guards) Brigade War Diary, TNA(PRO) WO 95/1341.

48 3rd Division General Staff War Diary, TNA(PRO) WO 95/1274.

49 4th (Guards) Brigade War Diary, TNA(PRO) WO 95/1341.

50 Messenger, Charles, *Terriers in the Trenches; The Post Office Rifles at War, 1914–1918*, Chippenham: Picton, 1982.

51 140th Brigade War Diary, TNA(PRO) WO 95/2727.

52 1st Division General Staff War Diary, TNA(PRO) WO 95/1227.

53 6th Brigade War Diary, TNA(PRO) WO 95/1352.

54 RE Institution, *Work of the RE in the European War, 1914–19, Military Mining*, Chatham: Institution of Royal Engineers, 1922, plate 2.

55 4th (Guards) Brigade War Diary, TNA(PRO) WO 95/1341.

56 Ibid.

57 First Army General Staff War Diary, TNA(PRO) WO 95/156.

58 4th (Guards) Brigade War Diary, TNA(PRO) WO 95/1341.

59 2nd Brigade War Diary, TNA(PRO) WO 95/1267.

60 Guards Brigade Report, in 1st Brigade War Diary, TNA(PRO) WO 95/1261.

61 4th (Guards) Brigade War Diary, TNA(PRO) WO 95/1341.

62 6th Brigade War Diary, TNA(PRO) WO 95/1352.

63 Graves, Robert, *Goodbye to All That*, London: Penguin Modern Classics, 1961, p. 96.

64 *Operation order No 18, 4 July 1915*, in 4th (Guards) Brigade War Diary, TNA(PRO) WO 95/1341.

65 6th Brigade War Diary, TNA(PRO) WO 95/1352.

PART ONE

113

66 Ibid.

67 Ibid.

68 *2nd Division Operation Order No 53, 21 September 1915*, in 6th Brigade War Diary, TNA(PRO) WO 95/1352.

69 Bales, Capt. P.G., *The History of the 1/4th Battalion, Duke of Wellington's (West Riding) Regiment, 1914-1919*, London & Halifax: Edward Mortimer, 1920, p. 14.

70 7th Division CRE War Diary, TNA(PRO) WO 95/1641.

71 MS additions to 1:10,000 map *Second Army Sheet 12, OSO 1915, o/p 1st Ptg Co RE (2) 785, Trenches ... 5 February 1916*, used by 2/Lt G. S. Dickinson, 7th Lincolns. Author's collection.

72 Bishop, A. & Bostridge, M. (eds), *Letters from a Lost Generation – First World War Letters of Vera Brittain and Four Friends*, London: Little, Brown and Co., 1998, pp. 78–80.

73 Names taken from 1:10,000 trench maps *28SW2* [Wytschaete] and *28SW4* [Ploegsteert], GSGS 3062, OSO 1915. Author's collection.

74 *The 'New Church' Times*, Monday, 22 May 1916, in: Roberts, F.J. (ed.), *The Wipers Times*, first complete facsimile edition, London: Eveleigh Nash & Grayson, 1930.

75 1:5,000 map of Hill 60 in: Cuthbert Keeson, Major C.A., *The History and Records of Queen Victoria's Rifles 1792-1922*, London: Constable, 1923.

76 27th Division General Staff War Diary, TNA(PRO) WO 95/2254.

77 Ibid.

78 Second Army GS War Diary, TNA(PRO) WO 95/270.

79 Edmonds & Wynne, 1927, op. cit., pp. 174–5, fn.

80 Ibid., p. 407.

81 Ibid., p. 190, fn.

82 Cuthbert Keeson, op. cit., pp. 105–10.

83 Documents quoted in Cave, Nigel, *Sanctuary Wood & Hooge*, Barnsley: Leo Cooper, Pen & Sword, Battleground Europe, Ypres, series, 2002, pp. 63–5. Unfortunately, this publication does not give archive references for these documents.

84 MS additions (dated 4/8/15) to 1:10,000 map *St Jean* in 14th Division War Diary, TNA(PRO) WO 95/1864.

85 8th Brigade War Diary, TNA(PRO) WO 95/1416.

86 *7th Brigade Operation Order No.1, September 1915*, in TNA(PRO) WO 95/1413.

87 1:10,000 duplicated trench map: *Right Half of A Sector, 12/8/15*, and MS sketch maps, mid-1915. Private collection.

88 MS sketch maps, mid-1915. Private collection.

89 1:10,000 demy trench map *St Jean*, dated 24 June 1915, printed by Second Army Printing Section, with MS additions. Institution of Royal Engineers Library.

90 1:10,000 trench map *28NW2 St Julien, Edn. 5A (Secret), Trenches corrected to 1 April 1917*, OS April 1917.

91 1:10,000 demy trench map *St Jean*, 24 June 1915, op. cit.

III

BRITISH TRENCH NAMING FROM THE BATTLE OF LOOS TO THE END OF THE SOMME BATTLE

Trench Maps and Naming Policy: July 1915 Onwards

Regular series 1:10,000 trench maps were introduced in mid-1915, being drawn in the field by the draughtsmen of the Army Maps & Printing Sections, and printed by the Ordnance Survey at Southampton, but at first they carried few if any trench names. As Army Topographical Sections were formed between July and September 1915, they absorbed the Maps & Printing Sections and took over the latter's functions. The same process was repeated in February 1916, when the Topographical Sections were enlarged into Field Survey Companies, one to each army. Names of British trenches were generally given by units, formations only laying down broad guidelines (e.g. an alphabetical framework). Names of German trenches, as these gradually, and then systematically began to appear on British trench maps in the period 1915–17, were given by the staff. Where the names given by the Germans to their own trenches were known, these were normally used in preference to British inventions. Occasionally the Field Survey Companies were directly involved in this naming process. In all cases, however, the draughtsmen of the Field Survey Companies (and later in addition the Corps Topographical Sections) were responsible for inscribing the trench names on to the trench-plate drawing before the map was reproduced.

Fire trenches were practically always designated by their sector letter and a number (e.g. *E.3*), but communication trenches were being rapidly named throughout 1915. Attempts were being made to standardise their nomenclature, the preferred general staff designation being the aristocratic 'avenue' (from the past participle of the French verb *avenir*; to come to, approach or draw near to), which in civilian life denotes the (often tree-lined) approach to a country house. This battlefield usage in fact had a military precedent; the *Shorter Oxford Dictionary* gives for avenue: 'A way of

Flat-bed lithographic printing presses at 3rd Field Survey Company RE headquarters in 1917–18. These were used to print special Army trench maps to supplement the regular series trench maps printed at the Ordnance Survey at Southampton. The drawings, including names, for all trench maps were produced by the Field Survey Company/Battalion draughtsmen.

approach; a passage or path of entrance or exit (Formerly a military term)'. The old siege warfare word for a communication trench was an 'approach', created by sapping forward in order to construct new parallels closer to the enemy position. On 22 July 1915 the Chief Engineer of 27th Division referred to 'Communication Avenues' in a letter to III Corps of Second Army.[1] This term, used in the 1911 *Manual of Field Engineering*, designated communication trenches formed by building up breastworks (avenues of sandbags, therefore, rather than trees) on either side of a duckboard track laid directly on the ground. By August 1915 a distinct policy of naming communication trenches 'avenues' appears to have been promulgated throughout the BEF, and this may well have been associated with the formation of Third Army and the taking over of a new frontage north of the Somme. In the very front part of the trench system, shorter communication trenches were named 'alleys' by the troops in the line, who preferred this more urban and plebeian terminology. The 'alley' designation survived in places, despite staff disapproval.

Promoted by the staff, the practice of designating communication trenches 'avenues' soon became widespread. On 7 August the 8th Division CRE (Commander, Royal Engineers) gave a lecture to the officers and NCOs of the 96th Field Company and the 20th Division. Entitled 'Trench Fortifications,' this included the location and design of 'Avenues'.[2] 8th Division used this designation for new communication trenches, and even changed some existing names to conform. A sketch diagram of the Le Bridoux sector dated 25 September 1915, showed *Boutillerie Avenue* and *Devon Avenue*,[3] while *Dead Dog Alley* became *Dead Dog Avenue*. For a while this usage became well-established (it was extensively used by Third Army – see below), but it was never consistently applied. In the northern section of the Ypres Salient, on Second Army front, the designations 'street', 'lane', 'road' and 'trench' were all used for communication trenches, while on First Army front 'alley' (or 'sap') remained popular, as it did with Fourth Army on the Somme in the Flers area.

Secrecy

Although the first trench maps freely showed all the German trenches, artillery batteries and other tactical features that could be identified from air photographs and other sources such as flash-spotting and sound-ranging, the depiction of the British trenches was rigorously embargoed for security reasons. These could only be shown on very limited 'secret' editions of trench maps, which were only issued to formation staffs and were not permitted to be taken forward of brigade headquarters, and certainly not into the front-line trenches where they might be captured. These 'Secret' edition trench maps showed all the British trenches with their names, and also other features of the British defensive organisation. Only small sections of these secret edition map sheets, and small sketch maps, could be taken into the front-line trenches as it was considered that the security risk was too high.

It was only gradually that the printing of British trenches (without names) was permitted on non-secret editions; in 1915 it was permitted to show the British front line, from the end of 1916 the front and support lines could be shown to a depth of some 200 yards, and the restrictive policy was dropped further in late 1917, when up to 600 yards could be shown, and completely in 1918, when all trenches could at last be shown (though not features that could not be already identified by the enemy from air photos). Thus British 1918 maps generally show all the German and British trenches, with names. However misplaced this policy of excessive secrecy – the Germans were quite capable of making their own maps of the Allied trenches from air photos – the fact remains that for most of the war the trace of the British trenches, and their names, was considered something that had to be kept from the enemy. This also applied to French practice.

Second Army Front, Mid- to Late 1915

In June 1915 the front trenches of the 19th Brigade in the Laventie sector included *Trench 59*. This brigade was part of 27th Division of III Corps (8th, 27th, 12th and Canadian Divisions), whose Trenches *60* to *89* ran from the left of 19th Brigade northward to the Lys river near Armentières.[4] This number sequence persisted, for in the Wez Macquart–Houplines area, east and south-east of Armentières, the British front trenches in early 1916 were still numbered from *67* to *80*, while the support trenches used the numbers of the trenches in front of them with an *S* suffix (*73S*, etc). This system had remained unchanged from 1915.[5] Robert Graves, joining the 2nd Royal Welch Fusiliers (19th Brigade) at Laventie at the end of July 1915, found himself in 'high command breastworks' in the *Red Lamp Corner* sector.[6] Nearby, the British rear position of the *Bois Grenier Line* existed by midsummer.

In mid-1915 Ian Hay, an officer in a New Army division, the 15th Scottish Division, which was entering the trenches for the first time, noted the following names in the Bois Grenier sector: *Old Kent Road* communication trench, *London Bridge*, *Jock's Joy*, *Piccadilly* and *Piccadilly Circus*, *The Haymarket*, *Artillery Lane*, *Cyclists' Rest*, *Shaftesbury Avenue*, *Trafalgar Square*, and the Anglesey tongue-twister *Llanfairpwllgwyngyllgogerychwyrndrobwll-llantysiliogogogoch Villa*,[7] probably the longest name on the Western Front. By August, *Queen's Avenue*, *City Road*, *Greatwood Avenue*, *Emma Post*, *Queer Street*, *Stanway Avenue* and *Safety Alley* existed in the Flamengrie–Bois Grenier area of 27th Division's sector, as did 'fortified localities' at Bois Grenier, La Vesée, Rue Flerie, Rue Allée, Gris Pot, L'Armée, *Halfway House* and Rue Marle.

Naming at this time was (subject to conformity to higher formation designation guidelines) clearly considered to be a prerogative of units and lower formations, as on 10 August 1915 a staff captain of III Corps (transferred in July to First Army) wrote to 27th Division:

1/10,000 map forwarded showing positions of trenches, fortified localities, etc, as we have them marked on a map at Corps HQ. Although the maps have been compiled from information forwarded from time to time from Divisions, I should be glad if you would verify their correctness and make any alterations or additions which are necessary either in positions of works or *names of places* [author's italics] and return to me.[8]

The names given above were soon joined by many further London names: *Oxford Circus, Down Street, Brick Street, Half Moon Street, Clarges Street, Berkeley Street, Albemarle Street* and *Dover Street*. Many non-London names also appeared in the trench system, including *Achi Baba* and *Sedd-el-Bahr* from Gallipoli, and *McGill Street, Toronto Street* and *Winnipeg Street* from Canada.[9]

Second Army Front, May 1916

The alphanumerical system used by Second Army to designate British trenches survived well into 1916. A large-scale (1:5,000) linen trace (*Secret, Plan No. 94 23-5-16*) of the Ridge Wood–Bois Quarante–Vierstraat area south of Ypres, apparently held by 24th Division at the time, showing the British trenches in green, topographical detail in back and water in blue, designated the British front trenches (from south to north) in sectors from *E* to *O*, retaining therefore the 1915 assignments.[10]

Extension of the British Front and the Battle of Loos, 1915

The growth of the BEF on the Western Front enabled it to take over considerable additional stretches of line. In the second half of May 1915, First Army extended its right for 5 miles from Cuinchy, just south of the La Bassée Canal, to near *Puits 16* opposite Lens; this was to be the frontage of the Battle of Loos. On 4 June Joffre sent a draft of his plan for a combined Artois–Champagne offensive to Sir John French, suggesting British participation. General French on 19 June stated that he intended to attack on the Loos front from Grenay to the La Bassée Canal.[11] At Saint-Omer on 11 July, French and Joffre discussed the plan. French, Haig (commanding First Army) and the latter's corps commanders had carefully reconnoitred the ground chosen by Joffre, between Loos and La Bassée, and had already agreed that it was unsuitable, preferring to attack north of the canal; a compromise was reached, but the date of the attack was repeatedly postponed.

British formations and units taking over from the French Tenth Army south of the La Bassée Canal were provided with French war *plans directeurs*, but for security reasons these did not show the French trenches. Special secret editions of the *plans directeurs* showing French trenches were, however, printed for the great Artois and Champagne battles in September. The trench system taken over, with trench names, was shown on French sketch maps

Scots Guards cleaning, and inserting detonators into, the new Mills hand grenades while holding trenches at the *Hohenzollern Redoubt*, in the closing stages of the Battle of Loos, September–October 1915. Trenches here were named *Big Willie* and *Little Willie* after the German Kaiser and Crown Prince.

supplied to incoming units in the Loos sector in May 1915. French trenches were renamed by British units, and *Old Boots Trench* appeared opposite the *Hohenzollern Redoubt* (shown on the *Auchy–Lens* map sheet of 11 June by that name, but also referred to by First Army on 13 June as *Fort Hohenzollern*[12]) a little farther to the south. The French numbered '*boyaux*' system for communication trenches was retained for a long time, although the word '*boyau*' was gradually replaced by 'sap'. Some of these '*boyau*' designations remained in use throughout the war. British trench map coverage of this front, redrawn from French sheets, followed immediately, but these new sheets again failed to show the British trenches. Two 1:10,000 demy sheets, *Haisnes* and *Loos*, were printed at GHQ at the end of May, and these were soon combined into the *Auchy–Lens* (GSGS 3073) sheet, printed at Southampton, with German trenches (very few of which were named) revised to 11 June.

A 6th Brigade defence scheme for Section *Y* (opposite Hulluch), dated 14 June, showed many numbered *boyaux* and 'Supporting Points' lettered *P* (Haie Triangulaire), *T* (Le Rutoire Farm) and *Q* (on *Boyau 1* between Le Rutoire Farm and Vermelles). It also stated that a new supporting point (*S*) was being constructed 500 yards south-east of Le Rutoire Farm, to replace *P*.[13] There were soon many of these keeps behind the immediate front system, in line with policy previously adopted; in the Vermelles area were *Railway Keep*, *Central Keep*, *Fountain Keep*, *Clarke's Keep*, *Inglis Keep*, *Brewery Keep*, *Water Tower Keep*, *Hulluch Road Keep*, *Junction Keep*, *Chapel Keep*, *Daly's Keep*, *Loos Road Keep* and *Quality Keep North*. Most of these were named after the Royal Engineer officers responsible for their construction or after features on the ground.

Communication trenches taken over from the French, many having formerly received only *boyaux* numbers, were among the first to be renamed, several of them with the same names as the keeps: *Railway Alley*, *Fountain Alley*, *Clarke's Alley*, *Gordon Alley*, *Mills Alley*, *Le Rutoire Alley*, *French Alley*, *Chapel Alley*, *Hulluch Alley*, *Hay Alley*, *Stansfield Road*, *Cross Way*, *Fosse Way*, *Daly's Passage*, *Northern Up* and *Southern Up*, *London Road* and *Finchley Road*. Rear lines were named *Sussex Trench* and *Lancashire Trench*. Dressing Stations were named *Bart's* and *Guy's*, after the famous London teaching hospitals, and these gave their names to *Guy's Alley* and *Bart's Trench*, communication trenches.

One of the most important positions in rear of the front line on the Loos battlefield was Le Rutoire, a fortified farm well-described during the Battle of Loos by Gilbert Frankau[14] who, together with Patrick MacGill,[15] incorporated much of the named topography of the Loos battlefield into their writing. MacGill named a dugout in the Loos sector *The Last House in the World*.[16] Other important localities were *Lone Tree*, the flowering cherry tree in no man's land, and the nearby features marked on the map *The Haie*, *Bois Carrée* and *Triangular Fence*. Further key localities were *Quality Street*, on the Béthune–Lens road, and the commanding observation positions on the slag heaps of *Fosse 3* at Annequin, *Fosse 5* at Grenay, and so on. The Germans held the key positions of the *Hohenzollern Redoubt*, protecting their observation posts on the dump of *Fosse 8*, the *Loos Road* and *Lens Road Redoubts*, various strongpoints in their second line known as *Stutzpunkt 1, 2*, etc., Loos itself with its commanding colliery winding towers known variously to the British as *The Pylons*, *Tower Bridge* or *Crystal Palace*, and behind all these the eminence of *Hill 70 Redoubt*.[17]

First Army's rear defences were also being elaborated before the Loos battle. In July Rawlinson's IV Corps was working on the *Grenay* and *Sailly Labourse Lines*, and on a new line east of Vermelles, as well as on the front system of defence. Haig held a conference on First Army's defences on 11 July at Hinges Château, one item on the agenda being a 'Uniform system of nomenclature for rearward lines of defence and supporting points'. More discussion on defensive organisation took place towards the end of the month, and on 27 July First Army issued its *Scheme of Defence*, which included the following instruction:

In order to avoid misunderstanding, the terms 2nd line, G.H.Q. line, etc., will not be used. The various systems of defence and groups of supporting points fall naturally into certain zones of defence which will in future be designated as follows:

(a) <u>front system</u> – includes Front trenches, support trenches, reserve trenches, communication trenches, keeps and all supporting points and defended localities immediately in rear.

(b) Grenay–Village–St Vaast–Croix Barbée–Fleurbaix system. With the following branches:

    (1) Vermelles branch

    (2) Noyelles branch

    (3) Tuning Fork branch

    (4) Bois Grenier branch

    (5) La Vesée branch

    (6) L'Armée branch

    (7) Erquinghem branch

(c) Houchin–Beuvry–Gorre–Essars–Vieille Chapelle–Bout Deville–Le Drumez and River Lys system. This includes all defensive works and bridgeheads on both banks of the Rivers Lawe and Lys, and the Steenwerke branch.

(d) The Canal system – Robecq–St Venant–Steenbecque.

<u>Note</u>: All defensive works, keeps, localities, and bridge heads will be known by their names.[18]

Three days later, following another conference at Hinges on 30 July to discuss the defence scheme, Haig issued further instructions to his corps commanders to drum in certain important principles, including knowledge of names:

Attention is drawn by the G.O.C. 1st Army to the following points … All officers commanding batteries and companies should be fully acquainted with the schemes of defence, the various systems of defence, the names of all keeps and supporting points in any area in which they may be used.

    <u>It is only by making the subordinate commanders acquainted with the principles and general scheme of defence, that you can expect them to use their initiative boldly in the right direction</u> [underlined for emphasis in the original].[19]

Haig was absolutely right in emphasising this contribution of knowledge and initiative. Local commanders could not exercise the latter unless they were thoroughly *au fait* with the layout of the defences and the names of all trenches and other features.

Certain of the German trenches were named by the British before or during the Battle of Loos in September–October 1915; it had been realised that naming the German trenches on the maps was of great assistance to the staff in writing orders, and also to brigade and battalion officers and NCOs when it came to carrying them out. *Quarry Trench* was referred to by First Army on

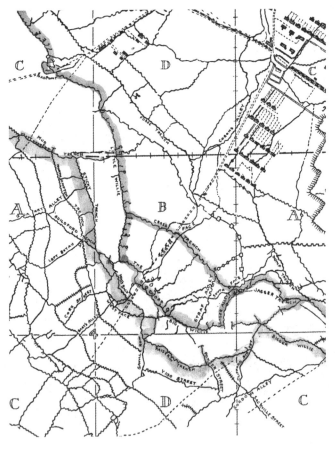

British trench map showing British (left) and German trench systems at the *Hohenzollern Redoubt*, 2 December 1915. *Big and Little Willie* form part of the German front line. The zig-zag feature on the right of the miners' cottages at the top is the Dump of *Fosse 8*. This map was drawn and lithographed in the field by First Army Printing Section RE.

21 July,[20] and over the next few weeks the following names appeared: *Brick Trench* (or *Les Briques Trench*), *Railway Trench*, *Mine Point*, *Mad Point*, *Fosse Trench*, *Corons Alley* and, at the *Hohenzollern Redoubt*, *Little* and *Big Willie*, *West*, *North* and *South Faces*, *The Dump* (*Fosse 8*), *Dump Trench*, *Slag Alley* and *Fosse Alley* were all named. South of *The Dump* were *The Pope's Nose*, *Hans*, *Fritz* and *Otto Redoubts*, *Goeben Alley* and *Breslau Avenue* (named after the German warships that escaped into the Black Sea), *The Window* and *The Slit*, *St Elie Avenue* and *Hulluch Road Trench*.[21]

The same went for the names of the British trenches, which were now printed in the field on lithographed 'secret' edition maps (blue trench plate for British trenches overprinted on cropped regular series sheets) for the first time. As part of its preparations for the Loos battle, First Army's Maps & Printing Section produced such maps showing the British trenches, with names, in blue, as well as the German trenches in red, some of them named. New assault trenches ('parallels') were dug in the wide no man's land north of Loos, connected with the old front line by saps, to reduce the distance to the German position. These were shown, with names, on the secret edition of the 1:10,000 trench maps.

The assault on 25 September captured key German positions such as Loos village, the *Loos Road Redoubt*, *Lens Road Redoubt* (*Jew's Nose*), and part of the *Hohenzollern Redoubt*. The *Hill 70 Redoubt* was temporarily overrun, but had to be relinquished. On 27 September the Guards Division attacked at *Hill 70*, and Lt Carrol Romer, commanding First Army's Printing Section, noted: 'Hill 70 is the key and it does not seem to be very clear what the situation is there. My show is working at full blast.'[22] Equipped only with hand-litho presses for map production, his Section was hard-pressed to supply the large-scale trench diagrams needed for the close-quarter fighting that had developed at *Fosse 8*, in the *Hohenzollern Redoubt*, at *Hill 70* and elsewhere.

On 5 October, while the battle continued, he wrote despairingly of the men in *Big Willie* and *Little Willie*, trenches on either flank of the *Hohenzollern Redoubt*, named after the Kaiser and the Crown Prince:

I ponder by the fire deeply – It is midnight and I am waiting for my work to be completed. I ponder of others, with no fire to warm their feet and who stand in mud in Little Willie or is it Big Willie, yes Big Willie, that trench near to Boche. Then there are those others in mud in hope or despair but in pain and discomfort – amongst bursting shell and bomb in the wet night. It is horrible ...[23]

In the event, the British managed to cling to the west face of the *Redoubt*. The battle dragged on for some weeks. On 13 October Robert Graves noted that his battalion was now ordered to the *Hohenzollern Redoubt*, and that they had been issued with new trench maps of this grim location.[24]

At the time of the Loos battle, a light railway or trench tramway was constructed from *Victoria Station* (behind the old British line) eastward to *Posen Station* (close to the old German first position). These names were perpetuated; in May 1916 Lieutenant John Staniforth (7th Leinsters) described the warren of trenches in the Loos sector in wired-up urban terms as:

> ... a world of moles, burrowing always deeper and deeper to get away from the high explosives: an underground city with avenues, lanes, streets, crescents, alleys and cross-roads, all named and labelled and connected by telegraph and telephone. 'No.3 Posen Alley' was my last address, and you reach it via 'Piccadilly', 'Victoria Station', and 'Sackville Street'.[25]

In his novel *Greenmantle* (1916), John Buchan, who was a war correspondent at the Battle of Loos, made a point of commemorating certain of the key names of that bloody field: *Lone Tree*, the *Hohenzollern Redoubt*, and the *Hairpin* trench near *The Quarries*. In the same breath, he also referenced another charnel house of the 1915 fighting, the 'ugly angle at Hooge' on Second Army's Front.[26]

Indian Names

We have already made reference to the Indian Army names given to tactical features in the Neuve Chapelle area and elsewhere earlier in 1915. Apart from secret edition sheets showing British trenches, and embryonic barrage maps, particular evidence of staff forethought for the Battle of Loos exists in the form of various 1:20,000 and 1:40,000 sheets of the Loos area prepared with names transliterated into Arabic, Nagari and Gurumulslie (or Urdu, Punjabi and Gujerati) characters for the use of the Indian Cavalry Corps. Though the Indian Corps was transferred to the Middle East after the 1915 campaign (except for the cavalry, which remained for the Somme battle), certain names associated with the Indian Army remained on the trench maps to the end of the war – for example the *Indian Village*, near Festubert.

1916 – Redesignation of Front Trenches by First Army

From the beginning of 1916, First Army introduced a new alphanumeric system of designating its front trenches; this was by map-square; for example, the front-line trenches in map-square *S 23* (a square with sides of 1,000 yards) were designated from right to left *S.23.1*, *S.23.2* and *S.23.3*. This system ignored the 500 yard sub-squares. Front trenches were generally unnamed or, if they were, the names did not appear on the secret editions of the trench maps.

Third Army 1915–16: Taking Over From the French on the Somme Front

British formations had been taking over portions of the front from the French since the end of 1914 but, apart from the Ypres Salient, the first really significant area to be taken over was that north of the Somme river, and astride the Ancre, in late July 1915. On 11 July Sir John French also agreed that his new Third Army, specifically formed complete with its own specialist

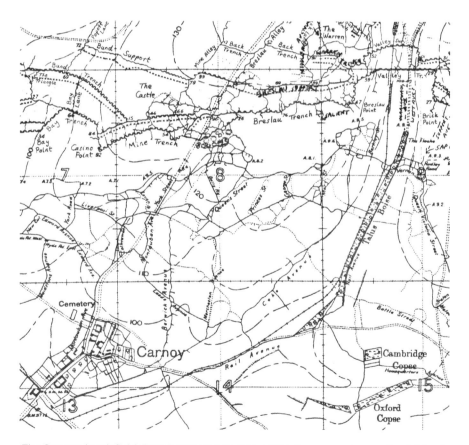

The Somme battlefield: British 1916 trench map of the Carnoy sector, south of Albert and north of the Somme. The British trench system is in the bottom two-thirds of the map, and the German front system at the top.

survey and mapping unit (3rd Topographical Section) for this purpose, should take over two French corps fronts astride the Somme, this relief being planned to take place between 18 July and 8 August.[27] In fact Third Army at first took over more than 15 miles of chalk downland front from Curlu on the Somme, northward past Albert and Thiepval, to Hébuterne. It later, in September, also briefly took over a frontage south of the Somme.

Trenches in the area north of the Somme had already been numbered and named by the French (see Chapter VIII), and many were renamed by their new inhabitants over the next few months. Third Army briefly extended south of the Somme on the Chaulnes–Curlu front in October 1915, and continued to take over more line northward from the French towards Arras. During this process of wholesale relief of French corps and armies, complete trench systems and defence schemes were taken over. The French trench names were retained, and only gradually replaced. Along certain stretches of the front, the French names survived the Somme battle, and in the Vimy Ridge sector some were still in use in 1918.

On taking over from the French, Third Army issued new Instructions with regard to tactical training and the organisation of works of defence. This document stated that:

The following nomenclature will be allocated with regard to defensive lines:

Front trench	for actual Fire Trench
Support trench	for Supporting Trench
Battalion Reserve trench	for Battalion Reserves
Brigade Reserve trench	for Brigade Reserves
Keep	for small post close up to support trench; Garrison up to one platoon
Supporting point	for works or defended localities anywhere in rear of keeps; Garrison from 1 Company to 1 Battalion
Shelter	Needs no explanation. This work is to be used in place of the slang term 'dugout'
Avenue	Main communication trenches. They should be named
Street	Minor communication trenches. They should be named
Forming up places	Trenches excavated in any part of the first line system for the purpose of screening infantry prior to an attack

Signboards and direction posts should be freely used to indicate the name of avenues, streets, and supporting points, and to show the way to neighbouring trenches.[28]

When 5th Division took over the Curlu–Fricourt front from the French, it also took over the French 1:20,000 *plan directeur*, or trench map, which showed German but not French trenches, and also larger-scale sheets that also only showed German trenches. Prior to the production of a new British trench map, the French map, with German trenches in blue corrected to 18 July 1915, was used as a base for adding in manuscript the French trenches taken over, and at the same time for entering the new British names for the communication trenches. The French front trenches had been numbered from *11* (at the Moulin de Fargny, on the Somme) to *104* east of Bécourt, south-east of Albert, and these numbers were retained for the time being by the British. French rear systems, elaborated by the British, were also unnamed.[29]

Third Topographical Section's officers gave some fascinating names to topographical features in and around the Somme valley (*Maricourt, Vaux* and *Péronne* sheets): *120 Millimètre Wood* (after a French battery of that calibre), *Limberlost Wood* (probably a reference not only to a German limber but also to the American authoress Gene Stratton-Porter's book *A Girl of the Limberlost*, first published in 1909), *Howitzer Wood* (behind which a German howitzer had been observed), *Walrus, Mimsey* and *Gimble Woods* and *Borogrove* [sic] *Trees*, (these last four from Lewis Carroll), *Observation Wood* (French *Bois des Observateurs*), *Salmon Wood* and *Yakko Copse* (both named by F.J. Salmon, 3rd Topographical Section's Trig and Topo Officer), etc.

In the Curlu sector, closest to the river, the names given by the British to the communication trenches running over the downland, and the occasional redoubt, were: *Suzanne Avenue, Crest Avenue, Head Quarter* [Trench], *Observation Avenue, Ravine Avenue, Fargny Wood Avenue* and *Péronne North Avenue*. In the area of the village and wood at Maricourt were *Privet Avenue, Main Avenue, Round Point Avenue, Orchard Avenue, Castle Avenue, Centre Avenue, Weston Avenue, Maricourt Avenue, Head Quarter Avenue* and *Support Avenue*. To the west and north, in the Carnoy and Mametz sector, were *Rail Avenue, Coke Avenue, Merchiston Avenue, Montauban Avenue, Edward Avenue, Francis Avenue, George Avenue, Péronne Avenue, Wellington Redoubt* and *Avenue, Portland Avenue, Weymouth Avenue, Redoubt A, Bonté* [Redoubt], *Rendel Avenue, Willow Avenue, Royal Avenue, King's Avenue, Bolzinger* [Trench] and *Queen's Avenue*.[30] These names were augmented by others as the trench system was further developed, and as new units moved into the sector. In accordance with the Third Army *Instructions*, 'avenue' designated a communication trench on this corps front.

Siegfried Sassoon and Robert Graves were here with the Royal Welch Fusiliers in early 1916, in the Morlancourt sector, opposite Fricourt and Mametz, and a map in Sassoon's possession, formerly used by the battalion intelligence officer, showed many names in addition to the above; as well as *Gibraltar*, *71 North* and *South*, and *The Citadel* for rear positions marked on the detail plate of the trench map, the following Kentish trench names appeared, several of which were mentioned in his fictionalised autobiographies *Memoirs of a Fox-Hunting Man* and *Memoirs of an Infantry Officer*: *Ashford Street*, *Dover Street*, *Tonbridge Street*, *Maidstone Street*, *Canterbury Avenue*, *Old Kent Road* and *Shooter's Hill*. In addition he spoke of *Crawley Ridge* [Redoubt], *Maple Redoubt*, *Bonté Redoubt*, *Wicked Corner*, *Watling Street*, *Albert Road*, *Portland Road* and the German *Bois Français Trench* and *Kiel Trench*, while Graves referred to the *Trafalgar Square* trench junction.[31]

In the La Boisselle sector east of Albert, many Scottish names were given in August 1915 by the 51st Highland Division to trenches taken over from the French. A French map from the 153rd Brigade War Diary, dated 28 July 1915, includes some Scottish names written alongside the original French names. It was reported that the Scots found it hard to pronounce the French names, hence the renaming.[32] English troops had the same problem with the Scots names when they subsequently took over the same trenches. Communication trenches in the La Boisselle sector were named, among others, *Arbroath Street*, *Tarvis Street*, *Lochnagar Street*, *Kirriemuir Street*, *Atholl Street*, *Scone Street*, *Methuen Street*, *Anstruther Street*, *Dunfermline Street*, *Largo Street*, *Kirkaldy Street*, *St Andrews Avenue*, *St Monans Street*, *Kilfauns Street*, *Pitlochry Street*, *Argyll Street*, etc. There were also *Burnt Island*, *Keats Redan*, *Market Cross* and *Joseph's Well*. Some topographical names in this sector were Irish: *Usna Hill*, *Tara Hill* (and their eponymous redoubts), *Avoca Valley* and so on. The 32nd Division, who arrived here in March 1916, mentioned Irish names in their War Diary.

Sausage Valley in the same sector (a companion of *Mash Valley*) may have derived its name from the large trench mortar bombs known as 'sausages', but another possibility is that the name derives from British observation balloons ('sausages' or ruder names) based in the valley, as shown in a sketch in the 17th Highland Light Infantry history. Farther north, at the eastern tip of Authuille Wood where the British line turned briefly west around the German *Leipzig Salient* and *Redoubt* before running north again past Thiepval Wood, a pronounced British salient was named *The Nab* – one of the many 'nose' euphemisms used for naming at the front.

Scottish naming continued through this sector, the Thiepval Wood trenches were mostly named by the Scots – *Gourock Street*, *Sauchiehall Street*, *Clyde Avenue*, *Greenock Avenue*, *Paisley Avenue*, *Forres Street*, *Elgin Avenue*,

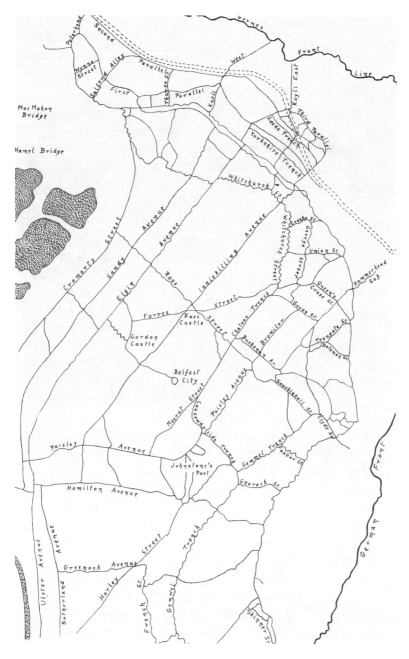

British sketch map of the British trench system, with names, in the Thiepval Wood sector, Somme battlefield, August 1916. The many Scottish names were given by the 51st Highland Division in 1915. Note the later First, Second and Third Parallels dug to close the distance to the German front line (top) prior to assaulting the Thiepval position in September 1916, after the failure of 1 July.

Cromarty Street, Thurso Street and the *Peterhead* and *Burghead* saps, etc. – but later there appeared here several Ulster names associated with the 36th Division: *Ulster Avenue, Belfast City, Inniskilling Avenue*, etc. At Hamel was *Shankhill Road*, and between here and Beaumont Hamel were the *William* and *Mary Redans*, fiercely redolent of Ulster. Yorkshire names also appeared at Thiepval Wood later in the Somme battle: the *Koyli* (King's Own Yorkshire Light Infantry) *West* and *East* saps, *Yorkshire Trench* and *Leeds Trench*. Edmund Blunden spoke at length of British and German trenches and positions in the Thiepval sector: the *Koyli* saps, *Paisley Avenue, Gordon Castle, St* [sic] *Martin's Lane*, the *Schwaben Redoubt, Thiepval Crucifix, Stuff Trench, Regina Trench* and so forth.

In the Beaumont Hamel sector, many of the trench names have become famous by association with Lieutenant Geoffrey Malins, the cinematographer, who on 1 July 1916 filmed the Lancashire Fusiliers fixing bayonets in *King Street*, and the mine explosion and 29th Division's attack at *Hawthorn Redoubt* from *Jacob's Ladder* (later renamed *Moving Staircase* to distinguish it from the *Jacob's Ladder* at Hamel). He later filmed returning wounded at *The White City*. Edmund Blunden spent months in the sector later in the Somme battle and described almost lovingly the other *Jacob's Ladder, Peche Street, Louvercy, Devial Avenue, Picturedrome* and *Kentish Caves* in the Hamel sector. Here also were *Dolly's Brae, Moss Side, Charles Avenue, Esau Alley, Macmahon Avenue, Foch Avenue* and *Buret Avenue*; the French legacy had, as Blunden would have said, contrived to linger.

Climbing up from the Ancre Valley at Hamel (*The Crow's Nest, Lancashire Post* and *Picturedrome*), the front lines ran to the west of Beaumont Hamel to the *Hawthorn Redoubt* on *Redan Ridge*. At Hamel was a large group of London names: *Long Acre, Charing Cross, Shaftesbury Avenue, St James's Street, Buckingham Palace Road, Hyde Park Corner, Piccadilly, Regent Street, Park Lane, Knightsbridge Barracks, Constitution Hill, Bond Street, Brook Street, Mount Street, Haymarket, Broadway, Praed Street, Marylebone Road, Harrow Road, Uxbridge Road, Shooters Hill*, etc. Ireland was recalled by *Limerick Junction* and *Clonmel Avenue*, while the massacre of the Newfoundland Regiment opposite *Y Ravine* on 1 July 1916 was commemorated by *Terra Nova Street*. Unbelievably, up on the Hawthorn Ridge opposite the German redoubt and on the site of the failure of the 29th Division filmed by Geoffrey Malins on 1 July was *Happy Alley* (later marked on maps as *Happy Valley*), an inversion in several senses of *Happy Valley* and undoubtedly one of the most ironic names on the Western Front.

Opposite Beaumont Hamel and over Redan Ridge to the front facing Serre, many other London names appeared: *Elephant and Castle, The Lyceum, High Holborn Avenue, Cheapside Avenue, Hyde Park Corner, Newgate Street, Bow*

Men of 1st Battalion, Lancashire Fusiliers, fixing bayonets at the junction of *King Street* and the Firing Line, prior to the attack on Beaumont Hamel, 1 July 1916. The sign on the right indicates the direction of 'Battle HQ'. (IWM Q744)

Street, *Haymarket*, *New Oxford Street*, etc., but also a miscellany of other derivations: *Minden Terrace*, *Tenderloin Street* and *The White City*, and the biblical *Esau's Way* and *Jacob's Ladder*. *Gabion Avenue* was a reminder of the methods of an older form of siege warfare. On the Redan Ridge, saps to a new forward line were called *Rat*, *Bear*, *Cat*, *Dog*, *Egg* and *New Egg Streets*. Support and reserve trenches were named in this zone, including *86th* and *88th Trenches*, *Essex Street*, *Cardiff Street*, *St Helens Street* and *Fethard Street*. Several old French trench names also survived in this area. North of here were the famous *Matthew*, *Mark*, *Luke* and *John Copses*, named after the four disciples, with a further group of associated biblical names for the communication trenches in their hinterland: *Palestine Avenue*, *Jordan*, *Babylon*, *Eden*, *Uriah* and *Excema*. The Sheffield City Battalion, one of the Pals Battalions that went over from this sector to attack Serre on 1 July 1916, was commemorated by *Wicker Trench*.

As British formations of Third Army took over from the French in the Hébuterne–Fonquevillers sector, opposite Gommecourt, French names, mostly of communication trenches, were replaced with British ones on an alphabetical system based on sector designation. Thus in '*W*' Sector, we find *Watson Street*, *Warrior Street*, *Welcome Street*, *Whiskey Street*, *Woman Street*, *Wood Street* and *Wurzel Street*, and north of these in '*Y*' Sector were *Yankee Street*, *Yellow Street*, *Yiddish Street*, *York Street*, *Young Street*, *Yussif Street* and *Yuz Street*. At the north end of '*Y*' Sector, fittingly enough, was *Z Hedge*, but this had been named from its plan view rather than from any allegiance to a naming scheme. That said, there were also *Z Road*, *Little Z* and *The Z* a little farther north. There was no '*X*' group of trenches, and perhaps the staff officer responsible for name allocation had suffered a lexicographic crisis. He may have thought that the artillery (or whoever) could not cope with *Xanadu*, *Xenophon*, *Xmas* and *X-Ray*; indeed the few works beginning with 'X' in the dictionary are mostly unpronounceable. There were many survivals here from the original French naming after Gallic cultural celebrities and battles: *Annibal* (Hannibal), *Pelissier*, *Kellerman*, *Solferino*, *Papin*, *Pasteur*, *Saalfeld*, *Jena*, *La Fayette*, *Gounod*, *Vercingetorix*, *Guesclin*, *Wagram*, *Jean Bart*, *Vauban*, *Delaunay*, *Taupin*, etc., for communication trenches. To receive this honour, Hannibal must have been made an honorary Frenchman. Most of these trenches were subsequently renamed by the British; for example, *Wagram* became *Nairn*. *Jean Bart*, on the other hand, was formerly known as *Auerstadt*, and the latter name was used on British trench maps as well as *Jean Bart*. Further, the trace of *Jean Bart* and *Auerstadt* differed by some 100 yards. This could be put down to poor copying from French *plans directeurs*, or the inaccurate survey of Allied trenches (it was the responsibility of the divisional engineers), or both.

At Fonquevillers there was a series of communication trenches beginning with '*R*': *Rotten Row*, *Roberts Avenue*, *Regent Street*, *Raymond Avenue*, but south of these were *Leicester Street* and *Nottingham Street*, clearly the result of occupation by a Midlands formation. Between Fonquevillers and Hannescamps, the communication trenches were ordered in a sequential alphabetical system from right to left: *Appleby Sap*, *Bristol Sap*, *Colchester*, *Durham Street*, *Exmouth Street*, *Falmouth Street*, *Hull Street*, *Ipswich Street*, *Kendal Street*, *Lime Street*. South of *Durham Street*, there were several beginning with '*C*': *Crawl Boys Lane*, *Conduit Avenue*, *Chiswick Avenue*, *Cork Street*, *Central Avenue*. Optimistically running into Hannescamps from the north-west was *Berlin Street*, the name reminiscent of the *Berlin Tunnel* being driven under Hill 60. North of Hannescamps, opposite Monchy-au-Bois, the front communication trenches were in an '*L*' group: *Landleague*, *Lille Street*, *Linton Road*, *Lime Street*, *London Road*, *Le Mere*, *Lily Road* and *Longwy Street*. To the north of these were a sequence numbered *79 Street* to *90 Street*, presumably a continuation of the old French *boyau* numbering, while the communication trenches farther back all began with the letter '*S*': *St Cross Street*, *Shell Street*, *Stoneygate Road*, *Sergeants Parade*.[33]

North of Monchy-au-Bois, all the communication trenches began with 'N', the sector designation: *Neverending Street*, *Nitrate Street*, *Newark Street*,

Ninety-Nine Street, Noodles Avenue, Nawful Street, Noss Walk, North Street, Nuts Walk and *Nullah Street*. Clearly some brigade staff officer was enjoying himself. North again, in the Berles-au-Bois sector they all began with 'F': *Francis Street, Fish Street, Farnborough Road*, etc., and then with 'R': *Renfrew Road, Rugby Road, Roscommon Road* and their associated redoubts *Renfrew Work* and *Rugby Work*. North of these, they were all 'L's: *Lincoln Lane, Lanark Lane, Limerick Lane, Llandaff Lane* and *Llandaff Work*. It is difficult to discern any overarching scheme here, other than the lettered sections and the mostly geographical associations (which were perhaps also regimental).

First and Third Army Take Over the Arras–Vimy Ridge Sector, March 1916

At the end of 1915, Third Army's left flank was south of Ransart, where it abutted the French Tenth Army in the Arras–Vimy Ridge sector. When, between 2 and 14 March, 1916 Third Army sidestepped northward, taking over the Arras front from the French, its place on the Somme front was taken by Rawlinson's new Fourth Army, which was given the task of attacking in the summer. At the same time, First Army extended its front to the right, south of Lens, to join up with Third Army on Vimy Ridge. As on the Somme front in 1915, many French trench names were changed by the British formations.

In the sector opposite Ransart, newly taken over from the French, the alphabetical naming according to sector designation which was used farther south did not apply; the naming here was alphabetically random. Between Ransart and Blairville, in the sector of *The Talus*, the German position known as *The Blockhouse*, and *The Osier Bed*, where a stream ran in the valley of no man's land, names of communication trenches clearly related to the local topography: *Hedge Street, Willows Street, Dyke Street, Osier Street*. At *Shrapnel Corner*, Bellacourt, a small British defence work was called *Starfish Post* from its plan view.[34]

In the Rivière–Agny sector, opposite Beaurains, south of Arras, alphabetical numbering was again the rule. Communication trenches in 'F' and 'G' Sectors all began with those letters: *Forest Street, Ficheux Street, Fox Street, Fuze Street, Fiddle Street, Factory Road, Fine Street, Foul Street, Folly Lane, Flag Street, Flood Street, French Street, Ferret Street, Francis Street, Frog Street, Farm Street, Farrow Street, Fenchurch Street, Fleet Street* and *Friary Street*; *Game Street, Gate Street, George Street, Gem Street, Grantham Street, Girl Street, Goat Street, Gun Street, Grouse Street, Grave Street, Granger Street, Grey Street* and *Green Street*.

'*H*' Sector ran north-east from Agny, curving around the south-eastern side of Arras; here the British formations renamed the trenches taken over from the French *Hopeless Street*, *Hope Street*, *Hardy Street*, *Hastings Street*, *Haig Street*, *Haymarket*, *Hume Street*, *High Street*, *Havannah Street*, *Havelock Street*, *Hull Street*, *Holborn*, *Het Sas Street*, *Halstead Street*, *Hooge Street*, *Halifax Street*, *Horace Street*, *Hulluch Street* and *Hunter Street*. It can be seen that some of these names were derived from the Ypres and Loos sectors. North of these was '*I*' Sector covering the eastern side of Arras and featuring, among others, *Iceland Street*, *Ice Street*, *Idle Lane*, *Inverness Lane*, *Italy Trench*, *Ideal Cutting*, *Imperial Street*, *India Street*, *Infantry Road*, *Ingot Lane*, *Ibex Lane*, *Ivy Street*, *Islington Street*, *Interpreter Street*, *Ivory Street*, *Iris Street*, *Income Tax*, *Inns of Court* and then *Invalid Street* and *Iron Street* at Blangy by the Scarpe river. When the British first took over here, *Boyau Vert* managed to survive among all those '*I*'s for a while. North of the Scarpe, the British communication trenches ran sequentially from right to left by months of the year from *January Avenue* to *December Avenue*, and then by days of the week: *Sunday Avenue* ... *Thursday Avenue*, *Friday Avenue*, etc., towards Roclincourt, *The Labyrinth* and Vimy Ridge. In the Roclincourt sector followed *Génie Avenue*, *Anzin Avenue*, *Béthune Avenue* (*Down* and *Up*), *Madagascar Avenue*, etc., in an apparently haphazard sequence.

There was not, therefore, a consistent naming policy for British trenches in Third Army area, but again it can be seen that it was primarily communication trenches that were named. Support and reserve lines were often, on the map, designated exactly that: *Support Line* and *Reserve Line*. It was presumably divisions and corps rather than army that dominated the naming process.

Very few German trenches were given names on British trench maps in 1915, and the practice only developed slowly during 1916. When Third Army took over the Arras sector in early 1916, it at first adopted the names given to German trenches by the French. These were later changed to German names, presumably taken from captured German maps. The Battle of Loos in September–October 1915, and more particularly the Battle of the Somme in the summer and autumn of 1916, emphasised the absolute necessity for naming the German trenches, especially when the names were used in conjunction with map square references and coordinates. Not infrequently the coordinates given in operation orders by the staff were incorrect, and without the trench name serious mistakes were liable to occur. In the Gommecourt sector (Fonquevillers and Hébuterne sheets), the German trenches were given British names for the attack of 1 July 1916, but by October of that year these had been replaced by their German names, clearly obtained from captured maps.

The rationale for using German names for their own trenches was clear: during a British attack, the discovery of a German trench nameboard among the general debris of shell-smashed positions would be of great assistance to the assaulting troops in determining their precise location. This rationale was made explicit during the Canadian preparations for the Vimy Ridge attack in April 1917 when, in the British rear training areas, facsimile German trench signs were positioned on the appropriate trenches on the terrain models used by the Canadian units training for the attack, so that these units could find their orientation on the actual battlefield. There were also other reasons for using the German names on British maps. This practice helped the intelligence staff to fit locations mentioned in intercepted and captured messages, orders, maps, photos, and other documents and prisoner interrogation reports, to their own maps.

Battle of the Somme, July–November 1916

Allied trenches in the Somme area had already been named by previous French and British occupants, and many of these names have been given above. However, the 36th Ulster Division managed, before 1 July 1916, to give some Belfast names to trenches in the Hamel and Thiepval Wood sub-sectors: *Royal Avenue*, *Great Victoria Street*, *Sandy Row*,[35] *Picturedrome* (the cinema on the Shankhill Road) and *Belfast City*. Certain key objectives in the German position were named after Ulster towns such as *Belfast* and *Derry*,[36] and the men of the Ulster Division referred to the notorious *Schwaben Redoubt* as the *Devil's Dwelling*, or *Hell's Corner*.[37] In the Thiepval Wood sector were also *Union Street* and *Jack Street*, while just north of the Ancre were *William* and *Mary Redans*.

In fact the trenches in Thiepval Wood went through at least four phases of naming: firstly French (1914–15), secondly Scottish (51st Highland Division, 1915) replacing French, thirdly Ulster (36th Division, 1916) additions, and fourthly Yorkshire (49th Division, 1916) additions in *Koyli East* and *West*, and in '*The Parallels*' (*Leeds Trench* and *Yorkshire Trench*). In July, following the failure of the initial assault on the Thiepval Ridge, older forms of siege warfare were revived, even in the naming, when advanced trenches in the form of the system of '*Parallels*' – *First Parallel*, *Second Parallel*, *Third Parallel* – were dug closer to the German front line, south of *The Pope's Nose*, prior to an all-out assault on the Thiepval fortress on 3 September. This attack also failed, and it was not until the end of that month that Thiepval was finally stormed. German occupation in 1918 introduced a fifth phase of naming in this sector.

Many other British positions and trenches in and behind the old front-line system on the Somme have passed into history – *Minden Post*, *Lochnagar Street*, *Usna* and *Tara Redoubts*, *Matthew*, *Mark*, *Luke* and *John Copses*,

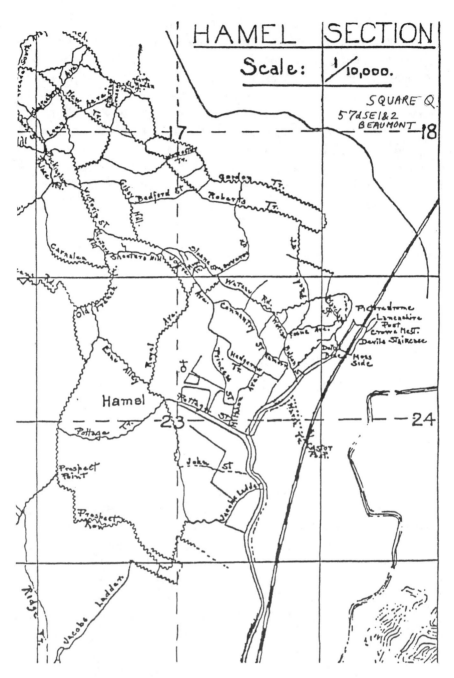

Duplicator sketch map of the British trench system at Hamel, on the River Ancre, during the Battle of the Somme. Notable names are Jacob's Ladder, Pottage Trench and Picturedrome, all of which Edmund Blunden describes in *Undertones of War*.

The White City, *The Tenderloin*, the two *Jacob's Ladders*, *Kentish Caves*, *Hammerhead Sap*, etc. The names given by the British to German trenches before the Battle of the Somme were a mixed bag. Among them were many German names, but Sassoon noted the pastoral quality of a group in the Fricourt–Mametz sector – *Apple Alley*, *Orchard Alley*, *Rose Trench* and *Willow Avenue* – which he identified with a 'topographical Arcadia'.[38] Reminders of the 1916 Easter Rising in Dublin, supported by shipments of German arms, were present here in *Dublin Trench* and *Redoubt*, and in *Casement Trench*, among the names given to enemy works.[39]

At Gommecourt Third Army's VII Corps, which assaulted that village as a diversion on 1 July, equipped the attacking divisions with maps identifying the German trenches by British names, notwithstanding that Third Army was generally pursuing a policy of using German names where these were known. But even if the German names were known, short British names were much easier to use and remember. The meticulous British preparations for the attack included giving names to every trench in the German defensive system, preparing painted name boards for these trenches and tasking troops with their erection as soon as the trenches were captured, and producing lithographed maps (drawn and printed by 3rd Field Survey Company) showing these names. The intention was that everyone involved would know exactly where they were.[40] The Official Historian noted that:

> The enemy trenches were given names by the VII. Corps on a system: first, on the right, words beginning with Fa, then blocks of Fe, Fi, Fo [but no Fu or Fum!]. The communication trenches had river names beginning with A, E, I, O to correspond. Thus behind Felon Trench was Elbe communication trench.[41]

Was there a specific naming vocabulary associated with the Somme battle? Not in the sense that it evoked a policy or practice of using names not used elsewhere, but of course, like all sectors, certain names (many of them taken over from the German names of redoubts and trenches) became forever associated with that battle and no other – *Hawthorn Redoubt* and *Y Ravine* at Beaumont Hamel, *Stuff Trench*, *Regina Trench*, the *Schwaben Redoubt*, *Wonderwork* and *Leipzig Redoubt* at Thiepval, the *Quadrilaterals* at Serre (*Heidenkopf*) and Ginchy, the *Switch Line* at Flers, *Gird Trench* taking its name from Gueudecourt, and a well-known group of trenches in the Flers area was named after newspapers and periodicals – *Bystander*, *Tatler*, *Time[s]*, *Mail*, *Punch*, etc. – while another, mentioned earlier in this book, was named after weather and meteorological conditions. This last group was immortalised by *The Daily Telegraph*'s war correspondent Perceval Gibbon, writing from

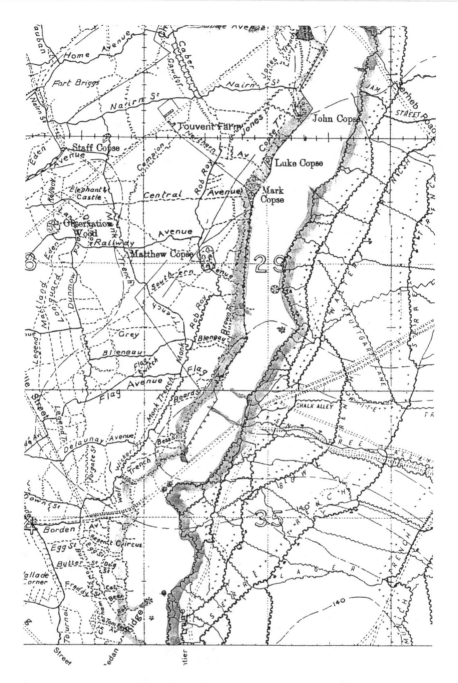

British trench map showing the British (left) and German (right) trench systems west of Serre in 1916. Note Matthew, Mark, Luke and John Copses in the British front line. The German salient near the bottom is the *Quadrilateral* or Heidenkopf, just north of Redan Ridge. The British attacked the German position at Serre unsuccessfully on 1 July 1916.

GHQ in France, in the issue of 26 October 1916, under the heading 'Typhoon of Death':

> West and north of Lesboeufs, the trenches, English and German, take their names from the weather – though none is named after fine weather. Here, upon an area of ground which has the general contour of a piece of crumpled paper, are Hazy, Frosty, Muggy, Rainy, Sleet, Thunder and Hail Trenches, shown upon the maps like fly legs drawn in red ink.[42]

He could have later added *Windy Trench*, *Stormy Trench*, *Cloudy Trench*, and others, near Flers. Of these the official historian remarked that 'the ingenuity of staffs, commanders and others was constantly exercised in finding names for new German trenches.'[43] It would be interesting to know who the 'others' were.

Through Sassoon[44] as well as the official history we remember the beery group in the Delville Wood sector of *Pilsen Lane* and *Bitter*, *Beer*, *Stout*, *Ale*, *Vat*, *Lager* and *Pint Trenches* and *Alleys*; the Official Historian laconically

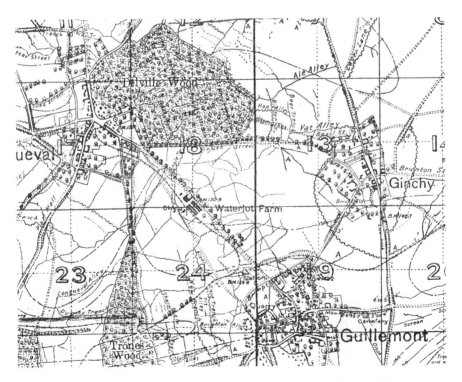

British trench map of the Longueval–Delville Wood–Ginchy–Guillemont–Trones Wood area, showing the British and German trench systems, including the 'beer' (Ale, Hop, Vat, Lager) group east of Delville Wood, and the 'London' group in the Wood itself.

noted that 'these German trenches, the position of which had been revealed by aeroplane photographs, had received simple and convenient names'.[45] Siegfried Sassoon attacked the *Quadrangle Trench* near Mametz Wood single-handed. David Jones and his 15th Royal Welch Fusiliers (London Welsh) jumped off from the little dry valley called *Queen's Nullah* over the same ground as Sassoon to attack Mametz Wood itself. *The Cough Drop* is particularly memorable, as is the sunken road named *Pilgrim's Progress* near Flers.

During the Somme battle, the British took to using a loose 'phonetic association' system based on village name nodes; thus we find a set of 'beefy' names (*Bully Trench*, *Beef Trench*, *Stew Trench*, etc.) appearing in the Lesboeufs area, *Gird Trench* at Gueudecourt, *Flare Alley* at Flers, *Till Trench* at Thilloy, *Devil's Trench* at Delville Wood, *Bark Trench* at le Barque, etc. Perhaps it would be going too far to call this a system, but it was certainly a significant phenomenon.

Strangely, the 1:10,000 trench maps issued by Fourth Army for the opening of the Battle on 1 July did not give names to the German trenches, and revision sheets printed in the field by 4th Field Survey Company, showing new German works, did not name these. The secret editions of the trench maps, printed in tiny editions and showing the British trenches did, however, give them names.

Towards the southern end of the British line the XV Corps, due to attack Fricourt and Mametz, ordered special sheets before 1 July, reproduced at the Ordnance Survey at 1:20,000, which named the German trenches. However, even as operations developed, many British trench maps did not name the German trenches. This situation changed rapidly during the battle, as it was soon realised that for successful operations it was necessary to name all the trenches on the battlefield, particularly those that formed attack objectives. It was essential that simple names, which could be easily and rapidly understood and transmitted in orders and which were marked on the daily trench maps and situation maps, should be used. From the early days of the Somme battle onwards, and in all future battles, naming of enemy as well as Allied trenches became the rule.

Furthermore, all trenches were now named, not just communication trenches. In the fluid conditions of attack and counter-attack, the old sectoral designations for front, support and reserve trenches had to go by the board. In trench and semi-open warfare, German trenches could become British, communication trenches could become fire trenches, and vice versa; all needed to be named. The old system of numbering fire trenches in the front, support and reserve lines from the right according to their sector designation (*C1*, *C2*, *C3*, or *J.29.1*, *J.29.2*, etc.), while suitable for a static front, was obsolete during a battle in which trenches were continually changing hands, being obliterated by bombardment, or simply falling into dereliction or dissolving into the porridge of the autumn and winter battlefield. However, when operations were in abeyance during the winter, sector numbering reappeared as the bureaucracy of the army defence scheme was reasserted.

Crucifix Corner is a name that recurs in accounts of the Somme battle, and there were many such locations on the Western Front, it being a French Catholic tradition to erect crucifixes by the roadside, at road junctions, etc. The three locations on the Somme were at Aveluy Wood (near Thiepval and Authuille Wood), at Bazentin (near Longueval), and at the Tambour (near Fricourt). Ivor Gurney, as Edmund Blunden noted in his introduction to *Poems of Ivor Gurney 1890–1937*, referred to *Crucifix Corner* in his work, as well as to *Dead End* (the canal cul-de-sac at Ypres) and La Gorgue (near Laventie).[46]

It was noticeable during the Somme battle that many changes of trench names occurred, so their identification during it is not as straightforward as it might appear, particularly as many of the names only appeared on the small, hastily duplicated maps produced by armies, corps or lower formations. These maps were by their nature ephemeral, and have not necessarily survived in archives as have the regular series sheets. The latter, however, appeared at far less frequent intervals and did not show all the names. Another difficulty is that several British trenches changed their names during the Somme battle – e.g. the Queen Victoria's Rifles, of the 56th (London) Division, named a new position near Leuze Wood *Victoria Trench*, subsequently changed by Divisional order to *Bully Trench*.[47] This battalion had previously given its name to *Queen Victoria Street* near St Eloi (south of Ypres) and at Maricourt. In the Pozières area the German trench *Kaiser Graben* was known to the British as *Western Trench* and *Pozières Trench*, and to the Australians as *K Trench*. Similarly, the German trench *Gierich Weg* was called *Ration Trench* and *Park Lane* by the British, and to the north of this, running towards Mouquet Farm, *Sixth Avenue* was also called *Skyline Trench*. Presumably trenches were first named by the troops on the ground, or by their immediate formation HQs, and the names were later changed by order of a higher formation (corps or army) to avoid confusion with trenches elsewhere in the same area carrying an identical name.

Famous signboards associated with the Somme battlefield include *Tattenham Corner*, from the road between Bécordel-Bécourt and Fricourt, later subtitled *The King's Horse Wins*. This outstandingly aesthetic sign, now in the Imperial War Museum, was painted in 1916 by the artist Oswald Birley. Nearby, overlooking Fricourt and Mametz, was *King George's Hill*, signed by a huge board after a visit by King George V in August during the Somme battle. Another well-known survivor was *Devil's Trench* at Delville Wood.

Devil's Trench, Delville Wood, 1917, taken after the tide of battle had moved on. (IWM Q 80270)

Tracks across the surface of the battlefield also had to be named or otherwise designated. In the undulating chalk terrain of the Somme and Arras areas, although it was often unnecessary to lay an artificial track on the ground, it was always important to mark routes very clearly and immense care had to be over this. A variety of devices were used for marking, the most usual being posts, notice boards or tapes. All markers and signs suffered damage or destruction from shellfire, and light wooden posts or boards were often damaged by weather or stolen by troops for firewood. Metal boards were occasionally used, but they were more difficult to make and erect. In zones of large troop concentration and a multiplicity of tracks, direction posts and boards had to be clearly and distinctively marked so that they could be easily recognised by units, as tracks could easily be lost or confused in foul weather, in the dust and smoke of heavy shelling or in the dark.[48] In the later stages of the Somme battle, and in 1917 in Flanders as we shall see in the next chapter, appalling ground conditions made plank roads for vehicles, and duckboard tracks for mules as well as men, absolutely indispensable, but the same imperative requirement for clear designation remained.

When Fourth Army extended its front to the south at the end of the Somme battle, taking over a sector previously held by the French, its trench maps continued for a while to maintain the French names. However, these were soon anglicised or changed. A marginal note on the St Pierre Vaast special sheet, trenches corrected to 28 December 1916, warned that: 'Trench names on this map cancel and supersede those shown on all previous maps.' This note was repeated on new editions into February 1917.[49]

Notes

1   27th Division General Staff War Diary, TNA(PRO) WO 95/2254.

2   8th Division CRE War Diary, TNA(PRO) WO 95/1671.

3   Ibid.

4   27th Division General Staff War Diary, TNA(PRO) WO 95/2254.

5   MS additions to 1:10,000 map *Second Army Sheet 12, OSO 1915, o/p 1st Ptg Co RE (2) 785, Trenches ... 5 February 1916*, used by 2/Lt G. S. Dickinson, 7th Lincolns. Author's collection.

6   Graves, Robert, *Goodbye to All That*, London: Penguin Modern Classics, 1961, p. 110.

7   Hay, Ian, *The First Hundred Thousand*, Edinburgh & London: Blackwood, 1916, pp. 203–5.

8   27th Division General Staff War Diary, TNA(PRO) WO 95/2254.

9   1:10,000 trench map, sheet *36NW4 Bois Grenier*, secret edition, December 1915.

10 1:5,000 trace of Ridge Wood – Bois Quarante – Vierstraat area, *Secret. Plan No. 94, 23-5-6*, TNA(PRO) WO 153 754 Divisional Trench Maps.

11 Edmonds, J.E., *History of The Great War, Military Operations, France and Belgium*, 1915, Vol. II, London: Macmillan, 1928, p. 113.

12 First Army General Staff War Diary, TNA(PRO) WO 95/156.

13 6th Brigade War Diary, TNA(PRO) WO 95/1352.

14 Frankau, Gilbert, *Peter Jackson, Cigar Merchant*, 3rd Edition, London: Hutchinson, 1920.

15 MacGill, Patrick, *The Great Push*, London: Herbert Jenkins, 1916; & *Soldier Songs*, London: Herbert Jenkins, 1917.

16 MacGill, *The Great Push*, op. cit., p. 38.

17 1:10,000 trench maps, sheet *36cNW3 & Part of 1* [Loos], August 1915, and subsequent editions of *36cNW3 & Parts of 1, 2 & 4*.

18 First Army General Staff War Diary, op. cit.

19 Ibid.

20 Ibid.

21 1:10,000 trench maps, sheet *36cNW3 & Part of 1* [Loos], August 1915, and subsequent editions of *36cNW3 & Parts of 1, 2 & 4*.

22 Romer, Carrol, typescript diary, present whereabouts unknown.

23 Ibid.

24 Graves, op. cit., p. 141.

25 Lieutenant John Staniforth papers, Imperial War Museum Dept of Documents.

26 Buchan, John (1916), *Greenmantle*, London: Hodder & Stoughton.

27 Graves, op. cit., pp. 118–19.

28 Third Army General Staff War Diary, TNA(PRO) WO 95/359.

29 1:20,000 gridded Second Army plan directeur, *feuille 4, 6e Tirage, 18 juillet 1915*, German trenches in blue, with MS British squaring and trenches. In 5th Division General Staff War Diary, TNA(PRO) WO 95/1512.

30 Ibid.

31 Graves, op. cit., p. 161.

32 153rd Brigade War Diary, TNA(PRO) WO 95/2869.

33 1:10,000 *Fonquevillers* trench map, secret edition,

34 1:10,000 *Ransart* trench map, secret edition, *Edn. 3A, OS 1916, British trenches corrected to 19 September 1916.*

35 Recordings by Tommy Russell, noted in Orr, Philip, *The Road to the Somme, Men of the Ulster Division Tell Their Story*, Belfast: Blackstaff Press, 1987, p. 136.

36 Orr (1987), op. cit., p. 144.

37 Ibid., p. 142.

38 Sassoon, Siegfried (1972), *Memoirs of An infantry Officer*, in *The Complete Memoirs of George Sherston*, London: Faber, p. 322.

39 1:20,000 trench map *Montauban, GSGS 3188, OS 1916, Trenches corrected to 2-6-16*. Author's collection.

40 Cuthbert, Keeson, Major C.A., *The History and Records of Queen Victoria's Rifles 1792–1922*, London: Constable, 1923, p. 144.

41 Edmonds, J.E., *History of The Great War, Military Operations, France and Flanders*, 1916, Vol I, London: Macmillan, 1932, p. 462fn.

42 Perceval Gibbon, in The Daily Telegraph, 26 October 1916.

43 Miles, Capt. Wilfred, *History of The Great War, Military Operations, France and Flanders*, 1916, Vol II, London: Macmillan, 1938, p. 435fn.

44 Sassoon, Siegfried, *Memoirs of An infantry Officer*, op. cit., p. 388.

45 Miles, 1938, op.cit., p. 193fn.

46 Blunden, Edmund, Introduction to *Poems of Ivor Gurvey 1890–1937*, London: Chatto & Windus, 1973, p.20.

47 Keeson, op. cit., p. 186.

48 Addison, Col. G.H. (compiler), *The Work of the Royal Engineers in the European War, 1914–1918, Miscellaneous*, Chatham: Institution of Royal Engineers, 1926, p. 187.

49 1:10,000 trench maps St Pierre Vaast, National Archives WO 297/2331, 2332 & 2333.

IV

BRITISH TRENCH NAMING IN 1917 AND 1918

Vimy Ridge and the Battle of Arras, April 1917

We have seen that the Vimy Ridge–Arras front was taken over by the British First and Third Armies in March 1916, many French trench names surviving into 1917, and even later. The systematic naming by the British of German trenches, in readiness for the Arras and Vimy Ridge operations, began early in 1917, but despite this many German trenches retained their German names

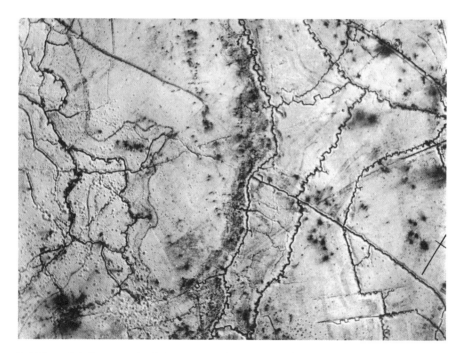

British aerial photograph of the British (left) and German (right) trenches on either side of no man's land west of Angres, at the north end of the Vimy Ridge; a 'snow photo' taken on 25 January 1917.

on British trench maps. Even in 1917 many of the German trenches in other sectors were unnamed by the British (though of course the Germans had their own names for their trenches, which the British might or might not know, depending on whether they had captured secret German maps showing the trenches and their names). Only in the first months of 1917 was a determined effort made by the British to name all (or most) of the German trenches, starting with sectors where large British offensives were planned – Vimy and Arras, Messines and Ypres.

The Canadian Corps took over part of the Vimy Ridge front at the end of 1916 and, despite the fact that the existing Allied trenches had been previously named by French and British units and formations, managed to impose its own naming on certain trenches and subways. However, most of the names in this area pre-dated the Canadian presence there. It was really later in 1917 that Canadian names made an impact, particularly in the Lens area.

Like every battlefield, that of Vimy Ridge and Arras became associated with certain key names apart from the village names such as Feuchy, Monchy-le-Preux, Gavrelle, etc., – the *Point du Jour*, the *Chemical Works* at Roeux, the Hindenburg Line, *The Harp* redoubt, *Greenland Hill*, *Orange Hill*, *Telegraph Hill*, *Wancourt Tower*, *Observation Ridge* and so on. These were nearly always, as the last demonstrates, associated with commanding positions on high ground, crucial for observation; consider how many actions and battles are named after hills and ridges – Aubers Ridge, Hill 60, Hill 70, Thiepval Ridge, Vimy Ridge, Messines Ridge, Menin Road Ridge, Passchendaele Ridge, etc.

German communication trenches north of Arras were given river names – *Cam*, *Clyde*, *Tees*, *Trent*, *Tweed*, etc. – and newly-dug trenches, which were either not named on captured German maps, not yet marked on captured maps or only just plotted from air photos, were given British names on an alphabetical system – for example in the Roeux and Greenland Hill area, east of the Chemical Works, *Corona Trench*, *Cupid Trench*, *Curly Trench*, *Charlie Trench* (and later *Chaplin Trench*) appeared early in 1917. This was not yet a map-square-based system, for the trenches in question were actually in square I. Later in the year, the map-square system was more in evidence. For example, in the *Oppy* map sheet for November 1917, the names of all German trenches in map square C began with that letter, and similarly for other letters. This reflected a policy begun earlier in 1917 in Second Army area.

In general, though, wherever possible, the British were now using German trench names obtained from captured maps. On 3 March 1917, before the German retirement to the new Hindenburg Line, VII Corps artillery were bombarding trenches north of Gommecourt that included *Schlangen Redoubt*, *Pigeon Trench* and *Pigeon Wood Trench*, *Riegel Stellung*, *First* and *Second Garde Stellung*, *Muller Graben* and *Burg Trench*.[1] In the Arras sector,

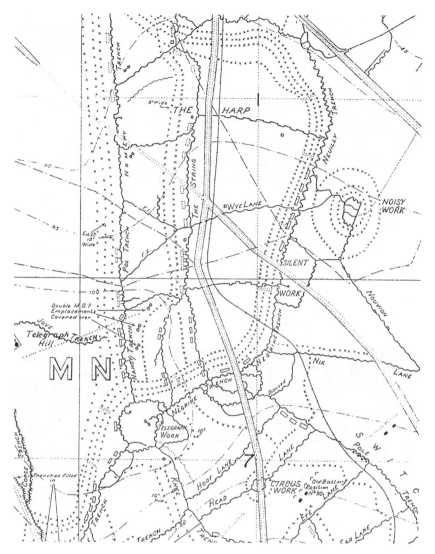

Detail of British 3rd Field Survey Company RE trench map, dated 3 April 1917, of the powerful German trench system at *The Harp* redoubt, the junction of the new Hindenburg Line with the old German defence position south-east of Arras. Note the names *The Harp*, *The String*, *Noisy Work* and *Silent Work*.

important features in the German defence system were given imposing names by the British – *Telegraph Redoubt*, *The Harp*, *Feuchy Work*, *Chapel Work*, *Hyderabad Redoubt*, and so on. The important new German rear defence systems – the Hindenburg Line (*Siegfried Stellung*), *Drocourt–Quéant Line*, *Wancourt–Feuchy Line* and so forth, presented new opportunities for British naming ingenuity, resulting in several memorable groups of names – the *Zoo*, *Aviary*, etc. Sassoon, in *Memoirs of an Infantry Officer*, described his experiences in the *Outpost Trench*, *Main Trench* and *Tunnel* of the Hindenburg Line, including leading bombing parties in an attack along the *Main Trench*.[2] Captain Dunn, of the Royal Welch, noted that on 8 May, while the battle was still raging, the battalion received a memo from GHQ about the use of the name *Drocourt–Quéant Line*. The GHQ staff were insistent that, as Quéant was on the right, the correct name should be *Quéant–Drocourt*. Yet, as Dunn pointed out, 'this topographical solecism' was on the maps hitherto issued and was still being printed subsequent to the memo.[3] Indeed, it remained in use to the end of the war.

The History of the Ninth (Scottish) Division noted that, as part of the preparations for the Arras battle on the training area near Monchy Breton, the German trench system was marked out accurately from aerial photographs using tapes and shallow-ploughed trenches, with the men making practice attacks over this course. In addition, exact and labelled clay terrain models of the ground to be attacked on 9 April were made, the men thus learning

British aerial photograph taken on 10 April 1917, of the terrain of the Bois de Givenchy area of the Vimy Ridge, after its capture, showing the 'confluent smallpox' effect of prolonged shellfire on the topographical features and the trench system.

not only the nature of the country, but also the names given to the German trenches. But, despite this thorough preparation, the men had the greatest difficulty in recognising the enemy trenches, so torn up by the British preliminary bombardment and creeping barrage that they could hardly be noticed in the zone of churned up earth that marked the devastating path of the British shells.[4] The battle itself gave rise to much new trench construction, and in the Fampoux–Monchy-le-Preux area (Vis-en-Artois map sheet) a sustained effort was made to create related groups themed around weapons, munitions and artillery equipment – *Shrapnel*, *Canister*, *Cordite*, *Saddle*, *Hook* and *Harness Trench*, etc. Those names that related to items of cavalry equipment were unsurprisingly grouped around *Cavalry Farm*. These groups are examined more closely in Chapter VI.

Systematisation of trench nomenclature continued, and in July–August 1917 Colonel Glubb (later to become famous in the Middle East as 'Glubb Pasha'), commanding the Royal Engineers of a division, described this process at some length in his war diary:

> Another divisional scheme was the methodical naming of all trenches. By this every front trench was to be called in sections O.13.1, O.13.2, etc., according to map reference [i.e. map square designation]. Support trenches were to be so called; thus, Ape Support not Ape Trench. Similarly Bison Reserve, not Bison Trench. All main C.T.s were to be called Avenues; thus: Shikar Avenue, not Shikar Lane, Kestrel Avenue not Kestrel Alley. Every trench junction was to be fully sign-boarded, as, at junction of Shikar and Egret:

Egret Trench to	Egret Trench to
Shikar Avenue	Kestrel Avenue
& Front Line	——>
<——	

> etc., etc. All this took some time in the way of notice painting; then a paper came round changing half the names, so we began again! Baldwin did this at first, and then Rebbeck took it over and also the boxes, and did it very well, though it did keep him busy.[5]

This example of the implementation of naming policy at divisional level was not an isolated one. It was clearly deriving from that laid down by GHQ and higher formations. We encounter in other armies during 1917 the adoption of the alpha-numerical section designations, and likewise the regularisation of the descriptors Trench, Support, Reserve and Avenue.

Ypres Salient 1916–17, and Messines and Third Ypres, June–November 1917

The images of mud and blood associated with the Third Battle of Ypres are inextricably linked to names, as witness the titles of several of Paul Nash's paintings, prints and drawings: *The Menin Road*, *Zillebeke Lake*, *Sanctuary Wood* (*We Are Making A New World*). While Wyndham Lewis was undoubtedly indulging in hyperbole when he said that the sight of the name Passchendaele on the map triggered a premonition that something nasty was going to happen, the name of that village (an objective for the first day of the battle – 31st July 1917), only finally captured after two ferocious assaults by the Anzacs and Canadians in October and November, was awarded in popular parlance to the whole three-and-a-half-month battle. By calling it *The Battle of the Mud*, Lloyd George gave voice to the common perception, which has become a national myth. A myth, of course, is not a matter of truth or untruth. The wild, howling and rain-lashed, swampy, nightmare of Third Ypres was ferociously described, and the high command damned, soon after the event by the journalist Philip Gibbs, in his *Realities of War*.

Hell Fire Corner, Menin Road, Ypres Salient, looking towards Hooge, during the Third battle of Ypres, 1917. The screens are to foil enemy observation from the high ground of the Bellewaarde Ridge and Gheluvelt Plateau. The sign on the right reads 'To Left Brigade Sector'. (IWM Q1889)

The names of *Hellfire Corner*, *Shrapnel Corner*, *Suicide Corner*, *Hellblast Corner*, *Dawson's Corner*, *Dirty Bucket Corner* and *Tattenham Corner* (*Dead End*), all for years under German observation and subject to ferocious shellfire, are forever associated with the Ypres Salient. Edmund Blunden, who spent a large part of 1917 in the Ypres Salient, referred to several of these frightful road junctions and to many trench names in his memoir. He spoke of *Hunter Street* and *Bridge Street* in the Boesinghe sector, and of *Haymarket* and *Piccadilly* communication trenches, *St James's Street* support trench and the reserve trench called *Half Moon Street*, in the Potijze sector. In the Hooge, Sanctuary Wood and Observatory Ridge sector (Mount Sorrel and Tor Tops) he encountered *The Great Wall of China* (also more prosaically known as *China Wall*), *Vince Street*, named after a Canadian officer, *Zillebeke Street*, a support trench named *Stafford Trench*, *Krab Krawl* (alternatively *Crab Crawl*), *Yeomanry Post* and the *Vancouver Street* communication trench – another memento of the Canadian occupation of this sector in 1916.

In the northern part of the Salient, he described the German position on Mauser Ridge (a westward offshoot of the Pilckem Ridge) known as *High Command Redoubt*, landmarks in the British rear area such as Vlamertinghe Château, Reigersburg, Pittsburg, Frascati and Les Briques, and the British trenches spread out underneath it near Cross Roads Farm at Wieltje – *Bilge Street* and *Hornby Trench* – from where his battalion would attack at the opening of Third Ypres. Second Army adopted a system of systematic naming for German trenches in early 1917, all names in particular zones starting with the same letter and proceeding according to an alphabetical system along the front. Thus in the St Julien sheet, German trench names in map square zone 'C' all began with the letter 'C' thus: *Caliban*, *Caledonia*, *Calendar*, *Cannabis* (a later addition), *Caramel*, *Camphor*, *Canadian*, *Calf*, and so on. The same process was repeated for square zones D, I, J, O, P, etc. These were the trenches of the German defensive system that had developed since 1914–15, and were the trenches that Blunden's battalion were to capture.[6]

In IX Corps *Instructions For The Offensive,* prepared for the Battle of Messines in June 1917, Corps Intelligence detailed the maps to be used in the forthcoming operation, and specifically referred to the naming of trenches: 'Trenches requiring names, both in our lines and the enemy's, will be named by corps. Divisions wishing to give a trench any particular name will notify corps headquarters as early as possible.'[7] There were also many cross-country tracks; IX Corps noted on 25 May, less than two weeks before the attack, that 'the signboarding of all tracks is not yet completed. Troops new to the area must reconnoitre all tracks before use.'[8] As in 1915–16, there was no indication in this of any censorship of names by higher formations, merely a notification that naming was considered essentially a corps matter. This was

British aerial photograph of the barrage fired at the Battle of Messines, June 1917. The German trenches and some topographical features can be seen among the smoke of shell bursts and the crater-pocked terrain.

significant, because corps were by now equipped with Corps Topographical Sections responsible for producing duplicator maps of their sectors and, during operations, daily situation maps, and it was important that all names be entered as soon as possible on all corps maps. These trenches and names were also entered on the maps produced by each army's Field Survey Company (FSC) and by the Ordnance Survey, which worked from drawings prepared by the FSC.

Trench names were relatively uncommon on the Third Ypres battlefield, partly because the prolonged heavy shelling, bad weather and flooded conditions were not conducive to trench warfare, but also for two other reasons. Firstly, the British had not bothered to name many of the trenches in the German rear zone before Third Ypres. A large number of trenches certainly existed in this area, including old French and British ones from the period before Second Ypres (22 April 1915), but it was equally the case that many of these had been allowed by the Germans to disintegrate as they did not form part of their defence scheme. Secondly, the new German policy of defence-in-depth was based on concrete strongpoints, shell-hole defences and counter-attack rather than on continuous trench lines.

While certain trench features were named – *Zonnebeke Redoubt*, *The Gravenstafel Switch*, *Deep Trench* and the unforgettable *Doom Trench*, etc. – it is to the names of these farms, therefore, that we should look for battlefield names rather than to trenches, and many of these farm/pillbox names are in fact immortalised in the maps, war diaries, operation orders and despatches of the period, and in the official and other histories that came later – *Vanheule Farm*, *Rat Farm*, *Spree Farm*, *Anzac*, *The Cockcroft*, *Springfield*, *Vancouver*, *Von Kluck*, *Dochy*, *Iron Cross*, *Potsdam*, *Vampir*, *Borry Farm*, *Schuler Farm*, *Gallipoli*, *Somme*, *Alma*, *Kronprinz*, *Albatross* and innumerable others. The author remembers, as a schoolboy in the early 1960s, reading in the school library Conan Doyle's history of the Flanders Campaign and being mesmerised by the unimaginable descriptions of the fighting among the pillboxes, remains of trenches and belts of barbed wire in the water and mud, and shivering at these spooky, alien and resonant names.[9]

The British regular series topographical and trench maps produced up to 1917 showed many unnamed features, and during the Third Ypres battle it became necessary to name as much as possible. Thus it happened that 2nd Field Survey Company overprinted in black on at least one regular series sheet (*FSC 1076 12-9-17, 28NE3 Gheluvelt*; *Edn. 6B(local)*) new names already given to cottages, farms and woods on Second Army's special sheets.

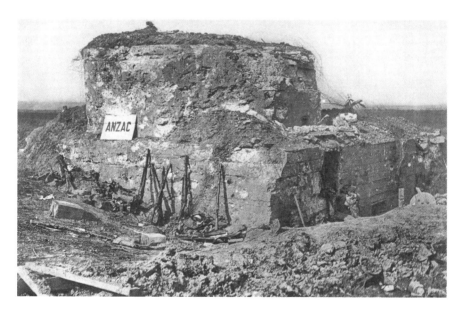

The captured German concrete pillbox at *Anzac*, south-west of Zonnebeke, after the Third Battle of Ypres, 1917. Many of the pillboxes were named after the farms within which they were constructed, while others were systematically numbered. (IWM E(Aus)2321)

During the Flanders offensives of 1917, the two existing layers of names on the map – topographical names (villages, farms, roads, streams, etc.) and trench names – were augmented by two more overlaid networks of names, superimposed on the trench maps to create a dense, often confusing, tangle of nomenclature. These two were both related to the special transport infrastructure created to get the guns, ammunition, supplies and men forward over ground turned into a quagmire by the shelling and rain. They were firstly the railway, light railway and 'foreway' networks, and secondly the plank road and duckwalk networks.

Railways were vital for bringing forward the heaviest, rail-mounted, artillery. Special gun and howitzer spurs were constructed off the existing standard gauge railways in the Ypres area, before and during the battle, and these took their name from local topographic features – *Railway Wood How. Spur*, *Spree Farm How. Spur*, etc., '*How.*' being the standard abbreviation for howitzer.

Many light railways, foreways and standard gauge sidings and spurs were constructed for and during the Messines and Third Ypres battles, and all stations, depots and sidings had to be named and signed. One spur in Ploegsteert Wood was given the very topical name *Rasputin*! It is therefore significant that, at this stage of the war, Transportation (Works) Companies RE carried three signwriters on their strength, and Foreway Companies RE, responsible for light tramlines in the foremost battle zone, one.[10] Towards the end of the war, contradicting established practice at the front where for years light railways and tramways had been named after British or Imperial railways, the Engineer in Chief noted that:

Such names as 'Great Eastern,' Great Central,' etc., should not be used, as they give no indication as to the locality of the line. The name adopted should be that of some point or points given on a map, in the neighbourhood of the line ... All traffic control or indicating posts should be painted on sheet iron or tin, and mounted on angle-iron pickets, otherwise they are likely to be burnt by troops in cold weather.[11]

The waterlogged state of the ground meant that communication trenches could not be dug during the battle, and their role was taken over by duckboard tracks, light railways and tramways known as foreways. The heavily laden men, mules and horses that had the misfortune to slip off the duckwalks or plank roads (their positions marked at night by hurricane lamps), or be blown off by shellfire, into the water-filled craters, often drowned where they sank into the mire. In the most advanced and exposed areas, there were no such tracks, and relieving and relieved troops had to pick their way, along the dryer rims of shell holes, along tracks of their own making. The vital forward duckboard tracks, plank roads and light railways were named, or at least designated, in a similar way to trenches – *Hunter's Trail*, *Plumer's Drive*, *M Track*, *X Track*, etc. A fascinating name bestowed on a plank road in the central sector of the Third Ypres battlefield was *Secauspion Road*, which the author has deciphered as deriving from <u>Sec</u>ond <u>Au</u>stralian <u>Pio</u>neers. The *A.T.N. Track* (a phonetic approximation to eighteen), constructed in July and August 1917 by the 18th Division's Royal Engineers, which ran from *Reninghelst* along the south side of Zillebeke Lake to *Clapham Junction*, was another example of these cross-country tracks.

A report by Colonel E.F.W. Lees RE, the CRE of the Guards Division (which attacked from Boesinghe in a north-easterly direction towards Langemarck, on the northern flank of Fifth Army), noted that track-tracing parties closely followed the advancing troops, through a zone beaten by German machine gun and artillery fire, in an attack.[12] The intended traces were chosen after close study of the trench maps and air photos, and the troops were informed of them prior to the attack. The function of the parties was to mark with white tapes raised on posts (or low pickets when under direct enemy observation) the routes or 'traces' of new duckboard tracks forward of the existing duck-walk heads. These traces were 'freely notice-boarded with place names, map references and objectives, the notice boards being prepared beforehand'. If the traces deviated from their intended route, notice boards had to be changed to pinpoint the new route. Lees stated that 'the greatest determination was shown by these track-tracing parties, and they never failed to arrive on the final objective, usually within 20 minutes to half an hour of its capture, unless the casualties were too great'. On the first day of the Third Ypres battle (31 July, the Battle of Pilckem Ridge), only one sapper of the party running the *Railway Street* trace survived, 'but with all his own carrying to do in the final stage, and with the aid of a sketch partially obliterated by the blood of his officer, who was killed, he got his trace through'.

Lees emphasised that the great value of these traces, and the duck-walks that quickly followed them over the crater field, 'was proved by the constant stream of traffic up and down them, as the tapes moved forward; the moves of supports and reliefs, the evacuation of the wounded, and the supply of ammunition were much facilitated'. He also referred to the problem of troops locating themselves in the featureless landscape resulting from the heavy shelling of this former farmland: 'The notice boards were especially valuable in enabling troops to locate themselves; the troops always seemed rather hazy as to their whereabouts on the battlefield, especially when it came to a question of identifying Green, Blue, etc., lines [the objectives] on the ground, such lines being usually in a devastated zone.' On 31 July, the parties erected forty-eight notice boards along the four traces pushed forward by the Guards Division. These name boards were particularly valued by battalion runners, who carried messages to-and-fro between battalion and company headquarters. The sappers also marked with name boards the captured pillboxes, often located in farm buildings, studding the battlefield.

A point that was often made was that the network of plank roads and tracks, light railways and foreways, with their accompanying sign boards, provided an indispensable means of location and orientation for troops in the otherwise featureless devastated area, where the landscape features shown on the maps had simply ceased to exist. In this context it should be emphasised that the troops engaged in operations were given aerial photographs and photo-mosaics as well as trench maps; the photographic imagery gave a much better picture of the actual state of the ground – often a sea of mud and confluent shell holes – than the maps, though the latter were often overprinted with flooded areas in blue. The maps showed the pre-war topography (contours, streams, roads, railways, villages, farms, woods, field boundaries and so on), overprinted with the Allied and German trenches and other tactical detail. As the battle went on, they also showed the fragile spider's web of surface communications we have noted (duckwalks, light railways, etc.), and also the extending sub-surface network of buried cable routes and junction boxes that provided crucial communications for the slowly advancing headquarters, artillery and observation functions).

The watery environment of the Passchendaele area was reflected in the names of many local features, including *Waterfields*, *Marsh Bottom*, *Riverside*, *Vapour Farm*, the ambiguous *Duck Lodge, Snipe Hall* and *Waterloo*, and the farms named after rivers, some of which have already been mentioned: *Alma*, *Aisne*, *Marne*, *Somme*, *Seine*, *Spree*, *Thames*, *Tyne*, *Tiber*, *Nile*, *Rhine* and *Scheldt*. It should be pointed out, though, that these names were given in 1916, well before this part of the Ypres battlefield became a swamp.

Many trenches were named after nearby farms or woods (themselves named by the British), and many of these were named alphabetically according to map zone. For example, in map zone 'D', between Zonnebeke and Passchendaele, were the level crossings across the Ypres–Roulers Railway called *Daring Crossing*, *Dash Crossing*, *Defy Crossing* and *Detect Crossing*, while in zone 'E', just east of Passchendaele, were *Exert Farm* and *Copse*, *Enlist Farm*, *Encore Wood*, *Entice Cottage*, *Erratic Farm*, *Exempt Wood*, *Exit Wood*, *Echo Copse* and *Evasion Farm*.

By December 1917, the British were numbering the captured pillboxes to aid their identification, and entering these names on the trench maps. Edition 9A of the Zonnebeke sheet showed pillboxes numbered up to 142, all to the south of the Ypres–Roulers railway; none was shown to the north. This was presumably because the railway formed the boundary between I Anzac

Corps and Canadian Corps on 5 December (the trench correction date for that edition), and only the former had numbered the concrete structures. The war diary of I Anzac Corps shows that a special job of its Topographical Section was the plane table survey of captured German pillboxes in the Corps area. This began on 22 October; by the end of the month ninety-seven had been fixed, forty-six more being surveyed in the first half of November.[13] This was a clear indication of the input of corps topographical sections to the production of trench maps by the army field survey companies.

If we recall Wittgenstein's point,[14] in the Introduction to this book, that the primary function of naming is *in preparation* for something, a weak point of British cartography before Third Ypres was undoubtedly the failure by 2nd Field Survey Company (and by implication by Second Army Intelligence) in 1916–17 to name all the buildings in the densely farmed German-fortified zone of the potential battlefield. Names of farms and other buildings were hurriedly added by 2nd and 5th Field Survey Companies in the final period of preparations and during the battle itself. Thus it came about that the regular series trench maps issued before and during the battle omitted many names, while the special sheets issued concurrently carried many not shown on the regular sheets – a recipe for confusion if nothing worse. Another case of slackness was the typing of a name near two or more buildings, leaving uncertainty as to which it actually designated. In such cases, a pinpoint map reference was essential to identify the intended location, but even when this was provided doubt often persisted.

Cambrai

The battlefield terrain of the surprise tank attack at Cambrai in November 1917 was relatively fresh and undamaged by war. The Germans had retired to the Hindenburg Line (*Siegfried Stellung*) in March 1917, and the new British front system facing this strong German position developed slowly during the spring and summer. The trenches of the British front system had been named as they were dug, and in the Havrincourt sector included many Welsh and other British regional names: *Merthyr Trench, Rhondda Trench, Mountain Ash Trench, Pentre Trench, Newport Trench, Oldham Alley, Blackburn Avenue, Burnley Alley, Tufnell Avenue, Derby Trench* and *Support, Bass Lane, Ashby Lane, Loughborough Lane, Coalville Lane, Grantham Lane, Brooksby Lane, Fern Trench, Frimley Trench, Gun Trench* and *Support, Glasgow Trench, Willis Avenue*, and so forth. Certain British trenches reflected the villages and rural economy of this area: *Trescault Trench* and *Support, Rat Lane, Village Trench* and *Support, Plough Trench* and *Support*. Certain names near villages were clearly related to the village name – e.g. *Glasgow Trench* and *Gun Trench* near Gonnelieu.

The German trenches of the Hindenburg Line system in the Havrincourt–Flesquières–Marcoing sector were individually named by the British: *Plush Trench* (named after Villers-Plouich), *Valley Trench*, *Valley Support*, *Unseen Trench*, *Unseen Support*, *Ridge Trench*, *Ridge Support*, *Mole Trench*, *Worm Alley*, *West* and *East Fork Avenue*, *George Street*, *Darwin Alley*, *Hughes Switch*, *Farm Trench*, *Corner Trench*, *La Vacquerie Trench*, *Vacquerie Support*, *Vacant Trench*, *Barrack Trench*, *Bleak Trench*, *Walk* and *Support*, *Quarry Trench*, etc. Several of these had been named from their topographical position (*Unseen*, *Valley*, *Ridge*, *Corner*), some from nearby villages, while others in this area were named after officers and men of 3rd Field Survey Company. As with the British trenches, some trench names near villages were related to the village name, as in the case of *Vacant Trench* near *La Vacquerie*.

Certain features on the map had been given striking names, and many of these had given their names to trenches in their vicinity – *Yorkshire Bank*, *Boggart Hole*, *Argyle Ridge*, *Highland Ridge*, *Bleak House*, *Pam Farm* (The Pam Pams were the 3rd Field Survey Company concert party), *Good Old Man* (or *Good Man*) *Farm*, *The Barracks*, *Sonnet Farm*, *Le Pavé*, *Fémy Chapel*, *Nine Wood*, etc.

The 1918 Battles: The German Offensives and Allied Counter-Offensives of 1918

As related in Chapter 1, British rear lines proliferated in the winter of 1917–18. Many of these dated from earlier years, and were incorporated into the new defence scheme. Important rear defence lines at this stage were one west of Arras; the *Sailly-Oostvleteren Line* west of Ypres; the *Béthune–Saint Omer Line* west of the canals, which formed a good defensive feature; and the *Boulogne-Calais-Dunkirk (BCD) Line* covering the vital Channel ports.[15] Farther south were the *GHQ Line* and the *Amiens Defence Line*. The usual practice was to name these extended lines according to the villages they embraced, from right to left. They only carried non-topographical names where earlier names already existed – e.g. *Gun Trench* at Loos, or *Haymarket Switch* at Laventie. The British did not indulge in the type of 'cultural' naming that the Germans showed a fondness for when naming their rear positions (*Siegfried*, *Wotan*, etc.).

Secret editions of First Army *Maps 'A'* and *'B'* of late February or early March 1918 – that is before the German offensive – showed a large and complex system of wired rear defence lines, defended localities, assembly points and posts. They showed *Cross Cut* south-east of Armentières, *Houplines Switch*, *Fleurie Switch*, *Greatwood Switch* at Bois Grenier, the *Nieppe System*, the *Bridgehead Line* covering the Lys crossings, *Erquinghem Switch*, the *Fleurbaix Defences* and *Switch Line*, *Support Line* and *Reserve Line*, *Haymarket Switch* east of Laventie, the *Locon-Beaupré-Estaires-Lys Line*, the *Lacouture* line, *Le Hamel Switch*, the *Village Line* (including *Lone* [Tree] *Locality*, *Le Rutoire Locality*, *Cambrin Locality*, *Pont Fix*[e] *Locality* and *Festubert Locality*), the *Richebourg-Laventie-Fleurbaix-L'Armée-Houplines* line, *Penin-Mariage Switch*, the *La Couture-Le Drumez-Nouveau Monde-Lys-Bridgehead System*, the *Canal Line* (at Hinges), *Le Hamel Switch*, the *Beuvry-Gorre Line*, the *Sailly-Labourse-Tuning Fork* line (including *Tuning Fork Locality*, *Preol Locality*, *Labourse Locality* and *Noeux Locality*), *Windy Corner Switch*, the *Annequin* line (including *Annequin Locality*), the *Grenay-Vermelles System* (including *Philosophe Locality* and *Vermelles Locality*), the *Maistre Line*, the *Bajolle Line*, the *Noulette-Maistre-Grenay-Noyelles System* (including *Noyelles Locality*), *German Switch* and *Gun Trench* at Loos, the *Bailleul-Chaudrière-Hirondelle-Riaumont-Loos* line, *Crassier Switch* (south-west of Loos), the *Farbus-Vimy-Liévin System*, the *Point du Jour-Thélus-Ridge Line*, the *Roclincourt-Targette-Marqueffles-Houchin-Vaudricourt-Locon-Beaupré-Estaires-Lys System* (perhaps the longest name on the Western Front apart from *LlanfairPG*?), the *Bouvigny Line*, the *St Aubin-Berthonval Line*, and *St Catherine Switch* (north-east of Arras).[16]

A secret map showing Second Army Lines of Defence 29 April 1918, indicated the following back lines west of Ypres: *Vlamertinghe*, *Brandhoek*, *East Poperinghe*, *Watou*, *Eecke*, *West Caestre*, *Kreuke*, *West Hazebrouck*, *Hondeghem*, *Winnezeele*, *Wallon Cappel* and *Watten*, with numbered junction points.[17] XV Corps Topographical Section produced maps of the *East* and *West Hazebrouck Lines*, and *Le Peuplier Switch*. A secret *Second Army Defence Lines* map dated 6 May 1918 showed the following back lines, some of which had appeared on the earlier map: *Abeele*, *Watou*, *Reninghelst*, *Steenvoorde*, *Eecke*, *West Caestre*, *Kreule*, *West Hazebrouck*, *Winnezeele*, *Terdeghem*, *Hondeghem*, *Wallon Cappel* and *Watten*.[18] These discrete elements were often regarded as sections of more extended lines; for example, maps and instructions show or refer to the *West Hazebrouck-Winnezeele Line*, the *Watten Bridge Head-Merckeghem Switch-St Omer-Sercus Line*, and the *Boulogne-Calais-Dunkerque (BCD) Line*.

To the west and south-west of Arras, rear defence lines, marked on a Third Army map dated 13 April 1918, incorporating the old trench systems of 1914-17, were named *Second System*, *Third System*, *Fourth System*, *Blaireville Switch* and *Humbercamp Switch*.[19] The old trenches of the Somme and other battles were often difficult to identify on the ground or in air photos, and on the palimpsest of the 1918 landscape, as represented by the air photos of the destroyed terrain and the incoherent cobwebs of pecked lines representing derelict trenches on the maps, it was considered easier to give new names to stretches of suddenly resurrected trenches rather than attempt to recreate the earlier identification. In any case, the trace of new trenches did not necessarily correspond exactly to that of the old; often only certain stretches would be reused, or joined up to other old trenches. Sometimes a new section would be added to make better use of the terrain or to conform to the new tactical situation. Thus in the area covered by the Wytschaete sheet, many of the old British names given to German trenches in early 1917 were discarded and new names given to trench features that could be identified on air photos. The old *Odd Trench*, for example, became *Oban Trench*. The old names for trenches of the old British defensive system existing before the Messines battle were, however, retained in 1918. Much the same goes for the Hébuterne sheet (Gommecourt–Serre sector), at the northern end of the old Somme and Ancre battlefields.

The German offensives of 1918 pushed back the Allied lines a considerable distance, in several areas far beyond the original trench systems from which the Allies had attacked in the 1915–17 period. Thus new trench systems developed in 1918, and again the necessity for trench naming arose. In the Somme area, the Australians now really made their mark, giving large numbers of trenches in the Albert–Villers-Bretonneux area unmistakably Australian names. In the Villers-Bretonneux, Hamel and Vaire Woods area, appeared *Australia Support*, *Barcoo Communication Trench*, *Diggers Support* and *Arawatta Trench*, while east and south of Albert in the Dernancourt–Morlancourt sector, north of the Somme, were *Diggers Avenue*, *Australia Street*, *Melbourne Trench*, *Sydney Street*, *Brisbane Trench*, *Possum*, *Dingo*, *Emu*, *Yarra* and *Warrego Trenches*, *Hobart*, *Cook*, *Culgoa*, *Ross*, *Coomac*, *Burke*, *Cooee*, *Coolbardie*, *Cootamundra*, *Conamulla*, *Coogee*, *Botany*, *Cloncurry*, and others.

A Third Army map, dated 20 May 1918, showed the new rear defence system in the Toutencourt area following the German offensives. Here trenches were named after the local villages; some names were composites of the village names; Leanvillers and Louvencourt supplied *Lealou Trench*, *Lealou Support*, *Lealou Reserve* and *Lealou 2nd Reserve*; there were also *Louvencourt Flank* (communication trench), *Lealvillers Trench*, *Lealvillers Support*, *Lealvillers Avenue*, *Lealvillers Flank* and *Lealvillers Reserve*, *Clairefaye Trench*, *Support*, *Avenue*, *Reserve* and *Flank*. Continuing this system to the south were *Harponville Trench*, *Support*, etc., *Valley Trench*, *Harp Valley Support*, *Harp Valley Reserve*, *Toutencourt Switch Trench*, *Toutencourt Switch Support* and *Reserve*, *Toutencourt Locality*, *Tout. St. Flank* and the composite name *Toutharp Trench* and *Toutharp Locality*. *Vadencourt Wood* gave its name to

Vad Wood Trench (at Hébuterne there was a *VAD Avenue*, commemorating the nursing contribution made by the women of the Voluntary Aid Detachment). There was also the *Baizieux System*. *Blab Wood* (near *Daily Mail Woods*) gave its name to *Blab Trench*.[20]

In the back area for which 4th Field Survey Company was responsible, west of the Ypres–Lys front, many of the twenty or so newly surveyed 1:10,000 sheets in the Hazebrouck area bore evidence of a certain slackness or dyslexia on the part of the officer (as yet unidentified – perhaps the drawing officer, Lieut. (Acting Capt.) K.S. Broad, of the Leinster Regiment) responsible for naming. There were not many clearly defined and named trenches in this zone, so the naming – on a remarkably idiosyncratic pattern perhaps related to the popular novels and westerns he read – was mostly confined to farms, road junctions and crossroads, and camps. By contrast with the omission of many farm names on the sheets covering the Ypres battlefield in early-to-mid 1917 (rectified during the Third Ypres battle), these were provided lavishly on 4th FSC's new 1918 sheets.

All along the front, the defence had hardened in this way following the German offensives, old trench systems were brought back into use and strengthened, and new ones were created. Sometimes the old names for the trenches were reused, and sometimes they had been forgotten and new ones given in their place. The Allies, fearing further German attacks, made their defensive systems particularly strong and elaborate, but those of the Germans were now much more tenuous. The German armies had suffered enormous casualties, and were exhausted. They had also lost the initiative, at a time when the Allies were being dramatically reinforced by vast American forces. The Allies continued to elaborate their rear defence lines, even when it was clear that the Germans were incapable of further advance, and Allied defence maps show successive named rear lines covering the zone right back to the coast.

As the Allies advanced from July to November 1918, they encountered the old trench systems of 1914 to early 1918, and old, resonant names came back into the news. On and after 8 August, in the Battles of Amiens and Albert, the British fought back across the old Somme battlefields, and at the end of September stormed the Hindenburg Line, known to the Germans as the *Siegfried Stellung*. Now the British had to consider the German defensive positions even further to the rear: the *Hunding Stellung*, *Brunnhilde Stellung*, *Kriemhilde Stellung*, *Michael Stellung*, *Wotan I Stellung* (which the British knew as the Drocourt–Quéant Line), *Wotan II*, *Wotan III* and *Hermann Stellung*. Behind these was the *Antwerpen–Maas* (*AM*) *Stellung* (the Antwerp–Meuse Line), and the final line was the *Grenz-Stellung*; few of these received British names, and the German designations are explored further in Chapter IX. The

Hermann Stellung along the Sambre and Oise Canal was breached by the British on 4 November, an operation in which Wilfred Owen was killed, and the Avesnes–Maubeuge line was breached by the British on 8 November.[21] Three days later came the Armistice.

Notes

1   Third Army General Staff War Diary, TNA(PRO) WO 95/361.

2   Sassoon, Siegfried, *Memoirs of An infantry Officer*, 1972, op. cit., pp. 429–46.

3   Dunn, Captain C.J., *The War the Infantry Knew*, London: Jane's, 1987, p. 342.

4   Ewing, John, *The History of the Ninth (Scottish) Division 1914–1919*, London: John Murray, 1921, pp. 189 & 194.

5   Commander, Divisional Royal Engineers War Diary, Royal Engineers Corps Library, Chatham, Ref: RE 80018.

6   Blunden, Edmund, *Undertones of War*, London: Cobden-Sanderson, 1928, p. 214.

7   IX Corps, *Instructions For The Offensive*, reprinted as *The Attack of the British 9th Corps at Messines Ridge*, Washington: Government Printing Works, 1917, p. 83.

8   Ibid, 1:20,000 map: *Cross Country Tracks – IX Corps Area, IX Corps Topo Section 29-5-17*.

9   Conan Doyle, Arthur, *The British Campaign in France and Flanders*, London: Hodder & Stoughton, 1919.

10 Addison, op. cit., pp. 177, 226.

11 Ibid, p. 240.

12 Report by Colonel Lees, quoted in Edmonds, J.E., *History of the Great War, Military Operations, France and Belgium,* 1917, Vol.2, London: HMSO, 1948, p. 213.

13 I Anzac Corps Topographical Section War Diary, PRO WO 95 1014.

14 Wittgenstein, L. (trans. G.E.M. Anscombe), *Philosophical Investigations*, Oxford: Blackwell, 1953, I, §26.

15 Edmonds, J.E., *History of the Great War, Military Operations, France and Belgium*, 1918, Vol.1, London: Macmillan, 1935, p. 44.

16 1:40,000 [First] *Army Map 'A', FSC RE 5740*, o/p *5839* [MS 23-3-18], and *'B', FSC RE 5741*, o/p *5865* both o/p red & blue: *Wire, Defended Localities, Assembly Points* and *Posts* [also shows rear defence lines]. Author's collection.

17 1:100,000 sheet [2nd] *Army Area No. 1*, [4th] *FSC RE (8142) 26-1-18*, o/p black *(8729) 30-4-18, Second Army Lines of Defence 29th April 1918*. Author's collection.

18 1:40,000 sheet *27, OS (OB) April 1918*, o/p purple-brown [4th] *FSC RE (8781) 6-5-18: Defence Lines Second Army 6.5.18*. Author's collection.

19 1:40,000 sheet *51c, OS(OB) March 1918*, o/p blue: [3rd] *FSC 10506 Rear Line Defences, April 13th 1918*. Author's collection.

20 1:20,000 sheet *57dSW, OS(OB) April 1918*, [3rd] *FSC 10556*, o/p black *10588 20-5-18, Secret, Third Army Defences, Provisional, Army Defence Line, From information to 20-5-18. All trenches approximate*. Author's collection.

21 Montgomery, Maj.-Gen. Sir A., *The Story of the Fourth Army in the Battles of the Hundred Days, August 8th to November 11th 1918*, London: Hodder & Stoughton, 1920, pp. 247–60.

V

BRITISH TRENCH AND TOPOGRAPHICAL NAMES – FURTHER CONSIDERATIONS

Having examined the development of trench naming during the war, we can turn our thoughts to naming themes. Names associated with the French and Flemish landscape and weather featured in the second part of Chapter I. This and the following two chapters continue this thematic treatment by examining aspects of British trench naming policy and practice. While this chapter introduces the subject, and deals with its broad aspect and general patterns of naming, the next two chapters deal respectively with names derived from Army organisation and practice, and with names taken from British urban or rural topographical contexts (which were often related to regimental recruiting areas).

The determinants and patterns of trench naming by the British throw an interesting sidelight on the nature of trench warfare conducted only initially by a regular army, and thereafter largely by a civilian army. It is worth considering whether the names were, consciously or unconsciously, determined or influenced by particular factors. At the outset there was no deliberate naming policy, as trench warfare was not expected; most soldiers and civilians believed that it would be a brief war of manoeuvre, not one of semi-permanent siege works and trench fighting. Even as trench

The *Suicide Corner* board, including its map reference, from the north side of Ypres. This board is now in the Imperial War Museum.

warfare developed, no clear policy emerged, and it was very much left to the soldiers on the spot to decide on names for their own trenches. Occasionally imagination failed; there was a *Nameless Trench* near Gouy, a *Nameless Farm* near Wytschaete, and a *Nameless Trench* and *Nameless Farm* together near Hébuterne. Literary and cultural theorists will be pleased to know that there was a *Text Trench* near Arras.

When it came to applying names to the enemy trenches, the same considerations at first apply; in general it can be said that in the first year or two this was done on a fairly random basis, though actual German names were used where these could be determined from captured maps. Later in the war, however, the sheer quantity of names required to designate the proliferating warren of enemy trenches extending back over many miles behind the front, together with a consideration of zoning imperatives for observation and target-designation purposes, led to 'dictionary trawling', linked to the notion that it might be as well to identify all the names of German trenches in a particular area, sector or map zone by the same initial letter. An alphabetical system was thus developed after 1916, in which all the German trenches within a 6,000 yard square zone designated on the map by a letter carried names (where they had not already been named) beginning with that letter. This led to sometimes desperate, but nevertheless poetic in outcome, scouring of the dictionary for names. Thus zone 'C' in Sheet 28, in the Ypres Salient, included *Calf Trench*, *Caliban Trench*, *Canopus Trench*, and so on.[1] Such dictionary trawling often resulted in tedious alliterative sequences, but was occasionally redeemed by a delightful, probably unintended, stream-of-consciousness creativity. A development of this systematisation was the use of the same name for the front, support, reserve, communication, switch and other trenches in narrow sectors of the enemy zone. Thus we find, again in the Ypres Salient, such sequences, denoting German trenches successively farther from the front line, as: *Idiot Trench*, *Idiot Support*, *Idiot Reserve*, *Idiot Drive*, *Idiot Crescent*, *Idiot Row*, etc.[2] The fact that these were close to a topographical feature named *Idiot Corner* by the British reminds us that there was often a close link between the names of trenches and the names of other tactical features nearby, such as farms, barns, crossroads, etc. Further examples in the same area were the British communication trenches *Haymarket*, which ran near *Hay Farm* and *Market Farm*, and *Piccadilly*, running past *Dilly Farm*.

As far as the British trenches were concerned, although the names were sometimes arranged alphabetically by sector (e.g. all the trenches in 'Y' Sector beginning with Y), the names were generally far more carefully chosen and intimate, often being concerned with regional, regimental and even personal associations. We need to consider whether the pattern of naming reveals anything about the men, mostly officers, who named them, and the institutions to which they belonged. Were they the sort of names to be expected of a strong military tradition, or of a largely civilian army? What sort of world did they reveal? What were their presuppositions? Were social and psychological necessities involved? Was there any censorship by senior officers? Or self-censorship? Some of the names were remarkably direct in describing the bloody realities of trench warfare and rotting corpses, and perhaps it was only the French who could name a trench *Tranchée des homosexuels*.[3] We have to be careful here; there were several British trenches named *Queer Street*, but the meaning then was not that of the later 20th century; it referred to an imaginary street where people in financial or other difficulties resided. Dickens used the term, and at least two books had been published before the war that included it in their titles.[4]

We have to transport ourselves back to the tough, cynical but sentimental world of Bruce Bairnsfather's archetypal regular army soldier, 'Old Bill', to identify the mindset of the civilian population and the British Army as it was in late 1914 when trench warfare first began, and trenches first began to be named, and to think carefully about the foreign country that was that lost past. Although that keynote song of 1914, 'It's a Long Way to Tipperary', rapidly fell out of favour with the troops, there was a *Tipperary Avenue* on the Somme (Beaumont). In particular, we should examine the culture of the 'officer class', whatever that was, as these were often the people who bestowed the names. We should also remember that the pre-war professional officer corps was tiny compared to the huge number of wartime commissions awarded to 'temporary officers', many of whom were of humble origins. Nevertheless, it contained a fairly broad cross-section of the middle and upper classes, while there were a certain number of officers who had risen from the ranks either, such as William Robertson (who rose to the rank of field marshal), through their own considerable abilities, or through the long-recognised path of the quartermasters' commissions that took warrant officers into the officers' mess. The aristocracy were concentrated in the cavalry and the guards, while the better line regiments insisted on a private income. Intelligent but relatively penniless candidates for commissions entered Woolwich rather than Sandhurst, destined for those technical corps, the Royal Artillery and the Royal Engineers. In many families there was a tradition of soldiering, and the same names crop up with remarkable frequency, but there was not an 'officer caste' as there was in Germany. Many British officers came from families that had succeeded in trade, industry and the professions, as well as those of the landed gentry, and the growth of empire had created many more opportunities for wealth creation.

We are very familiar with the poets and memoirists of the First World War, but should beware of viewing the events and experiences of trench warfare only through their eyes. They were not typical, even if their writings had a great appeal to later generations. Nevertheless, we could perhaps see them as grasping the *Zeitgeist* – as encapsulating some sort of poetic reality that has an eternal truth. And in fact the vocabulary of some of them, Sassoon and Owen for example, while a departure from accepted poetic norms, was very much in tune with some of the trench names they found around them, examples of which have been given in previous chapters. Other significant contributors to our folk memory of trench names, as has already been indicated, were David Jones, Edmund Blunden and Isaac Rosenberg, who each in his own way brought nomenclature to our attention. Jones's magnificent prose poem *In Parenthesis*,[5] Blunden's great 'Trench Nomenclature'[6] and Rosenberg's harrowing 'Dead Man's Dump'[7] are cases in point. Other, less literary, accounts are equally valuable in impressing trench names and vocabulary on our consciousness.

Trench names work on many levels and, as pointed out in the Introduction to this book, in many cases significance is inferred from juxtaposition; individual names may in any case possess a certain set of possible meanings and associations, but juxtaposition immediately limits these to a particular reading rather than to others. Many examples of this are given below.

Ironic Names

In the Introduction to this book, the point was made that irony as a dominant mode of 'front language' was explored in depth by Paul Fussell. This is not the place to cover the same ground, and readers are referred to that study. It was also stated in the Introduction that there is an unspoken sentiment of 'I don't think!' about many names, which highlights the immense discrepancy between an expected (or desired) and an actual state of affairs – *Rose Cottage*, *Thatched Cottage*, *Orchard Trench*, *Ritz*, *Savoy*, *Happy Valley*, *Lovers Lane*, *Lavender Walk*, etc. As an intelligence officer contributor to *The 'New Church' Times* (successor to *The Wipers Times*) remarked, speaking of the names of observation posts in or near the front line in the Neuve Eglise sector, south of Ypres:

> I like the way the O.P.'s are named ... Doesn't Thatched Cottage remind me or you of one up River with topping little girlies who loved the Brighton Métropole for occasional week-ends? ... Doesn't Heath Trench in name if not in smell remind one of Dartmoor? ... And then surely one must be happy at Rossignol with name and bird both with us contra punting a machine gun playing from Ash Road ... Even to be in Winter

Trench is like a breath of Adelboden, ski and snow shoes: doesn't that keep one cool this hot weather even if you are suddenly found by G.O.C. ignorant of the quantity of grenades Mills Mark V. stored there.[8]

Ironic humour was present from the very first; as we saw in Chapter II, the men of Hunter-Weston's 11th Brigade were naming their positions on the Aisne heights *Woodbine Villa*, *Wheatsheaf Inn*, or 'such and such a trench', while at Ploegsteert Wood in 1914, they established the *Café Royal*, *Carlton Restaurant*, *Maximes* and a score of other names, any one of which could be interpreted as ironic. Other examples of ironic names along the front, and there are hundreds, are *Safety Trench* (Quéant), *Safety Dugout*, *Friendly Trench*, *Quaker Alley* (Beaumont), *Wonderland*, *Peter Pan*, *Bellevue* and *Sans Souci* (Zonnebeke), *Paradise Alley* at St Jean (Ypres), *Peace Farm* (Westroosebeke), *Cosy Alley* and *Trench* (Lens), *Cosy Communication Trench* (Morlancourt), *Fun Trench* (Fonquevillers), *Fun Lane* (Bullecourt), *Funny Trench* (Oppy and Roclincourt), *Merry Trench* (Rouvroy), *Comedy Farm* (St Julien), *Happy Alley* (Beaumont), *Happy Trench* (Lens, Harnes and Longueval) and *Happy Valley* (Méaulte). Perhaps there was more of optimism in some of these names than irony; *Humanity Trench* (La Bassée) seems more of a mute appeal, while *Merciful Trench* (Rouvroy), *Hope Street* and *Trench* (Hébuterne), *Hopeful Trench* (Fampoux) and *Hope Street* (Neuville Vitasse) were offset by *Hopeless Street* (also Neuville Vitasse). *Rapture Trench* (Gonnelieu) seems particularly inappropriate.

We are so used to irony as a dominant mode for speech and nomenclature in the First World War that it is sometimes difficult for us to realise that frequently names that appear ironic were originally given non-ironically. They either became ironic during the war in the light of later events and experience – perhaps as idealism, patriotism and regimental spirit turned to disenchantment – or to later, more cynical, generations.

Appropriate Names

A huge number of trench names strike us as totally appropriate in their literalness. When we think of trenches we think of fighting, fear, mud and blood, and indeed there were *Hate Alley* (Vimy), *Fight Trench* (Hébuterne), *Quivering Trench* and *Support* (Bertincourt), *Mud Alley* (La Bassée), *Mud Corner* (Ploegsteert), *Mud Lane* (Ploegsteert and Vimy), *Mud Terrace* (Ploegsteert), *Mud Trench* (Fonquevillers and the Hohenzollern Redoubt), *Muddy Lane Post* (Fleurbaix), *Mudlark Alley* (Ploegsteert Wood), not to mention *Puddle Trench* (Bertincourt), *Bog Avenue* (Nieuport), *Bog Lane*

(Gouy), *Bog Trench* (Vimy), *Cesspool Trench* (Armentières), *Sticky Trench* (Hohenzollern Redoubt), *Slither Trench*, *Slimy Trench* and *Slimes Trench* (Lens and Harnes), *Worm Alley* (Marcoing), *Worm Trench* (Fampoux and Arras), *Louse Post* (Quéant), *Bug Alley* (Grugies), *Bug Trench* and *Bedbug Trench* (Vimy), and *Flea Alley* (Vendeuil), *Flea Trench* (Le Sars), *Slum Trench* (Arras), *Pest Trench* (Roclincourt), *Odour Trench* (Wytschaete and Combles) and *Odious Trench* (Wytschaete). In the same vein were *Vile Trench* (Comines), *Unclean Trench*, *Uncomfortable Crescent* (Ploegsteert), *Worry Trench* (Oppy) and *Wretched Way* (Beaumont). We also find *Gory Trench* (Vis-en-Artois), *Blood Trench* (Roclincourt) and *Bloody Farm* (Kemmel), as well as *Thud Trench* (Arras) and *Thunder Trench* (Combles). To emphasise the rotting rubbish-heap nature of this type of warfare, we find *Old Boot Street* (Vimy), *Old Boots Trench* (La Bassée) and *Old Toast Trench* (Vimy/Rouvroy).

Many names took the ghastly nature of the war surprisingly lightly – as though men used humour as a way of coping with the horrors – it became a defence against the daily stress and anxiety, which otherwise might have driven them to breakdown, which it sometimes did in the guise of madness, desertion or shell-shock. Many names were not merely appropriate, but were horrible, gruesome and grotesque: *Gas Alley* (Flers), *Gangrene Alley* (Gricourt), *Gory Trench* (Vis-en-Artois), *First Aid Trench* (Ovillers), *The Danger Tree* (Beaumont), *Last Hope Trench* (La Bassée), *Mad Trench* and *Mad Point* (Loos), *Loon Copse* (Wervicq and Combles), *Vampir* (Zonnebeke), *Vampire* (Wytschaete), *Vampire Farm* (Dixmude), *Hag Trench*, *Mud Terrace*, *Stink Post*, *Stormy Trench*, *Ominous Alley*, *Old Boots Trench* (La Bassée), *Worm Trench*, *Infernal Alley*, *Tremble Copse* (Vermandovillers), *Suicide Corner* (Ypres), *Wrath Copse*, *Hangman's Avenue* (Aubers), *Witch's Elbow* (Longueval), *Vulture House* (Westroosebeke), *Hellfire Corner* (Ypres), *Hell Trench* (Loos), and *Shell Trap Farm* (although the staff jibbed at this last one) near St Julien. Sheer fright was marked, in various locations, by *Windy Corner*. There was even a *Windy Corner* in the North Sea, named after a critical turning point during the Battle of Jutland.[9] To be 'windy', or to 'have the wind up', was an all too well known phenomenon when under fire.

When we think of the trenches, we also think of rats, as did T.S. Eliot when writing *The Waste Land*, that metaphor for the state of western civilisation, just after the war. The population of rats along the Western Front was probably similar to, or greater than, that of soldiers. And as they gorged on the flesh of the rotting corpses they became 'loathsome, bloated creatures'. Along all trenches, and over the men sleeping in dugouts, ran the rats, and what more appropriate name could there be than *Rats Alley*, *The Rat Hole*, etc. The name naturally occurred frequently along the line: *Rats Alley* (Berthenicourt), *Rat Alley* (Zillebeke), *Rat Farm* (St Julien), *Rathole* (Méaulte), *Rat House*

(Langemarck), *Rat Lane* (Neuville Vitasse), *Rat Pit* (in *Bovril Alley*, Angres), *Rat Post* (Quéant) and *Rat Trench* (Hébuterne, Roclincourt and Nieuport). Dugouts, where rats congregated as well as men, naturally attracted appropriate holey and subterranean names, and there was a plethora of *Rat Holes* and *Holes-in-the-Wall*. A variant on this was *Toad in the Hole* above Bray-sur-Somme, the headquarters dugouts of XIX Corps Heavy Artillery in mid-August 1916. Apostrophes were present or not, as the draughtsman liked, and sometimes appeared or disappeared with subsequent editions of the map sheet; thus *Rats Alley* might also be *Rat's Alley* or *Rats' Alley*, in an anarchistic lexicography that would have delighted T.E. Lawrence. Spelling also changed in a similar way, and even designation – an alley might become a street or an avenue, etc.

Queer Street, in the sense mentioned above of an imaginary street in which destitute people live, was a perfect name for a filthy slum of a trench. All soldiers, by the nature of exercising their permanent or temporary profession in wartime, resided there. The name *International Trench* appeared in at least four different locations along the British front, three of them being in the Ypres Salient – at *Caesar's Nose* (Boesinghe), on the Bellewaarde Ridge and near *The Bluff*. The other was near Longueval on the Somme, while there was an *International Post* near Gricourt and an *International Corner* near Elverdinghe north of Ypres. The *International* epithet was particularly apposite, for these trenches had been the subject of fierce fighting, and often the corpses – or their remains – of French, German and British soldiers lay there and thereabouts. In a similar vein was *Esperanto Terrace* near the Cuinchy *Brickstacks*.

As crossroads, road junctions and obvious bends were well-located on the enemy's artillery maps, and were subject to regular harassing fire, names such as *Anxious Cross Roads* (near Houthulst Forest), *Windy Corner* (mentioned above), *Idiot Corner* (north-west corner of Bellewaarde Lake, east of Ypres), *Idiot Street* (Arras), and a group of '*Idiot*' trench names awarded by the British to German trenches near *Idiot Corner* (Zillebeke) were well-merited, as were *Nonsense Trench* (Aubers), *Anxious Trench*, *Baffle Trench*, *Chaos Trench* and *Cyanide Trench* (all Vimy), *Crazy Redoubt* (Lens), *Cry Support* (Fampoux), *Howl Trench* (Loos), *Unbearable Trench* (Ploegsteert), *Doleful Post* (Epéhy), and *Dreary, Dredge, Dregs, Drench, Dribble, Drivel* and *Drizzle Trenches* near Rouvroy. Also appropriate were *Furies Trench* (Combles), *Fury Trench* (Fonquevillers), *Peril Avenue* (Gheluvelt) and *Hazard Trench* (Fampoux and Richebourg). *Lunatic Sap*, close to the Germans (too close), south of the *Brickstacks* at La Bassée, was another name that suited, while the name of *Lunatic Trench*, running past the asylum on the eastern outskirts of Armentières, was madly appropriate, being simultaneously ironically humorous and topographically accurate.

Haunted House appeared at Itancourt and Lens, *Ghostly Trench* at Loos and *Spook Lane* at Vis-en-Artois. There was a *Folly Lane* (Beaumetz) and at least five examples of *Folly Trench* (two near Oppy and one each near Le Sars, Longueval and Fonquevillers), while a *Fool Trench* appeared at Roclincourt and both *Fool* and *Foolery Trenches* at Fonquevillers. *Tragic Trench* (Richebourg) and *Sad Trench* (Lens and Roclincourt) also seemed right. Some road junctions were very graphic: *Hellfire, Hellblast* and *Shrapnel Corners* (as well as *Suicide Corner*), were found in the Ypres Salient. *Trap Trench* (Arras and Gueudecourt), *Abuse Trench* and *Abyss Trench* (Rouvroy) might well describe the soldier's condition. In watery conditions, what better name than *The Pump Room* north of Ypres, while in the late-1917 swamps of the Ypres Salient near Passchendaele there were *Waterfields* and *Marsh Bottom*, as well as the delightfully ambiguous *Duck Lodge* and *Snipe Hall*. The striking visual appearance of Havrincourt Wood from the air led to it being unofficially named *Mossyface Wood* by the RFC.

Obstacles or other features in no man's land reminded horsy officers of names from British topography with alarming associations, and also names perhaps associated with steeplechases, none more so than the *Devil's Jump* (Fromelles), with the not-so-hidden sub-text that the race across no man's land (in the face of murderous machine gun fire) might soon be theirs to undertake. Sporting metaphors – 'The Great Game', 'The Great Adventure' and so forth – were commonly used by generals, chaplains and the press. In 1916, various newspapers, including *The Wipers Times* at the front, referred in this vein to the coming offensive as 'the Spring Steeplechase' and 'the Spring Handicap'.

Death and its Associations

As one would expect, associations with death, and gallows humour, were ever present in trench naming. The earliest associations were with reference points and landmarks in the form of dead animals on the battlefield, and of course with soldiers' corpses. There are many examples: *Death or Glory Sap* (La Bassée), *Dead Boche Alley* or simply *Dead Alley* (Vis-en-Artois), *Dead Cow* (title of a poem by Robert Graves) *Trench* and *Post* (Richebourg), *Dead Cow Farm* (Ploegsteert and Bois Grenier), *Dead Dog Avenue* and *Tram* (Radinghem), *Dead Dog Farm* (Wytschaete), *Dead Horse Copse* (Aubers), *Dead Horse Corner* (Ploegsteert Wood), *Dead Man Farm* (St Julien), *Dead Hun Farm*, *Dead Man's Bottom* (Zillebeke), *Dead Man's Corner* (Arras and Gouzeaucourt), *Deadman's Trench* (Givenchy), *Dead Mule Corner* and *Dugouts* (Zillebeke), *Dodo Trench* (Bullecourt and Dernancourt) and *Dodo*

Wood (near Toutencourt), and *Doom Trench* (Zonnebeke). There was the *Mound of Death* at St Eloi. Between Bécourt and High Wood, on the Somme, the name *Death Valley* was used by the troops, although it never appeared on the trench maps, and a similarly named *Valley of Death* appeared south of Trônes Wood. Such valleys, likely approach routes for reinforcing British troops, were the subject of standing barrages from the German artillery during the Somme battle.

'Dead Man's Dump', the title of a poem by Isaac Rosenberg, was a real location that took its name from *Dead Man's Corner* (Gonnelieu) near Gouzeaucourt in the Cambrai sector. Rosenberg was here in April–May 1917, with 7 Platoon, 120th Brigade Works Company. This brigade was part of 40th Division (XV Corps), which occupied the Gouzeaucourt–Villers-Plouich–Beaucamp–Metz-en-Couture front, and *Dead Man's Corner* was plumb in the centre of the division's communications. Rosenberg was describing exactly what he saw and experienced, possibly during the night of 5 May 1917, when 8th and 40th Division made a large-scale raid on La Vacquerie and temporarily occupied that village. The Dump was for RE stores – barbed wire, duckboards, timber, etc., from which the Works Company took materials up to the front line.

In a situation where men living cheek-by-jowl with death were liable to shake the dangling hand of a corpse overhanging the parapet, it might be thought that the Western Front did not require additional *mementi mori*. Nevertheless we find *Carrion Trench* (Vimy), and *Skull Farm* next to *Paradise Copse* (Moorslede). These examples of what might be called *vanitas* cartography were not alone. Further reminders appeared in *Bone Point* (Wytschaete), *Bone Trench* (Neuville Vitasse and Roclincourt), *Bones Lane* (Gonnelieu) and *Bones Post* (Richebourg). There were also *Coffin Trench* (Lens), *Cemetery Salient* and *Post* (Bois Grenier), *Cemetery Avenue* (Bullecourt), *Cemetery Alley* (La Bassée), *Cemetery Avenue*, *Crescent* and *Drive* (Armentières) and many *Cemetery Trenches* along the front. *End Trench* (Roclincourt) was also a potentially alarming name, as were *Hemlock Alley* (Loos) and *Hemlock Trench* (Rouvroy). *Murder Alley* (Lens) was thoroughly alarming, as were *Suicide Corner* (Ypres and Kemmel) and *Suicide Road* (Wytschaete). Suicide in the trenches was not just the name of a poem. A phenomenon considered by Benjamin Franklin to be as inevitable as death[10] was brought to mind in *Tax Trench* (Roclincourt) and *Income Tax Trench* (Arras). Other names still shocked, though probably merely relics of pre-war use of buildings, such as *Butcher's Shop* (Armentières) and *Slaughterhouse* (Arras).

Pathos was ever-present, allied with pessimism and negativity. A prime example was the hopelessly poignant *Cheeroh Avenue*, a communication trench taking men from Colincamps towards the front line; one soldiers' song went: 'Bonsoir old thing, cheerio, chin-chin, napoo, toodle-oo, goodbyee.' In soldier's slang, 'napoo' meant nothing, all gone, finished, gone west. There were *Napoo Farm* (Wervicq) and *Napoo Avenue* and *Farm* in the Ploegsteert Wood–Armentières sector. In the same breath are *Napoo Avenue*, *Nix Lane* (Neuville Vitasse), *Nameless Trench* and *Farm*, *Nonsense Trench*, *No Man's Cott* (in no man's land), *Not Trench*, *Omit Trench*, *Incomplete Trench*, *Inconsistent Trench*, *Void Farm* (Westroosebeke) and, ominously, *Zero Avenue* and *Zero Wood* (referring to zero hour: 'over the top' at zero, also known as 'over the bags', 'over the plonk', etc.). In this context, the seconds ticking away to this moment 'when the barrage lifts' were recalled by *Tick Trench* (Arras, Roclincourt and Gueudecourt) and *Tok* [sic] *Trench* (Arras); 'tic-tocs' was also slang for signallers. *Last Hope Trench* was near La Bassée, reminiscent of the desperate 'Forlorn Hope' of earlier wars.

Apocalyptic

Trenches running through the battlefield naturally reminded men of Dante, Bunyan, Milton, Blake and other apocalyptic writers. *Pilgrim's Progress* was an appropriate name that appeared at the Hohenzollern Redoubt, and a *Pilgrim's Way* appeared on the Somme battlefield near Flers. Bruce Bairnsfather produced a calendar illustration for the year 1918, showing a soldier on a battlefield road, entitled 'The Pilgrim's Way'. A roadside shrine near Marquion was marked on the map as *Pilgrim's Rest*. The battlefield became such a sacred site to many that soldiers returning after the war took part in 'pilgrimages'. Apocalyptic naming was also conjured up by some of the names given to mine craters – *Etna* and *Vesuvius* near Cambrin, etc.

Religious

Although the British Army was a remarkably secular, or pagan, institution (in this it probably mirrored a large part of society), despite the efforts of the Chaplain General's Department, the conditions of war naturally made men's thoughts turn to the metaphysical. A certain amount of religious imagery appeared in trench naming. Many of the names derived from both the Old and New Testaments had a certain ironic intent. How appropriate was *Jacob's Ladder* (Hamel and Beaumont Hamel)! *Matthew*, *Mark*, *Luke* and *John Copses*, and their associated trenches, appear in the Serre sector at the northern end of the Somme battlefield, while nearby, in the Hébuterne map sheet, were: *Palestine Avenue*, *Isaiah*, *Hittite*, *Uriah Street*, *Eczema Avenue*, *Jeremiah Trench*, *Jericho Avenue*, *Babylon Trench*, two *Eden Trenches* and a *David Camp*.

Goliath Farm was many miles north, at Westroosebeke, near Passchendaele. Not far away from here was *Promised Land Corner* (Hooglede), an objective either desirable or not-to-be-thought-of, depending on the soldier's point of view! A German Army rhyme went something like: 'I can't give you a hand/you're for the promised land/my comrade good and true.' *Hebrew Trench* was at Harnes, *Esau's Way* appeared near Beaumont Hamel, while *Daniel's Den* was in the old German lines in the Nab Valley area (Ovillers). *Sabbath Trench* and *Sacred Trench* were near Lens, and *Resurrection Trench* near Achiet. This last was perhaps a promise to those who survived the battle, and perhaps a consolation to some; but it is difficult to feel that most did not regard it as ironic. There was another *Sacred Trench* near Berthenicourt, and a *Salvation Corner* near Ypres. *Zion Alley* was near Fampoux.

Heaven and Eden get their look in, and Hell occurs regularly as one would expect. *Heaven* and *Hell Trenches* appeared at Loos, *Hellfire Corner* occurred more than once (the most famous in the Ypres Salient), while the savage glee of *Hell's Delight* (Wervicq) sets one thinking. There were *Hell Farm* (Wytschaete), *Hell Quarry* (Vis-en-Artois), *Hell Trench* (Roclincourt) and *Hellblast Corner* (Zillebeke). The Prince of Darkness was quite popular, as witnessed by *Satan Trench* (Richebourg), *Lucifer Farm* (Moorslede), *Devil's Staircase* (Beaumont), *Devil's Trench* (Fampoux and Delville Wood), *Devil's Wood* (Arras and Delville Wood), *Devil's Jump* (Aubers), *Devil's Street* (Lestrem) and *Devil's Elbow* (Wervicq). We should remember, however, that a lucifer was, although obsolescent, a match used to light a fag (as in 'Pack up your troubles in your old kit-bag and smile, smile, smile/While you've a lucifer to light your fag, smile boys that's the style'). Even the pragmatic British made occasional references to deities of other cultures. Lieutenant Salmon of 3rd Topographical Section RE (later to command 3rd Field Survey Battalion RE), who had served with the Survey of Ceylon, noted that he named *Yakko Copse*, south of Méaulte, after a Sinhalese devil. *Rue Dante* was near Aubers, and *Purgatory* near Wytschaete. A whiff of all this could be found in *Sulphur Avenue* (Ovillers and Villers-au-Flos).

The Pope was the one religious figure or concept to make repeated appearances in the nomenclature. Was it the 36th Ulster Division, with its powerful Orange tradition, that named an enemy bastion in the Thiepval Wood sector, which they assaulted on 1 July 1916, the *Pope's Nose*? Crucifixes, chapels and shrines were a part of the Roman Catholic religion which was still a strong feature of republican France, and were equally prominent features of the rural landscape. Like the church spires, which were often used as artillery observation posts and trigonometrical survey stations, they made excellent reference points. There were innumerable *Crucifix Corners*, perhaps the most famous being those at Aveluy near Thiepval, and at Bazentin near High Wood, both on the Somme battlefield. By one such *Crucifix* near Bugnicourt, east of Arras, were *Barabas Mill* and *Robber Wood*.

The Roman Catholic religion was also strong in Belgian Flanders. In the Moorslede sheet, north-east of Ypres, were *Pope*, *Edict*, *Vatican*, *Papal*, *Paul*, *Tarsus*, *Luke*, *Miracle*, *Font*, *Lord*, *Lucifer*, *Nave* and *Cherub Farms*, *Epistle House*, *Gabriel Cross Roads* and *Preacher Point*. Elsewhere the New Testament predominated. In the Gomiecourt sheet: were *Judas* and *Iscariot Trenches*. South of Arras was *Judas Copse*, suspected of harbouring a German railway gun. In the Steenwerck area, south-west of Ypres, were *Jesus Farm*, *Reaper Farm* and *Gospel Villa*; near Bailleul, south of Ypres, were *Baptist Farm* and *Assisi Farm*, and in the Westroosebeke sheet, north-east of Ypres, were *Jordan Farm*, *Canaan Farm* and *Parable Cross Roads*.

Ungodly Trench and *Avenue* were near Ploegsteert. Neither God nor Jesus figured in British trench naming (as opposed to trench blaspheming – being often on the tongues of the troops), but when it came to naming German trenches, the Allies (and this was something that may have started with the French) were more profligate with the name of God – *Gott mit Uns Trench*, *Alle Gott Trench*, etc., in the Péronne sector of the Somme battlefield. For non-Christians, there were *Pagan Trench* and *Support* (Wervicq). There does not seem to have been an *Atheist Trench*.

Humour, Whimsy and Mimsy

Virginia Woolf opined, while speaking of Sir Thomas Browne, that: 'The English mind is naturally prone to take its ease and pleasure in the loosest whimsies and humours.'[11] This seems very true of a national tendency in trench naming. Many humorous names have already been cited, but some were outstanding. Among the best were the well-lubricated *Alf Cut* (Bouchavesnes), which managed simultaneously to refer to a soldier called Alf, a short entrenchment, and a semi-inebriated state. Similar cases were the punning names of *Cox Bank* (Cox & Co. were the officers' bank, into which their pay was credited) and *Ply Wood* south of Saint-Quentin. There are many similar examples. Bruce Bairnsfather, whom as we have seen did much to spread the soldier's humour through his characters Old Bill and Young Bert, gave rise to: *The Better 'Ole* (Ploegsteert and St Venant), and this was echoed by *Betterole Farm* (Bailleul). There were flights of fancy; in one group already mentioned – *Walrus*, *Borogrove* [sic], *Gimble* and *Mimsy Woods*, and in *Dum* and *Dee Copses*, on the Somme front – a homage was made to the surreal humour of Lewis Carroll. *Umpty Trench* was near Rouvroy, but no *Dumpty* is discernible nearby. What the British soldier did to French place names has already been remarked, but one such trench name noted by Blunden should be mentioned – *Tubular Trench*,[12] where the description Tourbières (peat bogs) was marked on the map north of Annequin, near Béthune.

Lyrical and Artistic

Lyrical and artistic themes do not naturally spring to mind when considering the Western Front, but in fact they made a significant contribution to naming. The large German redoubt, south-west of Arras, at the junction of the new Hindenburg Line with the old front system, was named *The Harp* by the British from its shape on the map. Its chord naturally became *The String*, and its smaller associated strongpoints were known as *Noisy Work* and *Silent Work*. Nearby, in a more prosaic vein, military music was represented by *Fife Trench* and *Whistle Trench* (Vis-en-Artois). There were two *Music Trenches* (Lens and Fonquevillers), while west of Festubert were the *Tuning Fork* and *Tuning Fork Switch*.

On the northern and eastern flanks of the Ypres Salient, a large number of musical names appeared. In the Houthulst Forest area, north of Ypres, a sustained fanfare to celebrate composers' names started with *Clairon* and *Trumpet Farms*, and continued with, among others, *Carmen* and *Toreador Farms*, *Massenet Junction*, *Berlioz*, *Verdi*, *Mozart*, *Paganini*, *Mayerbeer*, *Wagner*, *Palestrina* and *Salome Cross Roads*, *Strauss*, *Bach*, *Chopin*, *Lulli*, *St Saens* [sic], *Fauré*, *Weber*, *Schumann*, *Schubert*, *Brahms*, *Beethoven* and *Gounod Farms* and *Offenbach Corner*. Farm and other topographical names were often transferred to nearby trenches; in the same general area were *Delibes Trench*, *Donizetti Junction*, *Gluck Junction*, *Gounod Trench*, *Faust Trench*, *Gramophone Farm* (all Zwartegat), while further east, appeared *Bach Buildings*, *Tanze Wood*, *Gounod Wood*, *Chopin Farm*, *Handel Farm*, *Haydn Farm* and *Mozart Farm* (all Hooglede). *Opera Trench* could be found at Radinghem, Vis-en-Artois and Bouchavesnes. *Caruso Avenue* and *Copse*, named after the famous singer, appeared at Ayette, south of Arras, in 1918.

Instruments were also heard above the cacophony of the battlefield. In the Zwartegat sheet were *Trumpet Cross Roads*, *Euphonium Junction*, *Cello*, *Bugle*, *Cornet*, *Piccolo*, *Flute*, *Clarionet Farms*, *Trombone* and *Oboe Corners*. Some miles to the east, in the Moorslede sheet, several of these names were repeated; here we find *Crotchet*, *Quaver*, *Cello*, *Violin*, *Piccolo*, *Flute*, *Clarionet* and *Bugle Farms*, *Stave House*, *Trombone* and *Oboe Corners*, and *Trumpet Cross Roads*. On the Somme, a group of musical names appeared in the Combles sheet: *Schumann*, *Schubert*, *Beethoven*, *Gilbert*, *Sullivan* and *Mikado Trenches*, and a sub-group of Wagnerian significance: *Wagner*, *Bayreuth*, *Rhine*, *Ring*, *Tristan Trenches* and *Isolde Alley*.

The visual arts were less well covered, but there was evidence of a certain awareness of art practice and history in the Ypres Salient. In the Westroosebeke sheet were *Van Dyke*, *Rubens* and *Memling Farms*, while in the Moorslede sheet appeared *Artists' Cross Roads*, *Sculptors Fork*, *Mallet Buildings*, *Carvers Cross Roads*, *Chisel Farm*, *Model Farm*, *Palette Cottage*, *Rubens Wood* and *Rembrandt Buildings*. There was also a group of names relating to draughtsmen's practice, and these, being an army matter, are described in Chapter VI. It is worth noting that Stanley Cursiter, the Orcadian Printing Officer of 4th Field Survey Company, was not only an established artist but also a musician of some accomplishment, and may have had some influence in naming.

Hotels, Restaurants, Cafés, Pubs and Clubs

It was natural, perhaps inevitable, that dugouts and command posts should have names bestowed on them by the troops; these names almost always carried wry, ironic or humorous overtones; the contrast between the filthy, wet and spartan conditions of trench life and the cosy memories of home was too stark to ignore. Thus a grim hole in the ground, perhaps a company headquarters, if it was not named *The Better 'Ole* or *Rat Hole*, might become the *Ritz* or *Savoy*, *Carlton* or *Maxim's*. The Richebourg sector boasted two artillery observation posts in ruined buildings just behind the front trenches, known as the *Ritz* and *Savoy*. The best hotels and restaurants offered the best ironic contrast with the filthy, cramped dugout and the meal (served on a tin or aluminium plate) of bully and machonochie. *Claridge's*, the *Dorchester*, *Wheeler's*, *Scott's* ...

Soldiers were always willing to wet their whistles, and cafés occurred frequently enough near the firing line, or at least the reserve trenches – if not the Café Royal then at least *Café Belge*, *Café Farm*, and *Café Trench* – and their Franco–Belgian companion, l'estaminet, such as *La Polka* near Kemmel and *La Demi Lune*, near Ploegsteert. Pub names also appeared – the *Elephant and Castle*, *Cabbage Patch* (La Bassée), *Pig and Whistle* (Langemarck), *Pike and Eel* (Ypres), *Spotted Dog* (La Bassée), etc.

The Stage: Theatres, Music Halls, Actresses and Dancers

In a vein similar to that of luxury hotels, many trenches, dugouts and posts were named after actors, theatres and music halls. Kipling made the point in one of his poems about a soldier in the front trench standing up like children in boxes at the theatre better to see the play, and getting sniped as a result. The theatre image was well-founded, and theatrical artifice (e.g. camouflage, artificial trees, deception schemes) was everywhere.

From the 'theatre of war' on a global strategic level to the 'set-piece' battle on the operational, the 'dress rehearsal' for an assault and the choreography of infantry tactics (waves, worms, blobs, files, 'artillery formation', etc) on the micro level, theatrical imagery was always present. Significant groups of such names appeared on the Ypres, Vimy Ridge and Somme battlefields. In the last-named area during 1916 the French introduced the following names: *Tranchée de Tragédie, de Comédie, du Scaramouche, d'Actrice, d'Auteur, de Dame Blanche, d'Othello, de Lysistrata*. Theatre names – e.g. *Daly's* – were appearing in the trenches in the Loos area before the battle of September 1915 and the death of Kipling's son. When Third Army first organised a formal flash-spotting system on the Somme front at the end of 1915 for locating German batteries, its first survey posts were *The Tivoli, The Oxford, Grandstand, Coliseum, Alhambra, Empire, Wonderland* and *Palladium*. Another post was named *Zoo*, perhaps after the local fauna which moved in to share the accommodation.[13] There was a defended locality called *Alhambra* near Vimy, and an *Ambassadors Redoubt* near Itancourt. In 1918 it was still using several of these names, and others – *Hippodrome, Wonderland, Criterion, Daly's*, etc. East of Ypres, the Roulers sheet contains a group of theatre names: *Lyric Crossing* and *Farm, Playhouse, Garrick* and *Gaiety Cross Roads, Haymarket* and *Alhambra Farms, Coliseum Fork, Lyceum House* and *Regent Chateau*. Elsewhere were *Daly's Passage* and *Keep* (Loos), *Ambassadors Redoubt* (Itancourt) and *Gaiety* (Vimy); in the last-named sheet were many names with theatrical associations. The trench called *The Only Way* (Ploegsteert) was named after the 1899 adaption from Dickens's novel *A Tale of Two Cities*, staged at the Prince of Wales Theatre (between Piccadilly Circus and Leicester Square in London).

Many trenches were named after the artistes, actors, actresses and dancers. Most of these were grouped in the Vimy–Rouvroy area, which suggests that a staff officer of First Army had more than a passing interest in the West End: *Actress Trench, Maud Allan, Billy Burke Trench, Keane Trench, Daly's, Empire, Alhambra, Vesta Tilley, Teddie Gerrard, Gladys Cooper, Gaby Trench, Lily Elsie, Acrobat Trench* and *Drama Trench. Seldom Trench* referred to a music hall double act, 'The Seldoms', which appeared at the Coliseum. *Comedy Maze* and *Comic Trench* were nearby (Lens), and *Vaudeville Trench* was farther north (Comines). We could note that while popular dance is represented, the ballet is not.

Maud Allan was a Canadian 'free-style' dancer of the Isadora Duncan sort who made her reputation in a sensational interpretation of the Salome and John the Baptist story – *The Vision of Salome* – set to waltz music in the early years of the century. In April 1918 she appeared in Wilde's play *Salome*, for two private performances at the Royal Court Theatre, which triggered the sensational Pemberton Billing court case of May–June 1918, when Billing's weekly newspaper *The Imperialist* printed his article, with the notorious headline *The Cult of The Clitoris*, previewing the production and making accusations of depravity and treason in high places. This led Allan and her producer to bring an action against Billing for criminal libel.[14] *Billing Avenue* and *Salome Sap* (Fonquevillers) duly appeared in 1918. That said, *Salome*, as the name of a settlement near Lens, pre-dated the war.

One defensive position west of Loos, Lens and Vimy, consisting of such posts, was even called the *Music Hall Line*. *Oxford* and *Cambridge* on the maps often referred to the eponymous theatres rather than seats of learning. On the Vimy Ridge, observation posts were charmingly named *Fi-Fi* and *Tou-Tou*. The West End shows themselves featured in the nomenclature; 'Choo Chin Chow' was represented by *Chin* and *Chow Trenches*, which were close together in the Lens sector, and perhaps *Chin* was not far away. There was a *Chin Trench* near Fampoux, and a *Chin-Chin Trench* near Oppy, but the latter referred to the popular (originally Italian) saying immortalised in the popular song 'Goodbye-ee'.

London and provincial music halls were extremely popular with the troops on leave, and they had equivalents at the front with the various divisional concert parties that put on many music hall and pierrot turns – The Tivolies, The Roosters, The Red Roses, etc. One of the most disturbing war paintings, by Sickert, took as its subject pierrots performing to a meagre audience and a sea of empty deckchairs on the front at Brighton in 1915, and this vehicle for transmitting a message about the war was picked up again in 1963 by Joan Littlewood and Theatre Workshop in *Oh! What a Lovely War!*. Music hall artists were well represented at the front, both in person and by name. Basil Hallam served in the forces, and was killed while observing for the artillery from a captive balloon. Leslie Henson and Du Calion entertained the troops, while Charlie Chaplin films were shown from an early date. Chaplin even had a popular wartime song (derived from an earlier song 'Pretty Redwing') dedicated to him:

And the moon shines bright on Charlie Chaplin,
His boots are cracking for t' want of blacking,
And his old fusty coat is wanting mending,
Until they send him to the Dardanelles.

Or:

Oh, the sun shines bright on Charlie Chaplin.
His boots are cracklin for the want of black'nin
And his old baggy troosers they need mendin,
Before they send him to the Dardanelles.

Charlie and *Chaplin Trenches* were next to each other north of the Scarpe (Fampoux), while near *Dirty Bucket Corner*, north of Ypres, were *Charlie* [Chaplin] *Farm*, [George] *Robey Farm*, [Little] *Tich House*, [Leslie] *Henson House*, [George] *Formby Farm* and *Gaby Cottage*. The popular song 'Sister Susie's Sewing Shirts for Soldiers' provided *Sister Trench* and *Susie Trench* next to each other near Bailleul in 1918. The names of *Stop, Look* and *Listen Copses* near a railway near Amiens in 1918 referred simultaneously to the familiar warning signs by British railway lines, to Irving Berlin's 1915 West End revue (starring Gaby Deslys) called *Stop! Look! Listen!*, and to the nearby 'stop line' – the Amiens Inner Defence Line.

Dance halls also provided an important source of entertainment and opportunity while on leave, and trenches were even named after popular dances of the period: *Gaby Glide* (named after Gaby Deslys), *Cake Walk*, *Bunny Hug*, *Crab Crawl* (Zillebeke), *Tango Trench* (Roclincourt), *Quick Trench* and *Step Trench* (Bapaume). *Ragtime Villas* (Menin) reminds us of the song, sung to the tune of 'The Church's One Foundation', which the men of Kitchener's Army sang so proudly and mournfully:

We are Fred Karno's Army, the Ragtime Infantry,
We cannot fight, we cannot shoot, no bloody use are we,
And when we get to Berlin the Kaiser will agree
'Hoch, Mein Gott, what a bloody rotten lot
Are the Ragtime Infantry.'

The name also brings to mind Sassoon's bitterly satirical poem about the tank lurching over the music hall stalls.

J.M. Barrie's *Peter Pan*, also a popular pantomime, was commemorated by *Peter Pan* (Zonnebeke sheet), *Hook Copse* and *Wendy Cottage* (both in the Westroosebeke sheet) near Passchendaele. A huge number of other theatrical names – many of them remarkably appropriate – also appeared in the area of the Ypres salient; in the Moorslede map sheet were: *Mummers Cross Roads, Scimitar Farm, Mountebank Fork, Super Cross Roads, Dwarf Crossing* and *House, Stage House, Trick Farm, Acrobat Cross Roads, Balance Cottage, Freak Crossing, Tumbler Crossing, Spangle Farm, Trapeze Wood, Actor's Fork, Clown Crossing, Juggler Cross Roads, Showman Crossing, Comedian Crossing, Minstrel Cross Roads, Melody Buildings, Fair Farm, Critic*

Cross Roads, *Dramatist Cross Roads*, *Beerbohm Houses*, *Tree Farm* and *Irving Houses*. In the Steenwerck sheet was the grand and rich mixture (not all theatrical in the narrow sense) of: *Prompt Farm*, *Prospero Farm*, *Pistol Farm*, *Ossian Farm*, *Persia House*, *Pandora*, *Orpheus House*, *Ophir House*, *Onyx House*, *Domby House*, *Fum Farm* (but no *Fe*, *Fi* or *Fo*), *Jingle Fork*, *Virus Farm*, *Grand Slam*, *Owl Farm*, *Orca Farm*, *Orgy House*, *The Mutes*, *Darling House*, *Limbo Cottage*, *Dook Farm*, *Murder Farm*, *Thunder Cottages*, *Gringo Farm* and *Lupin Farm*, the last perhaps named after the flower, the son of Mr Pooter (in the Grossmiths' *Diary of a Nobody*), or the character in Dickens' *Martin Chuzzlewit*.

Cinema

The Army was an avid consumer of films for the entertainment of troops, but also arranged the filming of its own activities and operations, for propaganda rather than for record purposes. Its cinematographer Geoffrey Malins, for example, filmed the attack on Hawthorn Ridge Redoubt on 1 July 1916. The new technology of moving pictures was well-established before the turn of the century, and was eagerly embraced to record the events of the war for home audiences, to entertain the troops at the front (Charlie Chaplin and others), to film the battlefield from above for intelligence purposes, and even to locate enemy artillery as part of the Bull sound-ranging apparatus adopted by the British in 1915. Several cinema names were given to trenches: *Kino Street* (Vimy), *Cinema House* (Aubers) and *Cinema Trench* (Fampoux), *Cinema Road* (Wytschaete), *Picturedrome* (Beaumont) named after the Picture Drome on the Shankhill Road in Belfast[15] and *Film Trench* (Fonquevillers) near Gommecourt. *Charlie Chaplin* was commemorated in several locations, as we noted above.

Newspapers and Magazines

The Somme area (Longueval) in particular commemorated the double-edged contribution of newspapers and journals to the war effort. Here, in the vicinity of Flers, where tanks first hit the headlines, were found: *Sketch*, *Mirror*, *Tatler*, *Bystander*, *Mail*, *Time*[s] and *Punch Trenches*. Perhaps it was not a coincidence that *Truth*, war's first casualty, was also a trench name in this area. There was also a *Truth Trench* in the Arras sheet. *News Trench* appeared twice (Roclincourt and Rouvroy), and there was also a *Press Trench* (Sorel-le-Grand). The French journal *La Vie Parisienne* was very popular among British officers for its pictures of scantily clad women drawn by Kirchner (not Ernst Ludwig Kirchner, the German expressionist painter, who served on the other side of no man's land), which were pinned up in many a company headquarters dugout. His name was commemorated in *Kirchner Copse* in the Toutencourt area, west of Albert. The cartographers were perhaps giving their opinion of Lord Northcliffe's contribution to the war effort when they named *Daily Mail Woods*, *Blab Copse* and *Screecher Copse* near Toutencourt. It is possible that *Blast Trench* near Combles was named after Wyndham Lewis's vorticist publication, though explosions or expletives closer to home may have been a more likely explanation.

Many officers and men had the national and local newspapers sent out from home. Even the official historian deigned to mention the newspapers, and not just in the context of breaches of security. He noted that after the front had stabilised, the *Continental Daily Mail*, published in Paris, regularly reached the troops on the day of issue and achieved a large circulation, while the most popular weeklies were *John Bull*, *La Vie Parisienne*, the *Bystander* carrying Bairnsfather's cartoons, and *Punch*, 'whose artists, poets and "watchdogs" did much to keep up the spirits of the troops'.[16] Blunden quoted an apposite little rhyme about John Bull's editor with its: 'When you're in deep decline/Who provides the Number Nine?/Mr. Bottomley – John Bull.'[17] The 'No. 9 pill' was one of the medical officer's favourites, guaranteed to generate a rapid laxative effect.

Censorship by the GHQ Intelligence section, combined with evasive and tritely lyrical reporting (particularly when it came to larks singing in no man's land during the barrage) by Beech Thomas and other journalists, infuriated the troops, but there was little they could do to counteract it except through satire in their own trench newspapers, and also the time-honoured use of such publications in the latrines. One of the accredited journalists, Philip Gibbs, resisted censorship as far as he possibly could, and was moved to tell what he considered to be the truth about the war in his wartime and post-war books: *The Soul of the War* (1915), which covered the battle of Loos, *The Battle of the Somme* (1917), *From Bapaume to Passchendaele* (1918) and *The Realities of War* and *Now It can Be Told* (1920)

Philosophical

The pragmatic and reputedly unintellectual British (or at least the English) were less involved in the European 'culture wars' than the French and Germans. The French prided themselves on their rational intellectual tradition, their *Academie* and their *Philosophes*, while the Germans, more romantic and nationalistic, also valued their home-grown philosophers; the French named several German trenches after exemplars of German '*Kultur*', including *Boyau Heine*, *Boyau de Nietsche* and *Boyau de Kant*.

The war made philosophers of all soldiers, who pondered the reasons for their plight and the meaning of their experiences, and William Orpen even painted one such British soldier-philosopher – *The Thinker*. The soldiery would largely have been in sympathy with the Greek philosopher after whom *Diogenes Cross Roads*, near Passchendaele, was named. This humbug-hating philosopher, who searched in vain for an honest man, lived in a storage (rum?) jar, was the founder of the Cynics, believed in ignoring conventions and asked Alexander the Great to get out of his light. Conan Doyle named the Diogenes Club, to which Mycroft, Sherlock Holmes's unclubbable brother belonged, after him. Nearby was *Hippocrates Cross Roads*, named after the founder of a medical tradition for which soldiers had good reason to be thankful. An outlying suburb of coal miners' houses north-west of Loos was already named *Philosophe*, and there was a *Philosopher's House* west of Saint-Quentin.

Literary and Thespian

While the war made a vast impact on literature, literature had a smaller effect on the war. It did, however, contribute a certain number of names. We have already looked at the wide range of theatrical references in the naming of trenches and localities. Publishers were represented by *Harmsworth*, *Cassell*, *Hodder*, *Stoughton* and *Methuen Farms* (Dadizeele), but remarkably few authors or literary characters make their appearance. There was, however, a *Cowper Trench* (Lens), a *Dryden Trench* (Rouvroy) and a *Trollope Trench* (Gouy). Tobias Smollett's picaresque novel of 1751, *Peregrine Pickle*, was marked by *Peregrine Farm* and *Pickle House*, close together in the Wervicq sheet. There are certainly some biblical characters, and we might expect more from Bunyan's *Pilgrim's Progress*, if not from Milton or Dante. As we have seen, the name *Pilgrims Progress* itself appeared at the *Hohenzollern Redoubt*, while *Pilgrims Way* was a sunken road at Flers on the Somme. The Roulers sheet, east of Ypres, contains *Shelley's Farm*, *Milton Copse*, *Scott Farm* and *Shaws Farm*. *Keats Redan*, near La Boisselle on the Somme, named in 1915 by the 51st Highland Division, is unlikely to have been named after the romantic poet. There were few Shakespearean references along the front – *Caliban Trench* appears almost by accident, as the result of alphabetical sequencing, in the Ypres sector, but there seems little of the accidental about the juxtaposition of *Hamlet* and *Ghostly Trenches* north of Loos, and *Hamlet Trench* near Saint-Quentin. We have already noted *Prospero Farm* and *Pistol Farm* in the Steenwerck area. There was also an *Ophelia Alley* (Saint-Quentin) and a *Tempest Trench* (Rouvroy).

Robert Louis Stevenson's disturbing novel *The Strange Case of Dr Jekyll and Mr Hyde* is remembered in *Jekyll* and *Hyde Copses* (Fonsommes sheet) north-east of Saint-Quentin. This exploration of human nature and personality change provided a remarkably appropriate analogy to the soldier's condition – that strange split personality expected of him whereby he should be one moment a normal, good human being, and the next, having in the line of duty been authorised to lose control of his senses, a frenzied and berserk killer.

Seeing the names *Boon Farm*, *Blessing Farm*, *Pickwick House*, *Owl Barns* and *Pen Cottage* near each other in the Moorslede map sheet, we might suppose some random juxtaposition. But when we recall that Siegfried Sassoon found, during the war, a rhyme coming to him unbidden from a railway station's enamel advertising panel, 'They came as a boon and a blessing to men/The Pickwick, the owl and the Waverley pen', we suddenly know the significance of that battlefield group. The topographical trigger for this group was clearly the Belgian place name Boonhoek, which appeared here on the pre-war and wartime maps. In the same map sheet are *Author's Corner*, *Poets' Corner*, *Epic Cottage*, *Ode Farm* and *Marvel Mill*, while nearby in the Westroosebeke sheet are *Wordling Farm* and *Written Farm*. The cartographer responsible for these sheets was clearly also a 'literary gent'.

The Green Curve (the name of a trench near Loos), was the title of a pre-war military science-fiction book by Lieutenant Colonel Ernest Dunlop Swinton RE (Ole Luk'oie), who besides writing the official history of the Russo–Japanese War had also had a hand in the development of the tank. Kitchener appointed him to be the 'Eyewitness', or official war correspondent, with the British Army in France.

Those growing up in the late Victorian and Edwardian periods were great readers of Dickens, and it is unsurprising that many names associated with that great story-teller appeared on the Western Front. In the Comines sheet, south-east of Ypres, we encounter *Nickleby House*, *Dotheboys Hall*, *Squeers Farm* and *Twist Corner*. The Cambrai battlefield features *Bleak House* and its associated trench names, *Bleak Trench*, *Bleak Walk*, etc. In *Our Mutual Friend*, Fledgeby says 'Queer Street is full of lodgers just at present',[18] and *Queer Street*, the imaginary street where people live who have suffered misfortune, particularly financial, duly appeared in various locations on the Western Front – indeed in the Bois Grenier trench map sheet it featured twice, once as a British and again, a mile or two away, as a German trench.

A Dickensian group appeared west of Albert (sheet *57dSW*) in 1918, as part of a new defensive system to contain the German offensive: *Pickwick Avenue*, *Weller Avenue*, *Wardle Avenue*, *Winkle Avenue*, *Snodgrass Avenue*, *Stiggins Avenue*, *Bardell Avenue*, *Tupman Avenue*, *Buzfuz Avenue*, and *Jingle Avenue*. Other possible Dickensian allusions are *Pip Street* and *Trench* (Wytschaete,

Neuville Vitasse and Bertincourt) and *Jingle Trench* (Roclincourt) from *The Pickwick Papers*; *Lupin* appears in *Martin Chuzzlewit*, but was also the son of Mr Pooter in George and Weedon Grossmith's *The Diary of a Nobody*. The problem with all these is they are not in a definite Dickensian context, and could easily derive from quite other associations.

R.S. Surtees, author of the amusing 'Jorrocks' hunting novels, was an extremely popular author with horsy officers, of whom there were many, particularly in the cavalry and gunners, but also the infantry. However, the only obvious allusions are *Handley Cross* and *Hillingdon Hall* in the Toutencourt (Fifth Army HQ in 1916) area, with less obvious ones contained in *Jumper Wood*, *Image Wood* and the misspelt *Jarrocks Farm* (Zillebeke). The 'Image' reference is to the assertion that hunting is the image of war, with all of its danger and none of its guilt. Lewis Carroll's surreal world, which questioned the whole nature and assumptions of 'sane' adult society, threw up *Walrus*, *Gimble*, *Mimsy*, *Borogrove*, *Dum* and *Dee*. Daniel Defoe (and his inspiration in the form of Alexander Selkirk) was commemorated by *Defoe Farm*, *Crusoe Cross Roads*, *Castaway Corner*, *Friday Copse* and *Selkirk Farm* in the Zonnebeke and Moorslede sheets. George Borrow's 'wind on the heath' novels of gypsy life provided *Lavengro Farm*, *Gipsey*, *Romany*, *Rovers Cross Roads* and *Tinkers Fork* in the Staden and Hooglede sheets. Not far away, in the Comines area, were *Vagabond Trench* and *Avenue*, and *Vagrants Row*. Finally, it is very odd that although the two volumes of Compton Mackenzie's *Sinister Street* were published in 1913–14,[19] the title was not used as a trench name; it was however, according to H.M. Tomlinson, used for a street near the Cloth Hall in Ypres.[20]

As we have seen, a clear source of names, certainly in the map sheets of back areas produced by 4th Field Survey Battalion in the summer of 1918, was popular literature. This 'book code' can be broken once a clear indicating name is identified. One such name, that was literally 'no one' if not 'no name', was *Nemo Farm* (Borre sheet, south-west of Ypres), a clear reference to Jules Verne's *Twenty Thousand Leagues Under the Sea*, which someone in 4th FSB had been reading in 1918. This book may give the clue to other names in this and adjacent sheets, such as *Sepoy Mill*; Captain Nemo had lost his family in what was know to the British as the Sepoy Rebellion, or Indian Mutiny. It is fascinating to note that Verne was a native of Albert, on the Somme battlefield.

Women's and Girls' Names

The Army at the front was necessarily separated from its womenfolk, and although the number of British women immediately behind the front grew as the war went on (nurses, ambulance drivers, auxiliaries, etc.), relationships inevitably formed with French and Belgian women, and many officers and men, tormented by their unnaturally monastic, and probably brief, lives, resorted to prostitutes (at the blue lamps and red lamps respectively). Venereal disease became a serious problem for the military authorities.

As with Raphael Kirchner's prints from *La Vie Parisienne*, there was probably not a little wishful thinking associated with giving trenches female names, and those associated with femininity (and yearning and lust). Intriguing examples are *Flirt Trench* and *Fluffy Trench* (Vimy) and *Corset Trench* (Lens). We have already looked at the naming of trenches after actresses, particularly in the Vimy area. Many were also named after wives and girlfriends and, in that sense, had such private associations to the namers that the contexts are now generally not recoverable. Generic names were given, such as *Flapper Trench* (Vimy), *Girl Street* (Ficheux), *Female Trench* and *Woman Street* (Hébuterne), etc. Although a 'flapper' was originally a girl still young enough to be wearing flapping pigtails, the meaning of the word was clearly soon extended to include young women entering society; Gilbert Frankau wrote of 'Flappers I met at Tango Teas', in a context that clearly envisaged more intimate encounters. That said, flappers were also devices used to clear gas out of trenches, so we need to be careful in negotiating this world of multiple meanings.

Many women's names were used for British trenches and posts in the Bois Grenier sector and elsewhere. It is likely that the female names in the Vimy and adjacent sheets also referred to actresses. *Ada Trench* (Bois Grenier, Lens, Vis-en-Artois), *Agnes Street* (Ploegsteert), *Hilda Trench* (Loos), *Mina Avenue* (Aubers), *Fanny Trench*, *Gladys Trench* and *Gertie Trench* at Vimy, *Anna Trench* at Hébuterne, and *Fanny's Avenue* at Wytschaete. *Aileen*, *Alice* and *Amy Communication Trenches* appear in the Hamel–Vaire Wood sector in 1918, though *Alice* can also refer to Alice Springs, in Australia. *Wendy Alley* was near Saint-Quentin. The following women's names, in more or less alphabetical order from right to left, were given to British posts in the Bois Grenier sheet, south of Armentières: *Ada*, *Agnes*, *Alice*, *Amy*, *Annette*, *Annie*, *Augusta*, *Bertha*, *Betty*, *Caroline*, *Carrie*, *Catherine*, *Cis*, *Connie*, *Cynthia*, *Daisy*, *Decima*, *Dixie*, *Dolly*, *Dorothy*, *Dot*, *Emma*, *Esme*, *Eve*, *Evelyn*, *Eileen*, *Eunice*, *Florence* and *Flossie*. South of these were a few men's and boys' names: *Patrick*, *Percy*, *Paul*, *Peter* and *Robert*, but these were greatly outnumbered. German trenches were also given female names by the British, including some specifically German ones; there are many on British trench maps of the Bois Grenier–Aubers–Richebourg area: *Anna Switch* and *Trench*, *Nora Trench* and *Nora's Arm*, *Sally Trench*, *Sophia Trench*, *Susan's Trench*, *Eva Trench*, *Frieda Trench*, *Gretchen Trench*, *Lisl Trench*, *Margaret Trench*, *Maudlin Trench* and *Mitzi Trench*. Other pairs of names in the same series, such as *Dora Trench* and *Dora's Arm*, *Nora Trench* and *Nora's Arm*, *Clara Trench* and *Clara's Fan*, *Irma Trench* and *Irma's Elephant*, reflected the plan view of trench-features or strongpoints on the air photo and the trench map.

Scientific

A large group of scientists' names appears in the Somme area, near Picquigny, in May 1918, in sheet *62eNE, Edition 1A(local) Secret, FSC 3730 27-5-18*. Following the German offensive and consequent British retreat, these names were given to British communication trenches in the new defensive system known as *Vaux Trenches* and *Ferrières Trenches*: *Amundsen Avenue, Evans Avenue, Darwin Avenue, Wallace Avenue, Newton Avenue, Maxwell Avenue, Kelvin Avenue, Stokes Avenue, Huxley Avenue, Thomson Avenue, Faraday Avenue, Sedgwick Avenue, Murchison Avenue, Lapworth Avenue, Sorby Avenue, Woodward Avenue, Ramsey Avenue, Dewar Avenue, Pope Avenue, Davy Avenue, Joule Avenue, Adams Avenue, Dalton Avenue, Royle Avenue, Hutton Avenue* and *Lyell Avenue*.

Professional

Naturally the profession of soldiering was reflected in trench naming, and the various regiments and arms were well represented. Academic life was invoked in the Moorslede map sheet, north-east of Ypres, by *Academy Buildings, Scholar Cross Roads, Student Cross Roads, Varsity Farm, Professor Cross Roads, Dominie Farm* and *Exam Buildings*. The legal profession and judiciary was also represented in this area. The paucity of philosophers has been mentioned. The oldest profession, to which soldiers frequently resorted, was invoked by *Pimp Trench* (Bertincourt) and *Tart Trench* (Arras and Roclincourt), while its medical consequences are dealt with in Chapter VI together with the medical profession at war. The professions of architects, surveyors, draughtsmen and cartographers are also explored in Chapter VI.

Domestic and Familiar

Darby and *Joan Copses* (Fonsommes) north-east of Saint-Quentin, were named after the homely old couple with origins in the 18th century, and the associated Staffordshire mantelpiece figures. Soldiers could quench their thirst at *Tea House* (Aubers), *Tea Trench, Support* and *Lane* (Longueval), *Tea Farm*

(Wytschaete), *Tea Post* (Epéhy), *Tea Trench* (Arras and Le Sars), and *Lime and Juice Trenches* (Longueval and Le Sars) north of Flers. Alcoholic drinks are covered in Chapter VI. There was *Pie Alley* (Berthenicourt), and *Pie Trench* (Roclincourt and Wervicq), and also *Plum Duff Street* (Ploegsteert). *Streaky Bacon Farm Post* was near Bois Grenier. Large and small change were included in a group in the Dadizeele sheet, which included a delightful progression, primarily monetary, from sparkling diamond to base copper: *Kohinoor Cross Roads*, *Golden Cross Roads*, *Sovereign Wood*, *Crown Buildings*, *Silver Farm*, *Florin House*, *Shilling Farm*, *Copper Corner* and *Penny Corner*.

Public Schools

The names of the famous English and Scottish public schools, which supplied a high proportion of the officers of the Regular, New and Territorial Armies, were a feature of the Aubers sheet from September 1915, if not before, covering part of the Old Front Line north of Neuve Chapelle. The schools represented, giving their names to posts and roads in this area, were *Clifton* (Sir Douglas Haig's school), *Rugby*, *Winchester*, *Eton*, *Harrow*, *Charterhouse*, *Wellington* (a strong military connection), *Cheltenham* (also a military connection), *Haileybury*, *King Edward's Oxford*, *Fettes* and *Loretto*. In the Ypres Salient, *Winchester Farm* and *Wellington* (Zonnebeke) stood next to each other. Perhaps it is significant that such naming, like that of politicians, generals and subjects of military glory, was not a general feature of the British front.

Cyrano at the Front

The multiplicity of projecting features, or local salients, where the trench lines bulged out around a village, wood, farm or hill feature, gave rise to many noses, nebs, nabs, points, bills, beaks and so on in a nomenclature of protuberance. They were as important to trench warfare as to Sterne's *Tristram Shandy*, which in fact neatly encompassed trenches and anatomical addenda. These were key points for the defence, as machine guns sited in them could enfilade no man's land to either side, but they naturally formed obvious targets for mortar and shellfire. Among the many were *Blunt Nose*, *The Pope's Nose* (Thiepval, Loos, Richebourg), *Kaiser Bill*, *Caesar's Nose* (Boesinghe), *Leipziger Nase* (*Leipzig Redoubt*, Thiepval), *Casino Point* (Méaulte), *The Nab* (south of Thiepval), *The Neb* (Richebourg), *Nez Trench*, *The Duck's Bill* (Givenchy), *The Boar's Head* (Richebourg), *Jew's Nose*, *Jackdaw Beak*, *Mad Point* and *Mine Point* (Loos), *Nun's Nose*, or simply *The Nose*, are a few of the many names given to these small salients. Several such names were used more than once. *Big Willie* (the Kaiser) and *Little Willie* (the Crown Prince), German flanking trenches on either side of the enemy's *Hohenzollern Redoubt*, were perhaps named with an eye to anatomy as well as Teutonic personages, although they kept company with *Tirpitz*.

Pairs and Groups

David Jones's litany is a reminder that names may often form part of sets – pairs or groups – that are related in serious or playful ways. This kinship is something that setting the names out in alphabetical form destroys. In the Hébuterne sheet, for example, we find *Babylon, Eden, Palestine, Isaiah, Hittite* and *Eczema Trenches*, among others, in close proximity, while in the St Julien sheet are a large group of French military historical names: *La Belle Alliance, Marengo*, and nearby *Turco, Zouave* and *Spahi Farms*. In other sheets, clusters of names, clearly bestowed by the first British units to take over the sector, are derived from their home city or region, as in the Ovillers sheet on the Somme front that includes a lot of names given by the 51st (Highland) Division. We encountered groups of river, tree, fruit, flower, vegetable, animal, bird and fish names in Chapter I.

There were many pairs of names, some already mentioned: *Dum Copse* and *Dee Copse* (Gricourt), north of Saint-Quentin, *Plum Farm* and *Apple Villa* (St Julien), *Fag Alley* and *Match Alley* (Bullecourt), *Tip Work* and *Top Work* (Gueudecourt, Somme), *Ping* and *Pong Farms* (Hooglede), *Kit and Kat* (Ypres Salient), *Tick Trench* and *Tok* [sic] *Trench* (Arras), *Union Trench* and *Jack Trench* (Beaumont, near Thiepval Wood), *Lime* and *Juice Trenches*, north of Flers (Longueval and Le Sars), *Hook* and *Eye Trenches, Whiz Farm* and *Bang Farm, Bab Farm* and *Code Farm* (Bab was a field code), *Spud Farm* and *Murphy Farm* east of Oostaverne (Wytschaete), *Jack* and *Jill Farms, Wam Farm* and *Beek Farm* either side of the Wambeek, east of Oostaverne (Wytschaete), *Rag Point* and *Bone Point* (Wytschaete), *Jekyll* and *Hyde Copses* (Fonsommes), *Lucifer Farm* and *Match Spinney, Pip Farm* and *Squeak Farm, Apple Farm* and *Orange Farm*, and *Ink* and *Pen Farms* (all Wervicq).

Beyond pairs, diminishing returns set in as staff officers struggled to make connections. Fewer triads occurred, among them the German redoubts on the Messines Ridge known to the British as *Hop Point, Skip Point* and *Jump Point* (Wytschaete). *Jack, Jill* and *Pail Copses* ascending the hill towards Folemprise Farm at Ertrées, north of Saint-Quentin, *Faith, Hope* and *Charity Farms* (Wytschaete), *Tom's Cut, Dick's Cut* and *Harry's Cut* south of Cuinchy (La Bassée), *Nansen, Fram* and *Pemmican Farms* (Poperinghe), and *Stop,*

Look and *Listen Copses* east of Amiens. There were even fewer fours, for example *Matthew, Mark, Luke* and *John Copses* opposite Serre, and *Tinker, Tailor, Soldier* and *Sailor Woods* near Toutencourt. There were naturally even fewer groups of five, one being *Boon Farm, Blessing Farm, Pickwick House, Owl Barns* and *Pen Cottage* (from the Waverley pen advertising jingle) in the Moorslede sheet.

Some sets were naturally large but finite – e.g. the communication trenches north of Arras named after days and months, or the group of woods named after signs of the zodiac. There were, however, a large number of loosely related thematic groups, many of which have already been examined or will be encountered in the following chapters – for example the weather, newspaper and Lewis Carroll groups on the Somme, the Dardanelles and Egypt groups at Ypres, and animal, bird, plant, flower and vegetable groups (the last four occur together in the Hooglede sheet, north-east of Ypres) – and that with a nautical theme just north-west of Ypres: *Bilge Cottage, Windward House, Bobstay Castle* and *Leeward, Topsail, Scupper* and *Crojack Farms*. The boating theme (probably triggered off by the Belgian place name *Spinnekens*) also appears in the Hooglede sheet, with *Yacht Farm, Windlass Farm, Skiff Corner* and *Brig Corner*.

Games and Sport

If rugby is a brutish game played by gentlemen, football (soccer) a gentleman's game played by brutes, boxing a brutish game played by brutes, and foxhunting the unspeakable in pursuit of the uneatable, what is the profession of the soldier? The Army, of course, encouraged sports that developed physical fitness and courage, and a large proportion of the civilian soldiery had played sport of some sort in peacetime.

However, despite the highly publicised occasions when attacking troops kicked footballs towards the German lines, sporting references do not make up a significant proportion of trench names. Notwithstanding the sporting metaphors used by some politicians, generals, journalists and clergymen, the soldiers themselves were reluctant to see the war as a 'great game'. One of the most popular soldiers' games, along with cards, was commemorated by *Crown* and *Anchor Trenches* at *The Kink*, south of the *Hohenzollern Redoubt*.

Soccer and rugby football actually featured on the battlefield itself. Apart from friendly games with the Germans in no man's land during the 1914 Christmas truce, a few sporting officers started attacks at Loos and on the Somme by kicking (or drop-kicking) spherical (or oval) balls. The London Irish did this at Loos, and Captain Billy Neville of the East Surreys on the

Somme. Soccer references are occasionally found in trench names – e.g. *Kick-off Trench*, *Aston Trench* and *Villa Trench* on the Somme (Longueval), and *Football Crater* (Vimy) and *Football Trench* (Villers-Guislain).

There appears to have been only one group of cricketing names, that east of Passchendaele in the Ypres Salient. This commemorated two of the most famous cricketers of the pre-war period – W.G. Grace and Gilbert Jessop ('the croucher'). The group comprised: *Grace Farm*, *Jessop Buildings*, *Crouch Farm*, *Maiden Farm*, *Bat* and *Bail Copses*, *Wicket Buildings*, *Crease* and *League Woods*, *Lunge Farm*, *Lob Cottages* and *Yorker Houses*. There was also a *Cricket Trench* in the Villers-Guislain sheet, and a *Wicket Corner* in the Méaulte sheet but this, possibly referring to a wicket gate, was also called *Wicked Corner* by Sassoon[21] – a good example of poetic manipulation. Wicket and wicked, incidentally, are both derived from the same linguistic root.

Horse racing was commemorated by *Tattenham Corner* near Fricourt on the Somme (subtitled *The King's Horse Wins* in a later caption to the nameboard in the Imperial War Museum) and also at the *Dead End* at Ypres, where the Yser canal meets the edge of the town, while in the Ypres Salient itself (St Julien), there was a group of racecourses – *Racecourse Farm*, *Ascot Cottage*, *Sandown Farm*, *Hurst Park*, *Gatwick Cot* and *Kempton Park*. Racecourses were commemorated but for some reason not racehorses. Several observation posts along the front were called *Grandstand*. Foxhunting, despite its popularity among the pre-war officer corps, as attested by Siegfried Sassoon and Robert Graves, was little represented in trench naming, though there were many references to foxes – *Fox Lane* (Le Sars), *Fox Street* (Ficheux), *Fox Trench* (Neuville Vitasse, Fonquevillers, Vis-en-Artois). The proximity of *Foxy Alley*, *Foxy Trench* and *Belvoir Alley* in the Oppy sheet was unusual. There was also a *Forrard Trench* (Vis-en-Artois) and a *Tally Ho Lane* (Hermies). We have already noted the strange dearth of names from Surtees' novels – with only *Handley Cross* and *Hillingdon Hall* (Toutencourt), *Jarrocks* [sic] *Farm*, *Jumper Wood* and *Image Wood* (all Zillebeke) crossing the Channel. There were, however, as we have seen, many names relating to horses and their equipment.

As far as boxing, a popular regular Army sport, is concerned we should never forget that the powerful black German shell explosion called a '*Jack Johnson*' was named after the legendary American boxer. Boxing names included, in the Moorslede sheet, *Boxers Cross Roads*, *Punch Farm*, *Bout Farm*, *Bantam Copse*, *Carpentier Cottage*, *Gong Spinney*, *Time Farm*, *Muscle Houses*, *Knock Farm*, *Blow Buildings*, *Solar Farm*, *Plexus Farm*, *Glove Cottage*, *Purse Cottage*, *Bet House*, *Sweep Cottage* and *Ring Buildings*. There was also *Gym Farm* (Wytschaete) and *Upper Cut* (La Bassée).

In the Villers-Guislain sheet there was a general sport group: *Fives*, *Tennis*, *Racket*, *Football*, *Cricket* and *Squash Trenches*, and *Skittle Alley*. A golfing group appeared in the Hooglede and Roulers sheets: *Stymie*, *Bogey* and *Club Farms*, *Niblick Houses*, *Bunker House*, *Link Copse*, *Caddies Corner* and *Mashie Cottage*. There was also a *Links Wood* (Wervicq) and *Tee Trench* (Rouvroy), while there were of course many bunkers along the front. *The Wipers Times* drew a neat parallel between a golf course and no man's land, with the various holes and bunkers represented by saps and other military obstacles. *Hockey Trench* was at Loos. Tennis was represented in the Hooglede, Roulers and Moorslede sheets, with *Wimbledon*, *Deuce House*, *Sporty Fork*, *Tennis*, *Racquet* and *Net Farms*. The particular irony represented by shooting as a sport was brought home by the *Grouse Butts* (Richebourg and La Bassée), and many ambiguous references to snipe – e.g. *Snipe Hall* near Passchendaele and *Snipe Trench* (Wytschaete and Hermies). The names of other game birds and animals have already been noted in Chapter I. Fishing was poorly represented; one of its few appearances was in the pairing of *Rod Trench* and *Reel Trench* (Achiet), while *Speckle Farm*, *Trout Fork*, *Roach Farm*, *Pike Farm*, *Herring Farm* and others appear in the Hooglede sheet.

The next chapter looks at names that have a specific connection with the Army, while Chapter VII examines names associated with regions, cities, towns and other places in the British Isles and Empire.

Notes

1   1:10,000 trench map, sheet *28NW2 St Julien, Edn. 5A, April 1917.*

2   1:10,000 trench map, sheet *28NW4&NE3 (Parts of), Zillebeke, Edn. 5A, April 1917.*

3   In the Champagne area – see Chapter VII.

4   For *Queer Street* in titles see: Abbott, J.H.M., *Letters from Queer Street*, London: Adam & Charles Black, 1908; Hume, Fergus, *In Queer Street*, London: F.V. White, 1913; Mackenzie, Compton (n.d.), *Mabel in Queer Street*, Oxford: Basil Blackwell.

5   Jones, David, *In Parenthesis*, London: Faber & Faber, 1937.

6   In Blunden, Edmund, *Undertones of War*, London: Cobden-Sanderson, 1928.

7   In Rosenberg, Isaac, *Poems by Isaac Rosenberg*, London: Heinemann, 1922.

8   Anon, in *The 'New Church' Times*, Monday 29 May, 1916, in: Roberts, F.J. (ed.), *The Wipers Times*, first complete facsimile edition, London: Eveleigh Nash & Grayson, 1930.

9   Gibson, Langhorne, & Harper, Vice-Admiral J.E.T., *The Riddle of Jutland*, London, Cassell, 1934, Chapter XXXVI.

10   Franklin, Benjamin, letter to Jean-Baptiste le Roy, 13 November, 1789: 'In this world, nothing can be said to be certain, except death and taxes.'

11   Woolf, Virginia, 'Reading', in *Essays*, ed. A. McNeillie, London: Hogarth Press, 1986, III (pp. 141–61), p. 154.

12   Blunden, Edmund, *De Bello Germanico, A Fragment of Trench History, Written in 1918 by the author of Undertones of War*, Hawstead: G.A. Blunden, 1930, p. 77. I have been unable to find this trench on a trench map.

13   Chasseaud, Peter, *Artillery's Astrologers – A History of British Survey and Mapping on the Western Front, 1914–1918*, Lewes: Mapbooks, 1999, p. 128.

14   Andrew, C., *Secret Service, The Making of the British Intelligence Community*, London: Heinemann, 1985, pp. 188–9.

15   Orr, Philip, *The Road to the Somme, Men of the Ulster Division Tell Their Story*, Belfast: Blackstaff Press, 1987, p. 128.

16   Edmonds, J.E., *History of The Great War, Military Operations, France and Belgium*, 1916, Vol. I, London: Macmillan, 1932, p. 148.

17   Blunden, 1928, op. cit.

18   Dickens, Charles, *Our Mutual Friend*, Book 3, Chapter 1.

19   Mackenzie, Compton, *Sinister Street*, Vols I & II, London: Martin Secker, 1913–14.

20   Tomlinson, H.M., *Waiting for Daylight*, London, Cassell, 1922.

21   Sassoon, Siegfried, 'The Hero', in *The War Poems of Siegfried Sassoon*, London: Heinemann, 1919, p. 26.

VI

MILITARY NAMES

Readers of the late Richard Holmes's excellent book *Tommy*, on the British soldier of the Great War,[1] will be pleased to hear that there was a *Tommy Trench*, *Tommy Alley*, *Tommy Locality* and *Tommy Post* in the Roclincourt–Oppy area. Tommy, or Thomas Atkins, stood above all for the PBI (Poor Bloody Infantry), but in the minds of civilians and foreigners (even the Germans across no man's land) he stood for any British soldier.

We have seen from preceding chapters that many of the early trench names were created from the occupation of particular stretches of trench by a battalion that, of course, had a regimental name – for example *RB* [Rifle

Sentry of the 10th Battalion, Gordon Highlanders, at the junction of *Gourlay Trench* and *Gordon Alley*, south-east of Pozières and south-west of Martinpuich, on 28 August 1916 during the Battle of the Somme. (IWM Q4180)

Brigade] *Trench* at St Eloi. A large number of trenches were named after regiments, and these are often inseparable from county names: Surrey, Essex, Warwicks, Devon, etc. Sometimes the name was generic – e.g. *Guards Trench* (Richebourg). Similarly, the use of the cap badge emblem as a trench name may make it difficult to know which is being referred to. Most non-county regiments are easy to identify – particularly the Grenadier and Coldstream Guards, the Royal Fusiliers, etc. *Coldstream Lane* and *Road* (La Bassée) are unmistakable. In some cases, a former nickname had become incorporated in the formal regimental name – The Buffs (Royal East Kent), Greenjackets (Rifle Brigade), etc. Sometimes it is clear that a county regiment is being referred to rather than merely the county as a region – for example Yorks and Lancs.

It may be easier to spot a regimental association when the nickname is used – Gunners (Royal Artillery), Mudlarks (Royal Engineers), Bays (2nd Dragoon Guards), Death or Glory Boys (17th Lancers), Carabiniers (3rd Prince of Wales's Dragoon Guards), Pompadours (Essex), Invalids (41st Foot), Tigers (Hampshire), Yellow Bellies (Lincolnshire), Diehards (Middlesex), Shiners, Old and Bold and Fighting Fifth (Northumberland Fusiliers), Old Stubborns (Sherwood Foresters), Brickdusts, and Young Bucks and Old Bucks (Shropshire Light Infantry), Springers (Wiltshire), Snappers (East Yorkshire), Peacemakers (Bedfordshire), Bloody Eleventh (Devonshire), Faithful Durhams (DLI), Cherrypickers (11th Hussars), Pontius Pilate's Bodyguard (Royal Scots), Black Watch (Royal Highlanders), Steelbacks (Northamptonshire Regiment), Sweeps (Rifle Brigade), Rough and Ready (2nd Frontier Force), etc.

Thus we can perhaps locate some, if not all, of *Death or Glory Sap* (La Bassée), *Cherrypicker Copse* (Vermandovillers), *Mudlark Lane* (Ploegsteert Wood), *Tiger Lane*, *Tiger Pop* and three examples of *Tiger Trench*, *Buffs Bank* and *Tunnel* (Wytschaete), *Buffs Road* (St Julien), *Green Jacket Ride* (Zillebeke), *Greenjacket Trench* (Longueval), *Pompadour Trench* (Beaumont, and also Bixschoote), as well as *Pompadour Farm* north of Armentières, in this regimental category.

Cap badge (regimental badge) emblems and mottoes also give a clue to some trench names. For example, the white horse and 'Invicta' respectively in the case of the Royal West Kents may have given rise to *White Horse Trench* and *Invicta Alley* (Longueval) and *White Horse Crater* (La Bassée). We have to be careful, however, as the Royal Welch Fusiliers also used the white horse in their regimental arms. Other examples include the 'Bydand' motto for the Gordon Highlanders, the inscription appearing on the cap badge, meaning 'Stand Fast' (*Bydand Avenue*, *New Bydand Trenches* and *New Bydand Avenue*, near Sanctuary Wood), and many others.

Battle honours and battles forming an important part of a regiment's history, even if not official honours, similarly give a clue to the names:

Gibraltar for The Northamptonshire Regiment, Minden for the six British regiments that carved through a superior French cavalry force (*Minden Post, Minden Terrace*), Corunna (*Corunna Road*, La Bassée), Albuhera, Malplaquet (*Malplaquet Trench*, Neuville Vitasse, Bouchavesnes), Waterloo (*Waterloo Road*, La Bassée; *Waterloo Street,* Arras), etc. The problem with Waterloo, of course, is that the eponymous London railway station may have been intended. Many regiments boasted multiple battle honours; Robert Graves was proud of the fact that the Royal Welch Fusiliers (old 23rd Foot), besides being one of the Minden regiments, carried Malplaquet, Albuhera, Waterloo and Inkerman on its colours (David Jones added Oudenarde to these), in addition to having fought at The Boyne, Aughrim and Lille. The old British regimental numbers may also give clues to trench naming, but there are many possible sources of confusion here, including French numbering systems and British brigade numbers.

Many regimental names, even if in a bastardised or familiar form, appeared on the Somme battlefield, particularly in the High Wood–Delville Wood–Trônes Wood area: *Worcester Trench, Seaforth Trench, Greenjacket Trench, Sherwood Trench, Black Watch Trench, Koyli* [King's Own Yorkshire Light Infantry] *Redoubt, Irish Trench* and *Alley, Cheshire Trench, Ranger Trench, HLI*

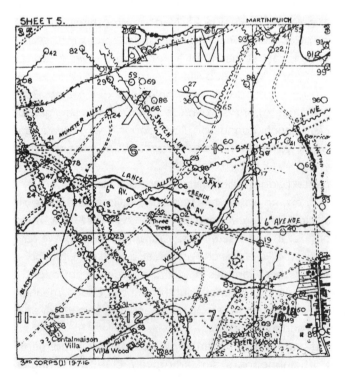

British III Corps duplicator map dated 19 July 1916, showing trenches and their names in the Bazentin-Martinpuich area, Somme battlefield. Several regimental names are represented: Munsters, Glosters, Lancs, Welch and Black Watch.

[Highland Light Infantry] *Trench, Wales Trench, Cornish Alley, Scotch Alley, Lancashire Trench* and *Lancs Trench, W. Yorks Alley, Northampton Street, Warwick Trench, Dorset Trench, Y.L.* [York and Lancaster] *Alley, Yorkshire Alley, Rifles Trench, Queens Trench, Argyle Trench, Bedford Street, Cameron Trench* and *Gloster Alley.* The Royal Engineers were also represented in this area, with *R.E. Alley* and *Sapper Trench,* as were the pioneers with *Pioneer Trench. Yeomanry Post* was near Zillebeke. The Germans had their *Grenadier-weg. Voltigeurs Alley* (St Gobain) referred to French skirmishers, the equivalent of the British light infantry.

Cavalry regiments were represented by *Bays Wood, Hussar* and *Dragoon Copses* (Homblières), by *Royal Dragoons Wood* (Vaux), *Hussar Horn* (Loos), and many other cavalry references, including many names relating to equipment, particularly around Fampoux and Vis-en-Artois, east of Arras (where we also find *Hussar, Dragoon* and *Lancer Lanes*). Moving beyond regiments, we come to the larger corps – Cavalry Corps, Corps of Royal Engineers, Tank Corps, Machine Gun Corps, Royal Flying Corps, Royal Army Medical Corps, etc. – and the broad classification of arms – cavalry, infantry, artillery, engineers. There were references to the arms generally: *Infantry Hill* (Vis-en-Artois), *Infantry Road* (Arras), *Artillery Valley,* and even to *Staff Copse* (Hébuterne), as well as auxiliary forces.

This pattern was repeated along the whole of the British front. A glance at the Gazetteer will show the frequency of regimental naming, particularly when the regional associations are taken into account.

All the line regiments grew enormously during the war, some to over twenty battalions, and a regiment could have battalions serving in many places simultaneously along the Western Front with different divisions. The following list suggests the regimental names found on the Western Front, as well as their county and regional associations.

Regimental Names of the BEF

Many or most of these were, in one way or another, incorporated into trench names.

I. British Infantry Regiments

Foot Guards: Coldstream, Grenadier, Scots, Irish, Welsh.
Infantry of the Line (including Territorial Army): Argyll & Sutherland Highlanders, Bedfordshire, Royal Berkshire, Black Watch, Border,

Cambridgeshire, Cameron Highlanders, Cheshire, Connaught Rangers, Cornwall, Devonshire, Dorsetshire, Royal Dublin Fusiliers, Duke of Cornwall's Light Infantry, Duke of Wellington's (West Riding), Durham Light Infantry, East Kent (Buffs), East Lancashire, East Surrey, East Yorkshire, Essex, Gloucestershire, Gordon Highlanders, Green Howards (Yorkshire), Hampshire, Hertfordshire, Highland Light Infantry, Honourable Artillery Company, Royal Inniskilling Fusiliers, Royal Irish Fusiliers, Royal Irish Rifles, King's (Liverpool), King's Own, King's Own Scottish Borderers, King's Own Yorkshire Light Infantry, King's Own Royal (Lancaster), King's Royal Rifle Corps, King's Shropshire Light Infantry, Lancashire Fusiliers, Leicestershire, Leinster, Lincolnshire, London Rifle Brigade, Loyal North Lancashire, Manchester, Middlesex, Monmouthshire, Royal Munster Fusiliers, Norfolk, Northamptonshire, North Staffords, Northumberland Fusiliers (including Tyneside Scottish and Tyneside Irish), Oxford & Bucks Light Infantry, Queen's (Royal West Surrey), Rifle Brigade (Prince Consort's Own), Royal (City of London) Fusiliers, Royal Irish, Royal Scots, Royal Scots Fusiliers, Scottish Rifles (Cameronians), Seaforth Highlanders, Sherwood Foresters (Notts & Derby), Somerset Light Infantry, South Lancashire, South Staffordshire, South Wales Borderers, Suffolk, Royal Sussex, Royal Warwickshire, Welch Regiment, Royal Welch Fusiliers, Queen's Own Royal West Kent, West Yorkshire, Wiltshire, Worcestershire, York & Lancaster.

The London Regiment (Territorial battalions): Artists Rifles, Royal Fusiliers, London Rifle Brigade, Rifles, Post Office Rifles, Rangers, Inns of Court, Kensington, London Scottish, Civil Service Rifles, Queen Victoria's Rifles, Queen's Westminster Rifles, Poplar & Stepney Rifles, Hackney, London Irish Rifles, St Pancras, Blackheath and Woolwich, Surrey Rifles, Finsbury Rifles and The Queen's.

Royal Marine Light Infantry: Anson, Drake, Hawke, Hood, Howe and Nelson Battalions.

II. Cavalry Regiments

Household Cavalry: Life Guards and Royal Horse Guards (Royals).
Cavalry of the Line (including Special Reserve & Yeomanry): Lancers: Royal Irish, Queen's Royal, The Queen's; Dragoon Guards: Queen's Bays, Prince of Wales's, Royal Irish, Princess Charlotte of Wales's; Dragoons: Royal (Blues); Hussars: Queen's Own, Prince of Wales's Own, Prince Albert's Own, The King's, Queen Mary's Own, Queen Alexandra's Own Royal; Special Reserve and Yeomanry: South Irish Horse, King Edward's Horse, Essex Yeomanry, Leicestershire Yeomanry, North Somerset Yeomanry.

III. Empire and Dominion Forces

Canadian Infantry: Prince of Wales's Leinster (Royal Canadians), Princess Patricia's Canadian LI, Royal Canadian Regt (Western Ontario, Eastern Ontario, Toronto, Western Cavalry, British Columbia, Winnipeg R, Royal H of Canada, Royal Montreal Regt, Highlanders of Canada, Canadian Scottish); Royal Newfoundland Regt.
Canadian Cavalry: Canadian Mounted Rifles, Canadian Hussars, Alberta Dragoons.
New Zealand: Auckland, Canterbury, Otago, Rifles, Wellington.
Australia: All Australian Imperial Force battalions were numbered.
South Africa: South African Infantry Brigade
Indian Infantry: Bhopal, Jats, Sikhs, Sikh Pioneers, Punjabis, Dogras, Garhwal Rifles, Pathans, Wilde's Rifles, Scinde Rifles, Napier's Rifles, Baluchis, Gurkha Rifles, Punjab Frontier Force (*Piffers*).
Indian Cavalry: Lancers (Fane's Horse), Deccan Horse, Poona Horse.

Military Abbreviations

These permeated Army discourse, and naturally turned up in trench names; in the Hébuterne sheet there appeared in 1918: *R.A.F. Avenue*, *V.A.D.* [Voluntary Aid Detachment] *Avenue*, and *WAAC* [Women's Auxiliary Army Corps] *Trench* and *Support*. There were also *RE Alley* (Longueval) and *RWF* [Royal Welch Fusiliers] *Sap* (La Bassée). *Sapper Trench* and *Pioneer Trench* have been referred to above. The Deputy Assistant Director of Ordnance Services was the source of *Dados Lane* and *Loop* (Villers-Guislain). *V.C. Avenue* and *V.C. Corner* appeared in the Aubers sheet, while the first Territorial winner of that decoration at Hill 60 was commemorated by *Woolley Walk* (Zillebeke).

Army Language and Soldiers' Slang

One of the pejorative words beloved of warrant officers and NCOs was, and is, 'Idle!' (expressed sharply and with contempt). As John Masters pointed out in *Bugles and a Tiger*, this can mean anything from dirty boots or rifle to sloppy appearance or behaviour. Sure enough, we find *Idle Lane* or *Street* (Arras) and *Idle Trench*, *Sap* and *Reserve* (Zillebeke). National Service after the Second World War kept this usage of the word alive, as the 1959 film *Idle on Parade*, staring Anthony Newley, proves. There is also *Look Slippy Lane*

(Ploegsteert). To intimidate the privates and corporals, there was *Sergeant Alley* (Saint-Quentin) and *Sergeants Parade* (Fonquevillers).

We have already noted the excellent study of soldiers' slang made by John Brophy and Eric Partridge, and we would expect that a proportion of trench names would derive from this source. Many examples of soldiers' slang appear in trench naming. The source of much of it was London, and appropriately we find *Cockney Trench* near Lens. There may even be examples of rhyming slang. Examples crop up in the naming of shell-bursts, etc, which are dealt with below, but some were derived from Urdu and Hindustani picked up during the Army's tours of duty in India, for example: *Blighty Bridge* and *Hall* at Ploegsteert, *Blighty Trench* near Longueval and Vimy, *Blighty Valley* near Ovillers, etc. We also find *Fag Alley* (Bullecourt), *Fag Trench*, *Support* and *Alley*, *Gasper Alley* (Epéhy), *Fag Trench* (Longueval and Vimy), etc.

Some slang was derived from French, e.g. *Napoo*. This corruption of the French 'n'y a plus' (meaning finished, no more, gone, nothing) gave *Napoo Avenue* (Armentières) and *Napoo Corner* (Liévin, near Lens). More generally, there were many *Windy Corners*, and *Funk Trenches* at Roclincourt (two) and Fonquevillers. On a higher social level, subalterns' banter provided *Cheero Trench* and *Chin-Chin Trench*, while *Fort Tosh* and *Tosh Keep* were near Loos. *Wart Trench* (Fampoux) may well have referred to a subaltern, as it did in the Royal Welch Fusiliers (Graves makes a point of it in *Good-bye to All That*) and indeed throughout the regular Army. Conscientious objectors to the war, many of whom were imprisoned and mistreated, were marked by *Conchie Farm* (St Sylvestre).

Equipment and Trench Stores

In the Longueval and Le Sars sheets are *Lime* and *Juice Trenches* (north of Flers), and *Hook* and *Eye Trenches*. Commonly used equipment and trench and vital dugout stores were recorded by *Candle Trench* (St Julien, Lens and Le Sars), *Thermos Trench* (Roclincourt), *Brasso Redoubt* (Péronne; in fact from the original French and Hungarian name for Brasov (Kronstadt) in Transylvania), and *Cape Blanco* and *Blanco Bay* (Bois Grenier). *Haversack Trench* appeared at Fampoux and Saint-Quentin. At Beaumont Hamel were *Cake Trench*, and *Leave Avenue* leading to *Hospital Trench*, while nearby in the Hébuterne sheet a visit to the barber was remembered with *Hair Alley*, *Hat Trench* and *Snuff Alley*. Important trench and dugout stores were emphasised in *Gramophone Trench* (Zwartegat), *Whiskey*, *Kirchner* (prints) and other items already mentioned.

Tobacco, Food and Drink

Cigarettes were inseparable from the trenches, and foul-smelling dugouts were made even fuggier by their smoke. David Jones remarked that there were many cigarette smokers for every pipe smoker, and this went for officers as well as men. Officers smoked more expensive cigarettes, and some had theirs handmade and specially sent out from London. There were *Fag Alley* and *Match Alley* (Bullecourt), *Fag Trench*, *Support* and *Alley*, *Gasper Alley* (Epéhy), *De Reske* [sic] *Copse* and *Abdulla Farm* (near Westroosebeke), *Capstan Farm*, *Goldflake* and *Woodbine House* (Dadizeele), *Gasper Trench* and *Hussar Trench* (Red Hussars), for cigarettes. There were also *Lucifer Farm* for a match as well as the Devil, as in the soldiers' song: 'Pack up your troubles', which exhorted the men: 'While you've a lucifer to light your fag, smile boys that's the style', and *Tobacco Trench* (Rouvroy).

Alcohol may have kept officers and men alive and the war on the move; it was well represented. *Alcohol Trench* and *Alehouse Trench* were near Lens. We have already encountered the trench delightfully named *Alf Cut*. In the Fonquevillers and Hébuterne sheets were *Beer*, *Stout*, *Rum*, *Gin* and *Guinness Trenches*. *Gin Trench* also appeared at Roclincourt and Fampoux, while *Gin Alley* was at Ovillers and *Gin Avenue* at Gonnelieu. In the Delville Wood–Ginchy area on the Somme, as Graves and Sassoon noted, was a group of beery names: *Hop*, *Vat*, *Ale*, *Lager*, *Pint*, *Pilsen*, *Stout*, *Porter*, etc. In the Ypres Salient were: *Bass Farm*, *Worthington Farm* (Hospital), *Tetleys Farm*, *Guinness House*, *Gilbey's Farm*, *Hennessey House*, *Martell Farm* (all Dadizeele), *Booze Farm*, *Cider Cottage*, *Port House*, *Cognac Cottage*, *Heidseick*, *Marsala Cottage*, *Vermouth Villa*, *Volnay House*, *Branby House*, *Gin Palace* and *Juice Farm* (all Elverdinghe), *Bass* (by the Bassevillebeek), *Stout* and *Bitter Woods*, near Tower Hamlets (Gheluvelt), and *Jimjam House* (delirium tremens) and *Rum Villa* balanced by *Baptist Farm* (both Bailleul). Farther away were *Tight Trench* (Saint-Quentin), *Tot* and *Toper Trenches* (Rouvroy), *Whiskey Corner* (Richebourg), *Whiskey Street* (Hébuterne) and *Whiskey Trench* (Ovillers). For those who preferred the dry canteen there was *Teetotal Corner* (Richebourg).

'Old soldiers live on bully and stew', the old song tells us, and there is no war story that does not mention tins of bully beef. Near *Bully Alley* (associated with the French village of Bully-Grenay) south of Loos, was *Bovril Alley* (Lens). On the Somme *Bully* and *Beef Trenches* were near the *Quadrilateral*, east of Ginchy (Longueval), and nearby were *Bovril*, *Veal*, *Calf*, *Cutlet*, *Hogs Back* and *Tail*. Perhaps this sequence stopped because the butcher's shop analogy was getting too close to the battlefield reality for comfort. At Beaumont Hamel were *Rump Trench* and *Steak Line*. *Bacon* and *Egg Copses* appeared near Fifth Army Headquarters at Toutencourt, and there were two *Bacon Trenches* on the Somme, one overlapping the Ovillers and Longueval sheets, and the other in the Gueudecourt sheet. *Fresh Egg Trench* appeared at Hébuterne, and *Fried Egg Crater* and *Poached Egg Crater* at Lens. In the La Boiselle–Ovillers area were *Sausage Valley* and *Mash Valley*, while near Hébuterne appeared *Sausage Trench* and *Redoubt*.

Other staples of the Army diet were bread, tea, cheese, plum and apple jam (Ticklers), biscuits, etc. Biscuit manufacturers were enumerated in *Jacob Farm*, *McVitie Farm*, *Huntley*, *Palmer*, *Peek Buildings* and *Frean Houses* and *Crawford House*. To go with the biscuits were jam and marmalade. In this category were: *Tickler Trench* (Rouvroy sheet), *Plum Farm* and *Apple Villa* (St Julien sheet) in the Ypres Salient (Plum was also the nickname of General Plumer, the Second Army commander), *Keiller Farm*, *Chivers Wood* and *Robertson House* (Dadizeele) (but the associated *Gollywog Lane* was a long way away in the Bullecourt sheet), *Marmalade Lane*, in the Hindenburg Line south-west of Arras (Bullecourt). Baked beans and various other preserved foods were commemorated by *Crosse Cottage* and *Blackwell Farm* (Dadizeele sheet). Christmas fare was commemorated in *Plum Duff Street* at Ploegsteert, perhaps a reminder of the 1914 truce, though a certain general loved to force duff on his men.

The Enemy

On many occasions, British trenches and positions were named after the enemy, and examples (not all complimentary) have already been given in previous chapters: *Hohenzollern Redoubt*, *Big Willie*, *Little Willie*, *Rupprecht Farm*, *Krupp Farm*, *Potsdam*, *Dead Hun Farm*, *Dead Boche*, *Huns Alley*, *Fritz Alley* and *Avenue*, *Kaisers Lane*, *Crown Prince Farm*, *Prince Eitel Fritz Farm*, *Von Kluck Cottage*, *Leipzig Redoubt*, *Otto Farm*, *Fokker Farm*, *Von Tirpitz Farm*, *Kultur Farm*, *Hindenburg Line* and *Farm*, *Boche House*, *Allemande Trench*, *Austrians Alley*, and so on. Many German trench names were also taken from captured maps, and appear in the Gazetteer.

Weapons, Firepower and Technology

Certain names were particularly memorable in a sensory way – for example the delightfully onomatopoeic *Bang Alley* (Zillebeke), *Noisy Trench* (Harnes), *Noisy Redoubt* (Neuville Vitasse), *Noisome Trench* (Harnes), *Stink Post* (at *Oder House*), *Pam Farm* (Gonnelieu), *Crump Farm* (St Julien) and *Thud House* (Bailleul). There were also *Crump Alley* (Bullecourt), *Crump Lane*

Boards such as this were shown in the trenches and behind the lines when there was a danger of cloud gas blowing over from cylinders placed in the German front trenches. At the same time the gas alarm would sound, by horn, bell or struck shell-case. This board is in the Imperial War Museum.

(Morlancourt), and four examples of *Crump Trench* (Fonquevillers, Fampoux, St Julien/Ypres and Oppy), referring to the bursts of German 5.9-inch howitzer shells. In addition, there were 'Jack Johnsons' and other larger-calibre howitzer shells, as well as the air bursts of 'woolly bears'. A British trench facing Gommecourt was called *Whizzbang Trench*, after the sound of the German 77mm field gun shell, and there was also a *Whizz Bang Corner* at Liévin, while Blunden spoke of *Whizzbang Keep* at Cuinchy.[2] This name, like that of the pipsqueak, a smaller shell, appealed to British soldiers, and not only adorned a concert party (The Whizzbangs) but was the theme of the soldiers' song: 'Hush, here comes a whizz – bang'.

All these remind us of the prime reason for the existence of trenches – the firepower of rifles, machine guns and artillery. In this connection we find *Artillery Trench* (Fonquevillers), *Gun Trench, Gunners Farm, Gunners Siding, Siege House* (Aubers), *Artillery Lane, Howitzer Avenue, Shrapnel Corner* and *Hellfire Corner* (*Ypres*), *Fuze Street* (Ficheux), *Shell Trench, Shell-Out Dugout* (St Julien), *Grape Trench* (Vis-en-Artois and Neuville Vitasse), *Fuze Trench* and *Friction Trench* (the friction tube was used for firing heavy guns) near Fampoux, *Mountain Gun Farm* (Ploegsteert), *Pompom Alley* at Serre (Hébuterne), *How Farm* and *Gun Farm* (Wytschaete). There was a *Fuzeville Fork* near Poperinghe, denoting a dump reserved for fuzes, and nearby an *Anti-Aircraft Camp*. A British heavy gunners' shelter near Méaulte on the Somme was named *Trembling Terrace*, while *Vibration Trench* was near Sorel-le-Grand.

Shell fillings and propellants, and other types of explosives, were also considered suitable subjects for trench naming: *Lyddite Lane, Cordite Trench* (Fampoux), *Ammonal Trench* (Lens). Cordite was a low explosive, used in rifle, machine gun and shell cartridges as a propellant, while lyddite was a high explosive used in shells as a bursting charge. Ammonal and gun cotton were used for the charges in mines tunnelled under enemy strongpoints; ammonal was the more powerful. Some of these great mines were charged with many tons of explosive. In this connection, we think of *Mine Point* (Loos), *Crater Lane* and *Smoke Trench* (Hébuterne), as well as the many named craters such as *Pulpit Crater*, *Hooge Crater*, *Jerusalem Crater*, *Red Dragon Crater*, *Etna*, *Vesuvius* and so on. In the same vein are *Flame Post* (Aubers), *Flame Trench* (Vimy and Bouchavesnes) and *The Flame* (Longueval) on the Somme, *Infernal Alley* (Saint-Quentin), *Inferno Trench* (Péronne) and *Incandescent Trench* (Bois Grenier), *Flare Alley* (Le Sars) and *Flash Trench* (Longueval). A bombardment, especially at night, was called from its firework effect a *Brock's Benefit*, and this name was used for a trench near Beaumont Hamel. Signalling and illumination were vital; near Fonquevillers in 1918 was the group *Rocket Trench*, *Very Trench* and *Flare Front Line*.

Besides artillery and mines, there were many other types of weapons utilised in trench warfare and contriving to make it even nastier; these are brought to mind by: *Mortar Copse* (Morlancourt), *Mortar Street* (Maricourt), *T.M. [Trench Mortar] Trench* (Epéhy), *Bois des Mortiers*, *Crapouillots Trench* (Grugies), *Minenwerfer Weg* (Neuville Vitasse), *Minen* and *Werfer Copses* (Morlancourt), *Minnie Road* (La Bassée) and *Stokes*, *Newton* and *Pippin Trenches* (Fampoux). Some types of mortar bombs were known as aerial torpedoes, and there was a *Torpedo Trench* (Richebourg). After the initial experiments with old Napoleonic mortars that had served in the Crimea, and with 'Toby' mortars of similar pattern, some early British patterns fired spherical bombs on sticks, known as 'footballs', 'toffee apples' and 'plum puddings'. The heaviest British mortar fired huge bombs known as 'flying pigs'. Stokes and Newton were both inventors of successful trench mortars, while Newton also invented the Pippin rifle grenade. The most successful British hand grenade was the Mills Bomb (the author remembers training with this, still in service as the 36 Grenade, in the 1960s), but there were many earlier and less successful varieties such as the 'hairbrush', 'cricket ball', etc. These are recalled by *Grenade Trench* (Loos and Fampoux), *Grenades Trench* (Gricourt), *Bomb Alley* (Loos) and *Bomb Row* (Richebourg). Grenadiers were represented many times: *Grenadier Loop* (Loos), *Grenadier Road* (a trench) near La Bassée, *Grenadier Trench* (Vimy and Roclincourt), *Grenadier Weg* (*Gas Alley*) near Longueval.

That mass killer of men, the machine gun ('Saul hath slain his thousands, and David his ten thousands',[3] or something very like it, is inscribed on the Machine Gun Corps memorial at Hyde Park Corner), gave its name to many trenches and battlefield features; we find: *Maxim Trench* (Serre), *Cartridge Trench* and *Belt Trench* (Fampoux), *German Machine Gun House*, *Machine*

Gun Wood, *Lewis Alley* and *Keep* (La Bassée), etc. The Lewis references, though, may well not be to the inventor of the eponymous light machine gun but quite another fellow.

The Vis-en-Artois sheet contained a full inventory of artillery equipment and ammunition (in those days all field batteries were horse-drawn) – *Shrapnel Trench*, *Canister Street*, *Case Trench*, *Grape Trench*, *Key Trench*, *Lanyard Trench*, *Spur Trench*, *Snaffle Trench*, *Hook Trench*, *Bridle Trench*, *Pick Lane*, *Tape Trench*, *Tool Trench*, *Shovel Trench*, *Spade Trench*, *Girdle Trench*, *Saddle Trench* and *Strap Trench*. The same sheet included an inventory of other weapons and projectiles: *Bullet Trench*, *Obus Trench*, *Bolt Trench*, *Pistol Trench*, and *Bow* and *Arrow Trenches* (the last pair also appeared near Fonquevillers). It also managed a *Tank Trench*. Derelict tanks were often marked on the map, forming prominent battlefield reference points, such as *Tank* (Bullecourt). This latest weapon of war also appeared in *Tank Trench*, *Support* and *Avenue* (Bullecourt), another *Tank Trench* (Hébuterne), *Tank Hole* and *Tank Farm* (Ypres) and *Tank Alley* (Beaumont).

Cross Bow Trench, *Halberd Trench*, *Bayonet Trench* and *Scabbard Alley*, *Trench* and *Support* appeared in the Fampoux sheet, adjoining Vis-en-Artois, and were part of the same weapons series. *Bayonet* and *Scabbard Trenches* also appeared on the Somme (Gueudecourt); nearby was *Bacon Trench*, indicating the use to which bayonets were commonly put in trench warfare. The Neuville Vitasse sheet included *Minenwerfer Weg*, *Battery Trench*, *Cordite Lane*, *Gunpit Lane*, *Fuse Trench* and *Artillerie Weg*, while in the Aubers sheet we find *Rifle Farm*, *Sniper's Corner* and *Snipers Post*. *Mauser Ridge* and *Krupp Farm* appear in the St Julien sheet. *Fuse Trench* also appeared at Fonquevillers.

Even the Army's two- and four-wheeled motor transport was called on to provide names in the Ypres Salient: in the Gheluvelt and Dadizeele sheets appeared *Triumph Junction*, *Crossley*, *Buick Farm*, *Wolsley Farm* and *Daimler House*. Other aspects of the new military technology were represented by *Radio Farm*, *Periscope House*, *Gyroscope Farm*, *Gas Alley* (Longueval) and *Gas Trench* (Ploegsteert), *Fume Trench* (Fonquevillers) and *Fumée Trench* (Gricourt).

Prisoners of War

A group of names around Fifth Army headquarters at Toutencourt, and its prisoner-of-war camp, suggested an unpleasant aspect of the treatment of prisoners – interrogation to extract information; the names *Blab*, *Screecher*, etc., were applied to woods in the vicinity.

Flying

Powered flight was itself a new technology that was rapidly adapted to many military purposes – reconnaissance, survey and mapping, artillery spotting, ground-strafing and so on. It is represented by *Aerial Trench* (Lens), *Airplane Switch* (Roclincourt/Oppy), *Aeroplane Trench* (Méaulte) and *Aerodrome Trench* (Gomiecourt). Not far from the last, a small group comprising *Aerodrome Switch, Aerodrome Support, Sopwith Sap* and *Farman Sap* appeared in 1918 (Boisleux). Different types of aircraft, mostly German, also appeared, such as *Albatross Trench* in the Vis-en-Artois and Bouchavesnes sheets. In the Zonnebeke sheet were *Albatross Farm, Adler, Fokker* and *Aviatik Farms*, while there was also a *Taube Farm*. *Immelmann Trench* (Homblières, east of Saint-Quentin) was named after the famous German ace who invented the eponymous turn that enabled a fighter pilot to get inside the turn of his opponent, while *Guynemer Alley* (Grugies) was named after the French ace. There was also an *Aviators Trench* near Grugies.

Balloons and airships were also recognised by the cartographers: *Zeppelin* and *Parseval* (Loos) were named after the airships, while *Zepp Copse*

The British 'A' Camera of early 1915 was the forerunner of a series of very effective air cameras taking photographs of the enemy area for intelligence and mapping purposes. Here it is shown mounted vertically behind the pilot.

(Fonsommes), next to *Mazeppa Wood*, probably derived from the name of the wood as well as the common British name for the Zeppelin. *Sausage Valley* and *Sausage Redoubt* on the Somme may well have been named after the captive balloons used for artillery observation, though as the former was partnered by *Mash Valley* something more culinary may have been intended. *Balloon Trench* appears in both the Roclincourt and Servais sheets.

Intelligence

Maps and survey were part of the Intelligence organisation, but there were understandably very few direct references to espionage and intelligence work, apart from *Spy Corner* (Ploegsteert) and *Spy Farm*, which occurred more than once, and *Cipher House* (Hooglede). It would hardly do to give the game away by printing revealing names on maps and orders. One of the few exceptions was the pair *Bab Farm* and *Code Farm*, relating to the 'Bab' field code.

Signalese

The phonetic language adopted by Army signallers was occasionally used for trench names. This developed slowly, and for much of the war many letters were pronounced as they were written. Near Dernancourt, south-west of Albert, in 1918 we find a group of 1918 trenches: *Ack* (A), *Beer* (B), *Don* (D) and *Emma* (M) *Trenches*. In this language, a trench mortar was a *Tock Emma* (TM), Talbot House in Poperinghe was *Toc H*, a machine gun was an *Emma Gee* (MG), the morning was *Ack Emma* (am) and the afternoon *Pip Emma* (pm). The Assistant Provost Marshall (Military Police officer) was an *Ack Pip Emma* (APM), an SOS call was '*Esses O Esses*', the Victoria Cross was the *Vic C*, and so on. It was not necessarily applied rigorously. The whole phonetic alphabet as it developed from 1914 to 1918 was:

A	Ack	B	Beer	C	Charlie	D	Don
E	Edward	F	Freddie	G	Gee	H	Harry
I	Ink	J	Johnnie	K	King	L	London
M	Emma	N	Nuts	O	Orange/s	P	Pip
Q	Queen	R	Robert	S	Esses	T	Toc
U	Uncle	V	Vic	W	William	X	X-ray
Y	Yorker	Z	Zebra				

Variants were Apples for A, Butter for B, Cork for C, Duff for D, Eddy for E, Freddy for F, George for G, Jug for J, Monkey for M, Pudding for P, Quad or Queenie for Q, Tommy for T, Xerxes for X, and Yellow for Y.

Medical

Firepower inflicted the most dreadful wounds, and these had to be dealt with by the Royal Army Medical Corps (RAMC – giving rise to the unfortunate alternative of Rob All My Comrades). The RAMC supplied the Medical Officer (MO) to each unit, and he, in turn, oversaw the battalion's stretcher-bearers, its regimental aid post (RAP) and the first stage of casualty evacuation. Behind the line were the advanced dressing stations (ADS) and field hospitals, and then, for those not merely lightly wounded, Blighty. Many regimental aid posts were given appropriate names, and even bearers' relay posts were sometimes named – for example the *Rat Pit* in *Bovril Alley* at Angres, south of Loos.

The medical profession, more relevant to the battlefield, conjured up *Hippocrates Cross Roads* (Westroosebeke) not far from Passchendaele, and *Harley Street* (La Bassée, Arras and Neuville Vitasse). *Wounded Trench* was near Lens. The agony of wounds was emphasised by *Morphia Street* at Cuinchy (La Bassée), while the treatment of the wounded and the evacuation process by *Barts* and *Guys* on the Loos battlefield, *Blighty Trench* (Vimy and Longueval), *First Aid Trench* and *Blighty Valley* (Ovillers), *Blighty Bridge* (Ploegsteert) and *Hospital Trench* (Beaumont). A 'blighty one' was a wound serious enough to ensure evacuation to England. Behind the Ypres Salient, railway evacuation sidings associated with field hospitals were given the wonderful pseudo-Flemish names of *Bandaghem*, *Dosinghem* and *Mendinghem*. *Scar Trench* was near Roclincourt, and *Septic* and *Scratch Trenches* near Vimy. There was at least one special hospital for venereal diseases; in the Bailleul sheet, strange associations and unpleasant medical conditions were presented by *Trouser Farm*, *Rag Farms*, *Wart Farm*, *Virus Villa*, *Gaspipe House* (gaspipe was also a slang term for the Stokes trench mortar). *Quinine Lane* was near Ovillers, and *Plague Trench* was near Fampoux. One of the horrifying, and usually fatal, results of a battlefield wound was reflected in *Gangrene Alley* (Gricourt).

Survey and Cartography

Draughtsmen, or their supervising officers, lacking inspiration for naming localities could fall back in desperation to the tools of their trade. A sheet

Accurate maps and artillery fire required very precise survey work to provide a dense trigonometrical framework. Here Field Survey personnel are using a theodolite, Lucas signalling lamp, plane table and telescope to fix points in the British area.

newly drawn by 2nd Field Survey Company, Roulers (east of Ypres) of July 1917, showed *Camera Farm* and *Lucida Corner* (the *camera lucida* was a prism apparatus used for plotting detail and trenches from air photos). The Moorslede sheet of the same date had *Map House, Parallel Houses, Ruler Buildings, Pencil Houses, Rubber Farm, Bottle Buildings, Cork Cottage* and *Pen Cottage*; nearby were *Metre Buildings, Yard Farm, Scale Cottage, Cadastral Farm* and *Grid House*. There was *Map Trench* (Roclincourt and Hébuterne). The heliograph, used for signalling and occasionally for survey purposes, was remembered by *Helio Trench* (Harnes and Rouvroy). The pre-war profession of several survey officers was remembered in *Architects Fork*. In a similar survey vein were *Angle* and *Kilo Farms* and *Datum House* in another 2nd FSC sheet (Wytschaete), and *Rowney* and *Whatman Copses* (Dadizeele). Many names of survey officers and men appeared in the last-named sheet, and 2nd FSC appears to have commemorated many of its personnel as well as beer (Westroosebeke area): *Reid* (Commanding Officer), *Gibb, Tarant, Bell, Barclay, Perkins, Watney, Coombe, Mason,* and *Mumford* (a Drawing Officer) *Farms,* and *Rimmer Copse* named after a regular Army topographer and draughtsman, who served with S.F. Newcombe in Sinai and southern Palestine just before the war.

Part of the war survey organisation, the Overseas Branch of the Ordnance Survey (OBOS) was recorded in *Obos Cottage* (Merville). Several officers and men of the other Field Survey Companies/Battalions were commemorated in trench names, and one, Lieutenant Frederick Salmon of 3rd Topographical Section, who came from the Survey of Ceylon, rose to the rank of lieutenant-colonel and commanded 3rd FSB in 1918, recorded that he named several features (e.g. *Yakko Wood*) and judging by some of the names appearing on 3rd FSC's maps – *Salmon Wood, Ceylon Wood, Fred's Wood*, etc. – some were named after him. *Keeling Copse* was named after Lieutenant-Colonel B.F.E. Keeling, of the Survey of Egypt, commanding 5th FSC, who was wounded on the Somme. He later returned to the front to command the Depot FSC, and then 3rd FSC; this company named various features after its own officers and men, particularly those killed or wounded. The Australian geologist Edgeworth David, who undertook a great deal of geological work

A Royal Engineers corporal using a sight-rule (alidade) on a plane table while fixing points of detail, either for mapping topographical detail or for fixing the position of a field battery.

for tunnel and dugout construction in the Ypres Salient, was commemorated by *Edgeworth* and *David Copses* (Westroosebeke).

Survey processes were recorded in *Topo Trench* and *Triangle Trench* (Gouy), by *Bench Farm* (Fampoux) named after a nearby benchmark, and by *Trig Post* on a hill north-west of Gouzeaucourt (Gonnelieu), while *Azimuth Alley* (La Bassée) sounds like the sort of name a survey officer would think of. The officers and NCOs of the Trigonometrical and Topographical sections of the FSC/Bs were also professionally interested in the heavenly bodies, taking observations on the sun, moon, planets and stars that, together with accurate time and tables, enabled them to give accurate line-of-fire to heavy batteries. They also used such observations to find azimuth (angle from true north) for terrestrial topographical surveys. Thus it is not entirely surprising that many features on the battlefield were named after such phenomena, or that one survey officer – Winterbotham – was known as 'The Astrologer'.

Stanley Cursiter, 4th FSC/B's Orcadian Printing Officer, was not only an experienced trade lithographer but an established artist in his own right and also an accomplished musician. He may have been responsible for many of the names appearing on 4th FSC/B sheets in 1917–18 in the Ypres area, as may Captain Broad, the drawing officer in charge of the draughtsmen.

Trench Construction

Many aspects of trench and mine warfare were immediately reminiscent of the siege warfare of earlier centuries. *Vauban Farm* (Bixschoote) was a reminder of this, and *Gabion Farm* and *Gooseberry Farm* (Ploegsteert; a gooseberry was a giant barbed-wire ball used for blocking trenches), *Gabion Avenue* (Beaumont), *Barricade Trench* (Roclincourt), *Bastion* at Fonquevillers and Arras, *Gabions Alley* and *Fascines Alley* (Grugies), *Fatigue Alley* (Le Sars), *Breastwork*, *Sandbag Alley* and *Sally Port* (Richebourg), *Shaft Switch* (Vis-en-Artois), *Plank Street*, *Board Trench* and *Trichter* (crater) *Stellung* (Neuville Vitasse), *Tunnel Trench* (Bullecourt and *The Bluff*), *Tunnel House* (Hooge), *Redoubt Alley* (Beaumont), *Dugout Lane*, and *Timber Trench* and *Street* (Hébuterne), *Sludge* and *Swill Farms* (Steenwerck). *Barbed Wire Square* was at Armentières, while the thorn barricade *Zareeba* was near Ploegsteert. The archetypical mud, apart from *Mud Alley*, *Corner*, *Farm*, *Lane* and *Terrace*, and so forth, gave *Greasy Trench* (Loos), and *Mudlark Alley* (Ploegsteert). Where the ground was particularly waterlogged or marshy, as in the Festubert–Givenchy area, short stretches of isolated breastwork were built, hence *The Islands*, *Grouse Butts* and *Grouse Butts Support* (Richebourg and La Bassée).

Railways and Trench Tramways

The Royal Engineers ('sappers') were responsible for all road, track, railway and tramway construction and maintenance. Their railway activities covered main lines and branches in the back areas, and also narrow gauge lines running right up to the front. Many railway troops were drawn from the personnel of British and Canadian railway companies. The naming of roads followed the same pattern as that of trenches – indeed in any locality they often shared the same names – but railway names, in particular those of the narrow gauge lines leading to the front, and trench tramways in the immediate frontal area, were almost always taken from the home railways. In the Aubers sheet, for example, we find *London & North Western*, *Great Northern*, *Great Central*, *Midland*, *South Eastern*, and *Great Eastern*. It was entirely appropriate that *Euston Post* was by the *London and North Western* tramway. In the Bois Grenier sheet to the north-east were *Tin Barn Tram*, *Breastwork Tramway* and *Mullewa Railway*, while in the Ploegsteert Wood area were *North British* and *Canadian Pacific*.

Railways, with their embankments, cuttings and station, were important topographical features on the battlefield, and it was natural that they should be named in their own right and also that nearby trenches and positions should be named after them. A delightful group of railway names appeared in the Gonnelieu sheet covering part of the Cambrai battlefield: *Midland Reserve*, *Railway Post*, *Soot Avenue* and *Smut Trench*. Marshalling yards and junctions on and behind the battlefield also took their names from British counterparts – *Crewe*, *Stafford*, *Willesden*, *Clapham Junction*, *Swindon* and so forth. In the Loos area were *Victoria Station* at one end of a trolley line, and *Posen Station* at the other. Also appearing in this sector were *Railway Alley*, *Railway Reserve Trench*, *Railway Avenue*, *White Disc* (railway signal), while nearby in the German-held La Bassée area were: *Railway*, *Turntable Alley*, *Roundhouse*, *Triangle Alley*, named after the locomotive shed and surrounding installations, including the railway triangle. On other parts of the front were another *Canadian Pacific*, *Tram Trench* (Fonquevillers), *White Disc Railway Sign* (Loos), *Footplate Buildings* (near Staden Station), *Railway*, *Engine* and *Station Trenches* (Beaumont) in the Beaumont Hamel – Beaucourt area, *Cowcatcher Trench* (Lens), and several London station names in the front line at Arras – *Paddington*, *Kings Cross*, *St Pancras*, etc. At Carnoy were *Rail Avenue* (British) and *Train Alley* (German).

As we saw in the previous chapter, the well-known British railway warning sign 'Stop, Look and Listen Before Crossing the Line' appeared in an unexpected context in 1918 just east of Amiens when its injunctions were borrowed for the names of *Stop Copse*, *Look Copse* and *Listen Copse*. But the namer also had in mind the West End show called *Stop! Look! Listen!*, and an altogether more dangerous type of line – the *Amiens Inner Defence Line* – that ran here. A veritable 'stop line', this had been constructed by the French in 1915, and the Germans, had they succeeded in overrunning it and capturing the city of Amiens with its railway junctions, may have split the French Army from the British and precipitated a Dunkirk-type evacuation.

Historical Campaigns and Battles

Another reason for trench naming was historical precedent – it had always been done, and had been picked up by regular soldiers and others from reading campaign and regimental histories. We have seen that permanent fortifications had always been named for identification (*Hadrian's Wall*, *Great Wall of China*, *Offa's Dyke*, etc.), and earlier wars had seen names given to temporary field works for the same reason – the *La Bassée Lines* of Marlborough's time, the *Ne Plus Ultra Lines*, the *Lines of Torres Vedras* in the Peninsula, the *Redan* and *Malakoff* in the Crimea, the *Chatalja* and *Bulair Lines* in Turkey, and so forth. The vocabulary of siege warfare was extensive, and much of it was echoed on the Western Front. Perhaps the earliest historical references, apart from the biblical *Jericho Street*, *Trench* and *Avenue* (Gheluvelt, Fampoux and Hébuterne respectively), were to *Troy Trench* (Fampoux) and *Troy Redoubt* (Richebourg), and to *Leonidas Trench* and *Alexander Trench* (St Gobain). Blunden actually noted that skulls dug up in the *Old British Line* at Festubert, near Richebourg, seemed as ancient as the ruins of Troy.[4] *Charlemagne Trench* commemorated the first Holy Roman Emperor in the St Gobain area, where many trench names were originally bestowed by the French. The Crimean War of 1854–55, with its long siege, was just within living memory, and the siege of Port Arthur during the Russo-Japanese War of 1904–05 was remembered by most who served in 1914–18. 1914 saw many permanent fortifications facing the German invader, and in key defensive zones such as Verdun–Belfort there were many named forts, *ouvrages*, *demi-lunes*, batteries and so forth. When these were augmented by temporary earthworks, it was natural that they should be similarly named. There were striking similarities between the siege warfare of earlier centuries and trench warfare, or semi-open warfare, on the Western Front, and natural connections were made when naming was occurring.

Various military historical names originally given by the French graced communication trenches in the Hébuterne sheet: *Annibal*, *Auerstadt*, *Austerlitz*, *Vercingetorix*, *Roman Road*, *Vauban*, *La Fayette*, *Jean Bart*, *Jena*, *Wagram*, *Solferino*, *Austerlitz*, etc. Conflicts of the 17th century and after were marked by *Condé House*, *Turenne Crossing*, *Bernadotte Farm* and *Colbert*

Cross Roads (all Westroosebeke), *Marlborough Trench*, *Malplaquet Trench* and *Magenta Lane* (Neuville Vitasse), and *Fontenay Trench* (Bouchavesnes). *Minden Avenue* and *Post* (Méaulte) and *Minden Terrace* (Beaumont Hamel) were named after the Battle of Minden in 1759; among the Minden Regiments were the 12th (later Suffolk), 20th (later Lancashire Fusiliers), 23rd (later Royal Welch Fusiliers) and the 37th (later Royal Hampshire), Regiments of Foot.

The Napoleonic Wars were commemorated by many names: *Wellington* and *Waterloo Farms* (Zonnebeke), *Corunna Trench* (La Bassée), *Raglan* (who also served in the Crimea) and *Picton Farms* (Westroosebeke area). A key feature of the Waterloo battlefield provided the name for *Hougomont Post* and *Hougoumont Lane* (Aubers) and *Hougomont Street* (Lens), while *Grognards Trench* (Fonsommes) was named after Napoleon's old soldiers, or 'grumblers'. The St Julien sheet contained a large cluster of martial names, many of them appropriately (given the parts the French played here in the First and Second Battles of Ypres) derived from French military history; the Napoleonic Wars provided *La Belle Alliance*, *Marengo House*, *Jena Farm*, *Austerlitz Farm*, *Saragossa Farm*, *Wagram Farm*, *Magenta Farm*, *Ulm Farm*, *Leipzig Farm*, *Murat Farm*, *Kleber Farm*, and *Soult Cottage*. The Crimean War was remembered by *Alma* (Zonnebeke), *Malakoff Farm* and *Trench* on the Cambrai battlefield and by *Malakoff Trench* and *Redan Lane* (Epéhy), while near Locre (Kemmel) were *Inkerman Farm*, *Alma Farm* and *Alma Lines*, and *Redan Wood*. *Redan Ridge*, *William* and *Mary Redans* appeared opposite Beaumont Hamel. Elsewhere there were *Malakoff* and *Redan Farms*, and also *Solferino* and *McMahon Farms*.

Politicians, Commanders and Celebrities (Famous and Infamous)

It was not usually the British habit, unlike the Germans or French, to glorify their leaders through trench naming, but there are occasional examples: *French*, *Haig Trench* (Arras), *Churchill*, *Wilson* or *Robertson* (La Bassée/Loos), and there was a *Winston Row* in the Bailleul sheet (after the Gallipoli debacle, Churchill served briefly here as a battalion commander in the winter of 1915–16). Such names were few and far between compared with the Hindenburgs, the Hohenzollerns, Bismarcks, Joffres, Fochs, and so on of the Germans and French. In 1918 a group of Allied commanders-in-chief appeared in the Courcelles area: *Haig*, *Foch* and *Pershing Trenches* (Foch was made the Supreme Allied Commander in that year). Army commanders were represented by *Horne Farm* (Westroosebeke) and *Plumer Trench* (Oppy) and *Plumer's Drive* (Zillebeke), and corps commanders by *Cavan Trench*

British communication trench signboard *Haig Street*, from the old British front system between Achicourt and Beaurains, south of Arras, and now in the Imperial War Museum.

(St Julien), while on Vimy Ridge there was *Wilson's Trench*, named after the IV Corps commander who was briefly responsible for that sector before taking over the new Fourth Army on the Somme. The Canadians named *Alderson Trench* (Ploegsteert) after their first divisional commander, and *Currie Avenue* (Ploegsteert) and *Currie Trench* (Villers-au-Flos) after their later corps commander. Various divisional, brigade and battalion commanders were commemorated along the front. Naval commanders were represented in *Jellicoe* (railway sidings and trench, Ypres) and *Beatty Alley* (Oppy).

In the Houthulst area were *Joffre*, *Pau*, *Foch*, *French* and *Castelnau Farms* and *Mangin Track*, and in the Oppy sheet the Italian C-in-C gave his name to *Cadorna Trench*. Statesmen associated with the Eastern and Balkan fronts were also commemorated: *Metaxas* Trench (Itancourt) for Greece, *Broussiloff Farm* (Houthulst) for Russia, *Enver Pasha Trench* (Combles) for Turkey and *Ferdinand Trench* (Combles) for the King of Bulgaria. The infamous Russian monk who notoriously influenced the Tsarina Alexandra, and was murdered for it, was remembered in the *Rasputin* light railway spur in Ploegsteert Wood and *Raputin Salient* (Servais). The many names for German royalty, leaders and commanders are dealt with in Chapter IX.

Other Sectors and Fronts

The 1915 fighting on the Gallipoli Peninsula was commemorated in the Bois Grenier sector by the names *Achi Baba* and *Sedd-el-Bahr* in the trench system, and in the Ypres Salient by a group of names given to farm buildings, which during the Third Battle of Ypres became the focus of severe fighting. In a savage twist of fate, some of the Australian and New Zealand veterans of the Gallipoli campaign found themselves in 1917 in action against points called *Gallipoli*, *Anzac* and *Helles*. The Salonica (Macedonia) front was commemorated by *Doiran Trench*. North of the Ancre river and east of Beaumont Hamel was *Suvla Lane*, while there was a *Suvla Wood* near Locre, south-west of Ypres.

In the Zonnebeke sheet, several names of battles (many in turn named after rivers) appeared attached to farms: *Alma*, *Aisne Farm*, *Loos*, *Somme*, *Gallipoli*, and also *Gallipoli Copse*, *Helles* and *Anzac*. In the Houthulst area, north of Ypres, a group of names associated with the Somme and other battlefields on the Western Front were given to tactical bridges: *Bécourt*, *Brie*, *Barleux*, *Contalmaison*, *Cérisy*, *Dompierre*, *Calonne*, etc.

The naval war was commemorated by *Jutland Alley* on the Somme (Longueval), by *Goeben* and *Breslau Alleys* (Loos), and by *Jellicoe* and *Beatty*, already mentioned. A large group of Royal Navy and Merchant Navy ships' (and other) names in the Ypres Salient was associated with the Dardanelles campaign: *Agamemnon*, *Lord Nelson*, *Canopus*, *Goliath*, *Albion*, *Hibernia*, *Euryalus*, *Bacchante*, *Manica*, *Venerable*, *Inflexible*, *Triumph*, *Swiftsure*, *London*, *Cornwallis*, *Vengeance*, *Amethyst*, *Implacable*, *Glory*, *Majestic*, *Endeavour* and *Ark Royal Farms*, *Lemnos* and *Helles Houses*, *Leonidas Farm* and *Sparta Cross Roads* (all Westroosebeke), and *Imbros House* (Bixschoote). To these might be appended a nearby group covering Egypt, the Suez canal and the route to India in the Bixschoote and Westroosebeke sheets: *Suez Farm*, *Cairo House*, *Egypt House*, *Aden House* and *Colombo House*.

The Bouchavesnes and Péronne sheets contained many names, probably originally given by the French, relating to the Balkans and south-eastern fronts: *Monastir*, *Florina*, etc., while south of the Somme, following the German offensive of March 1918 and the stabilisation of the line in the Villers-Bretonneux area, many trenches were named by the British and French after places in the Balkans, south-east Europe, and the Ottoman Empire, which were much in the news at the time: *Austrians Alley*, *Buda-Pest*, *Czechs*, *Slaves* [i.e. Slavs], *Croates*, *Bosnia* and *Herzegovina Trenches*, *Jaffa Trench*, *Sinai Alley*, *Syria Trench*, *Stamboul Trench*, *Angora Trench*, *Ararat Trench* and *Hebron Communication Trench*. Not to be left out, there were also *Allemande Trench* and *America Communication Trench* in the same sector.

There were also *Flanders Alley* (Grugies) and *Somme Alley* (Villers-Guislain), while the Vimy Ridge battlefield was commemorated by *Carency* and *Ablain Trenches* (Hébuterne). Battles farther south were remembered by *Eparges Trench* (Saint-Quentin) and a group of names relating to the Verdun battlefield (Dompierre) which, also being given by the French, are examined in Chapter VIII. At the extreme south of the British line in early 1918, in the Servais and St Gobain sheets, was a group of names (also probably originally given by the French) taken from the Vimy (*Artois Trench, Souchez Trench, Carency Trench*), Somme (*Somme Alley, Frise Trench, Biaches Trench, Barleux Trench*), and Verdun (*Verdun Trench, Fleury Trench*) battlefields.

For a transfer of names in the opposite direction – in this case from the Western Front to Egypt – we can do no better than observe that a camp at Heliopolis was named *Wytschaete*, a 1:20,000 scale map of the area being so-named.

Canadians

In 1915 the Canadians first took over the northern part of the Ypres Salient before the gas attack of 22 April, but had no time to name trenches in this sector. They were commemorated in the St Julien sheet by *Canadian Farm, Canadian Dugouts, Alberta, Regina Cross* and *Vancouver*, and in the Zonnebeke sheet by farms named *Quebec Farm, Calgary Grange, Toronto* and *Winnipeg*, by *Banff House* and the hill called *Abraham Heights* over which ran the old front-line trench position of 1914–15, occupied by the Canadians in April 1915.

They later fought in the Festubert battle in May, before moving to Ploegsteert Wood. In the Ploegsteert sector we find *Medicine Hat Trail, Regina Cut Off*, and *Alderson, Currie, Calgary, Winnipeg* and *Vancouver Avenues*. In the Locre area was *Canada Corner*. In late-1915 in the Bois Grenier sector appeared *McGill Street, Toronto Street* and *Winnipeg Street*. In 1916 they took over the trenches on Observatory Ridge and in the Sanctuary Wood area, east of Ypres; here, near *Crab Crawl* and *Vince Street* were *Vancouver Street, Winnipeg Street, Canada Street* and *Trench, Halifax Street*. Near Hill 60 was *Maple Copse*. Maple, in fact, was a recurring toponym along the British front, reflecting the ubiquity of the Canadian Corps.

On the Somme in 1916 they fought with Fifth Army at Courcelette in September 1916, and later captured *Regina Trench*. We should not forget the ill-fated Newfoundland Regiment, whose ordeal in front of *Y Ravine* at Beaumont Hamel on 1 July was commemorated by *Newfoundland Avenue* and *Terra Nova Trench. Maple Redoubt* was in the Méaulte sheet.

Following their ordeal in the Somme battle, they moved to the Lens–Vimy sector. In early 1917 the Canadian Corps formed its own Topographical Section, which gave it more scope for naming trenches in its sector. Long ensconced in the Lens and Vimy Ridge area, it was responsible for naming many trenches and other features – roads and railways behind the German lines in particular – which had not yet received designations: *Grand Trunk, Canadian Pacific*, etc. Trenches in the Lens–Vimy Ridge area included *Canada*

Trench, Canada Alley, Grand Trunk Trench, C.P.R. [Canadian Pacific Railway] *Trench, Ottawa North* and *South, Montreal Trench, Hudson, Brunswick* and *New Trenches, Quebec Trench, Winnipeg Trench* and *Yukon Trench.* Roads were named after *Saskatchewan, Manitoba, Winnipeg, Alberta, Moose Jaw, Montreal, Rupert, St John, Quebec, Calgary, Gaspé, Ottawa, Toronto, Canada, Fredericton, Galt, Regina, Hamilton* and *Kingston.* The Canadian Corps named even more trenches in the Vimy Ridge sector during the winter of 1917–18, and the first half of 1918. One of the trenches east of the Vimy Ridge, part of a group relating to dancers and actresses, was named after Maud Allan, the Canadian dancer who performed in Wilde's *Salome.*

The United States of America

Even before the United States entered the war in 1917, many of its citizens joined the British or Canadian forces. *America Communication Trench* (Hamel–Vaire Wood sector, 1918), and *America Trench* (Berthenicourt and Servais) appeared at the front, and *Pershing Trench* has already been mentioned. Evidence of transatlantic cultural influence appears in *Mutt* and *Jeff Trenches*, as well as *Connecticut* and *Hiawatha Trenches* in the Roclincourt–Arras area and *Hudson, Ohio, Mississippi* and *Missouri Trenches* towards Fampoux. There were many other examples. The popular culture of cowboys and westerns was reflected in at least one group of names on 1918 back-area sheets in Second Army Area – e.g. *Nix Farm, Chap Farm* and *Shot Farm* (all St Sylvestre), perhaps reflecting the reading habits of 4th Field Survey Battalion's drawing officer.

Anzacs (Australia & New Zealand Army Corps)

The acronym Anzac, first used at Gallipoli in 1915, was derived from the Australia & New Zealand Army Corps. There was a famous farm and pillbox called *Anzac* at Zonnebeke, *Anzac Cut* near Zillebeke and *Anzac Farm* near Wytschaete.

The Australians first arrived on the Western Front, together with the New Zealanders, with whom they had been grouped in the Anzac Corps, following the Gallipoli campaign and a rest period in Egypt, early in 1916. Their first experience of the Western Front was in a quiet sector at Fleurbaix. They fought fiercely at Pozières on the Somme in July 1916, and again the following year at Messines and Ypres. An interesting example of a cryptic-composite name is that of the plank road named *Secauspion Road* in the Ypres Salient, constructed and named during Third Ypres in 1917 by the Second Australian Pioneers.

For the most part, however, they occupied trenches already named by British troops, and it was not until 1918 that they were first able really to make a mark for themselves in terms of trench naming when, following the German March offensive and the fighting at Villers-Bretonneux, they occupied what amounted to a completely new trench system, east and south of Albert in the Dernancourt–Morlancourt sector, and north of the Somme. Here Australian names proliferated: *Diggers Avenue, Australia Street, Melbourne Trench, Sydney Street, Brisbane Trench, Possum, Dingo, Emu, Yarra* and *Warrego Trenches, Hobart, Cook, Culgoa, Ross, Coomac, Burke, Cooee, Coolbardie, Cootamundra, Conamulla, Coogee, Botany, Cloncurry,* and so forth.

South of the Somme, in the Villers-Bretonneux, Hamel and Vaire Woods area, were *Australia Support, Barcoo Communication Trench, Diggers Support, Arawatta Trench* and other Australian names. *Dinkum Alley* featured at Ovillers. In the Hindenburg Line system were *Adelaide, Brisbane, Hobart, Sidney* and *Melbourne Streets, Darwin Alley, Hughes Switch* and *Support* and *Collins Street* (Quéant and Marcoing). A beautiful example of Australian humour was *Roo-da-Kanga*, a street in Péronne named during the final advance in 1918.[5] No Waltzing Matilda, Swagman, Billabong or Coolabar Trenches have yet turned up.

The New Zealanders were represented by *Otago, Auckland, Canterbury, Wellington, Kiwi Wood, Kiwi Farm* and many other names brought from their islands.

Africa

South Africans are strongly associated with Delville Wood on the Somme, where they fought in 1916. *South Africa Trench* was at Armentières, and there were various South African names scattered around the British area, including some associated with the South African (Boer) War of 1899–1901, in which many British officers and men serving on the Western Front had fought. North of Ypres (St Julien) were *Colenso Farm, Talana Farm, Tugela Farm* and *Modder Farm*.

French North African troops gave their names to features and trenches that were subsequently taken over by the British – e.g. *Zouave Valley, Turco Farm, Spahi Farm, Algerian Farm,* etc. In a period when political correctness was an unknown concept, and the French had black colonial infantry units in their Army on the Western Front, it was not unusual to find British names such as *Kaffir* and *Zulu Copses* (Roisel), *Quadroon* and *Octoroon Corners, Nigger Farm, Nigger Fork, Zulu Cross Roads, Kaffir Fork, Kraal Farm* and *Moor Fork* (Moorslede). There were also black infantry units in the American Army but, although the British had black labour units, they did not use black infantry in the front line.

Indians

Native infantry units of the Indian Army – e.g. the 129th Baluchis (who fought at Messines/Wytschaete in October 1914) – were brought to the Western Front in 1914 in time to take part in the First Battle of Ypres. A building in Ploegsteert Wood was early named *Rough and Ready Villa*,[6] after the motto of 2nd Battalion, Punjab Frontier Force (Piffers).

The Indian Corps suffered enormously in the winter of 1914–15, and in the 1915 battles of Neuve Chapelle, Second Ypres, Aubers Ridge and Festubert, and Loos. Some Indian troops also fought at Gallipoli. Not being acclimatised to the cold and damp of northern Europe, all but the cavalry were soon sent from the Western Front to the warmer climate of Mesopotamia. They were commemorated by various names given to road junctions at Neuve Chapelle – *Gahrwal* [sic] *Cross*, *Gahrwal* [sic] *Road*, *Gurkha Cross*, *Gurkha Road* and *Kukri Cross* (named after the curved edge-weapon of the Gurkhas)[7] – and by *Gurkha* and *Baluchi Roads*, *Ludhiana Lane* and *Indian Avenue*, all in the Aubers sheet on the Old Front Line. Near here was also to be found the *Indian Village* (Richebourg). Farther south, maps of the Loos area were actually prepared in 1915 in three language scripts of the sub-continent for the use of the Indian cavalry in that battle. Indian cavalry also served in the Battle of the Somme, being in action on 14 July 1916 in the attack on High Wood. Several other names commemorated the Indian Army or its associations, including *Lucknow Redoubt* (Méaulte), *Pathan Cross Roads*, *Thug Farm*, *Wallah Farm*, *Ghoorka Fork* (Moorslede), *Kukri Valley* (Gouy), and *Hindu Cott* (Zonnebeke).

Chinese

The Chinese Labour Corps, recruited by the British in China for service in France and Belgium, gave rise to *Coolie Cross Roads* (Moorslede).

Notes

1   Holmes, Richard, *Tommy: The British Soldier on the Western Front 1914–1918*, London: HarperCollins, 2004.

2   Blunden, Edmund, *De Bello Germanico, A Fragment of Trench History, Written in 1918 by the author of Undertones of War*, Hawstead: G.A. Blunden, 1930.

3   *Old Testament*, 1 Samuel, 18:7.

4   Blunden, Edmund, *Undertones of War*, London: Cobden-Sanderson, 1928, p. 14.

5   IWM photo No. E.3412, dated 3 October 1918.

6   Marked on manuscript map in author's collection, dated March 1915.

7   8th Division War Diary, TNA(PRO) WO 95/1671.

VII

TOPOGRAPHICAL PLACE NAMES

This is probably the largest single class of trench names, and includes English, Scottish, Irish and Welsh place and street names, as well as those of certain countries of the Empire (some of which were mentioned in Chapter VI), reflecting the presence of national and county divisions and regiments, and also city regiments and battalions, of the United Kingdom and the overseas dominions. A study of the Gazetteer that forms the second part of this book will make clear the extent of this influence. It was natural that troops, whether from the Regular Army, Territorial Force or New (Kitchener) Army, or from overseas contingents, would want to stamp their identity on the alien environment in which they found themselves and, as was suggested in the introduction, naming was the obvious way of making their mark. Such a marking out of territory may have its origins in a remote tribal past but, whatever the impulse, it certainly created a cultural impact during the war and an enduring legacy in the history and literature of operations, not least in the survival and diffusion of trench maps and their wide reproduction.

The *Tattenham Corner* signboard from the road between Bécordel-Bécourt and Fricourt on the Somme battlefield. Subtitled 'The King's Horse Wins' in a caption added after the war, this outstanding sign, now in the Imperial War Museum, was painted in 1916 by the artist Oswald Birley. Nearby was *King George's Hill*.

The impressive series of books[1] written in recent years on the 'Pals Battalions' of Kitchener's Army – the Leeds Pals, Hull Pals, Barnsley Pals and Sheffield City Battalion of Yorkshire and the Accrington Pals, Manchester Pals, Salford Pals and Liverpool Pals of Lancashire, as well as other similar units – make clear the strong local identities and associations these carried with them throughout the war. Municipal pride was, at this stage of their industrial development, at a peak and, in a period before radio, television and the car had eroded local distinctions, community spirit and cohesion was a powerful force. Although they generally arrived at the front at a time when trenches had already been named by preceding units, wherever possible they tried to bestow their own names. This could be done in particular when they took over a new sector from the French.

No apology is made for looking first at the London names, as London influence dominated the Old Army and many of the Territorial battalions that went to the front in 1914–15 and thus formed the biggest single influence on trench naming.

London: West End to Western Front

It has to be said at the outset that the most striking feature here is the frequency with which significant groups of London's West End street names appear all the way along the front from Ypres to beyond the Somme. Time and time again, the same names recur: *Bond Street*, *Oxford Street*, *Regent Street*, *Piccadilly*, *The Strand*, *Haymarket*, *Jermyn Street*, *Grafton Street*, *Conduit Street*, *Bayswater*, *Rotten Row*, etc. We have seen how in Ploegsteert Wood, from October 1914, London names mushroomed: *Café Royal*, *Strand*, *Regent Street*, *Carlton Restaurant*, *Bunhill Row*, *Tothill Fields*, *Regent Street*, *Piccadilly Circus*, *Haymarket*, *Tower Bridge*, *Oxford Circus* and *Fleet Street*. It seemed natural to Siegfried Sassoon that clusters of shelters and dugouts should bear names such as *Elephant and Castle* (Hébuterne) or *Hampton Court*.[2] Blunden noted the London names of trenches in the Potijze sector: *Haymarket*, *Piccadilly*, *Half Moon Street*, etc.,[3] and these were just a small sample of a much greater representation in the Ypres Salient.

This practice undoubtedly began with the 'Old Army' – the Regular Army, or what was left of it, after the First Battle of Ypres in October–November 1914, and also by the Territorial battalions of the London Regiment. The original 'Old Front Line' of the winter of 1914–15 stretched from Ypres southward to Givenchy-lez-La Bassée, and was very soon associated with the names of St Eloi, Voormezeele, Kemmel, Le Rossignol, Neuve Eglise, Hill 63, St Yves, Ploegsteert Wood, Le Gheer, Armentières, Houplines, Rue du

Bois, Bois Grenier, La Cordonnerie, Grande Flamengrie Farm, La Boutillerie, Bailleul, Laventie, the Richebourgs, Festubert and Givenchy. To echo David Jones, this was the line of Bruce Bairnsfather and the regular 'old sweat', the traditional Christmas truce of old campaigners and football in no man's land, the Territorials and Eric Kennington's painting *The Kensingtons at Laventie*, the singing of 'Those Old Givenchy Trenches' to the tune of 'The Girl I left Behind Me', jam-tin bombs and 'Toby' mortars, and Tickler's plum and apple jam. There were few 'trench stores' in those days, little except sandbags and some barbed wire, and mortars, grenades, trench pumps, duckboards and periscopes had to be improvised.

So the Old Army, a high proportion of the men of which, and an even larger proportion of the officers, came from London or at least knew it intimately, indelibly stamped London's name on the original trench system, and some of these first trenches, from Armentières to Givenchy, remained the front line for four years. Occasionally the trench names move out of the West End of London, reaching north to the *Edgware Road*, east as far as *Mile End Road*, south-east along the *Old Kent Road* to Rotherhithe, Bermondsey and Woolwich, west to *Bayswater* and *Praed Street*. But the hard core was the West End; in the Aubers sheet, which can be considered typical, were: *Brompton Road*, *Haymarket*, *Piccadilly*, *The Bristol*, *Hyde Park*, *Bond Street*, *Burlington Arcade*, *Regent Street*, *Rotten Row*, *Northumberland Avenue*, *Strand*, *Drury Lane*, *Conduit Street* and *Vigo Street*. A similar pattern is found in the St Julien and Zillebeke sheets east of Ypres, at Hooge and in Sanctuary Wood, in Ploegsteert Wood, at Bois Grenier and many other places along the front. It was not just streets that were commemorated. The great railway stations also appeared with regularity: *Paddington*, *Euston*, *St Pancras*, *Kings Cross*, *Waterloo*, *Victoria*, *Clapham Junction*. Above all other regional name groupings, the London trench names were supreme.

A geographical analysis of these London groupings identifies them at the following nineteen locations, from north to south: Potijze–Railway Wood (Ypres), Hooge (Ypres), Sanctuary Wood (Ypres), opposite the Messines–Wytschaete Ridge, Ploegsteert Wood, Bois Grenier, Aubers, Richebourg, Givenchy-lez-La Bassée, Cambrin–Cuinchy (Brickstacks), Hohenzollern Redoubt sector, Loos–Maroc–Calonne (opposite Lens), Vimy Ridge (east of Hill 131), east of Roeux, south of the Scarpe river, Hermies–Havrincourt sector, Fonquevillers, opposite Serre and the *Quadrilateral*, Longueval-Delville Wood–Ginchy–Guillemont (Somme), and south of Fricourt, opposite Mametz. In addition, there was a group of West End street names at Lovie Chateau – Fifth Army Headquarters (see below).

This is precisely the old front line of 1914–16, with the exceptions of the Roeux and Hermies–Havrincourt sectors, which date from 1917 and are on the Arras and Cambrai battlefields. The Somme group in the Longueval–Delville Wood–Ginchy–Guillemont battlefield area dates from the fighting during the 1916 battle. It can be seen that the first ten groups in the list (Ypres southwards to the La Bassée Canal at Cambrin) date from the winter of 1914–15 – the oldest section of the old front line.

In a key passage in *The First Hundred Thousand*, Ian Hay described the route his battalion (of the 15th Scottish Division) took going up the line for the first time in mid-1915 in the Bois Grenier sector, noting that the trenches were not all named 'with strict regard for London geography'. Entering the *Old Kent Road* communication trench, after a mile across country, they crossed a stream at a point called *London Bridge*, where a side cutting, the place the Scots washed their knees, was called *Jock's Joy*. Continuing towards the front, they crossed the muddy hole of a complex trench junction known as *Piccadilly Circus*, remarking here on *The Haymarket* and *Piccadilly* but observing that *Artillery Lane* seemed misplaced in this London context. Where the *Criterion* should have been was a dugout named *Cyclists' Rest*. Turning into *Shaftesbury Avenue*, and crossing into a minuscule ('six feet by eight') *Trafalgar Square* (a geographical impossibility in London), they finally entered the front-line trench, where they found 'a well-furnished dugout' named *LlanfairPG Villa* (constructed by a Royal Welch Fusilier; the full name was given in Chapter III). Beside this nameboard, a placard outside the dugout prohibited 'Hawkers, Organs, and Street-cries'.[4]

Although Hay claims that the trenches so-named are not set out in their correct London relationship, he in fact plays fast and loose himself, as the layout in his account does not accord with the trench map.[5] He is, of course, changing their pattern to suit his creative purpose, but he has caught absolutely the spirit of the naming process.

Below the British front-line trench system in *Railway Wood*, east of Ypres, tunnelled galleries were dug, and off these branched a multiplicity of dugouts to shelter the troops holding the sector, constituting a veritable underground city. The galleries, like the trenches on the surface, were given London names – *Burlington Arcade*, *Albany*, *Coventry Street*.[6] Dugout complexes like this were a feature of the Ypres Salient, particularly the Observatory Ridge sector – *Tor Top*, *St Peter Street*, etc. Edmund Blunden gave an account of the huge system of *Hedge Street* and *Krab Krawl* dugouts under Observatory Ridge,[7] while Guy Chapman described the *Canada Street Tunnels*.[8]

The old Regular Army, even its county regiments, drew heavily on recruiting in the London area, and its officers were familiar with, if not drawn from, London society, the West End and its theatres and hotels. The 4th (Guards) Brigade, which early held the Cambrin–Cuinchy sector, was even more firmly London-based, and left its stamp, including its regimental names, on trenches in the area of the La Bassée Canal. Many of the officers of the Territorial and Kitchener's Armies, though perhaps not of the old officer class, were equally familiar with London haunts. Gilbert Frankau (an Etonian), a businessman who joined a New Army infantry battalion of the 24th Division before transferring to an artillery brigade of the same formation, wrote a novel about his wartime experiences, making clear these London connections,[9] as did the 24th Division's 'trench newspaper', *The Wipers Times, or Salient News*, to which he contributed. As Frankau, in common with many other writers (Sassoon, Blunden, etc.), often pointed out, there was also an overwhelming irony in being able to breakfast in London and the same day share supper with brother officers in a company headquarters dugout in the front line. This proximity and irony reinforced the natural pre-war connections. Officers and men on leave also naturally gravitated to the bright lights and pleasures of London, even if they were not natives of that city, thus further cementing the relationship between the Empire's capital and the trenches. Though some took the view that the trenches were the East End slums while the staff, of necessity in the back areas, represented the luxuries of the West End, the trench names reversed this connection.

At Fifth Army headquarters at La Lovie Chateau, west of Ypres, in the second half of 1917, the better class of London street names were given to the roads in the Chateau grounds, around which were scattered the headquarters huts and tents: *Oxford Street, Regent Street, Shaftesbury Avenue, Belgravia* (officers' quarters), *Berkeley Square* (officers' latrines!), *Park Lane, Cannon* [sic] *Row, Vine Street*; also present here were *Survey Avenue* (for 5th Field Survey Company), *Staff Corner, Tattenham Corner, Pat Lane, Rectory* (officers' quarters) and *Warts Walk* (officers' quarters and tent camp).[10] The last named referred to the common derisory regimental term for junior officers, as remarked by Robert Graves. South of Arras, in the Bullecourt–Hermies area, a more democratic group of London names, including both West End and City names, appeared, designating roads across the battlefield: *Cornhill, Poultry, Oxford Street, Park Lane, The Strand, Bond Street, Haymarket, Piccadilly, Barbican, Bishops Gate* [sic], *Houndsditch* and *Aldgate*.

An anonymous rhyme, entitled 'The Night Hawks', in the first issue of *The Wipers Times* on 12 February 1916, neatly drew the necessary familiar and ironic connections. Beginning thus: 'Talk not to me of vain delights/Of Regent Street or Piccadilly/A newer London, rarer sights/I visit nightly willy-nilly', it then perambulated, as night fell, 'clad in gum boots thigh', past *Gordon Farm, Oxford Street* and *Regent Street* to *Zouave Wood*, and then via *Grafton Street, Conduit Street* and *Bond Street*, 'Where memory ever fondly strays', concluding: 'So thus the London which we knew/Remembered is along the line.'[11]

In a real sense, the trench naming was designed precisely to create immediate recall of fond memories of home within the unpleasant environment of the front. Simultaneously the officer, if not the soldier, could be wading laden with spades, duckboards and sandbags as well as rifle and ammunition, through stinking mud (often intermixed with fragments of pulpy humanity), past latrine smells and chloride of lime, under sniper, shrapnel and trench mortar fire, and yet be transported back to oyster bars, grills and shows. This capability to co-exist physically and mentally in two quite different places made bearable the unbearable.

London hotels and grills savoured of pre-war pleasures, and were popular rendezvous for officers on leave. Many trenches, dugouts and observation posts were named after the *Savoy*, *Carlton* and *Ritz*. In 1915 artillery observation posts at Richebourg were named *The Ritz* (there was also a *Ritz* communication trench here) and *The Savoy*, and in 1916 *Carlton* and *Savoy Trenches* appeared on the Somme (Longueval).

To confuse matters, many London street names were echoed in other British and Irish towns, and it is not always easy to disentangle the references – context is all. For example, there is a *Piccadilly* in Manchester as well as London, while *Bachelors Walk* existed in London, but also in Lisburn. Which leads us to an examination of trench names deriving from the provinces.

Provincial Place Names

The Regular county regiments of England provided a rich source of place names that could be found up and down the front. These had their origins in the old numbered regiments of the line, which were based in the provinces for recruiting purposes – each had its recognised recruiting district. The Territorial Army, as its name implied, was also firmly based on local recruiting, and was in fact administered by county associations. Many Territorial infantry battalions wore the cap badges of Regular regiments, and these were numbered after the regular 1st and 2nd (home and foreign service) and 3rd (Special Reserve) battalions. London, being so large, was a special case and its Territorial battalions all formed part of the London Regiment, which was not a Regular entity. To complicate matters, in 1914 each Territorial battalion formed a new second line, and then a third-line battalion. When Kitchener called for his New Armies in 1914, these were not part of the Territorial Army (which he abhorred) but, as the name implied, were entirely new units and formations, like the Territorials wearing the cap badges of Regular regiments and numbered after the Territorial battalions as Service battalions. Thus there was a proliferation of new units and formations all over

Britain, and when the new divisions went to France they had the opportunity to stamp their regional identity – if this had not already been done by the Regular Army – on parts of the front line.

There is no space here to cover all the counties, let alone cities and towns. A vast number of such names will be found in the Gazetteer that forms Part Two of this book, and readers are referred to this. For example, the Westroosebeke sheet contains large groups of Cornish and Cambridge district names. To take just one county as an example, there were a huge number of Yorkshire names along the front; in the northern part of the Ypres Salient were *Yorkshire Trench*, *Skipton Road*, *Loop* and *Post*, *Halifax Road*, *Huddersfield Road*, *Headingly Lane*, *Barnsley Road*, *Knaresboro Castle*, and so on. Opposite Serre there was *Wicker Trench* from Sheffield. At Thiepval could be found *Yorkshire Trench*, *Koyli East* and *West* and *Leeds Trench*. At Fonquevillers were the Yorkshire names *Hull Trench*, and *Whitby* and *Bridlington Strong Points*, and later *Bradford Trench*, *Halifax Trench* and *Leeds Trench*, while in the Bullecourt and Vaulx-Vraucourt sheets occurred a further very large group of Yorkshire names.

In the Cordonnerie sector in June 1917, remarkable consideration was displayed when it came to naming new communication trenches to be dug across no man's land by the 5th Duke of Wellington's, a Yorkshire battalion, to connect new posts seized in the German front line with the old British front line as part of an XI Corps scheme. These were to be named *Halifax*, *Brighouse* and *Cleckheaton*, but the last was vetoed as it was believed that the artillery would not understand it, and replaced by *Hull*, which it was thought even gunners would comprehend.[12] In the event, the scheme was cancelled.

Scottish

A general Scottish presence at the front is remarked by the large number of names that include variations of *Jock*, *Scots*, *Scottish* and *Highland*, and of course the Scottish regimental names – *Black Watch*, *Argyles*, *Gordons*, *Seaforths*, etc. Thus we would expect a proliferation of Scottish place names, and indeed this is what we find. The cities and towns were well represented – *Edinburgh*, *Glasgow*, *Dundee*, *Aberdeen*, *Stirling*, *Dunfermline*, etc. Many Scottish names appeared on the major battlefields: *Inverness Copse* (Zillebeke), *Gourlay Trench and Gordon Alley* (Ovillers), *Highland Ridge* (Gonnelieu), etc.

The large number of Scottish regiments ensured a significant Scottish contribution to trench naming, as will be seen from the Gazetteer. One example will suffice: the 51st Highland Division took over the Albert sector, north of the Somme, from the French in 1915. In the La Boisselle area (where the Tyneside Scottish attacked on 1 July 1916) there was a large group of Scottish names in the Ovillers sheet, given by the 51st Highland Division, which replaced the original French trench names of the sector: *Largo Street*, *Burnt Island*, *Scone Street*, *Gowrie Street*, *Pitlochry Street*, *Methuen Street*, *Tummel Street*, *Fairmaid Street*, *Kirkcaldy Street*, *St Andrews Avenue*, *Kilfauns Street*, *Dunfermline Street*, *Lochnagar Street*, and so on. This pattern extended to the Thiepval Wood sector, where a large number of trenches were given names of Scottish towns and places. This pattern was repeated along the front.

Irish

A large number of Irish names appeared at the front, including *Shamrock Hill*, *Usna* and *Tara Hills* and *Redoubts*, *Avoca Valley* and *Chapes Spur* near Albert (Ovillers sheet) on the Somme front, and the wonderful *Ballynooky Road* (Fonquevillers). *Chapes Spur* is a very interesting name, as it relates to prehistoric bronzes found in abundance in Ireland[13] (and therefore perhaps named by O.G.S. Crawford, the archaeologist commanding 3rd Topographical Section's 'Maps and Printing section' in 1915–16).

In the Ypres Salient, *Birr Cross Roads* (Zillebeke sheet) was named in April 1915 by the 1st Battalion, Leinster Regiment, after their depot in Ireland.[14] A trig point called by the French the 'Arbre trèfle', between Albert and Bécourt, was mistranslated in British trig lists and on the map as the *Shamrock Tree* (the correct form would be clover), which gave its name to *Shamrock Hill*. This may well have led to further Irish names being used in the area: *Usna Hill*, *Tara Hill* and *Avoca Valley*. Thus the use by the French of the trefoil sign and name may have led to the cartographers creating an Irish landscape (in names at least) in Picardy. Many trenches were named after Dublin: *Dublin Street* at Ovillers, *Dublin Road* at Aubers, and *Dublin Alley*, *Trench* and *Redoubt* at Maricourt. It is significant, in view of the 1916 Easter Rising in Dublin, that these last three were grouped with *Casement Trench* and assigned to the enemy area. There was a *Curragh Copse* near Locre (Kemmel sheet).

Strife- and famine-torn Ireland was a traditional source of recruiting for the Old Army, and as well as supplying the Irish line regiments and the Irish Guards, provided men for many English regiments. The line regiments were the Royal Munster Fusiliers, the Connaught Rangers, the Royal Irish Regiment, the Leinster Regiment, the Royal Irish Fusiliers, the Royal Dublin Fusiliers, the Royal Irish Rifles and the Inniskilling Fusiliers. Battalions of all these regiments were represented in the 16th (Irish) Division, and of the last two in the 36th (Ulster) Division. Irish cavalry regiments were the 4th Royal Irish

Dragoon Guards, the 5th Royal Irish Lancers, the 6th Inniskilling Dragoons, the 8th King's Royal Irish Hussars, the South Irish Horse and the North Irish Horse.[15]

The heightened tension of 1914, when officers at the Curragh mutinied and civil war was feared, did not prevent New Army formations being raised. The protestant Ulster Volunteer Force became the core of the New Army's 36th (Ulster) Division, and a nationalist 16th Southern Irish Division was also created. The 36th Division first entered the trenches in October 1915 in the Touvent Farm sector, opposite Serre, later moving south to occupy the zone astride the Ancre river, where we have already seen that the Ulster Division gave certain trenches Belfast names – *Royal Avenue*, *Great Victoria Street*, *Sandy Row*, *Belfast City* – to positions in the Hamel and Thiepval Wood sub-sectors,[16] while key objectives for 1 July 1916 were named after Ulster towns[17] and the *Schwaben Redoubt* was called by the Ulstermen the *Devil's Dwelling*, or *Hell's Corner*.[18]

A small group of Irish (mainly Ulster) names also appeared in the Oostaverne area, east of the Messines–Wytschaete Ridge: *Irish Junction*, *Derry House*, *Antrim Road* and *Ulster House*, and these remind us that on 7 June 1917 at the Battle of Messines the 36th (Ulster) Division and the 16th (South Irish) Division went over the top side-by-side.

Welsh

Line Regiments from Wales had long existed in the pre-war Army, as had their associated Territorial battalions. The Welsh Guards did not exist before the war, but were formed following its outbreak. The Welsh non-conformist chapels were initially opposed to recruiting for the New Armies, but Lloyd George persuaded them that the war was also The Lord's battle, and the 38th (Welsh) New Army division was formed. David Jones served in the 15th (London Welsh) Battalion of the Royal Welch Fusiliers in this Division, and gave us a rich mixture of Welsh and London names (he himself was a south Londoner). The Welsh Regiment recruited in south Wales, and the Royal Welch Fusiliers in the north. Welsh miners were often to be found in the Tunnelling Companies of the Royal Engineers.

Welsh cities, towns and river names are well represented, including *Cardiff*, *Swansea*, *Newport* and *Cardigan*. To the Welsh, as we have already noted, goes the accolade for the longest name on the Western Front – that of *LlanfairPG*. Many Welsh names will be found in the Gazetteer. Some examples follow. In the Hindenburg Line area on the Cambrai battlefield, were *Welsh Ridge*, *Welsh Trench*, *Rhondda Post*, *Newport Avenue*, *Pentre Trench*, *Merthyr Trench*, *Mountain Ash Trench*, *Taff Post* and *Taff Vale Avenue* (all Gonnelieu).

There are many references to *Welsh*, *Welch*, *Red Dragon*, *Dragon* and so on, the classic example being the *Welsh Dragon Crater* blown by the Germans under the Welsh in 1916. The spelling 'Welch' was not necessarily specific to the Royal Welch Fusiliers who were not, of course, the only Welsh regiment. *Welch Trench* appeared at La Bassée, Lens and Dernancourt, and *Welsh Trench* at Loos and Bouzincourt as well as Gonnelieu, while *Welsh Avenue* was at Wytschaete. On the Somme, *Taffy Trench* was in the Beaumont–Ovillers area, *Welch Alley* between Ovillers and Longueval, while *Wales Trench* was at Bernafay Wood. In 1918, west of Albert, *Welsh Trench* and *Dragon Trench* were next to each other, and to the south was *Welch Trench*.

Notes

1   Series published by Leo Cooper, an imprint of Pen and Sword Books, Barnsley.
2   Sassoon, Siegfried, *Memoirs of an Infantry Officer*, part of *The Complete Memoirs of George Sherston*, London: Faber, 1972, p. 299.
3   Blunden, Edmund (1928), *Undertones of War*, London: Cobden-Sanderson, pp. 165–74.
4   Hay, Ian, *The First Hundred Thousand*, Edinburgh & London: Blackwood, 1916, pp. 203–5.
5   1:10,000 sheet *36NW4 Bois Grenier* (secret edition), in author's collection. Copies also in TNA(PRO) WO 297.
6   Barton, Peter et al, *Beneath Flanders Fields*, Staplehurst: Spellmount, 2004, p. 218.
7   Blunden, op. cit., pp. 184–92.
8   Chapman, Guy, *A Passionate Prodigality, Fragments of an Autobiography*, London: Nicholson & Watson, 1933.
9   Frankau, Gilbert, *Peter Jackson, Cigar Merchant*, 3rd Edition, London: Hutchinson, 1920.
10 Manuscript plan of Fifth Army Headquarters, La Lovie Chateau, 1917, author's collection.
11 Roberts, F.J. (ed.), *The Wipers Times*, first complete facsimile edition, London: Eveleigh Nash & Grayson, 1930.
12 Bales, Capt. P.G., *The History of the 1/4th Battalion, Duke of Wellington's (West Riding) Regiment, 1914-1919*, London & Halifax: Edward Mortimer, 1920, p. 138.
13 For chapes in Ireland, see Herity, Michael & Eogan, George, *Ireland in Prehistory*, Edn.2 reprint, London: Routledge, 1996.
14 Hammerton, Sir John, *The Great War, I Was There*, Vol.3, London, The Amalgamated Press Ltd., c.1938, p. 1388.
15 Harris, Henry E.D., *The Irish Regiments in the First World War*, Cork: Mercier Press, 1968.
16 Recordings by Tommy Russell noted in Orr, Philip, *The Road to the Somme, Men of the Ulster Division Tell Their Story*, Belfast: Blackstaff Press, 1987, p. 136.
17 Orr, op. cit., p. 144.
18 Ibid., p. 142.

VIII

FRENCH TRENCH NAMES

Glossary

Arbre	Tree
B. or Boy. = Boyau	Communication trench (C.T.). B. could also be used for Bois
Bois	Wood
Fortin	Small fort
Groupe de Canevas de Tir (GCTA)	French equivalent of British Field Survey Company, for survey and mapping of front area and of French and German trenches
Ouvrage	Work; important strongpoint; small fort
Plans directeurs	French equivalent of British trench maps (1:5,000, 1:10,000, 1:20,000)
Rdt. = Redoute/Reduit	Isolated redoubt/strongpoint/work/refuge
Saillant	Salient
T. or Tr. = Tranchée	Fire trench

General Observations

It is a useful cultural qualifier and contextualiser to be able to compare and contrast the trench names given by the armies of different nations. This and the following chapter deal with French and German names respectively, and while many appear straightforward and non-ironic, nevertheless great care has to be taken in making this sort of judgement. The author's linguistic ability is not equal to the task of recognising shades of meaning in foreign trench names; this is difficult enough with British names in some circumstances. Translations given in this and the next chapter should be treated with caution, and it should be made clear that this is only a preliminary and partial survey. The sample is relatively small, so again conclusions can only be tentative.

French trench nameboard from the Hébuterne sector. This area between Arras and the Somme was held by the French in 1914–15, but taken over by the British, who retained some of the French trench names, from July 1915. 'P.C.' refers to 'Poste de commandement' or command post, while 'P.C. Colonel' was the regimental headquarters. *Wagram Avenue* was a communication trench, hence the direction to the rear (l'arrière) where the Colonel's HQ was to be found.

There is plenty of room for specific expert studies. Trench names printed on *plans directeurs* and on British copies of these display many spelling errors and omitted accents – perhaps the fault of exhausted lithographic draughtsmen working and transcribing under pressure in bad light and, in the case of British transcriptions, ignorance of the French language.

A study of *plans directeurs 'avec organisations'* (i.e. trench maps showing the defensive organisation) makes it clear that the French, when they were naming their own trenches, frequently used the names of French (and French colonial) or Allied places and people. Into the latter category fell both illustrious French names from the present and past, and also officers, warrant officers and NCOs killed in action. When it came to the French naming the German trenches, the names of German and Central Powers (i.e. Germany's allies) personalities and places were used, and names with certain negative associations (e.g. sexual deviation or excess, pirates or unpleasant insects) also came into play to present German *Kultur*, and that of her allies, in an unfavourable light. In other words, for the French a particular propaganda or psychological warfare element can be discerned. Naming can be seen as part of a *Kulturkampf* (culture struggle, or 'clash of civilisations' in modern parlance) as the Germans might have said.

While the British official account of 1914–18 trench mapping made no reference at all to trench names (or indeed any other sort of names) or naming policy or practice, the French post-war report on wartime survey and mapping, the *Rapport de Guerre*,[1] contained several references to naming policy, and included many coloured extracts from trench maps of various scales, some of which included names. Other French documents relating to mapping also referred to naming policy. It is clear that the republican French Army, perhaps following Napoleonic precedent, had a much more prescriptive and bureaucratic approach to this, as to many other matters, as befitted a large conscript army that had for centuries been fighting major land wars and that had developed appropriate regulations to cover all aspects of training and operations. By contrast, the British Army had adopted a more ad hoc approach in certain matters.

Names did not necessarily develop immediately trench warfare set in. A French map of December 1914, giving details of an attack at the Main de Massiges, near St Ménéhould, showed the French trenches numbered and the German trenches lettered.[2] No trench names were given, and it is likely that none was in fact in use at this date. Very early on in the war, however, the French, like the British and Germans, began to name tactical points and trenches in an arbitrary way: *Bois en V*, *Bois en T*, *Bois en U*, *Bois Sabot*, *Bois du Sultan*, *Bois des Dardanelles*, *Bois du Crabe*, *le Trapèze*, *Ravin de la Mort*, *Tranchée des Bébés*, *Tranchée du Turkestan*, *Boyau de Hongrie*, *Boyau du Casque*, *Boyau des Valkyries* and others which, in Arthur-Lévy's words, 'had their moment of tragic celebrity'.[3]

Prominent trees were named, being important reference points or even trigonometrical points for mapping and artillery survey purposes. In the Albert sector on the Somme were *Arbre Trefoil* (Bushy Topped Tree), *Arbre Fourche* (Forked Tree) and *Arbre Filiforme* (Spindly Tree). Near Souain and Tahure (Champagne) there were *Arbre Plat* (Low Tree), *Arbre Durnerin*, *Arbre Mort* (Dead Tree), *Arbre Conique* (Conical Tree), *Pin Rouge* (Red Pine) and several *Grands Arbres* (Large Trees). The many vanished semaphore telegraph stations of the Napoleonic period also gave their name to features – '*Tél. détruit*' (Destroyed Telegraph) on Hill 132 north of Thélus on Vimy Ridge was associated with the nearby *Boyau du Télégraphe* – and similar names are found at Ginchy on the Somme and elsewhere. Much naming practice was common to all the belligerents; the many salients in the front lines were a case in point. The British had their *Duck's Bill* (Givenchy) and *Pope's Nose* (Thiepval), the French their *Bec de Canard* (Duck's Bill, at Navarin Farm on the Champagne battlefield) and *Bonnet d'Evêque* (Bishop's Mitre, at the Mort Homme), the Germans their *Enten Schnabel* (Duck's Bill, Givenchy) and *Heidenkopf* (Serre), and so on. In a similar vein, the elevation view of a cliff, reminiscent of a cocked hat, facing the Somme at Curlu, gave the name to the *Chapeau de Gendarme*.

The French trenches, with their names, began to be printed in red on secret editions of *plans directeurs* in August 1915; as with British practice, the names had been in use some months before the first of these maps were printed. The practice of naming French trenches as a way of commemorating French officers who had been killed in action began at a very early stage. This was noticeable in sectors from the Somme to the Vimy Ridge taken over by the British in 1915 and early 1916. The proliferation of communication trenches meant that in many sectors they were sequentially numbered rather than named, but this depended on the whim of corps or army commanders. In the Loos–Lens area numbering was the rule, while farther south, in the Hébuterne sector, names were more common. These were chosen to exemplify French military prowess over the ages. France had a long and 'glorious' military tradition, unlike Britain whose imperial expansion was more associated with her navy, and the names of Napoleonic battles were prominent on *plans directeurs*. In the Hébuterne area was found a veritable roll-call of historical military, naval and professional figures and the battles of Napoleon I and III: *Vercingétorix, Du Guesclin, Vauban, La Fayette, Jean Bart, Austerlitz, Jena, Wagram* and *Solférino*. *Annibal* (Hannibal) added lustre to this list by association. The 17th–18th-century physician Denis Papin, as well as the 19th-century biologist Louis Pasteur, were here represented by *Tranchées Papin* and *Pasteur*.

The war itself created many names, and there was much adoption of names from other sectors and fronts. We find Somme names at Verdun and vice versa. North of the commanding hill *Le Mort Homme* (a pre-war name), on the left bank of the Meuse, were the *Tranchées de Mametz, de Pozières, de Curlu, de Dompière, de Biaches, de Flaucourt* – all from the Somme battlefield. Near Belloy, south of the Somme, were *Tranchées Souville, de Verdun, du Mort Homme* and *de Damloup*. We also find names relating to the Ypres Salient – *Tranchée d'Ypres, Boyau St Julien* – near Vic-sur-Aisne and, in the Ypres Salient, names from the Marne, the Aisne, Verdun and other battle areas.

Names very often used for French trenches were those of French cities and towns, and dead, wounded or decorated officers. Classical names make frequent appearances, particularly those associated with death, such as *Caron* (Charon), *Styx*, etc. Death was naturally well to the fore; there were five *Ravines de la Mort* at Verdun, while *Le Mort Homme* was a key position on that battlefield. In the Champagne there was a hill called *La Fille Morte*. In the case of the last two, pre-war names had been embraced.

The French found rapidly, as did the British and Germans, that the widespread use of names and other designations for trenches and topographical features was necessary to ensure the most efficient use of *plans directeurs*. The front-line trench system formed a complex labyrinth (sometimes actually known by the name *Labyrinthe*, as was the case at Roclincourt below the Vimy Ridge) and, to enhance understanding and navigation of this maze of trenches, the French introduced area designations for localities, and within these gave particular designations to the most prominent points. For this purpose, as 'numbers spoke little to the spirit' in the French view, particularly if they were widely used, they preferred to name points or trenches in the French zone as well as in that of the German trenches. Adhering to Napoleon's dictum that 'the moral is to the physical as three is to one', they assumed that the psychological factor was important – that the soldier would be more willing to attack an enemy position designated by a grand name – for example *Tranchée de la Vistule* (Vistula) – than attack a knot of trenches that had been defined in his operation orders by a mere number. On a practical level, intelligence gleaned about the enemy was more valuable and more accurate if the designation of terrain features could be made more precise.[4]

Propaganda Considerations

When the French named German trenches, according to certain German commentators, they sometimes revealed their distaste for their enemy. This is certainly supported by some of the French names, notably in the Somme and Champagne sectors, where trench naming became one element of the 'culture war'. The French were more prone than the Germans to introduce names disparaging of their enemy – for example *Bois de Boche* (Boche meaning 'blockhead'). While there are certain names that clearly indicate contempt for the enemy – *Huns*, *Boche*, etc. – there is little sign, despite the occasional *Lucifer*, *Vampire*, *Diable* or *Satan*, of any real hatred or concerted effort to demonise the enemy. We find the *Bois des Vampires* near Roye, and *Tranchée du Vampire* by the Mont de Sapigneul, north of Reims. On the contrary, there are many references to German culture that seem positive, or at least neutral, rather than negative, and these may well have been taken directly from captured German trench maps. The Germans certainly used such names themselves. Names from Wagner's operas crop up along the front to designate German trenches – for example *Tranchées Siegfried* and *Brunehilde* near Vic-sur-Aisne, and *Tranchées Notung*, *Siegmund*, *de Sieglinde*, *Hagen*, *Fafner*, *Alberik*, *Hans*, *Sachs*, *du Roi Mark*, and *Boyaux de Tristan*, *d'Yseult*, and *Parsifal* near Roye, *Brunehilde* near the Somme, and *Lohengrin* near Ornes (Verdun). *Fafner* also appears at Vauquois. The Germans used many such names from *The Nibelungenlied* (see Chapter IX).

However, it was hardly surprising, given that their country had been invaded, that the French should despise the Germans, and there are several examples to substantiate this assertion. Max Eckert, the distinguished German geographer and survey officer, gave three – *Tranchée des Homo-Sexuels*, *Boyau du Harem*, *Boyau des Eunuques* – and sarcastically noted that these small French names for German trenches to the north of Souain were surely 'an eloquent testimony to high French culture'.[5] On the Tahure *plan directeur*, from 1915 to 1918, the *Tranchée des Homosexuels* can indeed be found in the German front system north-west of Souain, near the *Tranchée de Cattaro* and the *Tranchée des Invertis* (homosexuals), the *Tranchée de la Bohème*, the *Tranchée des Vandales*, the *Tranchée des Satyres*, *Tranchée de Nausicaa*, among a bevy of German place names and other German and Austrian associations – *Tranchée de la Kultur* (an ironic usage), *Boyau des Hohenzollern*, *Tranchée des Archiducs*, *Tranchée de Berlin*, *Tranchée des Habsbourg*, *Boyau de Gotha*, *Boyau de Gottingen*, *Tranchée de Dantzig* and a large number of other names – running past Navarin Farm to the Butte de Souain. It appears that Eckert had a point; the interweaving of names from Germany and her allies with those implying perverse and decadent practices cannot be ignored. The imputation that the House of Hohenzollern, and indeed the whole of German culture (*Kultur*), was depraved was unmistakable. Trench naming here entered the realm of propaganda, or psychological warfare.

This less than subtle interweaving extended for many kilometres across the Champagne battlefield. Farther east, the names *Tranchée du Harem*, *Tranchée des Eunuques* and *Boyau des Houris*, north of Vauquois in the Argonne, were part of a group of names, given by the French to German trenches, relating to the Ottoman Empire and the Balkans (*Tranchée de Constantinople*, *Tranchée des Balkans*, *Boyau des Turcs*, etc.). However, most names of German trenches to be found on French maps were names of German states, regions, cities, towns, royal families and generals. These were supplemented by place names from Eastern Europe, the Middle East and indeed most other parts of the world. Others were names clearly related to the topography of the locality of the trenches themselves. In the Souain sector, French trenches were named after French cities, towns, colonies, battles, etc.: *Tranchée de la Côte d'Azur* (perhaps an ironic usage), *Boyau de Sébastopol*, *Boyau de Solférino*, *Boyau Fleurus*, *Boyau Mistral*, *Boyau de Nîmes*, *Boyau de Madagascar*, *Boyau Béziers*, *Boyau d'Avignon*.[6]

Had Eckert looked farther north, to the Somme area, he would have found another group of French names for German trenches to support his thesis. As we shall see below, in the Curlu–Hem–Maurepas area, just north of the Somme, there was a group of names, given or inscribed by the *Groupe de Canevas de Tir* of the French Sixth Army, which by their sustained negativity must surely have been intended to demean the enemy. This pattern was repeated along the front.

General Headquarters (GQG) Policy

During 1915 the use of names and designations spread rapidly. After the 1915 Champagne battle, GQG extended the practice adopted by *GCTA2* to all other armies, so that all important elements of planimetry and relief (woods, valleys, hills, etc.), particularly in the enemy zone, received names. Where possible these were derived from those appearing on the 1:80,000 General Staff Map or on the large-scale cadastral plans, some of which had been first drawn up in the Napoleonic period and incorporated names that had already been in use for centuries. However, many were completely new names, given by the troops occupying the sectors, which had come into general usage. Finally, in default of all these, purely arbitrary names were bestowed by the Army cartographers or staff. In areas where small woods were very numerous, they were distinguished by two-figure numbers or by a locality letter followed by a two-figure number – e.g. K25.[7] Many French trenches were named after regions or towns in France and her colonies – a practice that was also followed by the British and Germans.

Following the Champagne battle, GQG published an official account of the operations, which extended to the cartographic and naming policy:

> We had information on the whole German defensive system, and plotted it on our maps. All defence works, fire trenches, communication trenches and copses were allotted special names, or an alphanumeric designation, according to their attack sectors. This minute precision in the details of the operations planning is particularly significant, as it emphasises an essential feature of this war, very much a siege war, in which the objectives have first to be recognised and clearly pinpointed, and every piece of terrain has then to be captured by heavy fighting, just as in earlier sieges each redan and curtain wall had to be assaulted.[8]

At the end of 1915, *Sections Topographiques des Corps d'Armées* (*STCA*), analogous to the later British Corps Topographical Sections, were formed, and an Instruction setting down their role and governing their relations with the *GCTA* was issued on Christmas Day. This stated that:

> The *GCTA* will supply the *STCA* with the information necessary to ensure that plans and sketch maps are created on a framework analogous to

that of the *plan directeur*, and in particular that the designations or names of new works and other elements on the plans and sketch maps follow the general conventions adopted in the Army.[9]

To avoid cluttering up the map with names, important points in the trenches or on the ground that were well-defined on the map, particularly in the front, support and reserve lines and in communication trenches, were given four-figure coordinates, each of which also served as a reference or artillery registration number (*matricule*) for a particular target.[10] Sections of the German trenches were designated by numbers or names, either taken from those already in use or purely arbitrary. It was deliberate policy to use names obtained from German sources – particularly from captured trench maps – for the same features. Where a different name had already been adopted, the German name was given in different characters, next to the existing French name, on the 1:5,000 trench map, but such additions remained subordinate to the clarity of the map. On the other hand, to facilitate communication and ensure that messages were properly understood, the French forbade the use of German general names such as *Graben*, *Stellung*, *Linie*, *Weg*, *Zug*, etc.[11] There were, however, important exceptions to this rule. While German names were retained, in brackets, after French names had been given to captured German trenches, the German names for certain positions, such as the *Kniestellung*, *Langestellung* and *Hangstellung* at the Butte de Vauquois, were clearly printed in 1918 on French maps.

The French made it a rule that all names and reference numbers printed on their 1:20,000 *plans directeurs* were also shown on the 1:10,000 and 1:5,000 plans, and that all those shown on the 1:10,000 (some of which did not appear on the 1:20,000) appeared on the 1:5,000. Conversely, the names printed on the 1:20,000 and 1:10,000 were selected according to their importance; at those scales there was not room for all those on the 1:5,000.[12] A 1918 *GQG* Instruction on mapping stated that:

> the experience of the present war has shown that it is advisable to increase the number of names and designations. In order to avoid their duplication, the *Instruction sur les Plans Directeurs* has specified that all new names, introduced by the Corps Topographical Sections (*STCA*) on their revision sheets or by the other services on their special sheets only become definitive after having been adopted by the Army Survey Companies (*GCTA*) and appearing on the maps published by them. It is appropriate to choose short names which are easy to pronounce and understand (telephone messages), and simple to write (orders and reports).[13]

French names were later adopted by the British (and subsequently American) troops, when they took over new sectors from the French. Many of the trench names on the Vimy, Arras and Somme fronts were merely taken over from the French with the trenches they applied to, and duly appeared on British trench maps. Some were later renamed, others not.

Naming in Specific Sectors – Some Case Studies

The case studies below are arranged geographically from north to south, but within them it will be seen that there has been little opportunity for an examination of chronological development, particularly as some of the sectors were subsequently taken over by the British.

Lorette, Vimy and Arras battlefield

By March 1915, as part of the preparations for an attack, the French had given names to the German trenches at Notre Dame de Lorette, west of Vimy Ridge, some of the designations being derived from the siege warfare of earlier centuries: *Parallèle Nord, Sape I, Sape II … Sape X, Ancienne Parallèle Allemande, Boyau de la Grande Mine*, etc. Others were: *Parallèle Vouaux, Tranchée Blanche, Boyau de l'escalier, Ancienne 1ère ligne Allemande, Boyau en S, Parallèle Brickert, Les Abattis, Tranchée des Saules* (Willows) and *Tranchée du Fonds du Buval*.[14] To the north was the *Ouvrage Blanc* at Angres. Farther south facing the ridge were the *Ouvrages Blancs* and the *Labyrinthe*, north of Roclincourt. This part of Artois was the scene of further French attacks in May and June 1915, and also in September. A secret 1:20,000 *plan directeur* of the Arras area, dated 15 August 1915, showed the French as well as German trenches, but the French trenches were not named. However, a 1:5,000 sketch map prepared for the 326th Infantry Regiment in the Neuville St Vaast sector, north of Arras, dated 29 August, showed the names of trenches that, officially adopted, were shown on subsequent *plan directeur* editions. These, with the name boards placed in the trenches themselves, helped the troops to locate themselves in the confusing tangle of trench lines on the map.[15]

Just south of the Scarpe river, east of Arras, the French Tenth Army in 1915 named some trenches *Tranchée de la Gloire* (Glory), and *Tranchée de M. le Maire* (Mayor), *Tranchée de l'Escarpe* (Scarpe river), *Boyau des Dames d'Avesne* (Women of Avesnes), *Boyau des Braves, Boyau de la Malterie* (Malthouse), *Tranchée de la Haie* (Hedge), *Boyaux Nord & Sud du Cimetière* (Cemetery), *Boyau Vert* (Green Alley), etc., reflecting the broad range of potential local sources of names, and the lack, at this early stage of the war, of any particular system of naming apart from other *boyaux* and trenches numbered from the south.[16]

Vimy Sector (1915)[17]

The following names given by the French to German trenches have been taken from various French *plans directeurs* of the Vimy Ridge sector in 1915 and early 1916. It is significant that a propaganda element enters into the naming of some trenches: *T. des Poux* (Lice Trench), *Boyau du Mensonge* (Lie CT), *Boyau de la Vérité* (Truth), *Tr. de la Justice* (Justice/Gallows), *Boyau de l'Œillette* (Poppy/Opium Poppy), *Boyau du Kaiser* (The Kaiser), *Tr. de Lemberg* (city), *Boyau Neuf* (New CT), *Tr. de Francfort* (city), *Boyau Keller*, *Boyau Compagnon* (Comrade CT), *Tr. & Boyau de la Garde* (Guard), *Boy. de Givenchy* (village of Givenchy-en-Gohelle), *Tr. de Potsdam* (town near Berlin), *Tr. Intermedian* (sic; Intermediate), *Tr. de la Lisière* (Edge/Boundary of village or wood), *Boyau Nord* (North CT), *Boyau Sud* (South CT), *B. de la Hofburg* (Citadel, Hill 145), *Tr. de la Folie* (La Folie Farm), *Boyau des Communs* (villages CT), *Tr. du Château*, *Boyau de l'Appendice* (Appendix CT), *Boyau de Layons* (Tracks CT), *Tr. & Boyau de Vimy*, *Tr. de la Station*, *Boyau du Télégraphe* (Napoleonic Semaphore Station), *Boyau du Champ Leley*, *Tr. de Thélus* (village), *Boyau du Kronprinz* (Crown Prince), *Tr. de la Chaudière* (Boiler Trench), *Boyau de l'Escalier* (Staircase), *Tr. de la Haie* (Hedge), *Boyau de la Ferme* (Farm), *L'hypoténuse* (The Hypotenuse), *Tr. & Boyau des 5 Saules* (5 Willows), *Le long Boyau* (Long CT), *Tr. du Garde* (Guard), *Boyau du Champ Baron* (sic; Baron Field), *Boyau de la Thieulloy*, *Boyau de Mariette*, *Boyau de la Cote 105* (Hill 105), *T. des Tilleuls* (Les Tilleuls village, Lime Trees), *Tr. des 3 Maisons* (3 Houses).

Somme Battlefield

The *GCTA2* of the French Second Army on the Somme front first printed 1:20,000 scale *plans directeurs* in the period November 1914 to July 1915, several editions of each sheet being produced during these months. They did not show the French trenches, and although the German trenches were overprinted in blue no names were given to these.[18] This did not mean that no names were given by the units holding those trenches; they did indeed give names, and these appeared on the manuscript sketch maps made by the units and formations in the line. For example, Second Army units named trenches after personalities, either distinguished cultural names from the past or officers and NCOs of more recent memory; the following names appear on a French engineers' manuscript sketch map of the La Boisselle area handed over to the British at the end of July 1915:[19] *Blanchard* (painter; pilot; naturalist; doctor/zoologist), *Donnet* (cardinal/archbishop), *Fistic, Caron* (navigator; soldier; singer), *Bécart, Follies, Durand* (physiologist/philosopher), *Musan, Le Binan, Cochereau, Mangin* (general), *Quémart* (*Nord & Sud*), *Ilot* (îlot: a small or isolated island), *Dohollou, Magnan, Lavice, Ridou, Joanny, Le Goff, Dutrieux, Le Berre, Namon, Le Jolléo, Renoal, Mercier, Masson, Ricou, Dutrieux, Lecuyader, Bodenés, Hérault* (President of Convention; département, part of Languedoc), *Delaunay* (mathematician and astronomer; actor; painter), *Chacks, Querrou, Bouchaud* (doctor, member of academy of sciences). These trenches were soon renamed by the Scots of the British 51st Division, who found the names difficult to pronounce. No doubt the French encountered the same problem when they took over British trenches.

French archives throw some light on the French regimental associations in trench naming of the trenches at La Boisselle. The French unit in this sector in 1915 until relieved by the 51st Highland Division at the end of July was the 19th Infantry Regiment. As this regiment pushed the Germans back on the outskirts of La Boisselle (where there was particularly savage mine warfare) they named the new trenches after their soldiers killed in the fighting. *Dohollou Trench* was named after Sous Lieutenant Jean Dohollou killed in action on 3 March 1915, and *Ridou* Trench after Sergeant François Marie Ridou killed on 10 February 1915. Sous Lieutenant Frédéric Hyacinthe Quémar (not Quémart) was killed at La Boisselle on 3 February 1915. The French trench map in the 51st Division War Diary shows *Quémart* and also has Scottish trench names in a different hand. This map also appears to have *Donollou*, although other maps include various spellings of *Dohollou*. Other French *plans directeurs* or sketch maps might show the transition from *Quémar* to *Quémart*.[20] The trench name board *TRANCHEE QUEMART NORD*, a rectangular white-washed wooden sign with black painted lettering was, in 2006–07, given privately to the Imperial War Museum. This seems to have been brought back from the Western Front in 1916 by Major Richard Norman Winstanley of the East Surrey Regiment.[21]

When the British 27th Division took over the Frise–Dompierre front south of the Somme in September 1915, it found itself occupying front trenches designated by the familiar letters (for sections) and numbers (for individual stretches of trench), and the *Redoute du Bois Vierge* (Virgin Wood), *Redoute de l'Arbre* (Tree), *Redoute du '99'* and *Redoute de Fontaine-le-Cappy* (village), as well as *Saillant Payan, Saillant Rajon, Saillant Jeanny* and *Saillant Filippi* in the Fay sector and *Galeries Peupliers* (Poplars) and *Sucrerie* (Sugar Factory) in the Dompierre sector[22] Here we have a mixture of topographical and personal names.

While the British often adopted French names, the practice also worked the other way round – when French troops took over sectors from the British. But sometimes it did not. Before the Battle of the Somme the French took over the sector north of the Somme river from the British. Here, in the Mametz–Montauban–Curlu area, they gave the German trenches names quite different from those given by the British, and some of these French names were later used by the British during the battle if they happened to designate a trench not in fact previously named by the British. An example is the *Tranchée des Chimpanzés* west of Hardecourt, a name soon adopted by the British for *Chimpanzee Trench* and *Chimpanzee Valley*.

French names given to German trenches in the Mametz–Montauban–Maricourt sector, and their subsequent British equivalents, need careful consideration; were the French names intended to convey the idea that the German occupants were merely a load of fruit and vegetables? North of Montauban was the *Boyau des Fuyards* (Runaway Soldiers), and between Bernafay Wood and Trônes Wood ran the *Tranchée des Parasites*, while not far to the south were the names of many unpleasant insects and other undesirables, as we saw above. The names given to German trenches in the Mametz–Montauban–Maricourt sector on 10 June 1916 were:[23]

French name	British name
Boyau des Abricots (Apricots)	*Bulgar Alley*
Tr. des Pruneaux (Prunes/Rifle Bullets)	*Black Alley*
Tr. des Poires (Pears)	*Pommiers Trench*
Ouvrage des Pommiers (Apple Trees)	*Pommiers Redoubt*
Boyau des Salades (Salads)	*Popoff Lane*
Tr. des Prunes (Plums)	*Bund Support*
Tr. des Pêches (Peaches)	*Bund Trench*
Tr. des Bananes (Bananas)	*Austrian Support*
Tr. des Pois (Peas)	*Bay Trench*
Boyau des Haricots (Beans)	*Mine Alley*
Boyau des Fèves (Broad Beans)	*Mine Alley*
Tr. des Figues (Figs)	*Breslau Alley*
Tr. des Raisins (Raisins)	*Breslau Support*
Tr. des Cerises (Cherries)	*Valley Support*
Tr. des Fraises (Strawberries)	*Train Alley*
Tr. des Choux (Cabbages)	*Alt Trench*
Tr. des Laitues (Lettuce)	*Train Alley & unnamed*
Tr. des Cornichons (Gherkin; also Idiot)	*unnamed*

Boyau des Céleris (Celery)	*Train Alley & unnamed*
Tr. Des Piments (Pimentos)	*unnamed*
Boyau du Pissenlit (Dandelion)	*Nord Alley*
Tr. des Groseilles (Redcurrants)	*Glatz Redoubt*
Tr. des Framboises (Raspberries)	*Casement Trench*
Boyau des Epinards (Spinach)	*Glatz Alley*
Tr. des Cassis (Blackcurrants)	*Favière Support*
Tr. des Carottes (Carrots)	*Horn Alley*
Boyau des Poireaux (Leeks)	*Franz Alley*
Tr. des Ananas (Pineapples)	*Favière Alley*

It can be seen that there was practically no correspondence between the British and French names, and this in a situation when the British and French armies were to advance side-by-side in this sector. Furthermore, even when different names could be collated, they did not necessarily correspond to the same stretch of trench. This lack of close liaison did not bode well for inter-Allied cooperation in the coming battle.

In the Maricourt–Hardecourt–Montauban–Curlu sector north of the Somme, further supporting Max Eckert's negative naming assertion outlined above, we find groups of names of fruit and vegetables, tools, commanders, unpleasant insects, diseases and latrine associations, etc: *Tranchée des Godiches* (stupid or hamfisted), *Tranchée des Cantharides* (Spanish Flies), *Tranchée des Crabes* (Crabs), *Tranchée des Cloportes* (Woodlice), *Boyau des Ecervelés* (Scatter-brained), *Tranchée de la Pestilence* (Plague), *Boyau des Feuillées* (Latrines), *Boyau du Défilement* (Running), *Tr. des Araignées* (Spiders), *Tranchée des Mouches* (Flies), *Tranchée des Moustiques* (Mosquitoes), *Tranchée des Fous* (Madmen), *Tranchée des Chétifs* (Puny or Sickly), *Tranchée du Petit Batignolles* and *Boyau de la Place Clichy* (both in the notorious Montmartre area of Paris), *Tranchée des Chimpanzés* (an uncomplimentary reference), and *Tranchée de Bacchanale* (Orgy, Drunken Revel). Not far away, on the south side of the Somme, was *Crotte Boche* (German Shit). We also find *Tranchée Gott mit Uns* and *Tranchée Uber Alles* (both names later adopted by the British) at Mont Saint-Quentin, just north of Péronne. The former was the motto inscribed on the belt-plates of Prussia and Baden, while the latter referred to the national anthem, *Deutschland Uber Alles* which properly translated was an exhortation to put Germany before everything, not a message about world domination. The French use of these names was clearly ironic.

Fruit, vegetables, spices and other sources provided names for some trenches in this sector: *Tr. des Ananas* (Pineapples), *B. de l'Ail* (Garlic), *Tr. du Gingembre* (Ginger), *Tr. du Carry,* (Curry), *B. d'Oseille* (Sorrel or Trick), *B. des Navets* (Turnips), *Tr. du Repos* (Rest), *B. du Défilement* (Cover or Running) and

B. de la Place Blanche. Four trenches here were named after French frontier garrison towns or barrier fortresses: *T. de Toul, T. de Lunéville, Tr. de Nancy* and *T. du Pont-à-Mousson.* The *Tranchée du Chapeau de Gendarme* was on a cliff of that name overlooking the Somme at Curlu. Four redoubts north-west of Curlu were named *T. du Bastion, Tr. Y. Nord, Tr. Y. Centre* and *Tr. Y. Sud.*

A large group of trenches in this sector were named according to a do-it-yourself theme: *Tr. des Panels* (Panels), *B. des Assemblages* (Gatherings), *B. des Tenailles* (Pincers), *Tr. des Marteaux* (Hammers), *B. des Vis* (Screws), *B. des Chevilles* (Pegs or Pins), *B. des Poinçons* (Bodkins or Bradawls), *B. des Crampons* (Clamps), *Tr. des Menuisiers* (Joiners), *B. des Clous* (Nails), *B. du Compas* (Compasses or Dividers), *B. de la Scie* (Saw), *Tr. des Equerres* (Set-squares), *Tr. du Vilebrequin* (Brace and bit), *Tr. du Rabot* (Plane), *Tr. de la Varlope* (Trying Plane) and *Tr. des Vrilles* (Gimlets).

Various other French names given to German trenches in the Curlu–Hem–Maurepas area, just north of the Somme, on the French Sixth Army front, are of more than passing interest. Many have a distinct propaganda element to them, portraying the Germans as lousy, treaty-breaking sausage-eaters: *Boyau du sauve qui peut* (every man for himself), *T. du Chiffon du Papier* ('Scrap of Paper' – the treaty guaranteeing Belgian neutrality, the German breaking of which was the reason for Britain going to war), *T. Kitchener* (British Secretary of State for War), *Tr. Galliéni* (French Commander of Paris Garrison), *Tr. du Nicolas* (Russian Tsar), *Tr. de l'Agence Wolf* (German Wolf News/Wireless Agency), *Tr. d'Attila* (Attila the Hun), *Tr. Barberousse* (Barbarossa, the ancient German invader of Russia), *B. des Larmes* (Tears), *Tr. du Kronprinz* (Crown Prince), *B. des Saucisses* (Sausages), *Tr. de Brunehilde* (heroine of Wagner's Ring Cycle), *Tr. de la Poule Verte* (Green Chicken/Tart?), *Tr. du Magot* (Barbary Ape or Figurine), *Tr. de la Misère* (Misery; near Miséry village), *Tr. Molasse* (Soft & Flabby or Slow & Lazy), *B. de la Peine* (Punishment), *B. de la Faim* (Hunger), *B. de la Soif* (Thirst), *Tr. des Phoques* (Seal, or Homosexual), *Tr. de Salzbourg* (Salzburg in Austria), *Tr. Rienzi* (Wagner Opera), *Tr. Léopold* (Leopold), and *T. du Sycophantes* (Sycophants, perhaps a reference to Germany's allies).

Several trenches in this area, and many in the sector south of the River Somme, carried names from classical history and mythology: *Tr. d'Annibal* (Hannibal), *Tr. d'Argus* (Argus, many-headed, observation posts?), *Tr. de Baucis* (wife of Philemon), *Tr. de Philémon* (husband of Baucis), *Fortin du Labyrinthe* (Labyrinth; Daedalus, Crete), *B. de Minos* (Minos, Cretan King), *B. du Minotaure* (Minotaur, Crete), *Tr. de Pythagore* (Pythagoras), *T. du Salmis* (sic; Salamis; a battle), *B. Salomon* (Solomon), *Tr. Sésostris* (Sesostris), *Tr. Sosthène, B. Zéphyrin* (Zephyr) and *Tr. Hélène* (Helen of Troy).

The section of front covering the villages of Dompierre, Marchelepot, Vermandovillers, Villers Carbonnel and Belloy-en-Santerre, south of the

Somme, included the following names given by the French (several names appearing north of the river were repeated, and these have been omitted; there was a clear alphabetical pattern, and several French colonial associations, and again there were frequent negative references to the Germans): Among the 'A' names were: *Tr. Abbé* (Abbot or Priest), *Tr. de l'Actrice* (Actress), *Tr. de l'Alhambre* (Alhambra), *B. de l'Anisette*, *Tr. des Annamites* (Vietnamese), *Tr. de l'Arrivée* (Arrival), *Tr. de l'Auteur* (Author), and *Tr. de l'Automne* (Autumn).

There was a very large group of 'C' names: *Tr. du Caïd* (Kaid, or Gang Leader), *B. du Caoutchouc* (Rubber), *La Caponnière* (Funk Hole), *B. de la Carafe*, *B. de Carisbah*, *Tr. de la Carpe* (Carp), *Tr. du Carso* (Italian River), *Tr. de la Casbah*, *B. du Casque* (Helmet), *B. du Cassis* (Blackcurrant or Head), *B. des Castagnettes* (Castanets), *B. du Cataplasme* (Poultice), *B. du Chagrin* (Grief), *T. du Chahut* (Noise), *Ouvrage du/de Chameau* (Camel), *B. du Chanteur* (Singer), *B. des Charcutiers* (Pork Butchers), *T. de Chat* (Cat), *T. du Chérif* (Sherrif), *B. de la Chicorée* (Chicory), *Tr. du Chocolat* (Chocolate), *B. de la Choucroute* (Sauerkraut), *B. des Choux* (Cabbages), *B. du Cimier* (Crest or Haunch), *B. du Cinéma*, *Tr. du Cirque* (Circus), *B. Citron* (Lemon), *T. du Cloporte* (Woodlouse), *B. de la Comell*, *Tr. du Coq* (Cock), *B. Cor* (Horn), *B. du Cornichon* (Gherkin or Idiot), *Tr. de Costin*, *Tr. du Coton* (Cotton or Trouble), *Tr. & Boyau du Couscous* (Couscous or Tabouleh), *Tr. Couteau* (Knife), *B. Couvert* (Covered), *Tr. des 5 Créneaux* (Loopholes), *T. du Crime* (Crime), *Tr. du Crocodil[e]*, *T. du Crocus*, *Crotte Boche* (German Shit), *B. Crotin* (Crottin = Dung), *Tr. Croûton* (Crust) and *B. des Cyclamens*.

Moving farther down the alphabet, we encounter: *Tr. de la Dame Blanche* (White Lady), *Tr. du Damloup* ('High Battery' at Verdun), *B. des Délicatesses* (Delicacy), *Tr. du Delta*, *B. du Départ* (Departure), *Tr. du Dragon* (Dragon or Dragoon) *Tr. & Boyau Engel* (Angel in German), *Tr. des Entonnoirs* (Mine craters), *Tr. d'Erfurt* (German town), *B. Fischer*, *Tr. de Flore* (Flora), *B. Fourche* (Fork), *B. Frenois/Fresnois* and *Tr. Fricke* (Wagnerian character).

The 'G' names included: *Tr. Gaby*, *B. de la Gaffe* (Gaffe or Boathook), *Tr. Gamelle* (Dixie or Mess-tin), *B. Gamin* (Child), *Tr. du Gange* (Ganges), *Tr. de la Gare* (Station), *T. du Gâteau* (Cake), *Tr. des Gaufres* (Waffles), *Tr. Gavai*, *T. du Gaz* (Gas), *Tr. de la Génisse* (Heifer), *B. de la Géométrie* (Geometry), *Tr. des Germains*, *Tr. Gigot* (Leg of mutton), *Tr. Givre* (Frost), *Tr. de Glatz* (Bald-headed), *Tr. du Goret* (Piglet or Dirty Child), *B. Gosse* (Youngster), *Tr. de Gotha* (German town), *B. de la Gourde* (Gourd, Water-bottle or Stupid), *Tr. de Gratz* (Austrian city), *B. Gredin* (Wretch), *B. du Griffon* (Gryphon, Gryphin or Vulture), *B. des Guêpes* (Wasps) and *Tr. Guetteur* (Lookout).

'H' to 'M' names were *Tr. du Haïphong* and *Tr. d'Hanoï* (Indo-China), *B. Harpies* (Harpies from classical mythology, or Shrews), *Tr. Heinrich*, *Tr. du Homard* (Lobster), *Tr. d'Honolulu*, *Réduit & Boyau d'Horgny* (village), *Tr. de l'Hyène* (Hyena), *T. d'Innsbruck* (Austrian town), *Tr. de l'Isar* (Bavarian River), *B. des Jambons* (Hams or Thighs), *B. de Jéricho* (Biblical town whose walls Joshua destroyed), *Tr. de la Jonction* (Junction), *Tr. Joseph*, *Tr. Juil*, *Tr. des Jumeaux* (Twins), *Tr. de la Licorne* (Unicorn), *B. des Lièvres* (Hares), *Tr. des Lisières* (Edges), *Tr. de Loge* (Lodge or Theatre Box), B. des *Macroures*, *B. de Magenta* (Napoleon II's battle), *B. Mare* (Pool), *Tr. de la Marmelade* (Stewed Fruit), *B. du Matou* (Tomcat), *Tr. des Maures* (Moors), *B. Maurice* (Mauritius), *B. de Mazes*, *Tr. de Minden* (Minden, battle), *B. du Mineur* (Sapper/Miner), *B. de la Motte* (Clod, Lump or Mound), *Tr. des Mouères*, *Tr. Mouise* (Poverty, Dire Straits or Gruel) and *B. Mund*.

'O' to 'W' names included *Tr. Octave*, *Tr. de l'Oeuf* (Egg), *Tr. de l'Omignon* (French river), *Tr. du Paragraphe*, *Tr. de Passau* (Napoleonic Battle), *B. de la Peine* (Punishment), *Tr. Placide* (Calm), *Tr. Pleyna* (Plevna), *Tr. du Prédicateur* (Preacher), *B. Rassov*, *B. Rosenberg*, *B. du Sainfoin*, *Tr. du Sansonnet* (Starling), *B. des Saucisses* (Sausages), *B. de la Séparation* (Separation or Partition), *Tr. de Soueb* (Soue = Pigsty; pun on Schwaben), *Tr. Scharff* (Scharf: German for Sharp), *B. de Sébastopol* (in Crimea), *B. du Soda*, *B. de la Soif* (Thirst), *Tr. Souffre* (Drudge or Laughing Stock), *B. de la Strypa*, *Tr. du Surin* (Knife), *Tr. de la Tarasque* (Monster), *Terres Noires* (lit. Black Earth), *Tr. Théodore*, *Tr. de la Tour* (near a Tower), *T. de la Trompelle*, *Tr. de Venise* (Venice), *Tr. Versen* and *Tr. Witterkind*. Certain names from the Verdun battlefield were also commemorated here: *Tr. de Verdun*, *Tr. de Vaux* (Fort Vaux), *Tr. du Morte Homme* (hill on Verdun's left bank), *Tr. Souville* (Fort Souville) and *Tr. du Poivre* (Côte de Poivre).

In the Mont Saint-Quentin–Péronne area the following names appeared towards the end of the Somme battle in 1916; here were the striking *Ouvrage de Brasso* (*Brasso Redoubt*, so called by the British), *Tr. Gott mit Uns* (God With Us, belt buckle motto) and *Tr. Uber Alles* (German national anthem: *Deutschland Uber Alles*). The frequency of place names from the Central European and Balkans area is noticeable: *Tr. de Rottweil* (German town), *Tr. de Kurillo*, *Tr. du Koros*, *Boyau de Radomin*, *Tr. Gottlieb*, *Boyau de Galatz*, *Boyau d'Agram*, *Tr. de Kholm*, *Tr. de Prague* (Czech capital, then part of Austro–Hungarian Empire), *Tr. Elsa*, *Tr. de Varna*, *Tr. de Transylvanie*, *Tr. de Danube*, *Tr. de Bania*, *Tr. Radégonde*, *Tr. d'Aluta*, *Tr. de Maros*, *Tr. du Pruth*. Also present were *Tr. Johannes* and *Tr. Jonathan*.

There was a variety of other names here including some local topographical names, personal names and classical deities: *Boyau de Moinville*, *Boyau de Toros* (Bulls), *Tr. du Canal* (Somme Canal), *Tr. du Bac* (Ferry over the Somme), *Tr. de Neptune* (God of the Sea), *Tr. de Zeus* (God), *Tr. Apollo* (Sun God), *Tr. de l'Astrologue* (Astrologer), *Tr. d'Assyrie* (Assyria), *Tr. Courrier*, *Tr. Henriot*, *Tr. de la Valse* (Waltz), *Tr. Valuel*, *Tr. Esposito*, *Tr. de l'Epée* (Rapier), *T. Callis*,

Boyau Dollfus (Austrian politician), *Tr. des Cyclistes* (Cyclists) and *Boyau Romain Desfosses*.

Literary names in the Nesle area, at the southern end of the Somme battlefield, included *Tranchée de Rabelais*, *Tranchée de Pantagruel* (from the former's 'Gargantua and Pantagruel'), and the relatively recent *Tranchée du Père Ubu* (from Jarry's anarchic 'Ubu Roi' of 1886). Many names on the Somme battlefield reflect cultural claims (e.g. *Kant Copse*) and the German military command (*Tranchée de Falkenhayn, Ludendorf, Hindenburg, Linsingen*, etc.), as well as topical events (e.g. *Tranchée de Jutland*, after the great naval battle of June 1916).

Aisne and Chemin-des-Dames Sector

On the Chemin-des-Dames Ridge above the Aisne river, the names given by the French to German trenches fell into two main categories; one group, relating to piracy, fell within the category of anti-German propaganda: *Boyau des Dames* (Chemin des Dames), *Boyau de l'Epervier* (Sparrowhawk), *Tr. de la Mouette* (Seagull), *Boyau de la Perdrix* (Partridge), *Tr. du Pirate* (Pirate), *Boyau du Corsaire* (Corsair or Privateer), *Boyau de la Baleinière* (Whaleboat), *Tr. du Canot* (Boat or Canoe), *Tr. Youyou* (Dinghy), *Tr. du Mât* (Mast), *Tr. de l'Artimon* (Mizzenmast), *Boyau des Haubans* (Rigging or Shrouds) and *Boyau du Beaupré* (Bowsprit). This nautical flavour reminds us that many of the officers of the *Groupes de canevas de tir* were drawn from the *Service hydrographique de marine*, but it is unlikely that they had much input into naming practice. The other group was the usual run of German and Central Powers' place names: *Tr. de Kassa, Eitel Trench* (a German royal family), *Tr. de Fiume* (Austrian city), *Tr. Krüger* (former Boer President), *Tr. Kant* (German philosopher), *Tr. d'Elberfeld* (German town), *Boyau de l'Oder* (German river), *Tr. de Buda-Pest* (Hungarian capital), *Tr. de Tokaï* (Hungarian wine), *Tr. de Vienne* (Austrian capital), *Tr. Klopstock* (German poet, dramatist), *Tr. de la Grève* (Strand, Strike, or Parisian Square where disgruntled workers gathered). An unusual name for a German trench on a French map dating from 1918 was the *Tranchée de la Social Démocratie*, near Vic-sur-Aisne. This could well be an ironic comment on the political turmoil in Germany in the summer and autumn of 1918 which culminated in the revolution of November, the abdication of the Kaiser and the proclamation of a republic.

In the Berry-au-Bac area, on the Aisne, the following names were given by the French to their own trenches and other features; it should be remembered that some of these trenches had been captured from the Germans, hence the disparaging names: *Tr. des Huns* (Huns Trench), *B. du Camp de César* (Caesar's Camp), *B. de la fuite* (Flight or Running Away), *Courtine du Dirigeable* (Airship),

Tr. de l'Aviatik (German aeroplane type), *Tr. devant le Vélodrome* (in front of the cycle-track), *B. Dumas* (possibly Alexandre Dumas, author of *The Three Musketeers*), *B. du Buffle* (Buffalo or Blockhead), *B. du Chacal* (Jackal or Shark), *B. de Tourville* (French town) and *Tr. des Lions* (Lions).

In the Nauroy–Prosnes–Moronvilliers–Le Mont St Nom–Aubérive sector, where the French Army attacked with tanks in April 1917, trench names included *Tr. Leopoldshöhe, Tr. Erfurt, Tr. Wahn, Tr. Offenburg, Boyau Düsseldorf, Boyau Hoenig, Tr. Goslar, Tr. Flensburg, Constanzlager, Tr. Fosse Froide, Tr. Gottingen, Tr. Rendsburg, Tr. Téton, Tr. Oldenburg, Tr. du Bois du Chien, Abris Hexen Kessen, Labyrinthe, Tr. Byzance, Boyau Main, Tr. Bethmann-Hollweg, Le Golf, Parallèles de Moronvilliers, Tr. Constantinople, Tr. Posnanie, Tr. Landtag, Tr. Beyrouth, Tr. Landsturm, Tr. Baden, Tr. Bayzance, Tr. Germains, Fortin Sud de Vaudesincourt, Tr. Prinz Eitel.* This reinforces the view that French names for German trenches, where they were not abusive, were principally related to the personalities and geographical names of Germany and her allies. Such names may well have been taken from captured German maps of the sector – in other words they may have been the names given by the Germans to the same lengths of trench.

Champagne Battlefield

In August and September 1915, before the Champagne attack in the Reims–Argonne area, the *Groupe de Canevas de Tir* of the French Second Army (*GCTA2*), which had just arrived in that sector from the Somme front, also began to print trench names on its *plans directeurs*. So that the use of rectangular coordinates could be confined to the designation of particular points, it adopted the rule of giving names, already established by common usage, to French trenches and other points on the map. At the same time it extended this principle to the German trenches, giving them 'purely conventional' names,[24] mainly those of personalities and places associated with Germany and her allies.

The Champagne battlefield provides a rich array of names. Those given before the massive French offensive, which began on 25 September 1915, to German trenches and strongpoints in the Aubérive–Souain–Tahure sector included *Tr. des Tantes* (Aunts), *Tr. de Gretchen, Tr. du Triangle, Boyau de l'Archiduchesse, Boyau de Fribourg, Saillant de Bois Sabot, Ouvrage d'Ulm, Rdt./Ouvrage du Palatinat, Rdt./Ouvrage de Magdeburg, Tr. d'Eckmühle, Boyau du Désespoir* (despair), *Boyau de Tahure, B. des Dardanelles, Saillant de Souabe, Saillant de Presbourg, Tr. de Hambourg, Boyau du Harem, Bois du Crabe, Tr. von Kluck, Tr. des Sapins* (pine trees), *Boyau de l'Elbe, Boyau du*

Danube, *Tr. du Rhin*, *Tr. des Entonnoirs* (craters), *Tr. Guillaume* (Kaiser William II), *Boyau du Kaiser*, *Tr. d'Hindenburg*, *Tr. François Joseph* (the Austrian Emperor, Franz Joseph), *Tr. de Lübeck*, *Rdt. Von Tirpitz* and *Rdt. Wilhelm II*. It can be seen that many of these related to the Central Powers.

On either side of Navarin Farm (where a relative of the author, George Chasseaud, was killed in September 1915 while serving with the French Foreign Legion), in the German second position, were the *Tranchée des Vandales* and *Tranchée de la Kultur*. In the Tahure sector were the *Camp de Sadowa* (a battle), *Tr. de la Vistule* (River Vistula), *Tr. Nouvelle*, *Tr. de la ferme de Ripont*, *Boyau de Leipzig*, *Tr. de la Prusse* (Prussia), *La Baraque* (a German earthwork) and *La Fille Morte* (a hill feature). We also find the *Parallèle de l'Epine de Védegrange*, *Epi du Parallèle de Bois Chevron*, the *Brosse à Dents* (toothbrush wood), *Tranchée de Constantinople*, *Tr. de Cologne*, *Boyau Heine* and *Boyau de Nietsche* (sic; a German poet and philosopher respectively), and *Mamelle* (breast) *Nord & Sud*. At Perthes was a system of German trenches known as *La Poche* (the pocket), and the *Tranchée d'York*. In the Le Mesnil–Butte de Mesnil sector was *Le Trapèze* (trapezium) on the *Mamelle Sud* (southern breast), the *Tr. de la Crête* (crest). In the Beauséjour sector

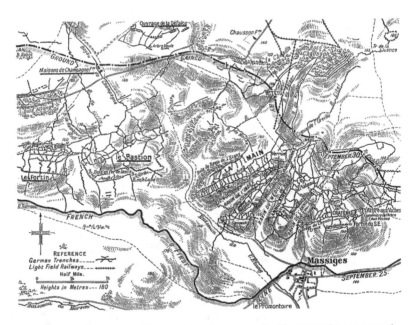

The German trenches on the Main de Massiges, so-called because its topography closely resembled the human hand. The French named the spurs or 'fingers' Index, *Medius*, *Annulaire*, etc., prior to attacking in September 1915. Other German positions were named *Le Fortin*, *Le Bastion*, etc. Ouvrage de la Défaite is at the top. The French front line is at the bottom.

were woods named *Fer de Lance* (spearhead) and *Demi-Lune* (half moon – an old fortification feature) after their shapes.

At the eastern end of the Champagne battlefield towards the Argonne was the aptly named Main de Massiges (a striking terrain feature whose plan view was the shape of a hand) where in 1915 the French gave German names to most of the enemy trenches: *Boyau Jung*, *Tr. Garnowski*, *Tr. Kreuter*, *Tr. Fischer*, *Boyau du Kaiser*, *Boyau du Kronprinz*, *Boyau de Moltke*, *Boyau Hindenburg*, *Boyau Eitel*, *Tr. de Nauen*, *Boyau Schumann*, *Tr. Schulz*, *Tr. Eichhorn*, *Tr. de la Justice* (Hill 166, site of an ancient gallows), *Tr. de Coblentz* [sic], *Tr. de la Briqueterie* (brickworks). For the jutting fingers of the hand, the appropriate anatomical names *Index*, *Medius*, *Annulaire*, etc., were given to the digits.[25] German strongpoints and trenches here and nearby at Maisons de Champagne were named *Ouvrage du Chemin Creux* (cross-roads), *Ouvrage de la Côte* (spot-height), *Le Fortin* (small fort), *Le Bastion* (stronghold), *S.-E. Fortin*, *Caponnière* (ancient defensive feature) *de l'Arbre aux Vaches*, *Boyau de Champagne*, *Boyau de Berlin*, *Boyau de Posen*, *Boyau de Hambourg* and *Ouvrage de la Défaite* (defeat – clearly a propaganda message).

Vauquois Sector (1916)[26]

In the Vauquois sector of the Argonne, one French trench was named *Grand Collecteur*, a name that also appeared at Vimy Ridge. The French names for German trenches at Vauquois included the usual place names relating to the Central Powers, a Wagnerian name and one or two derogatory names: *Tr. de Prague*, *Tr. de Brun*, *Tr. de Raouse*, *Ouvrage du Crotale* (rattlesnake), *Tr. de Pilsen*, *Boy. de Lemberg*, *Boy. de Gratz*, *Boy. des Houris*, *Le V de Vauquois* and *Boy. de Fafner* (Dragon in Wagner's Ring).

Verdun

The epic nature of the Verdun battle in 1916 produced many heroes for the French, and we naturally find these commemorated in trench names. Near the *Morte Homme* for example we find *Tranchée Robin*, a hero of the first days of the Verdun battle, fighting with Colonel Driant's Chasseurs-à-pied in the Bois des Caures. A *Tranchée du Colonel Driant* duly appeared between Douaumont and Vaux. The Verdun battle throws up few surprises in French naming practice.

In the crucial Douaumont, Vaux and Fleurie area of the Verdun battlefield were the usual mixture of typical French and enemy place and personal names, reflecting the capture and recapture of trenches during the 1916 battles: *Tr. de la Tour du Pin, Tr. Pernod, Tr. Bonnef, Tr. Charlier, Boyau Hanns, Boyau Aubry, Tr. de Leyris, Tr. Poggi, Boyau de la Fontaine, Boyau de la Fourche, Tr. de Douaumont, Tr. de l'Ouest* (of Fort), *Tr. de l'Est* (of Fort), *Tr. Olivier, Tr. du Styx* (the classical symbol of death), *Tr. d'Udine, Tr. Otto, Tr. de Thorn* (in East Prussia), *Tr. du Métro, Boyau Charles, Tr. de Buda-Pest, Tr. des Hongrois, Tr. des Bulgares, Boyau des Pirates* (a negative reference to the enemy), *Boyau Krupp* (of Essen) and *Boyau de Barmen* (both in the Ruhr), and *Boyau des Habsbourgs* (Hapsburgs).

In the Vaux–Fleury area in 1916 were:[27] *Tr. du Colonel Driant* (hero of the Bois des Caures), *Tr. de Sarajevo* (scene of the assassination which triggered the war), *Le Triangle, Tr. de Gotha, Tr. de Brandebourg, Tr. de Potsdam, Tr. de Berlin, Tr. de Magdebourg, Tr. de Belfort, Tr. de Vaux, Tr. des Huns, Ouvrage du Kronprinz, Tr. du Palatinat, Tr. Sophie, Tr. Vidal, Tr. Pauly, Ouvrage de Munich, Ouvrage Dardot* and *Tr. de la Bavière.*

Mort Homme Area (9 June 1917)

French Trenches: [28] The names given to French trenches included many personal names, as well as a few relating to local topography and French regiments: *Boy. Bentayou, Tr. Cattin* (Catin = Whore), *Tr. des Seigies, Ouvrage de la Station, Boy. de Cumières* (village), *Tr. des Blés* (Wheat), *Tr. de Doiran* (on Salonika front), *Tr. Robin* (a hero of the Verdun battle), *Boy. de St Brieuc, Tr. Murache, Bonnet d'Evêque* (Bishop's Mitre), *Tr. de Foix, Tr. Matteï* (Austria), *Tr. de Pamiers, B. du Ravin de Chattancourt* (village), *Boy. de Nantes* (city), *Tr. de Toulon* (city), *Tr. James, Avenue 2, Boy. Marguerite, Tr. Dupuy, Nord, Est & Ouvrage des Zouaves, Tr. Bourdel, Boy. Gillet, Tr. Lefrançois, Tr. Monge, Tr. Durel, Tr. Pasteur, Tr. Delaunay, Tr. du Ct. Riols, Tr. Roux* (Russet), *B. Sadoul, Tr. Marcouillard, Tr. des Abris Netter, Boy. Coignard, Tr. du Comt. Faure, Tr. du Cap. Fournery, B. Clément, Tr. Fontenoy* and *Tr. Sonnois.*

German Trenches: [29] In this much fought-over zone, many trenches had changed hands, so it is not surprising that names given to German trenches at this date by the French included many Allied names. Many were the names of Frenchmen, but there were also many place names taken from the Somme battlefield, and also from Italy, Germany, Austria–Hungary and the Eastern Front. The French personal names were *Tr. & Saillant Boivin, T. Sonnois, Tr. Cottin, Tr. Gilbert, Tr. Delaunay, Tr. Lavoisier, Tr. Chevreul, Tr. Moline, B. Bourre, B. Itasse, Tr. Guilbert, Tr. Bloch, Tr. Perrenet, Boy. Jacques, Boy. Paul* and *Tr. Delaperche.*

Trenches in the *Mort Homme* area named after villages on the Somme battlefield were *Tr. de Fay*, *Tr. de Biaches*, *Tr. de Dompierre*, *Tr. de Frise*, *Tr. de Curlu*, *B. Belloy*, *B. d'Estrées*, *B. des Foureaux* (High Wood), *Tr. de Mametz*, *Tr. de Pozières*, *Boy. de Longueval*, *Tr de Flaucourt*, *Boy. de Vaux* (also a village and fort at Verdun) and *Boy. d'Hem*. Other French place names were *Tr. de la Marne*, *Boy. de Bar* (Bar-le-Duc, south of Verdun) and *Tr. de Corse* (Corsica). Names from Italy, an ally, were *Tr. Tacana*, *Tr. de Lombardie*, *B. d'Altona*, *Tr. de Ravenne*, *Tr. de Parme*, *Tr. de Catane*, *Tr. du Piémont*, *Boy. de Vérone*, *Tr. de Turin*, *Tr. de Milan*, *Tr de Brindisi*, *Tr. de Pise* and *Ouvrage de Pavie*.

A variety of other names appeared in this area, several of them relating to fortifications: *Le Chapeau Chinois* (Chinese Hat), *Les Poutres* (Beams), *T. de Feuillères* (Grooves), *Tr. Servières*, *Le Trapèze* and *Boyau du Trapèze* (Trapezium), *Boyau de la Fausse Batterie* (Dummy Battery), *Boyau des Ouvrages blancs* (White Works), *Tr. des Ronces* (Brambles or Barbed Wire), *Tr. des Chardons* (Thistles or Spikes) and *Boyau des Orties* (Stinging Nettles). The *Boyau des Huns* speaks for itself, but *Tr. du Dee* is a mystery; this magus or Welsh river seems rather out of place.

Those named after places in enemy territories or from the Eastern Front included *Tr. de Posen*, *Tr. & Boyau de Brandebourg*, *Boyau de Pinsk*, *Tr. de Silésie*, *Boyau de Bayreuth*, *Tr. de Breslau*, *Boyau de Torgau*, *Boyau de Stettin*, *Tr. & Boy. de Hanovre*, *Tr. de Dantzig*, *Tr. & Boyau de Westphalie*, *Tr. de Hesse*, *Tr. de Darmstad*, *Tr. de Thuringe*, *Boyau de Gorizia*, *Tr. de Hassau*, *Tr. de Poméranie* and *Tr. d'Ulm*. *Bismarck Tunnel* and *Kronprinz Tunnel* were important German shelters and communications driven into the north slope of the ridge. Other German names were *Boyau Kiepert*, *Tr. de Waldeck* (wood corner in German), *Boyau de Raab* and *Tr. Braun*.

Les Eparges (South-East of Verdun)[30]

This vital high point and observation position was the key to the eastern flank of the Verdun salient, and was the site of savage assaults and mine warfare from 1914 onwards, and several of the names reflected siege warfare. Many of the names, as usual, were those of Frenchmen; others were named after allies. Among the French trenches were the *Parallèle des Quenottes* (teeth), *Le Trottoir* (walkway), *Tr. Ecochard*, *Boy. Dessirier*, *Boy. de Montaroux*, *Boy. Centrale*, *Tr. Bourgeois*, *Tr. Barthélemy*, *Tr. Baty*, *Tr. Antoine*, *Tr. Gunther Nord*, *Gabionnade Cuty*, *Gabionnade Annonsade*, *Tr. Lorthal*, *Tr. Ganne*, *Boy. Chast*, *Tr. du Japon* (Japan), *Tr. Baraja*, *Tr. Bouillaud*, *Boy. des Italiens*, *Boy. d'Isly*, *Tr. Dufour* and *Tr. Vacant* (unoccupied).

Names given by the French to German trenches here included a few derogatory ones, some place names, a few French names and a Wagnerian reference: *Tr. de la Brosse* (brush or crew-cut), *Boy. de la Choucroute* (sauerkraut), *Tr. de Genousevaux*, *Tr. du Crabe* (crab), *Saillant du Bois Brulé* (burnt wood), *Parc des Pionniers* (pioneer park), *Tr. de Breslau*, *Tr. & Boyau de Dantzig*, *Boy. Champlon*, *Tr. du Viseau*, *Tr. Wagner* and *Ouvrage Pierdet*.

Conclusion

From this brief and inevitably condensed tour of French trench names, we have to conclude that there were distinct themes to French trench naming, both for their own and for the enemy trenches. Their own trenches were commonly named after French personalities, both cultural and military, while the enemy's positions were frequently named after German and other Central Powers personalities, regions, cities, rivers, etc. There were also thematic groupings, such as occurred in British naming, with no obvious direct relationship to the battlefield; examples are those groups of trenches named after classical deities and characters, carpentry and tools, or after fruit and vegetables.

We also have to conclude that Max Eckert was right. There was a distinct and systematic, if understandable, hostile propaganda element present in the French naming of German trenches that was not reciprocated by the Germans (see Chapter IX), and was quite different from British practice. While the British did have their own hostile propaganda, it did not in general extend to trench naming, apart from a few trenches named 'Hun', 'Boche' or similar appellations. Trench naming for the French was a continuation of pre-war tribal rivalry. For their part, the Germans adopted nationalistic cultural names for their own trenches, as we shall see in the next chapter. They rarely named those of their enemies, and when they did these names were usually those already bestowed by their opponents. This in fact became a practice common to all belligerents as more and more trench maps (showing names) were captured as the war went on.

Notes

1   *Rapport sur les Travaux Exécutés du 1er août 1914 au 31 décembre 1919 (Rapport de Guerre)*, Paris: Service Géographique de l'Armee, 1924 & 1936.
2   Map reproduced by British 1st Printing Company, RE, GHQ (396), 17-12-14, in 7th Division War Diary, TNA(PRO) WO 95/1627.

3   Arthur-Lévy, *Les Coulisses de la Guerre, le Service Géographique de l'Armee 1914–1918*, Paris: Berger-Levrault, 1926, p. 33.

4   *Rapport de Guerre*, 1924, op. cit., pp. 172–4.

5   Eckert, Max, *Die Kartenwissenschaft,* Berlin & Leipzig: VWV, Mittler, Vol. 1 1921, Vol. 2 1925, p. 793.

6   1:5,000 plan directeur *Butte de Souain*, 11-4-1916, in collection of Service Historique de l'Armée de Terre, Vincennes.

7   *Rapport de Guerre*, 1936, op. cit., p. 97.

8   *La Bataille de Champagne* (French GQG official account). See also English translation from *The National Review* in John Buchan, *Nelson's History of the War*, Vol. X. London, Edinburgh, etc: Nelson, 1915, p. 290.

9   *Instruction sur l'Organisation et le fonctionnement des Sections Topographiques des Corps d'Armées (S.T.C.A.), Au G.Q.G. le 25 décembre 1915*, Grand Quartier Général des Armées, 1915, p. 7.

10 *Rapport de Guerre*, 1936, op. cit., p. 97.

11 *Rapport de Guerre*, 1924, op. cit., p. 173.

12 *Rapport de Guerre*, 1936, op. cit., p. 174.

13 Grand Quartier Général des Armées, Etat-Major (2e et 3e Bureaux) (1918), *Instruction sur les Plans Directeurs et les Cartes et Plans Spéciaux*, Annexes, Paris: Imprimerie Nationale, 1918, p. 50.

14 1:5,000 plan directeur *Secteur de Lorette* in collection of Service Historique de l'Armée de Terre, Vincennes, and 1:20,000 plan directeur of Lorette–La Targette area, May–June 1915. Author's collection.

15 *Du Paysage à la Carte – Trois siècles de cartographie militaire de la France*, Ministère de la Défense, Services Historiques des Armées; Vincennes (catalogue of an exhibition prepared under the direction of Marie-Anne de Villèle, Agnès Beylot and Alain Morgat), 2002, p. 158.

16 Sketch map originally handed to Lieut. Charles Whitley, Brigade Bombing Officer, by the French on taking over this sector in early 1916. Private Collection.

17 1:10,000 plan directeur *Secteur de Vimy*, 18-10-1915. Author's collection.

18 Author's study of *plans directeurs* in collection of Service Historique de l'Armée de Terre, Vincennes.

19 Sketch map dated 28 July 1915, in 153rd Brigade War Diary, TNA(PRO) WO 95/2869.

20 Information from Simon Jones of the Kings Liverpool Museum.

21 Information from Philip Dutton, IWM. The IWM reference number for the sign is FEQ 853.

22 27th Division General Staff War Diary, TNA(PRO) WO 95/2254.

23 1:20,000 plan directeur *Maricourt, 10 Juin 1916, Group des Canevas de Tir* [Sixth Army], compared with British 1:20,000 special trench map *Montauban, GSGS 3188, OS 1916, Trenches corrected to 2-6-16*. Both author's collection.

24 *Rapport de Guerre*, 1924, op. cit., p. 116.

25 1:5,000 plan directeur *La Main de Massiges*, 31-8-15, in collection of Service Historique de l'Armée de Terre, Vincennes.

26 1:5,000 plan directeur *Vauquois*, 20-5-16, in collection of Service Historique de l'Armée de Terre, Vincennes.

27 1:10,000 *plans directeurs* of Vaux–Fleury area, 1916, illustrated in Conrad, P & Laspeyres, A, *La Grande Guerre 1914–1918*, Paris: E.P.A., 1989.

28 Fragments of 1:10,000 plans directeurs *Bethincourt*, 9-6-17, and 1:10,000 *Cumières* 19-8-1917, in Rapport de Guerre, 1924, op. cit.

29 Ibid.

30 1:20,000 *plan directeur* of Les Eparges area in Royal Geographical Society Map Room.

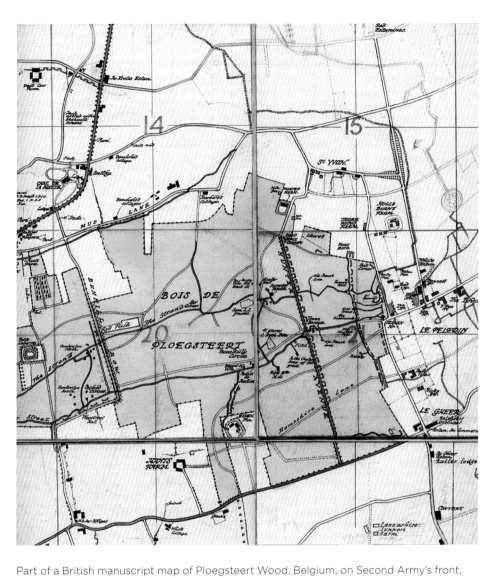

Part of a British manuscript map of Ploegsteert Wood, Belgium, on Second Army's front, dating from early 1915 (it carries the 'Revised System of Squaring' introduced on 1 January 1915). Ploegsteert was known as *Plug Street* to the British. The trenches, breastworks, duckboard or corduroy tracks, rides, headquarters, etc., are clearly marked. *Hunter Avenue* runs through the east end of the wood, and *Bunhill Row* (formerly *Bunter Avenue*) through the west end. *Mud Lane* borders the north edge of the wood. A point in the British breastwork near the east edge of the wood was called *The Tourists Peep*, being a popular place from which visitors could view the German line. The German trenches and breastworks lie to the east of the wood and Le Gheer, and take in Le Pelerin, where a strongly wired position was called *The Birdcage*.

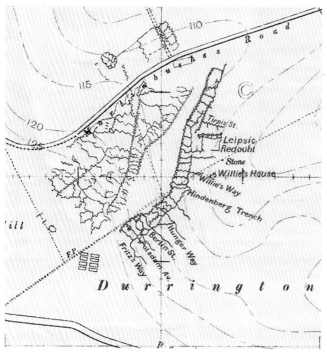

Detail from the 1:10,000 scale Artillery Training Map Durrington, printed at the Ordnance Survey (Southampton), showing the Larkhill ranges and training area on Salisbury Plain in 1916, with a practice Western Front-style trench system. The blue trenches are 'British' and the red, with appropriate names, are typically 'German'. *Hunger Way* is particularly interesting as it refers to the effect of the Royal Navy's blockade of Germany. In Germany the winter of 1916–17 was known as the 'turnip winter'.

Post-war oblique aerial photograph of the practice trench system, similar to the Larkhill one shown above, dug near Thundersbarrow on the Sussex downs north of Shoreham Camp, a divisional training area.

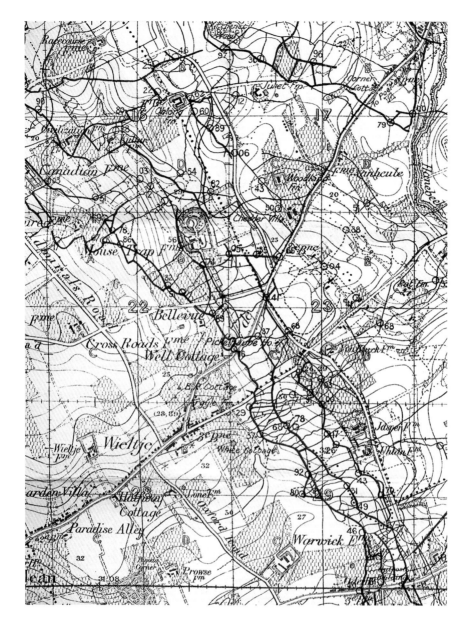

British Second Army trench map of the Wieltje sector, Ypres Salient, in late 1915. For security reasons, only the German trenches are shown. The Belgian map used as a background for overprinting the trenches has been augmented by the addition of many names given by the French and British – *Admiral's Road*, *Paradise Alley*, *Halfway Cottage*, *Warwick Farm*, *Canadian Farm*, *Mouse Trap Farm*, *Kultur Farm*, etc. The blue numbers by circles are artillery target numbers. Names were not yet being routinely given to the enemy's trenches.

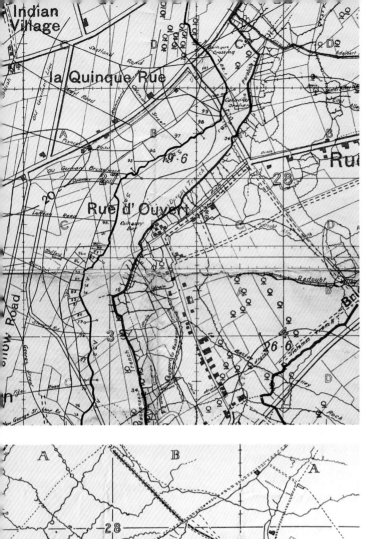

British First Army 'Brigade Trench Map' of the area east of Festubert in early 1916 showing the British trench system in schematised form, with trench names and numbers, in blue. This was an experiment to show British trenches on non-secret maps without giving vital evidence about precise position to the enemy, but ignored the fact that the Germans were taking perfectly good aerial photographs of the British positions and making very accurate maps of them. The German trenches, with names given by the British, are in red.

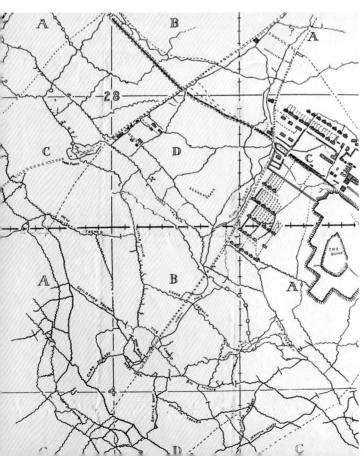

British First Army trench map of late 1915 showing the British (black) and German (red) trench systems in the area of the Hohenzollern Redoubt and The Dump of Fosse 8, north of Loos. During the Battle of Loos (September–October 1915) the British captured part of the redoubt, but were gradually expelled. The area was subsequently the scene of savage mine warfare. This map was drawn and lithographed in the field by First Army's Printing Section RE.

Part of the French 1:5,000 scale *plan directeur* (artillery and trench map) Fort de Douaumont, edition dated 18 May 1916, during the Battle of Verdun. The French trenches, with names, are in red, and the German trenches, with names given by the French, in blue. The ruined village of Douaumont is at top left. Fort Douaumont had been captured by the Germans in February 1916, a few days after the start of the battle, and was recaptured by the French later in the year. The map was drawn by draughtsmen of the *Groupe de Canevas de Tir* (field survey company) of the French Second Army.

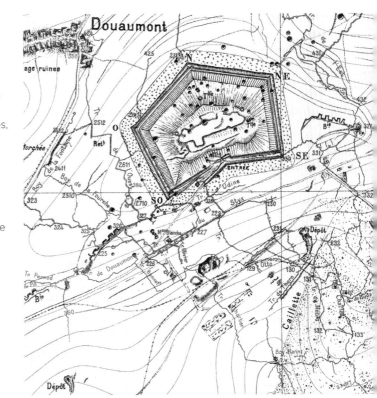

Part of French 1:10,000 scale *plan directeur* (artillery and trench map) Bethincourt, edition dated 9 June 1916, during the Battle of Verdun, showing the vital high ground of the Mort Homme on the left bank of the Meuse. The Mort Homme was captured by the Germans, as can be seen from this map in which the German trenches (blue, with names given by the French) occupy the heights previously held by the French. French trenches, with names, in red. The map was drawn by draughtsmen of the *Groupe de Canevas de Tir* (field survey company) of the French Second Army.

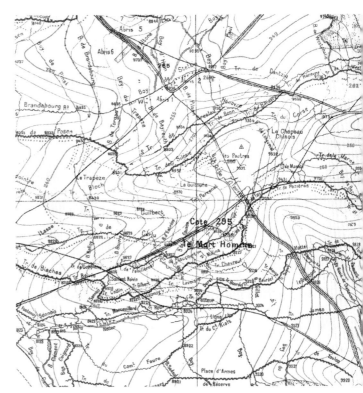

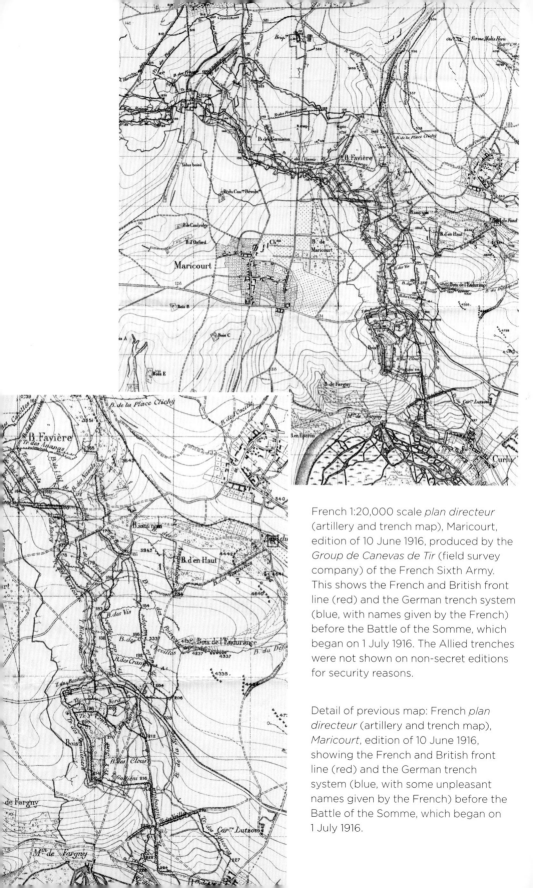

French 1:20,000 scale *plan directeur* (artillery and trench map), Maricourt, edition of 10 June 1916, produced by the *Group de Canevas de Tir* (field survey company) of the French Sixth Army. This shows the French and British front line (red) and the German trench system (blue, with names given by the French) before the Battle of the Somme, which began on 1 July 1916. The Allied trenches were not shown on non-secret editions for security reasons.

Detail of previous map: French *plan directeur* (artillery and trench map), *Maricourt*, edition of 10 June 1916, showing the French and British front line (red) and the German trench system (blue, with some unpleasant names given by the French) before the Battle of the Somme, which began on 1 July 1916.

German *Stellungskarte* (trench map) of the Thiepval–Pozières–Ovillers-la Boisselle area of the Somme front, before the start of the Battle of the Somme on 1 July 1916. The German trenches, with names, are in blue, and the British trenches in red. No names have been given to the British trenches, but points are designated by letters and numbers for artillery targets.

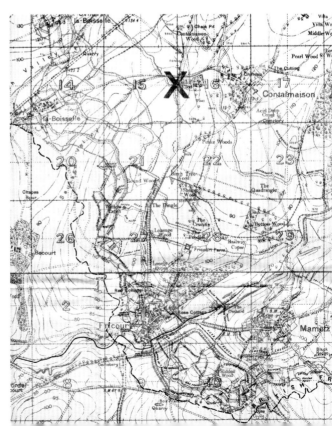

The Ovillers–la Boisselle–Contalmaison–Fricourt–Mametz area of the Somme battlefield. This is part of the British 1:20,000 trench map *Montauban* (GSGS 3188), drawn by draughtsmen of 4th Field Survey Company RE (with Fourth Army HQ) with trenches corrected to 2 June 1916, and printed at the Ordnance Survey (Southampton). German trenches are in red, with names given by the British in blue. The British front line is pecked blue. The British trench system is not shown for security reasons. The map shows the situation before the start of the Somme battle on 1 July 1916. This sector is described by Siegfried Sassoon, Robert Graves and David Jones in their respective memoirs.

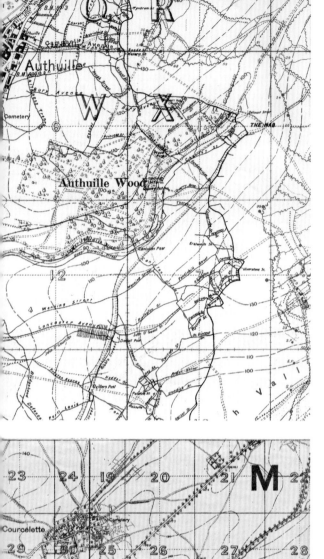

British 1:10,000 scale 'Secret' edition regular series (GSGS 3062) trench map of the Authuille–Mash Valley area of the Somme front, between Thiepval and Albert, showing the situation before the start of the Battle of the Somme on 1 July 1916. The German trenches are shown in red, without names, and the British trenches, with names, in blue. The German position at top centre is the southern part of the Leipzig Redoubt. The British position *The Nab* is one of very many 'noses', or small salients, along the Western Front. The map was drawn by draughtsmen of 4th Field Survey Company RE (with Fourth Army HQ) and printed at the Ordnance Survey (Southampton).

The Courcelette–Martinpuich–Pozières–Bazentins–High Wood–Contalmaison area of the Somme battlefield. Part of the British 1:20,000 scale trench map Area of Martinpuich (GSGS 3236) drawn by draughtsmen of 4th Field Survey Company RE (with Fourth Army HQ) with trenches corrected to 6 July 1916 and printed at the Ordnance Survey (Southampton), showing in red all the trenches (German and British) existing on that date, following the start of the Battle of the Somme, and new trenches, dug after that date during the battle as the British advanced, in manuscript with their names added by the officer, Major J. Best of the Machine Gun Corps, to whom this map belonged.

British 1:10,000 scale manuscript map, on tracing paper, of the area around Flers and Gueudecourt in late 1916 at the end of the Battle of the Somme. Trenches and tracks are shown with their names, along with the divisional and brigade boundaries, headquarters and landmarks such as 'wrecked tank'. Tanks, a new British invention, were first used on 15 September 1916 in the Battle of Flers-Courcelette, and helped in the capture of Flers. As part of a British local phonetic trench naming scheme, Flare Alley is near Flers, and Gird Trench near Gueudecourt.

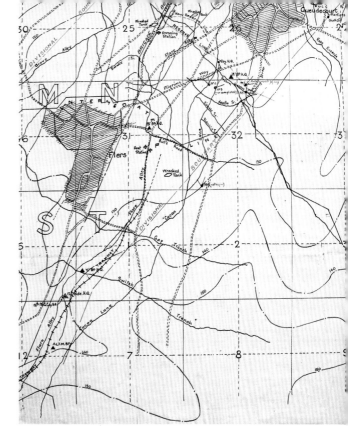

British 1:20,000 scale trench map, produced for Fifth Army by 5th Field Survey Company RE, of the Gommecourt–Hébuterne–Serre area at the end of the Somme battle. Gommecourt and Serre were both attacked by the British on 1 July 1916, but the attacks failed all along this northern part of the Somme battle front. German trenches, with names, are shown in red. Only the British front is shown, as a pecked red line, for security reasons.

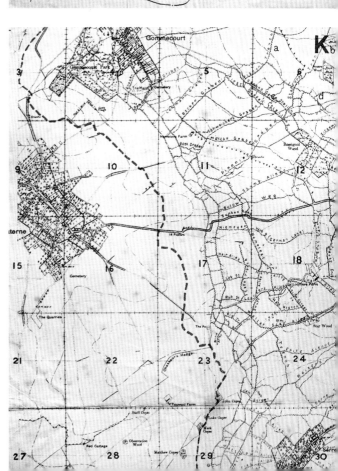

British trench map of the Zwarteleen–Hill 60–Battle Wood area in early 1917. German trenches are shown in red, with their names given by the British in blue. Note that all these names begin with the letter 'I'. Second Army had adopted a naming system for enemy trenches based on the map square system, and all these trenches fall within the 6,000 yard square 'I'. To the east of this was square 'J', in which all names of German trenches began with that letter. British trenches are not shown for security reasons. Massive mines were blown under Hill 60 and the Caterpillar on 7 June 1917, the start of the Battle of Messines.

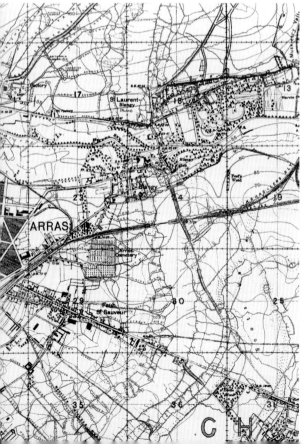

British 'Secret' edition 1:20,000 scale trench map, sheet 51bNW, dated 10 October 1916. British trenches, with their names, are in blue, and the German trench system in red. The British advanced in this sector on 9 April 1917 at the start of the Battle of Arras. Prior to this, however, the Germans had retired, in the area south of Arras, to their new rear position, the Hindenburg Line (*Siegfried Stellung*). British communication trenches north of the River Scarpe are named after months of the year, and those south of the river follow an alphabetical scheme, beginning with 'H' in the south and 'I' nearer to the river.

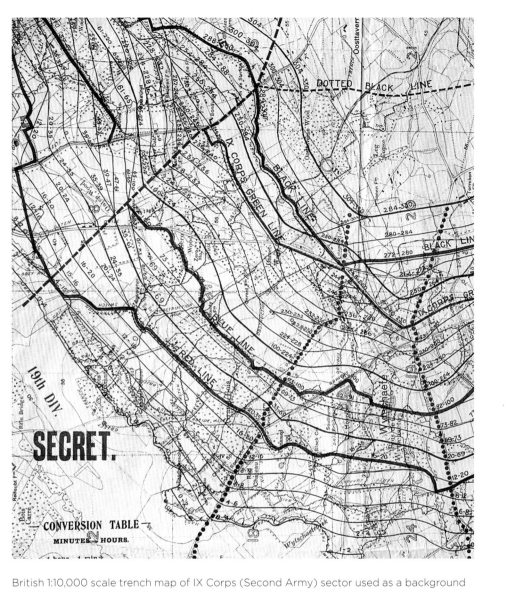

British 1:10,000 scale trench map of IX Corps (Second Army) sector used as a background for a blue 'Secret' overprint showing the Second Army field artillery creeping barrage map for the Battle of Messines, 7 June 1917. The thick blue lines, Red Line, Blue Line, IX Corps Green Line, Black Line, etc., are the successive objectives, the thick pecked and dotted lines are formation boundaries, and the more or less parallel thin blue lines show the timed lifts of the barrage from zero hour: 0–4 minutes, 4–6 minutes, 6–8 minutes, etc. up to 330 minutes. The background map shows the German trenches in red, with their names, given by the British, in blue.

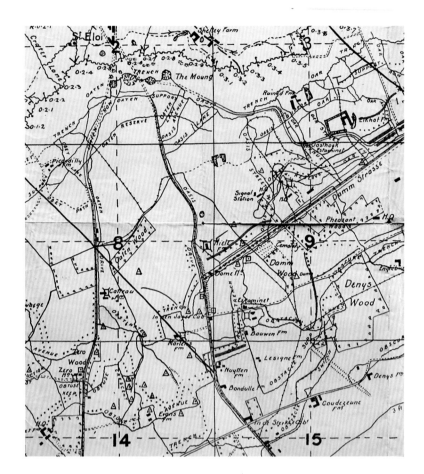

Simplified British trench map of the St Eloi sector and area to the south towards the high ground of the Wytschaete-Messines Ridge and the lower ground around Oostaverne to its east. This rather sketchy map was made as part of the preparations for the Battle of Messines (7 June 1917), and shows elements of the German rear organisation. While most of the British and German trenches, with their names, are in black, certain enemy positions have been overprinted in red. The British trenches are at the top of the map in the area St Eloi–Shelley Farm. Just south of St Eloi village, the German front trench system includes the large mine craters around Oaten Trench and The Mound.

Opposite: The Het Sas–Boesinghe–Pilckem Ridge area of the Ypres Salient, north of the city of Ypres. Part of the German 1:10,000 *Stellungskarte* (trench map) Langemarck, Geheim! (Secret), dated 3 May 1917, and produced by *Vermessungs-Abteilung 1* with the German Fourth Army, which held the Flanders front. The British trenches are in red, and the German trenches, with names, in blue. The Ypres–Nieuport Canal can be seen bottom left. The strong German Albrecht Stellung defensive position runs through Pilckem. German sector names, boundaries and artillery target numbers are in red. This was to become part of the battlefield of Third Ypres, the Allied attack being launched on 31 July 1917 after a prolonged artillery bombardment which, together with the heavy rain of early August, turned the terrain into a treacherous slough.

British 1:40,000 scale logistical map (1917–18) of the eastern part of the Ypres Salient as it was at the end of the Third Battle of Ypres. The destroyed village of Passchendaele is in top right, and the city of Ypres is off to the left. This map shows the British rear organisation, in particular the standard gauge, light railway and metre gauge railways (black), and roads (red), which were pushed forward as the battle progressed, and the associated railheads, dumps and howitzer spurs. It is significant that the railways could be pushed much further forward than the roads; plank roads had to be used over the boggy, shell-churned terrain east of Ypres. Of particular interest is the wealth of names given to the railway lines and localities. The high ground of the Gheluvelt Plateau and Passchendaele Ridge is in the darker yellow.

British 1:40,000 scale logistical map (1917–18) of the western part of the Ypres Salient as it was at the end of the Third Battle of Ypres (popularly known as the Battle of Passchendaele), showing the British rear organisation: railways (black), roads (red), dumps, etc. The plethora of names is of particular interest. The city of Ypres is towards the bottom left of the map, where the names Asylum, Barrack, Menin Gate and Moat Gun Spur can be seen.

Opposite: British trench map of the Monchy-le-Preux area, south-east of Arras, in 1918. Captured by the British in 1917, during the Battle of Arras, some of this area was recaptured by the Germans during their great offensives of March–April 1918. Where the situation was at all fluid, as here, all the trenches (with their names) were shown in red. Some groups of names can be seen, notably those associated with horsed artillery, with tools and utensils, and with animals and birds.

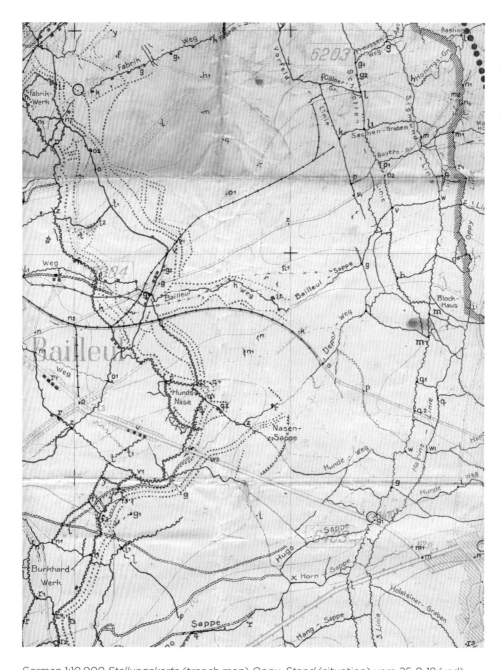

German 1:10,000 *Stellungskarte* (trench map) *Oppy*, *Stand* (situation) *vom 25-8-18* (red) overprinted *12-9-18* (blue), of the Bailleul area on the east side of the Vimy Ridge. British trenches in red, with names given by the Germans, as at 25 August 1918, and German trenches in blue, with names, as at 12 September. However, the *Vorderste feindliche Linie* (enemy front line) is given as the hatched blue line on the right (the *Oppy Linie*), and the *Vorderste deutsche Linie* (German front line) is designated by the line of heavy blue dots to its east. Thus many of the German trenches (blue) shown on this map have been relinquished. Map produced by *Gruppenkartenstelle A, bayr. Verm[essungs]. Abt[eilung]. 9.* (Group Map Section A, Bavarian Field Survey Company 9).

IX

GERMAN TRENCH NAMES

Glossary

Allee	Alley	*Riegel*	Switch/Covering Position
Bastion	Stronghold	*Sappe*	Sap
Bogen	Salient	*Schanz*	Entrenchments
Eck	Corner/Angle	*Steig/Steige*	Steep Track
Feste	Large Redoubt	*Stellung*	Position
Gabel	Fork	*Stiege*	Stairs/Staircase
Gasse	Alley	*Stollen*	Tunnel
Graben	Trench	*Strasse*	Street
Gut	Estate/Farm	*Stutzpunkt*	Strongpoint
Hof	Hotel/Inn/Farm	*Verbindungsgraben*	Communication Trench
Höhe	Hill	*Verbindungsweg*	Communication Trench
Laufgraben	Communication Trench	*Wald*	Wood
Linie	Line	*Wall*	Rampart
Mulde	Hollow/Valley	*Weg*	Lane or Way
Nase	Nose/Salient	*Werk*	Redoubt
Pfad	Path	*Zwischen-Stellung*	Intermediate Trench

German Naming in Context

Although this book is about British trench names it is impossible, for the same reasons that we have looked at French trench names, to discuss these without reference to names the Germans gave to the trenches on both sides of no man's land. We need to be aware of these because many German names for their own trenches were appropriated by the Allies, and often continued in use after the trenches in question had been captured. Many of the names given by the Germans to their own trenches, and to a lesser extent to their

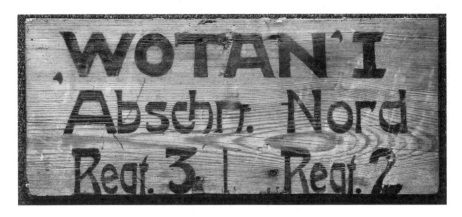

The Wotan Stellung (known to the British as the Drocourt–Quéant Line) was a German rear position in 1918. The Germans were particularly fond of names from Nordic mythology, This board is in the Imperial War Museum.

enemies' trenches, have already been encountered in earlier chapters on British and French naming. We should also note that spelling is not consistent on German maps (e.g. *Rupprecht* and *Ruprecht*), and that the same trench can be designated in different ways at different periods (e.g. *Hafen-Graben* and *Hafen-Weg*). Similar phenomena occurred in the Allied camp.

A study of German trench maps (*Stellungskarten*) makes it clear that, during the Battle of the Somme as well as earlier, German names for their own trenches were immediately appropriated (as soon as acquired through captured maps, orders, etc.) by the British and French, and used without delay on their own maps. For example, *Martinspfad* at Thiepval became *Martins Lane*. Many of these German trench names that appeared on British trench maps are included in the Gazetteer that forms the second part of this book. Secondly, it is important to be able to compare and contrast Allied and German patterns, policies and styles of naming. These were often shared, but there were striking cultural differences as we have already noted.

Max Eckert, the eminent German geographer who also served as a survey officer in Third Army in the Champagne–Argonne area, stated that German practice (perhaps he was only talking about Third Army) was generally only to name their own trenches.[1] There was a very good reason for this. Following the failure of the Schlieffen Plan to knock out France in 1914, German strategy in the 1915–17 period was to stand on the defensive in the west and to concentrate on defeating Russia. There was one major exception to this – Falkenhayn's offensive against Verdun in 1916. The Germans succeeded in their strategy to the extent that during 1917 Russia was eliminated as a military threat by her internal revolutions of that year. Germany was therefore able to force the Bolsheviks to sign the Treaty of Brest-Litovsk in January 1918 and shift most of her best formations to the west for the series of major offensives in France and Flanders, which were only held with great difficulty by the French and British Armies and defeated with the major assistance of the newly arriving Americans.

This mainly defensive strategy in the west implied that the Germans, unlike the Allies, were committed to staying put. The trenches of their defensive positions, amplified and elaborated by successive positions to the rear, were of supreme importance to them, and were appropriately named after German cities, towns, regions, local commanders and officers and also from the national memory bank of mythological, figurehead and territorial names. The names of members of royal families, and important military figures such as von der Tann, Moltke and von Kluck, occurred frequently. As they were not, in general, planning to advance in the west, it was not so important for them to name the Allied trenches. They did, however, plot these very accurately on their maps from air photos, using increasingly sophisticated and scientific photogrammetric techniques that were far ahead of those of the Allies.[2] They needed this accurate plotting for the precise direction of artillery fire.

Eckert wrongly believed that the British and French as a rule only named German trenches.[3] In fact they named their own trenches first, and only later the German ones, but when they did get around to this they did it very thoroughly and systematically. He presumably gained this impression by studying captured Allied trench maps, which only gave the names of the German trenches and in the 1914–16 period did not show their own trenches in any case.

An initial survey of names given by the Germans to their own trenches reveals little humour, and little out of the ordinary; as with the British, there were many descriptive and homely names, e.g. *Kaffeehausweg* (Coffee-House Lane) at Pilckem. The British view has traditionally been that the Germans lack subtle humour, their taste being for scatology and slapstick. Readers must make up their own minds in the face of such examples as *Nixen-Sappe* (Mermaids Sap) near Boesinghe, *Kummer-Weg* (Wretched Way) near Ploegsteert Wood, *Lach-Weg* (Laugh Way) at Thiepval, and *Wittwer-Strasse* (Widower Street) and *Krach-Strasse* (Crash/Bang Street) at Ovillers.

German trench names on the whole tended to be formal and descriptive. Perhaps this is only to be expected in a relatively undemocratic country which was newly industrialised, still dominated by traditional peasant agriculture, and with a small middle class. There was little spirit of independence as there was in Britain and France, and the centralising, military ethos was strong and coercive. On the other hand, one might expect a more subversive humour to be associated with large cities such as Berlin and Munich. Berlin in particular had a well-developed night club and cabaret culture, but both were significant centres of bohemianism and the avant garde.

The overwhelming impression given by a study of German trench maps is that German place names and the names of public and military figures were used. We should remember that Germany, and Prussia in particular, had a strong military tradition, and also a tradition of deference to authority, going back to the days of Frederick the Great, and that the Prussian Army had been undefeated since Blücher helped Wellington to defeat Napoleon at Waterloo. Most trenches were named after commanders, members of the royal families, German regions, cities, towns, rivers and other geographical features. The famous *Feste Schwaben* (*Schwaben Redoubt* to the British) at Thiepval was a good example of a regional name, while the *Leipzig Redoubt* south of Thiepval typified the city names.

Some commemorated regiments and their officers, or dealt with other military and naval associations. In a similar manner to the French, and to a lesser extent the British, the Germans commemorated the names of living or fallen commanders and other officers. *Feste Soden* and the *Heidenkopf* redoubt at Serre, were both named after local commanders, as was the *Feste Staufen* (known by the British as *Stuff Redoubt*) at Thiepval. Herbert Sulzbach confirmed this habit when he noted that particular positions were sometimes named after the COs of infantry units that held them.[4] The names of personalities and places associated with Germany's allies were also popular, and occasionally those of her enemies appeared as well. Girls' names also feature occasionally.

The officers of the Prussian State Survey (*Landesaufnahme*) and War Survey Organisation (*Kriegsvermessungswesen*) were commemorated by their maps officers in certain hill names: *Betrabhöhe*, *Bölckehöhe* and *Friedhöhe* in the Argonne, and *Eckerthöhe* and the *Hornberg* near Terron. Large numbers of German cities and towns also gave their names: *Berlin*, *Hamburg*, *Leipzig*, *Dresden*, *München*, *Düsseldorf*, *Köln*, *Koblenz*. Many original and graphic names were given to hill-features or mountains: *Lafettenschwanz* (Gun-carriage Trail; *der Schwanz* can also mean prick or cock), *Haubitzberg* (Howitzer Mount), *Nashorn* (Nose Horn), *Kanonenberg* (Cannon Mount), etc.[5] The name that appears to be *Alle Gott* Trench (Péronne), perhaps from the hymn: *Nun danket alle Gott* (Now thank we all our God), may have stimulated the French (and after them the British) to name two trenches in the same area *Gott mit Uns* Trench and *Uber Alles* Trench. German trench maps (*Stellungskarten*) of the Eastern (Russian) Front in the author's collection indicate that naming here followed the same pattern as in the west. Eastern Front maps and air photos show that in many areas trench systems (and mine warfare) were as fully developed as in the west.

The following survey takes sectors of the front from north to south. It is by no means comprehensive, but within each sector chosen as a case study it tries to give a true flavour. While it covers the more important trenches and many of the shorter and subsidiary ones, it may well omit certain trench names in the immediate area of the front and support lines which were only shown on the largest-scale plans. Tentative translations have been given for many names, or at least some indication of derivation – e.g. city or river – but no attempt has been made to provide a translation where the name appears to be that of a person; it is assumed that these are officers' names.

Ypres Salient (*Ypern Bogen*)

In 1916–17 the German defences in the northern sector of the Ypres Salient (Fourth Army) consisted of major positions behind the front line, called the *Albrecht Stellung* (second or main position), the *Wilhelm Stellung* (third position) and *Flandern I, II, III Stellungen*. These important positions were subdivided into stretches of trench or defended localities named after German historical military notables or, in some cases, places: *Bismarck, Moltke, Graf Haseler, Roon, Prinz Friedrich Karl, von der Tann, Werder, Alvensleben, Kronprinz I, Herzog Albrecht, Horn, Graf Tauentzien Nord, Mitte* and *Süd, Busse, Bredt, Hindenburg, Winterfeld, Prinz Heinrich, Wartenburg, Borbersburg*, etc. Between these key positions were the new zones of the defence-in-depth system, devised in principle by Colonel von Lossberg after the setback of the Somme; between the front (outpost) line and the *Albrecht Stellung* was the thinly held forward zone, between the *Albrecht* and *Wilhelm Stellungen* the battle zone, and between the *Wilhelm* and *Flandern Stellungen* the rear zone. At the back of the forward zone was the *Stutzpunktlinie* – a belt of strongpoints and fortified localities.[6]

There were also subsidiary positions and switch-lines, several of which took their names from places on the Belgian map: *Winterstellung, Langemarck-Nord & Süd, Koekuit Stellung, Wijdendrift Stellung, Bohne Wald-Stellung, Brucken Stellung, Kanal Stellung* (along the Yser Canal), *Nixen Linie, Werder Linie, Draaibank Linie, Hansa Linie, Tripp-Linie, Lützow-Linie Nord* and *Süd*.

Trenches in this sector included *Grunel-Hof Graben, Lebens-Ader* (Lifeline/ Artery), *Müller-Graben, Preussen-Graben* (Prussia Trench), *Sachsen-Graben* (Saxon Trench), *Minengraben* (Mine Trench), *Kronprinz-Graben* (Crown Prince Trench), *Ziegelei-Graben* (Brickworks Trench) and Bixschoote-Graben (after the village). Communication trenches included many personal and place names: *Kaffeehausweg* (Coffee-House Lane) at *Pilckem, Ost-Weg* and *West-Weg* (East and West Lanes), *Jäger-Weg* (Rifles Lane), *Botinenkampf-Weg*

(Messengers Battle Lane), *Wiedermann-Weg*, *Oberer Drigalski-Weg*, *Schneider-Weg*, *Hammerstein-Weg*, *Werder-Weg*, *Mainweg*, *Heynen-Weg*, *Benz-Weg*, *Weber-Weg*, *Erdwerk-Weg* (Earthwork Lane), *Leonhard-Weg*, *Knechtel-Weg*, *Sentsch-Weg*, *Versen-Weg*, *Sappe Edelshein*, *Beaulieu-Weg*, *Wartenburg-Weg*, *Laufgraben I*, *II* and *III* (Communication Trenches), *Waltersdorff-Sappe*, *Möller-Sappe*, *Beerstburg-Sappe*, *Flügelweg* (Wing Lane), *Nixen-Sappe* (Mermaids Sap), *Kolonnen-Weg* (Columns Lane) and *Laufgraben Bruhn*. Strongpoints here included *Riedel Stutzpunkt*, *Flankierend Schützen-Nest I*, *II* and *III* (Flanking Fire Nest I, II, III).

In the Mouse Trap Farm–Wieltje–St Julien area, were *Schrapnell-Weg* (Shrapnel Lane), *Herzog Albrecht Weg* (Duke Albrecht Lane), *Cecilien-Weg* (Cecilia Lane, after a queen), *Kronprinz-Weg* (Crown Prince Lane), *Schwarzhof-Weg* (Black Farm Lane), *von Hangessen-Weg*, *Regiments-Gut* (Regiment Estate), *Artillerie-Gut* (Artillery Estate), *Schloss-Stellung* (Castle Position, at Mouse Trap Farm), *Wasserschloss* (British *Mouse Trap Farm*), and *Engländer Hof* (British *Turco Farm*). In the Passchendaele area Hill 50, south of Westroosebeke, was called *Feldherrnhügel* (Commanders Hill), and north-west of Wallemolen was *Haus Kirchner* (Kirchner House). At Zonnebeke was *Brigade Hof* (Brigade Farm), and at Frezenberg were *Hindenburg-Gut* (Hindenburg Estate) and *Klein Engländer Wäldchen* (Little Englishman Copse).

The area east and south-east of Ypres saw some typical German names being given to buildings, topographical features and trenches. At Hooge was *Schlossruine Hooge* (Ruined Castle; Hooge Château), and towards Nonne Boschen were *Shrapnell-Allee* (Shrapnel Avenue) and *Nonnen-Weg* (Nuns Lane). The high point of the Menin Road ridge was named *Strassburger Tor* (Strassburg Gate). East of Zillebeke was *Trapez Wäldchen* (Trapezium Copse) and *Zuaven Waldchen* (*Zouave Wood* to the British), while east of Hill 60 was *Granat Hof* (Shell Farm). The feature called *The Bluff* by the British on the north side of the Ypres–Comines canal was named *Grosse Bastion* (Great Stronghold) by the Germans; over the canal was *Kleine Bastion* (Little Stronghold), and nearby was *Granat Wäldchen* (Shell Copse). South of the canal were *Engländer Schanz* (English Entrenchments), *Schotten Schanz* (Scottish Entrenchments), *Bayernschloss* (Bavaria Castle; Hollebeke Château) and *Fasanen-Wald* (Pheasant Wood).

From Railway Wood southwards past Hooge and Hill 60 ran the trenches *von der Decken-Weg*, *Leuthold-Weg*, *Ypern-Weg* (Ypres Lane), *Knörzer-Weg*, *Nördlich* and *Südlich See-Weg* (Lake Lane, at Bellewaarde Lake), *Jäger-Graben* (Riflemans Trench), *1.*, *2.* and *3. Linie*, *Hecken-Stellung* (Hedge Position), *Stein-Graben* (Stone Trench), the *Hecken-Höhe* (Hedge Hill) redoubt, *2. Stellung*, *Pionier-Weg* (Pioneer Lane), *Rekruten-Stellung* (Recruits Position), *Meissen-Gasse* (Meissen Alley), *Geier-Weg* (Vulture Lane), *Höhen-Linie*

(Heights Line), *Geler-Weg*, *Keller-Weg* (Cellar Lane), *Strassburger-Höhe* (Strassburg Hill), *Vossbein-Graben*, *Sack-Stellung* (Sandbag Position), *Stabs-Graben* (Staff-Officers Trench), *Kaiser-Friedrich-Weg*, *Bayern-Weg* (Bavaria Lane), *Kommandeur-Weg* (Commander Lane), *Schickfuss Linie*, *Königen Olga-Weg* (Queen Olga Lane), *Königen Charlotte-Weg* (Queen Charlotte Lane), *Preussen* (Prussia), *Köffner-Weg*, *Oberst Gluck Weg* (Colonel Gluck Lane), *Artur V.W.16* (Arthur CT 16), *Berthold-Weg*, *Breyer-Weg*, *Fallersleben* (a town), *Krummel-Weg*, *Bulgaren-Weg* (Bulgaria Lane), *Herzog Albrecht* (Duke Albrecht), *Alarm-Weg* (Alarm Lane), *Annäherungs-Weg* (Approach Lane), *Bereits.*, *Klein-Zillebeke* (Stand-by, Klein Zillebeke), *Langer-Weg* (Long Lane), *Kafferweg* (Thickhead Lane), *Kanal-Weg* (along canal, near the Bluff), *Strassen-Weg* (Street Lane, near the Damstrasse), *Knüppe[l] Damm* (Log Road), *Schiess-Weg* (Firing Lane), *Raab-Weg*, *Burkhardt-Weg*, *Müller-Weg*, *Frosch-Feste* (Frog Redoubt), *Raabriegel* (Raab Switch), *Engels-Weg* (Engels Lane), *Engels Feste* (Engels Redoubt), *Trichter-Riegel* (Crater Switch, as St Eloi), *Eder* and *Ems* (both rivers, CTs), and *Neuer-Bach* (New Stream).

Messines–Wytschaete Ridge (*Wytschaete Bogen*)

On the Messines–Wytschaete Ridge were *Granatenhof* (Shells Farm), *Mark-Wald* (Borderland Wood), *Hessen-Wald* (Hesse Wood), *Bayern-Hof* (Bavaria Farm), *Bayern-Wald* (Bavaria Wood), *Schützen-Hof* (Gunners Farm), *Nasen-Wald* (Nose Wood). In the *Bayernwald* sector the following trenches and features appeared on a large-scale plan of 1916:[7] *1a Linie* and *1b Linie* (1a and 1b Lines), *Bauer-Riegel* (Farmer Switch), *Bauern-Weg* (Farmers Lane), *Bauer-Eck* (Farmer Corner), *Bauern-Weg Eckboch* (Farmers Lane Corner Support), *Taleck* (Valley Corner), *Sandbach* (Sand Stream), *Elbe* (river), *Fürsten-Weg* (Prince Lane), *Bayern-Riegel* (Bavaria Switch), *Basel* (city), *Berlin* (city), *Breslau* (city), *Neckau*, *Bayer-Steig* (Bavaria Steep Track), *Hessen-Riegel* (Hesse Switch), *Kapellerie-Stellung* (Band Position), *Bayern-Weg* (Bavaria Lane), *Hessen Haus* (Hesse House), *Maas* (Meuse), *Cassel* (city), *Cöln* (Cologne), *Granathaüser* (Shell Houses), *Schweinter-Steg.*, *Keasy-Weg*, *Wennig-Wege* [sic], *Schweirle-Steig* (Difficult Steep Track), *Sachsen* (Saxon), *November Feste* (November Redoubt), *Breisig Linie* (town), *Wald-Weg* (Wood Lane), *Sterkte-Feste* (Strong Redoubt), *Donau* (Danube), *Jäger Feste* (Rifles Redoubt), *Zollern Feste* (Zollern Redoubt), *Pigge-Graben* and *Rupprecht-Feste* (Rupprecht Redoubt), named after the Crown Prince of Bavaria. German names given to British trenches on this plan included *Zick-Zack-Weg* (Zig-Zag Lane), *Casseler-Weg* (Cassel Lane) and *Eck-Weg* (Corner Lane).

From Wytschaete southwards past Messines, St Yves and Warneton to Ploegsteert many personal names appeared among others: *Füchselweg* (Little Fox Lane), *Paitsweg*, *Paifert-Weg*, *Beomans-Weg*, *Sonne-Linie* (Sun Line), *Stocksweg* (Sticks Lane), *Schütze-Graben* (Gun Trench), *Bayern-Graben* (Bavaria Trench) and *Bayern Stellung* (Bavaria Position). At Messines were *Tigergang* (Tiger Way) and *Lowengang* (Lion Way), and farther south by the Douve river were *Douve-Graben* (Douve Trench) and *Müller-Graben*. Around Ploegsteert Wood came *Berchen-Graben*, *Kummer-Weg* (Wretched Way), *Sity Promenade*, *Franke-Weg* (Franconian Lane), *Schinnerer-Weg* and *Rüben-Weg* (just north of Factory Farm, the moated ruins known to the Germans as *Wasser-Gut*).

Trenches and positions in the Ploegsteert–Armentières area included *Wasser-Gut* (Water Estate), the delightful *Bier-Gut* (Beer Estate), *Finken-Weg* (Finch Lane), *Jäger-Graben* (Riflemens Trench), *Kapital-Weg* (Royal Lane), *Schröder-Graben*, *Schmidt-Graben*, *Tonnen-Weg* (Barrel Lane), *Linden-Gut* (Lime Trees Estate), *Le Gheer-Str.* (hamlet name), *Laffert-Weg* [sic], *Prinzen-Weg* (Princes Lane), *Delbeque-Weg* (farm name), *Bühlau-Graben*, *Altes 104 Gut* (Old 104 Estate), *Liller-Weg* (Lille Lane), *Werder-Weg*, *Daons Gut*, *Welks-Weg*, *Klopres-Graben*, *Paver-Graben*, *Planitz-Str.*, *Bärenspring-blick* (Bears-Jump View, near Les Oursins Ferme), *Turm-Gut* (Tower Estate), *Despierre-Weg* (farm name), *Stapel-Platz* (Depot Square), *Westl. Bahngraben* (West Railway Trench, along railway), *Insof-Str.*, *Granaten-Garten* (Shells Garden), *Westgutweg* (West Farm Lane), *Kirchhof-Str.* (Churchyard Street), *Bomben-Graben* (Bombs Trench), *Waschenpost-Weg* (Washhouse Lane), *Lys-Str.* (Lys Street), *Linden-Str.* (Limes Street) and *Mühlen-Gut* (Mill Estate).

Armentières–Béthune Sector

Between Armentières and Béthune, German front trenches and sectors were named after cities – *Berlin*, *Crefeld*, etc.[8] In the Fromelles–Loos sector, largely overlapping the above, in the sector of the Bavarian Sixth Army, the names in use for German trenches at the beginning of 1918, many of which had been in use in October 1915, were largely topographical or related to German cities and regions, with an admixture of personal names. From Fromelles to just north of Neuve Chapelle were:[9] *Alte & Neue Franke Graben* (Old and New Franconian Trench), *Wiedermeier Graben* (an aesthetic style), *Schlossweg* (Castle Lane), *Ölgraben* (Oil Trench), *Scheinstellung* (Dummy Position), *Eichel-Graben* (Acorn Trench), *Rue d'Enfer* (trench parallel to road of that name), *Mühlen-Weg* (Mill Lane), *Münster-gasse* (Munster Alley), *Mecklenburger-Stiege* (Mecklenburg Steps), *Bauhof Weg* (Building Yard Lane), *Preussen-Graben*

(Prussian Trench), *Schmidt-Graben* (Smith Trench), *Kuh-Graben* (Cow Trench), *Petri-Graben* (Petri-Trench), *Tölzergraben* (Tölzer Land in Upper Bavaria), *Leierbach-Eck* (Leierbach Corner), *Iburg*, *Merkt-Graben* (Observed or Marked Trench), *Landsturm-Graben* (Militia Trench), *Augsburger-Graben* (Augsburg Trench), *Isarsteig* (Isar, a Bavarian river), *Schützen Haus Werk* (Gun House Redoubt), *Fürtherstr.* (Fürth Street), *Rupprecht-Graben* (Bavarian Crown Prince and Army Commander) and *Mittel-Weg* (Middle Lane).

In the Neuve Chapelle–Richebourg sector were: *Pietre-Weg* (Moulin du Pietre), *Nord-Weg* (North Lane), *Franzosen-Weg* (French Lane), *Russen-Weg* and *Ecke* (Russian Lane and Corner), *Brücken-kopf* (Bridgehead), *Engländer-Weg* (Englishman's Lane), *Depot-Weg* (Depot Lane), *Biez-Weg* (Bois de Biez), *Moltke-Weg* (commander), *Backungs-Wall* (Rampart), *Mindener-Weg* (Minden Lane), *Ruprecht-Weg* (commander), *Doubois-Weg* (Rue du Bois, Boar's Head), *Lipper-Weg*, *Dernald-Graben* and *Westliche-Weg* (Western Lane).

From Festubert to Givenchy appeared a similar range of names: *Apfel-Hof Weg* (Orchard Lane, Ferme du Bois), *Ulanen-Weg* (Uhlans Lane, cavalry), *Feldküchen-Weg* (Field Kitchen Lane), *Jägerhof-Weg* (Riflemens Yard Lane), *Damm-Weg* (Embankment Lane), *Friesen-Graben* (Friesian Trench), *Hameliner-Graben/Weg* (Hamelin, of Pied Piper fame), *Niedersachsen-Weg* (Lower Saxony), *Hildesheimer-Graben* (Hildesheim Trench), *Harzer-Graben* (Harz Trench), *Münchner-Haus* (Munich House), *Nollendorf* (a general), *Ouvert* and *Rue d'Ouvert-Stellung* (hamlet name), *Küchen-Gut* (Kitchen Estate), *Zimermans-Graben*, *Braunschweiger-Weg* (Braunschweig Lane) and *Weiden-Graben* (Willow Trench).

In the Givenchy area some names appeared to describe graphically the violent and fiery nature of the mine warfare in that sector: *Stn.labfall* or *Stella-Fall* (Position's End, Duck's Bill), *Enten Schnabel* (Duck's Bill), *Trichter-Stellung* (Crater Position, Duck's Bill), *Abschneider* (Cut-off, Duck's Bill chord), *Blinddarm* (Blind Alley, Givenchy), *Hohl-Weg* (Sunken Road, Duck's Bill), *Riegel-Stellung* (Switch Position, Duck's Bill), *Annäherungsgraben/weg 1 & 2* (Approach Trench or Lane), *Rauchhaupthöhe* (Smoke/Fumes Main Hill), *Schwefel Graben* (Sulphur or Brimstone Trench), *Nord-Weg* (North Lane), *Ulanen-Weg* (Uhlan Lane), *Grenz-Weg* (Boundary Lane) and *Senf-Graben* (Mustard Trench).

From Givenchy to the La Bassée Canal were: *Div.-Graben* (Division Trench), *Soelten-Weg*, *Rochus-Graben*, *Tal-Stellung* (Valley Position), *Pfalz-Graben* (Rhineland Trench), *Mittel-Stellung* (Middle Position), *Elfweiden-Graben* (11 Willows Trench), *Dorf-Graben/Weg* (Village Trench/Lane), *Westfalen-Graben* (Westphalia Trench), *Stützpunkt-am-Kanal* (Canal Strongpoint), *Kanal-Stellung* (Canal Position), *Kanal-Weg* (Canal Lane), *Stabs-Weg* (Staff Officers Lane),

Stützpunkt-Weg (Strongpoint Lane), *Brücken-Platz* (Bridge Square), *Damm-Weg* (Embankment Lane), *Stützpunkt-Weiderburg* (Pasture Hill Strongpoint), *Höhen-Stellung* (Hill Position), *Siegfried-Nord* (Siegfried North), *Rotes-Kreuz* (Red Cross), *Ziegelhaufen* (Brickstack), *Waldmann*, *Stützpunkt-Karl* (Karl Strongpoint), *Harzer-Weg* (Harz Lane), *Artillerie-Sicherungs-Stellung* (Artillery Protection Position), *La Bassée-Stellung* (La Bassée Position), *Pielbock/Prellbock-Weg*, *Mühlen-Weg* (Mill Lane), *Löwen-Schanze* (Lion Entrenchments), *Ziegel-Weg* (Brick Lane), *Weddigen-Weg* [sic], *1 Hauptkampf-Linie* (1st Main Battle Line) and *von der Tann* (19th century general).

In 1918 certain British positions were named on German maps, some names but not others being clearly derived from captured British originals: *Festubert-Islands* (same as British), *Waspen-Nest* (Wasps Nest), *Hindu-Graben* (Hindu Trench), *Beobachtungshof* (Observation Post), *Sieben-Gebirge* (Seven Mountains, Rhine) and *Flaggen-Stellung* (Flags Position).

South of the La Bassée Canal on the same maps was a variety of names, including many personal ones: *Pudding House* (from British map), *Feste Stammheim* (Stammheim Redoubt), *Hafen-Graben/Weg* and *Stellung* (Canal Basin Trench/Lane and Position), *Wiegand-Graben* (*Nordlich* and *Südlich*), *Kronprinzen-Eck* (Crown Prince Corner), *Ruprecht-Eck* (Rupert Corner), *Prinzen-Weg* (Princes Lane), *Bismarck-Weg* (Bismarck Lane), *Mühle-Weg* (Mill Lane), *Junkermann-Weg*, *Berthold-Weg*, *Kürzer-Weg* (Shorter Lane), *Kupke-Weg*, *Freund-Weg* (Friend Lane), *Hackertaüer-Weg*, *Seeman-Weg* (Seaman Lane), *Zechen-Bahn-Stellung*, *Zähringer-Weg*, *Peipe-Weg* (Pipe Lane), *Vorposten* (Advanced Posts), *Wartburg-Weg* (German mountain associated with Wolfram von Eschenbach who wrote part of *Parzifal*, and Walter von der Vogelweide, the medieval lyric poet who inspired Wagner's *Tannhäuser*), *Schubeiss-Weg*, *Kunke-Weg*, *Dohmann-Graben*, *Courtin-Graben*, *Handgranaten-Graben* (Hand Grenade Trench), *Feste-Manstein* (Manstein Redoubt), *Weiss-Weg* (White Lane), *Musikanten-Graben* (Musicians Trench), *Wenborn-Graben*, *Bober-Graben* (river), *Reichsgraf* (Imperial Count), *Schmandt-Graben* (mountain), *Spaar-Graben*, *Pionier-Weg* (Pioneer Lane), *Hohenzollern* (Hohenzollern Redoubt), *Flieger-Graben* (Airman Trench south of *The Dump*, Fosse 8), *Zeppelin-Graben* (Zeppelin Trench), *Schröer-Graben* and *Buchhotz-Graben*. Several of these names were used by the British after being obtained from captured German maps. There was also a trench or feature named *Schottisch* (Scottish) by July 1917 in the Loos sector; the British captured this nameboard.[10]

South of Lens, at the *Lorettohöhe* (Notre Dame de Lorette spur) at the north end of the Vimy Ridge, the site of savage battles in 1915 as the French struggled to capture the spur, were the *Totengraben* (Death Trench), the *Totenwiese* (Death Meadow) and the *Kanzel* (Pulpit) redoubt, the latter named after its commanding view. German trenches before their attack of 3 March 1915 also included *Sappe 1–15*, *Sappe A–E*, and *Steilhang 1–7* (steep slope or terrace). The depression east of the spur was named *Schlammulde* (Mud Valley), while that to the north was the *Krähenfussmulde* (Crowsfeet Valley). Roads on and near the spur were named *Barrikadenweg* (Barricade Way), *Kapellenweg* (Chapel Way) and *Höhenweg* (Hill Way). Important positions were the *Zuckerfabrikstellung* (Sugar Factory Position), *Lorettostellung* (Lorette Position), *Kapellenstellung* (Chapel Position) and *Kanzelstellung* (Pulpit Position), while the retrenchment on the east slope of the spur was the *Riegel-Stellung* (Switch Line).

Lens–Vimy Ridge–Arras Area (Sixth Army)

South of Lens and over the Vimy Ridge the following names had appeared by April 1917, and featured in the Battles of Vimy Ridge and Arras in April–May of that year; many were captured by the British and Canadians: *Fabarius-Riegel* (Fabarius Switch), *Magdeburg Schanze* (Magdeburg Entrenchments), *Hindenburg-Weg* and *Halberstädter-Weg* (Halberstadt Lane), while at Avion were *Avion-Riegel* (Avion Switch) and *Avion Stellung*, *Nord*, *West* & *Süd* (Avion Position). Continuing south were *Chausée-Stellung* (Road Position), *Glücksburg-Stellung* (Glücksburg Position), *Vimy Riegel* (Vimy Switch), *Einer-Weg* (Lane One), *Walpurgis-Weg* (woman's name), *Hasen-Weg* (Hare Lane), *Ruinen-Weg* (Ruins Lane), *Divisions-Weg* (Division Lane), *II & III Stellung*, *Kronprinzen Lager* (Crown Princes Camp), *K.T.K. Island Süd* & *Nord*, *Hanseaten-Lgr.* & *Weg* (Hanseatic Camp & Lane), *Fischer-Weg*, *Hannover-Weg* (Hanover Lane), *Koch-Weg*, *Kaiser-Weg* (Emperor Lane), *Pr. Heinrich-Weg* (Prince Henry Lane), *Sachsen-Lager* (Saxon Camp), *Berliner-Riegel* & *Haus* (Berlin Switch & House), *Prinz-Arnulf-Weg* (Prince Arnulf Lane), *Spandauer-Haus* & *Weg* (Spandau House & Lane), *Artillerie-Weg* (Artillery Lane), *Zwischen-Stellung*, *Nord* & *Süd* (Intermediate Position), *Schwaben-Weg* and *Tunnel* (Swabia Lane and Tunnel), *Riegel-Stellung* (Switch Position), *Landwehr-Graben/Weg* (Militia Trench/Lane), *Allgauer-Weg* (Allgau Lane), *Forster-Weg*, *Zehner-Weg* (Lane Ten), *Staubwasser-Weg* (Waterspray Lane), *Zollern-Lager* (Zollern Camp), *Grenadier-Weg* (Grenadier Lane), *Felsenketter* (Rock Chain), *Lindauer-Weg* (Lindau Lane), *Ulmer Haus* (Ulm House), *Graevewitz-Weg*, *Münchener-Weg/Hohl-Weg* (Munich Lane/Sunken Road), *Preussen-Weg* (Prussia Lane), *Poser-Weg* (Posen Lane), *Sanitäts-Weg* (First Aid Lane), *Gaul-Weg* (France Lane) and *Haselmayer-Weg*.

    In the area immediately north of the Scarpe river in April 1917 were *Scarpe-Riegel* (Scarpe Switch), *Gavreller-Weg* (Gavrelle Lane), *Gavrelle-Riegel*

(Gavrelle Switch), *Fresnes-Riegel* (Fresnes Switch), *Oppy–Riegel* (Oppy Switch), *Point du Jour Weg* and *Roeux-Weg*, which were all named after villages at the southern end of the Vimy Ridge. In addition were *Linhard-Weg*, *Mindel-Weg*, *Weissman-Weg*, *Polen-Werk* & *Weg* (Poland Strongpoint and Lane), *Festungs-Weg* (Fortress Lane) and *Brunnen-Weg* (Spring Lane).

Eckert stated that German practice (perhaps he was only talking about Third Army in the Champagne) was generally only to name their own trenches.[11] If this was the case, there were many exceptions. For example, north of Arras, German trench maps show that in 1915 they named the main French trenches forming successive defensive positions *1. Roclincourt-Stellung*, *2. Roclincourt-Stellung*, *Abdeckerei-Stellung* (Slaughterhouse Position, named after a pre-war building, not war humour), *St. Nicholas-Stellung Nord* and *Ost* (named after a suburb of Arras), and gave river names, including some from the Eastern Front, to French communication trenches in the Roclincourt and Labyrinthe sector. North of the Scarpe appeared successively *Meuse*, *Marne*, *Seine*, *Aube*, *Meurthe*, *Yonne*, *Loire*, *Garonne*, *Rhône*, *Somme*, *Pilica*, *Schelde*, *Düna*, *Weichsel*, *Nogat*, *Bug* and *Narew*.[12] German communication trenches in the same sector were named after German rivers – *Isar*, *Alz*, *Inn*, *Traun*, *Lech*, *Günz*, *Wehrlach*, etc., without any suffix. The British subsequently replaced these with the names of British rivers.

The names given in 1915 to German trenches in the Ecurie–Roclincourt–Blangy area[13] at the southern end of the Vimy Ridge are typical in that they are mostly tactical, geographical or commemorative: *Flankierungs-Anlage* (Flanking Position), *Sappe 1* (Sap I), *Feldweg Stellung* (Field Way Position), *Eiserner Kreuz Weg* (Iron Cross Lane), *Artillerie-Mulde* (Artillery Hollow), *Bastion A* (Strongpoint A), *Bereitschaft-Stellung* (Support Position), *Sachsen-W*eg (Saxon Lane), *Ruith-Weg*, *Augsburger-Weg* (Augsburg Lane), *Racke-Weg*, *Querschlag I* & *II* (Diagonal), *Günther-Pfad*, *Gabel-Sappe* (Fork Sap), *Kleines Dreieck* (Little Triangle), *2.*, *3.*, *4. Linie* (2nd, 3rd and 4th Lines), *Zehner-Graben* (Trench Ten), *Antwerpener-Graben* (Antwerp Trench), *Dreier-Graben* (Trench Three), *Mayr-Graben*, *Schnüzlein-Graben*, *Kommandeur-Graben* (Commander Trench), *Lutticher-Graben* (Liège Trench), *Metzer-Graben* (Metz Trench), *Gemersheim-Graben* (Gemersheim Trench), *Spatzen-Graben* (Sparrow Trench), *Gaul-Graben* (Old Nag Trench), *Hosen-Graben* (Trousers Trench), *Steinlein-Graben* (Little Stone Trench), *Hassimayr-Graben*, *Küchen-Graben* (Kitchen Trench), *Tal-Graben* (Valley Trench), *Lindauer-Graben*, *Maison blanche Graben* (named after hamlet), *Lemberger-Graben* (Lemberg Trench), *Helfer-Graben* (Helper Trench), *Strassburger-Graben* (Strassburg Trench), *Weissmann-Graben*, *Sebald-Graben*, *Obermayer-Graben*, *Salzach-Graben*, *Ziegelei-Graben* (Brickworks Trench), *Pauls-Graben* (Paul's Trench), *Schante...-Graben*, *Lille-Graben* (Lille

Trench), *Inn-Graben* (Inn river), *Benno-Graben*, *Mangfall-Graben* & *Westlich* & *Östlich* (Mangfall river), *Ost-Minne*, *Iller-Graben* (Ill river), *Sanitäts-Graben* (First Aid Trench), *West-Rinne* (West Channel), *Eigl-Graben*, *Isar Gabel* and *Graben* (Isar river, Fork and Trench), *Johanni-Graben* (John Trench). Several of these names, or variants of them, were still in use in 1917.

In the Oppy area, east of Vimy Ridge, in 1917–18, apart from trenches named after months of the year, first names of men and boys, and German states and cities, the Germans gave the following names, many of which are more human than the usual run of 'official' names, to their own trenches. From *The Nibelungenlied*, source for Wagner's Ring Cycle, were: *Brunhild-Graben* (Brunhild/Brunnhilde, Queen of Iceland, wife of Gunther), *Donner-Graben* (Thunder Trench; Thor), *Nibelungen-Graben* (Niebelungs Trench), *Krimhild-Graben* (Kriemhild Trench; wife of Siegfried, killer of Hagen) and *Sigmund-Graben* (Sigmund, father of Siegfried).

There was also here a great variety of other names, including possible references to British soldiers (Tommy), weapons, birds and animals: *Prusseit-Graben* (Prussite? an explosive), *Tomy-Sappe* (Tommy Sap), *Tomy-Graben* (Tommy Trench), *Hunds-Nase* (Dog's Nose), *Nasen-Sappe* (Nose Sap), *Hunde-Weg* (Dog Lane), *M.W. Graben* (Minenwerfer/Trench Mortar Trench), *Raben-Graben* (Raven Trench), *Adler-Graben* (Eagle Trench), *Reiher-Grabe* (Heron Trench), *Honings-Graben*, *Sachen-Graben* (Things/Objects Trench), *Maucksch-Graben*, *Schotten Linie* (Scots/Peas/Tall Story/Bulkhead Line), *Hang-Graben* (Slope Trench), *Kuh-Graben* (Cow Trench), *Küchen-Graben* (Kitchen Trench), *Kirche-Graben,* (Church Trench), *Schlangen-Graben* (Snaking Trench), *Aas-Graben* (Carrion Trench) and *Wasserholer-Weg* (Watercarriers Lane).

Divisional Sectors on the Lens–Arras front in April 1917 were named after commanders and notables: *Schwerin*, *Burg*, *Ansbach*, *Döberin*, *Fischer*, *Zollern*, *Arnulf*, *Loën*, *Rupprecht*, *Eberhardt*, *Schwaben* and *Habsburg*.

South of the Scarpe in April 1917 were many trenches named after French villages and German towns, regions, etc., among others: *Monchy-Riegel* (Monchy Switch), *Pelves-Riegel* (Pelves Switch), *Tilloy–Athies Riegel* (Tilloy–Athies Switch), *Die Ewigkeit* (Eternity or Eternal Rest) in *Artillerie-Mulde* (Artillery Valley), *Lemberg-Schanze* (Lemberg Entrenchments), *Wieland-Schanze* (Wieland Entrenchments), *Grenz-Weg* (Boundary Lane), *Sachsen-Weg* (Saxon Lane), *Wittelsbacher-Weg* (Wittelsbach Lane), the *Siegfriedstellung* (Siegfried Position, or Hindenburg Line), *Württemberger-Weg* (Wurtemburg Lane), *Artillerie-Schutzstellung* (Artillery Protection Position), *Pioneer-Weg* (Pioneer Lane), *Bayern-Weg* (Bavaria Lane), *Neuville-Nord* & *Süd* at Neuville-Vitasse, *Lange Gasse* (Long Alley), *Werk Altschul* (Old School Redoubt), *Potsdamer-Graben* (Potsdam Trench), *Sächsen-Weg*

(Saxon Trench), *Champagner-Graben* (Champagne Trench), *David-Graben* (David Trench), *Doktor-Graben* (Doctor Trench), *Edmund-Graben* (Edmund Trench), *Fulda-Graben* (Fulda, a city and river), *Kabel-Graben* (Cable Trench), *Mecklenburg* (city), *Schweriner-Weg* (Schwerin Lane), *Lumpen-Graben* (Rubbish/Rags Trench), *Münchener-Graben* (Munich Trench), *Cannstadter-Graben* (Cannstadt Trench) and *Calwer-Graben* (Calw Trench). A large number of other German trench names from the Arras and Somme areas can be found in the Gazetteer. In these areas, British trench maps often showed the German names obtained from captured maps.

Somme Area (First and Second Armies)

There were a huge number of trench names in the Somme area, more so as the operations of 1916 led to a proliferation of new trenches to a depth of many miles. The 1916 Battle of the Somme and subsequent operations before the German retirement in March 1917 also led to some fascinating appropriations of names by both sides. While the British and French took over German trench names from captured maps, the Germans used Allied names, sometimes with strange errors or adaptions. Thus the British *Starfish Line* becomes *Sarfish Line* on the German *Lagenkarte* of 13 February 1917, while *Pimple Alley* becomes *Pimpel Allee*, and we also find *Pine Trench*, *Sixth Avenue*, *Rutherford Allee*, *Maxwell Trench*, *Scotland Trench*, *Snag Trench*, etc., in the Le Sars area.[14]

In the Beaumont Hamel–Serre area were a large number of descriptive, regional and officers' names: *Ebelt-Graben*, *Bieber-Graben*, *Schloss-Stellung* (Castle Position), *Hindenburg-Weg* (Hindenburg Lane), *Junker-Graben* (Aristocrat Trench), *Irles-Graben* (Irles Trench), *Ellrichhauser-Graben*, *Geologen-Graben* (Geologists Trench), *Feste Alt-Württemburg* (Old Wurtemburg Redoubt), *Stations-Graben* (Station Trench), *Hang-Stellung* (Slope Position), *Lücke-Weg* (Breach/Gap Lane), *Neue-Weg* (New Lane), *Pflanz-Weg* (Plant Lane), *Sommer-Graben* (Summer Trench), *Landsturm-Graben* (Militia Trench), *Ziegesar-Graben*, *Steinbruch-Graben* (Quarry Trench), *Steinbruch-Stellung* (Quarry Position), *Schlucht-Graben* (Ravine Trench), *Leilung-Schlucht* (Y Ravine), *Langer-Graben* and *Riegel* (Long Trench and Switch), *Jahn-Graben*, *Brellauer-Weg*, *Serre-Riegel* (Serre Switch), *Mittel-Graben* (Middle Trench), *Flanken-St.* (Flank Street), *Rauch-Graben* (Smoke Trench), *Beaumont-Graben* (Beaumont Trench), *Soden-Graben* (officer's name), *Feste Soden* (Soden Redoubt), *Masken-Graben* (Mask Trench), *Kriegsminister-Graben* (War Minister Trench), *Artillerie-Graben* (Artillery Trench), *Rekruten-Graben* (Recruits Trench), *Küchen-Graben* (Kitchen Trench),

Landwehr-Stellung (Militia Position), *Bayern-Graben* (Bavaria Trench, at the *Heidenkopf*), *Kehl-Graben* (Throat Trench), *Gralsburg* (Grail Mount, Arthurian myth), *Bomben-Weg* (Bombs Way, near Falfemont Farm), *Röhrle-Graben*, *Tübinger-Stellung* and *St.*, *Sappen-Stellung* (Saps Position), *Fischer-Graben*, *Feldbahn-Graben* (Light Railway Trench), *Grevillers-Riegel* (Grevillers Switch), *R. Stellung* ('R' Position) and *Grandcourt-Riegel* (Grandcourt Switch).

A German trench map of the Ancre area, north of Albert, dated September 1916,[15] shows a large number of trench names, nearly every one of which later appeared on British maps. In the Thiepval and St Pierre Divion area were *Hansa-Weg* and *Stellung* (Hansa Lane and Position), *Serben-Weg* (Serbia

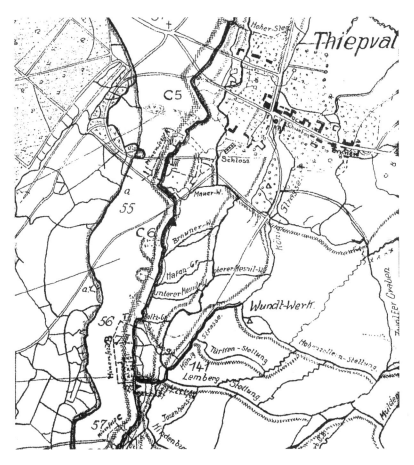

German trench map of the Thiepval–Leipzig Redoubt area, 1916, showing the British trenches on the left and the strong German positions on the right of no man's land. The Wundt-Werk was known to the British as the Wonder Work.

Lane), *Verbindungs-Riegel* (Communication Switch), *Stein-Weg* (Stone Lane), *Meisen-Gasse* and *Nest* (Titmouse Alley and Nest), *Münster-Graben* and *Gasse* (Munster Trench and Alley), *Teufel/Teufels-Graben* (Devil's Trench, from front line to Schwaben Redoubt), *Buck-Graben* (Hump Trench, from front line to Schwaben Redoubt), *Strassburger Stellung* and *Steige* (Strassburg Position and Steep-Track), *Steinweg* (Stone Lane, St Pierre Divion; Pierre = Stone), *Geheimweg* (Secret Lane), *Pfalzburger-Steige* (Pfalzburg Steep-Track), *Feste Schwaben* and *Schwaben-Graben* (British *Schwaben Redoubt* and Trench), *Hoher-Stellung* (High Position), *Markt-Gasse* and *Graben* (Market Alley and Trench), *Brauerei-Weg* (Brewery Lane), *Friedhof-Weg* (Cemetery Lane), *Schloss-Graben* (Château Trench, Thiepval), *Martinspfad* (British *Martins Lane*), *Josenhans-Graben* (Josenhans Trench), *Bulgaren-Graben* (Bulgaria Trench), *Grüne-Stellung* (Green Position), *Zollern-Graben* (British *Zollern Trench*), *Soden-Platz* (Soden Square), *Zwolfer-Graben, Flanken-Stellung* (Flank Position), *Kanonenwen* (Gun Lane), *Hessen-Weg* (Hesse Lane), *Feste Staufen, Staufen-Graben, Stellung, Riegel* and *Weg* (Staufen Redoubt, Trench, Position, Switch and Lane; British *Stuff Redoubt* and *Stuff Trench*), *Lach-Weg* (Laugh Way), *Rettberg-Weg* (Rettberg Way), *Oberer* and *Unterer Mesnilweg* (Higher and Lower Mesnil Lane), *König-strasse* (King Street), *Hafen-Graben* (Harbour Trench), *Brauner-Weg* (Brown Lane), *Mauer-Weg* (Wall Lane), *Park-Stellung* (Park Position, Park of Thiepval Château), *Kurzer-Weg* (Short Lane), *Holtz-Graben* (Timber Trench) *Schlüter-Graben* and *Tenfels-Graben* (?*Teufels Graben* = Devil's Trench).

In the Grandcourt–Courcelette area were *Grandcourt-Riegel* (Grandcourt Switch), *Courcelette-Riegel* (Courcelette Switch), *Below-Stellung* (Below Position, after the general), *Stump-Weg* (Stump/Tedium Way, British *Stump Road*), *Tal-Stellung* (Valley Position), *Biber-Kolonie* (Beaver Colony, by Ancre), *Braun-St.* (Brown Street), *Feste Zollern* (Zollern Redoubt), *Mouquet-Riegel* (Mouquet Switch), *Grosser-Riegel* (Greater Switch), *Artillerie Mulde* (Artillery valley; British *Battery Valley*), *Granat-Loch* (Shell Hole) and *Wundt-Werk* (British: *Wonder Work*).

Farther south on the Somme battlefield were various typical names for topographical features: *Schrapnell-Mulde* (Shrapnel Valley west of Mametz Wood, and another in Mametz–Montauban area), *Jäger-Höhe* (Riflemens Hill), *Küchenmulde* (Cooker Valley, La Boisselle), *Schwaben-Höhe* (Schwabia Hill, La Boisselle; site of Lochnagar crater), *Toten-Wald* (Death Wood, La Boisselle) and *Schrapnell-Wald* (Shrapnel Wood, Mametz–Montauban area). The feature south of Mametz Wood known to the British as *Caterpillar Valley* was divided by the Germans into two, *Granat-Schlucht* (Shell Ravine) and *Artillerie-Schlucht* (Artillery Ravine). There were also the following trenches: *Sachsen-Graben* (Saxon Trench), *Petersdorf-Riegel* (Petersdorf Switch),

British map of
the Flers area
showing 'Names
and Condition of
German Trenches
from captured
German Map',
September 1916. The
British first used
tanks in the Battle of
Flers–Courcelette on
15 September 1916.

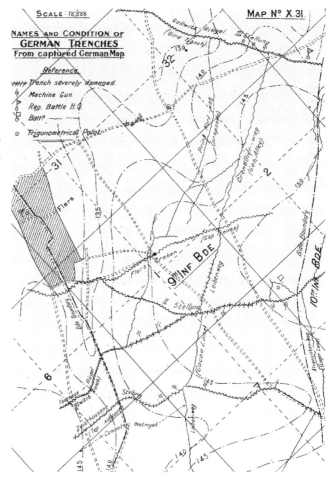

Gustav-Weg (Gustav Lane) and *Gallwitz-Riegel* (Gallwitz Switch). In the
Ovillers area ran *Leichen-Strasse* (Corpses Street), *Baum-Strasse* (Tree
Street), *Wittwer-Strasse* (Widower Street), *Krach-Strasse* (Crash/Bang
Street) and *Kronen-Strasse* (Crown Street).

A captured German map showed the following trenches and names in
the Delville Wood–Flers sector; *Foureaux Wald* (British *High Wood*),[16]
Foureaux-Riegel (British *Switch Trench*), *Zeischossene Stellung* (British
Tea Support), *Leiber-weg* (British *Cocoa Lane*), *Flers Graben* (British *Gap
Trench*), *Alvensleben-weg* (town near Hanover; British *Lager Lane*), *Prinz
Karl-weg* (proposed), *Grenadier-weg* (British: *Gas Alley*), *Gallwitz-Riegel*,
III Stellung (British *Gird Trench*). A German trench map of the High Wood–
Ginchy–Combles–Flers area, dated 10 September 1916,[17] showed in addition
Postierungs-Graben (Positions Trench), *Schenk-Weg*, *Sydow-Höhe*, *Karl-Weg*,

Below-Weg and *Stellung*, *Ginchy-Graben* (Ginchy Trench), *Württemburg-Graben*, *Zerschossene-Stellung* (Shot-to-bits Position), *Annäherungs-Weg* (Approach Lane), *Burstin-Weg*, *Kampf-Stellung* (Battle Position), *Oppen-Bereitschaft* (Oppen Support), *Combles-Graben* and *Riegel* (Combles Trench and Switch), *Quer-Riegel* (Cross Switch), *Rancourt-Riegel* (Rancourt Switch), and the poignantly-named *Herzbruch-Weg* (Heartbreak Lane) between Frégicourt and Combles.

A map of the Beaulencourt–Le Transloy–Morval area, dated 27 December 1916,[18] showed the following trenches: *Sachsen-Riegel* (Saxon Switch) and *Ludendorff-Riegel* (Ludendorff Switch) at Beaulencourt, *1. Linie*, *2. Linie (R.1.-Stellung)*, *Transloy-Riegel*, *Hindenburg-Riegel*, *Strohm-Stellung*, *R.2.-Stellung*, *R.3.-Stellung*, *Posten-Linie*, *Halbmond-Riegel* (Half Moon Switch, Sailly-Saillisel), *Zwischen-Stellung*, *Mesnil-Riegel*, *Mesnil-Etricourt-Riegel*, *Alter-Hanseaten-Riegel*, *Hohlweg*, *Verbindungsgraben (Heeres-Riegel)*, *Gouvernements-Riegel* (at Gouvernement Farm), *Wald-Riegel*, *Pionier-Graben* and *Vaast-Riegel* (at St. Pierre Vaast),

Other names on the Somme battlefield were: *Bayernwäldchen* (Bavaria Copse), *Tirpitzplatz* (Tirpitz Square, in the village of Combles), *Minenwäldchen* (Mine Copse, near Mametz), *Dreibaumhöhe* (Three Tree Hill, between Mametz and Montauban).[19] Farther south, in the Noyon sector in early 1916, Herbert Sulbach described the German tendency to name certain positions or ruins, citing the *Malerschlösschen* (Painter's Castle) and *der Kapellenberg* (Chapel Hill) as examples of names other than those of local infantry commanders, implying that the latter form of naming was commonplace.[20]

Champagne Area (Third Army)

Max Eckert, who served for years in the Champagne area, stated that the first tactical names were given by the Germans to woods, noting that when trench warfare developed in the winter of 1914–15, woods played an important role as tactical features, and in the Champagne, with its numerous small, fragmented woods, names were already being given in October 1914. From then on, names proliferated, and some remained in use during the whole war: *Zickzackwald* (Zig-Zag Wood), *Turcowald* (Turco Wood), the *Jahnwäldchen* (Johann's Copse) to the south of Ripont, and many more.[21] Other woods named by the Germans in this area were *Spandauwald* (Spandau, near Berlin) and *Kamerunwald* (Cameroon Wood). Many hill and valley features were also given the names of German topographical features, which in turn were often named after mythological characters – *Fichtelberg* (near Bayreuth), *Keilberg* (near Mannheim, Rhine), *Hochwald* (near Düren), *Rolandseck* (Roland's

Corner, Remagen, Rhine), *Drachenfels* (Dragon Rock in the Siebengebirge, Rhine), *Luginsland*, *Kanonenberg* (Gun Mount) – by the divisions or regiments that served in certain sectors for a long time. Others were named after high commanders – *Hindenburg*, *Ludendorff*, etc. – or army commanders: *Kluck*, *Einem*, *Lossberg*, *Oldershausen*, *Klewitz*, etc.[22]

Eckert estimated that in Third Army's Champagne–Argonne area, more than 3,000 new topographical names were given by the Germans, including those for woods, valleys, camps and stretches of road. As he was largely responsible for the cartography of this area, he was in a position to know. An example he gave was *Russenstrasse*, built by Russian prisoners-of-war. One famous crossroads called *Mazagran*, about 12km from Vouziers, where six roads intersected, was named by the airmen *die Spinne* (the Spider).[23] Such naming by airmen was reflected in the unofficial British name *Mossyface Wood* for Havrincourt Wood. The large number of trench names, some of which are given below, were in addition to this huge total.

Names of German Trenches in the Perthes-les-Hurlus–Tahure Sector (Champagne), December 1916–April 1917[24]

Many of the names given by the Germans in this sector were descriptive in nature, or referred to commanders. In the former category we have *Flanken-Weg* (Flank Lane), *Haupt-Graben* (Main Trench), *Kirch-Graben* (Church Trench), *Sanitäts-Weg* (First Aid Lane), *Verbindungs-Weg 6* (CT 6), *Grenz-Weg* (Boundary Lane), *Laufgraben 1–4* (CT 1–4), *Graben-gewir* (sic: Trench-maze), *West Wald* and *Ost Wald Graben* (West Wood and East Wood Trench), *Steilhang-Weg* (Steep Slope Lane), *Mittel-Weg* (Middle Lane), *Kabel-Graben* (Cable Trench), *Sehne* (Sinew) and *Nothelfer-Graben* (Auxiliary Trench), while in the latter are *Kluck-Weg* (von Kluck Lane), *Prinz Karl-Graben* (Prince Karl Trench), *Prinz Karl-Weg* (Prince Karl Lane), *Prinz Oskar-Weg* (Prince Oskar Lane), *Markgrafen-Weg* (Margrave Lane) and *Kronprinzen-Weg* (Crown Prince Lane).

Regimental names and numbers and other military references also appeared: *65er-Graben* (65th Trench), *114er-Graben* (114th Trench), *142er-Graben* (142nd Trench), *158er-Graben* (158th Trench), *Fusilier-Weg* (Fusilier Lane), *Grenadier-Graben* (Grenadier Trench), *Jäger-Graben* (Riflemens Trench), *Divisions-Weg* (Divisional Way), *Rekruten-Graben* (Recruits Trench) and *Kanonen-Weg* (Gun Trench).

Regional, city and town names were common in this as in other areas: *Rheinischer-Graben*, *Frankfurter-Weg*, *Hessen-Weg*, *Harburger-Weg*,

Dresdener-Weg, *Paderborner-Weg*, *Sachsen-Weg*, *Bayern-Graben*, *Rostock-Graben*, *Graudenzer-Weg*, *Braunschweiger-Weg*, *Frankfurter-Str.*, *Magdeburger-Weg*, *Bernberger-Weg*, *Wiesbadener-Str.*, *Bremer-Weg*, *Alvensleben-Weg*, *Zähringer-Graben*, *Schmitz-Weg*, *Eilenburg-Weg*, *Neu-Strelitzer* (near Berlin) and *Cottbruser-Weg* (near Berlin). There were also a number of smaller German place names, and personal (probably officers') names, plus a few more colloquial and indecipherable: *Turrey-Weg*, *Ensslin-Weg*, *Kettmann-Weg*, *Gelach-Weg*, *Folkersamb-Graben*, *Mann-Graben*, *Bonin-Weg*, *Kuhlmann-Graben*, *Ley-Graben*, *Geyer-Weg*, *Altluck-S.* or *Airrach-5*, *Lessing-Graben*, *Peirouitte-Weg*, *Götzer-Graben*, *Schorstehen/Schorschen-Eck*, *Riese-Weg* (Giant Lane), *Rüchen-Graben* (Rotten Trench), *Pro..zen-Weg* (Protze = Gun-limber) and *Wishen-Weg*.

In the Argonne Forest, between the Champagne and Verdun battlefields, was the Butte de Vauquois. This commanding feature was the site of savage mine warfare throughout the war. Nearby at Montfaucon was the *Rattenschloss* (Rats Castle) trench position.

Verdun Area

The Verdun battle raged from February 1916 through to the end of that year, and continued into 1917 as the French strained to push the Germans back and establish the front sufficiently far from the city to guarantee the security of their position. In particular, at the end of 1916 and in 1917, they were concerned to recapture Forts Douaumont and Vaux on the right bank of the Meuse, and the key hill positions of Mort Homme and Cote 304 on the left bank. This ebb and flow of battle meant that a large number of French trenches were initially captured by the Germans, and subsequently reoccupied by the French. Trench names were often appropriated along with the trenches, and many names used by the Germans were clearly of French origin, and vice versa. These trenches were often so pulverised by intense artillery bombardments that they ceased to be identifiable as continuous positions, and when recaptured and consolidated were on a rather different trace from the originals.

In the crucial operational area of Forts Vaux, Douaumont, Souville and the Damloup High Battery position, the following German trench names were in use. They showed a wide variety of sources, including territorial and personal names, as well as those derived from local topography and conditions. Local names and topographical references were: *Steinbruch-Graben* (Quarry Trench), *Chapitre-Weg*, *Westliche* and *Ostliche* (Chapter Way, West and East; Vaux-Chapitre), *Teich-Graben* (Pond Trench), *Fumin-Riegel* (Fumin Switch,

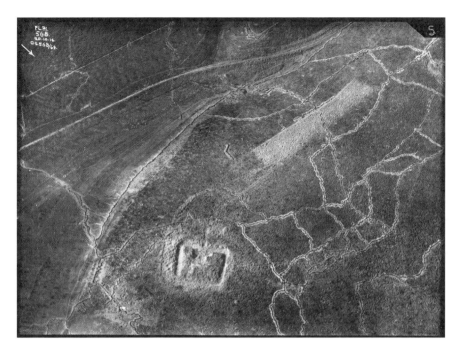

German aerial photograph of the Lauffée Redoubt and neighbouring trenches on the right bank of the Meuse on the Verdun battlefield, 20 October 1916.

Bois Fumin), *Alt Kirch-Graben* (Old Church Trench), *Lanz-Graben* (Lance Trench), *Pfeifen-Kopf* (Pipe Head), *Zick-Zack-Graben* (Zig-Zag Trench), *J Werk* (J Redoubt), *West-Sappe* (West Sap). Other names were *Morré-Graben*, *Cruse-Graben*, *Jäger-Graben* (Rifleman Trench), *Loren-Graben* (Wagon Trench), *Eidechsen-Graben* (Lizards Trench), and *Siebener-Graben* (Trench Seven).

Several names clearly indicated the relationship between the trenches and the terrain: *Schlangen-Graben* (Snake Trench), *Kreis-Graben* (Circle Trench), *Riegel-Graben* (Switch Trench), *Senkrechter-Graben* (Vertical Trench), *Grüner-Graben* (Green Trench), *Trapez-Graben* (Trapezium Trench), *Bogen-Graben* (Curve/Salient Trench), *Quer-Graben* (Cross Trench), *Waben-Gräben* (Honeycomb Trenches), *Filzlaus* (Crab Louse), *Spinne* (Spider), *Schunkspitze* (Linking Point), *Achselklappe* (Epaulette), *Tunnel-Graben* (Tunnel Trench), *Mittel-Graben* (Middle Trench), *Langer-Graben* (Long Trench), *Kap-Graben* (Headland Trench), *Kurzer-Graben* (Short Trench), *Drei-Fuss-Graben* (Three Foot Trench), *Geschoss-Graben* (Shot Trench), *Linien-Graben* (Lines Trench, along railway), *Irrgarten* (Crazy Garden), *Beil-Graben* (Axe Trench), *Nordost-Werk* (North-East Redoubt) and *Rechteck-Graben* (Right-Angle Trench).

Statesmen and generals were commemorated here by *Gambetta-Graben* (a French president), *Ludendorff-Graben* (Ludendorff Trench), *Joffre-Graben* (Joffre Trench, French C-in-C), *Garibaldi-Graben* (Garibaldi Trench) and *Wilhelm-Graben* (William Trench, Kaiser Wilhelm II), while on the Verdun left bank, in the Mort Homme–Côte 304 area two famous tunnels, *Kronprinz* and *Gallwitz*, were bored under the ridge. Some of the many names of territories and cities were *Verduner-Graben* (Verdun Trench), *Pariser-Graben* (Paris Trench), *Düsseldorfer-Graben* (Dusseldorf Trench), *Deutscher-Graben* (German Trench) and *Lothringer-Graben* (Lorraine Trench).

Various other names, possibly those of German officers, also appeared here: *Klöbe-Graben*, *Lindow-Stollen*, *Filslaus*, *Kiessling-Weg*, *Kutscher-Weg*, *Kellinghusen-Weg*, *Fressel-Weg*, *Engelhart-Weg*, *Walsemann-Weg*, *Putz-Graben* and *Herz-Graben*. Girls' names were *Kl. Lulu-Graben* (Little Lulu Trench), *Gr. Lulu-Graben* (Big Lulu Trench), *Dorotheen-Graben* (Dorothy Trench), *Mariannen-Graben* (Marianne Trench) and *Liese-S.* (Liese Sap/Street). One wonders about *Busen-Graben* (Bosom Trench).

There were four 'Wagnerian' trenches here, just west of Douaumont: *Walküren-Graben* (Valkyries Trench), *Donner-Graben* (Thunder Trench), *Wotan-Graben* (Wotan Trench) and *Blitz-Graben* (Lightning Trench). Perhaps *Rosencrantz-Stollen* (Rosencrantz Tunnel) was to remind the troops of a Shakespearean message.

South of Verdun and north of the St Mihiel Salient was the commanding hill position known, from the names of neighbouring villages, to the French as Les Eparges, and to the Germans as Combres-höhe. On this hill feature both sides fought with savage mine warfare, as at the Butte de Vauquois in the Argonne, for control of the splendid observation position afforded by the crest. Here the Germans had a trench position they called the *Stork-nest*.

The *Siegfried Stellung* and Other Defensive Positions

Called by the British the Hindenburg Line, the *Siegfried I Stellung*, running from south of Arras to north of the Aisne, was a powerful, heavily wired rear-defence system of field works dug in 1916–17 by forced labour of civilians and prisoners of war, strengthened by concrete shelters and emplacements, and completely surveyed for supporting artillery. Behind the Siegfried front and support lines was the fortified area called the Siegfried Zone.

In the Havrincourt area 1917 were: *Diestel-Weg*, *Rekruten-Weg*, *Bahr-Riegel*, *Riegel-Graben*, *Dossenbach-Graben*, *1a Linie*, *Stutzpunkt 7*, *Sappe d1* and *d2*, *Irr-garten*, *VI* (*Verbindungsgraben* – i.e. CT), *Stutzpunkt Hunding*, *Rosengarten*

(Rose Garden), *W5*, *Teich-W.* (Pool Lane) and *Walli-W.* (trench posts in wood), *S4* (Sappe), *V4* (*Verbindungsgraben*, i.e. CT), *W1*, *Philosophen-Weg*, *Stutzpunkt Preussen*, *Brandenburg* and *Preussen-*[Linie?].

In the Saint-Quentin sector, the following names appeared in the *Siegfried Stellung* on a 1:50,000 strategic trench map produced in March 1918 for the *Kaiserschlacht*:[25] *A. Stellung* (2nd line), *B. Stellung* (1st line), *Signalwald Riegel* (Signal Wood Switch), *Bellenglise Riegel* (Bellenglise Switch), *Zwischen Stellung* (Intermediate Position; many of these), *Höhen-Riegel* (Hills Switch), *Jungwald-Riegel*, *Trichter-Riegel* (Crater Position), *Rouvroy-Riegel* (Rouvroy Switch), *Boulevard-Linie* (Boulevard Line, in Saint-Quentin), *Elysee-Riegel* (Elysee Switch, Saint-Quentin), *Südrand-Riegel* (South Edge, Saint-Quentin), *Schul-Riegel* (School Switch), *Eisenbahn-Riegel* (Railway Switch), *Feldwach-Stellung* (Outpost Position), *Mesnil-Stellung I. 1 & 2 Graben* (Mesnil Position I, 1st and 2nd Trenches), *Mesnil-Stellung II. 1 Graben* (Mesnil Position II, 1st Trench), *Itancourt-Riegel* (Itancourt Switch), *Riegel E. II, III, E. IV, I.III & IV, S.I, II & III*, *Dressler-Riegel* (Dressler Switch), *II. Stellung* (2nd Position), *Lorival-Riegel* (Lorival Switch) and *Zwischen-Stellung Ost & West* (Intermediate Position East and West).

Still farther to the rear, covering Cambrai but not Saint-Quentin, were the *Hunding Stellung* and the *Brunnhilde Stellung*, partially completed in 1918. To the south and south-east, these latter were continued by the *Kriemhilde Stellung* and *Michael Stellung*, while to the north, beyond Quéant the *Wotan I Stellung* (called by the British the Drocourt–Quéant Line, covering Douai) and the *Hermann Stellung* (Le Cateau to Ghent) guarded the right flank. These names from the Wagnerian mythology suggested to the British staff the sarcastic comment that beyond them the Flying Dutchman (*Der fliegende Holländer*) would probably be found.[26] Behind these was the *Antwerpen–Maas* (*AM*) *Stellung* (the Antwerp–Meuse Line), and the final line was the *Grenz-Stellung* (the German frontier itself). The last feasible defence line along the Sambre and Oise Canal (*Hermann Stellung*) having been breached by the British on 4 November, the Germans were in full retreat by the following day, and the Avesnes–Maubeuge line was breached by the British on 8 November.[27] The war ended three days later.

Notes

1   Eckert, Max, *Die Kartenwissenschaft,* Berlin & Leipzig: VWV, Mittler, Vol. 1 1921, Vol. 2 1925, p. 790.

2   See Chasseaud, Peter, 'German Maps and Survey on the Western Front, 1914–18,' *The Cartographic Journal*, London, *38*(2), 2001, pp. 119–34.

3　Eckert, op. cit.

4　Sulzbach, Herbert, *With the German Guns – Four Years on the Western Front 1914–1918*, Barnsley: Pen and Sword, 2003, p. 77.

5　Eckert, op. cit.

6　Miles, Capt. Wilfred, *History of the Great War, Military Operations, France and Belgium,* 1917, Vol. III, *The Battle of Cambrai*, London: HMSO, 1948, p. 143.

7　1:5,000 *Stellungsplan [Bayernwald], Abschnitt II, Inf. Regt. 179.*

8　Author's study of German *Stellungskarten* in Bundesarchiv-Militärarchiv, Freiburg-im-Breisgau, Germany.

9　1:25,000 *Stellungskarte* (untitled) of Fromelles–Loos area, *Bayer. Kartenfeldruckerei. A.O.K.6. Vermessungs-Abtlg. A.O.K.6. 2.10.15*, in BA-MA, Freiburg-im-Breisgau.

10　IWM photographs (no refs) in Gaynor Kavanagh, *Museums and the First World War, A Social History*, London and New York: Leicester University Press, 1994.

11　Eckert, op. cit.

12　Author's study of German *Stellungskarten* in Bundesarchiv-Militärarchiv, Freiburg-im-Breisgau.

13　1:10,000 *Stellungskarte 1-IX-1915, Auswerung und Druck durch die bayr. Feld-Flieger-Abteil.4*. Bundesarchiv-Militärarchiv, Freiburg, Maps 3/198.

14　1:25,000 Gruppe A, *Lagenkarte v.13.2.17, Ausgabe A, Gehiem, Verm.-Abt. 23*, in Militärgeschichtliches Forschungsamt, Potsdam; also 1:25,000 Sonderkarte der Gruppe B, *Stand 21.XI.16, Gehiem, Ver.-Abt. 23*, in TNA(PRO) WO 153/968.

15　1:25,000 *Gruppe Armin. Zusammendruck - a - . Geheim, Ausgabe am 21-9-16; Stellungen am 20-9-16. Nach Fettabzügen der Vermessungs-Abtlg. 12 (1 Sachs), neue bearbeitet u. gedruckt von Vermessungs-Abtlg. 23.* Cambridge University Library, Maps 23.91.130. A captured map, deposited in 1916, probably by T.C. Nicholas, 5th FSC's Maps Officer.

16　*Map No X.31 (I.a. 19136), 1:10,000 Names and Conditions of German Trenches from captured German Map, 1st Printing Coy RE GHQ (3025)*, c. September 1916.

17　1:10,000 *Sonderkarte, Gruppe Kirchbach, Stand v. 10.9.16., Nach Fettabzügen der Vermessungs-Abtlg.23, Druck vom G.K. XII. R.-K., Stellungen nach Flieger Bildern u. Truppen-Angaben*, in Militärgeschichtliches Forschungsamt, Potsdam.

18　1:10,000 trench map, *Gruppe C., 27.12.16, Nicht in vordere Linie mitnehmen!*, in Militärgeschichtliches Forschungsamt, Potsdam.

19　Photographs in: Anon, *An Der Somme – Erinnerungen der 12. Infanterie-Division an die Stellungskämpfe und Schlacht an der Somme, Oktober 1915 bis November 1916*, Berlin: Ferdinand Dümmler, 1918.

20　Sulzbach, op. cit., p. 77.

21　Eckert, op. cit.

22　Ibid.

23　Ibid.

24 1:25,000 Stellungskarte *Perthes-les-Hurlus Blatt 19. Stand vom 15-12-1916. Hergestellt v.d. Vermessungs-Abteilung 19 (2 Sächs)*; similar for April 1917.

25 1:50,000 Übersichtskarte für die 18. Armee *(St. Quentin), Stand vom 9-3-18. Druck der Vermessungs-Abt. 26.*

26 Comment in carbon copy of postwar undated 'question and answer' typescript, provenance unknown but believed to derive from War Office, seen by author.

27 Montgomery, Maj-Gen. Sir A., *The Story of the Fourth Army in the Battles of the Hundred Days, August 8th to November 11th 1918*, London: Hodder & Stoughton, 1920, pp. 247–60.

X

AFTERTHOUGHTS

Patterns of Naming

This survey of British, French and German trench names appears to suggest that there were distinct differences in national naming policies and practices. Given that the French and German samples examined here are smaller than the British, we have to beware of too definite deductions, but it seems that we can make at least some tentative assertions.

Specimens of the signwriter's art in the Grand Place, Bailleul, south of Ypres, in the winter of 1918–19; left to St Jans Cappel, Berthen, Mont des Cats; centre to Meteren, Caestre, Cassel, and the Station. Bailleul was practically destroyed by shellfire in the German offensive of April 1918 and the Allied counter-offensive later in the year.

British trench names developed in a much more ad hoc way, were less susceptible to overall control and intervention by Army diktat and by formation commands, and displayed a refreshing variety of irony, humour, wit and popular cultural references. There were, of course, the usual run of regimental and place names, but these were more than leavened alternately by pastoral associations, delightful whimsy and high comedy, and those of almost unbearable tragic intensity. In this they extend to a coverage so broad in terms of human experience and emotions that it might be called Shakespearian. It should be borne in mind that in 1914 the British had the smallest regular army of the three nations, and the smallest number of reservists who had previously served with the colours. It did, however, possess a significant reserve of part-time soldiers in the Territorial Army, the units of which brought many local street and place names to the front. Even more significant numerically were the Kitchener or New Armies, men from all walks of life who brought with them (as did the Territorials) their civilian culture and, in a sense, opposed it to any pre-existing military culture. Proud of their country, the Empire and the traditions of their adopted regiments, these civilian soldiers stamped their indelible mark on the Western Front (and other fronts), not least through the names they bestowed on their trench environment.

The Regular Army was first in the field, and was the first to start naming its trenches. We should remember that the humour of Bruce Bairnsfather's cartoon character 'Old Bill' was the mournful humour of the 'old sweat' and was never far removed from cockney origins. It is no accident that in Ploegsteert Wood most names of trenches and corduroy or duckboard tracks were London names. Then there were all the English provincial, Scottish, Irish and Welsh regular regiments who simultaneously adopted the practice.

Names given by the French to their own trenches celebrated French cultural and military personalities and achievements and, like the Germans, commemorated local commanders and officers killed in action. The names of many French and colonial territories, cities and towns, rivers, etc., frequently cropped up. In several localities French trench names referred to high culture and to classical deities and mythology. In the names they gave to German trenches, regional and city names relating to enemy territories, and names of German and Central Powers royalty, statesmen and generals, predominated. It must be said that, in naming German trenches, the French often made clear their dislike; a certain disdain and negative propaganda element recurs, but this is understandable in that they were the invaded country and the enemy were sitting in French (and of course Belgian) territory. German names appear to have been the most rigidly subject to programmatic treatment. They consisted mostly of long litanies of regimental, river and place names, together with names from the pantheon of royalty, commanders, other military figures and, occasionally, high culture. Thus a certain picture of French and German naming practice emerges, but further, in-depth, studies of French and German trench names, covering their whole frontages (an immense task) need to be made before any definitive picture emerges.

It is perhaps a futile exercise to consider the classes of names that were not used for trenches or topographical features. There are many apparent lacunae, and it would be pointless to attempt to identify lessons here. But Conan Doyle's point about negative evidence – the dog that did not bark – was a good one. We can also observe that while many unpleasant names were used, convention and self-censorship ensured that obscenities did not appear.

Names on Maps of Training Areas

The Royal Engineers Training School was started in 1917 at Rouen, where an extensive trench system was constructed. The communication trenches being named *Buchanan Street*, *Moody Lane*, *Norman Avenue*, *Noyle* (or *Moyle*) *Street*, *Severs Street*, *George Street*, *Stoney Road*, *Lovers Alley*, *Lashmar Road*, *Strafe Street*, *West Street*, *Short Cut*, *Long Lane* and *Molloy Road*. Strongpoints were named *Fort Bangalore*, *Honeycomb Redoubt*, *The Keep*, *Fort Russe*, *Fort Tufut* and *Fort Grandpa*.[1] Although not all these names can be elucidated (several were probably names of RE officers), many are typical of those in use at the front, and the instructors at the school had all served at the front. As well as the trench system, the school incorporated trench board (duckboard) tracks, light railway (Decauville) tracks, metalled roads, mule tracks, matted tracks and plank and slab roads. All these, in addition to the trenches, had to be appropriately signboarded for easy identification at the front.

Artillery Training Maps at 1:20,000 and 1:10,000 scales, of selected training areas in the UK, were printed from 1914 onwards. A few of these, such as those covering the artillery ranges on Salisbury Plain and the Tank Corps training area at Bovington in Dorset, carried overprints of practice trench systems, including trench names. These names reflected those in use on the Western Front. One of these maps covering the Lark Hill and Durrington area showed a trench system some 700 yards long, and almost as wide, with the 'British' trenches printed in blue and the 'German' in red, as was the practice at the front. The 'German' trenches had been named *Tirpiz* [sic] *St.*, *Leipsic* [sic] *Redoubt*, *Willie's House*, *Willie's Way*, *Hindenberg* [sic] *Trench*, *Hunger Way*, *Berlin St.*, *Potsdam Av.*, and *Fritz's Way*. The 'British' trenches were unnamed. The name *Hunger Way* is indicative of the effect of the maritime blockade of Germany.[2]

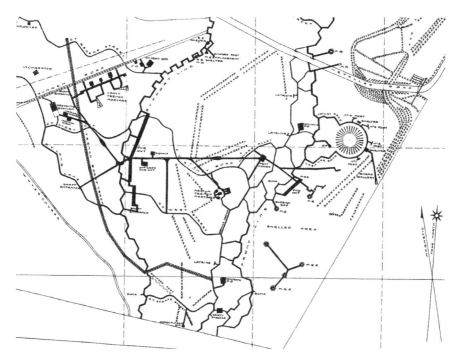

Map of the Royal Engineers Training School at Rouen – southern part. The sappers laid out a trench system here to instruct recruits in the techniques of trench construction and maintenance. This included wire entanglements, trench mortar and machine gun positions, and mine shafts, galleries and craters. Trenches were named – *Lovers Alley*, *Strafe Street*, *Short Cut*, etc. (Work of the Royal Engineers in the European War: Misc., Chatham 1926)

An even larger-scale map, at 1:5,000, entitled *Trenches at Bustard Inn* (on Salisbury Plain), took most of its names from the Bois Grenier sector of the Western Front, which as we have seen was also used as a model by Ian Hay in *The First Hundred Thousand*. This map was used by the Australian forces training in Britain, and the names clearly refer to the Australian occupation of this sector in early 1916 and their action at Fromelles in July of that year. The names shown were: *Bridoux Salient*, *Safety Alley*, *Queer Street*, *Stanway Avenue*, *Comb Street*, *The Haymarket*, *Oxford Circus*, *Regent Street*, *Bond Street*, *Fort Blanco*, *Cromwell Road*, *White City*, *Grispot*, *Cowgate*, *Bois Grenier*, *Wine Avenue* and *Leith Walk*.[3]

At Gallows Hill, Bovington Camp, a 1:10,000 Training Map showed a well-developed trench system, again including many well-known names from the Loos and Somme areas of the Western Front as well as a few local and invented names: *Potsdam Line*, *Berlin Line*, *Gallows Redoubt*, *Wilhelm Redoubt*,

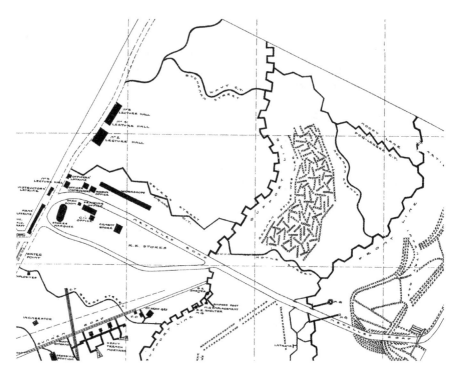

Map of the Royal Engineers Training School at Rouen – northern part. Trench names include *Moody Lane*, *Norman Avenue*, *Buchanan Street*, *Severs Street* and *Moyle Street*. (Work of the Royal Engineers in the European War, Misc., Chatham 1926)

Schwaber [sic] *Redoubt* (*Schwaben* was meant), *Serb Line*, *Kluck Redoubt*, *Hansa Line*, *Stuff Redoubt*, *Hohenzollern Redoubt*, *Mad Point*, *Wunder Work* [sic], *Colson Trench*, *Woods Trench*, *Hanley Trench*, *Willoughby Trench*, *Fritz Redoubt*, *Big Willie*, *Little Willie*, *Fort Anley*, *Three Sisters Redoubt*, *Flossie Trench*, *Hulke Trench*, *Boars Head*, *Kaiser Line*, *Roberts Trench*, *Gordon Trench*, *Piccadilly*, *Regent Street* and *Bond Street*. Topographical names added to the original 6-inch Ordnance Survey map that formed the base for the training map were *Lovers Valley*, *Blighty Valley* and *Happy Valley*.[4] Such trench systems occurred in many other locations in Britain, for example at Seaford Camp and Shoreham Camp on the Sussex Downs, and in the Ashdown Forest, and trenches in these systems may well have been named. Few maps have survived, but the trenches can often still be picked out on aerial photographs.

Trenches were also dug in the UK as a precaution against invasion – in particular the *London Defences* – and stretches were named. Outlying defences included those in Essex and Kent – including the *Maidstone–Swale* Line. One Artillery Training Map shows red and blue trench lines in Kent running south from the Thames estuary, possibly a Dartford–River Darent–Eynsford–Shoreham–Knockholt–Tatsfield line.[5] Little coordinated research has yet been done on the 1914–18 London Defences.

British Names on Other Fronts

While this book focuses on the Western Front, we should not ignore the similar naming patterns that arose in other theatres. Wherever British troops were operating, British names appeared. The same applies to French and German troops. In North Russia, during the 1918–19 operations, could be found *Oxford Circus* and *Strand*.[6] In Italy, British troops named *Tattenham Corner* on a mountain road leading to the Asiago Plateau.[7] Not to be outdone, the Germans put up a sign at Dar-es-Salaam proclaiming *Gott Strafe England*.[8]

Gallipoli: Perhaps the largest set of names outside France and Belgium was on the Gallipoli Peninsula in 1915. Mike Nolan has long been compiling a definitive listing, and its publication is eagerly awaited. Many resonant names were given at Helles, Anzac and Suvla that have found permanent places in history: *V Beach* and *W Beach*, *Lancashire Landing*, *Walmer Castle*[9], *Splinter Villa*,[10] *Fusiliers' Bluff*, *The Camber*, *Johnson's Jolly*, *The Nek*, the *Razor's Edge*, *Fort Doughty-Wylie*, *Quinn's Post*, *Lone Pine*, *Russell's Top*, *Chocolate Hill*, etc.

British 'trench diagram' (so-called because of the lack of planimetric accuracy and reliable heighting data) of the Krithia area, Helles sector, Gallipoli, 1915.

In view of the contribution of his brigade to naming on the Aisne and in the Ploegsteert area, it is appropriate that Hunter-Weston, who commanded the 29th Division and VIII Corps at Gallipoli, should have a feature on the Gallipoli Peninsula (*Hunter-Weston Hill*) named after him.

A Royal Naval Division map dated 14 June 1915 showed the following trenches at Helles: *Nelson Road*, *Plymouth Road*, *Trotman Road*, *Mercer Road*, *Backhouse Road*, and the communication trenches *Oxford Street* and *Regent Street*.[11] Another dated 21 June showed *Plymouth Avenue* and *Nelson Avenue*, both previously *Roads*. Perhaps Western Front designations were being applied. In the same month the trench diagrams prepared for the *Gully Ravine* action showed all Turkish trenches on *Gully Spur* numbered with the prefix 'J', while on *Fir Tree Spur* they were prefixed 'H', between Kirte and Kanli Deres 'G' and east of Kanli Dere 'F'.[12] The French also named a large number of features and trenches, while the Turks named the trenches from which they attacked on 29 June after an officer, Mahmed Tahouch, who had been prominent in the defence at the Allied landings in April and in subsequent operations.[13]

Other names used at Gallipoli were from various home countries: *Piccadilly Circus*, *Brighton Beach*, *Dublin Castle*, *Warwick Castle*, *Sauchiehall Street*. Some were descriptive: *The Pimple*, *Rhododendron Ridge*, *Scrubby Knoll* and *The Zig-zag*, or named after realities of warfare, e.g., *Dead Man's Ridge*, *Hell Spit*, *Sniper's Ridge* and *Rest Gully*.

Salonica: On the Salonica (Macedonia) front, the British and French continued the tradition started at Gallipoli, creating many trench and topographical names. There were *Park Lane*[14] and *The Birdcage Lane*[15] on the Langaza Plain, while on the Vardar front were the British names *Mulberry Hill*, *One Tree Hill*, *Cardiff Ravine*, *Bangor Ravine* and *Stoney Hill*. On the same front appeared the French names *Crête des Mitrailleuses*, *Piton des Mitrailleuses*, *Jumeau*, *Dome*, *Grand Mamelon*, *Grand Clou*, *Petit Clou*, *Crête des Tentes*, *Ravin du Dorsal*, *Chapeau de Gendarme*, *Grand Piton* and *Petit Piton*.

Palestine: In Palestine, British troops again named many features and trenches, and the solidification of the trench system on the *Gaza–Beersheba Line* created further opportunities; *Burnt Tank Trenches*, *Welsh Wadi*, *Whites Wadi*, *Tank Redoubt*, the *Labyrinth*, *Green Hill*, *Samson Ridge*, *El Arish Redoubt*, *Magdhaba Trench*, *Outpost Hill*, *Middlesex Hill*, *Anzac Ridge*, *The Warren*, *Jack and Jill*, *Dumb-bell Hill*, *Lambeth Wood*, *Queen's Hill*, *Lee's Hill*, *Blazed Hill*, *Bunker Hill*, *Hog's Back*, etc. There were *Ludgate Circus*,[16] *Kerry Road*[17] and *The Lyceum*[18] at Ludd, and elsewhere *Ongar Road*, *Brentford Redoubt*, *Ilford Road*, *Deacons Dyke* and *Brentford Road*,[19] as well as *Piccadilly*. The official historian noted that 'In the descriptions of the battles of Gaza new names appear with each new attack. Very few were on the maps for the first battle, a number were added prior to the second, and still more before the third. In some cases names previously in use were dropped out.'[20] On the other hand, many names were of local origin (e.g. the *El Buggar Ridge*, which must have caused the troops some amusement), and some of remarkable antiquity (e.g. *Abraham's Well*).

Mesopotamia: In Mesopotamia a similar naming situation existed. At Kut naming was reminiscent of traditional siege warfare practice. The main British positions were named *First Line*, *Middle Line* and *Second Line*, while the trenches of the Fort, with its *North East* and *West Bastions*, were named *River Communication Trench*, *Curtain Trench*, *Fire Trench*, *2nd Line*, etc. Nearby was *Woolpress Village*. At Ctesiphon were *Water Redoubt*, *High Wall*, and *Gurkha Mound*, and elsewhere were *Frazer's Post*, *Horse Shoe Marsh*, *Vital Point*, *Thorny Nala*, *Twin Pimples* and *The Triangle*.[21]

Beyond the World War

The trench names of the First World War continued to capture the imagination once the fighting had ended. The author's mother has told him that the next generation was intrigued by stories of trenches named *Piccadilly* and *Leicester Square*. They had passed into popular culture.

The naming of defensive positions was continued in the inter-war period and the Second World War. The Germans constructed their new *West Wall* (wrongly named by the British, who intended to hang out their washing on it, the *Siegfried Line*), while across the Rhine the French built their *Ligne Maginot*, modelled on the Verdun forts that had so impressed the French with their ability to withstand terrific artillery bombardment. Fearful of invasion in and after 1940, the British constructed a series of 'stop-lines' in the south-east of England. The widespread adoption of 'defence in depth' usually prevented the construction of linear defences in the old style, but unwillingness to cede territory often compromised the depth concept. In north Africa appeared *Knightsbridge* and the *Admin Box*, while tracks to bring up attacking troops at El-Alamein were named. There was the Axis *Mareth Line* position, and in Italy the *Gothic Line*. To defend the mainland of Europe, the Germans constructed their *Atlantic Wall*. In Burma, John Masters named sections of his defensive hill feature after cricket field positions.[22] In the post-Second World War period, during the prolonged French colonial struggle to retain Vietnam, the position at Dien Bien Phu was again modelled on the Verdun fortress concept. More recent conflicts such as the Falklands War and Iraq have again seen British and 'Coalition' names transposed to far-flung arenas. Lieutenant-Colonel Tim Collins, in his book *Rules of Engagement*, noted that the names *Shankhill Road*, *Newtonards Road* and *O'Connell Street* had been awarded by the men of the 1st Royal Irish Regiment to positions on the Kuwait–Iraq border in February 2003. Propagandist and ideological naming became an unfortunate feature of the questionable Bush–Blair 'wars on terror' in Iraq and Afghanistan, with 'Coalition' bases in Operation ENDURING FREEDOM being named *Freedom Camp*, *Camp Stronghold Freedom*, etc.

Survival of Trench Names

The names featured in formation and unit instructions, defence schemes and orders, and on sketch maps. From September 1915 they also featured on the very limited issues of secret editions of the regular series 1:10,000 trench maps. Many can be found scattered around the copious literature of the Great War. Perhaps the most obvious relic of the old trench names, apart from the few extant name boards, is their survival in some of the names of the cemeteries administered by the Commonwealth War Graves Commission. The most accessible source of information about these cemeteries is Rose Coombs' enduring book *Before Endeavours Fade*.[23] Many of the names were referred to in the unit war diaries, now to be found in the National Archives (formerly Public Record Office) at Kew (class WO 95). Large numbers of trench maps are also to be found in these archives, mostly in classes WO 153 and WO 297. The regimental, divisional and official histories are also a good source of information about minor trench operations and large-scale battles. Many of the names can be found on the maps in the author's trench map atlas, *Topography of Armageddon*,[24] and in the *Imperial War Museum Trench Map Archive* CD Rom[25] and later DVDs utilising the collections of the IWM and the National Archives. Some of the German names can be found on the *Captured German Trench and Operations Maps from The National Archives* CD Rom.[26]

Boards and Signs – the Material Culture of Trench Naming

Boards and signs were an integral and crucial part of the defensive systems, vital for the identification of precise locations within the often confusing labyrinth of old and new, used and disused trenches. What concrete form did the naming take? Names did not just appear on the maps, but were painted on boards by sappers of the RE Field Companies and nailed to the trench-side timbers, particularly at entrances and junctions. Several survive in the Imperial War Museum, often showing the effects of exposure to shellfire. Wooden boards were vulnerable in several ways; one of the greatest hazards apart from shell and mortar fire was soldiers scavenging for firewood – a scarce commodity in the trenches. One of the earliest official references to trench name boards and signs came in 4th (Guards) Brigade Orders of 28 April 1915; probably occasioned by scavenging, this stated: 'Notice Boards in Trenches. No signs or notice boards put up in the trenches are to be taken down except for renewal.'[27] These Brigade Orders were signed by the brigade major, Captain Gort, later to become famous as the Commander of the BEF, fighting again in this area, in 1939–40.

The production of sign boards of all kinds by the Royal Engineers was a huge industry. Output for August 1918, which a post-war official publication gave as typical, was 9,900 tin and 14,200 wooden boards. During the period June–August 1918 no fewer than 75,166 notice boards were issued to the British Armies on the Western Front.[28]

The signboards often carried information in addition to the name – sometimes it was the map reference, occasionally an instruction, such as *To*

Signboard for Bully Craters, very close to the German front line, hence the 'No Loud Talking' sign; Angres sector, south of Loos, 1916. (IWM 14744)

Mogg's Hole, No Loitering by Day, or *Bully Craters, No Loud Talking*. A few boards gave multiple names and directions; the most impressive example is the compendious *Thorpe Street* sign from Fonquevillers, now in the Imperial War Museum, which is illustrated in this book.

Most signs were made of wood, but occasionally sheets of metal, which would be punctured but not shattered by bullets or shell splinters, were pressed into service. Many were excellent specimens of the signwriter's art. These names found their way into the history, art and literature of the war, and the boards survive as *matériel*. Battlefield archaeologists occasionally find fragments of such boards, complete with lettering, during their excavations, but these are usually badly rotted.

Not all signboards carried the name of their location; some were exceedingly laconic (e.g. *Dump*), while others merely carried the map reference or gave directions. One, surviving in the Imperial War Museum, combined both these latter elements, with a directional arrow: *G.2.c.21* [arrow] *Ypres*. Another, rather illegible, in the National Army Museum, for *I.10.c.9.3 Hellfire Corner* also gave directions (with arrows) to *Ypres*, *Birr Cross Roads* and *Hooge*. This latter board had been brought to Edinburgh at the end of the war by Lieutenant W.S. Storie of the RASC, who displayed it in his shop window in Prince's Street as a way of attracting customers.

Some boards even gave the map sheet, which was always considered officially to be part of the reference; an example is another board now in the Imperial War Museum: *Suicide Corner I.1.c.1.6 Sheet 28*. Today these boards have a profound visual and emotional impact, triggering deep and extensive associations of a poetic type. That is to say they have acquired some magical, talismanic or shamanistic quality – like saints' relics – as a result of surviving several generations. The author remembers being first taken to the Imperial War Museum in the 1950s, and subsequently visiting frequently, and experiencing even then just such feelings, even at a time when many war veterans were very much alive. Some of these boards are featured in illustrations in this book.

Certain names became monumentalised in battlefield cemeteries (e.g. *Dud Corner* Cemetery, near Loos) and domestic war memorials. Jagger's magnificent Portland stone Royal Artillery memorial at Hyde Park Corner includes signposts indicating *Mole Track* (formerly *Mule Track*) and *Artillery Road* in the Ypres Salient. Very much in the public eye and much photographed by tourists, this memorial ensures that at least these names will survive to provoke questions.

Trench Names in Modern Memory

Popular culture has continued many of the stereotypes of the Great War. Joan Littlewood can be said to have started this in the early 1960s. In a more literary vein, Paul Fussell's study *The Great War in Modern Memory* of the 1970s has led to a serious examination of the cultural implications of the war's discourse, language and naming. Many of the names, as has been suggested in this book, lend themselves naturally to a humorous or ironic treatment. What are we to make, in the light of Rowan Atkinson's interpretation, of *Blackadder's Trench* (Richebourg), *Wibble Trench* (Oppy) or, following Allan Clark, of *Donkeys Trench* (Berthenicourt)? We can only look at them through modern eyes; we are inevitably influenced by these intermediating treatments, and must make a great effort to cut them out of our vision in an attempt to gain a glimpse of the original cultural mindset that bestowed these names. Some would argue, like Derrida, that this is impossible and that there is nothing outside the text. And in these days of the grotesquely misnamed 'reality television', when new trench systems are constructed for that medium, the old names are bound to re-emerge, with or without irony and humour, for our renewed consideration. Perhaps the most aptly named trench was that near Fampoux, on the Arras battlefield; it was called *Why Trench*. As Richard Jones, the director, commented a few years ago of Wagner's *Ring* cycle, there are no answers, only questions.

Notes

1   *Plan of R.E. Training School*, Rouen, in Addison, Col G.H. (compiler), *The Work of the Royal Engineers in the European War, 1914–1918, Miscellaneous*, Chatham: Institution of Royal Engineers, 1926.
2   Artillery Training Map, probably 1:10,000 GSGS 3417 *Durrington*, Ordnance Survey February 1917.
3   Blueprint *Trenches at Bustard Inn, Scale 1:5,000, Ref map Salisbury Plain 1:20,000*, in Australian War Memorial, Canberra.
4   1:10,000 GSGS 3374 *Bovington Camp*, OS February 1917, held at The Tank Museum, Bovington.
5   1:20,000 Artillery Training Map, *Woolwich, OS 1916*, in the British Library Map Library.
6   Both IWM Photo Q16911.
7   IWM Photos Q25956, Q26911 & Q25956.
8   IWM Photo Q46359/61.
9   IWM Photo Q13639.

10   IWM Photo Q13797.

11   Royal Naval Division War Diary, TNA(PRO) WO 95/4290.

12   Aspinall-Oglander, Brig.-Gen. C.F., *Military Operations, Gallipoli*, Vol. II, London: Heinemann, 1932, p. 83fn.

13   Anzac Intelligence War Diary, TNA(PRO) WO 157/681.

14   IWM Photo Q32246.

15   IWM Photo Q14683-4.

16   IWM Photo Q12876.

17   IWM Photo Q12880.

18   IWM Photo Q49796.

19   All IWM Photo Q37340.

20   Macmunn, G. & Falls, C., *History of the Great War, Military Operations, Egypt & Palestine*, Vol. I, London: HMSO, 1928, p. 341.

21   Moberly, F.J., *History of the Great War, Military Operations, The Campaign in Mesopotamia 1914–1918*, Vol. II, London: HMSO, 1924.

22   Masters, John, *The Road Past Mandalay*, London: Michael Joseph, 1961.

23   Coombs, Rose, *Before Endeavours Fade, A Guide to the Battlefields of the First World War*, London: Battle of Britain Prints International, 1976.

24   Chasseaud, Peter, *Topography of Armageddon, A British Trench Map Atlas of the Western Front 1914–1918*, Lewes: Mapbooks, 1991 & 1998.

25   *The Imperial War Museum Trench Map Archive on CD Rom*, The Naval & Military Press in association with The Imperial War Museum, Uckfield: The Naval & Military Press, 2000.

26   *Captured German Trench and Operations Maps from The National Archives*, CD Rom, The Naval & Military Press in association with The National Archives, Uckfield: The Naval & Military Press, 2003.

27   4th (Guards) Brigade War Diary, TNA(PRO) WO 95/1341, and 6th Brigade War Diary, TNA(PRO) WO 95/1352.

28   *The Work of the Royal Engineers in the European War, 1914–19, Supply of Engineer Stores and Equipment*, Chatham: Institution of Royal Engineers, n.d. (c. 1921), pp. 96–7.

BIBLIOGRAPHY

Published Books, Articles, etc.

Abbott, J.H.M., *Letters from Queer Street*, London: Adam & Charles Black, 1908.

Addison, Col. G.H. (compiler), *The Work of the Royal Engineers in the European War, 1914–1918, Miscellaneous*, Chatham: Institution of Royal Engineers, 1926.

Andrew, C., *Secret Service, The Making of the British Intelligence Community*, London: Heinemann, 1985.

Anon., *The Bible*, Authorised Version.

Anon., *The British Grenadier*.

Anon., *An Der Somme – Erinnerungen der 12. Infanterie-Division an die Stellungskämpfe und Schlacht an der Somme, Oktober 1915 bis November 1916*, Berlin: Ferdinand Dümmler, 1918.

Arthur-Lévy, *Les Coulisses de la Guerre, le Service Géographique de l'Armée 1914–1918*, Paris: Berger-Levrault, 1926.

Ashworth, Tony, *Trench Warfare 1914–1918, The Live and Let Live System*, London: Pan Books, 2000.

Aspinall-Oglander, Brig.-Gen. C.F., *Military Operations, Gallipoli*, Vol. II, London: Heinemann, 1932.

Bales, Capt. P.G., *The History of the 1/4th Battalion, Duke of Wellington's (West Riding) Regiment, 1914–1919*, London & Halifax: Edward Mortimer, 1920.

Barton, P.; Doyle, P. and Vandewalle, J., *Beneath Flanders Fields, The Tunnellers' War 1914–18*, Staplehurst: Spellmount, 2004.

Blunden, Edmund, *Undertones of War*, London: Cobden-Sanderson, 1928.

Blunden, Edmund, *De Bello Germanico, A Fragment of Trench History,* written in 1918 by the author of *Undertones of War*, Hawstead: G.A. Blunden, 1930.

Brophy, J. and Partridge, E., *Songs and Slang of the British Soldier 1914–18*, London: Scholartis Press, 1930.

Brophy, J. and Partridge, E., *The Long Trail – What the British Soldier Sang and Said in 1914–1918*, London: Andre Deutsch, 1965.

Brown, Malcolm, *The Imperial War Museum Book of The Western Front*, London: BCA, 1993.

Cave, Nigel, *Sanctuary Wood & Hooge*, Barnsley: Leo Cooper, Pen & Sword, Battleground Europe, Ypres, series, 2002.

Chapman, Guy, *A Passionate Prodigality, Fragments of an Autobiography*, London: Nicholson & Watson, 1933.

Chasseaud, Peter, *Topography of Armageddon, A British Trench Map Atlas of the Western Front 1914-1918*, Lewes: Mapbooks, 1991 & 1998.

Chasseaud, Peter, *Artillery's Astrologers - A History of British Survey and Mapping on the Western Front, 1914-1918*, Lewes: Mapbooks, 1999.

Chasseaud, Peter, 'German Maps and Survey on the Western Front, 1914-18', *The Cartographic Journal*, London, *38*(2), 2001.

Clausewitz, General Karl Maria von, *Vom Kriege*, Vols. 1-7, Berlin: Ferdinand Dümmler, 1832-37.

Conrad, Joseph, *The Secret Agent*, London: Penguin Modern Classics edition, 1971.

Conrad, P. and Laspeyres, A., *La Grande Guerre 1914-1918*, Paris: EPA, 1989.

Coombs, Rose, *Before Endeavours Fade, A Guide to the Battlefields of the First World War*, London: Battle of Britain Prints International, 1976.

Cuthbert Keeson, Major C.A., *The History and Records of Queen Victoria's Rifles 1792-1922*, London: Constable, 1923.

Dickens, Charles, *Our Mutual Friend*.

Dryden, John, *Absalom and Achitophel*.

Eckert, Max, *Die Kartenwissenschaft,* Berlin & Leipzig: VWV, Mittler, Vol. 1 1921, Vol. 2 1925.

Edmonds, J.E., *History of the Great War, Military Operations, France and Belgium, 1914*, Vol. II, London: Macmillan, 1925.

Edmonds, J.E. and Wynne, G.C., *History of The Great War, Military Operations, France and Belgium*, 1915, Vol. I, London: Macmillan, 1927.

Edmonds, J.E. *History of The Great War, Military Operations, France and Belgium*, 1915, Vol. II, London: Macmillan, 1928.

Edmonds, J.E., *History of The Great War, Military Operations, France and Belgium*, 1916, Vol. I, London: Macmillan, 1932.

Edmonds, J.E., *History of the Great War, Military Operations, France and Belgium,* 1918, Vol. I, London: Macmillan, 1935.

Eliot, T.S., *The Waste Land*, London: Faber & Faber, 1922.

Frankau, Gilbert, *Peter Jackson, Cigar Merchant*, 3rd Edition, London: Hutchinson, 1920.

Frege, Gottlob, 'On Sense and Meaning', in: P.T. Geach and Max Black (eds), *Translations from the Philosophical Writings of Gottlob Frege*, London: OUP, 1980.

Fussell, Paul, *The Great War and Modern Memory*, London: OUP, 1975.

Gordon, Professor Cyrus H., *Forgotten Scripts, The Story of their Decipherment*, London: Pelican, 1971.

Grand Quartier Général des Armées, *Instruction sur l'Organisation et le fonctionnement des Sections Topographiques des Corps d'Armées (S.T.C.A.), Au G.Q.G. le 25 décembre 1915*, 1915.

Grand Quartier Général des Armées, Etat-Major (2e et 3e Bureaux) (1918), *Instruction sur les Plans Directeurs et les Cartes et Plans Spéciaux*, Annexes, Paris: Imprimerie Nationale, 1918.

Graves, Robert, *Fairies and Fusiliers*, London: Heinemann, 1917.

Graves, Robert, *Goodbye to All That*, London: Penguin Modern Classics, 1961.

Griffith, Paddy, *Battle Tactics of the Western Front, The British Army's Art of Attack 1916–18*, New Haven and London: Yale University Press, 1994.

Hamilton, H.W.R., 'History of the 20th (Field) Company; Royal Bombay Sappers and Miners. Great War: 1914–1918', Part I, France, *Royal Engineers Journal*, December 1926

Harris, Henry E.D., *The Irish Regiments in the First World War*, Cork: Mercier Press, 1968.

Hatto, A.H. (transl.), *The Nibelungenlied*, London: Penguin Classics, 1975.

Hay, Ian, *The First Hundred Thousand*, Edinburgh & London: Blackwood, 1916.

Holmes, Richard, *Redcoat: The British Soldier in the Age of Horse and Musket*, London: HarperCollins, 2002.

Holmes, Richard, *Tommy: The British Soldier on the Western Front 1914–1918*, London: HarperCollins, 2004.

Hume, Fergus, *In Queer Street*, London: F.V. White, 1913.

The Illustrated London News, 4 Sept. 1915, London.

Innes, J.R., *Flash Spotters and Sound Rangers*, London, George Allen & Unwin, 1935.

IX Corps [British], *Instructions For The Offensive*, reprint by Washington: Government Printing Works, 1917.

Jack, Col. E.M., *Report on Survey on the Western Front*, Geographical Section, General Staff, War Office, London: HMSO, 1920.

Johnson, Dr Samuel, *Vanity of Human Wishes*.

Jones, David, *In Parenthesis*, London: Faber & Faber, 1937.

Josipovici, Gabriel, *The World and the Book, A Study of Modern Fiction*, London: Macmillan, 1971.

Kadmon, N, *Toponymy – The Lore, Laws and Language of Geographical Names*, New York: United Nations, 2000.

Kavanagh, Gaynor, *Museums and the First World War, A Social History*, London & New York: Leicester University Press, 1994.

Kripke, Saul A., *Naming and Necessity*, London: OUP, 1980.

Lamb, Charles, *Essays of Elia: Dream Children*.

Lewis, D., 'Truth in Fiction', *American Philosophical Quarterly*, 1978.

London, Jack, *The People of the Abyss*, New York: Macmillan, 1903.

Lucan, *Pharsalia*.

Lytton, Neville, *The Press and the General Staff*, London: Collins, 1920.

MacGill, Patrick, *Soldier Songs*, London: Herbert Jenkins, 1917.

Mackenzie, Compton, *Mabel in Queer Street*, Oxford: Basil Blackwell, n.d.

Mackenzie, Compton, *Sinister Street*, Vols. I & II, London: Martin Secker, 1913–14.

Macmunn, G. and Falls, C., *History of the Great War, Military Operations, Egypt & Palestine*, Vol. I, London: HMSO, 1928.

Malory, Sir Thomas, *Le Morte Darthur*, London: Caxton, 1485.

Masters, John, *The Road Past Mandalay*, London: Michael Joseph, 1961.

Messenger, Charles, *Terriers in the Trenches; The Post Office Rifles at War, 1914–1918*, Chippenham: Picton, 1982.

Miles, Capt. Wilfred, *History of The Great War, Military Operations, France and Belgium*, 1916, Vol. II, London: Macmillan, 1938.

Miles, Capt. Wilfred, *History of the Great War, Military Operations, France and Belgium,* 1917, Vol. III, *The Battle of Cambrai*, London: HMSO, 1948.

Moberly, F.J., *History of the Great War, Military Operations, The Campaign in Mesopotamia 1914–1918,* Vol. II, London: HMSO, 1924.

Montgomery, Maj.-Gen. Sir A, *The Story of the Fourth Army in the Battles of the Hundred Days, August 8th to November 11th 1918*, London: Hodder & Stoughton, 1920.

Moore, A.W. (ed.), *Meaning and Reference*, London: OUP, 1993, and Salmon, N., *Reference and Essence*, NJ: Princeton, 1982.

Orr, Philip, *The Road to the Somme, Men of the Ulster Division Tell Their Story*, Belfast: Blackstaff Press, 1987.

Pynchon, Thomas, *Gravity's Rainbow*, London: Picador (Pan Books), 1975.

Roberts, F.J. (ed.), *The Wipers Times*, first complete facsimile edition, London: Eveleigh Nash & Grayson, 1930.

Romer, Carrol, typescript diary, present whereabouts unknown.

Rosenberg, Isaac, *Poems by Isaac Rosenberg*, London: Heinemann, 1922.

Royal Engineers Institution, *The Work of the Royal Engineers in the European War, 1914–19, Supply of Engineer Stores and Equipment*, Chatham: Institution of Royal Engineers, n.d.

Royal Engineers Institution, *The Work of the Royal Engineers in the European War, 1914–19, Military Mining*, Chatham: Institution of Royal Engineers, 1922.

Sassoon, Siegfried, *The War Poems of Siegfried Sassoon*, London: Heinemann, 1919.

Sassoon, Siegfried, *Memoirs of a Fox-Hunting Man*, and *Memoirs of an Infantry Officer*, in *The Complete Memoirs of George Sherston*, London: Faber, 1972.

Scruton, Roger, *Modern Philosophy, A Survey*, London: Sinclair-Stevenson, 1994.

Service Géographique de l'Armée, *Rapport sur les Travaux Exécutés du 1er août 1914 au 31 décembre 1919 (Rapport de Guerre)*, Paris: Service Géographique de l'Armée, 1924, revised 1936.

Services Historiques des Armées, *Du Paysage à la Carte – Trois siècles de cartographie militaire de la France*, Ministère de la Défense, Services Historiques des Armées; Vincennes (catalogue of an exhibition prepared under the direction of Marie-Anne de Villèle, Agnès Beylot and Alain Morgat), 2002.

Shakespeare, William, *The Complete Works* (ed. Peter Alexander), London & Glasgow: Collins, 1961.

Shorter Oxford English Dictionary, 3rd Edition, Revised with Addenda, corrections, etc, Oxford: The Clarendon Press, 1965.

Sulzbach, Herbert, *With the German Guns – Four Years on the Western Front 1914–1918*, Barnsley: Pen and Sword, 2003.

Weekes, Alan, *The Royal Hampshire Regiment*, London, 1969.

Winter, J. & Baggett, B., *1914–18 – The Great War and the Shaping of the 20th Century*, London: BBC Books, 1996.

Wittgenstein, L. (trans. G.E.M. Anscombe), *Philosophical Investigations*, Oxford: Blackwell, 1953.

Wolff, Leon, *In Flanders Fields, The Flanders Campaign of 1917*, London: Corgi, 1966.

The National Archives (London (Kew))

1st Brigade War Diary, TNA(PRO) WO 95/1261.
2nd Brigade War Diary, TNA(PRO) WO 95/1267.
4th (Guards) Brigade War Diary, TNA(PRO) WO 95/1341.
6th Brigade War Diary, TNA(PRO) WO 95/1352.
7th Brigade War Diary, TNA(PRO) WO 95/1413.
8th Brigade War Diary, TNA(PRO) WO 95/1416.
11th Brigade War Diary, TNA (PRO) WO 95/1486.
11th Brigade War Diary (Appendices), TNA(PRO) WO 95/1487.
140th Brigade War Diary, TNA(PRO) WO 95/2727.
153rd Brigade War Diary, TNA(PRO) WO 95/2869.

Royal Naval Division War Diary, TNA(PRO) WO 95/4290.
1st Division General Staff War Diary, TNA(PRO) WO 95/1227.
3rd Division General Staff War Diary, TNA(PRO) WO 95/1274.

5th Division General Staff War Diary, TNA(PRO) WO 95/1510.
5th Division General Staff War Diary, TNA(PRO) WO 95/1512.
7th Division General Staff War Diary, TNA(PRO) WO 95/1627.
7th Division General Staff War Diary, TNA(PRO) WO 95/1628.
7th Division CRE War Diary, TNA(PRO) WO 95/1641.
8th Division General Staff War Diary, TNA(PRO) WO 95/1671.
8th Division CRA War Diary, TNA(PRO) WO 95 1683.
14th Division General Staff War Diary, TNA(PRO) WO 95/1864.
27th Division General Staff War Diary, TNA(PRO) WO 95/2254.
27th Division General Staff War Diary, TNA(PRO) WO 95/2255.
28th Division General Staff War Diary, TNA(PRO) WO 95/2267.

Anzac Corps Intelligence War Diary, TNA(PRO) WO 157/681.
II Corps GS War Diary, TNA(PRO) WO 95/629.

First Army General Staff War Diary, TNA(PRO) WO 95/156.
Second Army General Staff War Diary, TNA(PRO) WO 95/270.
Third Army General Staff War Diary, TNA(PRO) WO 95/359.
Third Army General Staff War Diary, TNA(PRO) WO 95/361.

Trench Maps 1914–18, Western & Other Fronts, TNA(PRO) WO 153.
Trench Maps 1914–18, Western Front, TNA(PRO) WO 297.

INDEX TO PART ONE

Note: Trench names, and towns and villages that gave their names to map sheets, are generally omitted from this index; British trench names are to be found in the Gazetteer.

PART TWO

GAZETTEER OF NAMES OF TRENCHES AND OTHER TACTICAL FEATURES

Abbreviations Used in the Gazetteer

All	Alley
Ave or Av	Avenue
Cres or Cr	Crescent
CT	Communication Trench
Dr	Drive
Ger	German
Gr	*Graben* [German for trench]
Ln	Lane
Lt Rly	Light railway
Rd	Road
Rdt	Redoubt
Res	Reserve
Rly	Railway
St	Street
Sup or Supp	Support
Sw	Switch
Tr	Trench
Wd	Wood

Finding Maps in the Gazetteer

Note on map sheet numbering: At the end of 1917, Sheet 36c was redesignated Sheet 44a; in the Gazetteer it is always given as 36c.

The references given are to the sheet-based system of reference squaring used by the BEF during the war years. The sheet name given is a general guide. Some sheets overlap; certain combined sheets overlapped the regular series sheetlines, and some of these can be identified on the index map. For example, *36NW2&NE1 Houplines* overlaps both *36NW2 Armentières* and *36NE1 Quesnoy*. If a trench cannot be found on one it might be found on the other. There were also many special sheets produced by Field Survey Companies/Battalions which overlapped two or four regular series sheets. These are listed alphabetically in The National Archives class WO 297. Many other trench maps can also be found in class WO 153. It is also worth looking at the 1:20,000 regular series sheets, each of which covers the area of four 1:10,000 sheets. However, their smaller scale makes reading the names more difficult, and a magnifying glass is sometimes necessary. The various Naval & Military Press/Imperial War Museum/National Archives trench map CD Roms and DVDs are invaluable in this respect, as their high resolution enables the zoom facility to be used to great effect.

Map square references were common to 1:40,000, 1:20,000 and 1:10,000 sheets. Where possible the 1:10,000 or 1:20,000 sheet is cited. Square references are given to the 500 yard sub-square (a, b, c or d) or some combination of these. Two- or four-figure coordinates with a sub-square are given where it is possible to pinpoint a trench or post.

The map references given in the listing are to the 500 yard sub-squares within which a trench was situated – e.g. K 17 d. Trenches frequently spread over two or more sub-squares, in which the reference might read K 17, c, d, 18 a, c. Some references taken from earlier maps – those of 1915 – are incorrect by up to 300m compared with later, more accurate maps, and the references must therefore only be taken as a rough guide; if the trench cannot be found in the sub-square given, it may be found in an adjacent sub-square. A further word of warning – not all trenches or trench names were entered on the maps, and a study of various sheets and editions might be necessary before a trench is finally located. If the date of a particular trench action is known, the trench may or may not be found on earlier or later sheets. Remember that British trench names were only shown on secret editions until 1918.

The Gazetteer includes trenches, breastworks, and certain paths and duckboard tracks in woods (e.g. Ploegsteert Wood and Delville Wood) which essentially served the same function and were similarly named. In addition named redoubts, works, strongpoints, craters and tunnels are included, and also certain important localities such as cross-roads and farms, etc. In the interests of brevity, some topographical names have been omitted. In fact, the names given to topographical features often came first, trenches later dug in their vicinity then taking their names.

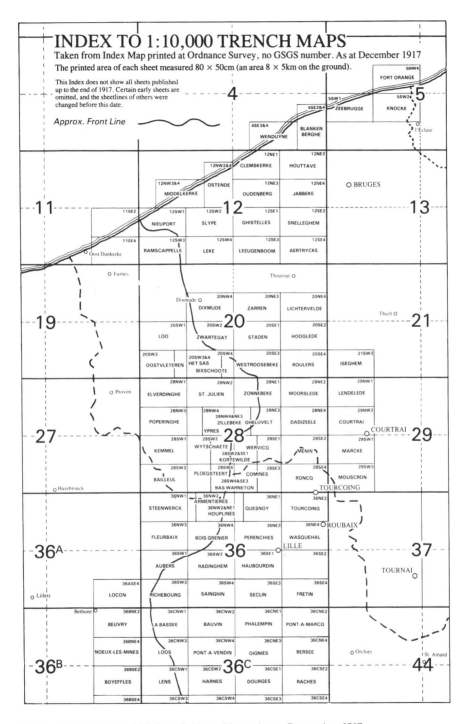

INDEX TO 1:10,000 TRENCH MAPS

Taken from Index Map printed at Ordnance Survey, no GSGS number. As at December 1917
The printed area of each sheet measured 80 × 50cm (an area 8 × 5km on the ground).

This Index does not show all sheets published
up to the end of 1917. Certain early sheets are
omitted, and the sheetlines of others were
changed before this date.

Approx. Front Line

Index diagram to 1:10,000 Trench Maps, Ypres–Lens, December 1917.

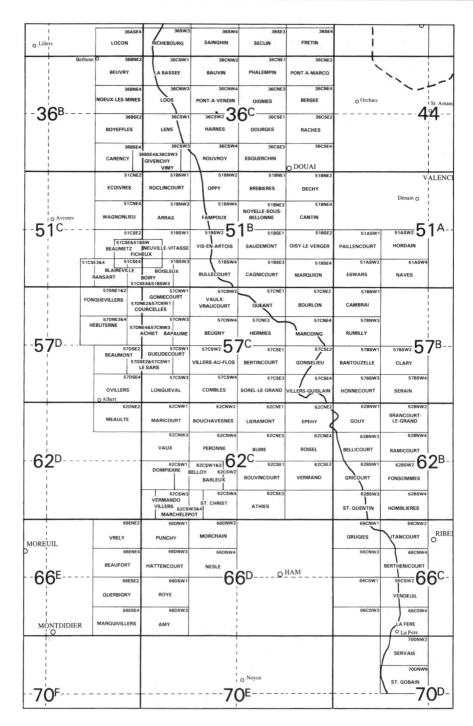

Index diagram to 1:10,000 trench maps, Vimy–St Quentin, December 1917.

Name	Map Sheet	Map Reference
1 Trench	51bNW3 Arras	G 30 a, c
1, Boyau [Mad Point]	36cNW1 La Bassée	A 28 c 8.1
101 Street	57dSE4 Ovillers	X 26 b
101 sud, Bois	66eNE4 Beaufort	L 32 b, 33 a
102nd Post	57dSE4 Ovillers	X 11 c 00.45
102nd Street	62dNE2 Méaulte	F 2 b
103rd Street	62dNE2 Méaulte	F 2 b
104 [French trench; Bécourt]	57dSE4 Ovillers	X 26 b, d
107, Boyau	36cNW3 Loos	G 4 d
11 [French trench; Moulin de Fargny]	62cNW1 Maricourt	A 29 a, b
110 [old French spot-height]	62dNE2 Méaulte	F 10 c 2.4
11th Street	57dSE2 Beaumont	R 24 c 7.9
120 Millimètre Wood	62cNW3 Vaux	G 9 b, 10 a
123, Boyau	36bSE4 Carency / 36cSW3 Vimy	X 23, 24, 29, 30, S 19
125 Street [N of St Yves / St Yvon]	28SW4 Ploegsteert	U 14 b, 15 a, c
126 Street [N of St Yves / St Yvon]	28SW4 Ploegsteert	U 14 b, 15 a
12th Division Cemetery	51bNW3 Arras	G 28 b 9.7
13, Boyau [Treize Alley]	36cSW1 Lens	M 9 a, b
130th Alley [Tranchée de la 130e D.I.]	36cSW3 Vimy	S 8 b, d, 14 a
13th Rifle Brigade Cemetery	57cNW3 Bapaume	G 4 c 5.5
14 bis, Puits No.	36cNW3 Loos	H 25 d 2.1
14 Camp	28NW3 Poperinghe	H 8 a, c
14 Tree Clump [le Piètre]	36SW1 Aubers	N 20 b 5.4
14 Willows Road	57cSE4 Villers-Guislain	X 14 d
140, Boyau du	57dNE3 & 4 Hébuterne	K 22 d, 23 a
143, Boyau du	36cSW1 Lens	M 9 c
16 Poplars	57dNE3 & 4 Hébuterne	K 17 a 5.8
18A Street	51cSE3 & 4 Ransart	W 17 d, 18 c
18B Street	51cSE3 & 4 Ransart	W 17 d, 18 c
18th Alley	36cNW3 Loos	G 6 c, d
19 Metre Hill	20SW4 Bixschoote	U 18 d 6.4
19 Street	51cSE3 & 4 Ransart	W 17 d, 18 c
1st Avenue	57dSE1 & 2 Beaumont	Q 9 d, 10 c, d
1st Entrance [CT east of Colincamps]	57dNE3 & 4 Hébuterne	K 27 c
1st Switch Line [Gommecourt 1916]	57dNE1&2 Fonquevillers/57dNE3&4 Hébuterne	E 29 a, c, K 5 a, b, d
2 / Scottish Rifles Cemetery	36SW1 Aubers	M 35 a 3.6
2 Maisons, les	20SW4 Bixschoote	T 17 b 2.4
20 Street	51cSE3 & 4 Ransart	W 17 b, 18 a
21 Street	51cSE3 & 4 Ransart	W 17 b, 18 a
22 Street	51cSE3 & 4 Ransart	W 17 b, 18 a
23 Street	51cSE3 & 4 Ransart	W 18 a
24 Street	51cSE3 & 4 Ransart	W 18 a
25 Street	51cSE3 & 4 Ransart	W 12 c, 18 a
25 Trench	57cSW4 Combles	T 5 a, c
25 Yards Trench	57cSW4 Combles	T 5 c
26th Avenue	57dSE2 & 57cSW1 Le Sars	M 21 c, d, 26 a, b, 27 a
27 Street	51cSE3 & 4 Ransart	W 12 c
29 Street	51cSE3 & 4 Ransart	W 12 c, d
2nd Avenue	57dSE1 & 2 Beaumont	Q 9 b, 10 a, b
2nd Entrance [CT east of Colincamps]	57dNE3 & 4 Hébuterne	K 27 a
2nd House [Le Pelerin]	28SW4 Ploegsteert	U 21 b 36.16
2nd Switch Line [Gommecourt 1916]	57dNE1&2 Fonquevillers/57dNE3&4 Hébuterne	E 24 a, b, d, 30 b, d, K 6 b, c, d

Name	Map Sheet	Map Reference
3 Farms, The	36aNE2 Vieux Berquin	F 15 a 6.7
3 Houses Street	51cSE3 & 4 Ransart	R 32 c, d
3 Inns [Corons de Pekin]	36cNW1 La Bassée	A 29 d 2.3
3 Maisons Farm	20SW4 Bixschoote	T 10 b 3.8
3 Tilleuls, les [farm]	36aNE2 Vieux Berquin	F 10 c
30 Street	51cSE3 & 4 Ransart	W 12 b, d
30th October Wood	62cNW3 Vaux	G 21 d / 27 b
36 Reserve	28NW4 & NE3 Zillebeke	I 28 d, 34 b
3rd Avenue	57dSE1 & 2 Beaumont	Q 3 c
3rd Entrance [CT east of Colincamps]	57dNE3 & 4 Hébuterne	K 27 a
3rd House [Le Pelerin]	28SW4 Ploegsteert	U 21 b 65.22
4 Extrémités, les	27NE1 Herzeele	E 3 c, d
4 Fils Aymon, les [farm]	27SE4 Meteren	X 3 c 05.10
4 Hallots Ferme, les	36NW2 Armentières	C 23 d 3.7
4 Huns Farm	28SW2 Wytschaete	O 26 c 9.0
4 Vents, Les	51bNW3 Arras	G 10 b 2.1
4th Avenue	57dSE1 & 2 Beaumont	Q 3 d, 4 a, b, c
5 Chemins Estaminet	28NW2 St Julien	C 14 a 85.85
5 Chemins, les [cross roads]	20SW4 Bixschoote	U 6 c 98.47
5.6 Farm	20SW3 Oostvleteren	T 9 d 2.2
500 Avenue	51bNW1 Roclincourt	A 16 c
500 Crater	51bNW1 Roclincourt	A 16 c 7.4
5th Avenue	57dSE1 & 2 Beaumont	Q 3 a, b, 4 a
5th Point [GFL, late 1915]	36SW2 Radinghem	O 1 a 50.85
6 k [kilometre] Farm [Broodseinde]	28NE1 Zonnebeke	D 23 c 3.0
6 Q [Br front trench, Aug 1915]	36NW4 Bois Grenier	I 31 c
6 R [Br front trench, Aug 1915]	36NW4 Bois Grenier	I 31 c
6 S [Br front trench, Aug 1915]	36NW4 Bois Grenier	I 31 c
64 Street	62dNE2 Méaulte	F 11 d
65 Metre Point Redoubt	36cNW3 Loos	G 28 b
66 Street [E of Mansel Copse]	62dNE2 Méaulte	F 11 d
67 Street	62dNE2 Méaulte	F 11 c
67 Support	62dNE2 Méaulte	F 11 c
68 Street	62dNE2 Méaulte	F 17 a
69 Street	62dNE2 Méaulte	F 17 a
6th Avenue	57dSE4 Ovillers / 57cSW3 Longueval	X 6 c, S 1 b, d, 2 a, c, d
6th Point [German Front Line, late 1915]	36NW4 Bois Grenier	I 31 d 85.30
7 Arbres, les	66eNE2 Vrély	F 11 a 5.5
7 Gables [house; Le Touquet]	36NW2 & NE1 Houplines	C 10 b 15.35
70 Street	62dNE2 Méaulte	F 16 b
70th Avenue	57cSW3 Longueval	S 1 b, d, 2 a, c
70th Trench	57cSW1 Gueudecourt	M 26 b
71 [old French spot-height]	62dNE2 Méaulte	F 15 c 9.9
71 North [Boyau; old French numbering]	62dNE2 Méaulte	F 15 a 5.5
71 South [Boyau; old French numbering]	62dNE2 Méaulte	F 15 d 0.8
71 Street	62dNE2 Méaulte	F 16 b
71 Street	62dNE2 Méaulte	F 16 b
72 Street	62dNE2 Méaulte	F 16 b
79 Street	57dNE1 & 2 Fonquevillers	E 5 c, 11 a
7e D.I., Tranchée de la [Horse Guards Ave]	36cSW1 Lens	M 15 a
80 Street [S of Bois Français]	62dNE2 Méaulte	F 9 d
81.B. Street [D1 Sub-sector]	62dNE2 Méaulte	F 10
84 Street [Boyau; old French numbering]	62dNE2 Méaulte	F 9 c
85 Street	57dNE1 & 2 Fonquevillers	E 4 d

Name	Map Sheet	Map Reference
85 Street [Boyau; old French numbering]	62dNE2 Méaulte	F 9 a
86 Alley	66cSW2 Vendeuil	N 12 d, O 7 c
86 Street	57dNE1 & 2 Fonquevillers	E 4 d
86th Trench [W of Beaumont Hamel]	57dSE1 & 2 Beaumont	Q 3 d, 4 c, 9 b
87 Street	57dNE1 & 2 Fonquevillers	E 4 b
88 Street	57dNE1 & 2 Fonquevillers	E 4 b
88th Trench	57dSE1 & 2 Beaumont	10 a, c
89 Street	57dNE1 & 2 Fonquevillers	E 4 b
9 Conspicuous Trees	36cSW4 Rouvroy	T 18 b 8.9
9 Kilo Farm [by kilometre stone]	20SW4 Bixschoote	T 11 d 75.40
9, Boyau [Cuinchy Sector, July 1915]	36cNW1 La Bassée	A 15 d, 21 b
9, Boyau [Neuf Alley]	36cSW1 Lens	M 9 a, b, d
90 Street	57dNE1 & 2 Fonquevillers	E 4 b
96 Piccadilly	36cSW3 Vimy	S 10 b
98, Boyau	36cNW3 Loos	G 5 d, 11 b
A & S Sap, North [Argyle & Sutherland]	36cNW1 La Bassée	A 21 b
A & S Sap, South [Argyle & Sutherland]	36cNW1 La Bassée	A 21 b
A [outlying trench, Fort 147]	51cSE3 & 4 Ransart	W 16 d 4.8
A 1 [Br, mid-1915, Gully Farm]	28NW4 & NE3 Zillebeke	I 5 d 7.0
A 2 [Br, mid-1915, SW of Gully Farm]	28NW4 & NE3 Zillebeke	I 11 b 2.8
A Lines [S of Neuve Chapelle 1914-15]	36SW3 Richebourg	S 4 d
A Sap	57cSE2 Gonnelieu	Q 4 b, 5 a
A Sap [Givenchy]	36cNW1 La Bassée	A 9 d
A Sector [4/15, N of R Douve]	28SW4 Ploegsteert	U 1 / 7
A Siding [railway, Ouderdom]	28NW3 Poperinghe	G 30 a, c
A Street	57dSE1 & 2 Beaumont	Q 16 b
A Trench	57cSW1 Gueudecourt	M 14 d, 15 c
A Work	51bNW3 Arras	G 17 d
A.1. Avenue (New Bond Street), & Post	36SW1 Aubers	N 8 a
A.b. [communication trench]	36cSW4 Rouvroy	T 12 a
A.c. [communication trench]	36cSW4 Rouvroy	T 12 a
A.d. [communication trench]	36cSW4 Rouvroy	T 12 c
A.g. [communication trench]	36cSW4 Rouvroy	T 12 c
A.h. [communication trench]	36cSW4 Rouvroy	T 12 c
A.I.F. Divisional Cemetery	62dNE [4 Bray-sur-Somme]	K 24 c
A.j. [communication trench]	36cSW4 Rouvroy	T 12 c
A.l. [communication trench]	36cSW4 Rouvroy	T 12 c
A.m. [communication trench]	36cSW4 Rouvroy	T 12 c
A.n. [communication trench]	36cSW4 Rouvroy	T 12 c
A.p. [communication trench]	36cSW4 Rouvroy	T 12 c
A.q. [communication trench]	36cSW4 Rouvroy	T 18 a
A.r. [communication trench]	36cSW4 Rouvroy	T 18 a, b
A.s. [communication trench]	36cSW4 Rouvroy	T 18 a, b
A.t. [communication trench]	36cSW4 Rouvroy	T 18 a, b
A.v. [communication trench]	36cSW4 Rouvroy	T 18 b
Aback Trench	36cSW4 Rouvroy	T 11 a, b
Abaft Trench	36cSW4 Rouvroy	T 11 b
Abancourt Line [1918]	62dSE [1 Hamel]	P 21 a, c, 27 a, c
Abash Trench	36cSW4 Rouvroy	T 11 b
Abattoir, Cité de l' [miners' cottages]	36cSW1 Lens	M 35 a
Abayette, l' [hamlet, Athies]	51bNW3 Arras	H 14 b 8.3
Abbaye Lane	57cSW1 Gueudecourt	M 23 a, b
Abbaye Trench [Eaucourt l'Abbaye]	57cSW1 Gueudecourt	M 17 c, d, 22 b, 23 a, b
Abbé Sector, L' [trenches, 1918]	62dSW [2 Villers-Bretonneux / 4 Cachy]	O 26, 31, 32, U 1

Name	Map Sheet	Map Reference
Abbé Trench	62cSW2 Barleux	N 17 b, c, d
Abbé Wood Trench, L' [1918]	62dSW [4 Cachy]	U 1 a, b, c, 7 a, c, 13 a
Abbé's Copse	20SE2 Hooglede	R 1 a 2.2
Abbé's Farm	20SE2 Hooglede	R 1 c 3.8
Abbey Road [road]	36aSE2 Lestrem	R 20 a, c
Abbey Road [road]	57dSE2 & 57cSW1 Le Sars	M 23 d, 24 c, 30 a, c, d, 36 b
Abbey Trench	36cSW1 Lens	M 20 b, d, 21 a
Abbey Trench	57cSW2 Villers-au-Flos	N 22 b
Abbot Corner [road jct]	28NE4 Dadizeele	L 22 d 7.1
Abbot Trench	36cSW1 Lens	M 22 a
Abbot's Lane	36SW2 Radinghem	N 6 a, b
Abeam Trench	36cSW4 Rouvroy	T 11 b
Abed Trench	36cSW4 Rouvroy	T 11 b
Abeele [village]	27NE4 Abeele	L 26 c, 32 a
Abeele Custom House	27NE4 Abeele	L 26 c 8.6
Abeele Line	27NE4 Abeele	extensive
Abeele Railhead / Refilling Point	27NE4 Abeele	L 27 c, 32 b, 33 a
Abeele Station	27NE4 Abeele	L 33 a
Aberdeen Avenue	28SW4 Ploegsteert	U 27 b, 28 a
Aberdeen Avenue	57dSE4 Ovillers	X 25 d, 26 a, c
Aberfeldy Trench	28SW4 Ploegsteert	U 27 b, 28 a
Abidjean [Trench]	66cNW2 Itancourt / 4 Berthenicourt	I 2 a, c, d
Abjure Trench	36cSW4 Rouvroy	T 11 d, 12 a
Ablain St. Nazaire [village]	36bSE4 & 36cSW3 Givenchy	X 10, 11
Ablain Trench	57dNE3 & 4 Hébuterne	K 16 d
Ablain Trench [1918]	57dNE2 & 57cNW1 Courcelles	F 28 a, b
Ablaincourt [village]	62cSW3 Vermandovillers	S 18 c, d, 24 a, b, T 13
Ablaze Trench	36cSW4 Rouvroy	T 11 d, 12 c
Aboard Trench	36cSW1 Lens	M 21 b
Abode Lane	62cNW2 Bouchavesnes	C 1 d, 2 c
Abode Trench	36cSW1 Lens	M 24 d
Abound Trench	36cSW4 Rouvroy	T 12 c
Above Trench	36cSW1 Lens	M 22 a
Aboyne Street	57dSE4 Ovillers	X 26 b
Abraham Alley [Abraham Heights]	28NE1 Zonnebeke	D 9 d, 15 b
Abraham Heights	28NE1 Zonnebeke	D 15 b
Abraham Trench	36cSW1 Lens	M 21 b, 22 a
Abrest Trench	36cSW4 Rouvroy	T 18 a
Abri Farm	20SW4 Bixschoote	U 26 a 35.25
Abri Wood	20SW4 Bixschoote	U 25 d, 26 c
Abricot Trench	20SW3 Oostvleteren	T 15 b, d
Abroad Trench	36cSW4 Rouvroy	T 18 a
Abrupt Trench	36cSW4 Rouvroy	T 12 d, U 7 a
Absalom Trench	36cSW1 Lens	M 22 d, 23 c, d, 24 c, d
Abschnitt D [Cake Trench]	28NW2 St Julien	C 14 a
Abscond Trench	36cSW1 Lens	M 27 a
Absent Trench	36cSW4 Rouvroy	T 12 d
Absinthe Trench	36cSW4 Rouvroy	T 6 c, 12 a
Absinthe Trench	62cNW2 Bouchavesnes	C 2 a, c, d
Absorb Trench	36cSW4 Rouvroy	T 6 c, d
Abuse Trench	36cSW4 Rouvroy	U 7 c
Abyss Trench	36cSW4 Rouvroy	T 18 b
Acacia Copse	62bNW4 Ramicourt	I 34 a, b
Acacia Trench	36cSW4 Rouvroy	U 18 d, 13 a, b, 14 a

Name	Map Sheet	Map Reference
Acacia Trench [1918]	62dSE [1 Hamel]	P 32 b
Academy Buildings	28NE2 Moorslede	F 28 c 75.90
Academy Trench	36cSW4 Rouvroy	U 13 a, c, d
Acajou Trench	36cSW4 Rouvroy	T 18 c, d
Accent Trench	36cSW1 Lens	M 22 a
Accent Trench	36cSW4 Rouvroy	T 18 c, d
Access Trench	36cSW3 Vimy	T 3 a, c
Access Trench	36cSW4 Rouvroy	T 18 d
Access Trench	62cNW2 Bouchavesnes	C 9 b
Accident Trench	36cSW1 Lens	M 21 d, 22 c, 27 b
Accloy Trench	36cSW4 Rouvroy	T 18 d, 24 b
Accord Trench	36cSW1 Lens	M 20 d
Accra Cottage	36aNE3 Haverskerque	J 7 a 15.10
Accroche Wood	62dSE [1 Hamel]	P 16 b, c, d, 22 a, b
Accrue Trench	36cSW1 Lens	M 20 c, d
Ace Lane	51bSW1 Neuville Vitasse	N 14 c
Ace Trench	36cSW3 Vimy	T 2 c
Acetic Trench	36cSW4 Rouvroy	T 24 b
Ache Trench	36cSW4 Rouvroy	U 18 d, 24 b
Acheville [village]	36cSW4 Rouvroy	T 18 d, U 13 c
Acheville Centre	36cSW4 Rouvroy	T 11 b, 12 a, c, d, 18 a, b
Acheville Maze	36cSW4 Rouvroy	U 13 c
Acheville Rear	36cSW4 Rouvroy	T 11 b, 12 a, c, d, 18 b
Acheville Road [road]	36cSW4 Rouvroy	T 17 a, c, d, 18 c, d, 22 b
Acheville Support	36cSW4 Rouvroy	T 11 b, 12 a, c, d, 18 a, b
Acheville Support Front [1918]	36cSW4 Rouvroy	T 11 a, b, 12 a, c, d, 18 a, b
Acheville Support Rear [1918]	36cSW4 Rouvroy	T 11 b, 12 a, c, d, 18 b
Acheville Trench	36cSW4 Rouvroy	T 11 a, b, d, 12 c, 18 a, c, d
Achi Baba	36NW4 Bois Grenier	I 25 d
Achicourt [village]	51bNW3 Arras / SW1 Neuville Vitasse	G 32 c, d, 33 c, M 2 a, b, 3 a
Achicourt Switch [1918]	51bNW3 Arras / SW1 Neuville Vitasse	G 33 d, 34 c, M 3 a, c
Achiet - Loupart Line	57dNE4 & 57cNW3 Achiet	G 14, 20, 26, 27, 33, 34
Achiet Trench	57dNE4 & 57cNW3 Achiet	G 20 a, c, d, 26 b, 27 a, c
Achille Alley	62cSW1 & 2 Belloy	N 5 a, b, d
Achilleion, l'	20SW4 Bixschoote	T 23 d
Acid Drop Alley	57dSE4 Ovillers	X 23 a
Acid Drop Trench [Grossherzog Graben]	57dSE4 Ovillers	X 17 c, 22 b, 23 a
Acid Trench	36cSW1 Lens	M 21 a
Acier, Tranchée de l'	70dSW [4 Vauxaillon]	U 12 d
Ack Street [1918]	62dNE [1 Dernancourt]	E 7 d
Ack Trench	36cNW1 La Bassée	A 6 b
Ack Trench	36cNW1 La Bassée	A 6 b
Acme Trench	36cSW1 Lens	M 20 d
Acme Trench	36cSW4 Rouvroy	U 1 c
Acne Trench	36cSW4 Rouvroy	T 18 d
Aconite Trench	36cSW1 Lens	N 19 b
Aconite Trench	36cSW4 Rouvroy	U 7 d, 13 b
Acorn Alley	51bSW1 Neuville Vitasse	N 13 a, b
Acorn Farm	28NE4 Dadizeele	L 34 b 2.3
Acorn Trench	36cSW1 Lens	M 20 d
Acorn Trench	36cSW4 Rouvroy	U 13 b, 14 a
Acorn Trench	62cNW2 Bouchavesnes	C 2 d, 3 c
Acquets Post	36NW4 Bois Grenier	H 11 d
Acre Farm	28NE2 Moorslede	F 22 d 20.95

Name	Map Sheet	Map Reference
Acrobat Cross Roads	28NE2 Moorslede	F 14 a 87.75
Acrobat Trench	36cSW4 Rouvroy	U 13 b, 14 a
Active Trench	36cSW1 Lens	M 20 d, 21 c
Acton Cross [cross roads]	36aNE2 Vieux Berquin	L 4 a 8.2
Actor's Fork [road jct]	28NE2 Moorslede	F 28 a 70.47
Actress Trench	36cSW3 Vimy	T 2 d, 3 c
Actress Wood	62cSW4 St. Christ	T 6 d, U 1 b, c, d
Actrice Trench	62cSW4 St. Christ	U 1 d, 7 a, b
Ada I & II Posts	36NW4 Bois Grenier	I 20 b; I 21 a
Ada Trench	36cSW1 Lens	M 20 d
Ada Trench	51bSW2 Vis-en-Artois	O 8 a, b
Adalbert Alley	36cSW3 Vimy	S 22 d
Adalbert Alley	36SW3 Richebourg	S 22 c, d, 23 c, 29 a
Adam / Adams Trench	57cSE2 Gonnelieu	R 29 c
Adam Corner	28SW3 Bailleul	T 2 b 8.1
Adam Post	57cNE3 Hermies	K 3 c
Adams Farm	28NW2 St Julien	C 10 b 8.3
Adamson Street	28NW4 & NE3 Zillebeke	I 33 d
Adda Farm	28NW3 Poperinghe	G 13 b 35.15
Adder Farm	28NE4 Dadizeele	L 36 c 4.8
Adder Trench	36aSW [2 Molinghem]	O 28 d, 34 a, b, 35 a
Addison Road [breastwork / track]	36bNE2 Beuvry	F 11 b, d, 12 c
Addle Mill [windmill]	20SE2 Hooglede	R 29 a 3.9
Addle Trench	36cSW1 Lens	M 20 c
Address Trench	36cSW1 Lens	M 27 a
Adela Trench [1918]	66eNW [4 Morisel]	H 36 d, I 31 a
Adelaide House	28NE4 Dadizeele	L 33 b 40.25
Adelaide Street	57cNE1 Quéant	D 5 d, 11 b, c, d
Adelpare Farm	66eNW [4 Morisel]	I 31 c 7.7
Aden House	20SE3 Westroosebeke	V 1 c 35.35
Aden Mound	51bSW2 Vis-en-Artois	O 34 b
Adept Dump	36cSW3 Vimy	N 31 d 5.8
Adept Trench	36cSW2 Harnes	N 25 d
Adept Trench	57cSW3 Longueval	T 2 a
Adinfer [village]	51cSE4 Blaireville	X 21 b, c, d
Adinfer Trench [1918]	51cSE4 Blaireville	X 22 a, c
Adinfer Wood	51cSE4 Blaireville / 57dNE1 & 2 Fonquevillers	X 26, 27, F 1, 2
Adinfer Wood Switch Trench [1918]	57dNE1 & 2 Fonquevillers	E 18, 24, F 7, 13
Adipose Trench	36cSW1 Lens	M 20 d, 26 b
Adjacent Trench	36cSW1 Lens	N 19 c, 25 a
Adjunct Trench	36cSW1 Lens	N 25 a
Adler Farm	28NE1 Zonnebeke	D 3 a 6.3
Admiral Farm	28NE4 Dadizeele	L 35 c 00.15
Admiral Trench	36cSW1 Lens	M 30 b
Admiral's Road	28NW2 St Julien	C 21, 22
Admirals Trench [Wieltje]	28NW2 St Julien	C 28 a, b
Ado Trench	36cSW1 Lens	M 27 a
Adobe Cottage	27SE2 Berthen	R 34 a 35.73
Adolf Trench, Support and Alley	62cNW1 Maricourt	A 11 b, 17 a, b
Adore Trench	36cSW1 Lens	N 19 b
Adorn Trench	36cSW1 Lens	M 24 d, N 19 c
Adrift Trench	36cSW1 Lens	M 24 d, N 19 c
Adroit Trench	36cSW1 Lens	N 19 a, c
Adult Trench	36cSW1 Lens	N 19 c

Name	Map Sheet	Map Reference
Advance Farm	28NE4 Dadizeele	L 36 a 9.9
Advance Trench	36cSW1 Lens	M 24 d
Advanced Estaminet	28SW4 Ploegsteert	U 14 a 5.4
Adze Trench	36cSW1 Lens	M 22 a
Aerial Trench	36cSW1 Lens	M 26 a
Aerodrome [Cambrai]	57bNW1 Cambrai	A 8 c, d, 14 a, b
Aerodrome [Grand Priel Farm]	62cNE4 Roisel	L 29 d
Aerodrome Support [1918]	51bSW3 Boisleux	S 25 b
Aerodrome Switch [1918]	51bSW3 Boisleux	S 26 a
Aerodrome Trench	57cNW1 Gomiecourt	A 2, 3, 8, 13, 14
Aeroplane Cemetery	28NW2 St Julien	I 5 a, b
Aeroplane Ravine	57cSE2 Gonnelieu	R 20 a
Aeroplane Trench	57cSW4 Combles	T 5 c, 11 a
Aeroplane Trench	62dNE2 Méaulte	F 9 b
Affica Junction [road jct]	28NE4 Dadizeele	L 32 d 65.25
Afghan Corner [road jct]	28NE2 Moorslede	E 22 b 2.1
Afghan Trench	36cSW1 Lens	M 26 a
African Support	57cSE2 Gonnelieu / 4 Villers-Guislain	Q 35 a, c, W 5 a
African Trench	27SE4 Meteren	X 16 c, 20 b, d, 21 a, b, 22 a
African Trench	57cSE4 Villers-Guislain	Q 35 a, c, W 5 b
Agadier Camp	28NW1 Elverdinghe	B 25 c 3.2
Agadier Farm	28NW2 St Julien	B 30 a
Agate Trench	36cSW1 Lens	N 32 b
Agency Farm	28NE4 Dadizeele	L 34 c 95.25
Agent Trench	57cSW3 Longueval	T 2 a
Agile Avenue	62cNW1 Maricourt	A 23 d
Agile Avenue	62cNW2 Bouchavesnes	B 17, 18, 22, 23, C 8, 9, 13, 14
Agnes Post	36NW4 Bois Grenier	I 20 d
Agnes Street	28SW4 Ploegsteert	N 36 c, d, T 6 b
Agony Lane [trench]	20NW4 Dixmude	I 13 a
Agra Cross [cross roads]	27NE4 Abeele	L 5 d 60.65
Agram Alley	62bSW4 Homblières	T 28 a
Agram Alley	62cNW4 Péronne	I 14 d, 15 a, c
Ague Trench	36cSW1 Lens	N 19 a, c, 25 a, b
Ahead Alley	62bSW4 Homblières	T 29 c, d
Ahead Trench	36cSW1 Lens	M 24 d, 30 b
Aid Post	28NE3 Gheluvelt	J 21
Aid Post [West Hoek]	36NW2 & NE1 Houplines	C 9 c 10.15
Aigle Trench	20SW3 Oostvleteren	T 15 c, d
Aigrette Trench [1918]	66eNW [2 Thennes]	C 7 c
Aileen Communication Trench [1918]	62dSE [1 Hamel]	P 21 c
Aileron Farm	36aNE2 Vieux Berquin	L 5 a 2.2
Ainette Trench	62cNE1 Liéramont	D 9 d, 15 b, 16 a
Ainslie [light rly locality, 1917]	28SW1 Kemmel	N 3 c
Aintree Street	57dSE4 Ovillers	X 1 a, c
Air Street	28NW4 & NE3 Zillebeke	I 5 d
Aircraft Farm	28SW1 Kemmel	N 32 b 2.2
Aire Trench	57cSW4 Combles	U 2 d, 8 b
Airpin, Tranchée de l'	70dSW [4 Vauxaillon]	U 12 a
Airplane Switch	51bNW1 Roclincourt / 2 Oppy	B 10 c
Airy Corner	51bSW1 Neuville Vitasse	N 9 a 8.7
Airy Trench	36cSW1 Lens	M 26 a
Aisne Alley	66cNW2 Itancourt	B 22 d, 23 c
Aisne Farm [Pill Box]	28NE1 Zonnebeke	D 13 c

Name	Map Sheet	Map Reference
Aisne Post	57cNE3 Hermies	K 33 c 3.3
Ajax Alley	62cSW2 Barleux	N 30 b, O 25 a, c
Ajax House	20SW4 Bixschoote	U 6 c 35.35
Ajax Trench	57cSE3 Sorel-le-Grand	V 27 b, 28c
Akba Cottage	28NW3 Poperinghe	G 25 b 3.2
Alabama Trench	51bNW4 Fampoux	H 28 d, 29 c
Alan Crater [Br, Zwarteleen]	28NW4 & NE3 Zillebeke	I 29 d 05.60
Alarm Trench	36cSW1 Lens	N 19 a
Alaska Houses	28NE3 Gheluvelt	J 33 b 5.6
Alban Trench	57cNE3 Hermies / 4 Marcoing	K 9 d
Albania [Farm]	28NE1 Zonnebeke	J 3 b 6.9
Albania Woods	28NE1 Zonnebeke	J 3 d, 4 c
Albany [tunnel, Railway Wood]	28NW4 & NE3 Zillebeke	I 11 b
Albany Group [craters]	36cSW3 Vimy	S 28 c
Albany Trench	36cSW3 Vimy	S 27 d, 28 c
Albatross Bank	51bSW2 Vis-en-Artois	N 23 d
Albatross Farm	28NE1 Zonnebeke	D 2 d 3.3
Albatross Lane	51bSW2 Vis-en-Artois	N 23 d, 24 c, 29 a, b
Albatross Trench	36aSW [2 Molinghem]	O 35 a
Albatross Trench	51bSW2 Vis-en-Artois	N 23 d, 24 c
Albatross Trench	62cNW2 Bouchavesnes	C 9 b, d
Albe Alley	62bSW1 Gricourt	N 1 a
Albemarle [light rly locality & huts]	28NW3 Poperinghe	H 26 d, 27 a, c
Albemarle House	28NW3 Poperinghe	H 27 a 2.3
Albemarle Street	36NW4 Bois Grenier	I 15 d
Albert [town]	57dSE3 / 4 / 62dNE1 / 2	W 27, 28, 29, E 3, 4, 5
Albert Alley	62cNW1 Maricourt	A 17 b
Albert Communication Trench [1918]	62dSW [2 Villers-Bretonneux] / SE [1 Hamel]	O 30 d, P 25 c, d, 26 c
Albert Hall	57dSE1 & 2 Beaumont	Q 22 a, c
Albert Lane	57dSE4 Ovillers	X 9 b, d
Albert Post	36SW3 Richebourg	S 8 d 5.4
Albert Redoubt	28NE3 Gheluvelt	J 9 a 8.9
Albert Redoubt [1918]	66eNW [2 Thennes]	B 22 b
Albert Road	36cSW4 Rouvroy	U 13 c
Albert Road / Albert, Rue	62dNE2 Méaulte	F 10 c
Albert Road [reserve trench]	28NW2 St Julien	I 4 d, 10 b
Albert Road [road]	36cSW4 Rouvroy	T 24 b, c, d, 30 a, c, U 13 b, c, 19 a
Albert Road [road]	36SW3 Richebourg	S 8 b, d
Albert Street	62dNE2 Méaulte	F 16 b
Albert Trench	12SW1 Nieuport	M 16 c
Albert Trench	36cSW1 Lens	M 26 a
Albert Trench	51bNW2 Oppy	B 6 d, 12 b, d
Albert Trench [1918]	62dSW [2 Villers-Bretonneux]	O 30 d
Alberta [farm]	28NW2 St Julien	C 11 c 9.6
Alberta Camp [1917-18]	28NW2 St Julien	C 11 d 2.9
Alberta Dugouts [row]	28SW2 Wytschaete	N 23 d 30.60 to 30.99; N 23 d 4.7
Alberta Line [tr tramway, La Polka-Irish House]	28SW2 Wytschaete	N 21 d, 22 c, d, 23 c, 28 b, 29 a
Alberta Road [road]	36cSW4 Rouvroy	U 13 b, c, 18 b
Alberta Track [1917-18]	28NW2 St Julien	C 11, 12, 17, 21, 25, 26, 27
Albessard Trench	62cNW3 Vaux	H 2 d, 8 b, 9 a
Albino Avenue	36aSW [4 Lillers]	U 5 d, 6 c
Albion Trench	36cSW1 Lens	M 26 b
Albrecht Avenue	51bNW1 Roclincourt	A 16 d, 17, 18
Albury Line [1918]	62dSE [1 Hamel]	P 19, 20, 25, 31

Name	Map Sheet	Map Reference
Alceste Trench	66dNW1 Punchy	A 6 c, 12 a, c
Alcock House	28SW3 Bailleul	T 8 b 4.8
Alcock Trench	57dNE3 & 4 Hébuterne	K 10 d, 16 b
Alcohol Trench	36cSW1 Lens	M 26 a
Alcove Trench	36cSW1 Lens	M 30 b
Alde Trench	62cNW2 Bouchavesnes	C 9 d, 15 b
Alder Trench	51bSW1 Neuville Vitasse	M 11 b
Aldershot	62cNW2 Bouchavesnes	C 8 d 35.60
Aldershot [post]	36cSW4 Rouvroy	T 24 c 45.15
Aldershot Camp	28SW3 Bailleul	T 19 b, d, 20 c
Alderson Avenue	28SW4 Ploegsteert	U 15 a
Aldgate [road]	57cNE1 Quéant	E 25 b, d
Aldgate Trench	62bSW3 St Quentin	T 19 c, 25 a
Aldwych Station	36cNW1 La Bassée	A 27 a 9.9 [approx]
Ale Alley	57cSW3 Longueval	T 7 c, d, 13 a
Ale Cottage	28NW3 Poperinghe	G 18 a 6.2
Ale Promenade [cottage or estaminet]	36aNE1 Morbecque	D 11 b 8.0
Alec Corons [miners' cottages]	36cSW3 Vimy	N 33 d
Alehouse Trench	36cSW1 Lens	M 26 a, b
Alembert, Rue d' [road in Calonne]	36cSW1 Lens	M 14 c, d
Aleppo Trench / Alep, Tranchée d'	66cNW2 Itancourt	B 12 c, d, 18 b, d
Alert Crossing [level crossing]	36aNE2 Vieux Berquin	F 7 c 8.9
Alert Trench	36cSW1 Lens	M 26 a
Alert Trench	62cNW2 Bouchavesnes	C 2 a
Alexander Camp	28SW3 Bailleul	T 7 b, d
Alexander Farm	28SW3 Bailleul	T 7 d 95.90
Alexander Trench	36cNW3 Loos	G 5 c, d
Alexander Trench	70dNW4 St Gobain	H 30 d, 36 b
Alexandra Farm	28NW1 Elverdinghe	B 19 a 3.7
Alf Cut	62cNW2 Bouchavesnes	C 8 c, d
Alford Cottages	27NE4 Abeele	L 4 c 5.5
Alfred Road [road]	57cSE1 Bertincourt / 2 Gonnelieu	Q 3 c, d
Alfred Trench	36cSW1 Lens	M 26 a
Algebra Trench	36cSW1 Lens	M 26 a
Algere Nord, Tranchée d' [Algiers Trench]	36cSW1 Lens	M 19 d
Algerian Cot.	28NW2 St Julien	C 15 c 6.1
Algiers Trench [Tranchée d'Algere Nord]	36cSW1 Lens	M 19 d
Algitha Farm	28NE4 Dadizeele	K 18 b 2.1
Algoma Central [railway]	36cSW4 Rouvroy	U 1 b, d
Alhambra [light rly loop]	36bNE2 Beuvry	F 8 c
Alhambra [Locality]	36cSW3 Vimy	S 13 d, 14 c
Alhambra, Tranchée de l'	62cSW3 & 4 Marchélepot	T 23 d, 29 b, 30 a, c
Alibi Lane [trench]	20NW4 Dixmude	I 19 a, b
Alice Communication Trench [1918]	62dSE [1 Hamel]	P 20 c
Alice Post	36NW4 Bois Grenier	I 21 a
Alight Trench	36cSW1 Lens	M 26 a
Alise Farm	28NE2 Moorslede	F 10 a 95.15
All Winds Mill	66cNW1 Grugies	B 2 a 3.0
Allaines [village]	62cNW2 Bouchavesnes / 4 Péronne	I 4 a, b, c, d
Alleaud, Tranchée	36cSW1 Lens	M 25 b
Allegre Alley	62cSW3 Vermandovillers	S 18 b, T 13 a
Allemande Trench [1918]	62dSE [1 Hamel]	P 25 b, 26 a
Alembert, Rue d' [road]	36cSW1 Lens	M 14 c, d
Allen Post	57cNE3 Hermies	K 3 d 8.0

Name	Map Sheet	Map Reference
Allen Street, & Crater [I 29 d 08.65]	28NW4 & NE3 Zillebeke	I 29 c
Allen Trench	36cSW1 Lens	M 29 a
Allendale Support [1918]	62dSE [3 Marcelcave]	V 1 a, c
Aller Golt / Gelt / Alle Gott Trench	62cNW4 Péronne	I 12 b, c
Alleux Trench	36cSW1 Lens	M 25 d
Alley 3 [Sept 1915]	36cNW3 Loos	G 17 b, 18 a, b
Alley 4 [Sept 1915]	36cNW3 Loos	G 17 d, 18 b, c, d
Alley Trench	62cNE2 Epéhy	F 29 b
Allgauer Weg	51bNW1 Roclincourt	A 24 b, c, d, B 19 a
Allgauer Weg Sud	51bNW1 Roclincourt	A 30 a, 24 c
Alliance Trench	20NW4 Dixmude	I 7 d, 13 a, b
Alliance Trench	51bNW1 Roclincourt	A 18 & 24
Alliance Trench	62cNW2 Bouchavesnes	C 15 b
Alliance Trench [1918]	51bNW1 Roclincourt / 3 Arras	A 18, 24, 30, G 6
Allies Avenue [1918]	62dSW [4 Cachy]	O 34 d, 35 c, U 3 b, 4 a, b
Allies Farm	20NW4 Dixmude	I 13 c 5.1
Allies Trench	36cSW1 Lens	M 26 c
Allies, Boyau des	62cSW1 Dompierre	M 4 b, c, d
Alligator Trench	36aSW4 [Lillers]	U 6 c
Allotment Copse	51bNW4 Fampoux	H 36 c
Allouette, l' [farm]	57bSW4 Serain	U 8 b 7.6
Allsopps Trench [1918]	57dNE1 & 2 Fonquevillers	E 28 b, c, d
Alma [farm]	28NE1 Zonnebeke	D 22 a 20.35
Alma [light rly siding, 1917-18]	28NE1 Zonnebeke	D 22 a 4.6
Alma Farm	28SW1 Kemmel	M 23 d 65.95
Alma Lines [camp]	28SW1 Kemmel	M 23 b
Almanac Trench	36cSW1 Lens	M 30 b, N 25 a, b
Almond House	36aNE1 Morbecque	D 15 a 40.65
Almond Trench	36cSW1 Lens	M 26 a, b
Aloe Trench	62cNW2 Bouchavesnes	C 9 d, 15 b
Aloof Trench	36cSW1 Lens	N 13 d
Alose, l' [trench]	66cNW2 Itancourt	C 25 a
Alosi Trench, d'	20SW3 Oostvleteren	N 33 c
Alouette Farm	20SW4 Bixschoote	U 29 a 8.6
Alouette, l'	51cSE4 Blaireville	W 12 a
Alouette, l' [farm]	28SW4 Ploegsteert	T 16 d 95.30
Alpaca Trench	36cSW1 Lens	N 20 c
Alpha [German Pillbox]	51bSW4 Bullecourt	U 1 d
Alpha [pillboxes, 1918-18]	28NE3 Gheluvelt	J 14 a 30.25
Alpha Lane	62cNW2 Bouchavesnes	C 8 d, 14 b, 15 a, b
Alphonso Trench	36cSW1 Lens	M 26 b, 27 a, c
Alpine Trench	36cSW1 Lens	M 26 a, c
Alsace Alley	66cNW2 Itancourt	B 22 c, d, 23 a
Alsace Trench	62bSW1 Gricourt	M 22 b, 23 a, c
Alston House	28SW2 Wytschaete	N 22 b 6.1
Alt Trench	62cNW1 Maricourt	A 3 d
Altar Cross Roads	36aNE1 Morbecque	D 13 a 70.35
Altar House	28NE2 Moorslede	F 25 b 2.9
Alte Jaeger Strasse	57dSE4 Ovillers	X 14 d
Altenkirchen Trench	66cNW1 Grugies	B 7 b, 8 a, b, d
Alternative Street	62cNW1 Maricourt	A 16 d, 23 a
Altona Support [1918]	62dSE [1 Hamel]	P 31 a, b
Alvensleben-weg	57cSW3 Longueval	T 7 d, 8 a
Alwine Trench	36cSW1 Lens	M 26 c

Name	Map Sheet	Map Reference
Alwyn Farm	27SE4 Meteren	X 21 c 9.8
Alz Trench	51bNW3 Arras	G 12 a, b, H 7 a
Amalgam Trench	36cSW1 Lens	N 13 d, 19 b
Amands Farm	20SE2 Hooglede	R 25 c 8.4
Amazon Alley	66cNW4 Berthenicourt	I 22 d
Amazon Trench	62cNW2 Bouchavesnes	C 3 c, 9 a
Ambassadors Redoubt	66cNW2 Itancourt	B 29 a
Amber Trench	36cSW1 Lens	M 27 c
Amber Trench	62cNW2 Bouchavesnes	C 9 b
Amberg Copse	62cSW3 Vermandovillers	S 22 c, 28 a
Ambert Trench	66cNW1 Grugies	B 14 d, 15 c
Ambilion / Ambition Trench	20NW4 Dixmude	I 26 a, c, 32 a, c, d
Amble Trench	36cSW1 Lens	M 26 c, d
Amble Trench	36cSW3 Vimy	T 2 b, d, 3 a
Amboises Trench	62bSW1 Gricourt	M 28 c, d
Ambrogi Trench	66cNW4 Berthenicourt	I 25 d
Ambrose Farm	28NE3 Gheluvelt	J 21 c 2.3
Ambrose Trench [1918]	28NE3 Gheluvelt	J 21 c
Ambulance Annexe	28NW3 Poperinghe	H 14 b 7.3
Ambulance Farm	28NW3 Poperinghe	H 14 b 65.25
Ambush Trench	36cSW1 Lens	M 27 b, c, d
Amedée, Tranchée	62cSW1 & 2 Belloy	O 1 d, 2 c
Amedes Trench	62cSW2 Barleux	O 1 d, 7 a, b
Ameer Farm	28NE2 Moorslede	E 22 b 6.6
Amélnagé, Talus [Gumboot Trench]	36cSW1 Lens	M 19 d
America Alley	66cNW3 Essigny / 4 Berthencourt	H 9 d, 14 c, d, 15 a, b
America Cabaret	28SE1 Wervicq	P 12 b 8.0
America Communication Trench [1918]	62dSE [1 Hamel]	P 25 b, d
America Trench	66cNW4 Berthenicourt	H 10 b, c, d, 11 a
America Trench	70dNW2 Servais	B 29 a
American Alley	62bSW3 St Quentin	M 33 a, c, d, 34 c, d
Amesbury [post]	36cSW4 Rouvroy	T 29 b 7.4
Amiens Defence Line [outer; S of Albert]	62dNE, SE	extensive
Amiens, Faubourg de [Arras]	51bNW3 Arras	G 25 b, 26 a, b
Amigny Trench	70dNW [1 Chauny]	H 3 a, b
Amity Trench	36cSW1 Lens	M 27 a, c
Ammonal Trench	36cSW1 Lens	M 21 c, d
Amont Wood [Nieppe Forest]	36aNE3 Haverskerque	J 7, 8, 9, 13, 14, 15, 19, 20, 21, 25
Amorous Trench	36cSW1 Lens	M 27 c
Amper Trench	51bNW3 Arras	H 7 c
Ampere Trench	36cSW1 Lens	M 26 d, 27 c
Ampphill Tunnel [sic]	36cSW1 Lens	M 14 d
Amulet Trench	36cSW1 Lens	N 13 a, b, c
Amulet Trench	62cNW2 Bouchavesnes	C 9 b
Amur Cottage	28NW3 Poperinghe	G 33 b 6.6
Amusoires, les [place name]	36aSE1 St Venant	P 17 d
Amusoires-Haverskerque-La Motte Line	36aSE1 St Venant	P 5, 11, 17, 23
Amy Communication Trench [1918]	62dSE [1 Hamel]	P 26 a
Amy Farm	20SE2 Hooglede	Q 23 c 65.75
Amy Post	36NW4 Bois Grenier	I 20 b
Amy Wood	62dSE [2 Proyart]	Q 23 c, 29 a
Anagram Trench	36cSW1 Lens	N 19 a
Ananas Lane [trench]	20NW4 Dixmude	I 13 a, b
Anchain Farm	36aNE3 Haverskerque	J 33 d 15.15

Name	Map Sheet	Map Reference
Anchin Farm	66eNW [4 Morisel]	H 11 b 2.1
Anchise Trench	57cSW4 Combles	U 5 d, 11 a, b, c
Anchor Lane	36cSW1 Lens	M 26 d
Anchor Trench	36cNW3 Loos	G 5 c
Anchor Trench	36cSW1 Lens	M 26 b, d
Anchor Trench	51bNW1 Roclincourt	A 4 b
Anchor Trench	57cSE2 Gonnelieu	R 15 a, b
Anchovy Farm	36aNE3 Haverskerque	K 26 b 95.40
Ancient Trench	66cNW3 Essigny / SW1 Remigny	H 27 d, 33 b, d
Ancona Farm	28NE4 Dadizeele	L 32 d 4.6
Ancre Trench	57dSE1 & 2 Beaumont	R 8 a, b, c
And Cottage	28NW1 Elverdinghe	A 16 b 7.5
Andauer Trench	51bNW1 Roclincourt	A 10 d
Andelain Alley	70dNW2 Servais	C 7 b, 8 a, b
Anderlu Wood	62cNW2 Bouchavesnes	B 5 c, d, 11 a, b
Anderson Trench [High Wood]	57cSW3 Longueval	S 4 c, d
Andes Alley / Lane	62cNW2 Bouchavesnes	C 2 d, 3 c, 7 b, d, 8 a, b
Andes Farm	28NW3 Poperinghe	H 21 b 8.3
Andouille, Tranchée de	70dSW [4 Vauxaillon]	U 5 b
Andover [post]	36cSW4 Rouvroy	T 29 a 35.20
Andover Place	62cNE1 Lieramont	D 3 b
Andover Place	62cNW1 Maricourt	A 23 d
Andover Place [wood]	62cNW2 Bouchavesnes	C 13 a
Andre Smit Farm	20SW4 Bixschoote	U 13 b 0.8
Andrea Ravine	66eNW [2 Thennes]	C 10 c, 16 a, b
Andrew Corons [miners' cottages]	36cSW3 Vimy	N 33 c, T 3 a
Andrews Post	57cSW4 Combles	T 5 c
Andros Camp	27NE4 Abeele	L 8 b
Andy Trench	36cSW1 Lens	M 26 c
Anes, Bois des [Donkeys]	62cSW3 & 4 Marchélepot	T 4 a, b
Angel Avenue	36cSW3 Vimy	S 15 c
Angel C.T. [1918]	62dSW [4 Cachy]	U 5 a
Angel Trench [also Angle]	51bNW4 Fampoux	I 25 d, 31 b
Angelus Orchard / Wood	57bSW3 Honnecourt	T 8 a
Anger Schlösschen [Angeschlössen?]	51bSW1 Neuville Vitasse	M 21 c
Anger Trench	51bNW1 Roclincourt	A 4 c
Anglais, Boyau des [English]	62cSW1 Dompierre	M 4 d
Angle Bank [lynchet]	62bNW3 Bellicourt	G 32 a, c
Angle Farm	28SW2 Wytschaete	O 36 a 8.6
Angle Lane	51bSW2 Vis-en-Artois	O 21 a, b, c
Angle Point [road junction]	20SW4 Bixschoote	U 6 d 55.38
Angle Post	36SW3 Richebourg	M 32 c, S 2 a
Angle Trench	57cSW3 Longueval	S 18 c
Angle Trench	57dSE2 Beaumont	R 9 c 8.1
Angle Trench [1918]	28SW1 Kemmel	M 29 a, b
Angle Wood	57bSW1 Bantouzelle	N 33 b
Angle Wood	62cNW1 Maricourt	B 1 d, 2 c
Angle, The / Angle Trench [The Bluff]	28NW4 & NE3 Zillebeke	I 34 c
Angle, The [GFL, late 1915]	36SW2 Radinghem	N 6 b 9.5
Angle, The [GFL]	36SW2 Radinghem	O 1 a
Angler Trench	36cSW1 Lens	M 26 c
Anglers Lane [canal path]	36aSE1 St Venant	P 5 a, b
Angles Chateau	57bSW3 Honnecourt	N 33 c 0.0
Anglian Trench	57cSW3 Longueval	S 18 d

Name	Map Sheet	Map Reference
Angora [farm]	27NE2 Proven	F 20 b 7.3
Angora Communication Trench [1918]	62dSE [1 Hamel]	P 25 b, 26 a
Angora Copse	27NE2 Proven	F 20 a, b
Angora Trench	62cNW2 Bouchavesnes	C 10 d, 16 b, c, d
Angres Alley [Angres, Boyau de la Route d']	36bSE2 Boyeffles / 36cSW1 Lens	R 29 d, 30 c, M 25 d
Angres, Boyau de la Route d' [Angres Alley]	36bSE2 Boyeffles / 36cSW1 Lens	R 29 d, 30 c, M 25 d
Angres-Liévin-Cité St Laurent Line	36cSW1 Lens	M 15, 16, 17
Angus [light rly sidings]	28NW3 Poperinghe	G 21 b, d
Angus Cottage	28NW3 Poperinghe	G 21 d 4.7
Angus Farm	20SE2 Hooglede	R 10 c 4.7
Anisette Alley / Boyau de l'Anisette	62cSW3 & 4 Marchélepot	T 13 c, 19 a, b
Anivorano Alley	66cNW2 Itancourt	B 24 d
Anjou Farm	28NW3 Poperinghe	G 20 b 5.3
Ankle Farm	36aNE2 Vieux Berquin	E 17 c 65.10
Ankle Lane	62dNE2 Méaulte	F 11 c
Ankle Trench	36cSW1 Lens	M 26 c
Anley Avenue	57dSE1 & 2 Beaumont	Q 15 a
Anna Switch	36SW1 Aubers	N 21 b
Anna Trench	36SW1 Aubers	N 15 d
Anna Trench	57dNE3 & 4 Hébuterne	K 11 b, d, 12 a
Annamites Trench	62cSW3 & 4 Marchélepot	N 34 c, d, T 4 a
Annandale Camp	28SW3 Bailleul	S 21 c, 27 a
Annandale House	28NE4 Dadizeele	K 23 d 3.5
Annandale House	28SW3 Bailleul	S 21 c 15.10
Annapolis Valley	36cSW3 Vimy	T 7 d
Annay [village]	36cNW4 Pont-à-Vendin	H 30 c, d, 36 a, b, I 25 c
Annequin - Laundry Line	36bNE2 Beuvry	E 23, 24, F 19, 20
Annequin [village]	36bNE2 Beuvry	F 23 d, 24 c, 29 b, 30 a, c
Annequin Fosse [Fosse No.9]	36bNE2 Beuvry	F 29 c 35.20
Annequin Locality	36bNE2 Beuvry	F 29 a, b, c, d, L 4 a, 5 a, b
Annette Post	36NW4 Bois Grenier	I 20 b
Annex Trench	36cSW1 Lens	M 26 c, d, 32 b, 33 a
Annexe 'B'	62dNE2 Méaulte	F 17 d
Annezin [village W of Béthune]	36bNE2 Beuvry	E 3 c, d, 9 a, b
Annibal Farm	20SW4 Bixschoote	U 10 c 65.80
Annibal Trench / Lane	57dNE3 & 4 Hébuterne	K 16 a
Annibal, Tranchée d'	62cSW3 & 4 Marchélepot	T 5 d, 6 a, c
Annie Post	36NW4 Bois Grenier	I 20 d, 21 c
Annie Trench	36cSW1 Lens	M 26 c
Anniversaire / Anniversary Avenue	51bNW1 Roclincourt	A 16, 19, 20, 21
Annscroft Avenue	28SW4 Ploegsteert	U 14 c, d
Anon Trench	36cSW1 Lens	M 26 c
Anson Crossing [bridge over river]	36aNE3 Haverskerque	J 33 d 1.9
Anson Trench	51bSW1 Neuville Vitasse	M 11 b
Anstruther Street	57dSE4 Ovillers	X 13 c
Ant Alley	57cNE1 Quéant	E 26 a
Ant Houses	28NE3 Gheluvelt	J 28 d 15.50
Ant Lane [1918]	57dNE2 & 57cNW1 Courcelles	F 16 b, 17 a
Ant Trench	57dNE3 & 4 Hébuterne	K 11 b
Anteater Trench	36cSW1 Lens	M 26 c, d
Antelope Alley	36cSW4 Rouvroy	T 28 d, 29 c
Antelope Alley [ride, Pacaut Wood]	36aSE1 St Venant/2 Lestrem/3 Gonnehem/ 4 Locon	Q 33 b, c, d
Antelope Trench	57cNE2 Bourlon	E 22 d, 28 b

Name	Map Sheet	Map Reference
Antelope Trench	57cSW4 Combles	T 5 c, d
Antelope Trench [1918]	36aSW2 [Molinghem]	O 29 c, 35 a, b
Antelope Trench [Green Crassier]	36cSW1 Lens	N 20 d
Antes, Bois des	62cSW3 & 4 Marchélepot	T 5 a, b
Antheaume, Boyau	36cSW3 Vimy	S 8 d
Anti Air Craft / Anti-Aircraft Camp	28NW3 Poperinghe	G 12 c, 18 a
Antic Trench	36cNW1 La Bassée	A 10 c, 16 a
Antigone Alley Trench	62cNW4 Péronne	I 6 d
Antigone Trench	62cSW1 & 2 Belloy	N 12 d
Antler Trench	51bSW1 Neuville Vitasse	M 6 c
Antoine Avenue	28SW4 Ploegsteert	U 10 d, 11 c
Antoine Support	28SW4 Ploegsteert	U 10 d, 16 b
Antoinette Junction [lt rly]	27SE2 Berthen	Q 23 b 8.7
Anton's House / Farm [N of Ploegsteert Wood]	28SW4 Ploegsteert	U 14 b 7.7
Antrim Road [road]	28SW2 Wytschaete	O 27 a
Antwerp Farm	20SW4 Bixschoote	T 16 c, d
Anvil Trench	36cSW1 Lens	M 26 c, d
Anvil Wood	28NE1 Zonnebeke	D 30 a
Anxious Trench	36cSW3 Vimy	S 5 d, 6 c
Anzac [farm / house & pill box]	28NE1 Zonnebeke	J 3 a 15.35
Anzac Avenue	28NW4 Ypres	H 30 a, c, 36 a, c
Anzac Camp	28NW4 Ypres	H 30 c
Anzac Cut	28NW4 & NE3 Zillebeke	I 33 c, d
Anzac Farm	28SW2 Wytschaete	O 28 a, c
Anzac Gr. [Graben? Dugout? Grave? 1918]	28NE3 Gheluvelt	J 3 c 43.63
Anzac Ridge	28NW4 & NE3 Zillebeke	J 3, 9
Anzin Avenue	51bNW1 Roclincourt	A 27, 28, G 2, 3
Ape Buildings	20SE2 Hooglede	R 16 a 5.8
Ape Trench	57cNE1 Quéant	E 26 c
Ape Trench [1918]	51bSW3 Boisleux	S 21 c, 27 a
Ape Trench [later Support]	51bSW2 Vis-en-Artois	O 20 a, c
Apes Wood	62cSW3 & 4 Marchélepot	T 4 a
Apex Farm	28NE2 Moorslede	F 6 c 8.8
Apex Trench [Sanctuary Wood, 1915]	28NW4 & NE3 Zillebeke	I 18 b, d, J 13 a, c
Apex, The	51bSW4 Bullecourt	U 4, 6, 10, 17 [area of]
Apolle / Apollo Trench	62cSW2 Barleux	O 3 c, 9 a
Apollo Support [1918]	62dSE [1 Hamel]	P 31 b, d
Apollo's Fork	20SE4 Roulers	W 6 a
Appam House	36aNE1 Morbecque	D 6 c 5.1
Appendix, The	57dSE2 & 57cSW1 Le Sars	M 17 c, d
Appendix, The [Sanctuary Wood, 1915]	28NW4 & NE3 Zillebeke	J 13 c 1.7
Appetite Farm	27SE4 Meteren	X 17 b 9.2
Apple Alley	51bSW1 Neuville Vitasse	M 29 d, 36 a
Apple Alley	62dNE2 Méaulte	F 10 a
Apple Farm	28SE1 Wervicq	P 19 a 9.3
Apple Farm	36aNE4 Merville	K 22 a 75.52
Apple House	36SW1 Aubers	M 18 b
Apple Lane	51bSW4 Bullecourt	U 7 d
Apple Lane Trench	62cNE4 Roisel	L 22 c, d, 28 b
Apple Trees	62cNW1 Maricourt	A 1 b
Apple Trench	36cSW1 Lens	M 26 c
Apple Villa	28NW2 St Julien	C 24 d 1.9
Appleby Sap	57dNE1 & 2 Fonquevillers	E 22 b
Approach Trench	36cSW1 Lens	N 19 d

Name	Map Sheet	Map Reference
Apricot Farm	20SE2 Hooglede	R 16 b 4.6
April Avenue	51bNW3 Arras	G 17 a, b
April Cottages	27NE2 Proven	F 20 c 4.3
Aqueduct Road [road]	57cSW1 Gueudecourt	M 8 a, b, d, 9 c, 15 a, b, d
Aquenne Switch [1918]	62dSW [2 Villers-Bretonneux / 4 Cachy]	O 28 c, 34 a, b, c, d, U 4 a
Arab Avenue	51bNW1 Roclincourt	A 29 a
Arab Cottages	36aNE4 Merville	K 10 a 80.15
Arab Farm	20SW4 Bixschoote	O 32 d 2.8
Arab Trench	36aSW [4 Lillers]	O 35 c
Arab Trench	36cSW1 Lens	M 26 c
Arabella Avenue [1918]	57dSW [3 Talmas]	S 24 a, c
Aragon Trench	57dNE3 & 4 Hébuterne	L 7 c, d
Aran Cottages	27SE2 Berthen	R 13 c 7.1
Aran Farm	28NW3 Poperinghe	G 15 d 3.2
Ararat Trench [1918]	62dSW [2 Corbie / Villers-Bretonn.] / SE [1 Hamel]	O 30 b, P 25 a
Arawatta Trench [1918]	62dSE [1 Hamel]	P 25 c, 31 a
Arbre de la Femme [crossroads]	51aSE3	V 21 d 95.95
Arbre en boule, Redoute de l' [bushy-top]	62cNW3 Vaux	G 34 a, b
Arbre en Chandelle [Candle Tree, trig point]	66eNE2 Vrély	F 10 d 05.20
Arbre Filiforme [Straggly / Filiform Tree, trig]	62dNE2 Méaulte	F 26 a
Arbre Fourche [Forked Tree, trig point]	62dNE [4 Bray-sur-Somme]	L 2 b 05.95
Arbre Touffu [at Quesnoy Farm, trig point]	57dNE1 & 2 Fonquevillers	F 13 b [name], F 14 a 2.6 [tree]
Arbre Trèfle [Shamrock Tree, trig point,]	57dSE4 Ovillers	W 30 c 45.15
Arbres, Bois des [Redoubt]	51bNW1 Roclincourt	A 9 a, c
Arbroath Farm	28SE1 Wervicq	P 9 a 3.7
Arbroath Street	57dSE4 Ovillers	X 20 c
Arcade Camp [Nieppe Forest]	36aNE3 Haverskerque	J 8 c
Arcade South	57dSE1 & 2 Beaumont	Q 16 b
Arcade, The	36SW1 Aubers	N 13 a, c
Arches, The	36NW2 Armentières	C 11 a
Archie Sector [trenches] [1918]	62dSW [2 Villers-Bretonneux / 4 Cachy]	N 36, T 6
Archie Trench	51bNW4 Fampoux	I 25 d
Architect's Fork [road jct]	28NE2 Moorslede	F 22 b 0.2
Arcot House	28NW3 Poperinghe	G 22 d 2.5
Arctic Buildings	27SE4 Meteren	X 14 b 2.7
Arcy Woods	62dSE [2 Proyart]	R 17 a, b
Ardath Fork	20SE4 Roulers	W 27 b 7.7
Ardee Copse	27NE2 Proven	F 10 c
Ardissart Copse	57bSW1 Bantouzelle	N 26 b
Ardissart Farm	57bSW1 Bantouzelle	N 26 d 25.15
Ardmore House	27NE2 Proven	F 29 d 60.85
Ardrishaig Street	57dSE4 Ovillers	Q 36 d
Ares, Bois des [Are = 100 sq. metres]	62cSW3 & 4 Marchélepot	T 4 c, d
Arethusa Trench [1918]	51bNW1 Roclincourt	A 24 b, c, d, 30 a
Arganautes, Tranchée des	70dSW2 [Coucy-le-Château]	O 22 c
Argent [farm]	57bSW1 Bantouzelle	M 2 a 4.7
Argonne Alley	62cSW1 Dompierre / 2 Barleux	N 13, 14, 20, 21, 27, 33, 34
Argonne Trench	62bSW1 Gricourt / 3 St Quentin	M 28 b, d, 34 b, d, S 4 b
Argousins, Tranchée des	66cNW2 Itancourt	C 26 d, 27 c, d
Argument Trench	57dSE2 & 57cSW1 Le Sars	M 21 c, 27 a
Argus [German M.G. Post; non-existent]	51bSW4 Bullecourt	U 14 d 75.80
Argus Trench	62cSW2 Barleux	N 36 b, O 25 c, 31 a
Argus, Tranchée d'	62cSW1 & 2 Belloy / 3 & 4 Marchélepot	N 36 b, c, d, O 25 c, 31 a, T 6 a

Name	Map Sheet	Map Reference
Argyle Avenue	57cSW3 Longueval	S 9 a, b
Argyle Farm	28NW2 St Julien	C 28 b 9.9
Argyle Group [Craters]	51bNW1 Roclincourt	A 16 a, c
Argyle Trench	36cSW1 Lens	N 19 b, 20 a
Argyle Trench	57cSW3 Longueval	S 8 b, 9 a, b, c
Argyll Lane	57cSE2 Gonnelieu	R 14 b
Argyll Road [road]	36aSE1 St Venant	P 6 b, d, 12 b, d
Argyll Street [cJuly 1915]	28NW2 St Julien	C 20 a
Argyll[e] Street	57dSE4 Ovillers	X 13 a, b
Argylle Trench, & Group [Craters]	51bNW1 Roclincourt	A 16 a
Ariane [Locality]	51bNW1 Roclincourt	A 20 d
Ariane Post	51bNW1 Roclincourt	A 26 b
Ark Farm	36aNE4 Merville	K 10 a 1.7
Ark Trench	57cSE4 Villers-Guislain	X 7 c
Ark, The	51bSW1 Neuville Vitasse	N 14 a
Arklow House	27NE2 Proven	F 10 a 50.15
Arkmolen [hamlet]	28NE4 Dadizeele	K 16 a, b
Arkmolen [windmill]	28NE4 Dadizeele	K 16 b 25.25
Arkwell [Thiepval Wood]	57dSE2 Beaumont	R 25 a
Arlette Communication Trench [1918]	62dSE [1 Hamel]	P 26 b, 27 a
Arlette O.P [1917-18]	51bNW1 Roclincourt	B 1 a 2.6
Arleux [village]	51bNE4 Cantin / SE2 Oisy-le-Verger	K 35 b, c, d, 36 a, c, Q 5 a, b, 6 a, b
Arleux Loop North	51bNW2 Oppy	B 5 a, c
Arleux Loop South	51bNW2 Oppy	B 5 c, d, 11 b, 12 a
Arleux Post	51bNW2 Oppy	B 6 b
Arleux Trench	36cSW4 Rouvroy	T 29 c
Arleux-en-Gohelle [village]	51bNW2 Oppy	B 5 a, b, d, 6 a, c
Arlington Street [Sept 1915]	36cNW1 La Bassée	A 15 d
Arloing Trench	66cNW1 Grugies / 2 Itancourt	B 16 a
Arm Trench	36cNW1 La Bassée	A 10 c, 16 a
Arm Trench	51bNW2 Oppy	I 2 a
Armadillo Trench	36aSW4 [Lillers]	O 35 d, U 5 b
Armagh House	28NW4 & NE3 Zillebeke	I 30 a 2.3
Armargh Wood	28NW4 & NE3 Zillebeke	I 29 b, 30 a
Armée Post, L'	36NW4 Bois Grenier	H 18 b
Armentières [town]	36NW2 Armentières	B 30, C 25, 26, H 6, I 1, 2
Armentières Railhead / Refilling Point	36NW2 Armentières	B 30 a, b
Armentières, Chapelle d' [village]	36NW4 Bois Grenier	I 8, 9
Armidale Communication Trench [1918]	62dSE [1 Hamel]	P 20 c, d
Armour Farm	28SW3 Bailleul	N 33 d 35.05
Armour Trench	51bNW1 Roclincourt	A 4 c
Army Dump C [Boyeffles]	36bSE2 Boyeffles	R 13 b 1.9
Arnay / Arnau, Boyau	36cSW3 Vimy	S 8 d, 9 c
Arnim Copse	66dNW1 Punchy	B 13 a
Arnim Cross [cross roads]	27SE4 Meteren	X 27 b 8.9
Arnim Trench	57dNE4 & 57cNW3 Achiet	L 10 a, b, 11 c, d
Arno House	27NE4 Abeele	L 29 c 7.2
Arnold Trench	36cSW1 Lens	M 26 d, 32 b
Arnott Copse	51bSE2 Oisy-le-Verger	Q 28 b
Arnould Quarry	57bSW3 Honnecourt	S 2 a
Arrangements Alley	66cNW4 Berthenicourt	I 28 a
Arras Alley	36cSW3 Vimy	S 13 d, 14 a
Arras East [Trench] [at the Citadel]	51bNW3 Arras	G 27 c, 31 b, 32 a, b, 33 a

Name	Map Sheet	Map Reference
Arras East Reserve	51bNW3 Arras	G 25 d, 26 c, d, 31 b
Arras East Support	51bNW3 Arras	G 31 b, 32 a, b
Arras Farm	36NW2 & NE1 Houplines	D 27 a 5.9
Arras Road Trench	36bSE4 Carency	R 36 c
Arras, Boyau de la Route d'	36bSE2 Boyeffles / 36cSW1 Lens	R 23 c, 29 a, b, d, 35 b, 36 a
Arrêt [Zillebeke]	28NW4 Ypres	I 22 c 6.3
Arret Trench [Hallu Station]	66dNW1 Punchy	A 21 d
Arrewage [hamlet]	36aNE4 Merville	K 10 a 80.85
Arriere Cour Wood, l'	66eNW [4 Morisel]	H 22, 23, 28, 29
Arrival Farm	28NW2 St Julien	B 28 d
Arrivé Trench	62cSW1 Dompierre	N 2 a, c
Arrivée Trench	62cNW3 Vaux	H 32 c
Arrol Wood	28NE4 Dadizeele	K 35 b, 36 a
Arrow Farm	28SW2 Wytschaete	O 30 c 5.7
Arrow Head Copse	51bSW2 Vis-en-Artois	O 2 a
Arrow Head Copse	57cSW3 Longueval	S 30 b 3.2
Arrow Lane	57dSE4 Ovillers	X 27 c
Arrow Trench	36cSW1 Lens	M 21 a
Arrow Trench	36cSW1 Lens	M 32 b
Arrow Trench [1918]	57dNE2 & 57cNW1 Courcelles	F 26 a, b
Arrow Trench [Arrow Head Copse]	51bNW4 Fampoux / SW2 Vis-en-Artois	I 32 c, O 2 a
Arroyo Trench / Arroyo, Tranchée de l'	66cNW2 Itancourt	B 30 b, C 25 a
Arsenic Trench	36cSW1 Lens	M 26 d, 32 b
Arsenic Trench	36cSW4 Rouvroy	T 18 b, c, d
Arson Trench	36cSW1 Lens	M 26 c, d
Art [Trench]	36cNW1 La Bassée	A 4 a, d
Artaud Trench [1918]	66eNW [2 Thennes]	B 23 b, 24 a
Artaxerxes Trench, Post & Alley	62cNE2 Epéhy	F 29 b
Artherbe Street	57dSE1 & 2 Beaumont	R 25 a
Arthur Corons [miners' cottages]	36cSW1 Lens	N 27 d
Arthur's Keep [SW of Mine Point]	36cNW1 La Bassée	A 27 b
Arthur's Seat Trench	36cSW3 Vimy	S 4 b
Artichoke Farm	20SE2 Hooglede	R 4 d 1.3
Artillerie Mülde [Battery Valley]	57dSE1 & 2 Beaumont	R 14 b, c, d
Artillerie Weg	36cSW3 Vimy	S 23 c, 28 b, 29 a
Artillerie Weg	51bSW1 Neuville Vitasse	M 15 c, 21 a, b
Artillery [sic] Graben	57dNE1 & 2 Fonquevillers	F 13 a, c, d
Artillery Alley	57dSE1 & 2 Beaumont	R 1 b, d, 2 a, b
Artillery Corner [St Aubin]	51cNE4 Wagnonlieu	L 5 d
Artillery Farm	28SW2 Wytschaete	N 10 a 9.3
Artillery Farm	36NW4 Bois Grenier	I 19 c
Artillery Hill	51bNW4 Fampoux / SW2 Vis-en-Artois	I 34 d, 35 c, O 5 a
Artillery House	28SW4 Ploegsteert	T 24 a 5.9
Artillery House [Feb 1916]	36cNW1 La Bassée	A 9 c, d, 15 a [approx]
Artillery Lane [road]	51bNW4 Fampoux	I 27 a, c, d, 33 b, 34 a, c, d
Artillery Lane [road]	57dSE1 & 2 Beaumont	R 1 a, c, 7 a
Artillery Road	36NW4 Bois Grenier	I 21 a, c
Artillery Road [road]	28SW1 Kemmel	M 30 b, d, 36 b, N 25 a, b
Artillery Road North [1917-18]	28NE1 Zonnebeke	D 21 a, c, d
Artillery Road South [1917-18]	28NE1 Zonnebeke	D 16 c, d, 21 c, d, 22 a, c, 27 a
Artillery Row	36cSW1 Lens	M 3 a, b
Artillery Row [ride, Nieppe Forest]	36aNE3 Haverskerque	J 18 d, K 19 a, c
Artillery Row [Sept 1915]	36cNW1 La Bassée	A 15 a
Artillery Siding [light rly, Vermelles]	36cNW3 Loos	G 7 b

Name	Map Sheet	Map Reference
Artillery Trench [1918]	57dNE2 & 57cNW1 Courcelles	F 20 a, c, d
Artillery Valley [Battery Valley]	57dSE1 & 2 Beaumont	R 14 b, c, d
Artillery Wood	28NW2 St Julien	C 1 c
Artilleryman's House	36NW4 Bois Grenier	I 21 a
Artists' Cross Roads	28NE2 Moorslede	F 28 c 90.45
Artois Trench	51bSW2 Vis-en-Artois	O 16 d, 17 c, d
Artois Trench	70dNW4 St Gobain	H 30 b, d
Artoishoek [place name]	28NE4 Dadizeele	K 30 c
Arun Trench [Bulow]	57dNE3 & 4 Hébuterne	K 11 d, 12 c, d
Arundel [farm]	28NW4 Ypres	I 33 c 5.5
Arva Trench	66cNW1 Grugies	B 8 a, c, d
Ascension Farm [by aerodrome]	62cNE4 Roisel	L 30 c
Ascension Posts	62bNW3 Bellicourt	G 31 b
Ascension Spur	62bNW3 Bellicourt	G 25 d, 31 b, d
Ascension Valley	62bNW3 Bellicourt	G 26 c, 32 a
Ascot Communication Trench [1918]	62dSE [1 Hamel]	P 20 d, 26 b
Ascot Cottage	28NW2 St Julien	C 10 c 3.0
Ascot O.P. [Hill 70, 1917-18]	36cNW3 Loos	H 32 c 0.5
Asfeld Alley	66cNW1 Grugies	B 8 a
Ash Avenue	51bNW1 Roclincourt	A 29 b
Ash Avenue [road]	28SW4 Ploegsteert	U 9 d, 10 c, 15 a, b
Ash Crater	28SW4 Ploegsteert	U 15 a 7.8
Ash Grove [Thiepval Wood]	57dSE1 & 2 Beaumont	R 25 c
Ash Lane	28SW2 Wytschaete	N 24 a
Ash Road / Ash Row	36cSW3 Vimy	M 32 c, S 2 a
Ash Street	36NW4 Bois Grenier	I 21 a, c
Ash Trench	36cSW1 Lens	M 26 d, 32 a, b
Ash Trench [1918]	57dNE3 & 4 Hébuterne	K 12 b, L 7 a
Ash Way Trench	28SW4 Ploegsteert	U 8 c
Ash Wood	62bSW1 Gricourt	M 30 b, N 25 a
Ashburton Trench [1918]	62dSE [1 Hamel]	P 25 c, 31 a
Ashcroft Buildings	28NE4 Dadizeele	L 9 c 7.9
Ashdown Street	57dSE4 Ovillers	X 19 d, 20 c
Ashford Street	62dNE2 Meaulte	F 8 d, 14 b
Ashmore Farm	28NE4 Dadizeele	L 15 c 8.1
Ashore Trench	36cSW1 Lens	M 26 c, 32 a
Ashton Alley / Sap [Havrincourt Wood]	57cSE2 Gonnelieu	Q 3 b
Ashton Trench	51bNW1 Roclincourt	A 9 b, 10 a
Ashway Trench [Hill 63]	28SW4 Ploegsteert	U 8 c, 14 a
Ashwell Wood	62dSE [2 Proyart]	R 35 a
Askew Trench	36cSW1 Lens	M 20 b, d
Asparagus Trench	36aSW2 [Molinghem] / 4 [Lillers]	O 34 b, d
Aspice Alley [1918]	66eNW [2 Thennes]	B 12 d, 18 b
Aspinall House	27NE2 Proven	F 19 d 6.5
Aspire Trench	36cSW1 Lens	M 21 c
Ass Alley	36cNW1 La Bassée	A 3 d
Assam Farm	28NW3 Poperinghe	H 22 a 3.6
Assegai Valley	62bNW1 Gouy	B 20 d, 26 b
Assembly Trench	28SW4 Ploegsteert	U 2 b
Asser Farm	27NE2 Proven	F 19 c 5.5
Assert Trench	36cSW1 Lens	M 29 a, c
Assign Trench	36cSW1 Lens	M 29 d, 30 a, c
Assisi Farm	28SW3 Bailleul	S 17 b 1.2
Assouan [pillbox]	28NE1 Zonnebeke	D 7 d 35.10

Name	Map Sheet	Map Reference
Assyria	28NE1 Zonnebeke	D 18 a, b
Assyrie Trench / Tranchée de l'Assyrie	62cSW2 Barleux	O 2 d, 3 c
Astill Farm	28SW3 Bailleul	T 7 b 6.8
Astin [?] [Tranchée, 1915] / Keats Redan	57dSE4 Ovillers	X 13 c
Aston Trench	57cSW3 Longueval	S 7 b, d
Astuce Trench [1918]	62dSW [4 Cachy / Gentelles]	U 5 d, 11 a
Asylum [light railway locality, 1917-18]	28NW4 Ypres	H 12 d
Asylum [Ypres]	28NW4 Ypres	H 12 d
Asylum Corner [Ypres; road jct]	28NW4 Ypres	H 12 d 3.4
Asylum Road [road]	36aSE1 St Venant	P 9 b, c, d, 14 b, d, 15 a
Athénée [railway sidings locality]	20SW3 Oostvleteren	S 18 a
Athies [village]	51bNW3 Arras	H 14 b, d, 15 c
Athies [village]	62cSW4 St. Christ / SE3 Athies	U 12 b, d, V 7 a, c
Athies Graben	51bNW3 Arras	H 8 a
Athlones Street	57dNE1 & 2 Fonquevillers	E 22 b
Atholl Street [Boyau Lavié, 1915]	57dSE4 Ovillers	X 19 b
Atila Trench	62cSW1 Dompierre	N 2 a, c
Atlantic Farm	28NW3 Poperinghe	G 9 c 5.4
Atlantic Siding	28NW3 Poperinghe	G 10 c 7.2
Atlas Trench	28NW2 St Julien	C 15 c
Atlas Trench	62cNW2 Bouchavesnes	C 1 d, 7 b
Atom Farm	36aNE4 Merville	K 18 c 99.55
Atom Mill [windmill]	27SE1 St Sylvestre	P 19 d 89.19
Atom Trench	57cSW2 Villers-au-Flos	N 16 c, 22 a, b, d
Attendorn Trench / Tranchée Attendorn	66cNW2 Itancourt	B 17 d, 18 c, 23 b, 24 a, c
Attila Trench	62cNW3 Vaux	H 32 c
Attila Trench / Alley	62cSW2 Barleux	O 2 c, d, 9 a
Attilly [village]	62cSE4 [Attilly]	X 9 b, d, 10 c
Aubencheul-au-Bac [village]	51bSE2 Oisy-le-Verger	R 15 b, d, 16 a, c
Aubencheul-aux-Bois [village]	57bSW3 Honnecourt	S 18 b, d, T 13 a, c,
Aubepines, Bois des	51bSW2 Vis-en-Artois	O 2 b
Aubert Alley	62cNW4 Péronne	H 30 c, d, 36 b, I 31 a, c
Aubigny Alley [1918]	62dSW [4 Cachy]	U 1 a, b, 2 a, b, 3 a, b
Aubigny Sector [trenches] [1918]	62dSW [2 Villers-Bretonneux / 4 Cachy]	O8,9,14,15,20,21,26,27,31,32, 33,U1,2
Aubigny, Marais d' [marsh / lake]	51bSE2 Oisy-le-Verger	R 8 a, b, c, d, 9 a, b, c, d
Aubigny-au-Bac [village]	51bSE2 Oisy-le-Verger	R 10 c, d, 16 a, b
Auchy Alley	36cNW1 La Bassée	A 23 d, 28 a, b, c
Auchy-lez-la Bassée [village]	36cNW1 La Bassée	A 23 c, d, 29 a
Auckland [light rly locality]	28NW3 Poperinghe	G 23 b 5.9
Auckland Avenue	36NW4 Bois Grenier	I 5 c
Auckland Farm	28NW3 Poperinghe	G 17 d 7.5
Auckland Trench	28SW4 Ploegsteert	U 1 d
Auckland Trench	57cSW3 Longueval	S 11 b
Auction Lodge	57dSE1 & 2 Beaumont	Q 10 a
Audley Street [Guillemont]	57cSW3 Longueval	T 19 c
Auerstadt Avenue	57dNE3 & 4 Hébuterne	K 21 b, 22 a
Auerstadt Trench [later Jean Bart]	57dNE3 & 4 Hébuterne	K 21 b, 22 a, c, d, 23 a, c
Augendre Alley	62bSW3 St Quentin / 66cNW1 Grugies	S 29 d, A 4 b, c, d, 5 a, b
Augias Trench	62cNE3 Buire	J 25 a, c
Augier [Boyau, W of Fricourt, 1915]	62dNE2 Méaulte	F 2 d, 3 c, 8 a, b
Augsberg Trench	66cNW1 Grugies	B 8 a, b
Augsburger Weg	51bNW1 Roclincourt	A 12 c
August Avenue	51bNW3 Arras	G 11, 16, 17

Name	Map Sheet	Map Reference
August City Road [road]	36cSW1 Lens	N 8 d, 9 a, c, 14 b
August Trench	36cSW3 Vimy	N 33 c
Augusta Battery	5SW1 Zeebrugge	N 7 d, 8 c, 13 b
Augusta Post	36NW4 Bois Grenier	I 20 b
Augusta Trench [1918]	66eNW [4 Morisel]	H 11 c, d, 17 b
Augustus [farm & pillbox]	28NE1 Zonnebeke	D 11 c 05.00
Augustus Wood	28NE1 Zonnebeke	D 11 c
Auk Alley	36cNW1 La Bassée	A 3 b
Auk House	36aNE2 Vieux Berquin	F 4 b 2.6
Auk Trench [1918]	36aSW4 [Lillers]	O 34 d, 35 c
Auloup Trench	62cSW1 & 2 Belloy	N 11 d, 12 a, c
Aunes, Bois des [Alders]	62cSW3 & 4 Marchélepot	T 6 a, b, c, d
Aura Fork [road jct]	27NE4 Abeele	L 19 b 45.90
Auray Trench	66cNW4 Berthenicourt	H 12 b
Aurillac Trench	66cNW1 Grugies	B 20 c, d
Aurora O.P. [Hill 70, 1917-18]	36cSW1 Lens	N 2 a 2.9
Aurore Alley	66dNW1 Punchy	B 2 a, b, 4 a, c
Ausbach Trench	62cNW2 Bouchavesnes	C 17 c, d, 23 a
Austerlitz Farm	28NW2 St Julien	B 29 b
Austerlitz Quarry	66eNW [2 Thennes]	B 12 b
Australia Street [1918]	57dSE [3 Bouzincourt]	V 30 b, W 25 a, b, 26 a
Australia Support [1918]	62dSE [1 Hamel]	P 20 d, 21 a, c, 26 a, b, c
Australia Trench	36NW2 Armentières	C 28 d, 29 c
Australian Road [road]	36cSW1 Lens	M 15 c, 21 a, b, d
Australian Trench	27SE4 Meteren	X10d, 11c, 14d, 15a,b,c, 16a,b, 20b
Austrian Trench, Support, & Junction	62dNE2 Méaulte	F 12 a
Austrian Way	36cNW1 La Bassée	A 9 b
Austrians Alley [1918]	62dSE [3 Marcelcave]	V 7 a, b, 8 a
Auterelle Alley	62cSW4 St. Christ	U 15 d, 16 c
Auteur Trench	62cSW4 St. Christ	U 1 b, d, 2 a
Author's Corner [road jct]	28NE2 Moorslede	F 5 d 83.00
Authuille [village]	57dSE4 Ovillers	Q 36 c, W 6 a
Authuille Post	57dSE4 Ovillers	Q 36 c
Authuille Wood [Blighty Wood]	57dSE4 Ovillers	W 6, 12, X 1, 7
Automne Trench	62cSW4 St. Christ	U 2 a, c
Autumn Reserve	57cNE1 Quéant	D 25 b, d, 26 c
Autumn Support	57cSW4 Combles	N 35 c
Autumn Trench	28SW4 Ploegsteert	U 8 a, c
Autumn Trench	57cSW4 Combles	N 35 c
Auvergne Track [1917-18]	20SW4 Bixschoote	U 1 b, c, d, 7 a
Auvergne Trench	66cNW1 Grugies / 2 Itancourt	B 15 a, b, 16 a, c, 17 c
Aval Wood	36aNE1 Morbecque	E 19, 20, 21, 22, 25, 26, 27, 28
Avelette [hamlet]	36aSE4 Locon	W 17 central
Avelu [hamlet]	57bSW4 Serain	U 4 d, 5 c, 10 b, 11 a
Aveluy [village]	57dSE4 Ovillers	W 17 a, b
Aveluy Chateau	57dSE4 Ovillers	Q 17 a 95.95
Aveluy Outposts [1918]	57dSE4 Ovillers	Q 34 d, 35 c
Aveluy Trench	57dSE4 Ovillers	X 26 d
Aveluy Wood	57dSE4 Ovillers	Q 34, 35, W 4, 5, 10, 11
Avenel Communication Trench [1918]	62dSE [1 Hamel]	P 31 a, b
Avenue 'A'	51bNW1 Roclincourt	A 23c, 28 b, 29 a
Avenue 'B'	51bNW1 Roclincourt	A 29 a
Avenue Centrale	51bNW1 Roclincourt	A 28 a
Avenue Charles	51bNW1 Roclincourt	A 22 d

Name	Map Sheet	Map Reference
Avenue des Mortices	51bNW1 Roclincourt	A 28
Avenue Farm	28SW4 Ploegsteert	U 9 c 3.8
Avenue 'G'	51bNW1 Roclincourt	A 23 c, 28
Avenue Road	36NW2 Armentières	I 4 b, d
Avenue Trench	20SW4 Bixschoote	T 17 d
Avenue, The	36cNW1 La Bassée	A 9 a, c, d
Avenue, The [road]	28SW4 Ploegsteert	U 9 a, c, 15 a
Avesnes-les-Bapaume [village]	57cNW3 Bapaume	H 26 central
Aviatik Farm	28NE1 Zonnebeke	D 8 a 5.2
Aviators Cross Roads	28NE2 Moorslede	F 30 a 35.40
Aviators Trench	66cNW1 Grugies / 2 Itancourt	B 27 b, 28 a, c
Avion [village]	36cSW1 Lens	N 26 d, 32 a, b, c, d, 33 a
Avion Support	36cSW3 Vimy	N 32 d, T 2 b, 3 a, b, c, d
Avion Switch	36cSW4 Rouvroy	T 4 b
Avion Trench	36cSW3 Vimy	N 32 c, d, T 2 b, 3 a, b
Avoca Valley	57dSE4 Ovillers	X 19, 25
Avoin, Tranchée de [W of Mametz Wood]	57dSE4 Ovillers	X 23 b, d
Avon [post]	36cSW4 Rouvroy	T 29 b 2.7
Avon Trench	51bNW3 Arras	G 12 d
Avon Wood	62cNW3 Vaux	H 14 a
Avondale Street / Road [trench]	36NW4 Bois Grenier	I 15 d
Avranches Trench	66cNW4 Berthenicourt	I 31 b
Awatuni Lines [camp]	28NW4 Ypres	H 23 c
Awenoe Trench	51bNW1 Roclincourt	A 5 c
Awkward Support [1918]	62dSW [2 Villers-Bretonneux / 4 Cachy]	O 35 c, d, 36 a, U 4 b, d, 5 a, b
Awoingt [village]	57bNW1 Cambrai	B 20, 26
Axe Alley	27SE4 Meteren	X 9 d, 10 c, 16 a
Axe Mill	27SE4 Meteren	X 16 a 2.9
Axe Trench	51bSW1 Neuville Vitasse	M 21 a, b
Axe Trench [Hatchet Wood]	51bNW4 Fampoux	I 34 a
Axholme Cross Roads	28NE4 Dadizeele	L 8 d 45.40
Ayette Switch [1918]	57dNE2 & 57cNW1 Courcelles	F 9 b, d, 10 a, c, d
Ayette Switch Support [1918]	57dNE2 & 57cNW1 Courcelles	F 9 b, c, d, 10 a
Aylward Street	57cSE4 Villers-Guislain	X 4 a
Ayr Street	28NW4 & NE3 Zillebeke	I 5 c, d
Ayr Street	28SW4 Ploegsteert	U 27 b, d
Ayres Cottage	28SW3 Bailleul	T 3 a 3.8
Ayrshire Camp	28SW3 Bailleul	M 35 d
Azimuth Alley	36cNW1 La Bassée	A 23 b, c, d, 24 a, b
Aztec Farm	27SE4 Meteren	X 13 c 9.4
Azur, Bois [Blue]	62cSW3 & 4 Marchélepot	T 5 a
B 10 [trench, Wieltje, May 1916]	28NW2 St Julien	C 22 d, 28 b
B 11 [trench, Wieltje, May 1916]	28NW2 St Julien	C 28 a, b
B 12 [trench, Wieltje, May 1916]	28NW2 St Julien	C 28 a, b
B 13 [trench, Wieltje, May 1916]	28NW2 St Julien	C 22 c
B 17 [trench, E of Turco Farm, May 1916]	28NW2 St Julien	C 15 c
B 9 [trench, Wieltje, May 1916]	28NW2 St Julien	C 28 b
B Camp	28NW3 Poperinghe	G 6 c, d
B Line [1918]	27SE3 Borre	extensive
B Lines [W of Neuve Chapelle 1914-15]	36SW1 Aubers / 3 Richebourg	M 34 b, c, 9, S 4 a
B Sap [Givenchy]	36cNW1 La Bassée	A 9 d
B Sap [Oldham Alley]	57cSE2 Gonnelieu	Q 4 b
B Sector [April 1915, N of R Douve]	28SW2 Wytschaete / 4 Ploegsteert	N 36 / T 6
B Street	57dSE1 & 2 Beaumont	Q 10 d

Name	Map Sheet	Map Reference
B Trench	57cSW1 Gueudecourt	M 14 d
B Work	51bNW3 Arras	G 11 b
B.B. Line	36aSW [1, 2, 4] / 36bNE [3] / SE [1, 3]	extensive
B.C.D. Line [Boulogne-Calais-Dunkerque Line]	19, 27 [both 1:40,000]	extensive
B.H.Q. Trench	57dNE1 & 2 Fonquevillers	E 9 d, 15 b, 16 a
Baart Buildings	28NE2 Moorslede	F 22 b 8.1
Bab Farm	28SW2 Wytschaete	O 23 d 6.9
Babble Junction [road jct]	28NE4 Dadizeele	L 28 c 35.40
Babel Trench	28NW2 St Julien	B 12 b
Babille Farm [nr Babillebeek]	28NE2 Moorslede	F 1 b 9.5
Baboo Drive	28NW2 St Julien	B 6 b, d, C 1 a
Baboo Lane	28NW2 St Julien	B 6 d
Baboon Avenue	28NW2 St Julien	B 6 a, b
Baboon Reserve	28NW2 St Julien	B 6 a, b, d
Baboon Row	28NW2 St Julien	B 6 a, b, c, d
Baboon Support	28NW2 St Julien	B 6 a, c, d
Baboon Trench	28NW2 St Julien	B 5 d, 6 c
Babs Post	57cNE3 Hermies	K 2 d
Baby Farm	36aNE3 Haverskerque	J 21 c 4.2
Baby Lane	28NW2 St Julien	B 5 b
Baby Reserve	28NW2 St Julien	B 5 b, 6 a
Baby Support	28NW2 St Julien	B 5 b, 6 a
Baby Trench	28NW2 St Julien	B 5 b, d
Baby Trench	36cSW3 Vimy	S 15 a, c
Baby Trench	51bNW2 Oppy	B 12 a
Babylas Alley	66dNW1 Punchy	B 8 b, d, 9 c
Babylon Trench	57dNE3 & 4 Hébuterne	K 22 d, 28 b
Bac St. Maur [village]	36NW3 Fleurbaix	G 18 d, H 13 c
Bacchantes Alley	62cSW4 St. Christ	T 29 a, b
Bacchus Trench	62cNW2 Bouchavesnes	C 4 c, d
Bach Buildings	20SE2 Hooglede	R 5 d 8.0
Bachelor Cross Roads	28NE4 Dadizeele	L 35 a 80.25
Bachelor Work	36NW2 Armentières	C 4 c
Back Estaminet	28SW4 Ploegsteert	U 14 a 65.15
Back House [Le Gheer]	28SW4 Ploegsteert	U 21 d 95.09
Back Lane	62cNW1 Maricourt	A 2 d, 3 c
Back Road [road]	36aNE3 Haverskerque	J 27 d, 33 b, 34 a, c
Back Street	36cNW1 La Bassée	A 21 d, 27 b, d, G 4 a
Back Trench	36cSW3 Vimy	S 15 b, c, d
Back Trench	51bNW2 Oppy	B 22 b, d, 23 c
Back Trench	51bSW1 Neuville Vitasse	N 14 c, d, 20 b
Back Trench	62cNW1 Maricourt	A 2 d, 3 c
Back Walk	12SW1 Nieuport	M 15 c
Back Wood	51bNW4 Fampoux	I 32 d
Bacon Camp	27NE4 Abeele	L 1 d, 7 b
Bacon Copse [Puchevillers]	57dSW [1 Puchevillers] / [2 Raincheval]	N 28 a, b
Bacon Trench	36cNW1 La Bassée	B 3 b
Bacon Trench	57cSW1 Gueudecourt	N 14 d, 20 b
Bacon Trench	57dSE4 Ovillers / 57cSW3 Longueval	X 6 a, S 1 b
Bacquencourt	66dNW4 Nesle	I 35 b, d, 36 c
Bacquerot Street	36SW1 Aubers	M 22 a, b, 16 d
Baddeck Trench	36cSW3 Vimy	T 7 a
Bade Trench	62cSE1 Bouvincourt	P 19 b, c, d, 25 b, d
Bade Trench [1918]	66eNW [2 Thennes]	C 6 c, 11 b, d, 12 a, 17 a, b

Name	Map Sheet	Map Reference
Baden Avenue [1918]	57dNE2 & 57cNW1 Courcelles	F 15 c, d, 21 b, 22 a, b
Baden Street	57dSE2 Beaumont	R 20 d, 27 a, b
Baden Trench	66cNW4 Berthenicourt	I 14 a, b, d
Baden-Baden Trench [1918]	66eNW [2 Thennes]	C 15 d, 21 a
Badener Graben	57dNE1 & 2 Fonquevillers	F 15 c, d, 21 a, b
Badger Copse	62bSW3 St Quentin	M 32 c, d
Badger Cross Roads	28NE4 Dadizeele	L 35 d 25.30
Badger Trench	51bSW2 Vis-en-Artois	O 8 d, 9 c
Badger Trench [1918]	36aSW [2 Molinghem]	O 22 a
Badminton Farm	28NE4 Dadizeele	L 25 c 3.9
Baeck Houck [farm]	27SE2 Berthen	Q 22 c 7.7
Baffin Row [buildings]	28NW3 Poperinghe	G 28 c 2.1
Baffle Trench	36cSW3 Vimy	S 15 a, b
Baguettes Track [1917-18]	20SW4 Bixschoote	N 36 c, d
Bahn Stellung	51bNW1 Roclincourt	H 1 b
Bahneinschnitt	51bNW1 Roclincourt	B 26 b, c, d
Bail Copse	28NE2 Moorslede	E 5 c 2.7
Bailbec Trench, de	57dNE3 & 4 Hébuterne	K 17 c
Bailiff Cross Roads	28NE4 Dadizeele	L 36 a 7.3
Baillescourt Farm [Grandcourt]	57dSE1 & 2 Beaumont	R 3 c 8.1
Bailleul [town]	28SW3 Bailleul	S 13, 14, 19 20
Bailleul [village]	51bNW1 Roclincourt / 2 Oppy	B 22 a, c
Bailleul Alley, Locality & Post [B 28 b]	51bNW2 Oppy	B 22 c, 28 a, b
Bailleul Asylum	28SW3 Bailleul	S 8 d, 9 c, 14 b, 15 a
Bailleul East Post	51bNW2 Oppy	B 23 a, b, c
Bailleul Old Aerodrome [northern]	28SW3 Bailleul	S 9 c
Bailleul Old Aerodrome [southern]	28SW3 Bailleul	S 14 b, 15 c
Baillie Farm	20SE2 Hooglede	R 29 c 6.1
Bain Trench	66dNW3 Hattencourt	G 12 b, H 7 a, b
Bainbridge Trench	57dSE1 & 2 Beaumont	R 20 d
Baird Avenue	57cNW2 Vaulx-Vraucourt	C 18 d, 24 a
Baird Trench	51bNW1 Roclincourt	A 16 a
Bairn Maze	36cSW2 Harnes / 4 Rouvroy	O 32 b, c, d
Bairn Trench	36cSW3 Vimy	S 15 a, c
Bairnsfather Dugout [Thorpe Street]	57dNE1 & 2 Fonquevillers	E 27 c, K 3 a
Bairnsfather's Cottage [St Yvon]	28SW4 Ploegsteert	U 15 c 6.6
Bairnsfather's Pond [St Yvon]	28SW4 Ploegsteert	U 15 c 4.9
Baisington Camp	28SW1 Kemmel	M 12 central
Bait Junction	28NE4 Dadizeele	L 35 a 7.6
Bait Trench	62bNW3 Bellicourt	G 1 d
Baita Farm	27NE4 Abeele	K 34 d 35.80
Bajalle / Bajolle Line	36bSE2 Boyeffles / 4 Carency	R 24, 30, X 10, 12, 17, 18, 23, 24
Bajalle / Bajolle Line [Ligne Bajolle]	36cSW1 Lens	M 8 c, d . . . 19 b
Bajalle Switch	36bSE4 Carency	X 5 d, 6 c
Baker Alley	51bSW2 Vis-en-Artois	O 26 c
Baker Street	36cNW1 La Bassée	A 15 a, b
Baker Street	51bNW2 Oppy	B 18 b, d
Baker Trench [1918]	36aSW [2 Molinghem]	O 12 a, c
Bakerloo [light rly locality, 1917-18]	28NW2 St Julien	C 5 b 8.9
Bakery, The, & Bakery Post [1918]	28SW4 Ploegsteert	U 14 a
Baku Copse	28NW3 Poperinghe	G 32 b, d
Bala [strongpoint]	36NW3 Fleurbaix	G 21 b
Bala Cottages	28NW3 Poperinghe	G 31 d 55.27
Balance Cottage	28NE2 Moorslede	F 20 a 8.3

Name	Map Sheet	Map Reference
Balbus Farm	28NW3 Poperinghe	G 12 a 1.0
Balcony Corner [road jct]	28NE4 Dadizeele	L 29 c 25.65
Balcony Trench [Balkon Stellung, Hind. Line]	57cNE1 Quéant	D 8 c, d, 9 c, 14 a, b, 15 a, b, 16 a
Bald Junction [road jct]	28NE4 Dadizeele	L 30 a 1.0
Bald Top Trench	36cSW3 Vimy	S 3 a, c
Baldry Fork [road jct]	28SW3 Bailleul	T 25 b 8.1
Bâle Ravine	66eNW [2 Thennes]	C 20 d, 21 c, 26 a, b
Balkon Stellung [Balcony Trench, Hind. Line]	57cNE1 Quéant	D 8 c, d, 9 c, 14 a, b, 15 a, b, 16 a
Ball Lane	57dSE4 Ovillers	X 26 b, 27 c
Ball Trench	36cSW3 Vimy	S 15 c
Ballast Fork [road jct]	28NE4 Dadizeele	L 5 d 9.4
Ballast Spur [light rly]	28NW3 Poperinghe	G 11 b
Balloon Avenue	51bNW1 Roclincourt	A 4 d, 5 c
Balloon Factory Shed	57cNE2 Bourlon	E 29 a
Balloon Trench	70dNW2 Servais	C 7 d, 8 c
Balloon Wood	66eNW [2 Thennes]	C 20 b, d, 21 a, c
Ballot, Ferme du gros	28SE1 Wervicq	P 5 a 4.2
Balls Farm	20SW4 Bixschoote	U 26 a
Balls Pond Farm	20SE2 Hooglede	R 31 b 2.7
Ballynooky Road	57dNE1 & 2 Fonquevillers	E 22 b
Balmoral Camp	28NW3 Poperinghe	G 17 b 9.3
Balmoral Street	57dSE4 Ovillers	X 26 a, b
Balsam Trench	36cSW3 Vimy	N 32 c
Balsam Trench	66cNW2 Itancourt	B 24 a
Balsoran Trench	66cNW4 Berthenicourt	I 13 b, 14 a
Balthazar Alley / Boyau de Balthazar	62cSW4 St. Christ / 66dNW2 Morchain	T 27 a, b, 28 a, c, d, B 4 b, 5 a, c
Baluchi Road [trench]	36SW1 Aubers / 3 Richebourg	M 28 c, 34 a, b, 35 c
Baluchi Trench	36SW1 Aubers	M 34 b
Bambecque Depot Railhead / Refilling Point	19SE4 [Beveren]	W 24, 29, 30
Bamberbridge Street	57dSE4 Ovillers	X 1 c, d
Bamboo Alley	66cNW1 Grugies	B 7 b
Bamburg Road [trench]	36cSW3 Vimy	S 14 b
Bamburgh Lane	12SW1 Nieuport	M 18 c
Bamburgh Trench	12SW1 Nieuport	M 24 a
Bamburgh Walk	12SW1 Nieuport	M 24 a
Ban, Tranchée de	62cSW1 & 2 Belloy	O 2 b, d
Banana Switch [1918]	62dSW [2 Villers-Bretonneux]	O 30 a, b
Banbury Avenue	57cSW4 Combles	T 18 d, 24 b, U 13 c
Banbury Cross	36cNW1 La Bassée	A 15 d
Banchory Street	57dSE4 Ovillers	X 26 c, d
Bancourt [village]	57cNW4 Beugny	H 36 a, b, c
Bancourt Line	57cNW3 Bapaume	H 13, 14, 20, 21
Band Trench	36cSW3 Vimy	S 15 c
Bandaghem Hospital & Railhead	19SE4 [Beveren] / 27NE2 Proven	W 28 d, E 4 b
Bandaghem Military Cemetery [Haringhe]	19SE4 [Beveren]	W 28 c 75.20
Bandika Wood	62cNW4 Péronne	H 35 c, d
Bandit's Fork [road jct]	28NE2 Moorslede	E 21 d 9.1
Bandon Road [road]	28SW1 Kemmel	M 18 d, 24 b, N 7 c, d, 13 a, c
Banff Dugouts [centre of row]	28SW2 Wytschaete	N 23 d 35.90
Banff House	20SE3 Westroosebeke	V 27 b 45.55
Banff Trench	36cSW3 Vimy	S 16 a, c
Bang Alley	28NW4 & NE3 Zillebeke	I 28 d, 29 c
Bang Farm	28SW2 Wytschaete	O 17 b 9.4
Bangle Farm	27SE2 Berthen	R 17 b 55.20

Name	Map Sheet	Map Reference
Bangor [strongpoint]	36NW3 Fleurbaix	G 21 a, c
Bania Trench	62cSW2 Barleux	O 2 b, d
Bank Farm	28NW2 St Julien	C 24 b 3.6
Bank Loop Station [lt rly, 1918]	51bNW2 Oppy	B 10 d
Bank Post	57cSE2 Gonnelieu	Q 21 d
Bank Street [1918]	62dNE [1 Dernancourt]	E 7 b, 8 a
Bank Trench	57cSW1 Gueudecourt	M 18 c, d, N 13 c
Bank Trench	62bNW3 Bellicourt	G 7 b, 8 a, c
Bank Trench [Puisieux-au-Mont]	57dNE3 & 4 Hébuterne	L 14 d, 15 c, 20 a, b
Bank, The [Trenches; Bois du Vert]	51bSW2 Vis-en-Artois	O 9 a, b, c
Bank, The, & Bank Sap	36cSW1 Lens	M 4 c
Bankhead Spur [light rly]	36cSW1 Lens	M 4 c
Banks Reserve	57cNW2 Vaulx-Vraucourt	B 5 a,c,d, 11 b, 12 a,c, 18 b, C 13 a,c
Banks Trench	57cNW2 Vaulx-Vraucourt	B4d, 10b, 11a,c, 17a,b,d, 18c, 24a,b
Banks Wood	57cNW2 Vaulx-Vraucourt	B 11 a
Bankside North & South	36cSW3 Vimy	S 8 b
Bannister Corner [road jct]	28NE4 Dadizeele	L 11 a 8.6
Banos Wood	66eNW [4 Morisel]	H 16 c, d
Banquise Trench	70dNW2 Servais	C 14 a, c, 20 a
Bantam Copse	28NE2 Moorslede	E 23 a 5.3
Banteux [village]	57bSW1 Bantouzelle	M 25 b, d
Banteux Ravine	57cSE2 Gonnelieu / 57bSW1 Bantouzelle	M 25 d, R 30 c, 35 a, b, 36 a
Banteux Spur	57cSE2 Gonnelieu	R 28 d, 29 c, d
Bantouzelle [village]	57bSW1 Bantouzelle	M 26 a, c, d
Bantry Cottage	27NE2 Proven	F 16 a 2.4
Bapaume - Rocquigny Line	57cNW3 Bapaume	G 1, 2, 8, 9, 15, H 16, 17, 23, 24
Bapaume [town]	57cNW3 Bapaume	H 27, 33,
Bapaume Post	57dSE4 Ovillers	W 24 c 8.1
Baptist Farm	28SW3 Bailleul	T 8 b 35.20
Bar Alley	57cSW2 Villers-au-Flos	N 23 c, d
Bar Support	57cSW4 Combles	U 20 a
Bara Farm	27NE4 Abeele	L 25 c 2.4
Barabas Mill	51bNE4 Cantin	L 30 a 4.3
Barakken [place name]	28NE4 Dadizeele	L 10 c, d
Baralle Wood	51bSE3 Cagnicourt	W 7 c, d
Baraques, les [place name]	36cNW1 La Bassée	H 3 b
Barastre [village]	57cSW2 Villers-au-Flos	O 15 a, b, d, 16 a
Baraudon Trench	66cNW1 Grugies	A 5 a, c, d
Barbary Coast	28SW4 Ploegsteert	T 12 a 3.7
Barbas, Boyau	36cSW3 Vimy	S 8 d
Barbe Alley	66cNW1 Grugies	B 9 c, 15 a
Barbed Wire Square [Armentières]	36NW2 Armentières	C 25
Barberousse Alley	66dNW1 Punchy	B 14 b, c, d, 15 a
Barberousse Trench	62cNW3 Vaux	H 26 c, d
Barbican [road]	57cNE1 Quéant	D 24 a, c
Barbour House	28NE4 Dadizeele	K 34 d
Barclay Farm	20SE3 Westroosebeke	V 4 c 35.65
Barclays Bank [1918]	51cSE4 Blaireville	W 24 d
Barcoo Communication Trench [1918]	62dSE [1 Hamel]	P 1 a, b, c, d, 2 a, c, d
Bard Cot.	28NW2 St Julien	B 24 b
Bard Lane	57cSE2 Gonnelieu	Q 18 b
Bardell Avenue [1918]	57dSW [3 Talmas]	S 29 a, b
Bardenbrug [bridge]	28SW1 Kemmel	N 4 c 05.55
Bardenbrug [light rly locality, 1917]	28SW1 Kemmel	N 4 c

Name	Map Sheet	Map Reference
Bardes Trench	51bNW1 Roclincourt	A 16 a
Bards Causeway [1917-18]	28NW2 St Julien	C 13 c 2.3
Bare Trench, Support, Avenue	12SW1 Nieuport	M 15 a, b, d
Bargain House	28NE2 Moorslede	F 8 d 00.35
Barge Trench	36cSW3 Vimy	S 15 c
Bargee Trench	20NW2	B 23 d
Barger Alley	62cNW4 Péronne	I 31 c, d
Barham House	27NE4 Abeele	L 2 c 15.15
Baricade Trench	51bNW1 Roclincourt	A 28 a
Baring Trench [1918]	36aSW [2 Molinghem]	O 18 a
Barisis [village]	70dNW4 St Gobain	H 22, 23
Barisis Trench	70dNW4 St Gobain	H 23 a, c, d
Bark Trench	36cSW3 Vimy	S 15 b
Bark Trench	57dSE2 & 57cSW1 Le Sars	M 6 d, 12 b
Barkenham Avenue	36NW2 Armentières	C 9 d, 10 c
Barking [locality N end Cndn. Farm, 1917-18]	28NW2 St Julien	C 15 d 6.6
Barleux [village]	62cSW2 Barleux	N 18 a, b
Barleux Trench	62cSW1 & 2 Belloy	N 12 c, 17 b, d, 18 a
Barleux Trench	70dNW [3 Sinceny] / 4 St Gobain	H 34 a, c
Barleux, Ouvrage de	62cSW1 & 2 Belloy	N 12 c, 17 b, 18 a
Barley Copse	20SE2 Hooglede	Q 5 d 1.6
Barley Corner [road jct]	28NE4 Dadizeele	L 18 c 40.15
Barley Trench	57cSW1 Gueudecourt / 2 Villers-au-Flos	N 7, 8, 14, 15, 16
Barlin [village]	36bNE[3]	K 26 d, 27 c, d, 32 b, d, 33 a, b, c, d
Barn Alley [1918]	57dSE1 & 2 Beaumont	Q 28 b, 29 a
Barn Avenue	36SW2 Radinghem	N 6 a
Barn Avenue	57cNE3 Hermies / 4 Marcoing	K 9 c, d, 10 a, 15 b
Barn Fork [road jct]	28NE4 Dadizeele	L 12 c 8.3
Barn Street [Mesnil]	57dSE1 & 2 Beaumont	Q 28 b, d
Barn Support [1918]	57dSE1 & 2 Beaumont	Q 22 d, 28 b, d
Barn Trench [1918]	57dSE1 & 2 Beaumont	Q 22 d, 28 b, 29 a
Barn, The	36aSE1 St Venant	Q 27 a 2.9
Barnacle, The	57cSE2 Gonnelieu	R 21 d 7.5
Barnacle, The [Tyne Cott, pillbox]	28NE1 Zonnebeke	D 16 b
Barnards Farm	20SE2 Hooglede	Q 5 a 1.6
Barnes Farm	28NW1 Elverdinghe	A 3 d 4.8
Barnet Post	36SW1 Aubers	N 13 c
Barney Cross Roads	62dSW [1 Longueau]	M 5 d
Barnole Trench	70dNW4 St Gobain	H 17 c, 23 a
Barnsley Road	28NW2 St Julien	C 7 c, 13 a
Barnton Road [Trench]	36cNW1 La Bassée	A 2 b, 3 a
Barocki Trench	57cSW4 Combles	U 10 d, 17 a, c
Baron Alley	62cSW3 Vermandovillers	S 8 b, d, 9 c
Baron Farm	27SE2 Berthen	Q 10 c 05.45
Baron Trench	51bNW2 Oppy	B 6 c, 12 a
Barosa / Barossa [house]	28SW4 Ploegsteert	U 8 c 1.6
Baroudon Trench	66cNW1 Grugies	A 4 d, 5 b, c, d, 6 a
Barque Switch [Le Barque]	57cSW1 Gueudecourt	M 11 c, d, 12 c, d
Barr Head	57dSE1 & 2 Beaumont	Q 30 d, R 25 c
Barrabas, Boyau	36cSW3 Vimy	S 8 d, 9 c
Barrack Junction [Ypres, light rly, 1917-18]	28NW4 Ypres	I 7 d 6.1
Barrack Support	57cSE2 Gonnelieu	R 22 c, 28 a
Barrack Trench	57cSE2 Gonnelieu	R 22 c, 28 a

Name	Map Sheet	Map Reference
Barracks, The	36NW2 Armentières	C 11 d 32.00
Barracks, The [German outpost]	57cSE2 Gonnelieu	R 21 d
Barrage Lane	57cSW2 Villers-au-Flos / 4 Combles	N 35 b, c
Barrasa Avenue / Boyau Barrasa	62cNW1 Maricourt	A 16 d
Barre Trench	62bSW3 St Quentin	S 29 b, d
Barre Trench	62cSW4 St. Christ	U 21 d, 27 b
Barrel House [OP; Hill 63]	28SW4 Ploegsteert	U 13 c 45.65
Barrers, Tranchée	70dSW [2 Coucy-le-Château]	N 18 d
Barricade	27SE4 Meteren	X 15 b, 16 a
Barricade	51bNW1 Roclincourt	A 28 a
Barricade	57cSE2 Gonnelieu	R 21 d 3.4
Barricade [across road]	27SE4 Meteren	X 16 a 2.8
Barricade Avenue [Avenue Farm]	28SW4 Ploegsteert	U 9 c
Barricade Avenue [road]	28SW4 Ploegsteert	U 9 a, c, 15 a
Barricade House [Le Gheer]	28SW4 Ploegsteert	U 22 c 08.19
Barricade Road	57cSE2 Gonnelieu	R 7 c
Barricade Trench	57cSE2 Gonnelieu	R 21 d
Barricades [across road]	27SE4 Meteren	X 15 a 20.03
Barricades [across road]	27SE4 Meteren	X 25 b 8.8
Barricades [Arrewage]	36aNE4 Merville	K 10 a
Barricades [W of Meteren]	27SE4 Meteren	X 15 a, c
Barrie [light rly sidings]	28NW1 Elverdinghe	H 1 b
Barrier Post	62bSW1 Gricourt	M 2 c
Barrier Trench	57cSE2 Gonnelieu	R 21 b, 22 a, c
Barriere Calverdans, la [west of Bailleul]	27SE4 Meteren	X 24 a
Barrière, Estaminet de la	36NW4 Bois Grenier	I 22 b 5.0 [in 1915]
Barrington Street [1918]	62dNE [1 Dernancourt]	E 2 a
Barrister's Corner [road jct]	28NE2 Moorslede	F 23 a 55.15
Barron Corner [road jct]	28NE4 Dadizeele	K 5 c 85.23
Barrow Fork [road jct]	28NE4 Dadizeele	L 17 d 20.35
Barrow Road	36cSW1 Lens	M 28 d
Barrow Street	57dSE4 Ovillers	X 7 c, d
Barrow Trench	36cSW3 Vimy	S 15 d
Barry [light rly locality, 1917-18]	28NW2 St Julien	C 16 a 3.1
Barry House	20SE3 Westroosebeke	V 27 b 45.45
Barry Post	28NW4 & NE3 Zillebeke	I 29 d 6.7
Barry Street	57dSE4 Ovillers	X 19 d
Bart O.P [1917-18]	36cSW1 Lens	M 22 b 6.5
Barter Trench	36cSW3 Vimy	S 22 c
Bartfield Trench	57cSW4 Combles	U 5 d, 6 c, d, 12 b
Barthélémy [Ouvrage, NW of Fricourt, 1915]	57dSE4 Ovillers / 62dNE2 Méaulte	X 26 d, F 2 b
Bart's [NE of Vermelles]	36cNW3 Loos	G 3 c
Barts Alley, & Post [G 9 a]	36cNW3 Loos	G 4, 8, 9, 10
Bas Hamel [hamlet]	36aNE3 Haverskerque	J 31 b, d, 32 a
Bascule Alley	66cNW3 Essigny	G 12 b, d, 18 a, H 1 c, d
Base Alley	12SW1 Nieuport	M 15 d
Basham Farm	36aNE3 Haverskerque	K 21 d 6.8
Basherville [copse]	62bSW2 Fonsommes	O 33 b, 34 a
Basil Street	57cSW3 Longueval	T 13 a, b
Basilide Alley [1918]	62dSW [4 Cachy]	U 11 c, d
Basin Trench	36cSW3 Vimy	S 15 d, 16 a, c
Basin Wood	57dNE3 & 4 Hébuterne	K 28 c
Basket Wood	57bSW3 Honnecourt	S 16 b, c, d, 17 a, c
Bass Farm	28NE4 Dadizeele	K 18 c 1.6

Name	Map Sheet	Map Reference
Bass Lane [trench]	57cSE2 Gonnelieu	Q 5 d
Bass Trench [1918]	57dNE3 & 4 Hébuterne	L 1 d, 7 a, b
Bass Wood	28NE3 Gheluvelt	J 20 b, d
Bassam [trench]	66cNW2 Itancourt	B 24 c, d
Basse Boulogne North Post	62cNE2 Epéhy	F 16 c
Basse Boulogne South Post	62cNE2 Epéhy	F 22 b
Basse Cour Ferme, La [Messines]	28SW4 Ploegsteert	U 2 b 95.45
Basse Ville, La [hamlet]	28SW4 Ploegsteert	U 17 b, d
Basseije [farm, March 1915]	28SW2 Wytschaete	N 16 b 6.6
Bassett Post	36SW1 Aubers	N 4 a
Basseville Cabaret	28SE1 Wervicq	P 2 b 12.77
Basseville Farm	28SE1 Wervicq	P 1 d 3.0
Basseville Wood	28NE3 Gheluvelt / SE1 Wervicq	J 32 d, 33 c, P 2 b
Bassevillebeek [stream]	28NE3 Gheluvelt / SE1 Wervicq	J 20, 26, 32, P 2
Bassevillebeek Trench	28SE1 Wervicq	P 1 d
Basso Trench	36cSW3 Vimy	S 15 c, d
Bastidon, le	20SW4 Bixschoote	T 23 b
Bastion	57dNE1 & 2 Fonquevillers	E 22 d
Bastion [Trench]	51bNW3 Arras	G 18 c
Basuto Fork [road jct]	28NE2 Moorslede	E 17 b 33.17
Bat Copse	28NE2 Moorslede	E 4 d 8.4
Bat Corner [road jct]	28NE4 Dadizeele	L 17 b 65.90
Bat Post [twin of Wom Post]	62cNE4 Roisel	L 29 d 90.35
Bat Trench	28NW4 & NE3 Zillebeke	I 11 b
Bat Trench	51bSW2 Vis-en-Artois	O 8 b, d
Batavia [place name]	20SE2 Hooglede	R 33 b 8.1
Bateman Trench [Thiepval Wood]	57dSE1 & 2 Beaumont	R 25 c
Bath Lane	57dNE3 & 4 Hébuterne	L 19 b
Bath Road [military road]	28NW1 Elverdinghe / 2 St Julien	H 3 b, 4 a, b
Batson Trench	36cSW3 Vimy	M 35 c
Battalion Trench [Beaumont Hamel]	57dSE1 & 2 Beaumont	Q 10 b, 11 a
Batter Trench	36cSW3 Vimy	S 15 d, 21 b
Battersea Farm	28NW4 & NE3 Zillebeke	I 23 c 8.2
Battery Copse	62cNW1 Maricourt	B 20 a, c
Battery Copse Trench [1918]	28NW2 St Julien	C 3 a
Battery Dugout [S of Canal]	28SW2 Wytschaete	O 4 a 4.8
Battery House [late 1915]	36SW2 Radinghem	O 2 c 10.25
Battery Lane [trench]	57cSE2 Gonnelieu	Q 22 a, b
Battery Post	28SW4 Ploegsteert	U 14 central
Battery Post	36SW2 Radinghem	N 5 b
Battery Post	57cSE2 Gonnelieu	Q 22 a
Battery Trench	51bSW1 Neuville Vitasse	M 12 a, c, d, 18 a
Battery Trench	62cNW1 Maricourt	B 14 d, 20 a, b, c
Battery Trench [Battery Valley]	51bNW3 Arras	H 27 c, 33 a, b, d, 34 c
Battery Valley	51bNW3 Arras	H 20, 26, 27, 33
Battery Valley	57dSE1 & 2 Beaumont	R 14 b, c, d
Batteuse Trench	57dNE3 & 4 Hébuterne	K 16 b
Battle [huts SE of Turco Farm, 1917-18]	28NW2 St Julien	C 15 c 9.1
Battle Street / Boyau de la Bataille	62cNW1 Maricourt	A 15 a, b
Battle Wood	28NW4 & NE3 Zillebeke	I 35 d
Batty Road	62cNW1 Maricourt	A 8 a, c
Battye Farm	27NE2 Proven	F 25 a 10.95
Bauble Trench	36cSW3 Vimy	S 15 d, 21 b
Bauchard Trench	66cNW1 Grugies	B 9 c, d, 15 b

Name	Map Sheet	Map Reference
Baucis, Tranchée de [wife of Philemon]	62cSW3 & 4 Marchélepot	T 28 b, 29 a
Baudimont, Faubourg de [Arras]	51bNW3 Arras	G 20 a
Bauer, Bois	62cSW3 & 4 Marchélepot	T 14 a
Baum Graben	57dNE1 & 2 Fonquevillers	F 7 a, b,
Baumans Support	51bSW4 Bullecourt	U 14 c
Bavaria / Bavarian Trench	57cSW4 Combles	N 36 c
Bavaria Alley	62bSW4 Homblières	T 29 a
Bavaria Forest	62dSE [2 Proyart]	R 23, 29
Bavaria House	28NW2 St Julien	C 30 c 60.35
Bavarians Trench [1918]	66cNW [4 Morisel]	I 1 c, 7 a, c, 13 a
Bavarois Trench	62cSW3 Vermandovillers	T 7 b, d
Bavaroise House	20SE3 Westroosebeke	V 25 c 8.5
Bavière Road [trench]	36bSE4 Carency	X 16, 17, 18
Bavière Trench	62cNE3 Buire	J 31 a
Bavière Trench	62cNW4 Péronne	I 30 b, d
Bavière Trench [1918]	66eNW [4 Morisel]	H 23 d, 24 c
Bax Cottage	28SW3 Bailleul	S 30 d 1.3
Bay Avenue	36NW4 Bois Grenier	H 36 d
Bay Farm	28SW2 Wytschaete	O 26 b 8.6
Bay Lane	62cNW1 Maricourt	A 7 b
Bay Point	62cNW1 Maricourt	A 7 b
Bay Road [road]	28SW2 Wytschaete	O 20 d, 26 b
Bay Trench	57dSE2 & 57cSW1 Le Sars	N 13 c
Bay Trench	62cNW1 Maricourt	A 7 b
Bayard, Tranchée	70dSW [2 Coucy-le-Château]	O 26 a
Bayern Nord	36SW2 Radinghem	N 23 c 0.3
Bayern Trench	57dSE2 & 57cSW1 Le Sars	M 21 d, 22 c
Bayern Weg	51bNW1 Roclincourt	A 12 b, B 7 a
Bayeux Trench	66cSW2 Vendeuil / 4 La Fère	O 31 a, T 6 b
Bayeux Trench	66cSW4 La Fère	N 36 d, T 6 b, d, U 1 a
Baylands Wood	20SE2 Hooglede	R 1 b
Baynes Bunk [Ploegsteert Wood 1914-15]	28SW4 Ploegsteert	U 21 b 02.30
Bayoncourt Switch [1918]	57dNE [1 Fonquevillers / 3 Hébuterne]	D 30, J 5, 6, 10, 11
Bayonet Trench	51bNW4 Fampoux	H 30 d, 36 b, d, I 25 a, c, 31 d
Bayonet Trench	57cSW1 Gueudecourt	M 18, 24, N 13, 14, 20
Bayreuth Trench	57cSW4 Combles	U 15 a, b, c
Bays Wood	62bSW4 Homblières	U 28 a, b
Bayswater	36cNW1 La Bassée	A 15 a, b, d
Bayswater Trench	36bNE2 Beuvry	F 15 a
Baza Cottage	28NW3 Poperinghe	G 33 a 85.07
Bazar Trench	66cNW2 Itancourt	C 14 a
Bazentin Trench	57cSW3 Longueval	S 9 a, c, d
Bazentin, Boyau du [SW of Villa Wood]	57dSE4 Ovillers	X 11 d, 17 b, c, d
Bazentin-le-Grand [village]	57cSW3 Longueval	S 15 a, b
Bazentin-le-Grand Wood	57cSW3 Longueval	S 14, 15
Bazentin-le-Petit [village]	57cSW3 Longueval	S 8 a, b, c, d
Bazentin-le-Petit Wood	57cSW3 Longueval	S 7, 8, 13, 14
Bazuel [village]	57bSE2 [Bazuel]	R 8
BB Line	36bNE [3] / 36aSW1, 2 & 4	extensive
BCD Line [Boulogne-Calais-Dunkerque Line]	19, 27 [both 1:40,000]	extensive
Beach Alley	12SW1 Nieuport	M 14 b
Beach Avenue	12SW1 Nieuport	M 14 b
Beach Avenue	57cSE4 Villers-Guislain	X 25 b
Beachville [light rly loop, Ploeg. Wd, 1917-18]	28SW4 Ploegsteert	T 24 d 9.9

Name	Map Sheet	Map Reference
Beadle Farm	28NE2 Moorslede	E 30 c 8.5
Beagle Trench [1918]	36aSW [2 Molinghem]	O 22 b
Beak Alley	70dNW2 Servais	C 20 a
Beale Farm	28SW3 Bailleul	T 9 a 05.05
Beale Trench	51bNW2 Oppy	B 12 d
Beam Trench	36cSW3 Vimy	T 2 b, 3 c
Beam Trench, & Lane	57cSW2 Villers-au-Flos	N 22 d
Bean Farm	28NW1 Elverdinghe	A 15 a 9.3
Bean, The [Der Helm]	28NW4 & NE3 Zillebeke	I 34 c, d
Beano Trench	36cSW3 Vimy	S 16 c
Bear Avenue	57cNE1 Quéant	D 26 d, 27 a, c
Bear Avenue [1918]	36aSW [2 Molinghem]	O 28 b
Bear Copse	20SW4 Bixschoote	U 17 c 8.9
Bear Support	20SW4 Bixschoote	U 17 c, d
Bear Trench	20SW4 Bixschoote	U 23 a, b
Bear Trench	57cNE1 Quéant	D 27 a
Bear Trench	57dNE3 & 4 Hébuterne	K 34 d
Bear Trench [1918]	51bSW3 Boisleux	S 21 b, c, d
Béarnais, Rue des [Hoxton Road]	36cSW1 Lens	M 15 a, b
Beast Alley	36cNW1 La Bassée	B 19 a, b, 25 c, H 1 a
Beatty [light rly locality, 1917-18]	28NW4 Ypres	H 29 b
Beatty Alley	51bNW2 Oppy	B 18 d
Beatty Post	51bNW2 Oppy	B 18 d
Beatty Post	57cNE3 Hermies	K 8 b
Beau Regard Alley	57dNE3 & 4 Hébuterne	L 32 b, 33 a, b
Beaucamp Ridge	57cSE2 Gonnelieu	Q 17, 18, 23, 24
Beaucamp Support	57cSE2 Gonnelieu	Q 12 a
Beaucourt Redoubt	57dSE1 & 2 Beaumont	Q 12 b, R 7 a
Beaucourt Road [road]	57dSE1 & 2 Beaumont	Q 5 d, 6 c, 11 b, 12 a, b, R 7 a
Beaucourt Switch	57dSE1 & 2 Beaumont	R 1 c, d, 7 a
Beaucourt Trench	57dSE1 & 2 Beaumont	Q 6 c, 12 a, b, R 7 a, c
Beaucourt-Hamel Station	57dSE1 & 2 Beaumont	Q 18 a 7.7
Beaucourt-Serre Road [road]	57dNE3 & 4 Hébuterne / SE1 & 2 Beaumont	K 30 c, 36 a, c, d, Q 6 c, d, R 7 a
Beaucourt-sur-Ancre [village]	57dSE1 & 2 Beaumont	R 7 b, c, d
Beaulencourt [village]	57cSW2 Villers-au-Flos	N 17 b, d
Beaulieu Farm	36aNE2 Vieux Berquin	E 28 d 3.3
Beaumetz [hamlet]	62cSE1 Bouvincourt	P 12 c
Beaumetz Woods No.1	62cSE1 Bouvincourt	P 16 central
Beaumetz Woods No.2	62cSE1 Bouvincourt	P 17 a
Beaumetz Woods No.3	62cSE1 Bouvincourt	P 11 c
Beaumont Alley	57dSE1 & 2 Beaumont	Q 5 d, 6 a, c, 11 b, 12 a
Beaumont Hamel [village]	57dSE1 & 2 Beaumont	Q 5 c, 11 a
Beaumont Road	36cSW4 Rouvroy	U 10 d
Beaumont Trench [1918]	57dSE1 & 2 Beaumont	Q 10 b, d, 16 b, 17 a, c
Beaumount [sic] Trench	57dNE3 & 4 Hébuterne / SE1 & 2 Beaumont	K 35 c, d, Q 5 a, c
Beaupré [house / farm]	36aNE4 Merville	L 32 d 05.75
Beauquesne [village]	57dSW [1 Puchevillers]	N 2, 3, 8
Beauquesne Support [1918]	57dSW [1 Puchevillers]	N 3 a, c, d, 8 b, 9 a
Beauquesne Trench [1918]	57dSW [1 Puchevillers / 2 Raincheval]	N 8 b, d, 9 a, b, 10 a
Beaurains [village]	51bSW1 Neuville Vitasse	M 4 d, 10 b, d, 11 a, b, c
Beauregard	62bNW4 Ramicourt	I 16 c 0.8
Beauregard [farm]	62bNW4 Ramicourt	I 15 d 95.87
Beauregard Alley	57dNE3 & 4 Hébuterne	L 32 b, 33 a, b
Beauregard Dovecote	57dNE3 & 4 Hébuterne	L 28 c

Name	Map Sheet	Map Reference
Beaurevoir [village]	62bNW1 Gouy / 2 Brancourt-le-Grand	B 9, 10
Beaurevoir Ridge	57bSW4 Serain / 62bNW2 Brancourt-le-Grand	T 28 c, d, C 4 a, b
Beaurevoir-Fonsomme Line	57bSW3 Honnecourt / 62bNW4 Ramicourt	extensive
Beauvoorde Farm	27NE4 Abeele	K 34 c 4.8
Beauvoorde Wood	27NE4 Abeele	K 33 b, d, 34 a, b, c
Beauvraignes Trench	62bSW1 Gricourt	M 23 c, 29 a
Beaver Corner	28SW1 Kemmel	N 15 c 3.3
Beaver Dell Valley	62bNW2 Brancourt-le-Grand	C 3 c, 9 a, b, c, 15 a
Beaver Hall	28SW1 Kemmel	N 31 a 95.35
Beaver Hat [light rly locality?]	28SW2 Wytschaete	N 23 c, d
Beaver Street	28SW2 Wytschaete	N 29 c
Beaver Trench	36cNW1 La Bassée	B 13 c, d, 19 b, d, 20 c, 26 a, c
Beaver Trench	36cSW3 Vimy	N 32 d
Beavers Trench	36cNW1 La Bassée	B 19 b
Bécart [Tranchée, 1915] / Largo Street	57dSE4 Ovillers	X 13 c, d
Beck House [farm & pill box]	28NE1 Zonnebeke	D 19 d 2.4
Becker [Epte] Trench / Becker Graben	57dNE3 & 4 Hébuterne	K 5 c, d, 11 a
Becker Alley [1918]	62dSW [4 Cachy]	U 27 d, 28 c
Becket Corner [road jct]	36aNE2 Vieux Berquin	F 26 b 2.0
Bècle, Boyau	36cSW3 Vimy	S 2 d, 8 b
Bècle, Tranchée [Allied front line 2/16]	36cSW3 Vimy	S 2 d
Bécourt [hamlet]	57dSE4 Ovillers	X 25 d
Bécourt Avenue	57dSE4 Ovillers	W 29 d, 30 c, d, x 25 c
Bécourt-Becordel [village]	62dNE2 Méaulte	F 7 a, b, c, d
Becque, la [farm]	36aNE2 Vieux Berquin	E 23 c
Becque, la [place name]	36NW1 Steenwerck	A 14 c, d
Becquigny [village]	57bSE [3 Busigny]	V 28, 29
Becquincourt [village]	62cSW1 Dompierre	M 6 a, b, c, d
Bedbug Trench [Hill 145]	36cSW3 Vimy	S 15 d, 16 c, 22 a
Bedcote [sic] House [early 1916, MS map]	28NW4 & NE3 Zillebeke	I 26 a 8.2
Bedding Cottages	27SE2 Berthen	Q 5 d 8.2
Bede Alley	36cSW3 Vimy	S 2 d, 8 b
Bedford Avenue	62dNE2 Méaulte	F 8 b, d
Bedford Camp	28NW1 Elverdinghe	A 12 a, c, d
Bedford Crescent	51bNW2 Oppy	B 12 d, 18 b
Bedford Farm	28NW1 Elverdinghe	A 12 d 6.6
Bedford Farm	36aNE3 Haverskerque	K 21 a 3.5
Bedford Farm [or Caribou] British Mil. Cmy.	28NW1 Elverdinghe	A 12 c 55.25
Bedford House	28NW4 & NE3 Zillebeke	I 26 a
Bedford House Camp	28NW4 Ypres	I 26 a, b
Bedford Road [road, late 1915]	36SW1 Aubers	M 17 d 18 c
Bedford Road [trench]	36bSE4 Carency	X 14, 15, 21, 22, 23
Bedford Row	51bNW2 Oppy	B 12 d, 18 b
Bedford Street	57cSW3 Longueval	S 9 b
Bedford Street / Boyau Bedford	62cNW1 Maricourt	A 16 a
Bedford Street [to new front line]	57dSE1 & 2 Beaumont	Q 17 c, d
Bedon Copse	28NE2 Moorslede	F 10 d 20.85
Bedouin Trench [1918]	28NE3 Gheluvelt	J 20 d, 26 b
Bedouin Triangle [road triangle]	28NE2 Moorslede	E 22 c 8.5
Bee Farm	20SE2 Hooglede	R 21 a 2.8
Bee Farm	28SW2 Wytschaete	O 23 b 20.55
Bee Hive / The Beehive	36cSW3 Vimy	T 27 d 2.6
Bee Lane	57dNE2 & 57cNW1 Courcelles	A 1 b

Name	Map Sheet	Map Reference
Bee Post	36SW1 Aubers	N 8 b
Bee Trench	57cNE1 Quéant	K 3 a
Bee Wood	57cNW1 Gomiecourt	B 25 c
Bee Wood Support	57cNW1 Gomiecourt	B 19 d, 25 b, d,
Bee Wood Trench	57cNW1 Gomiecourt	B 19 c, d, 25 b, c, d, H 1 b
Bee Work	57cNW1 Gomiecourt	A 30 b
Beech Avenue	57cSE4 Villers-Guislain	X 20 c, 25 b, 26 a
Beech Lane	57cSW4 Combles	U 26 b, d
Beech Trench	62bSW3 St Quentin	N 31 c
Beecham [farm & pillboxes]	28NE1 Zonnebeke	D 16 a 5.3
Beechbank Farm	20SE2 Hooglede	Q 24 d 1.1
Beef Alley	51bSW4 Bullecourt	U 21 b, d, 22 a
Beef Street	28NW4 & NE3 Zillebeke	I 34 c
Beef Trench	36cNW1 La Bassée	B 2 b, d
Beef Trench	57cSW3 Longueval	T 21 a
Beehive, The	36cSW3 Vimy	T 27 c
Beek Avenue	20SW4 Bixschoote	U 24 a, b
Beek Farm	28SW2 Wytschaete	O 29 b 1.9
Beek Houses	20SE3 Westroosebeke	V 20 d 1.0
Beek Street	20SW4 Bixschoote	U 18 c, 24 a
Beek Street	28NW4 & NE3 Zillebeke	I 11 a, c
Beel Avenue	62bNW1 Gouy	A 1 b
Beel Lane	62bNW1 Gouy	A 1 d
Beer Avenue	20SE3 Westroosebeke	V 19 c, 25 a
Beer Trench	20SE3 Westroosebeke	V 25 a, c
Beer Trench	36cNW1 La Bassée	A 6 d, B 1 a, c
Beer Trench	36cNW1 La Bassée	B 1 a
Beer Trench	36cSW3 Vimy	S 16 c, 22 a
Beer Trench	51bNW2 Oppy	B 6 b
Beer Trench	57cSW3 Longueval	S 12 d, T 7 c, 13 a
Beer Trench [1918]	57dNE1 & 2 Fonquevillers	E 22, 28, K 7, 8, 13
Beer Trench [1918]	62dNE [1 Dernancourt]	E 7 d
Beer Wood	66dNW1 Punchy	A 5 a
Beerbohm Houses	28NE2 Moorslede	F 4 c 8.0
Beersheba	28NE3 Gheluvelt	J 18 d 3.8
Bees Copse	51bNE4 Cantin	L 14 a, c
Bees Trench [1918]	51bNW1 Roclincourt	A 9 c, d
Beet Factory	57bSW1 Bantouzelle	M 19 d, 20 c
Beet Trench	57cNE4 Marcoing	L 13 a, c, d, 19 b, 20 a
Beet Trench	57cSE4 Villers-Guislain	X 8 a
Beethoven Trench [Beetoven, sic]	57cSW4 Combles	U 21 d
Beetle Alley	57cSW3 L'val/62cNW1 M'court/ 62dNE2 Méaulte	S 25 d, 26 c, A 1 b, F 6 a
Beetle Trench	51bSW2 Vis-en-Artois	O 8 d, 9 c, d, 10 c
Beetle Trench [1918]	36aSW2 [Molinghem]	O 22 d, 28 b
Beetroot factory [N of Etricourt]	57cSE3 Sorel-le-Grand	V 2 d 0.7
Bégard Wood No.1	62cSE1 Bouvincourt	P 19 d
Bégard Wood No.2	62cSE1 Bouvincourt	P 19 d
Bégard Wood No.3	62cSE1 Bouvincourt	P 19 d, 20 c, 25 b
Beggar Trench	57cSW4 Combles	U 26 c
Beggar Trench [Hill 145]	36cSW3 Vimy	S 16 c, 22 a, b, d
Beggars Rest	28SW2 Wytschaete	N 6 d 2.8
Begonia Trench	20SW3 Oostvleteren	T 16 a
Béhagnies [village]	57cNW1 Gomiecourt / 3 Bapaume	H 1 b, d, 2 a, c

Name	Map Sheet	Map Reference
Beira Farm	28NW3 Poperinghe	G 27 c 8.9
Beirut Trench / Beirout, Tranchée de	66cNW2 Itancourt	B 5 a, b, c
Bel Aise, Old Mill	57bSW1 Bantouzelle	M 12 a 65.30
Bel Trench	36cSW3 Vimy	S 15 d, 16 c
Bel-Aise [farm]	57bSW1 Bantouzelle	M 18 a 8.5
Belchiers Cottages [Le Gheer]	28SW4 Ploegsteert	U 21 d 75.05
Belfast [Walled Garden, Pozières]	57dSE4 Ovillers	X 4 b
Belfast City [Thiepval Wood]	57dSE1 & 2 Beaumont	Q 30 d
Belfort / Beloin Trench	70dNW4 St Gobain	H 30 b
Belgian Battery Corner	28NW4 & NE3 Zillebeke	H 24 a 3.8
Belgian Château	28NW4 Ypres	H 23 b
Belgian Wood	28NE3 Gheluvelt	J 31 d
Belgrade Trench [1918]	62dSW [4 Cachy]	U 12 a, c
Belgravia (Officers Quarters, Lovie Chateau)	27NE2 Proven	F 16
Belier, Tranchée du	70dSW2 [Coucy-le-Château]	N 24 c
Bélier, Tranchée du	66dNW2 Morchain	B 5 b, c, d
Bell Buildings	28SE1 Wervicq	P 2 d 95.95
Bell Copse	62bNW3 Bellicourt	G 33 b, 34 a
Bell Dugout	57dSE4 Ovillers	R 34 d 5.8
Bell Farm	20SE3 Westroosebeke	V 9 a 10.95
Bell Farm	28SW4 Ploegsteert	O 31 c 40.95
Bell Street [road]	36cSW1 Lens	N 19 b, d
Bell Trench	57cNE3 Hermies	K 20 b
Bella Cottages	27SE3 Borre	V 26 c 7.5
Bellacourt Street	51cSE3 & 4 Ransart	R 31 d, 32 c
Belle [light rly locality, 1917-18]	28NW2 St Julien	C 20 c 9.7
Belle Alliance, La [farm]	28NW2 St Julien	C 20 d, 21 c
Belle Bridge [1917-18]	20SW4 Bixschoote	U 28 d 3.4
Belle Croix Farm	27SE4 Meteren	X 27 d 1.7
Belle Vue, A la [Estaminet, Ploegsteert]	28SW4 Ploegsteert	U 25 a 5.4
Bellecourt Farm	62bSW2 Fonsommes	N 12 b 9.8
Bellegoed Avenue	28NW4 Ypres	H 24 c, d, 30 b, I 25 a
Bellegoed Camp	28NW4 Ypres	H 30 b, I 25 a
Bellenglise [village]	62bNW3 Bellicourt	G 34 d, 35 c
Belleville, Tranchée	70dSW2 [Coucy-le-Château]	O 7 c
Bellevue [farm]	28NW2 St Julien	C 22 d 75.80
Bellevue [pillboxes]	28NE1 Zonnebeke	D 4 d 6.1
Bellevue Ridge	57bSE [4 Wassigny] / 62bNE [1 & 2]	W 27, E 3, 4,
Bellevue Spur	28NE1 Zonnebeke	D 4 d, 5 c, 10 a, b
Bellewaarde Circuit [plank road, 1917-18]	28NW4 Ypres / NE3 Gheluvelt	I 11 d, 12 b, c, d, J 7 c, 13 a
Bellewaarde Farm	28NW4 & NE3 Zillebeke	I 12 a, c
Bellewaarde Lake	28NW4 & NE3 Zillebeke	I 12 d, J 7 c
Bellewaarde No 1 [dugout, 1917-18]	28NE3 Gheluvelt	J 7 a 2.7
Bellewaarde Ridge	28NW4 & NE3 Zillebeke	J 7 a, c
Bellicourt [village]	62bNW3 Bellicourt	G 4 c, d, 10 a, b
Bellicourt Road	62cNE2 Epéhy	F 23 c
Bellmont Street	57dSE4 Ovillers	X 1 b
Bellois Wood	66eNW [4 Morisel]	H 17, 18, 23
Bell's / Bells Redoubt [Contalmaison]	57dSE4 Ovillers	X 16 d
Belmont [farm]	28SW3 Bailleul	T 27 b 0.4
Belmont Lines [huts]	28SW3 Bailleul	T 27 a
Beloften, Land van	20SE2 Hooglede	R 7 b
Below Farm	28NW2 St Julien	C 15 a 7.8
Below Trench	57cSE4 Villers-Guislain	X 30 a

Name	Map Sheet	Map Reference
Below Trench, & Support	57dSE2 & 57cSW1 Le Sars	M 1, 7, 8, 14, 15, 21, 22
Belt Trench	51bNW2 Oppy	C 24 d
Belt, The	28NW4 & NE3 Zillebeke	I 29 b, 30 a
Belvoir Abbey	51bNW1 Roclincourt	B 19 c
Belvoir Alley	51bNW2 Oppy	B 24 d, C 19 c
Belvoir Trench	51bNW2 Oppy	B 12 d
Bel-Vue [hamlet]	20SE2 Hooglede	Q 18 b 85.60
Belzage Farm	36aSE4 Locon	W 22 d 8.7
Ben Cottages	20SE2 Hooglede	R 35 a 55.15
Ben Way	36cNW3 Loos	G 36 a, b
Bench Farm	51bNW4 Fampoux	I 35 d
Bench House	28NE2 Moorslede	F 25 d 45.85
Bench Trench	36cSW3 Vimy	T 2 d
Bendorf Trench	62cSW2 Barleux	O 16 d, 17 c, 22 b, d,
Benedetti Trench	66cNW1 Grugies	B 14 b, 15 a
Benedict Cross Roads	27SE4 Meteren	X 11 c 40.85
Benedictine Trench	51bNW2 Oppy	B 6 d
Benefit Row	36aNE2 Vieux Berquin	F 23 a 4.2
Bengal Cottages	27SE2 Berthen	R 18 a 6.9
Benger Copse	27SE2 Berthen	R 11 b, 12 a
Benger Corner [road jct]	27SE2 Berthen	R 12 a 60.35
Benifontaine [village, 1915 map]	36cNW3 Loos	H 13 d, 14 c
Benifontaine [village, 1917 map]	36cNW3 Loos	H 8 d, 9 c, 14 b, 15 a
Benifontaine Road [road]	36cNW3 Loos	H 15 a, b, d, 16 c, 22 a
Benin House	36aNE1 Morbecque	J 4 b 5.3
Benjamin Post	62cNE2 Epéhy	F 23 d
Benjamin Switch	62cNE2 Epéhy	F 23 a, c, 29 a, b
Benjamin Trench	62cNE2 Epéhy	F 23 b, d, 24 a, 29 b
Benjamin Trench [1918]	36aSW2 [Molinghem]	O 12 a
Bennet House [Le Pelerin, 1914-15]	28SW4 Ploegsteert	U 21 b 6.5
Bennett Street [trench]	57cNE4 Marcoing	K 18 a, b
Bennett Trench	57cSW4 Combles	T 5 b
Beno Graben	51bNW3 Arras	G 12 c, 18 a
Benoit Farm [Beaulencourt]	57cSW2 Villers-au-Flos	N 17 b 3.5
Benoit Trench / Tranchée Benoit	62cSW1 & 2 Belloy	O 1 d, 7 a, b
Bensham Avenue, & Road	28NW4 & NE3 Zillebeke	I 29 c
Benson Trench [1918]	36aSW2 [Molinghem]	O 18 a
Bensons Farm	28NW1 Elverdinghe	A 5 a 3.5
Bent Road [road]	28NW2 St Julien	C 26 a, b, d
Bent Road Camp [1917-18]	28NW2 St Julien	C 26 b, d
Bent Trench	51bSW2 Vis-en-Artois	O 10 c, d
Bentata Redoubt, & Trench & Sap [A 10 c]	51bNW1 Roclincourt	A 9 b, 10 c
Bents Avenue [1918]	57dNE1 & 2 Fonquevillers	E 29 a, c
Berceau Alley	66dNW3 Hattencourt	G 15 c, d, 16 c, d, 22 b, 23 a
Berceau, Maison du [Calonne]	36cSW1 Lens	M 13 d 4.6
Bereitschaft Stellung	51bNW1 Roclincourt	A 16 d, 17 c
Berg Graben [Rossignol Wood]	57dNE3 & 4 Hébuterne	K 12 c, d, L 7 c
Bergere, la [Bellenglise]	62bNW3 Bellicourt	G 35 d 5.2
Berghe Farm	28SW2 Wytschaete	N 17 c 9.8
Bergwerk	57dSE1 & 2 Beaumont	Q 5 c
Berkeley Square [Off's Latrines, Lovie Chateau]	27NE2 Proven	F 16
Berkeley Street	36cNW1 La Bassée	A 9 a, c, d
Berkeley Street	36NW4 Bois Grenier	I 15 d
Berkley [sic] Street / Boyau Berkley [sic]	62cNW1 Maricourt	A 9 a

Name	Map Sheet	Map Reference
Berks Fort	28SW4 Ploegsteert	U 19 b
Berks Houses	20SE3 Westroosebeke	V 27 a 4.4
Berkshire [strongpoint]	36NW3 Fleurbaix	H 7 a, b
Berkshire Avenue	57dSE4 Ovillers	W 30 b, c, X 19 d, 25 a, b
Berkshire Farm	36aSE1 St Venant	Q 14 c 5.7
Berkshire Road, & Lane [A 15 d]	36cNW1 La Bassée	A 15 c, d
Berle Alley	36cSW3 Vimy	S 2 d
Berles-au-Bois [village]	51cSE3 & 4 Ransart	W 15, 21, 22
Berlin [farm]	28NE1 Zonnebeke	D 9 d 5.5
Berlin Alley	57cSW4 Combles	U 20 a, b
Berlin Road [road]	36cSW4 Rouvroy	U 3 c, d, 8 b, 9 a
Berlin Street	57dNE1 & 2 Fonquevillers	E 9 b, d
Berlin Trench	57dNE3 & 4 Hébuterne	K 24, 25, 30, L 19
Berlin Tunnel [Hill 60 & Caterpillar]	28NW4 & NE3 Zillebeke	I 29 c, 35 a
Berlin Valley	62cNW2 Bouchavesnes	I 2 a
Berlin Wood	28NE1 Zonnebeke	D 10 c
Berlin Work [1918]	66eNW [2 Thennes]	H 4 b, 5 a
Berlincot Alley	66cNW1 Grugies	B 8 c
Bernadotte Farm	20SE3 Westroosebeke	V 9 c 3.9
Bernafay Wood	57cSW3 Longueval	S 28, 29
Bernagousse Alley	70dNW4 St Gobain	H 28 c, d, 29 c, 34 a
Bernard Alley	62bSW3 St Quentin	S 29 a
Bernard Maze	36cSW4 Rouvroy	U 14 b, d
Bernard Road, Bois [road]	36cSW4 Rouvroy	U 13 c, d, 14 c, d
Bernard Trench	36cSW4 Rouvroy	U 8 a, c, 14 a, b, d
Bernard, Bois [village]	36cSW4 Rouvroy	U 14 d, 15 c, 20 b, 21 a
Bernard, Bois [wood]	36cSW4 Rouvroy	U 15 c
Berne Trench	36cSW4 Rouvroy	U 21 c
Bernenchon, Mount	36aSE3 Gonnehem	W 1 a
Bernic Farm	20SE3 Westroosebeke	V 11 c 4.5
Bernie Maze	36cSW2 Harnes	O 32 b
Bernouis Alley	66cNW1 Grugies	B 8 d, 14 b
Bernsprungblick [Le Gheer]	28SW4 Ploegsteert	U 28 a 4.8
Berny-en-Santerre [village]	62cSW3 & 4 Marchélepot	N 32, 33, T 2, 3
Berry Cotts	28NE3 Gheluvelt	J 27 a 3.5
Berry Post	28NW4 & NE3 Zillebeke	I 29 d 6.8
Berry Trench	36cSW4 Rouvroy	U 15 a, c
Berry-au-Bac Trench [1918]	62dSW [4 Cachy]	U 16 a, c
Bersaucourt [village]	66dNW1 Punchy	B 21 a, b
Bertenacre [farm]	27SE2 Berthen	Q 29 a 1.7
Bertha Post	36NW4 Bois Grenier	I 20 d
Bertha Post	36SW1 Aubers	N 13 d, 14 a
Bertha Support	62cNW2 Bouchavesnes	C 16 c
Bertha Trench	36SW1 Aubers	N 14 c, 20 a, b, d
Bertha Trench	62cNW2 Bouchavesnes	C 16 c
Bertha Trench	70dNW4 St Gobain	H 11 d, 12 b
Bertha Trench [1918]	62dSW [4 Cachy]	U 10 a, b, c
Berthelot, Rue [trench]	36cSW1 Lens	M 14 c
Berthen [village]	27SE2 Berthen	R 22 c
Berthen Line [1918]	27SE2 Berthen	R 15, 16, 17, 20, 21, 22
Berthold Graben	57dNE3 & 4 Hébuterne	K 36 a
Berthonval Locality	36bSE4 Carency	X 22, 23, 29
Berthonval Wood	36bSE4 & 36cSW3 Givenchy	X 28 b, d, 29 a, c
Berthot, Cabaret de	28SW3 Bailleul	S 29 a 2.3

Name	Map Sheet	Map Reference
Bertie Trench	51bNW2 Oppy	B 30 d
Bertincourt [village]	57cSE1 Bertincourt	P 7 a, b, c, d, 8 a
Berwick [1918; light rly locality]	28NW2 St Julien	C 6 a 2.4
Berwick Avenue / Boyau Berwick	62cNW1 Maricourt	A 8 c, 14 a
Berwick Farm	20SE2 Hooglede	Q 4 c 8.8
Berwick Trench	36cSW4 Rouvroy	U 21 a
Berwick Trench / Street	36cNW1 La Bassée	A 27 c, G 3 a, b
Beryl Alley	36cNW1 La Bassée	B 1 d, 2 a
Beryl Trench	36cSW4 Rouvroy	U 20 b
Beryl Wood	62dSE [2 Proyart]	Q 29 a, c
Besace Farm	20SE3 Westroosebeke	V 13 b 95.80
Besace Farm, la	27SE4 Meteren	X 9 a 20.65
Besan / Bessan Trench	51bNW1 Roclincourt	A 9 d
Besancon [Boyau, NW of Fricourt, 1915]	57dSE4 Ovillers / 62dNE2 Méaulte	X 26 d, F 2 b
Besant Farm	28SW3 Bailleul	T 16 a 25.75
Besomte Trench [1918]	66eNW [4 Morisel]	H 16 a, b, d, 22 b
Bess Street	57dNE3 & 4 Hébuterne	K 35 a
Bessy Trench	36cSW3 Vimy	S 16 c, 22 a
Beston Farm	28SW3 Bailleul	T 21 b 35.05
Bet House	28NE2 Moorslede	E 30 a 40.55
Beta [German pillbox / strongpoint]	51bSW4 Bullecourt	U 7 b
Beta Copse	62bNW2 Brancourt-le-Grand	C 11 d, 12 a, c
Beta Hill	62bNW2 Brancourt-le-Grand	C 4 d, 5 c, 10 b, 11 a
Bethell Farm	28NW1 Elverdinghe	A 4 b
Bethell Sap [W of High Wood]	57cSW3 Longueval	S 3 a, b, c
Bethencourt [village]	66dNW2 Morchain	C 23 c, d, 29 a, b
Bethleem / Bethlehem Farm	28SW4 Ploegsteert	U 3 d 5.7
Bethleem Road [road]	28SW4 Ploegsteert	U 3 a, b, d
Béthune [town]	36bNE2 Beuvry	E 4, 5, 10, 11, 12, 16, 17, 18
Béthune Avenue (Up & Down)	51bNW1 Roclincourt / 3 Arras	A 26, G 1, 2
Béthune Locality	36bNE2 Beuvry	E 18a,b,c,d, 24b, F7c, 13a,b,c, 19a
Béthune Retrenchment	36aSE3 Gonnehem / 36bNE2 Beuvry	W 21, 27, E 3, 4, 10, 16, 22
Béthune Road [road]	36cSW1 Lens	M 5 a, b, d, 6 c, 12 a, b, d
Bethune Spur [light rly, Souchez]	36cSW3 Vimy	S 1 d, 7 b
Béthune Station [railway]	36bNE2 Beuvry	E 17 a 6.0
Bétricourt Farm	36cSW4 Rouvroy	U 2 c 9.1
Better 'Ole, The	28SW4 Ploegsteert	O 34 b 1.0
Better 'Ole, The	36aSE1 St Venant	P 6 b
Betterole Camp	28SW3 Bailleul	T 9 a
Betterole Farm	28SW3 Bailleul	T 9 a 3.1
Betty Avenue	57cNE3 Hermies	K 8 central
Betty Dump	36cSW3 Vimy	T 8 b 4.6
Betty O.P. [1917-18]	51bNW1 Roclincourt	A 6 d 9.9
Betty Post	36NW4 Bois Grenier	I 21 a
Betty Trench	36cSW3 Vimy	T 3 d, 9 a, b
Bettye Support	57cSW4 Combles	U 14 c, d
Beugnâtre [village]	57cNW4 Beugny	H 11 c, d, 17 b
Beugny [village]	57cNW4 Beugny	I 16 c, d, 21 b, 22 a, b
Beulemans House	20SW4 Bixschoote	T 24 a 25.25
Beurre Mill	57bNW1 Cambrai	G 5 a 40.55
Beurre, le [farm[	27SE4 Meteren	W 11 b 80.05
Beuvry [village]	36bNE2 Beuvry	F 14 a, b, c, d
Beux Trench	62bSW1 Gricourt	M 9 c
Bevel Farm	28NE2 Moorslede	E 18 a 4.1

Name	Map Sheet	Map Reference
Beveren [village]	20SE2 Hooglede	R 21 b, 22 a, c
Bevis House	28SW3 Bailleul	T 26 b 3.3
Bewicke Farm	28NW1 Elverdinghe	A 4 b 8.2
Bexhill Farm	20SE2 Hooglede	Q 29 d 8.6
Beythem [village]	28NE2 Moorslede	F 7 d
Biache St Vaast [village]	51bNW4 Fampoux	I 11 c, d
Biaches Trench	62cNW4 Péronne	I 25 d, 31 b
Biaches Trench	70dNW4 St Gobain	H 28 c, d
Bias Woods	62cSE1 Bouvincourt	P 15 b, d, 16 a, c
Bib Crossing	20SE2 Hooglede	R 4 b 6.7
Bibby Farm	27SE4 Meteren	R 31 c 7.6
Bibby Trench	36cSW2 Harnes	O 33 a
Bic-Bac, le	51bNE4 Cantin	L 33 b
Bicester Alley	57cSE2 Gonnelieu / 4 Villers-Guislain	R 34 a, c
Bichat Dump	62cSW1 Dompierre	M 25 d 95.05
Bichat Junction [light railway]	62cSW3 Vermandovillers	M 32 d
Bichecourt Wood	57cSE3 Sorel-le-Grand	W 1 c, 7 a
Bicks Farm	28NE2 Moorslede	F 21 c 6.2
Bicla Trench	57cSW4 Combles	U 11 c, 17 a
Biczer Trench	36SW3 Richebourg	S 11 d, 17 b
Bida Farm	28NW3 Poperinghe	G 32 a 4.6
Bidot Avenue	51bNW1 Roclincourt	A 22 d, 28 b
Bidot, The	51bNW1 Roclincourt	A 27
Bidstone Street [trench]	51bNW2 Oppy	B 18 a
Bienpensé Ditch	51bNW1 Roclincourt	A 4 d, 10 b
Bienvillers-au-Bois [village]	57dNE1 & 2 Fonquevillers	E 2, 3, 8, 9
Bienvillers-les-Bapaume [village]	57cNW3 Bapaume	H 19 central
Biez Support, & Switch [both 1918]	57dNE3 & 4 Hébuterne	K 5 d, 6 c, 12 a
Biez Trench [Biez Wood]	57dNE3 & 4 Hébuterne	L 1 d, 2 c, d
Biez, Bois de	36SW3 Richebourg	S 5, 6, 11, 12
Biez, Ferme du	36NW4 Bois Grenier	I 15 d 3.5
Biez, Ferme du	36SW3 Richebourg	S 11 d, 12 c
Biezer Trench	36SW3 Richebourg	S 12 c
Biff Trench	36cSW3 Vimy	S 22 a
Big Bill	62bNW3 Bellicourt	G 26 a
Big Bill Copse	62bNW3 Bellicourt	G 26 a
Big Bosun Hill	62bSW2 Fonsommes	O 21 d
Big Bull Cottages	28SW4 Ploegsteert	U 1 a
Big Clump	28NW2 St Julien	C 1 d
Big Redoubt, The [R'bourg St Vaast, Jan 1915]	36SW3 Richebourg	S 2 centre [Jan 1915]
Big Sap	51bSW2 Vis-en-Artois	O 26 a
Big Trench	51bSW4 Bullecourt	U 26 c
Big Willie [Hohenzollern]	36cNW3 & 1 Loos	G 4 d, 5 c
Bigamy Trench	36cNW1 La Bassée	B 1 b, 2 a
Bigger Willie	36cNW3 & 1 Loos	G 5 a, c
Bihucourt [village]	57dNE4 & 57cNW3 Achiet	G 11 d, 17 a, b
Bihucourt Line	57dNE4 & 57cNW3 Achiet	G 1,2,8,9,15,16,17,23,24, H19,25
Bijou Trench	36cNW1 La Bassée	B 1 c, d
Bile Trench	57dSE2 & 57cSW1 Le Sars	M 18 d, 24 b
Bilge Cottage	28NW4 Ypres	H 5 c 9.9
Bilge Street [Cross Roads Farm]	28NW2 St Julien	C 22 c
Bilge Trench	28NW2 St Julien	C 28 a, b
Bilge Trench	36cSW3 Vimy	T 2 d
Bilhem Avenue	57cSE4 Villers-Guislain	K 23 c

Name	Map Sheet	Map Reference
Bilhem Chapel Avenue	57cNE4 Marcoing	K 22 d, 23 a, b, c, 24 a
Bilhem Chapel Wood Switch	57cNE4 Marcoing / SE2 Gonnelieu	K 16, 22, 28, 29, 35, Q 5
Bill Corner [road junction]	20SE2 Hooglede	Q 18 b 90.95
Bill Cottage	28NW2 St Julien	I 6 b 3.8
Bill Extension	36cNW1 La Bassée	A 10 c, 16 a
Billaule, Boyau	62cSW1 Dompierre	M 10 a, c
Billet Farm	36NW4 Bois Grenier	I 19 b 6.3
Billiard Copse	62bNW3 Bellicourt	G 23 b, d
Billing Avenue [1918]	57dNE1 & 2 Fonquevillers	F 14 a, c, d
Billington Trench	36aSW2 [Molinghem]	O 11 d, 17 b, 18 a
Billon Avenue / Boyau Billon	62cNW1 Maricourt / 3 Vaux	A 20, 21, 26, G 2
Billon Copse [Redoubt]	62dNE2 Méaulte	F 24 c, 30 a
Billon Farm	62dNE2 Méaulte	F 24 c
Billon Farm Camp [1916-17]	62dNE2 Méaulte / 62cNW1 Maricourt	F 24 c, A 19 d
Billon Wood Valley	62cNW1 Maricourt / 3 Vaux	A 25 b, d, G 1 b, d
Billoquet Trench / Tranchée du Bil Boquet	66dNW3 Hattencourt	H 7 b, 8 a, b
Billot Wood	66eNW [4 Morisel]	H 6 d, 12 b
Billoter Alley	66cNW1 Grugies	B 9 c
Bill's Bluff	36cNW3 Loos	G 5 c
Bill's Lane [Hill 70]	36cNW3 Loos	H 32 c
Bills Trench	57dNE1 & 2 Fonquevillers	K 3 b, d
Billy [Trench / Post]	57cNE3 Hermies	K 2 c
Billy Alley	51bNW1 Roclincourt / 2 Oppy	B 28 a
Billy Burke Trench	36cSW3 Vimy	T 3 b, d, 9 b, 10 a
Billy Maze	36cSW2 Harnes / 4 Rouvroy	O 32 a, c
Billy Trench	36cSW2 Harnes	O 25 b, d, 31 b, 32 a
Billy Trench	36cSW3 Vimy	S 22 a
Bilstein Trench	36cNW4 Pont-a-Vendin	I 3 c
Bimbo [pill box / light rly locality, 1917-18]	28NE3 Gheluvelt	J 7 b 50.55
Bingen Trench	62cSW2 Barleux	O 22 d, 23 c, 29 a, b, d
Binney Farm	28SW3 Bailleul	T 1 b 65.00
Binting Trench	62cNW2 Bouchavesnes	B 6 a
Birbeck House	28SW3 Bailleul	N 32 d 05.50
Birch House	20SE2 Hooglede	Q 12 c 75.35
Birch Lane [ride in Pacaut Wood]	36aSE 1 St Venant / 2 Lestrem	Q 27 d, 28 c
Birch Tree Trench	57dSE4 Ovillers	X 21 d, 22 a, c
Birch Tree Wood	57dSE4 Ovillers	X 21 d
Bird Alley, & Post	51bNW2 Oppy	B 18 d
Bird Bridge [over stream]	36aNE3 Haverskerque	K 25 a 00.95
Bird Cage Street [late 1915]	36SW1 Aubers	M 22 b, d, 23 c, 29 b
Bird Cage Support	57cNE1 Quéant	D 14 a, b, c
Bird Cage Walk [Lère, Boyau de]	36cSW1 Lens	M 14 c
Bird Cage Walk [Sept 1915]	36cNW1 La Bassée	A 8 d, 9 a, c
Bird Cage, The	36SW1 Aubers	M 29 b, 30 a
Bird Lane	57cSE4 Villers-Guislain / 62cNE2 Epéhy	X 29 d, F 5 a
Bird Post	51bNW2 Oppy	B 18 d
Bird Post	57cSE4 Villers-Guislain	X 29 b
Bird Trench	62cNE2 Epéhy	F 4 b
Birdcage	57cSE4 Villers-Guislain	X 29 d
Birdcage	36SW1 Aubers	M 29 b, 30 a
Birdcage Lane [trench]	57cNE1 Quéant	D 14 a, c
Birdcage South Trench	57cNE1 Quéant	D 14 b, c, d
Birdcage Walk	36cSW1 Lens	M 14 c, d, 20 b
Birdcage Walk	36NW4 Bois Grenier	H 36 b, I 31 a

Name	Map Sheet	Map Reference
Birdcage Walk	36SW1 Aubers	M 29 b
Birdcage, The	36NW4 Bois Grenier	I 31 a
Birdcage, The [German; Le Pelerin 1914-15]	28SW4 Ploegsteert	U 21 b, 22 a
Birdcage, The [tree clump]	57cNE1 Quéant	D 14 a, b
Birdcage, The Quéant [tree clump]	57cNE1 Quéant	D 14 a, b
Birkin Trench, & Group [craters]	36cSW3 Vimy	S 28 a
Birma [farm]	28NE1 Zonnebeke	D 24 a 6.8
Birma Copse	28NE1 Zonnebeke	D 18 d, 24 b
Birmingham [light railway siding, 1917-18]	28NW4 Ypres	H 16 d
Birmingham [Locality]	36cSW3 Vimy	S 27 a, c
Birmingham [lt rly locality W of Pilckem 1917-8]	28NW2 St Julien	C 1 b
Birr Barracks	28SW1 Kemmel	M 29 a 9.8
Birr Cross Road / Roads	28NW4 & NE3 Zillebeke	I 17 b 2.8
Birr Trench	28SW2 Wytschaete	N 18 c
Birth Trench	36cNW1 La Bassée / 3 Loos	B 19 a, c, 25 a, c, H 1 a, c
Birthday Farm	28SW4 Ploegsteert	O 32 c 0.4
Birthday Road [road]	28SW4 Ploegsteert	O 31 b d, 32 c
Bis Post [NNE of Puits 14 bis]	36cNW3 Loos	H 25 d 3.7
Biscay House	27NE3 Winnezeele	J 32 d 6.7
Biscuit Trench	36cNW1 La Bassée	B 9 a, c
Biscuit Trench	57cSW1 Gueudecourt	N 20 d
Bise Trench	20NW4 Dixmude	I 13 a, c
Bishop Avenue	57cSW4 Combles	T 24 c, 30 b, U 25 a, b
Bishop Avenue Switch	57cSW4 Combles	T 24 c
Bishops Corner [road jct]	36aNE2 Vieux Berquin	L 3 a 4.0
Bishop's Gate	57cNE1 Quéant	D 30 b
Bishops Gate [sic; road]	57cNE1 Quéant	D 30 a, c
Bismarck Woods, No. 1	62cSW1 Dompierre	N 26 c
Bismarck Woods, No. 2	62cSW1 Dompierre	N 26 d
Bismarck Woods, No. 3	62cSW1 Dompierre	N 26 c, 32 a
Bison Trench [later Bison Reserve]	51bSW2 Vis-en-Artois	O 20 a, c
Bissel Trench	57dSE4 Ovillers	Q 36 d
Bissing Trench	66cSW2 Vendeuil	O 10 a, c
Bistro Trench	66dNW1 Punchy	A 5 c
Bit Lane [road]	51bNW4 Fampoux / SW2 Vis-en-Artois	I 26 b, d, 31 d, 32 a, b, c, O 1 b
Bit Trench	36cSW4 Rouvroy	O 32 d
Bit Trench [1918]	28NW2 St Julien	C 17 a, b
Bit Work	28NE1 Zonnebeke	D 25 b, d
Bite Trench	36cSW4 Rouvroy	O 32 d
Bite Trench	57dSE2 & 57cSW1 Le Sars	M 18 d, 24 b
Bitter Trench	36cSW3 Vimy	S 16 d, 22 a, b
Bitter Trench	57cSW3 Longueval	T 13 a
Bitter Wood	28NE3 Gheluvelt	J 26 a, b
Biville Trench	66cNW1 Grugies	B 15 b
Bixschoote [village]	20SW4 Bixschoote	T 18 b
Bixschoote Avenue	20SW4 Bixschoote	T 23 b
Bixschoote Fort	20SW4 Bixschoote	T 18 d
Blab Copse	57dSW [4 Toutencourt]	U 13 c
Black Adder / Blackadder's Trench	36SW3 Richebourg	S 10 b
Black Alley	12SW1 Nieuport	M 14 b
Black Alley	62dNE2 Méaulte	F 6 a, c, 12 a
Black Cotts	28NE3 Gheluvelt	J 33 a 7.1
Black Cut	28SW2 Wytschaete	O 13 c
Black Dune Alley	12SW1 Nieuport	M 15 a

Name	Map Sheet	Map Reference
Black Farm	20SE2 Hooglede	R 35 a 5.5
Black Horse Bridge [across Ancre]	57dSE4 Ovillers	W 5 b 9.1 / 6 a 3.2
Black Horse Road [road]	57dSE4 Ovillers	W 5 a, b, c, d
Black Jack [light rly siding]	36cSW1 Lens	M 8 d
Black Line	28SW4 Ploegsteert	O 33 d
Black Line	51bNW3 Arras	G 23 d
Black Shed [Ger FL opp Anton's Farm]	28SW4 Ploegsteert	U 15 a
Black Street	57cSW1 Gueudecourt	N 7 b
Black Street / Boyau Noir	62cNW1 Maricourt	A 23 c
Black Town	62bNW3 Bellicourt	G 22 b
Black Trench	36cSW3 Vimy	S 21 b
Black Trench	51bSW2 Vis-en-Artois	O 16 b, 17 a, b
Black Trench	62dNE2 Méaulte	F 6 c, 11 b, 12 a
Black Watch Alley	36cNW3 Loos	G 36 d, M 6 b
Black Watch Alley	57dSE4 Ovillers	X 10 d, 11 a, b, c
Black Watch Corner	28NE3 Gheluvelt	J 15 b 00.65
Black Watch Trench	57cSW3 Longueval	S 4 c, 10 a, b
Black Wood	62cNW3 Vaux	G 36 c, d
Blackbird Farm	20SE2 Hooglede	R 2 c 45.90
Blackbird Support [1918]	51bSW3 Boisleux	S 22 c, d
Blackbird Trench [1918]	62dSW [4 Cachy]	U 28 c
Blackburn Alley	57cSE2 Gonnelieu	Q 4 a
Blackfriars Bridge	57dNE3 & 4 Hébuterne	K 27 d 4.0
Blackfriars Bridge [road over canal]	36aSE1 St Venant	P 36 a 95.60
Blackfriars Bridge Post [Layes R.]	36NW4 Bois Grenier	I 25 b
Blackheath [Locality]	36cSW3 Vimy	S 27 a
Blacklock Trench	57dNE3 & 4 Hébuterne	K 17 a
Blackpool Street	57dSE4 Ovillers	X 1 a
Blacktown	62bNW3 Bellicourt	G 23 a
Blackwell Farm	28NE4 Dadizeele	K 11 c 45.00
Blackwood Camp	28NW1 Elverdinghe	A 5 c, 11 a
Blaimalle [Ouvrage, E of Bécourt Ch'eau, 1915]	57dSE4 Ovillers	X 26 c, d
Blainoy Trench	62bSW1 Gricourt	M 29 a, c
Blainville [Tranchée, 1915]	57dSE4 Ovillers	X 26 c, d
Blaireville Street	51cSE & 51bSW Ficheux	R 27 c, d
Blaireville Street	51cSE2 Beaumetz	R 27, 28, 34
Blake Copse	51bSE2 Oisy-le-Verger	Q 28 b
Blake Cross Roads	20SE3 Westroosebeke	W 26 b 05.25
Blakeley Crater [Bellewaarde Farm]	28NW4 & NE3 Zillebeke	I 12 a 2.2
Blamont Mill	51cSE2 Beaumetz	R 27 d
Blamont Reserve	57cSW4 Combles	U 19 b, d
Blamont Street	51cSE2 Beaumetz	R 27 d, 33 b, 34 a
Blanchard [Boyau, 1915, La Boisselle]	57dSE4 Ovillers	X 13 c
Blanchard Avenue	51bNW1 Roclincourt	A 28 a, b, 29 a
Blanche Maison [farm]	36NW1 Steenwerck	A 8 d 3.7
Blanco Bay [Bois Blancs]	36NW4 Bois Grenier	I 32 a
Blanco House [Bois Blancs]	36NW4 Bois Grenier	I 32 c
Bland Farm	28SW3 Bailleul	T 21 b 2.6
Bland Trench	62bSW4 Homblières	T 10 b, d
Bland, Tranchée du	70dSW4 [Vauxaillon]	O 33 c
Blandford Trench	51bNW2 Oppy	B 18 b, d
Blangy [village]	51bNW3 Arras	G 23 b, d, 24 a, c
Blangy Park	51bNW3 Arras	G 24 a, b
Blangy System [trenches, 1918]	62dSW [2 Villers-Bretonneux / 4 Cachy]	N 29, 34, 35, T 4
Blangy, Bois de	62dSW [1 Longeau / 3 Boves]	N 35, 36, O 31

Name	Map Sheet	Map Reference
Blangy-Tronville [village]	62dSW [1 Longeau / 3 Boves]	N 21, 22
Blangy-Tronville Line	62dSW [1 Longeau / 3 Boves]	N 22, 28, 34, T 3, 4, 8
Blanich Trench	66cNW3 Essigny	H 1 d, 2 c, 8 a, b, d
Blantyre Road	36NW4 Bois Grenier	I 21 a
Blarney Road [road]	28SW1 Kemmel / 2 Wytschaete	N 15, 16
Blast Trench	57cSW4 Combles	U 25 a, b
Blasthell [Tuilerie, Hallebast, 1918]	28NW4 & NE3 Zillebeke	I 22 a, b
Blauwe Poort Farm	28NW4 Ypres	I 27 b 5.4
Blauwen Molen [Blue Mill]	28SW4 Ploegsteert	O 33 c 7.7
Blauwentoren Farm	20SE2 Hooglede	R 34 a 30.95
Blauwhuis Farm	27NE4 Abeele	K 5 c 25.75
Blavet Alley	66cNW4 Berthenicourt	H 12 d
Blaze Lane	51bSW1 Neuville Vitasse	N 7 d
Blé, Tranchée du [SW of Acid Drop Copse]	57dSE4 Ovillers	X 17 c, 23 a
Bleak House	36aNE3 Haverskerque	K 20 a
Bleak House	36aNE3 Haverskerque	K 20 c 65.55
Bleak House	57cSE2 Gonnelieu	R 17 c 80.15
Bleak Quarry	57bSW1 Bantouzelle	M 19 b
Bleak Support	57cSE2 Gonnelieu	R 28 a, b, d
Bleak Trench	51bNW1 Roclincourt	A 18 d, 24 b
Bleak Trench	57cSE2 Gonnelieu	R 28 c, d
Bleak Walk	57cSE2 Gonnelieu	R 28 a
Bleary Trench	36cSW3 Vimy	S 21 b, 22 a
Bleekery [farms]	27NE2 Proven	F 13 a 3.3
Blegnaert Farm	28SE1 Wervicq	P 12 c 0.9
Bleneau Trench	57dNE3 & 4 Hébuterne	K 28 d, 29 c
Blery Trench	70dSW [2 Coucy-le-Château]	O 25 a
Blessing Farm	28NE2 Moorslede	L 3 a 6.0
Blessure Trench	20NW4 Dixmude	I 13 d, 19 b
Bletchley [light rly locality W of Canal, 1917-18]	28NW2 St Julien	B 18 a, b
Bleu [hamlet]	36aNE2 Vieux Berquin	F 19 b, d, 20 a, c
Bleuet Farm	28NW1 Elverdinghe	B 10 c 3.3
Bleuet Farm British Military Cemetery	28NW1 Elverdinghe	B 10 c 2.3
Blight Trench	36cNW1 La Bassée	B 13 a, c
Blighty Alley	28SW1 Kemmel	M 22 c
Blighty Bridge	28SW4 Ploegsteert	T 12 a
Blighty Hall [Ploeg. Wood]	28SW4 Ploegsteert	U 20, 21
Blighty Trench	36cSW3 Vimy	S 16 d, 17 c, d, 18 c, 22 a, b, 23 a
Blighty Trench	57cSW3 Longueval	T 2 a, b
Blighty Wood [Authuille Wood]	57dSE4 Ovillers	W 6, 12, X 1, 7
Blind Alley	36cSW3 Vimy	S 8 d
Blind Alley	57dNE3 & 4 Hébuterne	K 23 b
Blind Alley	62bSW3 St Quentin	T 1 b, 2 a
Blind Alley	62cNW1 Maricourt	A 2 b
Blind Alley	66dNW1 Punchy	A 6 c, 11 b, 12 a
Blind Trenches	57dSE2 & 57cSW1 Le Sars	M 17 b, d, 18 b
Bliss Crater [Railway Wood]	28NW4 & NE3 Zillebeke	I 12 a 0.4
Blizzard Post [1918]	57dNE2 & 57cNW1 Courcelles	F 17 a 8.2
Blizzard Trench	57cSW2 Villers-au-Flos	N 28 a, b
Bloater Trench	36cSW3 Vimy	S 17 c, d, 23 b, d
Bloater Trench	57dSE4 Ovillers	X 20 b, 21 a, c
Block House	51cSE3 & 4 Ransart	X 2 b
Block House	62bSW1 Gricourt	M 9 b
Block Houses	28SW4 Ploegsteert	O 34 c

Name	Map Sheet	Map Reference
Block Lane	51bSW2 Vis-en-Artois	O 32 a
Block Street Cabaret	28SE1 Wervicq	P 18 d
Blockhouse [at Pontruet]	62bSW1 Gricourt	M 9 b
Blockhouse Copse	62cSW3 Vermandovillers	S 21 a
Blogg Way	36cNW3 Loos	G 36 c
Bloke House [1918]	27NE3 Winnezeele	K 26 a 20.15
Blonde Corner [road junction]	20SE2 Hooglede	Q 30 b 4.8
Blondin House	28SW3 Bailleul	S 24 d 1.6
Blood Trench	51bNW1 Roclincourt	A 18 d
Bloody Farm	28SW1 Kemmel	N 9 a
Bloody Road [Mill Road]	57dSE1 & 2 Beaumont	Q 24 c, d
Bloomer Farm	28SW3 Bailleul	T 19 c 9.5
Bloomfield Avenue	57dSE1 & 2 Beaumont	Q 10 b
Blount Farm	28SW3 Bailleul	T 25 c 2.8
Blow Buildings	28NE2 Moorslede	E 30 b 7.3
Bloxham Farm	28SW3 Bailleul	T 20 c 6.6
Bludgeon Alley	62bSW3 St Quentin	S 29 a, c
Blue Alley	51bNW2 Oppy	B 24 b
Blue Alley	70dNW2 Servais	C 8 a, c, d, 9 c, 15 a, b
Blue Avenue	57cSW4 Combles	U 20 a
Blue Bird Alley	12SW1 Nieuport	M 15 a
Blue Bottle Alley [sunken road]	57cSW3 Longueval	S 17 a
Blue Bull Avenue	36cSW3 Vimy	S 14 d, 15 c
Blue Corner [road junction]	20SE2 Hooglede	R 23 a 3.7
Blue Cut [road SW of Le Barque]	57cSW1 Gueudecourt	M 18 a, c, d
Blue House	20SW4 Bixschoote	U 24 a 10.35
Blue Line	20SW4 Bixschoote	U 29 a
Blue Line	51bNW3 Arras	H 14 d
Blue Mill Cross Roads	20SW4 Bixschoote	T 18 d 9.3
Blue Pig Post [Crater]	57dNE3 & 4 Hébuterne	K 35 a
Blue Port [light rly sidings, 1917-18]	28NW4 Ypres	I 28 a
Blue Trench	36cSW3 Vimy	S 22 b, d
Blue Trench	57dSE2 Beaumont	R 14 c, d, 20 a, b
Blue Trench Line	36bNE2 Beuvry	F 5 c
Blue Trench, & Support	12SW1 Nieuport	M 15 a
Bluebell Copse	20SE2 Hooglede	R 3 c 3.4
Bluebottle / Blue Bottle Alley [sunk. rd]	57cSW3 Longueval	S 16
Bluenose Trench	36cSW3 Vimy	T 7 d, 13 b, d, 19 d
Bluff Junction [light rly locality, 1917-18]	28NW4 Ypres	I 33 d 65.80
Bluff Wynd [C.T., The Bluff]	28NW4 & NE3 Zillebeke	I 34 c
Bluff, The [Petit Miraumont]	57dSE2 & 57cSW1 Le Sars	R 10 b
Bluff, The, & Craters	28NW4 & NE3 Zillebeke	I 34 c
Blunt Nose	62bNW1 Gouy	A 13 b
Blunt Trench	36cSW3 Vimy	S 22 b
Blunt Trench	51bNW1 Roclincourt	A 18 c
Blush Farm	28SW3 Bailleul	S 30 b 8.9
Blush Trench	51bNW1 Roclincourt	A 18 c, d
Blyth [1918; light rly locality]	28NW2 St Julien	C 17 d 2.3
Boadicea Redoubt [SW of St Q]	66cNW1 Grugies	A 11, 17
Boar Copse [Le Bosquet]	57bSW1 Bantouzelle	M 5 c, d
Boar Copse [Oxford Lane]	57cSE2 Gonnelieu	Q 6 c
Boar Lane	28NW2 St Julien	C 20 b, d
Boar Trench	51bSW2 Vis-en-Artois	O 20 a, c
Board Street	57dNE3 & 4 Hébuterne	K 35 a

Name	Map Sheet	Map Reference
Board Trench	51bSW1 Neuville Vitasse	M 11 b
Boardman Trench	28SW2 Wytschaete	N 23 d, 29 b, d
Boar's Head	36SW3 Richebourg	S 16 a
Boast Trench	57cSW3 Longueval	M 34 c
Boat Trench	36cSW3 Vimy	S 16 c, d
Boat Trench	51bNW1 Roclincourt	A 18 d
Boaze's Farm	36aSE1 St Venant	Q 20 a 5.8
Bob Farm	62cNE4 Roisel	L 11 b
Bob Post	62cNE4 Roisel	L 34 b 20.25
Bob Street	28SW2 Wytschaete	O 26 d, 27 b, c, 28 c
Bob Trench	62cNE4 Roisel	L 34 b, d
Bobby Quarry	62cNE4 Roisel	L 11 a 25.25
Bobby Trench	36cSW3 Vimy	S 18 c, 23 b, 24 a
Bobstay Castle	28NW4 Ypres	H 11 b 8.3
Bobtail Post	62cNE4 Roisel	L 34 d 25.70
Bocage Alley	66dNW1 Punchy	A 10 d, 11 c, d, 12 c, d
Bocage Copse	62bSW1 Gricourt	M 8 d
Bochcastel Estaminet	28NW2 St Julien	C 10 d 05.62
Boche Cross Roads	20SW4 Bixschoote	T 24 d 40.55
Boche House	28NW2 St Julien	C 8 a 20.99
Boche Sap	57cSW1 Gueudecourt	M 36 a
Boche Trench	57dNE3 & 4 Hébuterne	K 16 a
Boches Wood	36bSE4 & 36cSW3 Givenchy	R 35 d
Bock Graben	57dNE3 & 4 Hébuterne	K 11 a
Bodger Farm	28SW3 Bailleul	T 1 b 1.4
Bodkin Trench	36cSW3 Vimy	S 24 a
Bodmin Avenue [1918]	51cSE4 Blaireville	X 28 a, b
Bodmin Copse	28NE3 Gheluvelt	J 19 d
Bodmin Trench	57cSW3 Longueval	T 9 d, 15 a, c, d
Bodmin Trench [29-9-16]	57cSW3 Longueval	T 15 c, d
Bodo Farm	27NE4 Abeele	L 28 b 1.4
Boerice, Boyau de	66dNW2 Morchain	B 6 c, d
Boeschepe [village]	27SE2 Berthen	R 9 b, d, 10 a, c
Boeschepe Ballast Spur [rly]	27SE2 Berthen	R 8 a, b
Boeschepe Line [1918]	27SE2 Berthen	R 4, 5, 10, 11, 15, 16
Boeseler Trench	62cNW2 Bouchavesnes	I 3 a, b, 4 a
Boesinghe How[itzer] Spurs	28NW1 Elverdinghe	B 9 b, d, 10 a, c
Boesinghe Point Junction [railway, 1917-18]	28NW4 Ypres	H 12 b 3.0
Boesinghe, Ecluse de	20SW4 Bixschoote	T 29 b
Boethoek [buildings]	28NE1 Zonnebeke	D 15 b 1.3
Boetleer	28NE1 Zonnebeke	D 8 b, d
Bog Avenue	12SW1 Nieuport	M 15 d
Bog Lane	62bNW1 Gouy	A 25 d
Bog Trench	36cSW3 Vimy	S 18 c, 24 a
Bogaert Farm	28SW2 Wytschaete	O 25 a 95.95
Bogey Avenue	51bNW1 Roclincourt	A 29 c, d
Boggart Hole [quarry]	57cNE3 Hermies	K 33 a, b
Boggart Hole Clough	57dSE4 Ovillers	X 1 a
Bogie Lane [1916]	51bNW3 Arras	H 31 b, 32 a, b
Bogie Lane [1918]	51bNW3 Arras	H 31 d, 32 c, d
Bognor [light rly locality]	28NW2 St Julien	C 15 b
Bogside [1918; light rly locality]	28NW2 St Julien	C 17 c 5.1
Bohain [town]	62bNE [1 Bohain] / [2 Mennevret]	D 14, 15, 16, 20, 21, 22
Bohème [farm]	36aSE2 Lestrem	Q 23 c 0.0

Name	Map Sheet	Map Reference
Bohemia Alley	66cNW4 Berthenicourt	I 8 a
Bohemia Trench [1918]	66eNW [4 Morisel]	I 19 c, d, 25 a, c
Bohemian's Trench	66cNW4 Berthenicourt	I 9 b
Boil Farm	27NE2 Proven	F 25 d 7.8
Boiry Lane	51bSW2 Vis-en-Artois	O 11 a
Boiry Notre Dame [village]	51bSW2 Vis-en-Artois	O 5 a, c
Boiry St. Martin [village]	51bSW3 Boisleux	S 14 d, 15 c, 20 b, 21 a
Boiry Ste. Rictrude [village]	51bSW3 Boisleux	S 14, 20
Boiry Trench	51bNW4 Fampoux / SW2 Vis-en-Artois	I 34 d, O 4 b, d
Boiry-Becquerelle Practice Trenches	51bSW3 Boisleux	T 8 a, b, c, d
Bois 11	36cSW3 Vimy	S 2 c
Bois 9	36cSW3 Vimy	M 31 d, S 1 b
Bois Allemande [Fricourt]	62dNE2 Méaulte	F 9 d, 10 c
Bois Bernard [village]	36cSW4 Rouvroy	U 14 d, 15 c, 20 b, 21 a
Bois Bernard [wood]	36cSW4 Rouvroy	U 15 c
Bois Bernard Road [road]	36cSW4 Rouvroy	U 13 c, d, 14 c, d
Bois Carré Trench	28SW2 Wytschaete	N 6 c
Bois Confluent	28SW2 Wytschaete	O 1 c, d, 7 a
Bois de Boulogne, au [Cabaret / Estaminet]	28SW4 Ploegsteert	U 19 a 7.8
Bois de Dix-huit	36cNW3 Loos	H 32 b, 33 a
Bois d'en Haut	62cNW1 Maricourt	A 18 a, c
Bois des Alleux Switch	36bSE4 Carency	X 25, 26, 27
Bois Farm	28NW2 St Julien	B 6 b 1.6
Bois Farm, du	36NW1 Steenwerck	A 19 b 6.5
Bois Français [Fricourt]	62dNE2 Méaulte	F 9 d
Bois Français Support	62dNE2 Méaulte	F 9 b, 10 c
Bois Français Trench	62dNE2 Méaulte	F 9 d, 10 c
Bois Grenier [village]	36NW4 Bois Grenier	H 29 b, 30 a, b, I 25 a
Bois Grenier Line	36NW4 Bois Grenier	H 29 b - I 9 c
Bois Grenier Work	36NW4 Bois Grenier	H 30 b
Bois Haché, Boyau du	62cNW3 Vaux	G 28 b
Bois Hugo	36cNW3 Loos	H 25 d, 26 c
Bois l'Abbé [W of Villers-Bretonneux]	62dSW [2 Villers-Bretonn. / 4 Cachy]	O 25, 26, 27, 31, 32, 33, 34, U 1, 3
Bois Line [E of B. de Gentelles & B. de Blangy]	62dSW [2 Villers Bretonn. / 4 Cachy]	O 1,7,14,20,27,32, U 1,7,13,24,30
Bois Mailard	57bSW3 Honnecourt	S 17 a
Bois Noir	62dNE2 Méaulte	F 12 a
Bois Rasé [Chalet Wood]	36cNW3 Loos	H 25 c
Bois Switch [1918]	62dSW [4 Cachy]	T 5 b, 6 a, c, d
Bois Touffu [railway locality]	62cSW1 Dompierre	M 16 c
Bois Trench	36SW3 Richebourg	S 16 a, c, 22 b
Bois Trench	62cNW4 Péronne	H 30 b, d
Bois Vilain	36cSW4 Rouvroy	U 19 b
Bois-en-Hache [E slope of Lorette Spur]	36cSW3 Vimy	S 2 a, b
Boisselet, P. [Poste]	36cSW3 Vimy	S 8 d
Boisselle Trench	57dNE3 & 4 Hébuterne	K 23 a, c
Boisselle Trench	57dSE4 Ovillers	X 13 a
Boissenard Trench [1918]	62dSW [4 Cachy]	U 22 b, d
Bolan Farm	27NE4 Abeele	K 30 c 30.05
Bold Street	62dNE2 Méaulte	F 16 b / 17 a
Bolide Trench	66dNW3 Hattencourt	H 8 b, c, d, 14 a, b, c, 20 a
Bollaartbeek Junction [light rly, 1917-18]	28NW4 Ypres	I 31 d 1.9
Bolo Farm [& trenches]	36NW2 Armentières	C 16 b 1.5
Bolo House [& trenches]	36NW2 Armentières	C 16 a
Bolsover Switch	62cNE2 Epéhy / 4 Roisel	L 3 b, d, 4 c

Name	Map Sheet	Map Reference
Bolt Alley	57cSW2 Villers-au-Flos	N 23 c, d
Bolt Trench	51bNW1 Roclincourt	A 18 d
Bolt Trench	51bSW2 Vis-en-Artois	O 8 b, 9 a
Bolton Abbey [trench / post]	51bNW2 Oppy	B 22 b
Bolton Alley	57cNW2 Vaulx-Vraucourt	C 11 d, 12 c
Bolton Bank [lynchet]	57cSE4 Villers-Guislain	X 10 d, 11 c
Bolton Farm	28NW4 Ypres	H 22 c 6.8
Bolton Keep	36NW2 Armentières	B 29 d 2.3
Bolton Street	36NW4 Bois Grenier	I 15 d
Bolus Cottage	28SW3 Bailleul	S 24 c 4.6
Bolzinger, Ouvrage [1915, Bécourt-Fricourt]	62dNE2 Méaulte	F 2 a, c
Bomb Alley	36cNW1 La Bassée / 3 Loos	G 3 b, d
Bomb Depot	36cNW1 La Bassée / 3 Loos	G 3 b
Bomb Farm	28SW2 Wytschaete	O 18 c 6.9
Bomb Row	36SW3 Richebourg	M 35 c, S 5 a
Bombardiers, The	12SW1 Nieuport	M 10 d, 11 c
Bombardment Trench	62dNE2 Méaulte	F 15 b, d
Bompard Trench	66cNW1 Grugies	B 15 a
Bompard Trench	70dNW2 Servais	B 23 c, 29 a
Bon / Bow Trench [1918]	57dNE2 & 57cNW1 Courcelles	F 26 a, b
Bon Accord Street	57dSE4 Ovillers	X 25 b, 26 a
Bon Fermier Cabaret, Au [Messines]	28SW4 Ploegsteert	U 2 b 3.4
Bon Gite, Au [SW of Langemarck]	20SW4 Bixschoote	U 28 d 20.99
Bon Post	28SW4 Ploegsteert	U 17 a 99.80
Bonabus Farm	57bSW3 Honnecourt	S 11 b 7.9
Bonaparte Farm	20SE3 Westroosebeke	V 5 c 1.3
Bonar Cross [cross roads]	36aNE4 Merville	K 16 a 33.61
Bonar Farm	36aNE4 Merville	K 16 a
Bonavis [farm]	57bSW1 Bantouzelle	M 13 b 45.25
Bonavis Ridge	57cSE2 Gonnelieu	R 17 d
Bond Street	28NW2 St Julien	I 4 b, 5 a
Bond Street	28NW2 St Julien / 28NW4 & NE3 Zillebeke	I 4 a, c
Bond Street	36cNW3 Loos	G 35 b, c, d
Bond Street	36SW3 Richebourg	S 9 d, 10 c
Bond Street	51bNW4 Fampoux	I 22 b, 23 a
Bond Street	57cNE3 Hermies	K 21 c, 26 b, 27 a
Bond Street	57dSE1 & 2 Beaumont	Q 16 b
Bond Street (A.1. Avenue) [New Bond?]	36SW1 Aubers	N 8 a, c, d
Bond Street [road]	57cNE1 Quéant	D 22 a, b, d
Bond Street [Sept 1915]	36cNW1 La Bassée	A 21 b
Bond Street [Zouave Wood - Hooge]	28NW4 & NE3 Zillebeke	I 17 d, 18 c
Bond Street A	28NW2 St Julien	I 5 a
Bond Street B	28NW2 St Julien	I 4 a, b
Bond Street, New [Zouave Wood - Hooge]	28NW4 & NE3 Zillebeke	I 18 a, b, c
Bond Street, Old [Zouave Wood - Hooge]	28NW4 & NE3 Zillebeke	I 18 a, b
Bond Street, Upper	28NW4 & NE3 Zillebeke	I 18 c
Bond Trench	51bNW1 Roclincourt	A 24 b, B 19 a
Bone Point [German Redoubt]	28SW2 Wytschaete	N 30 d, 36 b
Bone Trench	51bNW1 Roclincourt	A 24 b
Bone Trench	51bSW1 Neuville Vitasse	M 18 b
Bones Lane	57cSE2 Gonnelieu	Q 11 a
Bones Post	36SW3 Richebourg	S 2 b 1.1
Bonn Trench [1918]	66eNW [2 Thennes]	B 29 d
Bonnal Trench	51bNW1 Roclincourt	A 16, 21, 22, 23

Name	Map Sheet	Map Reference
Bonne Enfance Copse	57bSW1 Bantouzelle	N 19 c, d
Bonne Enfance Farm	57bSW1 Bantouzelle	M 30 a 8.5
Bonnet Trench	62cSW3 Vermandovillers	T 14 a
Bonnett House [Le Pelerin]	28SW4 Ploegsteert	U 21 b
Bonneuil Chateau Aerodrome [German, 1918]	66dSE [1]	P 29 b, d, 30 a, c
Bonnie Trench [1918] [see Bonnal]	51bNW1 Roclincourt	A 16 c, 22 a, d, 23 c
Bonnymuir Street	57dSE4 Ovillers	X 20 c
Bonté Redoubt	62dNE2 Méaulte	F 8 d
Bonton Alley	51bNW2 Oppy	B 24 d
Bonval Spur [light rly]	36cSW3 Vimy	S 30 c
Bony Avenue	62bNW1 Gouy	A 14 c, d
Bony Copse	62bSW1 Gricourt	N 10 b
Bony Point [trig point]	62bNW1 Gouy	A 10 c 61.21
Boo Farm	20SE2 Hooglede	R 17 b 95.65
Boodle Farm	27SE2 Berthen	R 5 a 60.05
Boom Ravine	57dSE2 & 57cSW1 Le Sars	R 10 d, 11 c, d
Boom Trench	36cSW3 Vimy	S 17 c
Boom Wood [Strooiboomhoek]	28NE2 Moorslede	K 5 b
Boomerang Copse	62cNE3 Buire	J 2 d, 8 b, 9 a
Boon Farm [Boonhoek]	28NE2 Moorslede	L 3 a 9.4
Boone Camp	27NE4 Abeele	L 13 c
Boonhoek	28NE2 Moorslede	L 3 a
Boose [sic] Trench	36cNW1 La Bassée	B 1 c, d, 7 b
Booth Farm	28NW1 Elverdinghe	A 14 b 2.4
Bootham Trench	51bSW2 Vis-en-Artois / 4 Bullecourt	N 35 d, 36 a, c, T 5 b
Boothoek [farm & pillboxes]	28NE1 Zonnebeke	D 15 b 0.4
Booze Farm	28NW1 Elverdinghe	B 25 d 8.0
Boqueteau Trench [1918]	62dSW [4 Cachy]	T 6 a, c, 12 a, c
Bordeau, Boyau	36cSW1 Lens	M 19 d
Borden Avenue	57dNE3 & 4 Hébuterne	K 34 c, d
Borden Camp	27NE4 Abeele	K 3 d, 4 c
Borden Trench	36cSW3 Vimy	S 6 b, T 1 c
Border Avenue	28SW4 Ploegsteert	U 26 c, d, 27 a, b, c
Border Camp	28NW1 Elverdinghe	A 30 a, b
Border Dugouts [Sanctuary Wood]	28NW4 & NE3 Zillebeke	I 24 c
Border House	28NW2 St Julien	C 18 b 0.8
Border Lane	36cNW3 Loos	G 5 c, d, 10 b, 11 a
Border Lane	51bSW2 Vis-en-Artois	O 25 d
Border Lane [Maple Copse]	28NW4 & NE3 Zillebeke	I 24 a, b
Border Lane [road]	51bNW4 Fampoux	H 17 a, c
Border Redoubt	36cNW3 Loos	G 5 d, 11 b
Borderer Lane	51bSW4 Bullecourt	U 21 c
Borderer Ridge	57cSE2 Gonnelieu	Q 23, 24
Borderers Road [road]	36aNE4 Merville	K 4 c, 10 a, c, d
Bordon [light rly, Vimy]	36cSW3 Vimy	T 25 c
Borinage Trench	20SW3 Oostvleteren	T 3 d, 4 c
Boris Post	36cNW3 Loos	G 23 d 5.0
Boriska Trench	57cSW4 Combles	T 5 a, b, d
Borlass Avenue	57cNE3 Hermies / 4 Marcoing	K 15 c
Borne, Boyau	62cNW3 Vaux	G 22 d, 23 c
Bornes Trench	20SW4 Bixschoote	T 17 c
Borogrove Trees [trig point]	62cNW3 Vaux	H 1 d 55.33
Borre [village]	27SE3 Borre	W 19 a, c, d
Borre Railhead / Refilling Point	27SE3 Borre	V 12, 18, W 7, 13

Name	Map Sheet	Map Reference
Borre Sidings [railway, military]	27SE3 Borre	W 7 a, b, c, d
Borries Graben	57dNE3 & 4 Hébuterne	K 24 c, d
Borry Farm [Pill Box]	28NE1 Zonnebeke	D 25 b
Borry Keep [1918]	28NE1 Zonnebeke	D 25 b
Bosch Walk / Bosche Walk	36cSW3 Vimy	M 32 c
Bosche, Abri	51bNW1 Roclincourt	A 3 c, d
Bosham Farm	36aNE4 Merville	K 21 d 60.82
Boshie Trench [1918]	62dSW [4 Cachy]	U 24 d
Bosky Redoubt	51bNW3 Arras	G 11 a
Bosky Trench	62dNE2 Méaulte	F 3 b, 4 a
Bosnia Trench	57cSW4 Combles	U 1 d, 2 c
Bosnia Trench [1918]	62dSE [3 Marcelcave]	V 19 a, c, 25 a
Bosquet Alley	62bSW1 Gricourt	M 35 a
Bosquet Alley / Boyau de Bosquet	66dNW1 Punchy	A 12 d, B 7 c, 13 a, b, 14 a, c
Bosquet Farm	20SW4 Bixschoote	T 5 b 10.05
Bosquet, le [hamlet]	57bSW1 Bantouzelle	M 4 d, 5 c, 10 a, b
Bossaert Farm	28NW2 St Julien	C 23 b 1.3
Bossaert Keep [1918; Bossaert Farm]	28NW2 St Julien	C 23 b 30.45
Bossy Quarry	62cNE4 Roisel	L 11 a 30.25
Boston [1918; light rly locality]	28NW2 St Julien	C 17 b 7.5
Boston [pillboxes, Verlorenhoek]	28NW2 St Julien	C 30 c 5.2
Boston O.P. [1917-18]	51bNW1 Roclincourt	B 14 a 6.6
Boston Trench	62cNW4 Péronne	I 32 c
Bosun Farm	62bSW2 Fonsommes	O 27 a 2.8
Bosun Hill, Big	62bSW2 Fonsommes	O 21 d
Bosun Hill, Little	62bSW2 Fonsommes	O 21 a, c
Bosun Valley	62bSW2 Fonsommes	O 15 c, d, 21 a, b, c
Botany Bend [cross roads, farm & road bend]	27NE3 Winnezeele	J 33 a 30.05
Botany Trench [1918]	62dNE [3 Morlancourt]	J 36 a, b, c
Botha Alley	66cNW2 Itancourt	B 5 b
Botha Farm	27SE4 Meteren	W 29 d 1.3
Botha Farm	28SW3 Bailleul	T 26 c 9.9
Botha Trench	57dNE3 & 4 Hébuterne	K 16 a
Bothcastel Estaminet	28NW2 St Julien	C 10 d 1.7
Bothmer Trench	62bSW4 Homblières	T 24 a, c, d, 30 b
Botte Wood	66eNW [4 Morisel]	I 12 c, d, 18 a, b
Botteuse Trench	57dNE3 & 4 Hébuterne	K 16 b
Bottle Buildings	28NE2 Moorslede	F 22 d 8.3
Bottom Alley	57dSE4 Ovillers	X 23 c, 28 b, 29 a
Bottom Bridge	51bSW2 Vis-en-Artois	O 27 b 8.2
Bottom Copse	62bSW3 St. Quentin	S 11 b
Bottom Trench	57cSE4 Villers-Guislain	X 24 c
Bottom Trench	57cSW3 Longueval	M 31 d, S 1 b, 2 a
Bottom Wood	57dSE4 Ovillers	X 28 b, 29 a
Bottom Wood	62bSW4 Homblières	T 17 a, b
Bottom Wood Road	57dSE4 Ovillers	X 29 b
Bouchaud [Tranchée, 1915, La Boisselle]	57dSE4 Ovillers	X 20 c
Bouchavesnes [village]	62cNW2 Bouchavesnes	C 14 b, d, 15 c, 20 a, b
Boucher Farm [Beaulencourt]	57cSW2 Villers-au-Flos	N 17 d 5.9
Boucher Wood	62cNW3 Vaux	G 24, H 19
Bouchot Alley	62cSW1 Dompierre / 2 Barleux	N 7, 13, 14, 20, 21, 28, 34
Boucle Avenue	20SW3 Oostvleteren	T 27 b, 28 a
Bouddha Trench	66dNW1 Punchy / 3 Hattencourt	H 3 b, c, d
Boudin Alley	66cNW2 Itancourt	B 5 b

Name	Map Sheet	Map Reference
Bouet Trench	66cNW2 Itancourt	C 25 b
Bouf Trench	62cSW4 St. Christ	U 21 d, 27 b
Bouillon Trench	57dNE3 & 4 Hébuterne	K 17 a
Bouillon, Boyau de [Bovril Alley]	36bSE2 Boyeffles / 36cSW1 Lens	R 11, 17, 18, M 19, 20
Boulder Communication Trench [1918]	62dSW [2 Villers-Bretonneux / 4 Cachy]	O 36 c
Bouleaux Copse	62bNW4 Ramicourt	I 31 d, 32 c
Bouleaux Trench	62cSW3 Vermandovillers	S 6 d, 12 a, b
Bouleaux Wood	57cSW3 Longueval	T 16, 21, 26, 27
Boulevard Frederic George [street, Béthune]	36bNE2 Beuvry	E 11 c, 17 a
Boulevard Inn, le	36aNE1 Morbecque	D 6 a 3.3
Boulevard Thiers [street, Béthune]	36bNE2 Beuvry	E 10 d, 11 c
Boulevard Trench	51bNW3 Arras	G 29 a
Boulogne Wood	62cSW1 & 2 Belloy	N 16 central
Boulogne Wood Alley	62cSW1 & 2 Belloy	N 10 b, d, 16 b
Boundary Farm	28NW4 & NE3 Zillebeke	I 10 b 95.51
Boundary Post	51cSE3 & 4 Ransart	R 31 c
Boundary Road [road]	28NW2 St Julien	C 15 c, 21 a, c, 27 a, c
Bourdeaux Farm [& pillboxes]	28NE1 Zonnebeke	D 15 d 5.7
Bourdon, Boyau [Corons d'Aix Alley, SE end]	36cSW1 Lens	M 25 d
Bourg Trench	66cNW1 Grugies	B 13 a, b, 14 a
Bourgas Trench	66cNW4 Berthenicourt	I 33 d
Bourgas Trench / Tranchée de Bourgas	62cSW2 Barleux	O 1 d, 2 c, 7 a, b
Bourgeat Trench	62cSW3 Vermandovillers	S 10 b, 11 a
Bourjane, Tranchée	66cNW2 Itancourt	B 18 a, b, c
Bourlon [village]	57cNE2 Bourlon	E 6 c, d, 11 d, 12, F 1 c, 7 a
Bourlon Wood	57cNE2 Bourlon	E 12, 18, F 7, 8, 13, 14
Bourne [light rly locality, 1917-18]	28NW2 St Julien	C 15 d 9.9
Bourne Farm [1918]	28SW1 Kemmel	M 35 a 40.75
Bourse, la [farm & place name]	28SW3 Bailleul	S 8 c 3.9
Boursies [village]	57cNE3 Hermies	J 5 c, d, 6 c
Bout Deville [hamlet]	36aSE2 Lestrem	R 17 d, 18 c, 24 a
Bout Deville Post	36aSE2 Lestrem	R 23 b, d
Bout du Pré [farm / hamlet]	57bSW2 Clary	N 4 b, d
Bout Farm	28NE2 Moorslede	E 23 c 7.8
Boutillerie Avenue, & Post [N 5 b]	36SW2 Radinghem	N 5 a, b, d
Bouvat Trench	57dNE3 & 4 Hébuterne	K 22 b
Bouvigny Hill [defended locality]	36bSE2 Boyeffles	Q24b,d, R19a,b,c,d, 20a,b, 25a,b, 26a
Bouvigny Huts	36bSE2 Boyeffles	R 25 d 5.5
Bouvigny Wood [defended locality]	36bSE2 Boyeffles	R 32 a, b, d, 33 a, c
Bouvincourt [village]	62cSE1 Bouvincourt	P 17 d, 18 c, 23 b, 24 a
Bouvincourt Aerodrome [German, 1918]	62cSE1 Bouvincourt	P 18 c, d
Bouvincourt Knoll	62cSE1 Bouvincourt	P 17 c, d, 23 a, b
Bouvines Farm	20SW4 Bixschoote	T 28 d 8.2
Bouzincourt [village]	57dSE [3 Bouzincourt]	W 7, 13
Bovent [village]	62cSW3 & 4 Marchélepot	S 12 d, T 7 c
Bovent Alley	62cSW1 Dompierre / 3 Vermandovillers	M 25, 31-5, S 5, 6, 12
Bovent, Bois de	62cSW3 & 4 Marchélepot	S 6 d
Boves [village]	62dSW [3 Boves]	M 6, 12, N 7
Bovet Trench	51bNW3 Arras	G 23 c, 29 a
Bovis Trench	51bSW4 Bullecourt	U 21 d, 22 c
Bovril Alley [Boyau de Bouillon]	36bSE2 Boyeffles / 36cSW1 Lens	R 11, 17, 18, 24, M 19, 20
Bovril House	27NE2 Proven	E 29 c 6.4
Bovril Trench	57cSW3 Longueval / 4 Combles	T 9 d, 10 c, 16 a

Name	Map Sheet	Map Reference
Bow Alley	51bSW2 Vis-en-Artois	O 2 a
Bow Farm	28SW2 Wytschaete	O 30 a 9.5
Bow Lane	36cNW3 Loos	G 35 d
Bow Lane	51bSW4 Bullecourt	U 11 c
Bow Lane	57cSW2 Villers-au-Flos	N 28 c
Bow Street	57dNE3 & 4 Hébuterne	K 34 a
Bow Street [cJuly 1915]	28NW2 St Julien	C 13 d, 19 b
Bow Trench	51bSW2 Vis-en-Artois	O 10 c, 16 a
Bow Trench, & Support	51bNW2 Oppy	B 4, 10, 16, 17, 23
Bow, The [N of High Wood]	57cSW3 Longueval	M 33 d, 34 c, S 3 b
Bow, The [S of Bazentin-le-Petit Wood]	57cSW3 Longueval	S 13 b
Bowdler Redoubt	57dSE2 & 57cSW1 Le Sars	M 1 d
Bower Lane	62bNW1 Gouy / 62cNE2 Epéhy	G 1 b, L 6 a
Bowery Cottages	36aNE4 Merville	L 8 c 6.9
Bowery, The [W of Beaumont Hamel]	57dSE1 & 2 Beaumont	Q 3 d
Bowl Trench	57dNE3 & 4 Hébuterne	K 29 d, 35 a, b
Bowline House [Vlamertinghe]	28NW3 Poperinghe	H 10 b 3.7
Bowls Lane	28SW2 Wytschaete	N 36 a
Box [Flers Practice Trenches]	57dSE2 & 57cSW1 Le Sars	N 25 c, 31 a
Box [light rly locality, 1917-18]	28NW2 St Julien	C 21 b 8.9
Box Alley [Box Wood]	57dNE3 & 4 Hébuterne	K 18 d, L 13 c, d
Box Camp	28NW1 Elverdinghe	A 11 a, b
Box Farm	36NW2 & NE1 Houplines	C 29 c 8.6
Box Lane	57dSE4 Ovillers	R 34 c, d
Box Trench	28NW2 St Julien	C 21 b
Box Trench	51bSW1 Neuville Vitasse	M 11 b, 12 a
Box Trench	57dNE3 & 4 Hébuterne	K 18 d, L 13 c
Box Tunnel	36cSW1 Lens	M 20 b
Box Wood	57dNE3 & 4 Hébuterne	L 13 c, d
Box, The	57cSE2 Gonnelieu	R 7 c
Boxers Cross Roads	28NE2 Moorslede	E 23 d 5.9
Boy Trench	36cSW3 Vimy	S 22 b, 23 a
Boyeffles Dump	36bSE2 Boyeffles	R 13 b 5.9
Boyeffles Locality	36bSE2 Boyeffles	R 13 a, b, c, d
Boyelles Reserve [1918]	51bSW3 Boisleux	T 20 a, b, d, 21 c
Boyle's Farm	28SW4 Ploegsteert	U 1 a 35.05
Boyles Farm C. T.	28SW4 Ploegsteert	U 1 c
Boyne Street [trench]	51bNW2 Oppy	B 18 a, b
Boynton Alley	51bNW2 Oppy	B 24 b, d
Brace Farm	27NE4 Abeele	K 27 d 95.60
Brace Trench	51bSW2 Vis-en-Artois	O 14 b, 15 a
Braces Trench	36cNW1 La Bassée	A 5 a, b
Braches [village]	66eNW [4 Morisel]	I 34 c, d
Braches Halt [railway]	66eNW [4 Morisel]	I 34 b 25.20
Bracken Farm	36aNE2 Vieux Berquin	F 19 c 3.1
Bracken Support [1918]	57dSE1 & 2 Beaumont / 4 Ovillers	Q 34 b, d
Bracken Trench	36cSW3 Vimy	S 23 a
Bracken Trench [1918]	57dSE1 & 2 Beaumont / 4 Ovillers	Q 34 b, d, 35 a
Bracquement [village]	36bNE4 Noeux-les-Mines	L 19 c, d, 26 a, b,
Bracquement Keep	36bNE4 Noeux-les-Mines	L 26 a
Bradawl House	27NE2 Proven	F 26 c 4.6
Braddel Trench [Sept 1915]	36cNW1 La Bassée	A 20 d, 26 b
Braddell Castle	36cNW1 La Bassée	A 20 d, 21 c
Braddell Point	36cNW1 La Bassée	A 20 d, 21 c

Name	Map Sheet	Map Reference
Bradford [1918; light rly locality]	28NW2 St Julien	C 17 b 1.7
Bradford Post	51bNW2 Oppy	B 24 b, C 19 a
Bradford Reserve	57cNW2 Vaulx-Vraucourt	C 18 c, 24 a, b
Bradford Trench	51bNW2 Oppy	B 24 b
Bradford Trench [1918]	57dNE2 & 57cNW1 Courcelles	F 20 b, d
Braemar Street	57dSE4 Ovillers	X 26 a, b
Braeton Post	62cNE2 Epéhy	F 5 a
Brag Farm	28NE2 Moorslede	F 29 b 6.8
Brahmin Bridge [road over stream]	27SE4 Meteren	X 20 c 8.8
Brain Cottage	28SW3 Bailleul	N 31 c 98.07
Brain Trench	36cNW1 La Bassée	B 1 a
Brain Trench	51bNW1 Roclincourt	A 24 a
Brains Trench	12SW1 Nieuport	N 13 c
Brains Way	36cNW1 La Bassée	A 21 d
Brake Camp	28NW1 Elverdinghe	A 30 c, d, G 6 a, b
Brake Wood	28NW1 Elverdinghe	A 30 c, d, G 6 a, b
Bram Copse	62cSW1 Dompierre	M 30 c
Bramble Trench	51bSW1 Neuville Vitasse	M 6 c, 12 a
Bran Lane [1918]	51cSE4 Blaireville	X 29 a
Branche Nord [trench]	62cSW1 & 2 Belloy	O 8 a, c
Brancourt-le-Grand	62bNW2 Brancourt-le-Grand	C 21, 22, 27, 28
Brandenburg Trench	66cNW1 Grugies	B 8 d, 9 c, d, 10 a
Brandhoek [light rly locality & camp]	28NW3 Poperinghe	G 12 b, H 7 a
Brandhoek [village]	28NW3 Poperinghe	G 12 a, b
Brandhoek Junction [railway]	28NW3 Poperinghe	H 7 b 0.8
Brandhoek Line [1918]	28NW1 Elverdinghe / 3 Poperinghe	A 24, 30, B 19, 25, G 6, 12, 18, 24
Brandhoek Switch [1918]	28SW1 Kemmel	N 1 a, c
Brandon Trench	36cSW4 Rouvroy	T 29 b
Brands Gully [E of Frezenberg]	28NE1 Zonnebeke	D 26 d, 27 c
Brandy House	28NW1 Elverdinghe	B 19 b 3.8
Brandy Trench	51bNW2 Oppy	B 6 a, b, d, 12 b
Brandy Trench	57dSE4 Ovillers	X 27 a
Brant Farm	28SW3 Bailleul	S 24 d 7.7
Brasserie [St Eloi]	28SW2 Wytschaete	N 6 a
Brasserie Farm [St Eloi]	28SW2 Wytschaete	N 5 b 85.05
Brasserie R.A.P.	28SW2 Wytschaete	N 11 a 7.6
Brasserie R.A.P. [Vierstraat-Ypres Rd]	28SW2 Wytschaete	N 6 a 1.1
Brasserie Trench	57dNE1 & 2 Fonquevillers	E 27 b
Brasserie, la	36aSE1 St Venant	P 21 d
Brasshat Farm	36aSE1 St Venant	Q 25 c 70.25
Brasso Redoubt	62cNW4 Péronne	I 13 b, 14 a, b
Brault, Boyau	62cSW1 Dompierre	M 4 a, b
Bravard Alley	66cNW1 Grugies	B 15 a
Brawford Crater	57cSE4 Villers-Guislain	X 17 b
Brawn Trench	57dSE1 & 2 Beaumont	R 31 a, b
Bray Farm	20SE3 Westroosebeke	V 27 b 3.4
Bray Keep [Annequin]	36bNE4 Noeux-les-Mines	F 30 c 95.05 to L 6 a 95.95
Bray Street	57dSE4 Ovillers	X 13 a, c
Bray Trench	36cNW3 Loos	H 25 a, b
Brayelle Avenue, La [1918]	57dNE1 & 2 Fonquevillers	E 23 b, 24 a, c, 30 a
Brayelle Farm, la	57dNE1 & 2 Fonquevillers	E 23 d 9.2
Brayelle Graben	57dNE1 & 2 Fonquevillers	E 24 d, 30 a, b
Brayelle Road, La [road]	57dNE1 & 2 Fonquevillers	E 22 c, d, 23 c, d
Brayelle Verb[indungs] Graben	57dNE1 & 2 Fonquevillers	E 23 d, 24 c, 30 a

Name	Map Sheet	Map Reference
Brazil Trench	20SW1 Loo	M 6 d, 12 b
Bread Lane	62bNW1 Gouy	A 13 d
Bread Street	28NW4 & NE3 Zillebeke	I 34 c
Bread Trench	36cNW1 La Bassée	B 9 a
Bread Trench	57cSW1 Gueudecourt	N 15 d
Bread Trench	57cSW2 Villers-au-Flos	N 18 a
Breakfast Post	57cSW3 Longueval	T 3 a
Bream Wood [later Sandford Wood]	57dSW [4 Toutencourt]	T 22 c, d, 28 a, b
Breastwork	57dSE1 & 2 Beaumont	Q 23 b
Breastwork Tramway	36NW4 Bois Grenier	I 14 b, 15 a, c, d
Breastwork, The [St Eloi]	28SW2 Wytschaete	O 2 d
Brebis, Les [village]	36bNE4 Noeux-les-Mines	L 35 a, b, c, d
Brecon Sap	36cNW3 Loos	G 12 d
Brecon Trench	51bNW1 Roclincourt	A 3 c
Brecon Trench	57cSW3 Longueval	S 3 c, d, 9 a
Breda Farm	27NE4 Abeele	L 23 b 5.7
Breda Farm	28NW1 Elverdinghe	A 16 d 6.6
Breeks Trench	36cNW1 La Bassée	A 5 b
Breemeerschen [farm]	28SW3 Bailleul	S 18 c 4.1
Breemeerschen [place name]	28SW3 Bailleul	S 18 c, 24 a
Breese Camp Wood [1918]	28SW1 Kemmel	M 10 d
Breezy Corner [road jct]	28NE4 Dadizeele	L 31 a 5.8
Breezy Walk [CT / track]	36bNE2 Beuvry / 36cNW1 La Bassée	F 11 b, 12 a, A 7 b
Breit Alley	57dSE4 Ovillers / 62dNE2 Méaulte	X 29 d, F 5 b
Breme Alley	66cNW4 Berthenicourt	I 9 b
Breme Work	66dNW1 Punchy	B 1 a
Bremen Alley	70dNW2 Servais	C 8 c, 13 b, 14 a
Bremen House, & Redoubt	28NE1 Zonnebeke	D 20 c, 26 a
Bremen Trench	62cNW2 Bouchavesnes	C 10 b, c, d
Bremen Trench	66cSW2 Vendeuil	O 15 a, c
Brent Cottage	27SE4 Meteren	X 6 a 95.05
Breslau Alley	62cNW1 Maricourt	A 2 d, 8 a
Breslau Avenue, & Sap	36cNW3 Loos	G 11 b, d, 12 a, c
Breslau Point	62cNW1 Maricourt	A 9 a
Breslau Support	57cSE2 Gonnelieu	R 23 d, 29 b, 30 a
Breslau Support	62cNW1 Maricourt	A 8 b, 9 a
Breslau Trench	57cSE2 Gonnelieu	R 23 c, d, 29 b
Breslau Trench	62cNW1 Maricourt	A 8 b, 9 a
Breslau Trench [1918]	66eNW [2 Thennes]	C 14 d, 20 b, c
Breslau Trench [Oct 1915]	36cNW3 Loos	G 11 b, d
Breslauer Graben	51bNW3 Arras	G 12 c
Brest Trench	62bSW3 St Quentin	S 5 b
Brest Trench	66cNW4 Berthenicourt	H 17 b
Bretencourt Street	51cSE & 51bSW Ficheux	R 32 b, d
Breton Alley	62bSW3 St Quentin	S 3 a, b, c, d, 4 a, b, 5 a
Breton Trench	66cNW1 Grugies	B 7 b, d, 8 c
Brett Switch [1918]	62dSW [2 Villers-Bretonneux / 4 Cachy]	O 36 c
Breuil [village]	66dNW4 Nesle	I 34 d, 35 c
Brew Lane [trench]	62bNW3 Bellicourt	G 14 c, d, 15 c
Brewer Fork [road jct]	28NE2 Moorslede	F 7 a 9.6
Brewery [Chez Bontemps]	36cSW4 Rouvroy	U 20 a 5.1
Brewery Corner	36SW3 Richebourg	S 25 b
Brewery Corner [Danger Corner]	36SW3 Richebourg	S 25 b 5.7 [1915], 7.7 [1916]
Brewery Dump	36cSW3 Vimy	N 31 c 5.0

Name	Map Sheet	Map Reference
Brewery Keep [Vermelles]	36cNW3 Loos	G 8 c
Brewery Post [two different posts]	36NW4 Bois Grenier	H 30 b, & I 31 a
Brewery Redoubt / Reduit de la Brasserie	62cNW1 Maricourt	A 22 a 9.5
Brewery Road	36SW3 Richebourg	S 5 a
Brewery Road [road]	36aSE1 St Venant	P 28a, b
Brewery Trench	36cNW1 La Bassée	B 1 c, 7 a, b, 8 a, b
Brewery Trench	51bSW1 Neuville Vitasse	M 16 b
Brewery, The [Bois Grenier]	36NW4 Bois Grenier	H 30 b 45.99
Brick Kiln & Yard [Zonnebeke]	28NE1 Zonnebeke	D 27 b 95.00
Brick Lane	62cNW1 Maricourt	A 3 d
Brick Pile Siding [light rly locality, 1917-18]	28NW4 Ypres	I 33 c
Brick Point	62cNW1 Maricourt	A 9 b
Brick Spur [lt rly, W of Canal 1917-18]	28NW2 St Julien	B 12 a
Brick Stack Trench	36cNW1 La Bassée	A 22 a
Brick Street	36NW4 Bois Grenier	I 15 b, d, 16 a, c
Brick Street	62cNW1 Maricourt	A 16 d
Brick Trench	36cSW1 Lens	M 30 d
Brick Trench	36SW3 Richebourg	S 28 d
Brick Trench [Briques Trench, Les; Sept 1915]	36cNW1 La Bassée	A 22 c, 28 a, b
Brick Walk	36cSW1 Lens	M 20 b
Brick Works	27SE2 Berthen	Q 12 d 4.8
Brick, The [Crater]	36cNW1 La Bassée	A 16 c
Brickbat Alley	36cNW1 La Bassée	A 22 a
Brickfield [Ginchy]	57cSW3 Longueval	T 14 c
Brickfield [near Angle Point]	20SW4 Bixschoote	U 6 d 5.1
Brickfield Terrace [Sept 1915]	36cNW1 La Bassée	A 15 d, 21 b
Brickfields Trench	36cNW1 La Bassée	A 30 d, B 25 a, c
Brickfields Trenches	57dNE4 & 57cNW3 Achiet	L 29 c, d, 35 a, b
Brickstack A [German, April 1915]	36cNW1 La Bassée	A 22 a
Brickstack B [German, April 1915]	36cNW1 La Bassée	A 22 a
Brickstack C [German, April 1915]	36cNW1 La Bassée	A 22 a
Brickstack D [German, April 1915]	36cNW1 La Bassée	A 22 a
Brickstack E [German, April 1915]	36cNW1 La Bassée	A 22 a
Brickstack F [German, April 1915]	36cNW1 La Bassée	A 22 a
Brickstack G [German, April 1915]	36cNW1 La Bassée	A 22 a
Brickstack H [German, April 1915]	36cNW1 La Bassée	A 22 a
Brickstack J [German, April 1915]	36cNW1 La Bassée	A 16 c
Brickstack K [German, April 1915]	36cNW1 La Bassée	A 16 c
Brickstack L [German, April 1915]	36cNW1 La Bassée	A 16 c
Brickstack M [German, April 1915]	36cNW1 La Bassée	A 16 c
Brickstack Walk	36NW4 Bois Grenier	I 8 b, 9 a
Brickstacks, The	36cNW1 La Bassée	A 22 a
Brickwork Lane	51bNW4 Fampoux	I 2 d
Brickworks Switch [1918]	51bSW1 Neuville Vitasse	M 4 d, 5 b, c, 10 b
Bride Farm	27SE2 Berthen	R 14 a 0.0
Bride Mill	27SE2 Berthen	R 13 d 57.43
Bridge Alley	66cSW2 Vendeuil	N 17 d, 23 b, 24 a, b, O 13 c, 14 a
Bridge Camp	28NW1 Elverdinghe	B 20 b
Bridge End	57dSE1 & 2 Beaumont	Q 10 b
Bridge End [Loos Pylons Tower]	36cNW3 Loos	G 36 d
Bridge House	28NW2 St Julien	C 24 a 3.5
Bridge House	36aNE4 Merville	K 16 d 15.50
Bridge House [Le Touquet]	36NW2 & NE1 Houplines	C 11 c 40.85
Bridge Junction [road junction]	28NW1 Elverdinghe	B 20 b 3.7

Name	Map Sheet	Map Reference
Bridge Keep [1918; Bridge House]	28NW2 St Julien	C 24 a 5.5
Bridge Lane	12SW1 Nieuport	M 24 d
Bridge Lane	51bSW2 Vis-en-Artois	O 16 c
Bridge Lane [road]	36aSE4 Locon	X 2 c, d
Bridge of Sighs [over stream]	36aNE3 Haverskerque	K 25 c 95.55
Bridge of Sighs Lock [St Venant]	36aSE1 St Venant	P 4 c 2.1
Bridge Street	28NW2 St Julien	B 6 c, 10 b - 12 a
Bridge Street / Boyau du Pont	62cNW1 Maricourt	A 22 d, 29 a
Bridge Street [1918]	57dNE2 & 57cNW1 Courcelles	F 25 d, 26 a
Bridge Wood [Riqueval]	62bNW3 Bellicourt	G 22 d
Bridgehead Defences	57dSE4 Ovillers	W 11 b, d, 12 c, 18 a, c
Bridges Camp	28NW1 Elverdinghe	A 5 c
Bridle Trench	36cSW3 Vimy	S 22 d, 23 c
Bridle Trench	51bSW2 Vis-en-Artois	O 8 c
Bridlington Strong Point [1918]	57dNE1 & 2 Fonquevillers	E 24 d
Bridoon Avenue / Alley	51bSW2 Vis-en-Artois	O 1 b
Bridoux Fort [late 1915]	36NW4 Bois Grenier	I 31 c 95.10
Bridoux Fort, & Salient	36NW4 Bois Grenier	I 31 c, d
Bridoux, Le [farm?]	36SW2 Radinghem	O 1 b
Brie [village]	62cSW2 Barleux	O 27 c, 33 a
Brief Houses	28NE2 Moorslede	F 23 a 25.25
Brielen [village]	28NW2 St Julien	B 29 a, c, d
Brielen Farm	28NW2 St Julien	B 28 b
Brielen Line [1918]	28NW2 St Julien / 4 Ypres	H 5 b, d, 6 c, 12 a
Brielle Farm, la [Doulieu]	36aNE2 Vieux Berquin	L 5 a
Brienne House	20SW4 Bixschoote	U 15 c 5.9
Brient Trench / Tranchée Brient	62bSW1 Gricourt	M 9 d, 10 c
Brierley Hill [1918]	51bNW1 Roclincourt	B 14 a, c, d
Brieuc Trench	66cNW4 Berthenicourt	H 12 d
Brig Corner	20SE2 Hooglede	Q 12 b 89.22
Brigade Farm	28NW3 Poperinghe	H 7 a 05.20
Brigand Lair [Sept 1915]	36cNW1 La Bassée	A 21 b
Brigand's Corner [road jct]	28NE2 Moorslede	E 27 b 95.45
Briggate	28NW2 St Julien	C 14 d, 20 c
Bright Alley	62dNE2 Méaulte	F 5 b
Brighton Alley	57cSW3 Longueval	S 24 c, d
Brighton Farm	20SE2 Hooglede	Q 21 d 7.9
Brimstone Trench	57cSW2 Villers-au-Flos	N 23 a, d
Brimstone Trench	57dSE4 Ovillers	R 33 c
Brindle Farm	20SE2 Hooglede	R 30 a 5.3
Briost [village]	62cSW4 St. Christ	U 2 c, d
Brique [light rly siding]	36cSW1 Lens	M 8 c, d
Brique Post, La	28NW2 St Julien	C 27 c 0.6
Brique, La [hamlet]	28NW2 St Julien	C 26 d
Briques Farm, Les	36cNW1 La Bassée	A 22 d 1.2 [Sept. 1915]
Briques Trench, les [Les Briques Farm]	36cNW1 La Bassée	A 28 a, b
Briquet Trench	70dNW2 Servais	C 25 c, d
Briqueterie	62cNW1 Maricourt	A 4 b
Briqueterie Trench	62cNW1 Maricourt	A 4 b
Brisbane [light rly]	28NW4 Ypres	H 24 a 7.6
Brisbane Dump	28NW4 Ypres	H 24 b 00.65
Brisbane Street	57cNE1 Quéant	D 12 c, d, 18 a, d
Brisbane Trench [1918]	57dSE [3 Bouzincourt] / 62dNE [1 Dernancourt]	W 25 d, 26 c, E 1 b, 2 a

Name	Map Sheet	Map Reference
Briseux Wood	57bSW1 Bantouzelle	N 9 c, d, 10 c, 15 a, b, 16 a
Briseux, Chateau	57bSW1 Bantouzelle	N 10 c 1.2
Brisoux Trench	57dNE3 & 4 Hébuterne	K 16 d, 22 b, 23 a
Brissein House	20SW4 Bixschoote	U 19 c 7.6
Brisson, Boyau	36cSW3 Vimy	S 8 d
Bristol [huts / camp, 1917-18]	28NW2 St Julien	B 30 a, b
Bristol Camp	28NW4 Ypres	H 35 d
Bristol Castle	28SW4 Ploegsteert	T 6 d
Bristol Fort	28NW2 St Julien	C 14 b 8.0
Bristol Sap	57dNE1 & 2 Fonquevillers	E 22 b, 23 a
Bristol, The	36SW1 Aubers	N 8 a
Britannia Castle	20SW2 Zwartegat	N 36 b
Britannia Farm	28NW2 St Julien	C 9 d 6.4
Britannia Trench	36cSW4 Rouvroy / 51bNW2 Oppy	T 30 c, B 6 a, b, d, 12 a
Britannia Work	51bNW3 Arras	G 17 a
Britling Cross [cross roads]	20SE2 Hooglede	R 16 a 25.50
Briton Street	62dNE2 Méaulte	F 2 c
Britt Trench	36cSW3 Vimy	S 23 c
Britten Farm	28NE4 Dadizeele	L 7 b 2.8
Brixen Graben	57dNE1 & 2 Fonquevillers	E 6 a, b, d,
Brizon, Boyau	36cSW3 Vimy	S 8 b
Broad Avenue	57dNE3 & 4 Hébuterne	K 3 c
Broad Street	36cSW3 Vimy	S 15 c, 21 a
Broad Street	57dNE1 & 2 Fonquevillers	K 3 c, d
Broad Street [road]	36cSW1 Lens	M 22 a, b
Broad Walk	51bNW3 Arras	G 29 b, d
Broadbridge Crater	36cSW3 Vimy	S 8 b
Broadmarsh Avenue	36cSW3 Vimy	S 21 d
Broadmarsh Crater	36cSW3 Vimy	S 21 d
Broadstreet [light rly locality S of Pilckem]	28NW2 St Julien	C 8 a
Broadway	28SW2 Wytschaete	N 24 c
Broadway	36cNW3 Loos	G 24 d
Broadway / Broad Way	57dSE1 & 2 Beaumont	Q 8 d, 9 c, d, 10 a, c
Broadwood Trench	36aSW [2 Molinghem]	O 11 d
Broccoli Trench	36aSW [2 Molinghem]	O 22 a, c, 28 a, d
Brock's Benefit	57dSE1 & 2 Beaumont	Q 28 d
Brockville Road	36cSW2 Harnes	N 24 b
Brocourt	62bSW4 Homblières	N 34 c, d
Broeken Road, De [road]	28SW3 Bailleul	S 30 b, T 25 a, b
Broeken, De [farm & place name]	28SW3 Bailleul	S 30 b
Broembeek Street / Broombeek Street	20SW4 Bixschoote	U 18 c
Broke Farm	27NE2 Proven	E 5 c 7.2
Broken Alley	57dNE3 & 4 Hébuterne	L 7 c, d
Broken Chimney [Pont-Rouge]	28SW4 Ploegsteert	U 29 d 95.82
Broken Mill	51bNW3 Arras	H 27 b 2.2
Broken Tree [E of Ploegsteert Wood]	28SW4 Ploegsteert	U 21 b 4.6
Broken Tree Farm [incorrect loc'n Nov 1915]	28SW4 Ploegsteert	U 15 b 4.3 (not U 15 b 3.1)
Broken Tree House [St Yvon]	28SW4 Ploegsteert	U 15 b 4.1
Bromdries [place name]	28NE4 Dadizeele	L 17 d
Bromdries [windmill]	28NE4 Dadizeele	L 17 d 40.55
Brome House [E of Poperinghe]	28NW3 Poperinghe	G 3 c 3.9
Bromilaw [Thiepval Wood]	57dSE1 & 2 Beaumont	R 25 a
Bromilow Support	57cSW4 Combles	U 14 a, b, c
Bromley Trench	51bSW2 Vis-en-Artois	O 15 b, 16 a

Name	Map Sheet	Map Reference
Brompton Road / Avenue	36SW1 Aubers	N 3 c, 9 a, b
Brompton Road [road & trench, Guillemont]	57cSW3 Longueval	S 24 d, T 19 b
Bronco Farm	36aNE4 Merville	K 18 b 15.10
Bronfay Camp [1916-17, near Bronfay Farm]	62dNE2 Méaulte	F 30 a
Bronfay Farm [Redoubt]	62dNE2 Méaulte	F 29 b
Bronfay Wood	62dNE2 Méaulte	F 30 a
Bronx Farm	62bNW2 Brancourt-le-Grand	C 7 a, c, d
Bronx Mill [windmill]	20SE2 Hooglede	R 10 d 63.01
Bronze, Tranchée du	70dSW4 [Vauxaillon]	U 12 c
Brooch Trench	36cNW1 La Bassée	B 1 b, c
Broodseinde [crossroads & hamlet]	28NE1 Zonnebeke	D 23 c 25.50
Broodseinde Cemetery [German, north]	28NE1 Zonnebeke	D 23 c 2.6
Broodseinde Cemetery [German, south]	28NE1 Zonnebeke	D 23 c 2.4
Broodseinde Crater [1914-15]	28NE1 Zonnebeke	D 29 c 6.7
Brook Lane	51bNW4 Fampoux	I 18 d
Brook Lane [road]	51bNE3 Noyelle-sous-Bellonne	J 19 a, c, d, 25 b, 26 a
Brook Street	36cSW1 Lens	M 6 a
Brook Street	57dSE1 & 2 Beaumont	Q 16 b
Brook Trench	36cSW3 Vimy	S 23 c
Brooklyn [1918; light rly locality]	28NW2 St Julien	C 6 c 3.4
Brooksby Lane [trench]	57cSE2 Gonnelieu	Q 6 d, 12 a, b
Brookwood Trench	36cNW3 Loos	G 12, H 7
Broome Communication Trench	62dSE [1 Hamel]	P 7 c, d, 13 a, b, 14 a
Brosse Alley	62cNW2 Bouchavesnes / 4 Péronne	H 4 a, c
Brosse Woods No. 1	62cNE4 Roisel	L 15 d, 21 a
Brosse Woods No. 2	62cNE4 Roisel	L 21 b, c, d, 22 a, c
Brouelle Trench	57cSE1 Bertincourt	P 21 a, c, d, 27 a, b, d
Brouette Alley / Boyau de la Brouette	66dNW1 Punchy / 2 Morchain	B 15 a, c, d, 16 c, 22 a, b, d
Brough Alley	51bNW2 Oppy	B 24 d, C 19 c
Broughs Redoubt [Sept 1915]	36cNW1 La Bassée	A 2 d
Broughty Ferry Street	57dSE4 Ovillers	X 19 d
Brousse Trench	62cNW2 Bouchavesnes	C 22 a, b, c
Brown Line	51bNW1 Roclincourt	A 30
Brown Line	51bNW3 Arras	G 12 c
Brown Line	51bNW3 Arras	H 33 a
Brown Line	51bSW1 Neuville Vitasse / 2 Vis-en-Artois	N 4
Brown Line	57cSW2 Villers-au-Flos / 4 Combles	N 35 a, d
Brown Line [1918]	36cSW3 Vimy	S 11 c, 17 a, b, d
Brown Quarry	62bSW3 St. Quentin	S 21 a
Brown Quarry (Manchester Hill Redoubt)	62bSW3 St Quentin	S 21 a, b
Brown Street	62dNE2 Méaulte	F 12 c
Brown Support	51bSW4 Bullecourt	N 36 d
Brown Switch	36cSW3 Vimy	S 4 b
Brown Trench	36cSW3 Vimy	S 4 b
Brown Trench	51bSW4 Bullecourt	N 36 c, d, O 31 c, T 6 a
Brown Trench	57cNE3 Hermies / 4 Marcoing	K 9 a, c
Brown Trench	57cSW3 Longueval	S 6 b, 12 b, d, T 7 c
Brown Trench	57dNE3 & 4 Hébuterne	K 29 c
Brown Trench / Drown Trench	36cSW4 Rouvroy / SE3 Esquerchin	U 23 b, 24 a, b, V 19 a
Browne Camp	28NW1 Elverdinghe	A 22 b, d, 23 c
Browne Camp, No.2	28NW1 Elverdinghe	A 22 d
Browne Camp, No.3	28NW1 Elverdinghe	A 22 b
Brownig Wood	66dNW1 Punchy	A 9 c, d, 15 a, b
Brownlow Farm	28SW3 Bailleul	T 20 c 2.0

Name	Map Sheet	Map Reference
Brownlow Lines & Bulford Camp [baths etc]	28SW3 Bailleul	T 26 a
Brownlow Lines [huts]	28SW3 Bailleul	T 20 c
Brown's Burrow	36cSW3 Vimy	S 14 b
Browns Farm	20SE2 Hooglede	R 33 b 30.75
Brubant [sic, farm]	28NW2 St Julien	B 29 d
Bruce Trench	28SW2 Wytschaete	O 14 d, 15 c
Bruet Wood	20SW4 Bixschoote	T 23 b, d
Brugerolles Alley	66cNW2 Itancourt	B 16 d
Bruges Trench	20SW3 Oostvleteren	T 3 a, b
Brugier Trench	66cSW4 La Fère	T 24 a, c
Brulle, le [Riencourt-lez-Cagnicourt]	51bSW4 Bullecourt	U 18 c
Brulooze [buildings]	28SW1 Kemmel	M 24 b 2.5
Brulooze [railway locality, 1917]	28SW1 Kemmel	N 19 c
Brulooze Cabaret, De	28SW1 Kemmel	M 24 a 7.3
Brulooze Line [railway, 1917]	28SW1 Kemmel	M 24 b, d, 30 b, d, 36 b, N 19 a
Brum Street	51bNW2 Oppy	B 18 d
Bruna Farm	36aNE3 Haverskerque	K 9 d 05.30
Brune Gaye [farm]	36NW2 Armentières	B 10 b 10.55
Brune Gaye Camp / Brue [sic] Gaye Camp	36NW2 Armentières	B 10 a
Brunehaut Trench	57cSW2 Villers-au-Flos / 4 Combles	O 34 a, b, d,
Brunehaut Trench	70dNW [3 Sinceny]	H 7 a, c, 13 a, c, 19 a, c
Brunehilde Trench	62cSW1 Dompierre	N 1 d, 2 c, 7 b, d
Brunemont [village]	51bSE2 Oisy-le-Verger	R 2
Brunemont, Marais de [marsh / lake]	51bSE2 Oisy-le-Verger	R 1 d, 2 c, 7 b, 8 a
Brunettes Corner [road junction]	20SE2 Hooglede	Q 24 a 7.1
Brunigardi Trench	57dSE1 & 2 Beaumont	Q 6 c, 12 a
Brünn Trench	62cNW4 Péronne	I 5 c, 11 a
Brunnen Weg	51bNW1 Roclincourt	B 26 b, 27 a
Bruno Copse	28NE4 Dadizeele	L 26 a, c
Brunswick Copse	28NE4 Dadizeele	K 18 d
Brunswick Line [light rly]	36cSW3 Vimy	T 19 d, 20 c, d
Brunswick Trench	57cSW4 Combles	U 8 b, 9 a
Brunswick Trench	66cSW2 Vendeuil	O 23 c, 29 a
Brunton Street [road, Ginchy to Quadrilateral]	57cSW3 Longueval	T 14 c, d
Brunwili, Tranchée	70dSW [4 Vauxaillon]	U 11 b
Brunz Trench	51bNW1 Roclincourt	A 3 a
Brush Copse	28NE2 Moorslede	F 5 b 3.4
Brushwood Drive	57dNE1 & 2 Fonquevillers	E 10 d, 11 c
Brute Trench	36cNW1 La Bassée	B 19 c, 25 a, b
Bruyere Copse	62bNW4 Ramicourt	I 34 a
Bruyère Ravine	62bNW3 Bellicourt	G 15 b, d, 16 a
Brykerie Farm	28SW2 Wytschaete	N 17 b 1.6
Bubble Cottage	28NW1 Elverdinghe	G 2 b 90.85
Bubbles Wood	28NW1 Elverdinghe	A 3 c
Bucaille Alley	66cNW1 Grugies	B 9 c
Buchan Farm	20SE2 Hooglede	Q 10 c 4.5
Buchan Street	57dSE4 Ovillers	X 26 c, d
Buchanan Avenue / Street [Thiepval Wd]	57dSE1 & 2 Beaumont	Q 30 d, R 25 c
Buchanan Farm	28NE4 Dadizeele	K 11 c 95.30
Buchanan Street [ride, Delville Wood]	57cSW3 Longueval	S 18 a
Buchanan's Cross	57cSW1 Gueudecourt	N 8 d
Buck Lane	62bNW1 Gouy	G 1 b, 2 a, c
Buck Trench	36cSW3 Vimy	S 23 b
Buck Trench [later Buck Reserve]	51bSW2 Vis-en-Artois	O 19 b, d

Name	Map Sheet	Map Reference
Bucket Trench	62dNE2 Méaulte	F 6 c
Bucket Trench	70dNW2 Servais	C 10 a, b, c
Buckingham Road / Buckingham Palace Rd	57dSE1 & 2 Beaumont	Q 17 c
Buckle Trench	51bSW2 Vis-en-Artois	O 8 b, d, 9 a
Buckley Crater	28NW4 & NE3 Zillebeke	I 12 a
Bucks Walk	36bSE4 Carency	X 28 b, 29 a
Buckshot Alley	66cNW2 Itancourt	C 23 c
Buckshot Ravine	62bNW3 Bellicourt	G 2 c, d, 3 c, d, 8 a, b, 9 a, b
Bucquet Mill	36cSW3 Vimy	S 3 a 57.90
Bucquoy Avenue [1918]	57dNE2 & 57cNW1 Courcelles	F 25 b, 26 c, d
Bucquoy Graben	57dNE1 & 2 Fonquevillers	F 25 a, b, 26 a, c, d
Bucquoy Trench	57dNE4 & 57cNW3 Achiet	L 2 d, 3 c, 9, 10, 11
Buda Pest Trench [1918]	62dSW [4 Cachy] / 62dSE [3 Marcelcave]	U 12 a, b, V 7 a, c
Buda Trench	62cNW4 Péronne	H 36 b, d, I 31 c
Buddha Farm	27SE4 Meteren	W 17 c 25.80
Buddon Street	57dSE4 Ovillers	X 19 d
Bude [locality SW of Cndn. Farm, 1917-18]	28NW2 St Julien	C 15 d
Budge Row	28NW4 & NE3 Zillebeke	I 34 a, c, d
Budget Copse	27SE2 Berthen	R 24 c
Bud's Farm	28NE2 Moorslede	L 1 b 65.20
Buff Lane	51bSW1 Neuville Vitasse	N 21 c, 27 a
Buffalo Trench [1918]	57dNE2 & 57cNW1 Courcelles	F 4 d, 5 c, 10 a, b
Buffalo Wood	62dSW [4 Cachy]	T 23 d, 29 b
Buffs [locality, S of Cross Rds Fm, 1917-18]	28NW2 St Julien	C 22 c
Buffs Bank Dugouts	28SW2 Wytschaete	O 5 a, b
Buffs Bank, & Tunnel	28SW2 Wytschaete	O 5 a, b
Buffs Road [road, St Julien]	28NW2 St Julien	C 21 c, d, 22 c
Bug Alley	66cNW1 Grugies	B 2 d, 3 a, c
Bug Farm	28SW2 Wytschaete	O 16 c
Bug Lane	57dNE2 & 57cNW1 Courcelles	F 11 d
Bug Trench	36cSW3 Vimy	S 22 c
Bug Trench	62cNW1 Maricourt	B 27 c, d
Bug Wood	28SW2 Wytschaete	O 16 a, c
Bugbags, Tranchée	70dSW4 [Vauxaillon]	O 31 c
Bugeaud Alley	62bSW1 Gricourt	M 23 c, 28 a, b
Bugeaud Trench	57dNE3 & 4 Hébuterne	K 16 d, 17 c
Bugginsville [E side of Ploegsteert Wood, 1915]	28SW4 Ploegsteert	U 21 b
Buggy Trench	36cSW3 Vimy	S 22 c
Bugle Farm	28NE4 Dadizeele	L 20 b 35.60
Bugle Trench	57cSW3 Longueval	S 11 c, d
Bugs Alley	36cSW1 Lens	N 1 c
Bugs Alley Spur	36cSW1 Lens	N 1 a
Buick Farm	28NE4 Dadizeele	K 6 c 35.45
Buisson Ridge	62cNE4 Roisel / 62bNW3 Bellicourt	L 23, 24, G 13, 14, 19
Buisson Trench	66cNW1 Grugies / 2 Itancourt	B 9 d, 10 c
Buisson-Gaulaine Farm [Gaulaine Ridge]	62bNW3 Bellicourt	G 20 a 9.5
Buissy Switch	51bSE / 57cNE	extensive
Bulford Camp	28SW3 Bailleul	T 20 c, 26 a
Bulford Trench	57dSE2 & 57cSW1 Le Sars	N 27 a, b
Bulgar Alley	62dNE2 Méaulte	F 5 d, 6 c, 11 b
Bulgar Lane	28NW4 & NE3 Zillebeke	J 31 b, 32 a
Bulgar Point	62dNE2 Méaulte	F 11 b
Bulgar Road [road]	28NE3 Gheluvelt	J 26 c, 32 b
Bulgar Support	62dNE2 Méaulte	F 11 a, b

Name	Map Sheet	Map Reference
Bulgar Trench	57cSW4 Combles	U 3 d, 10 a, c, d
Bulgar Trench	57dSE1 & 2 Beaumont	R 20 c, 25 b, 26 a
Bulgar Trench	62dNE2 Méaulte	F 11 b
Bulgar Wood	28NE3 Gheluvelt	J 25 d, 26 c, 31 b, 32 a, b
Bulgar, Maison [S of Langemarck]	28NW2 St Julien	C 5 c 85.80
Bulgaria Trench	66cSW4 La Fère	U 15 d, 21 b, c, d
Bulge, The [Sept 1915]	36cNW1 La Bassée	A 15 d
Bulge, The [W of Chapelle St Roch]	36cNW1 La Bassée	A 3 c
Bull Farm [Hooge, 1915]	28NW4 & NE3 Zillebeke	I 18 b
Bull Gunpits	57cNE4 Marcoing	K 10 b
Bull Post	62cNE4 Roisel	L 24 c 65.35
Bull Ring [trench]	28SW2 Wytschaete	N 30 c, 36 a
Bull Run Trench	57cSW1 Gueudecourt	N 26
Bull Trench	36cSW3 Vimy	T 1 d
Bull Trench	57cSW3 Longueval	T 9 b
Bull Trench [1918]	57dNE2 & 57cNW1 Courcelles	F 10 b, d, 11 a
Bulldog Reserve	57cSW4 Combles	U 13 c, d, 19 b
Bulldog Support	51bSW4 Bullecourt	U 22 b, 23 a, b
Bulldog Trench	51bSW4 Bullecourt	U 22 c, d, 23 c, d
Bulldog Trench [1918]	36aSW [2 Molinghem]	O 22 d
Bullecourt Avenue	51bSW4 Bullecourt / 57cNW2 Vaulx-Vraucourt	U 22 c, 28 a, C 3 a, b, c
Bullen Post	57cNE3 Hermies	K 8 b
Bullen Trench	57cSW3 Longueval	S 18 c, 24 a
Buller Trench [1918]	36aSW [2 Molinghem]	O 17 d, 18 a, c
Bullet Copse	62bNW3 Bellicourt	G 36 a
Bullet Cross Roads	57cSW4 Combles	U 20 a
Bullet Cross Roads, & Copse	62bNW3 Bellicourt	G 36 c
Bullet Trench	51bSW2 Vis-en-Artois	N 12 d, 18, b
Bullfinch Alley	51bSW2 Vis-en-Artois	O 25 d
Bullfinch Support	51bSW2 Vis-en-Artois	O 25 d
Bullfinch Trench	51bSW2 Vis-en-Artois	O 25 b, d, 26 a
Bullock Road	57dSE1 & 2 Beaumont	Q 29 c
Bullock Trench	36cSW3 Vimy	S 24 d
Bullrush Farm	20SE2 Hooglede	R 21 a 8.2
Bull's Road [road & trench]	57cSW3 Longueval	N 31 d, 32 c, d
Bulls Wood	62cNW3 Vaux	G 29 d, 30 c
Bullturn House [1918]	28SW1 Kemmel	M 17 a 4.9
Bullturn Post [1918]	28SW1 Kemmel	M 17 a 5.8
Bully Alley	51bNW1 Roclincourt / 2 Oppy	B 22 c
Bully Alley / Boyau de Bully	36bSE2 Boyeffles / 36cSW1 Lens	R 11 d, 17 b, 18 a, c, 24 a, M 19 b
Bully Craters [Angres]	36cSW1 Lens	M 20 c, 26 a
Bully Keep	36bNE4 Noeux-les-Mines	L 6 c central
Bully Switch	36bSE2 Boyeffles	R 14, 15, 16, 17, 23, 24
Bully Trench	57cSW4 Combles	U 20 b
Bully Trench [formerly Victoria Trench]	57cSW3 Longueval	T 15 c, 21 a
Bülow Farm [& pillbox]	28NW2 St Julien	C 6 a 8.8
Bülow Weg	57dNE3 & 4 Hébuterne	K 11 b, d, 12 c
Bülow Woods, No. 1	62cSW1 Dompierre	N 19 a
Bülow Woods, No. 2	62cSW1 Dompierre	N 19 b, d
Bülow Woods, No. 3	62cSW1 Dompierre	N 19 d
Bülow Woods, No. 4	62cSW1 Dompierre	N 20 c
Bülow Woods, No. 5 [??]	62cSW1 Dompierre	N 19 c, 25 a
Bulson Street	57dSE1 & 2 Beaumont	Q 23 b

Name	Map Sheet	Map Reference
Bumble Trench	36cSW3 Vimy	S 24 b, T 19 a, b
Bump Trench	36cSW3 Vimy	S 22 c
Bunbury Line [1918]	62dNE [3 Morlancourt]	J 12 a, c, d, 18 a, b, c
Bund Cotts	28NE3 Gheluvelt	J 33 c 4.5
Bund Support	62cNW1 Maricourt	A 1 d, 2 c
Bund Trench	62cNW1 Maricourt	A 7 b, 8 a
Bund, The [Zillebeke Lake dam dugouts]	28NW4 & NE3 Zillebeke	I 15d, 21 b
Bunder / Sander Sap [Sept 1915]	36cNW1 La Bassée	G 4 a
Bung Alley	57cSE2 Gonnelieu	Q 10 b, d, 11 c
Bung Trench	36cNW1 La Bassée	A 6 d, B 1 c
Bungle Farm	27NE2 Proven	E 5 d 70.65
Bunhill Row	51bSW4 Bullecourt	U 26 c
Bunhill Row [Bunter Avenue in 1914]	28SW4 Ploegsteert	U 20 a, c
Bunhill Row Breastwork	28SW4 Ploegsteert	U 14 c
Bunhill Row, & Reserve [both 1918]	51bSW4 Bullecourt	U 25 a, b, d
Bunhill Trench [1918]	51bSW4 Bullecourt	T 24 d, 30 b, d, U 25 c, d
Bunker, The [British strongpoint]	62dNE2 Méaulte	F 2 b 7.6
Bunny Alley [Mametz]	62dNE2 Méaulte	F 5 a, c
Bunny Hug Lane, & Trench	51bSW4 Bullecourt	U 23 c, 29 a
Bunny Hutch, & Shaft [Mine]	36cNW1 La Bassée	A 9 c 65.70
Bunny Trench [Mametz]	62dNE2 Méaulte	F 5 c
Bunny Wood	62dNE2 Méaulte	F 5 a
Bunting House	28SW3 Bailleul	T 1 a 4.3
Bunyan Farm	20SE2 Hooglede	R 6 c 15.90
Buquet Mill	36cSW3 Vimy	S 3 a 55.90
Burbach Trench	70dNW4 St Gobain	I 25 a, b, d
Burberry House	28NE4 Dadizeele	K 35 a 3.8
Burbure Alley	36cNW1 La Bassée	A 26 b, 27 a
Bureaux, Cité des [miners' cottages]	36cSW1 Lens	M 29 a
Burellier Trench	66cNW1 Grugies / 2 Itancourt	B 9 d, 10 c
Buret Avenue	57dSE1 & 2 Beaumont	Q 23 b
Burg [strongpoint]	57dNE1 & 2 Fonquevillers	E 24 d
Burg Support	51bSW4 Bullecourt	U 7 c, d
Burg Trench	51bSW4 Bullecourt	U 14 c, 20 a, b, 21 a, b, d
Burg Trench / Graben	57dNE1 & 2 Fonquevillers	E 24 a, c, d
Burge Farm	28NW1 Elverdinghe	A 13 d 05.10
Burgeon Trench	66cNW2 Itancourt	B 18 a
Burgermaster Farm Camp	28NW3 Poperinghe / 28NW4 Ypres	H 34 a
Burghead	57dSE1 & 2 Beaumont	Q 24 c
Burglars Rest	27NE2 Proven	F 27 c 6.0
Burgomaster Farm Camp	28NW3 Poperinghe / 28NW4 Ypres	H 34 a
Burgomaster Farm Camp [rly siding]	28NW3 Poperinghe / 28NW4 Ypres	H 27 d, 28 c, 34 a
Burke Farm	28NW1 Elverdinghe	A 12 d 5.7
Burke Line / Lane [1918]	62dNE [3 Morlancourt]	K 7 a, c, 13 a, c
Burkes [light rly siding]	36cSW3 Vimy	S 12 a
Burlington Arcade	36SW1 Aubers	N 7 b, 8 a, c
Burlington Arcade [tunnel, Railway Wood]	28NW4 & NE3 Zillebeke	I 11 b
Burlington Avenue	36SW1 Aubers	N 8 c
Burn Work	57dSE2 Beaumont	Q 4 d, 5 c
Burnaby Support	57cSW4 Combles	T 4 b
Burnaby Trench	57cSW2 Villers-au-Flos / 4 Combles	N 34 d, T 4 b
Burnham House	28NE4 Dadizeele	K 23 c 95.30
Burnie Communication Trench [1918]	62dSE [1 Hamel]	P 2 c, 8 a, b
Burning Bing	36cSW1 Lens	M 21 a

Name	Map Sheet	Map Reference
Burnley [light rly locality, 1917-18]	28NW2 St Julien	C 20 c 4.9
Burnley Alley	57cSE1 Bertincourt / 2 Gonnelieu	Q 3 a, b, 4 a
Burns Camp	28NW3 Poperinghe	G 12 c, d
Burns Farm	28NW3 Poperinghe	G 12 d 5.2
Burns House	20SE3 Westroosebeke	V 26 d 5.5
Burnt Copse	66dNW3 Hattencourt	G 34 c, d
Burnt Farm	28NW1 Elverdinghe	B 7 a 7.6
Burnt Farm	28NW2 St Julien	C 20 c 2.2
Burnt Farm	28SW4 Ploegsteert	T 5 b 3.9
Burnt Farm	36NW2 Armentières	C 17 c 85.95
Burnt Farm Street	51cSE2 Beaumetz	R 32 a, b, d
Burnt House	57dSE1 & 2 Beaumont	Q 24 a
Burnt House [near Maison Brulée Avenue]	20SW3 Oostvleteren	T 9 b 8.8
Burnt Island	57dSE4 Ovillers	X 13 c, 19 a
Burnt Mill	62bSW4 Homblières	T 4 d
Burnt Out Farm	28SW4 Ploegsteert	U 28 a 20.25
Burnt Out Farm	36NW2 & NE1 Houplines	C 9 d
Burnt Trench	51bNW1 Roclincourt	A 15 b
Burrel Road	57dSE1 & 2 Beaumont	Q 23 b
Burrow Trench	57dNE3 & 4 Hébuterne	K 34 d
Burr's Mill	51bSE4 Marquion	X 22 b 7.3
Burton [lt rly locality SW of L'marck 1917-18]	20SW4 Bixschoote	U 28 a, b
Burton Lane	57cSE2 Gonnelieu	Q 5 c
Bury [light rly siding, Vimy]	36cSW3 Vimy	S 24 c
Bury Avenue	57dSE4 Ovillers	W 6 a, b, X 1 a
Bury Post	28NW4 & NE3 Zillebeke	I 29 b 2.3
Bury Street / Boyau Bury	62cNW1 Maricourt	A 17 c
Bus [village]	57cSW2 Villers-au-Flos	O 24 a, b, c, d, 30 a
Bus Farm [Lindenhoek, March 1915]	28SW3 Bailleul	T 3 b 5.9
Bus Farm [Lind'hoek, Kemmel Defences, 1918]	28SW3 Bailleul	N 33 d 3.1
Bus House [St Eloi]	28SW2 Wytschaete	O 2 a 4.6
Bus Trench	36cSW3 Vimy	S 24 d
Bush Alley	57dNE4 [Hébuterne / Achiet]	L 31 d
Bush Trench	51bSW4 Bullecourt	N 36 a, O 31 c, U 1 a, b
Bush Trench [1918]	57dNE2 & 57cNW1 Courcelles	F 27 b, d, 28 a
Bush Valley	62bSW4 Homblières	T 11 d, 12 a, b, 17 a, b
Bushy [lt rly locality W of Canal 1917-18]	28NW2 St Julien	B 12 c
Busigny [village]	57bSE [3 Busigny]	V 10, 11, 16, 17
Busigny, Bois de	57bSE [3 Busigny]	V 23, 24
Busk Farm	28SW3 Bailleul	S 12 d 7.3
Busnes - Steenbecque Line [1918]	36aNE3 Haverskerque	J 1, 7, 13, 14, 20, 26, 32
Busnes - Steenbecque Line [1918]	36aSE1 St Venant	P 2, 8, 14, 20, 26, 32
Busnes [village]	36aSE1 St Venant	P 25 d, 26 b, c, d, 31 b, 32 a
Bussang Alley	66cNW4 Berthenicourt	H 12 b
Busschemeerschen [locality]	28SW4 Ploegsteert	T 18 c
Busseboom [railway sidings]	28NW3 Poperinghe	G 21 b
Busseboom [village]	28NW3 Poperinghe	G 16 c, 22 a
Busso Trench [Bussu]	62cNW4 Péronne	I 18 b
Bussu [village]	62cNW4 Péronne / 62cNE3 Buire	I 18 b, d, J 13 a, c
Bussu Wood	62cNW4 Péronne / 62cNE3 Buire	I 12 b, d, J 7 a, c
Bussus [farm]	62cSW1 Dompierre	M 12 c
Bussus Copse	62cSW1 Dompierre	M 10 b, d
Bussy, Poste de / du [Tambour craters]	62dNE2 Méaulte	F 3 c
Buster Trench	36cSW3 Vimy	S 24 d, T 19 a, b, c, d

Name	Map Sheet	Map Reference
Buster Trench	57dNE3 & 4 Hébuterne	K 34 d
Busty / Dusty Trench [1918]	57dNE2 & 57cNW1 Courcelles	F 22 b
Busy Wood	28NE1 Zonnebeke	D 23 b, 24 a, b
Butcher's Shop	36NW2 Armentières	C 10 c
Buterne Avenue	36NW2 Armentières	C 27 d, 28 c
Buterne, Ferme de la	36NW2 Armentières	C 28 c 65.15
Butlers Corner [road junction]	20SE2 Hooglede	Q 18 a 1.9
Butlers Cross	57cSE2 Gonnelieu	Q 3 b 2.2
Butlers Dump	57cSE2 Gonnelieu	Q 3 b 3.1
Butlers House	28SW4 Ploegsteert	U 19 d 05.90
Butlers Road	28SW4 Ploegsteert	U 19 c, d
Butlers Road [road]	57cSE2 Gonnelieu	Q 3 b, d
Buts Street	36SW3 Richebourg	S 10 a, c
Butt 7 [tr/breastwk, NW of Turco Fm, 1916]	28NW2 St Julien	C 20 b 2.9
Butt 8 [tr/breastwk, NW of Turco Farm, 1916]	28NW2 St Julien	C 20 b 0.9
Butt 9 [tr/breastwk, NW of Turco Farm, 1916]	28NW2 St Julien	C 20 a 8.9
Butt Lane [road]	36aSE4 Locon	X 8 a, c
Butt Post	62cNE2 Epéhy	F 24 c
Butt Trench	36cSW3 Vimy	S 24 d
Butt Wood	51bSE3 Cagnicourt	V 7 c
Butte [Polygone de Zonnebeke]	28NE3 Gheluvelt	J 10 a
Butte Alley [Warlencourt]	57dSE2 & 57cSW1 Le Sars	M 17 a
Butte de Warlencourt	57dSE2 & 57cSW1 Le Sars	M 17 a
Butte Trench [Warlencourt]	57dSE2 & 57cSW1 Le Sars	M 17 a, b
Butte, Boyau de la	36cSW3 Vimy	S 8 b
Butte, Tranchée de la [Allied front line 2/16]	36cSW3 Vimy	S 8 b
Butter Lane [road, la Pierre-au-Beure]	36aSE1 St Venant	Q 21 a, b, 22 a
Butter Trench	36cNW1 La Bassée	B 2 a, b, d, 3 c
Butter Trench	36cSW3 Vimy	T 19 a, b
Butter Trench	57dNE3 & 4 Hébuterne	K 34 d
Butterfly Farm	28SW1 Kemmel	M 19 a 65.90
Butterfly Walk / Butterly Street [?]	36cSW1 Lens	M 14 d
Butterfly Walk [Tas de Bois, Boyau de]	36cSW1 Lens	M 14 d
Butterworth Trench	57dSE4 Ovillers	X 6 c
Buttes de Rouy, les [trenches]	70dNW [3 Sinceny]	H 1 d, 2 a, b, c, 7 a, b, c
Button Trench	36cNW1 La Bassée	A 5 a, b
Buxton [light rly locality & huts, 1917-18]	28NW2 St Julien	C 20 b 1.3
Buxton Farm	28NW1 Elverdinghe	A 5 b 1.1
Buzfuz Avenue [1918]	57dSW [3 Talmas]	S 17 c, 23 a, b, d
Buzz Trench	36cSW3 Vimy	T 19 a
Buzzard Trench	51bSW2 Vis-en-Artois	N 24 a, b, c, d
Buzzer Alley	57cSW1 Gueudecourt	N 28 a
Buzzer Avenue	57cSW2 Villers-au-Flos	N 28 a
Bydand Avenue	28NW4 & NE3 Zillebeke	I 24 b
Byker Alley	51bSW2 Vis-en-Artois	O 25 b, 26 a
Byrne's Boulevard	36NW2 Armentières	C 28 c, d, I 4 b
Byron Farm	20SE2 Hooglede	Q 11 a 8.8
Byron Farm	28SW2 Wytschaete	N 18 a 3.4
Bystander Trench [Bouleaux Wood]	57cSW3 Longueval	T 21 b, d
C 1 [Hohenzollern Rdt]	36cNW3 Loos	G 4 d, 5 c
C 1 [trench 1915, E of Wulverghem]	28SW4 Ploegsteert	T 6 d, U 1 a
C 2 [Hohenzollern Rdt]	36cNW1 La Bassée / 3 Loos	G 4 b, d
C 2 [trench 1915, E of Wulverghem]	28SW4 Ploegsteert	T 6 b
C 3 [CT; Hohenzollern Redoubt]	36cNW1 La Bassée / 3 Loos	G 4 b, d

Name	Map Sheet	Map Reference
C 3 [trench 1915, NE of Wulverghem]	28SW4 Ploegsteert	T 6 b
C 4 [CT; Hohenzollern Redoubt]	36cNW1 La Bassée / 3 Loos	G 4 b, d
C 4 [trench 1915, NE of Wulverghem]	28SW4 Ploegsteert	N 36 d
C 6 [late-1915, Hooge Chateau]	28NW4 & NE3 Zillebeke	I 12 c 85.00
C 6 R[eserve] [late-1915, W of Hooge]	28NW4 & NE3 Zillebeke	I 18 a 80.75
C 6 S[upport] [late-1915, Hooge Chateau]	28NW4 & NE3 Zillebeke	I 18 a 8.8
C 7 [mid-1915, NW of Hooge]	28NW4 & NE3 Zillebeke	I 12 c 5.1
C 7 R[eserve] [late-1915, S of Y Wood]	28NW4 & NE3 Zillebeke	I 12 c 15.00
C 7 S[upport] [late-1915, NW of Hooge]	28NW4 & NE3 Zillebeke	I 18 a 70.85
C Camp / Camp C	28NW1 Elverdinghe	G 6 c 0.6
C Line [1918]	27SE3 Borre	extensive
C Line [1918]	36aNE1 Morbecque / 3 Haverskerque	D 6, 12, 17, 18, 22, 23, 27, 28, J 3
C Lines [NW of Neuve Chapelle 1914-15]	36SW1 Aubers	M 34 b
C Sap	28NW4 & NE3 Zillebeke	I 30 a
C Sap [Blackburn Alley]	57cSE2 Gonnelieu	Q 4 a
C Sap [Givenchy]	36cNW1 La Bassée	A 9 d
C Sector [4/15, N of R Douve]	28SW2 Wytschaete / 4 Ploegsteert	N 36, T 6, U 1
C Siding [railway, Ouderdom]	28NW3 Poperinghe	G 30 a, c, 36 a
C Street	57dSE1 & 2 Beaumont	Q 10 c, d
C Work	51bNW3 Arras	G 11 b
C.E. Spur [light rly, E of Canal 1917-18]	28NW2 St Julien	C 1 c 7.0
C.P.R. Trench [Canadian Pacific Rly]	36cSW3 Vimy	T 26 d, 27 c, d
C.T. 113	28SW4 Ploegsteert	U 21 d, 22 c
Cab Alley	51bNW4 Fampoux	I 1 d
Cabal Trench	66cNW1 Grugies	B 8 c
Cabaret Copse	62bNW1 Gouy	A 29 d 9.7
Cabaret Road / Avenue	36bSE4 Carency / 36cSW3 Vimy	X 17,18,21,22,23,25,26,27, S13,14
Cabaret Road [Messines - La Basse Ville road]	28SW4 Ploegsteert	U 17 a
Cabaret Rouge [Souchez]	36cSW3 Vimy	S 13 d
Cabaret Sector [trenches, 1918]	62dSW [2 Villers-Bretonneux]	N 23, 29, 34, 35
Cabaret Trench [Souchez]	36cSW3 Vimy	S 13 d
Cabaret Wood Farm	62bNW1 Gouy	A 29 c 8.7
Cabbage Cotts	28NE1 Zonnebeke	D 20 b 15.80
Cabbage Farm	20SE2 Hooglede	R 10 a 4.2
Cabbage Patch, & Redoubt	36cNW1 La Bassée	A 15 d
Cabbage Street	57dSE4 Ovillers	R 31 c
Cabbage Tree [Havrincourt]	57cNE3 Hermies	K 32 d 9.8
Cabbage Trench	36cSW3 Vimy	S 3 a
Cabbage Trench	51bNW2 Oppy	C 15 c, 21 a
Cabbage Trench	51bNW4 Fampoux	I 20 a
Cabbage Trench	70dNW2 Servais	C 25 b, d
Caber Trench	57dNE3 & 4 Hébuterne	K 23 a, c
Cabin Copse	28NE4 Dadizeele	L 35 b
Cabin Hill	28SW2 Wytschaete	O 27 c 92.02
Cabin Trench	36cSW1 Lens	M 28 a, b, c
Cabin Trench	51bNW4 Fampoux	I 15 b, d
Cable Avenue	51bNW4 Fampoux	H 5 d, 10 b, d, 11 a, b, 16 b, d
Cable Camp [1917-18]	28NW2 St Julien	C 7 a, b
Cable Copse	28NE4 Dadizeele	L 6 c
Cable Junction	28NW4 & NE3 Zillebeke	J 14 a 8.5
Cable Trench	36cSW1 Lens	M 33 b
Cable Trench	51bSW2 Vis-en-Artois	O 30 a
Cable Trench, Support, & Lane	28NW2 St Julien	C 7 a
Cabor Trench	57dNE3 & 4 Hébuterne	K 22 c

Name	Map Sheet	Map Reference
Cabri Copse	66dNW1 Punchy	B 9 a
Cacahuettes Alley / Boyau des Cacahuettes	62cSW3 & 4 Marchélepot	T 4 b, d
Cachy [village]	62dSW [4 Cachy]	U 2 d, 8 a, b
Cachy Salient Trench [1918]	62dSW [4 Cachy]	U 7 d, 8 b, c, d
Cachy Switch [1918]	62dSW [4 Cachy]	U 3 b, c, d, 7 d, 8 a, b, d, 9 a, 13 a
Cachy Switch [Cachy- Villers-Bretonneux]	62dSW [4 Cachy]	O 34, 35, U 3, 4, 8, 9, 13
Cachy Trench [1918]	62dSW [4 Cachy]	U 3 b, c, d, 4 a
Cackle Copse	28NE4 Dadizeele	K 22 c
Cactus Avenue	28NW2 St Julien	C 1 d, 7 b
Cactus Trench, Res, Point, Jct	28NW2 St Julien	C 7 b, c
Cadastral Farm	28NE2 Moorslede	F 21 c 3.6
Cadbury's Communication Trench	36SW3 Richebourg	S 15 a, c, d, 16 c
Caddie Tr, Supp, Res, Point, Lane, Ave	28NW2 St Julien	C 7 d, 8 a, c
Caddie Trench Camp	28NW2 St Julien	C 7 d, 8 c
Caddy Lane [S of Flers]	57cSW3 Longueval	S 6 d
Caddy Trench	36cSW1 Lens / 3 Vimy	M 33 d, 34 a
Caddy Trench	51bNW2 Oppy	C 1 c, 7 a
Cadet Trench	36cSW1 Lens	M 33 a
Cadger Trench	36cSW1 Lens	M 36 a
Cadic Trench	36cSW3 Vimy	M 33 d, 34 c
Cadiz Corner [road jct]	27SE2 Berthen	Q 11 c 1.9
Cadiz Trench / Reserve	51bNW4 Fampoux	H 12 d, 18 b
Cadmium Corner [road jct]	27SE2 Berthen	Q 4 c 7.8
Cadorna Trench	51bNW2 Oppy	B 18 d, 24 b, C 19 a
Caen Trench	66cSW2 Vendeuil	O 1 a, b
Caesar Support, Reserve & Lane	28NW2 St Julien	C 14 a
Caesar's Avenue	28NW2 St Julien	C 8 a
Caesar's Nose [Boesinghe]	28NW2 St Julien	C 13 b
Caestre Depot Railhead / Refilling Point	27SE3 Borre	Q 31, 32, W 1, 2
Cafard Cross Roads	20SE3 Westroosebeke	V 4 c 5.7
Café Belge	28NW4 Ypres	H 30 a 10.35
Café Belge [Vijverhoek]	28NW4 & NE3 Zillebeke	H 29 b
Café Belge Camp	28NW4 Ypres	H 29 b
Café Belge, Au [Estaminet, Ploegsteert]	28SW4 Ploegsteert	U 25 c 90.35
Café Farm	28NW4 Ypres	H 24 c 1.1
Café Trench	51bNW4 Fampoux	I 15 c, d
Cage Trench	57cNE3 Hermies	K 26 a
Cages Trench	36cSW3 Vimy	M 33 d
Cagnicourt Mill (Site of)	51bSE3 Cagnicourt	V 9 b 45.70
Caid Trench / Tranchée du Caid	62cSW3 & 4 Marchélepot	N 34 d, 35 c, T 4 b
Caillet Trench	66cNW1 Grugies	A 11 c, 17 a
Caillou, The [cross roads]	36NW2 Armentières	B 4 b 80.55
Cailloux Keep / North & South Keeps	36SW3 Richebourg	S 19 d, 20 c; S 26 a
Cain Alley [1918]	62dSE [4 Harbonnières]	X 27 d, 28 c, d, 29 c, d, 30 c
Cain Trench	66cNW4 Berthenicourt	I 31 d
Cairn Copse	27NE4 Abeele	L 19 d, 20 c
Cairo Alley	51bNW2 Oppy	C 19 c
Cairo Communication Trench [1918]	62dNE [3 Morlancourt]	K 19 c, d
Cairo Cut	51bNW2 Oppy	C 19 c 4.5
Cairo House	20SW4 Bixschoote	U 12 b 15.35
Cairo Junction [light rly]	36bNE3 [Bruay]	K 32 b
Caithness Trenches	57dSE4 Ovillers	W 6 a, c
Cake Lane	28NW2 St Julien	C 14 a
Cake Trench [Abschnitt D]	28NW2 St Julien	C 14 a

Name	Map Sheet	Map Reference
Cake Trench [Beaumont Hamel]	57dSE1 & 2 Beaumont	Q 5 b, c, d
Cake Trench, Support & Walk	28NW2 St Julien	C 14 a
Calabar Trench	51bNW4 Fampoux	I 7 c, 13 a
Calabash Trench, Ave, Lane & Walk	28NW2 St Julien	C 14 b
Calais Cabaret	28SW4 Ploegsteert	T 22 d 15.75
Calcutta Trench	51bNW2 Oppy	C 3 c
Calcutta Trench [1918]	57dNE2 & 57cNW1 Courcelles	F 16 b, 17 a
Caldron Trench	36cSW1 Lens	M 28 c, d
Caldron Trench	51bNW4 Fampoux	I 7 a, b, c
Caledonia Drive, & Avenue	28NW2 St Julien	C 9 c
Caledonia Tr, Sup, Res, Lane, New	28NW2 St Julien	C 14 b, 15 a
Caledonian Road	36cNW1 La Bassée	A 8 b, d, 9 a, c
Caledonian Trench / Avenue	51bNW4 Fampoux	H 6 c, d, 11 c
Caledonie Alley	62cSW1 Dompierre / 2 Barleux	N 14, 15, 21, 22 a, c, 28 a
Calendar Tr, Supp, Reserve, Lane, Ave	28NW2 St Julien	C 15 b, c
Calendar Trench	62bSW3 St Quentin / 66cNW1 Grugies	T 26 c, B 2 a, b
Calf Alley	57cSW3 Longueval	T 2 d, 3 a, c, 8 a, b
Calf Copse [Kalve]	20SE3 Westroosebeke	W 20 d
Calf Lane [road]	36aSE4 Locon	X 13 a, b, d
Calf Reserve	51bNW4 Fampoux	H 12 b, d
Calf Trench	36cSW1 Lens	M 18 d
Calf Trench	51bNW2 Oppy	C 9 a, c
Calf Trench, Support, Res, Ave, Row	28NW2 St Julien	C 16 c, d, 22 a
Calf Way	36cNW3 Loos	G 36 a
Calgary [light rly locality, 1917-18]	28NW4 Ypres	I 28 d
Calgary Avenue East	28SW4 Ploegsteert	U 1 c, d, 7 a
Calgary Avenue West	28SW4 Ploegsteert	T 6 c, d
Calgary Grange	28NE1 Zonnebeke	D 9 a 8.4
Calgary Road [road]	36cSW1 Lens / 3 Vimy / 4 Rouvroy	N 33 b, 34 a, c, d
Caliban Trench, Support, Reserve, Row	28NW2 St Julien	C 22 b
Calibration Range [light rly, Ablain St Nazaire]	36bSE4 Carency	X 2 c, d, 8 a, b
Calico Trench	36cSW1 Lens	M 36 b
Calico Trench	51bNW4 Fampoux	I 7 d, 13 b
California Drive [track, 1917-18]	28NW2 St Julien	C 17 a, c
California Tr, Supp, Res, Drive, Ave, Ln	28NW2 St Julien	C 17 c, 22 b, 23 a
California Trench	51bNW4 Fampoux	H 28 a, b, 34 a
Caliper Trench	36cSW1 Lens	N 8 c
Caliph Trench	36cSW3 Vimy	M 33 d, S 3 a, b
Call Trench, Reserve, & Row	28NW2 St Julien	C 23 c
Callaghans Corner [road junction]	20SE2 Hooglede	Q 23 b 95.42
Callanquin Trench [1918]	28SW1 Kemmel	N 9 d, 10 c
Callewaert Farm	20SE2 Hooglede	R 13 c 1.8
Calling Card Wood	51bSE3 Cagnicourt	V 13 a
Callis Trench	62cNW4 Péronne	H 24 a, b
Callous Trench	36cSW1 Lens	M 30 d, 36 b
Calm Trench	36cSW3 Vimy	S 2 d, 3 a, c
Calm Trench	57cSW4 Combles	T 5 c
Calmon Trench	62cSW2 Barleux	N 34 c, d
Calomel [pillbox / dugout / locality 1917-18]	28NE3 Gheluvelt	J 2 c 27.60
Calonne Alley [Calonne, Boyau de]	36cSW1 Lens	M 8 b, d, 9 c, d
Calonne Keep	36cSW1 Lens	M 9 a, c
Calonne North Trench [Calonne Nord]	36cSW1 Lens	M 7 b, 8 a, c, 14 a
Calonne South Trench [Calonne Sud, Boyau de]	36cSW1 Lens	M 8 c, 14 a
Calot Alley [1918]	66eNW [4 Morisel]	H 10 a

Name	Map Sheet	Map Reference
Calvaire Trench	66cNW1 Grugies	B 21 d, 27 b
Calvary Trench	36cSW1 Lens	M 29 c, d, 33 b, 34 a, b, 35 a
Calve Trench	36cSW3 Vimy	S 3 a, c
Calverley Copse	57dNE1 [Fonquevillers]	F 16 d
Calvert [Culvert] Farm [Nov 1914]	36NW4 Bois Grenier	I 25 c 3.3 [1915]
Calypso Alley	62cSW4 St. Christ	T 18 b, U 13 a, b, 14 a, b
Calypso Trench	62cNW2 Bouchavesnes	C 20 d, 21 c, 26 b
Cam Trench	51bNW3 Arras / 4 Fampoux	G 6, 12, H 7, 8, 16, 18, I 13
Cam Valley	51bNW4 Fampoux	H 15 b, c, d
Camblain Junction [light rly]	36bSE3 [Mingoval]	W 21 a
Cambrai [locality, Van Heule Farm]	28NW2 St Julien	C 24 c, d
Cambrai Tr, Supp, Res, Lane, Ave, Drive	28NW2 St Julien	C 23 c, d, 29 a
Cambrelin Trench	20SW2 Zwartegat	O 27 c, d
Cambrian Trench	51bNW4 Fampoux	I 7 d
Cambridge Avenue	36NW2 Armentières	C 17 c, 22 a, b
Cambridge Camp	28SW1 Kemmel	N 20 b 8.9
Cambridge Copse	62cNW1 Maricourt	A 15 a
Cambridge Road [road]	28NW4 & NE3 Zillebeke	I 5 c
Cambridge Siding [light rly, 1918]	28SW1 Kemmel	N 1 b 2.2
Cambridge Terrace	36cNW1 La Bassée	A 9 c, d, 15 b
Cambridge Trench	28NW4 & NE3 Zillebeke	I 5 c, 11 b
Cambrie [farm]	66cNW2 Itancourt	C 9 a
Cambrin [village]	36cNW1 La Bassée	A 14 b, d
Cambrin Alley [Sept 1915]	36cNW1 La Bassée	A 19 d, 20 c, 26 a
Cambrin Support Point	36cNW1 La Bassée	A 20 d
Cambrin Supporting Point [Sept 1915]	36cNW1 La Bassée	A 20 c, d
Cambrinus Alley	66cSW2 Vendeuil / 4 La Fère	O 34 a, b, c
Camden Road [Sept 1915]	36cNW1 La Bassée	A 8 b
Camden Street [1918]	62dNE [3 Morlancourt]	K 13 c
Camel Avenue	51bNW4 Fampoux	H 11 c, d, 16 b, 17 a, b, 18 a, b, I 13 a
Camel Cross Roads	51bNW4 Fampoux	H 17 a 80.95
Camel Lane	57cSW4 Combles	U 14 a, b
Camel Trench	51bNW4 Fampoux	H 11 d
Camel Trench, & Support [both 1918]	51bSW3 Boisleux	S 21 b, d, 22 a
Camel Trench, Supp, Res, Ave, Dr, Lane	28NW2 St Julien	C 29 a, b, 30 a
Camel Valley	62bSW3 St. Quentin	S 17 d, 18 a, c
Camelia Farm	20SW4 Bixschoote	U 13 b 4.6
Camelia Farm Cemetery	20SW4 Bixschoote	U 13 b 5.7
Cameo Trench	36cSW1 Lens	M 33 b, 34 a
Camera Farm	20SE4 Roulers	X 26 b
Cameron Alley	36cNW3 Loos	G 30, 31, 36, H 31
Cameron Covert	28NE3 Gheluvelt	J 16 a, b
Cameron Crater	36cNW3 Loos	G 31 c
Cameron House	20SE3 Westroosebeke	V 21 a 3.6
Cameron House	28NE3 Gheluvelt	J 16 a 2.8
Cameron Lane	36cNW3 Loos	G 4 d, 10 a, b
Cameron Road [road, 1917-18]	28NE1 Zonnebeke	D 25 d
Cameron Trench [later Post Trench]	57cSW3 Longueval / 57dSE4 Ovillers	S 1 b, d, X 6 a
Cameronian Street	57dNE1 & 2 Fonquevillers	E 22 b
Cameroon Tr, Supp, Res, Drive, Ave	28NW2 St Julien	C 29 d, 30 c
Cameroon Work	66cNW1 Grugies	B 2 a
Camouflage Copse	57cNW2 Vaulx-Vraucourt	B 16 b
Camouflaged Mound	36cSW4 Rouvroy	U 25 b 5.3
Camouflaged Mound	36cSW4 Rouvroy	U 25 b 6.3

Name	Map Sheet	Map Reference
Camoufle [trench]	66cNW2 Itancourt	C 26 c
Camouflé Alley	62bSW1 Gricourt	M 5 a
Camouflé/e / Camouflee [Trench]	66cNW2 Itancourt	C 25 d, 26 c, I 2 a
Camp 11	28NW3 Poperinghe	G 36 d
Camp C / C Camp	28NW1 Elverdinghe	G 6 b
Camp Trench	51bNW2 Oppy	C 1 a
Camp Trench	51bNW4 Fampoux	I 19 c
Camp Trench	57cNW3 Bapaume / SW1 Gueudecourt	G 34 b, M 3 d, 4 c, d
Campagne Drave [?] [farm]	27SE1 St Sylvestre	P 25 c 80.65
Campbell Avenue [trench & road]	57dSE4 Ovillers	Q 36 c, d
Campbell Street [Delville Wood]	57cSW3 Longueval	S 18 a, b
Campbell Trench	51bNW1 Roclincourt	A 16 a
Campbell's Cut	36cNW3 Loos	G 11 b
Campenet Trench	66cNW1 Grugies	B 8 c
Camperdown	57dSW [2 Raincheval]	O 26 a
Camphor Tr, Supp, Res, Ave, Lane	28NW2 St Julien	C 16 b, c, d
Campine Trench	20SW3 Oostvleteren	T 3 b, d
Campion Trench	57dNE3 & 4 Hébuterne	K 23 c, 28 b, 29 a
Can Farm	28NW2 St Julien	C 18 a
Can Pond	28NW2 St Julien	C 18 a
Can Trench	51bNW4 Fampoux	I 9 c, 15 a
Can Trench [1918]	28NW2 St Julien	C 17 a
Canada	51aSW3 Eswars	S 21 b 3.8
Canada [huts]	27NE2 Proven	F 15 c, d
Canada [locality]	27NE2 Proven	F 15 c
Canada Camp	28NW1 Elverdinghe	A 12 c 5.2
Canada Camp / Canada Corner Camp	28SW1 Kemmel	M 17 c
Canada Corner [near Hyde Park Corner]	28SW1 Kemmel	M 17 c 45.55
Canada Dump	36cSW3 Vimy	T 20 b 3.7
Canada Farm	28NW1 Elverdinghe	A 18 a 2.7
Canada Road [road]	36cSW1 Lens / 2 Harnes	N 21 a,b,d, 22 c,d, 28 b, 29 a,b, 30 a,b
Canada Street, Trench, & Tunnel	28NW4 & NE3 Zillebeke	I 30 a
Canada Trench	28NW2 St Julien	C 14 d, 15 a
Canada Trench	36cSW3 Vimy / 4 Rouvroy	T 20 b, 21 a, c, d, 22 c, d, 28 a
Canada Trench [CT, St Eloi Craters, 1916]	28SW2 Wytschaete	O 2 c, d
Canadian Avenue	28NW2 St Julien	C 15 d, 16 c
Canadian Dug Outs	28NW2 St Julien	C 14 d, 15 c
Canadian Farm [Cambrin]	36cNW1 La Bassée	A 13 b 95.67
Canadian Farm [previously Moated Grange]	28NW2 St Julien	C 15 d 8.5
Canadian Junction [trench]	28NW2 St Julien	C 15 d
Canadian Lane	28NW2 St Julien	C 15 b, d
Canadian Northern [railway]	36cSW4 Rouvroy	T 6 d, U 1 c, d, 7 b, 8 a, b, 9 a, b
Canadian Orchard	36SW3 Richebourg	S 28 a
Canadian Pacific [light rly / tr tramway, 1916]	28SW4 Ploegsteert	U 19 b, 20 a, b, 21 a
Canadian Pacific [railway]	36cSW2 Harnes	N 28, 29, 30, O 25
Canadian Reserve	28NW2 St Julien	C 15 b, 16 a, c
Canadian Siding [light rly, 1917-18]	28NW4 Ypres	H 5 c, d
Canadian Support	28NW2 St Julien	C 15 d, 16 c, 22 a
Canadian Trench	28NW2 St Julien	C 15 d, 22 a
Canal Alley	36cNW1 La Bassée	A 23 a, b
Canal Battery	5SW1 Zeebrugge	M 17 b
Canal Bridgehead Line [Béthune]	36bNE2 Beuvry	F 1, 2, 3, 9, 10, 11, 17, 18
Canal Copse	57cNE3 Hermies	K 26 b

Name	Map Sheet	Map Reference
Canal Dock [Béthune]	36bNE2 Beuvry	E 12 a, b
Canal Dock Locality [Béthune]	36bNE2 Beuvry	E 6 a, c, d, F 1 d
Canal du Nord Line	51bNE, SE, 57cNE	extensive
Canal Dugouts [N of Canal]	28SW2 Wytschaete	O 5 b
Canal House [Het Sas]	20SW4 Bixschoote	T 29 b
Canal Lane [road]	36aSE4 Locon	W 24 b, d, X 19 a
Canal Maze	36cSW2 Harnes	N 12 d, 18 b, O 7 c
Canal Res[erve] Alley	36cNW1 La Bassée	A 4 c, d, 10 b, d
Canal Reserve	36cNW1 La Bassée	A 16 d, 17 a, c
Canal Reserve Camp	28NW3 Poperinghe	H 27 b, d, 28 a, c
Canal Road [road]	36cSW1 Lens / 2 Harnes	N 15 a, b, 16 a
Canal Support [SE of Moeuvres]	57cNE1 Quéant	E 21 c, 27 a, c
Canal Switch	36aSE1 St Venant / 3 Gonnehem	P 36, Q 31, 32, 33, W 3
Canal Switch [1918]	36aNE1 Morbecque	D 18 a, c, 24 a, c, 30 a, c
Canal Tr, Supp, Res, Ave, Drive	28NW2 St Julien	B 12 b, C 7 a
Canal Trench	36cNW1 La Bassée	A 16 a, c
Canal Trench	57cNE1 Quéant	D 21 c, 27 a, c
Canal Trench	57dSE2 Beaumont	R 14 a, b, c, d 20 b
Canal Trench	62cNW4 Péronne	I 13 c, 19 a
Canal Trench	66cSW4 La Fère	T 28 d, 29 c, d
Canal Turn	36cNW1 La Bassée	A 17 d
Canal Walk [track, canal bank north]	28NW4 Ypres / SW2 Wytschaete	I 33 d, 34 c, O 4 a
Canal Wood	51bSE2 Oisy-le-Verger	Q 34 d
Canal Wood	62cNW4 Péronne	H 30 d
Canal Wood	57cSE4 Villers-Guislain / 57bSW3 Honnecourt	X 18 c, 24 a, S 13 d, 19 b
Canal Wood Trenches	57cSE4 Villers-Guislain	X 24 a
Canard Woods	62cSW1 Dompierre	M 7 d, 8 a, c
Canard, Bois du	62cSW3 & 4 Marchélepot	T 10 b
Canards Trenches	20NW4 Dixmude	H 24 b, d
Canary Farm	20SE2 Hooglede	R 26 c 7.9
Canary Trench	36cSW1 Lens	M 36 b
Canary Trench [1918]	66eNW [2 Thennes]	C 3 c
Canberra Farm	28SW4 Ploegsteert	U 4 d 7.8
Can-Can Trench	36cSW3 Vimy	S 3 a, c
Cancel Trench	36cSW1 Lens	M 30 d, 36 b
Cancer Farm	28NW1 Elverdinghe	G 5 b 8.9
Cancer Trench, Avenue, Drive	28NW2 St Julien	C 1 d, 2 c
Candas Trench	70dNW4 St Gobain	H 36 b, d
Cande Trench [1918, Kitchener's Wood]	28NW2 St Julien	C 10 c, d, 16 b
Candia Trench	51bNW2 Oppy / 4 Fampoux	H 6 b, d, 12 b
Candid Pig Cross Roads	57dSW [2 Raincheval]	N 36 a
Candid Trench	36cSW1 Lens	M 36 b
Candle Avenue	28NW2 St Julien	C 2 d
Candle Support	28NW2 St Julien	C 2 d
Candle Trench	28NW2 St Julien	C 8 b
Candle Trench	36cSW1 Lens	M 36 b, N 31 a
Candle Trench	57dSE2 & 57cSW1 Le Sars	N 25 b
Candre Trench [1918]	62dSW [4 Cachy]	U 16 a, b, d
Candy Trench	51bNW2 Oppy	C 13 c
Candy Trench	51bNW4 Fampoux	I 14 b, d
Candy Trench	57dSE2 & 57cSW1 Le Sars	R 30 c, 36 a, M 31 b
Cane Post [1918]	28NW2 St Julien	C 9 a 7.4 / 7.7
Cane Trench	51bSW2 Vis-en-Artois	O 2 c

Name	Map Sheet	Map Reference
Cane Trench [1918]	28NW2 St Julien	C 9 a, b, d
Cane Trench, & Avenue	28NW2 St Julien	C 9 a
Canine Trench	36cSW1 Lens	M 36 b
Canione Trench	62cSW2 Barleux	N 35 c
Canis Farm	28NW1 Elverdinghe	A 30 d 9.5
Canister Lane, & Street [O 2 c]	51bSW2 Vis-en-Artois	O 1 d, 2 c
Canister Trench	28NW2 St Julien	C 9 d
Canister Trench	51bSW2 Vis-en-Artois	O 1 d
Canlers Farm Trench	66cSW4 La Fère	N 34 d, 35 c, T 5 a
Cannabis Support [N of Cheddar Villa]	28NW2 St Julien	C 17 c
Cannabis Trench [N of Cheddar Villa]	28NW2 St Julien	C 17 c
Cannes Farm	20SW4 Bixschoote	U 22 a 3.8
Cannibal Fork [road jct]	27NE2 Proven	F 23 d 3.5
Cannibal Trench	51bNW2 Oppy	C 13 c, 19 b
Cannock [lt rly locality SW of L'marck 1917-8]	28NW2 St Julien	C 4 a
Cannon Corner	28SW2 Wytschaete	O 35 a 4.6
Cannon Row [road; Lovie Chateau]	27NE2 Proven	F 16 d
Cannon Street	36cSW3 Vimy	S 21 b
Cannon Street	51bNW3 Arras	G 11 b, 12 a
Cannon Trench	28NW2 St Julien	C 10 c, d
Cannon Trench [Thiepval, 1918]	57dSE2 Beaumont	R 25 b
Cannongate Crater	57cSE4 Villers-Guislain	X 17 b
Canoe Trench [Kitcheners Wood]	28NW2 St Julien	C 10 d, 16 b, 17 a
Canoe Wood	62cNW4 Péronne	I 23 a, b
Canon Farm	28NW2 St Julien	C 1 c 6.4
Canon Inn	27NE2 Proven	F 22 b 40.25
Canon Lane	28NW2 St Julien	B 6 d, C 1 c
Canon Trench	28NW2 St Julien	B 6 d, C 1 c
Canopus Support	28NW2 St Julien	C 17 a, b
Canopus Trench	28NW2 St Julien	C 17 a, b
Canords Trenches	20NW4 Dixmude	H 24 b
Canrobert, Tranchée	70dSW [2 Coucy-le-Château]	N 16 d
Cantaing Support	57cNE4 Marcoing	L 3 a, c, d, 9 b, 10 a, c, 16 a
Cantaing Trench	57cNE4 Marcoing	L 3 a, c, d, 9 b, 10 a, c, 16 a
Cantal Trench	66cNW1 Grugies	B 20 c, 26 a, b
Canteen Farm Post	36NW4 Bois Grenier	H 17 d, 23 b
Canteen Post	51bNW2 Oppy	C 13 c 02.46
Canteen Trench	28NW2 St Julien	C 17 b, 18 a
Canteen Trench, & Alley	36cSW1 Lens	N 8 a, b
Canteleux [hamlet]	36cNW1 La Bassée	A 11 c
Canteleux Alley North	36cNW1 La Bassée	A 10 c, d
Canteleux Alley South	36cNW1 La Bassée	A 10 c, d, 11 c, 16 b, 17 a
Canteleux Trench	36cNW1 La Bassée	A 11 c, 17 a, b, d
Canterbury Avenue	62dNE2 Méaulte	F 9 d, 15 a, b
Canterbury Cut	28SW4 Ploegsteert	U 1 d 2.8
Cantharides Trench	62cNW1 Maricourt	B 25 b, d, H 1 b
Canto Corner [road jct]	27SE2 Berthen	R 19 a 45.17
Canton Junction [lt rly, N of Larch Wd,1917-18]	28NW4 Ypres	I 28 b, 29 a
Canton Trench	28SW2 Wytschaete	N 23 b, d
Cantonnier, Bois du	66dNW2 Morchain	C 28 b
Cantrainne Locality	36aSE3 Gonnehem	V 7 a, b, c, d
Canute Trench	36cSW3 Vimy	S 3 a, c
Canvas Hill [hill]	28NW2 St Julien	C 18 a
Canvas Trench	28NW2 St Julien	C 18 a

Name	Map Sheet	Map Reference
Canyon Trench	36cSW3 Vimy	S 3 a, c
Caouchouc / Caoutchouc, Boyau du	62cSW3 & 4 Marchélepot	T 10 b, d, 11 c
Caours [village]	57fNE	L 5, 6, 11, 12
Cap de Pont / Capdepont Alley / Boyau / Tr	36bSE2 Boyeffles / 36cSW1 Lens	R 23 d, 24, 30, M 25
Cap Pond	28NW2 St Julien	C 18 c
Cap Trench	51bNW2 Oppy	C 7 a
Cap Trench	51bNW4 Fampoux	I 19 a
Cap Trench	51bNW4 Fampoux	I 33 b
Cap Trench	57cSW3 Longueval	T 1 a, b, d, 2 c
Cape Avenue	57dNE1 & 2 Fonquevillers	E 22 a, c
Cape Blanco	36NW4 Bois Grenier	I 32 a
Cape Trench	51bNW2 Oppy	C 2 b, d, 8 b
Cape Wood	28NE3 Gheluvelt	J 33 d, 34 c
Capelle Farm	28NW1 Elverdinghe	B 2 c 5.1
Capelle Farm [near Kappellehoek]	20SE2 Hooglede	R 11 a 2.9
Caperat Wood	62cNW3 Vaux	G 24 d
Capilano Trench	36cSW3 Vimy	S 11 b, d, 12 c, 18 a, b
Capital Farm	28NE3 Gheluvelt	J 27 c 5.9
Capital Trench	28NW2 St Julien	C 18 a
Capitol, The	28NE1 Zonnebeke	D 13, 14
Capper Lines [huts]	28SW3 Bailleul	S 30 c
Capper Road [road]	36cSW1 Lens	M 29 a, b, c
Cappy [village]	62dNE [4 Bray-sur-Somme]	L 30 a
Cappy Landing Ground [German, 1918]	62cSW1 Dompierre	M 3 b, 4 a
Capri House	27NE4 Abeele	K 36 b 7.4
Capri House Camp	27NE4 Abeele	K 36 b, d, L 31 a, b, c
Capricorn Junction [light rly, nr Spree Farm]	28NW2 St Julien	C 18 d 05.40
Capricorn Trench, Support, & Keep	28NW2 St Julien	C 18 c, d
Capron Copse	62cNE2 Epéhy	E 17 a, b
Capron Copse Line	62cNE2 Epéhy	E 17 a, b, 18 a, b, F 13 a, c, d
Capstan Farm	28NE4 Dadizeele	L 25 a 6.9
Capstan Trench	51bNW4 Fampoux	I 14 b, 15 a
Captain Avenue	28NW2 St Julien	C 24 a
Captain Avenue [1918]	57dNE1 & 2 Fonquevillers	E 23 c, d
Captain Lamargue Alley	62cNW3 Vaux	H 3 d, 4 c
Captain Post	28SW2 Wytschaete	N 5 d 55.30
Captain Trench	28NW2 St Julien	C 24 b
Captain Trench	62bSW3 St Quentin	N 31 c
Car Alley	36cSW1 Lens	N 13 b
Car Lane	28NW2 St Julien	C 20 b
Cara Trench	51bNW4 Fampoux	I 14 d, 20 b
Carafe, Boyau de la	62cSW3 & 4 Marchélepot	T 6 c, 11 d, 12 a
Caramel Copse	62bSW2 Fonsommes	O 26 d
Caramel Trench	28NW2 St Julien	C 16 b
Caravan [light rly sidings, 1917-18]	28NW4 Ypres	I 15 b
Caravan Trench	51bNW4 Fampoux	I 20 b, 21 a, b
Carbine Lane	51bSW2 Vis-en-Artois	O 8 b
Carbine Trench	62cNE2 Epéhy	F 30 c
Carbon Trench	51bNW4 Fampoux	I 14 b
Carcaillot, Le [Carcaillot Farm]	62dNE2 Méaulte	E 18 a
Carcass Trench	36cSW3 Vimy	S 3 c
Card Copse	62dSE [3 Marcelcave]	V 3 a
Card Trench	36cSW3 Vimy	S 3 c
Card Trench	51bNW4 Fampoux	I 14 b

Name	Map Sheet	Map Reference
Card Trench	51bSW1 Neuville Vitasse	N 14 c, 20 a
Cardiff [light rly locality, 1917-18]	28NW4 Ypres	I 34 d
Cardiff Sap	36cNW3 Loos	G 18 b
Cardiff Street	57dSE1 & 2 Beaumont	Q 10 a
Cardiff Trench	57cSW3 Longueval	S 8 a, b
Cardigan Alley	36cSW1 Lens	N 8 b, d
Cardigan Trench	51bNW4 Fampoux	I 7 a, c, 13 a, c
Cardinal Cottage	28NE2 Moorslede	F 13 d 42.20
Cardinal Wood	62cNW4 Péronne	I 23 a, b
Cardoen Camp	28NW1 Elverdinghe	A 18 a, b, d
Cardoen Farm	28NW1 Elverdinghe	A 18 b 1.8
Care Cross [cross roads]	36aNE4 Merville	K 30 b 20.25
Carency [village]	36bSE4 Carency	X 15 c, d
Carency Locality	36bSE4 Carency	X 14 b, 15 a
Carency Trench	57dNE3 & 4 Hébuterne	K 16 d
Carency Trench	70dNW4 St Gobain	H 16 a, c, d
Carency, Bois, de	36bSE4 Carency	X 17 a, b
Carentan Trench	66cSW2 Vendeuil	N 6 a, b, c, 12 a, c
Carew Farm	20SE2 Hooglede	R 19 d 8.6
Carew Trench	36cSW1 Lens / 3 Vimy	M 34 b, 35 a, c
Carey Trench	57cNE3 Hermies / 4 Marcoing	K 9 d, 10 c
Carey Trench	57dNE3 & 4 Hébuterne	K 10 c
Carey Trench [1918]	57dSE [3 Bouzincourt]	W 20 b, c, d, 26 a
Careys Farm	20SE2 Hooglede	R 23 b 2.9
Carfax Trench	36cSW1 Lens	N 8 a, b
Cargo Trench	36cSW3 Vimy	S 3 c
Cariboo Line [light rly]	36cSW3 Vimy	T 13 a, b, c, 14 a, b
Cariboo Trench, Lane, Avenue	28NW2 St Julien	B 6 d, C 1 a, b
Caribou [or Bedford Fm] Brit Mil Cemetery	28NW1 Elverdinghe	A 12 c 55.25
Caribou Camp	28NW1 Elverdinghe	A 11 d, 12 c
Caribou Hill	62bSW2 Fonsommes	O 12 a, b
Carieul Château	36bSE4 & 36cSW3 Givenchy	X 12 c
Carisbah, Boyau de [Casbah?]	62cSW3 & 4 Marchélepot	T 4 a, b
Carlin, Moulin	28SW4 Ploegsteert	U 17 d or 18 c
Carlisle Farm	28NE3 Gheluvelt	J 15 b 2.3
Carlisle Farm	28SW3 Bailleul	T 27 c 6.3
Carlisle Lines [huts]	28SW3 Bailleul	T 27 c
Carlisle Street	57dSE1 & 2 Beaumont	Q 16 a, b
Carlo Farm	28NW1 Elverdinghe	A 17 c 8.4
Carlsbad Trench [1918]	66eNW [2 Thennes]	C 13 b, 14 a
Carlsruhe Trench [1918]	66eNW [2 Thennes]	C 15 d, 21 b
Carlton Trench	57cSW3 Longueval	S 15 c, d, 16 a, b
Carlyle Street [road]	36cSW1 Lens	M 23 c, 29 a
Carmen Copse	62cSW4 St Christ	U 21 d
Carmen Trench	36cSW3 Vimy	S 3 c
Carnalea	57dSE1 & 2 Beaumont	Q 17 c
Carnation [1918; light rly locality]	28NW2 St Julien	C 24 a 5.2
Carnation Trench	28NW2 St Julien	C 23 b, d, 24 a
Carnia Trench / Tranchée de Carnie [?]	66cNW2 Itancourt	B 5 a
Carnival Copse	62cNE3 Buire	J 25 d, 26 c
Carnival Valley	62bSW2 Fonsommes	O 22 a, b, c, d, 28 a
Carnot Farm	20SW4 Bixschoote	T 6 d 15.05
Carnoustie Street	57dSE4 Ovillers	X 19 d, 20 c, 25 b
Carnoy [village]	62cNW1 Maricourt	A 13 b, d, 14 a

Name	Map Sheet	Map Reference
Carolina Trench	51bNW3 Arras / 4 Fampoux	H 16 a, c, 22 a
Caroline I & II Posts	36NW4 Bois Grenier	I 15 d & 16 c
Caroline Wood	62dSE [2 Proyart]	Q 22 d, 23 c, 28 b, 29 a
Carolus, Tranchée	62cSW1 & 2 Belloy	O 7 a
Caron [Tranchée, 1915] / St Andrews Avenue	57dSE4 Ovillers	X 13 c, 19 a
Caron Trench	57cSE1 Bertincourt	P 13, 14, 20, 21
Carot Trench	36cSW1 Lens	M 12 b
Carp Avenue	51bNW1 Roclincourt	A 21 b, 22 a
Carp Trench	36cSW1 Lens	N 8 b
Carp Trench	51bNW2 Oppy	C 25 b
Carp Trench [1918]	57dNE3 & 4 Hébuterne	K 12 b, L 1 c
Carpathian Trench	70dNW4 St Gobain	H 24 d, I 19 c, d
Carpe Trench	62cSW3 Vermandovillers	T 14 d, 15 c
Carpentier Cottage	28NE2 Moorslede	E 24 a 2.3
Carpet Trench	28NW2 St Julien	C 17 d
Carpet Trench	36cSW3 Vimy	S 3 c, 9 a
Carpet Trench	51bNW4 Fampoux	I 15 b, d
Carpeza Copse	62cNE4 Roisel	L 14 d, 15 c
Carr House	28NE4 Dadizeele	K 4 c 15.15
Carr Trench	57dSE1 & 2 Beaumont	R 5 d
Carré Farm	28SW2 Wytschaete	N 12 a 6.5
Carré Wood / Bois Carré	36bSE4 & 36cSW3 Givenchy	S 22 a
Carré, Bois	51bNW1 Roclincourt	B 7 c
Carré, Bois	66eNE4 Beaufort	L 27 b
Carré, Bois [Thélus]	36cSW3 Vimy	T 7 c
Carrée Farm	20SW4 Bixschoote	T 4 d 75.35
Carrée Farm	28NW2 St Julien	B 6 a 2.7
Carrefour de Londres [cross roads]	20SW4 Bixschoote	U 8 b 65.40
Carrefour Gambetta [cross roads]	20SW4 Bixschoote	U 9 b 80.02
Carrefour Richelieu [cross rds, Houthulst Forest]	20SW4 Bixschoote	O 35 c, d
Carrie Post	36NW4 Bois Grenier	I 21 a, b
Carrieg, Tranchée des Anc.	70dSW [2 Coucy-le-Château]	O 31 a
Carrière Trench	62cNW1 Maricourt / 3 Vaux	H 3 a, c
Carrière Trench	70dNW4 St Gobain	H 23 d, 24 c
Carrière, Tranchée de la	66cNW2 Itancourt	C 19 c, d, 20 c
Carrion Trench	36cSW3 Vimy	S 3 b, c, d, 9 a
Carrot Crater	36cSW1 Lens	M 6 b
Carrot House	27NE2 Proven	E 17 c 55.40
Carrot Trench	51bNW4 Fampoux	I 14 d, 20 b
Carry Trench	62cNW1 Maricourt	B 25 b, 26 a
Carso / Corso Farm	27NE4 Abeele	L 31 d 1.4
Carso Trench / Tranchée du Carso	62cSW1 & 2 Belloy	N 18 b, d, O 13 c
Carson Farm	28NE2 Moorslede	F 23 b 25.20
Cart Trench	62bNW3 Bellicourt	G 7 d, 13 b
Carte Keep [1918]	28NW2 St Julien	C 28 d, 29 c
Cartenoy Woods	62bSW1 Gricourt	M 26 b
Carter Copse	62cSW4 St. Christ	U 7 b
Carter Trench	36cSW3 Vimy	M 34 d
Carters Farm	36NW2 & NE1 Houplines	C 10 d 1.3
Carter's Post	36SW1 Aubers	M 2 c 8.2
Carthage [light rly locality & huts, 1917-18]	28NW4 Ypres	I 19 d
Cartier Trench	62cSW3 Vermandovillers	T 14 b
Cartmael Street	57dSE4 Ovillers	X 7 b
Carton House	28NE4 Dadizeele	K 30 a 3.7

Name	Map Sheet	Map Reference
Cartridge [light rly locality]	28NW4 Ypres	I 19 a
Cartridge Trench	51bNW4 Fampoux	I 32 b
Cartwright Trench	36cSW1 Lens	N 8 a
Caruso Avenue [1918]	57dNE2 [Courcelles]	F 10 d
Carve Trench	51bNW4 Fampoux	I 14 a, c
Carvers Cross Roads	28NE2 Moorslede	L 6 a 78.90
Carvin Road [road]	36cSW1 Lens / 2 Harnes	N 9, 10, 11, 15
Casa Blanca [house]	36aNE3 Haverskerque	J 25 c 5.9
Casa Duss [house]	36aNE3 Haverskerque	K 13 a 4.3
Casa Niente [1918]	28SW1 Kemmel	N 25 c 35.95
Casa Pin [formerly Foresters Home]	36aNE3 Haverskerque	J 8 d 72.01
Casablanca Farm	28NW1 Elverdinghe	B 9 b 99.90
Casan, le [farm]	36aSE4 Locon	X 8 b 3.6
Casbah Trench / Tranchée de la Casbah	62cSW3 & 4 Marchélepot	N 34 d, T 4 b
Case Alley	51bSW2 Vis-en-Artois	O 2 d
Casement Alley	62bSW4 Homblières	T 29 d
Casement Trench	62cNW1 Maricourt	A 10 a, b
Cash Alley	51bNW4 Fampoux	I 7 b, d, 8 c
Cash Farm	27NE2 Proven	E 11 b 1.1
Cash Trench	51bNW4 Fampoux	I 7 d
Cash Trench [Thiepval, 1918]	57dSE2 Beaumont	R 25 b
Casino Point	62cNW1 Maricourt	A 7 b
Casino Trench	36cSW3 Vimy	M 34 d, 35 c
Casket Trench	36cSW3 Vimy	M 35 c, d, S 4 b, 5 a
Caspar Trench [1918]	62dSW [4 Cachy]	U 27 d, 28 a, c
Casque House	20SW4 Bixschoote	T 23 b 5.4
Casque, Boyau du [Helmet]	62cSW3 & 4 Marchélepot	T 11 a, b, d
Cassel Farm	28NE4 Dadizeele	K 22 a 2.3
Cassell Street	57dNE1 & 2 Fonquevillers	E 10 d
Cassiopée Trench	62cSW3 Vermandovillers	T 4 c, 10 a
Cassis Alley	62cSW3 Vermandovillers	T 19 a
Cassis Alley / Boyau du Cassis	62cSW3 & 4 Marchélepot	T 19 a
Castagnettes, Boyau des	62cSW3 & 4 Marchélepot	N 34 d, 35 c, T 5 a, b, d, 11 b
Castaway Corner [road jct]	28NE2 Moorslede	E 4 c 75.50
Castel [village]	66eNW [2 Thennes]	B 24 central
Castel Halt [railway]	66eNW [2 Thennes]	C 19 a 2.3
Castelnau Alley [1918]	62dSE [4 Harbonnières]	X 17 b, 18 a
Castelnau, Tranchée [Essex Trench]	36cSW1 Lens	M 14 b, 15 a
Castle Avenue / Boyau du Château	62cNW1 Maricourt	A 16 a, c
Castle Bar Sap	62cNE2 Epéhy	F 12 a
Castle Lane	51bNW4 Fampoux	H 10 d, 16 a, b
Castle Lines [huts]	36NW2 Armentières	B 5 a, b
Castle Martin [Ploegsteert Wood, 1914-15]	28SW4 Ploegsteert	U 21 d 25.50
Castle O.P [1917-18]	36cSW1 Lens	M 22 b 3.7
Castle Street [Hooge 1915]	28NW4 & NE3 Zillebeke	I 16 b, 17 a, b
Castle, The	62cNW1 Maricourt	A 8 a
Castor Oil Alley	66cNW2 Itancourt	C 9, 13, 14, 15, 19
Castor Post	57dSE1 & 2 Beaumont	Q 23 b, d
Castor Trench	57cSW2 Villers-au-Flos	N 29 c
Castor Trench	66dNW1 Punchy	B 7 d, 8 a, c, 13 a, b, c
Castres [village]	66cNW1 Grugies	A 22 a
Castres Alley	66cNW1 Grugies	A 11, 16, 17, 18
Casualty Corner	57dSE4 Ovillers	X 16 a 40.55
Cat / Cot, The	51bSW1 Neuville Vitasse	N 27 b

Name	Map Sheet	Map Reference
Cat Alley	51bNW1 Roclincourt	B 1 d
Cat Alley [1918]	62dNE [3 Morlancourt]	K 7 c
Cat Copse	57dSW [4 Toutencourt]	T 28 c
Cat Copse	62cNE1 Liéramont	D 15 c, d
Cat Fort [1918]	57dNE3 & 4 Hébuterne	K 8 b
Cat Lane	51bSW1 Neuville Vitasse	N 13 b
Cat Mill	57dNE3 & 4 Hébuterne	K 8 b
Cat Post	62cNE2 Epéhy	F 24 a
Cat Running [Ploegsteert Wood, 1914-15]	28SW4 Ploegsteert	U 21 b 25.40
Cat Support	57cSW4 Combles	U 1 a, c
Cat Trench	36cSW1 Lens	N 14 c
Cat Trench	51bNW2 Oppy	C 8 d
Cat Trench	51bNW4 Fampoux	I 9 c, d
Cat Trench	57cNE4 Marcoing	K 4 c
Cat Trench	57dSE2 & 57cSW1 Le Sars	M 21 b, d
Cat Trench [Tr / Russian Sap /commn. tunnel]	57dNE3 & 4 Hébuterne	K 34 d
Cat Tunnel	57dNE3 & 4 Hébuterne	K 35 c
Catacombs Trench	66cSW4 La Fère	U 9 d, 10 c, 15 b, d
Catacombs, The [Wallangara, Hill 63]	28SW4 Ploegsteert	T 18 d, U 13 c
Cataplasme Trench	62cSW4 St Christ	T 10 a, b
Catapult Road	57cSW1 Gueudecourt	N 8 a
Catapult Trench	36cSW1 Lens	N 1 d, 7 b
Catapult, The [road junction]	27SE1 St Sylvestre	P 19 d 35.30
Cateau / Le Cateau Avenue	57dNE3 & 4 Hébuterne	K 28 b, 29 a
Catelet Alley	70dNW4 St Gobain	H 22 d
Catelet Copse	57cSE4 Villers-Guislain	X 28 d
Catelet Trench	57cSE4 Villers-Guislain	X 29 a
Catelet Valley	57cSE4 Villers-Guislain	X 27 c, d, 28 c
Catelets, le [Honnecourt]	57bSW3 Honnecourt	S 2 a
Caterpillar Copse [S end of Thiepval Wd]	57dSE1 & 2 Beaumont	Q 30 d
Caterpillar Trench	57cSW3 Longueval	S 26 a
Caterpillar Valley	57dSE4 Ovillers / 57cSW3 Longueval	X 29, 30, S 19 to 23
Caterpillar Wood	57cSW3 Longueval	S 20 c, d, 26 b
Caterpillar, The	28NW4 & NE3 Zillebeke	I 35 a
Catfish Trench	36cSW3 Vimy	M 35 d
Catherine Post	28SW4 Ploegsteert	U 23 c 9.2
Catherine Post	36NW4 Bois Grenier	I 21 a
Catillon [village]	57bSE [2 Bazuel] / 57aSW [1]	R 24, M 19
Catinat Farm	20SW4 Bixschoote	U 9 a 20.52
Catkin Trench	36cSW3 Vimy	M 34 d
Catley Farm	28SW3 Bailleul	S 30 d 1.9
Cato Copse	27SE2 Berthen	R 16 d
Cato Corner [road jct]	27SE2 Berthen	R 16 c 40.65
Cats Post	36SW3 Richebourg	S 15 a
Cats Trench	36cSW3 Vimy	M 34 d
Catteau Farm	28SW2 Wytschaete	O 8 c
Catteuw Farm	28NW1 Elverdinghe	B 7 b 2.3
Caucas Farm	20SE2 Hooglede	Q 28 d 7.9
Caudescure [village]	36aNE1 Morbecque / 3 Haverskerque	K 3 d, 4 a, c
Caudescure Station [rly]	36aNE3 Haverskerque	K 14 a 5.7
Caudron Road [road]	36aSE4 Locon	W 6 c, d, 12 a
Caulaincourt [village]	62cSE [4 Attilly]	W 4, 5
Caullery [village]	57bSW2 Clary	O 8 d, 9 c, d, 15 a, b
Caulquis, les	66dNW4 Nesle	I 16 c

Name	Map Sheet	Map Reference
Caumont, Cité de [miners' cottages]	36cSW1 Lens / 36cSW3 Vimy	M 33 b, c, d, 34 c, S 3 a, b
Caurrieres Trench [1918]	62dSW [4 Cachy]	T 18 b, U 13 a
Causeway [road]	57cSW1 Gueudecourt	N 26 d, 32 b, 33 a, c, d
Causeway Lane	62cNE2 Epéhy	F 12 c
Causewayside St / Tr [Thiepval Wood]	57dSE1 & 2 Beaumont	Q 30 d
Caution Dug Out	62cNE4 Roisel	L 17 b 35.30
Caution Paddock	62cNE4 Roisel	L 17 b
Cavalier Subway	36cSW3 Vimy	S 21 c
Cavalier Trench	36cSW3 Vimy	S 21 c
Cavaliers Alley	70dNW4 St Gobain	H 22 c, d 28 a
Cavalla Alley	66cNW4 Berthenicourt	I 2 c
Cavalry Farm	28NW4 & NE3 Zillebeke	I 10 a 05.50
Cavalry Farm	51bSW2 Vis-en-Artois	O 14 a 5.4
Cavalry Road [road / plank road, 1917-18]	28NW4 Ypres	I 4 c, d, 10 a, b,
Cavalry Road Trench [1918]	28NW4 Ypres	I 10 b
Cavalry Support	57cSE4 Villers-Guislain	W 18 b, d, X 13 c, 19 a, c
Cavalry Trench	36cSW1 Lens	M 12 d, 18 b
Cavalry Trench	51bSW2 Vis-en-Artois	O 13 d, 14 a, c
Cavalry Trench	57cSE4 Villers-Guislain	W 18 b, X 13 c
Cavalry Trenches	28SW4 Ploegsteert	T 17 a
Cavan Trench	28NW2 St Julien	C 22 c, 28 a
Cave Copse	62dSE [3 Marcelcave]	V 8 b
Cave Trench	36cSW3 Vimy	M 35 d, 36 c
Cavender House	28NE4 Dadizeele	K 29 a 95.60
Caves, Ferme des [Redoubt]	51bNW1 Roclincourt	A 28 a
Cawdor Trench	51bNW4 Fampoux	H 18 b
Cawdor Trench	57dNE3 & 4 Hébuterne	K 23 c
Cawnpore [light rly loop, 1917-18]	28NE3 Gheluvelt	J 1 c
Cawnpur Work	51bNW4 Fampoux	H 12 d, 18 b
Caxton Row [buildings]	36aNE3 Haverskerque	J 3 c 7.5
Cayouse Copse	62bSW2 Fonsommes	O 26 a
Cayuga [light rly siding, Vimy]	36cSW3 Vimy	S 24 a, c
Cazin Trench	66cNW1 Grugies	B 2 d, 3 c
Cecil Avenue	51bNW1 Roclincourt	A 29 d
Cecil Reserve	36NW2 Armentières	C 4 b
Cecil Support	28SW4 Ploegsteert	U 28 d
Cecil Trench	36NW2 Armentières	C 4 a
Cecil Trench	51bNW1 Roclincourt	B 19 c
Cecil Trench, & Support	51bNW2 Oppy	C 19 c
Cecile Trench	20SW4 Bixschoote	T 30 a, c
Cecilie Ravine	66eNW [2 Thennes]	C 16 a, b, c
Cedar Copse	62cSW1 Dompierre	M 17 b
Cedar Farm	20SE2 Hooglede	Q 18 b 7.9
Cedar Street [road]	36aSE4 Locon	X 14 b, 15 a
Cedar Trench	36NW2 Armentières	C 4 a, c, d
Cedar Trench	51bSW1 Neuville Vitasse	M 12 c
Cedilla Trench, Support, Reserve	36NW2 Armentières	C 4 d, 10 b
Cedric Farm	27SE4 Meteren	W 12 d 8.9
Ceinture Trench	66dNW3 Hattencourt	H 14 b, d, 15 a, c
Celery Copse	36aNE2 Vieux Berquin	E 12 d, F 7 c
Celestial Trench	36NW2 Armentières	C 10 b
Célestins, les	62dNE [3 Morlancourt] / [4 Bray-sur-Somme]	K 27 d, 33 b
Celia Tr, Supp, Ave, Street, Lane, Row	36NW2 Armentières	C 11 c, d, 17 a, b

Name	Map Sheet	Map Reference
Celibate Farm	27NE2 Proven	L 5 a 2.9
Cell Tr, Supp, Res, Ave, St, Lane, Row	36NW2 Armentières	C 17 a, b, c, d
Cellar Farm Avenue [Cordonnerie Fm]	36SW1 Aubers / 2 Radinghem	N 3 d, 4 c, 10 a, b, c
Cellar Marsh Craters	36cNW3 Loos	G 12 d 5.7
Cellars, The [Hill 63]	28SW4 Ploegsteert	U 13 a 53.65
Celle Trench	62cNW1 Maricourt	B 28 c, d
Cellin Avenue	62cNE2 Epéhy	F 6 c, 11 b, 12 a
Cello Farm	28NE4 Dadizeele	L 27 b 6.7
Celt Tr, Sup, Res, Sw, Dr, Row, Av, Ln	36NW2 Armentières	C 17 d, 18 c, 23 b
Celtic [farm & pill box]	28NE1 Zonnebeke	D 29 a
Celtic Park [farm]	28SW3 Bailleul	S 12 c 5.9
Celtic Park [locality & huts]	28SW3 Bailleul	S 12 c
Celtic Wood	28NE1 Zonnebeke	D 30 c
Cemetery	28NE1 Zonnebeke	K 1 a
Cemetery [civilian, E of Champaubert Fm]	20SW4 Bixschoote	U 15 a
Cemetery [E of St Julien]	28NW2 St Julien	C 12 b 7.0
Cemetery [near Cemetery Farm]	20SW4 Bixschoote	U 7 c 4.6
Cemetery [Neuville St Vaast]	51bNW1 Roclincourt	A 9 b, 10 a [centre: A 9 b 99.70]
Cemetery [Thélus]	51bNW1 Roclincourt	A 6 c 95.10
Cemetery Alley	36cNW1 La Bassée	A 29 a, b
Cemetery Alley [S of Flesquieres]	57cNE4 Marcoing	K 23 b, d
Cemetery Ave, Cres, Drive	36NW2 Armentières	C 11 b, d, 12 c, d, 18 b
Cemetery Avenue	51bSW4 Bullecourt	U 10 d
Cemetery Circle [Le Transloy]	57cSW2 Villers-au-Flos	N 29 d, 30 c, 35 b, 36 a
Cemetery Farm [NE of Bixschoote, near Cmy]	20SW4 Bixschoote	U 7 c 25.40
Cemetery Post	36NW3 Fleurbaix	G 22 c
Cemetery Post [Bois Grenier]	36NW4 Bois Grenier	I 30 b
Cemetery Road [road, Villers-Guislain]	57cSE4 Gouzeaucourt	X 2 a, b, d, 3 c
Cemetery Road [road]	36aSE1 St Venant	P 22 c
Cemetery Salient	36NW4 Bois Grenier	I 9 b
Cemetery Spur [light rly, Vermelles]	36cNW3 Loos	G 13 b, 14 a, c
Cemetery Trench	20NW4 Dixmude	H 12 d, 18 b
Cemetery Trench	20SE3 Westroosebeke	V 25 c, d
Cemetery Trench	36cNW1 La Bassée	A 29 d
Cemetery Trench	36cSW3 Vimy	S 13 b, 14 a
Cemetery Trench	51bNW3 Arras	G 29 b
Cemetery Trench	62bSW3 St Quentin	S 24 a
Cemetery Trench	62dNE2 Méaulte	F 10 b, 11 a, b
Cemetery Trench [Vis-en-Artois]	51bSW2 Vis-en-Artois	O 16 c, d, 22 a
Cemetery Wood	51bSE2 Oisy-le-Verger	Q 36 a
Cendrillon Trench / Tranchée Cendrillon	62cSW2 Barleux	O 19 b, c, d
Censor Trench, Supp, Row, Dr, Ave	36NW2 Armentières	C 23 b, c, d, 24 a, c
Censor's Nose	36NW2 Armentières	C 23 c, d
Census Trench, Supp, Res, Drive, Alley	36NW2 Armentières	C 23, 24, 29, 30
Centaur Fork [road jct]	28NE2 Moorslede	E 29 d 2.9
Centaur Trench, Sup, Lane, Sw, Cres, Row	36NW2 Armentières	C 29 a, b, c, d
Centaure Trench	62cSW3 Vermandovillers	S 8 a, b
Centaures Quarry	66eNW [2 Thennes]	C 13 a
Central Avenue	36cSW3 Vimy	S 21 a, b
Central Avenue	36NW2 Armentières	C 29 c, d
Central Avenue	36NW4 Bois Grenier	I 9 b, 10 a, b
Central Avenue	57cNE1 Quéant	D 21 c, d, 27 a, b
Central Avenue	57dNE1 & 2 Fonquevillers	E 16 c, d
Central Avenue	57dNE3 & 4 Hébuterne	K 27 d, 28a, b, c, 29 a

Name	Map Sheet	Map Reference
Central Boyau	36cNW3 & 1 Loos	G 3 c, d, 4 c
Central Camp	27NE2 Proven	F 14 d 5.6
Central Keep [SE of Bart's]	36cNW3 Loos	G 3 d, 9 b
Central O.P. [1918-18]	36cSW3 Vimy	S 29 a 8.9
Central Trench [Trônes Wood]	57cSW3 Longueval	S 23 d, 29 b
Central Trench, Supp, Drive, Cres, Switch	36NW2 Armentières	C 29 c, d, 30 d, 30 c, d
Central, Boyau	36cSW3 Vimy	S 20 b, c, d, 26 a
Central, Boyau	62cNW3 Vaux	G 27, 28, 34
Centrale, Abri	51bNW1 Roclincourt	A 28 b
Centrale, Avenue	51bNW1 Roclincourt	A 28 a, b
Centre Alley	66cNW2 Itancourt	B 18 d
Centre Avenue / Boyau du Centre	62cNW1 Maricourt	A 16 a
Centre Cross Roads	20SE3 Westroosebeke	V 4 c 55.70
Centre CT	28NW4 & NE3 Zillebeke	I 34 a, b
Centre Farm	28SW2 Wytschaete	O 18 c 4.2
Centre Keep [Fleurbaix]	36NW3 Fleurbaix	H 21 d
Centre Trench	36cSW3 Vimy	T 7 c
Centre Trench	57cNE4 Marcoing	L 33 b, 34 a, c, d, 35 c
Centre Way	57cSW3 Longueval	R 34 d
Centre Way	57dSE2 Beaumont / 4 Ovillers	R 28-9, 34-5, X 4, 9, 10
Centre, Du [trench] [Itancourt]	66cNW2 Itancourt	B 18 d,C 13 c
Century Drive	36SW2 Radinghem	O 24 d
Century Trench	36NW2 Armentières	C 24 c, 30 a
Cereal Trench	36NW2 Armentières	C 30 a, c
Cerebere Trench	57cSE1 Bertincourt	P 25 c, 31 a, c
Ceremony Trench	36NW2 Armentières	I 6 a
Cerise Trench	36NW2 Armentières	C 18 c, d, 24 a, b
Cerise Wood	62bNW4 Ramicourt	I 31 b, c, d
Cérisier Alley	62cSW3 Vermandovillers	S 10 c, 15 b, 16 a
Cérisier, Bois du [Cherrypickers Copse]	62cSW3 & 4 Marchélepot	S 10 c, d
Cert Farm	27NE2 Proven	L 3 b 7.1
Certain Trench, & Avenue	36NW2 Armentières	C 5 b, d
Certified Trench, Support, Switch	36NW2 Armentières	C 5 d, 11 b, 12 a
César, Trenchée	70dSW2 [Coucy-le-Château]	O 7 a
Cesspool Trench	36NW2 Armentières	C 6 a, b, d
Cetorix [sic] Trench [Vercingetorix]	57dNE3 & 4 Hébuterne	K 22 c
Ceylon Avenue	51bNW4 Fampoux	I 19 b, 20 a
Ceylon Lane [trench]	36NW2 & NE1 Houplines	D 1 c
Ceylon Trench	51bSW4 Bullecourt	U 8 a, c
Ceylon Trench, Support, Lane	36NW2 Armentières	C 6 d, 12 b
Ceylon Wood	62dNE [4 Bray-sur-Somme]	L 12 a, c
Chabord, Boyau	62cSW1 Dompierre	M 9 d
Chad Alley	66cNW2 Itancourt	B 18 d
Chafer Copse	36aNE1 Morbecque	D 16 b, d
Chaff Crescent	36NW2 & NE1 Houplines	D 7 c, 13 a, c
Chaff Trench	36NW2 & NE1 Houplines	C 18 b, D 7 c, 13 a
Chaff Trench	51bNW2 Oppy	C 25 b
Chaffinch Lane	57cSE4 Villers-Guislain	X 29 d
Chagford Corner	20SE2 Hooglede	Q 36 a 6.5
Chagrin Trench, Avenue, Alley	36NW2 & NE1 Houplines	D 13 a, c
Chahut Trench / Tranchée du Chahut	62cSW4 St. Christ	N 35 c
Chain Avenue	36NW2 & NE1 Houplines	D 7 a, b
Chain Lane [trench]	36NW2 & NE1 Houplines	D 1 c
Chain Row	36NW2 & NE1 Houplines	D 7 a, b

Name	Map Sheet	Map Reference
Chain Trench	51bNW3 Arras	G 18 b
Chain Trench / Support	51bNW4 Fampoux	I 31 d
Chain Trench, & Redoubt	36NW2 & NE1 Houplines	C 12 b, D 7 a
Chair Trench, Support, Switch	36NW2 & NE1 Houplines	C 24 b, D 13 c, 19 a
Chalet Wood [Bois Rasé]	36cNW3 Loos	H 25 c
Chalk Alley	57dNE3 & 4 Hébuterne	K 35 b
Chalk Alley	66cSW4 La Fère	U 15 d, 16 c
Chalk Cut	57dSE2 & 57cSW1 Le Sars	R 30 c, 36 a
Chalk Dugouts	62cNW1 Maricourt	B 1 b 8.4 or 9.4
Chalk Farm	28SE1 Wervicq	P 1 d 0.1
Chalk Farm	51bNW3 Arras	G 11 a 2.7
Chalk Lane	57dSE2 & 57cSW1 Le Sars	N 25 b, d, 26 a
Chalk Mound	57dSE2 & 57cSW1 Le Sars	R 29 a
Chalk Palace Dugouts	57dSE2 Beaumont	R 13 a
Chalk Pit	36cNW3 Loos	H 25 a, c
Chalk Pit [Contalmaison]	57dSE4 Ovillers	X 10 c
Chalk Pit Alley	36cNW3 Loos	G 29 b, 30 a, d, H 25 c
Chalk Pit Post	36cNW3 Loos	H 25 central
Chalk Pit Wood	36cNW3 Loos	H 25 a, c
Chalk Reserve	51bNW4 Fampoux	H 6 d, 12 b
Chalk Road	51bSW4 Bullecourt	U 4 b
Chalk Street	36cSW3 Vimy	S 8 d
Chalk Support	57cSW1 Gueudecourt	M 15 a, b
Chalk Trench	51bNW2 Oppy	C 20 a, b, 21 a, b
Chalk Trench	51bNW4 Fampoux	I 13 c
Chalmers Walk	28NW4 & NE3 Zillebeke	I 24 b, d
Chaluiteau [?] Trench [1918]	66eNW [2 Thennes]	B 29 b, d
Chamberry Trench	66cNW4 Berthenicourt	I 25 b
Chambers Alley	51bNW2 Oppy	B 24 d, C 19 c
Chameau, Ouvrage du	62cSW3 & 4 Marchélepot	N 34 c, d, T 4 a, b
Chameleon Alley [1918]	62dSW [4 Cachy]	T 30 b, d, U 25 c
Chameleon Alley [1918]	66eNW [2 Thennes]	C 1 b, d
Chamfor [sic] Trench	36cSW1 Lens	M 36 a, b
Champ de Manoeuvre [Cambrai Aerodrome]	57bNW1 Cambrai	A 8 c, d, 14 a, b
Champ de Mars [old training ground, Béthune]	36bNE2 Beuvry	E 4 d, 10 b
Champ Pourri, Bois de	36cSW3 Vimy	S 23 b
Champagne Alley	66cNW2 Itancourt	B 29 d, 30 a, H 5 b
Champagne Alley [1918]	62dSE [4 Harbonnières]	X 15 a, b, 16 a, c, d, 17 c
Champagne Trench	51bNW2 Oppy	C 13 c, 19 a
Champagne Trench	62bSW1 Gricourt / 3 St Quentin	M 27 d, 33 b, d
Champaubert Farm	20SW4 Bixschoote	U 15 a 0.4
Champignons Copse	62bNW4 Ramicourt	I 8 d
Champion Trench [1918]	62dSW [4 Cachy]	U 4 d, 5 c
Champs Elysées	62bSW3 St Quentin	T 14 b
Champs Grenotte, Cité de	36cSW1 Lens	M 21 d, 22 a, c
Chancel Houses	28NE2 Moorslede	F 25 d 1.9
Chancery Lane	36cNW3 Loos	G 36 b, H 31 a
Chancery Lane	51cSE2 Beaumetz	R 22, 23, 27, 28
Chancery Lane [road]	36SW1 Aubers	M 12 a
Chandron Trench / Tranchée Chandron	36cSW3 Vimy	S 15 c, d
Chantecler [Hellfire Corner]	51bNW3 Arras	G 6 d 0.2
Chantecler Cemetery	51bNW3 Arras	H 1 c 6.5
Chantecler Trench	62cSW4 St. Christ	U 7 a, c, 13 a, b
Chantes Alley	62cSW4 St. Christ	T 29 a, b

Name	Map Sheet	Map Reference
Chanteur, Boyau du [Singer]	62cSW3 & 4 Marchélepot	T 4 d, 5 c, 11 a
Chanticler [sic] Switch [Jan 1918]	51bNW1 Roclincourt / 3 Arras	A 30 d, B 19 b, d, 25 a, b, G 6 b, d
Chanzy, Tranchée	70dSW [2 Coucy-le-Château]	N 36 a
Chaos Trench	36cSW3 Vimy	M 36 a, c
Chap Farm	27SE1 St Sylvestre	P 26 c 30.55
Chap Street	36cNW1 La Bassée	A 21 b
Chapeau de Gendarme [trench on cliff]	62cNW1 Maricourt	A 29 d
Chapeau Siding [light rly]	36bNE4 Noeux-les-Mines	L 24 a
Chapeau Trench [Chapeau de Gendarme]	62cNW1 Maricourt	A 29 b, d
Chapeau, P.C. [Chapeau de Gendarme]	62cNW1 Maricourt	A 29 d 08.80
Chapel [N of Berles-au-Bois]	51cSE3 & 4 Ransart	W 16 c 2.9
Chapel [north of Oppy]	51bNW2 Oppy	C 7 b 1.1
Chapel Alley	36cNW3 Loos	G 8, 9, 10, 11, 12
Chapel Alley	51bSW2 Vis-en-Artois	N 4 a, b, d
Chapel Alley	57cSE4 Villers-Guislain	X 7 a, c
Chapel Alley	62bSW3 St Quentin	S 24 b
Chapel Alley [Dec 1915]	36cNW3 Loos	G 10 d, 16 b
Chapel Camp	27NE4 Abeele	K 35 d
Chapel Crossing	57cSE4 Gouzeaucourt	X 7 c 1.4
Chapel Hill [S of Gouzeaucourt]	57cSE4 Villers-Guislain	W 12 c, 18 a, b
Chapel Keep	36cNW3 Loos	G 10 c, 16 a
Chapel Post [N. D. de Consolation, Ch'elle de]	36cNW3 Loos	G 10 c 6.1
Chapel Redoubt [Chapel Hill]	57cSE4 Villers-Guislain	W 18 a, b
Chapel Road [road]	36aSE2 Lestrem	R 27 d, 34 a
Chapel Street	36cNW1 La Bassée	A 21 b
Chapel Street [road]	57cSE4 Gouzeaucourt	X 7 b, c, d, 8 a, b
Chapel Trench	51bNW2 Oppy	C 7 a, b, d
Chapel Trench	51bNW4 Fampoux	I 20 b
Chapel, The	28NE1 Zonnebeke	J 1 b 1.0
Chapelle Boom [farm]	36aNE3 Haverskerque	K 8 b 58.85
Chapelle Duvelle [hamlet]	36aNE4 Merville	L 26 a, b, c, d, 27 c
Chapelle Farm, La [Verbrandenmolen]	28NW4 & NE3 Zillebeke	I 33 b 4.9
Chapelle Nord Farm	20SW4 Bixschoote	N 35 c 15.10
Chapelle Sud Farm [no buildings]	20SW4 Bixschoote	T 11 c / 17 a
Chapelle, la [farm]	28NW4 Ypres	I 33 b 40.95
Chapellette, Ouvrage de la	62cSW1 & 2 Belloy	O 3 a
Chapels Farm Trench	20SW2 Zwartegat	N 29 b
Chapes [Boyau, Chapes Spur, 1915]	57dSE4 Ovillers	X 19 d
Chapes [Trench]	57dSE4 Ovillers	X 19 d
Chapes Spur	57dSE4 Ovillers	X 19, 20, 25, 26
Chapigny Farm	36SW1 Aubers	M 24 c 05.40
Chapigny Farm [post]	36SW1 Aubers	M 23 d, 24 c
Chapigny Farm [trenches / keep, late 1915]	36SW1 Aubers	M 23 d, 24 c
Chaplin Street	36SW1 Aubers	M 24 b, c
Chaplin Trench	51bNW4 Fampoux	I 7 b, d
Chaptal, Boyau	36cSW1 Lens	M 13 b, d, 14 a, c
Chapter Alley	36cSW1 Lens	M 20 a, c
Chapter Wood	62cNW3 Vaux	H 15 c, d
Charcoal Trench	36cSW1 Lens	M 13 d, 19 b
Chardonneret, Tranchée	70dSW [4 Vauxaillon]	U 5 d
Chardon-Vert [hamlet]	62bNW4 Ramicourt	H 36 c
Chards Farm [July 1915]	36NW4 Bois Grenier	I 16 a 9.2
Charent Trench	66cNW4 Berthenicourt	I 25 b
Charing Cross	28SW4 Ploegsteert	U 19 d 0.3

Name	Map Sheet	Map Reference
Charing Cross	57cSE2 Gonnelieu	Q 17 a
Charing Cross	57dSE2 Beaumont	Q 17 a
Charing Cross [Sanctuary Wood]	28NW4 & NE3 Zillebeke	I 24 b
Charing Cross Cemetery	57cSW4 Combles	U 19 d 2.8
Charing Cross Road	36NW4 Bois Grenier	I 25 d
Chariot Wood	62bSW4 Homblières	T 11 c
Charity Farm	28SW2 Wytschaete	O 11 c 6.7
Charity Wood	62bNW4 Ramicourt	I 33 b, 34 a
Charlemagne Trench	70dNW4 St Gobain	H 30 d, I 25 c, 31 a
Charleroy Trench	20SW1 Loo	N 2 a, c
Charles Avenue	57dSE1 & 2 Beaumont	Q 21 c,d, 22 c,d, 23 c
Charles Trench	51bNW1 Roclincourt	B 19 a
Charles Trench	51bNW2 Oppy	C 19 a
Charlie Farm	28NW1 Elverdinghe	A 28 a 9.1
Charlie Trench, & Support	51bNW4 Fampoux	I 7 b, d, 8 c
Charlot Alley	66cNW1 Grugies	B 8 c
Charlotta Weg	28NW4 & NE3 Zillebeke	J 25 b
Charm Trench	70dNW2 Servais	C 2 a, b, c, d
Charmes Alley	66cNW2 Itancourt	H 6 b
Charpentier Cross Roads	20SW4 Bixschoote	T 24 d 6.3
Charpentier Wood	20SW4 Bixschoote	T 24 c, d
Charpentier, Boyau	62cSW1 Dompierre	M 4 b
Charred Post	36SW1 Aubers	M 6 b, d, N 1 a, c
Charterhouse Post [Sept 1915]	36SW1 Aubers	M 20 a 85.60
Chartreux Avenue	36SW2 Radinghem	N 4 b, d, 5 c
Chasm Trench	36cSW3 Vimy	S 3 b, d, 4 a
Chass[eu]r. Cayzur, Tranchée	70dSW [2 Coucy-le-Château]	O 19 b
Chass[eu]r. Perpot, Tranchée	70dSW [2 Coucy-le-Château]	O 20 a
Chasse Farm [Beaulencourt]	57cSW2 Villers-au-Flos	N 17 d 65.95
Chassery Crater	36cSW3 Vimy	S 28 c
Chassery Trench / Boyau	36cSW3 Vimy / 51bNW1 Roclincourt	S 27, 28, A 1, 2, 3, 7
Chassery, Boyau [W of Bécourt, 1915]	57dSE4 Ovillers	X 25
Chassery, N. Boyau	51bNW1 Roclincourt	A 2 d
Chassery, Ouvrage	51bNW1 Roclincourt	A 2 b, d, 3 a, c
Chasseur Cabaret, Au	28SW4 Ploegsteert	U 17 a 2.4
Chasseur Trench	66cNW2 Itancourt	B 17 a, c, 23 a, b, d
Chasseurs Hedge	57dNE3 & 4 Hébuterne	K 22 d, 23 a, b, c
Chasseurs Trench	62cNW4 Péronne	I 31 c, d
Chasseurs Trench	62cSW3 Vermandovillers	S 7 b, 8 a
Chasseurs, Boyau des [1918]	28SW1 Kemmel	N 2 d, 3 c, 9 a
Chasseurs, Tranchée des	70dSW [2 Coucy-le-Château]	O 13 a
Chastel / Ghastel, Ferme du	36NW2 Armentières	C 18 d 2.1
Chat Maigre, le	51bSW1 Neuville Vitasse	M 27 a
Chat, Tranchée de	62cSW3 & 4 Marchélepot	T 10 a, b
Chataignies Wood	62bNW4 Ramicourt	H 17 c, d, 23 a, b
Château [near Au Luxemboug Cabaret]	28SW1 Kemmel	M 19 d 30.05
Château [W end of Hill 63]	28SW4 Ploegsteert	T 18 20.95
Château Alley	36cNW1 La Bassée	A 22 c, d, 23 a
Château Alley	70dNW2 Servais	C 2 b, d, 8 b
Château Alley [1918]	62dSE [4 Harbonnières]	X 30 c
Château Avenue	57cSW4 Combles	U 13 b, c, d
Château Belge	28NW4 Ypres	H 23 b
Château Bridge [Aveluy, across Ancre]	57dSE4 Ovillers	W 11 d 0.1
Château de la Haie Switch [1918]	57dNE1 [Fonquevillers] / 3 [Hébuterne]	D 24,30, E 19, J 6,12,24,30, K7,13,19

Name	Map Sheet	Map Reference
Château de la Hutte [Hill 63]	28SW4 Ploegsteert	U 13 d, 14 c
Château des Près Central Keep [S'y Labourse]	36bNE4 Noeux-les-Mines	F 27 d 5.4
Château des Près North Keep [Sailly Labourse]	36bNE2 Beuvry / 4 Noeux-les-Mines	F 27 b, d
Château Dugouts [Imperfect Copse]	28NW4 & NE3 Zillebeke	I 36 d
Château Farm [Hollebeke]	28SE1 Wervicq	P 7 a 95.70
Château Fort [La Hutte Château, Hill 63]	28SW4 Ploegsteert	U 13 d 91.25
Château Ghesquiere [Warneton]	28SW4 Ploegsteert	U 12 b
Château Keep / Redoubt	62cNW1 Maricourt	A 16 c, d
Château Redoubt [Sept 1915]	36SW3 Richebourg	M 35 c 85.35
Château Redoubt [Thiepval]	57dSE1 & 2 Beaumont	R 25 d
Château Road [CT, Sept 1915]	36SW3 Richebourg	M 35 c, d
Château Segard	28NW4 Ypres	H 30 a 3.0
Château Spur [Red Chateau]	28SW2 Wytschaete	N 18 b, O 13 a
Château Trench	20NW4 Dixmude	H 18 d, 24 b
Château Trench	28NW2 St Julien	I 4 a
Château Trench [Thiepval Wood]	57dSE1 & 2 Beaumont	Q 30 b, d, R 25 a
Château Wood [Hendecourt-lez-Ransart]	51cSE4 Blaireville	X 17 a, c
Château Wood [Hooge]	28NW4 & NE3 Zillebeke	I 12 d, 18 a, b, J 7 c, 13 a
Château Wood Road (Plank) [1917-18]	28NW4 Ypres / NE3 Gheluvelt	I 18 a, b, J 7 c, d, 8 c, 13 a
Château Work	51bNW1 Roclincourt	A 9 a
Château, Reduit de [Chateau Redoubt]	62cSW1 Dompierre	M 9 c, d
Château, The [Ploegsteert Wood 1914-15]	28SW4 Ploegsteert	U 21 c
Chateauroux, Tranchée de	70dSW [4 Vauxaillon]	U 11 a
Chatel Cuvon Alley / Chatel Guyon Alley [?]	66cNW1 Grugies / 2 Itancourt	B 15 d, 16 c, 20 d, 21 a, b, c
Chatham Cut	62dNE2 Méaulte	F 9 c
Chatham Trench	57dNE3 & 4 Hébuterne	K 34 d
Châtillon-sur-Oise [village]	66cNW2 Itancourt	C 30 c, d, I 6 a, b
Chatre, Tranchée de la	70dSW [4 Vauxaillon]	U 3 d
Chatsworth Castle	28NE3 Gheluvelt	J 32 a 7.8
Chaudie Alley	66cNW4 Berthenicourt	H 12 b
Chaudière Trench	36cSW3 Vimy	T 2 d, 3 a, c
Chaudière, Bois de la	36cSW3 Vimy	T 7 d, 8 c
Chaudière, la [farm]	36cSW3 Vimy	S 18 b 2.0
Chaufoures Wood	57cNW4 Beugny	I 12 c, d
Chaufoures Wood	66eNW [4 Morisel] / SW [2]	H 35 c, N 5 a
Chaulnes Trench	62bSW1 Gricourt / 3 St Quentin	M 35 a, c, d
Chaulnes Woods [central]	62cSW3 Vermandovillers	S 28 b 7.0
Chaulnes Woods No.1	62cSW3 Vermandovillers	S 28 b, 29 a
Chaulnes Woods No.2	62cSW3 Vermandovillers	S 29 a, b, c
Chaulnes Woods No.3	62cSW3 Vermandovillers	S 28 d, 29 c
Chaulnes Woods No.4	62cSW3 Vermandovillers	S 28 c, d
Chaulnes Woods No.5	66dNW1 Punchy	A 4 b
Chaulnes Woods No.6	62cSW3 Vermandovillers	S 28 c
Chaulnes Woods No.7	62cSW3 Vermandovillers	S 27 d
Chaulnes, South [village]	66dNW1 Punchy	A 11 c
Chaume Farm	20SW4 Bixschoote	U 19 a 6.4
Chaurrios Alley	62cSW3 Vermandovillers	S 14 d, 20 b
Chausseurs Trench [1918]	66eNW [4 Morisel]	H 17 d, 23 b
Chautel Alley	66cNW1 Grugies	B 8 c
Chavatte Salient	66dNW3 Hattencourt	G 13 d, 14 c, 19 b, d
Chavatte, La [village]	66dNW3 Hattencourt	G 19, 20
Chavattes Post	36SW3 Richebourg	S 13 b
Chavattes, rue des [road]	36aSE4 Locon	X 18 a
Cheap Lane	51bNW3 Arras / SW1 Neuville Vitasse	G 36 c, M 6 b

Name	Map Sheet	Map Reference
Cheapside	28NW2 St Julien	B 23 a 3.2
Cheapside	28NW2 St Julien	C 28 d, 29 c
Cheapside	28SW2 Wytschaete	N 10 d
Cheapside	51bNW2 Oppy	C 26 a, b, 27 a
Cheapside [farm & road jct]	28NW2 St Julien	B 18 a 05.05
Cheapside [light rly locality, 1917]	28SW1 Kemmel	N 15 a
Cheapside [road]	28SW1 Kemmel / 2 Wytschaete	N 9 d, 10 b, c, d, 15 b
Cheapside Avenue	57dNE3 & 4 Hébuterne	K 34 a, b
Cheapside Cemetery	28SW2 Wytschaete	N 10 a 95.45
Cheapside Line	28SW1 Kemmel / 2 Wytschaete	N 10 c -15 b
Check Trench	57cSW3 Longueval	S 21 a, b, 22 a
Cheddar Trench	51bNW2 Oppy	C 19 b
Chedder Villa	28NW2 St Julien	C 17 c 7.0
Cheeroh Avenue	57dNE3 & 4 Hébuterne	K 32 b, 33 a, b, 34 a
Cheery Trench	57dNE1 & 2 Fonquevillers	K 3 a, b
Cheese Copse	28NE2 Moorslede	E 11 c 7.6
Cheese Road [Gueudecourt]	57dSE2 & 57cSW1 Le Sars	N 26 a, b
Cheese Support	57cSW4 Combles	U 8 a, c
Cheese Trench	57cSW1 Gueudecourt	N 19 c, d
Cheese Wood	62cNW3 Vaux	H 2 d, 8 b
Cheesecake Trench	51bNW2 Oppy	C 19 a, b
Cheetham Reserve	57cNE3 Hermies	K 31 b, d
Cheetham Switch	57cNE3 Hermies	K 31 b, d, 32 a, b, c, d
Chef Alley	62cSW3 Vermandovillers	S 12 a, c, 18 a
Chelmsford Cottage	36NW2 & NE1 Houplines	C 3 c / d
Chelsea Bridge [road over canal]	36aSE3 Gonnehem	Q 32 c 7.9
Cheltenham Road	36SW1 Aubers	M 14 a
Chelwood Cotts [August 1915, N of Hay Farm]	28NW4 & NE3 Zillebeke	I 4 d 6.8
Chemical Trench [Roeux]	51bNW4 Fampoux	I 13 b, d, 14 a
Chemical Works [Roeux]	51bNW4 Fampoux	I 13 b, d
Chemin Creux, Boyau	36cSW3 Vimy	S 8 b
Chemin de Fer, Boyau du [Calonne]	36cSW1 Lens	M 8 a, b, d, 9 c, 15 a, b
Chemin des Dames [rd, heights N of R. Aisne]	75NE / 76NW	extensive
Chemin des Dames [road]	57dNE1 & 2 Fonquevillers	E 11 b, d, 12 c, 18 a
Chemin Militaire (Plank Road)	28NW1 Elverdinghe / 3 Poperinghe	A 30 a, c, d, B 25 c, d, H 1 b, 2 a, c
Chemin Trench, Avenue, Drive	28NW2 St Julien	C 8 a, c
Chemin Vert, le [hamlet]	57bSW2 Clary	O 14 a
Cheminade Alley	62cSW1 & 2 Belloy	N 6 c, 12 a, b
Cheminots Alley	66dNW1 Punchy	A 11 c, 17 a, b
Chemins Estaminet [1916, later Kempton Park]	28NW2 St Julien	C 15 b 4.5
Chemise Farm	28NW1 Elverdinghe	A 22 c 5.0
Chemsons Lane [road 1917-18]	28NW4 Ypres	I 28 b, 29 a
Chenalot Alley	62cSW3 Vermandovillers	S 12 c, d
Cheneaux Copse	57bSW1 Bantouzelle	M 10 d, 11 c, 16 b, 17 a
Cheneaux Woods	57bSW1 Bantouzelle	M 16 a, b, c, d
Chepstow Avenue	51bNW1 Roclincourt	A 3 c
Chequerbent Street	57dSE4 Ovillers	X 1 a
Cherbourg Trench	66cSW4 La Fère	T 10 d
Cherif Trench / Tranchée du Cherif [Sherrif]	62cSW3 & 4 Marchélepot	T 4 b, 5 a
Chérisy [village]	51bSW2 Vis-en-Artois	O 26 c, d, 32 a, b
Chérisy Lane [trench]	51bSW2 Vis-en-Artois / 4 Bullecourt	O 32 a, c, d, 33 a
Chérisy Trench	51bSW4 Bullecourt	O 32 d
Cherry Bridge [Chérisy]	51bSW2 Vis-en-Artois	O 32 b 95.45
Cherry Farm	20SE2 Hooglede	R 16 a 1.4

Name	Map Sheet	Map Reference
Cherry Lane	51bSW4 Bullecourt	U 7 d
Cherry Lane [Monchy-le-Preux]	51bSW2 Vis-en-Artois	O 1 c, d, 7 b
Cherry Wood [Chérisy]	51bSW2 Vis-en-Artois / 4 Bullecourt	O 32 b, d
Cherrypicker / Cherrypickers Copse	62cSW3 Vermandovillers	S 10 c, d
Cherrytree Woods No.1	62cSE1 Bouvincourt	P 14 b, d, 15 c
Cherrytree Woods No.2	62cSE1 Bouvincourt	P 14 c
Cherrytree Woods No.3	62cSE1 Bouvincourt	P 13 d
Cherub Farm	28NE2 Moorslede	L 1 a 1.3
Cheshire Avenue	28SW4 Ploegsteert	U 27 a, b, d
Cheshire Lane	28SW2 Wytschaete	N 35 b, 36 a
Cheshire Post [Bug Wood]	28SW2 Wytschaete	O 15 d, 16 c
Cheshire Quarry	57cSE2 Gonnelieu / 4 Villers-Guislain	R 34 a, c
Cheshire Road	36cNW1 La Bassée	A 2 d
Cheshire Street [road]	57cSE4 Villers-Guislain	R 33 d, 34 c, X 3 b
Cheshire Trench	57cNE4 Marcoing	L 27 b, d
Cheshire Trench	57cSW3 Longueval	T 21 c, d, 27 b
Cheshire Trench	57dSE2 Beaumont	R 21 c
Chesney Walk	57cSW3 Longueval	S 11 c
Chess board Wood	62dNE [3 Sailly-le-Sec]	J 21, 22
Chester Copse	62bSW4 Homblières	T 6 b
Chester Farm	28NW4 Ypres	I 33 a 7.6
Chester Road	36NW4 Bois Grenier	I 26 a
Chester Street	57cSW3 Longueval	S 9 a, c, d
Chester Street	62dNE2 Méaulte	F 11 d
Chesterman Farm	28NE4 Dadizeele	K 28 c 50.05
Chestnut Avenue	57cSE4 Villers-Guislain / 62cNE2 Epéhy	X 26 a, c, F 1 b, 2 a
Chestnut Avenue	62cNE2 Epéhy	F 1 b
Chestnut Farm	20SE2 Hooglede	Q 18 b 3.9
Chestnut Trench	51bNW2 Oppy	C 19 d
Chestnut Trench	51bSW1 Neuville Vitasse	M 12 a
Cheurot Farm	20SW4 Bixschoote	T 24 a 7.9
Cheurot Wood	20SW4 Bixschoote	T 24 b
Cheval Blanc Farm	20SW4 Bixschoote	U 13 b 45.05
Cheval Blanc, Au [Estaminet, Pl'steert, 1914-15]	28SW4 Ploegsteert	U 25 d 35.75
Cheval Noir Estaminet, Au [Pl'steert, 1914-15]	28SW4 Ploegsteert	U 25 a 6.7
Chevalier Alley	62cSW3 Vermandovillers	S 8 b, d, 9 c
Chevillard Trench	62bSW1 Gricourt	M 16 a, c
Cheviot Corner [road jct]	28NE4 Dadizeele	K 24 b 85.05
Chevogeon Trench	66cNW1 Grugies	A 18 b, B 13 a
Cheyne Row	57cNE4 Marcoing	K 28 a
Cheyne Row [houses]	27SE4 Meteren	X 1 a 1.1
Cheyne Walk	36cNW1 La Bassée	A 14 d, 15 c, d
Chez Bontemps [locality / earthworks]	36cSW4 Rouvroy	U 20 a, c
Chezal Alley	66cNW1 Grugies	A 18 b, d
Chib Wood	51bSE2 Oisy-le-Verger	Q 35 b
Chicago [light rly locality, 1917-18]	28NE3 Gheluvelt	J 7 c 1.8
Chicago Alley	66cNW4 Berthenicourt	H 11 b
Chicanery Trench	66cSW4 La Fère	U 15 d, 16 c, 21 b
Chicar Trench	36cSW3 Vimy	S 5 d
Chichester Camp	57dNE3 & 4 Hébuterne	K 27 b
Chicken Reserve	51bNW4 Fampoux	H 6 b, d
Chicken Row	36aSE1 St Venant	P 5 c
Chicken Run	36NW2 Armentières	C 17 a
Chico Support	51bNW2 Oppy	C 25 a

Name	Map Sheet	Map Reference
Chico Trench	51bNW2 Oppy	C 25 a
Chicoree Alley / Boyau de la Chicoree	62cSW3 & 4 Marchélepot	T 15 c, 20 b, 21 a
Chicory Lane	28SW2 Wytschaete	N 12 b, O 7 a
Chicory Trench	36cSW1 Lens	N 8 c, d, 13 b, 14 a
Chidd Support [Gavrelle]	51bNW2 Oppy	C 25 a
Chidd Trench [Gavrelle]	51bNW2 Oppy	C 25 a
Chien Blanc, le [hamlet]	36NW1 Steenwerck	A 21 d
Chien Farm	20SW4 Bixschoote	U 28 c 7.7
Chien, Boyau du [Dog]	62cSW3 & 4 Marchélepot	T 4 d, 10 b, 11 a
Chiens, Fontaine des	51bSW2 Vis-en-Artois	O 3 a
Chile Farm	27NE4 Abeele	L 34 b 5.3
Chili Avenue	51bNW4 Fampoux	H 6 b, c, d, 12 a, b, I 7 a
Chili Trench	20SW1 Loo	M 2 a, b, c
Chili Trench	51bNW4 Fampoux	H 6 c, 12 b, d
Chilly [village]	66dNW1 Punchy	A 19 d, 20 a, c
Chilly Alley	66dNW1 Punchy	A 20 d, 21 c, 27 a
Chilly Trench	62bSW1 Gricourt	M 35 b
Chilly Trench	66dNW1 Punchy	A 27 a
Chimney Crescent [road, Sept 1915]	36SW3 Richebourg	M 34 d
Chimney O.P. (Arras)	51bNW3 Arras	G 28 c 80.65
Chimney Trench	62cNW1 Maricourt	A 4 a, b
Chimpanzee Trench	62cNW1 Maricourt	A 5 d, 11 b
Chimpanzee Valley	62cNW1 Maricourt	A 5 d, 11 b
Chin Chin Trench / Chin Trench	51bNW2 Oppy	C 21 d, 27 b, d
Chin Corner [Tyne Cott]	28NE1 Zonnebeke	D 16 b 6.1
Chin Trench	51bNW4 Fampoux	I 15 a
China Lane	51bSW4 Bullecourt	U 22 c, 28 a
China Trench	51bNW4 Fampoux	I 19 a, c
China Wall [Wall of China]	28NW4 & NE3 Zillebeke	I 16 a, b, d, 17 c
China Wood	28NE1 Zonnebeke	D 24 c, 30 a
Chinese Camp [Nieppe Forest]	36aNE3 Haverskerque	K 9 c
Chinese House	20SW4 Bixschoote	U 23 b 5.8
Chinese Trench	28SW2 Wytschaete	N 12 b, c, d, 17 b, d
Chinese Wall [breastwork]	28SW2 Wytschaete	N 12, 17
Chink Trench	51bNW2 Oppy	C 25 d
Chinook Cemetery	36cNW1 La Bassée	A 12 d 35.25
Chinstrap Lane [road]	51bNW4 Fampoux	H 23 b, 24 c, 30 a, b, I 25 a, c
Chip Lane	57cSE2 Gonnelieu	Q 17 c, d, 23 a
Chip Trench	51bNW2 Oppy	C 15 c, 21 a
Chip Trench	51bNW4 Fampoux	I 15 c
Chipilly [village]	62dSE [2 Proyart]	Q 4 a, c, d
Chipilly Spur	62dNE [4 Bray-sur-Somme] / SE [2 Proyart]	K 29, 34, 35, Q 4, 5
Chipote, Boyau de la [Chips Trench]	36bSE2 Boyeffles / 36cSW1 Lens	R 30 a, M 19 d, 25 b
Chippawa Camp	28NW3 Poperinghe / 28SW1 Kemmel	G 35 b, 36 a, M 6 a, b
Chippawa Wood	28SW1 Kemmel	M 6 a
Chips Alley	51bNW4 Fampoux	I 1 c, d, 7 a
Chips Trench	36cSW1 Lens	M 19 d, 25 b
Chips Trench [Chipote, Boyau de la]	36bSE2 Boyeffles / 36cSW1 Lens	R 30 a, M 19 d, 25 b
Chiron Trench	66cNW1 Grugies	B 8 c, d, 9 c
Chirrup Farm	28NW1 Elverdinghe	A 23 a 9.2
Chisel Farm	28NE2 Moorslede	F 30 a 2.5
Chisholm Avenue	28NW4 & NE3 Zillebeke	I 29 d
Chiswick Avenue	57dNE1 & 2 Fonquevillers	E 16 d
Chiswick Farm	20SE2 Hooglede	Q 30 b 3.3

Name	Map Sheet	Map Reference
Chit Mill	27SE2 Berthen	R 15 b 30.53
Chivers Wood	28NE4 Dadizeele	K 17 a, c
Chocelprat, Tranchée [Middlesex Tr, part of]	36cSW1 Lens	M 15 a, b
Chocolat Menier Corner	36SW3 Richebourg	S 15 a 0.3
Chocolat Post	36SW3 Richebourg	S 14 b 9.1
Chocolat Trench / Tranchée du Chocolat	62cSW3 & 4 Marchélepot	T 15 c, 20 b, 21 a
Chocolate House	36SW2 Radinghem	O 13 d 0.9 [O 13 d 35.95 in late 1915]
Choir Farm	28NE2 Moorslede	F 25 b 7.4
Cholic Cottage	27SE4 Meteren	X 7 d 30.65
Cholic Trench	27SE4 Meteren	X 7 d, 8 a
Chop Trench	51bNW2 Oppy	C 19 d
Chopin Farm	20SE2 Hooglede	R 5 a 7.4
Chopin Farm [Beaulencourt]	57cSW2 Villers-au-Flos	N 17 b 2.3
Chopper Ravine	62bNW3 Bellicourt	G 33 b, 34 a
Choquaux Street [road; les Choquaux]	36aSE4 Locon	W 17 b, 18 a, b
Choquaux, les [farm / hamlet]	36aSE4 Locon	W 17 b, 18 a
Chord, The	51bNW2 Oppy	C 19 c
Chord, The [Hohenzollern Redoubt]	36cNW1 La Bassée / 3 Loos	G 4 b, c, d
Chorley Street	57dSE4 Ovillers	X 1 c, d
Choucroute Alley	62cNW3 Vaux	H 25 a, b, 26 a
Choux Alley / Boyau des Choux	62cSW3 & 4 Marchélepot	T 14 d, 15 c, 20 a, b
Chow Farm	20SE2 Hooglede	Q 5 a 1.1
Chow Trench	51bNW2 Oppy	C 21 d, 22 c, 27 b
Chowbart Street	57dSE4 Ovillers	X 1 a
Chrimes Junction [road jct]	28NE4 Dadizeele	K 5 c 1.9
Christian Cottage	27SE4 Meteren	X 20 b 2.9
Christiania Alley	62cNW4 Péronne	H 10 b, 11 a
Christo Alley	66cNW2 Itancourt	B 5 c
Christophe Alley	62cSW3 & 4 Marchélepot	T 2 d, 8 b, 9 a
Chrome Crossing [level crossing]	27SE2 Berthen	Q 12 d 8.7
Chronic Trench	62bSW4 Homblières	T 12 a, c, 18 a
Chub Trench [1918]	57dNE1 & 2 Fonquevillers / 3 & 4 Hébut.	E 30 d, F 25 c, K 6 b,c,d
Chuignes [railway locality]	62cSW1 Dompierre	M 8 c, d
Chuignes [village]	62dSE [2 Proyart] / 62cSW1 Dompierre	R 12 a, c, M 7 b, d
Chump Trench	51bNW2 Oppy	C 1 a
Church [isolated, S of Paradis]	36aSE2 Lestrem	Q 24 d 8.8
Church Bridge [Aveluy, across Ancre]	57dSE4 Ovillers	W 17 b 1.3
Church Cut	36cNW1 La Bassée	A 27 a
Church East Keep [Cambrin South]	36cNW1 La Bassée	A 25 b
Church End	28SE1 Wervicq	P 3 a 7.6
Church Keep [Vermelles South]	36cNW3 Loos	G 8 c
Church Lane [road]	36aSE2 Lestrem	Q 24 d, R 13 d, 19 a, b, c
Church Redoubt / Work [Feuchy Chapel]	51bSW1 Neuville Vitasse	N 4 c
Church Redoubt [Sept 1915]	36SW3 Richebourg	S 5 a 25.85
Church Road [CT, Sept 1915]	36SW3 Richebourg	M 35 c, S 5 a
Church Square [Guillemont]	57cSW3 Longueval	T 19 c
Church Street	51cSE3 & 4 Ransart	R 33 a, c
Church Street	57cSW2 Villers-au-Flos	N 30 b, c, d
Church Street	57dSE1 & 2 Beaumont	R 26 c
Church Street	57dSE1 & 2 Beaumont	R 7 c, d
Church Street / Boyau de l'Eglise	62cNW1 Maricourt	A 16 c
Church Trench	20SE3 Westroosebeke	V 25 a
Church Trench	51bNW4 Fampoux	I 14 d

Name	Map Sheet	Map Reference
Church Trench [Travecy]	66cSW4 La Fère	T 1 d, 7 a, b
Church West Keep [Cambrin]	36cNW1 La Bassée	A 25 b 3.6
Churchill Cut	36cNW1 La Bassée	A 27 a
Chutney Trench	51bNW2 Oppy	C 19 d, 25 b
Cicet Trench	57cSW4 Combles	T 11 a
Cider Cottage	28NW1 Elverdinghe	H 2 b 3.2
Cigale, Tranchée de la	66dNW2 Morchain	B 18 c, 2 d, 23 b, c, d, 24 a
Cigar Copse	51bNW4 Fampoux / SW2 Vis-en-Artois	I 32 d, O 2 b
Cigarette Copse	51bNW4 Fampoux / SW2 Vis-en-Artois	I 36 d, O 6 b
Cigarette Trench	62cSW3 Vermandovillers	T 13 c, 19 a
Cimier Alley / Tranchée du Cimier	62cSW4 St Christ	T 11 d
Cinder [track]	28SW4 Ploegsteert	U 19 c 6.2
Cinder Line [lt rly siding, Pl'steert Wd, 1917-18]	28SW4 Ploegsteert	U 19 c
Cinder Track / Path [Ritz - Boar's Head]	36SW3 Richebourg	S 9 d
Cinder Trench	36SW3 Richebourg	S 9 d, 16 a
Cinema Alley / Boyau du Cinema	62cSW3 & 4 Marchélepot	T 5 b, c, d, 11 a, c
Cinema Dump	28SE1 Wervicq	P 35 d
Cinema Dump [German]	28SW2 Wytschaete	O 25 d
Cinema House	36SW1 Aubers	M 24 a 08.23
Cinema Road [road]	28SW2 Wytschaete	O 36 a, b
Cinema Trench	51bNW4 Fampoux	I 7 d, 13 b
Cinnabar Trench	36cSW1 Lens	N 8 b, 14
Cinnamon Trench	51bNW2 Oppy	C 13 a
Cipher House	20SE2 Hooglede	R 27 a 6.1
Circe, Bois de	62cSW3 & 4 Marchélepot	T 12 a, b, c
Circle Farm	28SE1 Wervicq	P 31 a 4.8
Circle Lane	36NW2 Armentières	C 12 c, 17 b
Circle Point	36NW2 Armentières	C 12 c
Circle Trench [Monchy-le-Preux]	51bSW2 Vis-en-Artois	N 6 b, O 1 a, b, d
Circuit House	28SW3 Bailleul	S 17 a 4.2
Circular Wood	66eNW [4 Morisel]	I 24 d, 30 b
Circus Point [strongpoint]	28SE1 Wervicq	P 2 c 06.96
Circus Support	57cSE4 Villers-Guislain	X 4 d
Circus Trench	57cSW3 Longueval	S 14 b
Circus Trench	57dSE1 & 2 Beaumont	Q 17 b
Circus Trench	57dSE2 & 57cSW1 Le Sars	M 23 b, 24 a
Circus, The	62cNW1 Maricourt	A 16 b, d
Circus, The [German strongpoint]	57dSE2 & 57cSW1 Le Sars	M 23 b
Circus, The [road junction]	57cSW3 Longueval	S 14 b 95.90
Ciro Avenue	57cSW4 Combles	T 6 d, 11 a, b, 12 a, b, U 1 c
Ciros Copse	62bSW4 Homblières	O 32 d
Cirque, Tranchée du	62cSW3 & 4 Marchélepot	T 10 b, 11 a
Cirrus Trench	57cSW2 Villers-au-Flos	N 28 a
Cissi Post, & Cis I & II Posts	36NW4 Bois Grenier	I 15 d
Citadel [old citadel of Arras]	51bNW3 Arras	G 26 d, 27 c, 32 b, 33 a
Citadel, The	62dNE2 Méaulte	F 21 d 5.8
Cité Armand Voisin	36cSW4 Rouvroy	O 35 d
Cité Calonne	36cSW1 Lens	M 14 a, b, c, d
Cité Darcy	36cSW4 Rouvroy	O 34 d
Cité de la Plaine	36cSW1 Lens	M 16 c
Cité de la Plaine [1915]	36cSW1 Lens	M 16 a, b, c, d
Cité de Rollencourt	36cSW1 Lens	M 21 c, d, 27 a, b
Cité des Alouettes	36cSW1 Lens	M 1 d, 7 b
Cité des Cornailles	36cSW1 Lens	M 20 b, 21 a, c

Name	Map Sheet	Map Reference
Cité des Tabernaux [miners' cottages]	36cNW4 Pont-à-Vendin	H 10 central
Cité du No. 11	36cSW1 Lens	M 2 c, d, 3 c, 8 b, 9 a
Cité Jean Promper	36cSW4 Rouvroy	O 35 c, d
Cité Jeanne d'Arc	36cSW1 Lens	M 18 c
Cité Jeanne d'Arc [1915]	36cSW1 Lens	M 11 d, 12 c, 17 b, 18 a
Cité St Amé	36cSW1 Lens	M 22 b, 23 a
Cité St Auguste	36cSW1 Lens	N 3 a, b, c, d
Cité St Auguste [1915]	36cNW3 Loos	H 32 b, d, 33 a, c
Cité St Edouard	36cSW1 Lens	N 7 a, b, d
Cité St Edouard [1915]	36cSW1 Lens	M 6 d
Cité St Elie [miners' cottages]	36cNW3 Loos	G 6 d, 12 b, H 1 c, 7 a
Cité St Elizabeth	36cSW1 Lens	N 8 c
Cité St Emile	36cSW1 Lens	N 8 a
Cité St Lauent [1915]	36cSW1 Lens	N 1 c
Cité St Laurent	36cSW1 Lens	N 1 d, 7 a, b
Cité St Laurent-Hulluch-La Bassée Line	36cNW1 La Bassée / 3 Loos / SW1 Lens	extensive
Cité St Léonard [miners' cottages]	36cNW3 Loos / 4 Pont-à-Vendin	H 3 d, 4 c, 9 b, 10 a
Cité St Pierre	36cSW1 Lens	M 11 d, 12 a, c
Cité St Pierre [1915]	36cSW1 Lens	M 1 b, d, 12 a, c
Cité St Théodore	36cSW1 Lens	N 13 c, 18 b, d
Cité St Théodore [1915]	36cSW1 Lens	M 13 a
Cité Trench [Cité St Elie, 1915]	36cNW3 Loos	G 6 b, d
Cité, la [farm, by Poesele Farm]	20SW4 Bixschoote	N 34 d 65.40
Citron Alley	62cSW3 Vermandovillers	T 9 b, d, 10 c
Citron Trench	57cSW4 Combles	T 12 d, U 7 c, 13 a
City Post	36NW4 Bois Grenier	H 36 c, d
City Road	36NW4 Bois Grenier	H 29 b, d, 30 c, 36 a, c, d
City Road [Oct 1915]	36cNW3 Loos	G 17 b, d
City Support	57cNE3 Hermies	K 26 d, 27 c
City Trench	57cNE3 Hermies	K 26 b, 27 a
City Trench [Puisieux-au-Mont]	57dNE3 & 4 Hébuterne	L 14 c, d
Civic Trench	36cSW3 Vimy	S 4 d, 10 a
Civil Avenue	51bNW2 Oppy	H 6 a, b, I 1 a, b
Civil Farm [moated]	20SE2 Hooglede	Q 22 a 2.5
Civil Trench	51bNW2 Oppy	H 6 b, I 1 a, b
Civilisation / Civilization Farm	28NW2 St Julien	C 16 c 3.8
Cix. Marmuse, la [farm]	36aSE2 Lestrem	R 20 c 75.50
Clack Trench	36cSW1 Lens	N 20 d, 21 c
Claim Farm	27SE2 Berthen	Q 29 d 95.55
Clair Wood	62cSW4 St Christ	T 10 c
Clair, Bois	62cSW3 & 4 Marchélepot	T 10 d
Clairefaye Avenue	57dSW [2 Raincheval]	O 29 a, b, 30 a
Clairefaye Avenue Left	57dSW [2 Raincheval]	O 23 c, d
Clairefaye Flank	57dSW [[2 Raincheval]	O 29 b, d
Clairefaye Reserve	57dSW [2 Raincheval]	O 23 c, 29 a, b, c
Clairefaye Support	57dSW [2 Raincheval]	O 24 c, 29 b, 30 a
Clairefaye Trench	57dSW [2 Raincheval]	O 24 c, 29 d, 30 a, c,
Clairon, Bois du	62cSW3 & 4 Marchélepot	T 11 b, d, 12 a
Clams Trench	36cSW3 Vimy	S 3 b, 4 a
Clan Trench [Delbar Wood Spur]	51bNW4 Fampoux	I 14 d, 20 a
Clannish Trench	36cSW3 Vimy	S 3 d, 4 a
Clanusk Farm	28NE4 Dadizeele	L 1 d 9.7
Clapbanck [farm & cross roads]	27SE4 Meteren	X 29 b 1.3
Clapham Farm [Phosphate Factory]	62cNW1 Maricourt	A 18 b 5.5

Name	Map Sheet	Map Reference
Clapham Junction	28NW4 & NE3 Zillebeke	J 13 d
Clapham Junction [German position, late 1915]	36SW2 Radinghem	N 6 c 4.3
Clapham Junction [railway]	28SW3 Bailleul	S 11 b, d, 12 a
Clapham Junction RE Park [S of Dranoutre]	28SW3 Bailleul	S 12 a
Clapham Road [road]	28SW3 Bailleul	S 5 b, d, 6 c, 12 a, c, 18 a
Clara Trench	36cSW3 Vimy	S 4 a
Clara Trench	36SW1 Aubers	N 19 a, b, d
Clara's Fan	36SW1 Aubers	N 19 b
Clarborough House [Artoishoek]	28NE4 Dadizeele	K 30 c 6.7
Clare House	27NE4 Abeele	L 18 a 2.1
Clare Reserve [1918]	62dNE [3 Morlancourt]	J 12 b
Clare Trench	36cSW3 Vimy	S 10 c
Clarence Trench	51bNW2 Oppy	B 12 c
Clarence Trench, & Crater	51bNW3 Arras	G 12 a
Claret Trench	36cSW3 Vimy	S 3 d
Clarges Avenue	57cNE3 Hermies / 4 Marcoing	K 17 c, 21 c, d, 22 a, b, c, 23 a
Clarges Street	20SE3 Westroosebeke	V 20 d
Clarges Street	36NW4 Bois Grenier	I 15 d, 16 c
Clarges Street [military road / track 1917-18]	20SW4 Bixschoote / 28NW2 St Julien	U 10, 11, 15, 16, 20, 21, 25, 26, C 1
Clarges Street [road]	57cSW3 Longueval	S 17 a, b
Clarges Street [Sept 1915]	36cNW1 La Bassée	A 9 a
Clarionet Farm	28NE4 Dadizeele	L 26 d 4.6
Clarke Street [Zouave Wood]	28NW4 & NE3 Zillebeke	I 18 c
Clarke Trench	51bNW4 Fampoux	I 7 c, 13 a, c
Clarke Trench	57cSW3 Longueval	S 3 c, d
Clarke's / Clarks Alley	36bNE4 Noeux-les-Mines / 36cNW3 Loos	L 6 c, 12 a, G 7 b, 8 a, b
Clark's Dump	57cSW3 Longueval	S 3 d 3.7
Clarks Keep	36cNW3 Loos	G 8 a 7.4
Clarnico Buildings	28NE4 Dadizeele	K 16 d 1.9
Clary [village]	57bSW2 Clary	O 16 d, 17 b,c,d, 18 c, 22 b, 23 a,b,c
Clash Trench	36cSW3 Vimy	S 3 d, 4 c
Clasp Trench	51bNW4 Fampoux	I 7 a, c
Claud Trench [1918]	66eNW [2 Thennes]	H 4 a
Claude Crater	51bNW3 Arras	G 12 a
Claude Trench	36cSW3 Vimy	S 9 c, 15 a
Claude Trench	51bNW3 Arras	G 12 a
Claudot Avenue	51bNW1 Roclincourt	A 9, 10, 14, 15
Claudot Trench, & Group [Craters]	51bNW1 Roclincourt	A 10 c
Clavel Trench	36cSW3 Vimy	S 4 a, b
Claw Alley	51bNW4 Fampoux	I 1 d, 7 b
Claw Trench	36cSW3 Vimy	S 4 a, b
Claw Trench	51bSW4 Bullecourt	U 1 a, c
Clay Quarry [NE of Etricourt]	57cSE3 Sorel-le-Grand	V 3 c 0.7
Clay Trench	51bNW4 Fampoux	I 9 c
Clay Trench	57dSE2 Beaumont	R 20 a
Claymore Trench	62bNW1 Gouy	A 20 a
Claymore Valley	62bNW1 Gouy	A 13 d, 14 a, b, c, 19 b
Clear Farm	20SE3 Westroosebeke	V 16 d 5.2
Clear Trench	36cSW3 Vimy	S 4 a
Cleary Street [1918]	62dNE [3 Morlancourt]	K 19 a, c
Cleat Cottages	27SE2 Berthen	R 1 b 25.65
Clebert Wood	36aNE1 Morbecque	D 23, 28, 29, J 4, 5
Clement Farm	28NE4 Dadizeele	K 36 c 35.20
Clemson's Lane [track, 1917-18]	28NW4 Ypres	I 28 b

Name	Map Sheet	Map Reference
Cleo Trench	36cSW3 Vimy	S 4 a, c
Cler Trench	36cSW3 Vimy	S 4 a
Clermont Alley	66cNW1 Grugies / 2 Itancourt	B 15 b, d, 16 a
Cléry Station [railway locality 1917-18]	62cNW4 Péronne	H 10 d, 11 a
Cléry Trench	70dNW [3 Sinceny]	H 33 b, d
Cléry-sur-Somme [village]	62cNW4 Péronne	H 5 c, d, 6 c, d, 11 a, b, 12 b
Cleves Trench / Tranchée de Clèves	66cNW2 Itancourt / 4 Berthenicourt	C 27 d, 28 c, I 4 a, c
Click Trench	36cSW3 Vimy	S 4 b, d
Client Cottage	28NE2 Moorslede	F 23 a 65.00
Cliff Lane	62cNW1 Maricourt	A 23 d
Cliff Trench	36cSW3 Vimy	S 4 c
Cliff Trench	51bNW4 Fampoux	I 15 a
Cliff Trench	57dSE2 Beaumont	R 23 c, d, 29 a
Cliff Trench	57dSE4 Ovillers	X 29 b
Cliff Trench	62cNW1 Maricourt	A 23 d, 29 b
Cliff Trench	66cSW4 La Fère	T 6 b, c, d, 12 a
Cliff Trench	66cSW4 La Fère	U 21 d, 27 a, b, c
Cliffe Post	62cNE2 Epéhy	F 20 d
Clifford Avenue	57dSE1 & 2 Beaumont	Q 29 a, c
Clifford Craters	36cNW3 Loos	G 5 c
Clifford Street, & Craters	36cNW3 Loos	G 4 d, 5 c, 10 b
Clifford's Tower	28NW2 St Julien	C 15 c, 21 a
Clifton Bridge [rly over canal]	36aSE1 St Venant	P 13 a 25.35
Clifton Central Post	36aSE2 Lestrem	R 18 a, c
Clifton House	28NE1 Zonnebeke	D 7 b 8.4
Clifton North Post	36aSE2 Lestrem	R 18 a
Clifton South Post	36aSE2 Lestrem	R 18 c
Climber Cottage	27NE2 Proven	F 23 b 2.3
Climber Trench	36cSW3 Vimy	S 4 c
Clio, Bois	62cSW3 & 4 Marchélepot	T 10 b, 11 a
Clipper Trench	36cSW3 Vimy	S 4 c
Clissold Trench	57dNE3 & 4 Hébuterne	K 23 a
Clive House	27SE4 Meteren	W 11 a 20.05
Clive Road	36cNW1 La Bassée	A 21 b
Clive Trench	51bNW2 Oppy	I 1 a
Clock Trench	36cSW3 Vimy	S 3 d, 4 a, b, c, 9 a, b
Clock Trench	62bSW4 Homblières	T 5 a, b, d, 11 b, 12 a, b
Clocksky Avenue	57dSE2 Beaumont	R 14 a
Clod Trench	51bNW4 Fampoux	I 14 b, 15 a
Clog Trench	36cSW1 Lens	N 20 a
Clogher Farm	27NE2 Proven	L 29 c 3.5
Clogher Valley [trench]	28SW2 Wytschaete	N 29 d, 30 c
Clogs Trench	36cSW3 Vimy	S 4 a, b
Cloisters, The	28NW4 & NE3 Zillebeke	I 36 d 95.48
Cloncurry Trench [1918]	62dNE [3 Morlancourt]	K 13 b, d
Clonmel Avenue & Street	57dSE1 & 2 Beaumont	Q 10 c
Clonmel Copse	28NE3 Gheluvelt	J 19 c
Cloporte Trench / Tr. du Cloporte	62cSW3 & 4 Marchélepot	T 9 b, d, 10 a
Close Street [1918]	62dNE [3 Morlancourt]	K 19 d, 20 a, c
Cloud Support [1918]	62dNE [3 Morlancourt]	K 13 b, c, d
Cloud Trench	51bNW2 Oppy	C 7 a, c
Cloudy Trench	57cSW1 Gueudecourt / 2 Villers-au-Flos	N 21 d, 22 c, 28 a, b
Clover Trench	36cSW3 Vimy	S 3 d, 9 a, b
Clown Crossing [bridge / level crossing]	28NE2 Moorslede	F 26 d 45.85

Name	Map Sheet	Map Reference
Cloyne Farm	27NE2 Proven	F 9 c 9.9
Club [Béthune]	36bNE2 Beuvry	E 11 c 8.7
Club Avenue	51bNW4 Fampoux	I 14 a
Club Lane	51bSW1 Neuville Vitasse	N 14 c, d
Club Post	62bNW3 Bellicourt	G 7 b 2.5
Club Quarry	62cNE4 Roisel	L 12 a, c
Club Trench	36cSW3 Vimy	S 9 a, b, c
Club Trench	62cNE4 Roisel / 62bNW3 Bellicourt	L 12 a, b, c, d, G 7 b
Clucas Trench	36cSW3 Vimy	M 36, N 31, S 5 to 11
Cluck Trench	36cSW3 Vimy	S 15 a
Clue Trench	36cSW3 Vimy	S 15 b
Clump Trench	36cSW3 Vimy	S 9 c, d
Cluny Trench	36cSW3 Vimy	S 9 c, d
Cluster Houses	28NE1 Zonnebeke	D 7 d 5.8
Clusters, The [dugouts]	28NW4 & NE3 Zillebeke	I 36 d, J 31 c
Clutch Trench	36cSW3 Vimy	S 9 c, 15 a
Clutter Trench	36cSW3 Vimy	S 15 b
Clyde Alley	51bNW1 Roclincourt	B 10 a, c
Clyde Avenue / Trench	51bNW3 Arras	G 6 d, H 1 c
Clyde Avenue / Trench	51bNW4 Fampoux	H 12 c, d, I 7 c, d, I 7 a
Clyde Avenue [Thiepval Wood]	57dSE1 & 2 Beaumont	R 25 c
Clyde Farm	27NE4 Abeele	L 29 a 3.4
Clyde Locality	51bNW1 Roclincourt / 2 Oppy	B 10 a, b, c
Clyde Road [road]	36SW1 Aubers	M 7 b, d
Clydesdale Camp	28SW1 Kemmel	N 14 b 6.6
Clytte, La, Railhead / Refilling Point	28SW1 Kemmel	N 7 a, b
Coal Alley [Mur de Crassier, Calonne]	36cSW1 Lens	M 20 a, b
Coal Street	36cSW1 Lens	M 20 a, b
Coal Trench	36cSW1 Lens	M 11 a
Coalville Lane	57cSE2 Gonnelieu	R 7 a, c
Coast Trench	36cSW1 Lens	M 11 a
Coat Trench	36cSW1 Lens	M 4 d
Coax Trench	36cSW1 Lens	M 12 a, c
Cob Trench	36cSW1 Lens	N 8 a
Cob Trench	51bNW2 Oppy	C 15 b
Cob Trench	51bNW4 Fampoux	I 10 a, d
Coba Road	36cSW4 Rouvroy	U 14 b
Cobalt Cottage	36aNE4 Merville	L 16 c 9.7
Cobalt Cross Roads	20SE2 Hooglede	R 21 a 87.42
Cobalt Road [road]	36cSW4 Rouvroy	U 8 d, 14 b
Cobar Line [1918]	62dNE [3 Morlancourt]	J 18 b, K 7 c, 13 a, c
Cobham [house]	36aNE4 Merville	K 34 a 70.75
Cobham Trench	57cSW1 Gueudecourt	M 24 c
Cobley Cottage	36aNE1 Morbecque	E 21 b 80.15
Cobourg Alley	66cSW2 Vendeuil	O 16 d, 17 c, d
Cobourg, Boyau de	36cSW3 Vimy	S 8 d
Cobra Trench	36cSW1 Lens	M 4 d
Cobra Trench	51bNW2 Oppy	C 25 d
Coburg Alley	36cSW3 Vimy	S 8 d, 9 c
Coburg Street	36cSW3 Vimy	S 8 d, 9 c
Coburg Trench	57cSW4 Combles	U 15 a, b, d
Coburn Copse	27NE2 Proven	F 21 c
Cobweb Avenue	36NW2 Armentières	C 10 c
Cocatoo Trench	28SW2 Wytschaete	N 11 c, 17 a

Name	Map Sheet	Map Reference
Cocheneac / Cogmeneac [Tranchée, 1915]	57dSE4 Ovillers	X 19 b
Cochin Corner [road jct]	36aNE4 Merville	L 7 c 85.20
Cochon Copse / Bois du Cochon	62cSW4 St. Christ	T 11 a
Cochran Avenue	62bNW1 Gouy / 62cNE2 Epéhy	A 7 b, F 12 a
Cochran Cottage	27SE4 Meteren	X 14 d 9.1
Cochrane Alley	62cNW1 Maricourt	A 6 b
Cock Alley	51bNW4 Fampoux	I 14 a
Cockcroft, The [farm & pillbox]	28NW2 St Julien	C 6 a 2.3
Cockle Trench	36cSW1 Lens	M 12 a
Cockney Trench	36cSW1 Lens	M 12 a
Cockscomb Trench	36cSW1 Lens	M 10 b, d, 11 c
Cockshie / Cockshy, The [front line; 1915]	36cNW1 La Bassée	A 15 d
Cockshy Avenue	57dSE2 Beaumont	R 13 d, 14 a, c
Cockshy House Post	36SW1 Aubers	M 9 b, 10 a
Cockshy Lane [Sept 1915]	36cNW1 La Bassée	A 15 d
Cockspur Street	36SW3 Richebourg	S 9 d, 15 b
Coco Trench	36cSW1 Lens	N 14 c
Cocoa Alley	51bNW4 Fampoux	I 14 a
Cocoa Copse	62cSW4 St. Christ	U 1 c, 7 a
Cocoa Lane [Gas Alley / Leiberweg]	57cSW3 Longueval	S 12 d, T 1 c, d, 7 a
Cocoa Support	62cNE2 Epéhy	F 30 c
Cocoa Trench	36cSW1 Lens	M 16 a, c
Cocoa Trench, & Support	62cNE2 Epéhy	F 30 c
Cocret, Bois de	51bSE4 Marquion	W 11 d, 12 c, 18 a
Cod Farm	28SW2 Wytschaete	O 30 d 05.05
Cod Post	57cNE1 Quéant	J 5 b 95.50
Cod Trench	51bNW2 Oppy	C 25 b, d
Cod Trench	51bNW4 Fampoux	I 8 c
Cod Trench [1918]	57dNE3 & 4 Hébuterne	K 5 d, 6 c, 11 a, b
Code Farm	28SW2 Wytschaete	O 23 d 8.8
Codfish Trench	36cSW1 Lens	M 4 c, d
Coe Trench	51bNW2 Oppy	B 12 d, C 7 c
Coffee Lane	57cSW3 Longueval	S 5 d, 6 c
Coffee Redoubt	57cNW1 Gomiecourt	A 15 a, b
Coffee Spur [light rly]	36cSW1 Lens	M 10 central
Coffee Street Support	28NW4 & NE3 Zillebeke	I 34 b
Coffee Trench	36cSW1 Lens	M 4 d, 10 b
Coffee Trench	51bNW4 Fampoux	I 13 d, 19 b
Coffee Trench	57dSE2 & 57cSW1 Le Sars	R 10 c, d
Coffin Trench	36cSW1 Lens	M 11 a, b
Cog Lane	51bSW1 Neuville Vitasse	M 28 b, d
Cognac Cottage [farm]	28NW1 Elverdinghe	A 30 b 9.7
Cognon Trench	62cNW4 Péronne	H 30 d, 36 b, I 25 c
Cohen House	28NE4 Dadizeele	L 16 a 1.4
Cohort Trench	36cSW1 Lens	M 4 d, 10 b
Cohre [Boyau/Tranchée, W of Fricourt, 1915]	62dNE2 Méaulte	F 2 a, b, c
Coin Alley	51bNW4 Fampoux	I 7 b
Coin Lane	57dSE2 & 57cSW1 Le Sars	M 12 a, c, d
Coin Trench	36cSW1 Lens	M 12 d, N 7 d
Coin Trench	36cSW1 Lens	M 4 d
Coine Farm	27NE4 Abeele	L 23 d 7.0
Cojeul Alley [1918]	51bSW3 Boisleux	S 23 d, 24 c, d
Cojeul Switch [1917]	51bSW1 Neuville Vitasse	N 7 b, d, 8 c, 14 a, c, d, 20 b, 21 a
Cojeul Switch [1918]	57dNE2 & 57cNW1 Courcelles	F 2 c, d, 7 b

Name	Map Sheet	Map Reference
Coke Avenue / Boyau de Coke	62cNW1 Maricourt	A 8 c, d, 9 a, c, 14 b
Coke Street [Auchonvillers]	57dSE1 & 2 Beaumont	Q 3 d
Coke Trench	36cSW1 Lens	N 7 d
Coke Trench	51bNW2 Oppy	C 7 b, d
Cokes Cottage	28NE3 Gheluvelt	J 25 d 90.45
Colbert Cross Roads	20SE3 Westroosebeke	V 1 b 9.3
Colchester Camp	57dNE3 & 4 Hébuterne	K 28 a
Colchester Trench	57dNE1 & 2 Fonquevillers	E 16 d, 17 c
Cold Alley	51bNW4 Fampoux	I 7 d, 13 a, b
Coldstream Lane [Cuinchy; 1916]	36cNW1 La Bassée	A 15 c, d, 21 b
Coldstream Lane [Cuinchy; Sept 1915]	36cNW1 La Bassée	A 15 c, d
Coldstream Lane [Givenchy; Sept 1915]	36cNW1 La Bassée	A 8 b, d, 9 a
Coldstream Road	36cNW1 La Bassée	A 2 d, 8 b
Coldstream Trench [1918]	51cSE4 Blaireville	X 9 c, 14 b, d, 15 a, c
Coldstream Tunnel [Cuinchy; 1916]	36cNW1 La Bassée	A 15 c, d, 21 b, 22 a
Cole [sic] Trench [Cote Wood]	62cNE4 Roisel	L 10 b, d, 16 a, b
Cole O.P. [1917-18]	36cSW3 Vimy	S 16 a 3.4
Coleman Street	36SW3 Richebourg	S 21 d, 27 b
Colenso Farm	28NW2 St Julien	B 18 b 6.1
Colibri Farm	20SE3 Westroosebeke	V 1 d 2.0
Colic Trench	36cSW1 Lens	M 16 a
Colignon, Tranchée	70dSW [2 Coucy-le-Château]	O 19 a
Colin Communication Trench [1918]	62dSW [4 Cachy / Gentelles]	U 10 c, 16 a
Colin Trench [1918]	62dSW [4 Cachy / Gentelles]	U 10 c, 16 a
Coliseum [Locality]	36cSW3 Vimy	S 20 c, d
Collar Alley	66cSW4 La Fère	U 21 d, 22 c
Collar Trench	36cSW1 Lens	M 10 a, b
Colleague House	20SW4 Bixschoote	T 23 c 4.3
Collecteur Trench [Grand Collecteur]	51bNW1 Roclincourt	A 16 c
Collector Trench [Grand Collecteur]	51bNW1 Roclincourt	A 15, 16, 22, 23, 29
Colleen Cross [chapel & road jct]	28NE2 Moorslede	F 10 c 55.47
Colleen Post	62cNE2 Epéhy	F 16 d
Collège des Jeunes Filles [Béthune]	36bNE2 Beuvry	E 11 d 3.8
College Green	36NW4 Bois Grenier	I 20 c, d
Collegue Avenue	20SW3 Oostvleteren	T 27 d, 28 c
Collier Trench	36cSW1 Lens	M 10 a, c
Collingbourne Avenue	57dNE1 & 2 Fonquevillers	E 10 d, 16 b, 17 a
Collins Copse	62cNE4 Roisel	L 35 b 55.75
Collins Quarry	62cNE4 Roisel	L 35 b 55.75
Collins Street	57cNE3 Hermies / 4 Marcoing	K 15 d, 15 c
Collins Street	57cNE4 Marcoing	K 15 d, 16 c
Collins Street [1918]	62dNE [3 Morlancourt]	J 12 d
Colman Farm	27SE4 Meteren	W 9 d 7.6
Colne Trench	51bNW4 Fampoux	I 19 a, c
Colne Valley	28NW2 St Julien	C 13 a, b
Colntraive Street	57dSE4 Ovillers	Q 36 c
Cologne Alley	66cNW1 Grugies	B 3 b, c, d, 9 a
Cologne Farm	62cNE4 Roisel	L 6 c 48.63
Cologne Reserve	62cNE4 Roisel	L 6 c
Cologne Street	36NW4 Bois Grenier	I 26 a
Cologne Support	62cNE4 Roisel	L 6 c
Cologne Trench	62cSW2 Barleux	O 5 d, 11 a, b, d
Cologne Trench [1918]	66eNW [2 Thennes]	C 13 c, d
Colombe Wood	62bSW1 Gricourt	N 14 b, d

Name	Map Sheet	Map Reference
Colombo House	20SW4 Bixschoote	U 6 b 10.25
Colombo Trench, Switch	51bNW4 Fampoux	I 14 c, 20 a
Colon Avenue	51bNW4 Fampoux	H 18 d, I 13 c
Colon Mill [windmill]	27SE4 Meteren	W 4 a 87.02
Colonel's Farm	20SW4 Bixschoote	U 20 c 1.5
Colonel's House	36bSE2 Boyeffles	R 29 d
Colonels Road	36cSW1 Lens	M 25 b
Colonial, Boyau	62cNW3 Vaux	G 34 c, d
Colony [light rly siding]	36cSW1 Lens	M 12 b
Colony Trench	36cSW1 Lens	M 12 a, c
Colour Trench	51bNW2 Oppy	C 25 c
Colt Trench	36cSW1 Lens	M 21 b
Colt Trench	51bNW4 Fampoux	H 18 b, I 13 a, c
Colt's Avenue	57cSW1 Gueudecourt	M 14 d
Columbia Trench	36cSW1 Lens / 3 Vimy	M 36 d, N 31 a, b, c
Colvin [keep, late 1915]	36SW1 Aubers	M 29 d 75.10
Colvin Trench	36SW1 Aubers	M 29 d
Colza Trench	36cSW1 Lens	N 13 c, d
Comb Trench	36cSW1 Lens	M 4 c, 10 a
Combat Trench	36cSW1 Lens	M 12, N 7, 13, 14
Combe Trench	62cSW3 Vermandovillers	S 8 b, c, d
Combes, Boyau [Doran Alley, part of]	36cSW1 Lens	M 25 d
Combles [village]	57cSW3 Longueval / 4 Combles	T 28 a, b, c, d
Combles Trench	57cSW3 Longueval	T 27 a, b, d, 28 c
Combow Trench	51bNW1 Roclincourt	A 3 d
Comby Trench	66cNW1 Grugies	B 7 a, c, 13 a
Comedian Crossing [bridge / level crossing]	28NE2 Moorslede	F 26 d 25.12
Comédie Trench	62cSW3 & 4 Marchélepot	T 7 b, 8 a
Comedy Maze	36cSW1 Lens	N 16 a
Comedy O.P. [1917-18]	36cSW3 Vimy	M 36 c 3.7
Comet [light rly siding]	36cSW1 Lens	M 10 b, 11 a
Comet Trench	36cSW1 Lens	M 10 b, 11 a, b, d
Comet Trench	57SW4 Combles	U 7 c, d, 8 a, c
Comete Trench	62cSW3 Vermandovillers	S 8 a, c
Comic Trench	36cSW1 Lens	N 20 a
Command Post [Smith's Villa]	36NW4 Bois Grenier	H 29 central
Commandant's House	51bNW1 Roclincourt	B 7 d 6.2
Commerestraat [hamlet / place name]	28NE4 Dadizeele	L 20 b, 21 a
Commet Camp	28SW3 Bailleul	S 29 a
Commet Farm	28SW3 Bailleul	S 29 a 3.4
Common Lane [Thiepval, 1918]	57dSE2 Beaumont	R 19 a, c
Commons Crater	36cSW3 Vimy	S 28 a
Commons Trench	36cSW3 Vimy	S 28 a
Commotion Trench	36cSW1 Lens	N 7 d, 8 a, b
Commue, Boyau	36cSW1 Lens	M 20 c
Communication Trench	36bSE4 Carency	X 4 a, b
Communication, The [Ger, Ploeg. Wd 1914-15]	28SW4 Ploegsteert	U 22 a
Como Cross [cross roads]	28NW3 Poperinghe	H 8 a 4.8
Comox [light rly locality, 1917-18]	28NW4 Ypres	I 34 a
Comox Trench	36cSW1 Lens	N 2 c, 8 a, b
Comp Farm	28NE2 Moorslede	F 22 a 5.1
Company Trench	28NW4 & NE3 Zillebeke	I 29 c
Company Trench / Road	36cSW3 Vimy	S 1 b, 2 a, c
Compas Trench	62cSW4 St. Christ	U 7 a, b, c

Name	Map Sheet	Map Reference
Complaisance, A la [Estaminet, Ploegsteert]	28SW4 Ploegsteert	U 25 c 85.45
Compres Trench	36cSW1 Lens	M 10 c
Compromise Farm	20SE3 Westroosebeke	V 13 b 45.20
Compton Bridge [across Ancre]	57dSE4 Ovillers	W 23 a 5.9
Compton Corner	28NW2 St Julien	C 13 a
Comstock Trench	36cSW1 Lens / 2 Harnes	N 16 a
Conamulla Support [1918]	62dNE [3 Morlancourt]	K 19 a, c, 25 a, c
Concert Trench	36cSW1 Lens	M 4 c, d
Conchie Farm	27SE1 St Sylvestre	Q 9 b 1.8
Concord, A la [Estaminet, Ploegsteert]	28SW4 Ploegsteert	U 25 c 87.40
Concrete Post	28NW4 & NE3 Zillebeke	J 9 d 8.9
Concrete Reserve	51bSW4 Bullecourt	N 36 c
Concrete Shelter	28SW4 Ploegsteert	U 26 b
Concrete Tower	28NW4 & NE3 Zillebeke	J 14 d
Concrete Trench	51bSW2 Vis-en-Artois / 4 Bullecourt	N 36 a, b, c, T 5 b, 6 a
Condé House	20SE3 Westroosebeke	V 13 a 12.90
Condé Keep	36cSW1 Lens	M 1 d
Condé S Puits [coal mines]	36cSW1 Lens	N 9 c, d, 15 a, b
Condé, Tranchée	70dSW [2 Coucy-le-Château]	O 13 d
Condiment Cross [cross roads]	28NW3 Poperinghe	G 32 d 8.3
Conductor Alley	36cSW1 Lens	N 8 c
Conductor Trench	36cSW1 Lens	N 8 c, 14 a, b
Conduit Avenue	57dNE1 & 2 Fonquevillers	E 16 b
Conduit Street	36SW1 Aubers	M 28 b, 29 a
Conduit Street [Hooge 1915]	28NW4 & NE3 Zillebeke	I 17 b, 18 a, b
Conduit Street [Sept 1915]	36cNW1 La Bassée	A 21 b
Cone Trench	36cSW1 Lens	M 10 b
Coney Cottage	36aNE4 Merville	K 24 a 3.9
Coney Street	28NW2 St Julien	C 19 d, 20 c, d, 21 c
Coneys Farm	20SE2 Hooglede	Q 35 a 40.75
Conger [light rly siding]	36cSW1 Lens	M 10 a
Conger Farm	28NE2 Moorslede	F 1 d 25.60
Conger Trench	36cSW1 Lens	M 10 a, b
Conger Trench [1918]	62dNE [3 Sailly-le-Sec]	K 25 a
Congo Trench	51bSW2 Vis-en-Artois	N 6 a, c, d
Congress Trench	36cSW1 Lens	N 7 b
Congreve Walk	28NW2 St Julien	C 27 d, 28 c
Coniston Post	57dSE4 Ovillers	X 7 a
Coniston Street	57dSE4 Ovillers	X 7 a, c
Connantry Street / Avenue	57dSE1 & 2 Beaumont	Q 23 b
Connaught Road [road]	28SW3 Bailleul	T 26 c, d, 27 c, d
Connaught Street	36SW3 Richebourg	S 15 b
Connecticut Trench [1918]	51bNW1 Roclincourt	A 17,18,24, B 19,25,26
Connexion Trench	36cSW1 Lens	M 5 c, d
Connie Post	36NW4 Bois Grenier	I 21 a
Connie Trench	51bNW2 Oppy	C 1 b, d, 7 b, 8 a, b
Connor Switch	62cNE2 Epéhy	F 28 d
Conrad Trench, Support & Alley	51bNW4 Fampoux	I 1 d
Consett Dugouts	28NW4 & NE3 Zillebeke	I 24 b
Consetts Trench	36NW2 Armentières	C 28 b
Consolation Post [N.D. de Consolation]	36cNW3 Loos	G 10 c 3.4
Const.ne, Boyau [Constantine]	36cSW1 Lens	M 19 d, 25 b
Constable Trench	51bNW2 Oppy	C 14 b, 15 a, c, d
Constance Trench	57dSE2 Beaumont / 4 Ovillers	R 32 b, d, 33 a

Name	Map Sheet	Map Reference
Constantine Alley [1918]	62dSW [4 Cachy]	U 9 b, d, 10 a
Constitution Hill	57dSE1 & 2 Beaumont	Q 16 d
Constitution Hill [road]	36cSW1 Lens	M 17 b, c, d, 23 a
Constitution Hill [Sept 1915]	36cNW1 La Bassée	A 9 a
Constitution Line [light rly]	36cSW1 Lens	M 16 c, d, 22 a, b, c
Construction Spur [light rly]	36bSE2 Boyeffles	R 22 d
Consume Trench	36cSW1 Lens	M 12 b
Contalmaison [village]	57dSE4 Ovillers	X 16, 17
Contalmaison Chateau	57dSE4 Ovillers	X 16 b 80.15
Contalmaison Villa	57dSE4 Ovillers	X 11 d
Contalmaison Wood	57dSE4 Ovillers	X 10 c, 16 a
Contay [village]	57dSW [4 Toutencourt]	U 20, 21, 26, 27
Conte Trench [Tranchée de Conté]	57cSW4 Combles	T 6 a, b, c, d, U 1 c
Contescourt [village]	66cNW1 Grugies	A 21 b, d
Contescourt Alley	66cNW1 Grugies	A 23, 24, 28, G 4
Contest Trench	36cSW1 Lens	M 6 d
Contort Trench	36cSW1 Lens	N 7 b, d
Contour British Cemetery	57bNE1 [E of Cambrai]	E 15 b 4.0
Control Post	28SW4 Ploegsteert	T 18 a 6.8
Control Trench	36cSW1 Lens	N 7 b
Convent [Hooghe]	20SE2 Hooglede	Q 10 c 9.6
Convent [S of le Gheer]	28SW4 Ploegsteert	U 27 b 8.3
Convent [S of Lovie Chateau]	27NE2 Proven	F 22 d 05.90
Convent Avenue	36SW2 Radinghem	N 5 a, c
Convent Field [La Boutillerie]	36SW2 Radinghem	N 5 c, d, 11 a, b [approx, 1915]
Convent Lane	28SW4 Ploegsteert	U 28 a, c
Convent Lane [CT]	28SW2 Wytschaete	O 2 a, c
Convent Lane [track]	28NW4 Ypres / SW2 Wytschaete	I 32 a, c, O 2 a
Convent St. Sixte / Couvent des Trappistes	28NW1 Elverdinghe	A 1 a O.5
Convent Trench	36cSW1 Lens	M 11 a
Convent Wall [La Boutillerie]	36SW2 Radinghem	N 4 d, 5 c
Convent, The	36SW1 Aubers	M 18 d 15.25
Cooee Trench [1918]	62dNE [3 Morlancourt]	J 18 b, d
Coogee Trench [1918]	62dNE [3 Morlancourt]	J 30 d, K 25 a, c
Cook Copse	28NE2 Moorslede	F 25 d 95.95
Cook Street	57dSE1 & 2 Beaumont	Q 3 d
Cook Trench [1918]	62dNE [3 Morlancourt]	J 12 b, K 7 a
Cooker Alley [Cordonnier, Boyau]	36bSE2 Boyeffles / 36cSW1 Lens	M 25 d, 31 b, 32 a
Cooker Farm	28SW4 Ploegsteert	N 35 c 4.8
Cooker Quarry	62cSE2 Vermand	R 11 a, c
Cooker Trench	62cSE2 Vermand	R 5 c, d, 11 b
Cookers Farm	28SW4 Ploegsteert	N 35 c 3.8
Cookhouse Dugouts	57dNE3 & 4 Hébuterne	K 33 a
Cool Trench	36cSW1 Lens	M 10 a, b
Coolbardie Trench [1918]	62dNE [3 Morlancourt]	J 24 a, c
Coolie Cross Roads	28NE2 Moorslede	K 5 a 75.87
Coomac Trench [1918]	62dNE [3 Morlancourt]	J 18 b, K 13 a
Coombe Alley	62dNE2 Méaulte	F 10 b, d, 11 c
Coombe Farm	20SE3 Westroosebeke	V 3 d 4.6
Coombe Fork [road jct]	28NE4 Dadizeele	K 34 c 85.40
Coop Trench	36cSW1 Lens	M 11 a, b
Cooper Farm	20SE2 Hooglede	Q 28 d 3.1
Cooper Street	62dNE2 Méaulte	F 12 c
Cooper Trench	36cSW1 Lens	N 1 c, 7 a

Name	Map Sheet	Map Reference
Cooper Trench	57cNE3 Hermies	K 8 d, 9 c
Cooper Trench	62dNE2 Méaulte	F 3 b, d
Coot Trench	51bNW4 Fampoux	I 13 a, c
Cootamundra Street [1918]	62dNE [3 Morlancourt]	J 24 c, d
Coote Corner [cross roads]	27SE4 Meteren	X 23 a 80.35
Cope's Farm	28NE4 Dadizeele	L 25 a 85.40
Copper Corner [road jct]	28NE4 Dadizeele	L 23 a 1.4
Copper Trench	36cSW1 Lens	N 7 a, c
Copper Trench	51bNW2 Oppy	C 7 c, 13 a
Copper Trench	51bNW4 Fampoux	I 1 d, 7 a, b
Copper Trench	62dNE2 Méaulte	F 3 d, 9 b
Copper Wood	66dNW1 Punchy	A 11 d, 12 c
Coppernole Cabaret	28NW1 Elverdinghe	A 16 b 5.9
Coppernollenhoek [hamlet]	28NW1 Elverdinghe	A 9 a, b, 10 a
Copse A	62cNW1 Maricourt	A 20 c
Copse Alley	57dSE4 Ovillers	X 4 b, d, 5 c, 11 a
Copse Avenue	57dSE4 Ovillers	X 4
Copse B	62cNW1 Maricourt	A 21 a
Copse C	62cNW1 Maricourt	A 21 d
Copse Cemetery	62dNE [3 Morlancourt]	J 24 b
Copse Cotts	28NE3 Gheluvelt	J 28 a 4.6
Copse D	62cNW1 Maricourt	A 27 a
Copse E	62cNW1 Maricourt	A 20 d, 26 b
Copse F	62cNW1 Maricourt	A 26 b
Copse Farm	28SW2 Wytschaete	O 18 d 8.5
Copse G	62cNW1 Maricourt	A 26 a, b
Copse H	62cNW1 Maricourt	A 25 d
Copse J	62cNW1 Maricourt	A 26 d
Copse K	62cNW1 Maricourt	A 27 c
Copse Keep	36SW3 Richebourg	S 10 c
Copse L	62cNW3 Vaux	G 3 a
Copse Lane	51bSW2 Vis-en-Artois	O 23 a
Copse Lane	62cNW1 Maricourt	A 23 b, 24 a
Copse Lane [road]	51bSW2 Vis-en-Artois	O 17 d, 18 c, 23 a, b
Copse M	62cNW3 Vaux	G 2 b, d
Copse N	62cNW1 Maricourt / 3 Vaux	A 26 c, G 2 a
Copse O	62cNW3 Vaux	G 1 b
Copse P	62cNW3 Vaux	G 2 a
Copse Post [W of Loos]	36cNW3 Loos	G 34 b
Copse Reserve	57cSW4 Combles	U 7 a, b, d, 8 c
Copse Road	51bSW4 Bullecourt	U 9 c
Copse Road [road]	57cSE2 Gonnelieu	R 8 c, 13 b, 14 a
Copse S	62cNW3 Vaux	G 1 d
Copse Street	36SW3 Richebourg	S 10 b, c
Copse T	62cNW3 Vaux	G 2 c
Copse Trench	36SW3 Richebourg	S 10 a
Copse Trench	51bSW1 Neuville Vitasse	M 12 b, d
Copse Trench	51bSW4 Bullecourt	U 8, 9, 15, 16
Copse Trench	57dNE3 & 4 Hébuterne	K 23 d, 29 a, b
Copse Valley	62cNW1 Maricourt	A 20 d, 26 b, d
Coq de Paille, le [hamlet]	27SE2 Berthen	R 31 a 2.5
Coq Trench	20SW3 Oostvleteren	T 15 a, c
Coq Trench / Tranchée du Coq	62cSW3 & 4 Marchélepot	T 13 d, 19 b
Coquelicot Farm	20SW4 Bixschoote	T 18 a 3.2

Name	Map Sheet	Map Reference
Cor Alley	62cSW3 Vermandovillers	T 14 d
Cora Trench	36cSW1 Lens	M 10 d
Coral Trench	36cSW1 Lens	M 12 b
Coral Trench	51bNW4 Fampoux	I 13 c, 19 a
Corbeaux Copse	62cNE1 Liéramont	D 21 a
Corbeaux Trench	57cSE3 Sorel-le-Grand	V 10 a, c
Corbeaux Trench [1918]	62dSE [3 Marcelcave]	V 13 c, d
Corbie South [hamlet]	36aNE3 Haverskerque	J 36 a, b
Corbie, le [hamlet]	36aNE3 Haverskerque	J 30 d
Corbonne Ditch	36cSW3 Vimy / 51bNW1 Roclincourt	S 27 c, d, A 3 a, c
Corce Gut	51bNW4 Fampoux	I 19 b
Cord Alley	57cSW4 Combles	U 1 d, 2 c
Cord Trench	51bNW2 Oppy	C 1 c
Corded Road [1915-16]	28SW4 Ploegsteert	T 12 a, b
Cordiale Avenue	36cSW1 Lens	M 4 b, 5 a
Cordite Trench	51bSW1 Neuville Vitasse	M 6 a
Cordite Trench / Reserve	51bNW4 Fampoux	I 19 a, c
Cordonnerie Post	36SW2 Radinghem	N 10 a
Cordonnier, Boyau [Cooker Alley]	36bSE2 Boyeffles / 36cSW1 Lens	R 39 c, M 25 d, 31 b
Cordova [light rly siding]	28NW3 Poperinghe	H 19 c
Corduroy Road [Neuve Eglise]	28SW3 Bailleul	T 9 c, 14 b, 15 a
Corduroy Road [road, near Moated Grange]	28NW4 & NE3 Zillebeke	I 16 c
Corfu Avenue	51bNW4 Fampoux	H 24, I 13, 14, 19
Corfu Farm	27NE4 Abeele	L 22 d 6.5
Corin [farm]	36aNE2 Vieux Berquin	F 17 c 2.9
Cork Alley [E of High Wood]	57cSW3 Longueval	S 4 b, d, 5 a
Cork Copse	28NE4 Dadizeele	L 10 c
Cork Cottage	28NE2 Moorslede	F 23 c 15.20
Cork Cottages	28NW4 & NE3 Zillebeke	I 10 a 8.3
Cork Lane [trench]	28NW4 & NE3 Zillebeke	I 9 b, 10 a
Cork Street	28NW4 & NE3 Zillebeke	I 18 a
Cork Street	57dNE1 & 2 Fonquevillers	E 16 d
Cork Street [Hohenzollern, Oct 1915]	36cNW3 & 1 Loos	G 4 a, b
Cork Support	51bNW2 Oppy / 4 Fampoux	I 1 a, c
Cork Trench	28SW2 Wytschaete	N 18 c
Cork Trench	36cSW1 Lens	M 12 b, N 7 a
Corkscrew [Trench / Alley]	36cSW1 Lens	M 10, 11, 12, 16, 17, 18
Corkscrew Alley	36cSW1 Lens	M 15 b
Corn Hill [hill]	28NW2 St Julien	C 18 b, d
Corn Lane [1918]	51cSE4 Blaireville	X 29 c, d
Corn Lane [road, Long Cornet]	36aSE4 Locon	W 23 b, 24 c
Corn Lane [trench]	57cSW1 Gueudecourt	M 12 b, d
Corn Pond	28NW2 St Julien	C 18 d
Corn Trench	36cSW1 Lens	M 4 c, 10 a, c
Corn Trench	51bNW2 Oppy	C 15, 16 c, d, 21 b
Corn Trench	51bNW4 Fampoux	I 14 d, 20 a
Corncrake Cross Roads	20SE2 Hooglede	R 8 c 60.75
Corneilles Trench	62cSW3 Vermandovillers / 4 St Christ	T 4 c, 10 a
Corner Camp	28SW3 Bailleul	N 33 c
Corner Copse	20SE3 Westroosebeke	W 13 c, 19 a
Corner Copse	51bNW4 Fampoux/NE3 Noyelle/ SW2 Vis-en-Artois	I 36 d, J 31 c, O 6 b
Corner Cot.	28NW2 St Julien	C 17 b 60.36
Corner Cottage	36aSE1 St Venant	Q 14 c 85.20

Name	Map Sheet	Map Reference
Corner Fort [GFL]	36SW1 Aubers	N 6 b, d
Corner House [Zwarteleen]	28NW4 & NE3 Zillebeke	I 35 b 9.9
Corner Port [GFL, late 1915]	36SW2 Radinghem	N 6 d 5.9
Corner Support	57cSE2 Gonnelieu	R 15 a, c
Corner Trench	36cSW1 Lens	M 10 d, 11 c, 17 a
Corner Trench	57cSE2 Gonnelieu	R 15 b, d
Corner Work [La Vacquerie]	57cSE2 Gonnelieu	R 15 d
Cornet d'Or, le [farm & crossroads]	66cNW2 Itancourt	B 22 d
Cornet Farm	28NE4 Dadizeele	L 21 c 0.6
Cornet Malo, le [hamlet]	36aSE2 Lestrem	Q 28 a
Cornet Perdu, le	36aNE4 Merville	K 5 d
Cornet Trench	36cSW1 Lens	M 10 d, 11 c
Cornhill	28NW2 St Julien	C 21 c, 27 a
Cornhill [road]	57cNE1 Quéant	D 7 c
Cornhill B [trench, Nov 1915]	28NW2 St Julien	C 21 c, 27 a
Cornhill Valley	57cNE1 Quéant	D 7 c
Cornichon, Boyau de	62cSW3 & 4 Marchélepot	T 10 a, b
Cornish Alley	57cSW3 Longueval	S 23 d, 24 c, d
Cornouillers Alley	62bSW1 Gricourt	M 22 b, c, d
Cornu Copse	66dNW3 Hattencourt	G 21 d
Cornu Wood	66eNW [4 Morisel]	H 29 b, 30 a
Cornwall Avenue	28SW4 Ploegsteert	U 15 a, c
Cornwall Avenue	57cSE2 Gonnelieu	R 8 d, 14 b
Cornwall Avenue [1918]	51bSW3 Boisleux	S 22 c, 28 a
Cornwall Cut	57cSE2 Gonnelieu	R 14 b
Cornwall Lane	57cSE2 Gonnelieu	R 7 a
Cornwall Siding	36SW1 Aubers	M 35 b
Cornwall Support	57cSE2 Gonnelieu	R 14 b, 15 a
Cornwall Trench	36cSW1 Lens	N 7 c, 13 a
Cornwall Trench	57cSE2 Gonnelieu	R 14 d, 15 c
Cornwall Trench	57dSE2 Beaumont	R 17 c
Coron d'Aix [light rly]	36bSE2 Boyeffles	R 11 c
Corona Alley	51bNW4 Fampoux	I 19 c, d
Corona Support	51bNW4 Fampoux	I 14 c
Corona Trench	51bNW4 Fampoux	I 13 d, 14 c, 19 b
Coroner Houses	28NE2 Moorslede	F 12 c 3.2
Coronet Post	62cNE4 Roisel	L 30 c 8.8
Corons Alley	36cNW1 La Bassée	A 29 c, G 4 b, 5 a
Corons d'Aix Alley	36bSE2 Boyeffles / 36cSW1 Lens	R 17, 23, 24, 30, M 25 b, d
Corons d'Aix, Boyau	36bSE2 Boyeffles	R 30 a
Corons du No. 5 [Maroc]	36cNW3 Loos / 36cSW1 Lens	G 32 c, d, 33 a, M 2 a, b
Corons du Rutoire Keep	36cNW3 Loos	G 14 d, 20 b
Corot Trench	36cSW1 Lens	M 11 a
Corpo, Tranchée de la	62cSW3 & 4 Marchélepot	T 14 d, 15 c
Corporal Trench	36cSW1 Lens	M 10 a, b, 11 a
Corporale / Corporals Copse	62cSW4 St. Christ	U 15 d
Corrin Trench	36cNW3 Loos	G 4 d
Corsair Fork [road jct]	28NE2 Moorslede	K 5 a 05.08
Corsair Trench	36cSW1 Lens	M 11 c, d, 16 b, d
Corset Trench	36cSW1 Lens	M 10 c
Corsica Trench	51bSW2 Vis-en-Artois	N 5 a, c
Corsican Cross Roads	28NE2 Moorslede	E 10 c 50.55
Corton Cross [cross roads]	27NE4 Abeele	K 24 d 97.82
Corton House	27NE4 Abeele	L 19 a 05.15

Name	Map Sheet	Map Reference
Cortvriendt Chateau	20SW4 Bixschoote	O 36 c 70.99
Corunna Road [Sept 1915]	36cNW1 La Bassée	A 9 d
Corver Wood	20SW4 Bixschoote	O 34 c
Cosine Trench	36cSW1 Lens	M 10 c
Cossack Corner [road jct]	28NE2 Moorslede	E 16 b 80.75
Cossack Trench	36cSW1 Lens	M 10, 11, 12, 16
Cosson, Tranchée	70dSW [2 Coucy-le-Château]	O 27 c
Cost Trench	36cSW1 Lens	N 7 a
Cost Trench	51bNW4 Fampoux	I 8 d, 14 b
Costa Alley	51bNW4 Fampoux	I 7 b
Costa Trench	51bNW4 Fampoux	I 7 b, d
Coste Trench	62cSW1 & 2 Belloy	N 11 d
Costin, Tranchée de	62cSW1 & 2 Belloy	N 30 c, 36 a
Costly Lane [S of Flers]	57cSW3 Longueval	S 6 d
Cosy Alley	36cSW1 Lens	N 2 c
Cosy Communication Trench [1918]	62dNE [3 Morlancourt]	K 19 b
Cosy Copse	57cSE2 Gonnelieu	Q 3 d 4.3
Cosy Corner [W end of Montauban]	57cSW3 Longueval	S 27 c 7.4
Cosy Cotts	28NE3 Gheluvelt	J 6.3
Cosy Trench	36cSW1 Lens	N 2 c, d
Cot, The	51bSW1 Neuville Vitasse	N 27 b
Cote 99, Bois de la	66eNE4 Beaufort	L 32 a
Cote 99, Réduit [at spot-height]	62cSW1 Dompierre	M 3 d
Cote North [post]	62cNE4 Roisel	L 10 d 3.5
Cote South [post]	62cNE4 Roisel	L 16 a 8.7
Cote Wood	62cNE4 Roisel	L 10 c
Coton Trench, Tranchée du Coton	62cSW3 & 4 Marchélepot	T 14 d, 20 b, c, d
Cotta Crossing [bridge over rly]	27SE2 Berthen	Q 22 c 75.05
Cottage Alley	66cNW4 Berthenicourt	H 17 c, d, 23 a
Cottage Copse	62cNE4 Roisel	L 23 b
Cottage Trench	36cSW1 Lens	M 16 a
Cottage Trench	36cSW1 Lens	M 18 a, b
Cottage Trench	62dNE2 Méaulte	F 3 d
Cottage, The	36SW1 Aubers	N 7 d
Cottesmore Trench	57cSE4 Villers-Guislain	X 28 d
Cotton Farm	28NE4 Dadizeele	L 26 c 5.1
Cotton Trench	36cSW1 Lens	N 13 b, c
Cotton Trench	57cSE4 Villers-Guislain	X 10 d, 11 c, 17 a
Couché, Bois	66dNW2 Morchain	C 27 b, 28 a
Coudée Trench	62cSW2 Barleux	O 7 d, 8 c
Couesnon Alley	66cNW4 Berthenicourt	I 19 d
Cougar Trench	36cSW1 Lens	M 9 d, 10 c
Cougar Trench	57cSW1 Gueudecourt	M 35 a
Cough Drop Alley	57dSE2 & 57cSW1 Le Sars	M 35 a
Cough Drop, The	57dSE2 & 57cSW1 Le Sars	M 35 a
Couillet Alley	57cNE4 Marcoing	L 26 d, 32 b, 33 a
Couillet Avenue	57cNE4 Marcoing	L 27 c, 32 b, d, 33 a
Couillet Support	57cNE4 Marcoing	L 27 c, d
Couillet Trench	57cNE4 Marcoing	L 27 a, c, d
Coulee Trench	57dSE2 & 57cSW1 Le Sars	R 12 a, c, M 2 d, 7 b, d, 8 a, b
Coulee Trench	66cNW2 Itancourt	B 24 d
Counsel Buildings	28NE2 Moorslede	F 18 a 35.25
Count Avenue	51bNW2 Oppy	C 26 c, d, 27 b, c, d
Counter Alley	36cSW1 Lens	M 11 b, N 7 a, b, 8 a, c

Name	Map Sheet	Map Reference
Counter Copse	27NE2 Proven	F 20 a
Country Trench	36cSW1 Lens	M 18 a, b
County Cross Roads	20SE3 Westroosebeke	V 26 a 9.1
Coupe Gueule, le [hamlet / crossroads]	57dSE2 & 57cSW1 Le Sars	M 11 a
Coupe Trench	57dSE2 & 57cSW1 Le Sars	M 10 d, 11 a, b
Couperet Alley [1918]	66eNW [2 Thennes]	B 28 d, 29 c, d
Couperet Wood	66eNW [2 Thennes]	B 28 d, 29 c
Coupez Mill	57cNE2 Bourlon	F 1 a 95.75
Coupigny Chateau [W of Bully-Grenay]	36bSE2 Boyeffles	Q 11 b
Coupigny Locality	36bSE2 Boyeffles	Q 17 b, d, 18 a, c
Coupland Farm	28NE4 Dadizeele	L 2 d 4.2
Coupule [trench]	66cNW2 Itancourt	B 24 a, b
Coupy Alley	66cNW1 Grugies	B 7 b, d
Courbesseau	70dNW2 Servais	B 23 a, c, 29 a
Courcelette [village]	57dSE2 & 57cSW1 Le Sars	R 29 b, 30 a, c, M 25 b
Courcelette Trench	57dSE2 & 57cSW1 Le Sars	R 11 d, 12 c, 18 a, c, 24 a. c
Courcelles [village]	62bSW2 Fonsommes	O 15 b, d
Courcelles Alley	57cNW1 Gomiecourt	A 13 d, 14 c
Courcelles Alley [1918]	57dNE2 / 57cNW1 [Gomiecourt]	F 18 a, A 13 d, 14 c
Courcelles Trench	57cNW1 Gomiecourt	A 14 c, 19 b, 20 a
Courcelles-le-Comte	57cNW1 Gomiecourt	A 15 b, c, d, 16 a, c
Courier Alley	66cNW1 Grugies / 2 Itancourt	B 28 c
Courier Trench	66cSW4 La Fère	U 26 d, 27 a
Couronne Cabaret, La	28SW1 Kemmel	M 23 a 35.67
Couronne, La [cross roads]	28SW1 Kemmel	M 23 a 3.6
Couronne, la [cross roads]	36aNE2 Vieux Berquin	E 30 a
Couronne, la [hamlet]	36aNE2 Vieux Berquin	E 30 a, b
Courrier, Tranchée	62cSW1 & 2 Belloy	O 2 b, c, d
Courrières Road	36cSW4 Rouvroy	U 2 b
Courte Croix [cross roads & hamlet]	27SE4 Meteren	W 18 b 2.3
Courte Croix Switch	27SE4 Meteren	W 12, 18, 23, 24
Courte Croix Switch [1918]	27SE4 Meteren	extensive
Courte Dreve Farm	28SW4 Ploegsteert	T 24 a 4.5
Courtefroie Farm	36aNE3 Haverskerque	K 27 b 30 85
Courtine Alley	62cSW3 Vermandovillers	S 13 b, d
Courtine Trench	62cSW3 Vermandovillers	S 13 b
Couscous, Tranchée du	62cSW3 & 4 Marchélepot	T 4 d, 10 b
Cousin Farm	27NE1 Herzeele	E 13 b 50.55
Coutances Trench	66cSW2 Vendeuil	N 28 d, 34 b
Couteau Trench	62cSW3 Vermandovillers	T 14 c, d, 15 c
Couterel Street	51cSE3 & 4 Ransart	R 33 a, c, d
Couthove Camp	27NE2 Proven	F 14 d 3.4
Couthove Chateau [Canal Sector]	27NE2 Proven	F 21 a 5.5
Couthove Cross [cross roads]	27NE2 Proven	F 21 a 2.6
Coutts [farm]	20SE3 Westroosebeke	V 10 c 5.0
Coutts Trench	20SE3 Westroosebeke	V 10 c
Couturaud Trench	66cNW1 Grugies	A 6 d
Couture Copse	62cNE3 Buire	K 13 d
Couturée / Coutures Copse	62cNE1 Lièramont	D 25 b, d
Couve, Tranchée [S end of Spinney Trench]	36cSW1 Lens	M 25 d
Couvent des Trappistes / Convent St. Sixte	28NW1 Elverdinghe	A 1 a O.5
Couvent des Trappistes, St Sixte	28NW1 Elverdinghe	A 1 d
Couvert Alley	62cSW3 Vermandovillers	S 16 a
Couvert Alley	62cSW3 Vermandovillers	T 14 c

Name	Map Sheet	Map Reference
Cove Trench	36cSW1 Lens	M 10 c
Cove Trench	51bNW4 Fampoux	H 18 d
Covent Garden	36cSW1 Lens	M 14 b
Coventry [lt rly locality WSW of Langemarck]	20SW4 Bixschoote	U 27 b
Coventry Street	36cNW1 La Bassée	A 9 d
Coventry Street [tunnel, Railway Wood]	28NW4 & NE3 Zillebeke	I 11 b
Cover Trench, Right & Left	36SW3 Richebourg	S 22 c, 27 b, 28 a
Covered Trench	28SW2 Wytschaete	N 23 b, 24 a
Covered Way	36SW3 Richebourg	M 34 a - S 4 d
Covered Way [Loos Crassier]	36cNW3 Loos	G 36 c
Covering Trench	36NW2 Armentières	C 12 a, b
Covet Trench	36cSW1 Lens	M 11 c, d
Covs / Coys [post / trench]	36cNW1 La Bassée	G 3 a 1.7
Covs / Coys Alley	36cNW1 La Bassée	A 27 c, G 3 a
Cow Alley	36cSW1 Lens	M 12 c, N 7 c, d
Cow Alley	57cNE1 Quéant	D 26 d
Cow Lane	36cNW3 Loos	G 36 a
Cow Lane	36NW4 Bois Grenier	I 20 d
Cow Lane	51bNW2 Oppy	C 8 a, b, c
Cow Lane [road]	36aSE4 Locon	W 18 d, X 13 c
Cow Lane [road]	51bNE3 Noyelle-sous-Bellonne	J 26 a, b
Cow Post	62cNE4 Roisel	L 24 c 45.20
Cow Support	57cSW4 Combles	T 6 b, U 1 a, c
Cow Trench	51bNW4 Fampoux	I 9 c, 15 a, b
Cow Trench	57cSW3 Longueval	T 3 a, c, d, 9 b
Cowboy Corner [road jct]	28NE2 Moorslede	E 12 a 30.87
Cowboy Trench	36cSW1 Lens	M 9 d, 10 c, 15 b, 16 a
Cowcatcher Trench	36cSW1 Lens	M 15 b, 16 a, b
Cowden Trench	36cSW1 Lens	M 12, 15, 16, 17, N 1
Cowdray Trench	36cSW1 Lens	N 7 d, 13 b
Cowgate Avenue	36NW4 Bois Grenier	I 15 d
Cowgate Post	36NW4 Bois Grenier	I 9 c, 15 a, b, d, 16 c
Cowley Road [Sept 1915]	36cNW1 La Bassée	A 15 b
Cowley Trench	36cSW1 Lens	N 8 a, c
Cowper Trench	36cSW1 Lens	M 15 b, 16 a
Cowra Trench [1918]	62dNE [3 Morlancourt]	K 7 a
Cows Wood	62cNW3 Vaux	G 29 a
Cowshed Point	36NW2 Armentières	C 18 a
Cowslip Corner [road junction]	20SE2 Hooglede	R 9 c 75.50
Cowthorpe Road	28NW2 St Julien	C 21 a, c
Cox [Flers Practice Trenches]	57dSE2 & 57cSW1 Le Sars	N 31 a
Cox Bank, & Cox's Road	57cSE4 Villers-Guislain	X 23 a, b
Cox Trench	51bNW4 Fampoux	I 19 a
Coxs [farm]	20SE3 Westroosebeke	V 10 c 3.7
Cox's Bank [1918]	51cSE4 Blaireville	X 19 a, b, d
Cox's Trench	20SE3 Westroosebeke	V 10 c
Coy Farm	28SE1 Wervicq	P 4 b 5.6
Coy Trench	36cSW1 Lens	M 15 b, 16 a
Coyote Trench	36cSW1 Lens	M 15 b, 16 a
Cozet Trench	66cNW1 Grugies	B 14 a, b, 15 a, c
Crab Alley [1918]	51bNW1 Roclincourt	A 16 b, 17 a
Crab Apple Tree	28NW2 St Julien	C 8 b 90.13
Crab Crawl [trench]	28NW4 & NE3 Zillebeke	I 24 d
Crab Crawl Tunnel	28NW4 & NE3 Zillebeke	I 24 d 7.5

Name	Map Sheet	Map Reference
Crab Lane	62bNW1 Gouy	A 25 b
Crab Street	28NW4 & NE3 Zillebeke	I 24 b
Crab Trench	36cSW1 Lens	M 15 d
Crab Trench	51bNW2 Oppy	C 25 b
Crab Trench	57cNE3 Hermies	K 9 a
Crab Trench	57dSE1 & 2 Beaumont	Q 22 d, 23 a, c
Crabe Trench	62cSW2 Barleux	N 34 a, b, c
Crabes Trench	62cNW1 Maricourt	B 27 b, 28 a
Craddock / Cradock Trench	51bNW2 Oppy	C 1 b, d, 2 a
Cradle Trench [mistranscrip. of Credit Trench]	36cSW1 Lens	M 21 b
Craetsteen Copse	27SE2 Berthen	R 16 b
Craft Cottage	28NE2 Moorslede	F 25 a 15.40
Craft Trench [1918]	62dSW [4 Cachy]	U 5 d, 11 a, b
Craftsman Trench	36cSW1 Lens	M 18 a, b
Crag House	36SW1 Aubers	M 18 c
Craggy Trench	36cSW1 Lens	M 15 d, 16 c
Cragside Trench	51bSW4 Bullecourt	U 7 d
Craig Trench	36cSW1 Lens	M 15 d
Cranberry Trench	36cSW1 Lens	M 21 b, 22 a
Crane Cross Roads	20SE2 Hooglede	R 35 a 05.79
Crane Trench	51bNW2 Oppy	C 15 c, d
Crank Alley	51bNW4 Fampoux	I 8 c
Cranky Trench	36cSW1 Lens	M 16 c, 22 a
Cranleigh / Cranlegh Sap	36cSW1 Lens	M 15 a
Cranmer House	36aNE4 Merville	L 31 b 6.2
Cranny Trench	36cSW1 Lens	M 15 d
Cranz [Croix?] de Fer, la [X rds E of Béthune]	36bNE2 Beuvry	F 1 b 6.2
Craonne Farm	20SW4 Bixschoote	U 15 d 3.6
Crapaud, Bois de	62cSW3 & 4 Marchélepot	T 10 a
Crapouillots Trench	66cNW1 Grugies	B 7 b
Crapouillots, Bois des	28NW2 St Julien	B 6 c, d
Crash Trench	36cSW1 Lens	M 15 d
Crash Trench	51bNW4 Fampoux	H 18 d
Crash Trench	57cSW3 Longueval / 4 Combles	T 16 c
Crassier Trench [Maroc Sector]	36cSW1 Lens	M 4 a, c
Crate Wynd	51bNW1 Roclincourt	A 16 c
Crater A [Hohenzollern Rdt]	36cNW3 Loos	G 4 d 6.7
Crater Alley	62bSW3 St Quentin	M 36 c, S 6 a, b
Crater B [Hohenzollern Rdt]	36cNW1 La Bassée / 3 Loos	G 4 b 4.0
Crater C [Hohenzollern Rdt]	36cNW1 La Bassée	G 4 b 4.1
Crater Drive [Tunnel, 1916]	36cNW1 La Bassée	A 21 b
Crater Lane	57dNE3 & 4 Hébuterne / SE1 & 2 Beaumont	K 35, 36, Q 5 b, 6 a
Crater Lane [CT]	28SW2 Wytschaete	O 1 b, d, 2 a, c
Crater Leg [Hohenzollern]	36cNW3 Loos	G 4 d
Crater Loop [Hohenzollern Redoubt]	36cNW1 La Bassée / 3 Loos	G 4 b, d
Crater Sap	36cNW1 La Bassée	A 15 d
Crater Sap [Maroc Sector]	36cNW3 Loos / 36cSW1 Lens	G 34, M 5 [area of]
Crater Trench	28NW4 & NE3 Zillebeke	I 11 b
Crater Trench	36cNW1 La Bassée	A 9 b, d
Crater Trench [Fricourt]	62dNE2 Méaulte	F 3 a, c
Crater Trench [SW of Battle Wood]	28NW4 & NE3 Zillebeke	I 35 c
Craven Corner [road junction]	20SE2 Hooglede	R 7 d 5.8
Crawfish Trench	36cSW1 Lens	M 15 b, d
Crawford Crater	57cSE4 Villers-Guislain	X 17 b

Name	Map Sheet	Map Reference
Crawford House	28NE4 Dadizeele	K 10 b 5.2
Crawl Boys Lane	57dNE1 & 2 Fonquevillers	E 22 a
Crawl Trench	51bNW2 Oppy	C 25 d
Crawley Ridge [Redoubt]	62dNE2 Méaulte	F 9 c, d
Crayfish Trench [1918]	57dNE4 [Hébuterne / Achiet]	L 8 c, d, 14 a, c
Crayot Farm	28NE4 Dadizeele	L 13 d, 14 c
Crazy [Redoubt]	36cSW1 Lens	M 23 b
Cream Alley	51bNW2 Oppy	I 1 a, b
Cream Trench	36cSW1 Lens	M 15 b, d
Cream Trench	51bNW2 Oppy	C 19 a, b
Crease Wood	28NE2 Moorslede	E 4 d
Created Trench	36NW2 Armentières	C 6 a, c, d
Crèche, la [hamlet]	36NW1 Steenwerck	A 5 d
Crèche, La, Depot Railhead / Refilling Point	36NW1 Steenwerck	A 6 a, b, c, d
Crecy [dugout / light rly locality, 1917-18]	28NE3 Gheluvelt	J 1 c 3.8
Crécy, Fôret de	51dSW	extensive
Credit Trench	36cSW1 Lens	M 21 b
Creed House	28NE2 Moorslede	F 19 d 80.15
Creehy Street [Thiepval Wood]	57dSE1 & 2 Beaumont	R 25 a
Creel Trench	36cSW1 Lens	M 21 a, b
Creep Trench	51bNW2 Oppy	C 20 b
Creeping Trench	51bNW2 Oppy	C 1 b, 2 a, b
Crefeld Redoubt	62cSW2 Barleux	O 28 c, d, 34 a, b
Crellin Avenue	62cNE2 Epéhy	F 6 c, 11 b, 12 a
Crémery [village]	66dNW3 Hattencourt	G 36 a, b
Creole Fork [road jct]	28NE2 Moorslede	E 4 c 85.75
Crépey Wood [Creepy Wood]	62dSE [4 Harbonnières]	X 24c, 29 b, 30 a
Crepin Trench	62bSW1 Gricourt	M 28 b, d, 29 a, c
Crepule, Boyau de la	66dNW2 Morchain	B 10 b, 11 a, c, d, 12 c
Crépuscule, Tranchée du	66dNW1 Punchy / 2 Morchain	B 9 b, 10 a
Crescent Alley	57cSW1 Gueudecourt / 3 Longueval	M 22 d, 27 b, d, 28 a, b, 33 b, d, S 3 b
Crescent Avenue / Alley	57cSW1 Gueudecourt	M 22, 23, 27, 28
Crescent Communication Trench	36SW3 Richebourg	S 4 a, c, d, 10 b
Crescent Pond [ancient moat]	20SW4 Bixschoote	U 17 b 9.7
Crescent Redoubt [March 1915]	36SW3 Richebourg	S 10 b
Crescent Trench	36cSW1 Lens	N 7 d, 8 c
Crescent Trench	51bNW4 Fampoux	I 19 b, d, 20 a
Crescent Trench	51bSW2 Vis-en-Artois	O 8 c
Crescent Trench	57cNE1 Quéant	D 28 c
Crescent Trench	57dNE3 & 4 Hébuterne	K 33 c
Crescent, The	28NW4 & NE3 Zillebeke	I 28 d, 29 c, 35 a
Crescent, The	57dSE2 & 57cSW1 Le Sars	M 33 b, 34 a
Creslow [farm]	28SW4 Ploegsteert	U 25 b 0.9
Creslow [light rly siding, Ploeg. Wd, 1917-18]	28SW4 Ploegsteert	U 25 b 5.8
Cress Farm	20SE2 Hooglede	R 4 a 50.85
Crest Avenue / Boyau Crest	62cNW1 Maricourt / 3 Vaux	A 27 a, b, c, G 3 b, 4 a, c
Crest Farm [Passchendaele]	28NE1 Zonnebeke	D 6 c, 12 a
Crest House [Hill 63]	28SW4 Ploegsteert	U 13 d 3.6
Crest Street [1918]	62dNE [1 Dernancourt]	E 8 c
Crest Trench [E of High Wood]	57cSW3 Longueval	S 4 d, 5 c, d
Crest Trench [W of Pys]	57dSE2 & 57cSW1 Le Sars	M 1 d, R 6 c, 11 a, b, 12 a
Crête Farm, la	20SW4 Bixschoote	T 10 d 75.97
Crete Trench	51bNW4 Fampoux	H 18 d, 24 b, I 19 a

Name	Map Sheet	Map Reference
Crète Trench	62cSW3 Vermandovillers / 4 St Christ	T 4 c
Crete Trench [1918]	62dSW [4 Cachy]	T 6 d, 12 b
Crevillon [Tranchée, 1915]	57dSE4 Ovillers	X 26 b
Crewe [light rly locality NW of Langemarck]	20SW4 Bixschoote	U 22 d
Crewe Junction	57dNE3 & 4 Hébuterne	K 28 c
Crewe Trench	51bNW2 Oppy	I 1 a, b
Crib Cottage	36aNE1 Morbecque	E 7 d 58.24
Crib Trench	51bNW4 Fampoux	I 15 a, c, d, 21 b
Criccieth Farm	36SW1 Aubers	M 28 d 85.20
Criccieth Post	36SW1 Aubers	M 28 d
Cricket Trench	57cSE4 Villers-Guislain	X 19 a, b, d
Crime Corner	28SE1 Wervicq	P 14 a 2.4
Crime Trench	51bNW4 Fampoux	H 18 a
Crime, Tranchée du	62cSW3 & 4 Marchélepot	T 5 a, b, c
Crimson Trench	36cSW1 Lens	M 17 b, d, 18 a
Crinquette Lotte [house]	36aNE4 Merville	L 25 d 25.07
Cripps Cross Roads	20SE2 Hooglede	R 13 c 35.57
Critic Cross Roads	28NE2 Moorslede	F 3 d 6.6
Croates Trench [1918]	62dSE [3 Marcelcave]	V 13 c, d, 19 a
Crock Alley	51bNW4 Fampoux	I 13 b
Crock Trench	36cSW1 Lens	M 15 d, 21 b
Crocodile Track [1917-18]	20SW4 Bixschoote	N 35 b, c, d
Crocodile Trench	36cSW1 Lens	M 24 a, b, N 13 c, 19 a
Crocodile Trench / Tranchée du Crocodile	62cSW3 & 4 Marchélepot	T 5 d, 11 a, b
Crocus Trench	36cSW1 Lens	M 16 d, 17 c, 22 b, 23 a, c
Crocus Trench / Tranchée du Crocus	62cSW3 & 4 Marchélepot	T 10 a, c
Croft Lane	51bSW4 Bullecourt	U 8 b, 9 a
Croisilles [village]	51bSW4 Bullecourt	T 17, 18, 23, 24
Croisilles Switch [1918]	51bSW4 Bullecourt	T 22 b, 23 a
Croisilles Switch North	51bSW3 Boisleux	T 21 d, 22 c, 27 a, b
Croisilles Trench [1918]	51bSW4 Bullecourt	T 23 a, c, d, 24 a, b, c
Croix [Cranz?] de Fer, la [X rds E of Béthune]	36bNE2 Beuvry	F 1 b 6.2
Croix Barbée East Post	36SW1 Aubers	M 32 b
Croix Blanche Post	36NW3 Fleurbaix	H 33 a
Croix Blanche, Tranchée de	70dSW [4 Vauxaillon]	U 6 c
Croix de Poperinghe [hamlet & crossroads]	28SW1 Kemmel	M 32 b 6.4
Croix Marechal Post	36NW4 Bois Grenier	H 34 a, b
Croix Marraise [village]	36aNE3 Haverskerque	J 21 c, d
Croix, Ferme de la	28SW4 Ploegsteert	U 11 b 2.9
Croix, Tranchée de la	70dSW [2 Coucy-le-Château]	O 21 b
Croix-Fonsommes [village]	62bNW4 Ramicourt	I 35 c, d, O 5 a
Crojack Farm	28NW4 Ypres	H 11 b 9.7
Cromarty Street [Thiepval Wood]	57dSE1 & 2 Beaumont	Q 24 d, 30 b
Cromarty Trench	51bSW2 Vis-en-Artois	N 5 a, c
Cromer [railway locality]	20SW3 Oostvleteren	T 25 a
Crompton Corner	28NW4 & NE3 Zillebeke	I 29 d 7.4
Cromwell Road	36cNW1 La Bassée	A 28 c, G 4 a, b
Crony Trench	36cSW1 Lens	M 17 d, 18 c
Crook Trench	36cSW1 Lens	M 17 d, 18 c
Crooked Avenue [1918, Hendecourt]	51cSE4 Blaireville	X 17 b
Crooked Lane [road]	36cSW1 Lens	M 18 c, d, 23 a, b, c
Crop Trench	51bNW4 Fampoux	I 15 d, 21 b
Cropper Post	62cNE2 Epéhy	F 1 d
Croscolas / Groscolas Alley	66cNW1 Grugies	A 12 b

Name	Map Sheet	Map Reference
Cross Alley	36cNW3 Loos	G 29 c, d
Cross Bow Street / Trench	51bNW4 Fampoux	I 25 c
Cross Cotts	28NE1 Zonnebeke	D 13 b 5.3
Cross Cut	36NW2 Armentières / 4 Bois Grenier	I 2 d, 3 a, c, 8 b
Cross House	36cSW4 Rouvroy	N 35 c 3.1
Cross House [post]	36cSW3 Vimy	N 35 c 2.1
Cross Lane	57dNE3 & 4 Hébuterne	K 9 b, d
Cross Point [trench junction NW of Loos]	36cNW3 Loos	G 29 c 1.4
Cross Post [NW of Loos]	36cNW3 Loos	G 28 d, 29 c
Cross Road Support	57cSW1 Gueudecourt	M 16 c
Cross Roads Farm	20SW4 Bixschoote	T 24 c
Cross Roads Farm	28NW2 St Julien	C 22 c
Cross Roads Farm / Rabeque Farm, de la	36NW2 & NE1 Houplines	C 4 a
Cross Street	28NW4 & NE3 Zillebeke	I 24 d
Cross Street	36cSW3 Vimy	S 27 a
Cross Street	57dNE3 & 4 Hébuterne	K 10 c
Cross Street	62cNW1 Maricourt	A 23 c, 29 a
Cross Trench	57cSW3 Longueval	S 4 d, 5 c
Cross Trench	57dNE3 & 4 Hébuterne	K 9 b
Cross Trench	57dSE2 & 57cSW1 Le Sars	R 16 b, c, d, 22 a
Cross Trench	62cNW1 Maricourt	A 23 b, d
Cross Trench [1918]	57dNE2 & 57cNW1 Courcelles	F 26 d
Cross Trench [Hohenzollern]	36cNW1 La Bassée	G 4 b, 5 a
Cross Way	36cNW3 Loos	G 9 b, d, 10 c
Crossbill Road [road]	57cSE4 Villers-Guislain	X 29 c, d
Crosse Cottage	28NE4 Dadizeele	K 10 d 95.32
Crossing Lodge	28NW2 St Julien	B 18 a 3.7
Crossing Trench	36cSW4 Rouvroy / 51bNW2 Oppy	U 27 c, C 3 a
Crossley Farm	28NE4 Dadizeele	K 6 c 6.2
Crossway	36cNW3 Loos	G 36 a
Crotin Alley	62cSW3 Vermandovillers	T 15 a, c
Crotoir Trench	70dNW4 St Gobain	H 30 a, c
Crouch Farm	28NE2 Moorslede	E 10 b 6.6
Croup Post	62bNW3 Bellicourt	G 25 d 3.2
Crousaz Trench	62cSW1 & 2 Belloy	N 10 d, 11 a, c
Crousaz Trench	62cSW2 Barleux	N 11 a, c, 19 d
Crouton Trench	62cSW3 Vermandovillers	T 14 b, 15 a, c
Crow Alley	51bNW4 Fampoux	I 13 b
Crow Alley	66cNW4 Berthenicourt	I 8 a
Crow Dump	36cSW1 Lens	M 23 b 9.1
Crow Farm	28NW1 Elverdinghe	A 26 a 4.2
Crow Trench	51bNW4 Fampoux	I 13 b
Crow Trench	51bSW2 Vis-en-Artois	N 29 d, 30 a, c, 35 b
Crowbar Trench	28SW2 Wytschaete	N 18 c
Crowe Line [light rly]	36cSW1 Lens	M 23 a, b
Crown Alley [1918]	62dNE [3 Morlancourt]	K 19 b
Crown Buildings	28NE4 Dadizeele	L 16 b 8.6 to 17 a 1.8
Crown Copse	51bNW4 Fampoux	I 28 d
Crown Prince Farm [Le Touquet]	36NW2 & NE1 Houplines	C 10 b 8.5
Crown Prince Post	36NW4 Bois Grenier	I 1 b
Crown Prince Trench [1918]	66eNW [2 Thennes]	B 23 b, 24 a
Crown Support	57cSW4 Combles	U 1 c, d, 7 b, 8 a, 14 b
Crown Trench	36cNW1 La Bassée / 3 Loos	G 4 b, 5 c, 11 a, b
Crows Nest	51bSW4 Bullecourt	U 12 a

Name	Map Sheet	Map Reference
Crows Nest	57dSE1 & 2 Beaumont	Q 24 a
Crow's Nest	28SE1 Wervicq	P 5 a 1.6
Crow's Nest	51bNW3 Arras	G 24 a
Crow's Nest [Kennedy Crater]	36cSW3 Vimy	S 9 c
Crows Nest [railway]	36cSW4 Rouvroy	O 35 c, d
Crowsnest [farm]	28SE1 Wervicq	P 5 a 1.8
Crowsnest Farm	20SE2 Hooglede	Q 22 b 3.3
Croydon Farm	28SW3 Bailleul	S 5 a 1.1
Croydon Lines [huts]	28SW3 Bailleul	S 4 b, 5 a
Croydon Trench [1918]	62dNE [3 Morlancourt]	K 13 a, b
Crucifix [Thélus]	51bNW1 Roclincourt	A 6 c 95.00
Crucifix Alley	57cSW3 Longueval	S 17 d, 22 d, 23 a, b, c
Crucifix Corner	28SW3 Bailleul	S 18 a 65.20
Crucifix Corner	51bSW3 Boisleux	N 33 d 3.9
Crucifix Corner	57dNE2 [Fonquevillers]	F 19 c 7.3
Crucifix Corner [1918]	62dSW [4 Cachy / Gentelles]	U 6 c 5.5
Crucifix Corner [Aveluy]	57dSE4 Ovillers	W 11 d 9.2 or 9.9
Crucifix Corner [Bazentin]	57cSW3 Longueval	S 9 c.90.05
Crucifix Corner [near Lewis Farm]	28SW3 Bailleul	S 18 b 2.2
Crucifix Corner [Oppy]	51bNW2 Oppy	B 12 d 95.30
Crucifix Corner [Tambour, Fricourt]	62dNE2 Méaulte	F 3
Crucifix Dump	28NE3 Gheluvelt	J 4 c 0.0
Crucifix Lane [trench]	51bNW2 Oppy	C 7 a, c
Crucifix Street	57cSW3 Longueval	S 17 d
Crucifix Support	51bSW4 Bullecourt	U 27 a, b
Crucifix Track	28NE3 Gheluvelt	J 2 d, 3 c, d
Crucifix Trench	51bNW2 Oppy	B 18 b, C 7 c
Crucifix Trench [Bazentin]	57cSW3 Longueval	S 9 c 8.1
Crucifix Trench [Fricourt]	57dSE4 Ovillers	X 21 d, 27 b, 28 a
Crucifix Trench [Pall Mall]	57cSW3 Longueval	S 22 d, 23 a, c
Crucifix, The	28NE3 Gheluvelt	J 2 or 3
Crucifix, The [N of Fricourt Farm]	57dSE4 Ovillers	X 28 a 35.50
Cruciform Post	57cSE4 Villers-Guislain	X 28 d
Cruet Trench	36cSW1 Lens	M 16 c, 22 a, b
Cruet Trench	51bNW2 Oppy	C 19 d, 20 a, c
Crumb Trench	51bNW2 Oppy	C 19 b, 20 a
Crumlin Farm	28SW3 Bailleul	T 27 a 5.2
Crumlin Lines [huts]	28SW3 Bailleul	T 27 a
Crump Alley	51bSW4 Bullecourt	U 15 c
Crump Farm	28NW2 St Julien	I 5 a 9.5
Crump Lane [1918]	62dNE [3 Morlancourt]	K 19 c, 25 a
Crump Trench	28NW2 St Julien / 4 Ypres	I 5 a, c, d
Crump Trench	51bNW2 Oppy	C 1 a
Crump Trench	51bNW4 Fampoux	H 18 d, 24 b, d
Crump Trench [1918]	57dNE1 & 2 Fonquevillers	K 5 a, b, 6 a
Crumpet Trench	51bNW2 Oppy	C 19 d
Crumpet Trench	51bNW4 Fampoux	I 13 b, d
Crusoe Copse	62bSW2 Fonsommes	O 29 c, 35 a
Crusoe Cross Roads	28NE2 Moorslede	E 28 c 2.8
Crust Trench	51bNW4 Fampoux	I 14 c, 20 a, b
Crust Trench	57cSW4 Combles	T 16 c
Crusty Trench	36cSW1 Lens	M 16 c, 22 a
Crux Trench	51bSW4 Bullecourt	U 9 a, c, 15 b
Cry Trench / Support	51bNW4 Fampoux	I 1 d

Name	Map Sheet	Map Reference
Crysdale [light rly siding]	36cSW1 Lens	M 21 b, d, 22 a
Cub Trench	51bNW4 Fampoux	I 14 a, b
Cuba Trench	51bNW2 Oppy / 4 Fampoux	I 1 a, c, 7 a, b, d
Cuban Cross	27SE2 Berthen	Q 23 d
Cuban Cross [cross roads]	27SE2 Berthen	Q 23 d 75.30
Cuckoo Reserve	51bSW2 Vis-en-Artois	O 25 c, 31 a
Cuckoo Support [1918]	51bSW3 Boisleux	S 22 b, d, 23 a
Cuckoo Trench	36cSW1 Lens	M 16 c, 22 a
Cudgel Trench	36cSW1 Lens	M 16 d, 22 b
Cue Street [1918]	62dNE [3 Morlancourt]	J 12 c
Cuinchy [village]	36cNW1 La Bassée	A 15 c, 21 a, b
Cuinchy Keep	36cNW1 La Bassée	A 21 b
Cuinchy Support [Supporting Point, July 1915]	36cNW1 La Bassée	A 15, 21
Cuirassier Farm	20SW4 Bixschoote	U 13 c 2.9
Cuiscot [trench]	66cNW2 Itancourt	B 5 c, d
Culgoa Trench [1918]	62dNE [3 Morlancourt]	K 7 b, d, 13 a, b
Cullen Post	62cNE2 Epéhy	F 1 b
Culloden [railway, light rly & huts]	28NW1 Elverdinghe	B 26 c, d, H 2 a
Culloden Dump	28NW1 Elverdinghe	B 26 c, d, H 2 a [area of]
Cult Farm	27SE2 Berthen	Q 30 c 65.95
Culver Street / Boyau Culver	62cNW1 Maricourt	A 15 b, 16 a
Culverin Lane [road, Artillery Hill]	51bNW4 Fampoux	I 29 a, c, 35 a, c
Culvert Farm	36NW4 Bois Grenier	I 25 c 3.3
Culvert Position, The [Cuinchy, Feb 1915]	36cNW1 La Bassée	A 15 d
Culvert Position, The High [Cuinchy, Feb 1915]	36cNW1 La Bassée	A 15 d
Culvert Post [Cuinchy Sector, Feb 1915]	36cNW1 La Bassée	A 15 d
Culvert Road [Brickstacks]	36cNW1 La Bassée	A 15 d
Culvert Road [CT, Cuinchy Sector, Feb 1915]	36cNW1 La Bassée	A 15 d
Culvert, The	28NW4 & NE3 Zillebeke	I 18 a 1.7
Culvert, The [Cuinchy Sector, Feb 1915]	36cNW1 La Bassée	A 15 d
Culvert, The Big [Cuinchy Sector, Feb 1915]	36cNW1 La Bassée	A 15 d
Cumberland Dugouts	28NW4 & NE3 Zillebeke	I 24 d
Cummins / Cumming Trench [1918]	62dNE [3 Morlancourt]	K 13 d, 19 b, d, 25 a, b
Cup Alley [1918]	62dNE [3 Morlancourt]	K 19 a
Cup Trench	51bNW2 Oppy	C 19 b
Cupid Support	51bNW4 Fampoux	I 14 a
Cupid Trench	51bNW2 Oppy	C 20 c
Cupid Trench	51bNW4 Fampoux	I 7 d, 13 b, 14 a
Cupidon Copse	62bSW4 Homblières	T 7 d, 8 c
Cupola Alley	36cNW1 La Bassée	A 10 b, 11 a
Cupola Buildings	28NE4 Dadizeele	L 18 a 9.2
Cupola, The	36cNW3 Loos	G G 11 b, 12 a
Curb Switch, & Curb Switch North	51bNW4 Fampoux	I 31 b, c, d
Curb Trench / Lane	51bNW4 Fampoux	I 31 b, c, d
Curchy [village]	66dNW3 Hattencourt	H 3 c, d, 9 a, b
Curd Farm	27NE2 Proven	F 27 d 25.40
Curfew House	36aNE1 Morbecque	E 3 c 1.8
Curio Farm	20SE2 Hooglede	R 11 d 10.15
Curl Trench	57cSW3 Longueval	T 9 d
Curlew Trench	51bSW2 Vis-en-Artois	N 24 b, d
Curley Crescent	36cNW3 Loos	G 10 b, d
Curling Alley	57cNE3 Hermies / 4 Marcoing	K 21 d
Curlu Alley	62cNW1 Maricourt	A 30 a, c, d
Curlu Trench	62cNW1 Maricourt	A 24 c, 30 a

Name	Map Sheet	Map Reference
Curly Support	51bNW4 Fampoux	I 7 d
Curly Trench	51bNW4 Fampoux	I 31 b
Curly Trench	51bNW4 Fampoux	I 7 b
Curola Trench	66cNW2 Itancourt	B 24 a
Curragh Camp	28SW1 Kemmel	M 17 a, c [centre: M 17 c 4.9]
Curragh Copse	28SW1 Kemmel	M 16 d, 17 c
Curragh, The [Cuinchy; fortified house]	36cNW1 La Bassée	A 20 d
Currie Avenue	28SW4 Ploegsteert	T 12 b, U 7 a, b
Currie Trench	57cSW2 Villers-au-Flos	N 34 a, b
Currin Trench	36cNW1 La Bassée / 3 Loos	G 4 b, d
Curry Trench	51bNW2 Oppy	C 19 d
Curse Support	51bNW4 Fampoux	I 1 c, d
Curtain Trench	62bNW3 Bellicourt	G 1 d
Curtain Trench / Curtain Support	51bSW2 Vis-en-Artois	O 31 a, b, c
Curve Trench	57cSW4 Combles	U 13 a, c
Curzon Post	36cNW3 Loos	G 23 d, 24 c [G 24 c 05.70]
Curzon Post	36SW1 Aubers / 3 Richebourg	M 34 a, c
Curzon Post [Sept 1915]	36SW3 Richebourg	M 34 c 8.7
Curzon Street	36cNW3 Loos	G 23 b, d, 24 a, c
Curzon Street [Sept 1915]	36cNW1 La Bassée	A 9 a, c
Cushion Trench	51bNW4 Fampoux	I 7 c, 13 a
Cuslente Trench [1918]	66eNW [2 Thennes]	B 23 d, 24 a
Cusp Trench	51bNW4 Fampoux	I 13 c, 19 a
Custom House	27NE2 Proven	E 28 c 9.1
Custom House [Kortepyp]	28SW3 Bailleul	T 20 c 4.4
Custom House [Pont Rouge]	28SW4 Ploegsteert	U 29 b 4.4
Cut Trench	51bNW2 Oppy	C 1 a
Cut Trench	51bNW4 Fampoux	I 7 c, d
Cut, The	28SW2 Wytschaete	N 23 b, 24 a
Cute Farm	36aNE2 Vieux Berquin	F 28 a 05.40
Cute Trench	51bNW4 Fampoux	I 7 a, c
Cutey Trench	36cSW1 Lens	N 13 a
Cuthbert Avenue [1918]	57dSE1 & 2 Beaumont	Q 32 b, 33 a, b, 34 a, b
Cuthbert Crater	51bNW3 Arras	G 12 a
Cuthbert Trench	51bNW3 Arras	G 12 a
Cuthbert Trench	51bNW4 Fampoux	I 7 b, d
Cutlet Corner [road jct]	36aNE2 Vieux Berquin	F 21 a 4.5
Cutlet Trench	57cSW3 Longueval	T 9 d, 15 b
Cutoff Trench, & Alley	36cSW1 Lens	N 8 a, c
Cutter Farm	28NE2 Moorslede	E 18 c 7.8
Cutting Locality [E slope of Hill 70]	36cNW3 Loos	H 32 c, d
Cutting Trench	36cSW1 Lens	M 3 c
Cutting, The	28NE1 Zonnebeke	D 21 a, d
Cutting, The	28NW4 & NE3 Zillebeke	J 25 d
Cutting, The	28SW2 Wytschaete	O 17 c
Cutting, The	51bSW4 Bullecourt	T 27 a
Cutting, The [Contalmaison, sunken road]	57dSE4 Ovillers	X 17 a
Cuttle Farm	20SE2 Hooglede	Q 18 d 7.3
Cyanide Trench	36cSW3 Vimy	S 15 b
Cycamens, Boyau	62cSW3 & 4 Marchélepot	T 5 c, 11 a
Cycle Avenue [1918; old Radfahrer Graben]	57dNE2 Essarts	L 1 b, 2 a
Cycle Dump	36cSW3 Vimy	S 18 b 15.05
Cycle Trench	51bNW4 Fampoux	I 19 c
Cyclietes Trench	62cNW4 Péronne	I 31 b, d

Name	Map Sheet	Map Reference
Cyclist Lane [road]	51bSW2 Vis-en-Artois	O 13 a, b
Cyclist Trench	36cSW1 Lens	M 12 d, 18 b
Cyclist Trench	36cSW3 Vimy	S 16 a
Cyclone Corner [road jct]	28NE4 Dadizeele	L 32 c 07.77
Cyclops [farm & pill box]	28NE1 Zonnebeke	D 29 a
Cygnet Farm	20SE2 Hooglede	R 20 c 6.3
Cygnet Trench	36cSW3 Vimy	S 10 d, 16 a, c
Cymbal House	27SE4 Meteren	W 22 c 1.7
Cymbal Trench	36cSW3 Vimy	S 10 d, 11 c, 17 a, c
Cynic Trench	36cSW3 Vimy	S 10 c, 16 a
Cynthia Post	36NW4 Bois Grenier	I 16 c
Cyprian Farm	28SW3 Bailleul	S 11 c 7.3
Cyprus Trench	36cSW3 Vimy	S 15 b
Cyril Dump	36cSW3 Vimy	S 11 a 2.1
Cyril Trench	36cSW3 Vimy	S 6, 10, 11, 12, T 1, 2, 3
Cyril Trench	51bNW4 Fampoux	I 14 d, 15 c
Cyrille Vandamme Farm	28NW1 Elverdinghe	B 1 d 9.9
Cyrus Trench	36cSW3 Vimy	S 15 a
Cytises, Bois des [Laburnums]	62cSW3 & 4 Marchélepot	T 4 d, 5 c
Czar Trench	36cSW3 Vimy	S 16 a
Czechs Trench [1918]	62dSE [3 Marcelcave]	V 7 d, 8 c, 13 a, b
D [outlying trench, Fort 147]	51cSE3 & 4 Ransart	W 16 b 6.0
D 1 [trench 1915, NE of Wulverghem]	28SW4 Ploegsteert	N 36 c, d
D 2 [trench 1915, NE of Wulverghem]	28SW4 Ploegsteert	N 36 c
D 20 [trench, N of Turco Farm, May 1916]	28NW2 St Julien	C 15 c
D 21 [trench, NW of Turco Farm, May 1916]	28NW2 St Julien	C 14 d
D 3 [trench 1915, NE of Wulverghem]	28SW4 Ploegsteert	N 36 c
D Camp	28NW1 Elverdinghe	A 30 a, b
D Crater [S of La Bassee Road, 24-9-15]	36cNW1 La Bassée / 3 Loos	A 21
D Line [1918]	27SE3 Borre	extensive
D Line [1918]	36aNE1 Morbecque	D 5, 6, 11, 15, 16, 17, 21
D Lines [W of Pietre 1914-15]	36SW1 Aubers	M 28 d, 29 c, 34 b
D Sap [Burnley Alley]	57cSE2 Gonnelieu	Q 4 a
D Sap [Givenchy]	36cNW1 La Bassée	A 9 d
D Sector [4/15, N of R Douve]	28SW2 Wytschaete	N 29, 30, 35, 36
D Siding [railway, Ouderdom]	28NW3 Poperinghe	G 35 b
D Street	57dSE1 & 2 Beaumont	Q 10 c
D Work	51bNW3 Arras	G 5 d, 11 b
D, Post	51bSW2 Vis-en-Artois	O 26 a
Dab Farm	28NE4 Dadizeele	L 24 c 5.1
Dab Trench	28NE1 Zonnebeke	D 10 d, 16 b
Dab Trench	51bNE1 Brébières	D 20 a
Dab Trench, & Switch	36NW2 & NE1 Houplines	D 19 c
Dabble Avenue [Tyne Cott, Rly Cutting]	28NE1 Zonnebeke	D 17 a, c
Dace Trench, Supp, Street, Row	36NW2 & NE1 Houplines	D 25 d
Dachshund Avenue	51bSW4 Bullecourt	U 18 a, c
Dacia Trench	62bSW4 Homblières	T 29 d
Dacia Trench / Tranchée du Dacia	66cNW2 Itancourt	B 5 b, 6 a
Dad Trench	28NE1 Zonnebeke	D 10 b
Dad Trench	51bNE1 Brébières	D 19 d
Dadem Trench	57cSW2 Villers-au-Flos	O 33 b
Dadizeele [village]	28NE4 Dadizeele	K 12 c, d, 18 a
Dadizeele Chateau	28NE4 Dadizeele	K 12 c 6.2
Dadizeelehoek [cross roads]	28NE4 Dadizeele	L 14 b 1.4

Name	Map Sheet	Map Reference
Dadizeelehoek [hamlet / place name]	28NE4 Dadizeele	L 14 a, b
Dado Trench	36NW2 & NE1 Houplines	C 6 b, D 1 a
Dados Lane	57cSE4 Villers-Guislain	X 22 d, 28 a
Dados Loop	57cSE4 Villers-Guislain	X 22 d, 28 b
Dados Spur [light rly]	36bNE4 Noeux-les-Mines	L 2 c
Dagger Trench	28NE1 Zonnebeke	D 10 c, d, 16 b
Dagger Trench	36NW2 & NE1 Houplines	D 1 a, b
Dagger Trench	51bSW2 Vis-en-Artois	N 4 a, c
Dago House	57cNE4 Marcoing	L 21 d 4.9
Dago Trench	57cNE4 Marcoing	L 21 c, d, 27 b
Daily Mail Wood "A"	57dSW [4 Toutencourt]	T 23 c, d, 29 a, b
Daily Mail Wood "B"	57dSW [4 Toutencourt]	T 29 b, d, 30 a, c
Daily Mail Woods	57dSW [4 Toutencourt]	T 23, 24, 29, 30
Daily Trench	28NE1 Zonnebeke	D 27 d, 28 c
Daimler House	28NE4 Dadizeele	K 12 b 15.85
Dainty Copse	28NE1 Zonnebeke	D 18 d
Daird Trench	51bNW1 Roclincourt	A 16 a
Dairy Dugout / OP [1917-18]	28NE1 Zonnebeke	D 23 a 5.7
Dairy Farm	36aNE4 Merville	K 22 d 6.3
Dairy Wood	28NE1 Zonnebeke	D 23 b
Dairy Wood	36NW2 & NE1 Houplines	D 23 d
Daisy Farm	20SE2 Hooglede	R 3 a 90.75
Daisy Post	36NW4 Bois Grenier	I 15 c
Daisy Trench	36NW2 & NE1 Houplines	D 1 b, 2 a, c, d
Daisy Trench	51bNE1 Brébières	D 13 a, b
Daisy Wood	28NE1 Zonnebeke	D 23 central
Dakar Cottage	36aNE1 Morbecque	D 8 c 7.6
Dakar Trench	62bSW3 St Quentin	M 35 d
Dale Street	57cSE4 Villers-Guislain	X 4 b, 5 a
Dale Street	62dNE2 Méaulte	F 11 c, 17 a
Dale Trench	51bNE1 Brébières	D 19 b, d
Dale Trench	51bSW2 Vis-en-Artois	O 2 a, c, 8 a
Dalhousie Street	57dSE4 Ovillers	X 19 a, c
Dalkey Cottages	27NE2 Proven	F 3 b 6.2
Dalkey Trench	36cNW3 Loos	H 25 a
Dallas Cottage	36aNE1 Morbecque	D 1 c 75.95
Dallon [village]	66cNW1 Grugies	A 4, 10
Dalton Street	62cNW1 Maricourt	A 23 c
Daly's [Heavy Artillery OP]	36cNW3 Loos	G 29 c 1.4
Daly's Copse	62bNW4 Ramicourt	I 29 d
Daly's Keep	36cNW3 Loos	G 16 c
Daly's Passage	36cNW3 Loos	G 16 a, b, c
Dam Trench	36NW2 & NE1 Houplines	D 8 b
Dam Trench	51bNE1 Brébières	D 19 d, 25 b
Damas Trench	62bSW4 Homblières	T 22 d, 23 c, 29 a, c, d
Damas Trench	66cNW2 Itancourt	B 5 b
Damasette Trench	36cSW1 Lens	M 19 d
Dambre Camp	28NW1 Elverdinghe	B 27 c, d
Dambre Farm	28NW1 Elverdinghe	B 27 a 8.0
Dame Blanche Trench	62cSW4 St. Christ	T 18 d, 24 a, b
Dame Blanche, Tranchée de la	62cSW3 & 4 Marchélepot	T 18 c, d, 24 b
Dame House	28NE1 Zonnebeke	D 30 d 4.7
Dame Trench	36bNE [1 Labeuvrière]	D 4 c, 10 a
Dame Wood	28NE1 Zonnebeke	D 30 b, d

Name	Map Sheet	Map Reference
Dames Alley	62cSW3 Vermandovillers	T 8 c, d, 9 c
Dames, Bois des	36cNW3 Loos	H 21 b, d
Damiene, Moulin	51bSE1 Saudemont	P 28 a
Damier Farm [moated site]	28SW4 Ploegsteert	U 16 a 1.6
Damloup Alley	62cSW2 Barleux	N 34 a
Damloup Copse	62cSW1 Dompierre / 2 Barleux	N 34 a
Damm Strasse [road]	28SW2 Wytschaete	O 3 d, 4 c, 9 a, b
Damoclès Trench	62cSW3 Vermandovillers	T 8 a, b, d, 9 c
Damp Farm	28NE1 Zonnebeke	D 30 d 5.4
Damp Trench	51bNE1 Brébières	D 19 d
Damsel Trench	51bNE1 Brébières	D 19 b
Damson Trench	51bSW1 Neuville Vitasse	M 12 c
Dan House	28NE1 Zonnebeke	D 21 b 3.7
Dan Trench	51bNE1 Brébières	D 14 d
Dana Copse	62cSW4 St. Christ	U 22 d
Dance Support	36NW2 & NE1 Houplines	D 9 a, c
Dance Trench	36NW2 & NE1 Houplines	D 8 b, d, 9 c
Dance Trench	51bNE1 Brébières	D 19 d
Dancing Trench	66cSW2 Vendeuil	O 10 c, 16 a, c, d
Dancourt Trench	62bSW3 St Quentin	M 36 c, S 6 b
Dandelion Farm	20SE2 Hooglede	R 3 c 67.30
Dandy Trench [1918]	62dNE [1 Dernancourt]	E 7 b, 8 a
Dane Trench	51bNE1 Brébières	D 19 b
Danger Corner [Brewery Corner, R de Cailloux]	36SW3 Richebourg	S 25 b 5.7 [1915]
Danger Corner [Festubert]	36SW3 Richebourg	S 25 b
Danger Tree, The	57dSE1 & 2 Beaumont	Q 10 d
Daniel, Boyau	62cSW1 & 2 Belloy	N 12 b
Daniel's Den	57dSE4 Ovillers	R 32 c
Danizy Trench	66cSW4 La Fère	U 21 b, 22 a, c
Dank Cottage	36aNE4 Merville	L 11 a 9.2
Dantzig / Danzig Alley	62dNE2 Méaulte	F 5 c, d, 6 a, c, 10 b
Dantzig / Danzig Trench	62dNE2 Méaulte	F 10 b
Dantzig Alley	66dNW3 Hattencourt	G 2 c, d, 8 b, 9 a, c, d
Dantzig Trench	66cNW4 Berthenicourt	I 8 c
Dantzig Trench [1918]	66eNW [2 Thennes]	C 14 d, 15 c
Danube Alley	66cSW2 Vendeuil	O 15 d, 21 a, b
Danube Post	57dSE4 Ovillers	R 32 c 8.6
Danube Support	36NW2 & NE1 Houplines	D 15 a, b, d
Danube Trench	36NW2 & NE1 Houplines	D 15 a, c, d
Danube Trench	57dSE1 & 2 Beaumont / 4 Ovillers	R 32 b, c
Danube Trench, & Support	62dNE2 Méaulte	F 10 d, 11 c
Daours Sector [trenches, 1918]	62dSW [2 Villers-Bretonneux]	N 4, 5
Darby Copse [near Joan Copse]	62bSW2 Fonsommes	N 30 a
Darby Post	57cNE3 Hermies	K 2 d
Dardayrol / Darfayrol Trench	66cNW1 Grugies	B 9 c
Daring Crossing [level crossing]	28NE1 Zonnebeke	D 16 d 60.25
Daring Trench	51bNE1 Brébières	D 2 c, 7 b, 8 a
Dark Buildings	28NE4 Dadizeele	L 30 a 0.3
Dark Trench	51bNE1 Brébières	D 19 b, 20 a
Darling House	36NW1 Steenwerck	A 14 b 3.6
Darling Reserve [1918]	62dNE [1 Dernancourt]	D 18
Darling Trench	51bNE1 Brébières	D 26 b, 27 a, b
Darmstadt Alley	66dNW3 Hattencourt	G 14 b, 15 a
Darmstadt Trench	62cNW4 Péronne	I 17 a, c, 23 a, d

Name	Map Sheet	Map Reference
Darn Trench	51bNE1 Brébières	D 26 a
Dart House	27NE4 Abeele	L 15 a 05.40
Dart Lane	57dSE4 Ovillers	X 27 c
Dart Lane [1918]	51bSW3 Boisleux / 57cNW1 Gomiecourt	S 26 c, A 2 a
Dart Trench	51bNE1 Brébières	D 7 a, c
Dartford Wood	51bSE4 Marquion	W 11 b, d, 12 a
Dartmouth Trench	36cSW3 Vimy	T 8 a
Darwin Alley	57cNE4 Marcoing	K 16 b, 17 a, b
Darwin Cross [cross roads]	28NW3 Poperinghe	G 21 a 6.2
Darwin Reserve [1918]	62dNE [1 Dernancourt]	D 18
Dash Crossing [level crossing, Tyne Cott]	28NE1 Zonnebeke	D 17 c 25.85
Dash Trench / Road	28NE1 Zonnebeke	D 17 c
Date Trench	51bNW2 Oppy / NE1 Brébières	C 6 d, D 1 c
Date Trench	51bSW1 Neuville Vitasse	M 12 a, c
Dattier Alley	62cSW2 Barleux	N 34 b
Datum House	28SW2 Wytschaete	O 36 a 3.2
Datum House	36SW2 Radinghem	O 1 b 05.35
Dauley Trench	57dNE3 & 4 Hébuterne	K 17 c
Dauphin Road [road]	36cSW1 Lens	N 26 a, b, d
Davaar Avenue	57dSE4 Ovillers	Q 36 c, d
David Alley	70dNW4 St Gobain	H 36 b, I 31 a
David Camp	57dNE3 & 4 Hébuterne	K 27 c
David Trench	62bSW1 Gricourt	M 22 a
Davidson / Davison Street	28NW4 & NE3 Zillebeke	I 24 d, 30 b
Davidson Lane	28NW4 & NE3 Zillebeke	I 34 c
Davidson Trench	51bNE1 Brébières	D 20 c, 26 a, c
Davies Street	28NW2 St Julien	C 4 a
Davies Street [Sept 1915]	36cNW1 La Bassée	A 15 d
Davis / Doris / Dovis Street	36cNW3 Loos	G 36 c
Davison Camp	27NE4 Abeele	L 13 b
Davit Cottage	27SE4 Meteren	W 17 b 85.89
Davout Farm	20SE3 Westroosebeke	V 8 b 35.95
Davy's Corner [road junction]	20SE2 Hooglede	R 28 d 95.27
Dawes Copse	62cNE4 Roisel	L 23 c
Dawes Quarry	62cNE4 Roisel	L 23 d 15.30
Dawn Lane [trench]	51bSW2 Vis-en-Artois	O 26 d
Dawson	28NW4 Ypres	H 23 d 4.6
Dawson [light rly locality, 1917-18]	28NW4 Ypres	H 23 b, c
Dawson Alley	27SE4 Meteren	X 7 b, 8 a, c
Dawson Camp	27NE4 Abeele	L 9 a
Dawson City	28NW2 St Julien	C 14 d, 20 a, b
Dawson Farm	20SE2 Hooglede	R 3 d 85.40
Dawson Street	28NW4 & NE3 Zillebeke	I 30 b
Dawson Street	36cNW1 La Bassée	A 14 d, 15 c
Dawson's Corner	28NW2 St Julien	B 22 c
Day Street	28SW4 Ploegsteert	T 6 a
Day Trench	28SW4 Ploegsteert	T 6 b
Daylight Corner [Lindenhoek]	28SW1 Kemmel / 3 Bailleul	N 33 d 1.5 / 33 c 85.75
Daylight Corner [Wulverghem]	28SW4 Ploegsteert	T 4 a 8.7
Dayout, Tranchée	70dSW [2 Coucy-le-Château]	N 5 c
De Barre [Tranchée, 1915]	57dSE4 Ovillers	X 26 a
De Broeken Road [road]	28SW3 Bailleul	S 30 b, T 25 a, b, d
Dé Copse	66dNW1 Punchy	A 15 c
De Drie Goen Farm	28NW3 Poperinghe	G 24 b 6.8

Name	Map Sheet	Map Reference
De God [hamlet]	28NE2 Moorslede	F 11 a, b
De Salins [Tranchée, 1915] / Marischal Street	57dSE4 Ovillers / 62dNE2 Méaulte	X 26 c, F 2 a
De Seule [hamlet & road jcts]	36NW1 Steenwerck	B 1 central
De Vallon [trench]	66cNW2 Itancourt	B 24 b, d
De Villard Trench	66cNW1 Grugies	A 6 c, 12 a, b, B 7 a
De Vinke [hamlet]	28NE2 Moorslede	F 5 c, d
De Wippe [hamlet]	28NW1 Elverdinghe	A 11 b, d
De Wippe Camp	28NW1 Elverdinghe	A 11 a, b
Dé Wood	66eNW [2 Thennes]	C 30 d
De Zen Cabaret	28NW1 Elverdinghe	A 28 c 40.75
Deacon Mill [Proven]	27NE2 Proven	F 7 c 7.9
Dead Alley / Dead Boche Alley / Sap	51bSW2 Vis-en-Artois	O 25 d
Dead Cow Farm	28SW4 Ploegsteert	U 13 b 8.4
Dead Cow Farm	36NW4 Bois Grenier	I 20 b 9.0
Dead Cow Farm [July 1915]	36NW4 Bois Grenier	I 20 b 63.00
Dead Cow Farm [just N of Quinque Rue, 4/15]	36SW3 Richebourg	S 26
Dead Cow Farm [later Dilly Farm; Potijze]	28NW4 & NE3 Zillebeke	I 5 c 25.02
Dead Cow House	36SW3 Richebourg	S 14 d / 15 c
Dead Cow Post	36SW3 Richebourg	S 14 d, 15 c
Dead Cow Trench [Dec 1914]	36SW3 Richebourg	S 15 c
Dead Dog Alley / Avenue	36SW2 Radinghem	N 4 a, b, d
Dead Dog Bridge	36aSE1 St Venant	P 5 b 3.9
Dead Dog Dump	36NW3 Fleurbaix	H 33 d 90.65
Dead Dog Farm	28SW2 Wytschaete	N 6 b 2.1
Dead Dog Farm [La Boutillerie]	36SW2 Radinghem	N 4 central
Dead Dog Tram	36SW2 Radinghem	N 4 b, d, 5 c
Dead End Camp	28NW2 St Julien	I 2 c 1.8
Dead End Post	36SW1 Aubers	M 12 b
Dead End Road	36SW1 Aubers	M 12 b, d N 7 c
Dead End, The [Tattenham Corner / Kaaie]	28NW4 Ypres	I 8 a
Dead Horse [lt rly sidings, Ploeg. Wd, 1917-18]	28SW4 Ploegsteert	U 20 b 8.7
Dead Horse Copse	36SW1 Aubers	M 29 c, d
Dead Horse Corner [Ploeg. Wood, 1914-15]	28SW4 Ploegsteert	U 21 a 25.92
Dead Horse Fort [Hunter's Avenue]	28SW4 Ploegsteert	U 21 a
Dead Land	57dSE [3 Bouzincourt]	W 14, 15
Dead Man Farm	28NW2 St Julien	B 17 c 4.5
Dead Man's Bottom	28NW4 & NE3 Zillebeke	I 12 a, b
Dead Man's Corner	51bNW3 Arras	G 21 a
Dead Man's Corner [Gouzeaucourt]	57cSE2 Gonnelieu	Q 23 c 7.3
Dead Man's Dump [Gouzeaucourt]	57cSE2 Gonnelieu	Q 23 central
Dead Man's House [S of La Bassée Road]	36cNW1 La Bassée	A 20 d [approx]
Dead Man's Redoubt	57dSE1 & 2 Beaumont	Q 22 d, 23 c
Dead Man's Trench	36cNW1 La Bassée	A 3 c, 9 a, b
Dead Mule [pillboxes]	28NW4 & NE3 Zillebeke	J 8 b 7.2
Dead Mule Corner	28NW4 & NE3 Zillebeke	J 8 b
Dead Mule Dugouts	28NW4 & NE3 Zillebeke	J 8 b 83.24 or 99.20
Dead Mule Gully [1918]	28NE3 Gheluvelt	J 8 b
Dead Wood	66dNW3 Hattencourt	G 3 c
Dead Woods No.1	62cSE [4 Attilly]	X 3 c
Dead Woods No.2	62cSE [4 Attilly]	X 2 d, 3 c
Deal Farm	36aNE4 Merville	L 18 c 6.8
Deal Trench	51bNE1 Brébières	D 13 b
Deal Trench	51bSW1 Neuville Vitasse	M 12 a
Dean Hall	27NE4 Abeele	L 23 a 5.0

Name	Map Sheet	Map Reference
Dean Trench	62cSE2 Vermand	R 4 b, 5 a, c
Deane Street	36cNW3 Loos	G 35 b
Deanery [building / farm]	20SE2 Hooglede	Q 22 d 2.1
Deans Trench	66dNW1 Punchy	A 22 c, 28 a
Deansgate	62dNE2 Méaulte	F 12 c
Deansgate / Dean's Gate	28NW4 & NE3 Zillebeke	I 34 b
Dear House [Hill 32]	28NE1 Zonnebeke	D 8 c 5.8
Dear Street	28NE1 Zonnebeke	D 8 c, d
Dearborth Junction [light rly, 1917-18]	28NE3 Gheluvelt	J 7 c 6.3
Death Alley [Sept. 1915; later Dook Alley]	36cNW1 La Bassée	A 22 c, d
Death Corner / Carrefour de la Mort	66eNE4 Beaufort	L 9 a 4.3
Death Cross Road [Rouvroy-en-Santerre]	66eNE4 Beaufort	L 9 a 5.3
Death or Glory Sap	36cNW1 La Bassée	A 9 a 8.6 or A 16 c
Death Road [Albert - Pozières]	57dSE4 Ovillers	X 4, 9, 10, 13, 14
Death Valley [E of Mametz Wood to Bazentins]	57cSW3 Longueval	S 14 c, 19 b, d, 20 a
Death Valley [Gun Pit Alley/Gun Pit Rd]	57cSW1 Gueudecourt	M 28 b
Death Valley [SW of Grandcourt]	57dSE1 & 2 Beaumont	R 16 b, d, 17 a, c, 22 b
Death, The Mound of [St Eloi]	28SW2 Wytschaete	O 2 d
Debate House	28NE4 Dadizeele	L 34 a 4.3
Debeaux Alley	66cNW1 Grugies	A 16 c, d
Debenham House	28NE4 Dadizeele	K 23 d 7.1
Debris Farm [1915]	36NW2 Armentières	C 17 b 15.17
December Avenue	51bNW3 Arras	G 5, 10, 11 , 16
Decima Post	36NW4 Bois Grenier	I 15 c
Deck Wood	28NE1 Zonnebeke	D 11 b
Decline Alley	70dNW4 St Gobain	I 25 d, 26 c
Decline Copse	28NE1 Zonnebeke	D 18 a 5.6 [astride railway]
Deconfiture Trench	62cNW1 Maricourt / 3 Vaux	H 1 b, 2 a, c
Deconinck Farm	28SW2 Wytschaete	O 34 b 65.70
Decouck Camp	28NW1 Elverdinghe	B 13 b, 14 a
Decouck Farm	28NW1 Elverdinghe	B 13 b 2.7
Decoy Cross Roads	20SE2 Hooglede	R 13 d 80.35
Decoy Farm	28NE2 Moorslede	K 4 a 5.9
Decoy Wood	28NE1 Zonnebeke	D 18 a, c
Dee A. V.	51bNW1 Roclincourt	A 30 c 2.6
Dee Copse [twin of Dum Copse]	62bSW1 Gricourt	M 28 d
Dee Post	36SW1 Aubers	N 3 d
Dee Side	28NW4 & NE3 Zillebeke	I 34 b
Dee Trench	51bNE1 Brébières	D 14 c
Dee Trench	51bNW1 Roclincourt	A 24 b, d
Deelish Avenue	62cNE2 Epéhy	F 3 b
Deelish Post	62cNE2 Epéhy	F 8 d
Deep Drive	28NE1 Zonnebeke	D 14 c, d
Deep Living Trench	28NW4 & NE3 Zillebeke	I 29 c
Deep Moat Farm	28SW4 Ploegsteert	U 23 d 8.1
Deep Support	28NW4 & NE3 Zillebeke	I 29 c
Deep Trench	28NE1 Zonnebeke	D 14 b, d, 20 b
Deep Trench	51bNE1 Brébières	D 19 d, 20 a, c
Deer Lane	36cSW1 Lens	M 19 d
Defoe Farm	28NE2 Moorslede	E 28 c 2.5
Defontaine Farm [Beaulencourt]	57cSW2 Villers-au-Flos	N 18 c 2.7
Deft Trench	51bNE1 Brébières	D 14 c
Defy Crossing [level crossing, Nieuwemolen]	28NE1 Zonnebeke	D 17 b 3.3
Dehéries [hamlet]	57bSW4 Serain	N 36 d

Name	Map Sheet	Map Reference
Dejob Wood	66eNW [4 Morisel]	H 16 d, 17 c
Dekart Farm	28NW1 Elverdinghe	B 8 a 8.8
Dekort Farm	28NW1 Elverdinghe	B 3 a 2.1
Delanay [Tranchée, 1915] / Monikie Street S.	57dSE4 Ovillers	X 19 d, 25 b
Delaporte, Ferme	36SW1 Aubers	N 15 a
Delaunay Avenue	57dNE3 & 4 Hébuterne	K 34 b
Delbar Wood	51bNW4 Fampoux	I 21 a
Delbruck Alley	66cNW1 Grugies	B 1 d, 2 c
Delbske Farm	28SW2 Wytschaete	O 10 b 05.30
Delegate Farm	36aNE1 Morbecque	J 1 b 4.4
Delennelle Fme	36NW2 Armentières	C 1 d 35.15
Delennelle Siding [light rly]	36NW2 Armentières	C 1 d
Delettre Post	36NW4 Bois Grenier	H 23 c
Deleval, Ferme (Site of)	36SW1 Aubers	N 14 d
Delf Trench	51bNE1 Brébières	D 1 c
Delhi Farm	28NW3 Poperinghe	G 34 c 2.8
Delhi Road [Sept 1915]	36cNW1 La Bassée	A 9 d
Deliard Trench [1918]	66eNW [2 Thennes]	B 23 d, 29 b
Delibes Trench	20SW2 Zwartegat	O 11 b, 12 c, d, 18 b
Deligny Mill	57cNE2 Bourlon	E 4 a 75.20
Dell Lane	57cSE2 Gonnelieu	Q 24 a
Dell Trench	51bNE1 Brébières	D 19 d
Delloy Wood	51bNE2 Dechy	L 5 b
Delloy, Fosse	51bNE2 Dechy	F 29 a, c
Delpierre Post	36NW4 Bois Grenier	H 22 a
Delporte Farm	28SW2 Wytschaete	O 34 b 85.90
Delsaux Farm	57cNW4 Beugny	I 28 a 3.5
Delta House	20SE3 Westroosebeke	V 19 c 4.0
Delta House & Huts	20SW4 Bixschoote	U 30 a, b
Delta Trench	51bNE1 Brébières	D 25 b, 26 a
Delta Trench	62cSW4 St. Christ	T 23 d, 24 c
Delta, Tranchée du	62cSW3 & 4 Marchélepot	T 24 a, c, 23 d
Deluy Trench [1918]	62dSW [4 Cachy]	U 3 d, 4 a, b, c, 9 b, d
Delva Farm	28NE1 Zonnebeke	D 20 a 05.27
Delva Trench	62cNW2 Bouchavesnes	C 21 b, d
Delville Valley	57cSW3 Longueval	S 12, 16
Delville Valley [sunken road]	57cSW3 Longueval	T 1 a
Delville Wood	57cSW3 Longueval	S 11, 12, 17, 18
Delys Farm	20SE2 Hooglede	Q 22 d 60.35
Demars Alley	66cNW1 Grugies / 2 Itancourt	B 10 c
Demburg Lane	51bSW4 Bullecourt	U 8 a
Demi Lune Cabaret, A la	36NW2 Armentières	C 3 c 2.7
Demi Lune Siding [light rly]	36NW2 Armentières	C 3 c
Demicourt [village]	57cNE3 Hermies	J 12 d, 18 a
Demir Hissar Alley	66cNW2 Itancourt	B 12 b, d, C 7 a
Demi-Repos Wood [Armagh Wood]	28NW4 & NE3 Zillebeke	I 24 c, d
Demoles Trench	62cNW3 Vaux	H 3 d, 4 c
Demon Trench	51bNE1 Brébières	D 1 c, 7 a, b
Demon Trench [1918]	62dNE [1 Dernancourt]	E 1 d
Den Plas	28NE2 Moorslede	F 2 a, b
Denain Farm	20SW4 Bixschoote	U 21 b 4.1
Dene Farm	36aNE3 Haverskerque	K 15 b 60.95
Deniécourt [village]	62cSW3 & 4 Marchélepot	M 36, S 6
Deniecourt Alley	62cSW1 Dompierre / 3 Vermandovillers	M 25-9, 35, 36, S 6, T 1, 7

Name	Map Sheet	Map Reference
Denis le Rock Trench	51bNW1 Roclincourt	A 3 c
Denise Farm	36aNE3 Haverskerque	J 2 c 2.4
Denning Alley	57cSE4 Villers-Guislain	X 4 d, 5 c
Dennis Chord [trench]	51bSW4 Bullecourt	U 29 b, c, d
Dennis Cross [trench]	51bSW4 Bullecourt	U 29 d
Dent Street	57dNE3 & 4 Hébuterne	K 23 c, d
Dentist's Cross Roads	28NE2 Moorslede	F 16 c 85.25
Dent's Dump	51bSW2 Vis-en-Artois	N 24 c
Denver [house]	36aNE4 Merville	L 1 d 4.0
Denys Farm	28SW2 Wytschaete	O 15 b 6.6
Denys Wood	28SW2 Wytschaete	O 9 d, 15 b
Deodar Lane	51bSW1 Neuville Vitasse	M 18 b, d
Depart Alley	62cSW1 Dompierre	N 2 b, 3 a, b
Départ Alley	62cNW3 Vaux	H 32 c, d
Deploy Corner	27SE3 Borre	V 5 c 72.74
Deputy Trench	36bNE [1 Labeuvrière]	D 3 a, b
Depuydt [light rly locality, 1917]	28SW1 Kemmel	N 3 c 9.0
Derack Farm [1918]	28SW1 Kemmel	N 25 d 50.95
Derby [light rly locality, 1917-18]	28NW4 Ypres	H 24 b
Derby Camp	28NW3 Poperinghe	H 1 c
Derby Farm	28NW3 Poperinghe	H 1 c
Derby House	28NW3 Poperinghe	H 1 c 85.80
Derby Post	57cSE4 Villers-Guislain	X 9 d
Derby Redoubt	36cSW1 Lens	N 8 a
Derby Reserve	57cSE2 Gonnelieu	Q 5 c
Derby Road	28NW4 & NE3 Zillebeke	J 19 b
Derby Street	57dNE1 & 2 Fonquevillers	E 27 b
Derby Support	57cSE2 Gonnelieu	Q 5 c, d
Derby Support	57cSE2 Gonnelieu	R 9 b, d
Derby Switch	57cNE3 Hermies	K 20 c, 25 b, 26 a
Derby Trench	57cNE4 Marcoing	K 35 b
Derby Trench	57cSE2 Gonnelieu	Q 5 a, c, d
Derby Trench	57dNE3 & 4 Hébuterne	K 17 c
Derision Farm	28NE4 Dadizeele	L 29 d 6.8
Dermis House	28NE4 Dadizeele	L 33 d 05.45
Dermot House	36aNE2 Vieux Berquin	F 4 c 1.3
Dermot Mill	36NW1 Steenwerck	B 1 d 4.5
Dermy Copse	57cNW1 Gomiecourt	H 2 b
Deron Alley	62cSW3 Vermandovillers	S 8 c
Derrien Trench	57dNE3 & 4 Hébuterne	K 17 c
Derry Farm	28SE1 Wervicq	P 10 c 1.7
Derry House	28SW2 Wytschaete	O 27 a 3.6
Derry Huts	28SW1 Kemmel	N 32 central
Dervish Cross Roads	28NE2 Moorslede	E 21 d 9.3
Desaix Alley	66cNW1 Grugies	B 7 a
Desaix, Tranchée	70dSW2 [Coucy-le-Château]	O 26 c
Deseaux Alley	66cNW1 Grugies	A 16 c, d
Desert Corner [road jct]	28NE2 Moorslede	E 28 a 2.8
Deserted Farm	36aSE1 St Venant	Q 20 b 95.50
Desinet Farm	28SW2 Wytschaete	N 16 d 5.4
Desire Support	57cSW4 Combles	T 6 a
Desire Support Trench	57dSE2 & 57cSW1 Le Sars	M 7 d, 13 b, R 12 c, 17 a, b
Desire Trench [Dessauer Graben]	57dSE2 & 57cSW1 Le Sars	R 15 c, 16 c, d, 17 b, c, d
Desk Trench	51bNE1 Brébières	D 1 c

Name	Map Sheet	Map Reference
Desmond Trench	28NE1 Zonnebeke	D 22 b, d
Desmons Track [1917-18]	20SW4 Bixschoote	T 6 b, U 1 a, d
Desolation Alley	62cSW1 Dompierre / 3 Vermandovillers	N 25 c, 31 a, b, d
Despagne Farm [Spanish Farm?]	28SW2 Wytschaete	O 33 b 55.90
Despair Post [Serre Trench]	57dNE3 & 4 Hébuterne	K 35 b, d
Despot Farm	36aNE2 Vieux Berquin	F 15 b 85.50
Dessart Switch	57cSE3 Sorel-le-Grand	W 1, 2, 3 [vicinity of]
Dessart Valley	57cSE3 Sorel-le-Grand	W 1 c, d, 2 c, d, 3 c, d
Dessart Wood	57cSE3 Sorel-le-Grand	W 1 a, b, c, d, 2 a, b, c
Dessauer Graben [Desire Trench]	57dSE2 & 57cSW1 Le Sars	R 15 c, 16 c, d, 17 c
Destiny Buildings	28NE4 Dadizeele	L 29 a 1.8
Destremont Farm	57dSE2 & 57cSW1 Le Sars	M 21 a 5.3
Destremont Road [road]	57dSE2 & 57cSW1 Le Sars	M 14 d, 21 a
Destremont Trench	57dSE2 & 57cSW1 Le Sars	M 20 a, b, 21 a
Destroyed Mill	28SW4 Ploegsteert	T 4 b 40.15
Detect Crossing [level crossing]	28NE1 Zonnebeke	D 12 d 95.15
Deuce House	28NE1 Zonnebeke	D 14 b 90.65
Deuce Trench	51bNE1 Brébières	D 1 c
Deuillet Trench	70dNW2 Servais	C 13 b, d, 19 a, b
Deûlémont [village]	28SW4 Ploegsteert	U 24 c, d
Deûlémont, Pt. [Pont] de	28SW4 Ploegsteert	U 30 b 2.5
Deus Trench	62cNW4 Péronne	I 15 d
Deux Lucannes Farm	20SW4 Bixschoote	T 6 b 60.35
Deva Farm	28NE2 Moorslede	E 11 d 55.40
Devial Avenue	57dSE1 & 2 Beaumont	Q 23 b
Deviation Trench	36cSW1 Lens	M 20 a, c
Devies Camp	28SW1 Kemmel	M 17 c
Devillard Trench	66cNW1 Grugies	A 12 b
Devillers Farm	57cSE2 Gonnelieu	Q 36 a 9.8
Devil's Crossing [level crossing]	28NE1 Zonnebeke	D D 26 b 9.5
Devil's Elbow [road bend]	28SE1 Wervicq	P 7 b 5.2
Devil's Elbow [road, Dead End, Kaaie, Ypres]	28NW4 Ypres	I 2 c
Devil's Jump	36SW1 Aubers	N 19 a
Devils Staircase	57dSE1 & 2 Beaumont	Q 24 a
Devil's Street [road]	36aSE2 Lestrem	R 22 d, 23 b, c, d, 24 a
Devil's Trench	51bNW4 Fampoux	I 31 b, 32 a, c
Devil's Trench [Delville Wood]	57cSW3 Longueval	S 11 d, 12 c, 18 b
Devil's Valley	57cSW3 Longueval	S 12 b
Devil's Wood [Delville Wood]	57cSW3 Longueval	S 11, 12, 17, 18
Devil's Wood [Tilloy]	51bNW3 Arras	G 36 b, d, H 31 a, c
Devoi Repos Wood [April '15, Sanctuary Wd]	28NW4 & NE3 Zillebeke	I 24 c, d
Devon [Trench]	36cSW3 Vimy	S 28 a, c
Devon Avenue	36SW2 Radinghem	N 4 c, d, 10 b
Devon Bank [lynchet]	51bSW2 Vis-en-Artois	O 21 b, 22 a
Devon Crater	36cSW3 Vimy	S 28 a, c
Devon Lane	36cNW3 Loos	G 10 d, 11 c, d, 12 c, d
Devon Locality	36cNW3 Loos	G 19 d
Devon Trench	36cSW4 Rouvroy	T 30 b
Devonshire Camp	28NW3 Poperinghe	G 22 b, 23 a
Devonshire Farm	28NW3 Poperinghe	G 22 b 75.70
Dewar Farm	28NE2 Moorslede	F 7 c 1.2
Dewdrop Trench	57cSW4 Combles	N 34 d, 35 c, T 5 a
Dewsbury Trench	57cNW2 Vaulx-Vraucourt	C 10 b, 11 a, c
Diagonal	28NW4 & NE3 Zillebeke	I 29 c, 35 a

Name	Map Sheet	Map Reference
Diagonal	28SW4 Ploegsteert	T 6 b, U 1 a
Diagonal Trench	57cSW3 Longueval	S 18 d
Diagonal Trench [Snag Trench]	57dSE2 & 57cSW1 Le Sars	M 16 d, 17 c, d
Dial Cross Roads	20SE2 Hooglede	R 16 b 6.7
Diamond Copse	62bNW3 Bellicourt	G 8 b
Diamond Door Cottage [Sept 1915]	36cNW1 La Bassée	A 22 d 8.7
Diamond Lane	51bSW1 Neuville Vitasse	N 14 c, d
Diamond Lane / Trench [1918]	62dNE [1 Dernancourt]	D 18 d
Diamond Trench	36cNW3 Loos	G 11 a
Diamond Wood [Thiepval]	57dSE1 & 2 Beaumont	R 25 c
Diana Buildings	28NE2 Moorslede	F 9 c 5.2 to 15 a 7.8
Diana Trench	51bNE1 Brébières	D 13 d
Diana's Hill	62bSW4 Homblières	U 2 a, b
Diana's Valley	62bSW4 Homblières	O 32 c, d, U 1 b, 2 a
Diana's Wood	62bSW4 Homblières	O 32 d, 33 c, U 2 b, 3 a
Dibs Cottage	20SE2 Hooglede	R 9 d 55.90
Dibsland Farm	28NE4 Dadizeele	K 24 d 60.05
Dice Trench	51bNE1 Brébières	D 19 d
Dicharry, Tranchée [Pick Axe Road]	36cSW1 Lens	M 20 c, d
Dick Avenue	57cSE2 Gonnelieu	R 13 b, 14 a
Dick Hudson Post [1918]	57dNE1 & 2 Fonquevillers	F 19 b
Dick Post	62cNE4 Roisel	L 36 a 30.45
Dick Trench	51bNE1 Brébières	D 19 b, 20 c
Dickebusch [village]	28NW3 Poperinghe	H 33 a, b, 34 a
Dickebusch East [railway sidings, 1917-18]	28NW4 Ypres	H 28 c, d
Dickebusch Huts	28NW3 Poperinghe	H 26 b
Dickebusch Line [1918]	28NW3 Poperinghe	H 10, 16, 21, 22, 27, 32, 33
Dickebusch West [railway sidings]	28NW3 Poperinghe	H 26 d, 27 c
Dicker Farm	20SE2 Hooglede	Q 11 d 9.6
Dick's Cut	36cNW1 La Bassée	A 26 b
Dickson Cross Roads	28NE4 Dadizeele	L 1 c 8.1
Dicky Maze	36cSW4 Rouvroy	U 11 b, d
Die Trench	51bNE1 Brébières	D 19 d, 25 b
Diekirch Trench	62bSW3 St Quentin	S 18 d, T 13 a, c
Diemay Trench	70dNW4 St Gobain	H 18 c, 23 b
Dieppe Trench	66cSW3 Tergnier / 4 La Fère	T 22 c, 28 a, b, d
Dig Trench	51bNE1 Brébières	D 19 d
Digby Road [road]	36cSW1 Lens	N 26 b, d, 27 c
Digger Farm	27NE2 Proven	E 27 d 90.95
Diggers Avenue [1918]	62dNE [1 Dernancourt]	E 1 c, d
Diggers Support [1918]	62dSE [1 Hamel]	P 19 c, 25 a, c
Dijon Farm	27NE4 Abeele	K 30 b 3.5
Dijon House	28NW3 Poperinghe	G 13 d 2.4
Dike Trench	51bNW2 Oppy	C 6 b
Dilly Farm [formerly Dead Cow; Potijze]	28NW4 & NE3 Zillebeke	I 5 c 25.02
Dime Trench	51bNE1 Brébières	D 19 b, 20 a
Dimity Farm	36NW1 Steenwerck	A 2 a 4.3
Dimple Mines [dugouts, formerly named Arbre]	28NE1 Zonnebeke	D 7 a
Dimple Trench	28NE1 Zonnebeke	D 7 a, b, d
Dimple Trench	51bNE1 Brébières	D 13 d, 14 c
Din Trench	51bNE1 Brébières	D 20 a
Dinah Trench	51bNE1 Brébières	D 13 b, c, d
Dinde, Tranchée de la	66dNW2 Morchain	C 1 d, 2 c, 7 b, d
Dindon Trench	20SW3 Oostvleteren	T 14 b

Name	Map Sheet	Map Reference
Dinet Street	57dSE4 Ovillers	X 26 b
Ding Post [twin of Dong Post]	62cNE4 Roisel	L 30 c 60.35
Ding Trench	51bNE1 Brébières	D 26 c
Ding Trench	51bNW2 Oppy / NE1 Brébières	C 12 b, D 7 a
Dingle Cottages	27NE2 Proven	F 3 c 3.4
Dingle Trench	51bNE1 Brébières	D 1 a
Dingle Trench	57dSE4 Ovillers	X 21 d, 22 b
Dingle, The	57dSE4 Ovillers	X 27 b 3.9
Dingo Ditch [1918]	62dNE [1 Dernancourt]	D 24 b
Dingo Farm	28NW4 Ypres	H 16 a 5.5
Dingo Trench, & Support [1918]	62dNE [1 Dernancourt]	D 18 d
Dingwall Trench	51bNW4 Fampoux	H 16 d, 22 b
Dink Buildings	28NE2 Moorslede	F 27 c 2.7
Dinkum Alley	57dSE4 Ovillers	X 9 d
Dinky Alley	57dSE4 Ovillers	X 9 d
Dinky House	28SE1 Wervicq	P 10 a 4.3
Dinkyville [light rly]	36bSE4 Carency	X 13 b
Dinneford House	28NE4 Dadizeele	K 23 b 9.8
Dint Trench	51bNE1 Brébières	D 25 d, 26 a
Diogenes Cross Roads	20SE3 Westroosebeke	W 7 d 0.1
Dip Street [road]	36cNW3 Loos	G 36 d
Dip Trench	51bNE1 Brébières	D 19 b, d, 25 a
Dipper Bridge [road over stream]	36NW1 Steenwerck	A 28 d 90.05
Dire Trench	51bNE1 Brébières	D 25 b, 26 a
Director / Director's Farm	20SE3 Westroosebeke	V 5 a 7.2
Dirge Trench	51bNE1 Brébières	D 25 d
Dirk Alley	51bNW4 Fampoux	I 25 d, 31 b
Dirk Cottages	36aNE4 Merville	L 15 d 80.75
Dirk Trench	51bNE1 Brébières	D 7 a, c
Dirk Trench	51bSW2 Vis-en-Artois	N 4 c, d
Dirk Valley	62bNW1 Gouy	A 14 d, 15 c, 20 a, b, c
Dirt Trench	36NW2 & NE1 Houplines	D 7 b
Dirty Bucket Camp	28NW1 Elverdinghe	A 30 a, c
Dirty Bucket Corner	28NW1 Elverdinghe	B 19 c 3.7
Dirty Bucket Sidings [railway, 1917-18]	28NW1 Elverdinghe	A 24 b, B 19 c
Dirty Trench	51bNE1 Brébières	D 13 d
Dirty Trench [1918]	62dNE [1 Dernancourt]	D 6 d, E 1 c, 7 a
Disc Trench	51bNE1 Brébières	D 25 d
Distillery [N of Pont Fixe, Feb 1915]	36cNW1 La Bassée	A 14
Ditch Post	51bNW2 Oppy	B 28 d, H 4 b
Ditch Trench	28NE1 Zonnebeke	D 20 a
Ditch Trench	28NW2 St Julien	C 13 b
Dittelberger Graben	51bNW1 Roclincourt	G 6 b
Ditto Trench	51bNE1 Brébières	D 25 d, 26 b, c
Diver House	27NE2 Proven	E 24 c 25.40
Dives Copse	62dNE [3 Sailly-le-Sec]	J 24 b 6.8
Divide Lane	51bSW1 Neuville Vitasse	M 16 b
Divion Road [road]	57dSE1 & 2 Beaumont	R 19 a, b, d, 25 b
Dixie Post	36NW4 Bois Grenier	I 15 c
Dixmude [town]	20NW4 Dixmude	H 6 d, 12 a, b, d, I 1 c, 7 a
Dixmude Gate [Ypres]	28NW4 Ypres	I 8 a 4.9
Dixmude Trench	62bSW3 St Quentin	M 33 d, S 3 b
Dizzy Trench	51bNE1 Brébières	D 25 b
Dobbie Trench	36bNE [1 Labeuvrière]	D 10 b, d

Name	Map Sheet	Map Reference
Dobbin Farm	27NE3 Winnezeele	J 32 b 20.35
Dobie Ditch [1918]	62dNE [1 Dernancourt]	D 12 d, E 7 c
Doc [light rly siding]	36cSW1 Lens	M 8 a, b
Dochy [light rly loop, 1917-18]	28NE1 Zonnebeke	D 21 a 3.7
Dochy Farm [& pillboxes]	28NE1 Zonnebeke	D 15 c 1.1
Docile Trench	28NE1 Zonnebeke	D 22 d, 28 b
Dock Farm	20SE2 Hooglede	R 21 a 8.9
Dock Trench	51bNE1 Brébières	D 26 c
Doctor Trench	51bNE1 Brébières	D 7 a, b
Doctor's Corner [road jct]	28NE2 Moorslede	F 24 a 70.57
Dodo Copse	57dSW [4 Toutencourt]	T 5 b, d, 6 a, c
Dodo Trench	36NW2 & NE1 Houplines	D 1 a
Dodo Trench	51bSW4 Bullecourt	O 31 c
Dodo Trench [1918]	62dNE [1 Dernancourt]	D 6 d, 12 b
Dodo Wood	27NE2 Proven	F 10 b, 11 a
Dodo Wood	66eNW [2 Thennes]	C 10 b, d, 11 a, c, 16 b, 17 a
Doe Lane	62bNW1 Gouy	G 2 a, c
Doe Trench	51bNE1 Brébières	D 19 b, 20 a
Dog Copse	62bSW4 Homblières	U 7 c
Dog Hill	62bSW4 Homblières	U 7 a, c
Dog House / Houses	20SW4 Bixschoote	U 29 b 7.8
Dog Lane	51bSW1 Neuville Vitasse	N 7 d
Dog Street	57dNE3 & 4 Hébuterne	K 34 d
Dog Trench	51bNW2 Oppy / NE1 Brébières	C 6 d, D 1 c
Dog Trench	51bSW4 Bullecourt	U 21 b
Dog Trench	62cNE2 Epéhy	F 18 c
Dog Trench [1918]	62dNE [1 Dernancourt]	E 19 a
Dog Trench [near Fontaine des Chiens]	51bSW2 Vis-en-Artois	O 3 a, c
Dog Wood	62dSE [1 Hamel]	Q 24 c, 30 a, b
Dognon, Tranchée du	36cSW1 Lens	M 19 d, 20 c
Dogs Alley	36SW3 Richebourg	S 9 c, 15 a, b
Dogs Post	36SW3 Richebourg	S 9 c 2.7
Doignies [village]	57cNE3 Hermies	J 10 c, 16 a, b
Doignies Reserve	57cNE3 Hermies	J 10 a, c, d, 16 b, 17 a
Doingt ['Doing It', village]	62cNW4 Péronne	I 29 d, 35 b, 36 a, b, d
Doingt [railway locality & dump 1917-18]	62cNW4 Péronne	I 35 a, b, d, 36 c
Doingt Copse	62cNW4 Péronne	I 36 d
Doingt Wood [Rocogne Wood]	62cNW4 Péronne / NE3 Buire	I 24 c, 30 b, d, J 25 c, 31 a
Doiran Trench	66cNW4 Berthenicourt	I 8 c
Dolan Post	62bNW1 Gouy	A 7 b
Doleful Post	62cNE2 Epéhy	F 17 b 75.80
Dolfus Alley	62cNW4 Péronne	H 28 d, 29 c, 35 a, b, 36 a, c, d
Dolls House	36aNE3 Haverskerque	J 23 c 00.95
Doll's House	36SW2 Radinghem	N 11 c
Dolls House [1918]	57dNE2 & 57cNW1 Courcelles	L 3 b
Doll's House [Deulemont]	28SW4 Ploegsteert	U 24 c 7.2
Dolls House [Lock No. 9]	28NW4 Ypres	I 19 b 15.50
Dolls House Howitzer Spur [1917-18]	28NW4 Ypres	I 13 d, 14 c
Dolly Post	36NW4 Bois Grenier	I 15 d
Dolly Trench	51bNE1 Brébières	D 13 b, d
Dolly Trench [1918]	62dNE [1 Dernancourt]	E 13 a, b, c
Dolly's Bridge	57dSE1 & 2 Beaumont	Q 24 a
Dolmen [standing stones]	51bNE3 Noyelle-sous-Bellonne	K 32 a 2.7
Dolomite Trench / Dolomites, Tranchée des	66cNW2 Itancourt	B 6 b, d, C 1 a, 7 c

Name	Map Sheet	Map Reference
Dolphin Buildings	28NE4 Dadizeele	L 5 d 8.8
Domart-sur-la-Luce [village]	62dSW [4 Cachy / Gentelles]	U 26, 27
Dombarton [sic] Lakes [Dumbarton]	28NW4 & NE3 Zillebeke	J 20 a
Dombey Farm	36NW1 Steenwerck	A 2 c 8.7
Dome House	28SW2 Wytschaete	O 9 a 0.7
Dome Trench	51bNW2 Oppy	C 6 d
Domfront Alley	66cSW2 Vendeuil	N 6 d, O 1 c
Dominie Farm	28NE2 Moorslede	F 10 d 7.5
Dominion Camp	28NW3 Poperinghe	G 23 b, 24 a
Dominion Farm	28NW3 Poperinghe	G 24 a 2.4
Dominion House [SE of Knoll Farm]	28NW4 & NE3 Zillebeke	I 29 a 9.5
Dominique Trench	57dNE3 & 4 Hébuterne	K 23 a
Domino Dump	62cNW1 Maricourt	B 15 a 74.92
Domino Trench	28NW4 Ypres	H 24 c, d, 30 a
Dompierre [village]	62cSW1 Dompierre	M 5, 11
Dompierre, Boyau	62cSW1 Dompierre	M 16 a
Dompierre, Tranchée de	62cSW1 Dompierre	M 4 b
Don Camp, Le	36NW2 Armentières	B 4 b, 5 a
Don Trench	51bNE1 Brébières	D 19 d
Don Trench	51bNW2 Oppy / NE1 Brébières	C 12 b, D 7 a
Don Trench [1918]	62dNE [1 Dernancourt]	E 7 d
Donald Farm	20SE2 Hooglede	Q 9 b 62.93
Donald Trench	51bNE1 Brébières	D 7 a
Donald Trench	57cSW2 Villers-au-Flos	N 34 a
Donaueschingen Graben	57dNE1 & 2 Fonquevillers	E 12 b, d, F 7 a, c
Donegal Camp	28SW3 Bailleul	N 32 a, c
Donegal Farm	28SW3 Bailleul	N 32 c 3.5
Donegal Passage	57dSE1 & 2 Beaumont	Q 10 b
Done's / Dones Redoubt	62cNW1 Maricourt	A 15 d
Dong Post [twin of Ding Post]	62cNE4 Roisel	L 30 c 50.75
Dongarra Trench	36bNE [1 Labeuvrière]	D 17 b
Donizetti Junction	20SW2 Zwartegat	O 24 a
Donkeys Trench	66cNW4 Berthenicourt	I 8 a
Donnet [Tranchée, La Boisselle, 1915]	57dSE4 Ovillers	X 13 a, c
Donnet Post	57dSE4 Ovillers	W 12 d 8.2
Donnet Street	57dSE4 Ovillers	W 12 d, X 13 a
Donnington Hall	28SW4 Ploegsteert	U 8 c 3.9
Donny Brook Trench	36bNE [1 Labeuvrière]	D 11 c, d, 17 a
Donon Alley	66cNW2 Itancourt	H 6 b
Dont Trench	28NE1 Zonnebeke	D 13 c, 19 a
Don't Trench	28NE1 Zonnebeke	D 13 c
Doode Stappen Bridge	27NE4 Abeele	K 17 c 07.33
Dook Alley	36cNW1 La Bassée	A 22 c, d
Dook Farm	36NW1 Steenwerck	A 3 a 1.2
Dooley House	27NE3 Winnezeele	J 32 c 3.9
Doom Trench	28NE1 Zonnebeke	D 7 d, 8 c
Doon Copse	62bNW4 Ramicourt	I 9 a, b
Doon Hill	62bNW4 Ramicourt	I 9 a, b
Doon Mill	62bNW4 Ramicourt	I 8 b
Doone Farm [moated]	20SE2 Hooglede	Q 30 c 7.8
Doons Alley	57cNE3 Hermies	K 26 a
Door Trench	51bNW2 Oppy	C 6 d
Dora Farm	27SE1 St Sylvestre	Q 9 c 75.75
Dora Trench	36SW1 Aubers	N 19 c, 25 a

Name	Map Sheet	Map Reference
Dora Trench	51bNE1 Brébières	D 7 c, 13 a
Doran Alley [Oran, Boyau d']	36bSE2 Boyeffles	R 30 a
Dora's Arm	36SW1 Aubers	N 19 c, 25 a
Dorchester Trench	51bNE1 Brébières	D 14 c, d, 20 b, d, 21 c, 27 a
Dorchester, The [Rue d'Ouvert, June 1915]	36cNW1 La Bassée	A 3 a / c / d
Dore Wood	62cSW4 St Christ	U 21 b, d
Doré Wood	62cSW4 St Christ	U 21 b, d
Dorel House	36aNE3 Haverskerque	J 1 d 7.2
Doris Dump	36cSW3 Vimy	T 8 d 8.7
Doris Trench	36cSW3 Vimy	T 8 c, d
Dorking Trench	51bNE1 Brébières	D 7 c, d
Dorman Cottage	27SE4 Meteren	W 30 a 90.35
Dormy House	28NW4 & NE3 Zillebeke	I 23 a 6.4
Dormy House Lane	28NW4 & NE3 Zillebeke	I 23 a, b
Dormy Junction [light railway, 1917-18]	28NW4 Ypres	I 22 b 75.75
Dorothy Bridge [road over Heulebeek]	28NE4 Dadizeele	L 18 c 40.25
Dorothy Corons [miners' cottages]	36cSW4 Rouvroy	O 33 c, d, U 3 a, b
Dorothy Post	36NW4 Bois Grenier	I 15 c, 21 a
Dorothy Trench	57cNW1 Gomiecourt	A 21 d, 27 a, b
Dorset Street	57dSE4 Ovillers	X 13 a
Dorset Street / Trench	28SW2 Wytschaete	O 27 b, 28 a
Dorset Trench	57cSW3 Longueval	S 11 c
Dose Trench [Lempire]	62cNE2 Epéhy	F 10 c, d, 16 b
Doser Trench	66cNW2 Itancourt	B 6 c
Dosinghem Hospital & Railhead	27NE2 Proven	F 11 a, b, c, d
Dot Post	36NW4 Bois Grenier	I 15 d
Dot Trench	51bNE1 Brébières	D 19 d
Dot Trench	57dSE2 & 57cSW1 / 57cSW3	R 34 b, 35 c, d
Dot Trench	57dSE4 Ovillers	R 35 d, X 5 b, 6 a
Dot Way	36cNW3 Loos	G 35 b
Douage Wood	62cNW1 Maricourt / 2 Bouchavesnes	B 4 a
Douai Avenue	51bNW1 Roclincourt	A 15, 16
Douai Trench	51bNW1 Roclincourt	A 15 b
Douai Trench	62bSW3 St Quentin	M 33 d, S 3 b, c, d, 4 a, 9 a
Double Copse	20SE3 Westroosebeke	V 22 d, 23 c
Double Crassier	36cSW1 Lens	M 4 c, d
Double Crassier Road [road]	36cSW1 Lens	M 3 b, d, 4 a, c, 10 a, c
Double Crater [Kruisstraat]	28SW2 Wytschaete	N 36 a 6.4
Double Sap	36cSW1 Lens	M 32 a
Double Trench	51bNE1 Brébières	D 7 a, b, c
Double Trench	57dNE3 & 4 Hébuterne	K 35 b, 36 c
Doubno Alley	62bSW3 St Quentin	T 28 c
Doubt Trench	51bNE1 Brébières	D 2 c
Douce Crème Farm	36aSE1 St Venant	P 36 a
Doucet [Tranchée, SE of Bécourt Ch'eau, 1915]	57dSE4 Ovillers / 62dNE2 Méaulte	X 26 c, F 2 a
Douchy Avenue [1918]	51cSE4 Blaireville / 57dNE2 [Courcelles]	X 21, 27, F 3, 4, 9
Douchy-les-Ayette [village]	57dNE1 & 2 Fonquevillers	F 3 d, 4 c, d, 9 b, 10 a
Douddu Fme	36NW2 Armentières	B 5 c 7.6
Doudou [sic] Lines [huts]	36NW2 Armentières	B 5 c
Douglas Camp	27NE4 Abeele	L 14 c
Douglas Copse	62bSW3 St. Quentin	S 12 a
Douglas Trench	36cSW1 Lens	N 8 a
Douglas Villa [Ploegsteert Wood 1914-15]	28SW4 Ploegsteert	U 21 a 3.6
Douley Trench	57dNE3 & 4 Hébuterne	K 17 c

Name	Map Sheet	Map Reference
Doulieu [hamlet]	36aNE2 Vieux Berquin	F 29 d, 30 c, L 5 b
Doumenjou Trench	62bSW3 St Quentin	S 29 a, d
Dours Alley [1918]	66eNW [4 Morisel]	H 28 c
Douteuse House	28NW2 St Julien	B 6 d 80.55
Douve Farm, La	28SW4 Ploegsteert	U 9 a 1.1
Douve Farm, Site of Former [moated site]	28SW4 Ploegsteert	U 9 a 15.20
Doux Mont, le	51bNE3 Noyelle-sous-Bellonne	J 9 c
Dove Lane [trench]	57cSE4 Villers-Guislain	X 29 d
Dove Trench	51bNE1 Brébières	D 7 c
Dovecot Corner	20SE2 Hooglede	R 20 c 35.80
Dovecot, The [building]	20SW4 Bixschoote	T 17 d 5.7
Dover Camp	36NW2 Armentières	B 4 b
Dover Reserve	36SW3 Richebourg	S 28 c
Dover Street	28NW4 & NE3 Zillebeke	I 5 c, d
Dover Street	36NW4 Bois Grenier	I 15 d
Dover Street	62dNE2 Méaulte	F 15 a
Dover Street [road]	57cSW3 Longueval	S 17 d
Dover Trench	36SW3 Richebourg	S 27 d, 28 a, c
Dover Trench	51bNE1 Brébières	D 7 c, d
Down Alley	66cSW4 La Fère	U 10 c, 16 a
Down Street	28NW4 & NE3 Zillebeke	I 5 d
Down Street	36NW4 Bois Grenier	I 16 a, c
Down Street	57dNE3 & 4 Hébuterne	K 34 a, b
Down Street [Guillemont]	57cSW3 Longueval	T 25 a
Down Street [Sept 1915]	36cNW1 La Bassée	A 9 a
Down Trench [Mont Rouge]	28SW1 Kemmel	M 21 d, 22 c
Downhill Avenue [1918]	28SW1 Kemmel	M 21 d, 22 c
Downing Trench	28NE1 Zonnebeke	D 14 c, 20 a
Downshire Camp	28NW3 Poperinghe	G 30 d, H 25 c
Downshire Farm	28NW3 Poperinghe	G 30 d 5.8
Downshire Lines [camp]	28NW3 Poperinghe	G 30 b
Dowsett Drive	51bNW1 Roclincourt	A 3 a
Doyen, Tunnel de [Calonne]	36cSW1 Lens	M 14 c 9.2
Doze Trench	51bNW3 Arras	H 14 b
D-Q Line [Drocourt-Quéant]	36cSE / 51bNW / 51bSE	extensive
Draaibank [place name / farm]	20SW4 Bixschoote	U 2 c 5.7
Draaibank Farm	20SW4 Bixschoote	U 1 b 7.3
Drab Trench	36cSW2 Harnes	O 34 a
Drac Alley	66cNW4 Berthenicourt	H 18 a
Drackenburgh [sic] Post	57cNE1 Quéant	E 7 c, d
Draft Trench	36cSW4 Rouvroy	O 34 c
Drag Trench	36cSW4 Rouvroy	U 17 b
Dragoman Farm	28NE4 Dadizeele	L 22 d 7.0
Dragon Alley [1918]	66eNW [2 Thennes]	C 7 c, 13 a
Dragon Camp	28NW1 Elverdinghe	A 15 b
Dragon Grave	57cSW3 Longueval	S 10 d 5.7
Dragon Trench	36cSW4 Rouvroy	O 34 c
Dragon Trench	66cSW4 La Fère	O 33 d, 34 c, U 3 b, 4 a
Dragon Trench / Tranchée du Dragon	62cSW3 & 4 Marchélepot	T 9 d, 15 b
Dragon Trench [1918]	57dSE [3 Bouzincourt]	W 14 d, 15 c, 21 a
Dragon Wood	28NW1 Elverdinghe	A 9 d, 10 c, 15 b, 16 a
Dragon Wood	66cNW2 Itancourt	B 22 b, 23 a
Dragon Wood / Bois du Dragon	62cSW3 & 4 Marchélepot	T 15 a
Dragons Wood [Royal Dragoons Wood]	62cNW3 Vaux	G 16 a, b, d

Name	Map Sheet	Map Reference
Dragons, Tranchée des	70dSW [2 Coucy-le-Château]	O 13 b
Dragoon Alley	28NW4 & NE3 Zillebeke	I 4 c
Dragoon Copse	62bSW4 Homblières	U 27 a
Dragoon Farm [Potijze]	28NW4 & NE3 Zillebeke	I 4 c 4.2
Dragoon Lane [road]	51bSW2 Vis-en-Artois	O 7 a, c
Dragoon Post	62bNW3 Bellicourt	G 31 d 9.3
Dragoon Trench	51bNW4 Fampoux	H 30 d, 36 a
Drail Trench	66cNW1 Grugies	B 9 a
Drake Alley [1918]	57dSE1 & 2 Beaumont	Q 29 c, d
Drake Road	51bSW3 Boisleux	S 14 d
Drake Street [road]	57cSE1 Bertincourt	Q 3 a, b
Drake Trench	36cSW4 Rouvroy	U 4 a
Dram Trench	36cSW4 Rouvroy	U 11 d
Drama Trench	36cSW4 Rouvroy	U 4 a
Dramatist Cross Roads	28NE2 Moorslede	F 4 c 35.65
Dranoutre [village]	28SW3 Bailleul	M 35 d, 36 c
Drap / DripTrench	36cSW4 Rouvroy	U 11 c
Draper Trench	36cSW4 Rouvroy	U 4 a, c
Drapier Alley	66cSW2 Vendeuil	O 19 d, 25 a, b
Drapkin Crossing [road across rly]	28NE4 Dadizeele	L 20 a 8.9
Drastic Trench	36cSW4 Rouvroy	U 4 c
Drat Trench	36cSW4 Rouvroy	U 17 a
Draught House	28NE1 Zonnebeke	D 27 c 25.60
Draught Trench	28NE1 Zonnebeke	D 26 d
Draughty Junction [road jct]	28NE4 Dadizeele	L 2 c 35.40
Drave Trench / Drave, Tranchée de La	66cNW1 Grugies / 2 Itancourt	B 5 c, 9 a, b, 10 a, b, 11 a
Draw Trench	36cSW4 Rouvroy	U 4 c
Dray Trench	36cSW4 Rouvroy	U 4 c
Dread Trench	36cSW4 Rouvroy	U 4 c, 10 a
Dreadnought [keep, late 1915]	36SW1 Aubers	M 23 d
Dreadnought Post / Fort	36SW1 Aubers	M 23 d
Dreadnought Street [late 1915]	36SW1 Aubers	M 23 b
Dream Trench	36cSW4 Rouvroy	U 10 a
Dreary Trench	36cSW4 Rouvroy	U 4 c
Dredge Trench	36cSW4 Rouvroy	U 4 c
Dregs Trench	36cSW4 Rouvroy	U 17 a
Dreisbach Weg	51bSW1 Neuville Vitasse	M 16 b
Drench Trench	36cSW4 Rouvroy	U 4 c, d
Dresden Alley	66cNW4 Berthenicourt	I 14 d
Dresden Lane	57cSW4 Combles	U 21 b, d
Dresden Trench	36cSW4 Rouvroy	U 11 c
Dreslincourt [village]	66dNW2 Morchain	B 28 b, d, 29 a, c
Dreslincourt, Bois de	66dNW2 Morchain	B 29 d, 30 c, H 5 b, 6 a
Dress Farm	27NE2 Proven	E 29 a 35.70
Dressler Post	57dSE4 Ovillers	X 19 a
Dressy Trench	36cSW4 Rouvroy	U 4 c
Drew Trench	36cSW4 Rouvroy	U 4 c
Dribble Trench	36cSW4 Rouvroy	U 4 d, 10 b
Dried Trench	36cSW4 Rouvroy	U 4 d
Driest Trench	36cSW4 Rouvroy	U 4 d
Drift Trench	36cSW4 Rouvroy	U 10 b, d
Drill Trench	36cSW4 Rouvroy	U 11 c
Drink Trench	36cSW4 Rouvroy	U 11 c
Drip / Drap Trench	36cSW4 Rouvroy	U 11 c

Name	Map Sheet	Map Reference
Driscoll Trench	36cSW4 Rouvroy	U 17 d
Drive Cut	28NW4 & NE3 Zillebeke	I 34 a, b, d
Drivel Trench	36cSW4 Rouvroy	U 17 a
Driver Trench	36cSW4 Rouvroy	U 17 a, c
Drizzle Trench	36cSW4 Rouvroy	U 17 b, d
Drocourt Road [road]	36cSW4 Rouvroy	U 8 d, 9 c, d
Drocourt Support First	51bNE1 Brébières	D 7 a, c, 13 a, b, d, 19 b, d
Drocourt Support First, Second & Third	36cSW2 Harnes / 4 Rouvroy	O 34, 35, U 4, 5
Drocourt Support Second	51bNE1 Brébières	D 7 d, 13 b, 14 a, c, 20 a, c
Drocourt Support Third	51bNE1 Brébières	D 8 a, b, d, 14 b, 15 a, c, 21 a, c, d
Drocourt-Quéant Line / Switch	36cSE / 51bNW / 51bSE	extensive
Drocourt-Quéant Support Line	36cSE / 51bNW / 51bSE	extensive
Droll Trench	36cSW4 Rouvroy	U 17 d, 18 c
Dromana [farm]	36aNE2 Vieux Berquin	F 15 d 6.5
Dromore Corner	28NW1 Elverdinghe	A 18 d 2.7
Dromore Corner [railway siding]	28NW1 Elverdinghe	B 13 c
Dromore House	28NW1 Elverdinghe	A 18 d 9.6
Drone House	36aNE2 Vieux Berquin	F 11 a 4.3
Drone Trench	36cSW4 Rouvroy	U 17 d
Droogenbroodhoek	28NE1 Zonnebeke	E 19 b
Droogentek Farm	28NW1 Elverdinghe	A 21 a 9.3
Droop Trench	36cSW4 Rouvroy	U 11 a, b
Drop Alley	57dSE2 & 57cSW1 Le Sars	M 29 d, 35 a
Dropsy Trench	36cSW4 Rouvroy	U 11 b, d, 12 a, 17 b, 18 a, c, 24 b
Dross Trench	36cSW4 Rouvroy	U 17 c, d
Drossen Trench	62cNW2 Bouchavesnes	C 2 b, 3 a, c, d
Drought Trench	36cSW4 Rouvroy	U 17 d
Drouvin [village]	36bNE4 Noeux-les-Mines	K 4 c
Drove Trench	36cSW4 Rouvroy	U 23 b
Drown Trench	36cSW4 Rouvroy / SE3 Esquerchin	U 23 b, 24 a, b, V 19 a
Drowsy Trench	36cSW4 Rouvroy	U 23 d
Druce Trench	36cSW4 Rouvroy	U 30 c
Drudge Trench	36cSW4 Rouvroy	U 24 c
Druère Alley	62cSW1 Dompierre	N 20 a, d
Drug Trench	36cSW4 Rouvroy	U 24 c
Drugget Trench	36cSW4 Rouvroy	U 24 c
Druid Farm	28SW2 Wytschaete	O 23 a 15.35
Druid Trench	36cSW4 Rouvroy	U 30 b
Druids Camp	57dNE3 & 4 Hébuterne	K 26 d, 27 c
Drum Trench	36cSW4 Rouvroy	U 30 d
Drumez Post, le	36SW1 Aubers	M 3 a, c
Drumez, le [farm]	36SW1 Aubers	M 3 a 15.30
Drummond Trench	36cNW3 Loos	G 4 d, 10 b, 11 a
Drummond Trench	36cSW4 Rouvroy	U 30 a
Drunk Trench	36cSW4 Rouvroy	U 30 d
Drury Lane	36SW1 Aubers	N 13 a, c
Drury Trench	36cSW4 Rouvroy	U 30 b
Dry Trench	36cSW4 Rouvroy	U 17 d
Dryden Trench	36cSW4 Rouvroy	U 11 c
Du Quesnoy Post	36NW3 Fleurbaix	H 19 c, d
Du Ricin [trench]	66cNW2 Itancourt	C 9 d, 13 d, 14 a, b, c, 15 a, 19 a, b
Dubaile Trench [1918]	66eNW [2 Thennes]	B 17 d, 18 c
Dublin Alley	62cNW1 Maricourt	A 4 d
Dublin Camp	28NW1 Elverdinghe	A 10 d, 11 c

Name	Map Sheet	Map Reference
Dublin Redoubt [Lochner Werk]	62cNW1 Maricourt	A 10 b, 11 a
Dublin Road [road]	36SW1 Aubers	M 1 b, d, 7 b
Dublin Street	57dSE4 Ovillers	X 19 a
Dublin Street	62cNW1 Maricourt	A 4 b
Dublin Trench	62cNW1 Maricourt	A 4 c, d, 10 b
Dublin Trench [1918]	62dSW [4 Cachy]	U 26 a, b
Dubois Alley	66cNW1 Grugies	A 12 b
Dubois Alley, General [1918]	62dSE [4 Harbonnières]	X 23 b, 24 a
Dubois Trench	62cNW4 Péronne	I 31 d, 32 c
Dubois, Tranchée [Forest Alley]	36bSE2 Boyeffles / 36cSW1 Lens	R 30 a, M 19 d, 25 b
Dubreur Trench [1918]	62dSW [4 Cachy]	U 22 a
Ducasse Trench	62bSW3 St Quentin	S 29 d, 30 c
Duck Alley	57cNE2 Bourlon	E 28 b
Duck Alley	66cNW4 Berthenicourt	I 7 d
Duck Lodge [Puck Lodge: Belgian map 1918]	28NE1 Zonnebeke	D 5 c 85.20
Duck Trench	51bNE1 Brébières	D 25 b
Duck Trench	51bSW2 Vis-en-Artois	N 24 b, d, 30 a, b, O 19 c
Duck Trench [1918]	57dNE3 & 4 Hébuterne	K 11 b, d, 12 a
Duck Walk	28NW4 & NE3 Zillebeke	I 29 a
Duck Walk	36cSW3 Vimy	S 20 a, b
Duck Walk	57cSW3 Longueval	M 32 d
Duckboard Track	28NW4 & NE3 Zillebeke	I 5 c
Duckboard Track	28SW2 Wytschaete	O 4 b
Duckboard Track	57dSE2 Beaumont	R 9 b
Duckboards	28NW4 & NE3 Zillebeke	J 15 a
Duck's Bill	36cNW1 La Bassée	A 9 d, 10 c
Duck's Bill	36SW1 Aubers	M 35 b
Duck's Bill [Hörnchen]	28NW2 St Julien	C 15 c
Ducks Bill Extension	36cNW1 La Bassée	A 16 a
Ducks Walk	36bSE4 Carency	X 28 b, 29 a
Duck's Walk	36bSE4 & 36cSW3 Givenchy	X 30 a, c, S 25 b
Duck's Walk (1st Army)	36bSE4 & 36cSW3 Givenchy	X 12 c, S 7 d, 8 a, c
Duclos [Ouvrage, W of Fricourt, 1915]	62dNE2 Méaulte	F 3 a, c
Ducroux Trench	66cNW1 Grugies	A 6 d, B 1 c, 7 a
Dud Corner	36cNW3 Loos	G 34 a, b
Dud Corner [Lens Road Redoubt, 1915]	36cNW3 Loos	G 34 a
Dud House	36aNE4 Merville	K 15 b 9.4
Dud House	36SW1 Aubers	M 12 d 95.90
Dud Trench	51bNE1 Brébières	D 14 c
Dudgeon Wood	62dSE [2 Proyart]	Q 22 b, 23 a
Dudley Trench, & Lane	36cNW3 Loos	G 12 c, d
Duffield [Avenue]	36bSE4 & 36cSW3 Givenchy	S 21 d, 22 c, 27 b
Duffield [Trench]	36cSW3 Vimy	S 21 d, 22 c
Duffield Crater	36cSW3 Vimy	S 22 c
Duffield Road [road]	28NW1 Elverdinghe	A 14 a, c, d
Duffield Wood	28NW1 Elverdinghe	A 7 d, 8 c, d, 13 b, d, 14 a, c
Dug Trench	51bNE1 Brébières	D 19 b
Dugout Lane	36bSE4 Carency	X 6 a, c
Dugout Lane [trench, 1918]	57dNE3 & 4 Hébuterne	K 12 c, 18 b, d
Dugout Lane [trench]	57dNE3 & 4 Hébuterne	K 18 b
Dugout Row	36cSW1 Lens	M 4 a, c
Dugout Trench	62cNW1 Maricourt	A 3 c
Duguesclin Alley	62bSW3 St Quentin	M 35 c, d, 36 c, d
Duguesclin Redoubt	62bSW3 St Quentin	M 36 c

Name	Map Sheet	Map Reference
Duhallow A.D.S. [after southern Irish hunt]	28NW2 St Julien	C 25 d
Duhollou [Tranchée, 1915, La Boisselle]	57dSE4 Ovillers	X 13 d, 19 b
Duhollou Trench [Duhallow]	57dSE4 Ovillers	X 19 b, 20 a
Duizendzinnen	28NE2 Moorslede	F 16 a
Duke of Connaught [ammn. railhead; rly sidings]	28SW3 Bailleul	T 26 c
Duke of Connaught [camp]	28SW3 Bailleul	T 26 c
Duke of York [ammn. railhead; railway sidings]	28SW3 Bailleul	S 15 b, d
Duke Street	28NW2 St Julien	I 5 a, b
Duke Street	36cNW3 Loos	G 29 c, 35 a, b, d
Duke Street	51bNW2 Oppy	B 18 a
Duke Street	57dSE2 Beaumont	R 21 d, 27 b
Duke Street	62dNE2 Méaulte	F 16 b, 17 a
Duke Street [1918]	62dNE [1 Dernancourt]	D 18 d, 24 b, E 13 c
Duke Street [road]	57cSW3 Longueval	S 17 a
Duke Street [Sept 1915]	36cNW1 La Bassée	A 9 c
Duke Street, South	51bNW2 Oppy	B 18 a, c, 24 a
Duke Trench	51bNW2 Oppy / NE1 Brébières	C 6 b, D 1 a
Duke Trench	51bNW4 Fampoux	I 17 c, 23 a
Duke's Farm	28NE4 Dadizeele	L 27 c 8.5
Dukes Road [road]	36SW3 Richebourg	S 21 c, 27 a
Dum Copse [twin of Dee Copse]	62bSW1 Gricourt	M 29 c
Dumbarton Castle	57dSE4 Ovillers	W 6 d
Dumbarton Dump	28NE3 Gheluvelt	J 19 c, 20 a
Dumbarton Lakes	28NE3 Gheluvelt	J 20 a
Dumbarton Track [1917-18]	28NW4 Ypres	I 30 a, b
Dumbarton Trench	36aSE4 Locon	W 23 d, 29 b, d
Dumbarton Wood	28NE3 Gheluvelt	J 20 a, c
Dumbell Trench	36bNE [1 Labeuvrière]	D 3 c, d
Dummy Fork [road jct]	28NE4 Dadizeele	L 17 d 95.05
Dummy Trench	57cSW3 Longueval	S 23 c, d
Dump Avenue	36cSW3 Vimy / 51bNW1 Roclincourt	S 29 c, d, A 4 b
Dump House	28NE1 Zonnebeke	D 8 d 7.8
Dump Trench	36cNW1 La Bassée	G 4 b, 5 a
Dump, The	28NW4 & NE3 Zillebeke	I 29 c
Dump, The [Fosse 8]	36cNW1 La Bassée	G 5 a, b
Dumpy Trench	51bNE1 Brébières	D 25 b
Dunbar Trench	51bNE1 Brébières	D 13 d, 14 c
Dunblane Trench	51bNW3 Arras	H 32 d, 33 c, d
Duncan Avenue	62cNE2 Epéhy	F 17 d, 18 a, c
Duncan Post	62cNE2 Epéhy	F 17 d
Dunces Alley	36cNW3 Loos / SW1 Lens	G 35 d, M 5 b
Dundas Road [road]	36cSW1 Lens	N 20 d, 26 b, 27 a
Dundee Avenue	57dSE4 Ovillers	X 19 d, 25 b
Dundee Farm	28NE2 Moorslede	F 23 c 4.4
Dundee Trench	51bNE1 Brébières	D 20 a
Dundee Walk	36cNW1 La Bassée	A 27 d, G 3 b
Dune Trench, Lane, Alley, Avenue	12SW1 Nieuport	M 9 d, 15 a
Dunelm Avenue	57cNW2 Vaulx-Vraucourt	C 17 d, 22 a, b, 23 a, b
Dunfermline Street	57dSE4 Ovillers	X 13 c
Dungelhof Farm	20SW4 Bixschoote	O 32 d 85.30
Dunker Alley	66dNW1 Punchy	A 28 a, b, c, 29 a, c, d
Dunlop Farm	28NE4 Dadizeele	K 35 d 50.25
Dunlop Trench	51bNE1 Brébières	D 19 d, 20 c
Dunmow Trench	51bNE1 Brébières	D 20 a, b, 21 a

Name	Map Sheet	Map Reference
Dunmow Trench	57dNE3 & 4 Hébuterne	K 28 c, d
Dunn Trench	51bNE1 Brébières	D 1 d, 2 c
Dunraven Trench	57cSE2 Gonnelieu	R 19 a, b
Dunstable [lt rly locality E of Canal 1917-18]	28NW2 St Julien	C 13 a, c
Dunstable Trench	51bNE1 Brébières	D 14 a, b
Dunville Farm	28NE2 Moorslede	E 12 c 7.3
Dup Tunnel	36cNW3 Loos	G 18 a
Dupin Alley	66cNW1 Grugies	A 12 b, d, 18 b
Dupleix Farm	20SW4 Bixschoote	O 33 c 5.4
Duplex Farm	28NE3 Gheluvelt	J 28 c 1.8
Duplex Wood	20SW4 Bixschoote	O 33 d
Dupuise Trench / Dupuis [Tranchée / Boyau]	36cSW1 Lens	M 25 b
Duquesne House	20SW4 Bixschoote	U 3 d 55.25
Durand [Boyau, 1915, La Boisselle]	57dSE4 Ovillers	X 19 a, b
Durand Crater	36cSW3 Vimy	S 22 c
Durapec Trench	62bSW4 Homblières	T 30 d
Durazzo Trench	66cNW2 Itancourt	B 6 b
Durban Farm	28SW3 Bailleul	S 5 b 8.5
Durban Lines [huts]	28SW3 Bailleul	S 5 b
Durham Alley	51bSW2 Vis-en-Artois	O 13 d, 14 c
Durham Avenue	36NW2 Armentières	C 22 a, c
Durham Avenue [1918]	57dNE2 & 57cNW1 Courcelles	F 27 a, b, c
Durham Bridge [The Dump]	28NW4 & NE3 Zillebeke	I 29 c
Durham Cross [cross roads]	28SW3 Bailleul	S 5 b 90.45
Durham Keep	36cSW1 Lens	M 14 d, 15 c
Durham Lane	28NW4 & NE3 Zillebeke	I 24 a, c, d
Durham Lane	36cSW1 Lens	M 15 a
Durham Lane	36NW4 Bois Grenier	I 20 d
Durham Lane [trench]	51bSW4 Bullecourt	N 35 c, d, T 5 b
Durham Line [light rly]	28SW4 Ploegsteert	T 5 b, d, 6 a
Durham Lines	51bSW3 Boisleux	S 11 a
Durham Post [Fleurbaix]	36NW3 Fleurbaix	H 21 c
Durham Quad	36cSW1 Lens	M 15 a, c
Durham Road	28SW4 Ploegsteert	N 36 c
Durham Road	36cSW1 Lens	M 15 a
Durham Road / Street	57dSE4 Ovillers	Q 36 d, W 6 b
Durham Street	57dNE1 & 2 Fonquevillers	E 17 c
Durham Trench	57cSW1 Gueudecourt	M 24
Durham Trench	62dNE2 Méaulte	F 23 b, 24 a
Durnford Post	57cSE2 Gonnelieu	Q 24 b
Durnnford Road [road]	36aSE1 St Venant	P 3 a, b
Dury [village]	51bSE1 Saudemont	P 21, 22
Dury, Mont	51bSE1 Saudemont	P 27 b, d
Dury, Tranchée	62cSW1 Dompierre	M 9 d
Dusk Trench	51bNE1 Brébières	D 20 a
Dusseldorf Alley	66cNW2 Itancourt	B 17 d, 18 c, d
Dust Road [trench]	57dSE1 & 2 Beaumont	Q 35 a
Dust Trench	28NE1 Zonnebeke	D 19 a
Dusty Cottages	36aNE4 Merville	K 15 a 53.20
Dusty Trench	36bNE [1 Labeuvrière]	D 18 a
Dusty Trench	51bNW2 Oppy	C 19 c
Duteil Alley	66cNW2 Itancourt	B 16 c, 22 a
Dutiful Trench	28NE1 Zonnebeke	D 28 b, 29 a, c
Dutrieux [Tranchée, 1915]	57dSE4 Ovillers	X 19 d

Name	Map Sheet	Map Reference
Dutton Farm	27SE2 Berthen	R 7 b 3.5
Dutton Post	36NW4 Bois Grenier	I 13 b
Duveen Farm	28SW3 Bailleul	S 6 b 4.1
Duvernay Trench [1918]	66eNW [2 Thennes]	B 29 c, H 4 b, 5 a
Duvillard Trench [1918]	66eNW [2 Thennes]	B 23 b
Dwarf Bank [lynchet]	51bSW2 Vis-en-Artois	O 28 c
Dwarf Crossing [level crossing]	28NE2 Moorslede	F 2 d 2.4
Dwarf House	28NE2 Moorslede	L 1 a 8.2
Dyke Road [road]	57cSW1 Gueudecourt	M 14 c, d, 15 a, 19 b, d, 20 a
Dyke Street	51cSE3 & 4 Ransart	R 32 b, 33 c
Dyke Street	57dNE1 & 2 Fonquevillers	E 27 b
Dyke Street [road]	36aSE4 Locon	X 13 d, 14 c, 20 a, b
Dyke Trench	51bNE1 Brébières	D 25 d
Dyke Valley	57cSW1 Gueudecourt	M 14 c, d, 15 a, 19 b, d, 20 a
Dykes Farm	28NW1 Elverdinghe	A 4 b 00.50
Dynamite Road [road]	36cSW1 Lens	N 1 b, c, d, 2 a, b
Dynamite Wood	62cNE2 Epéhy	E 23 c, 29 a
Dynamo Farm	20NW4 Dixmude	I 15 c 7.8
E 1 [April 1915, opposite Messines]	28SW2 Wytschaete	N 30 c 3.0
E 2 [BFL trench, Wulverghem, March 1915]	28SW2 Wytschaete	N 29 d 9.3
E 3 [April 1915, opposite Messines]	28SW2 Wytschaete	N 30 c 1.0
E 3 [German trench, Givenchy, March 1915]	36cNW1 La Bassée	A 3, 9
E 4 [April 1915, opposite Messines]	28SW2 Wytschaete	N 35 b 8.9
E 4 [German trench, Givenchy, March 1915]	36cNW1 La Bassée	A 3, 9
E Lines [W of Fauquissart 1914-15]	36SW1 Aubers	M 18 d, 23 d, 24 a, c, 29 a, b,
E Lines [W of Pietre, early 1915]	36SW1 Aubers	M 28 d, 29 c, 34 b
E Sap	28NW4 & NE3 Zillebeke	I 30 a
E Sap, & Craters [Givenchy]	36cNW1 La Bassée	A 9 d
E Sector [4/15, N of R Douve]	28SW2 Wytschaete / 4 Ploegsteert	N 29, 30, 35, 36
E Street	57dSE1 & 2 Beaumont	Q 10 c
E Trench	51bSW2 Vis-en-Artois	O 8 c, 14 a
E Work	51bNW1 Roclincourt	G 5 b, 6 a
Eagle Avenue	57cSE2 Gonnelieu	R 4 b, c, d, 5 a
Eagle Lane [trench]	57cSE4 Villers-Guislain	X 29 d
Eagle Quarry	57cSE4 Villers-Guislain	X 29 d
Eagle Trench	28NE1 Zonnebeke	E 13 c
Eagle Trench	51bNW1 Roclincourt	A 16 c, d
Eagle Trench	51bSW2 Vis-en-Artois / 4 Bullecourt	O 25 c, d, 31 a, b, c
Eagle Trench	57cSE4 Villers-Guislain	X 29 d
Eagle Trench [later White Trench]	20SW4 Bixschoote	U 23 b, d
Ealing [farm]	27SE4 Meteren	Q 35 c 2.6
Ealing Trench	28NW2 St Julien	C 13 d, 14 c
Ear Lane	51bSW1 Neuville Vitasse	N 7 d
Ear Trench	57cSW1 Gueudecourt	N 8 d
Earl Street	51bNW2 Oppy	B 12 a, d
Earl Trench	51bNW1 Roclincourt	A 16 d
Earl Trench	51bNW1 Roclincourt	B 19 c
Earl Trench	51bNW2 Oppy	B 18 c
Earl's C.T.	51bSW1 Neuville Vitasse	N 21 c
Earls Court [trench]	51bSW2 Vis-en-Artois	N 35 a, c
Earl's Fork [road jct]	28NE4 Dadizeele	L 9 c 75.05
Earn Trench	51bNW1 Roclincourt	B 19 c, d
Earthworks Copse	62cNW1 Maricourt	B 3 b
Earwig Trench	51bNW1 Roclincourt	A 16 d

Name	Map Sheet	Map Reference
Easel Farm	28NE1 Zonnebeke	E 13 b 3.2
Easel Trench	28NE1 Zonnebeke	E 13 a, c
East Copse	36cSW4 Rouvroy	U 21 d, 27 b'
East Copse	36cSW4 Rouvroy	U 21 d, 27 b
East Farm	28NE3 Gheluvelt	J 32 d 4.4
East Fork Avenue	57cNE4 Marcoing / SE2 Gonnelieu	L 32 b, c, d, R 4 b, 5 a
East Fork Reserve	57cNE4 Marcoing / SE2 Gonnelieu	L 35 a, c, R 5 a, d
East Fork Support	57cNE4 Marcoing / SE2 Gonnelieu	L 35 a, c, R 5 a, c, 11 a
East Fork Trench	57cNE4 Marcoing / SE2 Gonnelieu	L 34 b, d, R 4 b, c, d
East K.O.Y.L.I.	57dSE1 & 2 Beaumont	R 19 c
East Lancs Trench [S of Plugstreet Wd]	28SW4 Ploegsteert	U 27 b
East Lane [N of railway, crossing to S]	28NW4 & NE3 Zillebeke	I 10 b, d, 11 a, b, c
East Poperinghe Line [1918]	28NW1 Elverdinghe	A 10, 16, 22, 27, 28, G 3
East Poperinghe Line [1918]	28NW3 Poperinghe	G 3, 4, 9, 10, 14, 15, 20, 21, 26, 32, 33
East Poperinghe Line [1918]	28SW1 Kemmel	M 1 d, 2 a, b, c, 7 b, d
East Street [road, Le Transloy]	57cSW2 Villers-au-Flos	N 30 b
East Trench	51bSW1 Neuville Vitasse	M 12 c
East Trench	57cSW3 Longueval	S 26 b, d
East Trench / Reserve [Monchy-le-Preux]	51bSW2 Vis-en-Artois	O 1 b, d, 7 b
East Trench [of Quadrilateral]	57cSW3 Longueval	T 15 c
Easter O.P. [1917-18]	51bNW1 Roclincourt	B 1 d 2.4
Easter Trench	36cSW1 Lens	N 8 a
Easter Trench	51bNW1 Roclincourt	A 16 d, 22 b
Eastern Lane	57cSW1 Gueudecourt	N 33 b, 34 a
Eastwood [farm]	28SW3 Bailleul	T 14 a 9.6
Easy Farm	28NE1 Zonnebeke	E 13 d 5.7
Easy Trench	51bNW1 Roclincourt	B 19 d
Eaton Hall	36SW1 Aubers	N 3 b
Eau, De la l' [suburb of Vendhuile]	57bSW3 Honnecourt	S 20 d, 26 b
Eaucourt l'Abbaye [old abbey, farm]	57dSE2 & 57cSW1 Le Sars	M 23 c
Ebarte Wood	66eNW [2 Thennes]	B 22 a, c
Ebb Cottage	28NE2 Moorslede	L 1 a 4.5
Ebb Trench	51bSW1 Neuville Vitasse	M 12 a, c
Ebelt Way	57dSE1 & 2 Beaumont	Q 18 a, b, d
Ebenezer Farm	36SW1 Aubers	M 34 b 55.95
Ebenezer Lane [road]	36SW1 Aubers	M 28 a, c, d
Ebenezer Street [trench]	36SW1 Aubers	M 27 b, 28 a, c, d, 34 b
Ebony Trench	62bSW1 Gricourt	N 1 b
Ebor Trench	51bNW1 Roclincourt	A 22 b
Ebro Farm	28NW3 Poperinghe	G 25 d 3.0
Eccles Fort [Hunter's Avenue]	28SW4 Ploegsteert	U 21 c
Eccles Trench	51bNW2 Oppy	B 30 d
Echalas Trench	62bSW1 Gricourt	N 2 a, b, c
Echo Copse	28NE1 Zonnebeke	E 7 a
Echo Trench	36bNE [1 Labeuvrière]	E 25 b, 26 a
Echuca Trench [1918]	62dNE [1 Dernancourt]	E 13 a, b
Eck Trench	57dNE3 & 4 Hébuterne	K 4 d
Eclème Locality, l'	36aSE3 Gonnehem	V 2 b, d, 3 c, d
Eclipse Trench	57cSW2 Villers-au-Flos	N 22 d, 28 b
Eclipse Trench	62cSW3 Vermandovillers	S 14 d, 15 c
Eclopes Trench	62bSW1 Gricourt	N 1 b, 2 a, c
Ecluse d'Essars [canal lock]	36aSE4 Locon	X 19 c 30.95
Ecluse Trench	28NW4 & NE3 Zillebeke	I 32 a

Name	Map Sheet	Map Reference
Eclusier [village]	62cNW3 Vaux	G 22 a
Eclusier Quarry	62cNW3 Vaux	G 28 b
Eclusier, Redoute d'	62cNW3 Vaux	G 21 b, d
Ecole [School; see Ecole de bienfaisance . . .]	28NW4 Ypres	I 9 c
Ecole Alley	28NW4 Ypres	I 8 d, 9 c
Ecole Communale [Vimy Ridge]	36cSW3 Vimy	S 23 c 05.30
Ecole de bienfaisance de l'Etat [Ypres]	28NW4 Ypres	I 9 c
Ecole Junction [light rly, 1917-18]	28NW4 Ypres	I 9 c 1.1
Ecole Switch	28NW4 Ypres	I 9 d, 15 a, b
Economy House	28NW4 Ypres	H 11 d 7.6
Ecossais, Boyau [Scots]	62cSW1 Dompierre	M 4 c, d
Ecosse Farm	20NW4 Dixmude	I 31 d 3.9
Ecoust Trench, Support, Reserve	57cNW2 Vaulx-Vraucourt	C 1, 2, 3, 7, 8
Ecuelle de Bois, l' [hamlet]	36aNE1 Morbecque	D 7 a
Ecume Trench	62bSW1 Gricourt / 2 Fonsommes	N 4 a, b, d, 5 c
Ecurie [village]	51bNW1 Roclincourt	A 21 d, 27 b
Ecurie Avenue	51bNW1 Roclincourt	A 22 a
Ecuriel / Ecureul Trench ??NAME	62bSW1 Gricourt	M 6 a, b, N 1 a
Eddy [light rly siding]	36cSW1 Lens	N 7 a
Eddy Farm	28NE1 Zonnebeke	E 13 c 1.9
Eddy Trench	28NE1 Zonnebeke	E 13 a, c
Eddy Trench	51bNW1 Roclincourt	B 19 d
Eden Trench	57dNE3 & 4 Hébuterne	K 11 b
Eden Trench	57dNE3 & 4 Hébuterne	K 22 d, 28 b
Edewaardhoek [hamlet]	28NW1 Elverdinghe	G 3 b, 4 a, b
Edge Copse	28NE1 Zonnebeke	E 19 c
Edge Farm	28SW2 Wytschaete	O 29 a 0.4
Edge Hill [station; Dernancourt area]	62dNE [1 Dernancourt]	E 20 b
Edge House [north]	28NE1 Zonnebeke	E 19 c 85.70
Edge House [south]	28NE1 Zonnebeke	E 19 c 8.2
Edge Street [Beaurains]	51bSW1 Neuville Vitasse	M 11 a
Edge Trench	70dNW4 St Gobain	I 21 c, d, 27 b
Edge Trench [Delville Wood]	57cSW3 Longueval	S 12 d, 18 b
Edgware / Edgeware [sic] Rd, & Laterals [tun'l]	36cNW1 La Bassée	A 21 b
Edgware / Edgeware [sic] Road [Calonne]	36cSW1 Lens	M 2 c, d, 8 b, 9 a, c, d
Edgware / Edgeware [sic] Road [road]	36SW3 Richebourg	S 4 b, d, 5 a, b
Edgware Keep	36cSW1 Lens	M 9 c, d
Edict Farm	28NE2 Moorslede	F 19 b 3.4
Edin Valley [trench]	51bNW4 Fampoux	I 7 b
Edinboro' Line	36aSE4 Locon	W 11 b, d, 17 b, 18 a, b, X 13 a, b
Edinboro' Support	36aSE4 Locon	W 17 b, 18 b, c, d, X 13 a, b
Edinburgh Castle	36aSE1 St Venant	P 5 c
Edinburgh Castle	57dSE4 Ovillers	X 22 b
Edinburgh Support, & Avenue	57cNE1 Quéant	D 19 a, b
Edit Cott.	28NE1 Zonnebeke	E 19 d 7.6
Edmeads Avenue	36NW2 Armentières	C 22 a, b
Edmeads Farm	36NW2 Armentières	C 23 a 05.45
Edmonton Crater	36cSW3 Vimy	S 28 c
Edouard VII, Boyau	62cSW1 Dompierre	M 4 b
Edwaarthoek [sic; railway sidings & huts]	28NW1 Elverdinghe	A 27 d, 28 c
Edward Avenue	51bSW2 Vis-en-Artois	O 5 c, d
Edward Avenue / Boyau Edouard VII	62dNE2 Méaulte / 62cNW1 Maricourt	F 12 c, A 7 d
Edward Post	36SW3 Richebourg	S 9 a, b
Edward Road / Trench	57cSW3 Longueval	S 24 b

Name	Map Sheet	Map Reference
Edward Road [road]	36SW1 Aubers / 3 Richebourg	M 32 b, d, S 3 a, c, 9 a
Edward Street [trench]	57cNE2 Bourlon	E 10 d, 11 a, c, 15 b, d, 16 a, b,
Edward Trench	36cSW3 Vimy	S 22 a
Edward Trench	51bNW2 Oppy	B 12 a, b
Edward Trench	51bSW2 Vis-en-Artois	O 5 c, 11 a, b
Edwards Trench	36cSW1 Lens	N 31 a, b
Edwards Trench	57cSW3 Longueval	S 30 b, d
Eecke Line [1918]	27SE2 Berthen	Q 21, 22, 28
Eel Alley [1918]	57dNE3 & 4 Hébuterne	K 5 c, d
Eel Copse	62bSW2 Fonsommes	O 31 a
Eel Farm	20SE2 Hooglede	R 17 c 4.3
Eel Farm	28SW2 Wytschaete	O 24 c 3.6
Eel Pie Fort [Hunter's Avenue]	28SW4 Ploegsteert	U 21 c
Eel Trench	57dNE3 & 4 Hébuterne	K 4 d
Eessen Trench	20NW4 Dixmude	I 9 a, c
Effect Copse	28NE1 Zonnebeke	D 24 d, 30 b, E 19 c, 25 a
Effie Switch North [1918]	51bNW4 Fampoux	H 4 d, 5 c, 10 b, 11 a
Effie Switch South [1918]	51bNW3 Arras / 4 Fampoux	H 9 b, 10 a, b
Effie Trench	51bNW3 Arras / 4 Fampoux	H 9 b, d, 10 c, 16 a, b, d
Egg Copse [Puchevillers]	57dSW [1 Puchevillers / 2 Raincheval]	N 22 c
Egg Farm	28NE1 Zonnebeke	E 25 b 3.3
Egg Post	62cNE2 Epéhy	F 11 d 85.65
Egg Post [in New Quarry]	62cNE4 Roisel	L 11 b 65.50
Egg Trench	51bNW1 Roclincourt	B 19 a, c
Egg Trench	57dNE3 & 4 Hébuterne	K 34 d
Egg, The	51bSW1 Neuville Vitasse	N 20 d
Egg, The [dugout / strongpoint in New Quarry]	62cNE4 Roisel	L 11 b 65.50
Egham House	27SE2 Berthen	R 22 c 35.45
Eglantine Trench / Tranchée de l'Eglantine	62cSW2 Barleux	O 19 d, 20 a, b, c, 25 b
Eglise North [keep, Fauquissart, late 1915]	36SW1 Aubers	M 18 d 6.1
Eglise Street, North [Fauquissart, late 1915]	36SW1 Aubers	M 18 d
Eglise Street, South [Fauquissart, late 1915]	36SW1 Aubers	M 24 b
Eglise, Reduit de l' [Church Redoubt]	62cSW1 Dompierre	M 9 c, d
Eglon Farms	27NE4 Abeele	L 14 a 15.40
Egmont Avenue	28SW4 Ploegsteert	U 11 a
Egress Farm	28NE1 Zonnebeke	E 25 d 3.9
Egret Loop	51bSW2 Vis-en-Artois	N 30 b, d, O 25 a
Egret Support [1918]	51bSW3 Boisleux	S 21 c, d
Egret Trench	51bSW2 Vis-en-Artois	N 30 b, O 19 c, 25 a
Egypt House	20SW4 Bixschoote	U 12 b 23.92
Eichhorn Trench	62bSW4 Homblières	T 30 b, d
Eider, Tranchée de l'	66dNW2 Morchain	C 2 b, c, d
Eiffel Farm	27NE2 Proven	F 9 a 3.1
Eight House	28NE1 Zonnebeke	E 25 c 4.9
Eighteen Street	51bNW3 Arras	G 35 b, 36 a
Eighth Avenue	57dSE4 Ovillers	X 1 a
Eighth Avenue [Oct 1915]	36cNW3 Loos	G 17 b, 18 a
Eighth Street	57dSE4 Ovillers	X 3 b, d
Eigl Weg	51bNW3 Arras	G 12 b, H 7 a
Eikhoek	27NE2 Proven	F 28 b, 29 a
Eikhof Farm	28SW2 Wytschaete	O 3 d 3.2
Eileen Post	36NW4 Bois Grenier	I 16 central
Eindner Farm	28NE2 Moorslede	F 25 d 95.55
Eisener Kreuz Weg	51bNW1 Roclincourt	A 16 b, c, d

Name	Map Sheet	Map Reference
Eisener Trench	36SW3 Richebourg	A 16 d
Eitel Alley	36SW3 Richebourg	S 29 a, b, d
Eitel Alley North	36SW3 Richebourg	S 22 c, d, 28 b, 29 a
Eitel Alley South	36SW3 Richebourg	S 28 a, b, 29 a
Eitel Fritz Farm	28NW2 St Julien	C 5 b 6.6
Eitel Post	57cSE4 Villers-Guislain	X 11 d
Eitel Trench	62cNE1 Liéramont	D 4 c, 10 a
Eksternest Farm	28SW2 Wytschaete	N 4 b 4.3
El Teb A Camp	28SW1 Kemmel	M 11 c 5.3
El Teb B Camp	28SW1 Kemmel	M 11 c 3.5
El Teb Farm	28SW1 Kemmel	M 11 c 15.70
El Teb Post [1918]	28SW1 Kemmel	M 10 d 9.6
El Teb Wood	28SW1 Kemmel	M 11 c, d, 17 b
Elam Copse	62bSW2 Fonsommes	O 2 d
Elam Copse	62cSE1 Bouvincourt	P 5 d, 11 b
Eland Farm	28NE2 Moorslede	F 20 a 4.7
Elank Farm	36aNE3 Haverskerque	K 9 a 05.12
Elate Trench	51bNW1 Roclincourt	B 20 d
Elba Alley [1918]	51bNW4 Fampoux	H 16 a, c, d
Elba Corner [road jct]	28NE4 Dadizeele	L 27 b 70.75
Elbe Alley	62bNW3 Bellicourt / SW1 Gricourt	H 31 c, N 1 a
Elbe Cottage	28NW1 Elverdinghe	A 24 b 1.6
Elbe Trench	51bNW1 Roclincourt	A 9 a, c, 15 a, b, d
Elbe Trench [1918]	66eNW [2 Thennes]	C 10 a, b
Elbe Trench [Schweikert]	57dNE3 & 4 Hébuterne	K 5 d, 6 c, 11 a, b
Elbe, Tranchée de	62cSW1 & 2 Belloy	O 3 a, b
Elbow Alley	51bNW4 Fampoux	I 25 c
Elbow Farm	28SW4 Ploegsteert	N 35 c 5.5 / 5.6
Elbow Farm	36NW4 Bois Grenier	I 28 c
Elbow Road [road]	36NW4 Bois Grenier	I 28 c, d, 34 b
Elbow Trench	51bNW4 Fampoux	I 25 b, c, d, 31 b
Elbow Work	36NW4 Bois Grenier	I 28 c
Elder Alley	57cSW1 Gueudecourt	N 21 d, 27 b
Elect Trench	51bNW1 Roclincourt	B 19, 26
Electric Power Station [Puits No. 7]	36cNW3 Loos	G 27 c
Elephant & Castle	57dNE3 & 4 Hébuterne	K 28 b
Elephant Trench	57cNE2 Bourlon / 4 Marcoing	E 28 d, K 4 b, d
Elephant Trench	62cSW3 Vermandovillers	T 13 c
Eleu dit Leauvette [hamlet]	36cSW1 Lens	N 25 b, d
Eleu Support	36cSW1 Lens	N 25 d, 26 c, d
Eleu Trench	36cSW1 Lens	N 25 b, d, 26 c, d
Elevator [east of Serain]	57bSW4 Serain	U 16 d 89.35
Eleven O'Clock Square [main square]	36NW2 Armentières	C 25 d
Eleven Trees	62bNW3 Bellicourt	G 33 c 6.7
Eleventh Street	57dSE2 & 57cSW1 Le Sars	R 24 a
Elf Copse	62bNW4 Ramicourt	I 28 d, 29 c
Elf Crossing [level crossing]	20SE2 Hooglede	R 8 b 1.4
Elfin Bank [lynchet]	51bSW2 Vis-en-Artois	O 27 d
Elger House [Le Pelerin]	28SW4 Ploegsteert	U 21 b 35.50
Elgin [keep, Fauquissart, late 1915]	36SW1 Aubers	M 24 a 6.6
Elgin Alley	57cSW3 Longueval	S 9 d, 10 a, c
Elgin Avenue [Thiepval Wood]	57dSE1 & 2 Beaumont	Q 30 b, c, d
Elgin Copse	28NW3 Poperinghe	G 16 d
Elgin Farm	28NW3 Poperinghe	G 16 d 45.75

Name	Map Sheet	Map Reference
Elgin Post	36SW1 Aubers	M 24 a
Elgin Street	36SW1 Aubers	M 17 d, 18 c, 24 a
Elgin Street (North & South)	36SW1 Aubers	M 24 b
Elgin Street, North [Fauquissart, late 1915]	36SW1 Aubers	M 24 a, b
Elgin Street, South	36SW1 Aubers	M 24 a, c, d
Elgin, Mount [light rly sidings]	28NW3 Poperinghe	G 16 d
Elie Street	57dSE4 Ovillers	X 13 a, c
Elincourt [village]	57bSW4 Serain	U 3 a, c, 9 a, b
Elise Trench	62bSW3 St Quentin	T 14 b, d
Elizabeth Bridge [road over Heulebeek]	28NE4 Dadizeele	L 17 d 15.15
Elizabeth, Chateau	28NW3 Poperinghe	G 8 a 4.1
Elk Farm	36aNE2 Vieux Berquin	E 22 a 5.2
Elk Trench	36cSW1 Lens	N 26 a, b
Elk Trench	51bNW1 Roclincourt	B 19 c
Ell Trench	51bNW1 Roclincourt	B 19 c
Ellarsyde [railway sidings]	28NW3 Poperinghe	G 21 c
Ellarsyde House	28NW3 Poperinghe	G 21 c 5.7
Elles / Ellis Square	57dNE3 & 4 Hébuterne	K 33 b
Elles Wood	20SE3 Westroosebeke	W 14 a, b
Ellinck [farm]	27NE1 Herzeele	E 2 a 8.3
Elliptic Work	20SW4 Bixschoote	T 30 a
Ellis Farm	20SE2 Hooglede	Q 10 a 2.5
Elm Street	36NW4 Bois Grenier	I 20 d
Elm Trench	51bNW1 Roclincourt	A 18 b, d, B 19 c
Elmina [farm]	27NE4 Abeele	L 8 d 95.10
Elverdinghe [railway sidings & huts]	28NW1 Elverdinghe	B 7 d, 8 c
Elverdinghe [village]	28NW1 Elverdinghe	B 14 b, d, 15 a, c
Elverdinghe Château	28NW1 Elverdinghe	B 14 b 2.1
Elverdinghe Château [grounds]	28NW1 Elverdinghe	B 14 b
Elverdinghe Old Mill	28NW1 Elverdinghe	B 15 a 1.9
Elverdinghe Pumping Station	28NW1 Elverdinghe	B 7 c 6.6
Elverdinghe White Mill [Old Mill]	28NW1 Elverdinghe	B 14 d 6.5
Elvis Copse	51bNE4 Cantin	L 20 a
Ely Passage	36NW4 Bois Grenier	I 26 a, c
Ely Way	62bNW1 Gouy	A 13 b
Elzenwalle [place name]	28NW4 Ypres	H 36 c
Elzenwalle Sidings [railway, 1917-18]	28NW4 Ypres	H 35 c, d
Elzenwalle Street	28NW4 & NE3 Zillebeke	H 36 d, I 31 c
Embankment Communication Trench	36SW3 Richebourg	S 9 d, 15 b, d
Embankment Dugouts	28NW4 & NE3 Zillebeke	I 36 c
Embankment Redoubt	36cNW1 La Bassée	A 16 c
Embankment, The	36cSW1 Lens	M 4 a, c
Embankment, The [feature S of Augustus Wd]	28NE1 Zonnebeke	D 17 a 2.9
Embassy Lane	57cSW1 Gueudecourt	N 33 a, b
Ember Farm	28NW4 Ypres	H 17 c 5.6
Emden Support	57cSE2 Gonnelieu	R 10 c, d, 16 b, d, 17 c, 23 a, c
Emden Trench	57cSE2 Gonnelieu	R 10 c, 16 a, b, d, 22 b, 23 a, c
Emden Trench	57dNE3 & 4 Hébuterne	K 4 d
Emden Trench	62dNE2 Méaulte / 62cNW1 Maricourt	F 12 a, A 7 b
Emile Camp	28NW1 Elverdinghe	B 9 c, d
Emile Farm	28NW1 Elverdinghe	B 9 c 9.5
Emily Road [road, Cité St Emile]	36cSW1 Lens	N 8 a, b, d
Emily Trench	36bNE [1 Labeuvrière / 3 Bruay]	K 2 b, d, 3 c
Emir Buildings	28NW3 Poperinghe	G 10 c 3.4

Name	Map Sheet	Map Reference
Emma Post	36NW4 Bois Grenier	I 31 a
Emma Trench [1918]	62dNE [1 Dernancourt]	E 13 a, b
Emmy Bridge [road over Wulfdambeek]	28NE4 Dadizeele	L 9 b 8.0
Emperor Road [road]	36aSE4 Locon	X 4 b, d, 10 b, d, 16 b
Empire [light rly loop]	36bNE2 Beuvry	F 8 b
Empire [Locality]	36cSW3 Vimy	S 26 b, d
Empire Lines [huts]	28SW3 Bailleul	T 15 c, d, 21 b
Empire Valley	62bSW4 Homblières	U 23 a, b, d, 24 c
Empire Villas	28SW3 Bailleul	T 15 c 0.4
Empire Wood	62bSW4 Homblières	U 22 d, 23 c, d, 24 c
Empress Trench, & Support	57dSE4 Ovillers	X 26 d, 27 c
Ems Trench	57dNE1 & 2 Fonquevillers / 3 & 4 Hébuterne	K 4 d, 5 a, c
Emu Alley	51bSW4 Bullecourt	U 18 d, 24 b, c, d
Emu Avenue [Pozières]	57dSE4 Ovillers	X 4 d, 5 c, 10 b
Emu Farm	28SW3 Bailleul	T 9 d 6.3
Emu Support [1918]	62dNE [1 Dernancourt]	D 24 d, 30 b
Emu Trench	28SW2 Wytschaete	N 11 c
Emu Trench [1918]	62dNE [1 Dernancourt]	E 19 a, b, d
Enclave de Messines [1915-16]	28SW4 Ploegsteert	T 6 d, 12 b, U 1 c, 7 a
Enclos Alley	62cSW3 & 4 Marchélepot	N 31 d, 32 c, T 2 a
Enclosure Avenue	36cSW1 Lens	M 5 b, 6 a
Enclosure, The [field]	27SE4 Meteren	X 21 b, d
Encore Wood	28NE1 Zonnebeke	E 1 d
End [light rly siding]	36cSW1 Lens	M 17 c
End Farm	28NE3 Gheluvelt	J 27 d 03.05
End Trench	51bNW1 Roclincourt	A 18 d
Endless Alley	57cSW2 Villers-au-Flos	N 28 d, 34 a, b
Endor Cottage	28NW3 Poperinghe	H 25 d 2.8
Energy Alley	57cSW1 Gueudecourt / 2 Villers-au-Flos	N 28 c, d, 33 b, 34 a, b
Energy Alley [1918]	62dNE [1 Dernancourt]	E 13 b
Energy Farm	28NW4 Ypres	H 17 c 9.5
Enfants Farm	20SW3 Oostvleteren	T 7 b 6.1
Enfer Wood	62cNE2 Epéhy	F 9 d
Enfer Wood Post	62cNE2 Epéhy	F 9 d
Enfer Wood, l'	28SW2 Wytschaete	O 25 d, 31 b
Enfer, l' [farm]	28SW2 Wytschaete	O 25 d 85.80
Enfer, Rue d' [hamlet]	57cSE4 Gouzeaucourt	Q 36 c
Enfilade Trench	62cNE2 Epéhy	F 6 a
Engern, Tranchée	70dSW4 [Vauxaillon]	O 35 d
Enghien Redoubt	62bSW3 St Quentin	S 3 d, 4 c
Enghien Trench	62bSW3 St Quentin	S 3 d, 4 a, c
Engine Houses	28NE2 Moorslede	F 21 b 75.05
Engine Trench	57dSE1 & 2 Beaumont	R 7 c
Engineer Corner [road jct]	28NE2 Moorslede	F 21 b 12.25
Engineer Farm	20SW4 Bixschoote	N 36 c 9.0
Engineer Street	51cSE & 51bSW Ficheux	R 32 b, 33 a, c
Engineer's Wood	20SW4 Bixschoote	T 30 a
England Alley	66cNW1 Grugies / 2 Itancourt / 3 Essigny	H 3, 4, 5, 8, 9, 14
Engländerhof [Turco Farm / Klokhof]	28NW2 St Julien	C 15 c 3.4
Englebelmer [village]	57dSE1 & 2 Beaumont	Q 19 b, c, d
English Alley	36cNW3 Loos	G 29 d, 35 b, 36 a, b, H 31 a, b
English Alley [1918]	62dSE [4 Harbonnières]	X 12 a
English Farm	20SW4 Bixschoote	U 19 a 9.1
English Farm	28NW2 St Julien	C 27 b 5.3

Name	Map Sheet	Map Reference
English Farm	28SW3 Bailleul	T 27 b 45.95
English Farm How[itzer] Spurs	28NW2 St Julien	C 27 b
English Lines [huts]	28SW3 Bailleul	T 21 c, d
English Trees	28NW2 St Julien	C 9 d 6.3
English Wood	28NW4 Ypres	H 29 d
Enlist Farm	28NE1 Zonnebeke	E 1 c 7.2
Ennemain [village]	62cSW4 St. Christ	U 17 b, d, 18 a, c
Ennis [house]	36aNE4 Merville	K 34 c 65.80
Entenschnabel [Duck's Bill, Le Pelerin]	28SW4 Ploegsteert	U 21 b 6.4
Entice Cott.	28NE1 Zonnebeke	E 1 d 7.3
Entrepot Trench	62bSW1 Gricourt	M 3 a, b
Enver Pasha Trench	57cSW4 Combles	U 10 d, 16 b
Envy Trench	51bNW1 Roclincourt	B 19 c
Eolian Farm	28NW2 St Julien	C 8 c 2.5
Eolienne [Tilloy]	51bNW3 Arras	H 31 d 23.45
Eolienne Trench	51bNW3 Arras	H 31 d
Eparges Alley	62cSW1 Dompierre	N 27 a, b, d, 33 b
Eparges Trench	62bSW3 St Quentin	S 5 a, b, c
Epénancourt [village]	66dNW2 Morchain	C 3 a, b
Epenancourt Aerodrome [German, 1918]	62cSW4 St Christ	U 26 c
Epervier Trench [1918]	66eNW [2 Thennes]	C 7 b, 8 a
Epic Cottage	28NE2 Moorslede	L 3 b 35.25
Epic Trench	51bNW1 Roclincourt	B 13 c
Epicure Alley	62bSW3 St Quentin	S 3 d, 4 c
Epinal Alley	66cNW2 Itancourt	H 6 b
Epine Alley	66cNW1 Grugies	A 3 b, d, 4 c
Epine d'Andigny Farm, l'	57bSW2 Clary	O 21 a 7.3
Epine de Dallon Redoubt, l'	66cNW1 Grugies	A 4 a, b, c, d
Epine Redoubt, l' [l'Epine de Dallon]	66cNW1 Grugies	A 4 b
Epinette Bridge	36aSE1 St Venant	P 20 b 1.1
Epinette East Post, l'	36SW3 Richebourg	S 19 b
Epinette Lane	36SW1 Aubers	M 10 a
Epinette North Post, l'	36SW3 Richebourg	S 13 d
Epinette Post, l'	36aSE4 Locon	X 24 a
Epinette Trench	62cNE1 Liéramont	D 9 d, 15 b, d, 16 a
Epinette, Ferme l'	36SW1 Aubers	M 16 d 7.6
Epinette, l'	36aSE1 St Venant	P 20 b
Epinette, l' [farm & place name]	36NW1 Steenwerck	B 27 b 7.1
Epinette, l' [farm]	36aNE4 Merville	K 11 a 5.5
Epinette, l' [farm]	57bSW2 Clary	O 36 b 5.9
Epinette, l' [SW of St Venant]	36aSE1 St Venant	P 20 b
Epinette, l' [village, WSW of Lestrem]	36aSE2 Lestrem	R 7 c, d
Epinette, l' [windmill]	57bSW2 Clary	O 36 b 50.63
Epistle House	28NE2 Moorslede	F 19 d 25.60
Eppeville Aerodrome [German, 1918]	66dNE [3] / SE [1]	J 36 c, d, P 6 a, b
Epsom Cross Roads	27SE4 Meteren	X 22 c 55.03
Epstein Farm	27NE1 Herzeele	D 6 d
Epte Trench [Becker]	57dNE3 & 4 Hébuterne	K 5 c, d, 11 a
Equancourt [village]	57cSE3 Sorel-le-Grand	V 4 c, d, 10 a, b, d
Equancourt Trench	57cSE3 Sorel-le-Grand	V 10 c, 16 a
Equarrissage [slaughterhouse]	51bNW3 Arras	G 11 a 2.6
Equateur Alley	62bSW1 Gricourt	N 2 b, c, d, 3 a, b, 4 a
Equerry Trench	20NW4 Dixmude	H 12 d
Ercheu East Aerodrome [German, 1918]	66dSW [2]	O 28 b, d, 29 c, 35 a

Name	Map Sheet	Map Reference
Erchin [village]	51bNE4 Cantin	L 4 d, 10 a, b
Erchin Wood	51bNE4 Cantin	L 9 d
Erebus Farm	28NW1 Elverdinghe	B 20 d 3.7
Erfurt Trench	62cSW4 St. Christ	O 33 c, d
Eric / Erie Trench [Gavrelle]	51bNW2 Oppy / 4 Fampoux	B 30 d, H 6 b
Erie Camp	28NW3 Poperinghe	G 11 c
Erie Farm	28NW3 Poperinghe	G 11 d 1.2
Erin Cottage	27SE4 Meteren	W 24 c 97.60
Erin Cottage	27SE4 Meteren	W 24 c 98.60
Erin Trench	57dNE1 & 2 Fonquevillers / 3 & 4 Hébut'ne	K 4 b, d
Erith Post	36SW1 Aubers	M 24 c
Erith Street	36SW1 Aubers	M 24 a, c, d
Ermine Trench	62bSW3 St Quentin	T 1 c
Ermitage [building]	27SE2 Berthen	R 30 c 93.05
Ermitage, l' [farm / hamlet]	51bNE3 Noyelle-sous-Bellonne	K 14 b
Erratic Farm	28NE1 Zonnebeke	E 7 b 3.3
Error Trench	36bNE [1 Labeuvrière]	E 26 c, K 2 a
Ersatz Avenue & Alley	36cSW3 Vimy	S 14 b, c, d, 15 a
Ersatz Crater	36cSW3 Vimy	S 14 b
Ersatz Point	57cSW4 Combles	N 36 c
Ersatz, Boyau de l'	36cSW3 Vimy	S 14 b
Erstwaite Street	57dSE4 Ovillers	X 7 b
Ervillers [village]	57cNW1 Gomiecourt	B 13 c, d, 19 a, b
Ervillers Trench	57cNW1 Gomiecourt	B 13 c, 14 c, 19 a, b, c, d, 20 a
Esau's Way	57dSE1 & 2 Beaumont	Q 4 c
Escarcuet / Escarguet Trench	66cNW1 Grugies	A 4 a, b
Escarpin Alley	62bSW1 Gricourt	N 3 a, c
Escaut Support	57cNE4 Marcoing	L 10 d, 11 c, d
Escaut Trench	57cNE4 Marcoing	L 10 d, 11 c, d, 17 b
Esche Weg	51bSW1 Neuville Vitasse	M 15 d, 21 a, b
Escrocs Trench	62bSW1 Gricourt	M 5 b
Esk Trench	51bNW3 Arras	G 18 a, b, H 13 a
Esme I & II Posts	36NW4 Bois Grenier	I 16 a
Esmond Farm	20SE2 Hooglede	R 11 d 7.3
Esnes [village]	57bNW4 Caudry / SW2 Clary	H 34 d, N 4 b
Esnes Mill	57bNW3 Rumilly	H 27 d 8.5
Espérance Cabaret, à l'	28SW2 Wytschaete	O 36 b
Espérance Farm	51bSE1 Saudemont	P 26 c, d
Espérance Farm, l'	66eNW [4 Morisel]	H 10 a 1.4
Espérance, l' [crossroads]	62bSW1 Gricourt	M 18 c 8.9
Esperanto Terrace / Street	36cNW1 La Bassée	A 15 d, 21 b
Espions Alley	62bSW1 Gricourt	N 1 a
Esplanade [Ypres, Ramparts]	28NW4 Ypres	I 8 b, d, 14 b
Esplanade Trench	66dNW1 Punchy	A 4 c, 10 a, c
Esposito / Exposito Trench	62cNW4 Péronne	I 32 d
Esquimalt Road [road]	36cSW1 Lens / 2 Harnes	N 16 d, 21 b, 22 a, b
Esquin Post	36SW1 Aubers	M 11 c
Essars [hamlet]	36aSE4 Locon	W 30 b, X 25 a
Essarts [village]	57dNE1 & 2 Fonquevillers	E 24 b, d, F 19 c
Essarts Graben	57dNE1 & 2 Fonquevillers	E 24 d, F 19 c
Essen Farm	28NW2 St Julien	C 14 a 7.3
Essen Trench	20NW4 Dixmude	I 9 c
Essen Trench	66cNW2 Itancourt	B 5 d
Essen Trench [1918]	66eNW [2 Thennes]	C 13 c, 19 a

Name	Map Sheet	Map Reference
Essen, Tranchée d'	66cNW2 Itancourt	B 11 b, 12 a
Essex [light rly sidings, 1917-18]	28NW4 Ypres	I 28 a, b
Essex [strongpoint]	36NW3 Fleurbaix	H 7 a
Essex Alley	36cNW3 Loos	G 4 c, d
Essex Avenue	62dNE2 Méaulte	F 16 b
Essex Central Farm	36NW2 & NE1 Houplines	C 4 a 6.0
Essex Cross Roads	36NW2 & NE1 Houplines	C 4 a 40.65
Essex Farm	28NW2 St Julien	C 19 c, 25 a
Essex Farm [Ploegsteert Wood 1914-15]	28SW4 Ploegsteert	U 20 d 75.15
Essex HQ	36NW2 & NE1 Houplines	C 2 d 65.40
Essex Lane	36cNW3 Loos	G 18 a, b, 24 b, H 19 a
Essex Street	57dSE1 & 2 Beaumont	Q 10 a, c
Essex Trench	28NW2 St Julien	C 7 c 3.3
Essex Trench	57dSE1 & 2 Beaumont	R 26 c
Essex Trench [1918]	51bNW1 Roclincourt	A 24 a, c
Essex Trench [Tranchée Castelnau]	36cSW1 Lens	M 14 b, 15 a
Esslin Alley	66cSW2 Vendeuil	O 27 d, 28 c, 34 a, b
Essling Alley	62cSE2 Vermand / 62bSW1 Gricourt	R24c, M1 c, 1 b,d, 20a,b, 21a,b, 22a
Esslingen Trench	62cSW2 Barleux	O 16 c, d, 22 a
Estaires [town]	36aNE4 Merville	L 29 , 30, 34, 35
Estaires-Lys Line [1918]	36NW3 Fleurbaix	extensive
Estaminet Au Gheer [Rutter Lodge]	28SW4 Ploegsteert	U 27 b 2.8
Estaminet Corner [Tilloy]	51bNW3 Arras	H 31 b 30.05
Estaminet du Commerce [Le Gheer]	28SW4 Ploegsteert	U 21 d 65.10
Estaminet Lane [trench]	28SW2 Wytschaete	O 3 b
Esther Bridge [road over stream]	28NE4 Dadizeele	L 7 c 75.75
Estrade, l' [place name]	36NW1 Steenwerck	A 30 b, d, B 25 a, c
Estrées Aerodrome [German, 1918]	62cSE1 Bouvincourt	P 27 d, 28 c, d, 29 c, 33 b
Estrees Railhead	62cSW1 Dompierre	M 29 c
Et Trench	57dNE3 & 4 Hébuterne	K 11 a
Etalon [village]	66dNW3 Hattencourt	H 14 b, d, 15 a, c
Etalon Château	66dNW3 Hattencourt	H 15 d, 21 b
Etang Farm [pond only]	20SW4 Bixschoote	T 11 c 00.21
Etch Trench [Lehmann]	57dNE1 & 2 Fonquevillers / 3 & 4 Hébuterne	K 5 a, c
Eternal Alley	57cSW1 Gueudecourt	N 27 d
Eterpigny Wood	51bSE1 Saudemont	P 7 c, d
Ethel Trench [1918]	62dNE [1 Dernancourt]	E 13 a, b, c
Ethel's Bridge [road over Heulebeek]	28NE4 Dadizeele	L 8 d 45.60
Ether Lane	57cSW2 Villers-au-Flos	N 16 d, 17 c, d, 22 b, 18 c
Etincelle Alley	62bSW1 Gricourt	N 3 c, 8 b
Etincelle Alley	62bSW1 Gricourt	N 3 c, 8 b
Etna Crater [Havrincourt]	57cNE3 Hermies	K 26 d 9.1
Etna Sap, & Crater [Cuinchy sector]	36cNW1 La Bassée	A 21 d
Etoile Alley	62cSW3 Vermandovillers	S 8 a
Etoile Trench	66cNW2 Itancourt	B 29 b, d, 30 c
Etoile Trench [Star / Starry Wood]	62cSW3 Vermandovillers	S 2 c, 8 a
Eton Lane [1918]	57dSE1 & 2 Beaumont	Q 16 b, 17 a, c
Eton Post [Sept 1915]	36SW1 Aubers	M 20 c 00.65
Eton Post, Old [Sept 1915]	36SW1 Aubers	M 19 d 70.45
Eton Road [road]	36SW1 Aubers	M 14 d, 19 d, 20 a, b
Etretat Trench	62bSW3 St Quentin	S 4 a, c
Etricourt [farm]	62bNW3 Bellicourt	G 18 d 9.2
Etricourt [village]	57cSE3 Sorel-le-Grand	V 7 b, d, 8 a, b, c, 13 b
Etricourt Trench	57cSW4 Combles	U 12 b, d

Name	Map Sheet	Map Reference
Eugène, Tranchée	62cSW1 & 2 Belloy	N 12 c, d
Eunice Post	36NW4 Bois Grenier	I 16 a, b
Euphonium Junction [road jct]	28NE4 Dadizeele	L 21 a 3.9
Euphrates Trench / Euphrate, Tranchée de L'	66cNW1 Grugies / 2 Itancourt	B 4 c, d, 5 c, 9 a, b, 10 a, c
Euston [road jct; also light rly?]	57dNE3 & 4 Hébuterne	K 33 a 2.7
Euston Dump	57dNE3 & 4 Hébuterne	K 33 a
Euston Post	36SW1 Aubers	M 34 a 2.8
Euston Road	28NW2 St Julien	C 21 d, 22 c
Euston Road	57dNE3 & 4 Hébuterne	K 32 d
Euston Road [CT, Sept 1915]	36SW3 Richebourg	M 34 c, d
Euston Road Tramway	36SW1 Aubers / 3 Richebourg	M 34 a, b, d, 35 c
Euston Sector	57dSE2 Beaumont	Q 4 a
Euston Trench	36bNE [1 Labeuvrière]	E 19 c, d, 25 a
Eva Farm	28NE2 Moorslede	F 16 a 95.20
Eva Sap	62bNW1 Gouy	A 14 a
Eva Street	57dSE1 & 2 Beaumont	Q 29 c, 35 a
Eva Trench	36SW1 Aubers	N 25 c, d
Evacuation Alley [1918]	62dSE [4 Harbonnières]	X 29 a, b, 30 a
Evacuation Avenue	20SW3 Oostvleteren	T 9 b, 10 a
Evacuation Trench	36cNW3 Loos	G 27 d, 28 c
Evans Farm	28SW2 Wytschaete	O 14 b
Evasion Farm	28NE1 Zonnebeke	E 8 a 9.9
Evasion Farm [Redoubt]	28NE1 Zonnebeke	E 8 b
Eve Alley	57dSE2 & 57cSW1 Le Sars	N 21 d, 27 b
Eve Copse	57cSE4 Villers-Guislain	X 17 d
Eve Farm	28NE3 Gheluvelt	J 26 a 1.9
Eve Post	36NW4 Bois Grenier	I 16 a
Evelyn Post	36NW4 Bois Grenier	I 16 b
Everest Farm	27NE1 Herzeele	D 4 a
Everest Flank [1918]	57dSW [3 Talmas]	S 6 b, T 1 a, b, d
Everest Flank Left [1918]	57dSW [1 Puchevillers / 3 Talmas]	N 31 a, b, d, 32 c
Everest Fort [Hunter's Avenue]	28SW4 Ploegsteert	U 21 a, c
Everest Loop [trench] [1918]	57dSW [3 Talmas]	N 32 d, T 2 b, c, d
Everest Reserve [1918]	57dSW [1 Puchevillers / 3 Talmas]	M 36 d, N 31 a, c, S 6 b, d
Everest Trench [1918]	57dSW [3 Talmas]	N 32 d, T 2 a, b, c
Everpuch Trench [Everest Tr - Puchevillers, '18]	57dSW [1 Puchevillers / 3 Talmas]	N 26 c, d, 32 a, c, d
Eversfield Copse	20SE2 Hooglede	Q 5 d 1.2
Evert Alley	66cNW2 Itancourt	B 12 a
Evescliff Copse	20SE2 Hooglede	Q 15 b 8.1
Ewe Farm	27SE4 Meteren	X 20 d 1.1
Ewe Post	62cNE4 Roisel	L 24 c 60.65
Ewell Farm	27SE4 Meteren	X 28 d 3.2
Exam Buildings	28NE2 Moorslede	F 10 d 95.10
Excellenzen Weg	51cSE4 Blaireville	W 24 b, X 13 b, c, d, 19 a
Excema Avenue	57dNE3 & 4 Hébuterne	K 27 c - 29 a
Exchange House	28NW1 Elverdinghe	A 27 c 9.7
Exchange Sidings [railway]	28NW1 Elverdinghe	A 27 c
Exe Post	36SW1 Aubers	N 8 a
Exe Trench	57dNE1 & 2 Fonquevillers / 3 & 4 Hébuterne	K 5 d, 6 a, c
Exempt Wood	28NE1 Zonnebeke	E 2 c, d
Exert Copse	20SE3 Westroosebeke / 28NE1 Zonnebeke	W 25 c, d, E 1 a
Exert Farm	28NE1 Zonnebeke	E 1 a 3.2
Exeter Avenue (Haymarket)	36SW1 Aubers	N 8 a, b
Exeter Trench	51bSW1 Neuville Vitasse	M 12 a

Name	Map Sheet	Map Reference
Exile Trench	36bNE [1 Labeuvrière]	E 19 a
Exit Wood	28NE1 Zonnebeke	E 2 b
Exmouth Street	57dNE1 & 2 Fonquevillers	E 17 a
Express Farm	27NE1 Herzeele	E 1 a 9.1
Eye Copse [by letter I on map]	57cNW2 Vaulx-Vraucourt	I 6 b
Eye Lane	51bSW1 Neuville Vitasse	N 7 d
Eye Trench	57cSW3 Longueval	S 2 b, 3 a, b
Eylau Trench	62bSW3 St Quentin	S 6 b, c, d, 12 a
Eylau Trench	62cSW2 Barleux	O 16 d, 22 a, b, c
Eylau Trench [1918]	66eNW [2 Thennes]	C 8 d, 14 b
F 10 [late-1915, N of Witte Poort Farm]	28NW4 & NE3 Zillebeke	I 11 b 2.0
F 11 [late-1915, NW of Witte Poort Farm]	28NW4 & NE3 Zillebeke	I 11 a 8.0
F 12 [late-1915, W of railway Wood]	28NW4 & NE3 Zillebeke	I 11 b 25.35
F 2 [Dec '14 to April '15, Spanbroekmolen Fm]	28SW2 Wytschaete	N 29 d 8.6
F 3 [Hooge, 1915]	28NW4 & NE3 Zillebeke	I 18 a
F 3 [late-1915, NW of Birr X Roads]	28NW4 & NE3 Zillebeke	I 11 d 02.30
F 30 [post / trench south of Fortin 17]	28NW2 St Julien	C 7 d
F 30 [trench, S of Fortin 17, June 1916]	28NW2 St Julien	C 7 d
F 4 [12/14 to 4/15, Spanbroekmolen Farm]	28SW2 Wytschaete	N 30 c
F 4 [late-1915, S of Witte Poort Farm]	28NW4 & NE3 Zillebeke	I 11 d 4.4
F 5 [late-1915, S of Witte Poort Farm]	28NW4 & NE3 Zillebeke	I 11 d 2.4
F 6 [late-1915, W of Witte Poort Farm]	28NW4 & NE3 Zillebeke	I 11 c 7.5
F 7 [late-1915, E of Witte Poort Farm]	28NW4 & NE3 Zillebeke	I 11 d 4.7
F 8 [late-1915, W of Witte Poort Farm]	28NW4 & NE3 Zillebeke	I 11 d 1.7
F Camp	28NW1 Elverdinghe	A 16 central
F Camp [Montreal Camp]	28NW3 Poperinghe	H 19 b
F Lines [NE of Rue Tilleloy 1914-15]	36SW1 Aubers	M 7 b, c, d, 8 a, 13 a
F Lines [SW of Rue d'Enfer early 1915]	36SW1 Aubers	M 34 b, d
F Sap	28NW4 & NE3 Zillbeke	I 30 b
F Sap [Givenchy]	36cNW1 La Bassée	A 9 d
F Sector [4/15, N of R Douve]	28SW2 Wytschaete	N 23, 24
F Street	57dSE1 & 2 Beaumont	Q 10 c
F Track	28NE1 Zonnebeke / 3 Gheluvelt	D 26 c, J 2 a, b, d
F Track (Duckboard) [1917-18]	28NW4 Ypres	I 5 c, d, 6 a, 9 a, b, 10 a, b
F Work	51bNW1 Roclincourt	G 5 b
FA Lines [SW of Rue d'Enfer April 1915]	36SW1 Aubers	M 35 b, d
Fabeck Graben	57dSE2 & 57cSW1 Le Sars	R 28 c, d, 29 a, b, c
Faber Farm	28NE4 Dadizeele	L 16 b 4.1
Fable Trench	51bNW2 Oppy	B 24 d
Fable Trench	57dNE3 & 4 Hébuterne	K 11 d
Fabric Trench	51bNW2 Oppy	B 24 d
Face Trench	57dNE3 & 4 Hébuterne	K 17 b
Facit Dump	57cSE1 Bertincourt	Q 3 c 2.8
Facons, les [farm]	36aSE4 Locon	X 15 c
Fact Trench	36cSW3 Vimy	S 22 c, d
Fact Trench	57dNE3 & 4 Hébuterne	K 11 c, d
Factory [post / trench]	36cNW1 La Bassée	G 2 a, b
Factory Avenue	51bSW4 Bullecourt	U 13 b, d
Factory Corner	57cSW1 Gueudecourt	N 19 c 95.05
Factory Corner	51bSW4 Bullecourt	U 13 d
Factory Farm [Reebrouck]	28SW4 Ploegsteert	U 16 c 0.3
Factory Keep, Post & Corner	36SW3 Richebourg	S 9 d
Factory Lane [Courcelette]	57dSE2 & 57cSW1 Le Sars	R 30 c, 36 a, M 31 b, 32 a
Factory Post	36NW3 Fleurbaix	G 22 c, d, 23 a, c

Name	Map Sheet	Map Reference
Factory Road	51cSE & 51bSW Ficheux	R 28 a, b, d
Factory Support	57cSW1 Gueudecourt	M 24 b, N 19 a
Factory Trench	36SW3 Richebourg	S 9 a, b, c, d
Factory Trench	51bSW2 Vis-en-Artois	O 9 d, 15 b, d
Factory Trench	57cSW1 Gueudecourt	M 24 a, b, N 19 a, c, d
Factory Trench	66cSW4 La Fère	O 34 c, U 5 a, b
Factory Trench [1918]	51bSW3 Boisleux / 51cSE4 Blaireville	S 19 b, X 24 a, c
Factory, The [Ritz OP, 1915]	36SW3 Richebourg	S 9 d 7.6
Facus Trench	36cSW2 Harnes	O 9 d
Fag Alley	51bSW4 Bullecourt	U 9 c,14 a, b, c, 15 a
Fag Support	62cNE2 Epéhy	F 11 b, d
Fag Trench	36cSW3 Vimy	S 22 c
Fag Trench	57cSW3 Longueval	M 36 c, d, S 6 a
Fag Trench	62cNE2 Epéhy	F 11 b, d
Fagan Alley	57cNE3 Hermies	K 14 b, 15 a
Fagan Avenue	57cNE3 Hermies / 4 Marcoing	K 14 d, 15 c
Fagan Support	57cNE3 Hermies / 4 Marcoing	K 14 d, 15 c
Fagan Trench	57cNE3 Hermies / 4 Marcoing	K 15 a, c
Fagan Trench	57cSW3 Longueval	S 30 a
Faggot Farm	36aNE4 Merville	L 23 b 3.0
Faggot Wood	62cNE4 Roisel	L 35 c
Faidherbe Alley [1918]	62dSE [4 Harbonnières]	X 11 d, 17 b, 18 a
Faidherbe Cross Roads	20SW4 Bixschoote	U 5 d 25.38
Faidherbe Post [1917-18]	20SW4 Bixschoote	U 5 d 35.50
Fair Cott	28NE3 Gheluvelt	J 28 a 5.5
Fair Trench	57dNE3 & 4 Hébuterne	K 11 d
Fairmaid Street	57dSE4 Ovillers	X 19 b
Fairy Copse	62cSW4 St Christ	U 29 b, c, d
Fairy House	28SW1 Kemmel	M 18 d 4.1
Fairy House Camp	28SW1 Kemmel	M 18 d
Fairy Wood	62bNW4 Ramicourt	I 26 b, 27 a
Faisan Trench [1918]	62dSW [4 Cachy]	U 28 b, d
Faith Copse	62bNW4 Ramicourt	I 32 b
Faith Farm	28SW2 Wytschaete	O 10 d 9.2
Faith Trench	57dNE3 & 4 Hébuterne	K 16 b
Fal Farm	36aNE4 Merville	K 17 b 00.88
Falaba House	27NE2 Proven	F 14 a 3.3
Falaise, Tranchée de la	62cNW3 Vaux	G 23 c, 29 a
Falcon Avenue	57cSE4 Villers-Guislain	X 30 a
Falcon Sap	57cSE4 Villers-Guislain	X 29 b
Falcon Trench	51bNW2 Oppy	B 24 c, 30 a
Falcon Trench	51bSW2 Vis-en-Artois	O 19 d, 25 b
Falcon Trench [1918]	66eNW [2 Thennes]	C 3 d, 4 c, 9 a, b
Falfemont Farm	62cNW1 Maricourt	B 2 a, b
Falkenhayn Redoubt [June 1916]	28NW2 St Julien	C 17 a, b
Falkenhayn Trench / Falkenhayn, Tranchée de	66cNW2 Itancourt	B 6 d, 12 b, C 7 a, c
Falkland Street	51bNW3 Arras	G 5 b, d
Falkland Trench	51bNW1 Roclincourt	A 16 c
Fall Trench	36cSW3 Vimy	S 22 d, 28 b
Fall Trench	57cSW2 Villers-au-Flos / 4 Combles	N 34 b, 35 c
Fall Trench	57dNE3 & 4 Hébuterne	K 11 a, c
Fallen Tree Post / Keep	36SW3 Richebourg	S 15 d, 16 c
Fallow Lane	51bSW1 Neuville Vitasse	M 11 c
Falmouth Street	57dNE1 & 2 Fonquevillers	E 17 a

Name	Map Sheet	Map Reference
Falter Trench	51bNW2 Oppy	B 24 c, 30 a
Falvy [village]	66dNW2 Morchain	C 5 a, b, c, d
Falvy Copse	62cSW4 St. Christ	U 29 b, c, d
Fame Trench	57dNE3 & 4 Hébuterne	K 11 a, d
Famine Alley	62bSW1 Gricourt	M 5 b
Famine Trench	36cSW3 Vimy	S 22 d
Famine Trench	51bNW2 Oppy	B 24 d
Fampoux [village]	51bNW4 Fampoux	H 17 b, c, d, 18 c, 23 a, b
Fan Tail [light rly, Aix Noulette]	36bSE2 Boyeffles	R 17 c
Fan Trench	57dNE3 & 4 Hébuterne	K 11 d
Fancy Trench	57dNE3 & 4 Hébuterne	K 11 d
Fanfarons Trench	62bSW1 Gricourt	N 7 a, c, d
Fanny Farm	28NE2 Moorslede	K 6 a 7.9
Fanny Mill	28NE2 Moorslede	K 6 a 57.82
Fanny O.P. [1917-18]	51bNW1 Roclincourt	B 14 b 3.5
Fanny Trench	36cSW3 Vimy	S 28 a, b
Fanny's Avenue	28SW2 Wytschaete / 4 Ploegsteert	O 33 a, b, 34 b, d, 35 c
Fanny's Farm	28SW2 Wytschaete	O 33 a 6.5
Fantasia Farm	28NW1 Elverdinghe	B 21 d 5.5
Fantasio Trench / Tranchée de Fantasio	62cSW2 Barleux	N 29 a, c
Fantasy Farm	36aNE2 Vieux Berquin	E 22 b 80.45
Farbus [village]	51bNW1 Roclincourt	B 1 d, 2 c, 7 b, 8 a
Farbus Post [S of Farbus]	51bNW1 Roclincourt	B 14
Farbus Wood	51bNW1 Roclincourt	B 8 a, b, c, d
Farbus-Vimy-Liévin Line	36cSW3 Vimy / 51bNW1 Roclincourt	extensive
Fargate [Trench]	28NW2 St Julien	C 7 c, 13 a
Fargate Street	57dNE3 & 4 Hébuterne	K 34 b
Fargny Mill	62cNW1 Maricourt	A 29 d
Fargny Wood	62cNW1 Maricourt	A 28 b, 29 a
Fargny Wood Avenue / Boyau du Bois Fargny	62cNW1 Maricourt	A 22 d
Farm Avenue	57cSE2 Gonnelieu	R 9 c, 15 a
Farm B	20NW4 Dixmude	I 13 c 3.5
Farm Corner [Br Front Line]	36SW3 Richebourg	S 16 c
Farm Ravine	57cSE2 Gonnelieu	R 20 a
Farm Road [road]	36cNW3 Loos / 4 Pont-à-Vendin	H 33 a, b, 34 a
Farm Street	51cSE2 Beaumetz	R 23 a, b, d, 24 c
Farm Support	62bNW3 Bellicourt	G 7 d
Farm Tram	36NW4 Bois Grenier	H 36 c
Farm Trench	51bSW2 Vis-en-Artois	O 14 a
Farm Trench	57cSE2 Gonnelieu	R 15 a, b
Farm Trench	57dNE3 & 4 Hébuterne	K 11 c, d, 12 d, 18 b, d
Farm Trench	62bNW3 Bellicourt	G 7 d, 13 b, 14 a, c, 20 a, b, d
Farm Trench [1918]	57dNE2 [Courcelles]	F 8 c, 13 c, d, 14 a
Farm Trench [Government Farm]	57cSW4 Combles	U 21 d, 22 c
Farm Wood	20SW4 Bixschoote	U 19 c
Farm, The	36SW1 Aubers	N 13 a
Farman Sap [1918]	51bSW3 Boisleux	S 25 b, 26 a, c
Farmer Lane	51bSW4 Bullecourt	T 6 a
Farmer Road [road]	57dSE2 & 57cSW1 Le Sars	M 14 a, b, d, 15 c, d
Farmer Trench	28SW2 Wytschaete	N 23 d, 24 a, c
Farmer Trench	57dNE3 & 4 Hébuterne	K 11 c
Farmer Wood	62dSE [1 Hamel / 2 Proyart]	Q 15 d, 16 c, 21 b, 22 a
Farmers Lane	36cNW3 Loos	G 11 b
Farmers Lane	51bSW4 Bullecourt	T 6 a

Name	Map Sheet	Map Reference
Farmers Rest [Ploegsteert Wood 1914-15]	28SW4 Ploegsteert	U 21 a
Farmyard Trench	57dNE3 & 4 Hébuterne	K 11 c
Farnborough Road	51cSE3 & 4 Ransart	W 17 c, d
Farney's Lane	36cNW3 Loos	G 36 a, c
Farrel Line [light rly]	36cSW1 Lens	M 18 a, b, c, 23 a, b
Farrow Street	51cSE2 Beaumetz	R 24 a, c
Farthing Trench	36cSW3 Vimy	S 28 b
Fascines Alley	66cNW1 Grugies	B 1 b
Fasker Farm	27NE1 Herzeele	E 25 b 7.3
Fast Lane	51bSW4 Bullecourt	T 6 a
Fast Trench	36cSW3 Vimy	S 28 a
Fast Trench	57dNE3 & 4 Hébuterne	K 11 d
Fat Lane	51bSW4 Bullecourt	T 5 a
Fat Trench	57cSW3 Longueval	M 36 c
Fat Trench	57dNE3 & 4 Hébuterne	K 11 d, 17 b
Fate Trench	57dNE3 & 4 Hébuterne	K 11 a, c
Father Trench	36cSW3 Vimy	S 28 a
Fatigue Alley	57dSE2 & 57cSW1 Le Sars	N 20 c
Fatimar Farm	28NE4 Dadizeele	L 11 d 05.40
Fatty Trench	51bNW2 Oppy	B 30 a
Faubourg d'Arras [suburb, Béthune]	36bNE2 Beuvry	E 11 d, 17 b
Faubourg de Paris [Péronne]	62cNW4 Péronne	I 33 a, b
Faubourg Trench	62bSW3 St Quentin	S 24 c
Faucille Trench	62bSW1 Gricourt	M 11 d
Faucon Trench	57cSE3 Sorel-le-Grand	V 21 d, 22 a, c
Faugh-a-Ballagh Bridge	57cNE3 Hermies	J 36 b
Fauna Farm	27SE4 Meteren	X 1 b 3.1
Fauquelun [place name]	36aSE1 St Venant	P 7 a
Fauquissart [hamlet]	36SW1 Aubers	M 18 c, d, 24 a, b, N 13 c
Fauquissart [keep, late 1915	36SW1 Aubers	M 18 d 90.55
Fauquissart Post	36SW1 Aubers	M 18 d
Faure Alley	62bSW3 St Quentin / 66cNW1 Grugies	S 23c, 28 b,c,d, 29 a, A1 d, 2 c,d, 3 b,c
Faussoires, Tranchée des	66cNW2 Itancourt	B 18 c, 24 a
Faust Trench	20SW2 Zwartegat	O 5 c, 11 b
Fauvette Alley	62bSW1 Gricourt	M 5 b
Favel Alley	66cNW1 Grugies	A 6 c, d, 12 a
Favière Alley	62cNW1 Maricourt	A 10 d, 11 c
Favière Support	62cNW1 Maricourt	A 10 c, d
Favière Trench	62cNW1 Maricourt	A 10 c, d
Favière Wood	62cNW1 Maricourt	A 11 a, b, d, 17 b
Favreuil [village]	57cNW3 Bapaume / 4 Beugny	H 10 c, 15 b, d, 16 a, c
Fawcus Avenue	57cSE4 Villers-Guislain	X 16 b, d, 17 a
Fayette Trench, la	57dNE3 & 4 Hébuterne	K 22 b, d
Fearon Camp	27NE4 Abeele	L 7 d, 8 c
Feast Trench	57dNE3 & 4 Hébuterne	K 4 d
Feather Farm	28SW2 Wytschaete	O 30 c 4.8
Feather Trench	36cSW3 Vimy	S 22 d, 28 b
February Avenue	51bNW3 Arras	G 16 d, 17 c, d
Fécamp Trench	66cSW3 Tergnier / 4 La Fère	T 16 c, 22 a, c
Fee Cottage	28NE2 Moorslede	L 4 b 85.23
Feeble Trench	51bNW2 Oppy	B 30 a, c
Feed Trench	57dNE3 & 4 Hébuterne	K 4 d, 5 c
Feint Trench	57dNE3 & 4 Hébuterne	K 5 c, 11 a

Name	Map Sheet	Map Reference
Feld Webel Trench	62bSW3 St Quentin	M 36 d, S 6 b
Fell Trench	57dNE3 & 4 Hébuterne	K 5 c
Fellah Trench	66cNW4 Berthenicourt	I 7 d
Fellow Trench	57dNE3 & 4 Hébuterne	K 5 c
Felon / Felon's Post [in Drury Lane]	36SW1 Aubers	N 13 c
Felon Cottage	28NE2 Moorslede	F 11 d 98..80
Felon Trench	57dNE3 & 4 Hébuterne	K 5 c, 11 a, b
Felons Alley	62bSW1 Gricourt	M 5 a
Felsen Trench	51bNW1 Roclincourt	A 10 b
Felt Farm	36aNE4 Merville	L 27 b 1.6
Felt Trench	57dNE3 & 4 Hébuterne	K 11 a
Female Trench	57dNE3 & 4 Hébuterne	K 4 d
Femur Farm [Estaires]	36aNE4 Merville	L 30 a 3.3
Fémy Line	57cNE4 Marcoing	K 35 a
Fémy Wood	57cNE4 Marcoing	K 34 d
Fen Trench	57dNE3 & 4 Hébuterne	K 4 d
Fenchurch Street	28NW2 St Julien	C 28 d, 29 c
Fenchurch Street	51cSE2 Beaumetz	R 23 b, 24 a, c
Fendal Trench	51bNW2 Oppy	B 30 a
Fennel Farm	28NW1 Elverdinghe	A 14 b 5.9
Fenton Farm	27NE2 Proven	E 12 c 2.5
Fer à Cheval Farm	28NW2 St Julien	B 4 b 2.6
Ferdan Trench	57dSE2 Beaumont	R 13 b, 14 a, c
Ferdinand [work / strongpoint]	57dNE1 & 2 Fonquevillers	F 1 c
Ferdinand Farm	28NW2 St Julien	C 5 c 05.50
Ferdinand Trench	57cSW4 Combles	U 10 a, c
Ferecourt Road [road]	62cNE4 Roisel	L 10 d, 11 a, c, 16 a, b
Ferguson Trench	57dSE2 Beaumont	R 14 c, 20 a
Ferme de la Moularderie [Hobbs Farm]	36NW2 Armentières	C 23 a 5.9
Ferme Graben	57dNE1 & 2 Fonquevillers	F 7 d, 13 a, b
Ferme Isolée	20SW4 Bixschoote	T 12 b 35.32
Ferme Rouge Trench	70dNW4 St Gobain	I 19 d, 20 c, d
Ferme Rouge, la	70dNW4 St Gobain	I 20 c 40.15
Ferme sans Nom	62cSW3 & 4 Marchélepot	S 11 d
Fermoy Farm	28SW1 Kemmel	N 13 a 2.0
Fermoy Trench	28SW2 Wytschaete	N 17 d, 18 c
Fern Trench	51bSW1 Neuville Vitasse	N 13 c, d
Fern Trench	57cSE2 Gonnelieu	R 20 d, 21 c, 27 a
Fern Trench	57cSW3 Longueval	N 31 d, 32 c
Fern Trench	57cSW3 Longueval	S 10 b, 11 a, b
Fern Trench	57dNE3 & 4 Hébuterne	K 4 d
Fern Wood	62bNW4 Ramicourt / SW2 Fonsommes	O 4 a, c
Fernes Farm	20SE2 Hooglede	Q 23 b 9.7
Fernie [light rly siding]	36cSW1 Lens	M 8 b
Fernie Road [road]	36cSW2 Harnes / 4 Rouvroy	O 31 a,b,d, 32 c,d, U 2 b, 3 a,c, 9 a,b
Ferns Camp [1918]	28SW1 Kemmel	N 7 a
Ferracci / Feracci, Tranchée [Br FL 3/16]	36cSW1 Lens	M 25 d, 26 c, 32 a
Ferret Left Post	62cNE2 Epéhy	L 6 a
Ferret Right Post	62bNW3 Bellicourt	G 1 d
Ferret Street	51cSE & 51bSW Ficheux	R 23 d, 29 b
Ferret Trench	57cSW3 Longueval	M 36 c, S 6 a
Ferret Trench	57dNE3 & 4 Hébuterne	K 4 d
Ferret Trench	62cNE2 Epéhy / 62bNW3 Bellicourt	L 6 a, G 1 b, d
Ferret Wood	62bSW4 Homblières	U 7 a, b

Name	Map Sheet	Map Reference
Ferrets Post [south Fleurbaix]	36NW3 Fleurbaix	H 27 d
Ferrure Farm	20SW4 Bixschoote	T 5 a 65.35
Ferry Camp	28SW1 Kemmel	N 7 a
Ferry Trench	36cSW3 Vimy	S 22 c, 28 a
Ferry Trench	51bNW2 Oppy	B 30 c
Fertile Farm	28NW1 Elverdinghe	A 28 b 7.1
Fervacque Farm	62cNE4 Roisel	L 16 c 8.8
Fervacque West [post]	62cNE4 Roisel	L 16 c 7.2
Fervaque Switch	62cNE4 Roisel	L 15 d, 16 c, 20 b, c, d, 21 a, b
Fervaque Trench [Fervaque Farm]	62cNE4 Roisel	L 16 a, b, c, 22 a
Fervaques Farm	62bSW2 Fonsommes	O 11 d 0.6
Feste Soden	57dNE3 & 4 Hébuterne	K 35 b
Festive Farm	27NE2 Proven	E 11 c 2.8
Festubert [village]	36SW3 Richebourg / 36cNW1 La Bassée	S 25 d, 26 c, A 1 b
Festubert East Keep	36SW3 Richebourg	S 26 c
Festubert Keep	36SW3 Richebourg	S 25 d
Festubert Switch	36aSE4 Locon	X 30 c
Fethard Street	57dSE1 & 2 Beaumont	Q 10 c
Fetlock Post	62bNW3 Bellicourt	G 31 b 5.5
Fetlock Trench	57dSE4 Ovillers	X 15 c, d
Fetter Trench	57dNE3 & 4 Hébuterne	K 11 a
Fettes Road [road]	36SW1 Aubers	M 26 c, 32 a
Fettle Farm	36aNE1 Morbecque	D 24 a 8.2
Feuchy [village]	51bNW3 Arras	H 21 a, c, d
Feuchy Chapel Redoubt / Work	51bSW1 Neuville Vitasse	N 3 b
Feuchy Copse	51bNW3 Arras	H 22 c
Feuchy Lane	51bNW3 Arras	H 20 a
Feuchy Switch	51bNW3 Arras	H 20 c, d
Feuchy Work / Redoubt	51bNW3 Arras	H 20 b, d, 21 a, c
Feud Trench	57dNE3 & 4 Hébuterne	K 5 c
Feve Redoubt	20SW2 Zwartegat	N 23 a
Fever Trench	57dNE3 & 4 Hébuterne	K 10 b, 11 a
Fez Alley [1918]	62dSW [4 Cachy]	U 15 a, b, 16 a
Fiasco Trench	62bNW4 Ramicourt / SW2 Fonsommes	O 3 a, c, d, 4 c, d, 10 a, b
Fibre Trench	57dNE1 & 2 Fonquevillers / 3 & 4 Hébuterne	K 4 a, b, d
Ficheux Street	51cSE2 Beaumetz	R 21, 27, 28
Ficheux Switch	51cSE2 Beaumetz / 51bSW1 Neuville Vitasse	R 30, 36, M 12, 19, 25
Fickle Trench	36cSW3 Vimy	S 29 a, c
Fiddle Street	51cSE & 51bSW Ficheux	R 28 a, c, d
Fiddle Trench	36cSW3 Vimy	S 29 d, 30 a, c, d
Fiddle Trench	51bNW2 Oppy	B 30 a, c
Fidget Farm	27SE2 Berthen	R 25 a 65.05
Field Camp	28NW1 Elverdinghe	B 15 c
Field Farm	28NW3 Poperinghe	G 10 d 8.4
Field Trench	57dNE1 & 2 Fonquevillers	K 4 a
Fielding Alley	27SE4 Meteren	X 13 b, d, 14 c, 20 a
Field's Lane	51bSW4 Bullecourt	T 5 b
Fiennes Street	57dSE1 & 2 Beaumont	R 19 c, d
Fieu Farm	28NW1 Elverdinghe	A 10 a 05.00
Fife Road, No.7 [Sap]	36cNW1 La Bassée	A 2 d, 3 c
Fife Trench	51bSW2 Vis-en-Artois	O 15 a, b
Fife Trench	57cSE4 Villers-Guislain	X 5 a, c
Fife Trench	57cSW3 Longueval	S 3 c, 9 a
Fifteen Alley	57cSE2 Gonnelieu	R 20 c, d

Name	Map Sheet	Map Reference
Fifteen Ravine	57cSE2 Gonnelieu	Q 24 b, R 19 a, b, d, 20 c
Fifteen Street	51bNW3 Arras	G 35 b
Fifteenth Street	36SW3 Richebourg	S 5 a, c
Fifth Avenue	57dNE1 & 2 Fonquevillers	K 3 a, b
Fifth Avenue [Oct 1915]	36cNW3 Loos	G 18 c, d
Fifth Avenue [Thiepval]	57dSE1 & 2 Beaumont / 4 Ovillers	R 31 c
Fifth Street	57dSE4 Ovillers	X 3 c, d, 9 a, b
Fifty Post	36NW4 Bois Grenier	I 9 d, 15 b
Fig Trench	57cSW3 Longueval	S 6 a
Fig Trench	57dNE3 & 4 Hébuterne	K 3 d, 4 c
Fig Wood	62bSW3 St. Quentin	S 5 c, d, 11 a
Fight Trench	57dNE3 & 4 Hébuterne	K 4 c
Figuier Trench	62bSW1 Gricourt	M 11 c
Fiji Road	36NW2 Armentières	C 28 b, 29 a
Fil de Fer, Ferme de	66dNW2 Morchain	B 11 a 3.6
Filanzanes [trench]	66cNW2 Itancourt	C 19 d, 25 a, b
Filatiers Avenue	51bNW1 Roclincourt	A 28 c
Filature	28SW4 Ploegsteert	U 18 c, d
Filbert Trench	51bNW2 Oppy	B 30 c
File O.P [1917-18]	51bNW1 Roclincourt	B 8 a 3.5
File Trench	51bSW1 Neuville Vitasse	M 22 c, d
Filet Trench	62bSW1 Gricourt	M 6 c, 12 a
Filettes [?] Woods	62dSE [2 Proyart]	R 8 b
Filey Forks [road junctions]	20SE2 Hooglede	Q 11 b 15.20 and 30.15
Filey Trench	57dNE1 & 2 Fonquevillers	K 4 a
Filiform Tree [Straggly Tree / Arbre Filiforme]	62dNE2 Méaulte	F 25 b 62.85
Fill Trench	57dNE1 & 2 Fonquevillers	E 29 c, K 5 a
Filler Work	62bNW3 Bellicourt	G 33 b 2.3
Fillet Farm	20SE2 Hooglede	R 29 a 3.9
Fillet Trench	57dNE1 & 2 Fonquevillers	K 5 a
Fillip Trench	36cSW3 Vimy	S 23 c, d
Filly Farm	28NE2 Moorslede	E 23 c 6.3
Film Farm	27NE1 Herzeele	D 14 c
Film Trench	57dNE1 & 2 Fonquevillers	E 4 b
Filmy Trench	51bNW2 Oppy	B 24 d, 30 a, b
Filous Trench	62bSW2 Fonsommes	O 7 a
Fin de la Guerre [place name]	36SW2 Radinghem	O 17 b
Finch Post	57cNE1 Quéant	D 26 d
Finch Street	28NW2 St Julien	C 21 d, 22 c
Finch Trench	57cSW2 Villers-au-Flos	N 29 c
Finchley Road	36cNW1 La Bassée	A 9 c, d, 15 b
Finchley Road	36cNW3 Loos	G 31 b, 32 a, d, 33 c
Find Trench	57dNE3 & 4 Hébuterne	K 3 d
Fine Air Farm	66dNW1 Punchy	B 25 a, c
Fine Street	51cSE2 Beaumetz	R 22, 28, 29
Fine Trench	57dNE1 & 2 Fonquevillers / 3 & 4 Hébuterne	K 4 a, c
Fins [village]	57cSE3 Sorel-le-Grand	V 12 a, b, c, d
Fins Ridge	57cSE3 Sorel-le-Grand / 4 Villers-Guislain	W 3, 4, 8, 9, 10
Fir Alley	51bSW1 Neuville Vitasse	N 13 a
Fir Lane	28NW4 & NE3 Zillebeke	I 34 c
Fir Support	57cSE4 Villers-Guislain	X 25 b, 26 a, b
Fir Trench	57cSW3 Longueval	S 6 a
Fir Trench	57dNE3 & 4 Hébuterne	K 4 c, d
Fire Trench	57cSW2 Villers-au-Flos	N 22 b, 23 a

Name	Map Sheet	Map Reference
Fire Trench F 101	62dNE2 Méaulte	F 10 d
Fire Trench F 102	62dNE2 Méaulte	F 10 d
Fire Trench F 103	62dNE2 Méaulte	F 10 d
Fire Trench F 114	62dNE2 Méaulte	F 11 c
Fire Trench F 115	62dNE2 Méaulte	F 11 c
Fireworks Post	36SW1 Aubers	N 13 b
Firm Trench	57dNE3 & 4 Hébuterne	K 4 c
Firsland Farm	20SE2 Hooglede	R 25 a 2.8
First Aid Corner [Richb'g -Festubert Jan 1915]	36SW3 Richebourg	S 15, 20, 26 [area of]
First Aid Trench	57dSE4 Ovillers	X 9 d, 10 a, b
First Avenue	51bSW2 Vis-en-Artois / 4 Bullecourt	N 35 b, 36 a, d
First Garde Stellung	57dNE3 & 4 Hébuterne	K 5 d, 6 c, 12 a, b
First Parallel [N of Thiepval Wood]	57dSE1 & 2 Beaumont	Q 19 c, 25 a, 24 c, d
First Street [German front line]	57dSE4 Ovillers	X 8 a, c
First Trench [German]	36cSW3 Vimy	S 15 a, c, 21 b
Fischer Alley	62cSW3 Vermandovillers	S 24 b, T 19 a, b, 20 a
Fischer Alley, Boyau Fischer	62cSW3 & 4 Marchélepot	T 19 a, b, 20 a
Fisener Trench	51bNW1 Roclincourt	A 10 d
Fish Alley	57cSW3 Longueval / Le Sars	M 36 a, c, N 19, 25, 31, S 6 a, c
Fish Alley [1918]	57dNE3 & 4 Hébuterne	K 5 c, 11 a, b, 12 a
Fish Avenue	51bNW1 Roclincourt	A 21 a
Fish Avenue	57cNE1 Quéant / 3 Hermies	J 5 a, b, c
Fish Bridge [over canal]	36aSE1 St Venant	P 5 a 25.05
Fish Lane	62bNW3 Bellicourt	G 1 d
Fish Pond	28SE1 Wervicq	P 1 b 70.95
Fish Street	51cSE3 & 4 Ransart	W 17 c, 23 b
Fish Support	57cNE1 Quéant / 3 Hermies	J 5 b, d
Fish Trench	57dNE3 & 4 Hébuterne	K 4 c
Fisher Crater	62bSW1 Gricourt	M 2 d 75.45
Fisher Wood	20SE2 Hooglede	R 8 c 60.75
Fishers Keep	62cNE2 Epéhy	F 1 a
Fishes Trench	20SW2 Zwartegat	N 35 b
Fishguard [post / strongpoint]	36NW3 Fleurbaix	G 26 a, b
Fishhook, The	28NW4 & NE3 Zillebeke	I 18 a 7.9
Fishtail No.1 & No. 2	36SW1 Aubers	N 13 d
Fist Trench	57cSW3 Longueval	M 35 d, 36 c
Fist Trench	57dNE1 & 2 Fonquevillers	K 4 a
Fit Lane	51bSW4 Bullecourt	T 6 d
Fit Trench	57dNE3 & 4 Hébuterne	K 3 d
Fitter Trench	36cSW3 Vimy	S 28 a
Fitz Lane	51bSW4 Bullecourt	T 6 d
Fitzclarence Farm [1917]	28NW4 & NE3 Zillebeke	J 14 d 4.9
Fitzclarence Farm [June 1915]	28NW4 & NE3 Zillebeke	J 14 b 2.3
Fitzpatrick Trench	57dSE2 Beaumont	R 27 b, d,
Fiume Trench [1918]	66eNW [2 Thennes]	C 15 b
Five Haystacks	28SW4 Ploegsteert	U 1 c 4.0
Five Points	57cSE3 Sorel-le-Grand	P 32 c 5.2
Five Roads, The [road junction/crossroads]	27SE3 Borre	V 25 b 06.03
Five Wood	62cNE3 Buire	J 25 c, 31 a
Fiver Wood	20SE3 Westroosebeke	V 12 b, d, W 7 a, c
Fives Trench	57cSE4 Villers-Guislain	X 7 d
Fix Trench	57dNE1 & 2 Fonquevillers	K 4 a
Fiz Farm	28NW1 Elverdinghe	A 26 c 9.7
Flabby Trench	51bNW2 Oppy	B 24 d

Name	Map Sheet	Map Reference
Flag Alley	57dNE3 & 4 Hébuterne	K 29 d, 30 c
Flag Avenue, & Switch	57dNE3 & 4 Hébuterne	K 28 c, d, 29 c
Flag Lane [Starfish Line]	57cSW3 Longueval	M 35 c, d
Flag Ravine	57cSE2 Gonnelieu	R 25 b, 26 a
Flag Street	51cSE & 51bSW Ficheux	R 28 b, 29 a, c
Flag Trench	36cSW3 Vimy	S 28 a, c
Flagon Farm	36aNE3 Haverskerque	K 27 d 6.2
Flagstaff Point	36cNW1 La Bassée	A 16 c
Flamanderie Farm, La [Grande Fl Fm, Nov '14]	36NW4 Bois Grenier	I 26 c 0.3 [1915]
Flambeau Trench	62bSW1 Gricourt	N 2 c, d, 8 b, 9 a
Flamborough Head [Oct 1915]	36cNW3 Loos	G 11 a, b
Flame Post	36SW1 Aubers	N 13 d
Flame Trench	36cSW3 Vimy	S 28 c
Flame Trench	62cNW2 Bouchavesnes	C 28 c, I 4 a
Flame, The	57cSW3 Longueval	N 25 c
Flamingo Trench	36cSW4 Rouvroy	U 13 d, 14 c, 20 a
Flanders Alley	66cNW1 Grugies	B 27 b, d, 28 c, H 4 a
Flange Trench	36cSW4 Rouvroy	U 13 b, 19 b
Flank Avenue	57cSW4 Combles	T 4 d, 5 c, 10 a, b
Flank Post	36SW1 Aubers	N 7 d, 8 c
Flank Post	36SW3 Richebourg	M 34 d 4.2
Flank Post [Le Bizet]	36NW2 Armentières	C 13 c, d
Flank Street	57dSE1 & 2 Beaumont	R 26 c, 31 b
Flanquement, Tranchée de	36cSW3 Vimy	S 8 d
Flap Trench	51bNW1 Roclincourt	A 22 b
Flapper O.P. [1917-18]	51bNW1 Roclincourt	B 8 d 0.4
Flapper Trench	36cSW3 Vimy	S 28 c
Flapper Trench [Flipo (Boyau)]	36cSW1 Lens	M 25 b
Flare Alley [Flers]	57dSE2 & 57cSW1 Le Sars	N 25 d, 26 c
Flare Front Line [1918]	57dNE2 & 57cNW1 Courcelles	F 16 d, 23 a
Flare Trench [1918]	57dNE2 & 57cNW1 Courcelles	F 16 d, 23 a
Flash [light rly locality E of Canal 1917-18]	28NW2 St Julien	C 13 a 8.7 and C14 a
Flash Cot.	28NW2 St Julien	C 14 a 2.6
Flash Junction [E of Canal, light rly]	28NW2 St Julien	C 14 a
Flash Trench	57cSW3 Longueval	S 6 b, d
Flat Farm	36SW3 Richebourg	S 29 d 53.10
Flat Line [light rly]	36cSW3 Vimy	S 6 b, c, d, 11 a, b, 12 a
Flatiron / Flat Iron Trench	57cSW3 Longueval	S 13 b, 14 a, b, d
Flatiron Copse	57cSW3 Longueval	S 14 c
Flatiron Wood	62bSW2 Fonsommes	N 11 a, b, c
Flatow Trench	62cNE3 Buire	J 1 d, 2 a, c
Flattened Farm [east of St Yvon]	28SW4 Ploegsteert	U 16 a 9.1
Flattened Road [road]	28SW4 Ploegsteert	U 15 d, 16 a, b, c
Flax Alley	28SW4 Ploegsteert	U 28 c
Flay Lane [part of Starfish Line]	57cSW3 Longueval	M 35 c, d, 36 c
Flea Alley	57cNE1 Quéant	E 26 d
Flea Alley	66cSW2 Vendeuil	O 10 d, 16 a, b
Flea Trench	57dSE2 & 57cSW1 Le Sars	N 31 b
Fleau Alley	62bSW1 Gricourt	M 5 d
Fleche Wood	62bSW1 Gricourt	N 3 a, c
Fleche Wood	62bSW1 Gricourt	N 3 a, c
Fleche, The	62cNW1 Maricourt	A 9 a
Fleeceall Lane	62cNE2 Epéhy	F 11 c
Fleeceall Post	62cNE2 Epéhy	F 11 b

Name	Map Sheet	Map Reference
Fleet Corner	28SW4 Ploegsteert	U 20 d, 21 c
Fleet Cott.	28NE1 Zonnebeke	D 10 a 3.3
Fleet Street	28NW2 St Julien	C 29 c
Fleet Street	36SW1 Aubers	N 13 a, c
Fleet Street	51cSE & 51bSW Ficheux	R 17, 18, 24, M 19
Fleet Street	62cNE2 Epéhy	F 17 b
Fleet Street [Hooge, 1915]	28NW4 & NE3 Zillebeke	I 18 b
Fleet Street [Ploegsteert Wood 1914-15]	28SW4 Ploegsteert	U 20 b, d, 21 c
Fleet Street [road]	36aSE4 Locon	W 11 a, b
Fleet Street [road]	57cSW3 Longueval	S 24 a, b, d
Fleet Trench	57dNE1 & 2 Fonquevillers	K 5 a
Fleming's Villa	28NW2 St Julien	C 28 c 35.92
Flemings Wood	28NW2 St Julien	C 10 b, 11 a
Flencque Ferme, la	36NW2 Armentières	C 14 d
Flenque [sic] Farm Post, la	36NW2 Armentières	C 14 b, d, 15 a, c
Flensburger Gang	51bNW1 Roclincourt	A 16 b, d
Flers [village]	57cSW1 Gueudecourt / 3 Longueval	M 36 b, d, N 31 a, c, S 6 b, T 1 a
Flers Avenue [sunken road]	57cSW3 Longueval	T 1 a, b
Flers Graben [Gap Trench]	57cSW3 Longueval	T 1 a, b, d, 2 c
Flers Line	57cSW1 Gueudecourt / 3 Longueval	M 23 c, 29 a, b, c, T 8 a
Flers Road [Sunken Road & trench]	57cSW3 Longueval	S 12 a
Flers Support	57dSE2 & 57cSW1 / 57cSW3	M 23 c, 29 a, b, c, 36 a, b, c, d
Flers Trench	57dSE2 & 57cSW1 / 57cSW3	M 23 c, 29 a, b, c, 36 a, b, c, d
Flêtre [village]	27SE4 Meteren	W 5 d, 6 a, c, 12 a
Fleurbaix Switch [1918]	36NW4 Bois Grenier	I 1, 2, 7, 13, 19
Fleurie Switch	36NW4 Bois Grenier	I 7 d, 13 b, d, 19 b
Fleury Trench	70dNW4 St Gobain	H 22 d
Flick Trench	36cSW3 Vimy	S 28 d
Flicker Trench	36cSW3 Vimy	S 30 b
Flicker Trench	36cSW4 Rouvroy	U 19 a, b, c
Flight Houses	28NE2 Moorslede	F 30 a 75.45
Flinders Support	57dSE2 & 57cSW1 Le Sars	N 20 d
Fling Trench	36cSW3 Vimy	S 30 b, d, T 25 a, b
Flinque Post, la	36SW1 Aubers	M 9 d
Flint Trench	36cSW3 Vimy	T 25 a
Flinte Copse	28NE1 Zonnebeke	D 29 b
Flinte Farm	28NE1 Zonnebeke	D 29 b 6.3
Flip Mill	28NE2 Moorslede	E 6 d 03.27
Flipo [Boyau] [Flapper Trench]	36cSW1 Lens	M 25 b
Flirt Trench	36cSW3 Vimy	S 28 d, 29 c
Flit Trench	36cSW3 Vimy	S 30 b, c, d
Flock Trench	36cSW3 Vimy	S 28 c
Flocon Trench	62bSW1 Gricourt	M 5 d, 11 b, 12 a
Flod Trench	36cSW2 Harnes	O 16 a
Flodden Lane [Calonne]	36cSW1 Lens	M 9 b
Flood Street	51cSE2 Beaumetz	R 22, 23, 29
Flood Street [road]	36aSE1 St Venant	Q 15 a, c
Flood Trench	36cSW3 Vimy	S 28 c
Flooded Land	36aNE3 Haverskerque	K 31 a, b
Flop Trench	51bNW1 Roclincourt	A 4 a
Flora [German strongpoint]	51bSW4 Bullecourt	U 7 d
Flora Cott.	28NE1 Zonnebeke	D 1 a 3.5
Flora Farm	28NE4 Dadizeele	L 34 c 05.60
Florand [sic] Siding [railway]	28NW1 Elverdinghe	B 14 c

Name	Map Sheet	Map Reference
Flore Trench	62cSW2 Barleux	N 29 a, c
Flore, Tranchée de	62cSW1 & 2 Belloy	N 29 a, c
Florence [farm]	27NE2 Proven	E 12 d 6.6
Florence Post	36NW4 Bois Grenier	I 15 b
Florend Farm	28NW1 Elverdinghe	B 13 b 3.4
Florin House	28NE4 Dadizeele	L 22 a 55.90
Florina Trench	62cNW4 Péronne	I 19 d, 20 a, b, c
Floss Farm	36aNE4 Merville	L 20 c 7.0
Flossie Post	36NW4 Bois Grenier	I 15 b
Flossie Trench	36cSW4 Rouvroy	U 13 c, 19 a
Flot de Wingles [stream]	36cNW3 Loos	H 3, 8, 9, 13, 14
Flot Farm	57bNW3 Rumilly	G 7 d 6.1
Flounce Trench	57cSW4 Combles	T 17 a, b, d
Flow Trench	36cSW3 Vimy	S 24 c, d
Flow Trench	51bNW1 Roclincourt	A 22 b
Flower Trench	36cSW3 Vimy	S 24 c
Flox House	28NE1 Zonnebeke	D 20 b 75.95
Fluff / Fluffy Trench	57cSW4 Combles	T 4 c, 10 a
Fluffy Trench	36cSW3 Vimy	S 30 b
Flume Copse	62bSW2 Fonsommes	N 4 d, 5 c, 10 b
Flume Trench	36cSW3 Vimy	S 30 b
Flung Trench	36cSW3 Vimy	S 24 c, d
Flung Trench	36cSW3 Vimy	S 30 b
Flunky Trench	51bNW1 Roclincourt	A 4 b
Flurry Trench	36cSW3 Vimy	S 30 b
Flurry Trench	51bNW2 Oppy	B 24 d
Fluster Trench	36cSW3 Vimy	S 30 d
Flute Farm	28NE4 Dadizeele	L 26 b 5.9
Flute Trench	36cSW3 Vimy	S 30 b
Flute Trench	62bNW3 Bellicourt / SW1 Gricourt	G 33 d, 34 c, M 4 a, b, 5 c
Flux Trench	36cSW3 Vimy	S 30 b
Fluxion Trench	62bSW2 Fonsommes	N 10 d
Fly Alley	57cNE2 Bourlon	K 4 b
Fly Buildings	28SW2 Wytschaete	O 23 b 65.95
Fly Trench	51bNW1 Roclincourt	A 4 a
Flycatcher Post	57cSE4 Villers-Guislain	X 29 a. b
Foal Copse	62bNW2 Brancourt-le-Grand	C 8 b, d
Foal Trench	51bSW2 Vis-en-Artois	O 2 b, d
Fob Trench	57dNE1 & 2 Fonquevillers	E 28 b
Focal Trench	36cSW2 Harnes	O 9 c, d, 15 b
Foch Alley, General [1918]	62dSE [4 Harbonnières]	R 34 d, 35 c, d, X 5 b, 6 a
Foch Avenue	57dSE1 & 2 Beaumont	Q 23 b
Foch Farm	20NW4 Dixmude	I 33 a 3.7
Foch Farm	28NW2 St Julien	C 20 d 15.90
Foch Trench [1918]	57cNW1 Gomiecourt	A 8 b, 9 a
Focus Farm	27NE2 Proven	L 1 a 75.65
Focus Trench	36cSW2 Harnes	O 9 d, 10 c, 16 a
Focus Trench	57dNE1 & 2 Fonquevillers	E 28 c, K 4 a
Fodder Trench	36cSW2 Harnes	O 9 d
Fodder Trench	51bNW1 Roclincourt	A 4 a
Foe Trench	57dNE1 & 2 Fonquevillers	E 28 d
Foerster Weg	51bNW1 Roclincourt	B 19 a
Foggy Trench	36cSW2 Harnes	O 9 d, 10 c, 15 b
Foggy Trench	36cSW3 Vimy	S 28 c

Name	Map Sheet	Map Reference
Foggy Trench	51bNW2 Oppy	B 24 d
Foggy Trench	57cSW4 Combles	T 4 b, 5 a, c
Foil Trench	36cSW2 Harnes	O 10 c, d
Fokker Farm [& pillboxes]	28NE1 Zonnebeke	D 14 a 4.3
Fokker Trench	62cSE1 Bouvincourt	P 7 c, 13 a
Folie Ferme, la	36cSW3 Vimy	S 29 a
Folie, Bois de la	36cSW3 Vimy	S 23 c
Folies, les [farm]	57bSW4 Serain	U 19 d 4.8
Folk Trench	57dNE1 & 2 Fonquevillers	E 28 b, d
Follow Trench	51bNW1 Roclincourt	A 4 b
Folly Lane	51cSE2 Beaumetz	R 22 d, 28 b, 29 a, c
Folly Quarry	66cNW4 Berthenicourt	H 17 d
Folly Trench	51bNW2 Oppy	B 24 d
Folly Trench	57cSW3 Longueval	S 17 c, d, 23 b
Folly Trench	57dNE1 & 2 Fonquevillers	E 28 b
Folly Trench	57dSE2 & 57cSW1 Le Sars	R 16 a
Folly Trench	51bNW2 Oppy	B 28 c, H 4 a
Folly, The [house]	66cNW4 Berthenicourt	H 17 b 6.7
Folus Trench	36cSW2 Harnes	O 9 d
Fonches [village]	66dNW3 Hattencourt	G 5, 6, 11, 12
Fonchette [village]	66dNW1 Punchy / 3 Hattencourt	G 9 b, d
Fonck Cottages	27NE1 Herzeele	E 26 d 6.7
Foncregoed Farm	20SE3 Westroosebeke	V 11 c 4.1
Fond Trench	51bNW1 Roclincourt	A 22 b
Fonquevillers [village]	57dNE1 & 2 Fonquevillers	E 21, 27
Fonquevillers Brewery	57dNE1 & 2 Fonquevillers	E 21 d
Fonquevillers Cemetery	57dNE1 & 2 Fonquevillers	E 27 a
Fonquevillers Gendarmerie	57dNE1 & 2 Fonquevillers	E 21 b
Fonquevillers Switch [1918]	57dNE [1 Fonquevillers] / [3 Hébuterne]	E 26 c, d, K 1 a, b, c, 2 a
Fonsommes [village]	62bSW2 Fonsommes	O 16 b, 17 a, b, c
Font Copse	62bSW2 Fonsommes	O 2 c
Font Farm	28NE2 Moorslede	F 25 d 1.7
Font Trench	57cSW1 Gueudecourt	M 30 d, 36 a, b, N 25 c
Fontaine Houck [hamlet & cross roads]	27SE4 Meteren	X 4 c
Fontaine Trench	51bSW2 Vis-en-Artois / 4 Bullecourt	O 32 a, c, U 1 b, 2 a
Fontaine Trench	66cNW1 Grugies	A 13 d, 14 c, d, 15 c, d
Fontaine Trench	66cSW1 Remigny / 2 Vendeuil	N 4 c, 10 b
Fontaine Wood	51bSW4 Bullecourt	U 2 a, b
Fontaine, la [hamlet]	51bNE4 Cantin	L 30 c, 36 a
Fontaine-le-Clercs [village]	66cNW1 Grugies	A 14 d, 15 c, d, 20 b, 21 a
Fontaine-lez-Croisilles [village]	51bSW4 Bullecourt	U 2 a, c, d, 8 a
Fontaines [hamlet]	27SE2 Berthen	R 14 d 3.2
Fontaines, les [farm]	27SE2 Berthen	R 30 a 8.7
Fontaine-Uterte [village]	62bNW4 Ramicourt	I 32 d, 33 c, O 2 b, 3 a
Fontenay Trench	62cNW2 Bouchavesnes	C 26 b
Fontenille Trench	66cNW1 Grugies / 2 Itancourt	B 10 c, 15 a
Food Trench	51bNW1 Roclincourt	A 22 b
Food Trench	57dNE1 & 2 Fonquevillers	E 23 c, 29 a
Fool Trench	51bNW1 Roclincourt	A 22 b
Fool Trench	57dNE1 & 2 Fonquevillers	E 28 b
Foolery Trench	57dNE1 & 2 Fonquevillers	E 28 c, d
Fooley Lane	51bSW4 Bullecourt	T 5 a
Fools Lane	28SW4 Ploegsteert	U 20 d, 21 c
Fools Path [CT, Sept 1915]	36SW3 Richebourg	M 35 c, S 5 a

Name	Map Sheet	Map Reference
Foolscap Copse	51bSE3 Cagnicourt	V 28 d
Fooly Lane	51bSW4 Bullecourt	T 5 b
Foot Alley	51bNW2 Oppy	C 1 b, c, d, 2 a
Foot Hill	51bNW2 Oppy	C 1 b, c, d, 2 a, b
Foot Trench	57dNE1 & 2 Fonquevillers	E 28 b, 29 a
Football Crater	36cSW3 Vimy	S 8 b
Football Trench	57cSE4 Villers-Guislain	X 13 c, d. 19 a
Football Trench [British front line 3/16]	36cSW1 Lens	M 9 d, 15 b
Fop Lane	51bSW4 Bullecourt	U 1 c
Fop Trench	36cSW3 Vimy	S 28 c
Fop Trench	51bNW1 Roclincourt	A 22 b
Forage Alley	57dSE2 & 57cSW1 Le Sars	N 19 d, 20 a, c
Forage Trench	57dNE1 & 2 Fonquevillers	E 29 b, d
Foray Post	36NW4 Bois Grenier	H 35 c, d
Forbes Trench	36cSW2 Harnes	O 9 b
Forbes Wood	62dSE [1 Hamel]	Q 14 a, b
Force Farm	27NE1 Herzeele	E 25 c 0.9
Force Trench	57dNE1 & 2 Fonquevillers	E 29 a
Ford [east of Serain]	57bSW4 Serain	U 16 d 90.33
Ford Dump	62cSW3 Vermandovillers	S 20 b 3.6
Ford Lane [Calonne]	36cSW1 Lens	M 9 b
Ford Lane [road]	36aSE4 Locon	W 5 a, d, 11 b
Ford Row	51bNW2 Oppy	C 12 d
Ford Street	62cNE2 Epéhy	F 12 c
Ford Trench	51bNW1 Roclincourt	A 22 b
Ford Trench	57dNE1 & 2 Fonquevillers	E 28 c, d
Fore Trench	51bNW1 Roclincourt	A 22 b
Fore Trench	51bNW1 Roclincourt	A 4 b
Fore Trench	57dNE3 & 4 Hébuterne	K 17 a, c
Foreats Trench	62bSW1 Gricourt	M 5 c, d, 11 b, 12 a, c
Foregate Street [Cuinchy]	36cNW1 La Bassée	A 21 b
Forehead Trench	57dNE1 & 2 Fonquevillers	E 29 a, c
Foreign Trench	51bNW1 Roclincourt	A 4 b, d
Foreign Trench	57dNE1 & 2 Fonquevillers	E 29 a
Forencille [hamlet]	57bNW3 Rumilly	H 8 c
Foresight Trench	57dNE1 & 2 Fonquevillers	E 29 a, b
Forest Alley	36cSW1 Lens	M 19 d, 25 b
Forest Alley [Dubois, Tranchée]	36bSE2 Boyeffles / 36cSW1 Lens	R 30 a, M 19 d, 25 b
Forest Corner [road jct, Nieppe Forest]	36aNE3 Haverskerque	J 23 a 1.5
Forest Hill	36bSE2 Boyeffles	R 30 a
Forest Hill Alley	36cSW1 Lens	M 25 b, d
Forest Hill Lane [road]	36cSW1 Lens	M 29 b, c, d, 30 a
Forest Road [road]	28NE3 Gheluvelt	J 26 c
Forest Street	51cSE & 51bSW Ficheux	R 27 c, d, 28 c
Forest Trench	36cNW3 Loos	H 25 b, d
Forest Trench [Bazentin-le-Petit Wood]	57cSW3 Longueval	S 7 d, 8 c, 14 a
Forest Wood, Le	62cNW2 Bouchavesnes	B 16 a, b, 17 a
Forest, Le [village]	62cNW2 Bouchavesnes	B 10 d, 16 b
Foreste Aerodrome [German, 1918]	66dNE [2 Roupy]	F 15 a
Foresters Home [later named Casa Pin]	36aNE3 Haverskerque	J 8 d 72.01
Foresters House [later named Palazzon]	36aNE3 Haverskerque	J 11 c 1.6
Foresters Lane	36SW3 Richebourg	S 3 d, 4 a
Foresters Post	28SW2 Wytschaete	O 21 d
Forestier / Forrestier Redoubt	51bNW3 Arras	G 17 a

Name	Map Sheet	Map Reference
Forestier Trench	62bSW1 Gricourt	M 17 b, 18 a
Forestry Trench	57cSW4 Combles	U 26 c, d
Forêt, le [hamlet]	36aNE3 Haverskerque	J 25 central
Foreway Camp	28NW1 Elverdinghe	A 3 b 9.5
Forez Trench	66cNW1 Grugies / 2 Itancourt	B 16 a, b, d
Forfait Alley	62bSW1 Gricourt	M 12 c, 17 b
Forgans Trench	62bSW1 Gricourt	M 4 a
Forgate Street	57dNE3 & 4 Hébuterne	K 34 b
Forgatt Alley	62bSW1 Gricourt	M 12 c
Forge Trench	51bNW1 Roclincourt	A 4 a
Forger Trench	66cNW2 Itancourt	B 18 c
Forges Trench	51bNW1 Roclincourt	A 10 c
Fork Alley	57cSW3 Longueval / 4 Combles	T 3 b, 4 a
Fork Avenue	57cNE4 Marcoing	L 26 d, 27 c, 32 b
Fork Redoubt	51bNW1 Roclincourt	A 15 a, b
Fork Trench	57dNE1 & 2 Fonquevillers	E 28 b
Fork Trench	57dNE3 & 4 Hébuterne	L 8 c, 13 b, 14 a
Fork Wood	57dNE3 & 4 Hébuterne	L 8 d
Fork, The	57cSW3 Longueval	T 7 b, 8 a
Forked Tree [Arbre Fourche, trig point]	62dNE2 Méaulte	L 2 b 02.92
Form Trench	57dNE1 & 2 Fonquevillers	E 29 a
Formby Farm	28NW1 Elverdinghe	G 5 b 5.3
Forrard Trench	51bSW2 Vis-en-Artois	O 32 a
Forres Street [Thiepval Wood]	57dSE1 & 2 Beaumont	Q 30 b, c, d
Forres Trench	36cSW2 Harnes	O 3 d, 4 c
Forrester Camp	28NW4 Ypres	I 25 a 1.1
Forrester Lane	28NW4 & NE3 Zillebeke	I 18 a
Forresters Lane	36SW3 Richebourg	S 3 d
Forret Farm	28SW2 Wytschaete	O 11 b 2.1
Forster Weg	51bNW1 Roclincourt	B 19 c
Forsyth Farm	28SW3 Bailleul	S 5 d 8.7
Fort 147	51cSE3 & 4 Ransart	W 16 b
Fort A	51bNW1 Roclincourt	A 21 b, d, 22 a, c
Fort Anley	57dSE1 & 2 Beaumont	Q 15 central
Fort B	51bNW1 Roclincourt	A 5 d
Fort Bell	62cNE4 Roisel	L 28 c 3.2
Fort Bismarck	36NW2 Armentières	C 12 c 2.1
Fort Boyd [Pl. Wd '14-15; SW of 3 Huns Fm]	28SW4 Ploegsteert	U 21 b 0.8
Fort Brandon [Hill 63]	28SW4 Ploegsteert	T 18 a 1.9
Fort Briggs	57dNE3 & 4 Hébuterne	K 22 d
Fort Briggs [Hill 63]	28SW4 Ploegsteert	U 13 c 10.63
Fort Buildings	28SW2 Wytschaete	O 18 d 65.90
Fort Caledonia	28NW2 St Julien	C 15 a
Fort Calgary	28SW2 Wytschaete	N 23 a 2.2 / O 23 a 2.2
Fort Clissold [Hill 63]	28SW4 Ploegsteert	T 18 b 05.20
Fort Cognac [Hill 63]	28SW4 Ploegsteert	T 18 b 5.2
Fort Cox	57dNE1 & 2 Fonquevillers	E 16 a
Fort de Liez	66cSW3 Tergnier	N 34 c
Fort d'Esquin	36SW1 Aubers	M 10 d
Fort Dick	57dNE3 & 4 Hébuterne	K 2 d
Fort Dyce	62cNE4 Roisel	L 34 a 4.7
Fort Eberle [Hill 63]	28SW4 Ploegsteert	T 18 a 8.6
Fort Edward	28SW2 Wytschaete	N 34 b 3.9
Fort Egal	36NW4 Bois Grenier	I 4 c

Name	Map Sheet	Map Reference
Fort Egal Evenue	36NW4 Bois Grenier	I 3 d, 4 c, d, 10 b
Fort Emma [Emma Post]	36NW4 Bois Grenier	I 31 a
Fort Estel Farm	51bSE2 Oisy-le-Verger	Q 6 a
Fort Garry [1917-18]	28NE3 Gheluvelt	J 14 a 03.02
Fort Garston S.P.	28SW2 Wytschaete	O 22 a, b
Fort Glatz [Sept 1915]	36cNW3 Loos	G 29 c, d
Fort Greathead [W edge of Le Verguier]	62cNE4 Roisel	L 34 a 5.0
Fort Grosvenor	57dNE3 & 4 Hébuterne	K 21 a
Fort Halifax	28SW2 Wytschaete	N 17 c 73.00
Fort Hector [1918]	57dNE3 & 4 Hébuterne	K 10 c
Fort Helen [1918]	57dNE3 & 4 Hébuterne	K 9 c
Fort Henry [1918]	57dNE3 & 4 Hébuterne	K 15 b
Fort Herod [1918]	57dNE3 & 4 Hébuterne	K 14 a
Fort Hill	28NW2 St Julien	C 18 b
Fort Hod [1918]	57dNE3 & 4 Hébuterne	K 21 a
Fort Horace [1918]	57dNE3 & 4 Hébuterne	K 19 a, b
Fort Horsted	57dNE3 & 4 Hébuterne	K 34 c
Fort Hugh [1918]	57dNE3 & 4 Hébuterne	K 10 d
Fort Jackson	57dSE1 & 2 Beaumont	Q 16 d, 22 b
Fort Lees [W edge of Le Verguier]	62cNE4 Roisel	L 33 b 8.3 / L 34 a 5.7
Fort Lindsay	28SW4 Ploegsteert	T 6 d
Fort Marie Louise	57dNE3 & 4 Hébuterne	K 16 c, 22 a
Fort Marshall [Hill 63]	28SW4 Ploegsteert	T 11 d 75.42
Fort Mayot Alley	66cSW2 Vendeuil	O 16 d, 17 c, 23 a, b, d, 24 c
Fort McLeod [1918]	28NE3 Gheluvelt	J 14 a, b
Fort Moulin	57dSE1 & 2 Beaumont	Q 21 b
Fort Mount Royal	28SW2 Wytschaete	N 23 a 2.5
Fort Osborne	28SW4 Ploegsteert	T 6 d 9.8
Fort Osborne Barracks	28SW4 Ploegsteert	U 1 c
Fort Paul	36NW2 Armentières	C 4 a
Fort Pinkie	28SW4 Ploegsteert	T 5 b, 6 a
Fort Prowse	57dSE1 & 2 Beaumont	Q 21 d, 27 b
Fort Raddel	28SW4 Ploegsteert	U 8 c
Fort Redoubt	51bNW1 Roclincourt	A 15 a
Fort Regina	28SW2 Wytschaete	N 28 a 8.5
Fort Rompu	36NW1 Steenwerck	A 17 a 55.20
Fort Rompu	36NW3 Fleurbaix	H 7 d 6.3
Fort Saskachewan	28SW2 Wytschaete	N 22 d 4.4
Fort Simmons [Hill 63]	28SW4 Ploegsteert	T 18 d 72.94
Fort Southdown [Fort Wagram]	57dNE3 & 4 Hébuterne	K 21 c
Fort Steel / Steele Dugouts	28NW4 & NE3 Zillebeke	J 8 d 4.3
Fort Stein	57dSE2 & 57cSW1 Le Sars	M 4 a, b, 5 a, b
Fort Stewart [1918]	57dNE3 & 4 Hébuterne	K 20 a, b
Fort Street	28NW4 & NE3 Zillebeke	I 24 b, d
Fort Toronto	28SW2 Wytschaete	N 11 a 35.33
Fort Tosh	36cNW3 Loos	G 36 a
Fort Trench	57dNE1 & 2 Fonquevillers	E 29 a
Fort Trench [Flers]	57cSW3 Longueval	M 36 d, N 31 c
Fort Vauban	20SW4 Bixschoote	T 29 b
Fort Vendeuil	66cSW2 Vendeuil	N 18 c
Fort Vendeuil Redoubt	66cSW2 Vendeuil	N 23 b, d, 24 a
Fort Victoria	28SW2 Wytschaete	N 28 c 1.3 / N 28 c 2.6
Fort Wagram [Fort Southdown]	57dNE3 & 4 Hébuterne	K 21 c
Fort Walter [E of Ploegsteert Wood]	28SW4 Ploegsteert	U 21 d

Name	Map Sheet	Map Reference
Fort Wiltington / Withington	57dSE1 & 2 Beaumont	Q 15 c
Fortait Alley	62bSW1 Gricourt	M 12 c, 17 a
Fortes Street [Thiepval Wood]	57dSE1 & 2 Beaumont	Q 30 b, d, R 25 a
Fortified Road [road & trench, S of Guillemont]	57cSW3 Longueval	T 25 a, c
Fortifs Alley	66cSW2 Vendeuil	O 8 d, 9 c
Fortin 17 [German front line, 1915]	28NW2 St Julien	C 7 c 6.8
Fortin Avenue	20SW4 Bixschoote	T 29 b, 30 a
Fortin House	20SW4 Bixschoote	T 29 b
Fortina Trench	66cNW1 Grugies	A 12 c
Fortress Trench	57dNE1 & 2 Fonquevillers	E 29 c
Fortuin [hamlet]	28NW2 St Julien	C 18 b
Fortune Trench	57dNE1 & 2 Fonquevillers	E 29 b
Fortune, la [Bailleul suburb]	28SW3 Bailleul	S 20 c
Forward Alley	36bSE4 Carency	X 12 a
Forward Cottage [New Cot]	28NW2 St Julien	C 21 b 8.5
Forward Farm	36aSE1 St Venant	Q 14 c 95.40
Forward Farm	36aSE1 St Venant	Q 26 d 20.65
Forward Trench	28NW2 St Julien	C 21 b, 22 a
Foss Lane	51bSW1 Neuville Vitasse	N 8 c, d
Fosse [hamlet]	36aSE2 Lestrem	R 22 a
Fosse [village]	36aSE2 Lestrem	R 21 b, 22 a
Fosse 1 de Liévin	36cSW1 Lens	M 22 c, d
Fosse 1 de Noeux, dite de Bracquement	36bNE4 Noeux-les-Mines	L 19 b, d
Fosse 10	36bSE2 Boyeffles	R 2 d 4.4
Fosse 10	36cNW4 Pont-a-Vendin	H 24 a
Fosse 11 Road [road]	36cSW1 Lens	M 8 a, b, d, 9 b, d, 10 c
Fosse 2 de Azincourt, Shaft	51bNE4 Cantin	L 12 a 8.4
Fosse 2 de Liévin	36cSW1 Lens	M 15 c
Fosse 3 de Lens	36cSW1 Lens	M 22 b
Fosse 3 de Noeux [conical dump]	36bNE4 Noeux-les-Mines	L 20 a 3.7
Fosse 3 de Noeux [flat-topped dump]	36bNE4 Noeux-les-Mines	L 13 d, 14 c
Fosse 4 de Béthune	36cNW3 Loos	G 9 c
Fosse 5 de Béthune [dite de Loos]	36cSW1 Lens	M 3 central
Fosse 5 de Liévin	36cSW1 Lens	M 20 a
Fosse 6 de Noeux	36bNE4 Noeux-les-Mines	F 26 c, d
Fosse 7 de Béthune [mine installations]	36cNW3 Loos	G 27
Fosse 7 de Béthune [tip]	36cNW3 Loos	G 27 c, d, 33 a, b
Fosse 7 Defences	36cNW3 Loos	G 27 b, d, 33 a, b
Fosse 7 Defences A [post]	36cNW3 Loos	G 33 a 3.3
Fosse 7 Defences B [post]	36cNW3 Loos	G 33 b 1.5
Fosse 7 Defences C [post]	36cNW3 Loos	G 27 d 3.3
Fosse 7 Defences D [post]	36cNW3 Loos	G 27 d 9.7
Fosse 7 Defences E [post]	36cNW3 Loos	G 27 b 2.0
Fosse 7 Junction [light rly]	36bSE1 [Hermin]	Q 2 d
Fosse 8	36cNW1 La Bassée	A 29 c
Fosse 8 de Lens [1915]	36cNW4 Pont-à-Vendin	H 34 c, d
Fosse Alley	36cNW3 & 1 Loos	G 5 b, 6 a, c, d
Fosse C. T.	28SW2 Wytschaete	N 17 c, d
Fossé Corbonne [sunken road]	51bNW1 Roclincourt	A 3 a
Fosse Delloy	51bNE2 Dechy	F 29 a, c
Fosse Labarre [moated enclosure; Ploeg. Wd]	28SW4 Ploegsteert	U 19 d 8.8
Fosse Lane [road]	36aSE2 Lestrem	R 20 b, c, d, 21 a, b
Fosse No.1 [Vimy]	36cSW3 Vimy	S 18 d
Fosse No.9 [Annequin]	36bNE2 Beuvry	F 29 c 35.20

Name	Map Sheet	Map Reference
Fosse Post	36aSE2 Lestrem	R 22 a, b
Fosse Post	62cNE4 Roisel	L 18 c 1.5
Fosse Post / Fosse Way Post	28NW4 & NE3 Zillebeke	I 29 d 65.80
Fosse Roucourt	51bNE2 Dechy	F 27 c, d
Fosse Trench	36cNW1 La Bassée	A 28 d, G 4 b
Fosse Way	28NW4 & NE3 Zillebeke	I 21 d - 29 d
Fosse Way	57cSW3 Longueval	T 1 d
Fosse Way [Sept 1915]	36cNW3 Loos	G 10 c, d, 15 b, 16 a
Fosse Wood	62bNW3 Bellicourt	H 20 c, d, 26 a, b
Fosse Wood	66dNW3 Hattencourt	G 17 d
Fosse Wood [1917; Square Wood in 1916]	28NW4 & NE3 Zillebeke	I 29 b
Fosse, The [CT]	28SW2 Wytschaete	N 16 d
Fossés Farm, les	51bSW2 Vis-en-Artois	N 11 b 95.40
Fosseway Alley	57cSW3 Longueval	T 1 b
Fossil Trench	51bNW4 Fampoux	I 26 c, d
Foster Avenue	51bSW2 Vis-en-Artois	N 23 d, 29 b, 30 a, b, d, O 25 c, d
Foster Camp	28NW3 Poperinghe	H 1 c
Foster Lane [trench]	57cSE2 Gonnelieu	R 20 d, 21 c
Foster Sap	57cSE2 Gonnelieu	R 20 d 45.20
Foster Trench	51bSW2 Vis-en-Artois	O 25 d
Fou Wood	66eNW [2 Thennes]	B 5 c
Foucard Trench	66cNW1 Grugies / 2 Itancourt	B 15 b, 16 a, c
Foul Street	51cSE & 51bSW Ficheux	R 28 b, d, 29 c
Fount Trench	57dNE1 & 2 Fonquevillers	E 28 b, c, d
Fountain Alley	36cNW3 & 1 Loos	G 1 d, 2 c, d
Fountain Keep [N of Vermelles]	36cNW3 Loos	G 2 c
Fouquescourt [village]	66eNE4 Beaufort	L 11, 12
Fouquières Maze	36cSW2 Harnes	O 20 a
Fouquières Trench	36cSW2 Harnes	O 20 c
Fouquières-les-Béthune [village]	36bNE2 Beuvry	E 15 c, 20 b, 21 a
Four a Chaux [farm]	20SW4 Bixschoote	T 6 a 8.2
Four Hundred, The [Cuinchy; OP, fortif. house]	36cNW1 La Bassée	A 20 d
Four Sheaves Wood	62cSW4 St. Christ	U 10 d, 16 b
Four Stones [S of Canal opposite Bluff]	28SW2 Wytschaete	O 4 a
Four Winds Farm [Quatre Vents]	57cSE3 Sorel-le-Grand	P 31 c 9.7
Fourche Alley	62cSW3 Vermandovillers	T 9 d, 10 c, 16 a
Fourche Farm	20SW4 Bixschoote	U 20 c 9.3
Fourche Trench	62cSW2 Barleux	O 8 b, 9 a
Fourche Trench, de la	51bNW1 Roclincourt	A 3 b, 4 a
Fourche, Boyau	62cSW1 Dompierre	M 4 d
Fourche, Tranchée de la	62cSW1 & 2 Belloy	O 8 b, d, 9 a, 14 b
Foureaux-Riegel [Switch Trench]	57cSW3 Longueval	S 6 c, d, T 1 c
Fourmi Trench	62bSW1 Gricourt	M 3 a, c, d
Fourmi, Tranchée de la	66dNW2 Morchain	B 18 d, 24 b
Fourmoy Alley	62bSW1 Gricourt / 62cSE2 Vermand	M 14 c, d, 15 a, b, c, 19 b, R 18 c, 24 a
Fournaise Alley	62cSW2 Barleux	N 29 a, b, d
Fournaise, Boyau de la	62cSW1 & 2 Belloy	N 29 a, b, d, 30 c
Fournier, Boyau	62cSW1 Dompierre	M 10 d
Fours a Coke [1915]	36cNW4 Pont-à-Vendin	H 34 d
Fourteen Trees Post	36NW3 Fleurbaix	H 19 c
Fourth Avenue / Ganter Weg [NE of Ovillers]	57dSE4 Ovillers	R 33 d, 34 c, X 3 a, b
Fourth Street	57dSE4 Ovillers	X 2 b, d, 8 b, d, 9 c, 15 b
Fous Alley	62bSW1 Gricourt	M 6 b
Fous, Tranchée des	62cSW1 & 2 Belloy	N 23 b, d

Name	Map Sheet	Map Reference
Fowl Trench	57dNE1 & 2 Fonquevillers	E 29 a
Fowl Wood	66cNW3 Essigny / 4 Berthenicourt	H 15 d, 16 c, 21 b, 22 a
Fowl-house, The [building]	20SW4 Bixschoote	T 17 d 4.9
Fox Copse	57bSW1 Bantouzelle	M 23 d, 29 a
Fox Cover and Berthonval Locality	36bSE4 Carency	X 22, 23, 29
Fox Farm	57bSW1 Bantouzelle	M 22 c 7.7
Fox Lane	57dSE2 & 57cSW1 Le Sars	M 36 a
Fox Street	51cSE & 51bSW Ficheux	R 28 c, d
Fox Support	51bSW4 Bullecourt	U 28 b
Fox Trench	51bNW1 Roclincourt	A 22 b
Fox Trench	51bSW1 Neuville Vitasse	M 16 b, 17 a
Fox Trench	51bSW2 Vis-en-Artois	O 2 d, 3 c, d
Fox Trench	57dNE1 & 2 Fonquevillers	E 23 c, 29 a
Fox Trench [1918]	57dNE2 & 57cNW1 Courcelles	F 16 a, b, c
Fox Trot Lane	51bSW4 Bullecourt	U 22 d, 28 b
Fox, Saillant, & Tranchée du	70dSW [2 Coucy-le-Chateau / 4 Vauxaillon]	O 34 d
Foxbar Street [Thiepval Wood]	57dSE1 & 2 Beaumont	R 25 c
Foxglove Farms	28SW3 Bailleul	S 5 c 8.3
Foxy Alley	51bNW2 Oppy	B 24 c, d, 30 b, C 25 a
Foxy Trench	51bNW2 Oppy	B 24 c, d, 30 a
Fracas Alley	62bSW2 Fonsommes	N 5 c, 10 b, d
Frail Trench	51bNW1 Roclincourt	A 4 d
Fraises Trench	62bSW1 Gricourt	N 1 c
Fram Farm	28NW1 Elverdinghe	B 25 b 7.2
Fram Trench	51bNW1 Roclincourt	A 4 a, b
Framework, The [German, 1916-17, Hénin Hill]	51bSW3&4 Croisilles	T 5 a 04.55
France [Trench]	36cSW3 Vimy	S 27 a
France Alley	66cNW1 Grugies / 2 Itancourt	B 22, 26, 27, 28, H 1, 2
Frances / Francis Avenue	62dNE2 Méaulte	F 11 d, 12 c, 18 a
Francilly-Selency Redoubt	62bSW3 St Quentin	S 5 a, b
Francis Street	51cSE & 51bSW Ficheux	R 23 d
Francis Street	51cSE3 & 4 Ransart	W 23 a, b
Francois [Tranchée]	62cSW1 & 2 Belloy	N 12 d
Francois Farm	28NW2 St Julien	C 4 c 5.4
Francois Trench	66cNW4 Berthenicourt	I 25 b
François Trench	62cSW2 Barleux	N 2 d
Frankfort / Frankfurt Trench	57dNE3 & 4 Hébuterne / SE1 & 2 Beaumont	K 36 c, Q 6 a, b, c
Frankfort Trench [1918]	66eNW [2 Thennes / 4 Morisel]	H 6 a, b, d
Franklin Farm	27NE3 Winnezeele	K 1 c 75.48
Franklin Trench	62bSW3 St Quentin	S 29 c, d
Franks Keep	36cNW1 La Bassée	A 22 c
Franks Keep [Sept 1915]	36cNW1 La Bassée	A 22 a 0.2
Frankton [light rly locality, 1917-18]	28NW4 Ypres	H 17 d, 18 c
Franque Wood	57bSW3 Honnecourt	S 8 c, d, 14 a, b
Franqueville [suburb of Honnecourt]	57bSW3 Honnecourt	S 7 d, 8 c, 13 b
Fransart [village]	66dNW3 Hattencourt	G 8, 9, 14, 15
Fransart Wood	66dNW3 Hattencourt	G 8 d
Fransart, Boyau de	66dNW3 Hattencourt	G 1 d, 2 c
Franz Alley	62cNW1 Maricourt	A 11 a, c
Frappier Trench	57dNE3 & 4 Hébuterne	K 17 c
Frascati [house]	28NW2 St Julien	C 26 c 7.6
Frascati Camp [1917-18]	28NW2 St Julien	C 26 central
Fraser Post	57dSE2 & 57cSW1 Le Sars	R 29 a 9.1
Fraser Trench	57cSW3 Longueval	S 4 d, 10 b

Name	Map Sheet	Map Reference
Fraser, Tranchée du	62cSW1 & 2 Belloy	N 29 c, d
Fraudeur Trench	62bSW1 Gricourt / 2 Fonsommes	N 9 d, 10 c
Fraudeurs Trench	62bSW2 Fonsommes	N 16 a, c
Freak Crossing [bridge / level crossing]	28NE2 Moorslede	F 8 d 45.65
Frean Houses	28NE4 Dadizeele	K 16 a 5.5
Freckles Wood	62cNW4 Péronne	I 7 c, 13 a
Freddy Maze	36cSW2 Harnes	O 20 a
Freddy Street	57dNE3 & 4 Hébuterne	K 34 d
Frederic [sic] Trench	62bSW3 St Quentin / 66cNW1 Grugies	T 25 d / B 1 b, 2 a, c
Frederick Trench	66dNW1 Punchy	A 21 a, c
Frederick's Copse	66dNW1 Punchy	A 15 c, 21 a
Fred's Wood	51bNW3 Arras	H 19 a
Freezing Trench	51bNW1 Roclincourt	A 5 b, d
Fregate Trench	62cSW2 Barleux	N 29 c, 35 a
Fregate, Tranchée de la	62cSW1 & 2 Belloy	N 29 c, 35 a
Frégicourt [hamlet]	57cSW4 Combles	T 30 a
Frelon Trench	62bSW1 Gricourt	N 1 c, 8 a, b, d, 9 c
Fremicourt [village]	57cNW4 Beugny	I 19 c, 25 a, b, 26 a
French Alley	36cNW3 Loos	G 14 b, 15 a, c, d
French Domart Wood	62dSW [4 Cachy]	U 19 b, 20 a, b, d
French Farm	28NW4 Ypres	I 27 a 7.7
French Farm [Givenchy, April 1915]	36cNW1 La Bassée	A 2 / 8
French Farm [later called Turco Farm]	28NW2 St Julien	C 15 c 2.4
French Post	36cSW3 Vimy	S 3 d
French Street	28NW4 & NE3 Zillebeke	I 18 b
French Street	51cSE2 Beaumetz	R 23 a, c, 29 b
French Street [Thiepval Wood]	57dSE1 & 2 Beaumont	Q 36 b
French Trench	28NW4 & NE3 Zillebeke	I 32 c, d, 33 c
French Trench	28SW2 Wytschaete	N 29 b, d
Frenchman's Farm [Pond Farm]	28SW2 Wytschaete	N 34 b 80.35
Frenois, Boyau	62cSW3 & 4 Marchélepot	T 9 d, 10 c
Frensham Trench	57cSE2 Gonnelieu	R 19 d, 20 c
Fresh Egg Trench	57dNE3 & 4 Hébuterne	K 34 d
Fresh Wood	66dNW1 Punchy	A 14 d, 15 c
Freshwater Wood	20SE2 Hooglede	Q 29 a 1.5
Fresnes [village]	62cSW3 & 4 Marchélepot	T 9, 10
Fresnes, Tranchée de	70dSW [2 Coucy-le-Château]	O 8 b
Fresnes-les-Montauban [village]	51bNW2 Oppy	C 22 c, d, 28 a, b
Fresnois Alley	62cSW3 Vermandovillers	T 3 c, 9 a, b, d, 10 c, 16 a
Fresnoy [village]	36cSW4 Rouvroy / 51bNW2 Oppy	U 25 c, C 1 a
Fresnoy Alley	36cSW4 Rouvroy	T 30 d, U 25 a, b, c
Fresnoy Support	36cSW4 Rouvroy	U 19 c, 25 a, c
Fresnoy Trench	36cSW4 Rouvroy / 51bNW2 Oppy	T 24 b,d, U 19 c, 25 a,c, B 12 b,d, C 1a,c, 7 a
Fresnoy Trench	62bSW1 Gricourt	M 27 b, 28 c
Fresnoy Village Redoubt	62bSW1 Gricourt	M 27 b, 28 a
Fresnoy Wood	51bNW2 Oppy	C 1 a
Fresnoy-le-Grand [village]	62bNW4 Ramicourt	I 17 b, d, 18 a, b, c, d, 24 a, b, d
Fresnoy-le-Petit [Redoubt]	62bSW1 Gricourt	M 21 d, 27 b
Fresnoy-le-Petit [village]	62bSW1 Gricourt	M 27
Fresnoy-les-Roye [village]	66dNW3 Hattencourt	G 32, 33
Fret Trench	51bNW1 Roclincourt	A 22 b
Freunds [sap]	36cNW3 Loos	G 12 d 0.0
Frey Trench	51bSW1 Neuville Vitasse	M 11 a

Name	Map Sheet	Map Reference
Freya Battery	5SW1 Zeebrugge	N 8 c
Freyburg Farm	27NE1 Herzeele	E 26 b 8.8
Frezenberg [locality]	28NE1 Zonnebeke	D 25 c
Frezenberg Keep [1918]	28NE1 Zonnebeke	D 25 c
Frezenberg Ridge	28NE1 Zonnebeke	D 25, J 1
Friant Post [1918]	20SW4 Bixschoote	U 3 d 09.55
Friary Street	51cSE & 51bSW Ficheux	R 17, 18 c, 24 a, M 19 a
Fribourg Trench	62cSW2 Barleux	O 27 b, d, 28 a, c
Fribourg Trench	66cNW1 Grugies	B 2 c
Fribourg Trench [1918]	66eNW [4 Morisel]	H 35 c, d
Fricassee Alley	62bSW2 Fonsommes	N 10 a, d, 11 a, c, 16 b
Fricourt [village]	62dNE2 Méaulte	F 3 a, b, c, d
Fricourt Farm	57dSE4 Ovillers	X 28 c 25.75
Fricourt Trench	62dNE2 Méaulte	F 3 c, d, 9 b
Fricourt Wood	57dSE4 Ovillers / 62dNE2 Méaulte	X 27 d, 28 c, d, F 3 b, 4 a, b
Friction Trench	51bNW4 Fampoux	I 26 a, c, 32 c
Frida Post	57cNE3 Hermies	K 9 a
Friday Avenue	51bNW1 Roclincourt / 3 Arras	A 28, 29, G 4
Friday Copse	28NE2 Moorslede	E 28 c 0.3
Fried Egg Crater	36cSW1 Lens	M 6 c
Frieda Trench	36SW1 Aubers	M 30 d, N 25 c, 31 a, b
Friedland Farm	28NW2 St Julien	B 24 a
Friedland Trench [1918]	66eNW [2 Thennes]	C 14 b, 15 a
Friedrich Lane	51bSW4 Bullecourt	T 5 b
Friendly Trench	57cSE2 Gonnelieu	R 20 a, b
Friesland [farm]	28NE1 Zonnebeke	D 11 a 7.9
Friesland Copse	28NE1 Zonnebeke	D 5 d
Frieze Alley	36cSW1 Lens	M 9 a, b
Frigate Work	62bSW1 Gricourt	M 5 c
Frigid Trench	51bNW2 Oppy	B 30 a, d
Frills Trench	51bNW1 Roclincourt	A 4 d
Frimley Trench	57cSE2 Gonnelieu	R 20 b, d, 21 c
Fringe Trench	51bNW1 Roclincourt	A 4 b, d
Fripons Trench	62bSW1 Gricourt / 2 Fonsommes	N 9 a, b, d, 10 d
Frisco Farm	36aNE2 Vieux Berquin	F 18 a 40.75
Frise [village]	62cNW3 Vaux	G 18, 24
Frise Trench	70dNW2 Servais	C 19 b, c, d
Frisk Trench	36cSW4 Rouvroy	T 30 b
Frisky Trench	51bNW2 Oppy	B 30 a
Fritter Trench	51bNW1 Roclincourt	A 5 a
Friture Trench	62bNW4 Ramicourt	O 2 b, 3 a
Fritz Alley / Avenue	57dNE3 & 4 Hébuterne	K 24 a, b, L 19 a
Fritz Cut	62cNW2 Bouchavesnes	C 10 c
Fritz Folly	57dSE2 & 57cSW1 Le Sars	N 20 d
Fritz Post	57cSE2 Gonnelieu	R 8 c 2.2
Fritz Redoubt [Oct 1915]	36cNW3 Loos	G 11 b, d
Fritz Structure [1918]	51bSW1 Neuville Vitasse	N 25 d 6.6
Fritz Trench	62cNW2 Bouchavesnes	C 10 c, 16 a
Fritz Trench	62dNE2 Méaulte	F 5 b, 6 a
Frivole Trench	62bSW1 Gricourt / 2 Fonsommes	N 9 b, 10 a
Frog Farm	27NE1 Herzeele	E 20 a 9.4
Frog Lane [Oct 1915]	36cNW3 Loos	G 10 d
Frog Post	62cNE4 Roisel	L 30 a 60.75
Frog Street	51cSE2 Beaumetz	R 23 b, d, 24 c

Name	Map Sheet	Map Reference
Frog Trench	51bNW1 Roclincourt	A 22 b
Frog Trench	51bNW1 Roclincourt	A 5 a
Froger Trench	51bNW1 Roclincourt	A 10 c
Froid Nid Farm	36NW1 Steenwerck	A 27 d 1.8
Froidmont [Nesle]	66dNW4 Nesle	I 19 d, 25 b
Froissy Beacon	62dNE [4 Bray-sur-Somme]	L 34 b
Fromage Farm	20NW4 Dixmude	I 15 a 1.3
Frome Farm	28NW3 Poperinghe	G 36 d 9.7
Fromme, Boyau	66eNE4 Beaufort	L 28 c, d, 34 b, 35 a, b
Frontier Lane [road]	57dNE3 & 4 Hébuterne / SE1 & 2 Beaumont	K 35 a, c, Q 5 a, c
Frost House	28NE1 Zonnebeke	D 25 a 7.1
Frost Trench	51bNW1 Roclincourt	A 5 a
Frosts Homestead [farm]	20SE2 Hooglede	R 25 c 4.7
Frosty Trench	51bNW2 Oppy	B 30 a, b
Frosty Trench / Reserve	57cSW4 Combles	T 5 a, b, d
Frugal Trench	51bNW2 Oppy	B 30 a
Fruge Avenue	20SW3 Oostvleteren	N 33 c
Fry Farm	27SE4 Meteren	X 15 b 30.85
Fry Pan	36NW2 Armentières	C 22 d
Fry Post	36NW4 Bois Grenier	I 13 a, b
Fry Trench	51bNW1 Roclincourt	A 22 b
Fry Trench	51bNW1 Roclincourt	A 5 a
Fry's Communication Trench	36SW3 Richebourg	S 15 d
FSC Trench [Demuin, March 1918]	62dSE [3 Marcelcave]	V 19
Ft. Hindenburg [Lemberg St.]	57dSE4 Ovillers	R 31 c, X 1 a, b
Ft. Lemberg [Türken St.]	57dSE1 & 2 Beaumont / 4 Ovillers	R 31 a, c, d
Fuchsbau	51bSW1 Neuville Vitasse	M 5 b
Fuddle Farm	20SE2 Hooglede	Q 4 a 45.10
Fudge Trench	51bNW1 Roclincourt	A 5 a, b
Fuel Trench	57dNE1 & 2 Fonquevillers	E 23 d
Fuel Way	57dSE2 Beaumont	Q 18 c
Fuite, Tranchée de la	66dNW2 Morchain	B 5 c, d, 10 b, 11 a
Fulda Alley	62cSW2 Barleux	O 27 d, 28 c
Fulda Trench	62cNW2 Bouchavesnes	C 16 c
Fuldner Lane	51bSW4 Bullecourt	T 5 b, 6 a
Fullerton Villas	28SE1 Wervicq	P 10 d 0.6
Fum Farm	36NW1 Steenwerck	A 2 c 80.55
Fume Trench	57dNE1 & 2 Fonquevillers	E 23 b, 24 a
Fumee Trench	62bSW1 Gricourt	M 6 d, 12 a, b
Fumistes / Fumiates Alley	62bSW1 Gricourt	M 18 a, b
Fun Lane	51bSW4 Bullecourt	T 6 d
Fun Trench	57dNE1 & 2 Fonquevillers	E 23 d, 29 b
Fungus Trench	57dNE1 & 2 Fonquevillers	E 24 c
Funk Street [road]	36aSE1 St Venant	Q 9 c, d, 14 b, d, 15 a
Funk Trench	51bNW1 Roclincourt	A 5 a, c
Funk Trench	51bNW1 Roclincourt	A 22 a, b
Funk Trench	57dNE1 & 2 Fonquevillers	E 24 a
Funke Farm	20SE2 Hooglede	R 6 a 8.8
Funnel Communication Trench	36SW3 Richebourg	S 21 a, b
Funny Farm	28NW4 & NE3 Zillebeke	J 32 c 9.6
Funny Trench	51bNW1 Roclincourt	A 5 a
Funny Trench	51bNW2 Oppy	B 30 c
Fur Trench	57dNE1 & 2 Fonquevillers	E 24 a, c
Furies Alley	62cSW1 Dompierre	M 19-23, 29, 30, N 25, 31

Name	Map Sheet	Map Reference
Furies Trench	57cSW4 Combles	O 32 c, U 2 a, b
Furnace Lane [road]	51bSW2 Vis-en-Artois	O 17 a, c, 23 a
Furness Street	57dSE4 Ovillers	X 7 d
Furrier Trench	57dNE1 & 2 Fonquevillers	E 23 d, 24 c
Fürst Farm	28NE1 Zonnebeke	D 5 a 3.1
Fury Trench	57dNE1 & 2 Fonquevillers	E 23 b, d
Furze Camp	28NW1 Elverdinghe	A 19 a 3.9
Fuse Meadow	62cSW3 Vermandovillers	S 25 b, 26 a
Fuse Trench	51bSW1 Neuville Vitasse	M 28 b
Fuse Trench	57dNE1 & 2 Fonquevillers	E 23 d
Fushia Farm	36aNE1 Morbecque	D 27 a 0.8
Fusilage Farm	36aNE1 Morbecque	D 11 c 2.1
Fusilier Alley	57cSE2 Gonnelieu	R 14 b
Fusilier Avenue	57dNE1 & 2 Fonquevillers	E 27 d
Fusilier Dugouts [Fusilier Wood]	28NW4 & NE3 Zillebeke	I 36 c
Fusilier Farm	28NW2 St Julien	C 14 c 4.4
Fusilier Farm	28SW3 Bailleul	T 3 c 95.70
Fusilier Farm	28SW4 Ploegsteert	U 8 c 3.2
Fusilier Lane	36NW2 Armentières	C 16 d, 22 b
Fusilier Lines [huts]	28SW3 Bailleul	T 3 c, d
Fusilier Ridge	57cSE2 Gonnelieu	R 20, 26
Fusilier Terrace	28SW4 Ploegsteert	U 27 a, b
Fusilier Trench	28NW2 St Julien	C 14 c
Fusilier Trench [Br. Supp. Line]	28SW4 Ploegsteert	T 6 b
Fusilier Wood	28NW4 & NE3 Zillebeke	I 36 c
Fuss Trench	57dNE1 & 2 Fonquevillers	E 24 a
Fussen Trench	62cNW2 Bouchavesnes	C 17 d, 23 a, b, c
Fusses, Tranchée des	70dSW2 [Coucy-le-Château]	O 2 a
Fusty Trench	51bNW1 Roclincourt	A 5 a, b
Fuze Cot.	28SW4 Ploegsteert	U 10 d 5.2
Fuze Street	51cSE & 51bSW Ficheux	R 28 d
Fuze Trench	51bNW4 Fampoux	I 26 a, b
Fuzeville [ammunition railhead]	28NW3 Poperinghe	G 34 b, d, 35 a
Fuzeville Fork [road jct]	28NW3 Poperinghe	G 34 b 6.8
G 1 [Hooge, 1915]	28NW4 & NE3 Zillebeke	I 18 d
G 10 [Hooge, 1915]	28NW4 & NE3 Zillebeke	I 18 a
G 2 [Hooge, 1915]	28NW4 & NE3 Zillebeke	I 18 b, d
G 3 [Hooge, 1915]	28NW4 & NE3 Zillebeke	I 18 b
G 4 [Hooge, 1915]	28NW4 & NE3 Zillebeke	I 18 b
G 5 [Hooge, 1915]	28NW4 & NE3 Zillebeke	I 18 b
G 6 [Hooge, 1915]	28NW4 & NE3 Zillebeke	I 18 b
G 7 [Hooge, 1915]	28NW4 & NE3 Zillebeke	I 18 b
G 8 [Hooge, 1915]	28NW4 & NE3 Zillebeke	I 18 b
G 9 [Hooge, 1915]	28NW4 & NE3 Zillebeke	I 18 b
G Camp	28NW1 Elverdinghe	A 16 d
G Sap	28NW4 & NE3 Zillebeke	I 24 b
G Sap [Givenchy]	36cNW1 La Bassée	A 9 b
G Sap [Triangle, S of Loos]	36cSW1 Lens	M 4 d
G Sector [April 1915]	28SW2 Wytschaete	N 24 30
G Trenches [+ no., July 1915, Br, Hooge & N]	28NW4 & NE3 Zillebeke	I 12 c, 18 a
G Trenches [Dec 1914, Spanbroekmolen]	28SW2 Wytschaete	N 30 a, c
G Work	51bNW1 Roclincourt	A 29 d
G.H.Q. Line	36bSE2 Boyeffles / 4 Carency	Q 36, R25,31, W5,6,11,17,22,23,28
Gaba, Maison	36bSE2 Boyeffles	R 12 c 87.50

Name	Map Sheet	Map Reference
Gabel [Graben]	51bSW1 Neuville Vitasse	M 21 c
Gabel Trench	51bNW3 Arras	G 18 a
Gabel Trench	51bSW1 Neuville Vitasse	M 21 c
Gabion Avenue	57dSE1 & 2 Beaumont	Q 15 d, 16 c, d, 21 a, b
Gabion Farm	28SW4 Ploegsteert	U 1 d 8.1
Gabionnade Trench	70dNW4 St Gobain	H 16 d, 17 c, 23 a
Gabions Alley	66cNW1 Grugies	B 1 b, 2 a
Gable Farm	28SW4 Ploegsteert	T 4 b 9.5
Gables Farm	20SE2 Hooglede	Q 33 b 7.8
Gabriel Cross Roads	28NE2 Moorslede	F 19 d 25.20
Gabriel, Boyau	36cSW3 Vimy	S 8 d
Gabriel, Boyau / Trench	36cSW3 Vimy	S 8 d
Gaby Cottage	28NW1 Elverdinghe	A 30 c 7.4
Gaby Trench	36cSW3 Vimy / 4 Rouvroy	T 3 b, d, 4 c, 10 a
Gaby Trench / Tranchée Gaby	62cSW1 & 2 Belloy	N 24 c, d
Gadfly Farm	28NW1 Elverdinghe	A 26 c 8.8
Gadget Crossing [bridge or level crossing]	27SE2 Berthen	Q 23 b 55.90
Gaffe Alley / Boyau de la Gaffe	62cSW3 & 4 Marchélepot	T 19 c, d, 25 a
Gaffer Trench	62bSW4 Homblières	N 36 c, d
Gaieté, la [farm]	62bSW1 Gricourt	N 33 c 9.3
Gaika Copse	57cNW4 Beugny/NE3 Hermies/ SW2 Villers-au-Flos	I 36 d, J 31 c, O 6 b
Gaillet Trench	66cNW1 Grugies	A 11 c, 17 a
Gairloch Trench	51bNW3 Arras	G 36 c, d
Gaites Farm	28SE1 Wervicq	P 11 d 5.3
Galatz Alley	62cNW4 Péronne	I 14 d, 15 a
Gale Alley	36cNW1 La Bassée	G 6 a, b, H 1 a, b, 2 a
Gale Junction [road jct]	28NE4 Dadizeele	L 31 b 0.7
Galere Trench	62bSW2 Fonsommes	N 23 a, c
Galilée Farm	20NW4 Dixmude	I 8 a 05.45
Gall Cottages [Nachtegaal]	28NE2 Moorslede	F 21 d 7.8
Gallant Alley	36cNW1 La Bassée	A 28 d, 29 a, c
Galley / Gallay / Galloy Wood	51bSE1 Saudemont	P 1 c, d, 2 a, c
Gallia Trench	57cSW4 Combles	U 2 a, c, d, 3 a, b, d
Gallichet Alley	62bSW1 Gricourt	M 8 c, d, 9 c, d, 13 b, 14 a
Gallipoli [farm / pill box]	28NE1 Zonnebeke	D 13 d 4.1
Gallipoli Copse	28NE1 Zonnebeke	D 14 c
Gallipoli Ridge	28NE1 Zonnebeke	D 13 d, 14 c
Gallow Gate	36cSW3 Vimy	S 20 b, 21 a
Gallow Gate [Sept 1915]	36cNW1 La Bassée	A 9 a
Gallowgate Avenue	36NW4 Bois Grenier	I 20 c, d
Gallowgate Post	36NW4 Bois Grenier	I 20 d
Gallows Corner	27NE1 Herzeele	D 1 c
Gallwitz Switch	57dSE2 & 57cSW1 Le Sars	M 3 c, d, 9 b, 10 a, c, 11 c
Gallwitz Trench	57cSW4 Combles	O 35 c, U 5 a, b, d
Gallwitz Trench	57dSE2 & 57cSW1 Le Sars	M 8, 9, 10, 11, 13, 14, 17
Gallwitz-Riegel, III Stellung [Gird Trench]	57cSW1 Gueudecourt / 3 Longueval	N 32 b, T 3 a
Galo Farm	27NE4 Abeele	L 13 c 6.4
Galoirs Trench	62bSW2 Fonsommes	N 16 b, d
Galopins Alley	62bSW1 Gricourt	M 23 d, 24 a, b, c, d
Galsriens Trench	62bSW2 Fonsommes	N 24 c, 30 a, b
Galt Road [road]	36cSW1 Lens	N 21 c, d
Galwall Lines [huts]	28SW3 Bailleul	S 30 c
Galway Trench	51bNW3 Arras	G 36 c

Name	Map Sheet	Map Reference
Gama [sic; pillbox near Polygon Butt (sic) 1918]	28NE3 Gheluvelt	J 10 a 70.73
Gamages	20SE3 Westroosebeke	V 16 b 3.5
Gambetta Trench	20SW4 Bixschoote	U 9 c, d, 10 c
Gambit Alley	36cNW3 Loos	G 12 b
Gamble Alley	36cNW3 Loos	G 4 b, 5 a
Gambler's Corner	28NE4 Dadizeele	L 2 d 35.10
Game Copse	28SE1 Wervicq	P 1 c
Game Street	51cSE & 51bSW Ficheux	M 13 d, 19 b
Game Support	57cSE2 Gonnelieu	R 20 b, d
Gamin Alley	62cSW3 Vermandovillers	T 20 a
Gamins Alley	62bSW2 Fonsommes	N 29 a
Gamma [German strongpoint]	51bSW4 Bullecourt	U 7 b 8.5
Ganaches Trench	62bSW1 Gricourt	N 20 b
Gand Trench	20SW3 Oostvleteren	N 33 c, T 3 a
Gander Trench	36cNW1 La Bassée	A 30 c, G 5 b, 6 a
Gander Trench	51bSW2 Vis-en-Artois	O 2 d, 3 c
Gandy Cottage	20SE2 Hooglede	R 29 d 1.3
Gange Trench	62cSW3 Vermandovillers	T 19 d, 20 c
Gange Trench / Tranchée du Gange [Ganges]	62cSW3 & 4 Marchélepot	T 19 d, 20 c
Ganger's Cot. [E side of rly]	28SW4 Ploegsteert	U 23 c 7.4
Gangers Hut [E of railway]	28NW4 & NE3 Zillebeke	I 28 b 75.35
Gangrene Alley	62bSW1 Gricourt	N 19 c, d, 20 c, d
Gangue Trench	62bSW1 Gricourt	M 30 d
Gannet Trench [later Reserve]	51bSW2 Vis-en-Artois	O 19 d, 25 b
Ganter Weg / Fourth Avenue [NE of Ovillers]	57dSE4 Ovillers	R 33 d, 34 c, X 3 a, b
Gap E [British FL south of Warnave Lodge]	28SW4 Ploegsteert	U 28 c 2.5
Gap F [British FL east of Rutter Lodge]	28SW4 Ploegsteert	U 28 a 2.8
Gap G [British FL N of Le Gheer]	28SW4 Ploegsteert	U 21 d 95.35
Gap Street	28NW4 & NE3 Zillebeke	I 30 a
Gap Trench	28NW4 & NE3 Zillebeke	I 29 b, 30 a
Gap Trench [Flers Line / Graben]	57cSW3 Longueval	T 1 a, b, d, 2 c
Gap, The	36SW2 Radinghem	O 2 d
Gapaard [hamlet]	28SW4 Ploegsteert	O 35 a, c
Gapaard Avenue	28SW4 Ploegsteert	O 34 b, 35 a, c
Gara Farm	27NE4 Abeele	K 35 a 95.95
Gard Wood	57bSW2 Clary	N 24, 30, O 19, 20, 25, 31
Garde Dieu	28SW2 Wytschaete	O 36 a
Garde Dieu Cabaret	28SW2 Wytschaete	O 36 b
Garde House	20SW4 Bixschoote	T 12 a 54.62
Garde Stellung	57dNE1 & 2 Fonquevillers	K 5 a, b, c, d
Garden / Green House	28NE1 Zonnebeke	D 13 b 8.6
Garden Block [houses]	28SW3 Bailleul	S 27 b 9.2
Garden Dump [Aix-Noulette]	36bSE2 Boyeffles	R 22 b 5.3
Garden Farm	66dNW1 Punchy	B 14 c
Garden Farm [1918]	28SW1 Kemmel	N 13 d 85.50
Garden Road	51bNW3 Arras	G 28 b
Garden Street [St Jean]	28NW2 St Julien	C 27 d, 28 a, c
Garden Trench	57cSW1 Gueudecourt	N 27 a
Garden Villa [Wieltje]	28NW2 St Julien	C 28 a 5.1
Gardens Trench	66cSW2 Vendeuil	O 3 a, c
Gardiner Bank [lynchet]	57cSE4 Villers-Guislain	R 35 c
Gare Trench	62cSW3 Vermandovillers	T 19 b, 20 a
Garenne Copse	66dNW1 Punchy	B 7 c, d
Garenne Wood	62dSE [2 Proyart]	R 5 b, d, 6 a

Name	Map Sheet	Map Reference
Garenne, La [wood]	51bNE4 Cantin	L 15, 16, 21, 22
Gargantua Alley	62bSW1 Gricourt	M 30 b
Garnville Trench	62bSW3 St Quentin	S 27 b
Gars Brugge [farm]	36aNE2 Vieux Berquin	K 5 b 9.8
Garstin Cottages	27NE1 Herzeele	E 2 b 8.3
Garter Copse	28NE2 Moorslede	E 12 c 4.1
Garter Corner	28SW3 Bailleul	T 3 a
Garter Point	28NE1 Zonnebeke	J 3 a 5.5
Gas Alley [Grenadier-Weg]	57cSW3 Longueval	T 1 c, d, 2 a, b, c, 7 a
Gas Bas Reserve [Gastineau & Basseux] [1918]	51cSE [2 Beaumetz / 4 Blaireville]	Q 35 a, c, W 5 a
Gas Bas Support [Gastineau & Basseux] [1918]	51cSE [2 Beaumetz / 4 Blaireville]	Q 35 b, d, W 5 b, d
Gas Bas Trench [Gastineau & Basseux] [1918]	51cSE [2 Beaumetz / 4 Blaireville]	Q 36 a, c, W 6 a, c
Gas Trench	28SW4 Ploegsteert	U 13 a, c
Gascon Alley	36cNW3 Loos	G 5 d, 6 c
Gascons, Boyau des	36cSW1 Lens	M 15 a, b
Gasometers [Passchendaele]	28NE1 Zonnebeke	E 7 a 3.8
Gaspé Road [road]	36cSW4 Rouvroy	N 35 c
Gaspe Trench	36cSW3 Vimy	T 7 b, 8 a
Gasper Alley	62cNE2 Epéhy	F 29 b
Gaspers Cliff	28SW2 Wytschaete	O 4 b 5.5
Gaspers Cliffe Tunnel	28SW2 Wytschaete	O 4 b 4.4
Gaspiard / Gaspillard Trench	62bSW2 Fonsommes	N 17 c, 23 a
Gaspipe House	28SW3 Bailleul	S 17 d 7.1
Gasthof House	20SW4 Bixschoote	T 24 a
Gastineau (Tuilleries)	51cSE4 Blaireville	W 11 b, 12 a
Gate / Gale Lane [trench, S of Flers]	57cSW3 Longueval	T 1 a, b, c
Gate Street	51cSE & 51bSW Ficheux	M 13 d, 14 c
Gate Trench	57dNE3 & 4 Hébuterne	K 17 b, d
Gate Walk [track, from Lille Gate]	28NW4 Ypres	I 14 c, d, 15 a, c, 16 a
Gâteau Trench / Tranchée du Gâteau	62cSW3 & 4 Marchélepot	T 21 a, b, d
Gatefield Farm	20SE2 Hooglede	Q 5 b 3.5
Gateshead Trench	51bNW3 Arras	G 36 b, c, d
Gattigny Wood	57bSW2 Clary / SE1 Bertry	O 24 b, d, P 19 a, c
Gatwick Cot.	28NW2 St Julien	C 15 b 8.9
Gauche Alley	57cSE4 Villers-Guislain	X 1 c, d, 7 a, b
Gauche Wood	57cSE4 Villers-Guislain	X 1 c, d, 2 c
Gauchy [village]	66cNW1 Grugies	A 6 c, d, 12 b
Gaudy Reserve [1918, Gaudiempré]	57dNE [1 Fonquevillers]	D 1 a
Gaudy Support [1918, Gaudiempré]	57dNE [1 Fonquevillers]	D 1 a, b, c
Gaudy Trench [1918, Gaudiempré]	57dNE [1 Fonquevillers]	D 2 a, c, 8 a
Gauffres Trench / Tranchée des Gaufres	62cSW3 & 4 Marchélepot	T 19 d, 20 c
Gaufre Trench	62bSW1 Gricourt	M 18 b
Gaul Avenue	57dSE1 & 2 Beaumont	Q 28 d, 29 c, 35 a, b
Gaul Farm	36aNE2 Vieux Berquin	F 16 c 6.0
Gaul Weg / Alley [later Poser Weg]	51bNW1 Roclincourt	A 30, B 25, 26
Gaulaine Ridge [Buisson-Gaulaine Farm]	62bNW3 Bellicourt	G 20 b, d
Gaulois, Boyau	70dSW [4 Vauxaillon]	U 10 d
Gaunt Farm [farm, railway & huts]	28NW1 Elverdinghe	A 28 a 2.7
Gauwy Mill	36NW1 Steenwerck	A 18 a 00.05
Gavail Trench	62cSW3 Vermandovillers	S 24 d
Gavardie [Boyau, 1915]	57dSE4 Ovillers	X 26 a, b
Gavrelle [village]	51bNW2 Oppy	B 30 b, C 25 a
Gavrelle Mill	51bNW2 Oppy	C 19 c 72.36
Gavrelle Support	51bNW2 Oppy	C 20 c, 26 a, c

Name	Map Sheet	Map Reference
Gavrelle Trench	51bNW2 Oppy	C 25 a, b, d
Gavrelle Trench, South	51bNW2 Oppy	C 25 d, I 1 b
Gavreller Weg	51bNW1 Roclincourt	B 26, 27, H 2, 3
Gawthorpe Road	28NW2 St Julien	C 15 c, 21 a, c
Gay Trench / Alley	66cNW1 Grugies	A 4 d
Gaye Trench	28SW2 Wytschaete	N 35 b
Gaz Trench / Tranchée du Gaz	62cSW3 & 4 Marchélepot	S 24 d, T 19 c
Gaza Cross Roads	27SE4 Meteren	X 22 a 1.1
Geddes Dump Siding	20SW3 Oostvleteren	T 27 c, d
Gee Trench [1918]	51bNW1 Roclincourt / 3 Arras	G 6 b, d
Geelfoort [farm]	27NE1 Herzeele	E 8 d 5.3
Gefreite Trench	62bSW3 St Quentin	M 36 d, S 6 b, T 1 a, b
Geikie Farm	20SE3 Westroosebeke	W 20 a 55.55
Geine Lines, De [huts]	36NW2 Armentières	B 10 b, d
Geleide Post	12SW1 Nieuport	M 16 d
Geleide, Tranchée	12SW1 Nieuport	M 16 d
Gem Farms	27SE2 Berthen	Q 23 c 7.6
Gem Street	51cSE & 51bSW Ficheux	M 14 a, c
Gemeenendriesch	27NE1 Herzeele	E 8 d, 9 c
Gemeenhof [farm]	20SE2 Hooglede	Q 35 b 1.2
Gemmel Trench [Thiepval Wood]	57dSE1 & 2 Beaumont	Q 30 d, R 25 c
Gen. Dubois Alley [1918]	62dSE [4 Harbonnières]	X 23 b, 24 a
Gen. Foch Alley [1918]	62dSE [4 Harbonnières]	R 34 d, 35 c, d, X 5 b, 6 a
Genay, Tranchée	62cSW1 & 2 Belloy	O 2 a, b
Gendarme Trench [Chapeau de Gendarme]	62cNW1 Maricourt	A 29 b
Gendarmerie [Watou]	27NE2 Proven	K 5 a 2.3
Gendarmerie Trench	57dNE1 & 2 Fonquevillers	E 15 d, 16 c
Gendarmery [Ypres]	28NW4 Ypres	I 7 b 85.70
General Farm	28NW2 St Julien	C 1 a 7.2
General's Farm	20NW4 Dixmude	I 26 d 2.2
Genermont [village]	62cSW3 & 4 Marchélepot	T 8, 9
Genet Corner [road jct]	36aNE4 Merville	L 7 a 3.7
Génie Avenue	51bNW1 Roclincourt	A 27, 28, G 23
Génie, Boyau du	36cSW3 Vimy	S 8 d
Génie, Boyau du	62cSW1 Dompierre	M 10 b
Génies Trench	62cSW1 & 2 Belloy	O 1 b, d
Genin Well Copse No.1	57cSE4 Villers-Guislain	W 17 a
Genin Well Copse No.2	57cSE4 Villers-Guislain	W 17 b, d
Génisse Trench / Tranchée de la Génisse	62cSW3 & 4 Marchélepot / 66dNW1 Punchy	T 26 b, c, d, 27 a, B 2 a, c
Genoa [farm / pillbox]	28NE1 Zonnebeke	D 1 c 5.2
Genonville Farm	66eNW [4 Morisel]	I 15 d 15.30
Genonville Wood	66eNW [4 Morisel]	I 16 b, 17 a, b, d
Genou Trench	62bSW2 Fonsommes	N 17 a, c
Gent House	36aNE4 Merville	K 12 d 0.6
Gentelles [village]	62dSW [4 Cachy]	N 12 c, d, U 7 c, 13 a
Gentelles Line [1918]	62dSW [4 Cachy]	U 13 a, c, 19 a, c
Gentelles Switch [1918]	62dSW [4 Cachy]	T 18 b, c, d, 23 b, d, 24 a, U 13 a
Gentelles Trench [1918]	62dSW [4 Cachy]	U 13 a, c, 19 a, c
Gentelles, Bois de	62dSW [4 Cachy]	T 10, 11, 16, 17
Géomètre Alley / Boyau du Géomètre	62cSW3 & 4 Marchélepot / 66dNW1 Punchy	T 19, 20, 26, B 2, 3, 9, 15, 16
George Avenue	51bSW2 Vis-en-Artois	O 6 c, 11 b, 12 a
George Avenue	62dNE2 Méaulte	F 18 a
George Post	51bNW1 Roclincourt	A 5 b
George Post	62cNE4 Roisel	L 36 c 80.75

Name	Map Sheet	Map Reference
George Street	51bNW2 Oppy	B 12 c
George Street	51cSE & 51bSW Ficheux	M 14 a, c
George Street	57cNE3 Hermies / 4 Marcoing	K 15 c, d, 16 c, d, 21 a
George Street	57cSE4 Villers-Guislain	X 4 c
George Street	57cSW3 Longueval	S 16 a, b
George Street	62cNW1 Maricourt	A 8 d
George Street [road]	36aSE4 Locon	R 33 d, 34 c, X 3 a, b
George Street [Sept 1915]	36cNW1 La Bassée	A 2 b, d
George Street [Thiepval Wood]	57dSE1 & 2 Beaumont	R 25 a
George Support	51bSW2 Vis-en-Artois	O 5 d, 11 b
George Trench	36cSW3 Vimy	S 15 a
Georges Trench	12SW1 Nieuport	M 16 c
Geoulzin Wood	51bNE4 Cantin	K 16 b, 17 a
Geranium Farm	20SE2 Hooglede	R 9 c 9.5
Gerard Trench	62bSW3 St Quentin	S 28 a, b
Gerbedoen Farm	36aNE2 Vieux Berquin	F 1 b, 2 a
Gerfaut Trench	62cSW3 Vermandovillers	T 19 d
Germain Wood Trench	62cNW2 Bouchavesnes	C 10 b, d, 16 b
Germains Trench	62bSW1 Gricourt	N 14 a, c, d
Germains Trench / Tranchée des Germains	62cSW3 & 4 Marchélepot	T 13 d, 19 b, d, 25 b
German Cemetery [N of Morchies]	57cNW2 Vaulx-Vraucourt	I 5 b 60.45
German Cemetery [NE of Bixschoote]	20SW4 Bixschoote	U 7 c 4.6
German House [July 1915]	36NW4 Bois Grenier	I 21 b 15.10
German House [Le Pelerin]	28SW4 Ploegsteert	U 21 b 27.15
German Lane [Niemeyer Weg]	57dNE3 & 4 Hébuterne	K 17 b, 18 a, b
German Lane [Sept 1915]	36cNW1 La Bassée	A 21 b
German M.G. House	36NW2 Armentières	C 10 b
German Redoubt [Givenchy, March 1915]	36cNW1 La Bassée	A 3, 9
German Reserve Trench	36cNW1 La Bassée	A 10, 16
German Road	36cSW3 Vimy	M 32 c
German Street	36cNW1 La Bassée	A 3 c
German Support Trench	36cNW1 La Bassée	A 9, 10, 16
German Switch	36cNW3 Loos	G 17 b, d, 23 b, c, d
German Tambour [Fricourt]	62dNE2 Méaulte	F 3 c
German Trench	57cSW4 Combles	T 5 c
German's / Germans' Wood	62cNW1 Maricourt	A 10 a
Germersheimer [sic] Graben	51bNW1 Roclincourt	A 30 c
Gerrard Trench	36cSW3 Vimy	T 15 b
Gertie House	28NW3 Poperinghe	G 5 c 2.8
Gertie Trench	36cSW3 Vimy	T 13 b, d, 14 c
Gervais Wood	66eNW [2 Thennes]	B 5 c, d
Geuss Farm [Geusschesmis]	28NE2 Moorslede	F 15 d 1.3
Geux Alley	62bSW1 Gricourt	N 21 a
Gheer Estaminet, Au [Rutter Lodge]	28SW4 Ploegsteert	U 27 b 75.85
Gheer, Le [hamlet]	28SW4 Ploegsteert	U 22 a, b, c
Gheluvelt - Langemarck Line	20SW4 Bix'te/28NW2 St Jul'n/NE1 Zonn./ 3 Ghel't	extensive
Gheluvelt [village]	28NE3 Gheluvelt	J 22 c, d
Gheluvelt Mill	28NE3 Gheluvelt	J 22 c, d
Gheluvelt Switch	28NE3 Gheluvelt	J 21, 22, 28, 29
Gheluvelt Wood	28NE3 Gheluvelt	J 21 d, 22 c
Ghent Cottages	28NW2 St Julien	B 22 d, 28 b
Ghilly Trench	62bSW1 Gricourt	M 35 b
Ghoorka Fork [road jct]	28NE2 Moorslede	K 4 b 75.80

Name	Map Sheet	Map Reference
Ghost Farm	27NE2 Proven	E 10 d 60.75
Ghostly Trench	36cNW3 Loos	G 12 a, b
Ghurka Road [road]	36SW1 Aubers / 3 Richebourg	M 29 c, 35 a, c
Giana Farm	27SE2 Berthen	Q 22 b 1.9
Giant, The [strongpoint]	28SW2 Wytschaete	O 12 c
Gibbon Trench	36cNW1 La Bassée	A 30 c, G 5 b, 6 a
Gibet, le [hamlet]	36NW1 Steenwerck	B 15 d, 16 c
Giblet House	27NE2 Proven	E 10 a 90.95
Gibraltar / Gibraltar Trench	62dNE2 Méaulte	F 26 d, 27 a
Gibraltar [Panzerturn, Pozières]	57dSE4 Ovillers	X 4 c 7.4
Gibraltar Farm [Potijze]	28NW4 Ypres	I 3 d 3.7
Gibraltar Mill	51bSE3 Cagnicourt	V 11 a 65.85
Gibson Croles	36cNW1 La Bassée	A 21 d
Gibus Trench	62bSW1 Gricourt	N 19 a
Gideon Alley	62cSW2 Barleux	N 24 b, d, O 19 c
Gierich Weg [Ration Trench]	57dSE4 Ovillers	R 33 c, d, X 2 b, 3 a
Giffécourt [village]	66cNW1 Grugies	A 11 c
Gig Farm	27NE1 Herzeele	E 19 b 15.50
Gigot Trench	62cSW3 Vermandovillers	T 13 d
Gilbert Alley	57dSE2 & 57cSW1 Le Sars	M 20 c, 21 a, c, 26 b
Gilbert Avenue	57cSW1 Gueudecourt	M 15 b, c, d, 20 b, d, 21 a
Gilbert Trench	57cSW4 Combles	U 15 c, 21 a
Gilbeys Farm	28NE4 Dadizeele	K 17 b 7.3
Gilders Farm	20SE2 Hooglede	Q 27 d 80.85
Giles Post	36NW4 Bois Grenier	H 12 b
Gilford Cross Roads	28NW1 Elverdinghe	A 11 b 3.2
Gillemont Crescent	62bNW1 Gouy	A 14 a
Gillemont Farm	62bNW1 Gouy	A 13 b
Gillemont Farm Post	62bNW1 Gouy	A 13 b
Gillemont Road [road]	62cNE2 Epéhy / 62bNW1 Gouy	F 17 c, A 13 b
Gillemont Switch	62bNW1 Gouy	A 13 b
Gillemont Trench, South	62bNW1 Gouy	A 13 d
Gilles Farm	20SW4 Bixschoote	N 36 d 7.2
Gillie Farm	36aNE2 Vieux Berquin	F 27 b 25.25
Gillingham Trench	51bNW3 Arras	G 36 b
Gillow Farm	28NE4 Dadizeele	K 29 d 0.3
Gimble Wood	62cNW1 Maricourt / 3 Vaux	H 1 b, d
Gimmel Trench	57dSE2 Beaumont	Q 36 b
Gin Alley	57dSE4 Ovillers	X 27 a
Gin Avenue	57cSE2 Gonnelieu	R 26 b, d, 27 a
Gin Palace [farm]	28NW1 Elverdinghe	A 30 a 7.7
Gin Trench	51bNW1 Roclincourt	B 20 a, c
Gin Trench	51bNW4 Fampoux	H 34 c, d
Gin Trench [1918]	57dNE1 & 2 Fonquevillers	E 28 b, c, d
Ginchy [village]	57cSW3 Longueval	T 13 b, d, 14 c
Ginchy Avenue	57cSW3 Longueval	S 18 d, T 13 c
Ginchy Farm	57cSW3 Longueval	T 13 d 5.3
Ginchy Telegraph	57cSW3 Longueval	T 14 d 0.7
Ginger Cut [sunken road S of Le Barque]	57cSW1 Gueudecourt	N 7 c
Ginger Road [road SE of Le Barque]	57cSW1 Gueudecourt	N 7 c, d
Gipsy Alley	36cNW3 Loos	G 5 d, 6 c
Gipsy Hill	57dSE1 & 2 Beaumont	Q 17 c
Girafe Trench	62bSW1 Gricourt	N 19 c, d, 25 b
Gird Trench [Gallwitz-Riegel, III Stellung]	57cSW1 Gueudecourt / 3 Longueval	N 32 b, T 3 a

Name	Map Sheet	Map Reference
Gird Trench, & Support Trench	57dSE2 & 57cSW1 Le Sars	M 17, 18, 24, N 19, 20, 26, 32, T 3
Girdle Trench	51bSW2 Vis-en-Artois	O 8 c
Girl Street	51cSE & 51bSW Ficheux	M 14 a, b, c, d
Girls Convent [late 1915]	36SW2 Radinghem	O 14 a 4.5
Giroud Alley	62cNW1 Maricourt	B 27 c, d
Girouettes Alley	62bSW1 Gricourt	M 24 c, d
Girton Cross [cross roads]	28NW3 Poperinghe	G 22 b 5.4
Gita Farm	28NW3 Poperinghe	H 19 a 7.1
Gits [village]	20NE4 Lichtervelde / 20SE2 Hooglede	K 36 d, Q 6 b
Gitsberg [hamlet]	20SE2 Hooglede	R 1 d, 7 b
Givenchy Camp	28NW3 Poperinghe	H 8 d, 9 c
Givenchy Farm	28NW3 Poperinghe	H 8 c 75.65
Givenchy Keep	36cNW1 La Bassée	A 9 c
Givenchy Shrine [April 1915]	36cNW1 La Bassée	A 3, 9
Givenchy Spur [light rly]	36cSW3 Vimy	S 4 c
Givenchy Wood / Bois de Givenchy	36cSW3 Vimy	S 3 a, b, c, d, 9 a
Givenchy-en-Gohelle [village]	36cSW3 Vimy	S 3, 4, 9, 10
Givenchy-lez-la-Bassée [village]	36cNW1 La Bassée	A 9 c, d
Givre Trench	62cSW3 Vermandovillers	T 21 a
Gk [sic; Greek?] Fm [Broodseinde]	28NE1 Zonnebeke	D 29 a 35.90
Glace Trench [1918]	36cSW3 Vimy	S 18 b, T 13 a
Glaciere Trench	62bSW2 Fonsommes	N 23 c, d
Gladiator Farm	28NW4 Ypres	H 18 a 05.65
Gladys Trench	36cSW3 Vimy	T 8 a, c
Gland Trench	62bSW1 Gricourt	N 26 b
Glasgow [locality]	51bNW1 Roclincourt	A 14 a
Glasgow Redoubt	28SW4 Ploegsteert	U 28 c
Glasgow Road [trench]	36cNW1 La Bassée	A 20 b, 21 a
Glasgow Spur [S of Zonnebeke]	28NE1 Zonnebeke	D 27 d, 28 c
Glasgow Street	36cNW1 La Bassée	A 9 c, 15 a, b
Glasgow Trench	51bNW3 Arras	G 36 b
Glasgow Trench	57cSE2 Gonnelieu	R 33 b, 34 a
Glasgow Trench [High Wood]	57cSW3 Longueval	S 4 c
Glasgow Trench [March 1915]	36cNW1 La Bassée	A 15 a, b
Glass Farm	28NE2 Moorslede	F 11 c 1.2
Glass House [Vimy Ridge]	36cSW3 Vimy	S 29 a
Glass Houses	28NE3 Gheluvelt	J 28 b 15.80
Glass Houses	57dSE2 Beaumont	R 22 d
Glass Street [road]	57cSE2 Gonnelieu / 4 Villers-Guislain	R 33 c, X 3 a, c
Glass Support [1918]	57dSE [3 Bouzincourt]	W 8 d, 14 b
Glass Trench [1918]	57dSE [3 Bouzincourt]	W 15 a, c
Glasshouse Street	57dSE2 Beaumont	R 22 d, 28 b
Glatignies, les [farm]	36aSE4 Locon	X 14 c 7.4
Glatz Alley	62cNW1 Maricourt	A 4 c, 10 a
Glatz Redoubt	62cNW1 Maricourt	A 3 d, 4 c
Gleam Trench	57cSW2 Villers-au-Flos	N 22 d, 28 b
Glebe Street [road]	57cSW1 Gueudecourt	N 25 b, c, d
Glen Farm	20SE2 Hooglede	Q 34 a 30.35
Glen Lane	62bNW1 Gouy	A 13 b, d
Glen, The [dugouts, Shrewsbury Forest]	28NW4 & NE3 Zillebeke	J 25 d
Glenarm Lane	51bNW3 Arras	G 24 d, 30 b, H 19 c
Glencorse Lane [beech slab road, 1917]	28NW4 & NE3 Zillebeke	J 14 a, b
Glencorse Lane [beech slabs, 1917]	28NW4 & NE3 Zillebeke	J 14 a, b
Glencorse Wood	28NW4 & NE3 Zillebeke	J 8 c, 14 a, b

Name	Map Sheet	Map Reference
Glenelg Lane	51bNW3 Arras	G 30 b, H 19 c, 25 c
Glenfield Farm	28NE4 Dadizeele	K 34 b 8.1
Glengarry Trench	51bNW3 Arras	H 25 c
Glengorse Avenue	28SW4 Ploegsteert	U 21 d, 22 c
Glentham Copse	28NE4 Dadizeele	L 13 c
Glim Farm	36aNE1 Morbecque	E 20 c 20.85
Glimpse Cottage Line	28NW2 St Julien	C 13 c, d, 19 a
Glimpse Farm	28NW2 St Julien	C 13 b
Glisy-Blangy Switch [1918]	62dSW [1 Longueau / 2 Villers-Bretonneux]	N 20, 21, 22, 26, 27
Glisy-Nicolas Switch [1918]	62dSW [3 Boves]	T 1, 2, 8
Gloriette, la	62bSW4 Homblières	T 4 b
Gloriole Alley	62bSW1 Gricourt	N 14 d, 15 a, b, c
Glory Hole, The	57dSE4 Ovillers	X 13 d
Glory Lane	57dSE1 & 2 Beaumont	Q 6 b, c, R 1 a
Glory Trench	51bSW2 Vis-en-Artois	O 17 c
Gloster / Gloucester Alley	57cSW3 Longueval / 57dSE4 Ovillers	S 1 d, X 6 c
Gloster / Gloucester Road	57cSE4 Villers-Guislain	X 9 d
Gloster Avenue Duckboard Track	28NW2 St Julien	C 10 a, b, c
Gloster Farm	20SE3 Westroosebeke	V 20 c 35.30
Gloster House	36SW1 Aubers	M 24 a 7.2
Gloster House [Ploegsteert Wood]	28SW4 Ploegsteert	U 20 c 5.9
Gloster Lane	36cNW3 Loos	G 35 d
Gloster Road [road]	36aNE3 Haverskerque	K 20 c, d, 26 b, 27 a
Gloster Trench	51bNW2 Oppy	C 28 b, d, 29 c
Gloster Wood	51bNW2 Oppy	C 29 a, b, d, 30 a, c
Gloucester Avenue	36NW2 Armentières	C 22, 27, 28
Gloucester Terrace	51bNW3 Arras	G 24 b, d
Gloutons Trench	62bSW1 Gricourt	M 18 a, c, 24 a, c, 30 a
Glove Cottage	28NE2 Moorslede	E 30 a 70.35
Glove Street	57cSW1 Gueudecourt	N 25 d
Glu Trench	62bSW1 Gricourt	M 12 c, d, 18 b, N 13 a, c
Gluck Trench	20SW2 Zwartegat	O 18 b
Glue Trench	51bNW1 Roclincourt	B 20 a
Glynde Corner [road junction]	20SE2 Hooglede	Q 28 d 9.7
Gnat Trench	57cSW1 Gueudecourt	N 27 c, d
Goat [Trench / Post]	57cNE3 Hermies	K 2 a
Goat Lane	51bSW2 Vis-en-Artois	O 20 c
Goat Lane	62bNW1 Gouy	G 2 b, c, d, 3 a
Goat Post	62cNE4 Roisel	L 24 a 4.6
Goat Redoubt [Feste Zollern]	57dSE1 & 2 Beaumont	R 21 d, 27 b
Goat Street, & Post [M 14 b]	51cSE & 51bSW Ficheux	M 9 d, 14 b, d
Goat Trench	36cNW1 La Bassée / 3 Loos	G 6 a, b, c
Goat Trench	57cSW1 Gueudecourt	N 26, 32
Gobelet Trench	62bSW2 Fonsommes	N 23 b, c, d
Gobelins, Boyau des	62cNW3 Vaux	G 34 b
Goblin Bank [lynchet]	51bSW2 Vis-en-Artois	O 28 c
Gobron Communication Trench	36cSW3 Vimy	S 14 b, 15 a
Gobron, Boyau	36cSW3 Vimy	S 14 b, 15 a
Godewaersvelde ['Gertie Wears Velvet', village]	27SE2 Berthen	Q 12 c, d, 18 a, b
Godewaersvelde [railway locality]	27SE2 Berthen	Q 12 d, 18 b
Godewaersvelde Line	27SE2 Berthen	extensive
Godezonne Farm	28SW2 Wytschaete	N 10 d 1.5
Godiches Trench	62cNW3 Vaux	H 1 d, 7 b
Godley Road [plank road]	28NW2 St Julien	C 24 a, c, 30 a, c, d

Name	Map Sheet	Map Reference
Godschalk Wood [Wytschaete Wd / B. de W.]	28SW2 Wytschaete	N 24 b, d, O 19 a, c
Godwin Farm	27NE1 Herzeele	E 7 a 3.3
Goeben Alley	36cNW3 Loos	G 11 b, d, 12 c
Goeben Battery	5SW1 Zeebrugge	M 17 c
Goed Moet Line [1918]	28NW3 Poperinghe	H 10, 14, 15, 16, 19, 20, 25
Goed Moet Mill	28NW3 Poperinghe	G 30 b 9.4
Goed ter Vesten Farm, 't	20SW4 Bixschoote	U 17 d 6.2
Goedbeek Farm	28NW3 Poperinghe	H 20 a 1.6
Goethals Farm	28SW2 Wytschaete	N 22 b 1.9
Goeulzin [village]	51bNE4 Cantin	K 4 d, 5 c, 10 b, d, 11 a, c
Goeulzin Chateau	51bNE4 Cantin	K 10 b 8.7
Gog [German M.G. Post]	51bSW4 Bullecourt	U 21 a 3.1
Golan Farm	28NW3 Poperinghe	G 35 b 0.3
Golancourt Aerodrome [German, 1918]	66dSE [1]	P 17 d, 18 c, 23 b, 24 a
Golden Cross Roads	28NE4 Dadizeele	L 22 c 1.9
Golden Farm	20SE2 Hooglede	R 18 c 95.05
Goldfish Chateau	28NW4 Ypres	H 11 a, b
Goldfish Line [1918]	28NW4 Ypres	H 10 b, c, d, 11 a, b, c, 12 a
Goldflake Farm	28NE4 Dadizeele	L 19 c 05.95
Goldneys Redoubt [Sept 1915]	36cNW1 La Bassée	A 2 b
Goldsmith Farm	28NE4 Dadizeele	K 29 a 3.0
Golfe Alley	62bSW1 Gricourt	M 18 d, N 13 a, b, c
Gollywog Lane	51bSW4 Bullecourt	U 20 b
Gombert Farm	36aNE2 Vieux Berquin	E 29 c 9.1
Gomiecourt [village]	57cNW1 Gomiecourt	A 23 b, d, 29 b
Gomiécourt [village]	62cSW3 & 4 Marchélepot	T 13 d, 14 c, 20 a
Gomiecourt Circle Trench	57cNW1 Gomiecourt	A 23 b, d, 29 a, b
Gommecourt [village]	57dNE1 & 2 Fonquevillers	E 28 c, d, K 4 a, b
Gommecourt Park	57dNE1 & 2 Fonquevillers / 3 & 4 Hébuterne	K 3 b, d, 4 a, c, d
Gommecourt Support [1918]	57dNE1 & 2 Fonquevillers	E 29 a, b
Gommecourt Trench [1918]	57dNE1 & 2 Fonquevillers	E 29, 30, F19, 20, 25, K5
Gommecourt Wood	57dNE1 & 2 Fonquevillers	E 28 b, c, d
Gondola Farm	20SE2 Hooglede	R 10 b 4.0
Gondole Trench	62bSW1 Gricourt	N 19 c, d, 25 b, d
Gondoles, Tranchée des	62cSW1 & 2 Belloy	N 18 a, b, d, 24 b
Gondrecourt Trench	66cNW3 Essigny / 4 Berthenicourt	H 15 a, b, d, 16 c
Gong Lane [trench]	57cSE2 Gonnelieu	R 27 a
Gong Spinney	28NE2 Moorslede	E 17 d 7.5
Gong Trench	57cNE3 Hermies	K 14 c, 20 b
Gonnelieu [village]	57cSE2 Gonnelieu	R 26 d, 27 c, d, 32 b, 33 a
Gonnelieu Ridge	57cSE2 Gonnelieu	R 22 d, 28 a, b
Gonning Avenue	57cSE4 Villers-Guislain	X 4 d, 5 c
Gontard Trench [1918]	66eNW [2 Thennes]	B 23 b, d
Gooch Street	57dNE1 & 2 Fonquevillers	E 27 d
Good Eye Spur [light rly, Vimy]	36cSW3 Vimy	S 24 d
Good Man Farm / Good Old Man Farm	57cSE2 Gonnelieu	R 9 a
Good Street	57cSW1 Gueudecourt	N 25 d, 26 c
Goodman Avenue	36cSW3 Vimy	S 27 c, d
Goodman Redoubt [Château de Pommery]	66dNE [2 Roupy]	F 9 c
Goodrich Junction [road jct]	28NE4 Dadizeele	K 35 a 95.20
Goods Trenches	57dNE4 & 57cNW3 Achiet	L 29 b, 30 a
Goodwin / Goodwin's Post [Grease Trench]	57dSE2 & 57cSW1 Le Sars	N 20 b
Goodwood House	36aNE3 Haverskerque	J 12 b 99.80
Goole Alley	57cNW2 Vaulx-Vraucourt	C 5 b, 6 a

Name	Map Sheet	Map Reference
Goose Alley	57cNE2 Bourlon	E 28 b
Goose Alley	57dSE2 & 57cSW1 Le Sars	M 24 b, c, d, 29 d, 30 a, c
Goose Foot Cross Roads	20SE3 Westroosebeke	V 10 b 55.50
Goose Support	57cSW1 Gueudecourt	M 24 a
Gooseberry Farm	28SW4 Ploegsteert	U 7 b 35.85
Gopher Alley	36cNW3 Loos	H 7 a
Gophir Cross Roads	27NE1 Herzeele	E 13 c 6.8
Gordon Alley	36cNW3 Loos	G 36 d, H 31 c
Gordon Alley	51bNW1 Roclincourt	B 13 a
Gordon Alley	51bSW1 Neuville Vitasse	N 13 a
Gordon Alley	51bSW2 Vis-en-Artois	N 18 b, O 13 a, b
Gordon Alley	57dSE4 Ovillers	X 6 a, c, 11 b
Gordon Alley [Dec. 1915]	36cNW3 Loos	G 4 d, 5 a
Gordon Alley [Sept / Oct 1915]	36cNW3 Loos	G 9 b, 10 a
Gordon Avenue	28SW4 Ploegsteert	U 27 b
Gordon Avenue	36cSW3 Vimy	S 14 d
Gordon Avenue	51bSW2 Vis-en-Artois	N 18, O 7, 8, 13, 14
Gordon Camp [Railway Triangle]	51bNW3 Arras	G 19 central
Gordon Castle [Thiepval Wood]	57dSE1 & 2 Beaumont	Q 30 b, d
Gordon Copse	62bNW4 Ramicourt	I 16 a
Gordon Corner [road junction]	20SE2 Hooglede	R 15 c 5.8
Gordon Crater	36cSW1 Lens	N 1 a
Gordon Crater [Railway Wood]	28NW4 & NE3 Zillebeke	I 12 a 1.3
Gordon Farm [near Ridge Wood]	28SW2 Wytschaete	N 5 a 2.7
Gordon Farm C.T.	28NW4 & NE3 Zillebeke	I 16, 17, 18
Gordon House How[itzer] Spurs [rly, 1917-18]	28NW4 Ypres	I 15 b, 16 a
Gordon House, Farm & Dump	28NW4 & NE3 Zillebeke	I 16 b
Gordon Line	36aSE3 Gonnehem / 4 Locon	Q 3, W 2, 3
Gordon Post	57dSE4 Ovillers	X 14 d
Gordon Post [Lock 7 bis, The Bluff	28NW4 & NE3 Zillebeke	I 33 d 51.40
Gordon Pump	36cNW3 Loos	G 10 b
Gordon Road [road]	36aSE1 St Venant	Q 1 a, c, 7 a
Gordon Support	51bSW2 Vis-en-Artois	O 13 b, d
Gordon Support, Reserve & Switch	51bSW4 Bullecourt	U 28 a
Gordon Terrace	28NW4 & NE3 Zillebeke	I 33 a 8.2
Gordon Trench	28NW4 & NE3 Zillebeke	J 13 c
Gordon Trench	36cSW3 Vimy	S 15, 16
Gordon Trench [new front line]	57dSE1 & 2 Beaumont	Q 17 a, c, d
Gordons Castle	57dSE4 Ovillers	X 20
Goret, Tranchée du	62cSW3 & 4 Marchélepot	T 19 c, d
Gorey Farm	27NE2 Proven	F 15 a 90.85
Gorgue, la [Estaires]	36aNE4 Merville	L 34 a, b, c, d
Gorioles Trench	62cSW1 & 2 Belloy	N 18 a, b, d
Goritz, Tranchée de / Gorsilz [sic] Trench	62cSW1 & 2 Belloy	N 12 c
Gorizia Trench	62cSW2 Barleux	N 22 b, d
Gorre [village]	36bNE2 Beuvry	F 3 b
Gorre Wood	36aSE4 Locon / 36bNE2 Beuvry	X 27 d, F 3 b
Gory Trench	51bSW2 Vis-en-Artois	O 16 d, 17 b, c
Gosford Terrace	51bNW3 Arras	G 24 b, d
Gosh Walk	36cSW3 Vimy	M 32 c
Gospel Villa	36NW1 Steenwerck	H 3 a 5.1
Gosport Trench	51bNW3 Arras	G 24 a, b
Gossart Farm [Beaulencourt]	57cSW2 Villers-au-Flos	N 18 c 05.95
Gosse Alley	62cSW3 Vermandovillers	T 19 b, 20 a

Name	Map Sheet	Map Reference
Gosset Street	57dSE4 Ovillers	W 6 b
Gossip Trench	70dNW [3 Sinceny]	H 27 a, b
Gostin Trench	62cSW2 Barleux	N 30 c, 36 a
Gotha Trench	57cSW4 Combles	U 9 c
Gotha Trench / Tranchée de Gotha	62cSW2 Barleux / 4 St. Christ	O 27 d, 33 b, d
Gothié Alley	62cSW3 Vermandovillers	S 6 b, d
Gott Mit Uns Trench	62cNW4 Péronne	I 15 d, 21 b
Gottlieb Trench	62cNW4 Péronne	I 8 b, d, 14 b, d
Goudberg	20SE3 Westroosebeke	V 29 d
Goudberg Copse	20SE3 Westroosebeke	V 29 a, b
Goudée, Tranchée	62cSW1 & 2 Belloy	O 8 c
Goudezeune Farm	28SW2 Wytschaete	O 15 b 10.35
Gough House	28SW3 Bailleul	S 30 a 1.4
Gough Lines [huts]	28SW3 Bailleul	S 29 b, 30 a
Goujet, Tranchée [Middlesex Trench, part of]	36cSW1 Lens	M 15 a, c
Goulot Wood	36cSW3 Vimy	T 1 a, c
Gounaris Trench	70dNW4 St Gobain	I 19 d, 20 c, 26 a
Gounod Trench	20SW2 Zwartegat	O 5 d, 11 b, 12 a, c
Gounod Trench	57dNE3 & 4 Hébuterne	K 22 b, d
Gounod Wood	20SE2 Hooglede	R 5 b
Gourbi Farm	20SW4 Bixschoote	U 8 a 75.15
Gourd Farm	20SE3 Westroosebeke	V 28 a 10.75
Gourde Trench / Boyau de la Gourde	62cSW3 & 4 Marchélepot	T 21 b, c, d, 22 a, 27 a
Gourdin Trench	62cSW3 Vermandovillers	T 20 c
Gourgandines / Sourgandines Trench	62cSW3 Vermandovillers	S 10 b, d
Gourlay Trench	57dSE4 Ovillers	X 11 b
Gournier Farm	28NW2 St Julien	C 9 d 2.7
Gournier Huts	28NW2 St Julien	C 9 a
Gourock Avenue	28NW4 & NE3 Zillebeke	I 28 b
Gourock Road	28NW4 & NE3 Zillebeke	I 24 b, J 19 a
Gourock Street	28NW4 & NE3 Zillebeke	I 24 b
Gourock Street [Thiepval Wood]	57dSE1 & 2 Beaumont	Q 30 d, R 25 c
Gourock Trench	51bNW3 Arras	G 24 d
Gouvernement Ferme, le	57cSW4 Combles	U 22 b, d
Gouy Junction [light rly]	36bSE4 Carency	W 5 c, d
Gouy Station [light rly]	36bSE4 Carency	W 5 a
Gouzeaucourt [village]	57cSE2 Gonnelieu / 4 Villers-Guislain	Q 30 d, 36a, b, R 25 c, 31 a, c
Gouzeaucourt Valley	57cSE2 Gonnelieu / 4 Villers-Guislain	R 25, 31, W 6, 12, X 1, 7
Gouzeaucourt Wood	57cSE2 Gonnelieu	Q21d, 22c,d, 27b,d, 28 a,c, 33b, 34a
Govan Dump [light rly, Bully Grenay]	36bSE2 Boyeffles	R 11 a, b
Govan Street [Thiepval Wood]	57dSE1 & 2 Beaumont	R 25 a, c
Government Farm	57cSW4 Combles	U 22 b
Government Trench [Government Farm]	57cSW4 Combles	U 22 b, c, d, 28 b
Gower Buildings	28NW3 Poperinghe	G 26 a 1.9
Gower Street	28SW2 Wytschaete	N 29 a, b
Gower Street	51bNW3 Arras / SW1 Neuville Vitasse	G 31, M 1, 2, 8
Gowers Trench	51bNW1 Roclincourt	A 4 d
Gowrie Street	57dSE4 Ovillers	X 19 a
Gowther [sic] Road [Gawthorpe]	28NW2 St Julien	C 15 c, 21 a
Gowthorpe Road [Nov 1915]	28NW2 St Julien	C 15 c, 21 a
Grab Trench	36cSW3 Vimy	M 32 c
Grab Trench	51bNW1 Roclincourt	A 16 b
Graben Trench	51bNW1 Roclincourt	A 5 a
Grace Farm	28NE2 Moorslede	E 4 b 9.5

Name	Map Sheet	Map Reference
Grace Trench [1918]	57dNE3 & 4 Hébuterne	K 33 d
Grace Wood	62dSE [2 Proyart]	Q 22 d
Graf [farm]	28NE1 Zonnebeke	D 5 d 50.65
Graf Wood [Passchendaele]	28NE1 Zonnebeke	D 5 d, 6 c
Grafton Copse	62bSW4 Homblières	U 2 c
Grafton Post	62cNE2 Epéhy	F 5 c
Grafton Street	36cNW1 La Bassée	A 21 a, b
Grafton Street	36cSW1 Lens	M 5 b
Grafton Street, Lower [S of Menin Rd]	28NW4 & NE3 Zillebeke	I 18 a
Grafton Street, Upper & Lower [Hooge]	28NW4 & NE3 Zillebeke	I 17 b, 18 a, b
Grafton Street, Upper [N of Menin Rd]	28NW4 & NE3 Zillebeke	I 18 a
Grafton Trench	62cNE2 Epéhy	F 11 d
Graham Post	62cNE4 Roisel	L 30 a 0.0
Grail Copse	62bSW4 Homblières	T 11 d, 12 c, 17 b
Graincourt Line	57cNE4 Marcoing	K 5, 6, 11, 12, L 1, 2, 8, 9, 15
Graincourt-lez-Havrincourt [village]	57cNE2 Bourlon / 4 Marcoing	E 29 d, 30 c, K 5 a, b, d, 6 a, c
Gralsburg Post	57cNE1 Quéant	E 1 d
Gramophone Farm	20SW2 Zwartegat	O 20 b
Gramophone Trench	20SW2 Zwartegat	O 20 b, 21 a
Grampus Cottage	28SW3 Bailleul	T 13 a 8.2
Granby Avenue	36cSW3 Vimy	S 14 d
Granby Street	57cSE2 Gonnelieu	Q 28 d
Granby Street / Avenue	36cSW3 Vimy	S 14 d, 15 c
Grand Avenue	51bNW1 Roclincourt	A 16 c
Grand Beaumart, le [hamlet]	36NW1 Steenwerck	A 22 a
Grand Bois	28SW2 Wytschaete	N 18 b, O 13 a, b, c, d
Grand Bretelle Trench	51bNW1 Roclincourt	A 10 b
Grand Canal [Givenchy, April 1915]	36cNW1 La Bassée	A 2 / 8
Grand Collecteur Trench	51bNW1 Roclincourt	A 15, 16, 22, 23, 29
Grand Condé, Cité du [miners' cottages]	36cSW1 Lens	N 9 d, 15 a, b
Grand Dam Lock	36aNE3 Haverskerque	K 2 c 3.9
Grand Fleet Street	28NW4 & NE3 Zillebeke	I 34 b
Grand Gardes Trench	62cSW3 Vermandovillers	T 14 a, b
Grand Haie Farm	28SW4 Ploegsteert	U 23 a 95.65
Grand Hasard, le [hamlet]	36aNE1 Morbecque	D 8 d, 9 c
Grand National, The [road, St Floris]	36aSE1 St Venant	P 6 a, b, c
Grand Pacaut, le [hamlet]	36aNE4 Merville	K 35 d
Grand Place [Béthune]	36bNE2 Beuvry	E 11 a 5.3
Grand Priel Chateau	62cNE4 Roisel	L 23 a 4.2
Grand Priel Farm	62cNE4 Roisel	L 29 b 40.55
Grand Priel Woods	62cNE4 Roisel	L 16 c, d, 17 c, 22 a, b, c, d, 23 a, c
Grand Ravine	57cNE4 Marcoing	K 29, 30, L 25, 26
Grand Sec Bois [village]	36aNE1 Morbecque	E 8 a, b, c, d
Grand Slam [farm]	36NW1 Steenwerck	A 30 c 4.8
Grand Stand [Tower Bridge / Pylons]	36cNW3 Loos	G 36 c
Grand Treille [farm]	36aNE3 Haverskerque	J 33 d 85.51
Grand Trunk Line [light rly]	36cSW3 Vimy	S 2 b, c, d, 3 a
Grand Trunk Pacific [railway]	36cSW2 Harnes	N 16 b, d, 22 b, d, 28 b
Grand Trunk Trench	36cSW3 Vimy	T 21 c, d, 25 b, 26 a, b, 27 a
Grand Wood	62cNW4 Péronne	H 36 b, I 31 a
Grandcourt [village]	57dSE1 & 2 Beaumont	R 8 d, 9 a, b, c, d
Grandcourt Trench	57dSE2 Beaumont	R 10 d, 11 c, d, 15 b, 16 a, b
Grande Ceinture, Boyau	62cSW1 Dompierre	M 3 b
Grande Devise, la [farm]	36aNE3 Haverskerque	K 14 d 50.65

Name	Map Sheet	Map Reference
Grande Flamengrie Farm	36NW4 Bois Grenier	I 25 d, 26 c
Grande Haie Ferme	28SW4 Ploegsteert	U 23 b 05.70
Grande Marquette Farm	36aNE1 Morbecque	E 7 b 20.65
Grande Munque Farm, La	28SW4 Ploegsteert	T 24 d 3.7
Grande Polka Cabaret, La	28SW1 Kemmel	N 21 d 5.4
Grandjean Trench	62cSW3 Vermandovillers	T 13 b, c
Grange Avenue, & Subway	36cSW3 Vimy	S 27 b, 28 a
Grange Group [craters]	36cSW3 Vimy	S 22 c
Grange Road	28NW4 & NE3 Zillebeke	I 15 d to 16 d
Grange Street	57dSE4 Ovillers	X 7 d
Grange, The	51cSE4 Blaireville	X 8 b
Granger Street	51bSW1 Neuville Vitasse	M 9 c, d, 15 b
Grant / Grant's Post	36SW1 Aubers	M 23 d
Grantchester Farm	20SE3 Westroosebeke	W 1 a
Grantham Alley	57cSE2 Gonnelieu	Q 12 b
Grantham Street	51bSW1 Neuville Vitasse	M 7 d, 13 b, 14 a
Grants [keep, late 1915]	36SW1 Aubers	M 23 d 2.4
Granville [light rly sidings & locality]	28NW3 Poperinghe	H 13 central
Granville Trench	62bSW3 St Quentin	S 21 d, 27 b, d
Grape Trench	51bSW1 Neuville Vitasse	M 29 c
Grape Trench	51bSW2 Vis-en-Artois	O 7 b, 8 a
Graphic Trench	57cSW3 Longueval	T 21 d
Graspers, The [farm]	20SE2 Hooglede	R 16 d 1.8
Grass Avenue / Street [Mesnil]	57dSE1 & 2 Beaumont	Q 28 a, b, d
Grass Farm	28SW2 Wytschaete	O 29 c 15.30
Grass Lane [Flers]	57dSE2 & 57cSW1 Le Sars	N 25 b, d
Grass Siding [light rly]	36cSW1 Lens	M 10 a, c
Grass Way	36cNW3 Loos	G 36 a
Grasset Lane	28SW4 Ploegsteert	N 35 d
Grate Trench	57dSE2 Beaumont	Q 5 a
Grate Weg	28NW4 & NE3 Zillebeke	J 25 c
Gratte-Panche Farm	57bSW1 Bantouzelle	M 35 a 20.45
Gratz Trench / Tranchée de Gratz	62cSW3 & 4 Marchélepot	T 15 b, 16 a
Graudenz, Boyau de	66dNW3 Hattencourt / 66eNE4 Beaufort	G 19 b, L 23 a, b, 24 a
Grave Copse	20SE2 Hooglede	Q 11 b 99.90
Grave Pit Trench	36cNW3 Loos	H 32 c
Gravel Copse	51bNE4 Cantin	L 3 d, 4 c, 9 b, 10 a
Gravel Farm	20SE3 Westroosebeke	V 7 b 95.05
Gravel Street	51bSW1 Neuville Vitasse	M 9 a, c, d, 15 b
Gravenstafel Switch, The	28NE1 Zonnebeke	D 7, 8, 9
Gravenstafel, s' [hamlet & crossroads]	28NE1 Zonnebeke	D 9 c 85.22
Graves Copse	28SW2 Wytschaete	O 6 c 8.8
Graves Cottage	28NW3 Poperinghe	G 4 d 3.8
Graveyard Cottage	28NW4 & NE3 Zillebeke	J 31 a 2.9
Gravier Inn	27NE2 Proven	F 7 d 6.7
Gravy Lane	57cSW4 Combles	T 10 c
Grayling Post	57cNE3 Hermies	J 12 b, K 7 a
Grayling Support	57cNE3 Hermies	K 7 a, c
Grayling Trench [1918]	57dNE1 & 2 Fonquevillers	K 4 b, 5 a
Graz Trench	62cNW2 Bouchavesnes	I 3 b, d, 4 a
Grease Trench	36cNW3 Loos	G 12 b, d, H 7 c
Grease Trench	57dSE2 & 57cSW1 Le Sars	N 20 d, 21 c
Great Bear [wood]	62bNW3 Bellicourt	G 33 d, 34 c
Great Bear [wood]	62dNE2 Méaulte	F 22 d, 23 c

Name	Map Sheet	Map Reference
Great North Road	36SW1 Aubers	M 12 b, N 7 a, c, d
Great North Road	57cSW3 Longueval	S 8 d, 9 c, 14 a, b
Great Northern [road / tramway]	57dNE3 & 4 Hébuterne	K 27 d, 28 c
Great Northern Trench [1918]	51bNW1 Roclincourt / 3 Arras	A 24, 30, G 6
Great Oak, The [trig point, Nieppe Forest]	36aNE3 Haverskerque	J 18 a 06.57
Great Peter Street [road]	36cSW1 Lens	M 17 a, b, 18 a, c, d, N 13 c, d
Great Wall of China [Wall of China]	28NW4 & NE3 Zillebeke	I 16 a - 17 c
Greatwood Avenue	36NW4 Bois Grenier	H 36 b, I 31 a, c, d,
Greatwood Switch [1918]	36NW4 Bois Grenier	H 30 a, b, c, d, 36 a
Gredin Alley	62cSW3 Vermandovillers	T 19 c, 25 a, b
Greek Fork [road jct]	28NE2 Moorslede	E 16 b 1.7
Greek House	20SW4 Bixschoote	U 13 c 0.2
Green Avenue	51bNW1 Roclincourt	A 22 a
Green Avenue [road, Le Barque]	57cSW1 Gueudecourt	M 7 a
Green Chasseur Alley	66cNW4 Berthenicourt / SW2 Vendeuil	I 31 c, N 6, 12, 17, 22, 28, O 1
Green Copse	66dNW3 Hattencourt	G 3 c
Green Crassier [The Green Dump]	36cSW1 Lens	N 20 c, d
Green Curve, The	36cNW3 Loos	G 18 c, d, H 13 c
Green Dump	57cSW3 Longueval	S 16, 22
Green Dump	57dSE2 Beaumont	Q 12 c 1.2
Green Dump	62cNW1 Maricourt	A 5 a
Green Egg	36cSW1 Lens	M 5 d, 6 c
Green Farm	28SW2 Wytschaete	O 17 b 3.4
Green Jacket Ride	28NW4 & NE3 Zillebeke	I 30 b, J 13 d, 19 a, b, c
Green Lane	57cSE4 Villers-Guislain	R 31 d, X 1 b, 2 a
Green Lane [road]	51bNW4 Fampoux / SW2 Vis-en-Artois	O 2 c, d, 3 c, 9 a, b, 10 a, b
Green Line	51bNW4 Fampoux	H 11 a
Green Line	57cSE2 Gonnelieu	R 19 d, 20 c
Green Mill	20SW4 Bixschoote	U 25 d 2.2
Green Mill Trench	20SW4 Bixschoote / 28NW2 St Julien	U 25 c, C 1 a, b
Green Mound [Crater]	36cSW1 Lens	M 6 b
Green Mound Line [light rly]	36cNW3 Loos / SW1 Lens	G 36 d, H 31 a, b, c, M 6 b
Green Street	51bSW1 Neuville Vitasse	M 3 c, 9 a, b, d, 10 c
Green Street	57dNE1 & 2 Fonquevillers	E 22 d
Green Street [1918]	57dNE3 & 4 Hébuterne	K 6 c, d
Green Street [road]	36aSE4 Locon	X 3 d, 4 a, c
Green Switch	57cSE2 Gonnelieu / 4 Villers-Guislain	R 26 c, 31 b, d, 32 a
Green Trench	57cSW3 Longueval	S 12 d, 18 b
Green Trench	62dNE2 Méaulte	F 3 c
Green Trench, & Street	57dNE3 & 4 Hébuterne	K 34 a
Green Wood	28SW2 Wytschaete	O 17 a, b, c
Green Wood	62cNW3 Vaux	G 36 b
Green Work	51bSW2 Vis-en-Artois	O 3 d, 9 b
Green-Jacket Ridge	57cSE1 Bertincourt	P 23, 24, Q 19
Greenjacket Trench	57cSW3 Longueval	S 11 c, d
Greenland Farm	27NE3 Winnezeele	K 1 d 30.05
Greenland Hill	51bNW4 Fampoux	I 8 b
Greenly Corner	20SE3 Westroosebeke	W 21 c 00.25
Greenock Avenue	57dSE1 & 2 Beaumont	Q 36 a, b
Greenwood / Green Wd / Vert Bois Lane [rd]	36aSE4 Locon	Q 35 d, W 5 a, b, c, 10 b, 11 a
Greg Trench	66cNW4 Berthenicourt	H 5 d
Gregory Cross Roads	28NE4 Dadizeele	K 27 b 95.75
Grenade Trench	36cNW3 Loos	G 6 c, d, 12 b
Grenade Trench	51bNW4 Fampoux	I 26 b, d

Name	Map Sheet	Map Reference
Grenades Trench	62bSW1 Gricourt	M 30 a, c
Grenadier Farm	20SW4 Bixschoote	U 13 d 9.7
Grenadier Loop	36cNW3 Loos	G 5 c
Grenadier Road [Trench]	36cNW1 La Bassée	A 8 a, b, c, d, 9 a
Grenadier Trench	36cSW3 Vimy	S 12 b, T 7 a
Grenadier Trench	51bNW1 Roclincourt	A 4 d
Grenadiers Trench	62cSW3 Vermandovillers	T 9 a, b
Grenadier-Weg [Gas Alley]	57cSW3 Longueval	T 2 a, b
Grenay - Noyelles Line	36bNE4 Noeux-les-Mines / 36cNW3 Loos	L12a,c, 18a,c, 24c, 30a, G25b,d, 31b,d
Grenay - Vermelles Line	36cNW3 Loos	G 14 b, d, 20 b, c, d, 26 a, c, 32 a
Grenay Keep	36cSW1 Lens	M 1 b, d
Grenay Line (Vermelles Branch)	36cNW3 Loos	G 20 a, c, 26 a
Grenay Road Keep	36cNW3 Loos	G 26 a
Grenay Siding [light rly]	36bSE2 Boyeffles	R 8 d
Grenilles [Alley / Trench]	62bSW2 Fonsommes	N 17 a, b, d, 18 c
Grenoble Trench	66cNW4 Berthenicourt	I 13 d
Grenouille / Grenquille Trench	62bSW2 Fonsommes	N 11 d, 17 b, 18 a, c, 24 a
Grenouille Trench	62cSW4 St. Christ	U 27 b, d
Grenouiller, La	62cNW3 Vaux	G 18 a
Grenouillères	57bSW1 Bantouzelle	M 20 a
Grenuseule Trench	66dNW1 Punchy	B 9 b, 10 a
Grenz Graben	57dNE1 & 2 Fonquevillers	E 23 d, 29 b
Grenz Weg	51bNW1 Roclincourt	A 24 a
Gresham Avenue / Alley	57cSE2 Gonnelieu	R 27 c, d, 32 b, 33 a
Gressaire Wood	62dNE [4 Bray-sur-Somme]	K 23 c, d, 28 a, b, 29 a
Gretchen Ravine	66eNW [2 Thennes]	C 17 c, 22 b, 23 a
Gretchen Trench	36SW3 Richebourg	M 36 a, b, N 31 a, b, d
Gretna Cross [cross roads]	28NW3 Poperinghe	H 32 b 45.90
Greve Farm	36aNE4 Merville	K 24 d 35.60
Greville / Greviller Trench	57dSE2 & 57cSW1 Le Sars	M 1 d
Grévillers [village]	57cNW3 Bapaume	G 30 central
Grevillers Line	57dNE4 & 57cNW3 Achiet	G 35 c, d
Grevillers Trench	57dSE2 & 57cSW1 Le Sars	M 1, 2, 3, 4, 5, 7
Grevillers Trench [Pys]	57dSE2 & 57cSW1 Le Sars	M 1 d, 7 b
Grey Avenue / Trench	57dNE3 & 4 Hébuterne	K 28 d, 29 c
Grey Corner [road junction]	20SE2 Hooglede	R 16 d 6.0
Grey Farm	28SW4 Ploegsteert	U 9 b 6.1
Grey Farm Reserve	28SW4 Ploegsteert	U 9 b, d, 15 b, 16 a, c
Grey Keep [1918]	28NW2 St Julien	C 30 d
Grey Ruin	28NW2 St Julien	C 30 a 9.2
Grey Street	51bSW1 Neuville Vitasse	M 9 a, c, d
Grey Street	51bSW2 Vis-en-Artois / 4 Bullecourt	N 35 b, c, d
Greyhound Avenue	51bSW4 Bullecourt	U 17 a, b, c, 18 a
Gric House	28NW1 Elverdinghe	A 16 b 00.20
Gricourt [village]	62bSW1 Gricourt	M 22 d, 23 c, 29 a
Grid House	28NE1 Zonnebeke	E 21 d
Grid House	28NE2 Moorslede	F 20 d 95.30
Grid Road	28NW4 & NE3 Zillebeke	J 13 d, 19 b
Grid Trench [1917-18]	28NE3 Gheluvelt	J 13 d
Grid Trench [incorrect form of Gird Trench]	57cSW1 Gueudecourt / 3 Longueval	see Gird Trench
Grid Walk	28NE1 Zonnebeke	D 25 d
Gridiron 1, 2 & 3	57cSW3 Longueval	S 24 b, T 19 a
Gridiron Lane	51bNW1 Roclincourt	G 6 a, b
Gridiron Trenches	36SW3 Richebourg	S 10 a

Name	Map Sheet	Map Reference
Gridiron, The	51bNW1 Roclincourt / 3 Arras	G 6 a, c
Griffin Alley	36cNW3 Loos	G 6 c, d, H 1 c
Griffon Alley / Boyau du Griffon	62cSW3 & 4 Marchélepot	T 20 b, d, 26 b, d
Grigou, Tranchée [Cooker Alley, SE end]	36cSW1 Lens	M 32 a
Grillons Trench	62bSW2 Fonsommes	N 16 b, 17 a, c
Grilse Trench [1918]	57dNE1 & 2 Fonquevillers / 3 & 4 Hébuterne	E 30 c, d, F 25 a
Grime Farm	36NW1 Steenwerck	B 27 c 95.75
Grimm Trench / Tranchée Grimm	66cNW2 Itancourt	B 12 b, d, 18 b
Grimwood Tunnel	36cNW3 Loos	G 12 c
Gringley Farm	20SE4 Roulers	Q 33 d 95.90
Gringo Farm	36NW1 Steenwerck	B 27 c 8.7
Gripp's Cut	57dSE1 & 2 Beaumont	Q 4 c, 10 a
Gris Pot ['Grease Pot', hamlet]	36NW4 Bois Grenier	H 18 d, 24 a, b
Gris Pot Post	36NW4 Bois Grenier	H 18 d, 24 b
Grive Alley	62bSW1 Gricourt	M 30 b
Grive Trench	62bSW2 Fonsommes	N 29 a, c
Grive, Tranchée de la	66dNW2 Morchain	B 18 d, C 7 d, 13 a, c
Grizel Junction [road jct]	28SW3 Bailleul	S 18 b 3.2
Grizzly Alley	36cNW3 Loos	G 12 a, b
Groenelinde Cabaret	28SW2 Wytschaete	O 17 c 85.85
Groenen / Grünen Jaeger, Den	28NW4 Ypres	H 16 d
Groenenburg Farm	28NE3 Gheluvelt	J 31 b 1.5
Grognards / Grounards Trench	62bSW2 Fonsommes	N 12 d, 18 a, b, O 7 c
Gropi Trench	57cSW3 Longueval	T 21 a, b
Gros Chêne, le [hamlet]	36aNE3 Haverskerque	J 11 b
Gros Hêtre Wood	66eNW [2 Thennes / 4 Morisel]	B 30, H 5, 6
Groseille Trench	20SW3 Oostvleteren	T 8 b, 9 a, c
Grosherz-Freier Graben	57dNE1 & 2 Fonquevillers	E 29 a
Grosse Bastion, Die [The Bluff]	28NW4 & NE3 Zillebeke	I 34 c
Grossen Battery	5SW1 Zeebrugge	M 19 d, 25 b
Grosvenor Cross Roads	28NE4 Dadizeele	K 18 d 7.6
Grotto Post	36SW3 Richebourg	S 2 a 8.8
Group Post	62bNW3 Bellicourt	G 25 d
Grouse Butt [near Lancashire Farm]	28NW2 St Julien	C 14 c
Grouse Butts [Givenchy]	36cNW1 La Bassée	A 2 d
Grouse Butts Support [Givenchy]	36cNW1 La Bassée	A 2 b, 3 a, c
Grouse Corner [road junction]	20SE2 Hooglede	R 2 b 80.75
Grouse Farm	28SE1 Wervicq	P 25 b 6.7
Grouse Street	51cSE & 51bSW Ficheux	M 9 c, 15 a
Grove Alley [Flers]	57dSE2 & 57cSW1 Le Sars	M 30 c, d, 36 a, N 19 d, 25 a, b, c
Grove Copse	51bNE1 Brebières	D 30 d
Grove Farms	27NE4 Abeele	L 14 c
Grove Wood	27NE4 Abeele	L 14 b, c, d
Groves Avenue / Boyau Groves	62cNW1 Maricourt	A 16 a
Grovetown [1916]	62dNE2 Méaulte	L 1 b
Grovetown Camp [1916]	62dNE [4 Bray-sur-Somme]	L 8, 14
Grub Alley	36cNW1 La Bassée	A 29 c, d
Grub Farm	20SE2 Hooglede	R 14 b 95.60
Grub Lane	62bNW1 Gouy	A 7 d
Grün [farm]	28NE1 Zonnebeke	D 12 d 4.9
Grundherr Lane	51bSW1 Neuville Vitasse	M 17 a, b, d
Grundy Road [road]	57dSE2 & 57cSW1 Le Sars	M 8 a, b, 9 a, b,
Grundy Trench	57dSE2 & 57cSW1 Le Sars	M 3 c, d, 8 b, 9 a
Gruyterszale Farm	20SW4 Bixschoote	U 16 b 7.7

Name	Map Sheet	Map Reference
Guadeloupe Alley	62cSW1 Dompierre / 2 Barleux	M 6, N 1, 2, 8, 9, 15, 16
Guarbecque Locality	36aSW2 [Molinghem]	O 11, 12, 17, 18
Guard Farm	28SW2 Wytschaete	O 29 d 5.1
Guard Trench	57dSE2 & 57cSW1 Le Sars	M 8 c, 13 b, 14 a
Guardian Reserve	51bSW4 Bullecourt	U 13 c
Guards Trench	36SW3 Richebourg	S 9 d, 10 a, c
Gudel House	20SW4 Bixschoote	T 30 b
Gudgeon Post	57cNE3 Hermies	J 12 a
Gudgeon Trench	57dNE4 & 57cNW3 Achiet	L 20 c, d, 21 c
Guelder Trench	62bSW3 St Quentin	T 8 a
Guémappe [village]	51bSW2 Vis-en-Artois	N 18 b, d, O 13 a, c
Guenon Alley	66cSW2 Vendeuil	O 22 c, d, 27 b
Guepe Trench	62bSW2 Fonsommes	N 22 b, d
Guepes Alley	62cSW4 St. Christ	T 24 c, d, 30 b, U 25 a
Guêpes, Boyau des	62cSW3 & 4 Marchélepot	T 24 c, d, 30 b
Guerre Wood, la [Carnoy]	62cNW1 Maricourt	A 13 d
Guerre, Fin de la [place name]	36SW2 Radinghem	O 17 b
Guerriers Alley	62cNW3 Vaux / 4 Péronne	H 21 c, d, 22 a, c, d, 23 c
Guesclin Trench, Du	70dSW [2 Coucy-le-Château]	O 1 a
Guesclin, Tranchée du	57dNE3 & 4 Hébuterne	K 22 a, c, d
Guet Trench	62bSW2 Fonsommes	N 17 a, c
Gueudecourt [village]	57cSW1 Gueudecourt	N 26 b, d, 27 a
Guex, Tranchée des	70dSW [4 Vauxaillon]	U 12 b
Guides Alley	62bSW1 Gricourt	N 13 c, d
Guidon Trench	62cSW2 Barleux	N 28 b, d
Guignard Alley	66cNW4 Berthenicourt	H 35 b, 36 a
Guildford Trench	36cNW1 La Bassée	G 4 a, b
Guildford Trench	51bNW3 Arras	H 25 a
Guildford Trench	57dSE4 Ovillers	X 26 d
Guille Trench	62cSW2 Barleux	N 22 d, 28 b, 29 a
Guilleaume Trench	20SW4 Bixschoote	T 17 c
Guillemin [hamlet]	57bSW2 Clary	N 17 a
Guillemont [village]	57cSW3 Longueval	T 19 a, c, d, 25 a, b
Guillemont Alley	57cSW3 Longueval	S 30 a, b
Guillemont Station	57cSW3 Longueval	S 24 d 8.9
Guillermot Avenue / Trench	51bNW1 Roclincourt	A 8 c, d, 9 a, b, c
Guilmant Trench	20SW2 Zwartegat	O 10 c, 16 a, c, 22 a
Guilmant Trench	66cNW4 Berthenicourt	H 36 a
Guilty Cottage	28NE2 Moorslede	F 12 c 15.77
Guimauve Trench	62bSW2 Fonsommes	N 23 c, 29 a
Guimbarde Alley	62bSW2 Fonsommes	N 23 d, 24 c, 29 a, b
Guinea Farm	20SE2 Hooglede	R 13 d 15.95
Guinea Fowl Wood	66cNW4 Berthenicourt	H 16 a
Guinness House	28NE4 Dadizeele	K 17 d 65.30
Guinness Trench [1918]	57dNE1 & 2 Fonquevillers / 3 & 4 Hébut.	E 27 b, K 3 b, 4 a, c
Guiriandes Trench	62bSW2 Fonsommes	N 22 b, d, 23 a
Guisancourt Farm	57bSW3 Honnecourt	T 27 c 0.5
Guiscard Trench	62bSW3 St Quentin	S 23 c
Guislain Trench	57cSE4 Villers-Guislain	X 8 b
Guizancourt Aerodrome [German, 1918]	62cSE3 Athies	V 21 b, c, d, 22 a, c, 27 b, d, 28 a, c
Guli Copse	62cSW1 Dompierre	N 31 b
Gully Farm [N of Railway Wood]	28NW4 & NE3 Zillebeke	I 5 d 57.03
Gully Farm Crater [N of Railway Wood]	28NW4 & NE3 Zillebeke	I 5 d 74.02
Gully Keep	36bNE4 Noeux-les-Mines	L 6 c 3.5

Name	Map Sheet	Map Reference
Gully Track	28NW4 & NE3 Zillebeke	J 8 b, 13, 14
Gully Trench	28NW4 & NE3 Zillebeke	I 5 d, 11 b
Gully, The	57dSE2 & 57cSW1 Le Sars	R 17 c
Gully, The [trench on N side of]	57dSE2 & 57cSW1 Le Sars	R 17 a, c
Gumboot Trench [Talus Amélnagé]	36cSW1 Lens	M 19 d, 20 c
Gun / Gan Alley	57cSW3 Longueval	T 1 b, 2 a
Gun Alley	36cNW3 Loos	G 29 d, 30 a, b, c
Gun Alley	51bSW4 Bullecourt	U 16 d, 17 a
Gun Alley	57cNE4 Marcoing	K 10 d
Gun Cotton Lane [road]	36SW1 Aubers	M 15 d, 16 c, d, 22 b
Gun Farm	28SW2 Wytschaete	O 27 a 8.8
Gun Hollow	57cSE1 Bertincourt	P 6 b, c, d
Gun Lane [road]	57cSE4 Villers-Guislain	X 7 a, b
Gun Pit Alley [Gun Pit Road; later Death Valley]	57cSW1 Gueudecourt	M 28 b
Gun Pit Road	57cSW1 Gueudecourt	M 28 b
Gun Post	36cSW3 Vimy / 4 Rouvroy	T 10 c
Gun Post	57cSE4 Villers-Guislain	X 7 b
Gun Post A	36cSW4 Rouvroy	T 10 d 4.4
Gun Post B	36cSW4 Rouvroy	T 10 c 9.7
Gun Post C	36cSW3 Vimy	T 10 c 3.9
Gun Post D [formerly C?]	36cSW4 Rouvroy	T 10 c 9.7
Gun Road [road]	28SW2 Wytschaete	O 27 a, b, d
Gun Street	51bSW1 Neuville Vitasse	M 9 c, 15 a
Gun Street [Cuinchy sector, 21-9-15]	36cNW1 La Bassée / 3 Loos	A 15 / 21
Gun Support	57cSE2 Gonnelieu	R 27 a, c, d
Gun Trench	36cNW3 Loos	G 12 b, d
Gun Trench	36cNW3 Loos	G 29 a
Gun Trench	51bNW4 Fampoux	I 32 a
Gun Trench	57cSE2 Gonnelieu	R 27 a, b, d
Gun Trench Switch	36cNW3 Loos	G 29 d, 30 a, b, c
Gun Valley	57cSW3 Longueval	S 12 b, T 7 a, c, d
Gunewele, la [hamlet]	36aNE1 Morbecque	D 1 d 8.8
Gunner Crater	36cSW3 Vimy	S 15 a
Gunner Farm / Gunners' Farm	36NW2 Armentières	C 2 d 5.3
Gunner Post	36NW4 Bois Grenier	H 18 d, I 13 c
Gunner/s Siding	36cNW1 La Bassée	A 15 a
Gunners Lodge	28NW4 Ypres	I 26 b 95.95
Gunners' Road	36cSW3 Vimy	S 3 b
Gunner's Walk	36NW4 Bois Grenier	H 35 b, d, 36 c
Gunpit Lane	51bSW1 Neuville Vitasse	N 19 c, 25 a
Gunpit Trench, & Road	57dSE2 & 57cSW1 Le Sars	M 25 d, 31 b, 32 a
Gunton Farm	27NE2 Proven	F 14 c 00.35
Gurkha Road [road, late 1915]	36SW1 Aubers	M 29 c, 35 a
Gurlu Wood Trench	62cNE1 Liéramont	D 22 a, c
Gurnard Cross [cross roads]	36aNE3 Haverskerque	K 21 b 7.5
Gurney Road [road]	36SW1 Aubers	M 8 d, 9 a, c, 14 a
Gusman Alley	66cNW2 Itancourt	B 12 a, c
Gustav Street	57cNE1 Quéant	D 1 d, 2 b, c, d
Gustave Trench / Tranchée Gustave	62cSW1 & 2 Belloy	N 12 c, 18 a
Gusty Support [Jan 1917]	57cSW2 Villers-au-Flos	N 28 c, d
Gusty Trench [misprinted Gosty & Gusly]	57cSW2 Villers-au-Flos	N 28 c, d
Gutemberg Trench	62cSW2 Barleux	O 28 a, c, 33 b, 34 a
Gutter Alley	66cNW2 Itancourt	B 24 a, c
Guy Farm	28SW2 Wytschaete	O 26 a 3.8

Name	Map Sheet	Map Reference
Guynemer Alley	66cNW1 Grugies	B 27 d
Guy's [dressing station, Sept 1915]	36cNW1 La Bassée	G 3 a 1.9
Guys Alley	36cNW1 La Bassée / 3 Loos	A 27 c, G 3 b
Guy's Alley	20SW2 Zwartegat	N 24 d
Gwalia Farm	28NW1 Elverdinghe	A 22 a 9.0
Gwalia Farm Hospital	28NW1 Elverdinghe	A 22 b, d
Gym Farm	28SW2 Wytschaete	O 17 b 3.9
H [outlying work, Fort 147]	51cSE3 & 4 Ransart	W 17 a 2.4
H 13 [late-1915, E of Y Wood]	28NW4 & NE3 Zillebeke	I 12 c 3.4
H 14 [late-1915, E of Y Wood]	28NW4 & NE3 Zillebeke	I 12 c 4.5
H 15 [late-1915, E of Y Wood]	28NW4 & NE3 Zillebeke	I 12 c 3.6
H 16 [late-1915, E of N end of Y Wood]	28NW4 & NE3 Zillebeke	I 12 c 15.65
H 17 [late-1915, WSW of Bellewaarde Farm]	28NW4 & NE3 Zillebeke	I 12 c 1.8
H 18 [late-1915, W of Bellewaarde Farm]	28NW4 & NE3 Zillebeke	I 12 a 1.1
H 19 [late-1915, WNW of Bellewaarde Farm]	28NW4 & NE3 Zillebeke	I 12 a 00.15
H 2 [Spring 1915]	28SW2 Wytschaete	N 18, 24
H 20 [late-1915, E end of Railway Wood]	28NW4 & NE3 Zillebeke	I 11 b 9.4
H 21 [late-1915, N of Railway Wood]	28NW4 & NE3 Zillebeke	I 11 b 8.6
H 22 [late-1915, astride Railway]	28NW4 & NE3 Zillebeke	I 11 b 8.8
H 3 [Spring 1915]	28SW2 Wytschaete	N 18, 24
H 4 Trench [E of Kemmel]	28SW2 Wytschaete	N 18, 24
H Camp	28NW1 Elverdinghe	A 9 b, 10 a
H Sap	57dSE4 Ovillers	R 31 c
H Sap [Givenchy]	36cNW1 La Bassée	A 9 b
H Sap [Triangle, S of Loos]	36cSW1 Lens	M 4 b
H Sector [4/15]	28SW2 Wytschaete	N 18, 24
H Track (double duckboards) [1917-18]	28NW2 St Julien / NE1 Zonnebeke	C 24, 29, 30, D 19, 20,
H Trenches [+ no, Jly '15, Br, opp Bell'de Lake]	28NW4 & NE3 Zillebeke	I 12 a, c
H Work	51bNW1 Roclincourt	A 29 b 7.1
H.L.I. Trench	57cSW3 Longueval	S 1 d
H.Q. Junction [road junction]	20SW4 Bixschoote	U 5 d 25.04
H.Q. Lane	57cSW2 Villers-au-Flos	N 30 c, d
Haalen [farm]	28NE1 Zonnebeke	D 11 a 9.6
Haalen Copse	28NE1 Zonnebeke	D 11 b
Haandekot [hamlet]	27NE2 Proven	E 4 d
Haanixbeek Farm	28NW2 St Julien	C 5 b 1.8
Haasmann Weg	51bSW1 Neuville Vitasse	M 20 d, 21 c
Habarcq Trench	51bNW3 Arras	H 25 d
Habben Weg	51cSE2 Beaumetz	R 35 a
Haboli / Napoli Street	36NW4 Bois Grenier	I 21 a
Haborn Alley	36cNW3 Loos	H 7 d, 13 a, b
Hache Copse	66dNW3 Hattencourt	G 15 d
Hache Trench	62bSW1 Gricourt / 3 St Quentin	N 31 b, d, 32 c
Hache Wood / Bois en Hache	36cSW1 Lens	S 2 a, b
Hack Trench	36cNW3 Loos	H 32 b, 33 a
Hack Trench	51bNW1 Roclincourt	B 25 c
Hackney Marshes	51bSW4 Bullecourt	U 22 c, 28 a
Hackney Villas [St Julien]	28NW2 St Julien	C 12 c 3.2
Hades Farm	28SW2 Wytschaete	O 18 d 5.4
Hadjopoulos Alley	62bSW1 Gricourt	N 31 b
Hadow House	27SE4 Meteren	R 31 d 55.12
Haecht Avenue	20SW3 Oostvleteren	T 9 d, 10 c
Haegedoorne [farm & place name]	28SW3 Bailleul	S 3 d 5.0
Haegedoorne Railhead / Siding / Refilling Point	28SW3 Bailleul	S 9 a

Name	Map Sheet	Map Reference
Hag Trench	36cSW2 Harnes	O 1 a, c
Hag Trench	51bNW1 Roclincourt	B 25 a, b
Hagebaert-St Jean [hamlet, S of Poperinghe]	28NW3 Poperinghe	G 8 c
Haggard Alley	36cNW3 Loos	H 7 c
Haggard Farm	36aNE4 Merville	L 24 c 5.8
Haggard Trench	51bNW4 Fampoux	H 6 a, c
Hagle [light rly locality]	28NW1 Elverdinghe	G 6 central
Hagle Dump	28NW1 Elverdinghe	G 6 a
Hague Farm	28NW3 Poperinghe	H 25 c 7.0
Haie / Hay Alley	36cNW3 Loos	G 17 b, 18 a, b
Haie Wood	57cSW4 Combles	T 23 b
Haie, La / The Haie	36cNW3 Loos	G 17 b
Haig Street	51bSW1 Neuville Vitasse	M 3 d, 4 a
Haig Trench [1918]	57cNW1 Gomiecourt	A 8 c, d, 14 b, 15 a
Hail Street	28NW2 St Julien	C 22 a
Hail Trench	57cSW2 Villers-au-Flos / 4 Combles	N 35 b, d
Haiphong Trench	62cSW2 Barleux	N 22 d, 28 b
Hair Alley	57dNE3 & 4 Hébuterne	K 17 b, 18 c, d
Hair Trench	51bNW1 Roclincourt	B 25 a
Hairpin Bend [& Trench]	36cNW1 La Bassée / 3 Loos	G 5 d, 6 c
Hairpin Crater	36cNW3 Loos	G 11 b
Hairpin System [British Defences]	57dSE [3 Bouzincourt] / 4 Ovillers	W 27, 28 approx; NW Albert
Hairpin, The [Oct 1915]	36cNW3 Loos	G 5 d, 6 c
Haisnes Alley	36cNW1 La Bassée	A 29 b, 30 a
Haisnes Trench	36cNW1 La Bassée	A 24 d, 30 b
Haitères, Tranchée des	66dNW1 Punchy / 2 Morchain	B 27 c, d, 28 a, c
Hake Alley	36cNW3 Loos	H 26 d
Hakim Alley	36cNW3 Loos	H 32 d
Hakim Trench	36cNW3 Loos	H 32 d, 33 c
Hal Trench	36cSW2 Harnes	O 1 c, d
Halberd Trench	51bNW4 Fampoux	I 31 b, d
Halberd Trench	62bSW1 Gricourt / 3 St Quentin	T 3 a, b, 4 a
Halcyon Trench	36cNW3 Loos	H 21 c, 27 a
Halcyon Trench	51bNW4 Fampoux	H 6 c
Halden House	28NE4 Dadizeele	K 27 b 65.65
Half Moon Street	36NW4 Bois Grenier	I 16 c
Half Moon Street [Givenchy; Sept 1915]	36cNW1 La Bassée	A 9 a
Half Moon Street [Potijze]	28NW2 St Julien	I 4 b, 5 a
Half Moon Trench	36cNW3 Loos	G 28
Half Moon Work [1918]	66eNW [4 Morisel]	H 10 c, 16 a
Half Moon, The [château park]	66dNW1 Punchy	A 10 a
Half Thatched Cottage/s	36NW2 Armentières	C 17 b 25.06
Half Trench	51bNW3 Arras	H 19 a
Halfway House	28NW4 & NE3 Zillebeke	I 17 c 4.7
Halfway House	36aSE3 Gonnehem	W 2 b 4.5
Halfway House	36NW2 & NE1 Houplines	C 10 c 7.8
Halfway House [dugouts]	28NW4 & NE3 Zillebeke	J 25 c
Halfway House Spur [light railway, 1917-18]	28NW4 Ypres	I 17 a, c
Halibut Trench	36cNW3 Loos / 4 Pont-à-Vendin	H 27 d, 28 c, 34 a
Halicz Trench	62cNW2 Bouchavesnes	C 4 c, d
Halifax [light rly locality, 1917-18]	28NW4 Ypres	H 23 b
Halifax Alley	36cNW3 Loos	H 13 a, b
Halifax Area (Vancouver Camp)	28NW3 Poperinghe	H 14 c
Halifax Camp	28NW3 Poperinghe	H 14 c

Name	Map Sheet	Map Reference
Halifax Keep [farm buildings]	28NW3 Poperinghe	H 14 c 9.2
Halifax O.P. [1917-18]	51bNW1 Roclincourt	B 20 b 1.2
Halifax Road	28NW2 St Julien	C 19 a, b
Halifax Street	28NW4 & NE3 Zillebeke	I 24 c, 30 a
Halifax Street	51bNW3 Arras	G 35 a, c
Halifax Support	57cNW2 Vaulx-Vraucourt	C 5 d, 11 b, d
Halifax Track [Halifax Camp to Dawson]	28NW4 Ypres	H 14 c 5.8 to H 23 d 4.6
Halifax Trench	28NW4 & NE3 Zillebeke	I 30 a, c
Halifax Trench	51bNW4 Fampoux / SW2 Vis-en-Artois	H 34 a, c, N 4 a, c
Halifax Trench [1918]	57dNE2 & 57cNW1 Courcelles	F 20 b, d, 21 a
Hall Farm	28SW3 Bailleul	S 23 a 80.55
Hall Road	36cNW3 Loos	H 10 c
Hall Trench	36cNW3 Loos	H 19 d, 26 a
Hall Trench	51bNW1 Roclincourt	B 25 b
Halle Station [railway locality 1917-18]	62cNW4 Péronne	I 13 c, d
Hallebast [hamlet]	28NW3 Poperinghe	H 32 d
Hallebast [Hellblast Corner]	28NW4 & NE3 Zillebeke	I 22 b
Hallebast Corner [Hellblast Corner]	28SW1 Kemmel	N 2 b
Hallebast Farm	28SW1 Kemmel	N 2 d 70.95
Hallebast, Chateau de	28SW1 Kemmel	N 2 b 7.8
Hallobeau, l' [place name]	36NW1 Steenwerck	B 25 c
Hallu [village]	66dNW1 Punchy	A 21 d, 22 c, 27 b, 28 a
Hallu Alley	66dNW1 Punchy	A 20 b, 21 a, b, d, 22 c, d, 23 c
Hallu Wood	66dNW3 Hattencourt	G 4 c, d, 10 a, b
Hallue Defences, L' [1918]	62dSW [2 Villers-Bretonneux]	N 5, 11
Hally Avenue	57cNW1 Gomiecourt / 2 Vaulx-Vraucourt	B 3 d, 4 c, d, 9 b, 10 a
Hally Copse	57cNW2 Vaulx-Vraucourt	B 10 a
Halo Trench	51bNW4 Fampoux	H 11 c
Halpegarbe Trench	36SW3 Richebourg	S 12 b, d, T 7 a
Halstead Alley	36cNW3 Loos	H 14 b, 15 a, b
Halstead Street	51bNW3 Arras	G 35 c
Halt Corner [road jct near rly]	36aNE3 Haverskerque	K 8 c 50.25
Halt Trench	57cSW4 Combles	T 5 a
Halte Trench	66dNW1 Punchy	B 27 d, 28 c, H 3 b
Halter Trench [1918]	57dNE3 & 4 Hébuterne	K 17 d, 23 b, 24 a
Halteres Trench	66dNW1 Punchy	B 27 c, d, 28 a, c
Ham Lane	36cNW4 Pont-à-Vendin	H 23 a
Ham Lane [1918]	57dNE2 & 57cNW1 Courcelles	F 9 b, d
Ham Trench	36cSW2 Harnes	O 1 d
Ham Trench	51bNW1 Roclincourt	B 25 b
Ham Trench	57cSW3 Longueval	S 2 a
Ham Trench	57dSE2 & 57cSW1 Le Sars	N 20 b
Ham Trench	62bSW3 St Quentin	S 17 c
Hamac Trench	62bSW1 Gricourt / 2 Fonsommes / 4 Homblières	N 27 d, 33 b, 34 a, c
Hamadan Trench	62bSW2 Fonsommes	N 29 d, 35 b
Hamage Farm	57bSW4 Serain	T 24 c 6.9
Hamblain-les-Pres	51bNW4 Fampoux	I 24 d, 30 b
Hamburg [farm & pillbox]	28NE1 Zonnebeke	D 16 b 2.7
Hamburg Battery	5SW1 Zeebrugge	N 9 c, 10 a
Hamburg Copse	66dNW1 Punchy	A 12 d, 18 b
Hamburg Trench	66dNW1 Punchy	A 12 d, 18 a, b, c
Hamburg Work [1918]	66eNW [4 Morisel]	H 11 b
Hameau Farm [Adinfer]	51cSE4 Blaireville	X 20 b 5.1

Name	Map Sheet	Map Reference
Hameau Switch Front Line [1918]	51cSE4 Blaireville	X 20 b, d, 21 a, b
Hamecon Trench	66dNW1 Punchy	A 18 d, B 13 c
Hamel [hamlet]	66cNW1 Grugies	A 25 d, G 1 b, 2 a
Hamel [village]	51bNE3 Noyelle-sous-Bellonne	K 33 a, c, d
Hamel [village]	57dSE1 & 2 Beaumont	Q 23 a, b, d
Hamel [village]	62dSE [1 Hamel]	P 9 b, 10 a, c
Hamel Bridge [across Ancre]	57dSE1 & 2 Beaumont	Q 24 c 4.0
Hamel Outposts [1918]	57dSE1 & 2 Beaumont	Q 23 c, 29 a
Hamel Switch	51bSW3 Boisleux / 57cNW1 Gomiecourt	S 23, 29, 30, A 6, b 1, 2, 8
Hamel Wood	62dSE [1 Hamel]	P 15 a, b, c
Hamel Work	51bNW3 Arras	H 25 a
Hamel Work	57cNW1 Gomiecourt	A 5 c, d
Hamelincourt [village]	51bSW3 Boisleux / 57cNW1 Gomiecourt	S 29 d, A 5 b
Hamelincourt Trench	51bSW3 Boisleux	S 29 a, b, c, 30 a
Hamerville Trench	57cNW1 Gomiecourt	A 6, 11, 12, 18
Hamet Billet [houses]	36aSE1 St Venant	P 13 b, 14 a
Hamet Bridge	36aSE1 St Venant	P 13 d 3.4
Hamhoek	27NE2 Proven	F 30 a
Hamhoek [hamlet]	28NW1 Elverdinghe	A 19 d, 25 a
Hamilton Alley [Trônes Wood]	57cSW3 Longueval	S 30 a
Hamilton Avenue	57dSE1 & 2 Beaumont	Q 30 c, d, 36 a, b
Hamilton Road [Sept 1915]	36cNW1 La Bassée	A 9 a
Hamilton Street	51bNW3 Arras / SW1 Neuville Vitasse	G 34 d, M 4 b
Hamilton Trench	36cNW3 Loos / 4 Pont-à-Vendin	H 27 c, d, 33 b, 34 a, c
Hamilton Wood	62dSE [1 Hamel]	Q 14 b, d
Hamilton Work	57dSE1 & 2 Beaumont	Q 11 a 85.25
Hamlet Trench	36cNW3 Loos	G 12 b, H 7 a, c, d
Hamlet Trench	62bSW3 St Quentin	N 32 c, T 2 a
Hammam Trench	62bSW1 Gricourt	N 26 b, d, 27 c
Hammer Trench	51bSW2 Vis-en-Artois	N 18 b, d, O 13 a
Hammerhead Sap [Thiepval Wood]	57dSE1 & 2 Beaumont	R 25 a
Hammonds Corner	28NW2 St Julien	C 21 c 29.36
Hammonds Corner Camp [1917-18]	28NW2 St Julien	C 21 c
Hamon Wood	66eNW [2 Thennes] / NE [1]	C 12 c, d, 18 b, D 7 c, 13 a
Hampden House	20SE2 Hooglede	Q 5 b 7.5
Hamper Farm	27NE1 Herzeele	E 3 c 5.0
Hampshire Farm	28NW2 St Julien	C 22 a 3.8
Hampshire Lane [ride, Ploeg. Wd. 1914-15]	28SW4 Ploegsteert	U 21 c, d
Hampshire Trench [E of Ploegsteert Wood]	28SW4 Ploegsteert	U 21 b, d
Hampton Alley	36cNW3 Loos	H 8 c, 13 a, b, 14 a
Hamshaw House	28NE4 Dadizeele	L 31 b 2.4
Hanbury CT	28SW4 Ploegsteert	U 1 c
Hanbury Support North	28SW4 Ploegsteert	U 1 c
Hanbury Support South	28SW4 Ploegsteert	U 1 d
Hancock Trench	51bNW3 Arras	H 7 c
Hancourt Aerodrome [German, 1918]	62cSE1 Bouvincourt	Q 2 b, d, 8 a, b
Handcuff Trench	36cNW4 Pont-à-Vendin	H 22 d, 23 c
Handel Farm	20SE2 Hooglede	R 5 c 6.8
Handel Road [road]	57dSE2 & 57cSW1 Le Sars	R 5 d, 6 c, M 1 d
Handle Copse	62cNE3 Buire	J 19 b, 20 a, c
Handley Cross	57dSW [2 Raincheval]	N 30 b
Hanebeke [sic, locality]	28NW4 & NE3 Zillebeke	J 2 d
Hang Stellung	36cSW3 Vimy	S 16 c, d, 22 b, 23 a
Hangan Trench	62bSW4 Homblières	T 4 b, d

Name	Map Sheet	Map Reference
Hangar Avenue	20SW4 Bixschoote	T 29 d, 30 a, c
Hangar Farm	20SW4 Bixschoote	T 30 a 4.2
Hangard [village]	62dSW [4 Cachy]	U 28, 29
Hangard Trench [1918]	62dSW [4 Cachy]	U 28 b, 29 a
Hangars Alley	66cSW4 La Fère	T 23 c, 28 b, 29 a
Hangest Trench	51bNW3 Arras	H 25 d, 31 b
Hangman Farm	28NE4 Dadizeele	L 35 a 7.1
Hangman's Avenue	36SW1 Aubers	M 18 b, N 13 a, c
Hanley [lt rly locality E of Pilckem 1917-18]	28NW2 St Julien	C 3 central
Hanley Cross Roads	28NE4 Dadizeele	K 16 b 55.53
Hannart Farm	28SW1 Kemmel	N 27 b 30.65
Hannescamps [village]	57dNE1 & 2 Fonquevillers	E 9 d, 10 c, 16 a
Hannetons Trench	62cNW4 Péronne	H 4 d, 10 b
Hanoi Trench	62cSW2 Barleux	N 28 d
Hanover Lane	57cSW4 Combles	U 21 b
Hanover Street [Sept 1915]	36cNW1 La Bassée	A 15 d
Hans Alley	66dNW1 Punchy	A 10 c, d, 16 a
Hans Crescent [Ginchy]	57cSW3 Longueval	T 13 d
Hans Redoubt	36cNW3 Loos	G 11 b
Hans Trench	51bSW4 Bullecourt	G 1 b, c, d, 12 a
Hansa Line	57dSE1 & 2 Beaumont	R 13 b, d
Hansa Road	57dSE1 & 2 Beaumont	R 13 b, 14 a
Hanszaeme Trench	20NW4 Dixmude	I 1 c
Hantee House	62cSW4 St. Christ	U 8 c
Hants Farm	28SW4 Ploegsteert	U 26 a 1.7
Hants Lane	36cNW3 Loos	G 35 b, d
Hants Trench	51bSW1 Neuville Vitasse	M 15 c, d
Haplincourt [village]	57cSW2 Villers-au-Flos	O 3 c, d, 4 c, 9 b, 10 a
Happy Alley / Happy Valley	57dSE1 & 2 Beaumont	Q 10 b
Happy Trench	36cSW1 Lens	N 2 d, 8 b
Happy Trench	36cSW2 Harnes	O 8 a, b, c, d, 9 a
Happy Trench	57cSW3 Longueval	S 11 d
Happy Valley	51bNW4 Fampoux	H 30 c, d, 35 b, 36 a
Happy Valley	51bSW3 Boisleux	S 18 c
Happy Valley [near Bray-Fricourt Rd]	62dNE2 Méaulte / 4 [Bray-sur-Somme]	F 26 b, 27 c, L 3 a, c
Haps Alley	36cNW3 Loos	H 26 d, 27 c
Hapsburger Weg	51bNW1 Roclincourt	A 11 c, d
Harbard's Cottage [N of Ploeg. Wd, 1914-15]	28SW4 Ploegsteert	U 14 d 50.35
Hard Trench	36cNW3 Loos	H 27 c
Hardecourt Alley	62cNW1 Maricourt	A 11 b, 12 a, c
Hardecourt Trench	62cNW1 Maricourt	A 12 b, d
Hardecourt-au-Bois [village]	62cNW1 Maricourt	A 12 d, 18 b
Hardmuth Cross Roads	28NE4 Dadizeele	L 10 d 9.9
Hardpye Hill	57dSW [4 Toutencourt]	U 3 c, 9 a, c
Hardwick Trench	57dSE1 & 2 Beaumont	Q 12 a, b
Hardy Lane	62cNE2 Epéhy	F 28 a
Hardy Street	51bSW1 Neuville Vitasse	M 2, 3, 4, 10
Hare Lane	62dNE2 Méaulte	F 3 a
Hare Trench	36cSW2 Harnes	O 8 a
Hare Trench	51bNW1 Roclincourt	B 25 a, b
Hare Trench [1918]	57dNE2 & 57cNW1 Courcelles	F 16 b, c, d
Harem Alley	62bSW1 Gricourt	M 30 d, 36 b
Haret Avenue	66cNW2 Itancourt	A 16 b
Harfleur Trench	51bNW3 Arras	H 31 c

Name	Map Sheet	Map Reference
Hargicourt Switch	62cNE4 Roisel	L 7 d, 8 c, d, 13 b, 14 b, 15 a, b, 16 a
Hargicourt Trench	62cNE2 Epéhy / 4 Roisel	L 4 a, b, c, 10 a, b
Hargival Farm	57bSW3 Honnecourt	S 27 d
Harisoirs, les	36aSE3 Gonnehem	W 2 b
Hark Trench	36cNW3 Loos	H 32 b, 33 a
Harker Farm	20SE3 Westroosebeke	W 14 a 2.0
Harlech [strongpoint]	36NW3 Fleurbaix	G 19 d
Harlech Castle [moated farm]	36SW1 Aubers	M 12 a 3.9
Harlech Road [road]	36SW1 Aubers	M 5 a, c, d, 6 c, d
Harlequin Copses	28SW1 Kemmel	M 32 a
Harley Street	36cNW1 La Bassée	A 20 a, b
Harley Street	51bNW3 Arras / SW1 Neuville Vitasse	G 34 c, M 4 a, c
Harley Street [road]	36cNW1 La Bassée	A 14 d, 20 a, b
Harly [village]	62bSW4 Homblières	T 23 a, b
Harmonie, Tranchée de l'	66dNW3 Hattencourt / SW1 Roye	G 36 a, c, M 1 a
Harmsworth Park [building]	28NE4 Dadizeele	K 21 b 6.7
Harnes Corons [miners' cottages]	36cSW2 Harnes	O 7 a, b, d
Harnes Fosses, Fosse 21	36cSW2 Harnes	N 6 c, d, 12 a, b
Harnes Support	36cNW4 Pont-à-Vendin / SW2 Harnes	H 36, N 6, O 1, 2, 8
Harness Alley	51bNW4 Fampoux	I 31 b
Harness Lane [road]	51bNW4 Fampoux / SW2 Vis-en-Artois	I 26 c, 31 b, c, d, O 1 a
Harnians Avenue	36NW2 Armentières	C 3 c, d, 4 c
Harold Trench	51bNW1 Roclincourt	A 27 a, c
Harp Trench	36cNW4 Pont-à-Vendin / SW2 Harnes	I 33 d, 34 c, d, O 2 c, d, 3 a, b, 8 b
Harp Trench	51bNW1 Roclincourt	B 25 a
Harp Trench	62bSW3 St Quentin	T 2 d, 3 c, d, 4 c
Harp Valley Reserve [Harponville]	57dSW [4 Toutencourt]	U 5 d, 11 b, c
Harp Valley Support [Harponville]	57dSW [4 Toutencourt]	U 5 d, 11 b, d
Harp Valley Trench [Harponville]	57dSW [4 Toutencourt]	U 6 c, 12 a, c
Harp, The [Redoubt]	51bSW1 Neuville Vitasse	N 1 a, b, c, d, 7 a, b
Harper Mill	27NE1 Herzeele	E 14 c 1.4
Harpies Alley / Boyau des Harpies	62cSW3 Vermandovillers / 66dNW1 Punchy	T 25 d, 26 c, B 2 a, b, d, 8 b, 9 a, c
Harpon Trench / Tranchée du Harpon	62cSW2 Barleux	N 29 c, 35 a
Harpon Wood	66eNW [4 Morisel]	I 26 a, b
Harponville Support	57dSW [[2 Raincheval / 4 Toutencourt]	O 35 b, c, d, U 5 b
Harponville Trench	57dSW [[2 Raincheval / 4 Toutencourt]	O 35 b, d, U 5 b
Harpoon Alley	36cNW3 Loos	H 21 c, d, 22 c
Harris Maze	36cSW2 Harnes	N 12 c, d
Harris Post	36NW4 Bois Grenier	I 1 b
Harrisburg Junction [light rly]	36NW2 Armentières	B 12 a 5.7
Harrismith Trench	51bNW3 Arras / 4 Fampoux	H 28 c, 34 a
Harrison Road [road, les Harisoirs]	36aSE3 Gonnehem	Q 31 d, 32 c, W 2 a, b, 3 a
Harrison's Crater / Craters	36cSW1 Lens	M 6 c
Harrod's / Harrods Stores	28SE1 Wervicq	P 3 d 2.9
Harrods Farm	28NE4 Dadizeele	K 35 a 8.3
Harrods Stores	62cNE4 Roisel	L 23 b 55.60
Harrogate / Harrowgate Post	51bNW1 Roclincourt / 2 Oppy	B 16 c, 22 a
Harrogate Avenue	57cNW2 Vaulx-Vraucourt / NE1 Quéant	C 24 b, D 13 c, 19 a
Harrogate Dump	57cNW2 Vaulx-Vraucourt	I 1 d central
Harrogate Support	57cNW2 Vaulx-Vraucourt	C 18 d
Harrow [light rly locality, 1917-18]	28NW4 Ypres	H 23 c, 29 a
Harrow Copse	20SE2 Hooglede	Q 6 d
Harrow Post [Sept 1915]	36SW1 Aubers	M 20 d 80.36
Harrow Road [road]	36SW1 Aubers	M 20 c, d, 21 a, c, 26 a

Name	Map Sheet	Map Reference
Harrow Road Corner	36cSW1 Lens	M 26 a 2.7
Harrow Row	57dSE1 & 2 Beaumont	Q 16 b
Harrow Trench	36cNW3 Loos	H 7 d
Harrow Trench	51bNW4 Fampoux	H 11 b, 12 a
Harry Road [road]	36cNW3 Loos / 4 Pont-à-Vendin	H 27 b, c, d, 28 a
Harry Trench	51bNW4 Fampoux	H 5 d, 6 c
Harry's Cut	36cNW1 La Bassée	A 26 b
Hart Copse	62cSW3 Vermandovillers	S 21 d
Hart Farm	28NE2 Moorslede	E 16 c 75.85
Hart Street	36cSW4 Rouvroy	T 29 b
Harte Vent [place name]	36aSE1 St Venant	P 2 b, 3 a
Harting Crater	36cSW3 Vimy	S 14 b
Hart's Crater / Craters	36cSW1 Lens	M 6 c
Hartung, Boyau	36cSW3 Vimy	S 14 b, 15 a
Harvest Trench	36cNW4 Pont-à-Vendin	H 23 c, 29 a, c
Has Trench	36cSW2 Harnes	O 1 a
Haselmeyer Weg / Trench	51bNW1 Roclincourt	A 30 d, B 25 c, d
Hassall Trench	62bSW3 St Quentin	S 24 d
Hassard Alley	66dNW1 Punchy	A 18 b, d
Hastings [huts]	28NW4 Ypres	H 29 c 05.95
Hastings [light rly locality, 1917-18]	28NW4 Ypres	H 28 b, 29 a
Hastings Alley	36cNW3 Loos	H 13 a, b
Hastings Farm	20SE2 Hooglede	Q 4 d 5.2
Hastings Lane	51bNW3 Arras	G 36 d
Hastings Street	51bSW1 Neuville Vitasse	M 4 c, 10 a, b
Hasty Alley	62bSW4 Homblières	T 23 c
Hasty Trench	36cNW4 Pont-à-Vendin / SW2 Harnes	I 31 b, c, d, 32 a, b, O 1 a
Hat Trench	36cSW2 Harnes	O 1 d, 2 c
Hat Trench	51bNW4 Fampoux	I 27 b
Hat Trench	57dNE3 & 4 Hébuterne	K 18 c, d
Hatch Farm	28NE3 Gheluvelt	J 34 d 1.4
Hatchet Wood	51bNW4 Fampoux	I 34 a, c
Hate Alley	36cSW3 Vimy	M 32 c
Hate Farm	36aSE3 Gonnehem	W 3 b 4.2
Hatfield Road / Street	36cNW1 La Bassée	A 9 c, d
Hattencourt [village]	66dNW3 Hattencourt	G 9, 10, 15, 16
Hattencourt Trench	66dNW3 Hattencourt	G 15 a, b, 16 a
Hatter Road [road]	36cNW3 Loos	H 14 d, 20 b, 21 a
Haucourt [village]	51bSW2 Vis-en-Artois	O 23 b, d, 24 a
Haucourt Trench	51bNW3 Arras	H 31 b
Haul Trench	51bNW1 Roclincourt	B 25 b
Haunted House	36cSW1 Lens	M 20 b 30.55
Haunted House	66cNW2 Itancourt	C 16 d
Haus Graben	51bNW3 Arras	G 6 d
Hausa Wood	51bNW4 Fampoux	I 15 c
Hause Trench	57dNE3 & 4 Hébuterne	K 4 c, d
Haussman Alley	62bSW3 St Quentin	S 16 d, 22 a, b
Haut Aly [sic] [1918]	57dSW [4 Toutencourt]	U 30 c
Haut Farm	57bSW1 Bantouzelle	N 27 c 6.2
Haute Maison [farm]	36aNE2 Vieux Berquin	F 14 d 1.4
Haute Maison [house]	36aNE2 Vieux Berquin	F 14 d 4.4
Haute Porte [locality; incorrect reference]	27SE4 Meteren	X 11 c 4.9
Haute Porte Farm [second, correct, reference]	27SE4 Meteren	X 11 c 75.90
Haute Porte Farm [wrongly given to Ike Farm]	27SE4 Meteren	X 10 a 2.2

Name	Map Sheet	Map Reference
Havana Street	62dNE2 Méaulte	F 16 b
Havana Trench [1918]	51bNW4 Fampoux	H 12 c, d, 18 b
Havannah Street	51bNW3 Arras / SW1 Neuville Vitasse	G 33, 34, M 4
Havant Lane	51bNW3 Arras	H 31 a, b
Havelock Street	51bNW3 Arras / SW1 Neuville Vitasse	G 34 b, c, d, M 4 a, b
Haversack Trench	51bNW4 Fampoux	I 33 a, c
Haversack Trench [Manchester Hill]	62bSW3 St Quentin	S 21 b
Haverskerque - La Motte Line [1918]	36aNE3 Haverskerque	J 6, 11, 12, 17, 23, 28, 29, 34
Haverskerque [village]	36aNE3 Haverskerque	J 27 b, d, 28 a, c
Havre Trench	66cSW1 Remigny	N 9 d, 10 c, 15 b, d
Havre Trench [Manchester Hill]	62bSW3 St Quentin	S 15 d, 21 b, d
Havrincourt Wood	57cNE3 / 4 / SE1 / 2	J, K, P, Q
Hawick Alley	51bNW1 Roclincourt / 2 Oppy	B 4 c, d
Hawk Alley	36cNW3 Loos	H 7 c, d, 8 a, c
Hawk Road [road]	36cNW3 Loos	H 7 b, d
Hawk Trench	57cSE4 Villers-Guislain	X 24 c
Hawk Trench [1918]	57dNE3 & 4 Hébuterne	K 17 b, 18 a, b
Hawke Alley [1918]	57dSE1 & 2 Beaumont	Q 29 c
Hawks Farm	20SE2 Hooglede	R 14 d 1.3
Hawkstreet Trench [E of Monchy-le-Preux]	51bSW2 Vis-en-Artois	O 2 d
Hawser House	28SW1 Kemmel	M 21 b 25.45
Hawser Lane [trench, 1918]	28SW1 Kemmel	M 17 a, b, d
Hawthorn Farm	20SE2 Hooglede	R 15 a 5.6
Hawthorn Ridge Redoubt	57dSE1 & 2 Beaumont	Q 10 b
Hawthorne Trench	51bNW4 Fampoux	H 6 c
Hay / Haie Alley, & Alley Keep [G 18 a]	36cNW3 Loos	G 17 b, 18 a, b, d
Hay Farm [Potijze]	28NW4 & NE3 Zillebeke	I 4 d 6.7
Hay Hill	36cSW1 Lens	M 6 a
Hay Houses	28NE3 Gheluvelt	J 34 d 45.40
Hay Locality	36cNW3 Loos	G 18 b, d, H 13 a, b
Hay Street [1918]	62dNE [3 Morlancourt]	K 7 a, b
Hay Trench	36cSW2 Harnes	O 1 d
Hay Trench	51bNW1 Roclincourt	B 26 c
Hay Trench	57cSW1 Gueudecourt	N 20 a
Haydn Farm	20SE2 Hooglede	R 4 b 8.4
Haye Farm	66dNW1 Punchy	B 9 d
Haye, la [place name]	36aSE1 St Venant	P 11 a, b
Hayettes Wood	57cSE1 Bertincourt	P 27 d, 33 b
Haymarket	28NW2 St Julien / 28NW4 & NE3 Zillebeke	I 4 d, 5 a, c
Haymarket	36cNW3 Loos / SW1 Lens	G 35 d, M 5 b
Haymarket	36NW4 Bois Grenier	I 25 d, 26 c
Haymarket	36SW1 Aubers	N 8 a
Haymarket	51bSW1 Neuville Vitasse	M 4 c, d
Haymarket	57dSE1 & 2 Beaumont	Q 10 c
Haymarket [CT, Ploegsteert Wood 1914-15]	28SW4 Ploegsteert	U 20 d
Haymarket [locality, 1917-18]	28NW2 St Julien	C 13 c
Haymarket [lt rly locality E of Canal 1917-18]	28NW2 St Julien	C 13 c
Haymarket [road & trench]	57cSW3 Longueval	S 18 b, T 13 a
Haymarket [road]	57cNE1 Quéant	D 23 a, c
Haymarket Switch [1918]	36SW1 Aubers	N 1 b, d, 2 c, 8 a
Haymarket, The [Langemarck]	20SW4 Bixschoote	U 28 b
Haystack Avenue	36NW4 Bois Grenier	I 14 b, d, 15 c, 21 a
Haystack Farm	36aSE1 St Venant	Q 19 a 6.1
Haystack Loop [light rly]	36bSE4 Carency	W 29 a, c

Name	Map Sheet	Map Reference
Haystack Post	36SW3 Richebourg	S 14 b, d
Haystack Post	36SW3 Richebourg	S 4 d 3.9
Haystack Post [NW of Loos]	36cNW3 Loos	G 28 b, 29 a
Hayter Trench [1918]	36cSW3 Vimy	T 8 c, 13 b, 14 a
Haywards Heath	36cNW1 La Bassée / 3 Loos	G 4 c
Hazard Street	36SW3 Richebourg	S 10
Hazard Trench	36SW3 Richebourg	S 10 a, c, d
Hazard Trench	51bNW4 Fampoux	H 11 a, b
Hazebrouck [southern part of town]	36aNE1 Morbecque	D 3, 4
Hazebrouck [town]	27SE3 Borre	V 21, 22, 26, 27, 28
Hazebrouck Station [railway]	27SE3 Borre	V 28 a 5.5
Hazebrouck Street	51bNW3 Arras	G 35 c, d
Hazel Wood	62dSE [1 Hamel]	P 24 b, d, Q 19 a, c
Hazelburg [sic; early 1916, MS map]	28NW4 & NE3 Zillebeke	I 26 d 6.7
Hazelbury / Hazelbury Farm	28NW4 Ypres	I 26 d 5.8
Hazelmere Alley	51bNW1 Roclincourt	A 30 d, B 25 c, d, 26 c
Hazera Trench	66cNW4 Berthenicourt	H 16 c, 22 a, c
Hazos Farm	27NE4 Abeele	K 23 b 0.5
Hazy Trench	57cSW4 Combles	T 5 a, b, d, 6 c
Head Farm	28SW2 Wytschaete	O 30 d 2.9
Head Lane	51bSW1 Neuville Vitasse	N 7 b, c, d
Head Street	62cNW1 Maricourt	A 16 a
Head Trench	36cNW3 Loos	H 31 d
Headingly Lane	28NW2 St Julien	C 20 a
Headquarter Street	36cSW1 Lens	M 14 b, d
Headquarter Trench	36cSW3 Vimy	S 1 b, d
Headquarters Alley / Avenue / Boyau du Q.G.	62cNW1 Maricourt	A 15 a, b
Headquarters Trench	36cSW1 Lens	M 31 b, d, S 1 b, d
Headquarters Trench	62cNW1 Maricourt	A 15 a, b
Headquarters Trench [Sept 915]	36cNW1 La Bassée	A 27 a, b, d
Headquarters Walk	36NW4 Bois Grenier	I 10 a, b, c
Heal House	27SE4 Meteren	X 15 a 1.1
Health Support [1918]	62dNE [3 Morlancourt]	J 12 c
Heart Copse	62cNE4 Roisel	L 35 c, d
Heart Lane	51bSW1 Neuville Vitasse	N 14 c
Heart Trench	36cNW3 Loos	H 31 d
Heath Farm	20SE2 Hooglede	R 4 c 4.4
Heath Hedge [Hill 63]	28SW4 Ploegsteert	U 13 d
Heath Trench [Hill 63]	28SW4 Ploegsteert	U 13 b, d
Heathcotes Bank [1918]	57dSE4 Ovillers	W 3 b, d, 4 a
Heather Copse	20SE2 Hooglede	R 3 c 95.30
Heather Support	57cSE4 Villers-Guislain	W 5 a, c, 11 a, c
Heather Trench	57cSE4 Villers-Guislain	W 5 b, d
Heaton Cross Roads	27SE4 Meteren	X 11 b 9.5
Heaton Road	57dSE1 & 2 Beaumont	Q 10 a
Heaton Road [mistranscription of Hoxton Road]	36cSW1 Lens	M 15 a, b
Heaven Trench	36cNW3 Loos	H 32 a, b
Heaven Trench [Le Transloy]	57cSW2 Villers-au-Flos	N 29 a, b, d
Hebe Post	62cNE4 Roisel	L 18 c 1.6
Hebe Trench	66dNW1 Punchy	A 12 d, 18 b, B 7 a, c
Hebrew Trench	36cSW2 Harnes	O 28 a, b
Hebron Communication Trench [1918]	62dSW [4 Cachy]	U 5 b
Hebule, The [quarry & trenches]	57cSW4 Combles	U 13 a
Hébuterne Graben	57dNE3 & 4 Hébuterne	L 1 c, d, 2 c

Name	Map Sheet	Map Reference
Heck Trench	36cSW2 Harnes	O 28 b
Hecken Stellung	57dNE1 & 2 Fonquevillers	F 7 a, c, 13 a
Hecker Weg	51bSW1 Neuville Vitasse	M 4 d, 10 b, 11 a
Heckle Trench	36cSW2 Harnes	O 22 d, 23 c, 28 b
Hecla Farm	28NW3 Poperinghe	H 25 d 8.0
Hecq Trench	51bNW3 Arras	H 20 c, d
Hectic Farm	28SW1 Kemmel	M 26 c 90.15
Hectic Trench	51bNW4 Fampoux	H 11 c
Hector Avenue	20SW3 Oostvleteren	T 3 a, b, c
Hector Trench	36cSW2 Harnes	O 23 c, 29 a
Hector Trench	62cNE3 Buire	J 7 b, d, 8 a
Hector Trench / Tranchée Hector	62cSW1 & 2 Belloy	N 12 c, 17 b, 18 a
Heddon Street	28NW4 & NE3 Zillebeke	I 5 d
Hedge [light rly siding]	36cSW1 Lens	M 16 d
Hedge Alley	57cSW3 Longueval	S 14 a
Hedge Row	57cNW2 Vaulx-Vraucourt	C 23 d
Hedge Row [Trench]	51cSE3 & 4 Ransart	R 32 d
Hedge Row Trench / C.T.	28NW4 & NE3 Zillebeke	I 34 a, c, d
Hedge Sap [Bellewaarde]	28NW4 & NE3 Zillebeke	I 12 a 4.1
Hedge Street / Boyau de la Haie	62cNW1 Maricourt	A 28 d, 29 a, c
Hedge Street [& Tunnel]	28NW4 & NE3 Zillebeke	I 30 b
Hedge Trench	28NW4 & NE3 Zillebeke	I 10 c
Hedge Trench	36cSW2 Harnes	O 29 a, c
Hedge Trench [1918]	57dNE [2 Fonquevillers / 4 Hébuterne]	F 27 c, L 2 b, c, d, 3 a
Hedgehog Trench	62bSW3 St Quentin	N 31 c, T 1 a, b
Hedgerow [lt rly locality, 1917]	28SW1 Kemmel	N 2 a
Hedgerow Trench	57dSE1 & 2 Beaumont	Q 23 b
Hedley Street [1918]	62dNE [1 Dernancourt]	E 1 d, 2 c
Heel Trench	36cNW3 Loos	H 25 d, 31 b
Heel Trench	51bNW1 Roclincourt	B 26 a, c
Heft Trench	51bNW1 Roclincourt	B 26 a, c
Hefty Trench	36cSW2 Harnes / 4 Rouvroy / SE3 Esquerchin	O 35b,d, U 6a,b,d, 12 b,d, 18b, V 13 a
Heidelberg Trench [1918]	66eNW [2 Thennes]	C 4 d, 5 c, 10 b
Heidengoed Copse	20SE3 Westroosebeke	W 13 c
Heidengoed Farm, Het	20SE3 Westroosebeke	V 18 d 2.8
Heidenkopf [Quadrilateral]	57dNE3 & 4 Hébuterne	K 35 a, c
Heider Trench	57cNE2 Bourlon	E 15 a, b, 16 a, b
Heidseick [farm]	28NW1 Elverdinghe	H 2 b 2.5
Heifer Farm	27SE4 Meteren	X 10 b 40.95
Heifer Trench	36cSW2 Harnes	O 29 a, c
Heilerons Trench	62cNW4 Péronne	H 10 a, b, c
Heilly Trench	51bNW3 Arras	H 25 a
Heine Street, & House	28NE1 Zonnebeke	D 11 c
Heinzman Park	57dSE2 Beaumont	R 13 b
Heksken [hamlet]	28SW1 Kemmel	M 3 c 10.15
Heksken Cabaret	28SW1 Kemmel	M 9 a 15.70
Heksken Depot Railhead / Refilling Point	28SW1 Kemmel	M 3 c, d, 4 a, c, 9 a, b
Helen Trench	36cNW3 Loos / 36cSW1 Lens	H 32 d, N 2 b
Helen Trench	36cSW4 Rouvroy / SE3 Esquerchin	U 6 b, V 1 a
Helen Trench	57cNE1 Quéant	D 13 b, 14 a, c
Hélène Alley / Trench	62cNE3 Buire	J 7 d, 8 a, b, c
Hélène Ridge	62bNW3 Bellicourt / SW1 Gricourt	G 33 b, c, d, M 3 a, b
Helfer Graben	51bNW3 Arras	G 6 d

Name	Map Sheet	Map Reference
Helford / Hellford Trench	51bNW2 Oppy / 4 Fampoux	H 6 a, c
Helice Trench	62bSW1 Gricourt	M 36 a
Helice Trench	66dNW1 Punchy	A 12 b, c, d
Heligo Lane	62dNE2 Méaulte	F 10 b, d
Heligoland Redoubt	57dSE4 Ovillers	X 20 b, d, 21 a, c
Helinke Trench	51bSW1 Neuville Vitasse	M 20 b
Helio Trench	36cSW2 Harnes / 4 Rouvroy / SE3 Esquerchin	O 35 b, 36 a, c, d, U 6 b, V 1 a
Hell Corner [Festubert]	36SW3 Richebourg	S 25 d
Hell Farm	28SW2 Wytschaete	O 31 b 5.6
Hell Fire Corner [Maricourt Wood, SE corner]	62cNW1 Maricourt	A 23 a 05.95
Hell Fire Corner [St Floris]	36aSE1 St Venant	P 6 a 15.25
Hell Lane	57dSE2 Beaumont	R 20 d, 26 b, d
Hell Quarry	51bSW2 Vis-en-Artois	O 21 b, d
Hell Trench	36cNW3 Loos	H 25 d, 31 b
Hell Trench	51bNW1 Roclincourt	B 26 a, c
Hell Trench	57cSW3 Longueval	M 35 d
Hellblast Corner [Hallebast]	28NW4 & NE3 Zillebeke	I 22 b 8.2
Hellblast Corner [Hallebast]	28SW1 Kemmel	N 2 b
Helle Trench	51bNW3 Arras	H 20 c
Helles [farm / pill box]	28NE1 Zonnebeke	J 3 b 55.40
Helles House	20SE3 Westroosebeke	V 14 c 5.4
Helles Track (Duckboard) [1917-18]	28NW4 Ypres / NE3 Gheluvelt	I 12 d, 17 b, 18 a, b, J 7 b, c, d, 8 a
Hellfire Alley [1918]	51bNW3 Arras	G 6 d, 12 a, b, H 1 c, 7 a, b
Hellfire Corner [Chantecler]	51bNW3 Arras	G 6 d 0.2
Hellfire Corner [crossroads & level crossing]	28NW4 & NE3 Zillebeke	I 10 c 9.3
Hellfire Junction [light railway, 1917-18]	28NW4 Ypres	I 16 b 15.70
Héllier [Boyau, 1915] / Kirriemuir Street	57dSE4 Ovillers	X 19 b, d, 20 a
Hell's Delight [farm]	28SE1 Wervicq	P 15 b 2.8
Helly Trench	62bSW3 St Quentin	T 1 b
Helm Trench	51bNW4 Fampoux	H 6 c
Helmer Trench, & Crater	36cSW3 Vimy	S 2 a
Helmer, Boyau	36cSW1 Lens	M 31 d, S 1 b, 2 a
Helmet House	27NE2 Proven	E 10 b 5.8
Helmet Trench	36cSW4 Rouvroy	O 35 d, 36 c, d
Helmke Weg	51bSW1 Neuville Vitasse	M 20 b, d
Helter Trench	36cSW4 Rouvroy	O 34 c, d
Helveys Homestead [building / farm]	20SE2 Hooglede	Q 22 c 65.80
Hem [village]	62cNW3 Vaux	H 7, 8
Hem Farm [Rolleghemcappelle]	28NE2 Moorslede	L 4 b 65.55
Hem Trench	51bNW3 Arras	H 26 a
Hem Trench	62cNW3 Vaux	H 1 d, 2 c, d, 3 c
Hem Wood	62cNW1 Maricourt	B 26 d, 27 c, H 3 a, b
Hême Trench	62cSW3 Vermandovillers	T 3 c, d
Hemel [light rly locality, 1917-18]	28NW4 Ypres	H 29 a
Hemel Cabaret, In den	20SW4 Bixschoote	O 32 c 8.9
Hemelhoek [place name]	28NE4 Dadizeele	L 9 a, b
Hemelryk Cabaret	28NW4 Ypres	H 29 c
Hemerie Chapel	36aNE4 Merville	L 19 b 8.9
Hemlock Alley	36cNW3 Loos	H 13 b, c, d, 14 a, c
Hemlock Trench	36cSW2 Harnes / 4 Rouvroy	O 34 a, c, d, U 4 b
Hemp Trench	36cSW4 Rouvroy	O 34 d
Hen Run [road]	36cNW3 Loos	H 14 b, d, 15 c, 21 a
Hen Trench	51bSW2 Vis-en-Artois	O 2 b, d

Name	Map Sheet	Map Reference
Hen Trench	62cNE2 Epéhy	F 6 c
Hendecourt Trench	51bSW4 Bullecourt	U 17 a, c, d, 18 c
Hendecourt Trench [1918]	51cSE4 Blaireville	X 11 d, 16 b, 17 a, c
Hendecourt-lez-Cagnicourt [village]	51bSW4 Bullecourt	U 11 c, d, 17 a, b
Hendecourt-lez-Ransart [village]	51cSE4 Blaireville	X 17 a, b
Hendon Alley	36cNW3 Loos	H 13 c, d
Hénencourt [village]	57dSE [3 Bouzincourt] / 62dNE [1 Dernancourt]	V 27, 28
Hengist Cross [cross roads]	28NW3 Poperinghe	G 27 d 8.7
Henham Road	36cSW3 Vimy	S 21 a
Hénin - Liétard Road	36cSW4 Rouvroy	U 14, 15, 19, 20, 25
Henin - Wancourt Line	51bSW1 / 2 / 3	N 21, 22, 26, 27, 31, 32
Hénin Hill	51bSW4 Bullecourt	N 34, 35, T 4, 5, 10, 11
Héninel [village]	51bSW1 Neuville Vitasse	N 28 b, d, 29 a, c
Héninel Trench	51bSW1 Neuville Vitasse	N 27 b, d, 28 c
Hénin-sur-Cojeul [village]	51bSW3 Boisleux	N 32 c, d, T 2 a, b
Henley Avenue	57cNE3 Hermies	K 31 b, d, 32 a, c
Henley Avenue [1918]	57dNE2 & 57cNW1 Courcelles	F 20 d, 26 b
Henley Bridge	36aSE1 St Venant	P 27 b 3.4
Henley Copse	51bSE3 Cagnicourt / 57cNE1 Quéant	V 29 c, D 5 a
Henley Lane	51bNW3 Arras	H 25 c
Henley Lane	57cNE3 Hermies	K 32 a
Henne Farm [Hennekot]	28NE2 Moorslede	F 27 c 7.5
Hennecion Redoubt [1918]	66eNW [4 Morisel]	H 28 a, b
Hennekot	28NE2 Moorslede	F 27 c, d
Hennessy House	28NE4 Dadizeele	L 13 c 40.05
Hennois, Bois du	57cSW4 Combles	U 24 a, b, c, d
Henriot Trench	62cNW4 Péronne / SW2 Barleux	I 33 c, O 2 b, 3 a
Henry Road [road]	36cNW3 Loos / 4 Pont-à-Vendin	H 27 d, 28 a, b, c, 33 a, b
Henry Street	51bNW2 Oppy	B 12 a, c
Henry Trench	20SW2 Zwartegat	O 26 a, b, d
Henry Trench	36cSW3 Vimy	S 16 c, 22 a
Henry Trench	51bNW1 Roclincourt	A 27 a, c
Hen's Post / Hens Post	36SW3 Richebourg	S 3 c, d
Henson House	28NW1 Elverdinghe	A 30 1.5
Hentz Trench	66cNW1 Grugies	B 7 d, 8 c
Henwood Houses	28NE2 Moorslede	F 27 a 35.10
Hera Alley	62cNW2 Bouchavesnes	I 5 b, 6 a, b, d
Herald Copse	27NE2 Proven	F 5 d
Herald Trench	36cSW2 Harnes / 4 Rouvroy	O 34 b, 35 a, c
Heralds Crossing [light rly]	36cSW3 Vimy	S 11 c
Heraulte Street	57dSE4 Ovillers	X 19 b
Herb Trench	36cSW4 Rouvroy	U 4 a
Herbert Trench	36cSW4 Rouvroy	U 4 a, b
Herbin Trench [1918]	62dSW [4 Cachy]	U 23 c, 29 a
Hercules Trench	36cNW3 Loos	H 32 b, d
Hercules Trench	36cNW3 Loos	H 8 c, 14 a, b, d, 20 b
Herd / Hero Trench	51bNW2 Oppy / 4 Fampoux	H 6 a, c
Herd Trench	51bNW1 Roclincourt	A 16 a
Heresy Trench	36cSW4 Rouvroy	U 5 a, b, 6 a
Herly [village]	66dNW3 Hattencourt / 4 Nesle	H 22 a, b, c, d
Herly Wood	66dNW3 Hattencourt	H 21 c, d, 27 a, b
Hermannstadt Alley	62bSW4 Homblières	T 30 c, d, U 25 c
Hermes Trench	51bNW3 Arras	H 19 c, 25 a

Name	Map Sheet	Map Reference
Hermies Switch	57cNE3 Hermies	J 17, 22, 23
Hermine Farm	20SW4 Bixschoote	O 31 c 4.4
Hermit Trench	36cSW4 Rouvroy	U 5 b, d, 6 c
Hermon Cottages [1918]	28SW1 Kemmel	M 15 a 4.4
Hero Trench	51bNW1 Roclincourt	A 16 a
Hérode Trench	62cSW2 Barleux	N 35 b, 36 a
Herodes Trench	36SW3 Richebourg	S 21 d
Heroes Wood	51bNW1 Roclincourt	B 1 c
Heroic Trench	36cSW4 Rouvroy / SE3 Esquerchin	U 5 a, b, 6 a, c, d, V 1 a,b
Heron Alley	62bSW3 St Quentin	T 1 c, d, 7 b
Heron Trench	51bNW4 Fampoux	H 11 a, c
Heron Trench	66dNW1 Punchy	A 4 b, 5 a
Heron Trench [later Heron Support]	51bSW2 Vis-en-Artois	O 20 c, 26 a
Heron Work	51bNW3 Arras	H 25 d
Herring Alley	36cNW3 Loos	H 13 c, d
Herring Farm	20SE2 Hooglede	R 17 a 5.8
Herring Support	57cNE1 Quéant	D 28 d, 29 c, J 5 a
Herring Trench	62bSW3 St Quentin	T 2 b, 3 a
Herring Trench [1918]	57dNE3 & 4 Hébuterne	L 1 c, 7 a
Hérrisart [village]	57dSW [4 Toutencourt]	T 10
Herron C.T. [1918]	62dSW [4 Cachy]	U 5 b
Herrot Alley	66cNW2 Itancourt	B 16 c
Hersfeld Trench	62cNW2 Bouchavesnes	C 26 a, c
Hertford Street [Cuinchy]	36cNW1 La Bassée	A 20 b, 21 a
Hertford Trench	51bNW3 Arras	H 25 a, c
Herthoek [hamlet]	28NE4 Dadizeele	L 28 a, c
Herts Avenue	36cNW1 La Bassée	A 8 c, d
Herts Cross Roads [Herthoek]	28NE4 Dadizeele	L 28 c 8.9
Herué [Tranchée, 1915]	57dSE4 Ovillers	X 20 c, 26 a
Hervé Trench / Tranchée Hervé	62cNW4 Péronne / SW2 Barleux	I 32 c, d, O 2 a
Hervilly Aerodrome [German, 1918]	62cNE4 Roisel	K 30 a, b
Hervin Farm	51bNW3 Arras	H 13 b, d
Herzeele Railhead / Refilling Point	27NE1 Herzeele	D 10 c
Herzegovina Trench [1918]	62dSE [3 Marcelcave]	V 8 c, 14 a
Hesperus Trench	36cSW4 Rouvroy	U 5 c, d, 6 a, c
Hesse Trench	62cNW4 Péronne	I 24 a, c
Hesse Trench	70dNW2 Servais	C 20 a, c, 25 b, 26 a
Hesse Trench / Tranchée de Hesse	66cNW2 Itancourt	C 20 c, d
Hessian Dump	57dSE2 Beaumont	R 28 b 2.8
Hessian Support	57dSE1 & 2 Beaumont	R 21, 22
Hessian Trench	57dSE1 & 2 Beaumont	R 20 d, 21 c, d, 22 c, d, 23 a, b, c
Hessian Wood	28SE1 Wervicq	P 1 a, c
Heston Road	57dSE1 & 2 Beaumont	Q 10 a
Het Kasteeltje Farm [moated]	20SE2 Hooglede	Q 30 a 8.6
Het Sas	20SW4 Bixschoote	T 29 a
Het Waterpachthof Farm	28NE2 Moorslede	L 5 b 3.9
Hetsas Street	51bNW3 Arras	G 34 c
Hetty Post	62cNE4 Roisel	L 18 c 15.95
Hetty Road [road]	36cSW1 Lens / 2 Harnes	N 4 a
Hetty Support	62cNE4 Roisel	L 17 b, d
Heudecourt [village]	57cSE3 Sorel-le-Grand	W 15 a, c, d, 20 b, d, 21 a, b, c
Heulebeek [stream]	28NE4 Dadizeele	extensive
Hew Trench	51bNW1 Roclincourt	B 25 d, 26 c
Hexham Junction [light rly, 1917-18]	28NW4 Ypres	I 9 c 10.95

Name	Map Sheet	Map Reference
Hexham Road [road; Eaucourt l'Abbaye]	57cSW1 Gueudecourt	M 23 a, b, d
Hexham Trench	57cSW1 Gueudecourt	M 23 d
Heyse Weg	57dNE1 & 2 Fonquevillers	E 28 d
Heythorp Lane	62cNE2 Epéhy	F 4 b
Heythorp Post	62cNE2 Epéhy	F 4 b
Hiawatha Trench [1918]	51bNW1 Roclincourt / 3 Arras	B 25 d, H 1 b, c, d
Hibou Farm	20SW4 Bixschoote	U 1 b 4.4
Hibou, Maison du [farm & pillbox]	28NW2 St Julien	C 6 c
Hiccup Trench	62bSW3 St Quentin	N 31 d
Hickory Farm	20SE2 Hooglede	R 19 a 9.6
Hicks Alley	36cNW3 Loos	H 13 d, 19 a, 20 a, b,
Hicks House / Houses [Le Gheer]	28SW4 Ploegsteert	U 21 d 64.43
Hidden Lane	62dNE2 Méaulte	F 10 a, b, c
Hidden Trench	62bNW1 Gouy	A 2 b
Hidden Way	57cSE2 Gonnelieu	Q 18 d
Hidden Wood	62dNE2 Méaulte	F 10 b
Hiele Farm	28SW2 Wytschaete	O 8 d 90.95
Higgins Wood	28NE4 Dadizeele	K 27 d, 28 c
High Alley	62cNW1 Maricourt	A 17 d
High Alley [W of High Wood]	57cSW3 Longueval	S 4 c, 9 b, d, 10 a
High Command Redoubt	28NW2 St Julien	C 14 b, 15 a
High Command Trench	36NW2 Armentières	C 4 c
High Farm	28SW2 Wytschaete	O 18 c 25.20
High Holborn	57cSW3 Longueval	S 18 c, d, 24 b
High Holborn Avenue	57dNE3 & 4 Hébuterne	K 32 d, 33 c
High Road [trench]	57cSW3 Longueval	T 8 d, 14 b
High Street	36cNW1 La Bassée / 3 Loos	A 21 d, 27 b, d, G 4 a
High Street	51bNW1 Roclincourt	A 27 a
High Street	51bSW1 Neuville Vitasse	M 4 c, d
High Street [CT]	36SW1 Aubers	M 34 b
High Street [road]	36cSW1 Lens	M 24 c, 30 a
High Street Trench	57dNE3 & 4 Hébuterne	K 6 d
High Street, & Support	57cSE4 Villers-Guislain	X 4 d
High Trees	57cNE2 Bourlon	F 2 a 0.3
High Trench	57cSE4 Villers-Guislain	X 5 c, 11 a
High Trench	57dSE1 & 2 Beaumont	R 27 d, 28 c
High Trench North	62cNW1 Maricourt	A 17 d, 18 c
High Trench South	62cNW1 Maricourt	A 24 a
High Wood [Foureaux Wald]	57cSW3 Longueval	S 3, 10
Highgate Trench	36cNW3 Loos	H 33 c, d, 34 c
Highland Cross [cross roads]	57cNE4 Marcoing	L 32 a 2.3
Highland Farm	28NW2 St Julien	C 19 b 4.5
Highland Ridge	57cNE4 Marcoing / 57cSE2 Gonnelieu	L 32, R 1, 2, 7, 8
Highland Road [road]	57cNE4 Marcoing	L 31 b, 32 a, c
Highland Street	36SW3 Richebourg	M 35 c
Highland Support	51bSW2 Vis-en-Artois	O 1 b, 2 a
Highland Support	57cSE2 Gonnelieu	R 1 b, d, 2 a, 7 b
Highland Switch	57cSE2 Gonnelieu	R 1 d, 2 c
Highland Trench	36cNW3 Loos	G 11 a
Highland Trench	57cSE2 Gonnelieu	R 2 a, b, c, 7 b, 8 a
Hignett Crossing [road across rly]	28NE4 Dadizeele	L 32 b 1.2
Hilarian Farm	28NW1 Elverdinghe	A 28 d 5.8
Hilary Junction [road jct]	28NE4 Dadizeele	L 27 d 3.2
Hilda Copse	62cSW1 Dompierre	M 24 b, N 19 a

Name	Map Sheet	Map Reference
Hilda Trench	36cNW3 Loos	H 19 a, b, d
Hilders / Hilda Redoubt [Givenchy]	36cNW1 La Bassée	A 9 c
Hilhoek	27NE4 Abeele	L 21 a
Hill / Hills Redoubt	36SW3 Richebourg	S 5 a 3.3
Hill 110	62cNW2 Bouchavesnes	B 23 c, d, 29 a
Hill 131 [south of Souchez]	36bSE4 & 36cSW3 Givenchy	S 19 b, d
Hill 142 [NW of Mesnil]	57dSE1 & 2 Beaumont	Q 27 a, b
Hill 145 [crest of Vimy Ridge]	36cSW3 Vimy	S 16 c, 22 a
Hill 150	62cNW2 Bouchavesnes	B 18 a, b
Hill 20 Post [Veldhoek]	20SW4 Bixschoote	U 5 c 35.30
Hill 32	28NE1 Zonnebeke	D 8 c
Hill 35 [S of Gallipoli Farm]	28NE1 Zonnebeke	D 19 b
Hill 37 [NE of Delva Farm]	28NE1 Zonnebeke	D 20 a
Hill 40 [summit; Zillebeke]	28NW4 & NE3 Zillebeke	I 16 d 25.85
Hill 40 [Windmill Hill, N of Zonnebeke Station]	28NE1 Zonnebeke	D 21 d
Hill 60 [Zwarteleen]	28NW4 & NE3 Zillebeke	I 29 c
Hill 61 [Tor Top]	28NW4 & NE3 Zillebeke	I 30 b 5.8
Hill 62 [Tor Top]	28NW4 & NE3 Zillebeke	I 24 d 8.4
Hill 63 [Huttenberg]	28SW4 Ploegsteert	T 18, U 13
Hill 63 Dugouts [Catacombs / Wallangara]	28SW4 Ploegsteert	T 18, U 13
Hill 65 [north of Vimy village]	36bSE4 & 36cSW3 Givenchy	T 7 c, d, 13 a
Hill 65 [Reservoir Hill]	36cSW1 Lens	M 30 b, N 25 a
Hill 70 [E of Loos]	36cNW3 Loos	H 31, 32
Hill 70 Redoubt	36cNW3 Loos	H 31 a, b, c, d
Hill 70 Road [road]	36cNW3 Loos	G 36 d
Hill 90 Work [1918]	62dSE [4 Harbonnières]	X 12 a
Hill Farm [Mount Bernenchon]	36aSE3 Gonnehem	W 1 a 30.75
Hill Farm [Sallaumines]	36cSW2 Harnes	N 29 c 6.3
Hill Metier	51bNE3 Noyelle-sous-Bellonne	J 8 a
Hill Post	62cNE2 Epéhy	F 29 a
Hill Side Work	51bSW2 Vis-en-Artois	O 21 a, b
Hill Street	28NW4 & NE3 Zillebeke	I 24 b, d
Hill Street [Guillemont]	57cSW3 Longueval	T 19 c
Hill Support	51bSW2 Vis-en-Artois	O 2 c, d
Hill Top Camp [1917-18]	28NW2 St Julien	C 21 d
Hill Top Farm	28NW2 St Julien	C 21 d 1.8
Hill Top Farm Dugout	28NW2 St Julien	C 21 d
Hill Top Work	51bSW2 Vis-en-Artois	O 21 c, d
Hill Trench	51bSW2 Vis-en-Artois	O 21 c
Hill Trench	57cSW1 Gueudecourt	N 20 d
Hill Trench	57dSE1 & 2 Beaumont	R 26 a
Hill Trench	62cNW2 Bouchavesnes	C 4 d, 5 a
Hill Trench [Infantry Hill]	51bSW2 Vis-en-Artois	O 2 c, d, 8 a
Hille [farm & place name]	28SW3 Bailleul	S 4 d 3.8
Hille [farm]	28SW3 Bailleul	S 9 b 7.4
Hillock Farm	28NW2 St Julien	C 12 a 5.6
Hill's Redoubt [Sept 1915]	36SW3 Richebourg	S 5 a 1.1
Hillsea House	28SW1 Kemmel	M 32 a 05.93
Hillside [light rly sidings]	36bSE1 [Hermin]	Q 9 c
Hillside North Camp	28SW3 Bailleul	T 14 c
Hillside South Camp	28SW3 Bailleul	T 14 c
Hilltop Camp	28NW2 St Julien	C 21 d
Hilly Trench	51bNW4 Fampoux	H 5 d, 6 c, 12 a
Hilt Lane [road]	51bSW2 Vis-en-Artois	N 6 a, c, d

Name	Map Sheet	Map Reference
Hilt Trench [Rainbow Trench]	57cSW1 Gueudecourt	N 20 d
Himalaya Trench	51bNW3 Arras / 4 Fampoux	H 28 a, c
Hinckley Avenue	57cNE4 Marcoing	K 23 c, d, 24 a, c
Hincksley Avenue	57cNE4 Marcoing	K 23 c, d, 24 a, c
Hind Avenue	51bSW4 Bullecourt	T 6 a
Hind Support	51bSW4 Bullecourt	T 6 d, U 1 c, 7 a
Hind Trench	51bSW4 Bullecourt	T 5 a
Hindenberg [sic] Trench	57dSE4 Ovillers	R 31 c, d
Hindenburg / Hindenberg [sic] Trench	57dSE2 Beaumont	R 3 a, b, 4 a
Hindenburg Farm	28NW2 St Julien	C 8 d 95.25
Hindenburg Line	51b, 57b, 57c, 62b etc	extensive
Hindenburg St.	57dSE4 Ovillers	R 31 c, d
Hindenburg Trench	36cNW1 La Bassée	G 4 b, 5 a
Hindleg Trench	62cNW1 Maricourt	B 25 b, d
Hindleg Wood	62cNW1 Maricourt	B 25 b, 26 c, d,
Hindoo Alley	36cNW3 Loos	H 19 b, d, 20 a
Hindoo Farm	28NE2 Moorslede	E 28 d 30.05
Hindu Cot. / Cott. [& pillbox/es]	28NE1 Zonnebeke	D 13 a, b
Hinges [village]	36aSE3 Gonnehem / 4 Locon	W 9 b, d, 10 a, c, 15 b, 16 a
Hinges Chateau	36aSE4 Locon	W 16 a 1.8
Hinges Road [road]	36aSE2 Lestrem / SE4 Locon	Q 28 d, 34 a, c, W 4 a, c
Hinges, Pont l' [over canal]	36aSE4 Locon	W 4 c 35.70
Hingette [hamlet]	36aSE4 Locon	W 10 d, 11 c, 16 b, 17 a
Hinks Farm	28SW1 Kemmel	M 33 a 3.9
Hinton Farm	20SE3 Westroosebeke	V 21 b 5.1
Hip Farm	27NE1 Herzeele	D 24 d 2.2
Hip Lane	62cNE2 Epéhy	L 6 c
Hip Trench	51bNW1 Roclincourt	B 25 d
Hip Trench	62bSW3 St Quentin	G 7 b
Hip Trench	62cNE4 Roisel	L 6 c, 12 a
Hippo Lane [trench]	51bSE3 Cagnicourt	V 19 c
Hippocrates Cross Roads	20SE3 Westroosebeke	V 6 d 85.05
Hipshoek	27NE2 Proven	L 2 a
Hirondelle Cabaret, à l'	28SW4 Ploegsteert	U 6 c 20.75
Hirondelle Mill, l'	36cSW3 Vimy	M 33 c 99.73
Hirondelle, Bois de l'	36cSW3 Vimy	M 35 c, d, S 4 b, 5 a, b
Hirson Lane	51bNW3 Arras	H 27 c, 33 a, b, d
Hitchenburg Trench	62bSW2 Fonsommes / 4 Homblières	T 34 b, d
Hitchin [light rly locality, 1917-18]	28NW4 Ypres	H 28 b, 29 a
Hitchin Road	36cNW1 La Bassée	A 8 a, b, c, d, 9 a, c
Hittite Farm	27NE1 Herzeele	K 2 b 4.0
Hittite Trench	57dNE3 & 4 Hébuterne	K 27 b, 28 c
Hive Alley	36cNW3 Loos	H 15, 16, 19, 20, 21
Hivite House	27SE4 Meteren	W 11 c 9.5
Hoary Trench	51bNW4 Fampoux	H 6 c, 11 b, d, 12 a
Hoax Farm	20SE2 Hooglede	R 23 c 05.95
Hobart Avenue	57cNW2 Vaulx-Vraucourt	C 11 a, b, c, 12 a
Hobart Communication Trench [1918]	62dNE [3 Morlancourt]	J 12 a
Hobart Street	57cNE1 Quéant	E 8, 9, 13, 14
Hobart Trench	36cNW3 Loos	H 19 d, 25 b, 26 a
Hobart Trench	51bNW4 Fampoux	H 10 d, 11 a, c
Hobbs Alley	36cNW3 Loos	H 20 c, 25 b, 26 a
Hobbs Farm [Ferme de la Moularderie]	36NW2 Armentières	C 23 a 5.9
Hobby Farm	36aSE1 St Venant	Q 26 c 95.60

Name	Map Sheet	Map Reference
Hobereaux Trench / Tranchée des Hobereaux	62cSW2 Barleux / 4 St. Christ	N 35 b, d
Hobo Fork [road jct]	28NE2 Moorslede	E 6 c 65.30
Hoche Alley	62bSW3 St Quentin	S 21 d, 22 b, c, d, 23 a
Hoche Alley	62cSW3 Vermandovillers	S 13 b
Hock Farm	28NE2 Moorslede	E 28 d 4.6
Hock Post	62bNW3 Bellicourt	G 31 d 6.8
Hock Trench	57dNE3 & 4 Hébuterne	K 24 b, L 19 a
Hockey Trench	36cNW3 Loos	H 33 a
Hod Trench	36cNW3 Loos	H 32 d, 33 c
Hodder House	28NE4 Dadizeele	K 22 b 2.7
Hodder Street	57dSE4 Ovillers	W 18 b
Hodge Street	62cNW1 Maricourt	A 28 d, 29 a, c
Hoe Trench [later Support]	51bSW2 Vis-en-Artois	O 8 c, 14 a
Hoekje Cabaret, In het	20SW4 Bixschoote	N 36 d 10.75
Hoekske [place name]	20SW4 Bixschoote	N 35 c
Hofland [farm]	27NE1 Herzeele	E 1 d 3.3
Hofland Windmill	27NE1 Herzeele	E 1 d 27.10
Hog Post	57cNE2 Bourlon	K 4 a 3.1
Hog Trench	36cNW3 Loos	H 32 b, 33 a
Hogan House	36NW4 Bois Grenier	I 21 a
Hogan Road	36NW4 Bois Grenier	I 21 a, c
Hogs Back	36cNW3 & 1 Loos	G 4 b, d
Hog's Back / Hogg's Back Trench	57cSW3 Longueval	T 8 d, 9 c
Hogs Back Crater	36cNW3 & 1 Loos	G 4 b
Hog's Head	57dSE2 & 57cSW1 Le Sars	N 31 b
Hohen Stellung [Ripley Trench; Thiepval]	57dSE1 & 2 Beaumont	R 25 b
Hohenzollern Redoubt	36cNW1 La Bassée / 3 Loos	G 4 b, d
Hohenzollern Trench [S of Thiepval]	57dSE1 & 2 Beaumont / 4 Ovillers	R 31 b, d, 32 c
Hoino Farm	28SW2 Wytschaete	N 29 c 2.9
Hoist Lane [trench]	51bSE3 Cagnicourt	V 1 a, c, d
Hokhoy Lane	51bNW3 Arras	H 20 d, 26 b
Holborn	51bNW3 Arras / SW1 Neuville Vitasse	G 34 d, M 4 b
Holden Farm [1918]	28SW1 Kemmel	M 27 a 75.50
Hole in the Wall	36cSW1 Lens	M 2 d
Hole in the Wall	36SW2 Radinghem	N 16 d
Hole in Wall	57dSE2 Beaumont	R 3 c 6.6
Hollan Wood	66eNW [2 Thennes]	C 17 c, d
Holland Park Road [road]	36cSW1 Lens / 2 Harnes	N 3 d, 9 b, 10 a, c
Holland Post	62cNE2 Epéhy	F 17 a
Holland Road [road]	36cSW1 Lens	N 3 d, 9 b
Hollande, Bois d'	57dSE1 & 2 Beaumont	R 8 a
Hollanderie [farm]	36aSE1 St Venant	P 26 a 50.95
Hollanderie [place name]	36aSE1 St Venant	P 19 d, 20 c
Hollanderie [Post]	36aSE1 St Venant	P 20 c
Hollandscheschuur Farm / Craters	28SW2 Wytschaete	N 18 b
Hollebeke Chateau	28SW2 Wytschaete	O 12 b
Hollebeke Junction	28SW2 Wytschaete	O 3 b, d
Hollebeque Farm	36NW1 Steenwerck	B 20 c 4.7
Hollow Copse	51bNW2 Oppy	C 27 c
Hollow Way / Holloway [trench]	36cSW3 Vimy	S 8 b
Hollow, The [Cuinchy, Feb 1915]	36cNW1 La Bassée	A 15 d
Holloway Street [Sept 1915]	36cNW1 La Bassée	A 21 d
Holly Lane [72, Boyau / Sap]	36cNW3 Loos	G 18, 19, 24, H 13, 19
Holly Post	62cNE4 Roisel	L 18 c 1.2

Name	Map Sheet	Map Reference
Holly Trench	51bNW4 Fampoux	H 6 c, 11 b, 12 a
Holly Trench	62bSW3 St Quentin	T 3 a, b
Hollywood [proposed Br strongpoint]	57dSE4 Ovillers	R 34 d 1.0
Holmes Redoubt [Contalmaison]	57dSE4 Ovillers	X 17 a
Holnon [village]	62bSW3 St Quentin	S 2 d, 8 a, b, c, d
Holnon Wood	62cSE4 [Attilly]	X 16, 17
Holstein Support	57cSW4 Combles	T 6 b
Holster Trench	36cNW3 Loos	H 1 c, d, 2 c
Holt Corner [Ploegsteert Wood, 1914-15]	28SW4 Ploegsteert	U 21 b 2.7
Holt Work	51bNW3 Arras	H 25 d
Holts [farm]	20SE3 Westroosebeke	V 9 d 8.3
Holts Trench	20SE3 Westroosebeke	V 9 d
Holts Trench	57cSE4 Villers-Guislain	X 28 b
Holyhead [Post]	36NW3 Fleurbaix	G 27 a
Holywell Farm	20SE2 Hooglede	R 13 b 6.7
Homard Trench	62bSW1 Gricourt	N 31 a
Homard Trench	66dNW1 Punchy	A 4 b, 5 a
Homard Trench, Tranchée du Homard	62cSW3 Vermandovillers	S 29 c
Homblières [village]	62bSW4 Homblières	U 14 a, b, c, d, 20 a, b
Home Avenue	57dNE3 & 4 Hébuterne	K 21 c, d, 22 c, d, 23 c, d
Home Farm	28NW4 Ypres	I 26 a 3.2
Home Farm	36aSE1 St Venant	P 5 d 1.6
Home Trench	57dSE2 Beaumont	R 20 c
Homer Alley	36cNW3 Loos	H 7 c
Homme Mort Farm, l'	51bNE1 Brebières	D 11 b, 12 a
Homme Mort, l' [crossroads]	57cNW2 Vaulx-Vraucourt	B 17 a
Homme Mort, l' [farm]	36cSW4 Rouvroy	U 2 d 4.5
Homme Sauvage, l' [farm]	27NE1 Herzeele	D 23 d 75.20
Hondo Farm	28NW3 Poperinghe	H 27 c 5.6
Honduras Alley	62bSW1 Gricourt	N 32 b
Hone Trench	51bNW1 Roclincourt	B 26 a, b
Honef Alley [Indian Wood]	62bSW1 Gricourt	M 36 a
Honey Alley	36cNW3 Loos	H 26 a, b
Honey Trench	51bNW4 Fampoux	H 11 b
Honey Wood	27NE2 Proven	F 19 b, c, d
Honeydew Farm	28NE4 Dadizeele	L 31 a 4.4
Hong Kong Trench	28SW2 Wytschaete	N 23 b
Honnecourt [village]	57cSE4 Villers-Guislain / 57bSW3 Honnecourt	X 12 a, c, S 1 b, d, 2 c, 7 b, d, 8 a, c
Honnecourt Wood	57cSE4 Villers-Guislain	X 11 b
Honolulu Trench	62cSW3 Vermandovillers	T 25 b, c, d
Honorat [Boyau, 1915] / Bon Accord Street	57dSE4 Ovillers	X 26 a, c
Honorat [Tranchée, E of Bécourt Ch'au, 1915]	57dSE4 Ovillers	X 26 c
Honore Farm	20SW4 Bixschoote	O 31 d 85.70
Hood Road [road]	36cNW3 Loos	H 14 b, c, d
Hood Trench	51bNW2 Oppy	H 6 a
Hoof Lane	51bSW1 Neuville Vitasse	N 7 a, b, d
Hoof Post	62cNE4 Roisel	L 30 a 65.30
Hoof Trench	36cNW3 Loos	H 32 b, 33 a
Hooge Inn	27NE2 Proven	L 4 b 7.2
Hooge Retrenchment	28NW4 & NE3 Zillebeke	I 18 b
Hooge Street	51bNW3 Arras	G 34 b, 35 a, c
Hooge Trench	36cNW3 Loos / SW1 Lens	H 31 d, N 1 b
Hooge, Chateau & 1915 Crater	28NW4 & NE3 Zillebeke	I 18 b

Name	Map Sheet	Map Reference
Hoogenacker [hamlet & ridge]	28SW3 Bailleul	M 33 c
Hoogenacker Mill	27SE4 Meteren	X 27 d 7.9
Hooggraaf [railway loop]	28NW3 Poperinghe	G 26 c
Hooggraaf Cabaret	28NW3 Poperinghe	G 26 c 5.8
Hooggraaf Camp	28NW3 Poperinghe	G 26 c
Hooggraaf Farm	28NW3 Poperinghe	G 26 a 8.4
Hooggraaf Windmill	28NW3 Poperinghe	G 26 a 8.1
Hooghe [village]	20SE2 Hooglede	Q 10 d
Hooghe Convent	20SE2 Hooglede	Q 10 c 9.6
Hooglede [village]	20SE2 Hooglede	Q 17 a, b
Hook Post	62bSW3 St Quentin	G 31 d
Hook Sap	57dSE2 & 57cSW1 Le Sars	M 17 b, d
Hook Street	36cNW3 Loos	G 36 c
Hook Trench	36cNW3 Loos	H 26 d, 32 a, b
Hook Trench	51bNW1 Roclincourt	B 20 d, 26 b
Hook Trench	51bSW2 Vis-en-Artois	O 2 c, d, 8 b
Hook Trench	57cSW3 Longueval	M 33 b, d, S 2 b, 3 a, b, 4 a
Hook Trench	57cSW3 Longueval	S 24 d, T 19 c
Hook, The	28NW2 St Julien	C 6 d, 12 b
Hook, The [N end of Hook Trench]	51bSW2 Vis-en-Artois	O 2 c, d
Hookey Trench	36cNW3 Loos	H 13 b, d
Hooley House	28NE4 Dadizeele	K 11 b 8.6
Hoop Lane	51bSW4 Bullecourt	U 15 b
Hoop Trench	36cNW3 Loos / SW1 Lens	H 33 c, N 3 a
Hoop Trench	51bNW1 Roclincourt	B 25 d
Hoop Trench	51bSW4 Bullecourt	U 9 c, 15 b, 16 a
Hoop, The	57dSE4 Ovillers	X 6 c
Hooper Farm	27NE1 Herzeele	E 7 c 3.1
Hoot Trench	36cNW3 Loos	H 26 d, 32 b
Hooter Road [road]	36cNW3 Loos	H 15 b, c, d
Hoover House	28SW1 Kemmel	M 33 a 7.8
Hop Alley	57cSW3 Longueval	T 13 a
Hop Lane	51bSW4 Bullecourt / SE3 Cagnicourt	U 6 d, V 1 c, 7 a, b, d
Hop Lane [trench] / Hop Trench	51bSW4 Bullecourt / SE3 Cagnicourt	U 6 d, V 1 c, 7 a, b
Hop Out [Hopoutre village]	27NE4 Abeele	L 17 d
Hop Point [German Redoubt]	28SW2 Wytschaete	N 30 d 7.7
Hop Trench	36cNW3 Loos	H 31 d, 32 d, 33 c
Hop Trench	51bNW1 Roclincourt	B 26 b
Hop Trench	51bSW1 Neuville Vitasse	N 7 c
Hope Copse	62bNW4 Ramicourt	I 33 a
Hope Cut [June 1916, Turco Farm]	28NW2 St Julien	C 15 c
Hope Farm	28SW2 Wytschaete	O 11 c 4.4
Hope House [Ploegsteert Wd; near front line]	28SW4 Ploegsteert	U 21 d
Hope Post [Serre Trench]	57dNE3 & 4 Hébuterne	K 35 b, d
Hope Street	51bSW1 Neuville Vitasse	M 2 d, 3 c, d, 10 a, b,
Hope Street	57dNE3 & 4 Hébuterne	K 16 b, d
Hope Trench	57dNE3 & 4 Hébuterne	K 10 d, 16 b
Hope Wood	62dSE [2 Proyart]	Q 29 b
Hopeful Trench	51bNW4 Fampoux	H 17 a
Hopeless Street	51bSW1 Neuville Vitasse	M 10 a, b
Hôpital pilier, Ferme	62cNW2 Bouchavesnes	B 18 a 85.65
Hôpital, Ferme de	62cNW2 Bouchavesnes	B 17 b
Hopoutre [village; 'Hop Out']	27NE4 Abeele	L 17 d
Hopoutre Railhead / Refilling Point	27NE4 Abeele	L 17 d

Name	Map Sheet	Map Reference
Hoquet Trench	62bSW1 Gricourt	N 31 a
Horace Street	51bNW3 Arras	G 35 b, d
Horas Trench	62bSW3 St Quentin	S 16 c, 22 a, c, d
Horgny [village]	62cSW2 Barleux / 4 St. Christ	N 35 central
Horgny Alley	62cSW2 Barleux	N 34 b, 35 a
Horgny, Boyau d'	62cSW1 & 2 Belloy	N 35 a
Horgny, Reduit d'	62cSW3 & 4 Marchélepot	N 35 c, d
Horn Alley	62cNW1 Maricourt	A 10 d, 11 a, c
Horn Trench	51bNW1 Roclincourt	B 26 b
Horn Trench	51bSW4 Bullecourt	U 1 a, c
Horn Werk	57dNE1 & 2 Fonquevillers	E 6 a
Hornby [hut]	28NW4 Ypres	I 25 a
Hornby Crater [Bellewaarde Farm]	28NW4 & NE3 Zillebeke	I 12 c 3.7
Hornby Trench	57dSE2 Beaumont	R 20 d 45.55
Hornby Trench [BFL Cross Roads Farm]	28NW2 St Julien	C 22 a, c
Hörnchen [Duck's Bill]	28NW2 St Julien	C 15 c
Horne Farm	20SE3 Westroosebeke	W 26 b 3.4
Horne Works [Ypres]	28NW4 & NE3 Zillebeke	I 8 d
Hornet Alley	36cNW3 Loos	H 7 d, 8 c, 13 b
Hornet Avenue	57dSE1 & 2 Beaumont	Q 29 b, d,
Hornet Trench [1918]	57dSE1 & 2 Beaumont	Q 29 a, c, 35 a
Hornet Wood	27NE2 Proven	F 4 c, 10 a
Hornet's Nest	36SW1 Aubers / 2 Radinghem	N 10 a
Hornsea Trench	51bNW3 Arras	G 36 b, H 31 a
Horse Alley	36cNW3 Loos	H 25 d, 26 c, d
Horse Guards Avenue [Trancheé de la 7e D.I.]	36cSW1 Lens	M 15 a
Horse Lane	51bSW1 Neuville Vitasse	N 13 b, 14 a
Horse Post	62cNE2 Epéhy	F 3 d
Horseshoe Dump	36aNE3 Haverskerque	K 8 d 40.35
Horseshoe Post	51bSW2 Vis-en-Artois	O 31 b 8.1
Horseshoe Redoubt / The Horse Shoe	51bSW4 Bullecourt	U 29 c
Horseshoe Support	51bSW4 Bullecourt / 57cNW2 Vaulx-Vraucourt	U 28 d, 29 c, C 5 a, b
Horseshoe Trench	57dNE3 & 4 Hébuterne	K 28 d
Horseshoe Trench / The Horseshoe	57dSE4 Ovillers	X 21 b, d
Horseshoe, The	62dNE2 Méaulte	F 11 d
Horthe / Hortle Trench [1918]	62dSW [4 Cachy]	U 17 a
Horton Trench	36cNW3 Loos	H 25 d, 26 c
Hosack Trench	51bNW4 Fampoux	H 11 d
Hosky / Bosky Trench	62dNE2 Méaulte	F 3 b, 4 a
Hospice [Locre]	28SW1 Kemmel	M 23 d 65.00
Hospice [Nieppe]	36NW1 Steenwerck	B 15 d 6.6
Hospice [Wytschaete]	28SW2 Wytschaete	O 19 a 7.8
Hospice Civil [Ploegsteert]	28SW4 Ploegsteert	U 25 d 5.8
Hospice Farm	36NW4 Bois Grenier	H 24 d 2.3
Hospice Wood	62cNW3 Vaux	G 24 d
Hospice, Moulin de l' [Messines]	28SW4 Ploegsteert	U 2 a 7.9
Hospital [Béthune]	36bNE2 Beuvry	E 10 d 8.8
Hospital Corner	36bSE4 Carency	X 16 d 9.5
Hospital Cross Camp	27NE4 Abeele	L 10 b
Hospital Farm	28NW1 Elverdinghe	B 19 d 1.0
Hospital Farm	62cNW2 Bouchavesnes	B 17 b
Hospital Farm Camp	28NW1 Elverdinghe	B 19 d, 25 b
Hospital Lane	57cSW2 Villers-au-Flos	N 30 d

Name	Map Sheet	Map Reference
Hospital Lane [road, Le Transloy]	57cSW2 Villers-au-Flos	N 30 b, d
Hospital Spur [light rly]	28NW3 Poperinghe	H 7 a
Hospital Spur [light rly]	36bNE3 [Bruay]	K 20 a
Hospital Trench [Beaumont Hamel]	57dSE1 & 2 Beaumont	Q 10 b, 11 a
Hospital Wood	62cNW2 Bouchavesnes	B 12 a, c, 17 b, 18 a
Hot Road [road]	36cNW3 Loos	H 21 d, 22 c, 27 a, b
Hotel de Luxe	36NW2 & NE1 Houplines	C 2 c 95.20
Hottentot Alley	36cNW3 Loos	H 2 d
Houart Farm	20SW4 Bixschoote	U 3 b 2.9
Houart Wood	20SW4 Bixschoote	U 3 a 6.8
Houchard Post [1918]	20SW4 Bixschoote	U 3 d 83.20
Houchin - Lillers - Steenbecque Line	36bNE [1, 3 & 4] / 36aSW [2 & 4]	extensive
Houchin [village]	36bNE3 / 4 Noeux-les-Mines	K 9 c, d, 15 a, b, 16 a
Houchin Hill Locality	36bNE4 Noeux-les-Mines	K 16 a, b, c, d
Houdain Lane	51bNW3 Arras	H 25 b
Hough Street	57dSE4 Ovillers	W 6 b
Houghton Road	36NW4 Bois Grenier	I 10 d, 16 b
Hougomont / Hougoumont Post	36SW1 Aubers	M 12 c
Hougomont Street	36cSW1 Lens	M 14 d
Hougoumont Lane [road]	36SW1 Aubers	M 5 d, 11 b, d
Houlette Work	51bNW3 Arras	H 31 b
Houndsditch [road]	57cNE1 Quéant	D 30 b, E 19 b, c, d
Houngas Trench	62cSW1 & 2 Belloy	O 7 a, b
Hounslow Camp	28NW1 Elverdinghe	A 11 c
Hounslow Road	57dSE1 & 2 Beaumont	Q 10 a
Houplines Line	36NW2 Armentières / 4 Bois Grenier	G 27 b,c,d, I 2 d, 3 a,c, 7 a,b,c, 8 a,b
Hour Trench	36cNW3 Loos	H 27 a, c, 33 a
Hourges [village]	66eNW [2 Thennes]	C 3 d, 4 c
Houri Alley	62bSW1 Gricourt	M 30 c, d
House A [Rue de Cailloux, April 1915]	36SW3 Richebourg	S 25
House B [Rue de Cailloux, April 1915]	36SW3 Richebourg	S 25
House of the Allies	62cSW2 Barleux	O 14 b
House Trench	36cNW3 Loos	H 27 a, c
Household Lane [road]	36aNE3 Haverskerque	J 27 a, b, d
Houston Fork [road jct]	28NE4 Dadizeele	K 36 b 8.3
Houthulst Forest	20SW2 / 4 / SE1 / 3	extensive
Houthulst Support	20SW4 Bixschoote	U 4 b, 5 a, c
Houthulst Trench	20SW4 Bixschoote	U 4 d, 5 c
Houtkerque [village]	27NE1 Herzeele	E 14 c, d, 15 c
Houtkerque Chateau	27NE1 Herzeele	E 20 d 2.7
Hove Avenue	36NW2 Armentières	C 10 a, c
Hove Copse	62bSW2 Fonsommes	N 12 a, b
Hove Trench	36cNW3 Loos	H 31 b, d
Hove Trench	51bNW3 Arras	H 25 c
Hovis Trench	36cNW3 Loos	H 31 b
How Farm	28SW2 Wytschaete	O 27 d 10.95
Howard Trench	36cNW3 Loos	H 33 a, c
Howe [light rly locality, 1917-18]	28NW4 Ypres	H 24 b
Howe Camp	28NW4 Ypres	H 24 c, d
Howitzer Avenue	57dSE4 Ovillers	X 10 a, b
Howitzer Wood	62cNW1 Maricourt	H 3 b, d, 4 a
Howl Trench	36cNW3 Loos	H 32 d, 33 a, c
Howson Road [trench]	57dSE1 & 2 Beaumont	Q 29 c, 35 a, b
Howson's Point [post]	36cNW3 Loos	G 22 b, 23 a

Name	Map Sheet	Map Reference
Hoxton Road [Béarnais, Rue des]	36cSW1 Lens	M 15 a, b
Hoy's Trench	57dSE4 Ovillers	X 1 d, 2 c
Hubert Avenue	57cNE3 Hermies / 57cSE1 Bertincourt	K 32 b, c, d, Q 2 a, c
Hubert Road [road]	36cNW3 Loos	H 7 d, 8 a
Hübner Avenue	28NE1 Zonnebeke	D 1 c
Hübner Farm	28NE1 Zonnebeke	D 1 c 4.6
Hübner Trench	28NW2 St Julien	C 6 d
Huck Trench	51bSW1 Neuville Vitasse	N 20 c
Huddersfield Road	28NW2 St Julien	C 13 d, 19 a, b
Huddle Trench	51bNW4 Fampoux	H 17 b, 18 a
Huddleston Camp [1917-18]	28NW2 St Julien	C 7 c, d
Huddleston Road [road]	28NW2 St Julien	C 7 b, d, 13 b, d
Hudson Alley	51bNW4 Fampoux	H 11 a, b
Hudson Bay	36NW4 Bois Grenier	H 36 d, I 31 c
Hudson Bay Post, & Bay Avenue	36NW4 Bois Grenier	H 36 d
Hudson Post [N of Arleux, 1918]	36cSW4 Rouvroy	T 24 c
Hudson Trench	36cSW3 Vimy / 4 Rouvroy	T 22d, 23c,d, 24c, 27d, 28b,c,d, 29a,b
Hudson Trench	51bNW4 Fampoux	H 5 d, 11 a, b
Hudson Trench	62cSW2 Barleux	N 29 d, 35 b
Hudson, Tranchée d'	62cSW1 & 2 Belloy	N 35 a, b
Hudson's Post	62cSE2 Vermand	R 6 a 5.5
Huff Trench	51bNW1 Roclincourt	B 26 b
Hug Trench	51bSW4 Bullecourt	U 23 c
Hugedoorn, l' [farm]	27SE2 Berthen	Q 23 a 3.3
Hugel Halles	28NW2 St Julien	C 11 b
Hugel Hollow	28NW2 St Julien	C 11 b
Hugers Graben	51cSE2 Beaumetz	R 35 b
Hugg Trench	51bNW1 Roclincourt	B 26 b
Hughes Farm	28SW3 Bailleul	S 15 d 10.15
Hughes Support	57cNE3 Hermies / 4 Marcoing	K 3 d, 9 b, 10 a, b
Hughes Switch	57cNE3 Hermies / 4 Marcoing	K 3 d, 9 b, 10 a, b
Hughes Trench	57cNE3 Hermies / 4 Marcoing	K 9 b, 10 a, b
Hugo Alley	62cSE [4 Attilly] / 62bSW3 St Quentin	X 24 , 28 , 29, 30, S 15, 16, 19, 20, 21
Hugo Lane	36cNW3 Loos	H 25 a, c
Hugo Locality [Bois Hugo]	36cNW3 Loos	H 25 d, 26 c
Hugo Trench	36cNW3 Loos	H 32 a
Huit Maisons Group [posts]	36aSE2 Lestrem	R 23 d, 24 c, 29 b, 30 a
Huitres Trench	62bSW2 Fonsommes	N 30 d, 36 b
Hull [light rly locality, 1917-18]	28NW4 Ypres	H 28 b
Hull Alley	36cNW3 Loos	H 25 d, 26 c
Hull Post	51bNW1 Roclincourt / 2 Oppy	B 16 a, c
Hull Road [road]	36cSW3 Vimy / 4 Rouvroy	T 9 d, 10 b, c, d, 11 a, 15 b
Hull Road [road]	36cSW3 Vimy / 4 Rouvroy	T 10 b, c, d, 11 a, 15 a, b, c, 16 a
Hull Road, & Post	36NW4 Bois Grenier	I 16 a
Hull Street	57dNE1 & 2 Fonquevillers	E 11 c
Hull Trench	51bNW1 Roclincourt	B 26 b
Hull Trench	51bSW1 Neuville Vitasse	M 4 b
Hull Trench	36cNW3 Loos	H 13 b, d
Hull Trench [1918]	57dNE1 & 2 Fonquevillers	E 24 d
Hullebert Farm	36aNE2 Vieux Berquin	F 19 b 9.9
Hulloa Trench	57dNE3 & 4 Hébuterne	K 34 a
Hulls / Hull's Burnt Farm	28SW4 Ploegsteert	U 15 d
Hull's Farm	28NW2 St Julien	B 18 c 8.3

Name	Map Sheet	Map Reference
Hulluch [village]	36cNW3 Loos	H 13 b, d [1915]
Hulluch Alley	36cNW3 Loos	G 7, 8, 9, 10
Hulluch Retrenchment	36cNW3 Loos	G 10 b, 11 a
Hulluch Road Keep	36cNW3 Loos	G 9 b
Hulluch Road Trench	36cNW3 Loos	G 11 d, 12 c, d [1915]
Hulluch Street	51bNW3 Arras	G 35 b, d
Hulluch Trench	36cNW3 Loos	H 7 d, 13 a, b, d, 19 b, 20 a, c, 26 a
Hulluch Tunnel	36cNW3 Loos	G 18 a
Hulst Trench	51bNW3 Arras	H 26 c
Humanity [Trench; Sept 1915]	36cNW1 La Bassée	A 27 c
Humber Support	51bSW4 Bullecourt	U 7 d
Humber Trench [La Folie Farm]	36cSW3 Vimy	S 29 a, b
Humbug Alley	36cNW3 Loos	H 26 d, 27 a, b, c, 28 a, b, 31 b, 32 a
Humbug Post	36cNW3 Loos	H 25 d, 26 c, 31 b, 32 a
Humbug Trench	36cNW3 Loos	H 31 b
Hume Trench	51bSW1 Neuville Vitasse	M 4 c, d
Humid Trench	51bNW4 Fampoux	H 17 b
Humid Trench	51bNW4 Fampoux	H 6 a, c
Humid Trench	62bSW4 Homblières	T 4 d
Humming Bird Wood	66cSW4 La Fère	U 4 d, 5 c
Humour Trench	62bSW1 Gricourt	N 25 b
Hump Alley Trench	51bSW4 Bullecourt	U 20 a
Hump Lane	51bSW4 Bullecourt	U 13 d
Hump Support, & The Hump	51bSW4 Bullecourt	U 13 d, 14 c
Hun Alley	57cSW3 Longueval	S 24 d
Hun Farm	36aSE1 St Venant	Q 20 d 95.55
Hun Street	36SW3 Richebourg	S 4 b, d
Hun Trench	36cSW3 Vimy	M 32 c
Hun Trench	62cSE2 Vermand	R 4 b
Hun Trench [1918]	66eNW [4 Morisel]	I 8 c, d, 14 a
Hungerford Lane	51bNW3 Arras	H 13 c
Hunk Houses	28NE2 Moorslede	L 1 b 35.05
Huns Farm	28SW2 Wytschaete	O 32 a 90.95
Huns Walk [1918]	62dSE [1 Hamel]	P 15 c, d, 16 c
Huns Walk [road]	28SW4 Ploegsteert	O 33 c, d, 34 d, 35 c, U 4 a, b
Hunt Avenue	57cNE3 Hermies	K 8 d, 14 b
Hunt Trench	36cNW3 Loos	H 32 d, 33 c
Hunter Avenue [& slit trs. 1-20, Ploeg. Wd]	28SW4 Ploegsteert	U 21 a, c, 27 a
Hunter Post	36SW3 Richebourg	S 8 a
Hunter Street	28NW2 St Julien	B 10, 11, 16
Hunter Street	36cNW1 La Bassée	A 15 d
Hunter Street	51bNW3 Arras	G 35 a, b, d
Hunter Street [1918]	62dSE [1 Hamel]	P 19 d
Hunter Street [Hawthorn Ridge]	57dSE1 & 2 Beaumont	Q 10 b
Hunter Street [military road / track 1917-18]	20SW4 Bixschoote / 28NW2 St Julien	U 11, 12, 16, 17, 21, 22, 26, 27, C 1
Hunter Street [sunken road]	57dSE1 & 2 Beaumont	Q 4 b, d
Hunter Trench [new front line]	57dSE1 & 2 Beaumont	Q 4 b, d
Hunters Post	36SW3 Richebourg	S 8 a 2.2
Hunters Trail [inf'y & lt horse transp't, June '17]	28SW1 Kemmel / 2 Wytschaete / 3 Bailleul / 4 Ploegsteert	M 29,30,32-36, N25,26,27,31, 32,33
Hunterston North, & South [Ploe. Wd '14-15]	28SW4 Ploegsteert	U 20 c
Huntingdon Trench	51bNW3 Arras	H 19 a
Huntley Avenue	57dSE4 Ovillers	X 25 a, 26 a
Huntley Farm	28NE4 Dadizeele	K 10 c 25.35

Name	Map Sheet	Map Reference
Hurdle Alley	36cSW1 Lens	M 14 a
Hurdle Trench	36cNW3 Loos	H 31 d, 32 a, c
Huron [light rly locality]	28SW2 Wytschaete	O 8 d
Huron Road [road]	36cSW4 Rouvroy	U 9 a, b, c
Huron Trench	51bNW1 Roclincourt / 2 Oppy	B 4 c
Hurrah Alley	36cNW3 Loos	H 31 b, 32 a, c
Hurricane Fork [road jct]	28NE4 Dadizeele	L 25 d 75.85
Hurrum Trench	51bNW4 Fampoux	H 5 d, 6 c
Hurst House	20SE2 Hooglede	R 2 a 3.8
Hurst Park [farm]	28NW2 St Julien	C 10 c 5.7
Hurst Street	57dNE1 & 2 Fonquevillers	E 27 c, d
Hurt Trench	51bNW1 Roclincourt	B 25 d
Hurt Trench	57dSE4 Ovillers	B 25 d
Hurtebise Copse	57bSW1 Bantouzelle	N 15 d, 21 b
Hurtebise Farm	57bSW1 Bantouzelle	N 20 b 8.9
Hurtevent farms	57bSW2 Clary	O 21 d 2.8
Husband Camp	27NE4 Abeele	L 7 d
Hush Alley	57cSE2 Gonnelieu	R 27 d, 33 b
Hussar / Huzzar Trench	51bNW4 Fampoux	H 5 d, 11 b
Hussar Alley	70dNW4 St Gobain	H 30 a, b
Hussar Copse	62bSW4 Homblières	U 27 b, 28 a
Hussar Farm [Potijze]	28NW4 & NE3 Zillebeke	I 4 c 7.6
Hussar Horn	36cNW3 Loos	G 5 c
Hussar Lane [road]	51bSW2 Vis-en-Artois	N 12 b, d, O 1 c
Hussar Lane [trench]	28NW4 & NE3 Zillebeke	I 3 d, 4 c
Hussar Post	62cNE2 Epéhy	F 29 b, d
Hussar Ride	28SW4 Ploegsteert	N 35 d, T 5 a, b
Hussar Road	62cNE2 Epéhy	F 22 d
Hussey Redoubt [Oct 1915]	36cNW3 Loos	G 11 b, d
Hussier Trench	62bSW1 Gricourt	N 25 d
Hussy's Corner	28NE4 Dadizeele	K 36 d 85.20
Hustlers Farm	20SE2 Hooglede	R 19 d 45.50
Hut Farm	28SE1 Wervicq	P 4 b 90.25
Hut Trench	36cNW3 Loos	H 32 b
Hutte Farm, la	36NW1 Steenwerck	D 26 a
Hutte, Château de la [Hill 63]	28SW4 Ploegsteert	U 13 d, 14 c
Hutteberg [Hill 63]	28SW4 Ploegsteert	T 18, U 13
Hutton Mill	36aNE4 Merville	K 18 b 9.7
Huxley Trench	36cNW3 Loos	H 31 b, d
Huzzah Trench [1918]	51bNW4 Fampoux	H 5 d, 11 b
Hyaena Trench	62bSW3 St Quentin	M 36 b, d
Hyde [copse, near Jekyll copse]	62bSW2 Fonsommes	O 19 c
Hyde Park	36cSW1 Lens	M 14 d
Hyde Park	36SW1 Aubers	N 7 a 7.5
Hyde Park Corner	28SW4 Ploegsteert	U 19 b 3.7
Hyde Park Corner	57dNE3 & 4 Hébuterne	K 34 a
Hyde Park Corner	57dSE1 & 2 Beaumont	Q 16 d
Hyde Park Corner [Brickstacks; Sep '15]	36cNW1 La Bassée	A 15 d
Hyde Park Corner [near Canada Corner]	28SW1 Kemmel	M 17 c 6.4
Hyde Park Corner [St Eloi]	28SW2 Wytschaete	O 2 a, b
Hyde Road East	62cNW1 Maricourt	A 7 d
Hyde Road West	62dNE2 Méaulte / 62cNW1 Maricourt	F 12 c, A 7 d
Hyderabad Trench [1918]	51bNW4 Fampoux	H 11 b, 12 a, c
Hyderabad Work / Redoubt	51bNW4 Fampoux	H 11 b, d, 12 a, b, c

Name	Map Sheet	Map Reference
Hyena Alley	36cNW3 Loos	H 3 c
Hyencourt-le-Grand [village]	66dNW1 Punchy	B 1 a, b, d
Hyencourt-le-Petit [village]	66dNW1 Punchy	B 20 c
Hyène Trench / Tranchée de la Hyène	62cSW3 & 4 Marchélepot	T 25 b, c, d
Hyènes Trench	62bSW1 Gricourt	M 36 b
Hyman Trench	36cNW3 Loos	H 33, 34
Hymen Trench	51bNW4 Fampoux	H 11 c
Hyson Alley	36cNW3 Loos	H 7 b, d, 8 a
Hythe Alley	36cNW3 Loos	H 32 c
I Sap [Givenchy]	36cNW1 La Bassée	A 9 b
I Work	51bNW1 Roclincourt	A 29 b
Iban Trench [Rettemoy Graben]	57dNE1 & 2 Fonquevillers	F 25 a, c, d
Iberia Trench, Support, Reserve, Avenue	28NW2 St Julien	I 5 b, 6 a
Iberian [farm & pill boxes]	28NE1 Zonnebeke	D 19 b
Ibex Cottage	27SE4 Meteren	X 4 a 75.55
Ibex Trench, Supp, Res, Lane, Dr, Ave	28NW2 St Julien	I 5 b, 6 a, b
Ibis Post	51bSW2 Vis-en-Artois	O 20 a
Ibis Trench	51bSW2 Vis-en-Artois	O 20 c, 26 a
Ice Street	51bNW3 Arras	G 35 b
Ice Trench	51bNW1 Roclincourt	B 27 a
Ice Trench, Support, Avenue, & Lane	28NW4 & NE3 Zillebeke	I 6 c
Icehouse Trench	66cNW4 Berthenicourt	I 25 b
Iceland Street	51bNW3 Arras	G 29 c, d, 35 b
Iceland Trench	51bNW3 Arras / 4 Fampoux	H 28 a, c
Icu Trench [Mont Rouge]	28SW1 Kemmel	M 22 a, c
Ida House	28NE4 Dadizeele	K 18 d 7.8
Ida Post	28SW4 Ploegsteert	U 29 c 05.30
Ida Trench	36SW1 Aubers / 3 Richebourg	M 36 a, d, N 31 c
Idea Tr, Supp, Res, Row, Ave, Lane, Sw	28NW4 & NE3 Zillebeke	I 6 c, 11 b, 12 a
Identity Tr, Supp, Res, Row, Ave, Lane	28NW4 & NE3 Zillebeke	I 12 a, c, d
Idiot Avenue	28NW4 & NE3 Zillebeke	I 12 c, d
Idiot Corner [NW corner of Bellewaarde Lake]	28NW4 & NE3 Zillebeke	I 12 d 2.6
Idiot Crescent	28NW4 & NE3 Zillebeke	I 12 a, b
Idiot Drive	28NW4 & NE3 Zillebeke	I 12 b, c, d, J 7 a
Idiot Lane	28NW4 & NE3 Zillebeke	I 12 b, d
Idiot Reserve	28NW4 & NE3 Zillebeke	I 12 b, d
Idiot Row	28NW4 & NE3 Zillebeke	I 12 b, J 7 a
Idiot Street	51bNW3 Arras	G 29 b, 30 a
Idiot Support	28NW4 & NE3 Zillebeke	I 12 c, d
Idiot Trench	28NW4 & NE3 Zillebeke	I 12 c
Idle Lane / Street	51bNW3 Arras	G 29 b, d, 30 c
Idle Trench, Reserve, Sap	28NW4 & NE3 Zillebeke	I 12 c, d, 18 a, b
Idol Trench	51bNW1 Roclincourt	B 27 a
Idol Trench	62bSW3 St Quentin	T 7 b
Ifs, Bois des [Yews Wood]	62cSW3 & 4 Marchélepot	N 31 d, T 1 a, b
Iggaree Corner [Noreuil]	57cNW2 Vaulx-Vraucourt	C 10 c 65.95
Iglau Trench	62cNW4 Péronne	H 30 d, 36 b, I 25 c
Ignis Trench, Support, Reserve [Hooge]	28NW4 & NE3 Zillebeke	I 12 d, 18 b
Ignoramus Trench	28NW4 & NE3 Zillebeke	I 18 b
Ignorance Trench, Sup, Res, Row, Cres, Lane	28NW4 & NE3 Zillebeke	I 18 b, J 13 a, c
Ignorant Trench	62bSW3 St Quentin	T 7 b
Iguana Trench, Support, Lane, Ave	28NW4 & NE3 Zillebeke	I 6 b, c, d, 12 a, b
II Stellung [SE of Flers]	57cSW3 Longueval	T 1, 8
III Stellung [Gird Trench, E of Flers]	57cSW3 Longueval	N 32 b, d, T 3 a

Name	Map Sheet	Map Reference
Ike Farm [originally misnamed Haute Porte Fm]	27SE4 Meteren	X 10 a 3.2]
Ikey Terrace	36cNW1 La Bassée	A 15 d
Iliad Trench, Supp, Res, Ave, Row, Ln, Switch	28NW4 & NE3 Zillebeke	I 24 d, 30 b, J 19 c, 25 a
Ilkley Support	57cNW2 Vaulx-Vraucourt	C 5 b, d
Illiesco Trench [Maewitz Weg]	66cNW2 Itancourt	B 6 c
Illusive Trench, Supp, Res, Drive, Ave	28NW4 & NE3 Zillebeke	I 30 b, d, J 25 a, c
Illustrious Trench	28NW4 & NE3 Zillebeke	I 30, J 25
Ilôt Trench [La Boisselle]	57dSE4 Ovillers	X 19 b
Image Dugouts	28NW4 & NE3 Zillebeke	I 30 c, d
Image Lane	51bNW3 Arras	G 24 c, 30 a
Image Tr, Sup, Res, Ave, Cres, Row	28NW4 & NE3 Zillebeke	I 30 a, b, c, d, 36 a, b, d
Image Wood	28NW4 & NE3 Zillebeke	I 30 d, 36 a, b
Imam Trench	62bSW4 Homblières	T 17 b, 18 a, c
Imbros House	20SW4 Bixschoote	U 18 d 63.13
Immaculate Lane / Trench	28NW4 & NE3 Zillebeke	I 30, 36
Immediate Trench, Support, Avenue	28NW4 & NE3 Zillebeke	I 29 d, 30 c
Immelmann Trench	62bSW4 Homblières	T 12 a, b, d, U 7 c, 13 a, b
Immodest Lane	51bNW3 Arras	G 23 b, 24 a
Immovable Tr, Sup, Row, Ave, Drive	28NW4 & NE3 Zillebeke	I 29 c, d, 35 a, b
Imp Bank [lynchet]	51bSW2 Vis-en-Artois	O 27 d
Imp Street	51bNW3 Arras	G 30 a
Imp Trench, Support, Reserve, Avenue	28NW4 & NE3 Zillebeke	I 29 d, 30 c, 35 b, 36 a
Impact Crescent [Battle Wood]	28NW4 & NE3 Zillebeke	I 35 b, d
Impact Tr, Sup, Res, Terr, Ave, Ln	28NW4 & NE3 Zillebeke	I 35 a, b, c, d
Impair Lane	28NW4 & NE3 Zillebeke	I 35 a
Impale Drive, Support, Reserve	28NW4 & NE3 Zillebeke	I 35 b
Impartial Trench, Avenue, Lane	28NW4 & NE3 Zillebeke	I 36 a, c, d
Imperfect Lane	51bNW3 Arras	G 29 d, 30 c
Imperfect Trench, & Row	28NW4 & NE3 Zillebeke	I 36 a, b, d
Imperial Dugouts [Fusilier Wood]	28NW4 & NE3 Zillebeke	I 36 c
Imperial Sap	51bNW3 Arras	G 36 a
Imperial Street	51bNW3 Arras	G 29 c, d, 30 c, 36 a
Imperial Tr, Supp, Sw, Lane, Ave	28NW4 & NE3 Zillebeke	I 34 b, d, 35 a, c
Imperial Track (Duckboard) [1917-18]	28NW4 Ypres	I 33 d, 34 b, c
Imperial Trench	57dSE1 & 2 Beaumont	R 31 b, d, 32 c
Impertinence Trench	36SW1 Aubers	N 2 d, 3 c
Impey Copses	27NE1 Herzeele	J 5 b
Impey Farm	27NE1 Herzeele	J 6 a 10.65
Import Lane, Support, Trench	28NW4 & NE3 Zillebeke	I 35 c
Impotent Avenue	51bNW3 Arras	G 24 c
Impudence Trench & Support [Bluff]	28NW4 & NE3 Zillebeke	I 34 c, d
Inadequate Trench	36NW4 Bois Grenier	I 12 c, 18 b, d
Inane Alley	36NW4 Bois Grenier	I 5 d, 11 b, 12 a
Inane Tr, Sup, Res, Sw, Row, Dr, Ave	36NW2 Armentières / 4 Bois Grenier	I 5 b, d, 6 a, b, c, 12 a, b
Incandescent Trench & Support	36NW4 Bois Grenier	I 5 c, d, 11 a, b
Incanto Farm	36aNE1 Morbecque	D 24 b 45.75
Incarnate Trench, Support, Avenue	36NW4 Bois Grenier	I 11 a, c, d, 17 b, d
Incense Corner [road junction]	20SE2 Hooglede	R 3 b 00.12
Incense Trench, Support, Avenue	36NW4 Bois Grenier	I 11 c, 17 a, c, d
Inch Houses	28NE1 Zonnebeek	D 3 a 9.9
Inch Street	57dSE4 Ovillers	X 19 b
Inch Trench, & Support	36NW4 Bois Grenier	I 16 b, d, 17 a
Inchy Mill	57cNE1 Quéant	E 7 c 45.35
Inchy-en-Artois [village]	57cNE1 Quéant	E 1, 7

Name	Map Sheet	Map Reference
Incident Tr, Sup, Row, Dr, Av, Ln, Alley	36NW4 Bois Grenier	I 16 d, 22 b, 23 a
Incision Avenue	36NW4 Bois Grenier	I 22 c, d, 29 a
Incision Reserve	36NW4 Bois Grenier	I 22 d, 23 c
Incision Trench, & Support	36NW4 Bois Grenier	I 16 d, 22 a
Inclement Trench, Support & Switch	36NW4 Bois Grenier	I 21 b, 22 a
Incline [pillbox, under cross in Tyne Cott Cmy]	28NE1 Zonnebeke	D 16 b 9.3
Incline Alley, & Avenue	36NW4 Bois Grenier	I 21 c, d, 27 b
Incline Row	36NW4 Bois Grenier	I 28 c
Incline Street	36NW4 Bois Grenier	I 27 b, d, 28 c, 34 a
Incline Trench, & Support	36NW4 Bois Grenier	I 21 b, d
Include Avenue	36NW4 Bois Grenier	I 27 a
Include Support	36NW4 Bois Grenier	I 21 c, 27 a
Include Trench	36NW4 Bois Grenier	I 21 c
Income Avenue	36NW4 Bois Grenier	I 27 a, c
Income Drive	36NW4 Bois Grenier	I 27 c, d
Income Lane	36NW4 Bois Grenier	I 26 b
Income Tax [Trench]	51bNW3 Arras	G 23 b, d, 24 a, c, 29 d
Income Trench	51bNW3 Arras	G 24 a
Income Trench, Support & Switch	36NW4 Bois Grenier	I 26 b, 27 a
Incomplete Avenue	36NW4 Bois Grenier	I 26 d, 27 c
Incomplete Drive	36NW4 Bois Grenier	I 27 d, 33 b
Incomplete Lane	36NW4 Bois Grenier	I 32 a, b
Incomplete Trench, & Support	36NW4 Bois Grenier	I 26 b, d
Inconsistent Alley	36NW4 Bois Grenier	I 32 a, b
Inconsistent Avenue	36NW4 Bois Grenier	I 32 b, d, 33 c
Inconsistent Reserve	36NW4 Bois Grenier	I 32 a, b, c
Inconsistent Trench, & Support	36NW4 Bois Grenier	I 32 a, c
Increase Avenue	36NW4 Bois Grenier	I 32 c, d
Increase Drive	36NW4 Bois Grenier	I 32 d, 33 c
Increase Lane, & Row	36NW4 Bois Grenier	I 32 c
Increase Trench, & Support	36NW4 Bois Grenier	I 31 d, 32 c
Incubator Avenue	36NW4 Bois Grenier	I 33 d, 34 c
Incubator Trench	36NW4 Bois Grenier	I 33 b, d
Incumbent Row	36NW4 Bois Grenier	I 18 d
Incumbent Trench, & Switch	36NW4 Bois Grenier	I 18 b, d
Incursion Trench	36NW4 Bois Grenier	I 18 d, 24 b
Indecent Trench	36NW4 Bois Grenier	I 30 d, 36 c
Indeed Alley	36NW4 Bois Grenier	I 29 a, b
Indeed Trench	36NW4 Bois Grenier	I 29 b
Indefinite Trench	36NW4 Bois Grenier	I 29 c, d
Indemnity Support, & Reserve	36NW4 Bois Grenier	I 35 a, b
Indemnity Trench	36NW4 Bois Grenier	I 29 c, 35 a
Indent Reserve, & Lane	36NW4 Bois Grenier	I 35 c
Indent Switch	36NW4 Bois Grenier	I 34 d, 35 c
Indent Trench	36NW4 Bois Grenier	I 34 b, d, 35 a
Index Avenue & Drive	36SW2 Radinghem	O 1 b
Index House [dugouts]	28NW4 & NE3 Zillebeke	I 30 c, 36 a
Index Street	36SW2 Radinghem	O 1 a
Index Trench, & Support	36NW4 Bois Grenier / SW2 Radinghem	I 31 c, d, O 1 a
India [pillbox]	28NE1 Zonnebeke	D 16 d
India Avenue	36SW1 Aubers	N 13 c
India Lane	51bNW3 Arras	G 29 d, 30 c
India Road	36NW4 Bois Grenier	I 13 d
India Trench	36NW2 Armentières	C 28 d, 29 c

Name	Map Sheet	Map Reference
India Trench	62bSW3 St Quentin	S 11 d, 12 a, c, 17 b
Indian Avenue	36SW1 Aubers	N 13 c
Indian Hill	62bSW2 Fonsommes	N 7 a, c
Indian Post	62cNE2 Epéhy	L 5 b
Indian Trench	51bNW4 Fampoux	H 23 c, 29 a
Indian Trench	62cNE2 Epéhy	L 5 b, d
Indian Village, The	36SW3 Richebourg	S 20 b, d
Indian Wood	62bSW1 Gricourt	M 36 a
Indigo Alley	62bSW4 Homblières	T 16 b, 17 a, b
Indigo Corner [road junction]	20SE2 Hooglede	R 12 a 99.05
Indre Trench [Kavallerie Graben]	57dNE1 & 2 Fonquevillers	E 30 c, d
Indre, Tranchée de l'	70dSW [4 Vauxaillon]	U 11 b
Indus Farm	28NW3 Poperinghe	H 28 c 2.9
Indus Trench	57dNE1 & 2 Fonquevillers	K 4 b, 5 a, b
Indus Trench [Radfahrer Graben]	57dNE1 & 2 Fonquevillers	E 29 d, 30 c, K 4 b, 5 a, b
Infantry Barracks [Ypres]	28NW4 Ypres	I 7 d
Infantry Hill	51bSW2 Vis-en-Artois	O 2 d
Infantry Lane [road]	51bSW2 Vis-en-Artois	O 1 b, 2 a, c, d
Infantry Road [ride, Nieppe Forest]	36aNE3 Haverskerque	K 13 b, d, 19 b, 20 a
Infantry Road [trench]	51bNW3 Arras	G 29 b, 30 a
Infants Alley	62bNW3 Bellicourt / SW1 Gricourt	G 36 a, c, M 6 a
Infernal Alley	62bSW3 St Quentin	S 6 b, T 1 a
Inferno Trench	62cNW2 Bouchavesnes / 4 Péronne	I 2 a, c, 7 b, 8 a
Informal Lane	51bNW3 Arras	G 30 c
Ingersoll Camp	36NW2 Armentières	B 4 c, 10 a
Inglenook [Hohenzollern]	36cNW3 Loos	G 4 d
Inglis Keep [Vermelles east]	36cNW3 Loos	G 8 b
Ingolstadt, Werk	51bNW1 Roclincourt	A 30 a, G 6 b
Ingon Trench / Tranchée d'Ingon	66dNW1 Punchy / 3 Hattencourt	H 2 d, 3 a, c
Ingon Wood	66dNW3 Hattencourt	G 12 b, H 7 a, b, 8 a
Ings Avenue	51bNW3 Arras	G 30 a, b
Ings, The	28NW2 St Julien	C 4 a 4.8
Ink Farm	28SE1 Wervicq	P 4 d 75.10
Ink Street	51bNW3 Arras	G 30 a
Ink Trench	51bNW1 Roclincourt	B 27 a
Inkerman Camp	28SW3 Bailleul	S 12 a, b
Inkerman Farm	28SW3 Bailleul	S 12 b 0.8
Inn Corner	28NW3 Poperinghe	H 14 b 40.75
Inn Trench	51bNW3 Arras	G 12 d
Inner Circle [Sept 1915]	36cNW1 La Bassée	A 8 d, 9 c
Inner Trench [Delville Wood]	57cSW3 Longueval	S 12 c
Innes Alley	51bSW2 Vis-en-Artois	O 26 c
Inniskilling Avenue [Thiepval Wood]	57dSE1 & 2 Beaumont	Q 24 d
Innocence Street	51bNW3 Arras	G 30 c, 36 a
Inns of Court Trench	51bNW3 Arras	G 23 d, 24 c
Inoubliables Trench	62cSW3 Vermandovillers	S 12 d, 18 b
Inquest Houses	28NE2 Moorslede	F 11 d 85.25
Inquiry Lane	51bNW3 Arras	G 24 c
Insect Trench	20SW2 Zwartegat	N 24 b, O 13 c, 19 a
Inside Road	36cNW3 Loos	H 13 c
Inspruck, Tranchée d' [Insbruck]	62cSW3 & 4 Marchélepot	T 10 c
Institution Royale [Messines]	28SW4 Ploegsteert	U 2 b 8.7
Intact Farm	20SW3 Oostvleteren	N 34 a 3.0
Intermediate Cross Roads	20SW4 Bixschoote	T 17 d 6.6

Name	Map Sheet	Map Reference
Intermediate Line [19-7-16]	57cSW3 Longueval	S 2 c, d, 3 c
Intermediate Line [Gommecourt 1916]	57dNE1 & 2 Fonquevillers / 57dNE3 & 4 Hébuterne	E 29 b, 30 a, c, K 5 d, 6 a
Intermediate Trench	51bNW1 Roclincourt	A 16 a, c
Intermediate Trench	51bNW3 Arras	G 36 b
Intermediate Trench / Line [International Tr.]	57cSW3 Longueval	S 2 c, d, 3 c
Intermediate Trench [29-9-16]	57cSW3 Longueval	S 2 c, d, 3 c
Intermediate Trench [E of Steenebeek]	28SW2 Wytschaete	O 31 b, 32 a, c
International Avenue	36cSW3 Vimy	S 14 d, 15 c
International Corner	28NW1 Elverdinghe	A 9 a 15.35
International Corner Railhead / Refilling Point	28NW1 Elverdinghe	A 2 d, 8 a, b
International Post	62bSW1 Gricourt	M 8 d 4.9
International Trench	28NW2 St Julien	C 7 c
International Trench [Bellewaarde]	28NW4 & NE3 Zillebeke	I 12 a 35.00
International Trench [Bluff]	28NW4 & NE3 Zillebeke	I 34 c
International Trench [Intermediate Trench]	57cSW3 Longueval	S 2 c, d, 3 c
International Trench [S of canal]	28SW2 Wytschaete	O 3 b, d
Interpreter Street	51bNW3 Arras	G 24 c
Invalid Road [trench]	51bNW3 Arras	G 23 b, 24 a
Invalide Trench	62bSW3 St Quentin	T 7 a, c
Invasion/s Trench / Street	51bNW3 Arras	G 24 a
Inverary Avenue	28NE2 Zonnebeke	D 11 d, 16 b, 17 a, b
Inverary Street	57dSE1 & 2 Beaumont	Q 36 b, R 31 a
Invergordon Trench [Orange Hill]	51bNW4 Fampoux	H 23 c, 28 d, 29 a, c, 34 b, 35 a
Inverness Avenue	51bNW4 Fampoux	H 23 c, d
Inverness Copse	28NE3 Gheluvelt	I 14 c, d
Inverness Lane	51bNW3 Arras	G 29 b, d, 30 a, c
Inverness Street [Thiepval Wood]	57dSE1 & 2 Beaumont	Q 30 b, R 25 a
Inverness Trench	36aSE4 Locon	W 23 b, 24 a, c, d
Inverness Trench	36cNW1 La Bassée	G 3 a, b
Inverted Alley	62bSW3 St Quentin	T 1 c, d
Invicta / Invite Trench	51bNW2 Oppy	C 25 c
Invicta Alley	57cSW3 Longueval	S 30 a, b
Iodine Trench	51bNW3 Arras	G 36 a
Iolanthe Street	51bNW3 Arras	G 36 a
Iona House	28NW3 Poperinghe	H 32 b 9.4
Iona Street	57dSE4 Ovillers	Q 36 d
Ionian Trench	51bNW3 Arras / 4 Fampoux	H 28 a, c
Ionic House	27SE4 Meteren	W 18 d 15.50
Ipswich Sap	36cNW1 La Bassée	A 21 d
Ipswich Street	57dNE1 & 2 Fonquevillers	E 11 c
Irawadi Trench	51bNW3 Arras	G 30 c
Ireton Street	62cNW1 Maricourt	A 15 b
Iris Copse	57bSW2 Clary / 4 Serain	O 35 b, d
Iris Farm	57bSW2 Clary	O 34 a 7.7
Iris Street	51bNW3 Arras	G 29 d, 30 c
Irish Alley	36cNW3 Loos	G 24 a, b
Irish Alley	36cSW3 Vimy	S 8 b
Irish Alley	57cSW3 Longueval	S 29 c, d
Irish Avenue	36NW2 Armentières	C 16 d, 17 c
Irish Avenue [1918]	57dNE1 & 2 Fonquevillers	E 29 a
Irish Crater	36cSW3 Vimy	S 8 d
Irish Farm	28NW2 St Julien	C 27 a 2.6
Irish Farm	28SW4 Ploegsteert	U 7 d 65.75

Name	Map Sheet	Map Reference
Irish Farm Camp [1917-18]	28NW2 St Julien	C 26 b, d, 27 a, c
Irish Farm How[itzer] Spurs	28SW4 Ploegsteert	U 7 c, d
Irish House	28SW2 Wytschaete	N 23 c 8.6
Irish Junction	28SW2 Wytschaete	O 21 c
Irish Lane	51bNW3 Arras	G 23 d
Irish Support	36cSW3 Vimy	S 6 d
Irish Trench	36SW3 Richebourg	S 20
Irish Trench [Leuze Wood]	57cSW3 Longueval	T 21 c
Irksome [Tyne Cott, pillbox]	28NE1 Zonnebeke	D 16 b
Irles [village]	57cNW3 Bapaume	G 26 c, 31 b, d, 32 a
Irles Road [rd E of Pys, W of Warlenc't-Eauc't]	57cSW1 Gueudecourt	M 3 a, c, d, 9 b, 10 a
Irma Post	36SW1 Aubers	N 14 a
Irma Trench	36SW1 Aubers	N 14 d, 15 c, 21 a
Irma's Elephant	36SW1 Aubers	N 14 b, d
Iron Bridge [bridge & light rly locality, 1917-18]	28NW4 Ypres	I 26 c 3.6
Iron Bridge Tunnel	28SW2 Wytschaete	O 4 a 99.90
Iron Copse	66dNW1 Punchy	A 12 a, c
Iron Cross [NE of Pilckem]	28NW2 St Julien	C 3 a 8.5
Iron Cross Redoubt [SW of Zonnebeke]	28NW4 & NE3 Zillebeke	J 3 a, c
Iron Cross Ridge [NE of Pilckem]	28NW2 St Julien	C 3 a
Iron Dugouts [Image Wood]	28NW4 & NE3 Zillebeke	I 36 b
Iron Gates [Grenay]	36cSW1 Lens	M 2 c
Iron Street	51bNW3 Arras	G 23 b, 24 a
Iron Trench	51bNW1 Roclincourt	B 27 a
Iron Tripod [trig, Abraham Heights, 1917-18]	28NE1 Zonnebeke	D 15 b 65.60
Ironside Trench	57dSE2 Beaumont	R 18 a, c, 24 a, c
Irving Houses	28NE2 Moorslede	F 4 d 3.3
Irwin Trench	57dSE1 & 2 Beaumont	R 14 c, 19 b
Isaacs Farm	28NE2 Moorslede	F 23 b 5.3
Isackere Farm, Van	28NE1 Zonnebeke	D 21 a 2.6
Isar Graben / Trench, & Gabel	51bNW3 Arras	G 18 a
Isar Trench	62cSW2 Barleux	N 24 d, 30 b, O 19 c
Isar, Tranchée de l'	62cSW1 & 2 Belloy	N 30 b, O 19 c
Iscariot Work	57cNW1 Gomiecourt	B 9 a
Iser [farm]	28NE1 Zonnebeke	D 9 a 5.6
Isigny Alley	62bSW3 St Quentin	S 11 b
Island Fork [road jct]	28NE2 Moorslede	E 28 a 8.0
Island Posts [Hooge, 1915]	28NW4 & NE3 Zillebeke	I 18 a, b
Island Trench	62bSW3 St Quentin	S 8 d, 9 c, 14 b, d, 15 c
Island Trench, & Traverse	62cNE2 Epéhy	F 12 c
Island, The [in river NE of Blangy]	51bNW3 Arras	G 24 a
Islands, The	36SW3 Richebourg	S 22 c
Islay Street	57dSE4 Ovillers	Q 36 d
Isle Trench	51bNW1 Roclincourt	B 27 a, c
Islington Road / Street [trench]	51bNW3 Arras	G 23 c, d, 29 a, d, 30 a
Isly Farm	28NW2 St Julien	B 29 d
Isob Trench [1918]	62dSE [3 Marcelcave]	V 2 a, c
Isolde Alley	57cSW4 Combles	U 21 b, c, d
Isolde Trench	57cNE1 Quéant	D 14 b, 15 a
Israel Farm [De God]	28NE2 Moorslede	F 11 b 25.20
Israel House	28NE1 Zonnebeke	D 21 a 7.7
Issigny Trench	66cNW4 Berthenicourt	H 36 b
Issoire Alley	66cNW1 Grugies	B 9 c, d, 15 a, b
Issoudun, Tranchée d'	70dSW4 [Vauxaillon]	U 9 b

Name	Map Sheet	Map Reference
Istria Junction [road jct]	28NE4 Dadizeele	L 4 d 45.90
Italian Trench	51bNW4 Fampoux	H 23 c, 29 a
Italy Alley	66cNW4 Berthenicourt	H 4 d
Italy Road	36NW4 Bois Grenier	I 13 b
Italy Terrace	51bNW3 Arras	G 30 a
Italy Trench	51bNW3 Arras	G 29 b, 30 a
Itancourt [village]	66cNW2 Itancourt	B 18, 24, C 13
Itchin Farm	36aNE4 Merville	K 10 d 60.75
Ivan Cottages	27NE1 Herzeele	D 24 d 80.95
Iveson Farm	28NE4 Dadizeele	L 9 b 55.65
Ivice Trench	66cSW2 Vendeuil	O 9 a, c
Ivory Corner	20SE2 Hooglede	R 4 b 35.30
Ivory Street	51bNW3 Arras	G 23 d, 24 c
Ivry Alley	62bSW3 St Quentin	S 9c,d, 10a,b,cd, 11c,d, 14d, 15a, 17b
Ivy Cottage	36cSW4 Rouvroy	T 6 d 3.2
Ivy Post	62cNE4 Roisel	L 18 a 30.25
Ivy Row	51bNW3 Arras	G 30 a
Ivy Street	51bNW3 Arras	G 29 a, b, 30 a
Ivy Tree Post	62cNW1 Maricourt	G 5 b
Ivy Trench [1918]	51bNW1 Roclincourt	A 10 a
Ivyland Corner [road junction]	20SE2 Hooglede	Q 24 a 55.90
Izel Street	51bNW3 Arras	G 30 c
Izel-Montigny-Courrières Line [pt of D-Q Line]	36aSW4 Rouvroy	extensive
Izel-Vitry-Quéant Line [D-Q Line]	51bNE / SE	extensive
J Camp	28NW1 Elverdinghe	A 8 b
J Sap	28NW4 & NE3 Zillebeke	I 30 b
J Sap [Givenchy]	36cNW1 La Bassée	A 9 b
J Sector [4/15]	28SW2 Wytschaete	N 18 a, c
Jabber Avenue	28NW4 & NE3 Zillebeke	J 7 c, d
Jabber Drive	28NW4 & NE3 Zillebeke	J 7 a, c
Jabber House	28NW4 & NE3 Zillebeke	J 4 a
Jabber Reserve [Westhoek]	28NW4 & NE3 Zillebeke	J 8 a, c
Jabber Support [Westhoek]	28NW4 & NE3 Zillebeke	J 8 a, c
Jabber Trench [Westhoek]	28NW4 & NE3 Zillebeke	J 7 b, d, 8 c
Jachmann Stellung	51bSW1 Neuville Vitasse	M 23 a
Jachmann Weg	51bSW1 Neuville Vitasse	M 21 a, c
Jack Farm	28SW2 Wytschaete	O 23 a 45.65
Jack Street [Thiepval Wood]	57dSE1 & 2 Beaumont	R 25 a
Jackdaw Avenue	28NW4 & NE3 Zillebeke	J 13 c, d, 19 a
Jackdaw Beak	28NW4 & NE3 Zillebeke	I 24 b, J 13 c, 19 a
Jackdaw Crater	28NW4 & NE3 Zillebeke	I 24 b, J 19 a
Jackdaw Post [1918]	28NE3 Gheluvelt	J 13 b
Jackdaw Reserve	28NW4 & NE3 Zillebeke	J 13 a, c, d
Jackdaw Row	28NW4 & NE3 Zillebeke	J 13 c
Jackdaw Support	28NW4 & NE3 Zillebeke	J 13 c
Jackdaw Switch [beech slab road, 1917]	28NW4 & NE3 Zillebeke	J 13 a, b, d
Jackdaw Switch [trench]	28NW4 & NE3 Zillebeke	J 13 a, b, d
Jackdaw Trench	28NW4 & NE3 Zillebeke	J 13 c, 19 a
Jackdaw Trench	51bSW2 Vis-en-Artois	O 20 c, 25 b, d, 26 a
Jackdaw[s] Tunnels	28NW4 & NE3 Zillebeke	J 19 a 2.8
Jackson Dump	28NW4 & NE3 Zillebeke	I 28 b
Jackson Street	28NW4 & NE3 Zillebeke	I 28 b, 29 c
Jackson Trench	28NE3 Gheluvelt	J 21 b, 22 a
Jackson Villa [1918]	28SW1 Kemmel	M 7 d 30.05

Name	Map Sheet	Map Reference
Jackson's Trench	57cSW3 Longueval	S 30 c, d
Jacob Bearer Post	28NW4 & NE3 Zillebeke	J 7 a, c
Jacob Farm	28NE4 Dadizeele	K 4 c 55.55
Jacob Trench	51bNW1 Roclincourt	A 11 c
Jacob Trench [Bellewaarde Ridge]	28NW4 & NE3 Zillebeke	J 7 a, c
Jacob's House	28NE1 Zonnebeke	D 21 a 4.5
Jacob's Houses [De God]	28NE2 Moorslede	F 11 b 7.5
Jacob's Ladder [Hamel]	57dSE1 & 2 Beaumont	Q 23 c, d, 29 a
Jacob's Ladder [west of Beaumont Hamel]	57dSE1 & 2 Beaumont	Q 4 c, d
Jacobus Trench	28NE3 Gheluvelt	J 3 c, d
Jacquemet Trench	62cSW2 Barleux	N 29 a, c
Jacqvenne Copse	57cSE4 Villers-Guislain	W 29 c
Jade Trench	51bNW1 Roclincourt	H 1 a
Jaffa [dugout / light rly locality, 1917-18]	28NE3 Gheluvelt	J 7 a 2.7
Jaffa Avenue	28NW4 & NE3 Zillebeke	J 1 d, 7 a, b
Jaffa Drive	28NW4 & NE3 Zillebeke	J 7 a, b
Jaffa Post [1918]	28NE3 Gheluvelt	J 8 a
Jaffa Trench	28NW4 & NE3 Zillebeke	J 1 d, 7 a, b
Jaffa Trench	66cNW4 Berthenicourt	I 9 a
Jaffa Trench [1918]	62dSE [3 Marcelcave]	V 1 b, d
Jaffa, Tranchée de	70dSW4 [Vauxaillon]	U 28 b
Jag Trench	51bNW1 Roclincourt	H 1 b
Jager Trench	28NE3 Gheluvelt	J 27 a, c, 33 a, c
Jager Trench	62bNW1 Gouy	A 1 b
Jager Weg	51bSW1 Neuville Vitasse	M 11 a, b
Jagged Trench	28NE1 Zonnebeke / 3 Gheluvelt	J 2 b, 3 c
Jagged Trench	57cNE3 Hermies	J 28 a, c, 34 a
Jagger Trench	36cNW3 Loos	G 5 c
Jago Farm	28NE4 Dadizeele	L 13 c 45.80
Jail Trench	28NW4 & NE3 Zillebeke	J 32 / 33
Jail Trench	51bNW1 Roclincourt	H 1 b
Jail Trench	57cNE3 Hermies	J 23 d, 29 b
Jallap House	28NE3 Gheluvelt	J 15 d 5.5
Jalon Trench	66dNW1 Punchy	A 10 c, d
Jam Avenue, Lane & Row	28NW4 & NE3 Zillebeke	J 19 a, b
Jam Reserve	28NW4 & NE3 Zillebeke	J 19 b
Jam Sap	57cSE2 Gonnelieu	R 21 c
Jam Sap	57cSE2 Gonnelieu	R 21 c
Jam Street	57dNE3 & 4 Hébuterne	K 23 d, 24 c
Jam Trench	51bNW1 Roclincourt	H 1 b
Jam Trench	57cSE2 Gonnelieu	R 21 b, c, d
Jam Trench, & Support	28NW4 & NE3 Zillebeke	J 19 a
Jamaica Trench	51bNW4 Fampoux	H 30 c, 36 a, b
Jambons Alley	62cNW3 Vaux	G 30 b, H 25 a, b
James Avenue	57dSE1 & 2 Beaumont	Q 28 c, d, 29 c
James Crater [Bellewaarde Farm]	28NW4 & NE3 Zillebeke	I 12 c 4.8
James Farm [Potijze]	28NW4 & NE3 Zillebeke	I 4 d 6.2
James Street	28NW4 & NE3 Zillebeke	I 5 d
James Street	57cSW3 Longueval	S 18 b, T 7 c
James Trench	36cSW3 Vimy	S 22 b
James Trench	51bNE3 Noyelle-sous-Bellonne	J 11 d
James Trench [Chateau Wood]	28NW4 & NE3 Zillebeke	J 7 c, 13 a
James Work	57cNW1 Gomiecourt	B 27 b
Jamet Trench	57cSW4 Combles	T 11 a

Name	Map Sheet	Map Reference
Jan House	36NW1 Steenwerck	B 1 c 38.55
Janet Avenue / Lane [trench]	51bSW4 Bullecourt	U 7 c, 13 a
Janet Cottages	27NE2 Proven	F 5 a 93.15
Janet Farm	28NW2 St Julien	C 12 d 3.4
Janet Trench	57cNE3 Hermies	J 30 d
Janet Wood	27NE2 Proven	F 5 a
Janitor Trench	57cNE3 Hermies	J 23 d, 29 a, b
Jap Avenue	28NW4 & NE3 Zillebeke	J 13 d, 14 c, d
Jap Row	28NW4 & NE3 Zillebeke	J 19 b, 20 a
Jap Trench	28NW4 & NE3 Zillebeke	J 14 b, d
Japan Avenue	36NW2 Armentières	C 28 d, I 4 b, 5 a
Japan House	20SW4 Bixschoote	U 17 c 40.15
Japan Road	36NW2 Armentières	C 28 d, I 4 b, 5 a
Japan Trench	51bNW4 Fampoux	H 30 c
Japan Trench	70dNW2 Servais	B 29 c
Jar Row	28NW4 & NE3 Zillebeke	J 19 b, 20 a
Jar Switch	28NW4 & NE3 Zillebeke	J 20 d
Jar Trench	28NW4 & NE3 Zillebeke	J 20 d
Jar Trench	51bNW1 Roclincourt	H 1 b
Jar Trench	57cNE3 Hermies	J 24 d, K 19 c
Jardin Public [Béthune]	36bNE2 Beuvry	E 10 d 3.7
Jardine Bridge [across Ancre]	57dSE4 Ovillers	W 11 b 5.7
Jardins, Cabaret des	36cSW1 Lens	M 22 c 1.4
Jargon Drive	28NW4 & NE3 Zillebeke	J 13 b, 14 a
Jargon Post [1918]	28NE3 Gheluvelt	J 8 c
Jargon Switch	28NW4 & NE3 Zillebeke	J 7 d, 8 c, 13 b
Jargon Track	28NW4 & NE3 Zillebeke	J 13 b, 14 a
Jargon Trench	28NW4 & NE3 Zillebeke	J 8 c, 14 a
Jargon Trench	57cNE3 Hermies	J 23, 24, 28, 29
Jargon Tunnel	28NW4 & NE3 Zillebeke	J 14 a
Jarhac Trench	62bSW4 Homblières	U 22 a, c, 28 a, b, 29 a, c, d, 30 c, d
Jarret, Tranchée du	70dSW2 [Coucy-le-Château]	O 3 c
Jarretiere Trench	66dNW1 Punchy	A 15 d, 21 a, b
Jarrocks [sic] Farm	28NE3 Gheluvelt	J 31 c 15.10
Jarvis Street	28SW2 Wytschaete	O 1 c, 7 a
Jas Farm	28NW1 Elverdinghe	A 25 b 95.77
Jasmin / Jasmine Alley	66cNW2 Itancourt	C 22 c,d, 23 c, 27 b,c,d, 28 a, I 2 b, 3 a
Jasmin Trench	20SW1 Loo / 3 Oostvleteren	N 32 a, c
Jason Trench	57cSW2 Villers-au-Flos	O 26 c, d
Jasper Avenue	28NW4 & NE3 Zillebeke	J 13 d, 14 c, 19 b
Jasper Drive	28NW4 & NE3 Zillebeke	J 19 b, 20 a
Jasper Farm	28NW2 St Julien	C 29 b 4.7
Jasper Farm	28NW4 & NE3 Zillebeke	J 19 b
Jasper Keep [1918]	28NW2 St Julien	C 23 d, 29 b; or C 29 a 2.9
Jasper Lane	28NW4 & NE3 Zillebeke	J 13 d, 14 c
Jasper Street	28NW4 & NE3 Zillebeke	I 23 a
Jasper Trench	28NW4 & NE3 Zillebeke	J 20 b, d
Jasper Trench	51bNE3 Noyelle-sous-Bellonne	J 11 b
Jaunt Copse	28NE1 Zonnebeke	D 30 d, J 6 b
Java Avenue	28NW4 & NE3 Zillebeke	J 19 b, d, 20 c
Java Drive	28NW4 & NE3 Zillebeke	J 25 b, 26 a
Java Trench	28NW4 & NE3 Zillebeke	J 20 c, 26 a
Jaw Trench	51bNW1 Roclincourt	H 1 b

Name	Map Sheet	Map Reference
Jaw Trench	57cNE3 Hermies	J 29 c
Jay Barn	28NE3 Gheluvelt	J 5 c 5.1
Jay Copse	20SE2 Hooglede	R 20 d 5.9
Jay Corner [trench junction]	28SW2 Wytschaete	N 29 c 60.13
Jay Cott	28NE3 Gheluvelt	J 5 d 25.65
Jay Farm	57bSW1 Bantouzelle	M 27 c 2.4
Jay Post [La Boutillerie]	36SW2 Radinghem	N 6 a
Jay Support [1918]	57dNE2 & 57cNW1 Courcelles	F 5 b, 6 a
Jay Trench	51bNW1 Roclincourt	H 1 a, b
Jean Bart Avenue / Boyau Jean Bart [Auerstadt]	57dNE3 & 4 Hébuterne	K 22 a, c, d, 23 a, c
Jean Bart House	20SW4 Bixschoote	U 4 c 82.56 / U 4 d 0.8
Jean Copse	62bNW4 Ramicourt / NE[3]	I 30 d, 36 b, J 25 c, 31 a
Jean Street	57dSE1 & 2 Beaumont	Q 23 b
Jean Trench / Tranchée Jean	62cSW1 & 2 Belloy	O 1 b, 2 a
Jean Wood	62dSE [1 Hamel]	Q 21 d
Jeanerod / Jeannerod [trench / salient]	36cSW1 Lens	M 32 a
Jeanne d'Arc Redoubt [NW of Urvillers]	66cNW1 Grugies	B 19 d, 20 c, 25 b, 26 a
Jeanne d'Arc, Tranchée	70dSW2 [Coucy-le-Château]	N 6 c
Jedhof Farm	28NW1 Elverdinghe	B 9 a 9.8
Jeer Trench	28NW4 & NE3 Zillebeke	J 25 c, d
Jeer Trench	51bNW3 Arras	H 1 d
Jeff Trench [1918]	51bNW1 Roclincourt	B 25 c, H 1 a
Jeffery Avenue	28NW4 & NE3 Zillebeke	J 19 c, d, 25 b
Jeffery Trench, Support, Reserve	28NW4 & NE3 Zillebeke	J 19 c
Jehova Trench	28NW4 & NE3 Zillebeke	J 31 a
Jehu Switch	28NE3 Gheluvelt	J 3 c
Jehu Trench	28NW4 & NE3 Zillebeke	J 25 b, d, 26 a
Jekyll [copse, near Hyde [copse]]	62bSW2 Fonsommes	O 19 c
Jellicoe [locality]	28NW4 Ypres	H 36 a, b
Jelly Trench	28NE3 Gheluvelt	J 32 d, 33 a, c
Jelly Trench	51bNW1 Roclincourt	H 3 a
Jemmy Trench	51bNW3 Arras	H 3 c
Jena Alley	62bSW3 St Quentin	S 13 d, 14 b, c, d, 15 a, b, 16 a, b, 17 a
Jena Avenue / Boyau Jena	57dNE3 & 4 Hébuterne	K13-15,19-23
Jena Farm	28NW2 St Julien	B 23 d
Jena Trench [1918]	66eNW [2 Thennes]	C 8 d, 9 a, c
Jenkins Farm	28NE3 Gheluvelt	J 18 c 1.6
Jenks Siding	36cSW3 Vimy	S 2 c
Jenks Siding [light rly]	36cSW3 Vimy	S 2 c
Jeremiah Trench	57dNE3 & 4 Hébuterne	K 27 c, d
Jeremy Switch	28NE3 Gheluvelt	J 3 c, 9 a
Jericho Alley	62cSW4 St. Christ	T 30 a, c, d
Jericho Avenue	57dNE3 & 4 Hébuterne	K 27 c, d, 28 a, b, c
Jericho Street [1918]	28NE3 Gheluvelt	J 16 c, 22 a
Jericho Trench	51bNW4 Fampoux	H 29 c, 35 a, c
Jericho, Tranchée de	62cSW3 & 4 Marchélepot	T 30 c, d
Jerk House	28NW4 & NE3 Zillebeke	J 15 b
Jerk Track (Duckboard) [1917-18]	28NE3 Gheluvelt	J 13 d, 14 b, c, d, 15 a
Jermyn Street	28NW2 St Julien / 4 & NE3 Zillebeke	I 5 a, b, c
Jermyn Street	36cNW3 Loos	G 4 d, 5 c
Jermyn Street	36cSW1 Lens	M 5 b, c
Jermyn Street	57cNE3 Hermies	K 20 b, 21 a
Jerry Farm	28NE2 Moorslede	F 28 a 6.4
Jerusalem [farm]	36cSE1 Dourges	P 7 a 5.4

Name	Map Sheet	Map Reference
Jerusalem Hill, Sap & Crater	36cNW1 La Bassée	A 22 a
Jerusalem Trench	51bNW4 Fampoux	H 29 c, d, 35 a, c
Jerusalem Trench [1918]	51bNW1 Roclincourt	A 11 a, b, c, 17 a, c
Jervis Post	57cNE3 Hermies	K 9 a
Jes Post	62cNE4 Roisel	L 36 c 65.90
Jesmond Road	36cSW3 Vimy	S 14 b
Jess Mill	28NE2 Moorslede	E 4 b 40.35
Jessop Buildings	28NE2 Moorslede	E 4 a 9.1
Jest Trench	51bNW1 Roclincourt / 3 Arras	H 1 b, c, d
Jester Farm	27NE2 Proven	E 6 c 7.8
Jesupol Trench	62cNW4 Péronne	I 2 d
Jesus Farm	36NW1 Steenwerck	B 26 d 4.0
Jet Trench	51bNW3 Arras	H 1 d
Jet Trench	57cNE3 Hermies	J 30 b
Jet Trench	66dNW1 Punchy	A 15 d, 21 b
Jetty Trench	28NE3 Gheluvelt	J 10 b
Jetty Warren [valley & wood]	28NE3 Gheluvelt	J 11 a, c
Jeu Trench	66dNW1 Punchy	A 16 a
Jeune Trench, le	66cNW1 Grugies	B 15 d
Jevington Farm	20SE2 Hooglede	R 1 c 1.9
Jew / Jew's Hill / [hill, St Julien]	28NW2 St Julien	C 12 c, d
Jewel Farm [1918]	28SW1 Kemmel	M 8 c 6.2
Jewel Trench	51bNW3 Arras	H 3 c, 9 a
Jewel Trench	57cNW1 Gomiecourt	B 8 a, c, d
Jewel Valley	57dNE2 Essarts	F 15 b, 16 a
Jew's Nose [Lens Road Redoubt]	36cNW3 Loos	G 34 a
Jew's Nose Trench [Sept 1915]	36cNW3 Loos	G 28 c
Jib Trench	57cNE3 Hermies	J 30 d
Jig Lane	36NW2 & NE1 Houplines	J 1 a
Jig Trench [Jigsaw Wood]	51bNW4 Fampoux	I 34 a
Jig Trench, Support, & Row	36NW2 & NE1 Houplines	J 1 b
Jigger Trench [1918]	57dNE4 [Hébuterne / Achiet]	L 7 d, 8 c
Jigsaw Wood	51bNW4 Fampoux	I 28 c, d, 34 a, b
Jill Farm	28SW2 Wytschaete	O 23 a 7.5
Jim Hill Line [light rly]	36cSW1 Lens	M 6, 11, 12, N 1, 2
Jim Post	62cNE4 Roisel	L 36 a 4.2
Jimjam House	28SW3 Bailleul	S 22 d 85.65
Jingle Avenue [1918]	57dSW [3 Talmas]	S 27 d, 28 c
Jingle Fork [road jct]	36NW1 Steenwerck	A 10 d 1.6
Jingle Trench	51bNW1 Roclincourt	H 3 a
Jingle Wood [1918]	28SW1 Kemmel	M 21 d, 27 b
Jingo House	28NE3 Gheluvelt	J 31 c 7.3
Jinks Row [houses]	28SW3 Bailleul	S 28 a 8.3
Joa Trench [1918]	62dSW [4 Cachy]	U 28 b, d, 29 a
Joan Copse [near Darby Copse]	62bSW2 Fonsommes	N 30 b
Joan Crater	36cSW3 Vimy	S 8 b
Joan Post	57cNE3 Hermies	K 2 d
Joan Street [1918]	62dSW [2 Corbie / Villers-Bretonneux]	O 30 d, 36 b
Joanny [Tranchée, 1915, La Boisselle]	57dSE4 Ovillers	X 19 b, 20 a, c
Joan's Bridge [road over Heulebeek]	28NE4 Dadizeele	L 16 d 8.1
Job Trench	51bNW1 Roclincourt / 3 Arras	H 1 b, d
Jobber Crossing [level crossing]	36aNE1 Morbecque	E 3 d 3.6
Jobot Trench	66dNW1 Punchy	A 10 c, 15 b, 16 a
Jocaste Alley	66dNW1 Punchy	A 10 d, 11 c

Name	Map Sheet	Map Reference
Jock Alley	51bNW1 Roclincourt	A 17 a
Jock Alley	57cSW1 Gueudecourt	M 16 a, c
Jock Alley	62bSW3 St Quentin	T 2 d, 8 b, d
Jock Farm	28NE3 Gheluvelt	J 18 d 6.8
Jock Keep [Dec 1915]	36cNW3 Loos	G 10 b
Jock Street	36SW1 Aubers	M 29 b
Jock Trench	57dSE2 & 57cSW1 Le Sars	M 10 c, 16 a
Jockey Trench	51bNW1 Roclincourt / 3 Arras	H 3 a, c
Jock's Joy	36NW4 Bois Grenier	I 25 d
Jock's Lodge	36SW1 Aubers	N 7 b 45.30
Jocks Redoubt	36SW1 Aubers	M 29 b, 30 a
Jocose Trench	51bNW3 Arras	H 3 c
Joe House	28NE3 Gheluvelt	J 31 c 82.12
Joe Post	62cNE4 Roisel	L 36 c 65.90
Joffre Avenue	57dSE1 & 2 Beaumont	Q 17 c, d, 23 b
Joffre Farm	20NW4 Dixmude	I 32 b 7.1
Joffre Farm	28NW2 St Julien	C 19 d 3.8
Jog Trench	51bNW3 Arras	H 1 d
Jog Trench	57cNE3 Hermies	J 30 d
Johannes Trench	62cNW4 Péronne	I 20 b, d, 26 b
John Alley	57dNE3 & 4 Hébuterne	K 29 b, 30 a
John Copse	57dNE3 & 4 Hébuterne	K 23 d
John O'Gaunt Street	57dSE4 Ovillers	W 12 c, d, W 18 a, X 7 c
John Street [1918]	62dSW [2 Villers-Bretonneux]	O 30 d, 36 b
John Street A & B	28NW2 St Julien	C 28 c
John Street C	28NW2 St Julien	C 28 d
John Trench	51bNW1 Roclincourt	A 11 d
John Trench	66cNW2 Itancourt	I 2 a
Johns Bridge [road over Canal de Poperinghe]	28NW1 Elverdinghe	A 22 b 5.6
Johnson Avenue	51bNW4 Fampoux	H 30 b, c, d, 36 a, I 25 c
Johnson Lane	51bNW4 Fampoux	H 30 d
Johnson Point	57dSE1 & 2 Beaumont	Q 30 d
Johnson Street	28NW4 & NE3 Zillebeke	I 28 b, d
Johnson Trench	28NE3 Gheluvelt	J 21 b, 22 a, c
Johnston Farm	28NE4 Dadizeele	K 36 a 8.1
Johnstone Avenue	57dSE1 & 2 Beaumont	Q 30 d, 36 b
Johnstone's Post [Thiepval Wood]	57dSE1 & 2 Beaumont	Q 30 d
Joiners Avenue	28NE1 Zonnebeke / 3 Gheluvelt	J 6 b, c, d
Joiners Rest [farm / buildings]	28NE3 Gheluvelt	J 6 c 25.25
Joiners Trench	62bNW1 Gouy	A 7 b
Joiners Wood	28NE3 Gheluvelt	J 6 d
Joist Farm	28NE3 Gheluvelt	J 27 a, b
Joist Trench	28NE3 Gheluvelt	J 27 a, b
Joke Trench	51bNW1 Roclincourt / 3 Arras	H 2 a, b, d, 8 b
Jolie Farm	28NW2 St Julien	C 9 a 3.8
Jollival Trench [1918]	62dSW [4 Cachy]	U 15 d, 21 b
Jolly Trench	51bNW3 Arras	H 1 d
Jolly Trench	51bNW3 Arras	H 3 c
Jolly Trench [1918]	66eNW [4 Morisel]	H 10 a
Jolly Trench [Basseville Wood]	28NE3 Gheluvelt	J 32 d
Jolt Trench	51bNW3 Arras	H 1 d
Jolting Houses	28NE3 Gheluvelt	J 11 a
Jolting Trench	28NE3 Gheluvelt	J 11 a
Jomini Farm [1918]	28SW1 Kemmel	M 7 b 2.7

Name	Map Sheet	Map Reference
Jonah Trench	28NE1 Zonnebeke	D 28 d, J 4 b
Jonas Trench / Tranchée de Jonas	62cSW2 Barleux	O 25 a, b, c
Jonathan Trench	51bNW1 Roclincourt	A 12 b, d
Jonathan Trench	62cNW4 Péronne	I 26 b, 27 a
Jonc Trench	66dNW1 Punchy	A 10 c, d
Joncourt [village]	62bNW3 Bellicourt	H 9 b, c, d, 15 a,
Joncourt Copse	62bNW3 Bellicourt / 4 Ramicourt	H 16 c
Jonction, Tranchée de	62cSW1 & 2 Belloy	N 17 c, d
Jones Trench	57dNE3 & 4 Hébuterne	K 23 c, d
Jonnecourt Farm	62bNW2 Brancourt-le-Grand	I 6 a
Joppa [farm / pillbox]	28NE3 Gheluvelt	J 16 c
Joppa Street [1918]	28NE3 Gheluvelt	J 16 c
Jordan [avenue;CT]	57dNE3 & 4 Hébuterne	K 23 c, 28 a, b, 29 a
Jordan Trench	28NE3 Gheluvelt	J 31 a, b, d
Jordan Trench	51bNE3 Noyelle-sous-Bellonne	J 12 c
Jos House	28NE3 Gheluvelt	J 31 c 8.1
Joseph Camp Lines	36NW2 Armentières	B 17 a
Joseph Trench	51bNW1 Roclincourt	A 11 c
Joseph, Tranchée	62cSW1 & 2 Belloy	N 18 c
Joseph/s Trench	57dSE1 & 2 Beaumont	R 31 b, 32 a, b
Josephine Farm	20SE3 Westroosebeke	V 5 c 55.40
Joseph's Well	57dSE4 Ovillers	X 19 b
Joshua Crossing [road & light rly, 1917-18]	28NW4 Ypres	I 35 a 1.8
Joss Trench	51bNW3 Arras	H 1 c, d, 7 a
Jot Copse	62dSE [3 Marcelcave]	V 13 a, c
Jot Farm	36NW1 Steenwerck	A 14 b 9.2
Jour Trench	51bNW1 Roclincourt	H 3 b
Journal Wood	28NE3 Gheluvelt	J 12 a, b
Jove [German M.G. Pillbox]	51bSW4 Bullecourt	U 20 b 5.7
Jove Lane	51bSW4 Bullecourt	U 20 b
Jove Trench	51bSW1 Neuville Vitasse	M 12 b, N 7 a
Jovotte Trench	66dNW1 Punchy	A 15 b, 16 a
Joy Ride [trench]	51bSW4 Bullecourt	U 21 d, 22 c, d, 23 c,d, 29 b
Joy Ride Support	51bSW4 Bullecourt	U 22 c
Joy Trench	51bNW3 Arras	H 1 c, d
Joye Farm	28SW2 Wytschaete	O 22 d 3.6
Joyous Trench [Point du Jour]	51bNW3 Arras	H 3 c, 9 a
Jubilee / Jubillee [sic] Trench	28NE3 Gheluvelt	J 4 d
Jubilee Croft	28NE3 Gheluvelt	J 11 a 12.98
Jubilee Farm	20SE2 Hooglede	R 4 a 35.75
Jubilee Track [1917-18]	28NE3 Gheluvelt	J 10 a, b
Jubilee Trench	51bNW1 Roclincourt / 3 Arras	H 3 b, c, d
Jud Fork [road jct]	28NE2 Moorslede	F 11 d 2.3
Judah House	28NE1 Zonnebeke	D 15 d 55.00
Judah Track (Double) [1917-18]	28NE1 Zonnebeke	D 16 b, c, d, 21 a, b, 22 a
Judah Track (Duckboard) [1917-18]	28NE1 Zonnebeke	D 16 b, c, 19 d, 20 c, d, 21 a, b, c, 22 a
Judas Copse	51bSW3 Boisleux	T 27 c, d
Judas Farm	28NE3 Gheluvelt	J 18 c 7.7
Judas Farm	51bSW3 Boisleux	T 26 d, 27 a, c
Judas Trench	28NE3 Gheluvelt	J 18 c, d, 24 a, b, c
Judas Trench	57cNW1 Gomiecourt	B 3 a, c, 9 a
Judge Alley	51bNW3 Arras	H 32 a
Judge Copse	28NE3 Gheluvelt	J 11 d 8.8

Name	Map Sheet	Map Reference
Judge Cot	28NE3 Gheluvelt	J 12 a 07.06
Judge Crater	28NE3 Gheluvelt	J 11 b 85.05
Judge Cross Roads	28NE3 Gheluvelt	J 12 a 55.40
Judge Trench	28NE3 Gheluvelt	J 6 c
Judson House	28NE4 Dadizeele	L 31 d 25.40
Judy Copse [1918]	28SW1 Kemmel	M 2 a
Judy Farm [1918]	28SW1 Kemmel	M 2 a 9.9
Judy's Passage [Support Point Cuinchy, 1915]	36cNW1 La Bassée	A 21 b
Juggler Cross Roads	28NE2 Moorslede	F 20 d 1.8
Jugnet [Tr / Boyau] [S end of Pyrenees Trench]	36cSW1 Lens	M 25 b, d
Juice Alley	57cSW1 Gueudecourt	N 13 d
Juice Farm	28NW1 Elverdinghe	H 1 a 3.4
Juil Trench	62cSW3 Vermandovillers	T 15 b, d
Ju-Ju Fork [road jct]	27SE2 Berthen	R 1 d 5.6
Jules Farm	28NE3 Gheluvelt	J 25 d 4.1
Jules Trench	51bNW1 Roclincourt	A 12 d
Julia Trench	57cNW1 Gomiecourt	B 27 a, d
Julia Trench	62bSW3 St Quentin	T 7 c
Julia Trench [1918]	28NE3 Gheluvelt	J 21 c, 27 a
Julien Switch Duckboard Track [1917-18]	28NW2 St Julien	C 12 c, d, 18 a
Juliet Farm	28NW2 St Julien	C 17 a 3.3
Julius Copse [1918]	28SW1 Kemmel	M 21 d, 22 c
Julius Farm [1918]	28SW1 Kemmel	M 28 a 3.8
Julius Farm [building to east of]	28SW1 Kemmel	M 28 a 6.9
July Avenue	51bNW3 Arras	G 11, 16, 17
July Farm	28SW2 Wytschaete	O 23 d 05.65
Jumble Trench	51bNW1 Roclincourt	H 3 a
Jumbo Avenue	57cNE3 Hermies	J 29 b
Jumbo Trench	57cNE3 Hermies	J 29 d, 30 c
Jumeaux Trench / Tranchée de Jumeaux	62cSW3 & 4 Marchélepot	T 15 b, c, d
Jump Point [redoubt]	28SW2 Wytschaete	O 25 a, b
Jumper Wood	28NE3 Gheluvelt	J 31 a, c
Junction Buildings	28SW2 Wytschaete	O 17 c 6.6
Junction Farm	28SE1 Wervicq	P 25 d 5.9
Junction Keep	57dNE1 & 2 Fonquevillers	K 2 a
Junction Keep [E of Vermelles]	36cNW3 Loos	G 9 b, d
Junction Post	36NW3 Fleurbaix	H 32 a
Junction Road	36SW3 Richebourg	S 4 d, 10 b
Junction Road [road, St Jean]	28NW2 St Julien	C 27 c, d, I 3 b
Junction Street	36SW3 Richebourg	S 10 c
Junction to Switch [19-7-16]	57cSW3 Longueval	S 2 a, c
Junction Trench	28NW2 St Julien	I 1 b, d
Junction Trench	28NW4 & NE3 Zillebeke	I 29 b
Junction Trench	51bNW1 Roclincourt	A 8 d
Junction Trench	57cSW3 Longueval	S 3 c, d, 4 c
Junction Trench	62cSW1 & 2 Belloy	N 17 c, d
Junction Trench [Railway Wood]	28NW4 & NE3 Zillebeke	I 11 d, 12 c
Junction Wood	62cNW1 Maricourt	B 13 c, d
Junction Wood	62cNW2 Bouchavesnes	B 28 a, b
June Avenue	51bNW3 Arras	G 11, 16, 17
June Copse	57bSW4 Serain	U 24 b
June Farm	28SW2 Wytschaete	O 23 c 65.65
June Wood	62bNW4 Ramicourt	I 30 d
Jungle Alley	51bSW2 Vis-en-Artois	O 19 b, 20 a

Name	Map Sheet	Map Reference
Jungle Houses	28SE1 Wervicq	P 2 d 55.65
Juniper Avenue	57cNE3 Hermies	J 24 c, d
Juniper Cott	28NE3 Gheluvelt	J 17 a 35.90
Juniper Support	28NE3 Gheluvelt	J 17 a, b, 18 a
Juniper Trench	28NE3 Gheluvelt	J 10 d
Juniper Trench	51bNW1 Roclincourt	A 12 d
Juniper Trench	57cNE3 Hermies	J 24 a, b, d
Juniper Wood	28NE3 Gheluvelt	J 11 d, 17 a, b
Junk Trench	57dSE1 & 2 Beaumont	Q 18 a, c
Junker Trench	51bNW4 Fampoux	H 29 d, 35 a, b
Juno Trench	51bSW4 Bullecourt	U 14 a
Juno Trench	57cNE3 Hermies	J 30 d, 36 b
Jupiter Alley	66dNW3 Hattencourt	G 16 b, 17 a, c, d
Jupiter Support	62cNW2 Bouchavesnes	C 3 d, 4 c, 10 a
Jupiter Trench	62cNW2 Bouchavesnes	C 3 d, 9 b, 10 a
Jupiter Wood	66cNW2 Itancourt	C 12 c
Jura Street	57dSE4 Ovillers	Q 36 d
Jury Alley	51bNW3 Arras	H 32 a
Jury Farm	28NW2 St Julien	C 12 d 8.6
Jussy [village]	66cSW1 Remigny	M 15
Justice Wood	28NE1 Zonnebeke	D 30 c, J 6 a, b
Justice Wood	62cNW3 Vaux	G 20 d
Justice Wood Cemetery	28NE1 Zonnebeke	J 6 a, b
Jut Farm	28NE3 Gheluvelt	J 16 a 3.1
Jute Cotts	28NE3 Gheluvelt	J 27 a 1.8
Jutland	28NE1 Zonnebeke	D 22 c
Jutland Alley	57cSW3 Longueval	S 2 b, d, 3 a
Jutland Trench	51bNW4 Fampoux	H 12 c, d, 18 a
Jutland Trench	62cNW4 Péronne	H 10 b, d
Jutland Trench	66dNW3 Hattencourt	G 16 a, b, 17 a
K 1 [Frise; Br tr S of Somme, 1915]	62cNW3 Vaux	G 18 / 24
K 10 Pill Box [Pilckem]	28NW2 St Julien	C 2 central
K 2 [Frise; Br tr S of Somme, 1915]	62cNW3 Vaux	G 18 / 24
K 3 [trench, NW of Fme Vandenberghe]	28SW2 Wytschaete	N 17 b 9.2
K 4 Redoubt [Festubert, May 1915]	36cNW1 La Bassée	A 2 b
K Camp [St Jan-ter-Biezen]	27NE2 Proven	L 2 a [area]
K Farm	28NE1 Zonnebeke	D 23 c
K House	20SW4 Bixschoote	T 30 a
K Sap	57dSE4 Ovillers	R 31 c
K Sector [Feb 1915]	28SW2 Wytschaete	N 17 b
K Track (Duckboard) [1917-18]	28NW4 Ypres / NE1 Zonnebeke	I 4 c,d, 5 c, D 15 b,c,d, 16 a, 20 b, 21 a
K Track (Treble) [1917-18]	28NE1 Zonnebeke	D 15 b, c, d, 16 a, 21 a
K.O. Lane	62bNW1 Gouy	A 13 b
Kaaie [Dead End, canal quays]	28NW4 & NE3 Zillebeke	I 2 c
Kaaie Salient [E of Canal]	28NW4 & NE3 Zillebeke	I 2 c
Kabul Avenue	57cNE4 Marcoing	L 26 d, 27 c, 32 b
Kabul Farm	28NE2 Moorslede	E 22 b 05.65
Kadssen Trench	62bSW3 St Quentin	S 24 a, b
Kaffir Copse	62cNE4 Roisel	L 16 b, 17 a
Kaffir Fork [road jct]	28NE2 Moorslede	E 17 c 65.85
Kaiser Bill [Wieltje]	28NW2 St Julien	C 29 central
Kaiser Copse	66dNW3 Hattencourt	G 3 c
Kaiser Graben	57dNE1 & 2 Fonquevillers	E 24 b

Name	Map Sheet	Map Reference
Kaiser Strasse	57dSE4 Ovillers	X 14 d, 15 c
Kaiser Support	57cNE4 Marcoing	L 19 b, 20 c, d
Kaiser Trench	57cNE4 Marcoing	L 19 a, b, 20 a, c, d
Kaiser Wilhelm Battery	5SW1 Zeebrugge	N 10 c
Kaiser Wilhelm II Battery	5SW2 Knocke	N 10 c, d
Kaiser/s Lane	57dNE3 & 4 Hébuterne	K 24 b, c, d, L 19 a, b, d, 20 c
Kaisergraben [2nd intermediate line]	57dSE4 Ovillers	X 4 a, c, 10 a, c, 16 a, b, d
Kaiserin Trench	36cNW3 Loos	G 4 d, 5 c
Kaiser's Oak, The	57dNE3 & 4 Hébuterne	K 3 d 7.6
Kaiserschantze [Hop Point: Ger. Switch Line]	28SW2 Wytschaete	N 30 d
Kaka Trench [1918]	57dNE4 [Hébuterne / Achiet]	L 7 d
Kaledine / Kaledin Alley	66cNW2 Itancourt	I 2 a, b
Kalve [place name]	20SE3 Westroosebeke	W 20 b
Kama Trench	66cNW1 Grugies	B 3 a, b
Kamwezi Copse	51bSE4 Marquion	W 6 a
Kandy Trench	51bSW4 Bullecourt	U 8 a
Kang Wang [beech rd, Hooge deviation, '17]	28NW4 & NE3 Zillebeke	I 18 a, b
Kangaroo Alley / Trench	57cNE1 Quéant / 2 Bourlon	E 27 d, 28 c, d, K 3 a, b
Kangaroo Avenue	20SW4 Bixschoote / SE3 Westroosebeke	U 24 d, V 19 a, c
Kangaroo Avenue	57cNE4 Marcoing	K 34 a, c
Kangaroo Huts	20SE3 Westroosebeke	V 13 c
Kangaroo Pond	20SE3 Westroosebeke	V 19 a
Kangaroo Trench	20SW4 Bixschoote	U 24 a, b, d
Kanoner Weg	57dNE1 & 2 Fonquevillers	E 28 b, d
Kansas Cross	28NE1 Zonnebeke	D 14 a 2.1
Kansas House	28NE1 Zonnebeke	D 13 b 8.2
Kant Copse	66dNW3 Hattencourt	G 5 c
Kanterhoek [farm]	28NE4 Dadizeele	L 7 a 2.7
Kanterhoek [place name]	28NE4 Dadizeele	K 12 b, L 7 a
Kantintje Cabaret [Menin Road]	28NE3 Gheluvelt	J 21 a 25.65
Kapel Hock Trench	20NW4 Dixmude	I 8 c
Kapel Hoek Trench [Kapelhoek]	20NW4 Dixmude	I 8 b, c, d
Kappelleehoek [place name]	20SE2 Hooglede	R 11 a, b
Kapper Farm [Klofkapperie]	28NE2 Moorslede	F 22 a 15.70
Kapple Farm [Slypskappelle]	28NE2 Moorslede	E 30 c 3.3
Karl Lane	51bSW4 Bullecourt	U 1 c
Karrier Cottage	28SW3 Bailleul	S 28 b 7.5
Karte Farm	28NW1 Elverdinghe	B 19 d 7.7
Karunga Farm	51bSE4 Marquion	X 27 b
Kasbah, la [farm]	20SW4 Bixschoote	O 33 d 8.8
Kaschau Trench	57cSW4 Combles	U 5 a, c
Kashmir Wood	51bNW4 Fampoux	I 36 b, c, d
Kassa Trench	62cNW2 Bouchavesnes	C 21 d, 27 b
Kasscub / Kasvotus Trench	62bSW3 St Quentin	T 7 d
Kast Copse [Kasteelhoek]	28NE2 Moorslede	F 1 a 7.2
Kast Farm [Kasteelhoek]	28NE2 Moorslede	F 1 c 0.9
Kasteelhoek	28NE2 Moorslede	E 6 b
Kasteelhoek Chateau	28NE2 Moorslede	E 6 b 10.65
Kasteeltje Farm, Het [moated]	20SE2 Hooglede	Q 30 a 8.6
Kasteethoek	28SE1 Wervicq	P 7 c
Kastenweg / Kasten Weg [German CT]	36SW2 Radinghem	N 10 c, d, 16 b
Kat Cabaret, De	20SE3 Westroosebeke	W 7 c 6.5
Kate Post	28SW4 Ploegsteert	U 29 a 6.4
Kate Trench, & Crater	51bNW3 Arras	G 6 c

Name	Map Sheet	Map Reference
Kate Wood	62dSE [1 Hamel]	Q 13 b, 14 a
Kathi / Kathie Trench	36SW3 Richebourg	M 36 c, S 6 a, b
Katipo Trench [1918]	57dNE4 [Hébuterne / Achiet]	L 13 b, d, 14 a
Katte Kerkhof [farm]	28SW1 Kemmel	N 20 d 66.28
Kaufmann Graben	57dSE4 Ovillers	X 20 a, b
Kavallerie Graben	57dNE1 & 2 Fonquevillers	E 30 c, d
Kavunge Copse	51bSE4 Marquion	X 27 b 7.2
Kay Alley	51bNW1 Roclincourt / 2 Oppy	B 28 c, d
Kay Buildings	28NE2 Moorslede	K 6 b 5.6
Kay Dump [Pozières]	57dSE4 Ovillers	X 3 b
Kay Trench [Pozières]	57dSE4 Ovillers	X 10 a
Kea Trench	51bNW3 Arras	H 7 a
Kea Trench [1918]	57dNE4 [Hébuterne / Achiet]	L 13 b, d, 14 c
Keane Trench	36cSW3 Vimy	T 8 d
Keane Trench [1918]	57dNE2 [Fonquevillers] / 4 [Hébuterne]	L 2 a, c
Keatings Lane	57cNE4 Marcoing	K 29 b, c, d, 35 a
Keats Redan [Galgen]	57dSE4 Ovillers	X 13 c
Keel Farm	28NE1 Zonnebeke	K 1 b 9.7
Keel Trench [Keeling Copse]	51bNW4 Fampoux	I 32 d, 33 c
Keeling Copse [Monchy-le-Preux]	51bNW4 Fampoux	I 32 d
Keen Trench	51bNW3 Arras	H 8 d, 9 a, c
Keep [Givenchy; Sept 1915]	36cNW1 La Bassée	A 8 d
Keep C [Loos]	36cNW3 Loos	G 36 a
Keep D [Loos]	36cNW3 Loos	G 35 b, 36 a
Keep E [Loos]	36cNW3 Loos	G 35 d
Keep Reserve [W of Mad Point]	36cNW1 La Bassée	A 27 d
Keep, The	57dNE3 & 4 Hébuterne	K 9 c, d
Keep, The [Souchez]	36cSW3 Vimy	S 8 b 8.2
Keepaway Farm	28SW4 Ploegsteert	T 11 c 6.3
Keepers Farm	20SE2 Hooglede	R 17 a 10.85
Keeper's House [St Quentin Wood]	62cSE4 [Attilly]	R 35 d 3.4
Keeper's Hut [Ploegsteert Wood]	28SW4 Ploegsteert	U 27 b 3.8
Keersebrom [farms & place name]	28SW3 Bailleul	S 10 d, 11 c
Keg Copse	28NE3 Gheluvelt	K 1 d 8.5
Keg Farm	28NE3 Gheluvelt	K 1 d 1.8
Keiberg	28NE1 Zonnebeke	E 25 b,
Keibergmolen	28NE1 Zonnebeke	E 26 a
Keiller Farm	28NE4 Dadizeele	K 16 b 35.30
Keilson Street	57dSE2 Beaumont	R 25 a
Keir Farm	28NE1 Zonnebeke	D 13 d
Keith Wood	51bSE3 Cagnicourt / 4 Marquion	W 21 b, d, 22 a, c
Keizer Inn	27NE2 Proven	E 22 c 0.9
Keller Street	51bNW3 Arras	G 18 c
Keller Weg	51bNW1 Roclincourt	A 11 a
Kellerman Trench	57dNE3 & 4 Hébuterne	K 3 c, 9 a
Kellet Trench	57cNE3 Hermies	K 8 a, b
Kellet/t Trench / Line / Kellets Line	36cSW3 Vimy	M 32 c, S 2 a
Kellow Crossing [level crossing & road jct]	36NW1 Steenwerck	B 14 c 9.4
Kelly Bridge [across Ancre]	57dSE4 Ovillers	W 5 d 6.1
Kelly Trench	28SW2 Wytschaete	N 23 d
Kelso Cottage	27SE4 Meteren	X 14 b 9.5
Kemmel Brewery	28SW2 Wytschaete	N 21 c 8.5
Kemmel Hall [1918]	28SW1 Kemmel	N 19 d 45.40
Kemmel Line [railway, 1917]	28SW1 Kemmel	N 13 b, c, d, 19 a, c, d

Name	Map Sheet	Map Reference
Kemmel Village	28SW1 Kemmel	N 21 a, c
Kemmel Windmill	28SW1 Kemmel	N 25 d
Kemmelbeke [railway locality & huts]	28NW1 Elverdinghe	B 20 d, 26 b
Kemmelberg [Mount Kemmel]	28SW1 Kemmel	N 26 a, b
Kemmelhof [farm]	27SE2 Berthen	Q 28 c 20.55
Kemp / Kempe Trench	57dSE1 & 2 Beaumont	R 20 a, c
Kemp [light rly, Vimy]	36cSW3 Vimy	T 25 a
Kemp Trench	36cSW3 Vimy	S 14 a, c
Kempfer Weg	51bNW1 Roclincourt	A 10 d
Kempton Park	28SW1 Kemmel	M 9 c
Kempton Park [Chemins Estaminet]	28NW2 St Julien	C 15 b 4.5
Ken Lane	62cNE2 Epéhy	F 17 a
Ken Trench	51bNW3 Arras	H 7 c, d
Kendal Trench	57dNE1 & 2 Fonquevillers	E 11 a
Kendal Trench	57dSE2 Beaumont	R 22 b, 23 a, c
Kendall House	20SE3 Westroosebeke	W 13 c 65.30
Kenilworth Copse	28NE4 Dadizeele	L 25 d
Kennebak Cabaret, De	28SW3 Bailleul	T 3 b 3.2
Kennebak Line, De [light rly locality]	28SW3 Bailleul / 4 Ploegsteert	T 4 c, d, 5 c, d,
Kennebak, De [railway sidings]	28SW3 Bailleul / 4 Ploegsteert	T 3 b, d, 4 c
Kennedy Crater	36cSW3 Vimy	S 9 c
Kennedy House	28NE4 Dadizeele	K 34 c 9.7
Kennel Support	57cSE4 Villers-Guislain	R 31 d
Kennel Trench	57cNE3 Hermies	K 26 c
Kennel Wood	28NE3 Gheluvelt	K 7 b 5.9
Kennet Cross [cross roads]	36aNE4 Merville	L 11 d 55.15
Kennet Wood	62cNW3 Vaux	H 9 b, d, 10 a, c
Keno [light rly siding]	36cSW1 Lens	M 3 d, 4 c
Kenora Camp [NE of Heksken]	28SW1 Kemmel	M 3 c 6.5
Kenora Trench	57dSE2 & 57cSW1 Le Sars	R 23 a, b, 24 a, c
Kent Avenue	36NW2 Armentières	C 3 d, 4 a
Kent Camp	28SW3 Bailleul	T 25 d
Kent Crater	51bNW1 Roclincourt	G 6 a
Kent Crossing [level crossing]	20SE2 Hooglede	R 8 d 2.4
Kent Farm	28NE3 Gheluvelt	J 33 a 2.1
Kent Lane [Oct 1915]	36cNW3 Loos	G 18 a
Kent Road [road]	36aNE4 Merville	K 9 b, d, 10 c, 16 a, c
Kent Road [trench]	28SW2 Wytschaete	O 3 b
Kent Road [trench]	51bNW2 Oppy	B 11 d, 12 c
Kent Street [1918]	62cSW [2 Corbie / Villers-Bretonn.] / SE [1 Hamel]	O 24 d, P 19 c
Kent Trench	51bNW1 Roclincourt	G 6 a
Kentish Caves	57dSE1 & 2 Beaumont	Q 23 b, 24 a
Kentish Villa	57dSE1 & 2 Beaumont	Q 23 b
Kerb Trench	51bNW3 Arras	H 7 a
Kerera Street	57dSE4 Ovillers	W 6 b
Kern Redoubt	57dNE1 & 2 Fonquevillers	K 4 b
Kerr Street	28SW2 Wytschaete	N 29 a, b
Kerry Alley	57cSW3 Longueval	S 3 c
Kersal Street	57dSE4 Ovillers	W 6 b, d
Kestrel Avenue	51bSW2 Vis-en-Artois	N 23, 24, O 19, 20
Kestrel Farm	28NW1 Elverdinghe	A 8 d 6.8
Kestrel Lane [later Avenue]	51bSW2 Vis-en-Artois	N 23 c, d, 24 c, d, O 19 c, d, 20 c, 26 a
Ketchen Avenue	28SW2 Wytschaete	N 23 d, 24 c

Name	Map Sheet	Map Reference
Kettering Junction [railway]	28NW3 Poperinghe	H 7 d 85.80
Kettle House	28NE3 Gheluvelt	J 28 a 3.8
Kew Cross [cross roads]	36aNE2 Vieux Berquin	E 30 d 6.1
Kewatin [buildings / camp / light rly loop]	28SW1 Kemmel	N 7 a
Key Trench	51bSW2 Vis-en-Artois	O 13 b, d
Key Trench	57cNE3 Hermies	K 14 a, b, 15 a
Kezelberg [hamlet]	28NE4 Dadizeele	L 19 b, d
Kezelberg Windmill	28NE4 Dadizeele	L 19 d 62.10
Khartoum Farm	28NE2 Moorslede	E 22 c 40.55
Kiboko Wood	62cNW4 Péronne	H 35 b, 36 a
Kick Trench	51bNW3 Arras	H 8 d
Kick Trench, & Crater	51bNW1 Roclincourt	G 6 a
Kick-off Trench	57dSE4 Ovillers	X 5 c, d, 11 a
Kid Lane	62bNW1 Gouy	G 1 b, 2 a
Kiduha Copse	51bSE4 Marquion	Q 36 a, c
Kiekeput	28SW2 Wytschaete	N 10 c, d
Kiel Cot.	28NW2 St Julien	C 7 d 6.6
Kiel Lane	62dNE2 Méaulte	F 10 c, d
Kiel Support	62dNE2 Méaulte	F 10 c, d
Kiel Trench	70dNW2 Servais	C 7 b, d
Kiel Trench	62dNE2 Méaulte	F 10 c, d
Kiel Trench [1918]	62dSW [4 Cachy]	U 16 b, d
Kilberry Street	57dSE4 Ovillers	Q 36 d
Kilby's Walk	36cNW1 La Bassée	A 9 c, d
Kildare Avenue	57cSE4 Villers-Guislain	X 21 c, d, 22 b, c, d, 23 a, c, 27 a
Kildare Lane [trench]	57cSE4 Villers-Guislain	X 22 c, 28 a
Kildare Post	57cSE4 Villers-Guislain	X 28 a 99.82
Kildare Trench	57cSE4 Villers-Guislain	X 22 c, 28 a
Kilfauns Street	57dSE4 Ovillers	X 19 a
Kilkerran Support	51bNW2 Oppy	B 28 b, d, H 4 b, 5 a
Kilkerran Trench	51bNW2 Oppy	B 28 b, d, 29 a, c, H 5 a
Killick Trench [1918]	28NW4 & NE3 Zillebeke	J 21 c
Kilmun Street	57dSE2 Beaumont	Q 36 b
Kiln Trench	51bNW3 Arras	H 7 d
Kilo Copse	66dNW3 Hattencourt	G 5 c
Kilo Farm	28SW2 Wytschaete	O 28 b 5.1
Kilo Farm [near 9 kilometre stone]	20SW4 Bixschoote	T 11 d 8.4
Kilometre Lane [road]	57dNE3 & 4 Hébuterne / SE1 & 2 Beaumont	K 33 d, 34 c, Q 3 a, b
Kilt Trench	51bSW2 Vis-en-Artois	N 4 b, c, d
Kim Road [road]	28SW1 Kemmel	N 7 d, 13 b, 14 a, c, d
Kimber Avenue	57cNE4 Marcoing	K 28 a, b
Kimber Trench	57cNE4 Marcoing	K 22 c, d, 29 a
Kin Lane	57cNE4 Marcoing	K 34 a, b
Kin Trench	51bNW1 Roclincourt	A 30 c
Kin Trench	51bNW3 Arras	H 7 a, b
Kine Farm	28NW1 Elverdinghe	B 28 b 10.95
King Castle	28NE3 Gheluvelt	J 25 d 6.4
King Copse [1918]	57dSW [3 Talmas]	S 23 c, d, 29 a
King Crater	51bNW1 Roclincourt	A 30 c 4.6
King Edward Trench	28SW4 Ploegsteert	T 6 d, U 1 c
King George's Hill [Fricourt, Aug 1916]	62dNE2 Méaulte	F 10 c
King George's Hill [IWGC reference]	62dNE2 Méaulte	F 9 c 2.2
King George's Road [road]	36aSE4 Locon	X 4 b, 5 a, c, d
King Street	28NW4 & NE3 Zillebeke	I 34 c

Name	Map Sheet	Map Reference
King Street	36cSW1 Lens	M 5 a, c, d
King Street	51bNW2 Oppy	B 12 a, c
King Street	57dSE1 & 2 Beaumont	Q 4 c, d
King Street	62dNE2 Méaulte	F 12 c
King Street / Boyau du Rois	62cNW1 Maricourt	A 23 c
King Street [1918]	57dSE [3 Bouzincourt]	W 8 c, d
King Street [1918]	62dNE [3 Morlancourt]	K 13 a
King Street [ride, Delville Wood]	57cSW3 Longueval	S 18 b
King Street [road, NW of Ginchy]	57cSW3 Longueval	T 13 b
King Street [road]	36aSE4 Locon	X 9 d, 10 c, 15 b
King Street West [1918]	57dSE [3 Bouzincourt]	W 8 a
King Trench	51bNW3 Arras	H 7 b, d
King's Avenue	62dNE2 Méaulte	F 1 b, d, 2 a, b, c, 3 a
Kings Copse	62cNE1 Liéramont	J 6 b
King's Cross	36cNW1 La Bassée	A 15 c, d
King's Cross	36cSW3 Vimy	S 8 a 1.4
Kings Cross [1918]	51cSE4 Blaireville	W 24 a
King's Cross [trench junction / strongpoint]	62dNE2 Méaulte	F 2 b 25.25
Kings Dump	36bSE4 Carency	X 11 b 8.2
King's Head	36cNW3 Loos	G 11 a
King's Hill	57cSE1 Bertincourt	P 15 d, 16 c, d, 22 a, b
King's Point	51bSW4 Bullecourt	U 7 b
King's Road	36cNW1 La Bassée	A 9 c, d
King's Road [1918]	57dNE1 & 2 Fonquevillers	E 28 b, 29 a
King's Street	36cSW3 Vimy	S 14 b, 15 a
King's Walk	57cSW3 Longueval	S 12 a
King's Way [northern canal bank]	28NW4 & NE3 Zillebeke	I 32 b
King's Way [track, N of Canal]	28NW4 & NE3 Zillebeke	I 32 b, 33 a
Kingsbridge [light rly siding]	36cNW3 Loos	G 20 c
Kingsclere / King's Claire [Cuinchy]	36cNW1 La Bassée	A 21 a 2.9
Kingsclere [farm]	28SW4 Ploegsteert	U 6 b 2.3
Kingsgate Street	57dSE4 Ovillers	X 20 a, c
Kingston Junction & Siding [rly & lt rly]	28SW3 Bailleul	T 28 a, c
Kingston Junction [railway]	28SW3 Bailleul	T 27 d 5.9
Kingston Quarry	57bSW3 Honnecourt	S 14 c
Kingston Road	62dNE2 Méaulte	F 8 b
Kingsway	28SW2 Wytschaete / 4 Ploegsteert	N 34 c, d, 35 b, c, d, 36 a
Kingsway	36cNW1 La Bassée	A 21 d, 27a, b
Kingsway	36cSW3 Vimy	S 15 d
Kingsway / King's Way [The Bluff]	28NW4 & NE3 Zillebeke	I 32 b, 33 a
Kingsway Station	36cNW1 La Bassée	A 27 a
Kingsway Support [Zouave Wood]	28NW4 & NE3 Zillebeke	I 18 c, d
Kink Corner	28NE1 Zonnebeke	D 26 a 55.50
Kink Crater	36cNW3 Loos	G 5 c 9.6
Kink Farm [by kink in road]	20SE2 Hooglede	Q 12 b 6.1
Kink, The	36cNW3 Loos	G 5 c
Kinkroo Keep	36SW3 Richebourg	S 21 d
Kinkroo Trench	36SW3 Richebourg	S 21 a, c, d
Kinky Roo [road: La Quinque Rue]	36SW3 Richebourg	S 21 d
Kino Street	36cSW3 Vimy	S 8 d, 14 b
Kint Crater	51bNW1 Roclincourt	A 30 c 4.5
Kintyre Trenches	57dSE4 Ovillers	Q 36 c, d
Kip Cottages	28NW1 Elverdinghe	A 25 b 1.2
Kipper Trench	57dSE4 Ovillers	X 20 d, 21 c

Name	Map Sheet	Map Reference
Kirby Street	28NW4 & NE3 Zillebeke	I 24 d, 30 b
Kirchhof Graben [Monchy-au-Bois]	57dNE1 & 2 Fonquevillers	E 6 c
Kirchner Copse	62bSW1 Gricourt	M 33 a, b
Kirk Trench	28NE3 Gheluvelt	J 12 b, d, 7 c
Kirkaldy Street	57dSE4 Ovillers	X 13 c
Kirlem, le [hamlet]	36NW1 Steenwerck	A 23 c
Kirriemuir Street	57dSE4 Ovillers	X 19 b, d, 20 c
Kirsch [Tranchée, W of Fricourt, 1915]	62dNE2 Méaulte	F 2 b, d
Kismet House	36aNE2 Vieux Berquin	F 9 b 10.35
Kiss Trench	51bNW3 Arras	H 7 d
Kit and Kat	28NW4 & NE3 Zillebeke	J 1 d
Kit Trench	51bNW4 Fampoux	I 27 d
Kit Trench	51bSW2 Vis-en-Artois	O 8 c
Kitchen Crater	57cSE4 Villers-Guislain	R 33 c 8.5
Kitchen Road	57dSE1 & 2 Beaumont	Q 29 c
Kitchen Street [road]	57cSE2 Gonnelieu	R 33 a, b, c
Kitchen Trench	62dNE2 Méaulte	F 3 d, 9 b
Kitchener's House	28NW2 St Julien	C 10 d 30.95
Kitchener's Wood	28NW2 St Julien	C 10 d, 11 c, 16 b, 17 a
Kite Alley	36cSW1 Lens	M 31 b, 32 a
Kite Copse	57dNE1 & 2 Fonquevillers	E 24 d, 30 b
Kite Crater	51bNW1 Roclincourt	A 30 c 4.1
Kite Farm	28NE2 Moorslede	F 21 a 95.95
Kite Lane	57cNE4 Marcoing	K 28 c
Kite Trench	51bNW3 Arras	H 7 d
Kite Trench / Crater	51bNW1 Roclincourt	A 30 c 4.1
Kitkat Post [1918]	28NE3 Gheluvelt	J 1 d 3.8
Kitten Street	57dSE4 Ovillers	R 31 c, X 1 a
Kitten Trench	57cNE3 Hermies	K 32 b, d
Kitty Copse	28NE2 Moorslede	F 26 d 15.10
Kiwi Avenue	36NW2 Armentières	C 4 a, b
Kiwi Farm	28SW4 Ploegsteert	O 36 c 5.5
Kiwi Lane	36NW2 Armentières	C 4 d
Kiwi Street	36NW4 Bois Grenier	I 26 a
Kiwi Wood	57dSW [2 Raincheval]	O 28 a, b
Klaxon House	27NE2 Proven	F 25 b 8.7
Kleber, Tranchée	70dSW2 [Coucy-le-Château]	O 19 c
Kleeman Stellung	51bNW1 Roclincourt	A 24 d
Klein Zillebeke	28NW4 & NE3 Zillebeke	I 36 b 3.1
Klein[e] Vierstraat Cabaret	28SW1 Kemmel / 2 Wytschaete	N 10 a 30.45
Kleine Vierstraat	28SW2 Wytschaete	N 10 a 9.9
Klephoek	28NE4 Dadizeele	K 12 d, L 7 c
Kliest Farm	28NW2 St Julien	C 9 b 9.8
Klite Hill Cross [cross roads]	27SE4 Meteren	W 23 b 05.35
Klofkapperie	28NE2 Moorslede	F 21 b
Klux Farm	36NW1 Steenwerck	A 29 b 85.90
Klythoek [place name]	28NE4 Dadizeele	L 26 c
Klytteput [farm]	27NE1 Herzeele	E 7 a 7.7
Knack Trench	51bNW3 Arras	H 7 d
Knaresboro Castle	28NW2 St Julien	C 14 d, 20 b
Knat [sic] Lane	57cNE3 Hermies	K 26 b, 27 a
Knat [sic] Trench, & Alley	57cNE3 Hermies	K 26 b, 27 a
Knat Avenue	57cNE3 Hermies / 4 Marcoing	K 27 c, d
Knave Trench	51bNW3 Arras	H 7 d

Name	Map Sheet	Map Reference
Knave Trench	57cNE4 Marcoing	K 6 c, d, 12 a, L 1 c
Knaves Road [trench]	66cSW2 Vendeuil	O 21 a, c, d, 27 b
Knead Trench	51bNW3 Arras	H 7 d
Knee Copse	66dNW1 Punchy	A 5 d
Knee Lane	57cSW2 Villers-au-Flos	N 33 a
Knee Trench	51bSW1 Neuville Vitasse	N 7 c
Knell Trench	51bNW3 Arras	H 7 d
Kneller Hall [Ploegsteert Wood, 1914-15]	28SW4 Ploegsteert	U 21 a 05.50
Knife Support	57cNE3 Hermies / 4 Marcoing	K 32 d, 33 c
Knife Trench	51bNW3 Arras	H 7 d, 13 b
Knife Trench	51bSW2 Vis-en-Artois	O 8 c, 14 a
Knife Trench	57cNE3 Hermies / 4 Marcoing	K 32 d, 33 c
Knife Trench	57dNE3 & 4 Hébuterne	L 8 c, 14 a
Knight's Farm	28NE4 Dadizeele	L 32 b 55.33
Knightsbridge	57dSE1 & 2 Beaumont	Q 16, 22
Knightsbridge / Knights Bridge	57cNE3 Hermies	K 20 b, 21 a, c
Knightsbridge Barracks	57dSE1 & 2 Beaumont	Q 16 c, d
Knit Trench	51bNW3 Arras	H 7 d
Knob Trench	51bNW3 Arras	H 7 a
Knob Wood [N of Bony]	62bNW1 Gouy	A 3 d, 9 a, b
Knob, The [NNW of Bony]	62bNW1 Gouy	A 9 b, d, 10 a, c
Knobkerry Ridge	62bNW3 Bellicourt	G 30 a
Knock Farm	28NE2 Moorslede	E 30 b 2.7
Knocke (Old Fort)	20SW1 Loo	N 8 a
Knoet Farm, De	28NE1 Zonnebeke	D 28 b 6.6
Knoll Farm	28NW4 & NE3 Zillebeke	I 29 a
Knoll Post	62cNE2 Epéhy	F 8 d
Knoll Road [metalled road, 1917]	28NW4 & NE3 Zillebeke	I 23 c, 29 a, c, d
Knoll Support	62bNW1 Gouy	A 7 b
Knoll Switch	62bNW1 Gouy	A 1 d
Knoll Trench	51bNW3 Arras	H 7 d
Knoll Trench	62bNW1 Gouy	A 7 b
Knoll, The [hill]	62bNW1 Gouy / 62cNE2 Epéhy	A 1 d, 7 b, F 6 c, 12 a
Knollys Farm	28NW3 Poperinghe	H 7 c 75.00
Knos Trench	51bNW3 Arras	H 1 c, 7 a
Knot Trench	51bNW3 Arras	H 1 d, 7 b
Knot Trench	57cSW3 Longueval	S 24 b, d, 30 b
Knotty Point [road jct, Thilloy]	57cSW1 Gueudecourt	N 2 c 25.80
Knox Street [1918]	57dNE3 & 4 Hébuterne	K 23 a
Knuckle Avenue	51bSW4 Bullecourt	U 14 c, 19 b, 20 a
Knuckle Redoubt	51bSW4 Bullecourt	U 20 a
Knuckle Trench	57cNE4 Marcoing	K 33 d, 34 a
Knuckle, The	51bSW4 Bullecourt	U 20 a
Kodak Farm	27SE4 Meteren	X 9 d 30.65
Koe Farm [Koekuitkapel]	28NE2 Moorslede	F 20 b 8.7
Koekuit [place name]	20SW4 Bixschoote	U 11 c, 17 a
Koekuit Junction [road junction]	20SW4 Bixschoote	U 11 c 64.04
Koekuithoek	28NE2 Moorslede	E 6 d
Koekuitkapel	28NE2 Moorslede	F 21 a
Kohinoor Cross Roads	28NE4 Dadizeele	L 17 a 5.9
Köln Farm	28NW2 St Julien	C 14 a 8.6
Kolomea Trench	66cNW1 Grugies	B 1 b
Kommandeur Graben	51bNW1 Roclincourt	A 30 c, d
Konieh, Tranchée de	66cNW2 Itancourt	B 11 b, 12 a, c

Name	Map Sheet	Map Reference
König Trench, Support & Lane	62dNE2 Méaulte	F 3 a
Königsberger Trench	51bNW3 Arras	G 12 c
Koningshoek [farm / hamlet]	20SE2 Hooglede	Q 17 c 2.1
Konitz Trench	62cSE1 Bouvincourt	P 13 b, d, 19 b
Kootenay [light rly]	36cSW3 Vimy	S 17 a, c
Kopje Farm	27SE4 Meteren	X 5 a 5.2
Kopp Wood	66dNW3 Hattencourt	G 5 c
Korek [farm / pillboxes]	28NE1 Zonnebeke	D 9 c 4.6
Koros Alley	62cNW4 Péronne	I 16 a, b, c, 17 a
Kortekeer Cabaret	20SW4 Bixschoote	U 13 d 8.3
Kortekeer, Halte de	20SE2 Hooglede	R 6 a 4.2
Kortepyp [place name]	28SW3 Bailleul	T 20 d
Kortepyp Cabaret	28SW3 Bailleul	T 20 a 95.15
Kortepyp Camp A	28SW3 Bailleul	T 26 b
Kortepyp Camp B	28SW3 Bailleul	T 27 a 2.3
Kortepyp Road	28SW3 Bailleul	T 20 d, 26 b, 27 a
Kortewilde Line [German]	28SW2 Wytschaete	O 18, 24 [through]
Koster Inn	27NE2 Proven	E 28 c 7.2
Koudekot [hamlet]	28SW3 Bailleul	M 34 d
Koulikord [trench]	66cNW2 Itancourt	B 24 d
Kovno Redoubt	62bSW3 St Quentin	T 13 c
Koyli Redoubt	57cSW3 Longueval	S 7 b 85.70
Koyli Trench	57cSW1 Gueudecourt	M 5
Koyli Trench	57dSE4 Ovillers	X 6 c, 12 a
Koyli, East	57dSE1 & 2 Beaumont	R 19 c
Koyli, West	57dSE1 & 2 Beaumont	Q 24 d, R 19 c
Kraal Farm	28NE2 Moorslede	E 17 d 2.7
Kraatenberg Cabaret, In den [S. Midland Fm]	28SW4 Ploegsteert	T 6 c 65.60
Krab Krawl [Crab Crawl]	28NW4 & NE3 Zillebeke	I 24 d
Krabbenhof Farm	28SW1 Kemmel	M 23 a 90.25
Kramer Weg / Kranmer Avenue	51bNW1 Roclincourt	A 11 d, 12 c, d
Krapina Copse	51bSE3 Cagnicourt	V 30 d
Kreidhohle	51bSW2 Vis-en-Artois	O 22 b
Kreuz Graben Ost	57dNE1 & 2 Fonquevillers	E 12 b, F 7 a
Kreuz Graben West	57dNE1 & 2 Fonquevillers	E 12 a, b
Kreuz Weg	51bNW1 Roclincourt	A 11 a
Krieger Stellung	51bSW1 Neuville Vitasse	M 5 a, c
Kron Wood	66dNW1 Punchy	A 6 a, c
Kronprinz Farm [& pillboxes]	28NE1 Zonnebeke	D 3 c 45.40
Kronprinz Trench	62cSW2 Barleux	N 29 b, d
Krosigk Weg	57dNE3 & 4 Hébuterne	K 24 a, c
Krossen Trench	62bSW3 St Quentin	S 24 b
Kruge Alley	66dNW3 Hattencourt	G 5 c, d, 9 b, 10 a, b, 11 a
Kruger Corner	20SE2 Hooglede	Q 28 d 2.5
Kruiseecke	28NE3 Gheluvelt / SE1 Wervicq	J 36 c, d, P 6 b
Kruiss Estaminet, Au [La Hutte]	28SW4 Ploegsteert	U 14 a 5.4
Kruisstraat [artillery OPs]	28NW4 Ypres	H 18 d 60.35
Kruisstraat Cabaret & crossroads	28SW2 Wytschaete	N 36 b
Kruisstraat Crater [1917]	28SW2 Wytschaete	N 36 a 9.7
Kruisstraat Craters	28SW2 Wytschaete	N 36 a
Krump / Crump Bank [W of Factory Corner]	57cSW1 Gueudecourt	M 24 d
Krupp Alley	66cNW2 Itancourt	B 30 b, d
Krupp Copse	66dNW3 Hattencourt	G 5 d
Krupp Farm	28NW2 St Julien	C 14 a 8.1

Name	Map Sheet	Map Reference
Krupp Trench [1918]	66eNW [4 Morisel]	I 13 b
Krutzer Trench	62bSW3 St Quentin	T 26 c
Kruystraete [farm]	27SE2 Berthen	Q 24 a 1.3
Küchen / Kuechen Weg	51bNW1 Roclincourt	B 25 c
Kuchen Graben	57dNE3 & 4 Hébuterne	K 30 c
Kuffner Weg	28NW4 & NE3 Zillebeke	J 25 a
Kukri Valley	62bNW1 Gouy	B 9 d, 14 b, d, 15 a, c, 20 b
Kulm, Bouay de	66eNE4 Beaufort	L 28 d, 34 b, d, 35 a
Kultur Farm	28NW2 St Julien	C 16 c 75.75
Kuntz Trench / Kuntz, Tranchée	36cSW1 Lens	M 25 b
Kupper Alley [1918]	62dSE [4 Harbonnières]	X 29 a, b
Kurilo Alley	62cNW4 Péronne	I 15 b, 16 a, b
Kurton Trench	36cSW3 Vimy	T 20 a, b
Kurz Graben	57dNE3 & 4 Hébuterne	K 24 c, d
Kurzer Weg	51bNW1 Roclincourt	A 30 b
Kusters Farm	20SE2 Hooglede	R 13 c 9.0
Kut Copse	28NE2 Moorslede	F 25 d 45.10
Kut Lane	57cNE4 Marcoing	K 34 b
Kut Trench	51bNW4 Fampoux	I 13 c, 19 a
Kutno Support	57cNE3 Hermies	K 25 a
Kutno Trench	57cNE3 Hermies	K 19 c, 25 a
Kwaebeek Trench	20SW2 Zwartegat	O 19 a, c, d, 25 b
L 1 [trench, N of Fme Vandenberghe]	28SW2 Wytschaete	N 18 c 4.8
L 2 [trench, N of Fme Vandenberghe]	28SW2 Wytschaete	N 18 a 5.1
L 2 [Wagram Farm]	28NW2 St Julien	B 23 central
L 3 [Brielen]	28NW2 St Julien	B 29
L 3 [trench, NE of Fme Vandenberghe]	28SW2 Wytschaete	N 18 a 7.2
L 4 [trench, NE of Fme Vandenberghe]	28SW2 Wytschaete	N 18 a 8.4
L 5 [Chateau des Trois Tours]	28NW2 St Julien	B 28 central
L 5 [trench, SW of Hollandscheschuur Fm]	28SW2 Wytschaete	N 18 a 8.6
L 6 [trench, SW of Hollandscheschuur Fm]	28SW2 Wytschaete	N 18 a 4.3
L 7 [trench, SW of Hollandscheschuur Fm]	28SW2 Wytschaete	N 18 a 7.6
L 8 [farm south of Brielen]	28NW2 St Julien	H 5 b
L Camp [St Jan-ter-Biezen]	27NE2 Proven	L 2 a [area]
L Line [just West of Ypres Canal]	28NW2 St Julien	B 18, 24, 30, I 1 [approx]
L Wood	66eNW [2 Thennes]	B 29 c, d
L Work	51bNW1 Roclincourt	A 29 b
L.R.B. Cottage [London Rifle Brigade]	28NW2 St Julien	C 23 a 0.3
L.R.B. Cottages [London Rifle Brigade]	36NW2 Houplines	C 1 b 1.1
La Bassée - Aubers - Fromelles Line	36SW1 / 2 / 3 / 36cNW1	extensive
La Bassée Alley	36cNW1 La Bassée	A 4 a, b, d, 5 c, d, 6 c
La Bassée Alley South	36cNW1 La Bassée	A 5 d, 6 c
La Bassée Trench	36cNW1 La Bassée	A 6 b, d, 12 a, b, c, 18 a, b
La Boisselle [Boyau, 1915]	57dSE4 Ovillers	W 18 b, X 13 a
La Boisselle [village]	57dSE4 Ovillers	X 13 d, 14 c
La Brique Camp [1917-18]	28NW2 St Julien	C 26 d
La Clytte [railhead, 1917]	28SW1 Kemmel	N 7 b
La Clytte [village]	28SW1 Kemmel	N 7 a, b, c, d
La Clytte Switch [1918]	28SW1 Kemmel	N 1 b, d, 7 b
La Fère [ramparts trenches]	66cSW4 La Fère	U 19, 20, 26
La Fone Street [Lafone Redoubt M 35 b]	36SW1 Aubers / 3 Richebourg	M 29 c, 35 a, b, d
La Motte [farm, E of Béthune]	36bNE2 Beuvry	E 1 b
La Motte Switch [1918]	36aNE1 Morbecque	D 30 b, d, E 19 c, 25 a, J 6 b
La Nave Trench	36aSW4 [Lillers]	U 12 b, d

Name	Map Sheet	Map Reference
La Targette [hamlet]	57bNW3 Rumilly	H 14 d, 15 c
La Vacquerie [defended village]	57cSE2 Gonnelieu	R 15 d, 16 a
Laamkeek [farm]	28NE1 Zonnebeke	D 10 b 6.6
Laare Farm [Tuimelaarehoek]	28NE2 Moorslede	E 18 d 65.40
Labe Wood Trench	62cNW2 Bouchavesnes	C 21 c, d
Labis Farm	36aNE2 Vieux Berquin	F 13 c 7.9
Lableu [Tr / Boyau, N end of Spinney Trench]	36cSW1 Lens	M 25 b
Labour Trench	57cNE4 Marcoing	L 15 c, d, 21 b
Labour Trench	57dNE3 & 4 Hébuterne	K 16 d, 17 c
Labourse [village]	36bNE4 Noeux-les-Mines	L 2 a, b
Labthi Trench	57cSW4 Combles	U 23 a, b
Labuissière - Houchin - Bouvigny Line	36bNE[1]/3 Bruay/4 Noeux-les-Mines/ SE2 Boyeffles	extensive
Laburnum Lodge	36aSE3 Gonnehem	P 36 d 5.8
Labyrinth, The	20SW1 Loo	M 11 d, 12 c, 17 b, 18 a
Labyrinth, The [redoubt]	51bNW1 Roclincourt	A 21 b
Labyrinth/e Avenue	51bNW1 Roclincourt	A 21 b, c, d, 26 b, 27 a
Labyrinth/e Redoubt	51bNW1 Roclincourt	A 21 b
Lac Trench	66dNW1 Punchy	A 26 b, 27 a
Lace Trench	51bNW1 Roclincourt	A 23 a
Lach Weg [Lucky Way, Thiepval]	57dSE1 & 2 Beaumont	R 14 d, 15 a, c, 19 d, 20 a, b, c
Lachaud, E. [Entonnoir (crater); BFL 3/16]	36cSW1 Lens	M 20 c
Lack Trench	51bNW1 Roclincourt	A 22 b, 23 a
Lackey Avenue	51bNW1 Roclincourt	A 29 b, d
Lacouture [Keep]	36aSE4 Locon	X 5 a
Lacouture [village]	36aSE4 Locon	X 5 a
Lacouture Post	36aSE4 Locon	X 4 b, d, 5 a, c
Ladbroke Grove	36cSW3 Vimy	S 20 b, 21 a
Ladder Farm	28NE2 Moorslede	F 12 a 3.7
Ladder Lane [CT / track]	36bNE2 Beuvry / 36cNW1 La Bassée	F 12 c, A 7 d
Ladder Trench	57cNE4 Marcoing	L 15 b, d
Ladies Lane	12SW1 Nieuport	M 17 d
Ladle Trench	51bNW3 Arras	H 9 a, c
Lady Grey Street	57dSE1 & 2 Beaumont	Q 23 b
Lady Lane	51bSW2 Vis-en-Artois	O 5 a, b, d, 6 c, 12 a
Lady Trench	51bNW1 Roclincourt	A 23 a
Lady's Leg [ravine, E of Irles]	57dNE4 & 57cNW3 Achiet	G 32 d, 33c
Laffitte Alley	62cSW1 Dompierre	N 20 a, c, 26 a, b, d
Lafone [keep, late 1915]	36SW1 Aubers	M 35 b 35.20
Lafone Redoubt	36SW1 Aubers	M 35 b
Lafone Street [late 1915]	36SW1 Aubers	M 28 d, 29 c, 35 a, b
Laft Trench	51bNW1 Roclincourt	A 23 b
Lagache Farm	28SW2 Wytschaete	N 23 d 1.2
Lagarde, Boyau	62cSW1 Dompierre	M 3 d, 4 c
Lager / Laager Alley [Hohenzollern]	36cNW3 Loos	G 5 c
Lager Alley	57dNE3 & 4 Hébuterne	K 35 c, d, 36 c, d, L 31 c
Lager Lane [Alvensleben-Weg]	57cSW3 Longueval	T 7 d, 8 a
Lager Trench [N of Ginchy]	57cSW3 Longueval	T 7 d, 8 a, c, 13 b
Lagnicourt [village]	57cNW2 Vaulx-Vraucourt	C 23 b, d, 24 a, c
Lagnicourt Switch	57cNW2 Vaulx-Vraucourt	C 23 b, d, 29 b, 30 a
Lagnicourt Trench	57cNW2 Vaulx-Vraucourt	C 16 b, d, 17 c, d
Lagoon Farm	36aNE3 Haverskerque	J 9 a 75.70
Lagoon Trench	66cNW4 Berthenicourt	I 13 b
Lagos Cottage	36aNE1 Morbecque	D 12 d 00.75

Name	Map Sheet	Map Reference
Lagouarde, E. [Entonnoir (crater); BFL 3/16]	36cSW1 Lens	M 20 c
Lahore Alley	66dNW1 Punchy	A 6 c, d, 7 a, 12 b
Lahou Trench	66cNW4 Berthenicourt	I 7 d
Laibach Trench	62cNW4 Péronne	I 10 b, d
Laid Alley	66dNW1 Punchy	A 26 b
Laiterie	28SW2 Wytschaete	N 16 d 00.35
Laiterie A.D.S.	28SW2 Wytschaete	N 16 d 1.4
Lake Copse	20SE3 Westroosebeke	W 13 a, b
Lake Farm	28SW2 Wytschaete	O 24 c 5.4
Lake Farm [N of Bellewaarde Lake]	28NW4 & NE3 Zillebeke	I 12 b 5.9
Lake Farm Spur [light rly, Bellewaarde, 1917-18]	28NW4 Ypres	I 12 b
Lake Left Post	62cNE4 Roisel	L 6 c 8.7
Lake Right Post	62bNW3 Bellicourt	G 1 d
Lake Trench	62bSW4 Homblières	T 22 b, d
Lake Trench	62cNE4 Roisel	L 6 c
Lake Trench	66cSW2 Vendeuil	N 24 b, d
Lake Wood [N of Bellewaarde Lake, June 1915]	28NW4 & NE3 Zillebeke	I 12 b
Lake, The [Redoubt, 1918]	51cSE 4 Blaireville	X 30 c
Lalaurie Trench	57dNE3 & 4 Hébuterne	K 17 c
Lalauze Alley	62cNW1 Maricourt	B 27 a, b
Laleau Bridge	36aSE1 St Venant	P 28 d 1.5
Lalost Alley	66cNW2 Itancourt	I 2 a
Lama Wood	62dSW [4 Cachy]	U 22 c, 28 a
Lamatte Farm	20SW4 Bixschoote	T 29 c 6.7
Lamb Post	57cNE1 Quéant	D 21 c
Lamb Post	62cNE4 Roisel	L 24 a 60.15
Lamb Support	57cNE1 Quéant	D 21 c
Lambart Avenue	12SW1 Nieuport	M 17 a
Lambart Lane	12SW1 Nieuport	M 16 d
Lambart Trench	12SW1 Nieuport	M 22 b
Lambart Walk	12SW1 Nieuport	M 22 b
Lambay Farm	66cNW4 Berthenicourt	H 10 d 0.2
Lambay Wood	66cNW3 Essigny / 4 Berthenicourt	H 15 b, d, 16 c
Lambert Alley	51bNW2 Oppy	C 8 c, 13 a, b, 14 a
Lambert Trench [1918]	28SW1 Kemmel	N 9 d, 10 c
Lambouver [sic] / Lanbouver Camp	28NW3 Poperinghe	G 21 a
Lambros Alley	66cNW2 Itancourt	C 15 d, 16 a, 20 b, d, 21 a, b
Lamcourt Trench	66cNW4 Berthenicourt	I 20 b
Lame Copse	62bSW2 Fonsommes	O 26 c
Lamp Post Corner [W of Wytschaete]	28SW2 Wytschaete	unidentified
Lamp Trench	36SW3 Richebourg	T 19 d, 20 c
Lampe Farm	57bSW4 Serain	T 12 d 3.7
Lampernisse [farm]	36NW1 Steenwerck	B 3 a 0.3
Lampions Trench	66dNW1 Punchy	B 1 c, d, 7 a
Lamplugh Farm	20SE3 Westroosebeke	W 7 c 4.4
Lamy Alley	70dNW4 St Gobain	H 30 a
Lanark Avenue [1918]	51bSW3 Boisleux	S 22 b, d
Lanark Lane	51cSE3 & 4 Ransart	W 6 d, 12 b
Lanark Work	51cSE3 & 4 Ransart	W 6 d
Lanbouver Farm	28NW3 Poperinghe	G 21 b 3.2
Lanbouver Farm Camp	28NW3 Poperinghe	G 21 b
Lancas Trench	57dSE4 Ovillers	X 6 c
Lancashire [strongpoint]	36NW1 Steenwerck	H 1 b 85.25
Lancashire Dump	57dSE1 & 2 Beaumont	Q 36 a

Name	Map Sheet	Map Reference
Lancashire Farm	28NW2 St Julien	C 14 c 1.2
Lancashire Farm	36aSE1 St Venant	Q 27 a 5.5
Lancashire Lane	36SW1 Aubers	N 7 c
Lancashire Lane [Zollern Graben]	57dSE1 & 2 Beaumont	R 26 a, b, c
Lancashire Line	36aSE3 Gonnehem / 4 Locon	W 8, 9, 15
Lancashire Post	57dSE1 & 2 Beaumont	Q 24 a
Lancashire Sap	57cSW3 Longueval	S 2 c
Lancashire Support Farm	28SW4 Ploegsteert	U 27 b
Lancashire Trench	57cSE4 Villers-Guislain	X 2 a, c, 8 a, c, d
Lancashire Trench	57cSW3 Longueval	S 1 b, 2 c
Lancashire Trench [Vermelles]	36cNW1 La Bassée / 3 Loos	G 2 b, d, 8 b, d
Lancaster Avenue	57dSE4 Ovillers	W 12 c, d
Lancaster Road	57cSE2 Gonnelieu	Q 11 b
Lancaster Street West & East	62dNE2 Méaulte	F 11 d
Lance Alley	66cNW2 Itancourt	C 25 c, d
Lance Bombe Farm [moat only]	20SW4 Bixschoote	T 10 d 6.3
Lancer Farm [Potijze]	28NW2 St Julien	I 4 b 00.05
Lancer Lane	36cNW3 Loos	G 11 b
Lancer Lane [road]	51bNW4 Fampoux	H 23 d, 29 b, d, 30 c, 36 a, c, d
Lancer Sap	36cNW3 Loos	G 12 c
Lancer Trench	51bNW4 Fampoux	H 23 b, d, 29 b, d, 30 c, 36 a
Lancet Farm	27SE2 Berthen	R 11 c 85.40
Lancier Farm	20SW4 Bixschoote	U 13 d 1.5
Lancing House	20SE2 Hooglede	Q 12 d 6.5
Lancs Trench	57dSE4 Ovillers / 57cSW3 Longueval	X 6 c, S 1 d
Land van Beloften	20SE2 Hooglede	R 7 b
Landerneau Trench	62bSW1 Gricourt / 3 St Quentin	M 36 a, c
Landerneau Trench	66cNW4 Berthenicourt	I 13 a
Landguard / Longuard Trench	57dNE3 & 4 Hébuterne	K 28 b, d
Landing Farm	20SE3 Westroosebeke	V 13 b 5.1
Landing Inn	27NE2 Proven	F 27 b 4.8
Landleague Trench	57dNE1 & 2 Fonquevillers	E 10 d
Lands End [trench / salient]	57cSE2 Gonnelieu	R 20 d 7.7
Landshut Trench	66dNW1 Punchy	A 12 b, d, B 1 c, 7 a
Landshut Wood	66dNW1 Punchy	A 12 b, d, B 7 a, c
Landsturm Graben	57dNE1 & 2 Fonquevillers	E 29 b, c, d, 30 a, b, F 25 a
Landsturm Trench	57cSW4 Combles	T 5 b, 6 a
Landwehr Avenue	36cSW3 Vimy	S 14 c, d
Landwehr Graben	57dNE1 & 2 Fonquevillers	E 12 b, c, d
Landwehr Stellung	57dNE3 & 4 Hébuterne	K 30 c, 36 a
Landwehr Trench	57cSW4 Combles	N 35 a, c, d
Landwehr Weg	51bNW1 Roclincourt	A 18 d
Landwehr, Boyau de la	36cSW3 Vimy	S 14 d
Lane Alley	36cNW1 La Bassée	A 28 b, 29 a
Lane, The [trench]	36cNW1 La Bassée	A 21 c, d
Lang Farm	28NE4 Dadizeele	K 3 d 70.65
Lange, De [tranchée]	66cNW2 Itancourt	C 25 c, d
Langemarck [village]	20SW4 Bixschoote	U 22 d, 23 c, 28 b, 29 a
Langemarck German Cemetery	20SW4 Bixschoote	U 16 d, 22 b
Langemarck Road [military road / track 1917-18]	20SW4 Bixschoote / SE3 Westroosebeke	U 17, 18, 23, V 7, 13
Langemarck Station	20SW4 Bixschoote	U 22 c
Langer Graben	57dNE3 & 4 Hébuterne	K 30 c, d, 36 a
Langewaade [place name]	20SW4 Bixschoote	T 6 b
Langouste Trench	66dNW3 Hattencourt	G 30 b, c, d, 36 a, H 20 c, 25 a,

Name	Map Sheet	Map Reference
		b, 26 a
Langton Barracks	62cNW2 Bouchavesnes	C 14 c 3.9
Langton Farm	28NE2 Moorslede	F 27 c 1.5
Languevoisin [village]	66dNW4 Nesle	I 26, 27, 33
Languid Cottage [1918]	28SW1 Kemmel	M 1 d 7.5
Lanka Farm	28NE4 Dadizeele	K 17 b 55.90
Lankhof Château	28NW4 Ypres	I 26 d 05.05
Lankhof Farm	28NW4 Ypres	I 26 d 00.15
Lannay / Lannoy Mill	51bSE1 Saudemont	P 7 a
Lannes Copse	20SW4 Bixschoote	U 9 c 5.0
Lannes Farm	20SW4 Bixschoote	U 9 d 80.88
Lannoy Switch (Projected)	36aSE3 Gonnehem	W 13, 19, 20
Lansdowne Communication Trench	36SW3 Richebourg	S 3 d, 4 c, d, 10 a, b
Lansdowne Post	36SW3 Richebourg	S 3 d, 4 a, c
Lanusse, Boyau	62cNW3 Vaux	G 28 c, d
Lanyard Trench	51bSW2 Vis-en-Artois	O 14 b, d
Lapin Farm	20SW4 Bixschoote	U 25 d 6.4
Lapins Trench	20SW4 Bixschoote	U 25 d, 26 c
Lappe [farm]	27SE2 Berthen	R 4 a 7.4
Laprade, Boyau	36bSE4 Carency	R 33 d, 34 c, d, X 4 b, 5 a, b, 6 a, c
Lapree Wood	62cNW1 Maricourt	A 14 c
Lapwing Post	57cNE1 Quéant	D 20 c
Larch Copse	62cSW1 Dompierre	M 18 a
Larch Lane	57cSW4 Combles	U 26 b, d
Larch Walk [Leith Walk]	57cSE4 Villers-Guislain	X 16 c
Larch Wood	28NW4 & NE3 Zillebeke	I 29 a, c
Larch Wood Duck Walk	28NW4 & NE3 Zillebeke	I 22 d, 29 a, c
Larch Wood Tunnels / Dugouts	28NW4 & NE3 Zillebeke	I 29 c
Lard Trench	51bNW1 Roclincourt	A 23 a
Lard Trench	57cSW1 Gueudecourt	N 20 b, d
Lard Trench	66dNW1 Punchy	A 4 b
Lardemelle, Tranchée	62cSW1 Dompierre	M 15 a, b
Largo Street	57dSE4 Ovillers	X 13 c, d
Lariat Buildings	28NE2 Moorslede	E 12 a 7.3
Laribeau, Boyau	36cSW1 Lens	M 19 d
Lark Corner	28SW2 Wytschaete	N 24 a
Lark Corner [road junction]	20SE2 Hooglede	R 14 d 12.05
Lark Lane	28SW2 Wytschaete	N 24 a
Lark Lane	51bSW2 Vis-en-Artois / 4 Bullecourt	O 31 a, b, d
Lark Post	57cNE1 Quéant	D 21 c
Lark Post	62cNE2 Epéhy	F 5 b
Lark Spur	57cSE4 Villers-Guislain	X 21, 26, 27
Lark Trench	62cNE2 Epéhy	F 6 a
Larkin Farm	36NW1 Steenwerck	A 6 d 4.6
Larkspur Street	57dSE4 Ovillers	Q 36 d
Larne Cottage	28SW3 Bailleul	T 27 b 4.7
Larne Lines [huts]	28SW3 Bailleul	T 27 b
Larrey Camp	28NW1 Elverdinghe	B 8 d, 9 c
Larrey Farm	28NW1 Elverdinghe	B 9 c 0.8
Larriken Fork [road jct]	28NE2 Moorslede	E 6 d 9.6
Larris / Lapris Trench	62cNE1 Liéramont / 62cNE3 Buire	D 25 d, 26 c, J 2 a, c
Larron Trench	66dNW1 Punchy	A 26 d, 27 a, c
Larve Trench	12SW1 Nieuport	N 14 c
Lasace Alley	66cNW4 Berthenicourt	I 14 b

Name	Map Sheet	Map Reference
Lasalle Farm	20SW4 Bixschoote	U 10 b 1.3
Lasange Trench	51bNW1 Roclincourt	A 10 a, b
Lassagne Alley	62bSW3 St Quentin	M 35 b, c, d
Lassalle Alley	70dNW4 St Gobain	H 29 b, 30 a
Lassalle Avenue	36cSW3 Vimy	S 21 c, d
Lassoo Houses	28NE2 Moorslede	E 12 a 70.65
Lassudie Trench	36cSW1 Lens	M 19 b
Last Hope Trench	36cNW1 La Bassée	A 30 d, B 25 c, d, 26 c, d
Lateau Support	57cSE2 Gonnelieu / 57bSW1 Bantouzelle	R 11 a,b,d, 12c, 18a, M 8c, 13b, 14a,b
Lateau Trench	57cSE2 Gonnelieu / 57bSW1 Bantouzelle	R 11 a,b,d, 17b, 18a,c, M 13b,d, 14 a,b
Lateau Wood	57bSW1 Bantouzelle	M 7 d, 8 c, 13 b, 14 a
Lath Trench	51bNW1 Roclincourt	A 23 a
Lathe Alley	57cNE4 Marcoing	L 9 c
Lathe Trench	57cNE4 Marcoing	L 8 b, d, 9 c, 15 a, b, d
Lather Trench	57cNE4 Marcoing	L 28 d, 29 c
Latin Farm	28NW3 Poperinghe	G 9 d 5.4
Latte Wood	66dNW3 Hattencourt	H 26 a, c
Laudetbeek Street	20SW4 Bixschoote	U 18 c, 24 a
Lauenbourg Trench	62bSW3 St Quentin	T 7 a, b, c
Lauenburg Riegel	51bSW1 Neuville Vitasse	M 20 d, 21 a, c
Laughton Farm	20SE2 Hooglede	Q 21 b 75.60
Laundes Avenue	36NW2 Armentières	C 2 a, b, d
Laundry & Baths [Brownlow Farm]	28SW3 Bailleul	T 28 a
Laundry Post [Blangy NW]	51bNW3 Arras	G 17 d 4.1
Laundry Post [south of Béthune]	36bNE2 Beuvry	E 23 b, d
Laurance [sic] Avenue [1918]	51bNW1 Roclincourt	A 29 c, d, G 5 b
Laurel Lane [1918]	51cSE [4] / 57dNE [2 Courcelles]	X 27 c, F 3 a
Laurel Trench	51bNW3 Arras	H 9 a, b, c
Laurels Alley	66dNW1 Punchy	A 27 a, b, d
Laurence Farm [Churchill's Bn HQ]	28SW4 Ploegsteert	U 27 c 4.9
Laurent House	20SW4 Bixschoote	T 24 a
Lauriers, les [farm]	36aNE3 Haverskerque	K 14 d 91.07
Lava Trench	36cSW3 Vimy	S 8 b
Laval Farm	27NE4 Abeele	L 21 c 4.0
Lavé Wood	66dNW3 Hattencourt	H 25 a
Lavender Bend [road jct]	27NE2 Proven	F 11 b 3.3
Lavender Lane [Sept 1915]	36cNW1 La Bassée	A 8 d
Lavender Road	57dNE1 & 2 Fonquevillers	E 11 a
Lavender Trench	36aSE1 St Venant / 3 Gonnehem	P 32 a, c, d, V 2 b
Laventie East Post	36SW1 Aubers	M 5 central
Laventie North Post	36NW3 Fleurbaix	G 34 b, 35 a
Laventie-Fleurbaix-Houplines Line [1918]	36NW3 Fleurbaix	extensive
Lavice [Boyau, 1915, La Boisselle] / Tay Street	57dSE4 Ovillers	X 19 b
Lavielle Trench / Alley [1918]	66eNW [2 Thennes]	B 23 c
Law Houses	28NE2 Moorslede	L 5 a 0.5
Law Lane [road]	36aSE2 Lestrem	R 8 b, d, 13 b, 14 a
Law Trench	51bNW1 Roclincourt	A 23 a
Law Trench	57cNE4 Marcoing	L 22 c, d, 28 b
Law Trench	66dNW1 Punchy	A 5 c
Lawrence [sic; Laurence] Farm [Churchill's Bn HQ]	28SW4 Ploegsteert	U 27 c 4.9
Lawrence Farm	28NW3 Poperinghe	G 11 c 6.5
Lawrence Trench	12SW1 Nieuport	M 17 c
Laws Lane [road]	36aSE2 Lestrem	R 8 d, 13 b, 14 a
Lawson O.P. [1917-18]	36cSW3 Vimy	M 36 c 3.7

Name	Map Sheet	Map Reference
Lawyers Corner [road jct]	28NE2 Moorslede	L 4 b 4.1
Lay Trench	51bNW1 Roclincourt	A 22 b
Layes Bridge Redoubt	36SW3 Richebourg	M 36 c
Layes Post	36SW1 Aubers	N 9 b
Laynbok Camp	28SW3 Bailleul	T 3 b 2.9
Lazarel Alley	70dNW4 St Gobain	I 25 b, 26 a
Lazy Trench	12SW1 Nieuport	M 17 c
Le Barque [village]	57cSW1 Gueudecourt	M 12 b, d, N 7 a, c
Le Barque Switch	57cSW1 Gueudecourt	M 11 c, d, 12 c, d
Le Berre [Tranchée, 1915] / Buddon Street	57dSE4 Ovillers	X 19 d
Le Binan [Tranchée, 1915] / Scone Street	57dSE4 Ovillers	X 19 b
Le Bosquet	57bSW1 Bantouzelle	M 4 d, 5 c
Le Bot [Tranchée, 1915] / Elie Street	57dSE4 Ovillers	X 13 a, c
Le Breton [Tranchée, W of Fricourt, 1915]	62dNE2 Méaulte	F 2 c
Le Cateau [town]	57bNE4 [Le Cateau]	L 34
Le Catelet - Nauroy Line	57bSW1 Bantouzelle/3 Honnecourt/ 62bNW1 Gouy	extensive
Le Cornet - Bourdois Locality	36aSW2 [Molinghem] / 4 [Lillers]	O 34, 35
Le Cornet - Brassart Locality	36aSW2 [Molinghem]	O 22, 28
Le Forest [village]	62cNW2 Bouchavesnes	B 10 d, 11 c, 16 b
Le Gheer Trench	28SW4 Ploegsteert	U 21 b, d, 27 b
Le Goff [Tranchée, 1915] / Dalhousie Street S.	57dSE4 Ovillers	X 19 c
Le Guyader [Boyau, 1915] / Scourinburn	57dSE4 Ovillers	X 19 d
Le Hamel [hamlet]	36aSE4 Locon	X 20 d, 21 c
Le Hamel N.W. [post]	36aSE4 Locon	X 19 b, 20 a
Le Joleo [Boyau, 1915] / Inch Street	57dSE4 Ovillers	X 19 b
Le Mere [Trench]	57dNE1 & 2 Fonquevillers	E 11 a
Le Mesnil-en-Arrouaise [village]	57cSW4 Combles	U 4 b, d, 5 a, c
Le Pavé	57cSE2 Gonnelieu	R 17 d
Le Peuplier Line [1918]	27SE3 Borre	extensive
Le Pire Locality	36aSW4 [Lillers]	U 5, 6
Le Plantin [village]	36cNW1 La Bassée	A 2 c, 8 a
Le Preol [hamlet]	36bNE2 Beuvry	F 10 c
Le Preol Keep	36bNE2 Beuvry	F 16 b 92.56 to F 17 a 1.6
Le Quennet Farm	57bSW1 Bantouzelle	M 7 b, d
Le Quesnoy [village]	36bNE2 Beuvry	F 8 b
Le Quesnoy Keep	36bNE2 Beuvry	F 8 b 7.3
Le Quesnoy-en-Santerre [village]	66eNE4 Beaufort	L 25 d, 26 c
Le Sars [village]	57cSW1 Gueudecourt	M 15 d, 16 c, 21 b
Le Sars Lane	57cSW1 Gueudecourt	M 16 c, d
Le Touquet Salient	36NW2 & NE1 Houplines	C 4, 10, 11
Le Touret [hamlet]	36aSE4 Locon	X 16 b, d
Le Touret Central Post	36aSE4 Locon	X 16 central
Le Touret North Post	36aSE4 Locon	X 10 b
Le Transloy [village]	57cSW2 Villers-au-Flos	N 30 a, b, c, d, O 25 a, c
Le Tronquoy [village]	62bSW1 Gricourt	N 2 d, 3 c, 8 b, 9 a
Le Verguier Switch	62cNE4 Roisel / SE2 Vermand	L 33 d, 34 c, R 9 d, 15 b
Lea Post	62cNE1 Lièramont	E 26 a 7.7
Lea Trench	51bNW1 Roclincourt	A 23 a
Leadhall Copse	28NE4 Dadizeele	K 23 b, 24 a
Leaf Lane / Trench	51bSW1 Neuville Vitasse	N 19 a
Leaf Lane [1918]	57dNE2 [Courcelles]	F 13 b, 14 a
Leaf Wood	62cSE4 [Attilly]	X 1 d, 2 c, 7 b, 8 a
League Wood	28NE2 Moorslede	E 5 c

Name	Map Sheet	Map Reference
Lealholm House	28NE4 Dadizeele	L 14 d 25.15
Lealou Reserve [Lealvillers & Louvencourt]	57dSW [2 Raincheval]	O 10 b, d, 17 a
Lealou Support [Lealvillers & Louvencourt]	57dSW [2 Raincheval]	O 11 a, c, 17 a, b, 18 a, c
Lealou Trench [Lealvillers & Louvencourt]	57dSW [2 Raincheval]	O 11 a, c, d, 17 b, 18 a, c
Leam Farm	36aNE4 Merville	L 17 c 65.00
Lean Sap	57cSW3 Longueval	S 1 d
Lean Trench	12SW1 Nieuport	M 17 b
Lean Wood	66eNW [4 Morisel]	H 16 c
Leaning Tower	28SW2 Wytschaete	O 23 c 3.7
Leaning Tree	57dNE3 & 4 Hébuterne	K 30 c 97.64
Leapfrog Wood	27NE2 Proven	F 4 a
Lear Copse	27SE2 Berthen	R 20 b
Leauwerk Farm	28SW4 Ploegsteert	T 10 d 4.3
Leave Avenue	57dSE1 & 2 Beaumont	Q 5 c, d, 6 c, d
Leaver Lane	36cSW1 Lens	M 25 d
Lebucquière [village]	57cNW4 Beugny	I 24 c, d, 30 a, b
Lechelle [village]	57cSE1 Bertincourt	P 25 c
L'Eclème - Hinges - Béthune Line	36aSE3 Gonnehem	V 5, 6, W 1, 7, 8, 9
Lécluse [village]	51bNE3 Noyelle-sous-Bellonne / SE1 Saudemont	J 36 b, c, d, K 31 c, P 6 a, b, Q 1 a
Lecoindre Alley	66cNW1 Grugies / 2 Itancourt	B 21 b, 22 a
Léda Trench	66dNW3 Hattencourt	H 14 d, 20 b, d, 26 a, b
Ledeghem [village]	28NE4 Dadizeele	L 2 c, 8 a, b, d
Ledeghem Station	28NE4 Dadizeele	L 8 a
Ledger Copses	27SE2 Berthen	Q 22 b
Leduc Trench	62bSW1 Gricourt	M 9 d, 15 b
Lee Farm	28SW3 Bailleul	S 21 b 60.25
Lee Farm Camp	28SW3 Bailleul	S 21 b, 22 a
Lee Trench	36cSW3 Vimy	S 6 a
Leech Alley	57cNE4 Marcoing	L 9 b, c, d
Leech Avenue	57cNE1 Quéant	D 20 c, 26 a, c
Leech Lane	57cNE1 Quéant	D 26 a, b
Leech Post	57cNE1 Quéant	D 20 c
Leech Trench	57cNE4 Marcoing	L 9 c, d
Leeds [locality]	51bNW1 Roclincourt	A 8 c
Leeds [Trench / Post]	51bNW1 Roclincourt	B 10 c
Leeds Avenue / Boyau Leeds	62cNW1 Maricourt	A 14 a
Leeds Reserve	57cNW2 Vaulx-Vraucourt	C 11 d, 17 b, 18 a
Leeds Trench [1918]	57dNE2 & 57cNW1 Courcelles	F 20 b, d, 25 b, 26 a
Leeds Trench [Thiepval Wood]	57dSE1 & 2 Beaumont	R 19 c, 25 a
Leek Farm	27NE2 Proven	E 10 c 4.4
Leek Trench	57cSW1 Gueudecourt	N 27 c
Leek Way	57dSE1 & 2 Beaumont	Q 11 d, 17 b
Leek Wood	51bSE4 Marquion	W 18 b, X 13 a
Leeming Lane	28SW2 Wytschaete	N 23 d
Leene Inn	27NE4 Abeele	L 17 d 8.4
Lees Redoubt [Sept 1915]	36cNW1 La Bassée	A 2 d
Leeuwerik Inn	27NE2 Proven	F 4 a 83.65
Leeuwerk Farm	28SW4 Ploegsteert	T 10 d 4.3
Leeward House	28NW4 Ypres	H 4 d 7.2
Lefebvre Trench	66cNW4 Berthenicourt	H 10 b
Left Alley [Bazentin-le-Petit Wood]	57cSW3 Longueval	S 7 d
Left Boyau [Hohenzollern]	36cNW1 La Bassée / 3 Loos	G 3 d, 4 a, b
Left Support Trench	36NW2 Armentières	C 10 c

Name	Map Sheet	Map Reference
Leg Copse	28SW2 Wytschaete	O 20 b
Leg Lane	51bSW4 Bullecourt	U 19 d, 25 a, b, c
Leg of Mutton Wood	62cNW2 Bouchavesnes	C 13 a
Leg Trench	51bNW1 Roclincourt	A 23 a
Leg Trench	51bNW2 Oppy / 4 Fampoux	I 2 a, c
Legal Farm	28NE2 Moorslede	F 13 b 5.1
Legal Trench	57cNE4 Marcoing	L 1 c, d, 2 c, d, 8 b
Legend Trench	57dNE3 & 4 Hébuterne	K 28 d, 34 b
Leger Farm	28NW3 Poperinghe	H 20 a 8.5
Leger Reserve [1918]	51bSW4 Bullecourt	T 22 a, b, d, 28 b, 29 a, c
Leger Trench [1918]	51bSW4 Bullecourt	T 22 c, 28 a, b, d
Legh Trench	51bNW3 Arras	G 18 a
Legret Trench	70dNW4 St Gobain	H 36 b, d
Lehaucourt [village]	62bNW3 Bellicourt / SW1 Gricourt	H 31 d, 32 c, N 1 b
Lehaucourt Ridge	62bNW3 Bellicourt	H 26, 31, 32
Lehmann Graben	57dNE3 & 4 Hébuterne	K 5 c
Lehrman [Etch] Trench	57dNE1 & 2 Fonquevillers / 3 & 4 Hébut'ne	K 5 a, c
Leiberweg [Cocoa Lane]	57cSW3 Longueval	T 7 a
Leicester [lt rly locality W of Pilckem 1917-18]	28NW2 St Julien	C 2 a, b
Leicester Farm	28NW3 Poperinghe	H 15 c 5.8
Leicester Square [Fosse Wood]	28NW4 & NE3 Zillebeke	I 29 b 3.8
Leicester Square [Sept 1915]	36cNW1 La Bassée	A 15 d
Leicester Street	57dNE1 & 2 Fonquevillers	E 28 a
Leich / Leigh Sap	36cNW1 La Bassée	A 21 d
Leidold Weg	57dNE1 & 2 Fonquevillers	E 28 b, d
Leinster [light rly terminus, 1917-18]	28NW4 Ypres	I 17 a
Leinster Farm	28NW4 & NE3 Zillebeke	I 17 a 8.3
Leinster Lane [Sap 73A]	36cNW3 Loos	G 19 c
Leinster Road [plank road, 1917-18]	28NW4 Ypres	I 17 a, c, 22 b, 23 a
Leinster Road [road]	28SW3 Bailleul / 4 Ploegsteert	T 15 c, d, 21 b, d, 27 b, d
Leinster Street	28NW4 & NE3 Zillebeke	I 17 a, b, d
Leinster Trench	28NW4 & NE3 Zillebeke	I 17 a
Leipzig Farm	28NW2 St Julien	B 23 c
Leipzig Redoubt	57dSE4 Ovillers	R 31 c, d, X 1 a, b
Leipzig Salient	57dSE4 Ovillers	R 31 c, d, X 1 a, b
Leipziger Nase	70dSW [2 Coucy-le-Château]	O 28 c
Leith Fort	57dSE4 Ovillers	X 16 d
Leith Post	36NW4 Bois Grenier	I 10 c
Leith Walk	36NW4 Bois Grenier	I 9 c, d, 10 c, 16 a
Leith Walk	57cSW3 Longueval	S 4 c, 10 a
Leith Walk [road]	57cSE4 Villers-Guislain	X 13 c, d, 14 c, d, 15 a, c, d
Lejeune Trench	66cNW1 Grugies / 2 Itancourt	B 15 c, d, 16 c, 22 a
Lemberg Trench	36cSW3 Vimy	S 15
Lemberg Trench	57dSE4 Ovillers	R 31 c, X 1 a, b
Lemberger Graben	51bNW3 Arras	G 12 a
Lemco Trench	36cSW1 Lens	M 19 b
Lemco Trench	57cSW3 Longueval / 4 Combles	T 16 a
Lemnos House	20SE3 Westroosebeke	V 19 a
Lemoel Alley	66cNW1 Grugies	B 7 a
Lemon Lane [1918]	57dNE2 [Courcelles]	F 2 d
Lemon Trench	51bNW4 Fampoux	H 10 d, 11 a, c
Lemon Valley	62bSW3 St. Quentin	S 16 b, c, d
Lempire Centre Post	62cNE2 Epéhy	F 16 b
Lempire East Post	62cNE2 Epéhy	F 10 d

Name	Map Sheet	Map Reference
Lempire Road [road]	62cNE2 Epéhy	F 4 b, c, 10 a, c
Lempire West Post	62cNE2 Epéhy	F 16 a
Lemur Cottage	28NW3 Poperinghe	G 18 a 4.9
Lena Wood	62dSE [1 Hamel]	Q 20 a
Lencif Trench	62cSW4 St. Christ	U 15 d, 21 b
Lenet House	20SW4 Bixschoote	T 24 a 7.6
L'Enfer [farm, hill & trenches]	28SW2 Wytschaete	O 25 d
Lennarré [Boyau, 1915] / Stonehaven Street	57dSE4 Ovillers	X 26 c
Lens [town]	36cSW1 Lens	N 14, 20, 21
Lens Road [road]	36cSW1 Lens	M 24 a, b, N 19 a, b
Lens Road Keep	36cNW3 Loos	G 20 c, d
Lens Road Redoubt	36cNW3 Loos	G 34 a
Lens Station	36cSW1 Lens	N 20 b
Lens Trench	28NE1 Zonnebeke	D 19 a, b
Lens Trench	57dNE1 & 2 Fonquevillers	E 11 a
Lens Trench	70dNW [3 Sinceny]	H 9 b, c, 15 a, c
Lensbeth Spur [light rly]	36cSW1 Lens	M 6 c
Lenthumy Salient	70dNW4 St Gobain	H 11 c, d
Lentil Farm	28NE2 Moorslede	E 12 b 5.4
Lenwick / Lerwick Street	57dSE1 & 2 Beaumont	Q 4 c
Leonards Farm	20SE2 Hooglede	Q 4 c 9.6 to Q 4 d 02.56
Leonidas Trench	70dNW4 St Gobain	H 30 c, 36 a
Leopard Avenue	20SW4 Bixschoote	U 17 a
Leopard Avenue	57cNE1 Quéant	E 21 c, 27 a, c
Leopard Huts	20SW4 Bixschoote	U 16 d 7.4
Leopard Lane	51bSW1 Neuville Vitasse	N 21 c
Leopard Post	57cNE1 Quéant	D 20 c
Leopard Support	57cNE1 Quéant	D 19 b, d, 20 c
Leopard Trench	20SW4 Bixschoote	U 16 d, 17 c, 23 a
Leopard Trench	36aSE3 Gonnehem	V 7 b, 8 a
Leopard Wood	62dSW [4 Cachy]	U 21 d
Leopold, Tranchée	62cSW1 & 2 Belloy	N 18 c, 24 a
Lepage, Boyau	70dSW [4 Vauxaillon]	U 27 b
l'Epinette Post	36aSE4 Locon	X 24 a
Leprince Farm [Béhagnies]	57cNW1 Gomiecourt	H 2 a 2.4
Lère, Boyau de [Bird Cage Walk]	36cSW1 Lens	M 14 c
Lère, Tranchée [Stafford Trench, SW end of]	36cSW1 Lens	M 20 b
Leroy Trench[1918]	66eNW [2 Thennes]	B 23 a, b
Les Brébis [village]	36bNE4 Noeux-les-Mines	L 35 a, b, c, d
Lesage Farm	36aNE2 Vieux Berquin	F 13 b 3.7
Lesboeufs [village]	57cSW3 Longueval / 4 Combles	T 4 a, b, c, d
Lesboeufs Road [road, Le Transloy]	57cSW2 Villers-au-Flos	N 30 c
Lesdain [village]	57bNW3 Rumilly / SW1 Bantouzelle	G 36 d, H 31 c, d, M 6 b, N 1 a, b
Leska Alley / Boyau de Leska	62cSW2 Barleux	O 1 d, 2 c
l'Esperance [farm / hamlet]	62bNW4 Ramicourt	I 22 b 9.0
Lesson Farm	28NE2 Moorslede	F 5 c 65.75
Lest Trench	51bNW1 Roclincourt	A 23 a
Lestrem Post	36aSE2 Lestrem	R 9 c
Lethbridge Road [road]	36cSW2 Harnes / 4 Rouvroy	N 28 c, 34 a, b, d
Lett Farm	36NW1 Steenwerck	B 25 c 3.6
Leuze Trench	20SW1 Loo	N 1 d, 7 a, b, c
Leuze Trench [Leuzenche Trench]	57cSW3 Longueval	T 27 a, c
Leuze Wood [Lousy Wood]	57cSW3 Longueval	T 20, 21, 26, 27
Leuzenche Trench	57cSW3 Longueval	T 27 a, c

Name	Map Sheet	Map Reference
Leval Cottage	28SW4 Ploegsteert	U 15 c 2.9
Levant Trench	66dNW1 Punchy	A 26 b, c, d
Level Farm	28NW3 Poperinghe	G 11 b 8.8
Leveque Alley [1918]	66eNW [4 Morisel]	H 4 c
Levergies [village]	62bNW4 Ramicourt	H 28 c, d, 34 a, b
Levergies Valley	62bNW3 Bellicourt	H 33 b, c, d
Leverrier [Tranchée / Boyau]	36cSW1 Lens	M 25 d
Levey House	28NW1 Elverdinghe	G 5 a 8.3
Levi Cotts	28NE1 Zonnebeke	D 21 a 8.3
Levis Road [road]	36cSW1 Lens	N 26 d, 32 a
Levrette, la [farm]	27SE2 Berthen	R 29 b 5.6
Lévy Alley	66cNW1 Grugies	B 7 a, c
Levy Camp	27NE4 Abeele	L 14 c, d
Lewen Street	62cNW1 Maricourt	A 8 c
Lewer Farm	36NW1 Steenwerck	A 24 a 75.95
Lewis Alley	36bNE2 Beuvry / 36cNW1 La Bassée	F 30 a, A 25 b, 26 a, b, d, 27 c, d
Lewis Farm	28SW3 Bailleul	S 18 a 3.0
Lewis House	28NE3 Gheluvelt	J 21 d 1.4
Lewis Keep [1917-18]	36cNW1 La Bassée	A 26 b 3.1
Lewis Keep [Sept 1915]	36cNW1 La Bassée	A 26 a, b
Lewisham Lodge	28SW4 Ploegsteert	U 20 b
Lexden Street / Boyau Lexde [sic]	62cNW1 Maricourt	A 16 a, b
Leyton Spinney	57dSW [2 Raincheval / 4 Toutencourt]	O 32, 33
Lezards Trench	66dNW1 Punchy	A 26 b, d
Liaison / Liason [sic] Avenue [1916]	28SW4 Ploegsteert	U 8 c, 14 a
Liaison Avenue	20SW3 Oostvleteren	T 21 b, d
Liaison Farm	20SW4 Bixschoote	U 5 b 05.55
Liaison, Boyau de [Link Alley]	36cSW1 Lens	M 32 a
Liancourt Wood	66dNW3 Hattencourt	G 24, H 13, 19
Lianes Wood	66dNW3 Hattencourt	H 25 d, 26 c
Liason [sic] Avenue	28SW4 Ploegsteert	U 14 a
Libel Houses	28NE2 Moorslede	F 17 a 9.8
Lichfield [light railway locality 1917-18]	28NW2 St Julien	L 18 b
Lichfield Crater	51bNW1 Roclincourt	A 4 c 9.9
Lichfield Trench	51bNW1 Roclincourt	A 4 c
Lick Trench	51bNW1 Roclincourt	A 23 a
Licorne Wood	66dNW3 Hattencourt	H 20 a, b, c, d
Licorne, Tranchée / Tranchée de la Licorne	62cSW3 & 4 Marchélepot	T 23 b, d, 24 a, 29 b, d
Licourt [village]	62cSW3 & 4 Marchélepot	T 30
Lid Trench	51bNW1 Roclincourt	A 23 a
Lid Trench / Lane	51bSW2 Vis-en-Artois	O 1 b, 2 a, c
Liddel Trench	57cSW3 Longueval	S 29 d, 30 c
Lie Trench	51bNW1 Roclincourt	A 23 a
Liége Farm	20SW3 Oostvleteren	T 16 a 2.5
Liéramont Trench	62cNE1 Liéramont	D 11 a, b, d, 12 c, 18 a
Lieutenant Alley	62bSW3 St Quentin	S 6 b, d, T 1 a
Lievens Farm	20SE2 Hooglede	R 11 d 15.30
Liévin - Lens Road [road]	36cSW1 Lens	M 23 b, c, d, 24 a, b
Liévin [mining town]	36cSW1 Lens	M 22, 23, 27, 28, 29
Lift Bridge [over Nieppe Canal]	36aNE3 Haverskerque	J 10 a 50.65
Light Trench	36SW3 Richebourg	T 2 c
Lightning Trench	57cSW3 Longueval	T 1 c, 7 a
Lightning Trench	57cSW4 Combles	T 18 a, b, U 13 a, c, d, 14 c
Ligny Street	57dNE3 & 4 Hébuterne	K 28 b, 29 a

Name	Map Sheet	Map Reference
Ligny-en-Cambresis [village]	57bNW4 Caudry / SW2 Clary	I 33 c, d, 34 c, O 3 a, b, 4 a
Ligny-Thilloy [village]	57cSW1 Gueudecourt	N 1 c, 7 a, b
Lihons [village]	62cSW3 Vermandovillers / 66dNW1 Punchy	S 26 c, A 2 a
Lilac Cotts	28NE1 Zonnebeke	D 20 b 25.95
Lilac Post	36NW4 Bois Grenier	I 9 d, 15 b
Lilac Trench	51bNW3 Arras	H 9 b
Lilas, les [farm]	20SW4 Bixschoote	U 7 d 7.0
Lille Gate [Ypres]	28NW4 Ypres	I 14 c
Lille Street	57dNE1 & 2 Fonquevillers	E 11 c
Lille, Poste de	51bNW1 Roclincourt	A 15 d, 16 c, 21 b, 22 a
Liller Graben	51bNW3 Arras	G 12 a
Lilly Farm	20SE2 Hooglede	R 21 c 8.7
Lilwall Farm	28NE2 Moorslede	F 27 d 8.6
Lily Elsie Trench	36cSW3 Vimy / 4 Rouvroy	T 10 c, 16 a
Lily Lane [1918]	57dNE2 & 57cNW1 Courcelles	F 2 b, 3 a
Lily Road	57dNE1 & 2 Fonquevillers	E 11 a
Lily Trench	62bNW3 Bellicourt	G 20 d, 21 c, 27 a
Limb Farm	28NE2 Moorslede	E 16 c 1.2
Limb Trench	51bNW1 Roclincourt	A 23 a
Limber Farm	27SE2 Berthen	R 28 d 35.50
Limberlost Wood	62cNW4 Péronne	H 18 b, d, I 13 a, c
Limbo Cottage	36NW1 Steenwerck	A 9 a 6.3
Limbourg Trench	20SW1 Loo	N 8 c, 13 b, d, 14 a, 19 a, b
Limbourg, Boyau	36cSW1 Lens	M 9 c
Lime Avenue	51bNW4 Fampoux	H 36 a, c, d
Lime Street	36cSW3 Vimy	S 14 b
Lime Street	57dNE1 & 2 Fonquevillers	E 11 a
Lime Street	57dSE4 Ovillers	X 1 a
Lime Street [road]	36aSE4 Locon	W 6 d, 12 b, X 7 a
Lime Trench	57cSW1 Gueudecourt	N 13 b, c, d
Limerick Junction	57dSE1 & 2 Beaumont	Q 10 c
Limerick Lane	51cSE3 & 4 Ransart	W 6 d, X 1 c
Limerick Lane	57cSE4 Villers-Guislain	X 21 b, c, d
Limerick Post	57cSE4 Villers-Guislain	X 21 d 5.3
Limerick Trench	57cSE4 Villers-Guislain	X 21 b, d
Limetree Corner [road jct]	28NE4 Dadizeele	L 24 a 6.1
Limpet Copse	27NE2 Proven	F 2 b, 3 a
Limpit Trench	51bNW3 Arras	H 9 b
Limpsfield Farm	28NE4 Dadizeele	K 23 c 55.65
Lincoln Avenue [Oct-Nov 1917]	57cSE2 Gonnelieu	Q 18 b, c, d, R 7 c, 13 a
Lincoln Lane	51cSE3 & 4 Ransart	W 12 a, b
Lincoln Lane	57dNE1 & 2 Fonquevillers	E 28 a
Lincoln Redoubt [La Boisselle]	57dSE4 Ovillers	X 15 c, 21 a
Lincoln Reserve	51bSW4 Bullecourt	U 13 b
Lincoln Reserve [1918; formerly Lincoln Avenue]	57cSE2 Gonnelieu	Q 18 b, c, d, 23 d, 24 a, c, R 7 c, 13 a
Lincoln Support	51bSW4 Bullecourt	U 13 a, b, d
Lincoln Switch	51bSW4 Bullecourt	U 13 b
Lincoln Switch	57cNE4 Marcoing	K 17 d, 18 a, c
Lincoln Trench	36cNW3 Loos	G 4 d
Lincoln Trench	57cSW4 Combles	T 6 a
Lincoln Work	51cSE3 & 4 Ransart	W 12 a
Lind Cott.	20SE3 Westroosebeke	V 22 a 45.25
Lindauer Weg	51bNW1 Roclincourt	G 6 b, d
Linde Goed Farm	28NW3 Poperinghe	G 17 c 5.7

Name	Map Sheet	Map Reference
Lindenhoek [hamlet]	28SW1 Kemmel	N 27 c, d
Lindenhoek A.D.S.	28SW1 Kemmel	N 27 d 0.8
Lindenhoek Cross Roads	28SW1 Kemmel	N 27 c 9.8
Lindenhoek Guard	28SW3 Bailleul	N 33 c 95.65
Line Alley	51bNW4 Fampoux	I 31 d
Line Farm	28NW3 Poperinghe	G 18 b 55.65
Linen Trench	57cSE4 Villers-Guislain	X 10 b
Ling Alley	62bNW3 Bellicourt	G 27 b, d
Lingard Farm	28NE4 Dadizeele	L 31 c 65.30
Linge Trench / Tranchée du Linge	62cSW2 Barleux	N 29 d, 30 a, b, c
Link Alley	51bNW4 Fampoux	I 31 d
Link Alley [Liaison, Boyau de]	36cSW1 Lens	M 32 a
Link Avenue	57cSW4 Combles	U 28 d
Link Avenue	62cNW2 Bouchavesnes	C 4 b, 5 a
Link Maze	51bNW2 Oppy	C 13 d
Link Trench	51bNW1 Roclincourt	A 23 a
Link Trench	51bNW2 Oppy	C 13 b, c, d, 14 a, b
Linke Graben	51bSW1 Neuville Vitasse	M 22 d
Links Wood	28SE1 Wervicq	P 9 a
Linnet Copse	20SE2 Hooglede	R 21 c 0.3
Linnet Post	57cNE1 Quéant	D 20 c, d
Linnet Valley	57cSE4 Villers-Guislain	X 19, 20
Linseed Trench	36cSW2 Harnes	N 10 b, d
Linsingen Trench	66dNW3 Hattencourt	G 11 b, c, d, 16 b, 17 a
Lint Farm	27SE2 Berthen	Q 24 d 0.7
Lint Trench	51bNW4 Fampoux	H 10 d
Lintel Villa	36aNE1 Morbecque	E 3 b 40.35
Linton Farm	36NW1 Steenwerck	A 4 a 5.2
Linton Road	57dNE1 & 2 Fonquevillers	E 11 a
Linx Trench	51bSW1 Neuville Vitasse	N 1 a, b
Lion d'Or, Au [Estaminet, Ploegsteert]	28SW4 Ploegsteert	U 25 c 85.65
Lion Lane	51bSW1 Neuville Vitasse	N 20 d
Lion Post	57cNE1 Quéant	D 20 d, 21 c
Lion Trench	51bNW3 Arras	H 9 a
Lion Trench	51bSW2 Vis-en-Artois	O 19 a, b, c
Lion Trench	57cNE1 Quéant	E 26 d, 27 a, b, c
Lion Trench	62bNW1 Gouy	A 1 d
Lion Trench	66dNW3 Hattencourt	H 26 a, c, 32 a, c
Lion Wood	62dSW [4 Cachy]	T 29 a, b, d
Lip Trench	51bNW1 Roclincourt	A 23 a
Lipa Trench	62cNW1 Maricourt	B 20 d, 26 b
Liscloghers Lane	57cNE3 Hermies	K 13 d, 14 c
Lisi Trench	36SW3 Richebourg	S 11 c
Lisieux Trench	66cSW2 Vendeuil	O 19 c, 25 a
Listen Copse [by Amiens Inner Defence Line]	62dSW [1 Longueau]	N 1 d
Listère Trench	62cSW3 Vermandovillers	T 3 d, 9 b
Litchfield [lt rly locality W of Canal 1917-18]	28NW2 St Julien	B 18 d
Litter Farm	36NW1 Steenwerck	B 1 d 95.40
Littie / Little House	57bSW1 Bantouzelle	N 13 d 7.5
Little Bear [wood]	62bNW3 Bellicourt	G 34 c
Little Bear [wood]	62dNE2 Méaulte	F 22 d, 28 b
Little Benjamin	62cNE2 Epéhy	F 23 d, 24 c
Little Benjamin Trench	62cNE2 Epéhy	F 23 d
Little Bill	62bNW3 Bellicourt	G 20 c

Name	Map Sheet	Map Reference
Little Bosun Hill	62bSW2 Fonsommes	O 21 a, c
Little Farm	57dNE1 & 2 Fonquevillers	F 8 b 3.2
Little Farm Trench [1918]	57dNE2 [Courcelles]	F 8 a, b, c
Little Gables [farm, near Gables Farm]	20SE2 Hooglede	Q 33 b 9.6
Little House	57bSW1 Bantouzelle	N 13 d 8.5
Little Street	57dSE1 & 2 Beaumont	Q 16 c
Little Trench	57dNE4 & 57cNW3 Achiet	G 13 d, 14 c
Little Warren	62cNW3 Vaux	H 19 c
Little Welsh Chapel	36cNW1 La Bassée	A 2 c 2.7
Little Willie [Hohenzollern Redoubt]	36cNW1 La Bassée	G 4 b
Little Wood	57cSE1 Bertincourt	P 26 a, b, c, d
Little Wood	62cNW4 Péronne / SW2 Barleux	H 36 d, N 6 b
Little Wood [W of Warlencourt-Eaucourt]	57dSE2 & 57cSW1 Le Sars	M 9 d, 10 c
Little Wyre Street / Boyau Petit Wyre	62cNW1 Maricourt	A 16 a
Little 'Z'	57dNE1 & 2 Fonquevillers	E 23 c
Little 'Z' British Cemetery	57dNE1 & 2 Fonquevillers	E 23 c 35.30
Livarot Trench	66cSW4 La Fère	T 29 b, d 30 a, c
Liver Trench	57dSE4 Ovillers / 57cSW3 Longueval	R 36 c, X 6 a, S 1 b
Liverpool [light rly locality]	36cSW3 Vimy	S 20 b
Liverpool [lt rly locality NW of P'cappelle '17-18]	20SW4 Bixschoote	U 12 d
Liverpool [west strongpoint; Petit Moulin]	36NW1 Steenwerck	H 3 a
Liverpool Avenue	57dSE4 Ovillers	X 1 c, d
Liverpool Camp	28NW4 Ypres	H 35 d
Liverpool Dump	36cSW3 Vimy	S 20 b, 21 c
Liverpool Street	28NW2 St Julien	C 21 d
Liverpool Street	36SW3 Richebourg	S 5 c
Liverpool Street	57cSW3 Longueval	S 10 d, 16 b
Liverpool Street	57dSE4 Ovillers	X 1 b
Liverpool Street / Boyau Liverpool	62cNW1 Maricourt	A 7 d
Liverpool Street [Br FL March 1916]	36cSW1 Lens	M 15 c
Liverpool Street [Sept 1915]	36cNW1 La Bassée	A 15 c
Liverpool Street [Zeude, Tranchée]	36cSW1 Lens	M 15 c
Liverpool Trench	57cSW3 Longueval / 62cNW1 Maricourt	S 29 d, A 5 b
Liverpool Trench	57dNE1 & 2 Fonquevillers	E 11 a, c
Liverpool Trench [Reserve Line]	28NW2 St Julien	C 20 d to C 27 d
Livesay Farm [1918]	28SW1 Kemmel	M 2 a 10.15
Lizard Alley	57cNE1 Quéant	E 26 a
Lizard Alley [1918]	62dSW [4 Cachy]	U 26 a, b, d, 27 a
Lizard Trench	57cNE1 Quéant	E 20 d, 26 b, d
Lizerne [locality]	20SW3 Oostvleteren / 20SW4 Bixschoote	T 22 a, b, c, d
Lizerolles [hamlet]	66cSW1 Remigny	M 6 c, d
Llama Post	57cNE1 Quéant	D 19 b, 20 a
Llandaff Lane	51cSE3 & 4 Ransart	X 1 a
Llandaff Work	51cSE3 & 4 Ransart	X 1 a
Lloyd O.P. [1917-18]	36cSW1 Lens	M 29 b 7.7
Lloyds [farm]	20SE3 Westroosebeke	V 10 c 25.20
Lloyds Avenue [Sept 1915]	36cNW1 La Bassée	A 2 a, b, c
Lloyd's Bank	57cSE4 Villers-Guislain	X 23 a
Lloyds Trench	36cNW3 Loos	G 35 d
Lloyd's Trench	20SE3 Westroosebeke	V 10 c
Load Trench	36cSW2 Harnes	N 10 d, 11 c
Loading Platform	57dSE4 Ovillers	X 1 c
Loaf Copse	62bSW1 Gricourt	M 19 c, 25 a
Loaf Farm	28NE2 Moorslede	E 29 c 3.5

Name	Map Sheet	Map Reference
Loaf Trench	51bNW1 Roclincourt	A 23 a
Loan Trench	51bNW1 Roclincourt	A 23 a
Lob Cottages	28NE2 Moorslede	E 4 b 60.15
Lob Street	57dNE3 & 4 Hébuterne	K 17 d
Lob Trench	51bNW1 Roclincourt	A 23 b
Lobelia Farm	20SE2 Hooglede	R 8 b 5.1
Lobster Farm	36aNE4 Merville	K 22 c 9.4
Lobster Trench	62bSW4 Homblières	T 6 a, c,
Locality 1	28SW4 Ploegsteert	U 14 c
Locality 2 [1916]	28SW4 Ploegsteert	U 14 a
Locality 3	28SW4 Ploegsteert	U 7 c
Loch Camp	57cNW4 Beugny	H 30 a
Lochaws Street	57dSE4 Ovillers	Q 36 d
Lochnagar Crater	57dSE4 Ovillers	X 20 a
Lochnagar Street	57dSE4 Ovillers	X 20 a, c
Locin House	20SW4 Bixschoote	T 30 b
Lock Alley	66cSW3 Tergnier / 4 La Fère	T 10 a, b, c, d, 12 a, b, c
Lock Barracks	62cNW2 Bouchavesnes	C 9 d
Lock de la Raint [on R. Lawes]	36aSE2 Lestrem	R 16 a 9.9
Lock de l'Etroa [on R. Lawes]	36aSE2 Lestrem	R 21 b 8.2
Lock Hospital [tunnel]	28NW4 & 28NE3 Zillebeke	I 32 a or b
Lock House	36cNW1 La Bassée	A 14 b
Lock Keeper's House [Het Sas]	20SW4 Bixschoote	T 29 a 9.5
Lock Lane [road]	36aSE2 Lestrem	R 13 d, 14 a, b, c, 15 a
Lock Lodge [dugout]	28SW2 Wytschaete	O 6 a
Lock No. 12 [Ypres]	28NW4 Ypres	I 1 d
Lock No. 5	28SW2 Wytschaete	O 12 b 3.6
Lock No. 6	28SW2 Wytschaete	O 6 d 95.05
Lock No. 6 bis	28SW2 Wytschaete	O 6 a 4.5
Lock No. 7	28NW4 Ypres	I 32 b 7.3
Lock No. 8	28NW4 Ypres	I 32 a 9.5
Lock No. 9	28NW4 Ypres	I 19 b
Lock Street [Moeuvres]	57cNE1 Quéant	E 20 b, d
Lock Trench	51bSW2 Vis-en-Artois	O 13 b, d, 14 a
Lock Trench	57cNE3 Hermies / 4 Marcoing	K 15 a, b, 16 a
Locks Nos. 10-11 [Ypres]	28NW4 Ypres	I 7 c
Lockyer Crossing [road across rly]	28NE4 Dadizeele	L 26 a 85.85
Locon [village]	36aSE4 Locon	X 7 a, b, c, d
Locon Road [road]	36aSE2 Lestrem	R 15 a, 21 a, c
Locon Road [road]	36aSE4 Locon	R 32 b, c, d, X 1 b, c, 2 a
Locre [village]	28SW1 Kemmel	M 23 a, c, 29 a
Locre Avenue [trench]	28SW1 Kemmel	M 22 d
Locre Chateau	28SW1 Kemmel	M 28 c 70.45
Locrehof Farm [1918]	28SW1 Kemmel	M 29 d 3.3
Locum Farm	28NE2 Moorslede	F 23 b 75.60
Locust Trench	36aSE3 Gonnehem	V 1 c, d, 7 b
Locust Trench	36cSW2 Harnes	N 10 d
Locust Trench	51bNW3 Arras	H 9 a, b
Locusts Farm, The	36aNE1 Morbecque	E 7 c 7.5
Locusts, The [farm]	36aNE1 Morbecque	E 7 c 7.4
Lodge [Ploeg. Wood 1914-15]	28SW4 Ploegsteert	U 21 b
Lodge Farm	28NE3 Gheluvelt	J 28 a 3.2
Lodi Farm	28NW2 St Julien	B 24 d
Log / Lag Trench	36cNW3 Loos	G 12 c

Name	Map Sheet	Map Reference
Log Avenue	57cNE4 Marcoing	L 15 b, d, 16 a
Log Lane [1918]	57dNE2 [Courcelles]	F 8 d, 14 b
Logeast Wood	57cNW1 Gomiecourt	A 25 d, 26 c, G 1 b, 2 a, b
Loges Copse	62cSW1 Dompierre	M 18 d
Logging Support [St Pierre Divion, 1918]	57dSE2 Beaumont	R 13 c, d, 19 a
Logging Trench [St Pierre Divion, 1918]	57dSE2 Beaumont	R 13 a, c
Logic Trench	51bNW4 Fampoux	H 10 d
Lohengrin Trench	66dNW3 Hattencourt	G 11 b, d, 12 a, b
Loire Alley	66cNW3 Essigny / 4 Berthenicourt	H 21 b, d, 22 a, b, 23 a, b
Loisne [farm]	36aSE4 Locon	X 28 a 3.6
Loisne Central Post	36aSE4 Locon	X 22 b, d
Loisne North Post	36aSE4 Locon	X 22 a
Loisne West Post	36aSE4 Locon	X 22 a
Loison Road [road]	36cSW1 Lens / 2 Harnes	N 15 b, 16 a
Lomax Farm	36NW1 Steenwerck	B 8 a 30.95
Lombard [lt rly locality & pillboxes, nr Bank Farm]	28NW2 St Julien	C 24 b 3.8
Lomond Copse	28NE2 Moorslede	F 16 d 45.60
Lomond Farm	28NE2 Moorslede	F 16 d 3.6
Lön Weg	51bNW1 Roclincourt	A 12 c, d, 17 a, b, 18 a, B 7 c
London Bridge Post [on River Layes]	36NW4 Bois Grenier	I 25 d
London Copse	36cSW4 Rouvroy	U 1 b
London Dump	62cSW3 Vermandovillers	S 14 a 3.8
London Farm, & trenches	36NW2 & NE1 Houplines	C 3 a
London Ridge [E of St Julien]	28NE1 Zonnebeke	D 7, 8, 9
London Rifle Brigade Cottages	36NW2 Houplines	C 1 b 1.1
London Road	36cNW3 Loos	G 25, 26, 32, 33, 34
London Road	36NW2 Armentières	C 28 d, 29 c
London Road	62dNE2 Méaulte	F 12 c
London Road / Street	57dNE1 & 2 Fonquevillers	E 11a, c
London Road [road & trench]	62cNE2 Epéhy	F 11 b, d
London Road [road]	36cSW4 Rouvroy	O 31 c, U 1 a, b, d, 7 b
London Road Keep [W of Loos]	36cNW3 Loos	G 33 d
London Support	51bSW4 Bullecourt	U 28 b, 29 a, b
London Support	57cNE3 Hermies	K 21 a, c
London Support Farm / Support Farm, & trenches	36NW2 Armentières	C 1 b
London Trench	36NW2 Armentières	C 28 d, 29 c
London Trench	51bSW1 Neuville Vitasse	M 5 b, d, 6 a
London Trench	51bSW4 Bullecourt	U 28 a, b
London Trench	57cNE3 Hermies / 4 Marcoing	K 15 c, 21 a, c, d
Londres, Boyau de [London]	62cSW1 Dompierre	M 4 b
Londres, Carrefour de [cross roads]	20SW4 Bixschoote	U 8 b 65.40
Lone Alley	36cNW1 La Bassée	A 28 b, d, 29 a
Lone Avenue	51bNW4 Fampoux	H 36 b, 31 a
Lone Copse	51bNW4 Fampoux	H 30 d
Lone Cottage	36cSW2 Harnes	N 35 a 4.9
Lone Cross Roads	28NE2 Moorslede	E 29 c 3.9
Lone Farm	28NW2 St Julien	C 28 b 35.05
Lone Farm	36cNW1 La Bassée	A 29 a 3.0
Lone Farm Cottage	36cNW1 La Bassée	A 28 b
Lone House	28NE3 Gheluvelt	J 15 a 4.3
Lone House	28NE3 Gheluvelt	J 20 c 3.4
Lone House [1916]	28SW4 Ploegsteert	U 15 d 00.85
Lone House [dugout, Battle Wood]	28NW4 & NE3 Zillebeke	I 35 a
Lone House Avenue	28SW4 Ploegsteert	U 15 c, d

Name	Map Sheet	Map Reference
Lone House Ruins	51bSW4 Bullecourt	O 34 d 4.4
Lone Keep North [S of Sailly-Labourse]	36bNE4 Noeux-les-Mines	L 9 a 4.3
Lone Keep South [S of Sailly-Labourse]	36bNE4 Noeux-les-Mines	L 15 b 1.7
Lone Lane	51bSW4 Bullecourt	U 13 d
Lone Lane [trench]	51bNW4 Fampoux	H 36 a, b, I 31 a
Lone Pine Cemetery	62dNE [3 Morlancourt]	J 24 d 9.0
Lone Sap	51bSW2 Vis-en-Artois	O 25 d
Lone Tree	36aNE3 Haverskerque	K 25 d 5.8
Lone Tree	36aSE4 Locon	W 4 b / W 5 a 15.80
Lone Tree	36cSW3 Vimy	T 27 c 00.75
Lone Tree	36cSW3 Vimy	S 2 a
Lone Tree	51bNW2 Oppy	C 7 a 2.8
Lone Tree	51bNW2 Oppy	B 24 d 6.6
Lone Tree	57cSW3 Longueval	S 10 b 1.8
Lone Tree [Givenchy, April 1915]	36cNW1 La Bassée	A 9 d 1.9
Lone Tree [Givenchy, lookout building, April 1915]	36cNW1 La Bassée	A 9 d
Lone Tree [October 1915]	36cNW3 Loos	G 17 c 9.3
Lone Tree Board	36cNW3 Loos	G 23 a 7.7
Lone Tree Cemetery	62dNE [3 Morlancourt]	J 24 d
Lone Tree Redoubt	36cNW3 Loos	G 17 d 8.3
Lone Tree Redoubt [St Eloi 1917-18]	28SW2 Wytschaete	O 4 a 65.25
Lone Tree Trench	62bNW1 Gouy	A 8 c
Lone Trees [two]	62dSE [1 Hamel]	P 3 c 60.05
Lone Trench	36cNW3 Loos	G 17 c, d
Lonely [keep, late 1915]	36SW1 Aubers	M 17 c, 23 a
Lonely Copse	57dSE4 Ovillers	X 27 b
Lonely Copse	62cNW2 Bouchavesnes	C 4 b, d
Lonely Erith Street [late 1915]	36SW1 Aubers	M 17 d, 23 b
Lonely House	62cSW3 & 4 Marchélepot	T 21 b 25.60
Lonely House [Rocquigny]	57cSW2 Villers-au-Flos	O 28 c 6.1
Lonely Lane	57dNE3 & 4 Hébuterne	L 25 a, b, 26 a
Lonely Lane	57dSE4 Ovillers	X 27 c, d
Lonely Mill [windmill]	20SW4 Bixschoote	U 10 d 35.91
Lonely Post	36SW1 Aubers	M 17 c
Lonely Street	36SW1 Aubers	M 17 c, d, 23 b
Lonely Support	57dSE4 Ovillers	X 27 d
Lonely Trench	20SW2 Zwartegat	N 28 b, 29 a
Lonely Trench	57dSE4 Ovillers	X 27 c, d
Lonely Trench	62bSW3 St Quentin	T 7 a, b
Lonely Trench [S of Guillemont]	57cSW3 Longueval / 62cNW1 Maricourt	T 25 c, B 1 a
Long Acre	57dSE1 & 2 Beaumont	Q 17 a
Long Avenue	36NW2 Armentières	C 4, 9, 10, 15
Long Copse	57dSW [4 Toutencourt]	N 35 c
Long Copse	62cNE4 Roisel	L 28 b, d, 29 a, c
Long Drive	57dSE4 Ovillers	X 4 d, 10 a, b, 11 a
Long Drive Valley	57dSE4 Ovillers	X 10 b, 11 a
Long Farm	28NE3 Gheluvelt	J 33 a 5.5
Long Island [Ploegsteert Wood 1914-15]	28SW4 Ploegsteert	U 21 a
Long Island [Ploegsteert Wood]	28SW4 Ploegsteert	U 21 a 99.30
Long Lane	28SW2 Wytschaete	N 29 d, 30 c, 35 b
Long Lane	51bSW4 Bullecourt	U 13 d
Long Lane [road]	51bNE3 Noyelle-sous-Bellonne / SE1 Saudemont	J 26 d, 32 b, c, d, P 2 a
Long Lane [road]	51bSW2 Vis-en-Artois	O 6d, 10c,d, 11b,c,d, 12a,b, 15b,d, 16a
Long Lane [trench alongside road]	51bSW2 Vis-en-Artois	O 15 d, 16 a

Name	Map Sheet	Map Reference
Long Ruin	28SW4 Ploegsteert	U 9 d 8.1
Long Sap	51bNW1 Roclincourt	A 4 d
Long Sap [to new front line]	57dSE1 & 2 Beaumont	Q 17 c
Long Trench	36cNW4 Pont-à-Vendin / SW2 Harnes	H 35 a, c, N 5 a, c, 10 b, 11 a
Long Trench	51bSW2 Vis-en-Artois	O 2 b, d, 8 b
Long Valley	57cSE1 Bertincourt	P 5 a, c, d, 11 a, b, c, d
Long Wood	51bNW1 Roclincourt	B 14 b, 15 a
Long Wood	51bSW2 Vis-en-Artois	O 11 c, d, 12 a, b, c, d
Long Wood	62bSW4 Homblières	T 18 d, 24 a, b, U13 b, c, d, 14 c, 19 a
Long Woods	62dSE [2 Proyart]	R 4 a, c
Longatte Support	57cNW2 Vaulx-Vraucourt	C 2 d, 3 c, 8 a, b
Longavesnes Aerodrome [German, 1918]	62cNE1 Lièramont	E 14 c, 19 b, d, 20 a, c
Longridge Street	57dSE4 Ovillers	X 7 b
Longueval [village]	57cSW3 Longueval	S 17 a, b, d,
Longueval Alley	57cSW3 Longueval	S 17 d, 23 b, c, d, 24 a
Longueval Trench	57cSW3 Longueval	S 18 c, 24 a
Longwy Street	57dNE1 & 2 Fonquevillers	E 11 a
Lonsdale Cemetery	57dSE4 Ovillers	X 1 b
Loobeek Farm	20SW4 Bixschoote	U 25 b 2.7
Look Copse [by Amiens Inner Defence Line]	62dSW [1 Longueau]	N 7 a
Look Slippy Lane	28SW4 Ploegsteert	U 14 d, 15 c
Look Trench	36cSW2 Harnes	N 16 b
Loon Copse	28SE1 Wervicq	P 9 a, b
Loon Copse	57cSW4 Combles	U 4 a
Loop North	36cSW4 Rouvroy	T 29 d
Loop Road [road]	36aNE3 Haverskerque	J 32 a, b, d
Loop Road [road]	36aSE1 St Venant	P 2 b, 3 a
Loop Road [Trench; Sept 1915]	36cNW1 La Bassée	A 2 d, 3 c
Loop Trench	57cSW3 Longueval / 62cNW1 Maricourt	S 26 c, A 2 a, c
Loop Trench [chord of Duck's Bill, Givenchy]	36cNW1 La Bassée	A 9 d
Loop Trench [Combles]	57cSW3 Longueval	T 21 c, d, 27 b, d
Loop Trench [The Bluff]	28NW4 & NE3 Zillebeke	I 34 c
Loop, The	28SW4 Ploegsteert	U 21 d
Loop, The	36cNW1 La Bassée	A 3 c
Loop, The	51bSW1 Neuville Vitasse	M 9 c
Loop, The	57cSE4 Villers-Guislain	X 19 a, b
Loop, The	57dSE4 Ovillers	X 5 d, 6 c
Loop, The [S of Hohenzollern Rdt, Oct 1915]	36cNW3 Loos	G 5 c
Loop, The [Sanctuary Wood, 1915]	28NW4 & NE3 Zillebeke	J 13 c, 19 a
Loop, The [trench]	62cNW1 Maricourt	A 2 c
Loophole / Loop Hole Farm	28SW4 Ploegsteert	U 22 d 1.2
Loos [pillboxes]	28NE1 Zonnebeke	D 13 c 85.95
Loos Alley	36cNW3 Loos	G 30 d, 36 a, c
Loos Crassier, & Pylons Tower	36cNW3 Loos	G 36 c
Loos Defences [German 2nd Line]	36cNW3 Loos / SW1 Lens	G 35 a, c, d, M 5 b, d
Loos Junction [light rly, Aix Noulette]	36bSE2 Boyeffles	R 17 c
Loos Line [light rly]	36cNW3 Loos / SW1 Lens	G 35 c, M 3, 4, 5, 9
Loos Road Keep	36cNW3 Loos	G 27 b, 28 a
Loos Road Redoubt	36cNW3 Loos	G 28 b, 34 a
Loos Trench	36cNW3 Loos	G 36 b
Loos Trench	36cSW2 Harnes	N 10 b
Loos Trench	57dNE1 & 2 Fonquevillers	E 11 a, c
Loose Trench	36cSW2 Harnes	N 10 b
Loot Trench	36cSW2 Harnes	N 10 b, d

Name	Map Sheet	Map Reference
Loot Trench	62bNW1 Gouy	A 13 d
Lord Farm	28NE2 Moorslede	F 25 d 4.4
Lord Raglan [trench]	57dNE3 & 4 Hébuterne	K 15 b, d, 16 a
Lord Street	62dNE2 Méaulte	F 16 b / 17 a
Lord Trench	36cSW2 Harnes	N 10 d
Lordship Lane [road]	36cSW1 Lens	N 13 a, c, d, 14 c
Loregreb House	20SW4 Bixschoote	T 24 a 5.2
Lorette Ridge	36bSE2 Boyeffles / 4 Carency	R 34, 35, X 5
Lorette, Notre Dame de, Ruined Chapel	36bSE4 Carency	X 5 a 2.2
Loretto Post	36SW1 Aubers	M 33 b
Loretto Road [road]	36SW1 Aubers / 3 Richebourg	M 27 d, 32 b, d, 33 a, b,
Lorien Alley	62bSW1 Gricourt	M 23 c
Lorival Farm	66cNW2 Itancourt	C 8 c
Lorne Street	57dSE2 Beaumont	R 18 c, 24 a, c
Lorraine Alley	66cNW2 Itancourt	B 17 c, 22 b, d, 23 a
Lorraine Trench	70dNW4 St Gobain	H 30 a, b
Lorry Avenue	12SW1 Nieuport	M 17 b
Lorry Trench	12SW1 Nieuport	M 23 a
Lorry Walk	12SW1 Nieuport	M 23 a
Losange Wood	66eNW [4 Morisel]	I 36 a, b, c
Lost Ravine	62cNW4 Péronne	I 13 a 4.2
Lost Trench	36cSW2 Harnes	N 10 d, 11 c
Lot Farm	27NE4 Abeele	K 10 c 95.35
Lot Trench	36cSW2 Harnes	N 10 b, 11 a
Lothian Avenue	36NW4 Bois Grenier	I 9 d, 10 c, d
Lothian Road	36SW3 Richebourg	S 27 c, d
Lothian Street	62cNW1 Maricourt	A 8 c
Lothian Trench [1918]	57dSE [3 Bouzincourt]	W 2 b, d, 3 a
Loto Trench	66dNW1 Punchy	A 25 d, 26 a, b, c
Lottie Trench	36cSW2 Harnes	N 4 d, 10 b
Lotus Lane [1918]	51cSE4 Blaireville / 57dNE2 [Fonquevillers]	X 27 c, d, F 3 b
Loubiere Alley [1918]	62dSW [4 Cachy]	U 27 b, d, 28 b
Loud Trench	36cSW2 Harnes	N 10 d
Louenburg Redoubt / Work	51bSW1 Neuville Vitasse	M 20 d, 21 a, c
Louis Farm	20SW4 Bixschoote	U 24 c 5.9
Lounge House	36aNE4 Merville	L 32 b 6.8
Lounge, The	36SW1 Aubers	M 18 d 3.0
Loupart Bastion [W of Loupart Wood]	57dNE4 & 57cNW3 Achiet	G 33 b, 34 c
Loupart Road [rd NNE of Warlencourt-Eaucourt]	57cSW1 Gueudecourt	M 5 a, c
Loupart Trench	57dNE4 & 57cNW3 Achiet	G 27 c, d, 33 b, 34 c, d
Loupart Wood	57dNE4 & 57cNW3 Achiet	G 34 a, b, c, d, 35 a, c
Loupart Wood Line [part of R.1 Line]	57dNE4 & 57cNW3 Achiet	G 20a,b,c,d, 26b, 27a,c,d, 33b, 34c,d
Louse Post	57cNE1 Quéant	D 27 b
Lousy Wood [Leuze Wood]	57cSW3 Longueval	T 20, 21, 26, 27
Lout Farm	27SE2 Berthen	R 10 d 7.2
Louvercy Street [Louvery; sic]	57dSE1 & 2 Beaumont	Q 17 d, 23 b
Louvercy Street Sap	57dSE1 & 2 Beaumont	Q 17 d
Louverval [hamlet]	57cNE3 Hermies	J 4 c
Louverval Chateau	57cNE3 Hermies	J 4 c 5.8
Louverval Reserve	57cNE1 Quéant / 3 Hermies	J 3 b, c, d, 9 b, 10 a
Louvière Alley [La Louvière Farm]	57dNE3 & 4 Hébuterne	K 17 d, 18 c
Louvière Farm, la	57dNE3 & 4 Hébuterne	K 18 d 3.7
Louvois Farm [moated]	20SW4 Bixschoote	U 11 a 60.45
Louwaege Farm	28SW2 Wytschaete	O 7 d 8.3

Name	Map Sheet	Map Reference
Lovats Lane [road]	36cSW1 Lens	N 19 c, d, 25 a
Love Crater	36cSW3 Vimy	S 15 a
Love Lane [trench]	51bNW4 Fampoux	I 31 a
Love Trench	36cSW2 Harnes	N 10 b, 11 a
Love Trench	36cSW3 Vimy	S 8 b
Love Trench	51bNW1 Roclincourt	A 23 a, b
Lover's Keep [July 1915]	36cNW1 La Bassée	A 15 d
Lovers Lane	36cNW1 La Bassée	A 15 d
Lovers Lane [E of Ravine Wood]	28NW4 & NE3 Zillebeke	I 34 a, b
Lovers Lane [Larch Wood - Hill 60]	28NW4 & NE3 Zillebeke	I 29 c
Lovers Lane [trench, 1918]	57dNE [2 Courcelles]	F 8 d, 14 b
Lovers Lane Drive	28NW4 & NE3 Zillebeke	I 34 a, b
Lovers Redoubt [Cuinchy]	36cNW1 La Bassée	A 15 d
Lovers Walk	12SW1 Nieuport	M 17 d
Lovers Walk	27SE4 Meteren	X 14 d, 20 a, b
Lovers Walk / Lane [south of The Ravine]	28NW4 & NE3 Zillebeke	I 34 a, b, d
Lovers Walk [Sanctuary Wood]	28NW4 & NE3 Zillebeke	I 24 b
Lovie Chateau	27NE2 Proven	F 16 d 45.85
Low Farm [dugout, 1917-18]	28NE3 Gheluvelt	J 1 d 60.65
Low Remains	28NW4 & NE3 Zillebeke	J 1 c, d
Low Road [trench]	57cSW3 Longueval	T 8 d, 14 b
Low Trench	51bNW1 Roclincourt	A 28 d
Low Trench	70dNW2 Servais	C 2 a, b, c, d
Low Trenches	28SW4 Ploegsteert	U 1 b 8.8
Löwen Schanze	51bSW1 Neuville Vitasse	M 5 d
Lower Cross [Monument]	62bSW3 St. Quentin	S 11 c
Lower Cut [Sept 1915]	36cNW1 La Bassée	A 9 a
Lower Fenchurch Street	51cSE & 51bSW Ficheux	R 23 b
Lower Gommecourt Road	57dNE1 & 2 Fonquevillers	E 27 d, 28 c
Lower Horwich Street	57dSE4 Ovillers	W 12, a, b, X 7 a
Lower Kent Road [Cuinchy]	36cNW1 La Bassée	A 21 a, b
Lower Oosthoek Farm	28SW2 Wytschaete	O 3 a 80.85
Lower Oxford Street [Zouave Wd, 1915]	28NW4 & NE3 Zillebeke	I 17 d, 18 c
Lower Road	28NW2 St Julien	C 14 c, 20 a
Lower Seine Trench	66cSW4 La Fère	U 1 a, b, c, d
Lower Star Post [June 1915, Shrewsbury Forest]	28NW4 & NE3 Zillebeke	J 25 b 2.1
Lower Trench	57dSE1 & 2 Beaumont	R 19 b
Lower Wood	57dSE4 Ovillers	X 18 a
Lowers Redoubt	36cNW1 La Bassée	A 15 d
Lowestoft Street / Boyau Lowestoft	62cNW1 Maricourt	A 16 b, 17 c, 22 b
Lowland Farm	36NW1 Steenwerck	B 19 c 35.85
Lowland Post	62bNW1 Gouy	A 7 b
Lowland Support	57cSE4 Villers-Guislain	W 11 c, d, 17 b, 18 a
Lowland Trench	27SE4 Meteren	X 9 d, 10 c
Lowland Trench	57cSE4 Villers-Guislain	W 11 b, 12 c
Lowndes Square	36cNW1 La Bassée	A 21 b
Lowndes Square [Sept 1915]	36cNW1 La Bassée	A 15 d
Lowrie Cemetery	57cNE3 Hermies	K 21 b 4.2
Loxley Farm [1918]	28SW1 Kemmel	M 14 a 25.75
Loxton House	36aNE4 Merville	K 22 c 33.15
Loye [farm]	27SE2 Berthen	R 5 b 1.8
Loyseau [Boyau, E of Bécourt Château, 1915]	57dSE4 Ovillers	X 26 d
Loyseau [Tranchée, 1915]	57dSE4 Ovillers	X 26 c, d
Lozenge Alley	57dSE4 Ovillers	X 27 c, d, 28 c

Name	Map Sheet	Map Reference
Lozenge Trench	57dSE4 Ovillers	X 27 a, b
Lozenge Wood	57dSE4 Ovillers	X 27 b
Lozenge, The	36SW1 Aubers	N 19 a
Lozenge, The [GFL, late 1915]	36SW2 Radinghem	O 1 a 2.7
Lubda Copse	57cSW2 Villers-au-Flos	O 13 c, d
Lubeck Work	66dNW1 Punchy	A 23 a, b, c
Lubecker Weg	51bNW1 Roclincourt	A 22 a, b
Lubricant House	27NE2 Proven	E 29 d 5.1
Luc Wood	62dSE [2 Proyart]	R 3 b, c, d
Lucas Crater	36cNW3 Loos	H 13 a 35.05
Lucian Fork [road jct]	28NE4 Dadizeele	L 4 d 35.20
Lucid Trench	51bNW4 Fampoux	H 10 d, 11 c
Lucida Corner	20SE4 Roulers	X 26 b
Lucifer Farm	28NE2 Moorslede	L 1 a 90.95
Lucifer Farm	28SE1 Wervicq	P 10 d 85.75
Lucifer Trench	36aSE3 Gonnehem	V 3 c, d
Lucifer Trench	57cSW1 Gueudecourt	N 21 b
Luck Farm	28NE2 Moorslede	F 7 c 65.75
Lucknow Avenue	62dNE2 Méaulte	F 16 d, 22 b, d
Lucknow Redoubt	62dNE2 Méaulte	F 22 b
Lucky Dugout	28NW4 & NE3 Zillebeke	J 19 b 1.7
Lucky Lane [1918]	57dNE [2 Courcelles]	F 13 b, 14 a, c
Lucky Trench	28NW4 & NE3 Zillebeke	J 19 b
Lucky Way [Lach Weg, Thiepval]	57dSE1 & 2 Beaumont	R 14 d, 15 a, c, 19 d, 20 a, b, c
Lucky Way Road	57dSE1 & 2 Beaumont	R 14 d, 15 a, c, 19 d, 20 a, b, c
Lucy Lane	51cSE2 Beaumetz	R 35 a
Ludendorf Lodge	27SE4 Meteren	X 21 d 55.05
Ludendorf Trench	57cNE1 Quéant	D 12 b, c, d, 18 a
Ludendorf Trench	66dNW3 Hattencourt	G 15 d 16 a, c
Ludford Farm	28SW1 Kemmel	M 26 b 20.35
Ludgate Circus	62dNE2 Méaulte	F 16 d 7.9
Ludgate Circus [Redan Ridge]	57dSE1 & 2 Beaumont	Q 4 b
Ludgate Hill [Double Crassier, S arm]	36cSW1 Lens	M 4 c
Ludhiana Lane [road]	36SW1 Aubers	M 34 a, b
Ludiana / Ludhiana Lodge	36SW1 Aubers	M 34 b 2.8
Ludwig Ravine	66eNW [4 Morisel]	I 3 d, 4 a, c
Luff Trench	51bNW1 Roclincourt	A 23 a
Lug Farm	36aNE2 Vieux Berquin	E 23 c 3.8
Lug Trench	51bNW1 Roclincourt	A 23 a, b
Lugano [farm]	27NE2 Proven	L 1 a 35.90
Lugger Farm	28SW3 Bailleul	S 28 a 80.25
Lugos Trench	62cNW4 Péronne	I 10 c, d
Luighem Trench	20SW2 Zwartegat	N 22 c, d
Luisen Trench	57dSE2 & 57cSW1 Le Sars	N 13 d, 14 c
Luisenhof Farm	57cSW1 Gueudecourt	N 13 d
Luke Alley	57dNE3 & 4 Hébuterne	K 29 b, 30 a
Luke Copse	57dNE3 & 4 Hébuterne	K 29 a, b
Luke Farm	28NE2 Moorslede	F 20 c 75.25
Lukers Houses [Le Touquet]	36NW2 & NE1 Houplines	C 10 c 9.9
Lulli / Lully Trench	20SW2 Zwartegat	O 22 c, d
Lulu Lane	57dNE1 & 2 Fonquevillers	E 10 c, d, 11 a, c
Lumber Trench	51bNW4 Fampoux	H 10 d, 11 c
Luminous Trench	57dSE1 & 2 Beaumont	Q 12 d, R 7 c
Lumley Fork [road jct]	28NE4 Dadizeele	K 12 d 70.25

Name	Map Sheet	Map Reference
Lumm Farm	28SW2 Wytschaete	O 26 d 1.7
Lump Farm	28NE2 Moorslede	L 1 a 35.60
Lump Lane	51bSW4 Bullecourt	U 7 b, c, d
Lumpy Trench	51bNW3 Arras	H 9 a
Lunar House	27SE4 Meteren	X 2 b 15.20
Lunar Terrace	57dSE1 & 2 Beaumont	Q 3 d
Lunatic Lane	36NW2 Armentières	I 2 b, 3 a, b
Lunatic Sap	36cNW1 La Bassée	A 21 b
Lundy Island Redoubt	51bNW1 Roclincourt	A 9 b
Lune Alley	62cSW3 Vermandovillers	S 14 d, 15 a, b
Lune Park [rly locality & dump / huts]	20SW3 Oostvleteren	T 13 a
Lunge Farm	28NE2 Moorslede	E 10 b 4.6
Lunge Wood	66dNW1 Punchy	A 6 a
Lunt Trench	57dNE3 & 4 Hébuterne	K 16 b
Luntin Farm	27NE2 Proven	E 29 b 2.1
Lupin Farm	36NW1 Steenwerck	A 27 b 55.80
Lupton Lane [Mesnil]	57dSE1 & 2 Beaumont	Q 28 a, b
Lure Trench	51bNW1 Roclincourt	A 23 b
Lurgan Switch	57cNE3 Hermies	K 19 c, d, 25 b
Lusty Trench	51bNW3 Arras	H 9 a, b
Lutin Copse	66dNW1 Punchy	B 9 c
Luton [light rly locality E of Canal 1917-18]	28NW2 St Julien	C 13 d
Luton Farm	20SE2 Hooglede	Q 22 c 0.1
Luxbourg Trench	70dNW4 St Gobain	I 25 a, c, d
Luxemboug Cabaret, Au	28SW1 Kemmel	M 19 d 85.15
Luxembourg Trench	20SW1 Loo	N 2 d, 3 a, 8 a, b
Luxmore Copse [1918]	28SW1 Kemmel	M 20 d
Luxmore House [1918]	28SW1 Kemmel	M 20 d 85.50
Luzerne Trench	66dNW3 Hattencourt	G 30 c, d, H 25 b, c, d, 26 a
Lyceum, The	57dNE3 & 4 Hébuterne	K 34 a
Lyddite Lane [road]	36SW1 Aubers	M 8d, 9c, 14 a,b, 15 a,c,d, 16 c, 22 a,b
Lyell Farm	20SE3 Westroosebeke	W 19 b 9.5
Ly-Fontaine [village]	66cSW1 Remigny	N 3 d
Lynde Farm	36aNE2 Vieux Berquin	F 13 a 1.7
Lyne Buildings	20SE2 Hooglede	Q 12 b 0.3
Lynn House	27NE4 Abeele	L 21 d 65.35
Lynn Trench	36cNW3 Loos	H 32 d
Lynx Post	57cNE1 Quéant	D 20 d
Lynx Support	57cNE1 Quéant	D 26 a, b
Lynx Trench	57cNE1 Quéant / 2 Bourlon	E 21 b, 22 a, c, d
Lynz Trench	51bNW3 Arras	H 9 a
Lyon Sap	57cSE2 Gonnelieu	R 9 d
Lyre Trench	20SW2 Zwartegat	O 4 a, c, d
Lyric [Heavy Artillery OP]	36cNW3 Loos	G 23 d 5.4
Lys Bridge [Estaires]	36aNE4 Merville	L 34 b 5.8
Lys Farm [Redoubt]	36NW2 Armentières	C 15 d
Lys Farm Avenue (abandoned)	36NW2 Armentières	C 15 b, d, 16 a
Lysa Trench	62cSW2 Barleux	O 7 c, d
Lysa Trench / Tranchée de Lysa	62cSW1 & 2 Belloy	O 7 c, d
Lysistrata Trench	62cSW4 St. Christ	U 21 b, 22 a
Lyssenthoek	27NE4 Abeele	L 24 c
Lytham Cot.	28NW2 St Julien	C 22 d 6.1
M 1 [trench, W of Hollandscheschuur Fm]	28SW2 Wytschaete	N 12 d 0.0
M 2 [trench, NW of Hollandscheschuur Fm]	28SW2 Wytschaete	N 12 d 1.2

Name	Map Sheet	Map Reference
M 3 [trench, N of Hollandscheschuur Fm]	28SW2 Wytschaete	N 12 d 3.3
M 4 [trench, NNW of Hollandscheschuur Fm]	28SW2 Wytschaete	N 12 d 2.4
M 5 [trench, W of Hollandscheschuur Fm]	28SW2 Wytschaete	N 12 c 5.1
M 6 [trench, W of Hollandscheschuur Fm]	28SW2 Wytschaete	N 12 c 4.2
M Camp [St Jan-ter-Biezen]	27NE2 Proven	L 2 a [area]
M Trench [St Eloi sector, Feb 1915]	28SW2 Wytschaete	O 3 / 4
M.G. Alley [CT, Sept 1915]	36SW3 Richebourg	M 35 c, d
M.G. House	36cNW1 La Bassée	A 21 b
M.G. House	36NW2 Armentières	C 4 c
M.O. House	36SW2 Radinghem	N 5 a
Ma Post [twin of Pa Post]	62cNE4 Roisel	L 36 a 2.7
Mabel Corons [miners' cottages]	36cSW4 Rouvroy	T 6 a, b
Mabel Lane	51cSE2 Beaumetz	R 30 c, 36 a
Mac Support	57cSE4 Villers-Guislain	X 5 a, c
Mac Trench [Moyenneville]	57cNW1 Gomiecourt	A 4 c
Mac. Brair Farm	28NE4 Dadizeele	K 5 c 10.25
Macaulay Avenue	57cNW2 Vaulx-Vraucourt	C 16 a, b, c, 17 a, b
Macaw Trench	28SW2 Wytschaete	N 16 d, 17 a, c
Macclesfield Lane	51cSE2 Beaumetz / 51bSW1 Neuville Vitasse	R 30 a, M 25 d, 31 b
MacDonnell Road	57dSE1 & 2 Beaumont	R 29, 35
Macdowell Trench	36cSW1 Lens	N 26 c, 31 b
Mace Trench	62bSW4 Homblières	T 10 d, 16 b
Mace Trench [Mace, Tranchée]	36cSW1 Lens	M 15 c
MacFarlane's Alley	57cSW3 Longueval	S 2 a, c, d
MacGregors [farm]	20SE3 Westroosebeke	V 10 d 05.25
Machiavel Farm	20NW4 Dixmude	I 17 c
Machine Gun Alley	57cSW3 Longueval	S 24 b, d
Machine Gun Farm	28NW4 Ypres	H 12 a 5.6
Machine Gun Farm Camp	28NW4 Ypres	H 12 a
Machine Gun Farm Depot [railway, 1917-18]	28NW4 Ypres	H 5 c, d
Machine Gun Farm Siding [railway, 1917-18]	28NW4 Ypres	H 12 a, b
Machine Gun House	36NW2 & NE1 Houplines	C 4 c
Machine Gun House	57cSW3 Longueval	S 24 b 75.40
Machine Gun House [Cuinchy Sector, Feb 1915]	36cNW1 La Bassée	A 15 c, d
Machine Gun Trench	51bNW2 Oppy	B 11 a, b, d
Machine Gun Wood	62cNW1 Maricourt	A 15 b
Mack House	28NE2 Moorslede	F 30 c 1.1
Mackensen Farm	28NW2 St Julien	C 8 c 5.7
Mackensen Trench, & Support to	36cNW1 La Bassée	A 3 b, d
Mackensen, Saillant	66eNE4 Beaufort	L 5 d
Mackenzie Trench	51bSW2 Vis-en-Artois	N 10 a, c, d
Maclaren Lane / Maclaren Land [sic]	57dSE1 & 2 Beaumont	Q 10 b
Macmahon Avenue	57dSE1 & 2 Beaumont	Q 23 b
MacMahon, Tranchée	70dSW [1 Folembray / 2 Coucy-le-Château]	N 10 a
Macquincourt Valley	62bNW1 Gouy	A 2 c, d, 3 c, 7 b, 8 a
Macroures, Boyau des	62cSW1 & 2 Belloy	N 23 b, 24 a, c, 30 b
Mac's Ruin	28SW4 Ploegsteert	U 13 b
Mad Alley	36cNW1 La Bassée	A 28 d, 29 a, c
Mad Point, & Craters	36cNW1 La Bassée	A 28 c 8.1
Mad Trench	51bNW1 Roclincourt	A 23 b, c
Madagascar [crossroads]	51bNW1 Roclincourt	A 26 d 8.2
Madagascar Avenue	51bNW1 Roclincourt	A 21 c, d, 26 d, 27 a, c
Madagascar Dump [Arras Road]	51bNW1 Roclincourt	A 21 c
Madagascar Redoubt	51bNW1 Roclincourt	A 27 c

Name	Map Sheet	Map Reference
Madagascar Trench	36cNW1 La Bassée	A 28 c
Madam Trench	57dNE3 & 4 Hébuterne	K 12 b
Madame Wood	62cSW3 Vermandovillers	S 13 b, d
Maddox Street [Sept 1915]	36cNW1 La Bassée	A 21 b
Madelaine Lane	51bSW1 Neuville Vitasse	M 21 c, 27 a
Madelaine Redoubt / Work	51bSW1 Neuville Vitasse	M 26 b, d, 27 a, c
Madeleine	62cNW2 Bouchavesnes	I 1 b 3.5
Madelin Trench	36bSE2 Boyeffles / 36cSW1 Lens	R 36 a, M 31 b, d, 32 c
Madelon Alley	66cNW1 Grugies	B 28 a
Madingley House	20SE3 Westroosebeke	V 6 b 5.7
Madrague Trench	51bSW1 Neuville Vitasse	M 27 a, b
Maedelstede Farm & Crater	28SW2 Wytschaete	N 24 c 9.4
Maès Trench	66cNW2 Itancourt	B 23 a, c, 29 a
Mag Trench	57cNW1 Gomiecourt	A 4 c
Magdeburg Trench / Tranchée de Magdebourg	66cNW2 Itancourt	C 20 c, d, 26 b, d
Magdeburg Trench [1918]	66eNW [2 Thennes]	C 9 d, 15 a, b
Magenta Alley	62cSW3 Vermandovillers	T 13 d, 14 c
Magenta Alley / Boyau de Magenta	62cSW3 & 4 Marchélepot	T 13 d, 14 c, 20 a
Magenta Lane	51bSW1 Neuville Vitasse	M 26 d, 33 a
Magenta, Passerelle de	57dSE1 & 2 Beaumont	R 26 c
Magilligan Camp / Macgilligan Farm Camp	28SW3 Bailleul	S 9 d, 15 b
Magilligan Farm	28SW3 Bailleul	S 9 d 8.0
Magnan [Tranchée, 1915] / Dalhousie Street N.	57dSE4 Ovillers	X 19 a, c
Magnet House	28SW1 Kemmel	M 11 d 25.60
Magny Wood	62bNW3 Bellicourt	H 25 b, c, d, 26 a, b
Magny-la-Fosse [village]	62bNW3 Bellicourt	H 25 a, b, d
Magog [German Pillbox M.G. Post]	51bSW4 Bullecourt	U 21 a 5.1
Magog Corner [road junction]	27SE3 Borre	P 31 c 35.43
Magot Trench / Tranchée du Magot	62cSW4 St. Christ	T 11 d, 12 a, b, c
Magpie Farm	20SE2 Hooglede	R 8 a 75.70
Magpie Trench	28SW2 Wytschaete	N 16 b, 17 a
Magpie's Nest [tree clump]	57cNE1 Quéant	D 13 a, b
Maguincourt Trench	62bNW1 Gouy	A 2 c
Magul, Tranchée	57dSE1 & 2 Beaumont	Q 17 d
Magyars Trench [1918]	66eNW [2 Thennes]	C 11 d, 17 b
Mahieu Farm	28SW2 Wytschaete	O 21 d 7.9
Mahutonga Farm	28SW3 Bailleul	T 19 b 5.5
Mahutonga Farm Camp	28SW3 Bailleul	T 19 b
Maid Trench	57dNE3 & 4 Hébuterne	K 12 b, d, 7 c
Maid Trench [1918]	28SW1 Kemmel	M 20 d, 21 a, c
Maida Camp	28NW4 Ypres	H 29 b, d, 30 a, c
Maida Vale [trench]	28NW4 Ypres	H 29 d, 30 c
Maida Vale [valley]	57cNW2 Vaulx-Vraucourt	B 12, 17, 18, C 1, 7
Maiden Farm	28NE2 Moorslede	E 11 b 4.4
Maiden, The	28SE3 Comines	V 25 a
Maidenhead Trench	51cSE2 Beaumetz	R 30c, 35 a, b, 36 a
Maidstone Avenue	62cNW1 Maricourt	A 7 d, 13 b
Maidstone Avenue	62dNE2 Méaulte	F 14 d, 15 c, d
Maidstone Farm [1918]	28SW1 Kemmel	M 2 a 7.2
Maidstone Lane	51bSW1 Neuville Vitasse	M 25 b, 26 a, c
Maience Trench [1918]	66eNW [2 Thennes]	B 29 a, b, c
Mail Trench	51bNW1 Roclincourt	A 23 d
Mail Trench	57cSW3 Longueval	T 2 a, b, d
Mailard, Bois	57bSW3 Honnecourt	S 17 a

Name	Map Sheet	Map Reference
Mailly-Maillet [village]	57dSE1 & 2 Beaumont	Q 7 a, b, c
Mailly-Raineval [village]	66eNW [4 Morisel]	H 24 c, d, 30 a, b
Main Avenue / Boyau Principal	62cNW1 Maricourt	A 16 b
Main Road Alley	66cNW2 Itancourt	B 22 b, d, 28 b, 29 c, H 5 a
Main Street	28NW4 & NE3 Zillebeke	I 30 a
Main Street [road]	36cSW1 Lens	M 24 c, 30 a
Main Trench	51bNW1 Roclincourt	A 23 d
Main Trench	57dNE3 & 4 Hébuterne	K 12 b, d
Main Trench [1918, Hendecourt-lez-Ransart]	51cSE4 Blaireville	X 17 a, b
Maine Trench	62cSW3 Vermandovillers	S 3 b, 4 a, M 34 c
Mainz Trench / Tranchée de Mainz	62cSW2 Barleux	O 21 b, d, 22 a, c, 27 b
Mairie Keep / Redoubt [Marie, sic] [Givenchy]	36cNW1 La Bassée	A 9 c, d
Maïs, Tranchée du [N of The Quadrangle]	57dSE4 Ovillers	X 23 c
Maisie Lane	57dSE1 & 2 Beaumont	R 19 a, c
Maison 1875	28SW4 Ploegsteert	U 26 c 75.46
Maison Blanche	51bNW1 Roclincourt	A 14 d 0.4
Maison Blanche [Redoubt]	51bNW1 Roclincourt	A 14 a, b, c, d, 20 a, b
Maison Blanche Graben	51bNW3 Arras	G 6 c, d
Maison Blanche, Bois de la	51bNW3 Arras	H 1 d
Maison Blanche, la	51bNW3 Arras	G 6 d 5.5
Maison Brulée Avenue [nr Burnt House]	20SW3 Oostvleteren	T 9 a, b, 10 a
Maison Bulgare	28NW2 St Julien	C 5 c 8.8
Maison Carrée Trench	20SW4 Bixschoote	T 29 d
Maison des Mitrailleurs [Aug 1915]	36cNW3 & 1 Loos	G 33 d 75.20
Maison du Hibou	28NW2 St Julien	C 6 c 2.3
Maison Gaba	36bSE2 Boyeffles	R 12 c 87.50
Maison Grise Sap [Thiepval Wood]	57dSE1 & 2 Beaumont	R 25 c
Maison Rouge	51bNW3 Arras	G 9 c 7.1
Maison Rouge [OP, fortified house]	36cNW1 La Bassée	A 20 d / 26 b
Maison Rouge Alley	36cNW1 La Bassée	A 26 b, 27 a
Maison Rouge Farm	51bSW3 Boisleux	T 25 c
Maison Rouge Post	36NW3 Fleurbaix	G 21 b, d
Maisonette Alley	62cSW3 Vermandovillers	S 18 d
Maisonette Wood	66eNW [2 Thennes]	B 18 b, d
Maisonnette [sic] Trench / Maisonnette, Tr. de la	62cNW4 Péronne / SW2 Barleux	I 31 d, O 1 b
Maistre (Ablain - Maroc) Line	36bSE2 Boyeffles / 4 Carency	R 11, 12, 17, 23, 29, 35, X 4, 5, 10, 16
Maistre Line / Ligne Maistre	36bSE2 Boyeffles / 4 Carency / 36cSW1 Lens	R 17-35, X 4-22, M 7, 8
Maitland Street	51bNW1 Roclincourt	A 10 b
Maitland Street & Trench	57dNE3 & 4 Hébuterne	K 28 b, d
Maitland Trench	57cSW4 Combles	N 34 c, d, T 4 b
Majdan Trench	62cNW2 Bouchavesnes	C 26 c, d, I 2 a
Major Alley	62bSW3 St Quentin	M 36 d, N 31 c
Major's Farm	20NW4 Dixmude	I 26 c 7.3
Major's Farm	20SW4 Bixschoote	U 25 b 6.8
Major's Post	28SW2 Wytschaete	N 11 a 8.9
Makay Camp	27NE4 Abeele	L 9 b, 10 a
Make Trench	36cSW2 Harnes	O 22 c, d, 28 a
Makerstone Farm	28NE4 Dadizeele	L 15 b 7.8
Mal Assise Farms / Fermes	57bSE [4 Wassigny]	W 29 b, d
Malabry Trench	51bSW1 Neuville Vitasse	M 22 c, d
Maladerie [house]	36aNE3 Haverskerque	J 34 c 75.80
Malakoff Farm	28NW2 St Julien	B 22 a 1.0
Malakoff Farm	62cNE2 Epéhy	F 30 c
Malakoff Trench [E & W trenches]	62cNE2 Epéhy	F 30 c

Name	Map Sheet	Map Reference
Malakoff Wood	62bNW1 Gouy	A 26 b, d
Malakoff, Garage de [railway station]	51bSE4 Marquion	W 18 c
Malard Communication Trench [1918]	62dNE [3 Morlancourt]	K 20 c, d
Malard Wood	62dNE [3 Morlancourt]	K 26, 27
Malassise Copse	57bSW1 Bantouzelle	N 20 d, 21 c
Malassise Farm	62cNE2 Epéhy	F 8 b
Malassise Farm East	57bSW1 Bantouzelle	N 20 b 1.2
Malassise, Epine de [trig point]	62cNW2 Bouchavesnes	C 16 c 9.7
Malbert, Boyau [Potters Bar]	36cSW1 Lens	M 20 a, c
Maldon Lane	51bSW1 Neuville Vitasse	M 26 a, c
Male Street [in Bullecourt]	51bSW4 Bullecourt	U 27 b
Male Trench	28SW3 Bailleul	S 2 a, b
Male Trench	57dNE3 & 4 Hébuterne	K 12 b
Malerant [?] Farm	27SE1 St Sylvestre	P 26 a 30.37
Malin House	28NW3 Poperinghe	G 14 c 9.7
Malincourt [village]	57bSW4 Serain	T 5 a, b, c, d, 6 c
Malincourt Wood	57bSW4 Serain	T 4 b, d
Mallard Road [near Duck Lodge]	28NE1 Zonnebeke	D 5 c
Mallard Trench [later Reserve]	51bSW2 Vis-en-Artois	O 25 b, c, d
Mallet Buildings	28NE2 Moorslede	F 30 c 0.5
Mallet Copse	20SE3 Westroosebeke	V 23 d
Mallet Farm	28SE1 Wervicq	P 25 d 4.2
Mallet Wood	20SE3 Westroosebeke	V 23 a, b, c
Malmaison Ferme	57bSE [2 Bazuel]	R 17 a 9.6
Malo Street	36aSE1 St Venant / 2 Lestrem	Q 27-30, R 19, 20, 21, 25
Malon Mill [watermill]	36bSE4 & 36cSW3 Givenchy	X 17 b 4.9
Maloon Street	62cNW1 Maricourt	A 15 b
Malplaquet Camp	28NW3 Poperinghe	H 33 a, b, c
Malplaquet Trench	51bSW1 Neuville Vitasse	M 27 a, b
Malt Trench	57dNE3 & 4 Hébuterne	K 12 a, c
Malt Trench	57dSE2 & 57cSW1 Le Sars	M 4 b, d, 5 c, 12 a, b, d
Malta House	20SE3 Westroosebeke	V 25 a 2.5
Malta Trench	51bSW2 Vis-en-Artois	N 10 d, 11 a, c
Malton Trench	57cNW2 Vaulx-Vraucourt	C 5 b
Maltz Horn Farm [Maltzkorn]	62cNW1 Maricourt	A 6 a 9.3
Maltz Horn Hill / Plateau	62cNW1 Maricourt	A 6 a, b, c, d, 12 a, b
Maltz Horn Trench	57cSW3 Longueval / 62cNW1 Maricourt	S 30 c, A 5 b, d, 6 a, 11 b
Maltzhorn Camp [1916-17, nr Maltz Horn Farm]	62cNW1 Maricourt	A 6 a
Mama Trench	57dNE3 & 4 Hébuterne	K 7 c
Mamelon Trench	20NW4 Dixmude	I 14 b, d, 20 b, 21 c
Mametz [village]	62dNE2 Méaulte	F 4 d, 5 c, d
Mametz Support	62dNE2 Méaulte	F 11 a
Mametz Trench	62dNE2 Méaulte	F 11 a, b, c, d
Mametz Wood	57cSW3 Longueval / 57dSE4 Ovillers	S 13, 19, X 17, 18, 23, 24
Mammoth Trench	57cNE2 Bourlon / 4 Marcoing	E 28 d, K 4 b, d
Man Reserve	51bSW4 Bullecourt	U 19 d
Man Trench	62cNW2 Bouchavesnes	C 25 b
Manancourt [village]	57cSE3 Sorel-le-Grand	V 13 a, b, c, d, 19 a
Manancourt Chateau	57cSE3 Sorel-le-Grand	V 13 d 1.9
Manancourt Mill	57cSE3 Sorel-le-Grand	V 19 c 3.1
Manawatu Camp	28NW4 Ypres	I 14 d, 15 c, 20 b, 21 a
Mance Road [road]	51bSW2 Vis-en-Artois	O 20 c, d, 21 c
Manche Copse, La	27SE2 Berthen	R 29 c
Manche Trench	51bSW1 Neuville Vitasse	M 17 d, 18 c

Name	Map Sheet	Map Reference
Manche Trench [misprinted as Nanche]	66cSW4 La Fère	T 12 b, d, 18 b, d
Manche, la [hamlet]	27SE2 Berthen	R 29 d 3.1
Manchester [lt rly locality NW of P'capp'le '17-18]	20SE3 Westroosebeke	V 13 c
Manchester Avenue	62dNE2 Méaulte	F 11 d
Manchester Cemetery	57cNW2 Vaulx-Vraucourt	N 12 b 1.7
Manchester Hill Redoubt / Manchester Redoubt	62bSW3 St Quentin	S 21 a, b
Manchester Keep [Pont de Nieppe]	36NW2 Armentières	B 23 c 8.4
Manchester Street	28SW2 Wytschaete	O 21 d, 22 c
Manchester Support	51bSW4 Bullecourt	U 19 b, d, 20 c
Manchester Trench	28SW2 Wytschaete	O 21 d, 22 c
Manchester Trench	51bSW1 Neuville Vitasse	M 15 c, 20 a, b
Manchester Trench [1918]	66eNW [2 Thennes]	B 6 b, d, 12 a
Mandalay Corner	28NW3 Poperinghe	G 20 a 4.4
Mandarin Alley	66cSW4 La Fère	O 34 c, d, 35 c, U 4 b, 5 a
Mandarine Lane [trench]	20NW4 Dixmude	I 13 c, d
Mandel Farm	20SE2 Hooglede	Q 36 a 9.2
Mandora Central	36cSW3 Vimy	S 14 d, 15 c
Mandora North	36cSW3 Vimy	S 14 d, 15 c
Mandora South	36cSW3 Vimy	S 14 d, 15 c
Mandrill Farm	27SE2 Berthen	R 18 c 75.55
Mandy Place	20SE2 Hooglede	Q 24 b 45.85
Mangabe Trench	66cNW1 Grugies	B 2 c, d, 8 b, 9 a
Mangel Cottage	28NW1 Elverdinghe	A 29 a 95.65
Mangelaere Post [1918]	20SW4 Bixschoote	U 4 c 86.02
Mangelare [place name]	20SW4 Bixschoote	U 10 a
Mangfall Trench	51bNW3 Arras	G 12 d, 18 b
Mangin [Tranchée, 1915, La Boisselle]	57dSE4 Ovillers	X 13 d
Mangin Track [1917-18]	20SW4 Bixschoote	U 13 c, 19 a
Mango Copse	62cSW4 St. Christ	T 24 b
Mangwatu Camp	28NW4 Ypres	I 14 d, 20 b
Manhattan Farm	28NE4 Dadizeele	L 8 c 15.50
Manhattan Trench [1918]	28SW1 Kemmel	M 27 d, 33 a, b
Mania House	27SE4 Meteren	X 13 b 65.25
Manicourt [village]	66dNW3 Hattencourt / 4 Nesle	H 10 c, 16 a
Manieu Farm	28SW2 Wytschaete	O 21 d 75.90
Manioc Trench	66cNW1 Grugies	B 1 a
Manitoba	66eNE2 Vrély	E 22 d 05.30
Manitoba Road [road]	36cSW4 Rouvroy	T 23 a, c, 29 a, b, d
Mannequin Hill	62bNW4 Ramicourt	I 13 d, 19 b
Mannequin Trench	70dNW2 Servais	C 10 c, 15 b, 16 a
Mannequin Wood	62bNW4 Ramicourt	I 25 b, d, 26 a
Manners Copse [1918]	28SW1 Kemmel	M 25 b
Manners Farm [1918]	28SW1 Kemmel	M 25 b 35.50
Manner's Junction [light rly, St Jean]	28NW2 St Julien	C 27 d 4.5
Mannheim Trench	62cNW4 Péronne	I 23 d, 29 b, 30 a, c
Manning's Mound [craters]	36cSW1 Lens	M 6 c 9.9
Manoir Trench	51bSW1 Neuville Vitasse	M 18 c, d
Manor Farm	28NW4 Ypres	I 22 c 6.5
Manor Halt [light rly locality, 1917-18]	28NW4 Ypres	I 22 c, d
Manor House Farm	28NW4 & NE3 Zillebeke	I 24 c 6.5
Manor Lane [road]	36aSE2 Lestrem	R 17 a, b, d,
Manse Street	57cSW4 Combles	T 11 c, d
Manseiger Weg	28NW4 & NE3 Zillebeke	J 19 a, b
Mansel Camp [1916-17, near Mansel Copse]	62dNE2 Méaulte	F 11 c

Name	Map Sheet	Map Reference
Mansel Copse	62dNE2 Méaulte	F 11 c
Mansfield Trench	51bSW1 Neuville Vitasse	M 15 c, d, 21 a
Mansion House	57dNE3 & 4 Hébuterne	K 34 b
Mansion House Dump	36cNW3 Loos	G 8 d 15.90
Manton Junction [railway]	28NW3 Poperinghe	H 8 a 8.7
Manufacture Farm	66cNW3 Essigny	H 1 d 3.8
Manx Corner [road jct]	28NE2 Moorslede	E 10 c 17.73
Map House	28NE2 Moorslede	F 23 d 45.72
Map Trench	51bNW1 Roclincourt	A 23 b, d
Map Trench	57dNE3 & 4 Hébuterne	K 12 c, d
Maple Copse	28NW4 & NE3 Zillebeke	I 23 b, d, 24 a, c
Maple Copse	62bSW4 Homblières	U 22 c
Maple Farm	20SE2 Hooglede	Q 18 c 25.97
Maple Leaf Cemetery	36NW2 Armentières	B 4 c 4.9
Maple Leaf Road [road]	57dSE2 & 57cSW1 Le Sars / 57dSE4 Ovillers	R 36 a, c, X 5 b, 6 a
Maple Lodge	28NW4 & NE3 Zillebeke	I 23 b 6.5
Maple Redoubt	62dNE2 Méaulte	F 9 d, 10 c, 15 b, 16 a
Maple Street	28NW4 & NE3 Zillebeke	I 23 b, 24 a
Maple Trench	62cNW1 Maricourt	A 2 a
Maple Trench	28NW4 & NE3 Zillebeke	I 23 c
Mar Street	28SW4 Ploegsteert	U 1 a, c
Mar Trench	66dNW1 Punchy	A 5 c, 11 a
Marais Alley	36SW3 Richebourg	S 28 b
Marais d'Aubigny [marsh / lake]	51bSE2 Oisy-le-Verger	R 8 a, b, c, d, 9 a, b, c, d
Marais de Brunemont [marsh / lake]	51bSE2 Oisy-le-Verger	R 1 d, 2 c, 7 b, 8 a
Marais de Palluel [lake / marsh]	51bSE1 Saudemont / 2 Oisy-le-Verger	Q 3, 4, 5, 9, 10, 11
Marais Dump [rly & light rly sidings]	36bNE2 Beuvry	E 24 d, F 19 a, c
Marais East Post, Le	36aSE2 Lestrem	R 11 c, 17 a
Marais South Post, Le	36aSE2 Lestrem	R 16 b
Marais South West Keep [N of Canal]	36bNE2 Beuvry	F 10 b 5.2
Marais Trench	70dNW [1 Chauny]	B 27 b, d, 28 a
Marais West Post, Le	36aSE2 Lestrem	R 10 c, 16 b
Marais Woods	62dSE [2 Proyart]	R 8 b
Marathon Road [Maroc Sector]	36cNW3 Loos / SW1 Lens	G 34, M 5 area
Marble Alley	36cSW1 Lens	M 6 c, d, 12 b
Marble Arch	36cSW1 Lens	M 14 d, 20 b
Marble Arch	36SW2 Radinghem	N 6 a, b
Marble Arch [light rly siding]	36cSW1 Lens	M 14 c
Marble Arch Road [road]	36cSW1 Lens	M 14 a, c, d, 20 b, d, 21 c, 27 a, b
Marceau, Tranchée	70dSW [2 Coucy-le-Château]	N 24 d
March Avenue	51bNW3 Arras	G 17 b, c, d
March Copse	57bSW4 Serain	U 16 d, 22 a, b
March Farm	28SW2 Wytschaete	O 23 c 6.8
Marchand Street	57dSE1 & 2 Beaumont	Q 18 c, 23 b, 24 a
Marchélepot [railway locality]	62cSW3 & 4 Marchélepot	T 22 a
Marchélepot [village]	62cSW3 & 4 Marchélepot	T 21, 22, 27, 28
Marcoing Line	57cNE2 Bourlon / 4 Marcoing	F 5-30, L 6-34
Marcoing Support	57cNE4 Marcoing / 57bNW3 Rumilly	L 1 a,c, 23 b,d, 24a, G 1d, 7b,d, 13b
Marcoing Switch	57cNE4 Marcoing / 57bNW3 Rumilly	L 18 a, c, 23 b, d, G 7 b, d
Marcovitch Crossing [road across rly]	28NE4 Dadizeele	L 14 c 75.40
Marcy [village]	62bSW4 Homblières	U 17 a, b, c, d
Mardon Farm	28NE4 Dadizeele	L 30 a 9.0
Mare Alley	62cSW3 Vermandovillers	T 21 a, b
Mare Lane	51bSW4 Bullecourt	U 21 d, 27 b

Name	Map Sheet	Map Reference
Marechal Farm	20SW4 Bixschoote	O 36 d 1.1
Marengo Farm	28NW2 St Julien	B 24 b 9.3
Marengo House	28NW2 St Julien	B 24 d 9.8
Maresfield Farm	20SE2 Hooglede	R 10 c 8.8
Maret Alley	66cNW2 Itancourt	B 16 b
Maretz [village]	57bSW4 Serain / SE3 Busigny	U 6 b, c, d, 12 a, b, V 1 a, c, 7 a
Maretz Wood	57bSW4 Serain / SE3 Busigny	U 18 b, d, V 13 a, c
Margaret Lane	51cSE2 Beaumetz	R 35 b
Margaret Trench	36SW3 Richebourg	N 31 d
Margate Farm	28NE3 Gheluvelt	J 27 d 4.9
Margate Trench	51bSW1 Neuville Vitasse	M 16 a, b
Marguerite Camp	28NW1 Elverdinghe	B 9 a, c
Marguerite Farm	28NW1 Elverdinghe	B 9 c 2.4
Maricourt [village]	62cNW1 Maricourt	A 15 d, 16 c, 21 b, 22 a
Maricourt Avenue / Boyau Marcourt [sic]	62cNW1 Maricourt	A 15 b
Maricourt Valley	62cNW1 Maricourt	A 27 a, b, c
Maricourt Wood	57cNW2 Vaulx-Vraucourt / 4 Beugny	I 4 b, d
Maricourt Wood	62cNW1 Maricourt	A 16 b, d, 17 c
Marie Jean Farm	28NW1 Elverdinghe	B 9 c 6.5
Marie Louise Farm	20SE3 Westroosebeke	V 11 b 2.7
Marin House	20SW4 Bixschoote	U 13 d 5.3
Marina Trench	36cSW4 Rouvroy	T 5 d, 11 a
Marine Alley	36cSW3 Vimy	S 8 d
Marine Terrace	28SW4 Ploegsteert	T 5 d
Marine Trench	51bNW2 Oppy	B 24 b, c, d, 30 a
Marine View	28NE1 Zonnebeke	D 7 a
Mariner Copse	62cSW4 St. Christ	T 17 c
Marinet Alley	66cSW4 La Fère	U 1 b
Marion Mound	51bNW2 Oppy	C 13 a 3.5
Maripet Trench	62bSW3 St Quentin	S 23 c
Marischal Street	57dSE4 Ovillers	X 26 c
Maritza Trench / Alley / Boyau de la Maritsa	62cSW2 Barleux	O 7 b, 8 a, c, d
Marjorie House	28SW1 Kemmel	M 18 c 6.6
Marjorie Lane [road]	28SW1 Kemmel	M 18 b, c, d, N 13 c
Marjorie Post [1918]	28SW1 Kemmel	M 18 c 30.78
Marjorie Trench [1918]	28SW1 Kemmel	M 17 b, d, 18 a, c
Mark Copse	57dNE3 & 4 Hébuterne	K 29 a
Mark Lane	28NW2 St Julien	C 21 b
Mark Lane [1918]	51cSE [4 Blaireville]	X 25 b, d
Mark Trench	51bNW1 Roclincourt	A 23 d
Marker Farm	20SE3 Westroosebeke	W 14 a 2.0
Market Cross	57dSE4 Ovillers	W 24 b, X 19 a
Market Farm [Potijze]	28NW4 & NE3 Zillebeke	I 4 d 7.6
Market Street	57cSW4 Combles	T 16 b
Market Street / Boyau du Marché	62cNW1 Maricourt	A 23 c
Market Trench [Thiepval]	57dSE1 & 2 Beaumont	R 19 d, 25 b
Markhill Avenue	36NW2 Armentières	C 8 c, d
Marks Farm	28NE2 Moorslede	F 19 b 80.15
Marlboro Trench	57cSW3 Longueval	S 20 b, d
Marlboro' Wood	57cSW3 Longueval	S 20 d
Marlborough Trench	51bSW1 Neuville Vitasse	M 15 d, 16 a, c
Marlborough Trench [new front line]	57dSE1 & 2 Beaumont	Q 4 c, d, 10 b
Marles Lane	51bSW1 Neuville Vitasse	M 28 a, c
Marlière [Wancourt]	51bSW2 Vis-en-Artois	N 17 d, 23 b

Name	Map Sheet	Map Reference
Marlow Bridge	36aSE1 St Venant	P 27 b 05.65
Marlow Farm	20SE2 Hooglede	R 18 c 05.70
Marlow Trench	51bSW1 Neuville Vitasse	M 4 d, 5 c
Marly Woods	62dSE [2 Proyart]	R 4 b, 5 a
Marmalade Lane	51bSW4 Bullecourt	U 7 d
Marmalade Trench	66dNW1 Punchy	G 1 b, d, 2 a
Marmelade Trench	62cNW1 Maricourt	B 19 c, 25 a
Marmelade Trench / Tranchée de la Marmalade	62cSW3 & 4 Marchélepot	T 15 c, d, 16 a, c
Marmons Alley	62cSW2 Barleux	O 13 b, 14 a
Marne [farm / pillbox]	28NE1 Zonnebeke	D 17 c
Marne Alley	66cNW2 Itancourt	B 29 d
Marne Post	62cNE4 Roisel	L 9 d 3.4
Maroc [village]	36cNW3 Loos / SW1 Lens	G 32, 33, M 2, 3
Maroc Alley [Calonne]	36cSW1 Lens	M 9 a, c, d
Maroc, Corons de [miners' cottages]	36cNW1 La Bassée	G 5 a
Maroc, Tranchée	62cNW3 Vaux	G 29 a
Maroon Copse	28NE2 Moorslede	E 28 c 95.40
Maros Trench	62cNW4 Péronne	I 7 d, 13 a
Marqueffles - Houssin - Vaudricourt Line	36bNE4 Noeux-les-Mines	K 10, 16, 22, 28, 34
Marquion Line	51bSE4 Marquion	extensive
Marquis Trench	51bNW2 Oppy	B 12 c, 18 a, c
Marquise Camp	28NW4 Ypres	H 17 d
Marquise Lane	51bSW1 Neuville Vitasse	M 23 b, d, 29 b
Marquise Redoubt / Work	51bSW1 Neuville Vitasse	M 29 b, 30 a, c
Marr Cross Roads	20SE3 Westroosebeke	W 19 d 55.95
Marrières Wood / Bois Marrières	62cNW2 Bouchavesnes	B 18 d, 24 b, C 13 c, 19 a, c, d
Marronier House	20SW4 Bixschoote	U 19 a 1.7
Mars [German MG & TM Pill Box]	51bSW4 Bullecourt	U 20 b 2.8
Mars Avenue	57cSW4 Combles	N 36 d, O 31 c
Mars Cottage	28NW4 Ypres	H 11 d 95.05
Mars Lane	51bSW4 Bullecourt	U 20 b
Marsala Cottage	28NW1 Elverdinghe	B 26 c 6.7
Marsaud Alley	66cNW4 Berthenicourt	I 13 a
Marsden Alley	36bNE4 Noeux-les-Mines / 36cNW3 Loos	L 17 b, 18 a, G 13 b
Marsden Keep	36SW3 Richebourg	S 21 b
Marsden Lane	28NE1 Zonnebeke	D 29 a, b
Marsden's Keep	36cNW3 Loos	G 13 b
Marsh Bottom [farm & pillboxes]	28NE1 Zonnebeke	D 10 b
Marsh Farm [railway sidings]	28NW1 Elverdinghe	H 3 a
Marsh Trench	57dNE3 & 4 Hébuterne	K 12 d
Marsh Trench	57dSE1 & 2 Beaumont	Q 23 b, d
Marsh Wood	62cNW4 Péronne	I 36 d
Marshal Trench	57dSE1 & 2 Beaumont	Q 18 a, c
Marshall Road	28NW4 & NE3 Zillebeke	I 29 c
Marshall Walk	28NW4 & NE3 Zillebeke	I 29 c
Marshalling Yard [Kortepyp]	28SW3 Bailleul	T 26 d
Marsh's Farm	28NW1 Elverdinghe	H 3 b 0.8
Marsouin Farm	28NW2 St Julien	C 8 b 6.2
Marsouins Trench	62cSW2 Barleux	O 1 c
Mart Trench	51bNW1 Roclincourt	A 23 c, d
Mart Trench	57cSW4 Combles	T 16 b
Martell Farm	28NE4 Dadizeele	L 19 b 0.2
Martell Wood	28NE2 Moorslede	E 15 b 16 a
Marten Lane [trench]	62cNE4 Roisel / 62bNW3 Bellicourt	L 18 a, G 13 b

Name	Map Sheet	Map Reference
Marten Post	62bNW3 Bellicourt	G 13 b 20.65
Marten's Farm	28SW2 Wytschaete	O 8 d, 14 b
Marteville [village]	62cSE4 [Attilly]	R 32 d, X 2 b
Martha House	28NE1 Zonnebeke	D 14 c 3.6
Martha House Dugout [Zonnebeke]	28NE1 Zonnebeke	D 14 c 5.5
Martin Alley	57cSW3 Longueval	M 33 a, c
Martin Road	62dNE2 Méaulte	F 10 c
Martin Trench	51bSW2 Vis-en-Artois	O 25 d
Martin Trench	57cSW3 Longueval	M 33 c
Martinique Alley	62cSW1 Dompierre / 2 Barleux	N 1, 7, 8, 14, 15, 16
Martinpuich [village]	57cSW1 Gueudecourt / 3 Longueval	M 27 c, 32 a, b, c, d, 33 a
Martins Corner [late 1915]	36SW2 Radinghem	O 7 b 0.6
Martin's Lane [Thiepval]	57dSE1 & 2 Beaumont	R 19 d, 25 b, d
Martin's Trench	57cSW3 Longueval	M 33 c
Martinsart [village]	57dSE [3 Bouzincourt]	W 3 a, b
Martinsart Wood	57dSE [3 Bouzincourt]	W 2 d, 3 a, b, c
Martyr's Alley	36cSW1 Lens	M 6 c, d, 12 b
Marwitz Weg	66cNW2 Itancourt	B 6 c, 11 b, 12 a
Mary Avenue	57cSW4 Combles	O 31 c
Mary Redan	57dSE1 & 2 Beaumont	Q 17 a
Mary Street	62cNW1 Maricourt	A 8 d
Maryland Buildings	20SE2 Hooglede	R 22 b 4.3
Marylebone Road	36cNW1 La Bassée	A 21 a, b, c
Marylebone Road	57dSE1 & 2 Beaumont	Q 16 b
Maryon Trench	62cNE4 Roisel	L 18 a
Mary's Bridge [road over Wulfdambeek]	28NE4 Dadizeele	L 9 c 65.60
Mash Alley	57cSW3 Longueval	S 6 b
Mash Valley	57dSE4 Ovillers	X 8 c, d, 13 a, b, c, d, 14 a
Mask Trench	51bNW1 Roclincourt	A 23 d
Masnières - Beaurevoir Line	57bNW3 Rumilly/SW1 Bantouzelle/ 62bNW1 Gouy	extensive
Masnières [village]	57bNW3 Rumilly	G 20, 26
Mason Cross Roads	20SE3 Westroosebeke	V 3 d 5.4
Mason's House	36cSW1 Lens	N 8 d
Mass Trench	51bNW1 Roclincourt	A 23 d
Masselot [keep; late 1915]	36SW1 Aubers	M 18 a
Masselot Fauquissart Street [late 1915]	36SW1 Aubers	M 18 a, b, d
Masselot Post	36SW1 Aubers	M 18 a
Masselot Street	36SW1 Aubers	M 18 a, d, N 13 c
Masselot Trench	36SW1 Aubers	N 13 c
Masson [Boyau, 1915] / Tarvis Street	57dSE4 Ovillers	X 20 c
Mast Trench	51bNW1 Roclincourt	A 23 d
Mastic Trench	70dNW2 Servais	C 21 c
Mastiff Trench	36SW1 Aubers	M 36 a
Masui Farm	20SW4 Bixschoote	T 4 a 75.35
Mat Double - Etinehem Road	62dNW [4 Querrieu]	I 29 b
Mat Trench	51bNW1 Roclincourt	A 23 d
Mat Trench	57dNE3 & 4 Hébuterne	K 12 c
Matadores Alley	62cSW2 Barleux	N 23 a, b, 24 a, c
Matai [trench, 1918]	57dNE4 & 57cNW3 Achiet	L 7 b, d
Matawati Camp	28NW4 Ypres	H 29 b
Match Alley	51bSW4 Bullecourt	U 15 a
Match Spinney	28SE1 Wervicq	P 11 b 2.9
Match Trench	57dNE3 & 4 Hébuterne	K 7 c

Name	Map Sheet	Map Reference
Mate Trench	51bNW1 Roclincourt	A 23 d
Matelot Farm	20SE3 Westroosebeke	V 9 b 6.4
Mater Mill [windmill]	20SE2 Hooglede	R 18 c 10.32
Matheson / Mathieson Cemetery	57cSW3 Longueval / 57dSE4 Ovillers	S 19 b, X 24 c
Matheson Road [road]	57cSE1 Bertincourt	P 10 d, 11 a, b, c
Matlock Fork [road jct]	36NW1 Steenwerck	H 1 b 50.65
Matou Alley, Boyau du Matou	62cSW3 & 4 Marchélepot	T 15 b, d, 21 b
Matthew Alley	57dNE3 & 4 Hébuterne	K 29 d, 30 c
Matthew Copse	57dNE3 & 4 Hébuterne	K 29 a, c
Matto Woods	62dSE [2 Proyart]	R 16 d, 17 c, 22 b, 23 a
Maucourt	66eNE2 Vrély	F 24, 30
Maucourt Wood	66dNW1 Punchy	A 13 d
Maud Allan Trench	36cSW3 Vimy / 4 Rouvroy	T 10 c, d, 16 b
Maud Villas [buildings]	36cSW4 Rouvroy	N 36 c, d, T 6 a
Maudlin Trench	36SW1 Aubers	M 30 d, 36 b
Mauer Street	51bNW3 Arras	G 18 c
Mauquissart Trench	36SW1 Aubers	M 30 c
Maurepas [village]	62cNW1 Maricourt	B 8 d, 9 c, 14 b, 15 a
Maurepas Alley	62cNW1 Maricourt	A 23 b, 24 a, b, B 13 c, d, 19 a
Maurepas Camp [1916-17, near Maurepas village]	62cNW1 Maricourt	B 8 d, 9 c, 14 b, 15 a [vicinity of]
Maurepas Ravine	62cNW1 Maricourt	B 8 a, b, c, 13 b, 14 a
Maurepas Trench North	62cNW1 Maricourt	B 8 d, 9 c
Maurepas Trench South	62cNW1 Maricourt	B 14 d, 15 c, 21 a, b, c
Maures, Tranchée des [Moors]	62cSW3 & 4 Marchélepot	T 10 c, d
Maurianne Farm	36aNE4 Merville	L 22 d 2.3
Maurice, Boyau	62cSW1 & 2 Belloy	N 23 b, 24 a
Mauser Cot.	28NW2 St Julien	C 14 a 5.9
Mauser Ridge	28NW2 St Julien	C 14, 15
Mauve Alley [1918]	62dSW [4 Cachy]	U 29 a, b
Mauxion Trench	66cNW4 Berthenicourt	I 25 c
Mavis Farm	20SE2 Hooglede	R 2 b 2.6
Mavis Trench	51bSW2 Vis-en-Artois	N 30 d, 36 b
Maw Trench	57dNE3 & 4 Hébuterne	K 12 b
Mawson House	28NW1 Elverdinghe	H 3 a 3.8
Max Trench	51bSW1 Neuville Vitasse	M 16 a
Max Wood	20SW4 Bixschoote	U 1 d 75.95
Maxim Farm [Maxim's: Ploegsteert Wood]	28SW4 Ploegsteert	U 21 b 25.94
Maxim Farm [Villeret]	62cNE4 Roisel	L 18 a
Maxim Road [road]	62cNE4 Roisel	L 18 a
Maxim Trench [Serre]	57dNE3 & 4 Hébuterne	K 30 d, L 25 c
Maximes / Maxim's [Ploegsteert Wood 1914-15]	28SW4 Ploegsteert	U 21 b 25.94
Maxse Redoubt	62dNE2 Méaulte	E 6 a
Maxwell Avenue	57cNE3 Hermies	K 25 c, d
Maxwell Junction [light rly]	36cSW3 Vimy	S 4 c
Maxwell Support	57dSE2 & 57cSW1 Le Sars	M 17 c, d
Maxwell Trench	57cSW3 Longueval	S 12
Maxwell Trench	57dSE1 & 2 Beaumont	R 25 d
Maxwell Trench	57dSE2 & 57cSW1 Le Sars	M 17 a, c, d
May Avenue	51bNW3 Arras	G 16 d, 17 a, b, c
May Copse	57bSW4 Serain	U 24 a
May Copse	62cNE2 Epéhy	F 9 c
May Copse Post	62cNE2 Epéhy	F 9 c
May Farm	28SE1 Wervicq	P 1 d 4.9
May Lane	62cNE2 Epéhy	F 8 d

Name	Map Sheet	Map Reference
May Trench	51bSW2 Vis-en-Artois	O 2 b
Mayence Trench	62cSW2 Barleux	O 5 b, d, 6 a, c,
Mayfair Avenue	28SW1 Kemmel / 3 Bailleul	M 26 d, 27 c, 32 b, 33 a, c, d, S 3 b
Mayo Corner	28NW3 Poperinghe	G 14 b 9.0
Mayo Trench	28SW2 Wytschaete	N 18 a
Mayot Fort	66cSW2 Vendeuil	O 24 c, d
Mayot Salient	66cSW2 Vendeuil	O 27 a, b, c, d
Mazancourt [village]	62cSW3 & 4 Marchélepot	T 10, 11, 16, 17
Maze [German, late 1915]	36SW2 Radinghem	N 11 a 8.3
Maze Trench	57dNE3 & 4 Hébuterne	K 4 d
Maze, The [1918]	57dSE [3 Bouzincourt]	V 24 d
Maze, The [ESE of Le Sars]	57dSE2 & 57cSW1 Le Sars	M 17 c, d, 18 c
Maze, The [Gommecourt]	57dNE3 & 4 Hébuterne	K 4 d
Mazeppa Farm	20SW4 Bixschoote	U 1 d 75.95
Mazeppa Wood [near Zepp Copse]	62bSW2 Fonsommes	N 24 d, 30 b
Mazera Trench	66cNW3 Essigny / 4 Berthenicourt	H 22 c
Mazes, Boyau des [at Mazancourt]	62cSW3 & 4 Marchélepot	T 16 a, b
Mazières Trench	66cSW2 Vendeuil	O 25 b, 26 a, c
Mazieu Trench	51bSW1 Neuville Vitasse	M 17 d
Mazingarbe [village]	36bNE4 Noeux-les-Mines	L 17 d, 22 d, 23 a, b, c
Mazingarbe Keep East	36bNE4 Noeux-les-Mines	L 24 c, 30 a
McCormick's Aid Post	57cSW3 Longueval	M 35 d 8.6
McCormick's Cemetery	57cSW3 Longueval	M 35 d
McCulloch Road [road]	36aSE1 St Venant	P 1 a, b, 2 a, b, c
McCullock Farm	20SE3 Westroosebeke	W 20 a 3.8
McDonell Road	57dSE2 & 57cSW1 Le Sars	R 29 c, 34 b
McDonnell Trench [Courcelette]	57dSE2 & 57cSW1 Le Sars	R 29 c, d, 34 b, 35 a
McDougal Trench	57cSW3 Longueval	S 10 b, d, 11 a
McGee Trench	28SW2 Wytschaete	O 1 a
McGhie Trench	57dSE4 Ovillers	R 36 c
McGill O.P. [1916]	51cNE4 Wagnonlieu	L 23 d 1.7
McGill O.P. [1917-18]	36cNW3 Loos	G 29 c 1.7
McGill Post	36cSW3 Vimy	S 9 d 2.0
McGill Street	36NW4 Bois Grenier	I 15 c, d, 21 b
McGovern Dump	36bSE2 Boyeffles	R 11 b 0.5
McGregor Trench	57cSW3 Longueval	S 10 b, 11 a
McGregor's Post	28NW2 St Julien	C 21 c 83.56
McIntyre Street	51bNW1 Roclincourt	A 16 a
McLaren Trench	51bNW3 Arras	H 13 a
McLean Post	57cSE4 Villers-Guislain	W 30 d
McMahon Avenue	57dSE1 & 2 Beaumont	Q 23 b
McPhee Post	57cSE4 Villers-Guislain	W 30 b
McPherson Trench	57dSE2 & 57cSW1 Le Sars / 57dSE4 Ovillers	R 36 a, c, M 31 b
McVitie Farm	28NE4 Dadizeele	K 4 d 6.5
Meadow Lane	51bNW4 Fampoux	I 29 b
Meadow Lane [road]	36aSE2 Lestrem	R 14 d, 14 c, 20 a, b
Meadow Lane [road]	51bNE3 Noyelle-sous-Bellonne	J 25 d, 26 c, d
Meadow Trench	57dNE3 & 4 Hébuterne	K 6 c
Meads Copse	20SE2 Hooglede	Q 5 c 8.4
Meagre Trench	36cSW3 Vimy	T 3 b
Meal Lane [1918]	57dNE2 & 57cNW1 Courcelles	F 5 b
Meal Trench	36cSW3 Vimy	T 3 a
Mealy Trench	36cSW3 Vimy	T 3 b
Mean Wood	66dNW3 Hattencourt	G 28 d, 29 c

Name	Map Sheet	Map Reference
Meander Street	36cSW1 Lens	M 14 b, d
Meander Trench	36cSW3 Vimy	N 33 c, T 3 a
Meant Trench	36cSW4 Rouvroy	T 5 a, c
Measle Trench	36cSW3 Vimy	T 3 b
Measure Trench	36cSW3 Vimy	T 3 b
Meat Trench	51bNW1 Roclincourt	A 23 d
Meat Trench	57cSW4 Combles	T 16 b, d
Meath Cemetery	57cSE4 Villers-Guislain	X 21 b 2.00
Meath Farm	28NW3 Poperinghe	G 35 d 7.4
Meath Lane	57cSE4 Villers-Guislain	X 20 b, 21 a
Meath Post	57cSE4 Villers-Guislain	X 21 b 4.8
Meath Trench	36cNW3 Loos	H 25 a, b, c
Meath Trench	51bSW1 Neuville Vitasse	M 16 a, b
Meath Trench	57cSE4 Villers-Guislain	X 15 d, 21 a
Meath Trench	57cSE4 Villers-Guislain	X 15 d
Méaulte [village]	62dNE2 Méaulte	E 16 d, 17 a, b, c, d, 22 b
Mebus Copse	28SE1 Wervicq	P 4 c
Mechanic / Mechanics Tr [Mecknès, Tranchée de]	36bSE2 Boyeffles	R 24 a, c
Mechanics Loop [light rly]	36bSE2 Boyeffles	R 24 b
Mecklenburg Trench / Mecklembourg, Tr. de	66cNW2 Itancourt	C 14 c, d, 20 b, d
Mecknès, Tranchée de [Mechanic/s Trench]	36bSE2 Boyeffles	R 24 a
Medicine Alley	62bSW4 Homblières	T 12 d, 18 b, c, d, 24 b
Medicine Hat Trail	28SW4 Ploegsteert	T 6 c, d
Medler Trench	36cSW4 Rouvroy	T 4 b
Medoc Farms	28NW3 Poperinghe	G 36 a 1.7
Medway Street	28SW4 Ploegsteert	U 1 a, c
Medway Trench	28SW4 Ploegsteert	T 6 b
Medway Trench	36cSW4 Rouvroy	N 34 c, d, T 4 a
Meed Trench	36cSW3 Vimy	T 3 b
Meed Trench	57dNE3 & 4 Hébuterne	K 6 c
Meek Trench	36cSW3 Vimy	T 4 a
Meerpillat Trench	51bNW1 Roclincourt	A 10 c
Meerut Street [Thiepval Wood]	57dSE1 & 2 Beaumont	Q 30 d
Meet Trench	36cSW3 Vimy	T 4 a
Meet Trench	57dNE3 & 4 Hébuterne	K 6 c, 12 a
Meetcheele / Meetscheele	28NE1 Zonnebeke	D 5 b, d
Meg Trench	36cSW4 Rouvroy	T 4 a
Megrim Trench	36cSW4 Rouvroy	T 4 a
Mehari Trench	62cNW4 Péronne	I 32 a, b
Méharicourt [village]	66eNE2 Vrély	F 16, 22
Meiboomhoek [farm]	20SE2 Hooglede	Q 24 c 65.60
Meillon, Tranchée	70dSW [2 Coucy-le-Château]	O 13 c
Mein Lane	57cNW2 Vaulx-Vraucourt	C 1 a, b, c
Meiningen Trench	62cSE1 Bouvincourt	P 7 c, 13 a, c
Meister Farm	20SE2 Hooglede	Q 30 d 2.6
Melbourne Avenue	57cNW2 Vaulx-Vraucourt	C 4 b, c, d, 5 a
Melbourne Street	57cNE1 Quéant	D 4 c, 10 a, c, 16 a
Melbourne Trench [1918]	57dSE [3 Bouzincourt]	V 30 d, W 19 d, 25 a, b, c
Meld Trench	36cSW3 Vimy	N 33 d
Melder Trench	36cSW4 Rouvroy	T 4 b, d
Mellins Farm	27SE4 Meteren	W 4 d 4.2
Mellow Farm	28NE2 Moorslede	F 4 c 80.85
Mellow Trench	36cSW4 Rouvroy	T 5 c
Melly Trench	36cSW3 Vimy	T 3 b

Name	Map Sheet	Map Reference
Melnik Trench / Tranchée de Melnik	62cSW1 & 2 Belloy	O 7 a, c, d, 13 b
Melody Buildings	28NE2 Moorslede	F 3 d 3.8
Melon Copse	28NW3 Poperinghe	H 20 d, 26 b
Melon Farm	28NW3 Poperinghe	H 26 b o.8
Melon, Tranchée du	70dSW [2 Coucy-le-Château]	O 2 d
Melt Trench	36cSW4 Rouvroy	T 4 b
Melton Fork [road jct]	27NE4 Abeele	L 8 d 85.75
Melton Street	51bSW1 Neuville Vitasse	M 11 c
Melville Road [road]	36cSW2 Harnes	N 28 c, d, 34 b, 35 a, c, d
Member Trench	36cSW1 Lens / 2 Harnes / 3 Vimy	N 34 a, b, c
Memorial Cross [Vimy Ridge, 1918]	51bNW1 Roclincourt	B 7 c 85.20
Menace Trench	36cSW4 Rouvroy	T 4 b, d
Menai [strongpoint]	36NW3 Fleurbaix	G 16 c
Mend Trench	36cSW4 Rouvroy	T 4 d, 5 c
Mend Trench	57dNE3 & 4 Hébuterne	K 6 c, d
Menden Trench	66cNW4 Berthenicourt	I 14 d
Mendinghem Hospital & Railhead	27NE2 Proven	E 5 d
Mendip Trench	36cSW4 Rouvroy	T 5 d
Mendip Trench	51bSW1 Neuville Vitasse	M 10 d
Mendoza Tractor Yard	20SW3 Oostvleteren	T 27 b
Menegat, le [place name]	36NW1 Steenwerck	A 24 d
Menelas Trench	66dNW3 Hattencourt	G 1 d, 2 c, 7 b
Menial Trench	36cSW4 Rouvroy	T 5 a, b
Menin Gate [Ypres]	28NW4 Ypres	I 8 b 10.06
Menox Trench	36cSW4 Rouvroy	T 5 c
Mensal Trench	36cSW4 Rouvroy	N 35 d
Mental Trench	36cSW4 Rouvroy	T 5 c
Menu Copse	51bNW4 Fampoux	I 36 d
Menu Trench	36cSW4 Rouvroy	N 36 c, d, T 6 a
Mer Post	62cNE4 Roisel	L 18 a 7.4
Mer Trench	62cNE4 Roisel	L 17 b, 18 a
Meraucourt Wood	62cNW3 Vaux	H 13 d, 14 c, 19 b, 20 a, b
Mercatel [village]	51bSW1 Neuville Vitasse	M 29 c, d
Mercatel Switch	51bSW1 Neuville Vitasse	M 27 a, d, 28 c, d
Mercedes Copse	62cNE3 Buire	J 21 c, d
Mercer Trench	36cSW4 Rouvroy	T 5 c
Merch Trench	36cSW4 Rouvroy	T 4 b
Merchant Trench	36cSW4 Rouvroy	T 4 b
Mercheston / Merchiston Ave / Boyau Mercheston	62cNW1 Maricourt	A 8 c, 14 a
Mercia Alley	51bNW1 Roclincourt	A 9 b, c, d, 10 a
Mercier Street [Boyau Mercier, 1915]	57dSE4 Ovillers	X 19 b, d
Mercier Trench	51bNW1 Roclincourt	A 9 a, b, c, d
Mercier Trench	57cSW4 Combles	T 6 a, b
Merciful Trench	36cSW4 Rouvroy	T 6 b
Merckem Trench	20SW2 Zwartegat	N 29 c, 35 a
Mercure Trench	62cSW3 Vermandovillers	S 14 a, b, d
Mercury [Pillbox]	51bSW4 Bullecourt	U 14 c
Mercury Lane	57cSW2 Villers-au-Flos	N 16 b
Mercury Trench	36cSW4 Rouvroy	T 6 a, c, 12 a
Mercury Trench	51bSW4 Bullecourt	U 14 c
Mere Farm	36aNE2 Vieux Berquin	E 16 a 3.7
Mere Trench	36cSW4 Rouvroy	T 4 d, 5 c
Mere Trench	57dNE3 & 4 Hébuterne	K 5 d, 6 c
Mere Trench, Le	57dNE1 & 2 Fonquevillers	E 11 a

Name	Map Sheet	Map Reference
Mereaucourt Wood	62cNW3 Vaux	H 13, 14, 19, 20
Mereig Trench	36cSW4 Rouvroy	T 5 c, 11 a
Merely Trench	36cSW4 Rouvroy	T 5 c, 11 a
Mericourt [village]	62bNW4 Ramicourt	I 22 c, d
Méricourt [village]	36cSW4 Rouvroy	T 5 a, b, c, d
Méricourt Maze	36cSW3 Vimy	N 33 d, 34 c
Méricourt Road [road]	36cSW4 Rouvroy	T 10 d, 11 a, b, c
Méricourt Support	36cSW3 Vimy / 4 Rouvroy	T 3 b, 4 a, b, 5 a, c
Méricourt Trench	36cSW3 Vimy / 4 Rouvroy	T 3 b, 4 a, b, d, 10 b, 11 a
Méricourt, Corons de [miners' cottages]	36cSW2 Harnes	N 30 a
Meril Trench	36cSW4 Rouvroy	T 11 a
Merino Trench	36cSW4 Rouvroy	T 11 a
Merit Trench	36cSW4 Rouvroy	T 11 a
Merit Trench	51bNW1 Roclincourt	A 23 d
Merkatel Weg	51bSW1 Neuville Vitasse	M 11 c
Merklen Alley	70dNW4 St Gobain	H 22 b, 23 a
Merlan Trench	70dNW4 St Gobain	I 26 b, d
Merle Brewery	28NE2 Moorslede	F 7 b 95.95
Merling Farm	28NE2 Moorslede	F 1 d 7.9
Mermaid House	28SW1 Kemmel	M 18 c 65.35
Merpillat Trench	51bNW1 Roclincourt	A 10 c
Merris [village]	36aNE2 Vieux Berquin	F 1 c, d
Merris Railhead / Refilling Point	36aNE2 Vieux Berquin	E 3 d, 4 c, 9 b, 10 a
Merris, Mont de	36aNE2 Vieux Berquin	E 5 d, 6 c
Merry Trench	36cSW4 Rouvroy	T 5 c
Mersea Street / Boyau Mersed [sic]	62cNW1 Maricourt	A 16 b
Mersey Alley	36cSW3 Vimy / 51bNW1 Roclincourt	T 26 d, A 6 d, B 1 c
Mersey Cross [cross roads]	28NW3 Poperinghe	G 23 c 8.5
Mersey Street	57dSE4 Ovillers	X 1 b
Mersey Street [sunken road]	57cSE2 Gonnelieu	R 33 b
Mersey Trench	36cSW4 Rouvroy	T 5 a, c
Mersey Tunnel	36cSW1 Lens	M 15 c
Merthyr Sap	36cNW3 Loos	G 12 d
Merthyr Trench	57cSE2 Gonnelieu	R 7 b, 8 c
Merton Mill	36NW1 Steenwerck	B 8 d 50.65
Merville [town]	36aNE4 Merville	K 29 a, b, c, d
Merville Old Mill	62bNW3 Bellicourt	H 26 d 25.75
Meseritz Trench	62cNE3 Buire	J 2 c, 8 a
Mesh Trench	36cSW4 Rouvroy	T 4 b
Mesh Trench	51bNW1 Roclincourt	A 23 d
Mesnil [village]	57dSE1 & 2 Beaumont	Q 28 c, d
Mesnil Outposts [1918]	57dSE1 & 2 Beaumont	Q 29 a, b, c, d
Mesnil-le-Petit [village]	66dNW4 Nesle	H 12 b, I 1 c, 7 a
Mesnil-St Laurent [village]	62bSW4 Homblières / 66cNW2 Itancourt	U 25 d, 26 c, C 1 a, b, c, 2 a
Mesnil-St. Nicaise [village]	66dNW4 Nesle	I 2 c, d
Mesopotamia Alley	62bSW3 St Quentin	S 24 c, d
Mesplaux [farm]	36aSE4 Locon	X 14 a 9.7
Mesplaux East Post	36aSE4 Locon	X 15 b
Mesplaux North Post	36aSE4 Locon	X 8 b
Mesplaux Shrine	36aSE4 Locon	X 14 b 12.75
Mess Trench	51bNW1 Roclincourt	A 23 d
Mess Trench	57dNE3 & 4 Hébuterne	K 5 d
Messéan Mill	36NW1 Steenwerck	A 24 c 20.65
Messelhoek [road jcts]	27SE2 Berthen	R 27 d 7.9 & 28 a 3.8

Name	Map Sheet	Map Reference
Messines Trench [1918]	51bNW1 Roclincourt	A 23 a, b, d
Mesure, Tranchée	36cSW3 Vimy	S 2 d
Metal Trench	36cSW3 Vimy	N 33 d
Metal Trench	57dNE1 & 2 Fonquevillers / 3 & 4 Hébuterne	K 6 b, d
Metaxas Trench / Tranchée Metazas [sic]	66cNW2 Itancourt	C 13 b, d
Meteor Redoubt	62bSW4 Homblières	T 29 a, b
Meteor Trench	57cSW2 Villers-au-Flos	N 23 c
Meteren [village]	27SE4 Meteren	X 15 a, b, c, d, 16 c
Meteren Veld [place name]	27SE4 Meteren	X 22 a, b
Methuen / Methven Street	57dSE4 Ovillers	X 19 b
Methuen Trench	57cSE4 Villers-Guislain	X 13 d, 19 b
Methuen Wood	28NE4 Dadizeele	K 22 b, d, 23 a, c
Methyl Trench	36cSW4 Rouvroy	T 6 b, d
Metier, Hill	51bNE3 Noyelle-sous-Bellonne	J 8 a
Metler Graben	51bNW1 Roclincourt	G 6 a
Metre Buildings	28NE2 Moorslede	F 22 d 2.5
Metro Trench	36cSW4 Rouvroy	T 6 b
Metropolitan Left	28NW4 & NE3 Zillebeke	I 29 a, c
Metropolitan Trench	28NW4 & NE3 Zillebeke	I 29 c
Mettle Trench	28SW1 Kemmel	M 22 a, b, c, 23 a
Metz Ravine	66eNW [2 Thennes]	C 15 b, c
Metz Switch	57cSE1 Bertincourt	Q 14, 20, 26 [vicinity of]
Metz-en-Couture [village]	57cSE1 Bertincourt	Q 19 b, d, 20 a, c, d
Meudon Wood	62cSW1 & 2 Belloy	N 11 a
Meudon Wood Alley	62cSW1 & 2 Belloy	N 4 d, 5 c, 11 a
Meuleheuck [hill]	28SW3 Bailleul	S 2 a
Meules Avenue	20SW3 Oostvleteren	T 2 b, 3 a, b
Meules Farm	20SW3 Oostvleteren	T 2 b 2.5
Meulewalle [cross roads]	27SE2 Berthen	Q 17 c 45.90
Meunier House	20SE3 Westroosebeke	V 20 b 1.2
Meunier House	57cSE4 Villers-Guislain	X 8 d 75.15
Meunier Trench	57cSE4 Villers-Guislain	X 8 d, 9 c, 15 a, b
Meuniers [place name]	36NW1 Steenwerck	B 7 c, d
Meunynck Farm	27NE1 Herzeele	E 8 c 8.3
Meurigny Wood	57bSW2 Clary	O 4 b
Meurillon [house]	36aNE4 Merville	L 31 c 35.95
Meuse Bridge [Estaires]	36aNE4 Merville	L 30 c 0.3
Mexico Trench	20SW1 Loo	M 6 b
Mezières Copse	57bSW1 Bantouzelle	N 13 d, 14 c, 20 a
Mezières Farm	57bSW1 Bantouzelle	N 20 a 0.3
Mica Farm	27NE2 Proven	E 28 a 6.6
Mice Trench [1918]	28SW3 Bailleul	S 1 b
Michael's Farm	28NE1 Zonnebeke	D 20 c 4.5
Michel Farm	28NW1 Elverdinghe	B 9 d 2.9
Michel Trench	62cNW2 Bouchavesnes	C 10 c, 16 a
Mick Buildings	28NE2 Moorslede	F 26 a 1.5
Micmac / Mic-Mac Camp	28NW3 Poperinghe	H 31 b
Micmac Farm	28NW3 Poperinghe	H 31 d 4.9
Mid Lane	57cSW4 Combles	T 4 d, 5 c
Middle Alley	36bSE4 Carency	X 6 c
Middle Alley	36cSW1 Lens	M 3 b, 4 a, b, d
Middle Alley [Bazentin-le-Petit Wood]	57cSW3 Longueval	S 7 d, 13 b
Middle Avenue	62cNW1 Maricourt	A 2 d, 8 b
Middle Copse	20SE3 Westroosebeke	V 22 b

Name	Map Sheet	Map Reference
Middle Copse	57bSW1 Bantouzelle	N 20 d, 26 b
Middle Farm	28SW2 Wytschaete	N 6 b 9.4
Middle Farm	28SW2 Wytschaete	O 32 b 1.4
Middle Road [road]	57dNE1 & 2 Fonquevillers	E 13 d, 14 a, c, 19 b
Middle Street [new front line]	57dSE1 & 2 Beaumont	Q 4 b, d
Middle Wood	57dSE4 Ovillers	X 12 c
Middlesex Avenue	62dNE2 Méaulte	F 1 b, d, 7 b
Middlesex Camp	28NW3 Poperinghe	H 32 c 5.5
Middlesex Cemetery	57cSE4 Villers-Guislain	X 15 b
Middlesex Lane	28NW4 & NE3 Zillebeke / SW2 Wytschaete	H 36 d, N 6 b, O 1 a, b
Middlesex Road [plank road]	28NW4 & NE3 Zillebeke	I 27 d, 28 a, b, c, 32 c, d, 33 a, b
Middlesex Trench	51bSW1 Neuville Vitasse	M 5 b, 6 a
Middlesex Trench [Br FL 3/16]	36cSW1 Lens	M 15 a, b, c
Middlesex Wood	28NW4 Ypres	H 35 b, 36 a
Middy Copse	62cSW4 St. Christ	T 16 d, 17 c
Midge Farm	28SW2 Wytschaete	O 24 a 05.77
Midinettes Trench	62cNE1 Liéramont	D 19 a, b, d, 25 b, d
Midland Alley [1918]	51bNW1 Roclincourt	A 17, 18, 24, B 13
Midland Reserve	57cSE2 Gonnelieu	Q 18 c, 23 b, 24 a
Midland Trench [Br]	28SW4 Ploegsteert	T 6 c
Midway Line	57dSE1 & 2 Beaumont	R 20 c, d, 26 b, 27 a, c, d
Mieg Wood	66dNW1 Punchy	A 9 a, b
Might Mill [windmill]	20SE2 Hooglede	R 15 d 80.37
Might Trench	57dNE1 & 2 Fonquevillers	E 30 c, K 6 a
Mignonette Alley	66cNW2 Itancourt	B 10 b
Mikado Lane	57cSW4 Combles	U 15 c, d, 21 b
Milan Trench	51bNW4 Fampoux	H 36 b, d, I 31 c
Mild Alley, & Trench	57dSE2 & 57cSW1 Le Sars	N 21 c, d
Mildesteimer Graben	57dNE1 & 2 Fonquevillers	E 18 b
Mildren Crater	36cSW3 Vimy	S 8 b
Mile Avenue [1918]	28SW3 Bailleul	M 32 c, S 2 a
Mile End Road	57cNE3 Hermies	K 27 b
Miles Avenue	62dNE2 Méaulte	F 14 a
Milk Run	36NW2 Armentières	C 4 c, d
Milk Trench, & Farm	51bNW1 Roclincourt	A 23 d
Milk Work	57cNW1 Gomiecourt	A 20 b
Milky Way [road]	28SW1 Kemmel	N 8 a, b, d, 14 b, 15 a
Mill [Boesinghe, E of Canal]	28NW2 St Julien	B 6 d 3.5
Mill [light rly siding]	36cSW3 Vimy	M 33 c
Mill [windmill, trig point, Neuville St Vaast]	51bNW1 Roclincourt	A 10 a 54.08
Mill [windmill, trig point, Thélus]	51bNW1 Roclincourt	A 6 c 71.95
Mill Alley	36cNW1 La Bassée	A 22 a, b, c
Mill Alley	66cSW4 La Fère	O 31 c, d
Mill Avenue / Boyau du Moulin	62cNW1 Maricourt	A 29 a, c, d
Mill Copse	51bSE2 Oisy-le-Verger	Q 22 b, d, 23 a, c
Mill Copse	51bSW3 Boisleux	T 27 b
Mill Cottages	28NW2 St Julien	I 5 a 0.7
Mill Cross	57cNW4 Beugny	I 27 a, c
Mill Hill / Windmill Hill [Pozières]	57dSE2 & 57cSW1 Le Sars	R 35, X 5
Mill Hill [Moulin de Villecholles]	62cSE2 Vermand	R 28 c
Mill Hill Road [road]	36cSW1 Lens	M 24 d, N 19 c, d
Mill House	28NE2 Moorslede	F 19 d 9.2
Mill Lane	51bNW3 Arras	H 26 c
Mill Lane	62cNE2 Epéhy	F 18 c

Name	Map Sheet	Map Reference
Mill Lane [near Steam Mill]	36aSE2 Lestrem	Q 18 c, d, R 13 c, d
Mill Post [Gavrelle]	51bNW2 Oppy	C 19 c, d
Mill Road (No.2) Cemetery [Thiepval]	57dSE1 & 2 Beaumont	Q 24 c, d
Mill Road [road]	57dSE1 & 2 Beaumont	Q 24 c, d, R 19 c
Mill Road Post	36SW2 Radinghem	N 4 d
Mill Sap	36cNW1 La Bassée	A 21 b, d
Mill Spinney	62cNE4 Roisel	L 34 b, 35 a, c
Mill Street	62cNW1 Maricourt	A 15 d
Mill Street [Morval]	57cSW4 Combles	T 10 d, 11 a
Mill Switch	51bSW3 Boisleux	S 26 a
Mill Trench	36SW1 Aubers	M 30 a, b
Mill Trench	51bNW1 Roclincourt	A 23 d
Mill Trench	57dSE1 & 2 Beaumont	Q 18 d, 24 b, R 13 a, b, c
Mill Trench	62cNW1 Maricourt	A 3 a
Mill Trench	66cSW2 Vendeuil	O 27 d, 33 b
Mill Wood [Walincourt]	57bSW2 Clary	N 30 a, b, c, d
Mill, The [Cuinchy Sector, Feb 1915]	36cNW1 La Bassée	A 15 c, d
Millbank [light rly siding]	36cSW1 Lens	M 14 a, c
Mille-Kapelleken Farm	28NW3 Poperinghe	H 19 d 7.8
Millekruisse [crossroads & houses]	28SW1 Kemmel	N 2 c 4.2
Millencourt [village]	57dSE [3 Bouzincourt] / 62dNE [1 Dernancourt]	V 29, D5
Miller Trench, & Support	28SW3 Bailleul	S 2 d, 3 c, d
Miller's Daughter	57cSW4 Combles	T 4 c
Millers Houses	20SE3 Westroosebeke	V 13 a 4.7
Millers Post [W of High Wood]	57cSW3 Longueval	S 3 d
Miller's Son	57cSW2 Villers-au-Flos	N 33 b, 34 a
Millet Mill	28NE2 Moorslede	F 17 c 47.12
Millo Trench	66cNW3 Essigny	H 14 b, 15 a
Mills Alley	36cSW1 Lens	M 6 c, 12 a
Mills Alley, & Keep [G 14 a]	36cNW3 Loos	G 13 b, 14a
Mills Post Tunnel	36cNW1 La Bassée	A 21 d 61.90
Mills Street [near Thorpe St]	57dNE1 & 2 Fonquevillers / 3 & 4 Hébuterne	E 27 c, K 3 a
Milner Lodge	36NW1 Steenwerck	B 21 d 70.99
Milton Copse	20SE2 Hooglede	R 35 b 1.6
Mimico [light railway sidings, 1917-18]	28NW4 Ypres	H 12 c, 18 a
Mimsey Trench	62cNW1 Maricourt	H 1 b
Mimsey Wood	62cNW1 Maricourt	H 1 b
Min Farm	36SW1 Aubers	M 22 a 8.2
Min Post	36SW1 Aubers	M 22 d
Min Street	36SW1 Aubers	M 22 d, 23 c, 29 a, b
Mina Avenue	36SW1 Aubers / 2 Radinghem	N 10 a, c
Mince Trench	57cSW4 Combles	T 16 a, b
Mince Trench	57dNE1 & 2 Fonquevillers	K 6 a
Mincing Lane [Metz-en-Couture]	57cSE1 Bertincourt	Q 20 c
Mindel Cemetery	51bNW3 Arras	H 13 a 7.7
Mindel Trench	51bNW3 Arras	H 13 a
Minden Avenue	57dSE1 & 2 Beaumont	Q 4 b, d
Minden Avenue	62dNE2 Méaulte	F 18 a
Minden Post	62dNE2 Méaulte	F 17 d, 18 c
Minden Trench / Minden, Tranchée de	62cSW3 & 4 Marchélepot	T 14 a, b, c, d, 15 a, b, c
Minden Trench / Terrace	57dSE1 & 2 Beaumont	Q 4 b, d
Mindin [sic] Trench [Minden]	57dSE1 & 2 Beaumont	Q 4 b
Mine Alley	36cSW1 Lens	M 3 b, d

Name	Map Sheet	Map Reference
Mine Alley	62cNW1 Maricourt	A 2 c, d
Mine Copse	28NE2 Moorslede	F 15 b 15.05
Mine House	28NE2 Moorslede	F 15 d 1.9
Mine Point	36cNW1 La Bassée	A 27 b
Mine Point [Sept 1915]	36cNW1 La Bassée	A 21 d 4.1
Mine Sap [Maroc Sector]	36cNW3 Loos / SW1 Lens	G 34, M 5
Mine Support	62cNW1 Maricourt	A 7 c, 8 a
Mine Trench	36cNW1 La Bassée	A 28 a
Mine Trench	51bNW1 Roclincourt	A 23 d
Mine Trench	62cNW1 Maricourt	A 7 c, 8 a
Minehead Sap	36cNW1 La Bassée	A 27 b
Minen & Werfer Copses [1918]	62dNE [3 Morlancourt]	K 26 c
Minenwerfer Weg	51bSW1 Neuville Vitasse	M 6 a
Miners Trench	28NW4 & NE3 Zillebeke	I 11 b
Miners Walk	36NW4 Bois Grenier	I 16 a
Minerva [German Pillbox]	51bSW4 Bullecourt	U 14 a
Minerve Trench	66dNW1 Punchy	A 26 c, G 1 b, 2 a
Mines, Boyau des [Mines]	62cSW1 Dompierre	M 4 b
Mineur, Boyau de [Sapper]	62cSW3 & 4 Marchélepot	T 17 a, b, d, 18 c
Ming Mill [windmill]	20SE2 Hooglede	Q 29 c 52.61
Minimum Wood	62bSW2 Fonsommes	O 35 a
Minnehaha Drain	36SW3 Richebourg	S 20 d 8.7
Minnie Road [road]	36cNW1 La Bassée	A 22 a, b
Minnow Post	57cNE3 Hermies	J 5 d 95.05
Minnow Trench	62bNW1 Gouy	G 1 b, d
Minny Trench	57dNE3 & 4 Hébuterne	K 16 b
Minor Trench	57dNE3 & 4 Hébuterne	K 34 b
Minorca Trench	51bSW2 Vis-en-Artois	N 10 d, 11 a, c, 16 b
Minos Alley / Boyau de Minos [nr Bois de Medée]	62cSW3 & 4 Marchélepot	T 16 c, d, 17 c, 23 a, b
Minotaure Alley / Boyau du Minotaure	62cSW3 & 4 Marchélepot	T 20 b, 21 a, b, 22 a
Minster [light rly siding]	36cSW1 Lens	M 8 d
Minston Post [draftsman's error: Minden]	62dNE2 Méaulte	F 18 c
Minstrel Cross Roads	28NE2 Moorslede	F 3 d 3.6
Mint Copse	20SE2 Hooglede	R 9 d 7.4
Mint Copse	28SE1 Wervicq	P 4 d
Mint Copse	62bNW1 Gouy	B 19 c
Mint Trench	51bNW1 Roclincourt	A 23 d
Mint Trench	57dNE1 & 2 Fonquevillers	F 25 a
Minto Farm	36NW1 Steenwerck	A 17 b 4.8
Minty Farm	28NW2 St Julien	C 10 c 1.5
Minty Farm Trench [1918]	28NW2 St Julien	C 9 d, 10 a, c
Minway	36cNW3 Loos	G 35 d
Minx Copse	57cNW1 Gomiecourt / 2 Vaulx-Vraucourt	B 16 a, c
Minx Dump	36bNE [3 Bruay]	K 20 a 5.5
Minx Locality [Verquin]	36bNE2 Beuvry / 4 Noeux-les-Mines	E 29 d, 30 c, K 5 b, d, 6 a, c
Minx Trench	57dNE1 & 2 Fonquevillers	E 30 a, c
Miracle Farm	28NE2 Moorslede	F 26 b 3.9
Mirage Trench	57cSW4 Combles	T 5 b, d
Miraumont [village]	57dNE4 & 57cNW3 Achiet / SE2 Beaumont	L 34 d, 35 c, R 4 b, 5 a
Miraumont Alley	57dSE2 Beaumont	R 3 a, b, c, 4 a, b
Miraumont Mill	57dSE2 Beaumont	R 4 d 4.7
Mire Farm	36NW1 Steenwerck	A 11 d 6.3
Mire Trench	51bNW1 Roclincourt	A 23 d
Mirecourt Trench	66cNW3 Essigny	H 6 d

Name	Map Sheet	Map Reference
Mirfield Cemetery	28NW2 St Julien	C 14 c 0.3
Mirfield Trench	28NW2 St Julien	C 13 d, 14 c
Mirror Trench	57cSW3 Longueval	T 3 c
Mirror Trench [1918]	28SW1 Kemmel	M 34 a, b
Mirvaux [village]	57dSW [3 Talmas]	T 26
Misère Trench	62cSW1 Dompierre	M 11 c,d, 12 c, d, 18 b, N 13 a
Misère, Tranchée de la [Misery]	62cSW3 & 4 Marchélepot	T 11 c, d
Misery [village]	62cSW4 St. Christ	T 11 d, 12 c, 17 b, 18 a
Miskin Farm	28NE4 Dadizeele	L 33 c 5.3
Mispelaere Cabaret, De	28NE1 Zonnebeke	D 24 d 3.8
Missiabi Trench	51bNW1 Roclincourt	A 4 c
Missing Link [Oct 1915]	36cNW1 La Bassée	A 28 c
Missing Link [Sept 1915]	51bNW3 Arras	G 5 d
Mission Buildings	28NE4 Dadizeele	L 1 d
Mission Farm	28NW1 Elverdinghe	B 27 c 2.3
Mission Junction [light rly]	28NW1 Elverdinghe	B 27 d 15.15
Mission Sidings [light rly]	28NW1 Elverdinghe	B 27 c
Mississippi Trench	51bNW3 Arras / 4 Fampoux	H 4 c, 10 a, b, d
Misson Buildings	28NE4 Dadizeele	L 1 d 95.40
Missouri Trench	51bNW3 Arras / 4 Fampoux	H 4 c, 10 a, b, d
Mist Trench	51bNW1 Roclincourt	A 23 d
Mist Trench	57dNE1 & 2 Fonquevillers	E 30 d, K 6 b
Misty Alley	57cSW2 Villers-au-Flos	N 28 a, c
Misty Trench	57cSW2 Villers-au-Flos	N 28 a
Misty Trench	57cSW4 Combles	T 4 b
Misty Trench [1918]	57dNE2 & 57cNW1 Courcelles	F 22 a, c, 28 a
Misty Way [road NW of Le Barque]	57cSW1 Gueudecourt	M 6 d, 12 b
Mit Cottage	36NW1 Steenwerck	A 11 b 5.4
Mitau [Trench]	66cNW2 Itancourt	C 25 a
Mitchell Street	57dSE4 Ovillers	X 7 d
Mitchell's Farm	28NE1 Zonnebeke	D 20 c 12.15
Mitchett Avenue	36cNW1 La Bassée	A 26 b
Mite Trench	51bNW1 Roclincourt	A 23 d, 24 c
Mitrailleurs Farm	28NW1 Elverdinghe	B 3 a 1.4
Mitre Trench	36SW3 Richebourg	M 36 c
Mittel Weg	51bNW1 Roclincourt	A 30 b
Mitzi Trench	36SW3 Richebourg	S 11 c
Mix Trench	51bNW1 Roclincourt	A 23 d
Mizen [sic] Farm	27NE4 Abeele	K 24 a 1.7
Mizpah [house]	36aNE3 Haverskerque	J 32 d 35.45
Moa Farm	28SW4 Ploegsteert	U 4 d 7.8
Moa Trench [E of Hébuterne, 1918]	57dNE3 & 4 Hébuterne / Achiet	unidentified
Moat Alley	36cSW1 Lens	M 6 c, 12 a, b
Moat Baths [Ypres Moat]	28NW4 & NE3 Zillebeke	I 14 a
Moat Copse	62bSW2 Fonsommes	O 27 c
Moat Farm	28SE1 Wervicq	P 1 b 8.8
Moat Farm Avenue	36NW4 Bois Grenier	I 25 a, c, 31 a
Moat House Redoubt [Givenchy, Sept 1915]	36cNW1 La Bassée	A 8 b, d
Moat Lane	28NW4 Ypres	I 14 b, 15 a, b, d, 16 c
Moat Lane	36cNW3 Loos	G 35 b, d
Moat Trench	51bNW1 Roclincourt	A 23 d
Moated Farm	36SW1 Aubers	N 7 a
Moated Farm [Ploegsteert Wood]	28SW4 Ploegsteert	U 15 c 3.2
Moated Grange	28NW4 Ypres	I 16 c 6.7

Name	Map Sheet	Map Reference
Moated Grange	28SW2 Wytschaete	O 1 a 6.3
Moated Grange	36aNE3 Haverskerque	K 26 d 4.7
Moated Grange [Fme Vanbesien]	36SW1 Aubers	M 29 c 85.90
Moated Grange [later called Canadian Farm]	28NW2 St Julien	C 15 d 8.5
Moated Grange Farm [Fme Vanbesien]	36SW1 Aubers	M 29 c 85.90
Moated Grange Street	36SW1 Aubers	M 28 d, 29 c, d
Moated Grange Street [late 1915]	36SW1 Aubers	M 22 d, 28 b, 29 a, c, d
Moated Grange, The [Fme Vanbesien, late 1915]	36SW1 Aubers	M 29 central
Mob Trench	36cSW2 Harnes	O 16 a
Mob Trench	51bNW1 Roclincourt	A 23 d
Mobbs Street	28SW4 Ploegsteert	T 6 b, d
Mobile Trench	36cSW2 Harnes	O 16 c
Mobray Wood	28SW1 Kemmel	M 34 b, 35 a
Mocassin S.P. [strongpoint; Montigny]	36cSW2 Harnes	O 22 b, d, 23 a, c
Moche, Tranchée	70dSW [2 Coucy-le-Château]	O 19 c
Model Farm	28NE2 Moorslede	F 29 b 45.30
Model Trench	36cSW2 Harnes	O 11 c, 16 b, 17 a
Modern Trench	36cSW2 Harnes	O 16 c, d
Modest Trench	36cSW2 Harnes	O 16 d, 17 c, d
Moertz Alley	62cSW3 Vermandovillers	S 9 a, c, d
Mogador Trench [1918]	62dSW [4 Cachy]	T 18 c, d
Mogg Farm	28NE2 Moorslede	F 26 a 75.25
Mogg's Hole	36SW3 Richebourg	M 35 c, d
Mogul Trench	36cSW2 Harnes	O 10 d, 11 c
Mogul Trench	57dSE1 & 2 Beaumont	Q 17 d
Mohair Trench	36cSW2 Harnes	O 22 c
Mohawk Trench	36cSW2 Harnes	O 22 c
Moinville Trench	51bSW1 Neuville Vitasse	M 27 c, 32 b, 33 a
Moise Wood	66dNW3 Hattencourt	G 22 a
Moislains [village]	62cNW2 Bouchavesnes	C 11 d, 12 a, c, d, 17 b, d, 18 a, b, c
Moislains Aerodrome [German, 1918]	62cNW2 Bouchavesnes	C 29 b, d, 30 a, c
Moislains Alley	62cNW2 Bouchavesnes	C 10 b
Moislains Trench	62cNW2 Bouchavesnes	C 11 d, 17 b
Moislains Wood	62cNW2 Bouchavesnes	C 4 c, d, 10 a, b
Moist Trench	36cSW2 Harnes	O 22 c
Moke Trench [1918]	28SW3 Bailleul	S 1 d, 2 c
Molar Cottage	28NE2 Moorslede	F 22 a 90.99
Molar Trench	36cSW2 Harnes	O 22 c
Molasse Trench	62cSW3 Vermandovillers	T 16 c, 22 a
Mole Hill Keep	36SW3 Richebourg	S 10 b 2.3
Mole Lane	51bSW4 Bullecourt	U 7 d
Mole Lane [Oct 1915]	36cNW3 Loos	G 10 d
Mole Street	36SW3 Richebourg	S 10 b
Mole Track (Duckboard) [1917-18]	28NW4 Ypres / NE3 Gheluvelt	I 6 c, d, 11 b, 12 a, J 1 c, d, 2 c, d
Mole Trench	57cNE4 Marcoing	L 31 a, b
Mole Trench [Brayelle Graben, east]	57dNE1 & 2 Fonquevillers	E 24 d, 30 b
Moleghein Farm	36aNE2 Vieux Berquin	E 10 c 3.5
Molen Lane [trench, 1918]	28SW1 Kemmel	M 17 b, d, 18 a
Molenhoek [hamlet, road bend]	28NE3 Gheluvelt	K 7 c
Molest Trench	36cSW2 Harnes	O 28 a
Moll Trench	57cNE4 Marcoing	L 31 a
Molly Post	62cNE4 Roisel	L 30 a 0.2
Molly Trench	36cSW2 Harnes	O 28 a
Molly Trench	36SW3 Richebourg	S 6 a

Name	Map Sheet	Map Reference
Molly Villas [buildings]	36cSW4 Rouvroy	N 36 d
Molsberg Alley	66cNW2 Itancourt	B 5 a, b, c, d
Molten Trench	57cSW2 Villers-au-Flos	N 29 a
Moltke Graben	57dNE3 & 4 Hébuterne	K 11 a, b, 12 a
Momber Crater [Bellewaarde Farm]	28NW4 & NE3 Zillebeke	I 12 a 3.1
Momber Crater [Railway Wood]	28NW4 & NE3 Zillebeke	I 12 b
Momber Crater [Vimy Ridge]	36cSW3 Vimy	S 15 a
Moment Trench	36cSW2 Harnes	O 28 c
Mon Farm	28NE2 Moorslede	F 13 c 9.7
Mona Trench	36cSW2 Harnes	O 4 b, d, 10 b, d, 11c, 17 a, c, 23 a
Monacu [farm]	62cNW3 Vaux	H 9 a
Monacu Trench	62cNW3 Vaux	H 3 c, 9 a
Monarch Trench	36cSW2 Harnes	O 28 c
Monastir Trench	62cNW2 Bouchavesnes / NE1 Liéramont	C 5, 6, 12, D 7, 8
Monchy Graben [Monchy-au-Bois]	57dNE1 & 2 Fonquevillers	E 12 a, b, F 7 a, b
Monchy Mill South	57dNE1 & 2 Fonquevillers	E 4 d 80.05
Monchy Switch Front Line [1918]	57dNE1 & 2 Fonquevillers	E 6, 9, 10, 11, 12, F 1
Monchy Switch Reserve Line [1918]	51cSE [4 Blaireville]	X 19 d, 20 a, c, 25 b
Monchy Switch Support [Monchy-au-Bois, 1918]	57dNE1 & 2 Fonquevillers	E 3, 4, 5, 6, 10, 11
Monchy Trench [Monchy-le-Preux]	51bNW4 Fampoux	H 36 b, I 31 a, c, d
Monchy-au-Bois [village]	51cSE3 & 4 Ransart / 57dNE1 & 2 Fonquevillers	W 29, E 5, 6
Monchy-Lagache [village]	62cSE3 Athies	V 12 c, d, 18 a
Monchy-le-Preux [village]	51bSW2 Vis-en-Artois	N 6 b, d, O 1 a, b, c, d
Moncrief Street	57dSE4 Ovillers	Q 36 d
Monday Avenue	51bNW1 Roclincourt / 3 Arras	G 5, 10 b, 11 a
Mondollet Trench [1918]	62dSW [4 Cachy]	U 9 d, 10 c, 15 b
Mondovi Farm [moated]	20SW4 Bixschoote	U 14 b 23.95
Mondovi Wood	20SW4 Bixschoote	U 8 d
Monestry Trench	57dNE3 & 4 Hébuterne	K 28 b, d
Money Trench [1918]	28SW1 Kemmel	M 22 c, d, 28 a
Monidée [farm]	62bSW1 Gricourt	M 24 b 1.9
Monikie Street	57dSE4 Ovillers	X 19 d, 25 b
Monirieth Street	57dSE4 Ovillers	X 19 b
Monitz Alley	62cSW3 Vermandovillers	S 14 a, b, 15 a
Monk Street	57cSW2 Villers-au-Flos / 4 Combles	N 34 central
Monk Trench	51bNW4 Fampoux	I 32 c
Monk Trench	57dNE1 & 2 Fonquevillers	E 30 b, d
Monk Trench	57dNE3 & 4 Hébuterne	K 22 d, 28 b, 29 c, 35 a
Monkey Lane	51bSW2 Vis-en-Artois	O 20 c, d
Monkey Lane	57cNE1 Quéant	E 26 d, 27 c, K 2 b
Monkey Puzzle, The [German trenches, 1915]	36NW2 Armentières	C 17 d, 18 c
Monkey Trench	57dNE1 & 2 Fonquevillers	E 30 b, d
Monkey Trench	66cNW1 Grugies	B 1 a, b, d
Monks Fork [road jct]	28NE4 Dadizeele	K 24 b 65.10
Monmouth Cot.	28NW2 St Julien	C 28 d 60.75
Monmouth House	36NW2 & NE1 Houplines	C 4 c 8.8
Monmouth Trench	36NW2 Armentières	C 4 a, c
Monmouth Trench	51bNW1 Roclincourt	A 3 a
Monmouth Trench [Wieltje]	28NW2 St Julien	C 28 b
Monnaart Copse	27NE2 Proven	E 23 b, d
Monnet, P.C. [Savernake Wood]	62cNW1 Maricourt / 2 Bouchavesnes	B 4 c 28.20
Monnier Alley	62bSW3 St Quentin / 66cNW1 Grugies	S 29 c, d, A 4, 5, 7 - 10
Monniken Farm	20SW2 Zwartegat	O 36 b 4.5

Name	Map Sheet	Map Reference
Monocle Trench	70dNW2 Servais	C 21 a, c
Monsieur, Bois	57dSW [1 Puchevillers / 3 Talmas]	M 32 a, b, c
Monsoon Trench	36cSW2 Harnes	O 11 a, c, d, 17 b, d, 23 b
Mont Bedu	51bNE3 Noyelle-sous-Bellonne	K 25 a
Mont de Lille [hill & farm]	28SW3 Bailleul	S 21 d 80.25
Mont des Cats [Katteberg]	27SE2 Berthen	R 19 b, 20 a
Mont des Cats [village]	27SE2 Berthen	R 19 b, d, 20 a, c
Mont des Cats Monastery	27SE2 Berthen	R 19 b 8.5
Mont des Recollets	27SE1 St Sylvestre	P 1 b, 7 b
Mont Forêt Line [light rly]	36cSW3 Vimy	T 15 c, d, 16 c, d, 20 a, b
Mont Forêt Quarries	36cSW3 Vimy / 4 Rouvroy	T 22 a 7.6
Mont Kemmel [Kemmelberg, summit]	28SW1 Kemmel	N 26 a
Mont Kokereele	27SE2 Berthen	R 16 d
Mont Kokereele [summit]	27SE2 Berthen	R 16 d 90.15
Mont Noir [summit]	28SW1 Kemmel	M 20 c, 26 a
Mont Notre Dame	51bNE3 Noyelle-sous-Bellonne	J 15 b, d
Mont Pierre	51bNE3 Noyelle-sous-Bellonne	J 15 a, b
Mont Rouge	28SW1 Kemmel	M 21 b, d, 22 a, b, c
Mont St Quentin [Hill 115 summit]	62cNW4 Péronne	I 10 c, d
Mont St Quentin [village]	62cNW4 Péronne	I 15 b
Mont Trench	51bNW1 Roclincourt	A 23 d
Mont Vidaigne [summit]	28SW1 Kemmel	M 20 d, 21 a, c
Mont Wood, le	51bNE3 Noyelle-sous-Bellonne	K 13 a, c
Mont, le [hamlet]	51bNE3 Noyelle-sous-Bellonne	K 13 b
Montagne Quarry	27SE2 Berthen	R 14 b, 15 a
Montagne, la [farm]	27SE2 Berthen	R 9 c 45.12
Montagnes Honnecourt, les	57bSW3 Honnecourt	S 8 a, b
Montauban [village]	57cSW3 Longueval	S 27 b, c, d
Montauban Alley	57cSW3 Longueval / 62cNW1 Maricourt	S 22 c, d, 26 d, 27 a, b, c, 28 a, A 1 b
Montauban Avenue / Boyau de Montauban	62cNW1 Maricourt	A 8 c
Montauban Mill	62cNW1 Maricourt	A 3 a 1.8 [approx]
Montauban Ridge	57cSW3 Longueval / 62cNW1 Maricourt	S 26, 27, 28, A 1, 2, 3
Montauban Trench [Fresnes-les-Montauban]	51bNW2 Oppy	C 28 a, c
Montbrehain [village]	62bNW2 Brancourt-le-Grand	C 25, H 6, I 1
Montecouvez Farm	57bSW3 Honnecourt	N 31 c
Montelle Copse	62cSE2 Vermand	R 20 c, d, 26 a
Montescourt [village]	66cSW1 Remigny	M 5, 6
Montfrenoy Trench	70dNW2 Servais	C 3 b, d, 4 c
Montigny [village]	57bSW2 Clary	O 6 c, 12 a, b, d
Montigny Copse	57bSW2 Clary	O 12 d
Montigny Farm Aerodrome [German, 1918]	62cNE4 Roisel / SE2 Vermand	K 35 d, 36 c, Q 5 a, b, c
Montigny Support	36cSW2 Harnes	O 16 b
Montigny Trench	36cSW2 Harnes	O 28 a
Montigny-Harnes-Annay Switch	36cNW4 Pont-à-Vendin / SW2 Harnes	H 36, N 6, O 1, 2, 8
Montlucon Trench	66cNW1 Grugies	B 8 c, d, 14 a, b, c
Montmirail Farm	20SW4 Bixschoote	U 15 c 8.3
Montolu Woods No.1	62cSE2 Vermand	R 8 c, 14 a
Montolu Woods No.2	62cSE2 Vermand	R 14 a, b
Montplaisir Trench	70dNW4 St Gobain	I 26 c, 32 a
Montreal	28SW [Kemmel Defences]	N 26 c 5.5
Montreal [light rly locality & huts]	28NW3 Poperinghe	H 7 d
Montreal Camp [F Camp]	28NW3 Poperinghe	H 19 b
Montreal Cemetery	36cSW3 Vimy	S 15 a 2.5
Montreal Crater	36cSW3 Vimy	S 15 a 60.15

Name	Map Sheet	Map Reference
Montreal Dump	28SW1 Kemmel	N 26 c 5.5
Montreal Road [road]	36cSW4 Rouvroy	T 11b, 12a,c,d, 18b, U13 a,c,d, 19b,d
Montreal Trench	36cSW4 Rouvroy	T 17 c, 23 a, c
Montrose Trench	36cSW2 Harnes	O 28 c
Monty Copse	62cNE3 Buire	J 20 a, b
Monument Commemoratif	57cNW3 Bapaume	H 15 c
Monument Wood	57cNW3 Bapaume	H 21 a, b
Monument Wood	62dSW [4 Cachy]	U 6 a, c
Monument, The	62dSW [4 Cachy]	U 6 a
Monument, The / The Needle	62bSW1 Gricourt	M 34 b 4.1
Monymusk Street	57dSE4 Ovillers	X 20 c
Moolenacker [hamlet]	27SE4 Meteren	X 19 b, d
Moon Quarry	51bSW4 Bullecourt	O 33 c
Moon Trench	57cSW4 Combles	N 36 a, b, d, O 31 c
Moon Trench	57dNE1 & 2 Fonquevillers	F 25 a
Moonray Trench	57cSW2 Villers-au-Flos	N 22 d, 23 c
Moonta Camp	28NW3 Poperinghe	G 22 a
Moonta Farm	28NW3 Poperinghe	G 22 a 2.5
Moor Alley	66cNW2 Itancourt	C 25 a
Moor Fork [road jct nr Moorslede]	28NE2 Moorslede	E 16 b 4.5
Moor Trench [1918]	57dSW [4 Toutencourt]	U 30 b, d
Moore Trench	36cSW2 Harnes	O 28 c, d, 34 b
Moorgate Street	28NW2 St Julien	C 21 d
Moorhen Farm	20SE2 Hooglede	R 13 d 9.7
Moorseele [village]	28NE4 Dadizeele	L 23 a, b, c, d
Moorslede [village]	28NE1 Zonnebeke / 2 Moorslede	E 9 d, 10 a, c, 15 b, 16 a
Moorslede-Dadizeele Line	28NE2 Moorslede / 4 Dadizeele	extensive
Moose Jaw [light railway locality]	28NW3 Poperinghe	H 8 d 5.2
Moose Jaw Fort [farm buildings]	28NW3 Poperinghe	H 8 c 6.1
Moosejaw Road [road; Acheville]	36cSW4 Rouvroy	T 12 d, 17 d, 18 a, b, c
Mop Trench [Brayelle Graben, west]	57dNE1 & 2 Fonquevillers	E 30 a, b
Moral Mill	27NE2 Proven	E 12 b 75.65
Morava Trench	62cNW4 Péronne	I 7 b, d
Moray Avenue	51bNW1 Roclincourt	A 22 a
Moray Copse	27NE4 Abeele	L 15 c, d
Moray Farm	27NE4 Abeele	L 15 d 9.0
Moray House	20SE3 Westroosebeke	V 21 d 05.70
Moray Trench	51bNW4 Fampoux	H 22 d, 28 b, d
Morbecque [village]	36aNE1 Morbecque	D 19 d, 20 a, b, c
Morbecque Chateau	36aNE1 Morbecque	D 14 d 0.0
Morbihan Trench	66cNW1 Grugies	B 7 c, d, 13 b, 14 a
Morchain [village]	66dNW2 Morchain	C 13, 14, 19, 20
Morchies [village]	57cNW4 Beugny	I 5 d, 6 c, 11 b, 12 a
Morcourt [village]	62bSW2 Fonsommes / 4 Homblières	N 34 b, 35 a, c
Mordacq Farm	28NW2 St Julien	B 17 c, d
Morden Trench	51bSW4 Bullecourt	U 16 d, 17 c, 23 b
Moreau, Boyau [Morrow Trench]	36cSW1 Lens / 3 Vimy	M 31 b, d, 32 c
Moreuil [village]	66eNW [4 Morisel]	I 2, 3, 8, 9
Moreuil Signal Pillar [trig]	66eNW [4 Morisel]	I 16 a 35.80
Moreuil Wood	66eNW [2 Thennes / 4 Morisel]	C 21, 22, 27, 28, I 3, 4
Morgan Cottage [1918]	28SW1 Kemmel	M 3 b 45.75
Morgan Post	57cSE4 Villers-Guislain	W 30 d
Morgan Trench [Mur de Calonne, Tranchée du]	36cSW1 Lens	M 14 d, 20 b
Morgan Wood	62dSE [2 Proyart]	Q 23 b, d

Name	Map Sheet	Map Reference
Moriebrug [cottage & bridge]	28SW3 Bailleul	T 1 d 4.7
Morisel [village]	66eNW [4 Morisel]	I 2 c, 7 b, 8 a
Morlaix Alley	62bSW3 St Quentin	S 5 b, 6 a, b
Morlaix Redoubt	62bSW3 St Quentin	S 6 a, c
Morland Avenue [plank road, 1917-18]	28NW4 Ypres	I 28 b, 29 a, b, 30 a, b
Morlemont [village]	66dNW4 Nesle	H 18 a, c
Morley House	28NE4 Dadizeele	L 31 d 90.75
Morman Fork [road jct]	27SE4 Meteren	X 3 c 05.40
Morny Farm	36NW1 Steenwerck	B 9 b 5.6
Morocco North [Tranchée Maroc Nord]	36cSW1 Lens	M 19 b
Morocco South [Tranchée Maroc Sud]	36bSE2 Boyeffles	R 24 c
Morocco Trench	51bSW2 Vis-en-Artois	N 12 b, d, O 7 a, c
Morocco Trench	66cNW3 Essigny / 4 Berthenicourt	H 4 c, 10 a, c
Morpeth Dump	28NW2 St Julien	I 4 d
Morphia Street [Cuinchy]	36cNW1 La Bassée	A 21 b
Morris Row [houses, 1918]	28SW1 Kemmel	M 20 d 3.7
Morris Wood [1918]	28SW1 Kemmel	M 20 b, d
Morrow Trench [Moreau, Boyau]	36cSW1 Lens / 3 Vimy	M 31 b, d, 32 c
Morse Copse	62cSE1 Bouvincourt	Q 14 d
Morse Farm	28SE1 Wervicq	P 20 b 9.5
Morshead House	28NE4 Dadizeele	L 1 d 55.35
Mortagne Alley	66cNW4 Berthenicourt	I 31 b
Mortar Copse [1918]	62dNE [3 Morlancourt]	K 31 a
Mortar Farm	28SW2 Wytschaete	N 36 d 7.3
Mortar Road [road]	36cNW3 Loos / 4 Pont-à-Vendin	H 28 c, d, 34 a
Mortar Street / Boyau du Mortier	62cNW1 Maricourt	A 23 c
Mortar Wood	36cNW4 Pont-à-Vendin	H 28 d
Morte Alley	62cSW3 Vermandovillers	T 15 d, 21 b
Morteldje Estaminet	28NW2 St Julien	C 15 c 9.5
Mortho Wood	57bSW3 Honnecourt	T 1 c, d, 7 a, b
Mortiers Avenue	51bNW1 Roclincourt	A 22 d, 28 b
Morval [village]	57cSW4 Combles	T 10 d, 11 c, 16 b, 17 a
Morval Mill	57cSW4 Combles	T 11 b 02.85
Morval Ridge	57cSW4 Combles	T 5, 10, 11, 12, 16, 17
Mory [village]	57cNW1 Gomiecourt / 2 Vaulx-Vraucourt	B 21 b, d, 22 a, c
Mory Copse	57cNW1 Gomiecourt / 2 Vaulx-Vraucourt	B 16 a, c
Mory Switch	57cNW1 Gomiecourt	B 8, 9, 15
Mosquito Alley	36cSW3 Vimy	S 14 c
Moss Farm	20SE2 Hooglede	R 15 d 35.80
Moss Side	57dSE1 & 2 Beaumont	Q 24 a
Moss Trench	51bSW1 Neuville Vitasse	N 14 c, 20 a
Moss Trench	57dNE1 & 2 Fonquevillers	E 30 b
Moss Trench	62bNW3 Bellicourt	G 13 b
Mosselmarkt [farm, Passchendaele]	28NE1 Zonnebeke	D 6 a 4.9
Mosselmarkt [village]	28SE3 Comines	V 30 c
Mossy Trench	36SW1 Aubers	N 14 c, d, 20 b
Mossy Wood	62cSW4 St. Christ	T 23 d, 24 c
Moth Copse	27SE2 Berthen	R 8 d
Moth Farm	27SE2 Berthen	R 8 c 85.55
Moth Street	51bSW1 Neuville Vitasse	M 21 a
Moti [trench]	66cNW2 Itancourt	C 25 a, b
Motor Car Corner	36NW2 Armentières	C 14 a 8.9
Motte au Bois Chateau, la	36aNE1 Morbecque	D 30 c 8.5
Motte au Bois, la [village]	36aNE1 Morbecque	D 30 a, b, c, d

Name	Map Sheet	Map Reference
Motte Baudet, la [hamlet]	36aNE3 Haverskerque	J 29 d, 30 c
Motte Marty Tree [trig point]	62bSW4 Homblières	O 36 d 72.03
Motte Valley, la	62bNW1 Gouy / 2 Brancourt-le-Grand	B 21 d, 27 b, 28 a
Motte, Boyau de la	62cSW3 & 4 Marchélepot	T 15 d, 21 b
Motte, la [farm, E of Béthune]	36bNE2 Beuvry	F 1 b 8.4
Mottes Trench	36SW1 Aubers	M 24 d
Mottes Way	36SW1 Aubers	M 24 d, N 19 c
Mouanza Trench	62bSW3 St Quentin	T 26 c
Mouchoir Copse	57cSW4 Combles	T 24 b 6.9
Mouere, Tranchée des [sic]	62cSW3 & 4 Marchélepot	T 10 d, 16 a, b
Mouettes Trench	57cSE1 Bertincourt / 3 Sorel-le-Grand	P 28 c, 34 a, c, d, V 4 b
Mouise Trench	62cSW3 Vermandovillers	T 13 d, 14 a, c
Moulin à Vapeur	28SW4 Ploegsteert	U 17 d or 18 c
Moulin Alley	66cNW1 Grugies	B 13 a
Moulin Avenue	57dSE1 & 2 Beaumont	Q 21 a, b, c
Moulin Brichembault	51bSE2 Oisy-le-Verger	Q 23 c 8.8
Moulin Carlin [La Basse Ville]	28SW4 Ploegsteert	U 17 d 5.7
Moulin Detruit	57dNE3 & 4 Hébuterne	K 3 c
Moulin du Roi	51bSW2 Vis-en-Artois	O 18 d
Moulin Farm	28NE1 Zonnebeke	D 22 d 5.6
Moulin Track [1917-18]	28NE1 Zonnebeke	D 22 c, d, 28 b
Moulin Vert Trench	20SW4 Bixschoote	U 25 c, d
Moulinet, le [Goeulzin]	51bNE4 Cantin	K 17 a, b
Mound [Jan. 1916]	36cNW1 La Bassée	A 4 c 7.7 [approx]
Mound Alley	51bSW2 Vis-en-Artois	O 2 d
Mound Keep	57dSE1 & 2 Beaumont	Q 35 b
Mound Keep	62cNW1 Maricourt	A 16 c
Mound Lane Trench	28SW2 Wytschaete	O 2 d 3.3
Mound O.P. [German]	57dSE2 Beaumont	R 3 a 2.5
Mound of Death / Mound, The [St Eloi]	28SW2 Wytschaete	O 2 d
Mound Street / Boyau du Remblai	62cNW1 Maricourt	A 29 a
Mound, The	57dSE2 Beaumont	Q 24 a
Mound, The	62dNE2 Méaulte	F 11 b, d
Mound, The [British OP, 3/15, St Eloi]	28SW2 Wytschaete	O 2 d 2.8
Mound, The [Eitel Fritz Farm. Verlorenhoek]	28NW2 St Julien	I 5 b 5.7
Mound, The [N of Bois du Vert]	51bSW2 Vis-en-Artois	O 3 c
Mound, The [Potijze Chateau]	28NW2 St Julien	I 4 a
Mound, The [Sapignies]	57cNW3 Bapaume	H 7 b 9.3
Mount Elgin [light rly sidings]	28NW3 Poperinghe	G 16 d
Mount Everest	57dSW [1 Puchevillers / 3 Talmas]	N 31, 32
Mount Everest [redoubt on Hunter Avenue]	28SW4 Ploegsteert	U 21 a 45.20
Mount Keep Cemetery	57dSE2 Beaumont	Q 35 b 8.2
Mount Olympus [NW of Bellicourt]	62bNW1 Gouy	A 27 c, G 3 a
Mount Pleasant Wood [Roeux]	51bNW4 Fampoux	I 19 a
Mount Sorrel	28NW4 & NE3 Zillebeke	I 30 a, b, c, d
Mount Street	57dSE1 & 2 Beaumont	Q 16 b, & Q 30 d
Mount Street	62dNE2 Méaulte	F 11 d
Mount Street [road, E of Guillemont]	57cSW3 Longueval	T 19 b, d
Mountain Alley	57dNE3 & 4 Hébuterne	L 19 d, 20 c
Mountain Ash Trench	57cSE2 Gonnelieu	R 8 c, d
Mountain Gun Farm	28SW4 Ploegsteert	U 27 c
Mountain Trench [Mont Noir]	28SW1 Kemmel	M 25 b, 26 a, b
Mountain Way [Loos Crassier]	36cNW3 Loos	G 36 c
Mounteagle Street	57dSE4 Ovillers	X 1 a, c

Name	Map Sheet	Map Reference
Mountebank Fork [road jct]	28NE2 Moorslede	F 7 b 3.1
Mountjoy Trench	57dNE3 & 4 Hébuterne / 57dSE 1 & 2 Beaumont	K 34 c, Q 4 a
Mouquet Farm	57dSE1 & 2 Beaumont	R 27 d, 33 b
Mouquet Fme.	36SW2 Radinghem	N 11 a 05.05
Mouquet Road	57dSE1 & 2 Beaumont	R 27 d, 28 c, 33 b
Moureaux Alley	62cSW1 Dompierre	N 14 c, 20 a, b, d, 26 b
Mouse Copse	62dSE [1 Hamel]	P 7 d
Mouse Post	57cNE3 Hermies / 4 Marcoing	K 3 d
Mouse Trap Avenue [1917-18; tr & rd / track]	28NW2 St Julien	C 16 d, 17 a, c, 22 b
Mouse Trap Farm [Shell Trap Farm until 1915]	28NW2 St Julien	C 22 b
Mouse Trap Track [1917-18; track]	28NW2 St Julien	C 16 d, 17 a, c, 22 b
Mouse Trap Trench [1918]	28NW2 St Julien	C 16 d, 22 b
Mouse Trench	36cSW1 Lens	M 6 c, d
Mouse Trench	57dNE1 & 2 Fonquevillers	E 24 d, 30 b
Mouse Trench	66cSW2 Vendeuil	O 21 b, d, 27 b
Mousetrap, The [opposite Gommecourt Park]	57dNE1 & 2 Fonquevillers	K 3 d
Mousse Farm	20SW4 Bixschoote	U 20 a
Mousses Trench / Tranchée des Mousses	66cNW2 Itancourt / 4 Berthenicourt	I 2 a, c
Moustiques Trench	62cNW4 Péronne	H 24 d, I 25 a
Mouton Avenue	51bNW1 Roclincourt	A 22 a, c, 28 a
Mouton Farm	28NW1 Elverdinghe	B 14 a 2.8
Mouton Trench	62cSW2 Barleux	N 28 d, 29 a
Mouton, Abri	51bNW1 Roclincourt	A 28 a
Moving Staircase [formerly Jacob's Ladder]	57dSE1 & 2 Beaumont	Q 4 c, d
Mow Cop	57cNE3 Hermies / 4 Marcoing	K 33 d
Mow Cop [Small Crater]	57cNE4 Marcoing	K 33 d 2.4
Mowbray Wood	28SW1 Kemmel	M 35 a
Mowcop [Redoubt]	51bNW1 Roclincourt	A 4 c
Moxon Farm	28SW1 Kemmel	M 26 b 95.65
Moy Alley	66cNW4 Berthenicourt	I 25 c
Moy Alley	66cSW1 Remigny / 2 Vendeuil	N 5, 10, 11, 15, 16
Moy Avenue	57dSE4 Ovillers	X 2 d, 3 a, b, c, 8 b
Moy Avenue [1918; Rettemoy Farm]	57dNE2 Essarts	E 30 b
Moyblain Trench	57dNE2 & 57cNW1 Courcelles	F 6 / 11 / A 1 b
Moyblain Trench [1918]	57cNW1 Gomiecourt	A 2, 3, 8, 13, 14
Moyen Wood [Nieppe Forest]	36aNE3 Haverskerque	J 24, 30, K 19, 20, 25
Moyenneville [village]	57cNW1 Gomiecourt	A 3 b, d, 4 a, b, c
Moyenneville Trench	57cNW1 Gomiecourt	A 3 b, d, 4 a, c
Mozart Copse	20SE2 Hooglede	R 5 a 0.3
Muck Trench	57dSE1 & 2 Beaumont	Q 6 d, R 1 c
Mucky Farm [Mouquet Farm]	57dSE1 & 2 Beaumont	R 27 d, 33 b
Mud [Lane] Cemetery	28SW4 Ploegsteert	U 19 c 9.3
Mud Alley	36cNW1 La Bassée	G 4 a
Mud Alley	57dNE3 & 4 Hébuterne	K 23 b
Mud Cemetery	28SE3 Comines	V 14 d 9.6
Mud Corner	20SW2 Zwartegat	O 20 a
Mud Corner	28SW4 Ploegsteert	U 14 d 7.4
Mud Farm	28NW3 Poperinghe	G 27 a 5.9
Mud Farm Camp	28NW3 Poperinghe	G 27 a
Mud Lane	36cSW3 Vimy	S 8 d
Mud Lane [N of Menin Road]	28NW4 & NE3 Zillebeke	I 10 d, 11 c, d, 12 c
Mud Lane [Ploegsteert Wood]	28SW4 Ploegsteert	U 14 c, d, 19 b, 20 a
Mud Track	51bSE3 Cagnicourt	P 32 d

Name	Map Sheet	Map Reference
Mud Trench	28NW4 & NE3 Zillebeke	I 11 d
Mud Trench	57dNE1 & 2 Fonquevillers	E 29 b, 30 a
Mud Trench [Hohenzollern]	36cNW1 La Bassée	G 4 a, b
Muddy Lane [trench]	36SW1 Aubers	M 3 a
Muddy Lane Post	36NW3 Fleurbaix	G 32 d, 33 c
Muddy Trench [1918]	28SW3 Bailleul	S 1 d, 7 b
Mudlark Alley [Ploegsteert Wood, 1914]	28SW4 Ploegsteert	U 20, 21
Muds Trench	62cSW2 Barleux	O 5 d, 11 b, d
Muffin Copse	27NE2 Proven	F 5 c, d
Muffin House	27NE2 Proven	F 5 d 5.0
Mug Trench [Burg]	57dNE1 & 2 Fonquevillers	E 24 d
Muggy Trench	57cSW4 Combles	T 5 c
Muguet Alley	62bSW1 Gricourt	M 15 b, 16 a
Muguets Trench / Tranchée des Muguets	66dNW1 Punchy/66eNE2 Vrély/66e NE4 Beaufort	A 25 d, G 1 b, L 6 a, c
Muiden Weg	51bNW1 Roclincourt	B 26 c
Muir Farm	36NW1 Steenwerck	A 23 c 95.08
Mula Cross [cross roads]	27NE4 Abeele	L 1 c 90.05
Mulatto Corner [road jct]	28NE2 Moorslede	E 24 b 05.45
Mulberry Farm	20SE2 Hooglede	R 4 a 15.00
Mulberry, Boyau	62cSW1 Dompierre	M 4 d
Muldoon Trench	28SW3 Bailleul	S 3 d, 4 a, b, c
Mule Copse	62bSW2 Fonsommes	N 4 c
Mule Lane	51bSW1 Neuville Vitasse	N 13 b, 14 a
Mule Track	28NE1 Zonnebeke	D 28 d
Mule Track	28SW4 Ploegsteert	U 2 a
Mule Trench	62cNE2 Epéhy	F 4 a
Mull Farm	20SE2 Hooglede	R 10 a 30.75
Mullah Farm	28NE2 Moorslede	E 21 b 7.2
Müller Cot.	28NW2 St Julien	C 15 b 1.5
Muller Farm	28NW2 St Julien	C 15 b 0.5
Müller Graben	57dNE1 & 2 Fonquevillers	E 23 c, 29 a
Mullet Farm	20SE3 Westroosebeke	V 23 b 2.9
Mummers Cross Roads	28NE2 Moorslede	F 1 d 80.35
Mummy Alley	66cNW4 Berthenicourt	I 21 a
Münchner Graben	51bNW1 Roclincourt	A 12 d, 18 b, c, d
Münchner Weg	51bNW1 Roclincourt	A 23 d, 24 a, c
Munich Lane	57cSW4 Combles	U 21 b, 22 a
Munich Trench	57dNE3 & 4 Hébuterne / SE1 & 2 Beaumont	K 30 c, 36 a, c, Q 6 a, c
Munich Trench	62cSW3 Vermandovillers	T 7 b, d, 8 a
Munster Alley	57dSE4 Ovillers	X 5 b, 6 a
Munster Crater	36cNW3 Loos	H 13 a 2.2
Munster Parade	36cNW1 La Bassée	G 3 a, b
Munster Parade North	36cNW1 La Bassée	A 27 d, G 3 b
Munster Parade, & North	36cNW1 La Bassée	A 27 d, G 3 a, b
Münster Trench [1918]	66eNW [2 Thennes]	C 10 a, c
Munster Tunnel	36cNW1 La Bassée	A 27 d, G 3 b
Mur de Calonne [Wall Street]	36cSW1 Lens	M 20 b
Mur de Calonne, Tranchée du [Morgan Trench]	36cSW1 Lens	M 14 d, 20 b
Mur de Crassier [Coal Alley, Calonne]	36cSW1 Lens	M 20 b
Mural Farm	27SE4 Meteren	X 17 b 50.75
Murat Camp	28NW2 St Julien	B 24 d
Murat Farm	28NW2 St Julien	B 30 b
Muratti Farm	28NE4 Dadizeele	L 31 d

Name	Map Sheet	Map Reference
Murchison Farm	20SE3 Westroosebeke	W 14 c 75.25
Murder Alley	36cSW1 Lens	M 5 c, 11 a
Murder Farm	36NW1 Steenwerck	A 18 d 55.20
Murder Hill [Bluff]	28NW4 & NE3 Zillebeke	I 34 b, c
Muriel Alley	36cSW1 Lens	M 5 c
Muriel House	27NE2 Proven	E 30 a 8.1
Murphy Farm	28SW2 Wytschaete	O 18 b 3.7
Murrati Farm	28NE4 Dadizeele	L 31 d 25.90
Murray House	28NE4 Dadizeele	L 26 a 9.1
Murray Trench [1918]	57dSE [3 Bouzincourt]	V 24 d, 30 b
Murray Wood	62cNW3 Vaux	G 9 a
Murray's Hut [Ploegsteert Wood 1914-15]	28SW4 Ploegsteert	U 21 b 15.05
Murrimbidgee Camp	28SW1 Kemmel	M 6 d, 12 b, N 1 c, 7 a
Muscle Houses	28NE2 Moorslede	E 30 b 8.9
Muse Trench [1918]	28SW1 Kemmel	M 17 c, d, 23 a
Muselhoek [place name]	28NE4 Dadizeele	L 12 a
Muses Wood	66eNW [2 Thennes]	B 6 b
Mush Farm	20SE2 Hooglede	R 28 d 05.15
Mushroom Alley	62dNE2 Méaulte	F 10 d
Mushroom Spur [light rly siding]	36bNE2 Beuvry	F 13 b, d, 14 c
Mushroom, The	36NW4 Bois Grenier	I 11 c
Music Hall Line	36cSW3 Vimy	S 14, 20, 26
Music Trench	36cSW1 Lens	M 5 d, 6 c, 11 b
Music Trench	57dNE1 & 2 Fonquevillers	E 30 a
Musk Trench	66cSW2 Vendeuil	O 16 d, 22 b
Musket Trench	51bNW2 Oppy	C 29 b
Musket Trench	51bNW4 Fampoux	H 36 b, I 31 a, c
Mussell Farm	20SE2 Hooglede	R 28 d 9.6
Mussin [Tranchée, 1915] / Dublin Street	57dSE4 Ovillers	X 19 a
Mustang Copse	27SE2 Berthen	Q 11 a
Mustard Corner	36cSW3 Vimy	M 32 c
Mustard Farm	36NW1 Steenwerck	A 12 b 82.65
Muston Farm	20SE2 Hooglede	R 31 a 3.8
Mute Trench	57dNE1 & 2 Fonquevillers	E 24 c, 30 a
Mutes, The [farm]	36NW1 Steenwerck	A 10 c 2.6
Muth Weg [Mutt Trench]	51bNW1 Roclincourt	A 30 d, G 6 b, H 1 a
Mutt Trench [1918]	51bNW1 Roclincourt	A 30 d, G 6 b, H 1 a
Mutton Avenue	51bNW1 Roclincourt	A 22 c, 28 a, c
Mutton Farm	36NW1 Steenwerck	A 11 a 3.3
Mutton Trench	57cSW4 Combles	T 17 c, d, 23 b
Mutwal Farm	28NE4 Dadizeele	L 33 b 4.7
Muzzle Trench [Burg Graben]	57dNE1 & 2 Fonquevillers	E 24 c, d
Mylchett Avenue	36cNW1 La Bassée	A 26 b
Myrtle Copse	62cSW4 St. Christ	T 23 b, d, 24 a
Myrtle Farm	20SE2 Hooglede	Q 24 a 2.2
Mysore Farm	27SE2 Berthen	R 31 b 65.20
N ["N" OP in ruined house, Givenchy]	36cNW1 La Bassée	A 9 c/d
N 1 [trench, NE of Hollandscheschuur Fm]	28SW2 Wytschaete	N 12 d 6.5
N 2 [trench, NE of Hollandscheschuur Fm]	28SW2 Wytschaete	N 12 d 7.6
N 3 [trench, W of Bois Quarante]	28SW2 Wytschaete	O 7 c 2.9
N 4 [trench, W of Bois Quarante]	28SW2 Wytschaete	O 7 a 2.0
N 5 [trench, W of Bois Quarante]	28SW2 Wytschaete	O 7 a 3.2
N 6 [trench, W of Bois Quarante]	28SW2 Wytschaete	O 7 a 5.3
N 9 [trench, E edge of Bois Carré]	28SW2 Wytschaete	N 12 b 7.7

Name	Map Sheet	Map Reference
N Branch Trench	62cSW2 Barleux	O 8 a, c
N Trench [St Eloi sector, Feb 1915]	28SW2 Wytschaete	O 3 / 4
N. House	20SW4 Bixschoote	T 23 d
N.F. Lane	62bNW1 Gouy	A 13 b
N.W. Fire Trench	62cNW1 Maricourt	A 15 b
Nab Junction [road jct]	57dSE1 & 2 Beaumont	R 32 b 9.7
Nab Lines [huts]	28SW3 Bailleul	T 28 c
Nab, The, & Nab Valley	57dSE4 Ovillers	X 1 b, d
Nabob Alley	36cSW1 Lens	N 8, 9, 10
Nabot Wood	66dNW1 Punchy	B 2 c
Naboth's Villa [1918]	28SW1 Kemmel	N 25 c 99.65
Nachte Farm [near Nachtegaal]	28NE2 Moorslede	F 21 d 6.2
Nachtegaal	28NE2 Moorslede	F 21 b, d
Nachtegaal Inn	27NE2 Proven	F 11 d 7.2
Nachtegaal Trench	20SW2 Zwartegat	O 21 b, c, d, 22 c
Nachtigall Cemetery [Vieux Chien]	28NE3 Gheluvelt	J 30 b 2.9
Nadaud [trench / salient, front line]	36cSW1 Lens	M 32 a
Nadeau [Boyau, NW of Fricourt, 1915]	62dNE2 Méaulte	F 2 b
Nadens Track (Duckboards) [1917-18]	28NW4 Ypres	I 30 b, c, d
Naeldoog Inn	27NE2 Proven	F 14 a 6.2
Nag Avenue	28SW2 Wytschaete	N 18 b, O 13 a, c
Nag Row	28SW2 Wytschaete	N 18 b, d
Nag Support, Reserve & Lane	28SW2 Wytschaete	N 12 d, 18 b
Nag Trench	36cSW1 Lens	N 8 d
Nag Trench, & Nag's Nose	28SW2 Wytschaete	N 12 d, 18 b
Nagpur Trench	51bSW1 Neuville Vitasse	N 32 b
Nail Row	28SW2 Wytschaete	N 18 b
Nail Street, Reserve & Drive	28SW2 Wytschaete	N 18 d, O 13 c
Nail Support	28SW2 Wytschaete	N 18 d
Nail Trench	36cSW1 Lens	N 8 b
Nail Trench	51bNW1 Roclincourt	A 24 c
Nail Trench	51bSW1 Neuville Vitasse	N 20 b
Nail Trench, & Switch	28SW2 Wytschaete	N 18 b, d
Nairn / Nairne Avenue [formerly Wagram]	57dNE3 & 4 Hébuterne	K 21 c, d, 22 a, c, 23 a
Nairn / Nairne Street	57dSE1 & 2 Beaumont	Q 30 a, b
Nairn Trench	36cSW1 Lens	N 3 a
Nairne Street	57dNE3 & 4 Hébuterne	K 22 d, 23 c, d
Naked Street	51cSE3 & 4 Ransart / 57dNE1 & 2 Fonquevillers	W 27 c, d, 28 c, d, E 3 a
Name Drive	28SW2 Wytschaete	N 18 d, 24 b, O 19 a
Name Support	28SW2 Wytschaete	N 18 d, 24 b
Name Trench	28SW2 Wytschaete	N 18 c, d, 24 a
Nameless Copse	62bSW1 Gricourt	M 35 a, b
Nameless Farm	28SW1 Kemmel	N 14 b 3.5
Nameless Farm	57dNE3 & 4 Hébuterne	K 11 a 8.8
Nameless House	28NE1 Zonnebeke	D 22 c 0.2
Nameless Road [road]	57dNE1 & 2 Fonquevillers	E 27 b
Nameless Trench	57dNE3 & 4 Hébuterne	K 11 a, d, 17 b, 18 a, c
Nameless Trench	62bNW1 Gouy	A 1 d
Nameless Wood	62cNW1 Maricourt	A 17 b
Nameless Wood	62cNW3 Vaux	G 28 d
Namon [Tranchée, 1915] / Monikie Street N.	57dSE4 Ovillers	X 19 d
Namur Crossing	20SW4 Bixschoote	U 18 a 4.7
Namur Trench	51bSW1 Neuville Vitasse	N 2 c, 8 a

Name	Map Sheet	Map Reference
Namur Trench	66dNW3 Hattencourt	G 3 d, 9 b, d
Nanaimo Road [road]	36cSW3 Vimy	S 12 b, d, 18 b, T 13 a, c
Nancy Avenue	28SW2 Wytschaete	N 24 b, d, O 19 a
Nancy Drive	28SW2 Wytschaete	N 24 b, O 13 c, 19 a
Nancy Reserve	28SW2 Wytschaete	N 24 b, O 19 a
Nancy Street [Petit Bois]	28SW2 Wytschaete	N 24 a, b
Nancy Support	28SW2 Wytschaete	N 18 d, 24 b
Nancy Switch [Petit Bois]	28SW2 Wytschaete	N 24 b
Nancy Trench	51bSW1 Neuville Vitasse	N 7 a
Nancy Trench	66cNW4 Berthenicourt	H 12 b
Nancy Trench [Petit Bois]	28SW2 Wytschaete	N 24 a, b, d
Nansen Farm	28NW1 Elverdinghe	B 26 a 7.5
Nantes Trench	66cNW4 Berthenicourt	H 24 d
Nanton [light rly siding, Vimy]	36cSW3 Vimy	T 19 b
Naome Keep	36SW1 Aubers	N 27 a
Naomi Trench	36SW1 Aubers	N 21 d, 27 a
Nap Avenue	28SW2 Wytschaete	N 24 d, O 19 c, 25 a
Nap Drive	28SW2 Wytschaete	N 24 c, d
Nap Reserve	28SW2 Wytschaete	N 24 d, O 19 c
Nap Trench	36cSW1 Lens	N 3 d
Nap Trench	51bNW1 Roclincourt	A 24 c
Nap Trench [Maedelstede Farm]	28SW2 Wytschaete	N 24 c, d
Napier	28SW4 Ploegsteert	U 1 d 2.8
Napier [light rly locality]	28NW3 Poperinghe	G 30 a
Napier Cottages	28NW3 Poperinghe	G 23 d 05.05
Napier Trench [1918]	57dNE3 & 4 Hébuterne	K 10 d
Napier Wood	62bSW2 Fonsommes	O 27 c, 33 a
Napier's / Napiers Redoubt	62cNW1 Maricourt	A 22 a
Napkin Farm	36NW1 Steenwerck	B 14 a45.75
Naples Avenue	28SW2 Wytschaete	N 30 a, b
Naples Drive	28SW2 Wytschaete	N 30 a, b, d
Naples Reserve	28SW2 Wytschaete	N 24 d, 30 b
Naples Row	28SW2 Wytschaete	N 30 a
Naples Support	28SW2 Wytschaete	N 24 c, 30 a, b
Naples Switch	28SW2 Wytschaete	N 30 b
Naples Trench [Peckham]	28SW2 Wytschaete	N 24 c, 30 a
Napoo Avenue	36NW2 Armentières	C 10 a
Napoo Corner [Stafford House, Lièvin]	36cSW1 Lens	M 28
Napoo Farm	28SE1 Wervicq	P 8 a 65.30
Napper House	36NW1 Steenwerck	A 4 c 6.6
Naptha Cottages	28SW1 Kemmel	M 26 d 85.80
Narborough Road (Boyau des Houris)	51cSE3 & 4 Ransart	W 17 c, d
Narcisses, Tranchée des	66eNE4 Beaufort	L 5 d, 6 c
Narcissus Farm	20SE2 Hooglede	R 21 d 0.4
Narew Alley	66dNW3 Hattencourt	G 19 d, 20 c, d, 25 b, 26 a
Narrow Alley	28SW2 Wytschaete	N 30 c
Narrow Alley	36cSW1 Lens	N 9 a, b
Narrow Lane	28SW2 Wytschaete	N 30 a, c
Narrow Reserve	28SW2 Wytschaete	N 30 c, d
Narrow Support	28SW2 Wytschaete	N 30 a, c
Narrow Support	51bSW2 Vis-en-Artois	O 26 c, d
Narrow Trench	28SW2 Wytschaete	N 30 a, c
Narrow Trench	51bSW2 Vis-en-Artois	O 21 c, d, 26 a, b, c, 27 a, 32 a
Narrow Wood	51bSW2 Vis-en-Artois / SE1 Saudemont	O 18 d, P 13 a, c

Name	Map Sheet	Map Reference
Narwal Trench	36cSW1 Lens	N 1 d, 7 a, b
Nasal Trench	36cSW1 Lens	M 22 c
Nash Alley	36cSW1 Lens	N 1 a, b, d
Nash Alley Spur	36cSW1 Lens	N 1 a, b
Nash Trench	36cSW1 Lens	N 1 d
Nassau Trench	62bSW3 St Quentin	S 24 c, d
Nassau Trench	62cSW2 Barleux	O 22 d, 28 b, d
Nassau Trench [1918]	66eNW [2 Thennes]	C 9 b, c, d
Nassau Work	66dNW1 Punchy	A 28 d, G 4 a, b
Natal Cottage	28SW2 Wytschaete	N 10 b 8.2
Natal Trench	36cSW1 Lens	M 6 b, N 1 a, b
Natal Trench	36SW1 Aubers	N 15 a, b
Natal Trench	51bSW1 Neuville Vitasse	N 26 d, 27 a, c
Natal Trench	66cSW2 Vendeuil	O 8 b, d
Natch Trench	36SW1 Aubers	N 25 a, b
Nathan Alley	28SW2 Wytschaete	N 36 a, b, O 31 a
Nathan Drive	28SW2 Wytschaete	N 36 d, O 31 a
Nathan Lane	28SW2 Wytschaete	N 36 a, b
Nathan Reserve	28SW2 Wytschaete	N 36 a, b
Nathan Support [Kruisstraat]	28SW2 Wytschaete	N 30 c, 36 a
Nathan Trench [Kruisstraat]	28SW2 Wytschaete	N 30 c, 36 a
Natil Trench	51bNW1 Roclincourt	A 24 c
Natron Trench	36cSW1 Lens / 2 Harnes	N 10 a, c
Natty Trench	36SW1 Aubers	N 15 c, d
Naudin Trench	66cNW1 Grugies	B 15 a
Nauroy [village]	62bNW3 Bellicourt	G 11 d, 12 a, c, 17 b
Nausicaa Trench	66dNW1 Punchy	A 22 a, b
Naval Reserve	57cSE2 Gonnelieu	R 9 a, b, c, 14 b, 15 a
Naval Trench	36SW1 Aubers	N 15 a
Naval Trench	51bNW2 Oppy	B 30 a, c, H 6 a
Nave Farm	28NE2 Moorslede	F 25 b 2.5
Nave Trench	51bNW1 Roclincourt	A 24 c
Navy Trench	36SW1 Aubers	N 13 c, 19 a
Navy Trench	51bNW1 Roclincourt	A 24 c
Nawful Street	51cSE3 & 4 Ransart	W 23 c
Nay Trench	51bNW1 Roclincourt	A 24 c
Naze, The [Nase]	57dSE4 Ovillers	R 31 c
Neaf Trench	36cNW4 Pont-à-Vendin	H 34 b, 35 a
Neame House [1918]	28SW1 Kemmel	M 30 b 35.40
Near Alley	36SW2 Radinghem	N 6 b
Near Avenue	36SW2 Radinghem	N 6 d
Near Crescent	36SW2 Radinghem	N 6 d
Near Drive	36SW2 Radinghem	O 1 c
Near Lane	36SW2 Radinghem	N 6 b
Near Row	36SW2 Radinghem	O 1 a
Near Street	36SW2 Radinghem	O 1 a
Near Support	36SW2 Radinghem	N 6 b
Near Trench	36SW1 Aubers	N 13 d
Near Trench	36SW2 Radinghem	N 6 b
Neat Lane	36SW2 Radinghem	N 6 c
Neat Street	36SW2 Radinghem	N 6 d
Neat Support	36SW2 Radinghem	N 6 d
Neat Switch	36SW2 Radinghem	N 12 b
Neat Trench	36SW2 Radinghem	N 6 d

Name	Map Sheet	Map Reference
Neb, The [Sept 1915]	36SW3 Richebourg	S 5 b, d
Nebula Alley	36SW2 Radinghem	N 12 a
Nebula Avenue	36SW2 Radinghem	N 12 a
Nebula Drive	36SW2 Radinghem	N 12 b
Nebula Support	36SW2 Radinghem	N 6 c
Nebula Switch	36SW2 Radinghem	N 12 b
Nebula Trench	36SW2 Radinghem	N 6 c
Nebula, The	57cSW4 Combles	U 7 c
Neck Avenue	36SW2 Radinghem	N 11 b
Neck Drive	36SW2 Radinghem	N 12 c
Neck Lane	36SW2 Radinghem	N 11 b
Neck Reserve	36SW2 Radinghem	N 11 b
Neck Road	36SW2 Radinghem	N 11 b
Neck Support	36SW2 Radinghem	N 11 b
Neck Trench	36SW2 Radinghem	N 5 d
Necklace Trench	36SW2 Radinghem	N 9 c, d
Necklace, The	28SW4 Ploegsteert	U 28 d, 29 a, c
Nectar Alley	66dNW1 Punchy	A 28 d, 29 c, G 5 a, c
Nectar Cottage	28SW2 Wytschaete	N 10 d 5.1
Ned Alley	36SW2 Radinghem	N 11 d
Ned Avenue	36SW2 Radinghem	N 11 a, c, d
Ned Drive	36SW2 Radinghem	N 17 b, 18 a
Ned Lane	36SW2 Radinghem	N 11 a, c, d
Ned Row	36SW2 Radinghem	N 11 d
Ned Support	36SW2 Radinghem	N 11 a, b
Ned Switch	36SW2 Radinghem	N 11 a
Ned Trench	36cSW2 Harnes	N 24 a
Ned Trench	36SW2 Radinghem	N 11 a
Neda Copse	20SE2 Hooglede	R 9 a 3.9
Needle [Ger FL, late 1915]	36SW2 Radinghem	N 5 d 85.15
Needle Drive	36SW2 Radinghem	N 10 d
Needle Dump [NW of Lesboeufs]	57cSW3 Longueval	N 33 c 2.0
Needle Keep	36SW2 Radinghem	N 10 b
Needle Support	36SW2 Radinghem	N 10 b, d
Needle Switch	36SW2 Radinghem	N 17 a, c
Needle Trench	36SW2 Radinghem	N 10 b, d
Needle Trench [part of Gird Trench]	57cSW1 Gueudecourt / 3 Longueval	N 26 c, 32 a, b, d, T 3 a
Needle Wood	62cNW2 Bouchavesnes	C 13 a
Needle; The Monument	62bSW1 Gricourt	M 34 b 4.1
Neer Farm [Neerhoek]	28NE2 Moorslede	L 4 b 2.5
Neerhof [hamlet]	28NE2 Moorslede	L 4 b
Negative Avenue	36SW2 Radinghem	N 10 d, 16 b, 17 a
Negative Drive	36SW2 Radinghem	N 10 d, 16 b, 17 a
Negative Street	36SW2 Radinghem	N 10 d
Negative Support	36SW2 Radinghem	N 10 d
Negative Switch	36SW2 Radinghem	N 10 d
Negative Trench	36SW2 Radinghem	N 10 d
Neglect Avenue	36SW2 Radinghem	N 18 a, c, d
Neglect Support	36SW2 Radinghem	N 24 a, b
Neglect Trench	36SW2 Radinghem	N 18 c, d, 24 a, b
Negrine Trench	51bSW1 Neuville Vitasse	N 7 a
Negro Avenue	36SW2 Radinghem	N 17 a, c
Negro Farm	28SW2 Wytschaete	N 10 b 6.3
Negro Post	12SW3 Ramscappelle	N 31 d

Name	Map Sheet	Map Reference
Negro Support	36SW2 Radinghem	N 23 a, b
Negro Switch	12SW3 Ramscappelle	N 31 b, d
Negro Switch	36SW2 Radinghem	N 16 b
Negro Trench	12SW3 Ramscappelle	N 31 c, d
Negro Trench	36cSW1 Lens	N 2 b, d, 3 c
Negro Trench	36SW2 Radinghem	N 23 a, b
Negro Trench [latterly Nero Trench]	36SW1 Aubers	N 14 b
Neighbour Lane	36SW2 Radinghem	N 22 d
Neighbour Support	36SW2 Radinghem	N 22 b, 23 a
Neighbour Trench	36SW2 Radinghem	N 22 b, d, 23 a
Neilson Street	57dSE1 & 2 Beaumont	R 25 a
Nell Farm	28SW2 Wytschaete	N 11 a 05.95
Nell Trench	36cSW1 Lens	N 2 d
Nelly Avenue	51bSW4 Bullecourt	T 18 d, U 13 a, b
Nelly Lane	51bSW4 Bullecourt	U 13 a
Nelly Switch	51bSW4 Bullecourt	U 13 b
Nelly Trench	36cSW2 Harnes	O 14 a
Nelson Camp	28NW4 Ypres	H 30 c
Nelson Copse	66dNW1 Punchy	A 16 a
Nelson Keep [Fosse 6 de Béthune]	36cNW3 Loos	G 25 d, 31 b
Nelson Lane	36cSW1 Lens	M 25 b
Nelson Support	57cSE2 Gonnelieu	R 3 d, 4 c, 9 b
Nelson Trench	36cNW3 Loos / SW1 Lens	H 32 c, N 1 b, d
Nelson Trench	57cSE2 Gonnelieu	R 4 c, 10 a
Nemo Farm	27SE3 Borre	V 9 b 10.45
Neo Trench	36cSW2 Harnes	N 24 a
Nepal Farm	28NW3 Poperinghe	H 26 c 2.9
Nepal Trench	51bSW1 Neuville Vitasse	N 21 b, c, d, 22 a
Nephew Trench	36SW1 Aubers	N 9 d
Neptune [German Pillbox M.G. Post]	51bSW4 Bullecourt	U 21 a 33.65
Neptune Trench	66dNW3 Hattencourt	G 3 d, 9 b, d
Néreides Trench	66dNW1 Punchy	A 28 d, G 4 a, b, c
Nero Alley	62cSW1 & 2 Belloy	N 5 d
Nero Trench	36cSW1 Lens	N 1 c
Nero Trench	57dSE4 Ovillers	X 2 c, d
Nero Trench [formerly Negro Trench]	36SW1 Aubers	N 14 b
Neron Trench / Tranchée de Néron	66dNW1 Punchy	A 27 d, G 3 b, d
Nesle [town]	66dNW4 Nesle	I 19 a, b, c, d
Nesles Alley	62bSW1 Gricourt	M 35 a
Nest Trench	51bNW1 Roclincourt	A 24 c
Nest, The [tree clump]	57cNE1 Quéant	D 21 a
Nest, The [trenches]	51bSW2 Vis-en-Artois	N 30 a
Nesta / Vesta Cottage	27SE4 Meteren	X 7 d 8.9
Nestor Alley	36cSW1 Lens	N 1 d
Nestor Trench	36cSW1 Lens	N 2 a, b, c
Net Farm	20SE4 Roulers	Q 34 c 7.2
Net Trench	36SW2 Radinghem	N 10 c
Net Trench	51bNW1 Roclincourt	A 24 c
Nether Farm	28SW2 Wytschaete	N 6 a 8.5
Netley Alley	36cSW1 Lens	M 6 d, N 1 a
Netley Farm	28SE1 Wervicq	P 15 b 9.1
Netley Trench	36cSW1 Lens	N 1 a, b, c
Nett Farm	27NE2 Proven	E 16 a 3.9
Nettle Farm	20SE2 Hooglede	R 21 a 3.5

Name	Map Sheet	Map Reference
Netzer Alley	66dNW1 Punchy	A 15 b, 16 a, c
Neuberger Weg	51bNW1 Roclincourt	A 10 b
Neuer Kreuz Graben	57dNE1 & 2 Fonquevillers	E 12 d, F 7 a
Neuf Alley [Calonne]	36cSW1 Lens	M 3 c, 9 a, b, c, d
Neuf Berquin [village]	36aNE4 Merville	L 13 b, d, 14 a, c, d
Neuf Keep	36cSW1 Lens	M 9 d
Neuf, Boyau	62cSW1 Dompierre	M 10 d
Neuf, Moulin	57dSW [4 Toutencourt]	T 17 a 0.8
Neufchâteau Trench	66cNW2 Itancourt	H 6 a
Neufchatel Lane [trench]	51bSW1 Neuville Vitasse	M 18 b, d, N 13 c
Neuilly Trench	51bSW1 Neuville Vitasse	N 1 b, d
Neuve Eglise [village]	28SW3 Bailleul	T 14 b, d, 15 a, b, c, d
Neuville Lane [trench]	51bSW1 Neuville Vitasse	M 24 a, b
Neuville Redoubt / Work	51bSW1 Neuville Vitasse	M 24 b, d, N 19 a, c
Neuville Vitasse Trench	51bSW1 Neuville Vitasse	N 19, 20, 26, 27
Neuville Wood	66eNW [4 Morisel]	I 21 d, 22 c, 27 a, b, c, d
Neuville-Bourjom [village]	57cSE1 Bertincourt	P 16 d, 22 b, c, d, 23 a
Neuville-Sire-Bernard [village]	66eNW [4 Morisel]	I 29 a, c
Neuville-St Vaast [village]	51bNW1 Roclincourt	A 2 d, 3 a, b, c, d, 9 a, b
Neuville-St. Amand [village]	66cNW2 Itancourt	B 5 c, d, 6 c
Neuville-Vitasse [village]	51bSW1 Neuville Vitasse	N 13 d, 19 a, b, c
Neuvireuil [village]	51bNW2 Oppy	C 8 c, d, 9 c, 14 b, 15 a
Neva Farm	36NW1 Steenwerck	A 16 a 95.05
Neva Lane	51bSW2 Vis-en-Artois	O 26 c, d
Nevada [farm]	27SE4 Meteren	W 17 d 35.85
Neverending Street	51cSE3 & 4 Ransart	W 22 d, 28 b, d
Nevilles Cross [cross roads]	62bNW4 Ramicourt	I 7 a 6.5
Nevis Trench	51bSW1 Neuville Vitasse	M 16 c, d
New Barkenham Avenue	36NW2 Armentières	C 10 c, d
New Beaumont Road [road]	57dSE1 & 2 Beaumont	Q 3 d, 4 c, 9 b
New Bond Street [Hooge, 1915]	28NW4 & NE3 Zillebeke	I 18 a, b, c, d
New Bond Street [Zouave Wood - Hooge]	28NW4 & NE3 Zillebeke	I 18 a, b, c
New Brunswick Road [road]	36cSW4 Rouvroy	T 20 c, d, 22 b
New Brunswick Trench	36cSW4 Rouvroy	T 16 c, d, 21 b, c, d
New Bydand Avenue	28NW4 & NE3 Zillebeke	I 24 b
New Communication Trench [Feb 1915]	36cNW1 La Bassée	A 9 d [Duck's Bill area]
New Cot. [June 1916, later Forward Cottage]	28NW2 St Julien	C 21 b 8.5
New Cots.	28NW2 St Julien	I 5 a 3.7
New Crater Work	51bNW1 Roclincourt	A 9 a
New Cross C.T.	28SW4 Ploegsteert	U 4 c, d, 5 c
New Cut	51bNW2 Oppy	B 24 d
New Cut	51bNW3 Arras	G 11 d
New Cut	57dNE3 & 4 Hébuterne	K 34 a
New Cut	57dSE1 & 2 Beaumont	Q 18 a, c
New Cut	62cNE2 Epéhy	L 6 a
New Cut	62cNW1 Maricourt	A 7 d
New Cut	62cNW2 Bouchavesnes	C 10 c 2.9
New Cut	62dNE2 Méaulte	F 9 a, d
New Cut [Givenchy]	36cNW1 La Bassée	A 8 b, 9 a, c
New Cut Alley	36SW3 Richebourg	M 35 c, d
New Cut Trench [Givenchy Sector, March 1915]	36cNW1 La Bassée	A 8 b, 9 a, c
New Cut, & Crater	36cSW3 Vimy	S 8 d
New Dickebusch Camp	28NW3 Poperinghe	H 33 a, c
New Douve Farm (Avenue Cottage)	28SW4 Ploegsteert	U 9 c 25.75

Name	Map Sheet	Map Reference
New Fantome Trench	51bNW1 Roclincourt	A 22 c
New Farm	28SW2 Wytschaete	N 6 b 5.4
New Gallwitz Support	57dSE2 & 57cSW1 Le Sars	M 8 d, 9 c
New Gallwitz Trench	57dSE2 & 57cSW1 Le Sars	M 8 d
New Hill Cemetery	57cNE4 Marcoing	K 10 c
New Houses	20SW4 Bixschoote	U 30 a 5.3
New Irish Farm Mil. Cemy. [Hammonds Corner]	28NW2 St Julien	C 21 c
New John Street	28NW2 St Julien	C 28 b
New Lincoln Lane	51cSE3 & 4 Ransart	W 12 b
New Mud Lane [Railway Wood]	28NW4 & NE3 Zillebeke	I 11 d, 12 c
New Munich Cemetery	57dSE2 Beaumont	Q 6 c
New Munich Trench	57dNE3 & 4 Hébuterne / SE1 & 2 Beaumont	Q 5 b, 6 a, c
New Oxford Street	57dNE3 & 4 Hébuterne	K 22 b
New Quarry	62cNE2 Epéhy	F 29 c 8.4
New Quarry [The Egg / Egg Post]	62cNE4 Roisel	L 11 b 65.50
New Reserve Line	57dSE2 & 57cSW1 Le Sars	N 25 b, 26 a, c
New Reserve Trench	28SW2 Wytschaete	N 11 b, 12 a
New Rope Keep [Sept 1915]	36SW3 Richebourg	S 21 d 1.7
New Rose S.P. [strongpoint]	36cNW1 La Bassée	A 9 a 55.60
New Rose Street [Givenchy]	36cNW1 La Bassée	A 9 a
New Strand [Ploegsteert Wood]	28SW4 Ploegsteert	U 21 a, b
New Street	28NW4 & NE3 Zillebeke	I 34 c
New Street	57dNE1 & 2 Fonquevillers	K 3 a, b
New Street	57dSE2 Beaumont	R 12 c, 18 a
New Street	57dSE4 Ovillers	R 33 c
New Street / Boyau Neuf	62cNW1 Maricourt	A 23 c
New Support	28SW2 Wytschaete	N 18 c
New Support	28SW4 Ploegsteert	U 28 a, c
New Support	36cSW1 Lens	M 14 d, 20 b
New Switch	51bNW2 Oppy	C 1 d, 7 b, 8 a
New Tea Trench	28SW2 Wytschaete	O 3 b
New Torr Top	28NW4 & NE3 Zillebeke	I 24 d
New Trench	20SW4 Bixschoote / 28NW2 St Julien	U 30 d, C 6 a
New Trench	28SW2 Wytschaete	O 5 c
New Trench	28SW4 Ploegsteert	U 15 a
New Trench	36cSW3 Vimy	S 20 a
New Trench	57cSW3 Longueval	S 24 a, c, d, 30 b
New Trench	57dNE1 & 2 Fonquevillers	K 3 a, c
New Trench	57dSE1 & 2 Beaumont	Q 17 a
New Trench	62cNE2 Epéhy	L 6 a
New Trench	66cNW1 Grugies	B 19 d
New Trench / Street [N of Monchy]	51bNW4 Fampoux	I 31 a
New Trench [1918]	57dNE1 & 2 Fonquevillers / 3 & 4 Hébuterne	K 5 d, 6 a, c
New Trench [Br, opp Bois Francais]	62dNE2 Méaulte	F 9 d
New Trench [Sept 1915]	36cNW1 La Bassée	A 9 a
New Trench, & Support	36cSW1 Lens	M 14 d
New Welcome Street	57dNE3 & 4 Hébuterne	K 11 c
New Whiskey Street	57dNE3 & 4 Hébuterne	K 11 c
New X Line	28NW4 & NE3 Zillebeke	I 10 a
New Year Crater [blown 2-1-16]	36cNW1 La Bassée	A 21 b
New Year Lateral [tunnel, 1916]	36cNW1 La Bassée	A 21 b, 22 a
New Year Sap	36cNW1 La Bassée	A 22 a
New Year Trench	57cSE2 Gonnelieu	R 8 d, 9 a, 14 a, b
New Year Trench [The Bluff]	28NW4 & NE3 Zillebeke	I 34 c 3.5

Name	Map Sheet	Map Reference
New Zealand Cemetery	28NE1 Zonnebeke	D 15 a
New Zealand Cemetery	57cNW3 Bapaume	G 30 d 3.8
Newark Street	51cSE3 & 4 Ransart	W 28 b, 29 a
Newburn [Trench]	36NW2 Armentières	C 28 b
Newbury Appendix	28SW4 Ploegsteert	U 5 b, 6 a
Newel Trench	36cSW1 Lens	N 2 d
Newfoundland Avenue [IWM board]	57dSE1 & 2 Beaumont	Q 5
Newgate Farm	28SW2 Wytschaete	N 10 b 6.7
Newgate Road	36cNW1 La Bassée	A 14 b, 15 a
Newgate Trench	36cSW1 Lens	N 3 d, 9 b, 10 a
Newland [farm, 1918]	28SW1 Kemmel	M 14 b 1.1
Newport [strongpoint]	36NW3 Fleurbaix	G 26 a
Newport Dugouts	28SW1 Kemmel	N 34 a 2.9
Newport Road	36cSW1 Lens	M 9 c, 15 a
Newport Sap	36cNW3 Loos	G 12 d
Newport Trench	57cSE2 Gonnelieu	R 14 b, d
News Trench	36cSW4 Rouvroy	T 6 a
News Trench	51bNW1 Roclincourt	A 24 c
Newt Farms	27NE2 Proven	F 18 c 3.3
Newt Lane [1918]	57dNE2 & 57cNW1 Courcelles	F 16 d, 17 c
Newton Cottage	36NW1 Steenwerck	B 8 c 15.85
Newton Post	57cSE2 Gonnelieu	R 34 a
Newton Road [road]	57cSE2 Gonnelieu	R 33 b, 34 a, b
Newton Trench	51bNW2 Oppy / 4 Fampoux	B 30 c, H 5 b, 6 a
Ney Copse	20SW4 Bixschoote	U 15 b
Ney Cross Roads / Carrefour	20SW4 Bixschoote	U 16 d 6.6
Ney Farm	20SW4 Bixschoote	U 16 a 6.8
Ney Wood	20SW4 Bixschoote	U 16 a, c
Nez Trench	20NW4 Dixmude	I 7 c
Nezot Avenue	51bNW1 Roclincourt	A 14, 15, 19, 20
Niagara	51aSW4 Naves	T 12 d 3.8
Nib Alley	36SW1 Aubers / 2 Radinghem	N 10 c, 16 a
Nib Support	36SW1 Aubers / 2 Radinghem	N 10 c
Nib Trench	36cSW1 Lens	N 3 c
Nib Trench	36SW1 Aubers / 2 Radinghem	N 10 c
Nib Trench	51bNW1 Roclincourt	A 24 c
Nib Trench	51bSW1 Neuville Vitasse	M 23 c
Nib Trench	62bNW3 Bellicourt	G 33 b
Nib Trench	62bNW3 Bellicourt	G 27 d, 33 b
Nice Trench	51bSW1 Neuville Vitasse	N 7 c
Nich Cottage	28NW3 Poperinghe	G 36 c
Nich Trench	62cNW4 Péronne	I 7 c, d
Nicholls Redoubt	51bNW3 Arras	G 11 c
Nichol's Farm	28NE4 Dadizeele	L 29 c 8.5
Nicholson Cross Roads	20SE3 Westroosebeke	W 20 a 10.55
Nicholson Trench	57dNE3 & 4 Hébuterne	K 16 b, c, d
Nicholson's Avenue	36NW2 Armentières	C 2 d, 3 c, d, 8 a, b
Nick Trench	36cSW1 Lens	N 3 d
Nick Trench	36SW1 Aubers / 2 Radinghem	N 22 c
Nickel Trench	36cSW1 Lens	N 3 a, b
Nickel, Tranchée du	70dSW [2 Coucy-le-Château]	O 15 b
Nicky Farm	36NW1 Steenwerck	A 12 c 25.60
Nicolas Sector [trenches] [1918]	62dSW [3 Boves / 4 Cachy]	T 3, 4, 8, 9
Nicolas Support [1918]	62dSW [3 Boves / 4 Cachy]	T 3, 4, 8, 9

Name	Map Sheet	Map Reference
Nicot Trench [1918]	66eNW [4 Morisel]	H 4 c
Nid Alley [1918]	28NE1 Zonnebeke	D 29 c, d
Nidd Trench	51bNW3 Arras	G 18 b, c, d
Niemen Trench	66cNW1 Grugies	B 1 d, 2 c
Niemeyer Weg (German Lane) [trench]	57dNE3 & 4 Hébuterne	K 17 b, 18 a, b
Nieppe [village]	36NW1 Steenwerck / 2 Armentières	B 15 b, d, 16 a, c
Nieppe System	36NW2 Armentières	B 4, 10, 11, 16, 17, 22, 28
Nieppe, Forêt de	36aNE1 Morbecque / 3 Haverskerque	extensive
Niergnies [village]	57bNW1 Cambrai / 3 Rumilly	A 30, G 6
Nieuwe Kruiseecke [hamlet & crossroads]	28NE3 Gheluvelt	J 29 d, 30 c [or J 30 c 05.80]
Nieuwe Kruiseecke Cabaret, De	28NE3 Gheluvelt	J 29 d 50.95 [or 9.9]
Nieuwe Stede Trench	20SW2 Zwartegat	O 13 b, d, 14 c
Nieuwemolen Dugout / OP [1917-18]	28NE1 Zonnebeke	D 17 c 7.4
Niger Farm	27NE4 Abeele	L 9 d 15.00
Niger Trench	51bSW2 Vis-en-Artois	N 16 a, b, d
Niggard Trench	36cSW1 Lens / 2 Harnes	N 4 c
Nigger Copse	62bNW3 Bellicourt	G 23 a, c
Nigger Farm	28NE2 Moorslede	E 16 d 05.15
Nigger Fork [road jct]	28NE2 Moorslede	E 22 b 15.90
Nigger Post	12SW3 Ramscappelle	T 1 a 8.9
Nigger Trench	36SW1 Aubers	N 14 b, d, 15 c
Nigger Trench	57cNE4 Marcoing	L 20 a, b
Night Lane	51bSW2 Vis-en-Artois	O 26 b, d
Night Trench	51bSW2 Vis-en-Artois	O 26 a, b
Nightingale Trench [1918]	66eNW [2 Thennes]	C 7 d, 8 c, 13 b
Nil Cottage	28SW2 Wytschaete	N 5 b 35.80
Nile [house]	28NE1 Zonnebeke	D 8 c 27.02
Nile [pillbox]	28NE1 Zonnebeke	D 8 c 32.05
Nile [trench]	28NW2 St Julien	C 13 d
Nile Trench	36cSW1 Lens	N 9 a
Nimble Cross Roads	20SE2 Hooglede	Q 17 c 15.50
Nine Elms [row of trees]	51bNW1 Roclincourt	A 17 a 85.15
Nine Elms Trench	51bNW1 Roclincourt	A 17 b, d
Nine Elms Trench [1918]	62dNE [1 Dernancourt]	D 18 b, d, E 13 a
Nine Wood	57cNE4 Marcoing	L 10, 16
Ninepin Trench	36SW1 Aubers	N 19 a, c
Nineteen Street	51bNW3 Arras	G 36 a
Ninety Nine Street	51cSE3 & 4 Ransart	W 22 d, 29 a
Ninfield Farm	20SE2 Hooglede	Q 6 d 1.8
Ninth Alley	57dSE2 & 57cSW1 Le Sars	M 17 c
Ninth Avenue	36cNW3 Loos	G 23 b, c, d
Ninth Avenue	51bSW2 Vis-en-Artois	N 35 b, 36 a
Niokle Farm	27SE4 Meteren	W 24 a 4.6
Nip Cottage	28NE2 Moorslede	E 18 b 5.9
Nip Trench	36cSW1 Lens	N 3 d
Nip Trench	51bNW1 Roclincourt	A 24 c
Nipper Farm	36NW1 Steenwerck	A 28 c 45.95
Nippon Bend [road bend]	36NW1 Steenwerck	B 19 b 4.5
Nirvana Farm	27SE2 Berthen	R 34 a 5.8
Niskol Trench	57cSE1 Bertincourt	P 26 a, c
Nit Trench	36cSW1 Lens	N 3 c, d
Nitrate Street	51cSE3 & 4 Ransart	W 29 a, c
Nitz Weg	51bNW1 Roclincourt	A 16 b
Nix Farm	27SE1 St Sylvestre	P 20 c 15.13

Name	Map Sheet	Map Reference
Nix Lane	51bSW1 Neuville Vitasse	N 7 b
Nix Trench	36cSW1 Lens	N 3 d
Nixon Fork [road jct]	36NW1 Steenwerck	A 2 c 9.1
Nizam Trench	36cSW1 Lens	N 2 a
No Man's Alley	57dSE4 Ovillers	R 31 c, X 1 a
No Man's Cot.	28NW2 St Julien	C 15 c 7.9
No Mans Land Siding [railway, 1917-18]	28NW4 Ypres	I 11 b, 12 a
No Trench	36cSW1 Lens	N 2 d
No. 1 Siding [trench]	36cNW1 La Bassée	A 27 a
No. 2 Siding [trench]	36cNW1 La Bassée	A 27 a
No. 3 Siding [trench]	36cNW1 La Bassée	A 27 a
No. 4 Siding [trench]	36cNW1 La Bassée	A 27 a
No. 5 Siding [trench]	36cNW1 La Bassée	A 27 a
No. 6 Siding [trench]	36cNW1 La Bassée	A 27 a
No.1 [Crater, Bellewaarde Farm]	28NW4 & NE3 Zillebeke	I 12 c 2.7
No.1 [Crater, Hohenzollern]	36cNW3 Loos	G 4 d 7.6
No.1 Cemetery [A.D.S. Duhallow]	28NW2 St Julien	C 25 d 1.0
No.1 Harley Street	36cNW1 La Bassée	A 20 d 1.8
No.10 Camp [Bois des Tailles]	62dNE [4 Bray-sur-Somme]	K 29 a 6.7
No.10 Copse	62cNE1 Liéramont / 3 Buire	J 5 b, 6 c
No.11 Copse A	62cSE1 Bouvincourt	Q 1 d, 7 b
No.11 Copse B	62cSE1 Bouvincourt	Q 12 b
No.1A [Crater, Bellewaarde Farm]	28NW4 & NE3 Zillebeke	I 12 c 3.7
No.2 [Crater, Bellewaarde Farm]	28NW4 & NE3 Zillebeke	I 12 a 1.1
No.2 [Crater, Hohenzollern Redoubt]	36cNW3 Loos	G 4 d 7.7
No.2 Browne Camp	28NW1 Elverdinghe	A 22 d
No.20 Copse	62cNE1 Liéramont	D 17 b
No.2A [Crater, Bellewaarde Farm]	28NW4 & NE3 Zillebeke	I 12 a 2.1
No.3 [Crater, Hohenzollern Redoubt]	36cNW3 Loos	G 4 d 5.7
No.3 Browne Camp	28NW1 Elverdinghe	A 22 b
No.4 [Crater, Hohenzollern Redoubt]	36cNW3 Loos	G 4 d 4.9
No.4 Camp [La Clytte]	28SW1 Kemmel	N 7 a
No.40 Copse	62cNE1 Liéramont	D 17 b
No.5 [Crater, Hohenzollern Redoubt]	36cNW1 La Bassée	G 4 b 4.1
No.5 [Sap; Sept 1915]	36cNW1 La Bassée	A 2 c, d, 8 a
No.5 Crater	36cSW3 Vimy	S 15 b
No.5 Crater [Railway Wood, S of rly]	28NW4 & NE3 Zillebeke	I 11 b 8.8
No.5 Track (Duckboard)	28NW2 St Julien / 28NE1 Zonnebeke	C 23, 24, 29, D 14, 15, 19, 20
No.6 Crater [Railway Wood, N of rly]	28NW4 & NE3 Zillebeke	I 11 b 70.95
No.6 Track [1917-18]	28NW2 St Julien / 28NE1 Zonnebeke	C 17 d, 18 b, c, d, 23 a, b
No.7 Sap [Cuinchy, July 1915]	36cNW1 La Bassée	A 27 d
Noah Trench	36cSW2 Harnes	N 24 a
Nob Trench	51bNW1 Roclincourt	A 24 c
Nob Villa [1918]	28SW1 Kemmel	N 25 c 70.95
Nobby Farm	36aSE1 St Venant	Q 26 d 0.6
Nobescourt Farm	62cNE3 Buire	K 32 b, d
Nobescourt Woods	62cNE3 Buire	K 26 a, c, d
Noble's Farm	20SE3 Westroosebeke	V 14 d 2.3
Nobs Walk	51cSE3 & 4 Ransart	W 22 a, d
Noc Farm [by Noc River]	36aSE1 St Venant	Q 19 b 90.55
Nod Trench	51bNW1 Roclincourt	A 24 c
Noeux Locality	36bNE4 Noeux-les-Mines	L 14 d, 20 b, 21 a
Noeux-les-Mines [village]	36bNE4 Noeux-les-Mines	K 18 b, c, d, L 13 a, c
Noggin Farm	28SW2 Wytschaete	N 5 c 3.0

Name	Map Sheet	Map Reference
Noggin Trench	36cSW1 Lens	N 2 b, d
Noif Trench	62cNW4 Péronne	I 32 a, c
Noir Wood	66eNW [2 Thennes]	H 5 b
Noise Trench	36cSW1 Lens	N 3 d
Noisome Trench	36cSW2 Harnes	N 18 c
Noisy Nook [farm]	36aSE3 Gonnehem	V 12 b 2.6
Noisy Redoubt / Work	51bSW1 Neuville Vitasse	N 1 d
Noisy Trench	36cSW2 Harnes	N 18 c
Nolan Trench	36cSW2 Harnes	N 23 b
Noll Maze	36cSW2 Harnes	O 13 b
Nom, Boyau Sans	62cSW1 Dompierre	M 4 a, b
Nomad Trench	36cSW1 Lens / 2 Harnes	N 4 a
Nome Locality	51bNW1 Roclincourt / 2 Oppy	B 4 a, b
Nome Trench	51bNW1 Roclincourt / 2 Oppy	B 4 a, b
Nomeny Trench	51bSW1 Neuville Vitasse	N 1 a, c
None Bosch [rly locality]	27SE2 Berthen	Q 4 d 5.0
None Bosch [wood]	27SE2 Berthen	Q 4 c, d, 10 a, b
None Bosch Line	27SE2 Berthen	extensive
Nonne Bosschen	28NW4 & NE3 Zillebeke	J 8 b, d
Nonnes Alley	66dNW3 Hattencourt	G 26, 27, 28, 29, 30, H 25
Nonsense Trench	36SW1 Aubers	N 20 c, d
Noodle Trench	36SW1 Aubers	N 32 a
Noodles Avenue	51cSE3 & 4 Ransart	W 22 d, 23 c
Nook Trench	36cSW2 Harnes	N 4 a, b
Nook Trench	36SW1 Aubers	N 15 b, d, 16 c
Noordhoek [place name]	28SW3 Bailleul	T 13 b, 14 a
Noordhoek [railway locality]	20SW3 Oostvleteren	S 30 b
Noose Trench	36SW1 Aubers	N 14 a, c
Noote Boom	36aNE2 Vieux Berquin	F 11 c, d
Noote Boom [farm]	27SE2 Berthen	R 26 d 15.45
Nootka Trench	36cNW3 Loos / SW1 Lens	H 31 d, N 1 b
Noppe [railway sidings & huts]	28NW1 Elverdinghe	B 7 a
Noppe Farm	28NW1 Elverdinghe	B 7 b 2.6
Nora Copse	28NE2 Moorslede	F 5 b, d
Nora Trench	36SW3 Richebourg	S 16 b, d, 17 c, 23 a
Norah Trench	36cSW1 Lens	N 8 b, 9 a
Norah's Arm	36SW3 Richebourg	S 16 b, d
Norbury Lines [huts]	28SW3 Bailleul	S 5 b
Norbury Villa	28SW3 Bailleul	S 5 b 2.4
Nord Alley	62cNW1 Maricourt	A 4 a, c
Nord Weg	51bSW1 Neuville Vitasse	M 4 d
Nord, Bois	66eNE4 Beaufort	L 17 a
Nord, Cité du [miners' cottages]	36cSW1 Lens	N 27 a, b
Nordad [light rly locality]	36NW2 Armentières	C 13 c 3.8
Nord-Helf [farm]	27SE4 Meteren	X 25 a 65.50
Nordwerk	57dSE4 Ovillers	R 2 b, 3 a
Nore Alley	36cSW1 Lens	N 1 c
Nore Trench	36cSW1 Lens	N 2 d
Noreuil [village]	57cNW2 Vaulx-Vraucourt	C 10 c, d, 16 a
Noreuil Switch	57cNW2 Vaulx-Vraucourt	C 9 d, 10 c, 14 a, b, c, d, 15 a, b
Norfolk Alley	57cNW2 Vaulx-Vraucourt	C 18 d
Norfolk Lodge [farm]	28NW4 Ypres	I 33 c 8.6
Norfolk Road / Street	28NW4 Ypres / SW2 Wytschaete	I 33 d, O 3 b, 4 a
Norfolk Road Cemetery	28SW2 Wytschaete	O 3 b 95.65

Name	Map Sheet	Map Reference
Norham House	27NE2 Proven	E 22 b 4.4
Normal Bridge Track [1917-18]	20SW4 Bixschoote	N 35 b, c, d, T 5 a
Norman Alley	66dNW1 Punchy	A 20 d, 21 c, d, 27 a
Norman Junction	20SW4 Bixschoote	U 27 d 1.1
Norman Street	28NW4 & NE3 Zillebeke	I 17 c
Norman Trench	36cSW1 Lens	N 2 b
Normands, Boyau	62cSW1 Dompierre	M 10 a
Normandy Trench	66cSW2 Vendeuil	O 1 a, c, 7 a, c
Norman's Cross [road over rly]	62bSW2 Fonsommes	N 24 b 7.1
Norris House	36NW1 Steenwerck	A 22 b 05.15
Norris Trench	36cSW2 Harnes	N 23 b
Norse Mill [windmill]	27SE4 Meteren	W 12 b 50.15
North Alley	36bSE4 Carency / 36cSW3 Vimy	X 6 a, S 1 b, d
North Alley	62bSW3 St Quentin	M 34 b, d, S 4 a
North Alley [to new front line]	57dSE1 & 2 Beaumont	Q 16 b
North Atlantic [trench & light rly locality]	28NW3 Poperinghe	G 9 b
North Barricade	36NW2 Armentières	C 10 b
North Breastwork [Ploegsteert Wood 1914-15]	28SW4 Ploegsteert	U 21 a 5.8
North Breastwork [S of Quinque Rue]	36SW3 Richebourg	S 27 a, b, c
North British [light rly / trench tramway, 1916]	28SW4 Ploegsteert	U 20 c, d, 21 c, 25 a, b, 26 a
North Copse [Sailly-Saillisel]	57cSW4 Combles	U 7 c, 13 a
North Crater	36cNW3 Loos	G 11 b
North Dump [Loos]	36cNW3 Loos	H 31 b 0.4
North Elgin Street	36SW1 Aubers	M 24 a, b
North End [Hexagon]	51bSW1 Neuville Vitasse	M 11 d, 17 b
North Face [Hohenzollern]	36cNW1 La Bassée	G 4 b
North Farm	28NE3 Gheluvelt	J 32 a 7.5
North Farm	28NW4 & NE3 Zillebeke	J 32 a
North Foreland	57dNE1 & 2 Fonquevillers	E 23 a
North Fork [Guillemont]	57cSW3 Longueval	T 19 c
North Gun Pits [E of Lesboeufs]	57cSW4 Combles	T 5 a
North House [Wytschaete village]	28SW2 Wytschaete	O 19 b 90.85
North Lane	62cNE2 Epéhy	F 2 c, d, 8 a, b
North Loos Alley	36cNW3 Loos	G 35 b
North Loos Avenue	36cNW3 Loos	G 23 c, d, 29 a, b
North Midland Farm	28SW4 Ploegsteert	T 6 c 7.8
North Practice Trenches	57dSE2 & 57cSW1 Le Sars	M 19 b, 20 a
North Road [road]	57cSW1 Gueudecourt	N 25 a
North Stampkot Farm	20SW4 Bixschoote	T 17 b 6.7
North Station Buildings	28NW4 & NE3 Zillebeke	J 1 a 4.5
North Street	28NW2 St Julien	C 14 d, 20 b
North Street	36cNW3 Loos	G 33, 34, 35, 36
North Street	51cSE3 & 4 Ransart	W 22 a, b, 23 a
North Street	57cSW1 Gueudecourt	N 30 a
North Street [Guillemont]	57cSW3 Longueval	T 19 c
North Street [new front line]	57dSE1 & 2 Beaumont	Q 4 b
North Street [road N from Longueval]	57cSW3 Longueval	S 5 d, 11 b, d
North Street [road, Le Transloy]	57cSW2 Villers-au-Flos	N 30 a, b, c
North Street [Tunnel: The Bluff]	28NW4 & NE3 Zillebeke	I 34 c
North Trench	36SW1 Aubers	N 15 b, d
North Trench	57cNE3 Hermies	K 26 a
Northampton [lt rly locality E of Canal 1917-18]	28NW2 St Julien	C 7 d
Northampton [strongpoint]	36NW3 Fleurbaix	G 18 b
Northampton Farm [1917]	28NW4 & NE3 Zillebeke	J 15 c 8.7

Name	Map Sheet	Map Reference
Northampton Farm [June 1915]	28NW4 & NE3 Zillebeke	J 14 d 9.7
Northampton Street	57cSW3 Longueval	S 3 c
Northampton Trench	36cNW1 La Bassée / 3 Loos	G 4 a, b, d
Northern Avenue	57dNE3 & 4 Hébuterne	K 23, 27, 28, 29
Northern Brickstack [Grand Bois]	28SW2 Wytschaete	O 13 c 27.84
Northern Craters	36cNW1 La Bassée	A 9 b, d
Northern Redoubt	20SE3 Westroosebeke	V 30 b
Northern Sap	36cNW3 Loos	G 22 b, 23 a, c
Northern Sap Redoubt	36cNW3 Loos	G 23 c
Northern Up	36bNE4 Noeux-les-Mines / 36cNW3 Loos	L 23, 24, G 19, 20, 21, 27, 28
Northumberland Avenue	36cSW3 Vimy	S 15 c
Northumberland Avenue	36cSW3 Vimy	S 2 a, b
Northumberland Avenue	36SW1 Aubers	N 13 b
Northumberland Avenue	51bNW4 Fampoux	H 11 a, c
Northumberland Lane [sunken road]	51bNW4 Fampoux	H 4 b, 5 a, c, 11 a, c,
Northumberland Lines	51bSW1 Neuville Vitasse	M 22 b
Northumberland Post	36cSW3 Vimy	S 2 a, b
Norton Farm	28NE4 Dadizeele	K 22 d 3.3
Nose Support	12SW1 Nieuport	M 22 b
Nose Trench	12SW1 Nieuport	M 22 b
Nose, The	51bNW4 Fampoux	I 1 d, 2 c
Nose, The	57dSE4 Ovillers	X 20 c
Nose, The [Snag Trench & The Tail]	57dSE2 & 57cSW1 Le Sars	M 17 c
Nosy Alley	62bSW4 Homblières	T 22 b, 23 a, b
Not Trench	36cSW2 Harnes	N 4 c, 10 a
Notamel Wood	62dSE [1 Hamel]	P 3 d, 4 c, 9 b, 10 a
Notary Cross Roads	28NE2 Moorslede	F 15 b 55.99
Notion Trench	36SW1 Aubers	N 25 a, c
Noto Trench	62bNW3 bellicourt	G 33 b, c, d
Notre Dame de Bon Secours	20NW4 Dixmude	I 7 d, 8 a
Notre Dame de Consolation, Chapelle de	36cNW3 & 1 Loos	G 10 c 95.09 [August 1915]
Notre Dame de Consolation, Chapelle de	36cNW3 Loos	G 10 c 5.2 [June 1915]
Notre Dame de Grâce, Chapelle de	28SW4 Ploegsteert	U 14 a 6.4
Notre Dame de Lorette Chapel	36bSE4 & 36cSW3 Givenchy	X 5 a 3.2
Notre Dame de Lorette Spur	36bSE4 & 36cSW3 Givenchy	X 4, 5, 6
Notre Dame de Lourdes, Chapelle de [M. Rouge]	28SW1 Kemmel	M 22 b 3.7
Notre Dame des Affliges [Touquet Berthe Farm]	28SW4 Ploegsteert	U 26 a 2.3
Notre Dame des Douleurs, Chapelle de	28SW4 Ploegsteert	U 22 b 60.53
Notre-Dame Trench	62cSW4 St. Christ	U 16 a, c, 22 a
Nottingham Camp	28SW2 Wytschaete	N 5 c
Nottingham Street	57dNE1 & 2 Fonquevillers	E 27 b
Noureil [trenches; front, support, reserve]	70dNW [1 Chauny]	A 4, 5, 10, 11, 16, 17
Nouveau Monde Post [strongpoint]	36NW3 Fleurbaix	G 27 c, 33 a
Nouveau Monde, le [farm & crossroads]	66cNW2 Itancourt	B 29 c
Nouveau Monde, le [farm]	28SW3 Bailleul	S 25 b 95.80
Nouveau, Bois de	62cSW3 & 4 Marchélepot	T 19 c
Nouvelle, Tranchée	51bNW1 Roclincourt	A 4 a, c
Nouvion Lane	51bSW1 Neuville Vitasse	N 1 d, 7 b, 8 a, c
Nova Scotia Trench	36cSW4 Rouvroy	T 24 c
Nova Scotia Trench	51bSW2 Vis-en-Artois	N 4 c, 10 a, c
Novel Alley	36cSW1 Lens	N 1 a, c
Novel Trench	36SW1 Aubers	N 26 c, d
Novel Trench	36SW1 Aubers	N 8 d, 9 c
November Avenue	51bNW3 Arras	G 5, 10, 11 , 16

Name	Map Sheet	Map Reference
Novi Bazar, Tranchée de	66cNW2 Itancourt	C 7 d, 13 b, 14 a
Now Trench	36cSW1 Lens / 2 Harnes	N 4 c, 10 a
Noyelles Centre Keep	36bNE4 Noeux-les-Mines	L 17 b
Noyelles Locality	36bNE4 Noeux-les-Mines	L 11 b, c, d, 17 b
Noyelles North Keep	36bNE4 Noeux-les-Mines	L 11 b
Noyelles South Keep	36bNE4 Noeux-les-Mines	L 17 c, d
Noyelles Trench	36cSW2 Harnes	N 17 d
Noyelles-les-Vermelles [village]	36bNE4 Noeux-les-Mines	L 11 b, c, d
Noyelles-sous-Lens [village]	36cSW2 Harnes	N 17 d, 18 c, 24 a
Nozzle Trench	36cSW1 Lens	N 32 b
Nozzle Trench	36SW1 Aubers / Richebourg	N 32 b, c, d
Nubia House	27NE4 Abeele	L 10 c 9.2
Nudge Trench	36cSW1 Lens	N 3 c, 9 a, c
Nudge Trench	36SW1 Aubers	N 27 c
Nugent Support	28SW4 Ploegsteert	T 6 d 9.3
Nuggin Trench	36cSW2 Harnes	N 24 b
Nullah Street	51cSE3 & 4 Ransart	W 23 a
Nullah Trench	36cSW2 Harnes	N 4 a, b, d
Numb Farm	20SE2 Hooglede	R 5 d 9.3
Numb Trench	36SW1 Aubers	N 27 b, d
Numides Trench	66dNW1 Punchy	A 28 d, G 4 a, b
Nun Alley	36SW1 Aubers	N 26 b
Nun Trench	36SW1 Aubers	N 26 b, 27 a
Nuneaton [W of Canal, light rly]	28NW2 St Julien	B 23 b
Nunnery Lane	36NW4 Bois Grenier	I 16 a, b
Nunn's Bearer Post	28NW4 & NE3 Zillebeke	J 8 b
Nun's Alley	36cSW1 Lens	N 2 a, d, 8 b, 9 c
Nuns Nose	36cSW3 Vimy	S 3 a, b
Nuns Trench	36cSW1 Lens	N 2 d
Nuphar Trench	36cSW1 Lens	N 3 d
Nuremberg Trench	62cSW3 Vermandovillers	S 13 b, 14 a
Nuremberg Trenchée, de	70dSW [2 Coucy-le-Château]	O 15 b
Nurlu [village]	57cSE3 Sorel-le-Grand / 62cNE1 Lièramont	V 28 c, d, 29 c, I 4 a, b
Nurlu Aerodrome [German, 1918]	62cNE1 Lièramont	D 4 d, 5 c
Nurlu Trench	57cSE3 Sorel-le-Grand	V 28 c
Nut Farm	28SE1 Wervicq	P 2 b 95.42
Nut Farm [1918]	28SW1 Kemmel	N 13 d 51.29
Nut Road [road]	28SW1 Kemmel	N 13 d, 14 c
Nut Support	51bSW2 Vis-en-Artois	O 20 d, 21 c, 22 b
Nut Trench	36cSW1 Lens	N 2 d
Nut Trench	36SW1 Aubers	N 14 a, b
Nut Trench	51bNW1 Roclincourt	A 24 c
Nut Trench	51bSW1 Neuville Vitasse	M 23 a
Nut Trench	51bSW2 Vis-en-Artois	O 20 b, d, 21 a, c, 26 b
Nutmeg Avenue	28SW4 Ploegsteert	N 36 d, O 31 c
Nutmeg Lane	28SW4 Ploegsteert	N 36 d, O 31 c
Nutmeg Reserve	28SW4 Ploegsteert	N 36 d
Nutmeg Support	28SW4 Ploegsteert	N 36 d
Nutmeg Trench	28SW4 Ploegsteert	N 36 d
Nutmeg Trench	36cSW1 Lens	N 3 a, c
Nuts Walk	51cSE3 & 4 Ransart	W 23 a
Nuttebilek [farm]	36aNE2 Vieux Berquin	F 10 a 3.5
Nyanza Cross Roads	27SE4 Meteren	R 32 c 30.35
Nymph Farm	28SW2 Wytschaete	N 5 d 9.7

Name	Map Sheet	Map Reference
Nymph Trench	36cNW4 Pont-à-Vendin / SW2 Harnes	H 35 c, N 5 a, c
O 1 [trench, W of Bois Quarante]	28SW2 Wytschaete	O 7 a 7.4
O 2 [trench, W of Bois Quarante]	28SW2 Wytschaete	O 7 b 0.5
O 3 [trench, W of Piccadilly Farm]	28SW2 Wytschaete	O 7 b 3.9
O 4 [trench, W of Piccadilly Farm]	28SW2 Wytschaete	O 7 b 5.7
O 7 [trench, Redoubt Farm]	28SW2 Wytschaete	O 7 a 2.7
O 8 [trench]	28SW2 Wytschaete	O 1 c 9.5
O Camp	28NW1 Elverdinghe	A 30 c, d
O Trench [E of St Eloi, Feb 1915]	28SW2 Wytschaete	O 3 b
O.B. 1 [Old British Line]	36cNW3 Loos	G 4
O.B. 1 [Old British Line]	36cSW1 Lens	M 3 b, d
O.B. 2 [Old British Line]	36cSW1 Lens	M 3 b, d
O.B. Front Line [1918]	57dNE2 Essarts	E 11, 16, 17, 22
O.B.4 [Old British]	36cNW3 Loos	G 9, 10, 11
O.B.L. Avenue	57cNE3 Hermies	K 7 c, d, 13 b, 14 a
O.G. [Old German Line]	36cSW1 Lens	M 4 b
O.G. 1 [Old German Line]	36cSW1 Lens	M 4 a
O.G. 2 [Old German Line]	36cSW1 Lens	M 4 b
O.G. Trench [Old German]	57cNE3 Hermies	J 30 d
O.G.1	36cNW3 Loos	G 11 d, 17 b
O.G.1	57dSE2 Beaumont / 4 Ovillers	R 14, 34, 35, X 5, 11, 12
O.G.2	36cNW3 Loos	G 11 d, 17 b
O.G.2	57dSE2 Beaumont / 4 Ovillers	R 14, 15, 34, 35, X 5, 6, 12
Oaf Alley	28SW2 Wytschaete	O 5 a, b
Oaf Avenue	28SW2 Wytschaete	O 4 b
Oaf Drive	28SW2 Wytschaete	O 5 a
Oaf Keep	28SW2 Wytschaete	O 6 a, b
Oaf Lane	28SW2 Wytschaete	O 5 a, b
Oaf Row	28SW2 Wytschaete	O 5 b, 6 a
Oaf Street	28SW2 Wytschaete	O 5 b
Oak Alley	28SW2 Wytschaete	O 4 c
Oak Alley	36cSW4 Rouvroy	T 29 d, 30 c
Oak Alley	57cSW4 Combles	U 26 d
Oak Avenue	28SW2 Wytschaete	O 4 a, d
Oak Crescent	28SW2 Wytschaete	O 4 c, d
Oak Dump	28SW2 Wytschaete	O 3 b
Oak Dump Cemetery	28SW2 Wytschaete	O 3 b 9.6
Oak Lane	51bSW1 Neuville Vitasse	M 18 c
Oak Post [NE of Arleux, 1918]	36cSW4 Rouvroy	T 30 c
Oak Reserve	28SW2 Wytschaete	O 4 a, c
Oak Row	28SW2 Wytschaete	O 4 a
Oak Street	36NW4 Bois Grenier	I 21 a, c
Oak Street	51cSE2 Beaumetz	R 28 c, 34 a
Oak Support	28SW2 Wytschaete	O 3 d
Oak Support	36SW2 Radinghem	O 12 d
Oak Switch	28SW2 Wytschaete	O 4 b, c, d
Oak Trench	28SW2 Wytschaete	O 4 a
Oak Trench	28SW2 Wytschaete	N 23 b, 24 a
Oak Trench	36SW2 Radinghem	O 12 d
Oak Trench	51bNW3 Arras	H 13 b
Oak Trench	57cSE4 Villers-Guislain	X 26 b, d
Oak Trench [1918]	57dNE4 [Hébuterne / Achiet]	L 1 c, d, 7 b, 8 a
Oak Walk	28SW2 Wytschaete	O 4 a, b
Oakham Trench	57dNE1 & 2 Fonquevillers	E 28 b

Name	Map Sheet	Map Reference
Oakhanger [house & farm]	28NW1 Elverdinghe	G 3 a, b
Oakhanger [railway sidings]	28NW1 Elverdinghe / 3 Poperinghe	G 3 b, d
Oakhanger Trench	62cNW1 Maricourt	B 2 b, d, 8 b, 9 a
Oakhanger Wood	62cNW1 Maricourt	B 2 d, 3 c, 8 a, b
Oakington Farm	20SE3 Westroosebeke	V 6 d 4.4
Oaklands Farm	20SE2 Hooglede	Q 35 b 1.3
Oakling Lane	28SW2 Wytschaete	O 4 b, 5 a
Oakling Reserve	28SW2 Wytschaete	O 4 b, 5 a
Oakling Support	28SW2 Wytschaete	O 4 b, 5 a
Oar Alley	28SW2 Wytschaete	O 3 d
Oar Avenue [1917]	28SW2 Wytschaete	O 3 c, 9 a, b, d
Oar Avenue [1918]	28SW2 Wytschaete	O 9 d, 10 c
Oar Lane	28SW2 Wytschaete	O 3 d, 4 c
Oar Reserve	28SW2 Wytschaete	O 3 d, 4 c, 9 b
Oar Row	28SW2 Wytschaete	O 3 d, 4 c
Oar Street	28SW2 Wytschaete	O 3 d, 9 b
Oar Support	28SW2 Wytschaete	O 3 d, 4 a, c
Oar Trench	28SW2 Wytschaete	O 3 b, c, d
Oar Trench	51bNW3 Arras	H 13 b
Oasis [locality, 1917-18]	28SW2 Wytschaete	O 2 d
Oasis Avenue	28SW2 Wytschaete	O 2 d
Oasis Drive	28SW2 Wytschaete	O 2 d, 8 b, d
Oasis Lane	28SW2 Wytschaete	O 2 d, 3 c, 8 b
Oasis Reserve	28SW2 Wytschaete	O 9 a, b
Oasis Row	28SW2 Wytschaete	O 9 a
Oasis Street	28SW2 Wytschaete	O 3 c, 9 a
Oasis Support	28SW2 Wytschaete	O 3 c
Oasis Trench	28SW2 Wytschaete	O 2 d, 3 c
Oat Avenue	28SW2 Wytschaete	O 9 b, d
Oat Lane [1918]	51cSE4 Blaireville	X 23 a
Oat Lane [trench]	57cSW1 Gueudecourt	M 12 d, 18 b, N 13 a, b, d
Oat Trench	51bNW3 Arras	H 13 c
Oat Trench [1918]	57dSW [1 Puchevillers]	M 36 a
Oaten Tr, Supp, Res, St, Row, Lane, Dr	28SW2 Wytschaete	O 2 c, d, 8 a, c
Oaten Wood	28SW2 Wytschaete	O 8 b, c, d
Obadiah Trench	36SW2 Radinghem	O 9 d
Oban Avenue	57dSE4 Ovillers	W 6 a, b
Oban Trench	28SW2 Wytschaete	O 28 c, 34 a
Obeaux, Ferme des	28SE1 Wervicq	P 10 b 1.8
Obelisk Trench	20SW2 Zwartegat	O 2 a, c
Obermayer Graben	51bNW3 Arras	G 12 b
Obey Tr, Supp, Lane, Path, Row	28SW2 Wytschaete	O 2 c, 7 b, 8 a
Obit Tr, Supp, Alley, Row, Street, Lane	28SW2 Wytschaete	O 7 b, d
Object Tr, Supp, Res, Ave, Switch, Alley	28SW2 Wytschaete	O 7 a, b, c, d, 13 b
Oblige Tr, Supp, Res, Ave, Lane, Alley	28SW2 Wytschaete	N 12 d, 18 b, O 7 c, 13 a
Oblique Alley	36cNW1 La Bassée	A 4 a, c
Oblique Avenue	20SW4 Bixschoote	T 23 a, b
Oblique Trench, & Row	28SW2 Wytschaete	O 5 a, b, d, 6 a
Oblong Farm	28NW2 St Julien	C 16 b 5.3
Oblong Farm	28SW2 Wytschaete	O 22 b 7.3
Oblong Trench, Reserve & Alley	28SW2 Wytschaete	O 4 d, 10 a, b, d
Oblong Wood	57dSE1 & 2 Beaumont	R 25 c
Oboe Corner	28NE4 Dadizeele	L 20 c
Oboe Trench	62bSW3 St Quentin	N 32 c, d, T 2 b

Name	Map Sheet	Map Reference
Oboe Trench, & Avenue	28SW2 Wytschaete	O 4 c, 10 a, b, d
Obos Cottage	36aNE4 Merville	L 20 d 1.8
Obos Cottage	36aNE4 Merville	L 20 d 1.8
O'Brien Post [1918]	57dNE4 [Hébuterne / Achiet]	K 19 b
Obscure Trench, Supp, Row, Alley	28SW2 Wytschaete	O 9 d, 10 a, c, 15 b
Observation Avenue / Boyau de l'Observation	62cNW1 Maricourt / 3 Vaux	A 28 d, G 4 a, b, c
Observation Farm [Reserve Farm]	36NW2 & NE1 Houplines	C 3 b 7.1
Observation Ridge	51bNW3 Arras	H 20, 25, 26, 31, 32
Observation Trench	36cNW1 La Bassée	A 9 b
Observation Trench [1918]	51bSW3 Boisleux	S 28 a, b
Observation Wood	57dNE3 & 4 Hébuterne	K 28 b
Observation Wood	62cNW1 Maricourt	H 2 a, c
Observatoire Anglais, Boyau de l'	62cNW3 Vaux	G 22 d
Observatoires Alley	62cNW3 Vaux / 4 Péronne	H 15 c, d, 16 c, d
Observatoires, Tranchée des	62cNW3 Vaux	G 22 a, c
Observatory Dump	28NW4 & NE3 Zillebeke	I 24 d 2.4
Observatory Farm	28SW4 Ploegsteert	T 4 a 7.8
Observatory Redoubt	51bNW3 Arras	G 5 d
Observatory Ridge	28NW4 & NE3 Zillebeke	I 24 c
Observatory Ridge Road [metalled, 1917]	28NW4&NE3 Zillebeke	I 23 c, d, 24 c, d
Observatory Trench	28NW4 & NE3 Zillebeke	I 24 c
Observatory Trench [1918]	62dSW [4 Cachy]	U 1 a, c, 7 a
Observers Work	66cNW2 Itancourt	B 28 d
Obstacle Trench, Supp, Switch, Ave	28SW2 Wytschaete	O 9 c, d, 15 a, b, c
Obstinate Trench	28SW2 Wytschaete	O 8 c, d, 14 b
Obstruction Supp, Alley, Ave, Ln, Drive	28SW2 Wytschaete	O 13 a, b, c, d, 14 c
Obstruction Tr, Sw, St, Row, Ave	28SW2 Wytschaete	O 7, 8, 13, 14
Obtuse Ave, Crescent, & Keep [O 14 a]	28SW2 Wytschaete	O 14 a, b
Obtuse Bend [in road]	20SW4 Bixschoote	U 11 b 3.0
Obus Farm	66dNW1 Punchy	B 26 a
Obus Trench, Support, Avenue	51bSW2 Vis-en-Artois	O 27 d, 28 b, c, 34 a
Obus Wood	62cNW2 Bouchavesnes	C 5 a
Obusiers Farm	20SW4 Bixschoote	O 31 d 15.10
Obvious Trench, Drive, Row, Ave, Alley	28SW2 Wytschaete	O 13 c, d, 14 c, 19 a, b
Occasion Trench, Sw, Ave, Alley	28SW2 Wytschaete	O 19 a, b, c, d, 20 c
Occident Lane	51bSW2 Vis-en-Artois	O 28 b, c, 33 b, 34 a
Occult Trench, Row, Avenue	28SW2 Wytschaete	O 25 a, c, d, 31 a
Occur Trench, Support, Avenue	28SW2 Wytschaete	O 31 a, b
Ocean Trench [1918]	28NE3 Gheluvelt	J 5 d
Ocean Trench, Sw, Ln, Av, Cres, Alley	28SW2 Wytschaete	O 19 c, d, 25 a, b
Ocean Work	51bSW2 Vis-en-Artois	O 29 a, b
Ochre Trench, Drive, Ave, Alley	28SW2 Wytschaete	O 19, 20, 25, 26
Ockenden Trench	62cNE2 Epéhy	F 3 a
Ocklynge Corner [road junction]	20SE2 Hooglede	R 13 d 30.75
Octave, Tranchée	62cSW1 & 2 Belloy	N 24 a, b
October Avenue	51bNW3 Arras	G 11, 16
October Trench, Supp, Alley, Ave, Drive	28SW2 Wytschaete	O 26 c, d, 32 a, b
Octoroon Corner [road jct]	28NE2 Moorslede	E 9 b 8.7
Octroi Ravine	62bSW3 St Quentin	S 16 b
Oculist Trench, Alley, Row	28SW2 Wytschaete	O 32 b, 33 a, b, 34 a
Odd Trench	28SW2 Wytschaete	O 28 c, 34 a
Odde Alley	62cNW2 Bouchavesnes / 4 Péronne	H 4 b, 5 a, c
Ode Farm	28NE2 Moorslede	L 3 b 75.55
Oder House	28NW2 St Julien	C 29 d 3.0

Name	Map Sheet	Map Reference
Oder Trench	62cNW4 Péronne	I 8 b, d, 14 b, d
Odiham Trench	57dNE1 & 2 Fonquevillers	E 28 b, d
Odious Trench	28SW2 Wytschaete	O 22 c, 28 a, c
Odol Cottages	27SE2 Berthen	R 25 b 5.3
Odonto House	28SW2 Wytschaete	O 22 a 2.9
Odonto Trench	28SW2 Wytschaete	O 16 c, 22 a
Odour House	28SW1 Kemmel	M 17 a 55.42
Odour Lane	57cSW4 Combles	T 4 c
Odour Trench	28SW2 Wytschaete	O 22 a, c
Odour Trench	57cSW4 Combles	T 4 c
Odyssey Trench	28SW2 Wytschaete	O 10 c, 16 a, c
Oerg Farm	27NE2 Proven	E 5 b 6.4
Oestres [village]	66cNW1 Grugies	A 5 b, 6 a
Oeuf Trench / Tranchée de l'Oeuf	62cSW4 St Christ	T 12 a, b
Offa Dump	36bSE4 Carency	X 11 b 6.1
Offal Farm	27NE2 Proven	F 13 d 05.55
Offer Trench	28SW2 Wytschaete	O 21 a, b
Offoy Aerodrome [German, 1918]	66dNE[3]	J 15 a, c
Og [German Pillbox]	51bSW4 Bullecourt	U 20 b
Og Corner [road jct]	27SE4 Meteren	W 22 b 6.4
Ogden Fork [road jct]	28NW3 Poperinghe	G 26 c 4.5
Ogle Farm	20SE2 Hooglede	R 34 b 8.8
Ogle Trench	28SW2 Wytschaete	O 23 c, 29 a
Ogre Pit	51bSW4 Bullecourt	U 5 c
Ogre Trench / Tranchée de l'Ogre	66dNW3 Hattencourt	G 7 d, 13 b, 14 a, b
Ohio Trench	51bNW4 Fampoux	H 36 c, d
Ohio Trench	57dNE1 & 2 Fonquevillers	E 29 a
Oil Avenue	36SW2 Radinghem	O 2 c, d, 8 b, 9 a
Oil Drive	36SW2 Radinghem	O 2 a, c, d
Oil Factory [post]	51bNW3 Arras	G 17 c 5.6
Oil Factory British Cemetery	51bNW3 Arras	G 17 c 3.7
Oil Lane	36SW2 Radinghem	O 1 b, 2 a, c
Oil Mill	28SE2 Menin	Q 30 d
Oil Street	36SW2 Radinghem	O 9 c, 15 a
Oil Switch	36SW2 Radinghem	O 8 d, 9 c
Oil Trench	28SW2 Wytschaete	O 21 a
Oil Trench	36SW2 Radinghem	O 2 c
Oil Trench	51bNW3 Arras	H 13 c
Oily Lane	57dSE2 & 57cSW1 Le Sars	N 20 d, 21 c
Oise Alley, L'	66cNW4 Berthenicourt	H 18 c, d, 24 a
Oisy-le-Verger [village]	51bSE2 Oisy-le-Verger	Q 24 b, d, R 19 a, b, c
Olaf Avenue	28SW2 Wytschaete	O 4 b, 5 a, b, c, 6 b
Old (Water) Comm. Tr. [Feb '15, Duck's Bill area]	36cNW1 La Bassée	A 9 d
Old Avenue	36SW2 Radinghem	O 7 c
Old Battery Trench [1918]	66eNW [4 Morisel]	H 10 d, 16 b
Old Beaumont Road [road]	57dSE1 & 2 Beaumont	Q 4 c, 9 b, 10 a
Old Block	28SW2 Wytschaete	O 33 a 25.45
Old Boche Alley	66dNW1 Punchy	B 9 c, 15 a, c, 21 a, c, 27 a, c, H 3 a
Old Bond Street [Hooge, 1915]	28NW4 & NE3 Zillebeke	I 18 a, b, c
Old Bond Street [Zouave Wood - Hooge]	28NW4 & NE3 Zillebeke	I 18 a, b
Old Boot Street / Old Boots Street	36cSW3 Vimy	S 21 a, b
Old Boots Trench	36cNW1 La Bassée	A 27 c, d, G 3 b
Old Bread Street [Ploegsteert Wood]	28SW4 Ploegsteert	U 20 b 98.50
Old Bridge Street [1917-18, plank road]	20SW4 Bixschoote	U 5 b, c, d

Name	Map Sheet	Map Reference
Old British Line (O.B.L.)	36SW3 Richebourg / 36cNW1 La Bassée	S 15, 20, 21, 26 , A 2
Old British Line [Feb 1915, Duck's Bill area]	36cNW1 La Bassée	A 9 d
Old British Post	51bSW4 Bullecourt	U 1 c 9.9
Old Communication Tr. [Feb '15, Duck's Bill area]	36cNW1 La Bassée	A 9 d
Old Communication Trenches	36bSE4 Carency	R 33 c, d, 34 c, X 3 d , 4 a, b
Old Crown [building]	28NW1 Elverdinghe	G 6 a 5.0
Old Eton Post [Sept 1915]	36SW1 Aubers	M 19 d 70.45
Old Factory St. Gobain	62cNW3 Vaux	G 17 c
Old Fantome	51bNW1 Roclincourt	A 22 c
Old Farms	28SW2 Wytschaete	N 6 c
Old Fort (Knocke)	20SW1 Loo	N 8 a
Old French Street	57dNE1 & 2 Fonquevillers	E 27 d, K 3 b
Old French Trench	28SW2 Wytschaete	O 1 b, c, d, 2 a
Old French Trench	57dSE1 & 2 Beaumont	Q 23 a
Old German Alley	57cSW3 Longueval	S 24 a
Old German Breastwork	36SW3 Richebourg	S 27 a
Old German Front & Support Lines	57cSW3 Longueval	S 14, 15, 16
Old German Front Line [late 1915]	36SW1 Aubers	M 29 b, c, d, 35 a
Old German Line	36cNW1 La Bassée	A 3 c, 9 a
Old Hindenburg Line [1918]	51bSW1 Neuville Vitasse	extensive
Old House	28SW4 Ploegsteert	O 32 d 4.6
Old Kent Road	28NW4 & NE3 Zillebeke / SW2 Wytschaete	I 33 d, O 3 a, b
Old Kent Road	62dNE2 Méaulte	F 10 c, 16 a
Old Kent Road [Sept 1915]	36cNW1 La Bassée	A 15 c, 21 a, b
Old Kent Tunnel [1916]	36cNW1 La Bassée	A 21 b
Old M & N [trench]	28SW2 Wytschaete	N 12 b, O 7 a
Old Man's Corner [German front line]	36cNW1 La Bassée	A 3 b 2.6
Old Mill [E of Spriet Copse]	20SE3 Westroosebeke	V 17 d 1.9
Old Mill [Itancourt]	66cNW2 Itancourt	B 17 d 95.90
Old Mill [south of Monchy-au-Bois]	57dNE1 & 2 Fonquevillers	E 9 c 1.5
Old Mill of Lesdain	57bNW3 Rumilly	G 36 b 3.4
Old Mill Signal [NW]	62bSW1 Gricourt	M 16 c 4.6
Old Mill Signal [SE]	62bSW1 Gricourt	M 36 a 12.15
Old Mill, Bel Aise	57bSW1 Bantouzelle	M 12 a 65.30
Old Mill, Elverdinghe	28NW1 Elverdinghe	B 15 a 1.9
Old Mill, Pypegaale	20SW3 Oostvleteren	T 14 d
Old Quarry [quarry & wood]	62cNW4 Péronne	H 11 a
Old Reserve Trench	28SW2 Wytschaete	N 6 c, 11 b, 12 a
Old Roman Road [road]	62bSW3 St Quentin	S 16 b, 17 a, etc.
Old Rope Keep [Sept 1915]	36SW3 Richebourg	S 21 d 25.90
Old Sarum Camp	57dNE3 & 4 Hébuterne	K 28 a, c
Old Snipers House [Le Touquet]	36NW2 & NE1 Houplines	C 10 b
Old Subsidiary Line [Ploegsteert Wood]	28SW4 Ploegsteert	U 21 a, b, c
Old Toast Trench	36cSW3 Vimy / 4 Rouvroy	T 10 d, 16 a, b, c
Old Torr Top	28NW4 & NE3 Zillebeke	I 24 d
Old Tower [Moulin Fm, 1917-18]	28NE1 Zonnebeke	D 22 d 1.3
Old Trench	36SW2 Radinghem	O 7 a
Old Trench / Old Trench Avenue	20SW4 Bixschoote	T 17 d, 18 c
Old Trench Line [Ploeg. Wood 1914-15]	28SW4 Ploegsteert	U 21 a, c
Oldenbourg Trench	62cNW2 Bouchavesnes	B 28 d, H 4 b
Oldenbourg Trench	70dNW4 St Gobain	H 17 b, 18 a, c
Oldenburg Lane	51bSW4 Bullecourt	U 7 d, 8 a, c
Oldham [lt rly locality SE of Langemarck 1917-18]	20SW4 Bixschoote	U 29 a, b
Oldham Alley	57cSE2 Gonnelieu	Q 4 b, d

Name	Map Sheet	Map Reference
Oldham Street	57cSE4 Villers-Guislain	X 30 c
Oldham Street [road]	57cSE4 Villers-Guislain	X 29 d, 30 c
Oldham Trench	28SW2 Wytschaete	O 29 a, c
Oldham Trench	62dNE2 Méaulte	F 11 d
Olga / Olgar Trench	28SW2 Wytschaete	O 23 c, 29 a
Olga Houses	20SW4 Bixschoote	U 18 b 6.2
Olga Trench	51bSW2 Vis-en-Artois	O 28 a, c, d
Olga Trench, Switch, Drive & Lane	36SW2 Radinghem	N 12 b, 18 a, O 7 c
Olive Farm	28SE1 Wervicq	P 10 d 90.99
Olive House	28NE1 Zonnebeke	D 7 d 9.8
Olive House	28SW2 Wytschaete / 4 Ploegsteert	O 33 a 9.1
Olive Street	28NE1 Zonnebeke	D 7 d, 8 c
Olive Tr, Supp, St, Row, Ave, Lane	36SW2 Radinghem	O 4 a, b, d,
Olive Trench	51bNW3 Arras	H 14 d
Olive Trench	51bSW2 Vis-en-Artois	O 24 c, 29 b, 30 a
Olive Trench, & Track	28SW2 Wytschaete	O 9, 10, 11, 15
Oliver Farm	28SE1 Wervicq	P 10 b 8.0
Olivia Farm	28NE4 Dadizeele	L 10 d 1.6
Oliviers, Tranchée des	66eNE4 Beaufort	L 5 d, 11 a, b, c
Oliyiers Copse	62bNW4 Ramicourt	I 33 d, O 3 b
Olmutz Trench	62cNW4 Péronne	H 30 a, b
Olney Farm	27NE4 Abeele	K 4 d 4.2
Olympia Tr, Supp, Keep, Drive, Ave	36SW2 Radinghem	O 3 b, 4 c, 9 b, 10 a
Omar Farm	28NE2 Moorslede	E 17 b 87.75
Omar Trench	28SW2 Wytschaete	O 16 a
Ombre Trench	36SW2 Radinghem	O 9 d
Omeara Trench, & Support	36SW2 Radinghem	O 12 c, d
Omega Trench	28SW2 Wytschaete	O 22 a, c
Omelette / Omelete [sic] Trench	28SW2 Wytschaete	O 24 c, 30 a
Omelette Support	28SW2 Wytschaete	O 24 c, d, 30 b
Omelette Trench, Reserve & Switch	36SW2 Radinghem	O 8 c, d, 14 b
Omelt Trench [sic, 1918]	28SW2 Wytschaete	O 11 a, c
Omiécourt [village]	66dNW1 Punchy	B 8, 14
Omiécourt Wood	66dNW1 Punchy	B 8 a, c
Omignon Trench	62cSW4 St. Christ	O 33 d, U 3 b
Ominous Tr, Keep, Sw, Drive, Av, Alley	36SW2 Radinghem	O 7 d, 8 c, 13 a, b
Omissy [village]	62bSW2 Fonsommes	N 28 c, 34 a
Omit Trench, & Support	36SW2 Radinghem	O 13 c
Omlette [sic] Farm	36aNE4 Merville	K 22 a 65.10
Omniecourt Trench	70dNW2 Servais	B 29 c, H 5 a
Ondank [hamlet]	28NW1 Elverdinghe	A 5 c, d, 11 a, b
Ondank Cabaret	28NW1 Elverdinghe	A 12 a 1.7
Ondank Dump	28NW1 Elverdinghe	A 5 c, d
One Tree Hill	57dSE1 & 2 Beaumont	Q 3 b, 4 a
Onesime Trench	62cSW2 Barleux	N 12 c, d, 24 b
Onia Trench	66cNW2 Itancourt	B 12 c
Onion Lane [trench]	62cNE3 Roisel / 62bNW3 Bellicourt	L 6 c, G 1 d
Onion Street	28SW2 Wytschaete	O 28 a, c
Onion Trench	28SW2 Wytschaete	O 28 a, c
Onion Trench	36SW2 Radinghem	O 21 b
Onion Trench	51bNW3 Arras	H 14 b, 15 a
Onion, The	28SW2 Wytschaete	O 33 b 4.4
Only Way, The	28SW4 Ploegsteert	U 8 d, 9 c, d, 14 a
Onoto Trench	62bNW3 Bellicourt	G 33 c

Name	Map Sheet	Map Reference
Onraet Dugouts	28SW2 Wytschaete	O 14 c 55.65
Onraet Farm	28SW2 Wytschaete	O 14 a 25.05
Onraet Wood	28SW2 Wytschaete	O 14 a, c
Onslow Trench [BFL]	28SW4 Ploegsteert	T 6 b 62.70
Ontario Avenue	28SW4 Ploegsteert	U 14 b, d
Ontario Camp [Reninghelst]	28NW3 Poperinghe	G 34 a, b, d [Vicinity of]
Ontario Farm	28SW4 Ploegsteert	U 1 a 4.7
Ontario Loop	28SW4 Ploegsteert	U 14 b, d
Ontario Trench	36cSW1 Lens	N 25 c, 31 a
Onyx House	36NW1 Steenwerck	A 16 d 8.2
Onyx Trench	51bNW3 Arras	H 14 b, 15 a
Oosels, The	36cSW1 Lens	M 14 a
Oostaverne [village]	28SW2 Wytschaete	O 21 b
Oostaverne Line	28SW2 Wytschaete / 4 Ploegsteert	O 5, 10, 11, 16, 22, 28, 34, U 4 10
Oostaverne Trench, Support, Track	28SW2 Wytschaete	O 14 c, d, 20 a, b
Oostaverne Wood	28SW2 Wytschaete	O 11 b, 14 d, 15 c, 20 b, 21 a
Oosthoek [hamlet]	28NW1 Elverdinghe	A 23 d, 24 c
Oosthoek [place name]	28SW2 Wytschaete	O 3 a, b
Oosthoek Farm, Lower	28SW2 Wytschaete	O 3 a 80.85
Oosthoek Trench	28NW4 & NE3 Zillebeke / SW2 Wytschaete	I 33 c / O 3 a
Oosthove Farm	28NW1 Elverdinghe	A 20 c 5.4
Oostnieuwkerke [village]	20SE3 Westroosebeke	W 3 d, 9 a, b
Oostvlode [farm]	27SE4 Meteren	Q 34 c 55.30
Oothove [hamlet]	27NE2 Proven	F 14 c, d
Ooze Copse	62bSW4 Homblières	O 32 c
Opaka Trench	57cSW4 Combles	U 5 c, 11 a
Opal Trench	51bSW2 Vis-en-Artois / 4 Bullecourt	O 35 a, b, U 6 a, b
Opal Trench, Support, Reserve, Walk	28SW2 Wytschaete	O 4 , 5 , 10, 11
Opaque Keep	28SW2 Wytschaete	O 6 a, b
Opaque Wood	28SW2 Wytschaete	O 6 a, b
Opawa Avenue [1918]	28NE3 Gheluvelt	J 5 d, 6 c
Open House	36NW1 Steenwerck	A 4 d 4.9
Opera Spur [light rly]	36cSW1 Lens	M 12 a
Opera Trench	36SW2 Radinghem	O 16 a
Opera Trench	62cNW2 Bouchavesnes / NE1 Liéramont	C 18 b,d, D 13 c, 19 a, b
Opera Trenches	51bSW2 Vis-en-Artois	O 29 a, b
Opérateur Trench	62cSW4 St. Christ	U 3 b, d, 4 c, d
Ophelia Alley	62bSW3 St Quentin	S 24 c
Ophir House	36NW1 Steenwerck	B 13 a 4.8
Ophir Trench	51bSW2 Vis-en-Artois	O 21 d, 27 b, 28 a
Opium Farm	28NW3 Poperinghe	H 21 c 9.7
Opium Trench	51bNW3 Arras	H 8 d, 14 b
Opossum Trench	36SW1 Aubers / 2 Radinghem	N 16 c
Opoux Trench [1918]	62dSW [4 Cachy]	U 23 a, c, 29 a
Oppy [village]	51bNW2 Oppy	C 7 c, 13 a, b
Oppy Post	51bNW2 Oppy	B 12 d
Oppy Support Trench	51bNW2 Oppy	C 7 a, c, d, 13 b, d, 20 a
Oppy Wood	51bNW2 Oppy	B 18 b, C 13 a
Oppy-Méricourt-Vendin Line	36aSW4 Rouvroy	extensive
Optic Avenue	28SW2 Wytschaete	O 4, 5, 6, 10, 11
Optic Support	28SW2 Wytschaete	O 5 d, 6 c, 11 a, b
Optic Trench	28SW2 Wytschaete	O 5 c, d, 11 a
Optic Trench, & Support	36SW2 Radinghem	O 30 d
Option Farm	36NW1 Steenwerck	G 5 a 20.46

Name	Map Sheet	Map Reference
Or, Tranchée de l'	70dSW [4 Vauxaillon]	U 12 a
Oracle Trench, & Support	36SW2 Radinghem	O 30 b
Oracles Alley / Boyau des Oracles	66dNW3 Hattencourt	G 7 d, 8 c, d, 14 b
Oraki Support [1918]	28NE3 Gheluvelt	J 5 d, 11 b
Oram Farm	28NE4 Dadizeele	L 15 d 3.4
Oran Alley [1918]	62dSW [4 Cachy]	U 4 c, d
Oran, Boyau d' [Doran Alley]	36bSE2 Boyeffles	R 30 a
Orange Alley	66cNW4 Berthenicourt	I 14 b, d
Orange Avenue	51bNW4 Fampoux	H 36 c, d, I 31 c
Orange Cemetery	51bNW4 Fampoux	H 36 a
Orange Farm	28SE1 Wervicq	P 19 c 5.8
Orange Hill	51bNW3 Arras / 4 Fampoux	H 34 b, d, 35 a, c
Orange Trench	36SW2 Radinghem	O 10 b
Orange Trench	51bSW1 Neuville Vitasse	M 29 c, 35 a
Orange Trench	51bSW2 Vis-en-Artois	O 29 b, d
Orange Trench	57dNE1 & 2 Fonquevillers	E 29 a
Orange Trench	51bNW4 Fampoux	H 34 b, d, 35 a
Orange Trench, & Street	28SW2 Wytschaete	O 27 b, c, d
Orb House	36aNE2 Vieux Berquin	F 18 c 7.1
Orb Trench	51bNW3 Arras	H 14 a
Orbit Support [1918]	57dSW [4 Toutencourt]	U 22 b, d, 23 c, 29 a
Orbit Trench	28SW2 Wytschaete	O 22 d, 28 b
Orbit Trench [1918]	57dSW [4 Toutencourt]	U 23 a, c, 29 a
Orca Farm	36NW1 Steenwerck	A 15 c 8.4
Orchard [Trench / Redoubt; Sept 1915]	36cNW1 La Bassée	A 9 a
Orchard [Trench]	36NW2 Armentières	C 28 b
Orchard Alley	62dNE2 Méaulte	F 4 d, 10 a
Orchard Alley	66cSW4 La Fère	O 31 c, d, 32 c
Orchard Alley [Puisieux-au-Mont]	57dNE3 & 4 Hébuterne	L 20 a, b, 21 a
Orchard Avenue / Boyau du Verger	62cNW1 Maricourt	A 16 b, c, d, 21 b, d, 22 a, 27 b
Orchard Barn	36SW1 Aubers	N 15 a 2.4
Orchard Cemetery	51bNW2 Oppy	B 18 b
Orchard Communication Trench	36SW3 Richebourg	S 3 d, 4 c, 10 a
Orchard Dugout	51bNW2 Oppy	B 11 a 6.7
Orchard Dump	51bNW1 Roclincourt / 2 Oppy	B 4 c, 10 a
Orchard Farm	36aSE1 St Venant	Q 14 d 8.5
Orchard Farm Keep [Orchard Redoubt, Givenchy]	36cNW1 La Bassée	A 15 a
Orchard Farm Trench [Government Farm]	57cSW4 Combles	U 21 b, 22 a, c, d
Orchard Hedge	36NW3 Fleurbaix	G 14 c 8.8
Orchard House	36SW1 Aubers	N 14 b 95.30
Orchard House	51bNW2 Oppy	B 10 a 8.3
Orchard Keep / Redoubt	36SW3 Richebourg	S 10 a, b
Orchard Lane [trench, Government Farm]	57cSW4 Combles	U 22 a, b
Orchard Post	36SW3 Richebourg	S 4 c - 10 d
Orchard Post	51cSE & 51bSW Ficheux	R 27 c
Orchard Post	62cNE2 Epéhy	F 22 c 9.4
Orchard Post	62cNE4 Roisel	L 28 c 9.2
Orchard Redoubt [Orchard Farm Keep]	36cNW1 La Bassée	A 15 a
Orchard Road	36cNW1 La Bassée	A 14 b, 15 a, b
Orchard Street	62dNE2 Méaulte	F 11 d
Orchard Street [1918]	62dSW [2 Villers-Bretonneux]	O 29 a, b
Orchard Street [Sept 1915]	36cNW1 La Bassée	A 14 b
Orchard Terrace	36cNW1 La Bassée	A 14 b, 15 a, b
Orchard Trench	57cSW3 Longueval	S 11 c, d

Name	Map Sheet	Map Reference
Orchard Trench	62cNE4 Roisel	L 28 c, d, 34 a
Orchard Trench	62dNE2 Méaulte	F 4 d, 10 b
Orchard Trench [Monchy-le-Preux]	51bSW2 Vis-en-Artois	O 1 a, b
Orchard Trench North	62dNE2 Méaulte	F 4 d
Orchard Trench South	62dNE2 Méaulte	F 4 d
Orchard, The	36NW4 Bois Grenier	I 15 c
Orchard, The [Hannescamps]	57dNE1 & 2 Fonquevillers	E 16 c 1.8
Orchard, The [north of Rouvroy]	62bSW4 Homblières	T 11 a
Orchard, The [Petawawa Farm]	28SW4 Ploegsteert	T 11 a 3.9
Orchid Avenue	57cNE4 Marcoing / SE2 Gonnelieu	L 33 b, c, d, R 3 a
Orchid Switch	57cSE2 Gonnelieu	R 3 a, c
Orchid Trench	28SW2 Wytschaete	O 28 b
Orchid Trench	36SW2 Radinghem	O 24 d
Ordnance Siding [light rly, Hersin]	36bSE2 Boyeffles	Q 5 c, d
Ore Farm	20SE2 Hooglede	Q 10 b 9.5
Ore Trench	51bNW3 Arras	H 14 b, d
Orford House	27SE2 Berthen	R 25 d 7.0
Org, Boyau	62cSW1 & 2 Belloy	O 2 a, b
Organ Farm	28NE2 Moorslede	F 25 d
Organ Farm	28NW1 Elverdinghe	A 16 c 6.0
Organ Farm	36NW1 Steenwerck	B 2 a 7.1
Organ Trench	51bNW3 Arras	H 13 b
Organise Alley	62cSW2 Barleux	O 2 a, b
Orgy House	36NW1 Steenwerck	A 9 d 8.4
Oriel Trench	28SW2 Wytschaete	O 15 c, d, 21 a
Orient Avenue [1918]	28NE3 Gheluvelt	J 5 d, 6 c, 11 b, 12 a
Orient Lane	51bSW2 Vis-en-Artois / 4 Bullecourt	O 33d, 34 a, b
Origny, Tranchée d' [BFL 3/16]	36cSW1 Lens	M 25 b, d
Orion House	28NW1 Elverdinghe	A 23 a 3.8
Orion Trench	36SW2 Radinghem	O 26 b, c, d, 32 a
Orion Trench	57cSW2 Villers-au-Flos	N 35 a
Orionoco Trench	57dNE1 & 2 Fonquevillers	E 29 a
Orival Wood	57cNE4 Marcoing	L 7 central
Orix Trench	51bSW2 Vis-en-Artois / SE3 Cagnicourt	O 35 a, b, V 1 a
Orkney [light rly, Bully Grenay]	36bSE2 Boyeffles	R 11 d
Orkney Road	36SW3 Richebourg	S 27 c, d
Orkney Support	28SW2 Wytschaete	O 18 d, 24 a, b
Orkney Trench	28SW2 Wytschaete	O 18 d, 24 a, b
Orkney Trench	36SW2 Radinghem	O 20 d, 21 a, c, 26 b
Orkney Trench	57dNE1 & 2 Fonquevillers	E 28 b
Orleans Trench	57dNE1 & 2 Fonquevillers	E 28 b, d
Orlet Road [Mesnil]	57dSE1 & 2 Beaumont	Q 28 d
Orme Street	28SW2 Wytschaete	O 27 d
Orme Trench	28SW2 Wytschaete	O 27 d
Ormes Copse	62bNW4 Ramicourt	I 28 c
Ormes, les [farm]	27SE4 Meteren	X 14 a 3.1
Orne Alley	66cNW4 Berthenicourt	I 19 d
Ornes Alley	62cSW3 Vermandovillers	S 11 a, b, 12 a, b
Orphans Rest [farm]	36NW1 Steenwerck	B 25 c 7.9
Orpheus House	36NW1 Steenwerck	G 5 b 4.3
Orr Avenue	51bNW1 Roclincourt	A 22 a
Orr Crater / Group [of craters]	51bNW1 Roclincourt	A 22 a
Ors [village]	57bSE2 [Bazuel]	R 5
Orsova, Tranchée d'	62cSW1 & 2 Belloy	O 8 d, 14 b

Name	Map Sheet	Map Reference
Orviato [sic, farm] [Orvieto]	27NE2 Proven	F 28 b 1.3
Orville Junction [road jct]	36NW1 Steenwerck	B 27 d 25.80
Orwell Farm	28NW3 Poperinghe	G 19 d 3.8
Osborne Avenue [1918, Hendecourt-lez-Ransart]	51cSE4 Blaireville	X 16 b, 17 a, c
Oscar Trench [1918]	66eNW [4 Morisel]	H 10 b, 11 a
Osier Street	51cSE3 & 4 Ransart	R 33 c
Osier Trench	28SW2 Wytschaete	O 11 c, d
Oskar Farm	28NW2 St Julien	I 5 d 95.95 to I 6 c 00.95
Osprey House	36NW1 Steenwerck	A 15 d 7.8
Ossian Farm	36NW1 Steenwerck	B 13 c 4.9
Ossus [farm]	57bSW3 Honnecourt	S 19 d 1.9
Ossus Wood	57cSE4 Villers-Guislain	X 24 c, 29 b, 30 a
Ossus Wood Road	57cSE4 Villers-Guislain	X 28 d, 29 a, b
Oste Track [1917-18]	20SW4 Bixschoote	N 36 d, O 31 c, T 6 a, b
Oster Graben	57dNE1 & 2 Fonquevillers	E 28 b, d
Ostgraben	57dNE1 & 2 Fonquevillers	F 7 b, d
Ostler Siding [light rly]	36cSW1 Lens	M 11 a, c
Ostrich Avenue	51bSW4 Bullecourt	U 23 b, d, 24 a
Ostrich Avenue	57cSE2 Gonnelieu	R 10 a, b
Ostrich Lane	57cSE2 Gonnelieu	R 9, b, 10 a
Ostrich Support [1918]	51bSW3 / 57cSE4 / 57dNE2	S 25, 26, X 29, 30, F 5, 6
Ostrich Trench	51bSW2 Vis-en-Artois	O 29 d, 30 a
Osvillers Lake	51bSE1 Saudemont / 2 Oisy-le-Verger	Q 20 d, 21 c, 27 a
Otago Avenue	28SW4 Ploegsteert	U 1 c 5.0
Otago Camp	28NW4 Ypres	I 14 d, 15 c
Otago Trench	57cSW3 Longueval	S 4 d, 5 c, 11 a, b
Othello Trench	62cSW4 St. Christ	O 33 d, U 3 b, 4 a, c
Otira Support	28SW2 Wytschaete	O 30 d, 36 a, b
Otira Trench	28SW2 Wytschaete	O 30 c, 36 a
Otley Reserve	51bSW4 Bullecourt	U 27 a, b
Ottawa [light rly locality, 1917-18]	28NW4 Ypres	H 22 d
Ottawa Camp	28NW3 Poperinghe	G 24 c
Ottawa Farm	28NW3 Poperinghe	G 24 c 8.6
Ottawa Trench	36cSW3 Vimy / 4 Rouvroy	T 28 a, c
Otter Copse	62bSW1 Gricourt	M 32 b
Otter Lane	51bSW4 Bullecourt	O 32 c
Otter Lane [trench, 1918]	28NE3 Gheluvelt	J 11 c 8.2
Otterberg Alley	62bSW3 St Quentin	T 7 c, d, 13 b
Otto Farm [& pillboxes]	28NE1 Zonnebeke	D 15 a 1.1
Otto Redoubt [Oct 1915]	36cNW3 Loos	G 11 d
Otto Sap	51bSW2 Vis-en-Artois	O 26 a
Otto Trench	28SW2 Wytschaete	O 15 b, d
Otto Weg	51bNW1 Roclincourt	A 22 b
Oude-Kruiseecke [hamlet & crossroads]	28NE3 Gheluvelt	J 36 a 4.4
Oudenmolen [place name]	28NE4 Dadizeele	L 22 a
Oudenmolen [windmill, at Shilling Farm]	28NE4 Dadizeele	L 22 b 15.70
Ouden-Roudbaart	28NE2 Moorslede	F 17 a, b
Ouderdom [railway sidings]	28NW3 Poperinghe	G 36 a, b
Ouderdom [village]	28NW3 Poperinghe	G 30 c
Ounce Trench	51bSW4 Bullecourt	U 2 c, d, 8 a
Oundle Trench	57dNE1 & 2 Fonquevillers	E 28 d
Ourcq Alley	66cNW4 Berthenicourt	H 35 a, c, d
Ours Alley	62cNW3 Vaux / 4 Péronne	H 9 b, 10 a
Oursins Ferme, les	36NW2 Armentières	C 24 a 35.40

Name	Map Sheet	Map Reference
Ouse Alley	51bNW2 Oppy	B 16, 17, 18, 23, 24
Ouse Alley / Valley Cemetery	51bNW2 Oppy	B 17 c
Ouse Cemetery	51bNW2 Oppy	B 17 c
Ouse Dump [N of Kitchener's Wood]	28NW2 St Julien	C 10 b
Ouse Lane	51bSW4 Bullecourt	U 3 b, c, d
Ouse Siding	51bNW2 Oppy	B 16 c, d
Ouse Trench	28SW2 Wytschaete	O 21 c, d, 27 b
Ouse Trench	51bNW1 Roclincourt	B 15, 16, 19, 20, 21
Ouse Trench	57dNE1 & 2 Fonquevillers	E 29 a
Outer Point	28SW4 Ploegsteert	O 34 c 9.6
Outlook, The [Philosophe]	36cNW3 Loos	G 20 c 8.8
Outpost Buildings	28NW2 St Julien	C 29 d
Outpost Buildings	28SW2 Wytschaete	N 29 d 70.35
Outpost Farm	28NW4 & NE3 Zillebeke	I 17 b 55.85
Outpost Line	51bSW1 Neuville Vitasse	N 8 a
Outre-Tombe, Boyau d' / Tomb Alley	66dNW3 Hattencourt	G 7 c, d
Outskirt Farm	28NW2 St Julien	I 2 b 1.8
Outtersteene [village]	36aNE2 Vieux Berquin	F 8 b, 9 a
Outtersteene Railhead / Refilling Point	36aNE2 Vieux Berquin	F 8 c, d
Ouvrage en Losenge [Neuville St Vaast]	51bNW1 Roclincourt	A 10 b
Ouvrages Blancs [Casino Point - Mine Tr]	62cNW1 Maricourt	A 7 b, 8 a
Oval Wood	62cNW3 Vaux	G 35 a
Oval Work	66cSW4 La Fère	U 26 d
Oval, The	51bSW1 Neuville Vitasse	N 19 b
Overheule [hamlet / place name]	28NE4 Dadizeele	L 17 a, b
Overland Track [Ploegsteert Wood, 1918]	28SW4 Ploegsteert	U 14 d
Oversea Avenue [1918]	28NE3 Gheluvelt	J 4 c, d
Ovillers Alley [1918]	62dSE [4 Harbonnières]	X 6 c, 12 a
Ovillers Huts	57dSE4 Ovillers	X 7 d
Ovillers Post	57dSE4 Ovillers	W 18 b
Ovillers-la-Boisselle [village]	57dSE4 Ovillers	X 8 a, b, c, d
Owen Support	57cNE4 Marcoing	K 10 d, 11 c
Owen Trench	57cNE4 Marcoing	K 10 b, d, 11 c
Owen Way	36cNW3 Loos	G 35 d
Owl Alley	62bSW2 Fonsommes / 4 Homblières	N 35 b, c, d
Owl Barns	28NE2 Moorslede	F 27 c 5.3
Owl Corner [road junction]	20SE2 Hooglede	R 20 c 85.57
Owl Farm	36NW1 Steenwerck	B 21 a 25.10
Owl Support	28SW4 Ploegsteert	O 34 d
Owl Trench	28SW4 Ploegsteert	O 34 c, d
Owl Trench [1918]	57dNE3 & 4 Hébuterne	K 11 d, 12 c
Owl Trench [1918]	66eNW [2 Thennes]	C 3 d, 4 c
Owls Wood	20SW4 Bixschoote	U 5 b, 6 c
Owston Farm	28NE4 Dadizeele	L 8 a 5.8
Ox Alley	57cNE1 Quéant	E 26 b
Ox Trench	51bSW2 Vis-en-Artois	O 22 d, 28 b, 29 a, c
Ox Trench	57cSW3 Longueval	T 9 b
Oxford Alley	57dNE3 & 4 / 57dNE4 & 57cNW3	L 21 a, b, 22 a, b
Oxford Circus	36NW4 Bois Grenier	I 25 d, 26 c
Oxford Circus	57dSE2 Beaumont	R 17 a 0.0
Oxford Circus [Ploegsteert Wood]	28SW4 Ploegsteert	U 20 c 5.4
Oxford Copse	62cNW1 Maricourt	A 15 c
Oxford Crossing [level crossing]	20SE2 Hooglede	R 20 d 8.1
Oxford Fort	28SW4 Ploegsteert	U 19 b

Name	Map Sheet	Map Reference
Oxford Houses	20SE3 Westroosebeke	V 26 b 4.5
Oxford Houses	36aSE1 St Venant	Q 13 d
Oxford Lane	57cSE2 Gonnelieu	Q 6 c, 12 a
Oxford Road [road]	28NW2 St Julien	C 28 b, d, 29 c, I 5 a
Oxford Road [road]	36SW1 Aubers	M 26 a
Oxford Road [trench / breastwork]	28NW2 St Julien	C 28 b, d, 29 c
Oxford Road Corner [Wieltje]	28NW2 St Julien	C 28 b 2.4
Oxford Spur [light rly]	36bNE2 Beuvry	F 19 d, 20 c, 25 b
Oxford Street	28SW2 Wytschaete	O 1 b, 2 a
Oxford Street	36cSW1 Lens	M 14 c, d
Oxford Street	36NW4 Bois Grenier	I 26 c
Oxford Street	36SW3 Richebourg	S 4 b, d, 5 c
Oxford Street	57dNE3 & 4 Hébuterne	K 23 a
Oxford Street	62dNE2 Méaulte	F 11 d
Oxford Street [Cuinchy; Sept 1915]	36cNW1 La Bassée	A 15 d, 21 b
Oxford Street [Givenchy; Sept 1915]	36cNW1 La Bassée	A 9 a, c, d
Oxford Street [Hooge]	28NW4 & NE3 Zillebeke	I 16 a, c, d, 17 c, d
Oxford Street [road; Lovie Chateau]	27NE2 Proven	F 16 a, b, c, 22 a
Oxford Street [road]	57cNE1 Quéant	D 19 b, c, d
Oxford Street, Lower [Zouave Wd, 1915]	28NW4 & NE3 Zillebeke	I 17 d, 18 c
Oxford Terrace	36cNW1 La Bassée	A 9 c, 15 a, b
Oxford Trench	28SW2 Wytschaete	O 28 b, d
Oxford Trench	51bNW4 Fampoux	I 22 b, d, 28 b
Oxford Valley	57cSE1 Bertincourt	Q 2 d, 3 a, c
Oxley Cottage	27SE4 Meteren	W 22 c 85.20
Oxonian Row	28SW4 Ploegsteert	O 33 c
Oxonian Trench	28SW4 Ploegsteert	O 32 d, 33 c
Oxus Cottage	28NW1 Elverdinghe	B 25 d 9.4
Oxus Trench	57dNE1 & 2 Fonquevillers	E 28 d, 29 c, d
Oxus Trench [Landsturm Graben]	57dNE1 & 2 Fonquevillers	E 30 a, b
Oxygen Trench	28SW4 Ploegsteert	O 34 c
Oyster Avenue	28SW4 Ploegsteert	O 32 c, d, U 2 a
Oyster Farm	36aNE4 Merville	K 22 d 3.4
Oyster Farm	36NW4 Bois Grenier	I 32 c 2.4
Oyster Reserve	28SW4 Ploegsteert	O 32 d, U 2 b
Oyster Row	28SW4 Ploegsteert	O 32 c
Oyster Support	28SW4 Ploegsteert	O 32 c
Oyster Trench	28SW4 Ploegsteert	O 31 d, 32 c, U 2 a
Ozone Alley	28SW4 Ploegsteert	O 31 d
Ozone Avenue	57cSW4 Combles	N 34 c, d
Ozone Strongpoint	28SW2 Wytschaete	O 31 d
Ozone Trench	36SW2 Radinghem	O 24 b
Ozone Trench	57cSW3 Longueval	T 3 central
P & O Avenue [1918]	28NE3 Gheluvelt	J 5 c, 11 a, b
P & O Trench	28SW2 Wytschaete	N 6 a, d, O 1 c, d
P [+ number, Ger trs, 8/15, Hooge & N]	28NW4 & NE3 Zillebeke	I 12, 18
P 1 [trench, W of Piccadilly Farm]	28SW2 Wytschaete	O 7 b 6.9
P 10 Avenue	20SW3 Oostvleteren	N 32 d, 33 c
P 2 [trench, NW of Piccadilly Farm]	28SW2 Wytschaete	O 1 d 7.1
P 2a [trench, NW of Piccadilly Farm]	28SW2 Wytschaete	O 2 c 05.30
P 3 [trench, NW of Piccadilly Farm]	28SW2 Wytschaete	O 2 c 05.20
P 4a [trench, SW of St Eloi]	28SW2 Wytschaete	O 2 c 3.5
P 4b [trench, SW of St Eloi]	28SW2 Wytschaete	O 2 c 4.6
P 5 [trench, NW of St Eloi]	28SW2 Wytschaete	O 2 a 4.4

Name	Map Sheet	Map Reference
P 6 [trench, W of St Eloi]	28SW2 Wytschaete	O 1 d 9.9
P Camp	28NW1 Elverdinghe	A 15 d
P Redoubt [Bois Carré]	28SW2 Wytschaete	N 6 d
P Trench [E of St Eloi, Feb 1915]	28SW2 Wytschaete	O 3 b / 4 a
Pa Post [twin of Ma Post]	62cNE4 Roisel	L 36 c 85.60
Pacaut [hamlet]	36aSE2 Lestrem	Q 23 c
Pacaut Lane [road]	36aSE2 Lestrem	Q 23 a, b, c, 24 a
Pacaut Wood / Bois de Pacaut	36aSE1 St Venant / 2 Lestrem	Q 27 d, 28 c, 33 a, b, c, d
Pacaut Wood [Bois de Pacaut]	36aSE1 St Venant / 2 Lestrem / 3 Gonnehem	Q 27 d, 28 c, d, 33 a, b, c, d, 34 a, c
Pacha Support	28SE1 Wervicq	P 8 c
Pacha Trench	28SE1 Wervicq	P 8 c
Pacht Houses [Het Waterpachthof Farm]	28NE2 Moorslede	L 6 a 00.75
Pacific [railway sidings, E of Poperinghe]	28NW3 Poperinghe	G 10 a
Pacific Avenue [1918]	28NE3 Gheluvelt	J 11 b
Pacific Dump	28NW3 Poperinghe	G 10 a
Pacific Farm	28NW3 Poperinghe	G 10 a 7.8
Pacific Siding	28NW3 Poperinghe	G 10 a
Pack Farm	28NE3 Gheluvelt	J 33 a 4.7
Pack Horse Farm	28SW4 Ploegsteert	T 5 a
Pack Horse Farm [March 1915]	28SW4 Ploegsteert	N 34 c 1.7
Pack Horse Shrine	28SW4 Ploegsteert	T 5 a
Pack Trench	57cSE1 Bertincourt	P 15 a, b
Packs Folly [late 1915]	36SW2 Radinghem	O 7 b 4.9
Paddington Junction [railway]	28SW3 Bailleul	S 12 b 6.9
Paddington Street	51bNW3 Arras	G 6 c
Paddy Farm	36NW1 Steenwerck	A 11 c 20.65
Paderborn Trench	66cNW4 Berthenicourt	I 2 c
Padre Farm	27SE4 Meteren	X 29 a 3.3
Pads Post	62cNE4 Roisel	L 30 a 60.75
Pagan Support	28SE1 Wervicq	P 9 c, 15 b, 16 a
Pagan Trench	28SE1 Wervicq	P 9 c, 15 a, b
Page Copse	62cSW3 Vermandovillers	S 9 b
Pages, Tranchée	36cSW1 Lens	M 25 d, 31 b
Paget Street	57dSE4 Ovillers	X 20 c
Pagoda Corner [Potije Chateau]	28NW2 St Julien	C 28 c 96.17
Pagoda Post [Neuve Chapelle]	36SW1 Aubers	M 35 a 65.50
Pagoda Walk [Potije Chateau]	28NW2 St Julien	C 28 d, 29 a
Pah Trench [1918]	57dNE4 [Hébuterne / Achiet]	L 13 b
Paidherse, Tranche	70dSW [2 Coucy-le-Château]	N 30 b
Paint Lodge	28SE1 Wervicq	P 3 c 85.15
Paint Trench	51bNW3 Arras	H 9 c, 15 a
Pair Farm	28NE2 Moorslede	F 3 d 3.1
Paisley Avenue [Thiepval Wood]	57dSE1 & 2 Beaumont	Q 30 d
Palace Farm	28NW2 St Julien	C 4 d 4.4
Palace Row [buildings]	36NW1 Steenwerck	B 1 a 0.7
Palace Siding [light rly, Annequin]	36bNE2 Beuvry	F 29 c
Palace Trench	57cSE1 Bertincourt	P 4 a, b, d
Palais de Justice [Ploegsteert Wood]	28SW4 Ploegsteert	U 20 d 98.70
Palaric Trench	62bSW1 Gricourt	M 9 b, d, 10 c
Palatine Street	57dSE4 Ovillers	X 13 a
Palazzon [formerly Foresters House]	36aNE3 Haverskerque	J 11 c 1.6
Pale Trench	57dSE1 & 2 Beaumont	R 32 c, d
Palestine Avenue	57dNE3 & 4 Hébuterne	K 27 a, b, 28 a, b
Palestine Trench [1918]	28NW4 & NE3 Zillebeke	J 20 d, 21 c

Name	Map Sheet	Map Reference
Paliasse Wood	62bSW2 Fonsommes / 4 Homblières	O 31 b, d, 32 a, c
Palissade Farm	28NW2 St Julien	C 1 d 05.75
Palissandre, Tranchée du	66cNW2 Itancourt	B 24 c, 30 a, b
Palisse Alley	66cNW1 Grugies	B 14 b
Palk Villa [Le Gheer]	28SW4 Ploegsteert	U 21 d 55.60
Pall Mall	28SW2 Wytschaete	N 29 c, d
Pall Mall	36cSW1 Lens	M 2 b, d, 3 a, b, 5 a, b
Pall Mall	36SW3 Richebourg	S 9 d, 15 b
Pall Mall [Sept 1915]	36cNW1 La Bassée	A 15 d
Pall Mall [Sunken Road]	57cSW3 Longueval	S 17 c, d, 23 a, c
Pall Mall Keep	36SW3 Richebourg	S 15 b, 16 a
Pallas Alley	62cNW2 Bouchavesnes	C 10 a
Pallas Support	62cNW2 Bouchavesnes	C 9 d, 10 a, c
Pallas Trench	62cNW2 Bouchavesnes	C 9 d, 10 a, c, 15 b, 16 a
Pallette Cottage	28NE2 Moorslede	F 28 d 8.7
Palliasse Farm	28NE2 Moorslede	F 9 b 8.7
Palliasse Wood	62bSW2 Fonsommes	O 31 b, d, 32 a, c
Palluel [village]	51bSE2 Oisy-le-Verger	Q 5 c, 11 a, b, c, d
Palluel, Marais de [marsh / lake]	51bSE1 Saudemont / 2 Oisy-le-Verger	Q 3, 4, 5, 9, 10, 11
Palm Trench	66cNW2 Itancourt	B 24 d
Palma House	27NE4 Abeele	K 22 b 05.80
Palmer Farm	28NE4 Dadizeele	K 10 c 9.1
Palmier Alley	62cSW2 Barleux	N 34 b
Palmier, Tranchée du	66cNW2 Itancourt	B 24 d, 30 b, C 25 a
Palmy Trench	51bNW3 Arras	H 14 d, 15 c
Palz Trench	57cSW4 Combles	U 8 d, 9 b
Pam Pam Farm	57cSE2 Gonnelieu	R 18 a
Pan Cotts	28SE1 Wervicq	P 2 d 75.30
Pan Lane [trench]	62bNW3 Bellicourt	G 14 a
Pan Post	36NW4 Bois Grenier	I 20 d
Pan Trench [by Pan Cotts]	28SE1 Wervicq	P 2 d, 8 b
Panama Canal	36NW2 Armentières	C 22 d
Panama House	20SW4 Bixschoote	U 5 b 12.10
Panama House Pill Box	20SW4 Bixschoote	U 5 b 1.1
Panda Stone Siding	20SW3 Oostvleteren	T 26 b
Pandora [farm]	36NW1 Steenwerck	B 8 c 5.4
Panemolen [place name]	28NE4 Dadizeele	K 23 c
Panet Dump	36bSE4 Carency	X 11 b 1.4
Panet Road [road]	28NE1 Zonnebeke	D 14 b, c, d,
Pang Trench	51bNW1 Roclincourt	A 30 a
Panic House	27NE2 Proven	E 23 d 50.05
Panmuir Street	57dSE4 Ovillers	X 19 a
Pannell Hall	28SW1 Kemmel	M 18 c 4.8
Pannerie North, la	57bSW3 Honnecourt	S 16 d, 17 c
Pannerie South, la	57bSW3 Honnecourt	S 29 b 0.4
Pansy Trench	51bNW4 Fampoux	H 16 c, 22 a
Pantagruel, Tranchée de	66eNE4 Beaufort	L 17 a, c, 23 a
Panther Alley [1918]	28NE3 Gheluvelt	J 5 d
Panther Lane	51bSW1 Neuville Vitasse	N 21 c, 27 a
Panther Trench	20SW4 Bixschoote	U 16 c, d
Panther Trench	51bSW2 Vis-en-Artois	O 19 a, c
Pantilochi, The	51bNW1 Roclincourt	A 28
Panton Camp	27NE4 Abeele	L 14 a
Pantoufle Trench / Tranchée Pantoufle	62cSW2 Barleux	O 13 c, 19 a

Name	Map Sheet	Map Reference
Panzerturn [Gibraltar, Pozières]	57dSE4 Ovillers	X 4 c 7.4
Paon Trench	20SW3 Oostvleteren	T 8 c, d, 14 b
Papa Farm	20SE3 Westroosebeke	V 21 b 05.30
Papakura Support [1918]	28NE3 Gheluvelt	J 10 c, 15 b, 16 a
Papal Fork [road jct]	36aNE1 Morbecque	J 4 a 4.9
Papal Woods No.1	62cSE4 [Attilly]	W 29 b, d
Papal Woods No.2	62cSE4 [Attilly]	W 30 c
Papal Woods No.3	62cSE4 [Attilly] & 66dNE2 [Roupy]	W 30 c, E 6 a
Papanui Switch [1918]	28NE3 Gheluvelt	J 11 a, b, c
Papegoed Farm	20SW4 Bixschoote	U 3 c 2.9
Papegoed Post [1918]	20SW4 Bixschoote	U 3 c 2.9
Papegoed Wood	20SW4 Bixschoote	U 2 b, d
Papel Farm [nr Papelandbeek]	28NE2 Moorslede	F 14 c 35.50
Papen Trench	62dNE2 Méaulte	F 4 c, 10 a
Papin Trench	57dNE3 & 4 Hébuterne	K 15 d
Papot [farm]	36NW1 Steenwerck	B 3 c 7.3
Papote [farm]	36aNE1 Morbecque	D 16 d 4.2
Paquemont, Tranchée	70dSW [2 Coucy-le-Château]	O 34 b
Paquerettes, Tranchée des	66eNE4 Beaufort	L 16 d, 17 a, c, 22 b
Para Farm	27SE4 Meteren	X 30 a 40.25
Parabola, The	36SW3 Richebourg	S 22 c, 28 a
Paraclet Wood	62dSW [3 Boves]	S 30, T 25
Paraclet, le [hamlet]	62dSW [3 Boves]	T 25 b
Parade Trench	36NW2 Armentières	C 4 c
Parade, The [Sept 1915]	36cNW1 La Bassée	A 21 d
Paradine Copse	62bSW4 Homblières	U 16 b
Paradis / Paradise Trench [1918]	66eNW [2 Thennes]	C 4 c, d
Paradis [farm]	36aSE2 Lestrem	Q 24 a 3.8
Paradis End	36aSE2 Lestrem	Q 24 a 5.0
Paradise Alley	36NW4 Bois Grenier	I 15 b, d
Paradise Alley	57dSE2 Beaumont	R 27 a, c
Paradise Alley [Wieltje, buildings]	28NW2 St Julien	C 28 c
Paradise Copse	28NE2 Moorslede	F 16 a 3.7
Paradise Inn	36aNE2 Vieux Berquin	E 11 a 4.2
Paradise Road [road]	36aSE2 Lestrem	Q 18 a, c, 24 a
Paradise Road [road]	36NW4 Bois Grenier	I 22 d, 28 b, 29 a, c
Paradou Farm	28NW1 Elverdinghe	B 10 c 2.7
Paragon Wood	62bSW4 Homblières	U 11 a
Parallel Houses	28NE2 Moorslede	F 22 d 75.40
Parallel V	51bNW1 Roclincourt	A 8 b
Parallel VI	51bNW1 Roclincourt	A 2 d
Parallel VIII	51bNW1 Roclincourt	A 3 d
Parallele des Cuirassiers	70dSW [2 Coucy-le-Château]	O 20 c
Parallelogram, The [Quadrilateral]	57dNE3 & 4 Hébuterne	K 35 a, c
Parallels, The [Thiepval Wood]	57dSE1 & 2 Beaumont	Q 19 c, 24 c, d, 25 a, R2 d, 3 b, c
Parasite Trench	66cNW2 Itancourt	B 5 d
Parasol Trench	66cNW2 Itancourt	C 28 a
Paratonnere Trench	62dSW [4 Cachy]	T 29 b, d
Paratonnerres Farm	20SW4 Bixschoote	T 28 d 1.8
Parc, le [hamlet]	36aNE3 Haverskerque	J 10 a, b, d
Paree Trench	62cNW1 Maricourt	A 30 b, B 25 a, c
Pargny [village]	66dNW2 Morchain	C 10 b, d
Paricot / Parigot Trench	66cNW1 Grugies	A 11 c, 17 a, b, d, 18 c, 24 a, b
Paris Copse	57bNW1 Cambrai	A 25 b, 26 a

Name	Map Sheet	Map Reference
Paris Crater Group	51bNW1 Roclincourt	A 16 a
Paris Lane	36cSW1 Lens	M 4 b, 5 a
Paris Plage [river bend]	36aNE3 Haverskerque	J 31 b, 32 a
Paris Redoubt	51bNW1 Roclincourt	A 16 a
Paris Trench	51bNW1 Roclincourt	A 15 b, 16 a
Paris, Boyau	62cSW1 Dompierre	M 4 d
Paris, Faubourg de [Cambrai]	57bNW1 Cambrai	A 21 d
Park Alley	36cNW3 Loos	G 4 d
Park Avenue	28SW2 Wytschaete	N 24 a
Park Avenue	36NW2 Armentières	C 10 a
Park Drive Buildings	28NE4 Dadizeele	L 19 d 7.0
Park Lane	28NW4 & NE3 Zillebeke	I 5 d
Park Lane	36SW1 Aubers	N 13 a, c
Park Lane	57dSE1 & 2 Beaumont	Q 16 b
Park Lane	62cNW1 Maricourt	A 23 d
Park Lane	62dNE2 Méaulte	F 15 b
Park Lane [Cuinchy]	36cNW1 La Bassée	A 21 b
Park Lane [Givenchy]	36cNW1 La Bassée	A 9 a
Park Lane [Guillemont]	57cSW3 Longueval	S 24 d, 30 b
Park Lane [road; Lovie Chateau]	27NE2 Proven	F 16 d
Park Lane [road]	36aSE4 Locon	Q 35 c, W 4 b, d, 5 a
Park Lane [road]	57cNE1 Quéant	D 20 a, b, d
Park Lane Redoubt [Cuinchy]	36cNW1 La Bassée	A 21 b
Park Lane, & Avenue	28SW2 Wytschaete	N 24 a
Park Row Avenue	36NW4 Bois Grenier	I 20 a, c, d
Park Row Post	36NW4 Bois Grenier	I 20 d
Park Stellung	51bSW1 Neuville Vitasse	M 10 d
Park Street	28SW2 Wytschaete	N 24 a
Park Street	51cSE3 & 4 Ransart	X 1 a
Park Trench	51bNW1 Roclincourt	A 30 a
Park Trench	66cSW4 La Fère	U 16 a, c
Park Work	51bNW4 Fampoux	I 28 b, d
Parkdrive Buildings [at Kezelberg Windmill]	28NE4 Dadizeele	L 19 d 7.0
Parker Copse	62cSE2 Vermand	R 5 d
Parker Post	62cSE2 Vermand	R 4 d
Parker's Walk	36NW2 Armentières	C 23 a, b
Parma Railhead / Refilling Point	28SW2 Wytschaete	N 12 c
Parma Trench	28SW2 Wytschaete	N 12 c
Paroo Farm	27NE4 Abeele	K 15 d 75.10
Parques Trench	66dNW1 Punchy	B 1 b, d, 2 c, 8 b
Parrain Farm	28SW2 Wytschaete	N 28 b 7.9
Parret Farm	28SW2 Wytschaete	N 17 a 3.4
Parrot Camp [1918]	28SW2 Wytschaete	N 16b / 17 a
Parrot Farm	20SE2 Hooglede	R 20 a 3.6
Parrot Trench	28SW2 Wytschaete	N 17 a
Parrot Trench	51bNW4 Fampoux	H 16 d
Parrot Trench [1918]	66eNW [2 Thennes]	C 13 a, b
Parrot's Beak	51bNW3 Arras	G 18 a
Parrs Trench	57cSE4 Villers-Guislain	X 21 b, d
Parseval / Parsival / Parsifal Alley	36cNW1 La Bassée / 3 Loos	G 5 a, b, d
Parseval St. [Strasse?]	70dNW2 Servais	I 2 b, 3 a
Parsley Farm	20SE2 Hooglede	R 9 c 40.05
Partial Support	28SE1 Wervicq	P 16 a, c, d, 22 b, 23 a
Partial Trench	28SE1 Wervicq	P 15 b, d, 16 c, d

Name	Map Sheet	Map Reference
Partridge Trench	36cSW3 Vimy	M 36 c, S 6 b, T 1 d, 2 c
Partridge Wood	20NE4 Lichtervelde / 20SE2 Hooglede	L 32 d, R 2 b
Partynje Farm	28SW2 Wytschaete	O 24 d 75.30
Parvillers [village]	66eNE4 Beaufort	L 28, 29
Pas de l'Oie, Tranchée du	66dNW2 Morchain	B 22 d, 23 c, d
Pascal Farm	20SW4 Bixschoote	U 12 c 5.2
Pascal Trench	20SW4 Bixschoote	U 11 b, d, 12 c
Pascal Trench [1918]	66eNW [2 Thennes]	B 17 d, 18 a
Passant House	20SW4 Bixschoote	T 24 d 4.6
Passau, Tranchée de	62cSW3 & 4 Marchélepot	T 25 a, c
Passchendaele [village]	28NE1 Zonnebeke	D 6 a, b, c, d, 12 a, b
Passchendaele Alley [1918]	28NE1 Zonnebeke	D 6 a, b, c, d
Passchendaele-Terhand Line [1917-18]	28NE1 Zonnebeke / 3 Gheluvelt / 4 Dadizeele	extensive
Passerelle de Magenta [SW of Thiepval Wd]	57dSE1 & 2 Beaumont	Q 29 8.4
Passerelle Farm	20SW4 Bixschoote	U 21 c 3.9
Passerelle Post	36aSE4 Locon	X 3 d
Passeur Avenue	20SW3 Oostvleteren	T 3 d, 4 c, 9 b
Passmore House	28NE4 Dadizeele	L 3 d 85.55
Pastel Farm	28SW1 Kemmel	M 5 d
Pastern Post	62bNW3 Bellicourt	G 25 d
Pasteur Sap	57dNE3 & 4 Hébuterne	K 15 d
Pasteur Trench	57dNE3 & 4 Hébuterne	K 15 b, 16 c, d, 17 c
Pasture Post	36NW3 Fleurbaix	G 17 c, d
Pasture Siding [light rly]	36bNE4 Noeux-les-Mines	L 3 d
Pat Alley	66dNW1 Punchy	A 15 b
Pat Farm	28SW2 Wytschaete	O 18 b 4.5
Pat Lane [road; Lovie Chateau]	27NE2 Proven	F 16 c
Pat Spur [light rly, Loos]	36cNW3 Loos	G 35 b, d
Pat Trench	36cNW3 Loos	H 19 c, 25 a
Pat Trench	51bNW1 Roclincourt	A 30 a
Pat Trench	51bNW4 Fampoux	H 11 c
Pat Trench	57cSE1 Bertincourt	P 10 c, d
Patates Trench	62cSW3 Vermandovillers	T 8 b, 9 a
Patch Alley	57dSE4 Ovillers	X 27 a, b
Paternoster Row	36NW2 Armentières	C 3 d
Paters Bridge [road across Sperrewevensbeek]	28NW1 Elverdinghe	A 9 a 9.0
Path Post	36SW3 Richebourg	S 14 b 1.3
Pathan Cross Roads	28NE2 Moorslede	K 4 a 5.7
Patoka Trench [1918]	28NE3 Gheluvelt	J 11 c
Patricia Crater	36cSW3 Vimy	S 28 a
Patrick Post	36NW4 Bois Grenier	I 26 a
Patrick Trench	36cSW3 Vimy	N 31 d
Patter Farm	27NE2 Proven	F 26 d 3.0
Patty Copse	62bSW4 Homblières	U 2 d
Patu Support [1918]	28NE3 Gheluvelt	J 10 d, 11 a, c
Patu Switch [1918]	28NE3 Gheluvelt	J 5 c, 11 a
Pau Farm	20NW4 Dixmude	I 33 a 1.3
Pau, Boyau	36cSW1 Lens	M 20 c
Paul Burgrave House [1918]	28SW1 Kemmel	N 19 c 05.45
Paul Farm	28NE2 Moorslede	F 19 d 5.5
Paul Farm	28NE3 Gheluvelt	J 34 c 50.85
Paul Graben	51bNW3 Arras	G 12 c, d
Paul Post	36NW4 Bois Grenier	I 31 b
Paul Trench	62bNW1 Gouy	A 20 c

Name	Map Sheet	Map Reference
Paul Wood	66eNW [4 Morisel]	H 16 d
Paul-Jacques Farm	28SW1 Kemmel	M 5 d 2.2
Pauper Support	28SE1 Wervicq	P 9 a, b
Pauper Trench	28SE1 Wervicq	P 2 d, 8 b, 9 a
Pauper Trench	57cSE1 Bertincourt	P 4 d, 10 b, d
Paupers Alley	66cSW2 Vendeuil	O 3 b, 4 a
Pauvre, Ferme du	20SW4 Bixschoote	N 34 d 4.5
Pauvres Mill [Mont des Cats]	27SE2 Berthen	R 19 b 05.90
Pave Trench	51bNW1 Roclincourt	A 30 a
Paviland Wood	51bSE3 Cagnicourt	W 25 d, 26 c
Pavillion Siding [light rly, Annequin]	36bNE2 Beuvry	F 30 c
Pawn Copse	62cSE1 Bouvincourt	Q 14 d, 20 b
Paynesley Trench	51bNW1 Roclincourt	A 4 c
Paytis Farm	28NE3 Gheluvelt	J 20 d 8.5
Paytis Suport [1918]	28NE3 Gheluvelt	J 20 b, d
Paytis Trench [1918]	28NE3 Gheluvelt	J 20 d
Pea Trench	57cSW3 Longueval	S 11 a, b
Peach / Peachy Trench	57cSW3 Longueval	S 11 b
Peach Farm	20SE3 Westroosebeke	W 26 b 1.8
Peach Street	36SW3 Richebourg	S 10 a, b
Peach Street [1918]	62dSW [2 Villers-Bretonneux]	O 28 b
Peach Trench	51bSE1 Saudemont	P 25 a, c, d, 31 b, d
Peacock Close Street	57dSE4 Ovillers	X 20 c
Peacock Farm	36aSE3 Gonnehem	Q 32 c 3.0
Peak, The [farm]	36SW1 Aubers	M 22 b
Peake Street	57dSE1 & 2 Beaumont	Q 17 d, 23 b
Peake Wood British Cemetery	57dSE4 Ovillers	X 22 a
Peake Woods	57dSE4 Ovillers	X 22 a
Pear Lane	51bSW4 Bullecourt	U 7 d
Pear Lane [trench]	51bSE1 Saudemont	P 19 c, d, 20 a, c, 25 a
Pear Street	36SW3 Richebourg	S 10 a, b
Pear Street	57cSW3 Longueval	S 11 c
Pear Tree [trig point]	62dNE [4 Bray-sur-Somme]	F 19 c 65.70
Pear Tree Avenue	28NW4 & 28NE3 Zillebeke	I 33 d, 34 c
Pear Tree Farm	36NW4 Bois Grenier	I 16 b 2.7
Pear Tree Walk	28NW4 & NE3 Zillebeke	I 33 d, 34 c
Pear Trench	51bNW4 Fampoux	I 33 c
Pear Trench	57dSE4 Ovillers	R 32 c
Pear Trench	62dNE2 Méaulte	F 10 a
Pear Trench [1918]	62dSE [1 Hamel]	P 8 d
Pearl Alley	57dSE4 Ovillers	X 11 d, 12 c, 17 a, b, c
Pearl Trench	51bNW4 Fampoux	I 26 b
Pearl Trench	62bNW3 Bellicourt	G 20 a, b
Pearl Wood	57dSE4 Ovillers	X 17 b
Pearl Wood	62bNW3 Bellicourt	G 14 d
Pearson Cross Roads	28NE4 Dadizeele	K 22 c 9.6
Pease Corner [road jct]	28NE4 Dadizeele	K 17 b 65.85
Peasmarsh Houses	20SE2 Hooglede	Q 4 b 6.6
Peat Copse	62bSW2 Fonsommes	N 11 d
Peat Trench	51bNW1 Roclincourt	A 30 a
Pebble Trench	51bNW4 Fampoux	H 16 d
Pêche Street	57dSE1 & 2 Beaumont	Q 23 b
Peche Trench	20SW3 Oostvleteren	T 9 c, 15 b
Pêcher Alley	62cSW3 Vermandovillers	S 11 d, 17 b, 18 a

Name	Map Sheet	Map Reference
Pechine Trench	66cNW2 Itancourt	B 29 c
Peckham Craters [Peckham Farm]	28SW2 Wytschaete	N 30 a
Peckham Farm	28SW2 Wytschaete	N 30 a
Pedigree Villa	28NW1 Elverdinghe	A 29 c 65.55
Peek Buildings	28NE4 Dadizeele	K 16 a 2.8
Peel Trench	51bNW1 Roclincourt	A 30 a
Peel Trench	57dSE2 Beaumont	R 20 a, c
Peel Trench [1918]	57dNE1 & 2 Fonquevillers	E 29 d, K 5 b, 6 a
Peer Trench	51bNW4 Fampoux	H 22 b, 23 a
Peerless Camp	28NW3 Poperinghe	G 8 a, b, d
Peg Copse	62bNW3 Bellicourt	G 21 b
Peg Cottage	28NE2 Moorslede	F 26 b 8.2
Peg Lane [trench]	62bNW3 Bellicourt	G 14 a, c
Peg Trench	51bNW1 Roclincourt	A 30 a
Peg Trench	57dSE4 Ovillers	X 5 b
Pegasus Farm	28SW3 Bailleul	S 29 d
Peggie Trench [1918]	36cSW3 Vimy	S 24 b, T 14 d, 15 a, 19 a, b, 20 a
Peggy Dump	36cSW3 Vimy	T 19 b 3.9
Peggy Junction [light rly, Vimy]	36cSW3 Vimy	T 19 a 1.8
Peggy Trench	36cSW3 Vimy	T 9 d, 10 c, 15 b
Pein, Tranchée	36cSW3 Vimy	S 8 d
Peiriole Alley	66cNW1 Grugies	B 8 c, 14 a
Pekin / Peking Support	36cNW1 La Bassée / 3 Loos	A 30 b, G 6 b, H 1 a
Pekin / Peking Trench	36cNW1 La Bassée / 3 Loos	A 30 b, d, G 6 b, d
Pekin Alley	36cNW1 La Bassée	A 29 d, 30 c
Pekin Trench	28SW2 Wytschaete	N 17 d, 23 b
Pekin, Corons de [miners' cottages]	36cNW1 La Bassée	A 29 c
Pekly Bulge	62cNW4 Péronne	I 7 b, d, 8 a [part of]
Pekly Trench	62cNW4 Péronne	I 7 b, d, 8 a
Pelew Junction [light rly]	28NW4 Ypres	H 30 area
Pelf Farm	28NW3 Poperinghe	G 12 c 9.3
Pelican Alley / Boyau de Pélican	66dNW3 Hattencourt / 66eNE4 Beaufort	G 13 b, 14 a, b, L 18 a
Pelican Avenue	51bSW2 Vis-en-Artois	N 36 b 8.0
Pelican Avenue / Lane	51bSW4 Bullecourt	U 21 c, 26 b, c, 27 a
Pelican Avenue / Trench	57cSE2 Gonnelieu	R 23 d, 24 a
Pelican Lane / Pelican Trench	51bSW2 Vis-en-Artois / 4 Bullecourt	N 36 b, O 31 c
Pelissier Farm	28NW1 Elverdinghe	B 21 a 15.05
Pelissier Trench	57dNE3 & 4 Hébuterne	K 16 a, b
Pelletier Alley	36cSW3 Vimy	S 8 b
Pelletier, Tranchée [Allied front line 2/16]	36cSW3 Vimy	S 2 d
Pelman House	27SE4 Meteren	X 5 c 2.7
Peloponese Alley	66dNW3 Hattencourt	G 13 d, 14 c
Pelt Farm	20SE2 Hooglede	Q 12 a 5.7
Pelt Trench	51bNW1 Roclincourt	A 30 a
Pelu Wood	57bSW1 Bantouzelle	N 2 c, d, 8 a, b
Pelves Alley	51bNW3 Arras	H 31 b, 32 a
Pelves Lane [road]	51bNW4 Fampoux	H 29 c, d, 30 c, d, I 25 b, c, d, 26 a, b
Pemmican Farm	28NW3 Poperinghe	H 7 c 2.6
Pen Cottage	28NE2 Moorslede	F 29 a 05.93
Pen Farm	28SE1 Wervicq	P 4 d 65.20
Pen Lane	57cSW3 Longueval	T 8 b
Pen Trench	57cSW3 Longueval	N 32 c, d, T 2 b
Pen Trench	62bNW3 Bellicourt / SW1 Gricourt	G 33 d, M 3 b

Name	Map Sheet	Map Reference
Pencil Houses	28NE2 Moorslede	F 23 c 35.80
Pendant Alley East	57dNE3 & 4 Hébuterne	L 25 c, d, 26 c
Pendant Alley West	57dNE3 & 4 Hébuterne	K 30 d, 36 a, b, L 25 c
Pendant Copse	57dNE3 & 4 Hébuterne	L 31 a
Pendant Trench, North	57dNE3 & 4 Hébuterne	L 25 a, c
Pendlehill Street	57dSE4 Ovillers	X 7 a, b, c
Pendu House	66dNW3 Hattencourt	G 10 a, c
Pendulum Alley	66cNW2 Itancourt	C 25 c
Penelope Alley	66dNW1 Punchy	B 19 a, c, d, 25 b, 26 a, c, d
Pengan [Boyau, SE of Bécourt Château, 1915]	57dSE4 Ovillers	X 26 c
Penge Villa	36NW1 Steenwerck	B 26 a 8.6
Penguin Camp	28SW3 Bailleul	S 29 b
Penguin Farm	28SW3 Bailleul	S 29 a 7.1
Penin Mariage Post	36aSE4 Locon	R 36 c
Penin Mariage Switch [1918]	36aSE4 Locon / 36SW3 Richebourg	R 36 c, X 5, 6, 11, 17, S 31 d
Penley Farm	20SE2 Hooglede	Q 29 c 8.8
Penny Corner [road jct]	28NE4 Dadizeele	L 16 d 60.65
Pensam Post	36NW4 Bois Grenier	I 32 a
Pension Farm	20SE2 Hooglede	Q 30 d 4.0
Pent House	36aNE2 Vieux Berquin	F 23 b 85.00
Pentagon Redoubt [N of Dump, Oct '15]	36cNW1 La Bassée	A 29 c 5.3
Pentagon, The [Redoubt, N of Dump, Oct '15]	36cNW1 La Bassée	A 29 c 5.3
Pentre Trench	57cSE2 Gonnelieu	R 8 c, d, 14 b
Penury Farm	27SE2 Berthen	R 7 d 5.1
Penzance [light rly locality, 1917-18]	28NW4 Ypres	I 31 c
Penzance [railway locality, 1917]	28SW1 Kemmel	N 19 a
Penzance Lines [huts]	28SW3 Bailleul	T 20 b, d
Pep Trench	36cNW3 Loos	G 29 d
Pepinière Alley	62cNW1 Maricourt	B 26 d, H 2 b, 3 a
Pepinière, Boyau de la	62cSW1 Dompierre	M 4 b
Pepper Trench	51bNW4 Fampoux	H 16 d, 22 a
Pepperbox / Pepperack, The [1918]	51bSW3 Boisleux	S 30 b
Péra Trench / Tranchée de Péra	62cSW1 & 2 Belloy	N 12 b, c, d
Perch North Post	57cNE3 Hermies	J 6 c
Perch South Post	57cNE3 Hermies	J 6 c
Perch Support / The Perch	57cSE4 Villers-Guislain	X 29 d
Perche Trench	66cSW2 Vendeuil	O 26 c, 32 a
Percy Post	36NW4 Bois Grenier	I 26 c
Perdrix Cabaret, Les [Mont Rouge]	28SW1 Kemmel	M 22 a 75.53
Père Ubu, Tranchée du	66dNW3 Hattencourt / SW1 Roye	G 35 d, 36 a, c, M 1 a
Peregrine Farm [near Pickle House]	28SE1 Wervicq	P 14 c 50.95
Perey Street, & North & South	57dNE3 & 4 Hébuterne	K 29 c
Peril Avenue [1918]	28NE3 Gheluvelt	J 20 b, d, 21 c
Periscope [trench]	66cNW2 Itancourt	B 30 b
Periscope House [pill box, Pilckem]	28NW2 St Julien	C 2 d 10.95
Perjury Farm	28NE2 Moorslede	F 17 d 75.95
Perkins Farm	20SE3 Westroosebeke	V 4 c 7.4
Péronne [town]	62cNW4 Péronne	I 27 b, c, d, 28 a
Péronne Avenue	62dNE2 Méaulte	F 17 c, d
Péronne Chateau	62cNW4 Péronne	I 27 a
Péronne Road	62cNW1 Maricourt	A 21 b, 22 a
Péronne Road North Ave / B'au Nord de Péronne	62cNW1 Maricourt	A 22 b, 23 a
Péronne Road South Ave / Boyau Sud de Péronne	62cNW1 Maricourt	A 22 b, 23 a
Péronne Trench	62bSW1 Gricourt	M 28 d, 34 b, 35 a

Name	Map Sheet	Map Reference
Péronne Trench	62cSW3 Vermandovillers	N 33 d, T 2 d, 3 a, b, c
Perrée Alley	66cNW1 Grugies	B 7 a, c
Perret Alley	62bSW1 Gricourt	M 23 c
Perrier Avenue	36cSW3 Vimy	S 21 a, c
Perrin Farm	28NW1 Elverdinghe	B 3 c 2.6
Perron Camp	27NE4 Abeele	L 13 b
Perry Street	57dNE3 & 4 Hébuterne	K 29 c
Persée Trench	62cNE3 Buire	J 7 d, 8 a, b, c
Pershing Trench [1918]	57cNW1 Gomiecourt	A 13 b, d, 14 c
Persia House	36NW1 Steenwerck	B 9 d 6.2
Pert House	36NW1 Steenwerck	A 9 b 5.8
Pertain [village]	66dNW1 Punchy / 2 Morchain	B 10 a, b, c, d
Perth Avenue	57dSE4 Ovillers	W 24 b, c, d, X 19 a
Perth Avenue (Duckboard) [1917-18]	28NE3 Gheluvelt	J 19 a, b, 20 a, b
Perth Avenue [1918]	28NE3 Gheluvelt	J 20 b, 21 a
Perth Road [military road]	28NW1 Elverdinghe / 2 St Julien	B26b, 27a,b, 28a,b, 29a,b, 30a,b, C25a
Perth Trench	36aSE4 Locon	W 18 c, 24 a, b
Peru Crater [Hollandscheshuur Farm]	28SW2 Wytschaete	N 18 b 2.8
Peru Trench	28SW2 Wytschaete	N 18 b
Peru Trench	51bNW4 Fampoux	H 16 d, 22 b
Pervenches House	20SW4 Bixschoote	T 18 b 5.2
Pescade, Petite [trench]	66cNW2 Itancourt	B 24 d, 30 b
Peselhoek [hamlet]	28NW1 Elverdinghe	A 20 c, d, 26 a, b
Peselhoek [railway sidings & huts]	28NW1 Elverdinghe	A 21 a
Peselhoek Depot Railhead / Refilling Point	28NW1 Elverdinghe	A 20 b, d, 21 a, c
Peselhoek Farm	28NW1 Elverdinghe	A 22 a 3.4
Pest Trench	51bNW1 Roclincourt	A 30 a
Pest Trench	62cNW4 Péronne	H 36 d, I 31 c
Pestle Alley	57cSE1 Bertincourt	P 24 d, Q 19 c
Pestle Avenue	57cSE1 Bertincourt	P 23 b, 24 a, c
Pestle Farm	27SE2 Berthen	Q 5 a 7.8
Pestle Trench	57cSE1 Bertincourt	P 24 b, c, d, 30 a, c
Pétain Farm	20SW3 Oostvleteren	T 9 c 3.6
Petard Farm	27NE2 Proven	F 8 a 2.8
Petawawa Farm	28SW4 Ploegsteert	T 11 a 3.9
Peter Farm	28NE3 Gheluvelt	J 34 b 3.4
Peter Graben	51bNW3 Arras	G 12 c, 18 a
Peter Pan [farm & pillbox]	28NE1 Zonnebeke	D 4 c 3.2
Peter Post	36NW4 Bois Grenier	I 31 b
Peter Street	28NW4 Ypres	I 24 d
Peter Street	62dNE2 Méaulte	F 11 d
Peter Trench	62bNW1 Gouy	A 26 b
Peterhead [sap]	57dSE1 & 2 Beaumont	Q 24 c
Petersbank Copse	20SE2 Hooglede	R 19 c 5.8
Peterson House	28NE4 Dadizeele	L 25 d 05.15
Petillon	36SW1 Aubers	N 2 d
Petit Bois	28SW2 Wytschaete	N 24 a, b
Petit Bois	36cSW3 Vimy	S 8 b
Petit Bois [trenches]	62cSW1 Dompierre	M 3 d
Petit Bois Bridge [over Meteren Becque]	36aNE4 Merville	L 17 d 4.8
Petit Bois Craters	28SW2 Wytschaete	N 24 a 9.7 & 9.9
Petit Bois Trench	36bSE4 & 36cSW3 Givenchy	S 8 b
Petit Bois, Boyau du	62cSW1 Dompierre	M 3 d

Name	Map Sheet	Map Reference
Petit Brocourt	62bSW3 St Quentin	T 3 b, 4 a
Petit Chateau [Houtkerque]	27NE1 Herzeele	E 19 c 3.9
Petit Haie Farm	28SW4 Ploegsteert	U 23 c 9.8
Petit Miraumont [village]	57dSE2 & 57cSW1 Le Sars	R 5 a, c
Petit Mortier, le [hamlet]	36NW1 Steenwerck	G 4 a, b
Petit Moulin [east strongpoint; Wigan]	36NW1 Steenwerck	H 3 b 5.6
Petit Moulin [farm & place name]	36NW1 Steenwerck	H 3 a 3.5
Petit Moulin [north strongpoint]	36NW1 Steenwerck	B 27 c 9.1
Petit Moulin [west strongpoint; Liverpool]	36NW1 Steenwerck	H 3 a 4.5
Petit Moulin Keep	51cSE & 51bSW Ficheux	R 22 d
Petit Sains	36bSE2 Boyeffles	R 2 b 5.8
Petit Saut Ravine [Villers-Guislain]	57cSE4 Villers-Guislain	X 3 d, 4 c, 9 b
Petit Sec Bois [village]	36aNE1 Morbecque	E 9 c
Petit Toreken Farm	28SW2 Wytschaete	O 20 d
Petit Vanuxeem [farm]	36NW1 Steenwerck	A 29 c 45.20
Petit Verger Farm	57bSW4 Serain	T 22 d
Petit Villers [Aubencheul-aux-Bois]	57bSW3 Honnecourt	T 13 a
Petit Vimy Junction [light rly]	36cSW3 Vimy	T 25 c 1.2
Petit, Tranchée	70dSW [4 Vauxaillon]	U 28 d
Petite Ceinture, Boyau	62cSW1 Dompierre	M 4 a
Petite Douve Farm, La	28SW4 Ploegsteert	U 8 a 9.5
Petite Farm	20SW4 Bixschoote	T 5 c 2.7
Petite Folie Farm	57bSW4 Serain	U 19 c 1.3
Petite Marquette [farm]	36aNE1 Morbecque	E 19 d 00.85
Petite Munque Farm, La	28SW4 Ploegsteert	T 23 d 8.8
Petit-Pont [farm]	28SW4 Ploegsteert	T 22 b 2.1
Petra Trench	66cNW1 Grugies	A 12 a, c
Pétri, Boyau	62cNW1 Maricourt	A 23 c
Petrograd Trench	36NW2 Armentières	C 28 b, 29 a
Petrol Lane	57dSE2 & 57cSW1 Le Sars	N 20 d
Petticoat Lane [Ravine Wood]	28NW4 & NE3 Zillebeke	I 34 b
Petticoat Lane [Sept 1915]	36cNW1 La Bassée	A 15 d
Petticoat Trench	66cSW2 Vendeuil	O 9 c, 15 a, c
Petworth Camp [Proven]	27NE2 Proven	unlocated
Peultevin [place name]	28NE4 Dadizeele	K 22 b, d
Peuplières Farm	20SW4 Bixschoote	U 25 a
Peupliers Trench [Poplar Copse]	62cSW3 Vermandovillers	T 1 d, 2 c
Peupliers, Bois des [Poplars Wood]	62cSW3 & 4 Marchélepot	T 1 d
Peupliers, Gallerie	62cSW1 Becquincourt / Dompierre	M 4 d
Peupliers, Saillant de	62cSW1 Becquincourt / Dompierre	M 4 d
Peuter Farm	28SW3 Bailleul	S 23 d 5.6
Pewter Farm	20SE2 Hooglede	Q 6 a 4.6
Phalempin Trench	66dNW1 Punchy	B 7 a, b, 8 a, b, 9 a
Pharm Street	36NW4 Bois Grenier	I 31 b, 32 a
Pheasant Dump	28SW2 Wytschaete	O 9 b
Pheasant Farm	20SW4 Bixschoote	U 30 b 1.7
Pheasant Post	57dNE3 & 4 Hébuterne	K 29 c
Pheasant Trench	20SW4 Bixschoote	U 30 a, b, d
Pheasant Trench [1918]	62dSW [4 Cachy]	U 28 b, d
Pheasant Wood	28SW2 Wytschaete	O 9 b
Phelan Trench	36cSW3 Vimy	A 10 b
Philemon, Tranchée de [husband of Baucis]	62cSW3 & 4 Marchélepot	T 23 c, d, 28 b
Phillip Group [Craters]	51bNW1 Roclincourt	A 10 b
Philosophe [village]	36bNE4 Noeux-les-Mines / 36cNW3 Loos	L 18 c, G 13 d

Name	Map Sheet	Map Reference
Philosophe Keep	36cNW3 Loos	G 20 c, d
Philosophe Triangle [light rly, Vermelles]	36cNW3 Loos	G 13 d
Philosopher's House / Maison du Philosophe	62cSW3 & 4 Marchélepot	T 15 b 95.15
Phil's Farm	28NE2 Moorslede	L 1 b 35.85
Phincboom	27SE4 Meteren	X 8 b 4.1
Phincboom [farm]	27SE4 Meteren	X 8 c 9.9
Phincboom Trench	27SE4 Meteren	X 7 d, 8 b, c, d, 9 a, c, d,13 b
Phipps Post [1918]	57dNE2 & 57cNW1 Courcelles	F 17 a 9.4
Phoques, Tranchée des	62cSW1 & 2 Belloy	N 23 a, c
Physic Trench	51bNW4 Fampoux	H 16 d, 22 a, b
Piano House	36SW3 Richebourg	S 24 c 35.00
Pic Alley	66cNW1 Grugies	B 9 d, 15 b
Picantin [hamlet]	36SW1 Aubers	N 7 b, d
Picantin Avenue	36SW1 Aubers	N 7 d, 8 c
Picantin Post	36SW1 Aubers	M 6 d, N 1 c
Picardy Alley	66cNW4 Berthenicourt	H 6 c
Piccadilly	36cNW3 Loos / SW1 Lens	G 34, 35, 36, M 3, 4
Piccadilly	36SW1 Aubers	N 1 c, 7 b
Piccadilly	57dSE1 & 2 Beaumont	Q 16 b
Piccadilly	62dNE2 Méaulte	F 12 c
Piccadily [CT]	28SW2 Wytschaete	N 29 c, d, 35 a
Piccadilly [Givenchy]	36cNW1 La Bassée	A 9 a, c, d
Piccadilly [Longueval, road & trench]	57cSW3 Longueval	S 17 b
Piccadilly [road]	57cNE1 Quéant	D 29 a, b, c
Piccadilly [SE of Potijze]	28NW4 & NE3 Zillebeke	I 4 c, d, 5 c, d
Piccadilly Bridge [1917-18]	20SW4 Bixschoote	U 28 c 8.8
Piccadilly Circus	36SW3 Richebourg	S 27 b
Piccadilly Circus	57cSW1 Gueudecourt	M 20 a 9.9
Piccadilly Circus	57dSE2 & 57cSW1 Le Sars	R 28 c, d, 34 b
Piccadilly Circus [Ploegsteert Wood 1914-15]	28SW4 Ploegsteert	U 20 d 87.63
Piccadilly Circus [Ploegsteert Wood]	28SW4 Ploegsteert	U 21 c 10.65
Piccadilly Circus [road jct, Langemarck]	20SW4 Bixschoote	U 28 b 85.65
Piccadilly Farm [St Eloi]	28SW2 Wytschaete	O 8 a 3.7
Piccadilly Post	36cSW1 Lens	M 3 b, 4 a
Piccadilly Trench	51bNW4 Fampoux	I 22 b, 23 a, c, 29 a, c
Piccadilly, & Piccadilly Circus	36NW4 Bois Grenier	I 25 d, 26 c
Piccolo Farm	28NE4 Dadizeele	L 21 c 25.15
Pick Avenue	51bSW2 Vis-en-Artois	N 12 b, O 7 a, b, c, 8 a, b
Pick Axe Road [Tranchée Dicharry; BFL 3/16]	36cSW1 Lens	M 20 c, d
Pick House	28SW2 Wytschaete	O 26 a 4.5
Pick Lane	36cSW1 Lens	M 14 b, d
Pick Trench	51bNW1 Roclincourt	A 30 a
Pick Trench	51bSW2 Vis-en-Artois	O 7 b, 8 a
Pick Wood	28SW2 Wytschaete	O 25 c
Pickaxe Corner	36cSW1 Lens	M 20 b
Pickelhaube House	28NW2 St Julien	C 23 c 5.6
Pickelhaube Keep	28NW2 St Julien	C 22 d, 23 c
Pickering [light rly siding]	28NW2 St Julien	I 2 a, b
Picket House [Le Gheer]	28SW4 Ploegsteert	U 22 c 13.22
Pickle House [near Peregrine Farm]	28SE1 Wervicq	P 14 c 3.6
Pickwick Avenue	57dSW [3 Talmas]	S 21 d, 22 c, 28 a
Pickwick House	28NE2 Moorslede	L 3 a 25.53
Picton Avenue [1918]	28NE3 Gheluvelt	J 11 c
Pictou Trench	36cSW3 Vimy	T 7 b

Name	Map Sheet	Map Reference
Picturedrome	57dSE1 & 2 Beaumont	Q 24 a
Pie Alley	66cNW4 Berthenicourt	H 24 a
Pie Farm	28SE1 Wervicq	P 2 c
Pie Trench	28SE1 Wervicq	P 2 c, d
Pie Trench	51bNW1 Roclincourt	A 30 a
Piebald Farm	28NE2 Moorslede	E 29 a 75.00
Pielbrouck [hamlet]	27SE2 Berthen	R 27 a 4.8
Pienne [farm]	57bSW3 Honnecourt	S 23 a
Pierre Mill (in ruins) [Villers Outreaux]	57bSW3 Honnecourt	T 8 d 65.45
Pierre Mill [windmill]	57bSW2 Clary	O 10 a 95.55
Pierregot [village]	57dSW [3 Talmas]	T 25
Pierremande [trench to east of]	70dNW [3 Sinceny]	G 28 b, d, 29 a, c
Pierrot Alley	62cSW1 Dompierre / 3 Vermandovillers	M 25-9, 33-5, S 5, 6, 12
Pierson's Post	57dSE4 Ovillers	X 12 c
Pietre Mill, le [Moulin du Pietre]	36SW1 Aubers	N 25 c
Piètre, le [hamlet / locality]	36SW1 Aubers	N 20 b, d
Pieumel Post	62cNE4 Roisel	L 28 d 2.8
Pieumel Trench	62cNE4 Roisel	L 28 d
Pieumel Wood	62cNE4 Roisel	L 28 a, b, c, d
Pig and Whistle [Langemarck]	20SW4 Bixschoote	U 28 b
Pig Avenue	57cNE3 Hermies / 4 Marcoing	K 3 d
Pig Trench	57dNE3 & 4 Hébuterne	K 17 d, 23 b
Pigeon Lane	57dNE4 & 57cNW3 Achiet	L 34 a, b
Pigeon Quarry	57cSE4 Villers-Guislain	X 17 c
Pigeon Ravine	57cSE4 Villers-Guislain	X 21 b, c, d, 22 c
Pigeon Trench	57cSE4 Villers-Guislain	X 17 a, c, d
Pigeon Trench [German]	57dNE1 & 2 Fonquevillers	E 30 a
Pigeon Wood	57dNE1 & 2 Fonquevillers	E 23 d, 29 b, 30 a
Pigeon Wood Trench [German]	57dNE1 & 2 Fonquevillers	E 30 a
Pigeonhouse, The [building]	20SW4 Bixschoote	T 17 d 6.3
Pigment Farm	28NW3 Poperinghe	H 13 d 05.50
Pigsty Farm [1918]	28SW1 Kemmel	M 13 d 6.6
Pike and Eel, The [HQ, Canal Bank]	28NW2 St Julien / 4 Ypres	I 2 c
Pike Copse [Pike Wood]	62bNW3 Bellicourt	G 22 c, 28 a
Pike Farm [moated]	20SE2 Hooglede	R 11 b 6.3
Pike House	28SW2 Wytschaete	O 30 a 45.05
Pike Post	57cNE3 Hermies	J 6 c 75.75
Pike Support	57cNE3 Hermies	K 7 a
Pike Trench	51bNW4 Fampoux	H 16 d, 22 b
Pike Trench [1918]	57dNE3 & 4 Hébuterne	K 5 c, d, 11 a
Pike Wood	62bNW3 Bellicourt	G 22 c, 28 a
Pilcher Farm	36NW1 Steenwerck	A 24 a 6.4
Pilckem Mill	28NW2 St Julien	C 2 c
Piley's Copse	20SE2 Hooglede	R 1 a 90.85
Pilgrim's Progress	36cNW3 Loos	G 12 c
Pilgrim's Rest	51bSE4 Marquion	X 25 b
Pilgrims Way [Sunken Road]	57cSW1 Gueudecourt / 2 Villers-au-Flos	N 26 c, 31 b, 32 a
Pilk Street	57dSE1 & 2 Beaumont	Q 10 a
Pill Farm	28SW2 Wytschaete	O 24 a 45.25
Pill Sap	57cSE1 Bertincourt	P 11 a
Pill Trench	57dNE1 & 2 Fonquevillers	E 26 a, b
Pill Work	51bNW1 Roclincourt	A 3 d
Pillage Alley	62bSW4 Homblières	T 28 b, c, d, 29 a
Pillage Alley	66cNW1 Grugies	B 3 d, 4 a, c, 9 b

Name	Map Sheet	Map Reference
Pillbox [light rly loop]	28NE1 Zonnebeke	D 20 b 5.5
Pillbox Junction [light rly]	28NE1 Zonnebeke	D 20 b 7.5
Pillegrems Farm	28SW2 Wytschaete	O 24 c 95.25
Pilsen Lane [road]	57cSW3 Longueval	S 18 b, T 13 a
Pilsen Place	57cSW3 Longueval	S 18 b, T 13 a
Piltdown Copse	51bSE4 Marquion	W 18 a
Pimp Trench	57cSE1 Bertincourt	P 15 d
Pimpernel [light rly locality, 1917-18]	28SW2 Wytschaete	O 7 a
Pimple Alley	12SW1 Nieuport	M 9 c
Pimple Alley	57cSW1 Gueudecourt	M 17 c, 22 b
Pimple Alley	57dSE2 & 57cSW1 Le Sars	M 16 d
Pimple Hill [The Pimple]	36cSW3 Vimy	S 9 a, b
Pimple Post	62cNE2 Epéhy	F 28 c, d
Pimple, The	57dSE2 & 57cSW1 Le Sars	M 16 d
Pimple, The [Givenchy-en-Gohelle]	36cSW3 Vimy	S 9 a, b
Pin Copse	62bNW3 Bellicourt	G 16 c
Pin House	28SE1 Wervicq	P 1 c 6.2
Pin Lane	62bNW3 Bellicourt	G 1 d
Pinch Cut	28NW4 & NE3 Zillebeke	I 24 d
Pinchier Graben	57dNE3 & 4 Hébuterne	K 11 b, d, 12 a
Pinder Copse	51bSE2 Oisy-le-Verger	Q 28 b
Pine Avenue	28SW4 Ploegsteert	U 4 a, b, 5 a
Pine Lane [trench]	51bSW1 Neuville Vitasse	N 13 a, c
Pine Trench	57dSE2 & 57cSW1 Le Sars	M 33 a
Pine Wood	66eNW [4 Morisel]	H 16 a
Pineapple Switch [1918]	62dSW [2 Villers-Bretonneux]	O 28 b, 29 a, b, 30 a
Pinepark Farm	20SE2 Hooglede	R 25 a 90.65
Pinero Farm	28NE2 Moorslede	F 4 d 3.7
Ping Farm [near Pong Farm]	20SE2 Hooglede	R 7 d 50.15
Pingouin, Tranchée du	66dNW2 Morchain	C 2 b, c, d
Pink Chateau	28NW4 Ypres	I 9 c 7.8
Pink Farm	20SE2 Hooglede	R 35 b 7.4
Pink Farm	28NE2 Moorslede	F 9 d 7.7
Pink Lane [road in Le Barque]	57cSW1 Gueudecourt	M 12 b 8.5
Pink Trench	57cSW2 Villers-au-Flos	O 7 b
Pink Trench	62bNW3 Bellicourt	G 27 a, b
Pinnace Cottage	27SE2 Berthen	R 29 d 25.90
Pinner [light rly locality & huts]	28NW1 Elverdinghe	B 21 a, b
Pinney's Avenue	36SW1 Aubers	N 9 a, c
Pinney's Post	62cNW1 Maricourt	B 15 a
Pinon Woods	57bSW4 Serain	O 34 c, d, U 3 b, 4 a, b
Pinonier Graben	57dNE3 & 4 Hébuterne	K 11 b, d, 12 a
Pinson Farm	20SW4 Bixschoote	U 21 c 2.7
Pint Street	57cSW3 Longueval	S 7 a, c, d
Pint Trench	57cSW3 Longueval	S 7 a, b, c,
Pint Trench [north of Ginchy]	57cSW3 Longueval	T 7 d, 13 b
Pintade Trench [1918]	66eNW [2 Thennes]	C 2 d, 8 b
Pinx Trench	62bNW3 Bellicourt	G 27 a, c, d
Pioneer Alley	51bSW2 Vis-en-Artois	O 31 a, b
Pioneer Alley	57cSW3 Longueval	S 16 a
Pioneer Alley / Avenue	57cSW1 Gueudecourt	M 23 b, d
Pioneer Area Cemetery	28NW3 Poperinghe	H 21 d, 27 b
Pioneer Avenue	57cSW1 Gueudecourt	M 17 d, 23 b, d, 29 a, b
Pioneer Avenue	62dNE2 Méaulte	F 1 c, d

Name	Map Sheet	Map Reference
Pioneer Camp	28NW3 Poperinghe	H 21 a, b
Pioneer Communication Trench	36SW3 Richebourg	S 4 a, c, d
Pioneer Farm	28NW1 Elverdinghe	B 21 d 85.80
Pioneer Farm	28NW3 Poperinghe	H 21 b 2.2
Pioneer House	28SE1 Wervicq	P 1 a 37.74
Pioneer Junction [light rly, 1917-18]	28NW3 Poperinghe / 4 Ypres	H 16 c, 22 a
Pioneer Keep	36SW3 Richebourg	S 10 b 55.85
Pioneer Lane	28SW2 Wytschaete	O 15 d, 16 c
Pioneer Lane	57cSW1 Gueudecourt	M 30 b, d
Pioneer Line	36aSE3 Gonnehem / 4 Locon	W 15 d, 16 c
Pioneer Post	57dSE4 Ovillers	X 12 c
Pioneer Road [road]	57dSE4 Ovillers	W 10 c, d
Pioneer Support	57cSW1 Gueudecourt	M 17 d
Pioneer Switch [1918]	62dSW [2 Villers-Bretonneux]	O 16, 20, 21, 22, 23, 24
Pioneer Track (Duckboards) [1917-18]	28NW4 Ypres	I 15 a, b, 16 a, b, 17 a
Pioneer Trench	12SW1 Nieuport	M 11 c
Pioneer Trench	36SW3 Richebourg	S 16 a 3.7
Pioneer Trench	36SW3 Richebourg	S 4 d, 10 b
Pioneer Trench	57dSE2 & 57cSW1 Le Sars	N 32 a
Pioneer Trench	57dSE4 Ovillers	X 10 b, 11 a
Pioneer Trench [1918]	62dNE [1 Dernancourt]	E 7 b, c, d
Pioneers Alley	57cSW3 Longueval	S 2 a, c
Pionier [sic] Track: see Pioneer Track	28NW4 Ypres	I 15 a, b, 16 a, b, 17 a
Pionniers, Tranchée des	70dSW [2 Coucy-le-Château]	O 22 b
Pip Farm	28SE1 Wervicq	P 19 c 1.5
Pip Street	28SW2 Wytschaete	O 33 b
Pip Street	36cNW3 Loos	G 29 a
Pip Trench	51bSW1 Neuville Vitasse	M 5 c, 11 a
Pip Trench	57cSE1 Bertincourt	P 15 a, b
Pipe Lane [trench]	62bNW3 Bellicourt	G 14 a
Pipe Street / Communication Trench	36SW3 Richebourg	S 21 b
Pipe Trench	57dSE2 Beaumont	R 20 d, 21 c
Pipe, Bois	66dNW2 Morchain	C 25 d, 26 c
Pippin Trench	51bNW4 Fampoux	H 11 b, d
Pirate Farm	62cSW1 Dompierre	M 36 a
Pirate Trench	57cSE1 Bertincourt	P 10 d, 17 a
Pire Aller, Le [farm & crossroads]	66cNW1 Grugies	B 8 b
Pirie [Trench]	36NW2 Armentières	C 28 d, 29 c
Pissenlits Alley	62cSW3 Vermandovillers	T 3 a, c, d
Pistes Trench	62cSW3 Vermandovillers	T 8 b, 9 a, c
Pistol Farm	36NW1 Steenwerck	B 19 c 5.0
Pistol Trench	51bSW2 Vis-en-Artois	O 16 b
Pit Alley	57cSW3 Longueval	S 24 d
Pit Lane	62bNW1 Gouy	A 26 d
Pit Prop Corner [Tas de Bois]	36cSW1 Lens	M 21 a 1.9
Pit Trench	51bSW2 Vis-en-Artois	O 15 c, d
Pitaut Alley	66cNW1 Grugies	B 7 b, d
Pitch Bend [road & farm]	36NW1 Steenwerck	A 5 a 5.1
Pitch Farm	36NW1 Steenwerck	A 5 c 1.9
Pitch Trench	36SW3 Richebourg	T 1 b, 2 a, c
Pitcher Farm	28NW1 Elverdinghe	A 9 b 1.8
Pith Trench	51bNW4 Fampoux	H 16 d
Pithie Post	57dSE4 Ovillers	X 6 c
Pitlochry Street	57dSE4 Ovillers	X 19 a

Name	Map Sheet	Map Reference
Pittsburg [house]	28NW2 St Julien	C 26 c 30.25
Pivone Trench	20SW3 Oostvleteren	T 3 a
Pixie Farm [1918]	28SW1 Kemmel	M 4 c 4.0
Pixie Wood [1918]	28SW1 Kemmel	M 10 a
Placid Farm [1918]	28SW1 Kemmel	M 28 a 6.3
Placide Trench / Tranchée Placide	62cSW2 Barleux	N 18 a, c
Plague Trench	51bNW4 Fampoux	H 16 c, d, 17 c
Plaid Trench	51bSW2 Vis-en-Artois	N 4 a
Plain Alley	36cNW1 La Bassée	A 16 a, b, 17 a, b
Plaine, Cité de la [miners' cottages]	36cSW1 Lens	M 16 c, 22 a
Plaintiff Farm	28NE2 Moorslede	F 17 b 65.30
Plaisir Farm, Mon	57bNW3 Rumilly	G 27 d
Plaisir Support	57bNW3 Rumilly	G 27 b, 28 a, b, 29 a
Plaisir Trench	57bNW3 Rumilly	G 27 d, 28 c, d, 29 c
Plane Trench	57cSE4 Villers-Guislain	X 19 d, 20 c, 26 a
Planet Dump [light rly, Ablain St Nazaire]	36bSE4 Carency	X 11 a, b
Planet Trench	57cSW4 Combles	U 2 c, 8 a, b, d
Plank Avenue / Road [trench]	36NW2 Armentières	I 4 b, d, 5 c
Plank Road Bridge [bridge over river]	36aNE3 Haverskerque	J 27 c 9.3
Plank Street	51bSW1 Neuville Vitasse	M 5 d, 12 a
Plantin East [Post], Le [Sept 1915]	36cNW1 La Bassée	A 2 d
Plantin North [Post], Le	36aSE4 Locon	A 2 c
Plas Farm	27NE4 Abeele	L 29 d 8.5
Plas Farm [at Den Plas]	28NE2 Moorslede	F 2 b 9.4
Plassey Terrace	57dNE1 & 2 Fonquevillers	E 4 d
Plateau Farm	28SW2 Wytschaete	N 18 b 5.6
Plateau Siding	62cNW1 Maricourt	A 20 a, b
Plateau Station	62cNW1 Maricourt	A 20 a, b
Plateau Woods	62dSE [2 Proyart]	R 29 b, 30 a, c
Platoon Fork [road jct]	27SE2 Berthen	R 25 b 15.95
Platter Farm [1918]	28SW1 Kemmel	M 21 c 30.75
Playden Farm	20SE2 Hooglede	Q 29 c 3.2
Pleasant Row [houses]	28SW1 Kemmel	M 3 c 8.6
Pleasure Copse	28NW3 Poperinghe	G 26 d, 32 b
Pleiades Trench	12SW1 Nieuport	N 14 c
Plevna Trench	62cNW4 Péronne	I 9 b, d
Plevna, Tranchée de	62cSW1 & 2 Belloy	N 17 c, d, 18 c, 23 a
Plexus Farm	28NE2 Moorslede	E 30 d 40.85
Ploegsteert [village]	28SW4 Ploegsteert	U 25 c, d
Ploix [Ouvrage, NW of Fricourt, 1915]	57dSE4 Ovillers	X 26 d
Plot Alley	62bSW3 St Quentin	T 3 c, 9 a, b
Plot Farm Military Cemetery	57cNW3 Bapaume	G 7 d 2.0
Plot Trench	51bNW1 Roclincourt	A 30 b, B 25 a
Plough Support	57cSE2 Gonnelieu	R 7 c, d
Plough Trench	51bNW4 Fampoux	H 16 d
Plough Trench	51bSW2 Vis-en-Artois	O 14 a
Plover Farm	27NE2 Proven	F 8 b 2.2
Plugstreet Hall [Ploegsteert Wood]	28SW4 Ploegsteert	U 20 c 35.40
Plum Duff Sap	28SW4 Ploegsteert	T 12 c
Plum Duff Street	28SW4 Ploegsteert	T 12 a, c, 18 a
Plum Farm	28SW2 Wytschaete	O 22 b 9.6
Plum Farm [strongpoint]	28NW2 St Julien	C 24 c 6.4
Plum Keep [1918]	28NW2 St Julien	C 24 c 5.2
Plum Lane	51bSW4 Bullecourt	U 7 d

Name	Map Sheet	Map Reference
Plum Street	36SW3 Richebourg	S 10 a
Plum Trench	51bNW4 Fampoux	H 17 c
Plum Trench	57cSW3 Longueval	S 11 c
Plumbers Cross Roads	20SE3 Westroosebeke	V 6 c 30.85
Plumer Road [Hill 63, Catacombs]	28SW4 Ploegsteert	T 18 d / U 13 c
Plumer Road [Plumers Drive]	28NW4 Ypres	I 23 c
Plumer Trench	51bNW2 Oppy	B 4 b, d
Plumer Trench [1918]	28NE3 Gheluvelt	J 11 c, d
Plumer's Drive	28NE3 Gheluvelt	J 13 c, d
Plumer's Drive (North) [beech slab road, 1917]	28NE3 Gheluvelt	J 13 b, d, 14 a
Plumer's Drive South	28NW4 Ypres	I 23 c, d, 24 b, c, d
Plumpton Farm	20SE2 Hooglede	R 7 c 8.6
Plus Douce [sic] Farm, la [1914-15]	28SW4 Ploegsteert	T 12 a 6.1
Plus Douve Farm, la	28SW4 Ploegsteert	T 12 a 6.1
Plush Trench	57cSE2 Gonnelieu	Q 6 a, b, R 1 a, c, d
Pluto [German Pillbox M.G. Post]	51bSW4 Bullecourt	U 20 b 95.65
Pluton Trench	57cSE1 Bertincourt	P 1 c, d, 2 c, 7 b
Plymouth Junction [light rly, 1917-18]	28NW2 St Julien	C 20 c 7.5
Poach Trench	51bNW4 Fampoux	H 16 d
Poached Egg Crater	36cSW1 Lens	M 6 b
Poacher's Post	28SW2 Wytschaete	O 22 c 5.2
Pocklington Loop	28NW4 Ypres	H 11 a, c
Pocran Street	57dSE4 Ovillers	X 20 c
Podge Farm	36aNE1 Morbecque	D 28 b 75.70
Podufaly Trench	70dNW4 St Gobain	H 30 b, d
Poe Cross [cross roads]	27SE4 Meteren	X 17 a 50.05
Poelcappelle [village]	20SE3 Westroosebeke	V 14 c, 19 a, b, d, 20 a
Poelcappelle Brewery	20SE3 Westroosebeke	V 14 c, 20 a
Poesele [place name]	20SW4 Bixschoote	N 34 c, T 4 a
Poesele Farm	20SW4 Bixschoote	N 34 c 1.1
Poet's Corner [road jct]	28NE2 Moorslede	L 3 b 6.6
Poezelhoek [farms]	28NE3 Gheluvelt	J 17 c
Poinsot Trench	62cNW2 Bouchavesnes	I 2 b, 3 a, c
Point 110 [old French spot-height]	62dNE2 Méaulte	F 10 c 2.4
Point 127 [NE of Monchy-au-Bois]	51cSE3 & 4 Ransart	W 24 d 95.55
Point 147 [NE of Berles-au-Bois]	51cSE3 & 4 Ransart	W 16 d 1.7
Point 71 [old French spot-height]	62dNE2 Méaulte	F 15 c 9.9
Point Cross [cross roads]	36aNE1 Morbecque	E 8 c 5.5
Point du Jour - Farbus Ridge Line	51bNW1 Roclincourt	A 6, B 1, 7, 14, 20
Point du Jour - Thélus - Ridge Line	36cSW3 Vimy / 51bNW1 Roclincourt	extensive
Point du Jour Post [1918] [N of Athies]	51bNW3 Arras	H 3 c, d
Point du Jour Redoubt	51bNW3 Arras	H 3 c
Point du Jour, le	51bNW3 Arras	H 3 c, d
Point G	36bSE4 Carency	X 23 a 5.1
Point No. 6 [North Maroc, 1915]	36cNW3 Loos	G 32 d 9.3
Point No. 7 [North Maroc]	36cNW3 Loos	G 32 d 8.9
Point X Avenue	20SW3 Oostvleteren	T 9 d, 10 c
Point, The [German front line]	57dNE3 & 4 Hébuterne	K 23 b 1.8
Pointer Alley	51bSW4 Bullecourt	U 16 c
Poitiers Farm	20SW4 Bixschoote	U 2 a 40.05
Poitou Alley	62cSW3 Vermandovillers	S 11 b, d, 12 c
Poivre Trench	62cSW2 Barleux	N 22 d
Poker Street [Heohenzollern Redoubt]	36cNW3 Loos	G 4 d, 5 c
Pol Trench	51bSW1 Neuville Vitasse	N 1 c

Name	Map Sheet	Map Reference
Pola Mill	36aNE2 Vieux Berquin	F 29 b 1.2
Polder Lane	12SW1 Nieuport	M 16 a
Polder Trench	12SW1 Nieuport	M 15 b
Polderhoek	28NE3 Gheluvelt	J 16 c
Polderhoek Chateau	28NE3 Gheluvelt	J 16 d 2.3
Polderhoek Reserve [1918]	28NE3 Gheluvelt	J 15 a, c, 21 a
Polders Trench	20SW3 Oostvleteren	N 33 c, d
Polders Wood	20SE3 Westroosebeke	V 5 d
Pole Trench	51bSW1 Neuville Vitasse	N 7 b, d
Pole Trench	51bSW2 Vis-en-Artois	O 8 b, 9 a
Pole Trench [Gueudecourt]	57dSE2 & 57cSW1 Le Sars	N 21 c, d, 27 b
Pole Trench [Thiepval]	57dSE4 Ovillers	R 32 c, d, X 2 b
Polegate Farm	20SE2 Hooglede	Q 28 a 4.2
Police Station [Westroosebeke]	20SE3 Westroosebeke	V 12 c 1.1
Polish Trench	57dSE2 & 57cSW1 Le Sars	N 21 d, 27 b
Polka Cabaret, La Grande	28SW1 Kemmel	N 21 d 5.4
Polka Estaminet	28SW2 Wytschaete	O 22 a 3.2
Polka La [light rly locality, 1917]	28SW1 Kemmel	N 21 d
Polka Trench	62cSW1 Dompierre	M 36 a, b
Polka, La [farm, Kemmel]	28SW1 Kemmel	N 22 c 05.65
Polka, La [hamlet, Kemmel]	28SW1 Kemmel	N 21 d
Poll House	28SW2 Wytschaete	O 18 a 75.50
Poll Trench	28SW2 Wytschaete	N 17 a
Pollard Support	28SW4 Ploegsteert	U 5 c
Pollen Farm	28SE1 Wervicq	P 20 a 5.9
Pollock Street [north of Bluff]	28NW4 & NE3 Zillebeke	I 34 d
Pollock Trench	28NW4 & NE3 Zillebeke	I 34 c
Pollox Trench	66dNW1 Punchy	B 7 d, 8 c, 13 b, c, d
Pollux Trench	57cSW2 Villers-au-Flos	N 35 a
Polo Copse	62bNW4 Ramicourt	I 32 a
Polo Road [Sunken Road]	57dSE4 Ovillers	X 10 b, d
Poltrons, Tranchée des	70dSW [2 Coucy-le-Château]	O 15 d
Polygon [1918]	28NE3 Gheluvelt	J 3 c
Polygon Butte	28NE3 Gheluvelt	J 10 a 7.8
Polygon Crucifix	28NE3 Gheluvelt	J 3 c
Polygon Reserve [1918]	28NE3 Gheluvelt	J 4 d, 10 a, b
Polygon Track	28NW4 & NE3 Zillebeke	J 13, 14
Polygon Wood	28NE1 Zonnebeke	J 9, 10, 11
Polygon Wood [Triangular Wood]	62cSW3 Vermandovillers / 66dNW1 Punchy	S 27 d, A 3 b, d, 4 a, c
Polygon Wood Dugout	28NE3 Gheluvelt	J 9 a 35.60
Polygon/e Trench	28NE3 Gheluvelt	J 9 a, c
Polygone de Zonnebeke [Polygon Wood]	28NE3 Gheluvelt	J 9 a, b, c, d, 10 a, b, c, d
Polygoneveld / Polygon Veld [hamlet]	28NE3 Gheluvelt	J 9 a
Polyheme / Polyhene Alley/Boyau Polyphème	62cSW3 Vermandovillers	S 18 b, d
Pom Alley	51bSW4 Bullecourt	U 22 b
Pom Cottage	36aNE4 Merville	L 6 c 4.0
Pom Support	36SW3 Richebourg	N 32 c
Pom Trench	28NE1 Zonnebeke	D 7 d, 8 c, 14 a
Pom Trench	36SW3 Richebourg	N 31 d
Pomba Farm	27NE4 Abeele	K 10 d 3.6
Pomerania Trench	70dNW2 Servais	C 25 a, b, c
Pomerania Trench [1918]	66eNW [4 Morisel]	H 35 b, d
Pomeraniens, Tranchée des	70dSW [2 Coucy-le-Chateau]	O 22 a
Pomfret Farm	36NW1 Steenwerck	H 2 a 25.33

Name	Map Sheet	Map Reference
Pommard [farm]	27NE2 Proven	E 15 d 8.6
Pomme Trench	20NW4 Dixmude	H 12 d, 18 b, I 7 c, 13 a
Pommel Alley	51bSW2 Vis-en-Artois	O 8 c
Pommereau Support	36SW1 Aubers / 3 Richebourg	N 31 d, 32 a, c
Pommereau Trench	36SW1 Aubers	N 31 d, 32 a, c
Pommern Castle	28NE1 Zonnebeke	D 19 a
Pommern Junction [light rly]	28NW2 St Julien	C 18 c 7.1
Pommier Copse	62bSW4 Homblières	U 18 c
Pommier Trench	62bSW3 St Quentin	S 28 a, b, d, 29 c
Pommier Trench	62cSW3 Vermandovillers	S 15 d, 21 a, b
Pommiers Lane [trench]	62cNW1 Maricourt	A 1 b, d, 2 c
Pommiers Redoubt [Jamin Werk]	62cNW1 Maricourt	A 1 b
Pommiers Trench	62cNW1 Maricourt	A 1 d
Pommiers Trench	62cSW1 & 2 Belloy	N 12 a, b
Pommiers, Boyau des	62cNW3 Vaux	G 28 d, 29 c
Pommiers, Tranchée des	62cNW3 Vaux	G 29 c, 35 a
Pomone, Tranchée de	66eNE4 Beaufort	L 17 b, 18 a
Pompadour Farm	20SW4 Bixschoote	T 30 d 7.9
Pompadour Farm	36aSE1 St Venant	P 24 d 6.5
Pompadour Farm	36NW2 & NE1 Houplines	C 3 b 25.00
Pompadour Siding [light rly]	36NW2 & NE1 Houplines	C 3 a 90.45
Pompadour Trench	20SW4 Bixschoote	T 30 a, b, c
Pompadour Trench	57dSE1 & 2 Beaumont	Q 10 c
Pompier Estaminet, Au	28SW1 Kemmel	N 14 c 5.9
Pompiers Alley	66dNW1 Punchy	A 24 c, d, 30 b, B 25 a, c, d
Pompom Alley	57dNE3 & 4 Hébuterne	K 30 b, L 25 a
Pompon [sic] Trench	66dNW1 Punchy	A 24 a, c
Pomponius Lane	62cNE2 Epéhy	F 11 d
Ponch Post, Rue de	36aSE2 Lestrem	·R 16 d, 22 b
Pond [pond, late 1915]	36SW1 Aubers	M 18 c 3.3
Pond Cottage Cemetery	28NW2 St Julien	B 24 b
Pond Farm	28SW4 Ploegsteert	N 34 d 65.95
Pond Farm [& pillbox]	28NW2 St Julien	C 18 b 9.0
Pond Farm [Frenchman's Farm, March 1915]	28SW2 Wytschaete	N 34 b 8.3
Pond Farm Military Cemetery	28SW2 Wytschaete	N 34 b 5.6
Pond Farm Salient	28NW2 St Julien	C 19 d, 25 b
Pond Street / Boyau de l'Etang	62cNW1 Maricourt	A 15 d
Pond Street [Bluff]	28NW4 & 28NE3 Zillebeke	I 34 c
Pond Support	62bNW3 Bellicourt	G 1 d, 7 b
Pond Trench	62bNW3 Bellicourt	G 1 d, 7 b
Ponder Reserve	57cSE1 Bertincourt	P 16 d, 22 b
Ponder Trench	57cSE1 Bertincourt	P 17 a, c, 23 a
Pondhurst Farm	20SE2 Hooglede	Q 28 b 95.95
Pong Farm [near Ping Farm]	20SE2 Hooglede	R 7 d 85.65
Ponkershot [farm, La Polka]	28SW1 Kemmel	N 21 d 65.10
Ponsonby House	28NE4 Dadizeele	K 30 d 90.55
Pont d'Achelles [hamlet]	36NW1 Steenwerck	B 8 b
Pont de St Quentin [Wulverghem]	28SW4 Ploegsteert	T 5 d 75.37
Pont des Vaches [E of Sailly]	51bNE3 Noyelle-sous-Bellonne	J 29 c 65.05
Pont des Vaches [W of Sailly]	51bNE3 Noyelle-sous-Bellonne	J 26 a 3.3
Pont du Hem Post	36SW1 Aubers	M 15 c
Pont Fixe [canal bridge]	36cNW1 La Bassée	A 14 d
Pont Fixe South [Post]	36cNW1 La Bassée	A 14 d
Pont le Pierre [road over stream]	36NW1 Steenwerck	A 10 b 1.1

Name	Map Sheet	Map Reference
Pont Leveque Trench	66cSW4 La Fère	T 23 a
Pont Logy	36SW3 Richebourg	M 34 c
Pont Logy Street [CT, Sept 1915]	36SW3 Richebourg	M 34 c, S 4 a, b, d
Pont Perry	36aSE1 St Venant	P 20 a
Pont Riquel / Riqueul Post	36aSE2 Lestrem	R 10 a
Pont Rondin [hamlet]	36aNE4 Merville	K 6 d, L 1 c
Pont Street	36cNW3 Loos	G 23 b, d
Pont Street	36cSW3 Vimy / 51bNW1 Roclincourt	S 26, 27, 28, A 1
Pont Street	51cSE3 & 4 Ransart	Q 36 b, W 6 a, b
Pont Street [Ginchy]	57cSW3 Longueval	T 13 d, 19 b
Pont Street [road]	57cSW3 Longueval	S 11 c, 17 a
Pont Wemeau [farm]	36aNE2 Vieux Berquin	F 23 c 4.0
Pontchu Quarry & Redoubt, Le [SE of St Q]	66cNW1 Grugies	B 22 a
Pontchu, Le [farm]	66cNW1 Grugies / 2 Itancourt	B 22 a
Pontefract Trench	57cNW2 Vaulx-Vraucourt	C 3 c, 9 a, b, 10 a, b
Pont-Rouge [hamlet]	28SW4 Ploegsteert	U 29 b
Pontru [hamlet]	62bSW1 Gricourt	M 7 b, d
Pontruet [village]	62bSW1 Gricourt	M 9 b, d, 10 a, c
Pontruet Trench	62bSW1 Gricourt	M 9 b, d
Ponts, Boyau des	36cSW3 Vimy	S 26 c, d
Pony Copse	62bSW2 Fonsommes	N 10 a
Pony Copse	62cSW4 St. Christ	U 22 b
Pony Trench	51bNW4 Fampoux	H 16 d
Pood Kruis Inn	27NE4 Abeele	L 17 b 3.1
Poodle Trench	51bSW2 Vis-en-Artois	O 2 b, 3 a
Poodles, The [tree clump]	57dSE4 Ovillers	X 28 a 2.1
Poop Farm	20SE2 Hooglede	R 16 d 75.15
Poosner Street	36bSE4 & 36cSW3 Givenchy	S 15 c
Pop Trench	51bNW1 Roclincourt	A 30 b, d
Pope Alley	57cSE2 Gonnelieu	Q 30 b, R 19 b, c, d, 25 a
Pope Avenue	57cSE2 Gonnelieu	R 14 c, d, 19 b, d, 20 a
Pope Farm	28NE2 Moorslede	F 19 a 4.4
Poperinghe [town]	27NE2 Proven / 4 Abeele / 28NW1 Elverdinghe / 3 Poperinghe	L 6 a, c, 12 a, c, G 1 b, d, 2 c, d, 7 b, 8 a
Poperinghe Line, East [1918]	28NW1 Elverdinghe / 3 Poperinghe	A 10-28, G 3-33
Poperinghe Line, West [1918]	28NW1 Elverdinghe	A 20, 21, 22, 25, 26
Poperinghe Railhead	27NE4 Abeele	L 5 c, d, 11 a, b
Poperingue [sic], Croix de	28SW1 Kemmel	M 32 b
Pope's Crater	51bNW1 Roclincourt	G 6 a
Pope's Nose [Br, S of Neuve Chapelle]	36SW3 Richebourg	S 10 b 9.4-7
Pope's Nose [Ger FL, SW Les Briques, Sept '15]	36cNW1 La Bassée	A 27 b 95.35
Pope's Nose [German FL]	51bNW1 Roclincourt	G 6 a 6.6
Pope's Nose [Thiepval]	57dSE1 & 2 Beaumont	R 19 c
Pope's Nose Redoubt	36cNW3 Loos	G 11 a, b
Poplar [tree in No Man's Land]	57dNE1 & 2 Fonquevillers	E 23 c 22.94
Poplar Avenue [road]	66dNW1 Punchy	A 10 b, 11 a, c
Poplar Copse	62cSW3 Vermandovillers	T 1 d
Poplar Keep [Calonne]	36cSW1 Lens	M 9 c
Poplar Spur [light rly]	36bNE2 Beuvry	F 25 b
Poplar Street	57cSW3 Longueval	N 31 c
Poplar Trench	51bSW1 Neuville Vitasse	N 7 c, 13 a
Poplar Trench	57cSE4 Villers-Guislain	X 26 a, b, c, d
Poplar Trench	57cSW3 Longueval	N 31 c
Poplar Trench	66eNE2 Vrély	F 16 a

Name	Map Sheet	Map Reference
Popoff Lane	62cNW1 Maricourt	A 1 d
Popote, Tranchée de la	66dNW2 Morchain	B 18 c, 24 a, c
Poppy Lane	28SW2 Wytschaete	N 11 b, d, 12 c
Poppy Lane [1918, Ficheux]	51cSE4 Blaireville	R 36 c, X 5 a, b, 6 a
Poppy Post	57cSE4 Villers-Guislain	X 2 b
Poppy Redoubt [Givenchy]	36cNW1 La Bassée	A 9 a, c
Poppy Trench	57cSW3 Longueval	S 11 a, b, c, d
Porcupine Wood	62cSE1 Bouvincourt	P 6 b, Q 1 a
Pork Trench	28SE1 Wervicq	P 22 b, d
Pork Trench	51bNW1 Roclincourt	A 30 b
Pork Trench	57dSE2 & 57cSW1 Le Sars	N 14 c, 20 a, b
Porridge [light rly locality, 1917-18]	28SW2 Wytschaete	O 8 central
Port Arthur Keep	36SW3 Richebourg	S 4 d
Port Arthur Trench	36SW3 Richebourg	S 4 b, d
Port Bouet, Tranchée de	66cNW2 Itancourt	C 25 a, c, d
Port Epic, Tranchée du	66eNE4 Beaufort	L 17 d, 23 a
Port House	28NW1 Elverdinghe	B 20 a 5.3
Port Louis [Trench]	57dSE4 Ovillers	W 18 a, b, c, X 13 a, c
Port Trench	51bNW4 Fampoux	H 16 b, d
Portage Avenue	20SW3 Oostvleteren	T 10 c, 16 a
Portage Road [road]	36cSW4 Rouvroy	U 7 c, d
Portage Road [road]	36cSW4 Rouvroy	T 12 d, U 7 c, d
Porter Trench	57cSW3 Longueval	T 13 c, 19 a
Porthcawl Road [Trench]	36cSW1 Lens	M 9 d, 15 a, b
Portique, La	51bNW1 Roclincourt	A 3 c
Portland Avenue	62dNE2 Méaulte	F 16 a
Portland Road [front line; Sept 1915]	36cNW1 La Bassée	A 15 d
Portland Street	62dNE2 Méaulte	F 12 c
Ports Farm	62bNW2 Brancourt-le-Grand	C 9 b
Portsdown Lane	57cNE3 Hermies	K 25 c, d
Portsea Corner [road junction]	20SE2 Hooglede	Q 9 d 80.85
Posen Alley	36cNW3 Loos	G 23 d, 24 c, d, H 19 c, 25 a
Posen Crater	36cNW3 Loos	H 19 d 2.1
Posen Line [light rly]	36cNW3 Loos	G 19, 20, 21, 22. 23
Posen Locality	36cNW3 Loos	H 19 c, 25 a
Posen Station	36cNW3 Loos	G 23 c 9.9
Posen Street [Oct 1915, formerly Alley 4]	36cNW3 Loos	G 18 b, c, d, 23 b, 24 a
Posen Trench	66dNW3 Hattencourt	G 14 a, c
Poser Weg [formerly Gaul Weg]	51bNW1 Roclincourt	A 23, 24, 30, B 25, 26
Posina Alley	66cNW4 Berthenicourt	I 14 d
Posmania Trench	70dNW4 St Gobain	H 11 b, 12 a
Possum Farm	28NW3 Poperinghe	G 11 b 8.2
Possum Lane [trench]	51bSE3 Cagnicourt	V 19 c, d, 20 c, 25 b
Possum Reserve	57dSE2 & 57cSW1 Le Sars	N 26 c, 32 a, b
Post A [W of Guémappe]	51bSW2 Vis-en-Artois	N 18 c
Post B [NW of Guémappe]	51bSW2 Vis-en-Artois	N 18 a
Post du Buffy / Bugny	62dNE2 Méaulte	F 3 c
Post G [SE of Guémappe]	51bSW2 Vis-en-Artois	O 20 c
Post H [SE of Guémappe]	51bSW2 Vis-en-Artois	O 20 c
Post Office Rifles Cemetery	36aSE4 Locon	X 30 c 0.1
Post Office Trench	57cNE4 Marcoing	K 16 a
Post Road [road]	36cSW1 Lens / 2 Harnes	N 9 b, d, 10 a
Post Trench	51bNW1 Roclincourt	A 30 b, B 25 a
Post Trench	51bNW1 Roclincourt / 2 Oppy	B 22 a, b, c, 28 a, c

Name	Map Sheet	Map Reference
Post Trench [Cameron & Sanderson Trenches]	57dSE4 Ovillers / 57cSW3 Longueval	X 6 a, S 1 b
Postick [Trench]	62dNE2 Méaulte	F 11 c
Poston Farms	36NW1 Steenwerck	B 20 b 35.05 & 20 d 35.95
Pot Alley	62cSW3 Vermandovillers	T 1 b, d
Pot Avenue [1918]	57dSW [3 Talmas]	S 23 d, 24 c
Pot Farm	28NE3 Gheluvelt	J 28 a 27.97
Pot Lane	62cNE2 Epéhy	F 23 b
Pot Street [road]	36cNW3 Loos	G 35 b, 36 a
Pot Trench	28SE1 Wervicq	P 15 b
Pot Trench	51bNW1 Roclincourt	A 30 a
Pot Trench	62cNE2 Epéhy	F 18 c
Pot Trench	51bSW1 Neuville Vitasse	N 20 b
Potato Farm	20SE2 Hooglede	R 10 a 25.95
Potence Trench	20SW2 Zwartegat	N 17 c, 22 b, 23 a
Potijze [village]	28NW4 & NE3 Zillebeke	I 4 c
Potijze Chateau	28NW2 St Julien	I 4 a
Potsdam [farm & pillbox]	28NE1 Zonnebeke	D 26 c 7.8
Potsdam Farm	28SE1 Wervicq	P 1 b 0.6
Potsdam Keep [1918]	28NE1 Zonnebeke	D 26 c
Potsdam Trench	57cSW4 Combles	U 8 b, d
Potsdam Trench	57dSE2 Beaumont	Q 6 b, d
Potsdam, Tranchée de	70dSW [2 Coucy-le-Château]	O 15 d
Pottage Street	57dSE1 & 2 Beaumont	Q 23 b, d
Pottage Trench	57dSE1 & 2 Beaumont	Q 23 a, c
Potte [village]	66dNW2 Morchain	B 24 b
Pottegemsgoed Farm	20SE3 Westroosebeke	W 26 d 4.6
Potten Farm	28NW1 Elverdinghe	H 3 b 5.3
Pottenhoek [railway & light rly sidings]	28NW1 Elverdinghe	B 27 a, c
Pottenhoek [Vlamertinghe]	28NW3 Poperinghe	H 3 d
Potterie Farm, La	28SW4 Ploegsteert	U 10 a 9.0
Potterijebrug [place name]	28NE4 Dadizeele	K 10 a
Potters Bar [Malbert, Boyau]	36cSW1 Lens	M 20 a, c
Potts Lane	57cSE2 Gonnelieu	Q 16 b, 17 a
Pouget Alley	66cNW1 Grugies	A 12 a
Poule Trench	20SW3 Oostvleteren	T 14 b, 15 a
Poule Verte, Tranchée de la	62cSW3 & 4 Marchélepot	T 12 d, 18 a, b, c
Poules Verts [sic] Trench	62cSW4 St. Christ	T 12 d, 18 a, b, c
Poulton Farm	28NE4 Dadizeele	K 35 b 75.95
Poultry [road]	57cNE1 Quéant	D 13 c
Poupore Trench	36cSW1 Lens	N 31 b
Poux, Tranchée des	70dSW [2 Coucy-le-Château]	O 15 b
Povlain [Tranchée, 1915]	57dSE4 Ovillers	X 20 d
Powder Mill Trench	66cSW2 Vendeuil	O 28 c, 34 a, c
Powder Trench	51bNW4 Fampoux	I 32 a
Powell Wood	51bNW4 Fampoux	I 36 a, b
Power House	28NE4 Dadizeele	K 11 a 65.20
Power Trench	57cSE1 Bertincourt	P 23 a, c, 29 a, b
Pozières [village]	57dSE4 Ovillers	X 4 a, b, c, d, 5 a
Pozières Trench	57dSE4 Ovillers	X 4 a, c, d, 5 c, d
Pozières Windmill	57dSE4 Ovillers	R 35 c 9.3
Pracomtel, Boyau	36cSW3 Vimy	S 14 d
Practice Road	57dSE2 & 57cSW1 Le Sars	M 19 b, d, 20 a, c
Practice Trenches [E of Saulzoir]	51aSE [1Verchain / 3 Haussy]	P 23, 24, 29, 30, 36, Q 25, 31
Practice Trenches [N of Haussy]	51aSE [3 Haussy]	V 5, 6, W 1

Name	Map Sheet	Map Reference
Practice Trenches [NE of Haspres]	51aSE [1 Verchain]	P 1 d, 2 c, 7 b, d, 8 a
Practice Trenches [North]	57dSE2 & 57cSW1 Le Sars	M 19 b, 20 a
Practice Trenches [SE of Haussy]	51aSE [3 Haussy]	W 13 d, 19 b
Practice Trenches [South]	57dSE2 & 57cSW1 Le Sars	M 19 b, d, 20 a, c
Praed Street	28NW2 St Julien	C 21 d, 22 c
Praed Street	36cNW1 La Bassée	A 21 b
Praed Street	57cSW3 Longueval	S 10 d, 16 b
Praed Street	57dSE1 & 2 Beaumont	Q 16 b
Prague Trench	62cNW4 Péronne	I 14 c, d, 19 b, d, 20 a
Prague Trench / Trench de Prague / Tranchée de	66cNW2 Itancourt	C 25 a, c, d
Prague Trench [1918]	66eNW [4 Morisel]	H 35 b, d
Prat Trench	57dNE3 & 4 Hébuterne	K 16 b
Pratt Dump [Loos]	36cNW3 Loos	H 31 c 9.8
Pratt Street	28NW2 St Julien	C 22 c, 28 a
Prattle Trench	57cSE1 Bertincourt	P 29 b, d, 30 c
Prawn Farm	20SE2 Hooglede	R 29 a 2.2
Pré à Vin, le [hamlet]	36aNE1 Morbecque	J 6 d, K 1 c
Preacher Point [road jct]	28NE2 Moorslede	F 25 b 25.95
Prémont [village]	57bSW4 Serain	U 28 a, b, d, 29 a, b, c, d
Prémont Wood	57bSW4 Serain	U 30 b, d
Prémont, Chapelle du	51bNE3 Noyelle-sous-Bellonne	J 12 c 85.70
Premy Avenue	57cNE4 Marcoing	L 15 c, d, 19 d, 20 b, c, d, 21 a, 25 a, b
Premy Chapel	57cNE4 Marcoing	L 16 c
Premy Road [road]	57cNE4 Marcoing	L 15 d, 21 a, c
Premy Support	57cNE4 Marcoing	L 20 b, 21 a, c
Premy Switch	57cNE4 Marcoing	L 20 a, b
Premy Trench	57cNE4 Marcoing	L 14 d, 15 c, 21 a, b
Premy Wood	57cNE4 Marcoing	L 20 d 35.90
Preol Locality, Le	36bNE2 Beuvry	F 10 b, 11 a
Preole Keep, Le	36bNE2 Beuvry	F 17 a
Prés des Vaux	57bSE [3 Busigny / 4 Wassigny]	W 22 a, b
Prés, Ferme des	51bNE3 Noyelle-sous-Bellonne	J 25 d 2.8
Presbytery Garden	28NW2 St Julien	C 27 c 05.25
Preselles Farm	62bNW4 Ramicourt	H 17 c 8.1
President Cross [cross roads]	36aNE2 Vieux Berquin	E 11 c 8.3
Press Trench	57cSE3 Sorel-le-Grand	P 36 d, Q 31 c
Pressoire [village]	62cSW3 & 4 Marchélepot	S 24
Preston Avenue	57dSE4 Ovillers	W 18 a, b
Preston Camp	28NW4 Ypres	H 35 d
Preston Farm	36NW1 Steenwerck	B 9 c 4.6
Preston House	28NW2 St Julien	C 2 b 98.05
Preston Road [trench]	28SW2 Wytschaete	O 15 d, 22 a
Preston Support	57cSE4 Villers-Guislain	R 34 a, b, d
Preston Trench	57cSE4 Villers-Guislain	R 34 a, b, d
Pret Trench	57dNE3 & 4 Hébuterne	K 16 b
Pretoria Cemetery	20SW4 Bixschoote	U 27 a 4.2
Pretoria House	28NE1 Zonnebeke	D 7 b 4.2
Pretoria Trench	36NW2 Armentières	C 28 b, 29 a
Preussen Graben	57dNE1 & 2 Fonquevillers	F 21 c, d, 27 b
Preussen Redoubt / Work	51bSW1 Neuville Vitasse	M 12 d, 18 b
Preussen Weg	51bSW1 Neuville Vitasse	M 5, 11, 12, 18
Previte Castle	36cNW3 Loos	G 28 b, d
Previte Passage	36cNW3 Loos	G 28 d

Name	Map Sheet	Map Reference
Previte Point	36cNW3 Loos	G 28 d
Price Farm	28NE4 Dadizeele	K 10 b 8.7
Price Street	57dSE1 & 2 Beaumont	R 19 d
Price Trench	57dSE2 & 57cSW1 Le Sars	N 20 c
Prickle Puss Trench	57cSE1 Bertincourt	P 36 a, b, d
Priel Copse	62cNE4 Roisel	L 29 b, d
Priel Crater	62cNE4 Roisel	L 29 b 1.8
Priel Farm Posts	62cNE4 Roisel	L 24 a, c, 30 a
Priel North Post	62cNE4 Roisel	L 17 d, 18 c
Priel Road Post	62cNE4 Roisel	L 17 d 9.7
Priel Wood Trench	62cNE4 Roisel	L 22 a, c, 28 a, b, c
Prieles Road [road]	62cNE4 Roisel	L 17 b, d, 23 b
Priez Farm / Ferme	62cNW2 Bouchavesnes	B 6 a 3.3
Priez Farm Camp [near Priez Farm]	62cNW2 Bouchavesnes	B 6 a
Prig Trench	51bNW4 Fampoux	H 16 b
Prim Support	57cSE1 Bertincourt	P 15 b
Prim Trench	51bNW4 Fampoux	H 16 b
Prim Trench	57cSE1 Bertincourt	P 15 b, d
Primrose Cotts	28NE1 Zonnebeke	D 20 b 3.7
Primrose Farm	20SE2 Hooglede	R 3 a 75.00
Primula Copse	20SE2 Hooglede	R 14 b 35.99
Primus Dugout & OP [Passchendaele]	28NE1 Zonnebeke	D 12 c 2.7
Primus Trench	57cSE1 Bertincourt	P 10 c, 15 b, 16 a
Prince Copse	57dSW [3 Talmas]	S 22 d
Prince Copse	62bSW1 Gricourt	N 15 b, d
Prince Eitel Fritz Farm	28NW2 St Julien	I 5 b 7.6
Prince Farm	36aNE4 Merville	L 3 d 3.7
Prince Oskar Farm	28NW2 St Julien	I 6 c 00.95
Prince Reserve	57cSE4 Villers-Guislain / 62cNE2 Epéhy	X 25 a, c, F 1 b, 2 c
Prince Rupert's Dug Out [Oostaverne]	28SW2 Wytschaete	O 21 b
Prince Street	57dSE1 & 2 Beaumont	R 31 a, b, c
Prince Trench	51bSW4 Bullecourt	U 7 b, 8 a
Prince Trench, & Support	57cSE1 Bertincourt	P 9 b, 10 a
Princes House	28NE3 Gheluvelt	J 31 d 05.70
Prince's Island	36cNW1 La Bassée	A 3 c, 9 a
Princes Road [road; Sept 1915]	36SW3 Richebourg	S 14 b, d, 20 d, 21 a, c
Princes Road [road]	36aSE1 St Venant	Q 1 b, d, 7 b
Princes Road [road]	36SW3 Richebourg	S 15 c, 21 a
Princes Street	62cNW1 Maricourt	A 8 d
Princes Street [1918]	57dSE4 Ovillers	W 4 a
Princes Street [Delville Wood]	57cSW3 Longueval	S 18 a, b
Princes Street [Sept 1915]	36cNW1 La Bassée	A 3 a
Princess Street	57dSE1 & 2 Beaumont	Q 23 b
Princess Street	57dSE4 Ovillers	W 6 d
Princess Trench	57cSE1 Bertincourt	P 10 a, c, d
Princeton [light rly jct]	36NW2 Armentières	B 4 d 8.2
Pringle Farm	36NW1 Steenwerck	B 9 c 2.6
Prinz Arnolf Graben	36cSW3 Vimy	S 28 c, d, 29 c, d
Prinz Karl-weg [proposed]	57cSW3 Longueval	T 1 b, 2 a, b
Priory Cott	28NE3 Gheluvelt	J 19 d
Priory Loop [light rly]	36bNE1 [Labeuvrière] / 2 Beuvry	E 21 d
Pripet Alley	66cNW2 Itancourt	B 24 d
Pripet, Tranchée de	66cNW2 Itancourt	B 24 d
Prism Trench	51bNW4 Fampoux	H 16 d

Name	Map Sheet	Map Reference
Prison [Béthune]	36bNE2 Beuvry	E 5 c 3.7
Prison [Ypres]	28NW4 Ypres	I 7 b 15.15
Prisoner of War Camp [Toutencourt]	57dSW4 [Toutencourt]	T 6 d
Pritchard Trench	57dSE2 Beaumont	Q 5 b, 6 a, c
Privet Avenue / Boyau Privé	62cNW1 Maricourt	A 16 d
Privet Cot.	28SW4 Ploegsteert	T 4 b 3.3
Privet Farm	20SE2 Hooglede	Q 18 c 5.5
Procuste, Boyau	66dNW3 Hattencourt / 66eNE4 Beaufort	G 13 d, 25 b, L17 d, 18 c
Prod Farm	36NW1 Steenwerck	B 9 c 75.15
Professor Cross Roads	28NE2 Moorslede	F 10 d 99.78
Profond Val	51bNW1 Roclincourt	A 13 d, 14 a, b, 19 b
Proggins Lane	62bNW1 Gouy	A 7 d
Progress Row [buildings; Le Touquet]	36NW2 & NE1 Houplines	C 10 b 3.3
Promenade, The [Zillebeke Lake south]	28NW4 & NE3 Zillebeke	I 21 b - 22 d
Promethius Trench	57cSW2 Villers-au-Flos / 4 Combles	O 32 c, d, 33 a
Promised Land Corner [road junction]	20SE2 Hooglede	R 2 c 45.47
Prompt Farm	36NW1 Steenwerck	B 9 b 6.3
Pronville [village]	57cNE1 Quéant	D 9 a, b, c, d
Pronville Switch	57cNE1 Quéant	D 9 a, c
Prop Trench	51bNW4 Fampoux	H 16 b, d
Property Support	57cSE1 Bertincourt	P 9 d, 15 a, b
Property Trench	57cSE1 Bertincourt	P 9 c, d, 15 a
Prose Farm [1918]	28SW1 Kemmel	M 28 d 70.75
Prospect Farm	27SE4 Meteren	X 1 b 3.1
Prospect Hill	57cNE3 Hermies / SE1 Bertincourt	K 31, P 1
Prospect Hill	62bNW1 Gouy	B 1 b
Prospect Point	57dSE1 & 2 Beaumont	Q 23 c
Prospect Row	57dSE1 & 2 Beaumont	Q 23 c
Prosper Trench	57cSE1 Bertincourt	P 15 a, c, d
Prospero Farm	36NW1 Steenwerck	B 10 c 1.7
Protector Post	57cSE4 Villers-Guislain	X 25 c
Proud Lane [trench]	57cSE1 Bertincourt	P 24 b
Proud Trench	57cSE1 Bertincourt	P 24 a, b
Proven [village]	27NE2 Proven	F 7 a, b, d
Proven Flying Field	27NE2 Proven	F 13 a 9.9
Proven Railhead / Refilling Point	27NE2 Proven	F 7 a, b
Provost Trench	12SW3 Ramscappelle	T 10 a
Prowl Trench	57cSE1 Bertincourt	P 3 c, d, 9 b
Prowse Boyd Line [lt rly / trench tramway, 1916]	28SW4 Ploegsteert	U 19 b, d, 20 a, b, 21 a
Prowse Farm	28NW2 St Julien	C 28 d 3.2
Prowse Point	28SW4 Ploegsteert	U 14 b 95.90
Prude House	27SE4 Meteren	W 5 c 3.9
Prudence Farm	28SW1 Kemmel	M 22 d 2.6
Prue Copse	57dSE2 & 57cSW1 Le Sars	M 34 b
Prue Copse	62bSW1 Gricourt	M 9 b
Prue Trench	57dSE2 & 57cSW1 Le Sars	M 33 a, b, 34 a, b, 35 a
Prune Trench	20SW3 Oostvleteren	T 2 b, d
Prunier Alley	62cSW3 Vermandovillers	S 10 d, 11 a, c
Prussian Avenue [1918]	57dNE2 & 57cNW1 Courcelles	F 20 d, 21 c, 27 b
Prussian Trench	57cSW4 Combles	N 36 c, d
Prussian Way	36cNW1 La Bassée	A 9 d, 10 a, c
Prussiens, Tranchée des	70dSW [2 Coucy-le-Château]	O 9 c
Pry's Post	36NW4 Bois Grenier	I 31 c
PS 1 [Br trench, late-1915, SE of Dead Cow Fm]	28NW4 & NE3 Zillebeke	I 11 a 5.7

Name	Map Sheet	Map Reference
PS 2 [Br trench, late-1915, S of Dead Cow Farm]	28NW4 & NE3 Zillebeke	I 11 a 25.85
Pub Street	57dNE3 & 4 Hébuterne	K 17 d
Puchevillers [village]	57dSW [1 Puchevillers] / [2 Raincheval]	N 21, 22, 27, 28
Puchvill 1st Reserve [1918]	57dSW [1 Puchevillers]	N 13 b, 19 d, 25 b, d
Puchvill 1st Support [1918]	57dSW [1 Puchevillers]	N 20 c, 26 a, c
Puchvill 2nd Reserve [1918]	57dSW [1 Puchevillers]	N 13 a, 19 c, 25 a, b, c
Puchvill 2nd Support [1918]	57dSW [1 Puchevillers]	N 20 c, 26 a, c
Puchvill Trench [1918]	57dSW [1 Puchevillers]	N 20 d, 26 b, d
Puck Trench	57cSE1 Bertincourt	P 15 a, b
Pudding Lane	36cNW1 La Bassée	A 15 c, d
Pudding Support	28SE1 Wervicq	P 8 a
Pudding Trench	28SE1 Wervicq	P 8 a
Pudding Trench	51bNW4 Fampoux	H 16 b, d
Pudding Trench	51cNE2 Ecoivres	E 28 a
Puddle Trench	57cSE1 Bertincourt	P 9 d, 15 b
Pudefort [farm]	28SW1 Kemmel	M 19 b 3.2
Pudsey Post	51bSW4 Bullecourt	U 29 a, b, d
Pudsey Support	51bSW4 Bullecourt	U 29 a, b, d
Puff House	20SW4 Bixschoote	U 22 d 3.1
Puff Trench	57cSE1 Bertincourt	P 9 b, d
Puffer Lines	20SW4 Bixschoote	U 23 d 1.3
Puffin Avenue	51bSW2 Vis-en-Artois / 4 Bullecourt	N 36 b, O 31 c
Pug Avenue	51bSW4 Bullecourt	T 6 b
Pug Lane	51bSW4 Bullecourt	T 6 b, U 1 a, b
Pug Trench	51bNW4 Fampoux	I 33 c
Puhallo Alley	66cNW2 Itancourt	C 16 d, 21 c, d, 22 a, b, c, 26 b, d, 27 a
Puisieux Alley	57dNE3 & 4 Hébuterne	L 31 d, 32 b, c
Puisieux Farm	66cNW4 Berthenicourt	H 18 a, b
Puisieux Road [road]	57dNE3 & 4 Hébuterne / SE1 & 2 Beaumont	L 31 d, R 1 b, d,
Puisieux Trench	57dNE3 & 4 Hébuterne / SE1 & 2 Beaumont	L 20, 26, 32, R 2, 8
Puits (Fosse) No. 12 [1916]	36cSW1 Lens	M 6 d
Puits Farm	20SW4 Bixschoote	T 29 b, 30 a
Puits No. 11 (Fosse) [E end Double Crassier, '15]	36cSW1 Lens	M 5 c, 11 a
Puits No. 11 bis [1915]	36cSW1 Lens	M 10 a, b
Puits No. 12 bis [1915]	36cSW1 Lens	M 12 b
Puits No. 13 [Cité St Elie]	36cNW3 Loos	H 7 a
Puits No. 13 bis	36cNW3 Loos	H 14 c
Puits No. 13 bis [Benifontaine, 1915]	36cNW3 Loos	H 14 c
Puits No. 14 bis Keep	36cNW3 Loos	H 25 c, d
Puits No. 15 [Loos, Tower Bridge]	36cNW3 Loos	G 36 a, c
Puits No. 16 [1915]	36cSW1 Lens	M 10 a, b
Puits No. 3 [Philosophe]	36cNW3 Loos	G 19 b, 20 a
Puits No. 7	36cNW3 Loos	G 27 a, c, d
Puits No. 7 bis	36cNW3 Loos	G 26 d
Puits Trench	36cNW3 Loos	G 12 b, H 7 a, c, d
Puits Trench [Puits No. 13, 1915]	36cNW3 Loos	G 12 b, H 7 a, c, d
Puits, Bois de	51bSE2 Oisy-le-Verger	R 25 d
Pukka Support	28SE1 Wervicq	P 23 c, d, 29 b, d
Pukka Trench	28SE1 Wervicq	P 23 c, 29 a, d
Puku Trench [1918]	57dNE4 [Hébuterne / Achiet]	L 8 b, c, d
Pullet Farm	36aNE4 Merville	L 13 d 10.05
Pulpit Crater	51bNW1 Roclincourt	A 4 d 25.15
Pulpit Trench	51bNW1 Roclincourt	A 4 d

Name	Map Sheet	Map Reference
Pulse Farm	28NW3 Poperinghe	H 15 a 2.6
Pulzic Trench	62cNE3 Buire	J 31 a, c
Puma Trench	62bNW1 Gouy	A 1 d
Pump Farm	28SW2 Wytschaete	O 12 b 25.15
Pump House	20SW4 Bixschoote	U 23 d 3.1
Pump House [late 1915]	36SW1 Aubers	M 29 d 1.0
Pump House Keep	36SW1 Aubers	M 35 b 4.8
Pump House Post	36SW1 Aubers	M 29 d 30.05
Pump Room, The	28NW2 St Julien	C 14 d
Pump Trench	51bNW1 Roclincourt	A 30 b, B 25 a
Pun Trench	51bSW2 Vis-en-Artois	O 8 d
Punch Farm	28NE2 Moorslede	F 25 a 4.3
Punch Row [buildings]	36NW1 Steenwerck	A 18 c5.2
Punch Trench	12SW1 Nieuport	M 16 b
Punch Trench	57cSW3 Longueval	T 1 d, 2 b, c, d, 3 a
Punchy [village]	66dNW1 Punchy	A 23, 29
Punchy Alley	66dNW1 Punchy	A 16 d, 22 b, 23 a, c
Punchy Copse	66dNW1 Punchy	A 30 c
Pungent Farm	36NW1 Steenwerck	B 26 a 2.5
Punkah Farm	27SE4 Meteren	R 35 c 5.2
Punters Copse	20SE2 Hooglede	Q 11 a 2.9
Pup Trench	51bSW4 Bullecourt	U 23 d, 24 c
Puppy Trench [near Fontaine des Chiens]	51bSW2 Vis-en-Artois	O 3 c
Purdy Road [road]	36cSW2 Harnes	N 4 b, d, 5 a
Puresbecques, les [hamlet]	36aNE4 Merville	K 16 d
Purfleet [British salient]	62dNE2 Méaulte	F 2 b, 3 a
Purgatoire, le [farm]	27SE2 Berthen	R 23 c 97.80
Purgatory [lt rly locality 1918]	28SW2 Wytschaete	O 7 c 0.7
Purlin House	28SW1 Kemmel	N 27 c 00.75
Purnses, Tranchée des	62cSW1 & 2 Belloy	N 17 d, 18 c, 23 b
Purple Corner	20SE2 Hooglede	R 17 d 95.80
Purple Cut Off [1918]	51cSE [4 Blaireville]	X 27 d, 28 a, c
Purple Front Line [1918]	51cSE [4 Blaireville] / 57dNE [2 Fonquevillers]	X 22-3, 27-8, F 2, 3, 8, 9, 14, 20
Purple Reserve Line [1918]	51cSE [4 Blaireville]	X 25 b, d
Purple Reserve Line [1918]	57dNE1 & 2 Fonquevillers	E 12, 18, F 1, 7
Purple Support Line [1918]	51cSE [4 Blaireville] / 57dNE [2 Fonquevillers]	X 22-3, 27-8, F 2, 3, 8, 9, 14, 20
Pursuit Trench	66cNW2 Itancourt	B 30 d
Purvis Farms	36NW1 Steenwerck	B 2 d 35.10 & 45.30
Push Alley	57dNE3 & 4 Hébuterne	L 26 c, 31 b, d
Push Alley	57dSE2 & 57cSW1 Le Sars	M 26 d, 32 a, b
Push House	28NW1 Elverdinghe	G 3 a 1.4
Push Trench	36SW3 Richebourg	T 1 a, b, d
Push Trench	57cSE1 Bertincourt	P 9 d, 10 c
Putney [suburb of Vendhuile]	57bSW3 Honnecourt	S 26 b, d, 27 a, c
Putney Hill [Double Crassier]	36cSW1 Lens	M 4 d
Putney Trench	57cNE3 Hermies / 4 Marcoing	K 21 d, 22 c, 27 a, b
Putois Cross Roads	20SW4 Bixschoote	U 4 d 65.48
Puxton Cross [cross roads]	36aNE4 Merville	L 5 c 4.2
Puzeaux [village]	66dNW1 Punchy	A 24 a, b, c, d
Puzeaux Alley	66dNW1 Punchy	A 18 c, d
Puzeaux Wood	66dNW1 Punchy	A 24 d, B 19 c
Puzzle Wood	20SE3 Westroosebeke	V 17 a, b
Pylon Avenue	57dNE3 & 4 Hébuterne	K 21 a - 27 c
Pylon Trench	20NW4 Dixmude	I 21 d, 27 a, b, c, d

Name	Map Sheet	Map Reference
Pylone Woods No.1	62cSW1 Dompierre	M 8 b, d
Pylone Woods No.2	62cSW1 Dompierre	M 8 d
Pylone Woods No.3	62cSW1 Dompierre	M 8 d
Pylone Woods No.4	62cSW1 Dompierre	M 8 c
Pylones Trench	51bNW1 Roclincourt	A 3 a
Pylons, The [Tower Bridge]	36cNW3 Loos	G 36 a
Pyne Farm	28NE4 Dadizeele	K 36 b 4.9
Pypegaale	20SW3 Oostvleteren	T 14 d
Pypegaale Old Mill	20SW3 Oostvleteren	T 14 d
Pypegaale Redoubt	20SW3 Oostvleteren	T 14 d, 15 c
Pyrenees Trench [Pyrénées, Boyau des]	36cSW1 Lens	M 19 d, 20 c
Pyritz Trench	57cSE3 Sorel-le-Grand	V 19 b, 20 a, c, d, 21 c, d, 27 b
Pyrmont Alley	70dNW2 Servais	C 8 c, d, 13 b, 14 a
Pys [Village]	57dSE2 & 57cSW1 Le Sars	M 1 d, 2 c
Pytchley [farm]	36NW1 Steenwerck	B 13 b 05.25
Pythagore Trench / Tranchée de Pythogore	62cSW3 & 4 Marchélepot	T 15 b, d, 16 c
Q [+ number, Ger trs., Aug 1915, Hooge & N]	28NW4 & NE3 Zillebeke	I 12, 18
Q 1 [trench, St Eloi]	28SW2 Wytschaete	O 2 c 8.8
Q 17 [Hooge, 1915]	28NW4 & NE3 Zillebeke	I 18 b
Q 2 [trench, St Eloi]	28SW2 Wytschaete	O 2 c 6.9
Q 3 [St Eloi]	28SW2 Wytschaete	O 2 b, d
Q 4 [trench, Voormezeele]	28SW2 Wytschaete	O 1 b 7.9
Q Camp	28NW1 Elverdinghe	G 5 b, 6 a
Q Trenches [+ no, 7/15, Br, Sanctuary Wood]	28NW4 & NE3 Zillebeke	I 18, 24
Quack Trench, & Support	57cSE1 Bertincourt	Q 21 c, d
Quad Farm	28SW2 Wytschaete	O 30 d 3.9
Quadrangle Avenue	57cSE1 Bertincourt	Q 7 b, 8 a, c, d
Quadrangle Cemetery	57dSE4 Ovillers	X 33 b
Quadrangle Reserve	57cSE1 Bertincourt	Q 1 a, c
Quadrangle Support	57dSE4 Ovillers	X 17 c, 23 a, b, 24 a
Quadrangle Trench	57cSE1 Bertincourt	Q 8 b, d, 9 a, c
Quadrangle Trench [Zwischenstellung]	57dSE4 Ovillers	X 22 b, d, 23 c, d
Quadrangle Wood	57dSE4 Ovillers	X 23 c
Quadrangle, The	28SE3 Comines	V 13 d
Quadrangle, The [wood]	57dSE4 Ovillers	X 23 c 9.2
Quadrilateral	36cNW3 Loos	G 17 b, 18 a
Quadrilateral	57dNE1 & 2 Fonquevillers	E 5 a
Quadrilateral [E of Ginchy]	57cSW3 Longueval	T 14 d, 15 c
Quadrilateral [German position, May 1915]	36SW3 Richebourg	S 21 b
Quadrilateral [Le Touquet; 1915]	36NW2 & NE1 Houplines	C 10 b
Quadrilateral [NNW of Zandvoorde]	28NE3 Gheluvelt	J 32 b, d, 33 a, c
Quadrilateral [Tower Hamlets]	28NE3 Gheluvelt	J 27 a
Quadrilateral Redoubt [Heidenkopf]	57dNE3 & 4 Hébuterne	K 35 a, c
Quadrilateral, The	62bSW3 St Quentin	S 3 d, 4 a, c
Quadrilateral, The [March 1915]	36SW1 Aubers	M 30 a
Quadrilateral, The [NW of Le Sars]	57dSE2 & 57cSW1 Le Sars	M 8 d, 14 b
Quadroon Corner [road jct]	28NE2 Moorslede	E 10 c 17.99
Quaestraete [Queer Street]	27SE1 St Sylvestre	P 7 a
Quaff Avenue [Havrincourt Wood]	57cSE1 Bertincourt	Q 13 a, b, 14 a
Quaff Lane	57cSE1 Bertincourt	Q 8 d
Quaff Support	57cSE1 Bertincourt	Q 8 d, 14 b
Quaff Trench	57cSE1 Bertincourt	Q 14 b, d, 15 a
Quail Lane	57cSE4 Villers-Guislain	X 29 d
Quail Quarry	57cSE4 Villers-Guislain	X 29 d

Name	Map Sheet	Map Reference
Quake Post	57cSE1 Bertincourt	Q 19 c
Quake Trench	57cSE1 Bertincourt	Q 19 c, 25 a
Quaker Alley [1918]	57dSE1 & 2 Beaumont	Q 22 b, 23 a
Quality Keep East	36cNW3 Loos	G 27 d
Quality Keep North	36cNW3 Loos	G 27 b
Quality Keep South	36cNW3 Loos	G 33 b
Quality Street	36cNW3 Loos	G 27 c, d
Quality Street	36NW2 Armentières	I 4 a
Quality Trench	57cSE1 Bertincourt	Q 15 c, 21 a, c
Quarante, Bois [Bayern Wald]	28SW2 Wytschaete	O 7 a, b, c, d
Quarantine Farm	28SE2 Menin	Q 10 a 5.2
Quarries [German position, W of St Elie]	36cNW3 Loos	G 12 a
Quarries [St Quentin Wood]	62cSE4 [Attilly]	R 35 d, X 5 b
Quarries Alley	36cNW1 La Bassée / 3 Loos	G 3 b, c
Quarries Road [road]	36cSW4 Rouvroy	T 10 d, 11 a, c, 16 b, c, d
Quarries Trench	51bNW1 Roclincourt	A 3 a
Quarries, The	57dNE3 & 4 Hébuterne	K 15 d, 21 b
Quarries, The [N of Grand Seraucourt]	66cNW1 Grugies	A 27 c
Quarry [at Tergnier]	66cSW3 Tergnier	T 13 a, b
Quarry [trench]	36cSW3 Vimy	S 27 a
Quarry Alley	66cNW2 Itancourt	C 19 d
Quarry Alley	66cSW4 La Fère	T 24 c, d
Quarry Alley / Boyau, & Loop [G 4 a]	36cNW1 La Bassée	G 3 b, 4 a, b
Quarry Bay	36cNW3 Loos	G 12 c
Quarry Brae	57dSE4 Ovillers	X 1 c, d
Quarry Camp	28SW1 Kemmel	M 21 b, 22 a
Quarry Cemetery	57cSW3 Longueval	S 22 c 0.6
Quarry Lane	51bSW4 Bullecourt	T 18 b
Quarry Lane [trench]	62cNW2 Bouchavesnes	C 11 c, d, 16 b, 17 a
Quarry Locality [Fouquières]	36bNE2 Beuvry	E 21 b, 22 a, b, c, d
Quarry Post	57cSE2 Gonnelieu	R 29 d
Quarry Post	57dSE4 Ovillers	X 1 c
Quarry Post Cemetery	57dNE3 & 4 Hébuterne	K 7 a 4.8
Quarry Ravine	62bNW3 Bellicourt	G 8 d, 9 c, d, 14 b, 15 a
Quarry Redoubt [S of Contescourt]	66cNW1 Grugies	A 27 d
Quarry Redoubt [Tergnier Redoubt]	66cSW3 Tergnier	T 13 a, b, c
Quarry Road [road]	28SW3 Bailleul / 4 Ploegsteert	T 27 b, d, 28 a
Quarry Street	51cSE & 51bSW Ficheux	R 26 d, 27 c, d
Quarry Street	62dNE2 Méaulte	F 9 d
Quarry Trench	36cSW1 Lens	M 3 d
Quarry Trench	57cSE2 Gonnelieu	R 28 d, 29 c
Quarry Trench	57dSE1 & 2 Beaumont	R 33 a, b
Quarry Trench	62cNW2 Bouchavesnes	C 11 d
Quarry Trench	66cSW2 Vendeuil	O 19 a, c, d, 25 b, 26 a, c
Quarry Trench	66dNW1 Punchy	A 5 c, d, 11 a, b
Quarry Trench [S of The Window]	36cNW3 Loos	G 5 d
Quarry Trenches [Hell Quarry]	51bSW2 Vis-en-Artois	O 21 b, d, 22 a, c
Quarry Wood	51bNW4 Fampoux	I 28 b
Quarry Wood	57cNE1 Quéant	E 9 b, 10 a, c
Quarry Wood	62bNW3 Bellicourt	G 8 c
Quart Farm	27SE1 St Sylvestre	Q 27 b 15.85
Quash Farm	36NW1 Steenwerck	G 2 b 6.5
Quatorze, Bois de	36cNW3 Loos	H 27 a, c
Quatre Rois Cabaret, Les	28SW4 Ploegsteert	O 35 c 8.3

Name	Map Sheet	Map Reference
Quatre Vents [farm]	57cSE3 Sorel-le-Grand	P 34 c 9.7
Quatre Vents, les [cross roads & hamlet]	36aSE4 Locon	X 22 c 9.1
Quay Avenue	57cSE1 Bertincourt / 3 Sorel-le-Grand	Q 31 c, d, 32 a, c
Quay Trench	57cSE1 Bertincourt / 3 Sorel-le-Grand	Q 32 a, c, d
Quéant [village]	57cNE1 Quéant	D 1 d, 2 c, d, 7 b, 8 a
Quéant Tower (In Ruins)	57cNE1 Quéant	D 8 c
Quéant-Drocourt Line / Switch [see D-Q]	36cSE / 51bNW / 51bSE	extensive
Quéant-Drocourt Support Line [see D-Q]	36cSE / 51bNW / 51bSE	extensive
Quebec [Trench]	36NW2 Armentières	C 29 c
Quebec Avenue	28SW4 Ploegsteert	U 14 a, b
Quebec Camp	28NW3 Poperinghe	G 35 c
Quebec Farm	28NE1 Zonnebeke	D 1 b 4.7
Quebec Road [road]	36cSW3 Vimy / 4 Rouvroy	N 33 c, d, 34 c, T 4 a, b
Quebec Trench	36cSW4 Rouvroy	T 16 a, b, c, d, 17 a, c, d, 23 b
Queen Avenue [1918]	28SW1 Kemmel	M 26 b, 27 a, c, d, 33 b, 34 a
Queen Copse	57dSW [3 Talmas]	S 23 a, c
Queen Lane	57cSE2 Gonnelieu	Q 5 d, 11 b
Queen Mary Road [road]	36SW3 Richebourg	S 2 c, 8 a
Queen Street	36cNW1 La Bassée	A 15 c
Queen Street	36cSW1 Lens	M 5 a
Queen Street	36NW4 Bois Grenier	I 15 c
Queen Trench	28SW1 Kemmel	M 20 d, 26 b, 27 a, c, d
Queen Trench	51bNW2 Oppy	B 6 c, 12 a
Queen Victoria Street	28SW2 Wytschaete	O 1 b, 2 a, c
Queen Victoria Street	62cNW1 Maricourt	A 9 c, d, 15 b
Queen's / Queens Road	62dNE2 Méaulte	F 11 d
Queen's Avenue	36NW4 Bois Grenier	I 15 c, 21 a
Queen's Avenue	57dSE4 Ovillers / 62dNE2 Méaulte	X 26 c, F 2 a, b
Queen's Avenue [junction with FL, Aug 1915]	36NW4 Bois Grenier	I 31 c 3.6
Queens Cross	57dSE1 & 2 Beaumont	R 25 a
Queens Cross Redoubt	57dSE1 & 2 Beaumont	Q 28 d, 34 b
Queens Gate	28SW2 Wytschaete	N 28 a, b
Queens Lane	51bSW4 Bullecourt	U 19 b, 20 a
Queen's Lane [Sept 1915]	36cNW3 Loos	G 10 b, 11 a
Queen's Nullah	57dSE4 Ovillers	X 29 d
Queen's Redoubt [Ouvrage Bouzinger]	62dNE2 Méaulte	F 2 a 35.35
Queens Road	36cNW1 La Bassée	A 9 c, 14 b
Queens Road [military road]	28NW1 Elverdinghe	H 3 a, b, 4 a
Queen's Street	62cNW1 Maricourt	A 8 c, d
Queens Trench [High Wood]	57cSW3 Longueval	S 4 c, d
Queensland Road	36NW2 Armentières	C 28 c, d
Queer Street	36NW4 Bois Grenier	I 31 a, c
Queer Street	51bSE3 Cagnicourt	V 17, 18, 22, 23, 27, 28
Queer Street [later Inclement Alley; Ger tr]	36NW4 Bois Grenier	I 21 d, 22 c
Queer Street [Quaestraete]	27SE1 St Sylvestre	P 7 a
Queer Street [road]	36NW4 Bois Grenier	I 21 a, b, 22 a
Quémart (N) [Tranchée, 1915, La Boisselle]	57dSE4 Ovillers	X 19 b
Quémart (S) [Tranchée, 1915, La Boisselle]	57dSE4 Ovillers	X 20 a, c
Quemont Street	57dSE4 Ovillers	X 19 b
Quenaou [Tranchée, 1915] / Arbroath Street	57dSE4 Ovillers	X 20 c
Quenesson Farm	51bNE4 Cantin	L 28 a 4.6
Quennemont Farm	62bNW1 Gouy	A 20 c 4.3
Quennemont Trench	62bNW1 Gouy	A 20 c, 26 b, d, G 2 b
Quennet Copse	62bNW1 Gouy	A 19 d

Name	Map Sheet	Map Reference
Quennet High Trench	62cNE2 Epéhy	F 24 c; F 30 a
Quennet Low Trench	62cNE2 Epéhy	F 30 a
Quentin Alley	57cSE4 Villers-Guislain	R 31 c
Quentin Mill [Gouzeaucourt]	57cSE4 Villers-Guislain	R 31 d 10.25
Quentin Redoubt	57cSE4 Villers-Guislain	X 1 b
Quentin Ridge	57cSE4 Villers-Guislain	R 31 b, d, 32 a, b, c
Quer Graben III	57dSE4 Ovillers	X 14 b, 15 a
Quergraben	66dNW3 Hattencourt	G 8 b, c
Query Camp	28NW3 Poperinghe	G 11 a 2.3
Query Farm	28NW3 Poperinghe	G 11 a 2.2
Quesnoy Farm	57dNE1 & 2 Fonquevillers	F 14 a
Quesnoy Trench [1918]	57dNE1 & 2 Fonquevillers	F 10 a
Queue de Vache [farm]	27SE2 Berthen	Q 11 d 10.95
Queue de Vache Line	27SE2 Berthen	extensive
Quibble Trench, Switch & Post	57cSE1 Bertincourt	Q 19 b, c, d, 25 b
Quick Trench	57dNE4 & 57cNW3 Achiet	G 13 d, 14 c, 19 b, 20 a
Quid Copse	62cNE2 Epéhy	F 15 a
Quid Farm	27NE1 Herzeele	E 15 d 2.3
Quid Post	62cNE2 Epéhy	F 14 b, 15 a
Quiery-le-Vert [hamlet / farm]	66eNW [4 Morisel]	I 29 c
Quill Trench	62bNW3 Bellicourt	I 227 d, 9 c
Quimper Trench	66cNW3 Essigny / 4 Berthenicourt	H 22 c, 27 b, d, 28 a
Quincaillerie [Rouvroy-en-Santerre]	66eNE4 Beaufort	L 9 a
Quinconce [railway locality & dump 1917-18]	62cNW4 Péronne	I 20 a, b, c, d
Quinconce, le [place name]	62cNW4 Péronne	I 21 c
Quinine Lane	57dSE4 Ovillers	X 26 b, 27 a, c
Quinneys Avenue	57cSE2 Gonnelieu	Q 16 a, b, c, d
Quinny's [farm]	36NW1 Steenwerck	A 29 a 66.60
Quinque Trench, & Crossing [S 22 c]	36SW3 Richebourg	S 22 a, c
Quinquebus	36SW4 Sainghin	O 34 d 9.2
Quinquine, Tranchée du	66eNE4 Beaufort	L 22 a, b, c
Quinten/Quintin/Quinlan [Poperinghe, rly sidings]	28NW3 Poperinghe	G 7 b, d
Quiquery [hamlet]	66dNW4 Nesle	I 21 d
Quit Lane [trench]	57cSE1 Bertincourt	Q 27 a
Quit Support	36cNW1 La Bassée	A 3 a
Quito Farm	27NE4 Abeele	K 11 a 4.3
Quiver Farm	27SE1 St Sylvestre	Q 14 d 4.4
Quivering Support	57cSE1 Bertincourt	Q 26 a, b
Quivering Trench	57cSE1 Bertincourt	Q 26 b, d, 32 a, b
Quorn Farm	27SE1 St Sylvestre	Q 21 a 2.3
Quorn Street [trench]	57cNE4 Marcoing	K 18 a, c, d
Quotient Avenue	57cSE1 Bertincourt	Q 13, 14, 20
Quotient Lane	57cSE1 Bertincourt	Q 20 b, d, 21 c
Quotient Trench	57cSE1 Bertincourt	Q 21 c, 27 a
R 1 [Br trench, St Eloi, 1915]	28SW2 Wytschaete	O 2 d 5.9
R 18 [Br redoubt, late-1915, S side of Rly Wd]	28NW4 & NE3 Zillebeke	I 11 b 55.20
R 2 [Br trench, St Eloi, 1915]	28SW2 Wytschaete	O 2 a 7.5
R 20 [Br redoubt, late-1915, SE side of Rly Wd]	28NW4 & NE3 Zillebeke	I 11 b 7.3
R 3 [Br redoubt, late-1915, N side of Rly Wd]	28NW4 & NE3 Zillebeke	I 11 b 55.48
R 3 [Br trench, St Eloi, 1915]	28SW2 Wytschaete	O 2 d 3.9
R 4 [Br redoubt, late-1915, N of Y Wood]	28NW4 & NE3 Zillebeke	I 11 d 67.50
R 4 [Br trench, St Eloi, 1915]	28SW2 Wytschaete	O 2 a 8.4
R 5 [Br trench, St Eloi, 1915]	28SW2 Wytschaete	O 2 b 2.6
R 6 [Br redoubt, late-1915, Y Wood]	28NW4 & NE3 Zillebeke	I 11 d 70.65

Name	Map Sheet	Map Reference
R 7 [Br CT, June 1915]	28SW2 Wytschaete	I 31 d, 32 c, O 2 a
R 8 [Br trench, Voormezeele, 1915]	28NW4 & NE3 Zillebeke	I 31 d 9.2
R Line, The [Zouave Wood]	28NW4 & NE3 Zillebeke	I 18 c, d
R Redoubt [German, N of Givenchy, April 1915]	36cNW1 La Bassée	A 3, 9
R Works	62cNW1 Maricourt	A 28 a
R.1 Line / Stellung	57dNE4 & 57cNW3 Achiet	extensive
R.2 Line / Stellung	57cNW3 Bapaume / 57cSW1 Gueudecourt	extensive
R.A.F. Avenue [1918]	57dNE3 & 4 Hébuterne	L 1 c, 7 a
R.B. Trench [Rifle Brigade; St Eloi]	28SW2 Wytschaete	O 2 c
R.E. Alley	57cSW3 Longueval	S 16 d, 17 c
R.E. Farm	28SW1 Kemmel	N 15 c 1.5
R.E. Farm [later Shamus Farm]	28SW4 Ploegsteert	N 35 d 85.65
R.E. Farm Line [tr. tramway; Kemmel - La Polka]	28SW1 Kemmel	N 15 c, d, 21 b, 22 a
R.E. Lane / Trench	62bNW1 Gouy	A 8 c, 13 b
R.E. Park [rly sidings, Hersin]	36bSE2 Boyeffles	Q 11 d, 12 a, c
R.F.A. Cemetery	28NW4 Ypres	I 1 c
R.I.R Graveyard	36SW1 Aubers	M 12 c 5.8
R.I.R. Cemetery	36NW2 Armentières	C 2 d
R.N.D. Cemetery	57dSE2 Beaumont	Q 17 central
R.W.F. Sap	36cNW1 La Bassée	A 27 b
Rabbi Farm	20SE2 Hooglede	R 4 b 50.85
Rabbit Alley	57cNE1 Quéant	D 28 c, d, 29 a, c, J 3 b, 4 a
Rabbit Bank [1918]	51cSE4 Blaireville	X 19 c
Rabbit Hutch [house]	36aNE3 Haverskerque	J 32 b 25.12
Rabbit Lane	62dNE2 Méaulte	F 3 c
Rabbit Post	57cNE1 Quéant	D 28 b, d, 29 c
Rabbit Support	57cNE1 Quéant	D 22 d, 28 b, 29 a, c
Rabbit Warren [Sept 1915]	36cNW1 La Bassée	A 9 a
Rabbit Wood	51cSE4 Blaireville	X 19 d, 25 b
Rabecaigne Ravine	57bSW2 Clary	O 2 d, 3 c, 8 b, 9 a
Rabelais, Tranchée de	66eNE4 Beaufort	L 22 b, c, d
Rabèque Avenue	36NW2 Armentières	C 3, 4, 8, 9
Rabhfriland Support	27SE4 Meteren	X 10 b, 11 a
Rabigeau / Rabineau Trench	36cSW3 Vimy	S 8 b, d
Rabot [hamlet]	36NW1 Steenwerck	B 7 d
Raby Street	36bSE4 Carency	X 23 a
Race Course Redoubt [S of Grugies]	66cNW1 Grugies	A 24 b
Race Trench	12SW1 Nieuport	N 19 c
Racecourse Farm	28NW2 St Julien	C 16 a 6.8
Racine [light rly loop, Ploegsteert Wood, 1917-18]	28SW4 Ploegsteert	U 20 b 2.6
Rack Support	51bSW4 Bullecourt	U 29 d
Rack Trench	51bNW1 Roclincourt	A 30 c
Racket Trench	57cSE2 Gonnelieu / 57bSW1 Bantouzelle	R 17 d, 18 c, 23 a, b, M 13 d
Racket Trench	57cSE4 Villers-Guislain	X 7 d, 13 b, d
Racket Wood	20SE3 Westroosebeke	V 24 b, W 19 a
Racquet Farm	20SE4 Roulers	Q 34 d 2.3
Radfahrer Graben	57dNE1 & 2 Fonquevillers	E 29, 30, K 4, 5, 6, L 1, 2
Radford Trench [1918]	57dNE2 [Fonquevillers] / 4 [Hébuterne]	L 2 a, b, d
Radio Farm	20SE3 Westroosebeke	V 9 c 9.0
Radley Road	62cNW1 Maricourt	A 9 a, b
Radomir Alley [Mt St Quentin, Hill 115]	62cNW4 Péronne	I 10 c, d, 15 b, 16 a
Rafia Farm	36aNE3 Haverskerque	K 20 d 00.15
Rag Farms	28SW3 Bailleul	S 16 b 5.2
Rag House	36SW1 Aubers	M 18 c 90.35

Name	Map Sheet	Map Reference
Rag Point [German strongpoint]	28SW2 Wytschaete	N 30 d 2.8
Rag Reserve [Rag Trench]	57cSE4 Villers-Guislain	X 16 b, 17 a
Rag Support [Cotton Trench]	57cSE4 Villers-Guislain	X 10 d, 11 c, 17 a
Rag Trench [Satin Trench]	57cSE4 Villers-Guislain	X 10 d, 11 c, 17 a
Ragged Trench	27SE4 Meteren	X 4 b, c, d, 5 a
Rags Post	36SW3 Richebourg	S 2 c 95.80
Rail Avenue	62cNW1 Maricourt	A 9, 14, 15
Rail C.T. / Trench [1918]	62dSW [2 Villers-Bretonneux / 4 Cachy]	O 36 c
Rail Trench	51bNW1 Roclincourt	A 30 c
Rail Trench	57dSE4 Ovillers	X 4 a
Rail Trench [1918]	57dNE3 & 4 Hébuterne	K 15 b, 16 a
Railhoek [rly sidings, W of Poperinghe]	27NE4 Abeele	L 5 c, d, 11 a, b
Railroad Alley	36cSW1 Lens	M 1, 7, 8, 9, 15
Railton [cross roads]	57cSE4 Villers-Guislain	W 22 b 90.95
Railway [light rly siding]	36cSW3 Vimy	S 3 a
Railway Alley	36bSE4 & 36cSW3 Givenchy	X 12 a, c, S 7 b
Railway Alley	36cNW1 La Bassée	G 2 b, 3 a, b, 4 a
Railway Alley	36cNW3 Loos	G 29 c, d, 30 c, d, 36 b, H 25 c
Railway Alley	51bNW1 Roclincourt / 2 Oppy	B 22 b, c, d, 23 a
Railway Alley	57dSE1 & 2 Beaumont	Q 18 b, R 7 c
Railway Alley	57dSE4 Ovillers	X 28 c, d, 29 c
Railway Avenue	36NW4 Bois Grenier	I 14 d, 20 b
Railway Avenue	57dNE3 & 4 Hébuterne	K 28 b, c, d, 29 a
Railway Barricade	36NW2 Armentières	C 4 d
Railway Bridge [across Ancre]	57dSE4 Ovillers	W 23 c 2.3
Railway Camp	28SW3 Bailleul	T 26 d
Railway Cliff [bank]	36cSW1 Lens	N 21 c, 27 a
Railway Copse	51bNW2 Oppy	C 27 b, d, 28 a, c
Railway Copse	51bSE2 Oisy-le-Verger / 4 Marquion	Q 34 c, d, W 4 b
Railway Copse	57dSE4 Ovillers	X 28 b
Railway Cottage	36cNW1 La Bassée	A 22 d
Railway Cottage	36cSW4 Rouvroy	U 1 c 7.1
Railway Dugouts	28NW4 & NE3 Zillebeke	I 20 d, 21 c
Railway Dump	28NE1 Zonnebeke	D 25 d 8.1
Railway Farm [July 1915]	36NW4 Bois Grenier	I 21 a 1.1
Railway Keep	36cNW1 La Bassée	G 3 a, b
Railway Loop	36bSE4 Carency	X 12 a, c
Railway Outposts [1918]	57dSE1 & 2 Beaumont	Q 35 a, b
Railway Post	57cSE2 Gonnelieu	Q 22 b
Railway Post [1918]	28NE1 Zonnebeke	D 25 c, J 1 a
Railway Redoubt, & Craters [A 28 c]	36cNW1 La Bassée	A 28 a, c
Railway Reserve	51bSW4 Bullecourt / 57cNW2 Vaulx-Vraucourt	U 27 c, d, C 4 b, 5 a
Railway Reserve Trench	36cNW1 La Bassée	G 3 b
Railway Ridge	62bNW1 Gouy	A 16 d, 17 c, d, 22 b, 23 a
Railway Road [road, Beaucourt-sur-Ancre]	57dSE1 & 2 Beaumont	Q 18 b, R 7 c
Railway Sign White Disc	36cNW3 Loos	G 9 a 1.5
Railway Street	28NW2 St Julien	B 12 c
Railway Street [military road / track 1917-18]	20SW4 Bixschoote / 28NW2 St Julien	U 12, 17, 18, 21, 22, 23, 26, 27, C 1, 2
Railway Support	51bNW2 Oppy	B 24 d
Railway Support	62bNW3 Bellicourt	G 7 b, d
Railway Switch	36NW2 Armentières	C 15 a, b, c
Railway Switch	51bNW3 Arras	G 24 d, H 19 a, b, c
Railway Trench	28NW4 & NE3 Zillebeke	I 36 c

Name	Map Sheet	Map Reference
Railway Trench	28SW2 Wytschaete	O 6 a
Railway Trench	51bNW2 Oppy	B 24 b, C 19 c
Railway Trench	51bNW3 Arras	H 13 d, 19 b
Railway Trench	51bSW4 Bullecourt	U 27 d, 28 c, d
Railway Trench	57cNE3 Hermies	K 21 c, 27 a, c
Railway Trench	57dSE1 & 2 Beaumont	R 1 c, 7a
Railway Trench	62bNW3 Bellicourt	G 7 b, d
Railway Trench [Sept. 1915]	36cNW1 La Bassée	A 27 b, 28 a
Railway Trench [W of Rly]	28SW2 Wytschaete	O 6 a, c
Railway Triangle	36cNW1 La Bassée	A 16 c, d
Railway Triangle	51bNW3 Arras	H 19 a, b, c, d
Railway Triangle Cemetery	51bNW3 Arras	H 19 c 5.8
Railway View [ravine]	57dSE1 & 2 Beaumont	Q 29 c, d
Railway Wood	28NW4 & NE3 Zillebeke	I 11 b
Railway Wood Howitzer Spur [railway, 1917-18]	28NW4 Ypres	I 11 b
Railway Wood Track (Duckboard) [1917-18]	28NW4 Ypres	I 11 b, d, 12 a
Rain Trench	51bNW1 Roclincourt	A 30 a, c
Rainbow Trench	57cSW1 Gueudecourt / 2 Villers-au-Flos	N 27 b, 28 a, c, d, 34 b
Rainy Corner [road jct]	28NE4 Dadizeele	L 19 b 25.55
Rainy Cross Roads	62dNW [3 Allonville]	G 3 d
Rainy Trench	57cSW4 Combles	N 34 c, d, T 4 b
Raisin Trench	20SW3 Oostvleteren	T 2 d, 8 b
Rake Trench	51bSW2 Vis-en-Artois	O 7 d, 13 b, d
Rally Support	27SE4 Meteren	X 5 c, d, 6 c, 11 a
Ralph Farm	27NE1 Herzeele	E 19 c 6.1
Ram Trench	51bNW1 Roclincourt	A 30 c
Ramicourt [village]	62bNW4 Ramicourt	H 5 c, d, 11 b, d
Rammer Farm	28SW3 Bailleul	M 32 d 7.4
Ramp Alley	62bSW3 St Quentin	T 3 a, d
Ramp Farm	27NE1 Herzeele	E 27 b 1.8
Ramp Trench	51bNW1 Roclincourt	A 30 c
Ramparts	28NW4 Ypres	I 8 b, d, 14 a, b, c, d
Ramparts Military Cemetery [Lille Gate]	28NW4 Ypres	I 14 a
Ramsay Corner	20SE3 Westroosebeke	W 14 d 1.4
Ramsay's / Ramsey's Hill [hill]	28SW2 Wytschaete	N 28 c, d, 29 a, 34 a, b
Rancourt [village]	57cSW4 Combles / 62cNW2 Bouchavesnes	U 25 d, 26 c, C 1a, b, c, d, 2 a
Rancourt Copse	57bSW3 Honnecourt	N 35 c
Rancourt Farm	57bSW3 Honnecourt	S 4 d 0.0
Rand Trench	57dSE4 Ovillers	X 2 c, d, 8 a
Range Wood	57bNW1 Cambrai / 3 Rumilly	G 1 b, d, 2 a, c
Ranger Trench	57cSW3 Longueval	T 15 d, 16 c
Rangers Trench [Sept 1915]	36SW3 Richebourg	S 15 b, 16 a
Rangoon [lt rly spur, Ploegsteert Wd, 1917-18]	28SW4 Ploegsteert	U 20 b 5.3
Rank Buildings	28SW3 Bailleul	S 27 a 6.4
Rank Post	12SW1 Nieuport	N 26 a
Rank Trench	12SW1 Nieuport	N 26 d
Ransart [village]	51cSE4 Blaireville	X 7 b, d, 8 c
Ransome Trench	57dSE1 & 2 Beaumont	R 19 d, 20 c
Raoul Trench / Tranchée Raoul	62cSW2 Barleux	O 3 c, d, 9 a, c
Rap Trench	51bNW1 Roclincourt	A 30 c
Raperie Alley	66dNW1 Punchy	A 16 a, b, c, 15 d
Raperie Switch [SW of Ronssoy]	62cNE2 Epéhy	F 20, 25, 26
Rapier Trench	57cSE2 Gonnelieu	R 17 a, b, 18 a
Rapiere Trench	66cNW4 Berthenicourt	I 26 a

Name	Map Sheet	Map Reference
Rapture Trench	57cSE2 Gonnelieu	R 29 b
Rasée, Ferme	20SW4 Bixschoote	N 34 c 1.7
Rasputin [light rly spur, Ploegsteert Wd, 1917-18]	28SW4 Ploegsteert	U 20 a 4.6
Rasputin Salient	70dNW2 Servais	C 19 a, c, d
Rasta, Maison de/du [pillbox]	28NW2 St Julien	C 5 a 75.10
Rat Alley	28NW4 & NE3 Zillebeke	I 34 b
Rat Farm	28NW2 St Julien	C 23 b 9.2
Rat Farm [pillbox group]	28NW2 St Julien	C 23 b, 24 a
Rat Hole / Rathole	62dNE2 Méaulte	F 11 d 80.15
Rat House [Langemarck]	20SW4 Bixschoote	U 29 b 85.15
Rat Keep [1918; at Rat Farm]	28NW2 St Julien	C 23 b 90.13
Rat Lane	51bSW1 Neuville Vitasse	N 13 b, 14 a
Rat Pit [Bovril Alley, Angres]	36bSE2 Boyeffles / 36cSW1 Lens	R 11, 17, 18, M 19, 20
Rat Post	57cNE1 Quéant	D 28 b
Rat Trench	51bNW1 Roclincourt	A 30 c
Rat Trench	62cNE4 Roisel	L 6 c
Rat Trench [originally Russian Sap/commn. tunnel]	57dNE3 & 4 Hébuterne	K 34 d
Rat Trench, & Post	12SW1 Nieuport	M 24 d
Rat Wood	62dSE [1 Hamel]	Q 24 b
Rathlin Reserve	27SE4 Meteren	R 34 d
Ratinau Trench	66cSW2 Vendeuil	N 24 d, O 19 a, c
Ration Corner [1915]	36NW3 Fleurbaix	H 33 c 3.6
Ration Dump	28NW4 Ypres	I 16 d 6.6
Ration Dump [Ration Farm]	28SW4 Ploegsteert	T 12 a
Ration Farm	36NW4 Bois Grenier	I 19 b 9.4
Ration Farm [Wulverghem]	28SW4 Ploegsteert	T 12 a 55.20
Ration Spur [light rly sidings, 1917-18]	28NW4 Ypres	I 15 d
Ration Trench	28SW4 Ploegsteert	U 8 d
Ration Trench	36bSE4 & 36cSW3 Givenchy	R 36 c, X 6 a, M 31 b
Ration Trench [Gierich Weg]	57dSE4 Ovillers	R 33 c, d, X 2 b, 3 a
Rats Alley	66cNW4 Berthenicourt	I 28 c
Rats, Boyau des	62cSW1 Dompierre	M 10 b
Rattekot	27NE4 Abeele	K 16 b
Rattekot Custom House	27NE4 Abeele	K 16 d 5.3
Rattekot Inn	27NE4 Abeele	K 16 b 75.80
Raulieu Alley	66cNW1 Grugies / 2 Itancourt	B 16 a, c, d
Raulieu, le [hamlet & wood]	66cNW2 Itancourt	B 10 c, d
Rause, Cse. du [farm]	36aSE4 Locon	X 23 a 8.9
Ravelaere Avenue	20SW3 Oostvleteren	T 3 c, d, 8 b, 9 a
Ravelaere Bridge	20SW3 Oostvleteren	T 8 a 95.30
Ravelaere Farm	20SW3 Oostvleteren	T 8 b 6.5
Ravelsberg [hill & hamlet]	28SW3 Bailleul	S 16 d
Ravelsberg Camp	28SW3 Bailleul	S 17 central
Ravelsberg Rest Station	28SW3 Bailleul	S 16 d
Ravelsberg Road [road]	28SW3 Bailleul	S 15 c, d, 16 c, d, 17 b, c, d
Raven Lane	12SW1 Nieuport	N 19 c
Raven Trench	12SW1 Nieuport	N 19 c
Raven Trench	57cNE1 Quéant	D 28 c, d
Ravenna [hamlet]	27NE2 Proven	L 3 a, b
Ravin Alley	62bSW3 St Quentin	T 26 d
Ravin Alley	66cNW1 Grugies	B 2 b, c
Ravin Alley [1918]	66eNW [2 Thennes]	B 28 d, H 4 b
Ravine [Albert-Bapaume road NW of Le Barque]	57cSW1 Gueudecourt	M 6 b, d
Ravine [S of Beaumont Hamel]	57dSE1 & 2 Beaumont	Q 11 c, d

Name	Map Sheet	Map Reference
Ravine [south of Boom Ravine]	57dSE2 & 57cSW1 Le Sars	R 11 c, 17 a
Ravine Alley	66cSW4 La Fère	T 6 b, U 1 a, c, d
Ravine Avenue	57cNE4 Marcoing	K 24 b, c, d, 29 b, 30 a
Ravine Avenue / Boyau du Ravin	62cNW1 Maricourt	A 28 b
Ravine Copse	62dNE2 Méaulte	F 30 d
Ravine Copse [Redoubt]	62dNE2 Méaulte	L 6 a
Ravine Road [road]	28NE3 Gheluvelt	J 25 b, d
Ravine Shelters / Abris du Ravin	62cNW1 Maricourt	A 28 b
Ravine Track	28SW2 Wytschaete	O 14, 15
Ravine Wood	28NW4 & NE3 Zillebeke	I 34 a, b, c
Ravine Wood Cemetery	28NW4 & NE3 Zillebeke	I 34 a 7.9
Ravine Wood Dugout	28NW4 & NE3 Zillebeke	I 34 a
Ravine Wood Spurs [railway, 1917-18]	28NW4 Ypres	I 28 a
Ravine, The	28NE3 Gheluvelt	J 25 c
Ravine, The	28NW4 & NE3 Zillebeke	I 34 b
Ravine, The	57dSE2 & 57cSW1 Le Sars	R 11 c, 17 a
Ravka Trench	62cNE3 Buire	J 19 d, 20 b, c, d, 25 a, b
Ravoire Trench	62cSW2 Barleux	N 6 d, O 1 c
Rawson Camp	28SW3 Bailleul	T 20 a, c
Rawson Farm	28SW3 Bailleul	T 20 a 50.35
Rawson Trench	51bNW1 Roclincourt	A 16 a, c
Ray Trench	51bNW1 Roclincourt	A 30 c
Raymond Avenue	57dNE1 & 2 Fonquevillers	E 21 b, 22 c
Raymond Farm	28NE4 Dadizeele	L 7 d 3.6
Raymond Farm	28NW1 Elverdinghe	B 3 d 1.3
Razor Alley	66cNW1 Grugies	B 1 b, 2 a
Razor Wood	66dNW1 Punchy	B 19 a
Reading Fort [Hunter's Avenue]	28SW4 Ploegsteert	U 27 a
Reading Trench	28SW4 Ploegsteert	U 21 c, 27 a, b
Ream Farm	27NE1 Herzeele	E 27 a 25.10
Reaper Farm	36NW1 Steenwerck	B 26 d 7.6
Rëau, Boyau [SE end of Bovril Alley]	36cSW1 Lens	M 19 b, d, 20 c
Rebel Alley	66cNW4 Berthenicourt	I 34 a
Rebel Avenue	57cSE2 Gonnelieu	R 11 b, c, d, 16 b
Rebshank Avenue	27SE4 Meteren	X 5 d, 6 c, 11 b, 12 a
Record Wood	62dSE [1 Hamel]	P 12 a
Rectangle Support	62dNE2 Méaulte	F 9 b, 10 a
Rectangle, The	62dNE2 Méaulte	F 9 b
Rectory (Officers Quarters, Lovie Chateau)	27NE2 Proven	F 16
Rectory, The	28NE1 Zonnebeke	J 1 d 30.95
Red Chateau	28SW2 Wytschaete	N 18 b 9.1
Red Copse	57bSW1 Bantouzelle	N 25 a
Red Cottage	57dNE3 & 4 Hébuterne	K 28 a 4.3
Red Cottage	62dNE2 Méaulte	F 3 a, b
Red Cross Corner	57cNW4 Beugny	I 20 b, 21 a
Red Cross Corner	57dSE4 Ovillers	X 9 b 7.6
Red Cross Farm	20SW4 Bixschoote	T 12 b 5.0
Red Cut [sunken road N of Le Barque]	57cSW1 Gueudecourt	N 1 a, c
Red Dog Dump	36NW3 Fleurbaix	H 33 d 90.65
Red Dragon Crater	36cNW1 La Bassée	A 9 d 7.5
Red Dyke Farm	20SE2 Hooglede	R 13 a 3.4
Red Estaminet	28SW4 Ploegsteert	U 15 b 2.9
Red Farm	28NW3 Poperinghe	G 5 d 95.20
Red Farm	28SW1 Kemmel	M 6 d

Name	Map Sheet	Map Reference
Red Farm [Bantouzelle]	57bSW1 Bantouzelle	M 26 b 9.1
Red Farm Military Cemetery	28NW3 Poperinghe	G 6 c 10.20
Red Farm Trench	66cSW4 La Fère	T 5 c, 11 a, c, 10 d
Red Flag	36cNW3 Loos	G 22 a
Red Hand Avenue	28SW2 Wytschaete	N 36 a
Red Hand Reserve	27SE4 Meteren	X 4 a, b
Red Horse Farm	28NW3 Poperinghe	G 28 b 5.3
Red Horse-Shoe Camp	28NW3 Poperinghe	G 28 a, b, c
Red House	36cNW1 La Bassée	A 9 a 6.4
Red House	36NE3 Perenchies	J 23 c 1.9
Red House	36NW2 & NE1 Houplines	C 4 d 2.3
Red House	51bNW3 Arras / 4 Fampoux	H 4 c
Red House	57bNE2 Vendegies	E 17 c 2.7
Red House [Givenchy, April 1915]	36cNW1 La Bassée	A 2, 8
Red House [Laventie sector]	36SW1 Aubers	M 6 d 25.05
Red House [Le Pelerin]	28SW4 Ploegsteert	U 21 b 4.4
Red House Post	36NW4 Bois Grenier	H 24 b
Red Lamp Corner / Lamp Corner	36SW1 Aubers	N 13 d
Red Line	28NE3 Gheluvelt	J 5 a
Red Line	51bNW2 Oppy	B 23 a
Red Line Trench	51bNW2 Oppy	B 28 d
Red Lion [Trench]	36cSW3 Vimy	S 15 d, 21 b
Red Lodge	28NE3 Gheluvelt	J 1 c 5.2
Red Lodge	28SW4 Ploegsteert	T 18 d 60.45
Red Mill	20SW4 Bixschoote	U 13 c
Red Mill	36cSW1 Lens	M 27 d 7.8
Red Patch [Hindenburg Line]	51bSW4 Bullecourt	U 27 b
Red Road [track: Citadel-Morlancourt]	62dNE2 Méaulte / 4 [Bray-sur-Somme]	K 8 b to F 21 b
Red Rock [light rly locality, 1917]	28SW1 Kemmel	N 1 a
Red Rose Camp	28NW3 Poperinghe	H 1 d, 2 c
Red Support	36cSW3 Vimy	S 5 d, 11 b, 12 a
Red Tile House	36NW2 Armentières	C 10 b
Red Tile House [Le Touquet]	36NW2 & NE1 Houplines	C 10 b 6.3
Red Trench	36cSW3 Vimy	S 5 d, 12 a, b, T 7 a, b, a
Red Trench	51bNW1 Roclincourt	A 30 c
Red Trench	57dSE4 Ovillers	R 34 c
Red Trench, Lane & Cottage	62dNE2 Méaulte	F 3 a
Red Wood	62bNW3 Bellicourt / SW1 Gricourt	G 31 d, M 1 b
Redan Avenue	28SW2 Wytschaete	N 36 a
Redan Farm	28NW2 St Julien	B 22 d 1.8
Redan Lane, & Post	62cNE2 Epéhy	F 30 c
Redan Ridge	57dNE3 & 4 Hébuterne	K 34 d, Q 4 b
Redan Wood	28SW1 Kemmel	M 24 c
Redeemed Huts	20SW4 Bixschoote	U 30 a
Redoubt A / Réduit A	62dNE2 Méaulte	F 14 b
Redoubt Alley	57dSE1 & 2 Beaumont	Q 7 a, 12 b, d
Redoubt Alley North	36SW3 Richebourg	S 28 c, d, 29 c, d
Redoubt Alley South	36cNW1 La Bassée	S 28 c, 5 a
Redoubt de l'Arbre [Br, S of Somme, 1915]	62cNW3 Vaux / 62cSW1 Becquincourt	G 34 a
Redoubt du Bois Vierge [Br, S of Somme, 1915]	62cNW3 Vaux	G 28 d, 34 b
Redoubt Farm	28SW2 Wytschaete	N 12 b 90.95
Redoubt Road [trench]	36bSE4 Carency	X 17 c, d, 18 c, 23 a
Redring Farm	28NE4 Dadizeele	L 20 c 45.65
Reduit d'Eclusier [Br, S of Somme, 1915]	62cNW3 Vaux	G 21, 22

Name	Map Sheet	Map Reference
Réduit, Boyau du [Redoubt]	62cSW1 Dompierre	M 4 b
Reed Alley	57cSE2 Gonnelieu	R 17 b, d
Reed Trench	51bNW1 Roclincourt	A 30 c
Reef Trench	51bNW1 Roclincourt	A 30 c
Reel Trench	51bNW1 Roclincourt	A 30 c
Reel Trench [1918]	57dNE2 [Fonquevillers]	L 2 b
Refuse Trench	27SE4 Meteren	X 4 d
Regal Lodge [house]	36aNE4 Merville	L 9 b 4.6
Regent Avenue	36NW2 Armentières	C 3 b, d, 4 a
Regent Circus	57dNE3 & 4 Hébuterne	K 34 d
Regent Crater	57cSE2 Gonnelieu	Q 4 d
Regent Dugouts [Kemmel Defences]	28SW2 Wytschaete	N 29 c 3.0 - 3.3
Regent Dump	28SW2 Wytschaete	N 29 c
Regent Flats Dugouts	28NW4 & NE3 Zillebeke	I 17 d
Regent Fort [Hunter's Avenue]	28SW4 Ploegsteert	U 20 c, d
Regent Lane	57cSE2 Gonnelieu	Q 12 a
Regent Line [tr. tramway; Lindenhoek-Store Farm]	28SW2 Wytschaete	N 27 d, 28 b, c, d, 29 a
Regent Street	28NW4 & NE3 Zillebeke	I 17 b, d, 18 a
Regent Street	28SW4 Ploegsteert	U 20 c, d
Regent Street	36cSW1 Lens	M 5 b, d, 6 a, b, c
Regent Street	36NW4 Bois Grenier	I 25 d, 26 c
Regent Street	36SW1 Aubers	M 12 d, N 7 c, 13 a
Regent Street	57dNE1 & 2 Fonquevillers	E 21 b, 22 c
Regent Street	57dSE1 & 2 Beaumont	Q 17 a, c
Regent Street [CT]	28SW2 Wytschaete	N 28 c, d, 29 c
Regent Street [Delville Wood]	57cSW3 Longueval	S 12 c, 18 a
Regent Street [Ploeg. Wood 1914-15]	28SW4 Ploegsteert	U 19 c, d, 20 c, d
Regent Street [road; Lovie Chateau]	27NE2 Proven	F 16 c, d
Regent Street [Sept 1915]	36cNW1 La Bassée	A 21 b
Regent Street [Sept 1915]	36cNW1 La Bassée	A 9 c
Regent Street Dugouts	28SW2 Wytschaete	N 29 c 4.2 to 5.5; N 29 c 4.3
Regent Street East	28NW4 & NE3 Zillebeke	I 17 d, 18 a
Regent Street Line [light railway 1917]	28SW1 Kemmel	N 27 c, d, 28 c
Regent Street Villa [Ploegsteert Wood]	28SW4 Ploegsteert	U 20 d 8.7
Regent Street West	28NW4 & NE3 Zillebeke	I 17 b, d
Regent Tram [light rly]	28SW2 Wytschaete	N 28 b, c, d, 29 a, c
Regent Trench	36cNW1 La Bassée / 3 Loos	A 30 d, G 6 b, H 1 a, b, d, 2 c
Regent Trench	51bNW4 Fampoux	I 22 b, d, 28 b, d
Regent Work	51bNW4 Fampoux	I 22 b, 23 a, c
Reggie Post [La Boutillerie]	36SW2 Radinghem	N 6 b
Reghier le Clerc [hamlet]	36aNE4 Merville	K 34 d, 35 c
Regiment Battle H.Q. [German]	36SW3 Richebourg	S 29 d
Regiments Weg	51bNW1 Roclincourt	B 19 b, d, 25 b
Regina Avenue	28SW4 Ploegsteert	U 7 d
Regina Cross	28NW2 St Julien	C 11 a 5.7
Regina Cut Off	28SW4 Ploegsteert	U 7 c, d
Regina Trench	57dSE2 & 57cSW1 Le Sars	R 21 a, b, 22 a, b, 23 a
Reginald Wood	62dSE [1 Hamel]	Q 14 d, 20 b
Regnault Redoubt [1918]	66eNW [2 Thennes]	B 17 c, d
Regulus Alley / Boyau de Régulus	66dNW3 Hattencourt / 66eNE4 Beaufort	G 25 d, 32 a, L 29 d, 30 c
Reid Farm	20SE3 Westroosebeke	V 3 d 90.75
Reid's Alley	57cSW3 Longueval	S 1 d
Reigersburg	28NW2 St Julien	H 6 b
Reigersburg Chateau	28NW2 St Julien	H 6 b

Name	Map Sheet	Map Reference
Reigersburg Railhead / Refilling Point	28NW2 St Julien	H 5 d, 6 c
Reindeer Post	57cNE4 Marcoing	K 11 a 2.5
Reine Alley	62cSW3 Vermandovillers	S 3 d, 4 c, d
Rêitres Farm	20SW4 Bixschoote	U 22 c 9.2
Relève Avenue	20SW4 Bixschoote	T 23 d
Relève House	20SW4 Bixschoote	T 23 d 4.5
Relic Farm	27NE2 Proven	L 5 b 1.9
Relief House	51bNW3 Arras	H 32 c 85.37
Rembrant [sic] Buildings	28NE2 Moorslede	F 24 c 25.23
Remigny [village]	66cSW1 Remigny	N 13, 14
Remirement Alley	66cNW4 Berthenicourt	H 6 d
Rempart Mill	20SW3 Oostvleteren	T 27 b
Remus Wood	28NE1 Zonnebeke	D 28 d, 29 c
Remy [village]	51bSW2 Vis-en-Artois	O 18 b, c, d
Remy Lane [road]	51bSW2 Vis-en-Artois	O 11 c, 17 a, b, c
Remy Railhead / Refilling Point	27NE4 Abeele	L 22 b, d, 23 a, c
Remy Siding [railway]	27NE4 Abeele	L 22 b, d, 23 a, c
Remy Valley	51bSW2 Vis-en-Artois	O 17 d, 18 c, 23 a, b
Remy Wood	51bSW2 Vis-en-Artois	O 18 a, c
Renard Farm	20SW4 Bixschoote	O 35 c 90.05
Renaud Trench	66cNW1 Grugies	B 15 a
Rendal / Rendall Avenue	57cSW3 Longueval	S 9 c
Renfrew Road	51cSE3 & 4 Ransart	W 11 d, 17 b
Reninghelst [village]	28NW3 Poperinghe	G 34 a, b, d
Reninghelst Line [1918]	28NW3 Poperinghe	G 28, 29, 32, 33, 34
Reninghelst Road [railway sidings]	28NW3 Poperinghe	G 21 a, b, c
Rennes Trench	66cNW4 Berthenicourt	H 18 d
Rennet Farm	36aNE4 Merville	K 16 b 7.4
Rennie Trench	57dSE4 Ovillers	R 35 d, X 5 b
Reno Farm	27NE4 Abeele	K 23 c 2.1
Renoal [Tranchée, 1915, La Boisselle]	57dSE4 Ovillers	X 19 b, d
Renty Farm	28SW2 Wytschaete	O 13 b 95.55
Repair Alley	66cNW1 Grugies / 2 Itancourt	B 10 a
Reply Alley	66cNW1 Grugies / 2 Itancourt	B 10 a
Report Mill	27SE2 Berthen	R 15 a 5.3
Repos des Voyageurs, Au [Estaminet, Ploegsteert]	28SW4 Ploegsteert	U 19 b 65.95
Reptile [light rly spur, Ploegsteert Wood, 1917-18]	28SW4 Ploegsteert	U 19 a 5.0
Reptiles Alley	66cNW4 Berthenicourt	I 28 a
Requete Farm	20SE3 Westroosebeke	V 14 c
Rerner Alley	28SE3 Comines	W 1 d
Reserve Avenue	36NW2 Armentières	C 8 b, d, 9 c
Reserve Farm [Observation Farm]	36NW2 & NE1 Houplines	C 3 b 65.05
Reserve Line	27SE4 Meteren	W 11, 12, 16, 21, X 2, 3, 7, 8
Reserve Line	28SW2 Wytschaete	N 23 c, 29 a, b, d
Reserve Line	36cNW3 Loos	G 18 a, c
Reserve Line	36cSW1 Lens	M 3, 4, 9
Reserve Line	36SW2 Radinghem	N 5 b
Reserve Line	51bNW3 Arras	G 29 d
Reserve Line	51bSW1 Neuville Vitasse	M 4 a, c
Reserve Line	51cSE & 51bSW Ficheux	R 23, 24
Reserve Line	57cSE2 Gonnelieu / 4 Villers-Guislain	R 26, 32, 33, X 3
Reserve Line	57dSE2 & 57cSW1 Le Sars	N 25 b, d, 26 c, 32 b
Reserve Line [1918]	27SE4 Meteren	extensive
Reserve Line [1918]	36aNE1 Morbecque / 3 Haverskerque	E 3, 8, 9, 13, 14, 19, 25, 26, K 2

Name	Map Sheet	Map Reference
Reserve Line [late 1915]	36SW1 Aubers	M 23 b, c, d, 24 a
Reserve Machine Gunners House	36NW2 Armentières	C 9 c
Reserve Trench	28SW2 Wytschaete	N 29 a, b
Reserve Trench	36cNW1 La Bassée	A 3 a
Reserve Trench	36cNW3 Loos	G 18, 24, 30, 36
Reserve Trench	36SW3 Richebourg	S 27 c
Reserve Trench	51bSW4 Bullecourt	T 12 d
Reserve Trench	62dNE2 Méaulte	F 16 b, 17 a
Reserve Trench [Sept 1915]	36cNW1 La Bassée	G 3 b
Reserve Weg	51bNW1 Roclincourt	A 11 d
Reservoir Hill [Hill 65]	36cSW1 Lens	M 30 b, N 25 a
Resin House	36aNE1 Morbecque	D 17 d 0.5
Rest & Be Thankful Farm	28SW1 Kemmel / 2 Wytschaete	N 15, 16
Rest-For-The-Weary	36aSE4 Locon	X 30 c 6.2
Resurrection Trench	57dNE4 & 57cNW3 Achiet	L 5, 11, 17, 18, 24, 19, 25, 31
Retaliation Farm	28NE1 Zonnebeke	D 28 d 45.75
Retape Alley	66cNW2 Itancourt	B 10 b
Retour Cross Roads	20SE3 Westroosebeke	V 19 d 05.50
Retour des Châteaux Estaminet, Aux [Ploegsteert]	28SW4 Ploegsteert	U 19 c 8.3
Retraite Trench	62cSW4 St. Christ	U 22 a, c, 28 a, c
Retraite Trench	66dNW3 Hattencourt	H 8 b, d, 9 a, 14 b, c, d, 20 a
Retrenchment Line	36cSW3 Vimy	S 2 a
Retrenchment, The	36NW2 Armentières	I 5 a, c
Rettemoy Avenue [1918]	57dNE2 [Fonquevillers] / 4 [Hébuterne]	F 25 d, 26 c
Rettemoy Farm	57dNE1 & 2 Fonquevillers	F 25 c 0.6
Rettemoy Graben	57dNE1 & 2 Fonquevillers	F 25 a, c, d
Reuce Trench	12SW1 Nieuport	M 9 d
Reunion Alley	62cSW1 Dompierre / 2 Barleux	N 1, 7, 8, 14, 15, 22 a, b
Reuss Trench	57cSW4 Combles	U 26 a
Reutel [hamlet]	28NE3 Gheluvelt	J 11 c
Reveillon - Choques Line	36aSE3 Gonnehem / 36bNE [1 Labeuvrière]	V 24 d, W 19 c, D 6, E 1, 2, 7, 8, 9
Revel Farm	27NE4 Abeele	K 11 b 60.85
Revel Trench	57dNE3 & 4 Hébuterne	K 16 a, b, 17 a
Revel Trench	62cSW1 & 2 Belloy	N 11 d
Revelon [farm]	57cSE4 Villers-Guislain	W 17 a 0.5
Revelon [road junction]	57cSE4 Villers-Guislain	W 16 b 8.5
Revelon Ridge	57cSE4 Villers-Guislain	W 16 a, b
Revelon Switch	57cSE4 Villers-Guislain	W 11 a
Revolver Range [Higgins Wood, Chesterman Fm]	28NE4 Dadizeele	K 28 c, 33 b, 34 a
Rex Trench	57dSE2 Beaumont	R 22 a, b, 23 a, c
Rexpoede Railhead / Refilling Point	19SE [3 Rexpoede]	P 33 c, d
Reynaud Alley	66cNW2 Itancourt	A 16 b, d, 17 a
Reynolds Farm	20SE4 Roulers	W 27 b 95.30
Rhine Alley	66cNW2 Itancourt	B 17 c
Rhine Copse	28NE1 Zonnebeke	D 18 c
Rhine Trench	57cSW4 Combles	U 21 a, b
Rhine Trench	57dNE3 & 4 Hébuterne	K 24 b, L 13 c, 19 a, c
Rhine Trench	66cNW1 Grugies	B 7 b, 8 a
Rhino Trench	51bSW4 Bullecourt / SE3 Cagnicourt	U 24 d, 30 b, V 25 a
Rhino Wood	27NE2 Proven	F 3 c, d, 9 b
Rhinocéros, Tranchée du	66dNW3 Hattencourt / 66eNE4 Beaufort	G 19 d, L 24 c, 29 d, 30 a
Rhodes Corner [road jct]	27NE4 Abeele	L 7 d 75.15
Rhondda Sap	36SW1 Aubers	N 8 c, d
Rhondda Trench	57cSE2 Gonnelieu	R 7 d, 8 c

Name	Map Sheet	Map Reference
Rhone Alley	66cNW4 Berthenicourt	H 11, 12, 16, 17
Rhone Farm	27NE4 Abeele	L 7 b 1.2
Rhume Trench	62cSW2 Barleux	N 29 d, 30 c, 36 a
Rhyl Farm	27NE4 Abeele	K 6 c 9.1
Rialto Bridge [road over stream]	27SE4 Meteren	X 13 b 1.1
Riault Trench [1918]	62dSW [4 Cachy]	U 5 d, 11 a, b, c, d, 17 a
Rib Trench	51bNW1 Roclincourt	A 30 c
Ribble Street	57dSE4 Ovillers	W 18 b, d
Ribble Trench	57cSE2 Gonnelieu	R 29 c, 34 b, 35 a
Ribbon, The [copse]	62bSW4 Homblières	O 31 d,
Ricardo Redoubt [W of Contescourt & Canal]	66cNW1 Grugies / 66dNE2	A 25, F 30
Rice Trench	51bNW1 Roclincourt	A 30 c
Rich Trench	51bNW1 Roclincourt	A 30 c
Richard Trench [Richen, Boyau]	36cSW1 Lens	M 19 d
Richard's Post [La Boutillerie]	36SW2 Radinghem	N 6 a
Richebourg l'Avoué [village]	36SW3 Richebourg	S 9 d
Richebourg Post	36SW3 Richebourg	S 2 c, 8 a
Richebourg Redoubt [R'bourg St.Vaast, Jan '15]	36SW3 Richebourg	S 2 centre
Richebourg St Vaast [village]	36SW3 Richebourg	M 32 c, S 2 a, c
Richen, Boyau [Richard Trench]	36cSW1 Lens	M 19 d
Richlieu [sic] [light rly, Vimy]	36cSW3 Vimy	S 30 b, T 25 a
Richmond Copse	57bSW3 Honnecourt	S 27 d, 28 a, c
Richmond Cross Roads	28NE4 Dadizeele	L 7 c 85.15
Richmond Quarry	57bSW3 Honnecourt	S 28 a
Richmond Terrace / Trench	36SW3 Richebourg	S 21 d, 27 b
Richmond Wood	62dSE [2 Proyart]	Q 29 b, d
Rick Trench	51bNW1 Roclincourt	A 30 c
Rick's Folly	36SW2 Radinghem	O 7 b 4.9
Ricochet Trench	66dNW1 Punchy	A 15 d, 16 a, c, 21 b
Ricou [Tranchée, 1915, La Boisselle]	57dSE4 Ovillers	X 20 c
Rid Trench	51bNW1 Roclincourt	A 30 c
Ridge Camp	28NW3 Poperinghe	G 11 a
Ridge Farm	28SW2 Wytschaete	O 16 d 70.55
Ridge Redoubt [Redan Ridge]	57dSE1 & 2 Beaumont	Q 5 a
Ridge Reserve North, Central, & South	62cNE2 Epéhy	F 2 a; F 8 b; F 15 a
Ridge Road [road]	51cSE4 Blaireville	W 6, 11, 12, 16, 17, X 1
Ridge Street Tunnel	28NW4 Ypres	I 17 c
Ridge Support [Highland Ridge]	57cNE4 Marcoing / 57cSE2 Gonnelieu	L 31d, 32 c, d, R 2 b
Ridge Trench	57dSE1 & 2 Beaumont	Q 16 d, 22 b, d, 28 b, d, 29 a
Ridge Trench [Highland Ridge]	57cNE4 Marcoing / 57cSE2 Gonnelieu	L 31d, R 1 b, 2 a
Ridge View [OP, ruined house, Feb 1916]	36cNW1 La Bassée	A 20 d, 26 b [approx]
Ridge Wood	28SW2 Wytschaete	N 5 a, b, c
Ridge Work	57cNW1 Gomiecourt	A 14 a, c, d
Ridley Walk [July 1915]	36cNW1 La Bassée	A 21 b
Ridou [Tranchée, 1915, La Boisselle]	57dSE4 Ovillers	X 19 b
Riegel Stellung	51bNW1 Roclincourt	B 27 c, H 3 a
Riegel Stellung	57dSE4 Ovillers	R 34 d, X 4 a, b
Rieger Graben	57dNE1 & 2 Fonquevillers	E 12 d, 18 b, F 7 c
Riencourt Trench	51bSW4 Bullecourt	U 24 c, d
Riencourt-les-Bapaume [village]	57cSW2 Villers-au-Flos	N 5 d, 6 c, 11 b, 12 a
Riencourt-lez-Cagnicourt [village]	51bSW4 Bullecourt	U 23 b, 24 a, c
Riest, le [farm]	36aNE1 Morbecque	D 10 c 3.8
Rietz Avenue	51bNW1 Roclincourt	A 4 c, 9 a, b
Rietz Trench	51bNW1 Roclincourt	A 8, 9

Name	Map Sheet	Map Reference
Rietz, au [crossroads]	51bNW1 Roclincourt	A 8 c
Riez Bailleul [hamlet]	36SW1 Aubers	M 7 b, d, 8 c
Riez Bailleul [keep / defended locality]	36SW1 Aubers	M 7 d, 8 c
Riez Bailleul [north post]	36SW1 Aubers	M 8 a 2.1
Riez Bailleul [south post]	36SW1 Aubers	M 13 b 40.65
Rifle Alley	51bNW4 Fampoux	I 31 d
Rifle Bridge [across Wytschaetebeek]	28SW2 Wytschaete	O 7 a 3.8
Rifle Brigade HQ [Rifle House] [Ploegsteert Wd]	28SW4 Ploegsteert	U 21 c 2.6
Rifle Camp	51bNW3 Arras	G 24 b
Rifle Dump	57dSE2 Beaumont	R 28 b 8.2
Rifle Farm	28NW4 & NE3 Zillebeke	I 10 d 95.50
Rifle Farm	28SW2 Wytschaete	O 23 d 15.95
Rifle Farm	51bNW4 Fampoux	I 31 d 75.60
Rifle Farm Spur [light railway, 1917-18]	28NW4 Ypres	I 16 b
Rifle House [Ploegsteert Wood]	28SW4 Ploegsteert	U 20 d 95.70
Rifle House [Rifle Brigade HQ, Ploegsteert Wd]	28SW4 Ploegsteert	U 21 c 2.6
Rifle House Cemetery	28SW4 Ploegsteert	U 21 c
Rifle Pit South	62cNE2 Epéhy	F 30 c, L 6 a
Rifle Pit Trench	62cNE2 Epéhy	F 29 d, 30 a, c, L 6 a
Rifle Post	12SW1 Nieuport	N 26 c
Rifle Road [road]	28NE3 Gheluvelt	J 26 b, d, 32 b
Rifle Row [CT, Sept 1915]	36SW3 Richebourg	M 35 c, d
Rifle Trench	57dSE2 Beaumont	R 22 a, c, 28 a, c
Rifle Trench, & Support	51bNW4 Fampoux	I 31 a, b
Rifleman Trench	27SE4 Meteren	X 11 b, d, 12 a
Rifleman's Avenue	36SW1 Aubers	N 7 d, 13 b, 14 a
Riflemans Post	62cNE2 Epéhy	F 29 b
Riflemans Redoubt	36cNW1 La Bassée	A 9 a
Rifles Trench	57cSW3 Longueval	S 10 b, d
Rig Farm	36NW1 Steenwerck	A 30 a 5.6
Riga [light rly spur]	36NW2 Armentières	B 6 b 0.3
Rigale Wood	66dNW3 Hattencourt	G 6 c
Right Alley [Bazentin-le-Petit Wood]	57cSW3 Longueval	S 7 d, 13 b
Right Boyau	36cNW3 & 1 Loos	G 4 c
Rigi Farm	28NW3 Poperinghe	G 6 d 05.25
Riley Avenue	57cSE2 Gonnelieu	R 20 a, b
Rill Works [factory]	36aNE4 Merville	L 33 b 2.7
Ring Buildings	28NE2 Moorslede	E 23 b 7.0 to E 24 a 0.0
Ring Copse	62dSE [3 Marcelcave]	V 19 a
Ring Trench	57cSW3 Longueval	T 2 b, 3 a
Ring Trench	57cSW4 Combles	U 20 d, 21 a, c
Rink Corner	28NE1 Zonnebeke	D 26 a
Rio House	27NE4 Abeele	K 18 a 90.85
Riom Trench	66cNW1 Grugies	A 12 b, B 7 a, b
Ripe Street	57cSW3 Longueval	T 13 b
Ripley Trench [Hohen Stellung]	57dSE1 & 2 Beaumont	R 25 b
Ripon Alley	57cNW2 Vaulx-Vraucourt	C 18 a, c
Ripon Lane	51bSW4 Bullecourt	U 29 b
Rippert, Avenue	51bNW1 Roclincourt	A 23 c, 29 a
Ripple Alley	57cSE2 Gonnelieu	R 16 c, d, 17 a
Ripple Trench	57cSE2 Gonnelieu	R 11 c, 17 a, c
Riqueul Post / Pont Riquel	36aSE2 Lestrem	R 10 a
Riqueval [hamlet]	62bNW3 Bellicourt	G 16 a
Riqueval Farm	62bNW3 Bellicourt	G 22 b 1.6

Name	Map Sheet	Map Reference
Riqueval Ravine	62bNW3 Bellicourt	G 10 b, d, 11 a
Risk Farm	27NE1 Herzeele	E 14 b 80.85
Rissole Trench	27SE4 Meteren	X 11 b, d
Ritter Wood	62cSW3 Vermandovillers	S 16 c
Ritter, Bois	62cSW3 & 4 Marchélepot	S 16 c
Rittmeister Alley	62bSW3 St Quentin	N 31 d, 32 c, T 1 a, b
Ritz Street / Ritz Street Trench	28NW4 & NE3 Zillebeke	I 17 c, 23 a
Ritz Street [plank road, 1917-18]	28NW4 Ypres	I 22 b, 23 a
Ritz Trench [1918]	66eNW [4 Morisel]	H 17 b
Ritz Trench [CT], & The Ritz [S 9 d 7.6]	36SW3 Richebourg	S 9 d, 15 b
Riva Farm	27NE4 Abeele	L 27 a 05.25
River Alley	36cSW3 Vimy	S 8 a, b
River Avenue	36NW2 Armentières	C 16 b, d
River Jordan Avenue	57dNE3 & 4 Hébuterne	K 23 c, 28 b, 29 a, b
River Lane	12SW1 Nieuport	N 19 d
River Lane	51bNW4 Fampoux	I 21 c
River Road [road]	36cSW1 Lens / 2 Harnes	N 10 d, 16 c, d, 17 c, 21 b
River Road [road]	51bSW4 Bullecourt	T 12 b, U 1 c, d, 7 a
River Road [road]	51bSW2 Vis-en-Artois	N 24 a, b, c
River Road Cemetery No.2	51bSW2 Vis-en-Artois	N 23 d 9.6
River Support	28SW4 Ploegsteert	U 11 a, b, c
River Terrace	36cSW3 Vimy	S 2 d, 8 b
River Trench	12SW1 Nieuport	N 19 d
River Trench	28NW4 & NE3 Zillebeke	I 11 d, 17 a
River Trench	57dNE3 & 4 Hébuterne / SE1 & 2 Beaumont	L 26, 32, R 2, 8
Riverside [farm & pillboxes]	28NE1 Zonnebeke	D 14 b 5.6
Riverside Trench	20SE3 Westroosebeke	V 25 a, c
Riverside Wood	57cSE3 Sorel-le-Grand	V 19 b, c, d, 20 c, 25 a, b, c, d, 26 a, c
Riviere, Boyau de la [1918]	28SW1 Kemmel	N 2 c, 8 a, b
Rivington Street, & Tunnel	57dSE4 Ovillers	X 7 b, c, d
Rivoli Farm	28NW2 St Julien	B 24 a 8.0
Roach Avenue	57cNE3 Hermies	J 11 d, 12 c, d, 17 b
Roach Farm	20SE2 Hooglede	R 11 b 4.6
Roach Post	57cNE3 Hermies	J 11 b 85.77
Roach Trench	51bSW1 Neuville Vitasse	M 6 c, d
Roach Trench [1918]	57dNE3 & 4 Hébuterne	K 6 c, 12 a
Road Avenue / Boyau de la Route	62cNW1 Maricourt	A 28 a
Road Bend [keep, Fauquissart, late 1915]	36SW1 Aubers	M 18 c 05.50
Road Bend Elgin Street [late 1915]	36SW1 Aubers	M 17 d, 18 c, 24 a
Road Bend Post	36SW1 Aubers	M 17 d, 18 c
Road Camp [Vlamertinghe]	28NW3 Poperinghe	H 9 c, d
Road Farm [Vlamertinghe]	28NW3 Poperinghe	H 9 d 1.5
Road House	28NE1 Zonnebeke	D 13 b 9.4
Road Post	57cSE1 Bertincourt	Q 32 a
Road Spur [light rly locality W of Canal 1917-18]	28NW2 St Julien	B 12 c, d
Road Trench	66cNW4 Berthenicourt	I 28 a
Road Wood	62bSW1 Gricourt	M 12 c
Road Wood	62cNW2 Bouchavesnes	C 25 a, b
Roadside Redoubt [La Basse Cour Fm, Messines]	28SW4 Ploegsteert	U 2 b, d, 3 a, c; U 3 c 1.8
Roadway Street	51cSE3 & 4 Ransart	R 31 d, X 1 b
Roanne Trench	66cNW1 Grugies	B 7 a, b, c, d, 8 c
Rob Roy Trench	57dNE3 & 4 Hébuterne	K 23 c, 29 a
Rob Trench	51bNW1 Roclincourt	A 30 d

Name	Map Sheet	Map Reference
Robber Wood	51bNE4 Cantin	L 29 b, d
Robe Trench	51bNW1 Roclincourt	A 30 c
Robecq Switch	36aSE1 St Venant	Q 13, 19, 25, 26, 32
Robermetz [farm]	36aNE4 Merville	K 24 d 6.9
Robert Maze	36cSW4 Rouvroy	U 3 c, 9 a
Robert Post	36NW4 Bois Grenier	H 36 d
Robert Wood	62dSE [2 Proyart]	R 16 c
Roberts Avenue	57dNE1 & 2 Fonquevillers	E 21 b, 22 c
Roberts Avenue / Lane	57cSE4 Villers-Guislain	X 4 d, 10 b, 11 a
Roberts Maze	36cSW4 Rouvroy	U 3 c
Roberts Post	62cNE2 Epéhy	F 1 d
Roberts Trench [new support / reserve line]	57dSE1 & 2 Beaumont	Q 17 c, d
Robertson House	28NE4 Dadizeele	K 16 d 25.40
Robertson's Alley	36cNW1 La Bassée	A 21 c, d
Robey Farm	28NW1 Elverdinghe	G 4 b 4.3
Robida Copse	62cNE3 Buire / 4 Roisel	K 27 b, 28 a
Robin Alley	57cNE1 Quéant	D 21 d, 27 b
Robin Post	57cNE1 Quéant	D 27 b
Robin Support	57cNE1 Quéant	D 21 d, 27 b, 28 a, b, 29 c
Robin Trench	36cSW4 Rouvroy	U 8 c, 14 a
Robin Trench	51bSW2 Vis-en-Artois	O 25 b, d
Robin Trench	57cSE2 Gonnelieu	R 9 b
Robineau, Boyau	36bSE4 & 36cSW3 Givenchy	S 8 d
Robinson Trench	57cNE4 Marcoing	K 5 c
Robinson Trench	57dNE1 & 2 Fonquevillers	E 22 d
Robson [light rly locality]	28NW3 Poperinghe	G 29 c, d
Robson Buildings	28NW3 Poperinghe	G 29 c 80.65
Roc Gris [light rly, Grenay]	36bNE4 Noeux-les-Mines	L 36 c
Rocade Trench	51bNW1 Roclincourt	A 15 b, 16 a
Rocade, Boyau	51bNW1 Roclincourt	A 27 c
Roch Alley	36cNW1 La Bassée	A 3 d, 4 c, d, 5 c, 11 a, b, 12 a, b
Roch Trench	12SW1 Nieuport	N 19 b
Roch Trench	36cNW1 La Bassée	A 4 d, 10 b, d
Roche Trench	66cNW1 Grugies	B 7 b
Rochester House	28NE4 Dadizeele	L 13 a 4.5
Rock [light rly siding]	36cSW1 Lens	M 14 a
Rock Alley	36cNW1 La Bassée	A 11 b
Rock Street	57dSE4 Ovillers	X 1 c
Rocket Alley	66cNW1 Grugies	B 1 d
Rocket Reserve	27SE4 Meteren	R 34 d, X 4 a
Rocket Trench [1918]	57dNE2 & 57cNW1 Courcelles	F 16 b, d, 22 b, d
Rocklington [railway locality, 1917-18]	28NW4 Ypres	H 11 c
Rockstone Farms	28NE4 Dadizeele	L 15 a 2.0
Roclincourt Avenue	51bNW1 Roclincourt	A 28 a, b, c, d
Roclincourt-Targ.-Mar.-Houchin-Vaudricourt Line	36bSE2 Boyeffles / 4 Carency	extensive
Roclincourt-Targette-Marqueffles-[contd above]	36bSE2 Boyeffles / 4 Carency	extensive
Rocogne Wood [Doingt Wood]	62cNW4 Péronne / NE3 Buire	I 24 d, 30 b, d, J 25 c, 31 a
Rocourt Salient	62bSW3 St Quentin	S 23 b, d, 24 a, c
Rocquigny [village]	57cSW2 Villers-au-Flos	O 27 a, b, c, d
Rocquigny Trench	57cSW2 Villers-au-Flos	O 27 c
Rod Trench	51bNW1 Roclincourt	A 30 d
Rod Trench [1918]	57dNE2 [Fonquevillers]	L 2 b
Rodgers Farm [moated]	20SE2 Hooglede	R 25 a 00.05
Rodney [light rly jct 1917-18]	28NW4 Ypres	I 32 b

Name	Map Sheet	Map Reference
Rodney R. E. Dump [1917-18]	28NW4 Ypres	I 32 b 56.81
Roe Trench	27SE4 Meteren	X 11 c, d
Roerle Graben	57dNE3 & 4 Hébuterne	K 29 d
Roeux [village]	51bNW4 Fampoux	I 19 b
Roeux Chemical Works	51bNW4 Fampoux	I 13 b
Roger Farm	28NW1 Elverdinghe	B 10 c 2. 9
Roi, Ferme du [Béthune, N of Canal Dock]	36bNE2 Beuvry	E 6 c 8.5
Roitelet Trench [1918]	62dSW [4 Cachy]	T 24, 30 b, c, d
Roland Posts	57cNE1 Quéant	E 7 d
Roland Trench	57dNE3 & 4 Hébuterne	K 22 d, 28 b
Rolands Farm	20SE2 Hooglede	R 23 b 9.9
Roll Trench	51bNW1 Roclincourt	A 30 c
Rolland Trench	57dNE3 & 4 Hébuterne	K 22 d, 28 b
Rolleg Farm [Rolleghemcappelle]	28NE2 Moorslede	L 5 a 3.8
Rolleghemcappelle [village]	28NE2 Moorslede	F 28 c
Rollen [light rly siding]	36cSW1 Lens	M 21 c, 27 a
Rollencourt [hamlet]	36cSW1 Lens	M 27 d
Rollencourt, Bois de	36cSW1 Lens	M 27 c, d
Rollencourt, Cité de	36cSW1 Lens	M 21 c, d, 27 a, b
Rollin Trench	62cNW2 Bouchavesnes	C 27 c, I 3 a, b, c
Rollo Farm	27NE1 Herzeele	E 21 c 9.7
Rom Graben	57dNE3 & 4 Hébuterne	K 4 d
Roma Farm	27NE4 Abeele	L 26 d 65.80
Roman Road [road]	66cNW2 Itancourt	C 15 d
Roman Road Trench	57dNE3 & 4 Hébuterne	K 33, 34 c, d
Roman Trench	62bSW3 St Quentin	S 18 b, T 13 a
Romanche Alley	66cNW4 Berthenicourt	I 13 a
Romarin [railway & light rly locality]	28SW3 Bailleul	T 28 a
Romarin Camp	36NW2 Armentières	B 4 a
Romarin Desfosses Alley	62cNW3 Vaux / 4 Péronne	H27c,32b,33a,b,34a,b,35a,c,d,36c
Rome Farm	28NW1 Elverdinghe	H 4 a 5.5
Romer Alley	28SW4 Ploegsteert	U 1 d
Rommens Farm	28SW2 Wytschaete	O 25 b 9.7
Romp Farm	28SW1 Kemmel	M 35 a 75.55
Romulus Road	28NE1 Zonnebeke	D 28 b
Romulus Wood	28NE1 Zonnebeke	D 28 b, d, 29 a, c
Ronce, Tranchée	62cNW3 Vaux	G 29 a
Rondal Avenue	62dNE2 Méaulte	F 8 b, 9 a
Ronde Trench	66dNW1 Punchy	A 15 c, d, 16 c
Rondin Alley	66cNW1 Grugies	B 2 a, c
Rondins, Tranchée des	66dNW3 Hattencourt / SW1 Roye	H 33 c, d, N 3 b
Ronquenet Trench	66cSW1 Remigny / 2 Vendeuil	N 15 d, 22 a, c, 28 a
Ronville Tunnel	51bNW3 Arras	G 28, 34, 35
Ronville, Faubourg [Arras]	51bNW3 Arras	G 28 c, d, 34 a, b, d
Rood Farm	28NE2 Moorslede	F 22 b 4.3
Roodbart	28NE2 Moorslede	F 23 a, b
Roof Lane	51bSW4 Bullecourt	O 32 c
Roof Trench	51bNW1 Roclincourt	A 30 d
Rook Alley	57cNE1 Quéant	D 22 c, 28 a
Rook Avenue	57cNE1 Quéant	D 27 d, 28 a, c
Rook Farm	20SE2 Hooglede	R 20 b 4.6
Rook Post	57cNE1 Quéant	D 28 a, b
Rook Trench	51bNW1 Roclincourt	A 30 c, d
Rook Trench	51bNW3 Arras	G 30 d

Name	Map Sheet	Map Reference
Rookery [Givenchy]	36cNW1 La Bassée	A 9 a, c
Rookery, The	51bSW2 Vis-en-Artois	N 30 c, d
Room Trench	57cSE4 Villers-Guislain / 62cNE2 Epéhy	X 26 c, d, F 3 a
Roome's Trench	36SW3 Richebourg	S 10 b
Rooney Farm [1918]	28SW1 Kemmel	M 30 b 2.5
Rooney's Sap	57dSE1 & 2 Beaumont	Q 10 b
Roosemberg [hamlet; Hill 63]	28SW4 Ploegsteert	T 18 a, b
Roosemberg [windmill / OP]	28SW4 Ploegsteert	T 18 b 05.72
Roosemberg Hedge	28SW4 Ploegsteert	T 18 b
Roost Farm	28NE2 Moorslede	F 27 d 3.0
Rooster Cabaret, In den	28SW4 Ploegsteert	U 18 a 2.9
Rooster Farm	36aNE2 Vieux Berquin	F 25 d 7.5
Rooster Trench	36cSW4 Rouvroy	U 9 b, d, 10 a, c
Roozendaal Inn	27NE4 Abeele	K 18 a 6.1
Rope [Alley / CT / Trench; Sept 1915]	36SW3 Richebourg	S 21 a, c, d
Rope Lane [trench]	62bNW3 Bellicourt	G 8 a, b
Rope Trench	36SW3 Richebourg	S 21 a, b, d
Rope Walk	28SE3 Comines	V 11 a
Rory Farm	27NE1 Herzeele	D 23 b 9.4
Roscoe Trench	62bSW3 St Quentin	M 25 b, 36 a, c
Roscommon Road	51cSE3 & 4 Ransart	W 12 a
Rose [?] Farm [Ross Farm?]	20SE2 Hooglede	R 9 c 2.7
Rose Alley	62dNE2 Méaulte	F 3 d, 4 c
Rose Camp [1917-18]	28NW2 St Julien	C 1 d, 7 b
Rose Cottage	36cSW2 Harnes	N 36 b 4.3
Rose Cottage [Fricourt]	62dNE2 Méaulte	F 3 d 95.85
Rose Farm	36NW1 Steenwerck	A 14 d 15.30
Rose House	20SW4 Bixschoote	U 24 d 95.20
Rose House	36aSE1 St Venant	P 36 b 2.3
Rose Reserve	57cSW1 Gueudecourt	N 27 a, c, 33 a, b, 34 a
Rose Street	20SW4 Bixschoote / SE3 Westroosebeke	U 24 d, V 19 c
Rose Street	36cNW1 La Bassée	A 3 a, c
Rose Support	57cSE4 Villers-Guislain	R 34 d, X 4 b, d
Rose Trench	20SE3 Westroosebeke	V 19 c
Rose Trench	51bNW1 Roclincourt	A 30 c
Rose Trench	57cSE4 Villers-Guislain	R 34 d, 35 c, X 5 a
Rose Trench	57cSW1 Gueudecourt	N 33 a
Rose Trench	62bNW3 Bellicourt	G 27 a
Rose Trench	62cNE2 Epéhy	F 10 c
Rose Trench	62dNE2 Méaulte	F 4 c, 10 b
Rose Wood	28SW2 Wytschaete	O 16 a
Rose, Bois de	62cSW3 & 4 Marchélepot	F 10 c, c, d
Rose, Tranchée de la	66eNE4 Beaufort	L 22 c, 27 b, 28 a
Rosenberg Alley	62cNW3 Vaux / 4 Péronne	H 14 b, c, d, 15 a, b, 16 a
Rosenthal [May 1915, Bedford House]	28NW4 & NE3 Zillebeke	I 26 a, b
Rosetta Farm	28NE4 Dadizeele	L 10 b 55.60
Rosewood Trench	66cNW2 Itancourt	B 24 d
Rosher Farm	28NW3 Poperinghe	H 13 a 4.7
Rosie [light rly siding]	36bSE4 Carency	W 6 b
Rosières-en-Santerre [village]	66eNE2 Vrély	F 1, 2, 7, 8
Rosing Bridge [road over Wulfdambeek]	28NE4 Dadizeele	L 4 d 65.35
Roslyn Street	28NW4 & NE3 Zillebeke	I 17 d
Ross [sic] Farm [Rose Farm?]	20SE2 Hooglede	R 9 c 2.7
Ross Camp Siding [light rly]	36bSE4 Carency	X 3 c

Name	Map Sheet	Map Reference
Ross Castle [Thiepval Wood]	57dSE1 & 2 Beaumont	Q 30 b, c, d
Ross Communication Trench [1918]	62dNE [3 Morlancourt]	J 18 a
Ross Street	36cSW3 Vimy	S 27 d, 28 c
Ross Street	57dSE1 & 2 Beaumont	Q 30 b, d
Ross Street	57dSE2 & 57cSW1 Le Sars	M 13 d
Ross Trench	36cSW3 Vimy	S 28 c
Rossi [Tranchée, 1915] / Carnoustie Street	57dSE4 Ovillers	X 25 b, 26 a
Rossignol [farm]	28SW1 Kemmel	N 21 b
Rossignol Avenue [CT]	28SW2 Wytschaete	N 22 b, 23 a, b, 24 a
Rossignol Cabaret, Au	28NE3 Gheluvelt	K 31 a 7.5
Rossignol Camp, Le	36NW2 Armentières	B 10 d 8.9
Rossignol Farm	20SW4 Bixschoote	T 22 a 7.9
Rossignol Farm	57dNE [3 Hébuterne]	J 3 c 8.5
Rossignol Line [tr. tramway; La Polka - Byron Fm]	28SW2 Wytschaete	N 17 d, 18 a, 22 a, b, 23 a, b
Rossignol Road [trench]	28SW2 Wytschaete	N 22 b, 23 a, b; N 23 a 8.8
Rossignol Trench	57dNE3 & 4 Hébuterne	L 7 c, 13 a, b, d
Rossignol Wood	28SW2 Wytschaete	N 22 a, b
Rossignol Wood	57dNE3 & 4 Hébuterne	K 12 b, c, d
Rossignol, Le [farm / hamlet, Hill 63]	28SW4 Ploegsteert	U 13 a 90.75
Rossignol, le [farm]	36NW1 Steenwerck	A 21 a 75.40
Rossignol, le [farm]	36NW2 Armentières	B 10 d 8.9
Rossignol, le [hamlet]	27SE2 Berthen	R 20 d 7.7
Rost Trench	51bNW3 Arras	H 1 c
Rostrum Trench [Auchonvillers]	57dSE1 & 2 Beaumont	Q 3 c, d
Rot Trench	51bNW1 Roclincourt	A 30 d
Roter Haus Graben	51bNW3 Arras	G 6 d
Roth Trench [Ems Trench]	57dNE3 & 4 Hébuterne	K 4 d
Rothard Alley	66dNW3 Hattencourt	G 14 c, d, 15 c, 20 a
Rotherham Alley	51bSW4 Bullecourt	U 29 d
Rotherham Road [CT, 1915]	28NW2 St Julien	B 12 d
Rothesay Bay	36SW3 Richebourg	S 27 d
Rott Trench	51bNW3 Arras	G 12 d
Rotten Ravine	57dNE1 & 2 Fonquevillers	F 2 c, 7 b, 8 a
Rotten Row	36cSW3 Vimy	M 32 c, S 2 a
Rotten Row	36SW1 Aubers	N 13 a, b, d
Rotten Row	51bSW4 Bullecourt	U 1 b
Rotten Row	57dNE1 & 2 Fonquevillers	E 21 b, 22 c
Rotten Row	57dSE1 & 2 Beaumont	Q 16 b
Rotten Row [Delville Wood]	57cSW3 Longueval	S 18 a, b
Rotten Row [road]	36cSW2 Harnes	N 6 c, d
Rotten Row [sunken road]	28SW4 Ploegsteert	U 15 c
Rotten Row [sunken road]	51bSW4 Bullecourt	O 31 c, U 1 a, b
Rotten Row Dugouts [Ploegsteert Wd]	28SW4 Ploegsteert	U 15 c
Rotten Trench	51bSW4 Bullecourt	U 1 b, d
Rouble Trench	36cSW4 Rouvroy	U 8 d, 14 b
Roucli Trench	62cNW4 Péronne	H 17 a, b
Roucourt [village]	51bNE2 Dechy	F 27 c, d, L 3 a, b
Roucourt Aerodrome [German]	51bNE2 Dechy	F 26 d, 27 c
Roucourt, Fosse	51bNE2 Dechy	F 27 c, d
Rouen Trench	66cSW2 Vendeuil	N 28 a, c, d
Rouge [light rly siding]	36cSW1 Lens	M 3 d
Rouge Croix [defended locality]	27SE4 Meteren	W 9 d, 10 c, 15 b, 16 a
Rouge Croix [hamlet & cross roads]	27SE4 Meteren	W 10 c 2.0
Rouge Croix East [keep, late 1915]	36SW1 Aubers	M 27 b 4.5

Name	Map Sheet	Map Reference
Rouge Croix Switch	27SE4 Meteren	W 10, 16, 17, 23
Rouge Croix Switch [1918]	27SE4 Meteren	extensive
Rouge Croix West & East Posts	36SW1 Aubers	M 27 a; M 27 b
Rouge Farm	28NW2 St Julien	B 4 c 65.30
Rouges Bancs [farm / locality]	36SW1 Aubers	N 15 b
Rough and Ready Villa [Ploegsteert Wood]	28SW4 Ploegsteert	U 20 b 98.50
Rougny Trench	62cSW2 Barleux	O 1 d, 2 c
Rougy, Tranchée	62cSW1 & 2 Belloy	O 2 a, c
Roukloshille Line	27SE4 Meteren	R 31 c, d, X 1 a, b, c, d, 7 a
Roukloshille Support	27SE4 Meteren	R 31 c, W 6 d, 12 b, X 1 a, c
Roukloshille, le [road jct]	27SE4 Meteren	X 1 a 7.9
Roulers [town]	20SE2 Hooglede / 20SE4 Roulers	R 31 b, d, 32 a, b, c, d, 33 a, c
Roumanie Alley	62cSW2 Barleux	N 16 a, b, 17 a
Round Hill	62bSW3 St Quentin	S 14 a, b
Round House, The [railway]	36cSW1 Lens	N 27 b, d
Round Point, & Avenue / Boyau de Rond Point	62cNW1 Maricourt	A 16 d
Round Trench	57cNE1 Quéant / 2 Bourlon	E 21 b, d
Round Wood	57dSE4 Ovillers	X 21 d
Round Wood Alley	57dSE4 Ovillers	X 21 c, d
Rousbrugge Railhead / Refilling Point	19SE [3 Rexpoede]	W 20 a, b, c, d
Roussel Camp	28NW1 Elverdinghe	B 13 a central
Roussel Farm	28NW1 Elverdinghe	B 13 a 2.6
Roussel Farm	36aNE3 Haverskerque	K 8 d 15.60
Roussillonnais Alley	62cSW2 Barleux	N 16 d, 17 a, c
Roussky Trench	62cNW1 Maricourt	B 27 b, d
Route A [road]	36aSE4 Locon / 36SW3 Richebourg	X X 29 a, b, 24 c, 30 a, R 19 d
Route B [road]	36aSE4 Locon / 36SW3 Richebourg	X 23 a, b, 24 a, S 19 b
Rouvroy [village]	62bSW4 Homblières	T 10 d, 16 b, 17 a
Rouvroy Road [road]	36cSW4 Rouvroy	U 7 d, 13 a, b, c
Rouvroy Trench	36cSW4 Rouvroy	U 2 c
Rouvroy-en-Santerre [village]	66eNE4 Beaufort	L 8 a, b, c, d
Rouy-le-Grand [village]	66dNW4 Nesle	I 10 b, 11 a, b
Rouy-le-Petit [village]	66dNW4 Nesle	I 10 a, b, c, d
Row Avenue	36NW4 Bois Grenier	I 20 d
Row Trench	51bNW1 Roclincourt	A 30 d
Rowdy Trench	36cSW4 Rouvroy	U 8 d
Rowney Copse	28NE4 Dadizeele	K 28 d
Roy Trench / Boyau	51bNW1 Roclincourt	A 2, 3, 7, 8
Royal Alley	27SE4 Meteren	X 4 c, 10 a
Royal Avenue	36cSW3 Vimy	S 21 d
Royal Avenue	36SW2 Radinghem	N 6 a, b
Royal Avenue	57cNE2 Gonnelieu / 57bSW1 Bantouzelle	R 17 d, 18 a, c, M 13 b
Royal Avenue	57cSW3 Longueval	S 7 b
Royal Avenue	57dSE1 & 2 Beaumont	Q 23 a, b
Royal Avenue	62dNE2 Méaulte	F 2 d
Royal Dragoons Wood [Dragons Wood]	62cNW3 Vaux	G 16 a, b, d
Royal, Bois	62cSW3 & 4 Marchélepot	T 11 c
Royat Trench	66cNW2 Itancourt	B 16 b, d
Roykens Akker [hamlet]	27SE2 Berthen	R 3 b, d
Royston Farm	20SE2 Hooglede	R 23 b 05.30
Rualt Trench	57dNE3 & 4 Hébuterne	K 17 c
Ruault, Tranchée [Stafford Trench, NE end of]	36cSW1 Lens	M 20 b
Rub 1st Support [Rubempré, 1918]	57dSW [3 Talmas]	S 12 b, d, 18 a, b
Rub 2nd Support [Rubempré, 1918]	57dSW [3 Talmas]	S 12 b, d, 18 a, b

Name	Map Sheet	Map Reference
Rub Reserve [Rubempré, 1918]	57dSW [3 Talmas]	S 11 b, d, 17 b
Rub Trench [Rubempré, 1918]	57dSW [3 Talmas]	T 7 c, 13 a
Rubber Farm	28NE2 Moorslede	F 22 d 9.9
Rubbish Trench	27SE4 Meteren	X 4 d
Rubempré [village]	57dSW [3 Talmas]	T 13, 14
Rubempré, Moulin de	57dSW [3 Talmas]	T 19 d 0.5
Rubens Wood	28NE2 Moorslede	F 23 d
Rubever 1st Support [Rubempré - Everest, 1918]	57dSW [3 Talmas]	T 1 c, d, 7 a
Rubever 2nd Support [Rubempré - Everest, 1918]	57dSW [3 Talmas]	S 12 b, T 1 b, c, d, 7 a
Rubever Reserve [Rubempré - Everest, 1918]	57dSW [3 Talmas]	S 6 b, c, d, 12 a
Rubever Trench [Rubempré - Everest, 1918]	57dSW [3 Talmas]	T 7 a, b, c
Ruby Farm	62cNE2 Epéhy	L 6 a 8.2
Ruby Lane [trench]	62bNW1 Gouy / 62cNE2 Epéhy	G 1 b, L 6 a
Ruby Wood	62bNW1 Gouy	G 1 b, 2 a
Rudder Copse	62bNW1 Gouy	A 29 b
Rudkin House	28NW4 & NE3 Zillebeke	I 24 c
Rudolphe Farm	28NW2 St Julien	C 3 d 4.4
Rudolph's Rise Crater	36cSW1 Lens	M 6 c
Rue Allée Post	36NW4 Bois Grenier	I 7 b, d, 8 a, c
Rue Bataille Post	36NW3 Fleurbaix	H 15 d, 16 c
Rue Dante [road]	36SW1 Aubers	N 20 d
Rue de Bois [Trench]	36NW4 Bois Grenier	I 21 a
Rue de Bruges Post	36NW3 Fleurbaix	G 24 a
Rue de Lillers [street, Béthune]	36bNE2 Beuvry	E 5 c 3.7
Rue de Puits Post	36SW1 Aubers	M 26 d
Rue de Sac [hamlet]	36NW1 Steenwerck	B 3 c, d
Rue des Morts, la [hamlet]	36aNE3 Haverskerque	J 11 b, d
Rue d'Hordain [hamlet]	57bSW4 Serain	T 6 c
Rue d'Ouvert [village]	36SW3 Richebourg / 36cNW1 La Bassée	S 29 c, d, A 3 b, d
Rue du Bois [road]	36aSE4 Locon	X 17 c, d, 18 c
Rue du Bois Trench	36NW4 Bois Grenier	I 21 a
Rue du Ponch Post	36aSE2 Lestrem	R 16 d, 22 b
Rue du Puits Post [Sept 1915]	36SW1 Aubers	M 27 c 2.7
Rue Fleurie Post	36NW4 Bois Grenier	I 13 a
Rue Marle Post	36NW4 Bois Grenier	H 12 b
Rue Masselot [road]	36SW1 Aubers	M 10 d, 11 c, d, 18 a, b, d, N 13 c
Rue Montigny [hamlet]	36aNE4 Merville	L 15 a
Rue Provost [farm / hamlet]	36aNE4 Merville	L 8 b
Rue Tilleloy [road]	36SW1 Aubers	M 18, 24, N 2, 7, 8, 13
Rues des Vignes, les [village]	57bSW1 Bantouzelle	M 4 b, c, d, 5 a, c
Rues, Vertes, Les	57bNW3 Rumilly	G 26
Rufus House	28NE2 Moorslede	F 23 a 55.58
Rug Trench	51bNW1 Roclincourt	A 30 d
Rugby [keep, late 1915]	36SW1 Aubers	M 22 c 2.1
Rugby [light rly locality E of Canal 1917-18]	28NW2 St Julien	C 1 a, c
Rugby [locality]	36cSW3 Vimy	S 19 d
Rugby Corner	28NW2 St Julien	C 1 d 2.5
Rugby Road	51cSE3 & 4 Ransart	W 11 d, 12 c
Rugby Road Cemetery	28NW2 St Julien	C 1 c 4.3
Rugby Work	51cSE3 & 4 Ransart	W 11 d, 12 c
Rugen Trench	62bSW3 St Quentin	T 2 d
Ruin, The [OP, Cuinchy; La Bassée Road]	36cNW1 La Bassée	A 20 d
Ruined Farm	20SW4 Bixschoote	U 7 b 40.56
Ruined Farm [WNW of Eikhof Farm]	28SW2 Wytschaete	O 3 c 8.3

Name	Map Sheet	Map Reference
Ruined House [Broken Tree Farm]	28SW4 Ploegsteert	U 15 b 30.15
Ruisseau Farm	20SW4 Bixschoote	U 21 c 7.2
Ruitz Crossing [standard gauge & light rly]	36bNE3 [Bruay]	K 25 b
Ruler Buildings	28NE2 Moorslede	F 22 d 65.10
Rum Camp	28SW3 Bailleul	T 3 c, d
Rum Corner [road junction]	36SW3 Richebourg	S 14 d
Rum Lane	28SW2 Wytschaete	N 29 d, 35 b
Rum Lane	57dSE4 Ovillers	X 26 b, 27 a
Rum Lane [road]	36aSE2 Lestrem	R 23 c, d, 29 b, d
Rum Road [military road]	28NW1 Elverdinghe / 2 St Julien	B 22, 23, 24, 27, 28, 30, C 25
Rum Trench	57dSE2 & 57cSW1 Le Sars	R 10 c
Rum Trench [1918]	57dNE2 Essarts / 4 Puisieux-au-Mont	E 28, 29, K 3, 4, 8, 9,14
Rum Villa	28SW3 Bailleul	T 3 c 95.45
Rumbold Farm	28SW1 Kemmel	M 35 b 60.55
Rumilly [village]	57bNW3 Rumilly	G 15, 21
Rumilly Support	57bNW3 Rumilly	G 13 b, 14 c, d, 20 b, 21 a, c, 27 a, b
Rumilly Trench	57bNW3 Rumilly	G 13 b, d, 14 c, 20 b, 21 a, c, 27 a, c, d
Rummage House [1918]	28SW1 Kemmel	M 2 a 1.7
Rump Trench	57dSE1 & 2 Beaumont	Q 5 a, b, d
Runcorn [lt rly locality NE of Langemarck '17-18]	20SW4 Bixschoote	U 17 c, d
Rupert [light rly locality, 1917-18]	28NW4 Ypres	H 17 d
Rupert Road [road]	36cSW4 Rouvroy	U 8 c, d, 14 b
Rupert Trench	36cSW4 Rouvroy / 51bNW2 Oppy	U 25 b, d, C 2 a
Rupert's Copse	28SE1 Wervicq	P 3 d
Rupert's Cot	28SE1 Wervicq	P 3 d
Rupprecht Farm	28NW2 St Julien	C 30 c 3.4
Rupprecht Keep [1918]	28NW2 St Julien	C 29 d, 30 c
Ruprecht Trench	62cNW4 Péronne	I 11 c, d
Rusk Farm	28NE3 Gheluvelt	J 28 a 50.05
Russell Row	36cSW3 Vimy	S 15 a, c, d
Russell Wood	51bNW4 Fampoux	I 36 b
Russells / Russels Keep	36cNW1 La Bassée	A 21 d, 27 b
Russia Alley	66cNW1 Grugies	H 3 b
Russia Trench	12SW1 Nieuport	N 20 c
Russian Sap	36cNW1 La Bassée	G 4 b
Russian Sap	36cSW1 Lens	M 5 c
Russian Sap	51bSW4 Bullecourt	U 1 b, 2 a
Russky Farm	27NE1 Herzeele	E 25 a 85.20
Rust Farm	36aNE4 Merville	L 25 a 65.65
Rustres Trench	62cNW1 Maricourt	B 25 b, d
Ruswarp Farm	27SE2 Berthen	R 27 c 95.65
Rut Farm	27SE1 St Sylvestre	Q 3 b 4.8
Rut Lane [trench]	57cSW3 Longueval	N 32 d, T 2 a, b
Rutherford Alley	57dSE2 & 57cSW1 Le Sars	M 22 d, 28 b, d
Rutland Row [CT]	36SW1 Aubers	M 29 a
Rutoire Alley, Le	36cNW3 Loos	G 8 d, 9 c, 14 b, 15 a, b, d, 22 a
Rutoire Keep, Le	36cNW3 Loos	G 15 b
Rutoire, Le [Farm]	36cNW3 Loos	G 15 b
Rutter Lodge [Au Gheer Estaminet, Le Gheer]	28SW4 Ploegsteert	U 27 b 75.85
Rutter Lodge [Estaminet Au Gheer]	28SW4 Ploegsteert	U 27 b 2.8
Ruyaulcourt [village]	57cSE1 Bertincourt	P 9 b, 10 a, c, d, 15 b, 16 a
Ryan Cotts	27NE4 Abeele	K 24 c, 30 a
Ryan's Alley	36cNW1 La Bassée	A 28 a, b

Name	Map Sheet	Map Reference
Ryan's Keep	36cNW1 La Bassée	A 28 a
Ryans Keep [Sept 1915]	36cNW1 La Bassée	A 22 c, 28 a, b
Rycroft Alley	57dSE2 Beaumont	Q 6 a, b
Rycroft Street	57dSE4 Ovillers	X 7 c, d, 13 a
Ryde Camp	28NW1 Elverdinghe / 3 Poperinghe	G 3 b, d, 4 a, c
Ryder Farm	20SE2 Hooglede	Q 29 b 8.2
Ryder Street	57cNE3 Hermies / 4 Marcoing	K 15 a, b, d
Rye Farm	20SE2 Hooglede	Q 10 b 9.1
Rye Lane [1918]	51cSE4 Blaireville	X 23 c
Rye Trench	51bNW1 Roclincourt	A 30 d
Rye Trench	57cSW1 Gueudecourt	N 7 c, d
Rygerie [place name]	20SE2 Hooglede	Q 29 d 7.1
Rygerie Farm	20SE2 Hooglede	Q 29 d 7.1
S & S 2 [Hooge, 1915]	28NW4 & NE3 Zillebeke	I 18 b
S 1 - S 9 [Saps numbered N to S]	62cSW1 Dompierre	M 10 b, d
S 1 [Br, Hooge, 1915]	28NW4 & NE3 Zillebeke	I 18 b, d
S 12 [Br support tr, late-1915, N of Birr X Roads]	28NW4 & NE3 Zillebeke	I 11 d 2.1
S 13 [Br support tr, late-1915, Y Wood]	28NW4 & NE3 Zillebeke	I 12 c 15.30
S 14 [Br support tr, late-1915, Y Wood]	28NW4 & NE3 Zillebeke	I 12 c 0.2
S 15 [Br support trench, late-1915, E of Y Wood]	28NW4 & NE3 Zillebeke	I 12 c 15.50
S 16 [Br support trench, late-1915, Y Wood]	28NW4 & NE3 Zillebeke	I 11 d 5.3
S 16 [trench, N of Hill Top Farm, May 1916]	28NW2 St Julien	C 21 a, b
S 18 [Br suppt tr, late-1915, E of Witte Poort Fm]	28NW4 & NE3 Zillebeke	I 11 d 6.8
S 18 [Y & L Trench, E of Turco Farm, May 1916]	28NW2 St Julien	C 15 c
S 21 [Br support tr, late-1915, Railway Wood]	28NW4 & NE3 Zillebeke	I 11 b 6.3
S 22 [Br support tr, late-1915, Railway Wood]	28NW4 & NE3 Zillebeke	I 11 b 5.4
S 23 [Br support tr, late-1915, Railway Wood]	28NW4 & NE3 Zillebeke	I 11 b 3.4
S 3 [Br, Hooge, 1915]	28NW4 & NE3 Zillebeke	I 18 d
S 3 a [Br, Hooge, 1915]	28NW4 & NE3 Zillebeke	I 18 a
S Bend [German posn. N of Givenchy, April '15]	36cNW1 La Bassée	A 3
S Street	62cNW1 Maricourt	A 22 c
S Trench [St Eloi sector, Feb 1915]	28SW2 Wytschaete	O 3, 4
S Works	62cNW1 Maricourt	A 22 c
S. Redoubt	28SW2 Wytschaete	N 12 b
S.1	62cNW1 Maricourt	A 22 c
S.2	62cNW1 Maricourt	A 22 c
S.3	62cNW1 Maricourt	A 22 d
S.4	62cNW1 Maricourt	A 22 d
S.5	62cNW1 Maricourt	A 22 d
S.6	62cNW1 Maricourt	A 22 c
S.P 11 [Strong Point 11]	28SW2 Wytschaete	N 23 d 25.50
S.P. [Strongpoint, hill N of Wulverghem]	28SW4 Ploegsteert	T 5 a 8.7
S.P. 10 [Strong Point 10]	28NW4 & NE3 Zillebeke	I 28 b 4.6
S.P. 10 [Strong Point 10]	28SW2 Wytschaete	N 29 a 60.35
S.P. 12 [Strong Point 12]	28SW2 Wytschaete	N 23 b 5.2
S.P. 13 (new) [Strong Point 13]	28SW2 Wytschaete	N 17 d 6.3
S.P. 13 (old) [Strong Point 13]	28SW2 Wytschaete	N 17 d 8.1
S.P. 6 [Strong Point 6]	28SW2 Wytschaete	N 35 b 65.37
S.P. 7 [Strong Point 7]	28NW4 & NE3 Zillebeke	I 33 b 65.93
S.P. 7 [Strong Point 7]	28SW2 Wytschaete	N 35 b 45.80
S.P. 8 [Strong Point 8]	28NW4 & NE3 Zillebeke	I 28 c 51.03
S.P. 8 [Strong Point 8]	28SW2 Wytschaete	N 29 c 80.25
S.P. 9 [Strong Point 9]	28NW4 & NE3 Zillebeke	I 28 d 35.85
S.P. 9 [Strong Point 9]	28SW2 Wytschaete	N 29 c 65.65

Name	Map Sheet	Map Reference
S.P. X. & Y [Strong Points X & Y]	36NW2 Armentières	I 4 b
Saalfeld Trench	57dNE3 & 4 Hébuterne	K 15 d
Sabat House	20SW4 Bixschoote	T 30 b 25.70
Sabbath Trench	36cSW1 Lens	M 32 b
Sabines Alley	62cSW3 Vermandovillers	S 15 d, 16 b, d, 22 b, 23 a, b
Sable Copse	62bSW4 Homblières	U 23 a
Sable Pit	51bSW4 Bullecourt	U 5 b
Sable Trench	36cSW1 Lens	M 32 b
Sabliers, Abri des	51bNW1 Roclincourt	A 28 b
Sabot Copse	57cSW3 Longueval	S 14 c, d
Sachet Farm	36aNE4 Merville	K 23 a 15.40
Sachsen Weg	51bSW1 Neuville Vitasse	M 10 d, 11 c
Sack Spur [light rly]	36bNE4 Noeux-les-Mines	L 3 c
Sack Trench	36SW3 Richebourg	S 28 a
Sack Trench	51bSW2 Vis-en-Artois	O 24 c, d
Sackville Dump	57dNE3 & 4 Hébuterne	K 28 c
Sackville Street	28NW4 & NE3 Zillebeke	I 24 d
Sackville Street	36cNW1 La Bassée	A 14 d, 15 c, d
Sackville Street	36cNW3 Loos	G 4 d, 5 c, 11 a
Sackville Street	57dNE3 & 4 Hébuterne	K 28 a, c, 34 b
Sackville Street [road]	28SW1 Kemmel / 2 Wytschaete	N 10 c, 15 d, 16 a, 21 b
Sacred Trench	36cSW1 Lens	M 32 b
Sacred Trench	66cNW4 Berthenicourt	I 15 b
Sad Trench	36cSW1 Lens	M 32 b
Sad Trench	51bNW1 Roclincourt	G 6 a
Saddle Copse	27NE2 Proven	E 23 b, 24 a
Saddle Lane [road]	51bSW2 Vis-en-Artois	O 7 d, 8 a, c, d, 14 b, 15 a
Saddle Trench / Support	51bSW2 Vis-en-Artois	O 8 a, c
Saddler Lane	51bSW4 Bullecourt	U 22 c
Sadie Trench	36cSW1 Lens	M 32 b
Safety Alley	36NW4 Bois Grenier	I 31 a, c
Safety Trench	57cNE1 Quéant	D 6 c, 11 b, 12 a
Safety Trench	57dNE3 & 4 Hébuterne	L 32 b, 33 a, c
Saffron Farm	20SE2 Hooglede	R 25 b 1.4
Saga Farm	28NE2 Moorslede	E 11 a 25.35
Sagra Farm	27NE4 Abeele	L 7 a 0.1
Saigon Trench	62cSW2 Barleux	N 28 d, 34 b
Sail Trench	51bNW1 Roclincourt	G 6 a
Saillant de Prague	70dSW [2 Coucy-le-Château]	O 15 c
Saillant Fox	70dSW [4 Vauxaillon]	O 34 d
Saillisel [village]	57cSW4 Combles	U 14 b, d, 15 a, c
Sailly Junction [light rly]	36bNE4 Noeux-les-Mines	L 4 c
Sailly Keep	36bNE4 Noeux-les-Mines	L 3 b, d
Sailly Labourse - Tuning Fork Line	36bNE2 Beuvry/4 Noeux-les-Mines/ SE2 Boyeffles	extensive
Sailly Labourse [village]	36bNE2 Beuvry	L 3 a, b
Sailly Labourse Locality	36bNE2 Beuvry	L 3 a, b
Sailly Lane	51bNW4 Fampoux	I 36 d
Sailly Lane [road]	51bNE3 Noyelle-sous-Bellonne	J 26 d, 31 b, c, d, 32 a, b
Sailly Station [Post]	36NW3 Fleurbaix	G 29 b
Sailly-en-Ostrevent [village]	51bNE3 Noyelle-sous-Bellonne	J 26 b, d, 27 a, b, c, d
Sailly-Labourse [village]	36bNE4 Noeux-les-Mines	F 27 c, d, L 3 a, b
Sailly-Saillisel [village]	57cSW4 Combles	U 8 a, c, 14 a, b
Sailly-Saillisel Chateau	57cSW4 Combles	U 13 b, 14 a

Name	Map Sheet	Map Reference
Sailor Alley	57cNE4 Marcoing	L 33 d
Sailor Copse	57dSW4 [Toutencourt]	O 33 d
Sailor Reserve North	57cNE4 Marcoing	L 33 d, 34 c
Sailor Reserve South	57cSE2 Gonnelieu	R 3 b, d
Sainfoin, Boyau du	62cSW3 Vermandovillers	S 28 d, 29 c
Sains Dump	36bSE2 Boyeffles	R 7 d 1.3
Saint - see St	all sheets	
Saizieu Alley	70dNW4 St Gobain	H 30 b, d
Salaam Trench	36cSW1 Lens	N 27 c, 32 b
Salad Trench	36cSW1 Lens	N 26 b, 27a, c
Salad Trench	36SW3 Richebourg	S 16 b
Salamander Alley [1918]	62dSW [4 Cachy] / 62dSE [4 Harbonnières]	T 30 b, U 25 a, b, X 24 a
Salami Trench	36cSW1 Lens	N 32 a
Salary Trench	36cSW1 Lens	N 27 a
Sale Trench	66dNW1 Punchy	A 4 b, d, 5 c
Salem Farms	27NE4 Abeele	K 12 a 1.3
Salers Trench	66cNW1 Grugies	B 9 c, d
Salford Alley [Thiepval Wood]	57dSE1 & 2 Beaumont	Q 24 c, d
Salford Road [road]	36SW1 Aubers	M 27 d, 28 c, 34 b
Salford Siding [light rly]	36NW2 Armentières	C 2 c
Salford Trench	57dNE3 & 4 Hébuterne	K 35 d, 36 c
Salford Village	36NW2 & NE1 Houplines	C 2 a
Salient [Breslau]	62cNW1 Maricourt	A 8 b, 9 a
Saline Trench	36cSW1 Lens	N 33 a
Sallaumines [village]	36cSW2 Harnes	N 22, 23, 28, 29
Sallaumines Cemetery [civil]	36cSW2 Harnes	N 29 b 7.7
Sallaumines Circus [crossroads]	36cSW2 Harnes	N 29 a 6.5
Sallaumines Hill [hill]	36cSW1 Lens / 2 Harnes	N 21, 22, 27, 28
Sallaumines Support	36cSW2 Harnes	N 29 c, 34 b
Sallaumines Trench	36cSW2 Harnes / 4 Rouvroy	N 22 b, d, 28 b, d, 29 c, 34 b, d, T 4 b
Sallow Cross [cross roads]	20SE2 Hooglede	R 24 c 85.75
Sallow Trench	36cSW1 Lens	N 27 c, 33 a
Sally Alley	57cNE4 Marcoing	K 16 b, d
Sally Maze	36cSW2 Harnes	O 19 c
Sally Port [Ypres]	28NW4 Ypres	I 8 d 1.2
Sally Port, The	36SW3 Richebourg	S 10 b 95.70
Sally Trench	36cSW1 Lens	N 33 a
Sally Trench	36SW3 Richebourg	S 10 d, 11 a, c
Salmis Trench / Tranchée du Salmis	62cSW3 Vermandovillers	S 29 b, 30 a, b
Salmon Farm	20SE2 Hooglede	Q 24 c 1.4
Salmon Farm	28SW2 Wytschaete	O 30 d 05.55
Salmon Post	57cNE3 Hermies	J 17 a
Salmon Trench	36cSW1 Lens	N 27 d, 33 b
Salmon Trench	51bSW1 Neuville Vitasse	M 6 c
Salmon Trench	66dNW3 Hattencourt	G 26 b, c, d
Salmon Trench, & Pt. [1918]	57dNE1 & 2 Fonquevillers	K 6 a
Salmon Wood	62cNW3 Vaux	G 28 a
Salmon's Tree [Hill 131]	36cSW3 Vimy	S 19 d 60.75
Salome Sap [1918]	57dNE2 & 57cNW1 Courcelles	F 11 c, 17 a
Salomon Alley	62cSW3 Vermandovillers	S 30 a
Saloon Trench	36cSW1 Lens	N 27 d
Salop Avenue	36NW4 Bois Grenier	I 14 d, 15 c, 21 a
Salt Road [road]	36SW3 Richebourg	S 9 d, 10 c, 15 b, 16 a, c, d

Name	Map Sheet	Map Reference
Salt Trench	36cSW1 Lens / 3 Vimy	M 32 b, d
Salt Trench	51bNW1 Roclincourt	G 6 a
Salt Trench	57cNE4 Marcoing	K 10 c, d, 16 a, b
Salt Trench	62bSW1 Gricourt	M 1 b, d
Salter Corner	20SE3 Westroosebeke	W 19 c 7.3
Salty Trench	36cSW1 Lens	N 27 d, 33 b
Salute Trench	36cSW1 Lens	N 27 d
Salvat Trench	62cNW4 Péronne	H 17 c, d, 23 b
Salvation Corner	28NW4 Ypres	I 1 d 00.75
Salve Farm	27SE4 Meteren	X 12 a 85.90
Salve Trench	36cSW1 Lens	N 27 d, 33 b, 34 a
Salzach Trench / Graben	51bNW3 Arras	G 12 a
Salzbourg, Tranchée de	62cSW3 & 4 Marchélepot	T 10 a, c
Sammy Farm	28SW3 Bailleul	S 2 a 8.7
Sammy Trench [1918]	28SW3 Bailleul	S 2 a
Sampson Trench	62bSW1 Gricourt	M 16 a, c
Samson Trench	36SW3 Richebourg	S 5 b, 6 a
Samuel Alley	66dNW1 Punchy	A 16 b, d, 17 c, d
Sanction Trench	36cSW3 Vimy	N 32 c
Sanctuary Crater	28NW4 & NE3 Zillebeke	J 13 c
Sanctuary Dump [Sanctuary Wood]	28NW4 & NE3 Zillebeke	I 24 c 9.5
Sanctuary Track [1917-18]	28NW4 Ypres	I 18 d, 23 b, 24 a b
Sanctuary Trench	36cSW1 Lens	M 32 b
Sanctuary Wood	28NW4 & NE3 Zillebeke	I 18 d, 24 b, d, J 13 a, c, 19 a, c
Sand Banks	36cSW3 Vimy	S 3 c, d
Sand Lane	57cNE1 Quéant	E 20 c, 25 b, 26 a
Sand Siding [light rly, W of Canal 1917-18]	28NW2 St Julien	B 18 c
Sand Trench	51bNW1 Roclincourt	G 6 a
Sanda Street	57dSE4 Ovillers	Q 36 d, R 31 c
Sandale Trench	62cSW3 Vermandovillers	S 17 d, 23 b
Sandar's Cross Roads	28NE4 Dadizeele	L 9 a 9.8
Sandbag Alley [Sept 1915]	36SW3 Richebourg	S 4 b
Sandbag Br. [Bridge]	28SW2 Wytschaete	O 4 b 3.4
Sandbag Camp	28SW1 Kemmel	N 15 a
Sandbag Corner [near Neuve Chapelle]	36SW3 Richebourg	S 4 b, d
Sandbag Cottage	28SW4 Ploegsteert	U 28 c 1.8
Sandbag Track	28NW4 & NE3 Zillebeke	I 26 b, 27 a, c
Sandeman's Trench	57cSW3 Longueval	S 1 d, 2 a, c
Sander Trench / Graben	51bNW1 Roclincourt	A 10 d
Sanders Keep	57cNE4 Marcoing	K 10 c 5.4
Sanderson Trench [later Post Trench]	57cSW3 Longueval	S 1 b, 2 c
Sandford Banks	57dSW [4 Toutencourt]	T 21 d
Sandford Wood [formerly Bream Wood]	57dSW [4 Toutencourt]	T 22 c, d, 28 a, b
Sandgate Road	28NW4 & NE3 Zillebeke	I 24 d
Sandown Avenue	62dNE2 Méaulte	F 8 d, 9 a
Sandown Farm	28NW2 St Julien	C 15 b 75.60
Sandpit Camp	62dNE2 Méaulte	E 18 d
Sandpit, Méaulte	62dNE2 Méaulte	E 24 b 7.9
Sandsfield Farm	28NE4 Dadizeele	K 24 c 5.3
Sandy Avenue [Thiepval Wood]	57dSE1 & 2 Beaumont	Q 30 a, b
Sandy Trench	36cSW2 Harnes	O 25 a
Sandy Trench	36SW3 Richebourg	S 5 d
Sanitas Corner [road jct]	36aNE1 Morbecque	E 15 a 75.85
Sanitats Graben	51bNW3 Arras	G 18 b

Name	Map Sheet	Map Reference
Sanitats Graben	57dNE1 & 2 Fonquevillers	F 19 c
Sanitats Weg	51bNW1 Roclincourt	A 30 a
Sankey Farm	27NE1 Herzeele	K 1 a 9.4
Sans Souci [farm]	28NW4 & NE3 Zillebeke	J 2 a 30.55
Sans Souci Valley [E of Frezenberg]	28NE1 Zonnebeke / 3 Gheluvelt	D 26 c, J 2 a, b, d
Sansonnet Trench	62cSW2 Barleux	N 34 b
Sans-Souci Work	62cSW4 St. Christ	U 15 a, b
Santerre Trench	62cSW3 Vermandovillers	T 3 d, 4 a, c
Sap 1 [British, Auchy Sector, June 1916]	36cNW1 La Bassée	G 4 a
Sap 1 [High Wood]	57cSW3 Longueval	S 4 c
Sap 1 [Hohenzollern]	36cNW3 Loos	G 4 d
Sap 10	36cNW3 Loos	G 27 d, 33 d
Sap 10	36cSW1 Lens	M 25 b
Sap 10 [British, Auchy Sector, June 1916]	36cNW1 La Bassée	A 27 d
Sap 10 [Hohenzollern Redoubt]	36cNW1 La Bassée / 3 Loos	G 4 b, d
Sap 10 [Hohenzollern]	36cNW3 Loos	G 4 d
Sap 10a [British, Auchy Sector, June 1916]	36cNW1 La Bassée	A 27 d
Sap 11	36cSW1 Lens	M 25 b
Sap 11 [British, Auchy Sector, June 1916]	36cNW1 La Bassée	A 27 b
Sap 11 [Grenay]	36cNW3 Loos	G 33 d
Sap 11 [Hohenzollern Redoubt]	36cNW1 La Bassée / 3 Loos	G 4 b, d
Sap 11A [Hohenzollern Redoubt]	36cNW1 La Bassée / 3 Loos	G 4 b, d
Sap 12	36cNW1 La Bassée	A 21 b
Sap 12	36cNW3 Loos	G 19 - 33
Sap 12	36cSW1 Lens	M 25 d, 31 b, 32 a
Sap 12 [Boyau]	36cNW3 Loos	G 4 c
Sap 12 [British, Auchy Sector, June 1916]	36cNW1 La Bassée	A 27 b
Sap 12 [Hohenzollern Redoubt]	36cNW1 La Bassée / 3 Loos	G 4 b, d
Sap 12X	36cNW3 Loos	G 22 c
Sap 13	36cNW3 Loos	G 34 a
Sap 13	36cSW1 Lens	M 25 d, 31 b, 32 a
Sap 13 [British, Auchy Sector, June 1916]	36cNW1 La Bassée	A 27 b
Sap 14	36cNW3 Loos	G 21, 22, 27
Sap 14	36cSW1 Lens	M 25 d, 31 b, 32 a
Sap 14 [British, Auchy Sector, June 1916]	36cNW1 La Bassée	A 27 b
Sap 14A	36cNW3 Loos	G 22 c
Sap 15	36cNW3 Loos	G 20, 21, 22
Sap 15	36cSW1 Lens	M 32 a
Sap 15 [British, Auchy Sector, June 1916]	36cNW1 La Bassée	A 27 b
Sap 16	36cNW3 Loos	G 22 a
Sap 16	36cSW1 Lens	M 32 a
Sap 16 [British, Auchy Sector, June 1916]	36cNW1 La Bassée	A 27 b
Sap 17	36cNW3 Loos	G 22 a
Sap 17	36cSW1 Lens	M 26 c
Sap 17 [British, Auchy Sector, June 1916]	36cNW1 La Bassée	A 27 b
Sap 17A	36cNW3 Loos	G 22 a
Sap 18	36cNW3 Loos	G 22 a
Sap 18	36cSW1 Lens	M 25 d
Sap 18 [British, Auchy Sector, June 1916]	36cNW1 La Bassée	A 27 b
Sap 19	36cNW3 Loos	G 22 a
Sap 19 [British, Auchy Sector, June 1916]	36cNW1 La Bassée	A 21 d, 27 b
Sap 1A	36cNW3 Loos	G 33 a, b
Sap 1B	36cNW3 Loos	G 34 a
Sap 2	36cNW3 Loos	G 33 b

Name	Map Sheet	Map Reference
Sap 2 [British, Auchy Sector, June 1916]	36cNW1 La Bassée	G 4 a
Sap 2 [High Wood]	57cSW3 Longueval	S 4 c
Sap 20	36cNW3 Loos	G 22 a, c
Sap 20	51bNW1 Roclincourt	A 23 c
Sap 20 [British, Auchy Sector, June 1916]	36cNW1 La Bassée	A 21 d
Sap 21	36cNW3 Loos	G 22 c, 28 a, 33 b
Sap 21	51bNW1 Roclincourt	A 23 c
Sap 21 [British, Auchy Sector, June 1916]	36cNW1 La Bassée	A 21 d
Sap 22	36cNW3 Loos	G 28 a
Sap 22	51bNW1 Roclincourt	A 23 a, c
Sap 22 [British, Auchy Sector, June 1916]	36cNW1 La Bassée	A 21 d
Sap 23	36cNW3 Loos	G 28 a
Sap 23	51bNW1 Roclincourt	A 22 d
Sap 23 [British, Auchy Sector, June 1916]	36cNW1 La Bassée	A 21 d
Sap 24	36cNW3 Loos	G 27 b, d
Sap 24 [British, Auchy Sector, June 1916]	36cNW1 La Bassée	A 21 d
Sap 25	36cNW3 Loos	G 27, 28, 33
Sap 25 [British, Auchy Sector, June 1916]	36cNW1 La Bassée	A 21 d
Sap 26	36cNW3 Loos	G 22, 28, 33
Sap 26	51bNW1 Roclincourt	A 22 b, d
Sap 26 [British, Auchy Sector, June 1916]	36cNW1 La Bassée	A 21 d
Sap 27	36cNW3 Loos	G 28 c, 33 d
Sap 27 [British, Auchy Sector, June 1916]	36cNW1 La Bassée	A 21 d
Sap 27a [British, Auchy Sector, June 1916]	36cNW1 La Bassée	A 21 d
Sap 27b [British, Auchy Sector, June 1916]	36cNW1 La Bassée	A 21 d
Sap 28	36cNW3 Loos	G 27 b, 33 c, d
Sap 28 [British, Auchy Sector, June 1916]	36cNW1 La Bassée	A 21 d
Sap 29	36cNW3 Loos	G 33 d
Sap 29 [British, Auchy Sector, June 1916]	36cNW1 La Bassée	A 21 d
Sap 3	28SW4 Ploegsteert	U 15 a
Sap 3	36cNW3 Loos	G 33 b
Sap 3 [British, Auchy Sector, June 1916]	36cNW1 La Bassée	G 4 a
Sap 3 [High Wood]	57cSW3 Longueval	S 4 c
Sap 30	36cNW3 Loos	G 21 d, 22 c, 33 b
Sap 30 [British, Auchy Sector, June 1916]	36cNW1 La Bassée	A 21 b, d
Sap 31	36cNW3 Loos	G 33 b
Sap 31 [British, Cuinchy Sector, June 1916]	36cNW1 La Bassée	A 21 b
Sap 31A	36cNW3 Loos	G 33 b
Sap 31a [British, Cuinchy Sector, June 1916]	36cNW1 La Bassée	A 21 b
Sap 32	36cNW3 Loos	G 33 b
Sap 32 [British, Cuinchy Sector, June 1916]	36cNW1 La Bassée	A 21 b
Sap 33	36cNW3 Loos	G 33 b
Sap 33 [British, Cuinchy Sector, June 1916]	36cNW1 La Bassée	A 21 b
Sap 34 [British, Cuinchy Sector, June 1916]	36cNW1 La Bassée	A 21 b
Sap 35	36cNW3 Loos	G 33 b, 34 a
Sap 35 [British, Cuinchy Sector, June 1916]	36cNW1 La Bassée	A 21 b
Sap 36 [British, Cuinchy Sector, June 1916]	36cNW1 La Bassée	A 21 b
Sap 37 [British, Cuinchy Sector, June 1916]	36cNW1 La Bassée	A 21 b, 22 a
Sap 38 [British, Cuinchy Sector, June 1916]	36cNW1 La Bassée	A 21 b, 22 a
Sap 39 [British, Cuinchy Sector, June 1916]	36cNW1 La Bassée	A 15 d, 16 c
Sap 3a [British, Auchy Sector, June 1916]	36cNW1 La Bassée	A 28 c
Sap 4	28SW4 Ploegsteert	U 15 a
Sap 4	36cNW3 Loos	G 33 b
Sap 4 [British, Auchy Sector, June 1916]	36cNW1 La Bassée	A 28 c

Name	Map Sheet	Map Reference
Sap 4 [High Wood]	57cSW3 Longueval	S 4 c
Sap 40 [British, Cuinchy Sector, June 1916]	36cNW1 La Bassée	A 15 d
Sap 41 [British, Cuinchy Sector, June 1916]	36cNW1 La Bassée	A 15 d
Sap 42 [British, Cuinchy Sector, June 1916]	36cNW1 La Bassée	A 15 d
Sap 43 [British, Cuinchy Sector, June 1916]	36cNW1 La Bassée	A 15 d
Sap 44 [B, S of canal, Cuinchy Sector, June 1916]	36cNW1 La Bassée	A 15 d
Sap 45 [Br, N of Canal, Cambrin Sector, June '16]	36cNW1 La Bassée	A 15 d
Sap 46	36cNW3 Loos	G 33 c, d
Sap 46 [British, Cambrin Sector, June 1916]	36cNW1 La Bassée	A 15 d
Sap 46 [N of Canal]	36cNW1 La Bassée	A 15 d
Sap 47 [British, Cambrin Sector, June 1916]	36cNW1 La Bassée	A 15 d
Sap 47 [N of Canal]	36cNW1 La Bassée	A 15 d
Sap 48 [British, Cambrin Sector, June 1916]	36cNW1 La Bassée	A 15 b
Sap 48 [N of Canal]	36cNW1 La Bassée	A 15 b
Sap 49 [N of Canal]	36cNW1 La Bassée	A 15 b
Sap 4a [British, Auchy Sector, June 1916]	36cNW1 La Bassée	A 28 c
Sap 4b [British, Auchy Sector, June 1916]	36cNW1 La Bassée	A 28 c
Sap 5	28NW2 St Julien	C 22 b
Sap 5	36cNW3 Loos	G 33 b, 34 a
Sap 5 [British, Auchy Sector, June 1916]	36cNW1 La Bassée	A 28 c
Sap 50 [N of Canal]	36cNW1 La Bassée	A 15 b
Sap 51 [N of Canal]	36cNW1 La Bassée	A 15 b
Sap 52 [N of Canal]	36cNW1 La Bassée	A 15 b
Sap 54 [Givenchy]	36cNW1 La Bassée	A 9 d, 15 b
Sap 55 [Givenchy]	36cNW1 La Bassée	A 9 d
Sap 56 [Givenchy]	36cNW1 La Bassée	A 9 d
Sap 57 [Givenchy]	36cNW1 La Bassée	A 9 d
Sap 58 [Givenchy]	36cNW1 La Bassée	A 9 d
Sap 59 [Givenchy]	36cNW1 La Bassée	A 9 d
Sap 5A	36cNW3 Loos	G 27 d
Sap 5a [British, Auchy Sector, June 1916]	36cNW1 La Bassée	A 28 c
Sap 5b [British, Auchy Sector, June 1916]	36cNW1 La Bassée	A 28 c
Sap 6	36cNW3 Loos	G 27 d, 28 c
Sap 6 [British, Auchy Sector, June 1916]	36cNW1 La Bassée	A 28 c
Sap 60 [Givenchy]	36cNW1 La Bassée	A 9 d
Sap 61 [Givenchy]	36cNW1 La Bassée	A 9 d
Sap 62 [Givenchy]	36cNW1 La Bassée	A 9 d
Sap 63 [Givenchy]	36cNW1 La Bassée	A 9 d
Sap 64 [Givenchy]	36cNW1 La Bassée	A 9 b
Sap 6A	36cNW3 Loos	G 28 c
Sap 7	36cNW3 Loos	G 27 b, d, 28 c
Sap 7	36cSW1 Lens	M 25 b, d
Sap 7 [British, Auchy Sector, June 1916]	36cNW1 La Bassée	A 27 d
Sap 72 [Holly Lane]	36cNW3 Loos	G 19 c
Sap 72A	36cNW3 Loos	G 19 c
Sap 72Z	36cNW3 Loos	G 19 c
Sap 73	36cNW3 Loos	G 19 c
Sap 73A [Leinster Lane]	36cNW3 Loos	G 19 c
Sap 74 [6th Avenue]	36cNW3 Loos	G 18 d, 19 a, c
Sap 76	36cNW3 Loos	G 18 b
Sap 77	36cNW3 Loos	G 18 b
Sap 78	36cNW3 Loos	G 12 d
Sap 79	36cNW3 Loos	G 12 d
Sap 7A	36cNW3 Loos	G 28 c

Name	Map Sheet	Map Reference
Sap 7B	36cNW3 Loos	G 28 c
Sap 8	36cNW3 Loos	G 27 d, 28 c, 33 d
Sap 8 [British, Auchy Sector, June 1916]	36cNW1 La Bassée	A 27 d
Sap 8 Vassauz / Vasseaux Lane	36cSW1 Lens	M 25 b, d
Sap 80	36cNW3 Loos	G 12 d
Sap 81	36cNW3 Loos	G 12 d
Sap 82	36cNW3 Loos	G 12 d
Sap 84	36cNW3 Loos	G 12 d
Sap 85	36cNW3 Loos	G 12 c
Sap 8A	36cNW3 Loos	G 28 c
Sap 8a [British, Auchy Sector, June 1916]	36cNW1 La Bassée	A 27 d
Sap 8B	36cNW3 Loos	G 28 c
Sap 8C	36cNW3 Loos	G 28 a
Sap 8D	36cNW3 Loos	G 28 a
Sap 8E	36cNW3 Loos	G 28 a
Sap 9	36cNW3 Loos	G 28 a, 33 d
Sap 9 [British, Auchy Sector, June 1916]	36cNW1 La Bassée	A 27 d
Sap 9 [Hohenzollern]	36cNW3 Loos	G 4 d
Sap 90	36cNW3 Loos	G 12 c
Sap 91	36cNW3 Loos	G 12 c
Sap 92	36cNW3 Loos	G 12 c
Sap 9A	36cNW3 Loos	G 28 a
Sap 9B	36cNW3 Loos	G 22 c
Sap A1	36cNW3 Loos	G 16 c
Sap A2	36cNW3 Loos	G 16 d
Sap A3	36cNW3 Loos	G 16 d
Sap A4	36cNW3 Loos	G 16 d
Sap A5	36cNW3 Loos	G 16 d
Sap B	36cNW3 Loos	G 16 d
Sap B1	36cNW3 Loos	G 16 d
Sap B2	36cNW3 Loos	G 16 d
Sap B3	36cNW3 Loos	G 17 c
Sap B4	36cNW3 Loos	G 17 a
Sap B5	36cNW3 Loos	G 17 a
Sap C	36cNW3 Loos	G 17 a
Sap D.D.	36cNW3 Loos	G 17 a
Sap F	36cNW3 Loos	G 10 d, 11 c
Sap F1	36cNW3 Loos	G 10 d
Sap F2	36cNW3 Loos	G 10 d
Sap K1	36cNW3 Loos	G 4 d
Sap K2	36cNW3 Loos	G 4 c
Sap K3	36cNW3 Loos	G 4 c
Sap K4	36cNW3 Loos	G 4 c
Sap K5	36cNW3 Loos	G 4 c
Sap K6	36cNW3 Loos	G 4 c
Sap L1	36cNW3 & 1 Loos	G 4 a
Sap L2	36cNW3 & 1 Loos	G 4 a
Sap M	36cNW3 & 1 Loos	G 4 a
Sap M2	36cNW3 & 1 Loos	G 4 a
Sap M3	36cNW3 & 1 Loos	G 4 a
Sap M4	36cNW3 & 1 Loos	G 4 a
Sap M5	36cNW3 & 1 Loos	G 4 a
Sap M6	36cNW3 & 1 Loos	G 4 a
Sap No.5	62cNW1 Maricourt	A 9 a 87.40

Name	Map Sheet	Map Reference
Sap No.6	62cNW1 Maricourt	A 9 b 02.15
Sap, The [Sanctuary Wood, 1915]	28NW4 & NE3 Zillebeke	J 13 c
Sapignies [village]	57cNW3 Bapaume	H 2 c, 8 a, b, c, d
Sapignies Switch	57cNW3 Bapume / 4 Beugny	G 11, 12, H 1 to 6, 7
Sapper Camp	28NW4 Ypres	I 3 c, 9 a, b
Sapper Lane [road]	51bNW4 Fampoux	I 30 a, c, 25 b, c, d, 36 a
Sapper Road	51bNW1 Roclincourt	A 3 d
Sapper Street	36cSW1 Lens	M 14 c
Sapper Trench	36cSW2 Harnes	N 30 c
Sapper Trench	36SW3 Richebourg	S 10 c, 16 a
Sapper Trench [W of Guillemont]	57cSW3 Longueval	S 24 d
Sappho Trench	36cSW3 Vimy	M 32 d, 33 c
Saps A, B & C [High Wood]	57cSW3 Longueval	S 3 c
Sarah Farm	20SE2 Hooglede	Q 21 d 80.55
Sarah Trench	36SW3 Richebourg	S 6 c, 12 a, c
Sark Post	57cNE4 Marcoing	K 10 a, b
Sarments Trench	62cSW3 Vermandovillers	S 16 a, b, c
Sars Alley	57cSW1 Gueudecourt	M 15 c, d
Sars, Le [village]	57dSE2 & 57cSW1 Le Sars	M 15, 16
Sarson House	36NW1 Steenwerck	B 14 c 0.1
Sart Post [Sart Farm]	62cNE2 Epéhy	F 11 c, 17 a
Sart Sart	62cNE2 Epéhy	F 11 c, 17 a
Sart, le [village]	36aNE3 Haverskerque	K 27 c, d
Sash Trench	51bNW1 Roclincourt	G 6 a
Saskatchewan Road [road]	36cSW4 Rouvroy / 51bNW2 Oppy	T 22 a, b, d, 29 a, c, B 5 a
Saskatoon Support	36cSW1 Lens	N 25 d, 31 b
Saskatoon Trench	36cSW1 Lens	N 25 d, 26 c, 32 a
Satan Trench	36SW3 Richebourg	S 12 a
Satellite Trench	62cSW3 Vermandovillers	S 17 a, b
Satin Support, & Avenue	57cSE4 Villers-Guislain	X 10 b, c, d
Satin Trench	36cSW3 Vimy	M 33 c
Satin Trench	57cSE4 Villers-Guislain	X 10 b, d, 11 c, 17 a
Satrape Alley	62cSW3 Vermandovillers	S 13 d, 14 c, d, 15 c, 21 a, b
Sauchiehall Reserve [1918]	57dSE3 [Bouzincourt]	W 2 d, 8 a, b, c, 14 a
Sauchiehall Street [Thiepval Wood]	57dSE1 & 2 Beaumont	R 25 c
Sauchiehall Support [1918]	57dSE3 [Bouzincourt]	W 3 c, 8 b, d, 9 a
Sauchiehall Trench [1918]	57dSE3 [Bouzincourt]	W 9 a, c, 15 a
Sauchy-Cauchy [village]	51bSE2 Oisy-le-Verger	Q 34 b, 35 a
Saucisse Wood Trench	62cNW4 Péronne	H 4 d, 10 b, 11 a
Saucisses Alley	62cNW3 Vaux	H 19 c, d, 25 a, b, 26 a
Saucy Trench	36SW3 Richebourg	S 30 a
Saudemont Mill	51bSE1 Saudemont	P 24 b 8.6
Saufre Trench	66dNW1 Punchy	A 5 a
Sauge, Tranchée de la	66eNE4 Beaufort	L 27 d, 33 b, d
Saule Fork [road jct]	36NW1 Steenwerck	A 16 a 95.55
Saule Inn	36NW1 Steenwerck	A 16 a 9.5
Saules Farm	20SW4 Bixschoote	U 25 b 3.2
Saules, Boyau des [Willows]	62cSW1 Dompierre	M 9 a, b
Saunders Copse	66dNW3 Hattencourt	G 28 a, c
Saurien Alley	62cSW3 Vermandovillers	S 7 b,d, 8 c,d, 9 c,d, 14 b, 15 a,b, 16 a
Saurus Lane [trench]	51bSE3 Cagnicourt	V 19 a, b
Saurus Trench	51bSE3 Cagnicourt	V 19 b, 20 c
Sausage Lane	51bNW3 Arras	H 26 d
Sausage Redoubt	57dNE1 & 2 Fonquevillers	F 19 a

Name	Map Sheet	Map Reference
Sausage Redoubt / Work	51bSW1 Neuville Vitasse	M 16 b, 17 a
Sausage Redoubt [Heligoland Redoubt]	57dSE4 Ovillers	X 20 b, d, 21 a, c
Sausage Rise [road]	57dNE1 & 2 Fonquevillers	F 13 c, 19 a
Sausage Support, South	57dSE4 Ovillers	X 20 d, 21 c, 26 b, 27 a
Sausage Trench	57dNE1 & 2 Fonquevillers	F 19 a, b
Sausage Trench, South	57dSE4 Ovillers	X 20 d, 26 b
Sausage Valley	57dSE4 Ovillers	X 14, 15, 20, 21, 26
Sauterelle Alley	62cSW4 St. Christ	U 15 d, 16 c
Sauvage Alley	62cSW3 Vermandovillers	S 18 c, d
Sauvage House	20SW4 Bixschoote	T 30 d
Sauve Alley	62cNW1 Maricourt	H 1 b, 2 a
Sauvillers Wood	66eNW [4 Morisel]	I 26, 31, 32, 33
Savage Farm	28NE2 Moorslede	E 24 d 2.9
Savage Street	57dNE1 & 2 Fonquevillers	E 9 a, b
Savatte Alley	66dNW3 Hattencourt	G 20 d, 21 c,d, 22 c,d, 23 c,d, 28 a,b
Savatte Copse	66dNW3 Hattencourt	G 28 a
Save Trench	66cNW4 Berthenicourt	I 33 d
Savernake Wood	62cNW1 Maricourt / 2 Bouchavesnes	B 3 b, c, d, 4 a, c
Savile / Saville Road [road]	28NW4 Ypres	I 2 d, 3 c, 9 a
Savile Row [Hooge 1915]	28NW4 & NE3 Zillebeke	I 17 b, 18 a
Saville Row	36cNW1 La Bassée / 3 Loos	G 4 b, d
Saville Row Tunnel	36cNW1 La Bassée / 3 Loos	G 4 d
Savour / Savoury Trench	36SW3 Richebourg	S 16 d
Savoury Bridge [road over canal]	36aNE1 Morbecque	D 6 c 90.15
Savoy Cottages	27NE4 Abeele	L 22 a 5.7
Savoy Trench	57cSW3 Longueval	S 15 a, b, 16 a, b
Savoy, The [Langemarck]	20SW4 Bixschoote	U 23 c
Savoy, The [O.P.]	36SW3 Richebourg	S 2 c
Savvy Trench	36cSW3 Vimy	M 32 d
Saw Trench	51bNW1 Roclincourt	G 6 a
Saw Trench	51bSW1 Neuville Vitasse	M 22 c, 28 a
Saw Wood	51bNE4 Cantin	L 20 b, d, 21 c
Sawmill Alley	66cNW4 Berthenicourt	I 25 b
Sawyer Fork [road junction]	20SE2 Hooglede	R 25 d 1.1
Saxe Trench	57cSW4 Combles	U 15 d, 21 b, 22 a
Saxe Trench	62cSE1 Bouvincourt	P 7 a, c, d
Saxe Trench [1918]	62dSW [4 Cachy]	U 17 a
Saxon Trench	57cSW4 Combles	N 36 d
Saxon Way	36cNW1 La Bassée	A 9 d, 10 c
Saxony Alley	62bSW4 Homblières	T 23 c, 29 a
Saxony Trench [1918]	62dSW [4 Cachy]	U 16 b, d, 17 a, c
Scabbard Alley	51bNW4 Fampoux	I 31 a, b
Scabbard Trench	57cSW1 Gueudecourt	N 14 d, 19 b, 20 a, b
Scabbard Trench / Support	51bNW4 Fampoux	I 25 c, 31 a
Scale Cottage	28NE2 Moorslede	F 27 b 75.80
Scallop Farm	36aNE1 Morbecque	D 23 d 15.85
Scamp Farm	27NE2 Proven	E 4 b 2.5
Scandal Crossing [level crossing]	36aNE2 Vieux Berquin	F 9 c 30.65
Scanlan Cross [cross roads]	36NW1 Steenwerck	A 22 d 5.9
Scantling Farm	28SW3 Bailleul	S 4 d 4.7
Scapa Trench	51bNW3 Arras / 4 Fampoux	H 27 d, 28 c
Scar Trench	51bNW1 Roclincourt	G 6 a
Scarabes Trench	62cSW3 Vermandovillers	S 17 c, d, 23 a
Scaramouche Trench	62cSW3 Vermandovillers	S 10 d, 11 c

Name	Map Sheet	Map Reference
Scarlet Copse	62bSW4 Homblières	T 30 d
Scarp Cottage	27SE4 Meteren	X 26 d 3.5
Scarpe Valley	51bNW3 Arras / 4 Fampoux	extensive
Scawby [Ploegsteert Wood]	28SW4 Ploegsteert	U 21 d 05.80
Schaaf Trench / Tranchée Schaaf	62cSW3 & 4 Marchélepot	T 20 c, 26 a
Schaaf, Bois	62cSW3 & 4 Marchélepot	T 26 a, c
Schaexken [hamlet & cross roads]	27SE4 Meteren	R 35 c 5.9
Schantekler Graben	51bNW3 Arras	G 12 a, b
Schein Stellung	51bSW1 Neuville Vitasse	M 5 b, d
Scheldt [farm]	28NE1 Zonnebeke	J 6 b 15.30
Scherpe Post [1918]	28SW1 Kemmel	M 11 d 4.6
Scherpe Post [N of Scherpenberg, 1918]	28SW1 Kemmel	M 10 d
Scherpenberg [hill, & dugouts]	28SW1 Kemmel	M 17, 18
Scherpenberg Mill / Molen	28SW1 Kemmel	M 17 b 9.4
Scherpenberg North Camp	28SW1 Kemmel	M 17 b, 18 a
Scherpenberg South Camp	28SW1 Kemmel	M 17 b, 18 a
Scherpenberg-Cheapside Line	28SW1 Kemmel	M 18, N 13, 14, 15
Schierveld Farm	20SE2 Hooglede	Q 36 a 0.5
Schiethoek [place name]	20SE2 Hooglede	Q 30 a 2.3
Schinngen Weg	51bSW1 Neuville Vitasse	M 21 b, d
Schlangen Redoubt / Work	51bSW1 Neuville Vitasse	M 28 a
Schlangen Weg	51bSW1 Neuville Vitasse	M 21 a, b, d, 22 c
Schleswig Trench	62bSW3 St Quentin	T 2 c, 7 b, 8 a
Schloss Weg	36cSW3 Vimy	S 23 c
Schloss Weg	51bSW1 Neuville Vitasse	M 10 b, 11 a
Schmidthohle	51bSW2 Vis-en-Artois	O 30 c
Schnitzel Farm	28SW4 Ploegsteert	U 3 c 8.2
Schofield Fork [road jct]	28NE4 Dadizeele	L 21 b 4.9
Scholar Cross Roads	28NE2 Moorslede	F 5 c 95.37
School [Ecole de bienfaisance de l'Etat]	28NW4 Ypres	I 9 c
School Camp	27NE4 Abeele	L 3 c, d
School House	28NW4 Ypres	I 15 a 10.95
School House [light railway locality, 1917]	28SW1 Kemmel	N 21 a
School Keep [Fleurbaix]	36NW3 Fleurbaix	H 21 d
School Trench	66dNW1 Punchy	A 5 a, c
Schoudemonthoek	27NE4 Abeele	L 16 b
Schout Farm [Schouthoek]	28NE2 Moorslede	F 19 c 65.70
Schouthoek	28NE2 Moorslede	F 19 c, d
Schreiboom	20SW4 Bixschoote	U 23 b
Schubert Trench	57cSW4 Combles	U 26 a, b
Schüler [pillbox locality]	28NE1 Zonnebeke	D 7 c, d
Schüler Farm	28NE1 Zonnebeke	D 13 a 8.8
Schüler Galleries	28NE1 Zonnebeke	D 13 a
Schumann Trench	57cSW2 Villers-au-Flos / 4 Combles	O 31 b, d, 32 c
Schwaben Höhe [Lochnagar Crater site]	57dSE4 Ovillers	X 20 a
Schwaben Nest	57dNE1 & 2 Fonquevillers	E 23 c, d
Schwaben Redoubt	57dSE1 & 2 Beaumont	R 19 d, 20 c
Schwaben Trench	57dSE1 & 2 Beaumont	R 26 c, d, 32 b, 33 a
Schwaben Tunnel	36cSW3 Vimy	S 28 c, d, 29 c
Schwarzwald Graben	57dNE1 & 2 Fonquevillers	F 19 a, b, 20 a
Schwarzwald Graben / Third Ave [W of Pozières]	57dSE4 Ovillers	X 2 d, 3 b, c, 4 a
Schweickert Graben	57dNE3 & 4 Hébuterne	K 5 d, 6 c,11 a, b
Schwerin Alley	66dNW1 Punchy	A 26 b, d, 27 a
Schwerin Copse	66dNW1 Punchy	A 26 b, d

Name	Map Sheet	Map Reference
Schweriner Weg	51bNW1 Roclincourt	B 25, G 6, H 1
Schwetz, Boyau	66dNW3 Hattencourt / 66eNE4 Beaufort	G 19 d, L 23c, d, 24 c
Scimitar Farm	28NE2 Moorslede	F 2 c 3.9
Scone Street	57dSE4 Ovillers	X 19 b
Scorer Junction [road jct]	28NE4 Dadizeele	K 11 b 5.7
Scorn Trench	57cNE4 Marcoing	K 24 b, L 19 a
Scot Farm	36aSE1 St Venant	Q 27 a 5.7
Scotch Alley	57cSW3 Longueval	S 7 b
Scotch Row	57cSW3 Longueval	S 12 a, b
Scotch Street [road]	57cNE3 Hermies	K 7 c, d, 13 b, 14 a
Scotland Support	57cSW1 Gueudecourt	M 15 b, 16 a
Scots Alley	27SE4 Meteren	X 10 b, d
Scots Alley	36cNW3 Loos	G 30 d, H 31 c
Scots Guards [farm, June 1915]	28NW4 & NE3 Zillebeke	J 14 d 05.70
Scots House	28NW2 St Julien	C 1 a 1.6
Scots Lane [road]	36cSW1 Lens / 2 Harnes	N 3 d, 4 c
Scots Redoubt	57dSE4 Ovillers	X 21 c
Scots Trench	27SE4 Meteren	X 16 b, c, d, 21 c, d, 22 a, c
Scots Valley	51bNW3 Arras	H 19, 25, 31
Scott / Scott's Farm	28SW2 Wytschaete	O 25 a 4.6
Scott Dump	36cSW1 Lens	M 30 d 2.1
Scott Farm	20SE2 Hooglede	R 28 d 42.25
Scott Line [light rly]	36cSW1 Lens	M 30 a, c, d
Scott Post	36SW3 Richebourg	S 2 a 05.05 or S 8 a, c
Scott Post	57cNE4 Marcoing	K 10 a
Scott Post [1918]	28NE3 Gheluvelt	J 9 b 99.15
Scottish Alley	36cNW3 Loos	G 24 a, b, d
Scottish Camp	28NW3 Poperinghe	G 23 a, b
Scottish Farm	28NW3 Poperinghe	G 23 b 0.6
Scottish House	20SW4 Bixschoote	U 13 c 5.7
Scottish Trench	57cSW3 Longueval	S 30 a, c, d
Scottish Trench [Givenchy]	36cNW1 La Bassée	A 9 a, b
Scottish Wood Camp	28NW4 Ypres	H 35 b
Scott's Post [Polygon Wd]	28NE3 Gheluvelt	J 9 b, d
Scott's Redoubt	57dSE4 Ovillers	X 21 c 9.9
Scourinburn	57dSE4 Ovillers	X 19 b
Scout Lane	57cNW2 Vaulx-Vraucourt	B 4 b, 5 a
Scrabo Camps	28NW3 Poperinghe	G 21 c, d
Scratch Trench	36cSW3 Vimy	M 33 c, S 2 b
Screecher Gorse	57dSW [4 Toutencourt]	T 18 b, U 13 a
Screech-Owl Trench [1918]	66eNW [2 Thennes]	C 7 d, 13 a, b
Screed Farm	27NE2 Proven	E 4 a 75.50
Screen Avenue	36NW2 Armentières	C 9 d
Screw Trench	57cNE4 Marcoing	K 24 a, b
Scrip Farm	28SW3 Bailleul	S 3 a 5.7
Scrub Valley	57cSE1 Bertincourt / 2 Gonnelieu	Q 21, 22, 27, 28
Scrum Trench	57cSW4 Combles	U 15 d
Scull Support	57cNE4 Marcoing	K 24 b, L 19 a
Scully Trench [Sully Trench]	20SW2 Zwartegat	O 25 b
Sculptors Fork [road jct]	28NE2 Moorslede	F 30 c 20.86
Scupper Farm	28NW4 Ypres	H 11 b 8.9
Scutari Alley / Trench	62cNW2 Bouchavesnes	C 22 c, 27 b, 28 a, c
Seaford House	20SE2 Hooglede	R 1 b 6.5
Seaforth Alley	36cNW3 Loos	G 36 d, M 6 b

Name	Map Sheet	Map Reference
Seaforth Avenue	28SW4 Ploegsteert	U 8 c, d
Seaforth Cottage	28SW4 Ploegsteert	U 8 d 3.3
Seaforth Craters	36cSW1 Lens	M 6 b
Seaforth Farm	28SW4 Ploegsteert	U 8 d 1.4
Seaforth Trench	57cSW3 Longueval	S 4 d, 10 b
Seaforth Trench	57dSE2 Beaumont	Q 10 b
Seagull Farm [1918]	28SW1 Kemmel	M 15 c 3.7
Seal Lane	57cNE1 Quéant	E 19 c
Seal Trench	36cSW3 Vimy	M 33 c
Seal Trench	51bNW1 Roclincourt	G 6 a
Seal Trench	57cNE4 Marcoing	K 16 b, d, 17 c
Seal Trench	66cSW2 Vendeuil	O 4 a, b
Seamew Farm [1918]	28SW1 Kemmel	M 11 a 6.4
Sear Trench	51bNW1 Roclincourt	G 6 a
Searchlight Lane [German CT, E of Mushroom]	36NW4 Bois Grenier	I 11 c
Seatle Farm	27NE1 Herzeele	E 2 c 6.7
Sebald Graben	51bNW3 Arras	G 6 d, 12 b
Sebastopol Alley / Boyau de Sebastopol	62cSW3 & 4 Marchélepot	T 13 c, d
Sebastopol Farm	66eNW [4 Morisel]	H 28 b 3.5
Sebastopol Trench	36cSW3 Vimy	M 32 c
Secauspion Road [plank, Bellewaarde-Westhoek]	28NW4 & NE3 Zillebeke	J 7 a, b
Seclin [farm]	36aNE2 Vieux Berquin	E 22 c 9.3
Second Garde Stellung	57dNE3 & 4 Hébuterne	K 5 d, 6 c, 12 a, b
Second Parallel [S of Mill Road, Thiepval Wood]	57dSE1 & 2 Beaumont	Q 24 d
Second Street [German support line]	57dSE4 Ovillers	X 8 c, 14 a
Second Trench [German]	36cSW3 Vimy	S 15 a, c, d, 21 b
Sect Farm	27SE2 Berthen	Q 29 c 3.4
Section Bend [road]	28NW3 Poperinghe	H 8 a 5.2
Sedd-el-Bahr	36NW4 Bois Grenier	I 25 d
Sedgewick Farm	20SE3 Westroosebeke	W 20 b 7.7
Sediment House	36aNE1 Morbecque	D 11 d 5.7
Seed Trench	51bNW1 Roclincourt / 3 Arras	G 6 a, c
Seed Trench	57cSE4 Villers-Guislain	X 29 d
Seegar Cut	62dNE2 Méaulte	F 9 a
Seek Trench	51bNW1 Roclincourt	G 6 a
Seer Farm	28NE2 Moorslede	F 28 a 4.8
Seesaw Support	36SW3 Richebourg	S 16 d, 22 b
Segard Ridge	28NW4 Ypres / SW2 Wytschaete	H 24, 29, 30, 35, 36, I 19, N 4, 5
Segard Wood	28NW4 Ypres	H 30 a, b, d
Segard, Château	28NW4 Ypres	H 30 a 3.0
Seguir Trench	36cSW3 Vimy	S 3 a
Seigle, Tranchée du	57dSE4 Ovillers	X 23 d
Seigneurie Ferme, la	28SW4 Ploegsteert	U 24 d 5.5
Seine [farm & pillbox]	28NE1 Zonnebeke	D 16 d 4.4
Seine [light rly siding 1917-18]	28NE1 Zonnebeke	D 16 c, d
Seine Alley	66cNW4 Berthenicourt	H 29 c
Seine Corner	28NE1 Zonnebeke	D 16 d 3.5
Seine Dump	28NE1 Zonnebeke	D 16 d 2.6
Selby Lane	51bSW4 Bullecourt	U 23 d, 29 b
Selby Row [houses]	27NE4 Abeele	L 9 b, 10 a
Seldom Trench	36cSW3 Vimy	M 32 d
Selency [Redoubt]	62bSW3 St Quentin	S 10 a
Selency [village]	62bSW3 St Quentin	S 9 a, b
Selfridge's [farm buildings]	28NE2 Moorslede	F 8 c 5.9

Name	Map Sheet	Map Reference
Selkirk Farm	28NE2 Moorslede	E 27 d 65.75
Selsey Farm	36aNE4 Merville	L 11 c 1.6
Selvigny [village]	57bSW2 Clary	O 13 a, b, c, d
Selvigny Mill [windmill]	57bSW2 Clary	O 14 a 4.1
Sénateurs Trench	62cSW3 Vermandovillers	S 10 d, 11 c, d, 16 b
Senator Bridge [road over watercourse]	36aNE1 Morbecque	D 17 a 15.20
Senecat Wood	66eNW [2 Thennes]	B 22, 23, 28, 29
Senegal Farm	20SE3 Westroosebeke	V 7 c 9.2
Senercy Trench	66cNW4 Berthenicourt	I 22 b
Senlac Farm	27SE2 Berthen	R 32 b 50.95
Senlis [village]	57dSE3 [Bouzincourt]	V 10, 11, 16, 17
Sensée Avenue	51bSW4 Bullecourt	T 12 b
Sensée Reserve	51bSW4 Bullecourt	T 12 d
Sensée River & Valley	51bSW3 Boisleux/4 Bullecourt/ 57cNW1 Gomiec't	extensive
Sensée Trench	51bSW4 Bullecourt	U 1 d, 2 a, c
Sen-Sen Trench	36cSW3 Vimy	M 33 c, S 2 d, 3 a
Sentence Houses	28NE2 Moorslede	F 11 d 4.7
Sentier Farm	20SW4 Bixschoote	U 20 d 5.8
Sentinel Ridge	62bNW3 Bellicourt	G 8 a, b, c, d, 9 a, b, c
Sentry Tree [E of Ploegsteert Wood]	28SW4 Ploegsteert	U 21 b 25.60
Separation Alley	62cSW1 Dompierre	N 2 c, d, 3 c, d
Sepoy Mill [windmill]	27SE3 Borre	P 32 c 50.35
September Avenue	51bNW3 Arras	G 11, 16, 17
September Post	28NW4 & NE3 Zillebeke	I 31 b
Septenville [hamlet]	57dSW [3 Talmas]	S 18 c, 23 b, 24 a
Septenville 1st Support	57dSW [3 Talmas]	S 18 a, c, 23 d, 24 a, c
Septenville 2nd Support	57dSW [3 Talmas]	S 18 c, 23 b, d, 24 a
Septenville Flank Left	57dSW [3 Talmas]	S 17 b, 18 a, b
Septenville Reserve	57dSW [3 Talmas]	S 17 b, c, d
Septenville Trench	57dSW [3 Talmas]	S 18 d, 24 b, c, d, T 13 c, 19 a
Sept-Fours [village]	66dNW3 Hattencourt	H 32 a, c
Septic House [1918]	28SW1 Kemmel	M 24 d 25.40
Septic Trench	36cSW3 Vimy	M 33 c
Septième Barn	28SW4 Ploegsteert	U 4 a 4.7
Sepulcre Trench	66dNW1 Punchy	A 10 b, d
Sequehart [village]	62bNW4 Ramicourt	H 29 d, 30 c, 35 b, 36 a
Séquenteau, le [place name]	36NW1 Steenwerck	A 29 c, d
Serail Alley	66cNW1 Grugies	B 7 b
Serail Trench	66cNW1 Grugies	B 7 b, 8 a
Serain [village]	57bSW4 Serain	U 14 b, c, d, 15 c, 20 a, b, 21 a
Serain Farms	57bSW4 Serain	U 21 b 8.1 and 21 d 6.9
Seranvillers [village]	57bNW3 Rumilly	H 14, 19, 20
Seraphim Cottages	27SE2 Berthen	Q 18 d 7.0
Serb Road [trench]	57dSE2 Beaumont	R 13 c, d, 19 a
Serb Switch	57dSE2 Beaumont	R 19 a, b
Serbes Alley	62cSW3 Vermandovillers	S 18 c, d
Serbia Alley	66cNW1 Grugies/2 Itancourt/3 Essigny/ 4 Berthenic't	B 28, H 2, 3, 4, 8
Serbie, Tranchée	62cNW3 Vaux	G 29 a
Serces Alley	62cSW3 Vermandovillers	S 18 c, d
Sere, Tranchée	62cSW1 & 2 Belloy	O 2 b
Sereta Trench	66cNW1 Grugies	A 12 c
Sereth Alley / Boyau du Sereth	62cSW1 & 2 Belloy	O 7 b, d, 13 b

Name	Map Sheet	Map Reference
Sergeant Alley	62bSW3 St Quentin	T 1 c
Sergeants Parade	57dNE1 & 2 Fonquevillers	E 10 b
Serheb Road [Serre-Hébuterne]	57dNE3 & 4 Hébuterne	K 23 d, 24 c, 30 a
Serious Trench	28SW4 & SE3 Bas Warneton	U 24 b, d, V 13 a, 19 b, d
Serjevo Trench [1918]	66cNW [2 Thennes]	C 15 b, d
Serlie Trench	66dNW1 Punchy	A 4 a
Serpent Trench	36SW3 Richebourg	S 22 b, d, 23 a
Serpentin Alley	62cSW3 Vermandovillers	S 16 c, d, 17 c, d, 18 c, 24 a
Serpentine Trench	57cSW3 Longueval	T 8 a, b, d
Serpentine, The [lake]	51bSE1 Saudemont	Q 1, 2, 3, 7, 8, 9
Serre [village]	57dNE3 & 4 Hébuterne	K 30 central
Serre Alley	57dNE3 & 4 Hébuterne	K 30 b, L 19 c, d, 25 a
Serre Trench	57dNE3 & 4 Hébuterne	K 24, 30, 35, 36, L 19
Sers Trench	62cSW3 Vermandovillers	T 13 c, 19 a
Servins Trench	51bSW2 Vis-en-Artois	O 24 a, d
Sésostris Alley / Boyau Sésostris	62cSW3 Vermandovillers	S 30 a, b, d
Setter Trench	36cSW3 Vimy	S 2 b
Seven Dials [crossroads]	57cNE4 Marcoing	K 33 c 9.8
Seven Dials [road junction]	57cSW1 Gueudecourt	N 26 a 1.9
Seven Elms	57cSW1 Gueudecourt	M 28 d
Seven Farm	28NW3 Poperinghe	H 7 a 90.25
Seven Sisters [hamlet]	36SW3 Richebourg	S 11 a
Seven Trees Avenue	36NW2 Armentières	C 3 c, d, 9 b
Seven Trees Redoubt	36NW2 Armentières	C 9 b 6.8
Seventh Avenue	36cNW3 Loos	G 18 a, b, c
Seventh Avenue	36cSW1 Lens	M 3, 4
Seventh Avenue Keep	36cNW3 Loos	G 18 c
Seventh Street	36cNW1 La Bassée	A 21 a
Seventh Street	57dSE4 Ovillers	X 3 a, b
Severn Alley	51bNW2 Oppy	B 6 c, d, 12 a
Severn Spur [light rly, 1918]	51bNW2 Oppy	B 10 d, 11 a, b, d
Sexton [dugout / light rly locality, 1917-18]	28NE3 Gheluvelt	J 1 c 55.56
Sexton House	28NE1 Zonnebeke	J 1 b 6.1
Sexton Post [1918]	28NE1 Zonnebeke	J 1 a, b
Seydel Alley	66dNW1 Punchy	A 20 d, 21 c, d
Seymour Street [front line; Sept 1915]	36cNW1 La Bassée	A 21 b
Shack Trench	36cSW3 Vimy	S 2 b
Shaft Alley	51bSW2 Vis-en-Artois	O 2 a
Shaft Avenue	51bSW4 Bullecourt	T 6 a
Shaft Switch	51bSW2 Vis-en-Artois / 4 Bullecourt	N 28 d, 34 b, 35 c
Shaft Trench	51bSW4 Bullecourt	U 1 c
Shaftesbury Avenue	36NW4 Bois Grenier	I 19 c, 25 a, b, d, 26 c, 32 a
Shaftesbury Avenue	57cSE2 Gonnelieu	Q 11 b, c, d, 16 b, c, d, 17 a, 22 a
Shaftesbury Avenue	57dSE1 & 2 Beaumont	Q 17 a
Shaftesbury Avenue [road; Lovie Chateau]	27NE2 Proven	F 16 c
Shaftesbury House	36NW4 Bois Grenier	I 19 c 5.2
Shaftesbury Shaft [tunnel entrance]	36cNW1 La Bassée	A 9 d
Shag Trench [1918]	57dNE4 [Hébuterne / Achiet]	L 7 d
Shagg Trench	36cSW3 Vimy	S 2 b, 3 a
Shame Trench	62bSW3 St Quentin	N 32 c
Shamrock Farm	20SE2 Hooglede	R 2 d 45.15
Shamrock Hill	57dSE4 Ovillers	W 30 c
Shamrock Tree [trig point, Arbre Trèfle]	57dSE4 Ovillers	W 30 c 45.15
Shamrock Trench	57cSW4 Combles	T 4 b, c, d, 10 b, 11 a

Name	Map Sheet	Map Reference
Shamrock Trench	62cNE2 Epéhy	F 16 c, d, 22 b
Shamus Farm [R.E. Farm]	28SW4 Ploegsteert	N 35 d 8.6
Shand Copse	51bSE2 Oisy-le-Verger	Q 28 d
Shandy Trench	36cSW3 Vimy	S 2 b
Shankhill Camp	28SW3 Bailleul	T 15 b
Shankhill Farm	28SW3 Bailleul	T 15 b 3.2
Shankhill Road	57dSE1 & 2 Beaumont	Q 23 b, 24 a
Shankhill Terrace [BFL]	57dSE1 & 2 Beaumont	Q 24 a
Shannon Trench	28SW2 Wytschaete	N 18 a
Shantung Trench	28SW2 Wytschaete	N 17 d
Shark Avenue	57cNE1 Quéant	D 29 c
Shark Support	57cNE1 Quéant	D 29 c, J 5 a
Sharp House	28SW1 Kemmel	M 11 d 8.1
Sharp Post	62cNE2 Epéhy	F 1 c
Sharpe Post [1918]	28SW1 Kemmel	M 11 d 9.3
Shaumberg Weg	51bNW1 Roclincourt	A 10 d
Shave House	27NE2 Proven	E 17 b 1.8
Shaw Cross [cross roads]	27NE4 Abeele	L 33 c 2.4
Shaw Street [1918]	57dNE1 & 2 Fonquevillers	E 29 a
Shawk Street [later Avenue]	51bSW2 Vis-en-Artois	N 23 d, 24 c, 30 a, b, O 25 a, b
Shaws Farm	20SE2 Hooglede	R 23 c 1.3
Shea O.P. [Fosse 11 Puits, 1917-18]	36cSW1 Lens	M 11 b 3.5
Sheba's Breasts / Sheeba's Breast	51bNW1 Roclincourt	A 4 d
Shed Alley	66cNW2 Itancourt	C 25 a
Sheep Post	62cNE4 Roisel	L 24 a 45.35
Sheffield Avenue / Boyau Sheffield	62cNW1 Maricourt	A 14 c, 20 a, c
Sheffield Support	51bSW4 Bullecourt / 57cNW2 Vaulx-Vraucourt	U 29 d, C 5 b
Shelac Cottage	28NW3 Poperinghe	H 7 c 9.5
Shelf Trench	51bNW1 Roclincourt	G 6 a
Shell Avenue	36NW2 Armentières	C 8 a, c
Shell Farm	28SW4 Ploegsteert	N 36 c 1.8
Shell Hole Trench [1918]	57dSE3 [Bouzincourt]	W 15 a, c, d
Shell Lane [CT]	28SW2 Wytschaete	O 2 b, d
Shell Street	57dNE1 & 2 Fonquevillers	E 9 b, 10 a, b
Shell Trap Farm [Mouse Trap Farm from 1915]	28NW2 St Julien	C 22 b
Shell Trench	51bNW4 Fampoux	I 32 a
Shelley Dump	28NW4 Ypres	I 33 c
Shelley Farm [St Eloi]	28SW2 Wytschaete	O 2 b 8.1
Shelley Lane	28SW2 Wytschaete	O 2 d
Shelleys Farm	20SE2 Hooglede	R 34 b 4.2
Shelleys Farm Mill [windmill]	20SE2 Hooglede	R 34 b 78.23
Shellhoek [railway siding]	28NW1 Elverdinghe	A 28 a
Shell-Out Dugouts [Canal Dugouts]	28NW2 St Julien	C 25 a, c, d, I 1 b
Shelter Alley	57dSE4 Ovillers	X 22 a, b, c
Shelter Wood	57dSE4 Ovillers	X 22 c
Shepherd Post	62cNE4 Roisel	L 24 c 9.2
Shepherds Copse	62cNE4 Roisel	L 23 d
Shepherd's Redoubt	36SW3 Richebourg	S 17 a
Sherbrook Road [road]	36cSW1 Lens	N 26 d, 32 a, b
Sherwood Avenue	57cSE2 Gonnelieu	Q 5 c, d, 10 b, c, d, 11 a, 15 b, 16 a
Sherwood Lane [road]	57cSE4 Villers-Guislain	X 9 d, 10 c, 16 a
Sherwood Switch	57cNE4 Marcoing	K 18 b, d, L 13 c, 19 a
Sherwood Trench	62cNE2 Epéhy	F 27 d, L 3 b, 4 a
Sherwood Trench [E of Trônes Wood]	57cSW3 Longueval	S 24 c, 30 a

Name	Map Sheet	Map Reference
Shetland Alley	57cSW3 Longueval	S 1 b
Shetland Road [CT]	36SW3 Richebourg	S 21 c, d, 22 c
Shetland Street	57dSE4 Ovillers	Q 36 d
Shikar Lane	51bSW2 Vis-en-Artois	N 24 b, d
Shikar Trench [later Avenue]	51bSW2 Vis-en-Artois	N 24 c, d, O 19 c, d, 20 c
Shilling Farm	28NE4 Dadizeele	L 22 b 1.6
Shindy Villa	28SE1 Wervicq	P 14 d
Shine Trench	57dSE2 & 57cSW1 Le Sars	N 21 d
Shingle Trench	36SW3 Richebourg	S 28 c
Shingler Support	57cNE4 Marcoing	K 11 c, 17 a, b, 18 a
Shingler Trench	57cNE4 Marcoing	K 11 c, d, 17 b
Shink Farm	28NW1 Elverdinghe	A 13 d 7.4
Ship Trench	51bNW1 Roclincourt	G 6 a
Ship Trench	57cNE4 Marcoing	K 10 d, 16 a, b
Shirt Trench	51bSW2 Vis-en-Artois	O 7 b
Shiver Farm	27NE1 Herzeele	E 2 d 95.40
Shoddy Farm	28SW3 Bailleul	S 8 a 7.5
Shoe Trench	51bNW1 Roclincourt / 3 Arras	G 6 a, c
Shoolbred Corner [road jct]	28NE4 Dadizeele	K 22 b 80.85
Shooters Hill	57dSE1 & 2 Beaumont	Q 17 c
Shooters Hill	62dNE2 Méaulte	F 9 d
Shop Trench	51bNW1 Roclincourt	G 6 b
Shoreditch Crater	36cSW1 Lens	M 6 b
Shoreham Farm	20SE2 Hooglede	Q 12 d 8.8
Short Alley	51bSW2 Vis-en-Artois	O 25 d
Short Cut	36cNW3 Loos	G 4 d, 10 b
Short Cut	36cSW3 Vimy	M 32 c
Short Cut [Sept 1915]	36cNW1 La Bassée	A 21 b
Short Sap	51bNW1 Roclincourt	A 4 d
Short Strand	57dSE1 & 2 Beaumont	Q 17 a
Short Street	36cNW1 La Bassée	A 15 b
Short Street	36cSW1 Lens	M 14 b
Short Street	57cNE1 Quéant	E 13 d, 19 b
Short Street	57dSE1 & 2 Beaumont	Q 23 b
Shot Farm	27SE1 St Sylvestre	P 25 b 3.4
Shot Trench	57cNE4 Marcoing	K 16 a
Shout Trench	36SW3 Richebourg	S 28 c
Shovel Camp	28SW3 Bailleul	T 13 c, d
Shovel Cottage	28SW3 Bailleul	T 13 d 1.4
Shovel Trench	51bSW2 Vis-en-Artois	O 7 b, c, d
Showery Cross Roads	28NE4 Dadizeele	L 13 d 15.30
Showman Crossing [bridge / level crossing]	28NE2 Moorslede	F 20 d 7.8
Shrapnel Corner [Bellacourt]	51cSE & 51bSW Ficheux	R 31 d 2.5
Shrapnel Corner [S of Ypres]	28NW4 Ypres	I 20 a 6.6
Shrapnel Corner How Spur [1917-18]	28NW4 Ypres	I 13 d, 14 c
Shrapnel Crossing [near Goldfish Chateau, rd/rly]	28NW4 Ypres	H 11 central
Shrapnel Farm [near Shrapnel Corner]	28NW4 & NE3 Zillebeke	I 20 a
Shrapnel Street	57dSE2 Beaumont	R 26 d, 27 c, 32 b
Shrapnel Trench	51bSW2 Vis-en-Artois	O 2 a, c, 7 d, 8 a
Shrapnel Trench	57dSE2 Beaumont	R 27 a, c
Shrewsbury Forest	28NW4 & NE3 Zillebeke	J 25 a, b, c, d
Shrimp Alley	28SW1 Kemmel	M 23 a, b
Shrine [Busschemeerschen]	28SW4 Ploegsteert	T 18 c 4.8
Shrine [Mesplaux]	36aSE4 Locon	X 14 b 12.75

Name	Map Sheet	Map Reference
Shrine Alley	62dNE2 Méaulte	F 5 c, d, 10 b, d, 11 a
Shrine Camp	27NE4 Abeele	L 14 b
Shrine Farm	36SW3 Richebourg	M 34 c 4.5
Shrine Trench	62dNE2 Méaulte	F 11 a
Shrine Trench [1918]	62dNE [1 Dernancourt]	E 7 a, c, d
Shrine, The	36SW3 Richebourg	N 32 c
Shropshire Line	36aSE3 Gonnehem / 4 Locon	W 8, 14, 15
Shropshire Reserve	57cNE3 Hermies / SE1 Bertincourt	K 32 c, d, Q 2 b, 3 a
Shropshire Spur [Havrincourt Wood]	57cSE1 Bertincourt	Q 3 c, d, 9 a
Shropshire Support	57cNE3 Hermies / SE1 Bertincourt	K 32 c, d, Q 2 b, 3 a
Shropshire Trench	28NW2 St Julien	C 15 c
Shropshire Trench	57cNE3 Hermies / SE1 Bertincourt	K 32 c, d, Q 2 b, 3 a
Shuttle Farm	27NE1 Herzeele	E 9 a 95.15
Shuttle Lane	57dSE4 Ovillers	X 26 a, b
Siam Cottage	36aNE1 Morbecque	D 21 d 80.65
Sibyl Trench	36cSW1 Lens	N 22 c
Sicile Trench	66dNW1 Punchy	A 4 a
Sickly / Sickley Alley	36cSW1 Lens	M 4 a, b
Sidbury [N of Pont Fixe]	36cNW1 La Bassée	A 14 b
Siddon Wood	62cNW3 Vaux	H 20 b
Side Street	57cNE1 Quéant	D 6 c, d, 11 d, 12 a, c
Sidney Street [see also Sydney St]	51bSE3 Cagnicourt / 57cNE1 Quéant	V 27 c, D 3 a
Sidney Trench	36cSW3 Vimy	T 1 d
Sieben House	28NE3 Gheluvelt	J 7 a 9.1
Siege [light rly siding]	36cSW1 Lens	M 9 a
Siege Camp	28NW1 Elverdinghe	B 20 d, 21 c, d, 27 a
Siege Camp No.1	28NW1 Elverdinghe	B 20 d 6.7
Siege Camp No.2	28NW1 Elverdinghe	B 21 c 2.1
Siege Camp No.3	28NW1 Elverdinghe	B 27 a 5.7
Siege Camp No.4	28NW1 Elverdinghe	B 21 c 3.7
Siege Camp No.5	28NW1 Elverdinghe	B 21 c 9.5
Siege Farm	28NW1 Elverdinghe	B 20 d 7.2
Siege Farm	28SW1 Kemmel	N 16 c 25.90
Siege House	36SW1 Aubers	N 13 a
Siege Junction [road junction]	28NW1 Elverdinghe	B 20 d 5.7
Siegfried Copse / Bois Siegfried	62cSW3 Vermandovillers	S 5 d
Siegfried Stellung [Hindenburg Line]	51b, 57c, 62b, etc.	extensive
Siena Cross [cross roads]	27NE4 Abeele	L 34 d 0.4
Sienna Alley	66cNW1 Grugies	A 17 a, b, d
Sierra Farms	27SE4 Meteren	R 32 d 7.3
Siesta Cottage	27SE4 Meteren	X 7 c 55.88
Sifflet Alley	62cSW3 Vermandovillers	S 17 a, c
Sight House [dugout, Fusilier Wood]	28NW4 & NE3 Zillebeke	I 36 c
Sight Trench	57dSE2 Beaumont	R 14 d, 15 c
Sign Post / Signpost Lane [road]	36SW1 Aubers	M 34 b, 35 a
Signal Alley	57cSW3 Longueval	S 24 a
Signal Copse	62cNE1 Liéramont	D 8 a
Signal Cottage	28NW2 St Julien	B 18 a 2.5
Signal Farm	20SW4 Bixschoote	U 21 c 20.05
Signal Post [Hill 130]	57dSE2 Beaumont	R 11 b
Signy Farm, la	57dNE3 & 4 Hébuterne	K 27 d
Silas Crossing [road over railway]	36NW1 Steenwerck	A 12 a 5.3
Silene Trench	66dNW1 Punchy	A 23 c, d
Silent Work	51bSW1 Neuville Vitasse	N 1 d, 7 b

Name	Map Sheet	Map Reference
Silesia Alley	62cNW1 Maricourt	A 3 d, 9 b
Silesia Sap	36cNW3 Loos	G 11 d
Silesia Support	62cNW1 Maricourt	A 9 b, 10 c
Silesia Trench	62cNW1 Maricourt	A 9 b, d, 10 c
Silesie Trench	62cNW4 Péronne	I 17 b, 18 c, 24 a
Silesie, Tranchée de	70dSW [2 Coucy-le-Château]	O 3 c
Silk Trench	51bNW1 Roclincourt	G 6 b
Silk Trench	57cSE4 Villers-Guislain	X 10 c, 16 a
Silver Farm	28NE4 Dadizeele	L 22 b 4.2
Silver Street [trench]	57cNE4 Marcoing	K 18 a, b
Silver Wood	66dNW1 Punchy	A 11 b
Silvery Trench	66cNW4 Berthenicourt	I 31 a
Simmer Farm	36aNE1 Morbecque	E 2 c 60.05
Simon Corons [miners' cottages]	36cSW1 Lens / 2 Harnes	N 22 c, 28 a
Simon House	28SW3 Bailleul	S 1 d 8.6
Simplon Farm	27NE2 Proven	F 22 c 2.0
Simpson Corons [miners' cottages]	36cSW2 Harnes	N 22 b, d, 23 a, c
Simpson Trench	36cNW3 Loos	G 22 c, d
Sims Keep	36cNW1 La Bassée	A 27 d
Sinai Alley [1918]	62dSE [3 Marcelcave]	V 1 d, 2 c
Sinbad Farm	36aNE4 Merville	K 17 b 10.55
Sinbad Trench	57cSW2 Villers-au-Flos	O 27 a, c
Sinceny [trench to east of]	70dNW [3 Sinceny]	G 11 b, d, 17 b
Sinew Trench	57cSW4 Combles	T 16 d, 22 b
Singe Trench	62cSW3 Vermandovillers	S 16 c
Singleton's Alley [road]	36aSE1 St Venant	P 6 c, 12 a, c
Sinister Street [road in Ypres]	28NW4 Ypres	I 8 c
Sinner Farm	28NE4 Dadizeele	K 12 a 5.8
Sinope Trench	62cNW2 Bouchavesnes	C 16 c, d, 22 b
Siorret Trench	51cSE3 & 4 Ransart	W 17 b
Sioule Alley	66cNW1 Grugies	A 24 b, d, B 8 c, 13 b, c, d, 14 a, 19 a
Sire Alley	62cSW3 Vermandovillers	S 1 b, d, 2 c, d, 3 c, 9, 10
Siren Trench	36cSW1 Lens	N 22 c
Sirène Alley	62cSW3 Vermandovillers	S 17 a, c, 22 b, 23 a
Sirius House	28NW1 Elverdinghe	A 17 d 8.3
Sisera Switch	27SE4 Meteren	X 9 a, b, 10 a
Sissy, Arbre de [trig point]	66cNW2 Itancourt	C 24 a 42.75
Sister Trench [1918]	28SW1 Kemmel	M 33 a, d
Sivas Alley	66cNW1 Grugies	B 3 a, c, 8 b, 9 a
Sixteen Road [road]	57dSE2 Beaumont	R 10 c, d, 16 a, c, 22 a
Sixth Avenue	36cNW3 Loos	G 18 d, 19 c
Sixth Avenue	57dNE3 & 4 Hébuterne	K 3 c
Sixth Avenue [SW of Mouquet Farm]	57dSE1 & 2 Beaumont / 4 Ovillers	R 32 d, 33 a, c, X 2 b
Sixth Street	57dSE4 Ovillers	X 3 d
Sixth Street	57dNE1 & 2 Fonquevillers / 3 & 4 Hébuterne	K 3 a, c
Skagway [light rly locality]	28NW4 Ypres	H 23 b 3.5
Skelter Cross [cross roads]	36aNE4 Merville	L 20 c 1.1
Sketch Trench	57cSW3 Longueval	T 2 d, 3 c, 9 a, b
Skevington Avenue	57cNE3 Hermies	K 20 b, c, d
Skew Trench	51bNW1 Roclincourt	G 6 a, b
Skewbald House	28NE2 Moorslede	E 29 c 9.7
Skiff Corner [road junction]	20SE2 Hooglede	Q 12 d 4.9
Skin Trench	51bNW1 Roclincourt	G 6 a
Skin Trench	62bNW3 Bellicourt	G 2 c, 8 a, c

Name	Map Sheet	Map Reference
Skinflint Farm	36NW1 Steenwerck	B 27 d 7.1
Skinner Street	57dSE1 & 2 Beaumont	Q 36 b, R 31 a
Skip Point [Redoubt]	28SW2 Wytschaete	O 25 b 1.2
Skip Trench	51bNW1 Roclincourt	G 6 a, b
Skip Wood	28SW2 Wytschaete	O 25 c, d
Skipton Alley	57cNW2 Vaulx-Vraucourt	C 24 d
Skipton Loop	28NW2 St Julien	C 13 c
Skipton Post	28NW2 St Julien	C 13 d 4.8
Skipton Reserve	57cNW2 Vaulx-Vraucourt / NE1 Quéant	C 24 b, d, D 19 c
Skipton Road	28NW2 St Julien	C 13 c, d
Skittle Alley	57cSE4 Villers-Guislain	X 13 a, b
Skot Farm [Zwijnskot]	28NE2 Moorslede	F 29 d 03.80
Skouloudis Trench / Tranchée Skouloudis	66cNW2 Itancourt	C 13 d, 19 b, 20 a, c
Skull Farm	28NE2 Moorslede	F 15 b 7.8
Skunk Copse	27SE2 Berthen	Q 10 c
Sky Farm	28SE1 Wervicq	P 3 d 2.1
Sky Trench	51bNW3 Arras	G 6 c
Skye Trench	51bNW4 Fampoux	I 32 b
Skyline Trench	57dSE1 & 2 Beaumont / 4 Ovillers	R 32 d, 33 a, c, X 2 b
Slab Trench	36cSW1 Lens	N 21 d, 22 c, 27 a, b
Slab Trench	51bNW3 Arras	G 6 c
Slack Trench	36cSW1 Lens	N 20 d, 21 c, 26 b
Slade Trench	36cSW1 Lens	N 21 c, N 22 a, b
Slag Alley [The Dump]	36cNW1 La Bassée	G 5 a, b
Slag Avenue	57cNE3 Hermies	K 8 d, 14 b, d, 20 a, b, c
Slag Quarry	62cNE4 Roisel	L 6 c 0.2
Slag Street	57cNE3 Hermies	K 14 b
Slag Trench	51bNW3 Arras	G 6 c
Slag Trench	62cNE4 Roisel	L 6 c, 11 b
Slam Trench	51bSW1 Neuville Vitasse	M 5 c
Slander Trench	36cSW1 Lens / 2 Harnes	N 21 d, 28 a, c
Slang Lane [trench]	51bSW2 Vis-en-Artois / SE1 Saudemont	O 24 d, P 19 c, 25 a
Slang Trench	36cSW2 Harnes	N 22 b
Slap Trench	36cSW2 Harnes	N 22 b
Slash Trench	36cSW2 Harnes	N 22 b
Slate Castle	12SW1 Nieuport	M 6 d
Slate Copse	57bSW1 Bantouzelle	M 21 a
Slate Farm [Bantouzelle]	57bSW1 Bantouzelle	M 27 a 0.2
Slate Quarry	57bSW1 Bantouzelle	M 21 a
Slate Trench	36cSW2 Harnes	N 22 b, d
Slaughterhouse [Equarrissage]	51bNW3 Arras	G 11 a 2.6
Slave Trench	36cSW2 Harnes	N 22 d
Slaves Trench [1918]	62dSW [4 Cachy] / SE [3 Marcelcave]	U 18 d, 24 b, V 13 c
Slavey Farm	36NW1 Steenwerck	A 30 b 33.95
Sleat [houses]	27NE4 Abeele	L 9 b 2.2
Sled Trench	36cSW2 Harnes	N 22 d
Slede Farm [near Moorslede]	28NE2 Moorslede	E 11 c 05.05
Sleep Trench	36cSW2 Harnes	N 22 d
Sleeper Road, The	28NW3 Poperinghe / 4 Ypres	H 3 d, 4 c, d, 5 c, d, 6 c, d, I 1 c
Sleet Trench	57cSW4 Combles	N 35 d
Sleeve Trench	36cSW2 Harnes	N 28 b
Slender Trench	36cSW2 Harnes	N 28 b
Slew Trench	36cSW2 Harnes	N 16 d, 17 c
Slice Trench	36cSW2 Harnes	N 28 b

Name	Map Sheet	Map Reference
Slick Trench	36cSW2 Harnes	N 28 b
Slight Trench	36cSW2 Harnes	N 29 c
Sligo Cottages	27NE4 Abeele	L 16 d 9.4
Slim Farm	36NW1 Steenwerck	B 2 c 8.6
Slim Street	57dNE3 & 4 Hébuterne	K 18 c, d, 24 b
Slim Trench	36cSW2 Harnes	N 34 b
Slimes Trench	36cSW2 Harnes	N 28 b, d, 29 c
Slimy Trench	36cSW1 Lens / 2 Harnes	N 27 d, 28 c, d, 34 b
Slink Farm	28SW3 Bailleul	S 21 a 4.4
Slink Trench	36cSW2 Harnes	N 35 a
Slip Farm [Slypshoek]	28NE2 Moorslede	F 25 c 1.8
Slip Trench	36cSW1 Lens	N 34 a
Slip Trench	57cNE1 Quéant	D 5 d, 6 c
Slip Wood	28NE2 Moorslede	E 30 d, F 25 c
Slipper Farm	36NW1 Steenwerck	G 5 b 98.91
Slipper Trench	36cSW1 Lens / 2 Harnes	N 34 a
Slit Redoubt [Oct 1915]	36cNW3 Loos	G 11 b
Slit, The [Oct 1915]	36cNW3 Loos	G 11 b
Slither Trench	36cSW2 Harnes	N 34 b, 35 a
Sloane Farm	28NW1 Elverdinghe	A 3 a 0.3
Sloane Square	28NW1 Elverdinghe	A 2 b
Sloane Square [farm]	36aSE4 Locon	X 11 b 3.4
Sloane Street	57cNE3 Hermies	K 20 b, d
Sloane Street	57dSE1 & 2 Beaumont	Q 17 d
Sloane Street [road]	57cSW3 Longueval	S 17 a, c, d
Slogan / Sloggan Trench	36cSW2 Harnes / 4 Rouvroy	N 35 a, c
Slogan Farm	36aNE2 Vieux Berquin	F 10 b 35.70
Slop Farm	36NW1 Steenwerck	B 3 d 93.85
Slop Trench	36cSW1 Lens	N 33 a, b
Slop Trench	51bNW3 Arras	G 6 c
Sloping Roof Farm	28SW4 Ploegsteert	O 32 c 0.9
Sloping Trench	36cSW2 Harnes	N 35 a
Sloppy Trench	36cSW2 Harnes	N 24 c, d, 30 a, b
Slot Farm	27NE1 Herzeele	E 19 a 05.75
Sloth Trench / Slouth [sic] Trench	36cSW2 Harnes	N 24 d
Slough Trench	36cSW2 Harnes	N 36 b
Slow Trench	36cSW2 Harnes	N 36 b
Slow Trench	57cSW3 Longueval	T 21 d
Sludge Farms	36NW1 Steenwerck	B 20 d 4.2
Slug Farm	27NE1 Herzeele	E 3 c 9.5
Slug Street	57dNE3 & 4 Hébuterne	K 12 d, 18 b, d
Slug Trench	36cSW2 Harnes	N 29 c
Slum Trench	51bNW3 Arras	G 6 c
Slumber Trench	36cSW2 Harnes	N 36 a, b, c, d
Slump Trench	36cSW2 Harnes	N 36 a
Slush Alley	57cSE2 Gonnelieu	R 27 d
Slush Trench	36cSW4 Rouvroy	N 35 d
Slush Trench	57cSW4 Combles	T 5 d
Slut Trench	36cSW4 Rouvroy	N 34 d
Sly Trench	36cSW1 Lens / 2 Harnes	N 28 c
Sly Trench	51bNW1 Roclincourt	G 6 b
Slypshoek	28NE2 Moorslede	E 30 d
Slypskappelle	28NE2 Moorslede	E 29 d
Small Foot Wood	62cSE2 Vermand	R 8 b

Name	Map Sheet	Map Reference
Small Street	28NW4 & NE3 Zillebeke	I 34 c, d
Small Wood	51bSW2 Vis-en-Artois / SE1 Saudemont	O 24 d, P 19 c
Smart Street [1918]	28NE3 Gheluvelt	J 16 c
Smart Support	28NE3 Gheluvelt	J 16 c
Smelt Trench	28SW2 Wytschaete	O 11 a, c
Smile Trench	57cNE4 Marcoing	K 17 c, d
Smiske Cabaret, 't	20SW4 Bixschoote	T 11 d 69.13
Smisson Lane, & Post	62bNW1 Gouy	A 1 d
Smith Road	28NE1 Zonnebeke	D 27 c, b, d, J 3 a
Smith-Dorrien Trench	36SW1 Aubers	M 29, 35
Smiths Crater	36cNW3 Loos	H 13 c 40.65
Smith's Villas	36NW4 Bois Grenier	H 29 c
Smithy [La Hutte]	28SW4 Ploegsteert	U 14 c 35.55
Smoke Trench	57dSE1 & 2 Beaumont	Q 5 a, b, d
Smoke Trench	57dSE2 & 57cSW1 Le Sars	N 25 c, d
Smorgon Trench	62cSW4 St. Christ	U 15 b, d
Smut Trench	57cSE2 Gonnelieu	Q 23 d
Smyrna Farm	36aNE2 Vieux Berquin	E 5 b 75.75
Smyth Camp	28NW3 Poperinghe	H 21 d
Smyth Farm	28NW3 Poperinghe	H 21 d 8.3
Smyth Valley	57dSE4 Ovillers	X 10 a, c
Smythe Avenue	36NW2 Armentières	C 9 b, d
Snaffle Trench	51bSW2 Vis-en-Artois	O 2 a
Snag Alley	57dSE2 & 57cSW1 Le Sars	M 17 d
Snag Trench [Diagonal Trench]	57dSE2 & 57cSW1 Le Sars	M 17 c, d
Snail Copse	27NE2 Proven	F 2 b
Snail Farm	27NE2 Proven	F 2 a 80.15
Snake House	36aSE1 St Venant	P 3 a 3.2
Snake Trench	57cNE4 Marcoing	K 16 a, b, d, 17 c
Snap Reserve	57cSE2 Gonnelieu	Q 10 d, 16 b, d, 17 c, 23 a, c, d
Snap Trench	57cSE2 Gonnelieu	Q 11 a, c, 17 a, c, d, 23 b, d
Snargate Street	36cSW3 Vimy	S 14 d, 21 a
Sneaton Farm	27SE2 Berthen	R 11 a 30.55
Snelgrove Farm	28NE4 Dadizeele	K 29 b 5.9
Snip Lane	57cSE2 Gonnelieu	Q 10 b, 11 c
Snipe Avenue [Br CT]	28SW2 Wytschaete	N 24 a
Snipe Copse	62dSE [3 Marcelcave]	V 18 c
Snipe Farm	28NE2 Moorslede	F 17 b 20.55
Snipe Hall	28NE1 Zonnebeke	D 5 c 53.04
Snipe Quarry	57cSE4 Villers-Guislain	X 29 d
Snipe Trench	28SW2 Wytschaete	N 24 a
Snipe Trench	51bSW4 Bullecourt	O 31 d
Snipe Trench	57cNE3 Hermies	K 26 a
Snipers / Sniper's Alley	36NW4 Bois Grenier	I 26 a
Snipers Barn	28SW2 Wytschaete	O 1 c 30.45
Sniper's Corner	28NW2 St Julien	C 13 d 05.59
Snipers Den [1917-18]	20SW4 Bixschoote	U 28 c
Snipers House	36aNE4 Merville	K 17 a 4.6
Sniper's House	28SW4 Ploegsteert	U 2 a 35.35
Sniper's House	36NW4 Bois Grenier	I 22 a
Sniper's House [Bellewaarde]	28NW4 & NE3 Zillebeke	I 12 c 8.5
Snipers Post	36SW1 Aubers	M 24 a
Snipers Tree [No Man's Land]	36cNW1 La Bassée	A 16 c
Snippet Farm	20SE2 Hooglede	R 28 b 50.65

Name	Map Sheet	Map Reference
Snodgrass Avenue [1918]	57dSW [3 Talmas]	S 22 d, 28 b
Snout Trench	51bNW4 Fampoux	H 5 d, 11 b
Snout, The [S tip of Bazentin le Grand Wood]	57cSW3 Longueval	S 14 d
Snout, The [Zwarteleen]	28NW4 & NE3 Zillebeke	I 29 d
Snow Hill [Double Crassier, N arm]	36cSW1 Lens	M 4 c
Snow Trench / Reserve	57cSW4 Combles	T 5 a
Snowden House	36SW1 Aubers	N 7 c
Snowdon Crater	57cNE3 Hermies	K 27 d 3.2
Snuff Alley	57dNE3 & 4 Hébuterne	K 18 c, 23 b
Snuff Alley [1918]	57dNE3 & 4 Hébuterne	K 17 d, 18 a, c, 23 b
Snuff Trench	51bNW3 Arras	G 6 c
Snug Trench	51bNW1 Roclincourt / 3 Arras	G 6 b, d
Soap Alley	57dNE3 & 4 Hébuterne	L 19 b
Soap Trench	57cNE4 Marcoing	K 10 d, 16 b
Soap Trench	66dNW1 Punchy	A 17 d, 18 c
Soar Trench	51bNW3 Arras	G 6 c, d
Sock Wood	51bNE4 Cantin	L 20 b, 21 a
Sod Trench	51bSW2 Vis-en-Artois	O 7 b, d
Soda Alley	62cSW3 Vermandovillers	T 13 d, 19 a, b
Soda Alley / Boyau du Soda	62cSW3 & 4 Marchélepot	T 13 d, 19 a, b
Soda Trench	57dSE4 Ovillers	X 21 d, 27 a
Sofia House	27NE4 Abeele	L 15 b 9.0
Sofia Trench [1918]	66eNW [2 Thennes]	C 5 c, 10 b, 11 a
Soft Lane [trench]	51bSW2 Vis-en-Artois	O 24 d, 30 b
Soft Trench	62bSW3 St Quentin	T 3 b, d
Sogny Post	36cSW1 Lens	M 14 b
Sogny, Boyau de [West Ham Lane, part of]	36cSW1 Lens	M 14 b, 15 a
Solace Trench	36SW3 Richebourg	S 22 d
Solace Wood	62bSW4 Homblières	T 6 b, d
Solar Farm	28NE2 Moorslede	E 30 d 05.85
Solar Lane	57cSW2 Villers-au-Flos	N 28 c
Solard Trench	66dNW1 Punchy	A 4 d
Soldaten Friedhof [cemetery]	51bNW1 Roclincourt	B 25 c
Soldier Copse	57dSW [4 Toutencourt]	U 9 b
Soldin Trench	62cNE3 Buire	J 1 c, 7 a
Sole Post	57cNE1 Quéant	J 4 a
Sole Trench	51bNW3 Arras	G 6 c, d
Soleil Trench	62cSW3 Vermandovillers	S 14 d
Soleil Trench	66cNW2 Itancourt	B 30 c
Solferino Farm	28NW2 St Julien	B 23 a 1.4
Solferino Trench	36cSW3 Vimy	M 32 c
Solferino Trench	57dNE3 & 4 Hébuterne	K 9 a, b
Solitary Elm	62cNE3 Buire	J 21 a 19.43
Sollas Farm	20SE3 Westroosebeke	W 19 b 8.2
Solomon's Way	36SW3 Richebourg	S 6 a, b, d
Somali Farm	28NE2 Moorslede	K 4 b 0.1
Sombart Trench	36cSW3 Vimy	S 21 a, c, d, 27 b, 28 a
Somer Farm	28SW2 Wytschaete	O 14 c 90.25
Somerby Farm	28NE4 Dadizeele	K 30 b 40.55
Somerset Bank [lynchet]	51bSW2 Vis-en-Artois	O 21 b
Somerset House [Ploegsteert Wood]	28SW4 Ploegsteert	U 21 a 09.23 or 2.4
Somerset L.I. Military Cemetery	28SW4 Ploegsteert	U 20 b 9.2
Somerset Spur [Havrincourt Wood]	57cSE1 Bertincourt	P 12 b, d,
Somerville Wood	62bNW3 Bellicourt	G 32 c, d

Name	Map Sheet	Map Reference
Somme [farm / pill box]	28NE1 Zonnebeke	D 13 c 5.3
Somme [pillboxes]	28NE1 Zonnebeke	D 13 d 1.5
Somme Alley	57cSE4 Villers-Guislain	X 1 c, d, 2 a
Somme Alley	66cNW2 Itancourt	B 29 a, b, c
Somme Alley	70dNW4 St Gobain	H 30 a, b, c
Somme Post	28NE1 Zonnebeke	D 13 c 5.2
Somme Redoubt	28NE1 Zonnebeke	D 13 c 5.2
Somme Sector [trenches] [1918]	62dSW [1 Longueau / 2 Villers-Bretonneux]	N 11, 12, 13 to18
Somme Street	28NW4 & NE3 Zillebeke	I 34 c
Somme, Bois de la	66dNW2 Morchain	C 11 d, 12 c
Somme, Source of the	62bSW2 Fonsommes	O 10 a
Sommet / Sommeil Trench	62cNW1 Maricourt	B 25 d, H 2 a, b
Son Trench	51bNW3 Arras	G 6 c
Sonda House	27NE4 Abeele	K 9 b 85.40
Sonen Farm	28SW2 Wytschaete	O 20 b 1.4
Sonia Corons [miners' cottages]	36cSW2 Harnes	N 29 b, d
Sonia Wood	62bNW2 Brancourt-le-Grand	C 2 a
Sonis Trench	57dNE3 & 4 Hébuterne	K 15 b, 16 a, b, d
Sonnet Farm	57cSE2 Gonnelieu	R 22 a 8.1
Sonnet Trench	57cSE2 Gonnelieu	R 22 b, c, d
Sonnet Wood	27NE4 Abeele	L 20 a, b
Sonning Bridge	36aSE1 St Venant	P 27 b 7.1
Sonore Alley	62cSW3 Vermandovillers	S 16 b, 17 a, b, 18 a
Sonore Trench	62cSW3 Vermandovillers	S 17 d, 23 b
Soo Line [railway; Montigny]	36cSW2 Harnes	O 22 b, d
Sool Spur [light rly, Loos]	36cNW3 Loos	G 36 c
Soot Avenue	57cSE2 Gonnelieu	Q 17 d, 18 c, 23 b
Soot Farm	28SW3 Bailleul	S 8 a 95.22
Soot Trench	51bNW3 Arras	G 6 c, d
Sop Trench	51bNW1 Roclincourt / 3 Arras	G 6 b, d
Sophia Trench	36SW3 Richebourg	S 11 b, 12 a
Sopwith Corons [miners' cottages, Sallaumines]	36cSW1 Lens	N 23 c, 29 a
Sopwith Sap [1918]	51bSW3 Boisleux	S 25 d
Sorby Farm	20SE3 Westroosebeke	W 13 d 9.2
Sordid Farm	20SE2 Hooglede	Q 23 a 2.1
Sorel Wood	57cSE3 Sorel-le-Grand	W 25 a, c
Sorel Wood	62cSW4 St. Christ	U 1 a, b
Sorel-le-Grand [village]	57cSE3 Sorel-le-Grand	V 18 d, 24 b, W 13 c, 19 a
Sornettes Alley	66dNW3 Hattencourt	G 15 d, 20 d, 21 a, b, d
Sorrels Rest [dugouts, Mount Sorrel]	28NW4 & NE3 Zillebeke	I 30 c
Sorrowitz Trench	62cNW2 Bouchavesnes	C 5 a, b, c, 11 b
Sort / Soft Trench	51bNW3 Arras	G 6 c
Sorval Chateau	57bSW2 Clary	O 20 c 6.7
Sosthène Trench / Tranchée Sosthène	62cSW1 & 2 Belloy	O 14 c, 19 b, 20 a
Sottises Alley	66dNW3 Hattencourt	G 19 d, 20 c, d, 21 a, c
Soubie Reserve [1918]	57dNE [1 Fonquevillers]	D 12 d, 17 b, d, 18 a, b, c
Souchal Alley	66cNW1 Grugies	B 15 a, c
Souchez [village]	36bSE4 & 36cSW3 Givenchy	S 7, 8
Souchez Alley	36cSW3 Vimy	S 8 d
Souchez Trench	70dNW4 St Gobain	H 4 d, 10 b, d
Souchez Wood	36bSE4 & 36cSW3 Givenchy	X 12 c, S 7 d
Souchez, Bois de	36cSW3 Vimy	S 7 d
Souchez, Tranchée de la	36cSW3 Vimy	S 2 d
Soudan Farm	28NE2 Moorslede	E 21 d 75.70

Name	Map Sheet	Map Reference
Soudards Trench	66dNW1 Punchy	A 17 a, b, d, 18 c
Soufflard Street	51bSW2 Vis-en-Artois	O 18 d, 24 b, d
Soufflard, Bois	51bSW2 Vis-en-Artois	O 18 d, 24 b
Souffre / Soufre, Tranchée du	62cSW3 & 4 Marchélepot	S 29 c, d
Soult Camp	28NW2 St Julien	B 23 a, c
Soult Cot	28NW2 St Julien	B 23 a 28.13
Soult Valley	62bNW1 Gouy	A18 c, d, 23 b, d, 24 a, c
Soup Trench	51bNW3 Arras	G 6 c
Soup Trench	51bSW2 Vis-en-Artois	O 24 d, 30 b
Sour Trench	51bNW3 Arras	G 6 d
Source Farm	20SE3 Westroosebeke	V 28 d 7.7
Source of the Somme	62bSW2 Fonsommes	O 10 a
Source Trench	20SE3 Westroosebeke	V 28 c
Source Wood	66cNW2 Itancourt	B 29 b
Sourd Farm	20SE3 Westroosebeke	V 28 a 1.6
Souris Trench	36cSW3 Vimy	T 3 a, c
Sourit [Trench]	57dNE3 & 4 Hébuterne	K 15 d
Sousa [house / farm]	36SW1 Aubers	N 14 d 95.45
South Africa [Trench]	36NW2 Armentières	C 23 c, 28 b, 29a
South Alley	36bSE4 Carency	X 5 d, 11 b
South Alley	70dNW4 St Gobain	H 22 d, 23 c, 28 b
South Alley [to new front line]	57dSE1 & 2 Beaumont	Q 16 b, 17 a
South Atlantic [light rly siding & huts]	28NW3 Poperinghe	G 9 d, 10 c
South Avenue	62dNE2 Méaulte	F 7 d
South Barricade	36NW2 Armentières	C 10 b
South Block	36NW2 Armentières	C 10 c
South Canal Post	28SW2 Wytschaete	O 4 a
South Copse [Sailly-Saillisel]	57cSW4 Combles	U 13 a 7.1
South Crater	36cNW3 Loos	G 5 d
South Dump [Loos]	36cNW3 Loos	H 31 d 1.8
South End [Hexagon]	51bSW1 Neuville Vitasse	M 17 b
South Face [Hohenzollern Rdt]	36cNW3 & 1 Loos	G 4 b, d, 5 c
South Foreland	57dNE1 & 2 Fonquevillers	E 22 d
South Gun Pits [E of Lesboeufs]	57cSW4 Combles	T 5 a, c
South Hill Camp	28SW1 Kemmel	M 17 c, 23 a
South Lane	62cNE2 Epéhy	F 8 a, b
South Lane, & Dugout	28NW4 & NE3 Zillebeke	I 10 d
South Midland Farm [In den Kraatenberg Cabaret]	28SW4 Ploegsteert	T 6 c 65.60
South Miraumont Trench	57dSE2 & 57cSW1 Le Sars	R 5 d, 6 c, 10 b, 11 a
South Practice Trenches	57dSE2 & 57cSW1 Le Sars	M 19 b, d, 20 a, c
South Sausage Support	57dSE4 Ovillers	X 20 d, 27 a
South Sausage Trench	57dSE4 Ovillers	X 20 d, 26 b
South Skirt [Morval]	57cSW4 Combles	T 17 a
South Stampkot Farm	20SW4 Bixschoote	T 17 c 3.6
South Station Buildings	28NE1 Zonnebeke	J 1 a 7.4
South Street	36cNW3 Loos / SW1 Lens	G 35, M 3, 4, 5, 6
South Street	57dSE1 & 2 Beaumont	Q 10 a
South Street [Delville Wood]	57cSW3 Longueval	S 18 d
South Street [road, Le Transloy]	57cSW2 Villers-au-Flos	N 30 d, O 25 c
South Trench	57cNE3 Hermies	K 26 a
Southend [reserve trench]	28NW2 St Julien	I 10 a
Southern Avenue	51bSW2 Vis-en-Artois	N 16, 17, 18, O 13, 14
Southern Avenue	57dNE3 & 4 Hébuterne	K 27 d, 28 c, d, 29 c, 33 b
Southern Brickstack [Wytschaete Wood]	28SW2 Wytschaete	O 13 c 7.0

Name	Map Sheet	Map Reference
Southern C.T. [later Avenue]	51bSW2 Vis-en-Artois	N 18 a, b, c, O 13 a, b, 14 a
Southern Extension [light rly]	36cSW3 Vimy	S 17 a
Southern Redoubt [NE of Passchendaele]	20SE3 Westroosebeke	W 25 c
Southern Sap	36cNW3 Loos	G 22 d
Southern Up	36cNW3 Loos	G 25 b, 26 a, c, d, 33 a, b
Soutien, de	51bNW1 Roclincourt	A 4 c
Soutien, Tranchée	36cSW3 Vimy	S 8 b
Soutiens Trench	51cSE3 & 4 Ransart	R 32 d
Souvenir Dump	28SW4 Ploegsteert	T 5 d 3.3
Souvenir Farm	20NW4 Dixmude	I 14 d 7.9
Souvenir Farm	28SW4 Ploegsteert	T 5 d 5.6
Souvenir House	20SW4 Bixschoote	U 18 c 30.65
Souville Alley	62cSW1 Dompierre	N 26 b, 27 a
Souville Trench	70dNW [3 Sinceny]	H 27 a, c, d
Sovereign Wood	28NE4 Dadizeele	L 10 d, 11 c, 16 b, 17 a
Soviet Farm [1918]	28SW1 Kemmel	M 20 a 15.80
Sow Avenue	57cNE4 Marcoing	K 4 c
Sow Lane	62cNW1 Maricourt	A 23 b
Sow Trench	36cSW1 Lens / 2 Harnes	N 27 d, 28 c
Soyécourt [village]	62cSW3 & 4 Marchélepot	M 34, S 4
Soyer [light rly spur]	36NW2 Armentières	B 6 d 00.55
Soyer Farm	36NW2 Armentières	B 6 d 35.35
Spade Lane	51bSW1 Neuville Vitasse	N 20 a, b
Spade Lane [trench]	62bNW3 Bellicourt	G 7 b, d
Spade Trench	51bSW2 Vis-en-Artois	O 7 b, c, d
Spade Trench [Spade Lane]	62bNW3 Bellicourt	G 7 b, d
Spadgers Lane [sunken watercourse]	28SW2 Wytschaete	O 4 d
Spahi Farm	28NW2 St Julien	C 19 b 9.6
Spahis Trench	70dNW4 St Gobain	H 30 b, d
Spain Avenue	36NW2 Armentières	C 28 a, b, d
Span Trench	51bNW3 Arras	G 6 d
Spanbroek Cabaret	28SW2 Wytschaete	N 30 c 35,75
Spanbroek Crater [1917-18]	28SW2 Wytschaete	N 30 c 2.7
Spanbroek Mill [Spanbroekmolen]	28SW2 Wytschaete	N 30 c 20.85
Spanbroekmolen Craters	28SW2 Wytschaete	N 30 a, c
Spangle Farm	28NE2 Moorslede	F 14 b 25.20
Spaniel Alley	51bSW4 Bullecourt	U 16 b, d
Spanner Houses	28NE2 Moorslede	F 22 a 0.4
Spare Farm	27NE2 Proven	E 16 b 0.3
Spark Farm	28NE2 Moorslede	F 26 d 5.0
Spark Trench	57cSW2 Villers-au-Flos	N 23 b
Sparrow Lane	51bSW2 Vis-en-Artois	O 31 a, b
Sparrow Support [1918]	57dNE2 & 57cNW1 Courcelles	F 11 c, 16 b, d
Sparta Cross Roads	20SE3 Westroosebeke	V 6 d 7.9
Spartan Trench	36SW3 Richebourg	S 23 d, 24 c, 29 a
Sparte Alley	62cSW3 & 4 Marchélepot	T 1 a, b, d, 2 c
Sparte Alley	62cSW3 Vermandovillers	T 1 a, b, d, 2 c
Spavin Houses	28NE2 Moorslede	E 29 c 45.65
Spear Lane [road]	51bSW2 Vis-en-Artois	N 12 c, 18 a, c
Spearmint Corner [road jct]	36aNE1 Morbecque	E 13 a 00.24
Spec Lane	57cSW2 Villers-au-Flos	N 34 b
Speckle Farm [near Trout Fork]	20SE2 Hooglede	R 12 c 35.70
Spectrum Trench	57cSW2 Villers-au-Flos	N 34 b, d
Speed Farm	20SE2 Hooglede	R 12 c 5.1

Name	Map Sheet	Map Reference
Speedwell Spur [light rly]	36bNE2 Beuvry	E 22 d
Spence Trench	57cSW1 Gueudecourt	M 21 d, 27 b, 28 a
Spender House	36aNE1 Morbecque	E 13 c 1.3
Speyside Road	57dSE1 & 2 Beaumont	Q 30 a, c
Sphinx Quarry	62dSW [4 Cachy]	U 25 a
Sphinx Trench	62cNE3 Buire	J 25 a, b
Sphinx Wood	66cNW2 Itancourt	B 17 a, c
Sphinx Wood / Bois du Sphinx	62cSW3 & 4 Marchélepot	T 15 b
Spider Corner [road jct, Feuchy]	51bNW3 Arras	H 20 d 8.7
Spider Cross Roads	20SE3 Westroosebeke	V 14 b 95.80
Spider Dump	36cSW3 Vimy	S 6 c 3.1
Spider House	28SW2 Wytschaete	O 17 c 93.10
Spike Trench	51bNW3 Arras	G 6 d
Spin Alley	57cNE4 Marcoing	K 10 d
Spinach Cottages	28NE2 Moorslede	L 1 a 10.05
Spinet House	28NE4 Dadizeele	L 25 b 2.3
Spinnekens [place name]	20SE2 Hooglede	R 24 c
Spinney 'B'	62cNW1 Maricourt	B 21 b, d
Spinney Post	36SW1 Aubers	N 7 c 2.5
Spinney 'R'	62cNW1 Maricourt	B 22 a, c
Spinney Sap	36cSW1 Lens	M 31 b, 32 a
Spinney Trench	36cSW1 Lens	M 25 b, d
Spinney, The	62dSW [1 Longueau]	N 8 d
Spinning Mill [Warneton]	28SW4 Ploegsteert	U 18 d 0.8
Spit Trench	57cNE4 Marcoing	K 17 c, d
Spite Cottage	36NW1 Steenwerck	B 14 d 85.90
Splendid Farm	36NW1 Steenwerck	A 7 d 8.4
Splinter Copse	51bNW4 Fampoux	I 34 a
Splutter Road [trench]	57dSE1 & 2 Beaumont	R 19 d, 20 c
Splutter Trench	57dSE2 Beaumont	R 19 d, 20 c
Spoil Bank	28NW4 & NE3 Zillebeke	I 33 c, d
Spoil Bank [light rly locality, 1917-18]	28NW4 Ypres	I 32 b, 33 a
Spoil Bank [N of Canal]	36cNW1 La Bassée	A 15 c, d
Spoil Bank E Tunnel	28SW2 Wytschaete	O 4 a
Spoil Heap	57cNE3 Hermies	K 20 central
Spoil Heap	57cNE3 Hermies	J 35 a, b & J 35 c, d
Spoil Heap [Yorkshire Bank]	57cNE3 Hermies	K 32 a, b
Spook Cottage	36aNE1 Morbecque	D 24 a 1.3
Spook Lane	51bSW2 Vis-en-Artois	O 20 c, d, 26 b
Spook Trench	36SW3 Richebourg	S 22 b, 23 a, c
Spool Farm	36NW1 Steenwerck	A 3 a 6.4
Spoon Trench	51bSW2 Vis-en-Artois	O 8 b
Spooner Avenue	51bNW1 Roclincourt	A 15 d, 16 c
Spooners Farm	20SE2 Hooglede	Q 12 c 5.9
Spoor Lane / Spoor Trench	51bSW2 Vis-en-Artois	O 20 c, d
Spot Farm	28NW2 St Julien	C 12 b 8.3
Spot Trench	51bNW3 Arras	G 6 c, d
Spotted Dog Alley	36cNW1 La Bassée	A 22 a, b
Spotted Dog P.H. [Public House]	36cNW1 La Bassée	A 22 b 6.4
Spotterhe [farm]	27SE2 Berthen	R 15 d 05.35
Spouse Farm	20SE2 Hooglede	Q 27 b 7.2
Sprat Post	57cNE1 Quéant	J 5 b
Spratt Trench	28SW2 Wytschaete	O 10 b, d, 11 a
Spree Farm [& pillbox]	28NW2 St Julien	C 18 d 1.3

Name	Map Sheet	Map Reference
Spree Farm How[itzer] Spurs	28NW2 St Julien	C 18 c
Spree Lane	62cNE2 Epéhy	F 6 a
Spresiano Camp [Nieppe Forest]	36aNE3 Haverskerque	J 14 b
Spriet [hamlet]	20SE3 Westroosebeke	V 16 c
Spriet Copse	20SE3 Westroosebeke	V 16 b, 17 a
Spriethoek	28NE2 Moorslede	E 28 b
Spring Copse	27NE2 Proven	E 24 a
Spring Farm	27NE2 Proven	E 18 d 30.05
Spring Gardens [road E of Ovillers]	57dSE4 Ovillers	X 8 b, 9 a, c
Spring Post	36NW4 Bois Grenier	I 7 d, 13 b
Spring Reserve	57cNE1 Quéant	J 2 b, 3 a
Spring Street	28SW4 Ploegsteert	U 7 b
Spring Trench	57cNE1 Quéant	J 2 b, 3 a
Spring Walk	28SW4 Ploegsteert	T 6 a, b
Springbok Valley	62bNW3 Bellicourt	H 15 a
Springfield [farm & pillbox]	28NW2 St Julien	C 12 b 4.6
Springfield [farm & pillboxes]	28NE1 Zonnebeke	D 16 a 0.0
Sprint Lane / Trench	57cSE4 Villers-Guislain	X 28 b
Spruce Farm	20SE2 Hooglede	Q 18 b 15.40
Spud Farm	28SW2 Wytschaete	O 18 b 2.9
Spud Road [road]	28SW2 Wytschaete	N 28 c, d, 34 b, 35 a
Spud Trench	51bNW3 Arras	G 6 d
Spun [?] Trench	51bNW3 Arras	G 6 d
Spur 194 [lt rly, E of Canal 1917-18]	28NW2 St Julien	C 7 c 7.9
Spur 21 [lt rly, E of Canal 1917-18]	28NW2 St Julien	C 13 a
Spur 243 [lt rly, W of Canal 1917-18]	28NW2 St Julien	B 18 b
Spur Alley [Lorette Spur]	36bSE4 Carency	X 5 c, d, 11 a, b
Spur Point	57cSE1 Bertincourt	Q 21 d
Spur Trench	51bNW3 Arras	G 6 c
Spur Trench	51bSW2 Vis-en-Artois	O 9 a
Spur Trench	66cSW2 Vendeuil	O 29 d, 35 b
Spur Wood	62cNW1 Maricourt	A 28 d
Spurn Head Sap, & Trench	36cNW3 Loos	G 5 c, 11 a
Spy Corner [Ploegsteert Wood]	28SW4 Ploegsteert	U 20 b 4.3
Spy Farm (Coesteker)	28SW2 Wytschaete	N 28 c 8.5
Square Alley	66cNW1 Grugies	B 1 b, d
Square Copse	62bNW3 Bellicourt	G 33 a
Square Farm	28NW2 St Julien	C 30 b 8.8
Square Farm	28SW2 Wytschaete	O 30 b 5.3
Square Keep [1917-18]	28NW2 St Julien	C 24 b 9.1
Square Keep [strongpoint SW of Goldfish Ch'au]	28NW4 Ypres	H 10 d 95.45 to H 17 a 05.95
Square Quarry Trench	36cSW3 Vimy	S 9 b
Square Trench [1918]	62dNE [1 Dernancourt]	D 12 b, d, E 7 c
Square Wood	51bNW2 Oppy	C 26 d, 27 c
Square Wood	57dNE1 & 2 Fonquevillers / 3 & 4 Hébuterne	K 6 b, d
Square Wood [1916; Fosse Wood in 1917]	28NW4 & NE3 Zillebeke	I 29 b
Square Wood [Cappy]	62dNE [4 Bray-sur-Somme]	L 35 b
Square Wood [E of St Eloi]	28SW2 Wytschaete	O 3 c 8.8
Square Work	51bNW1 Roclincourt	A 3 b
Square, The	57dNE3 & 4 Hébuterne	K 16 a
Square, The / Le Square	62cNW1 Maricourt	A 16 b
Square, The [Le Barque village]	57cSW1 Gueudecourt	M 12 b 8.3
Squash Trench	57cSE4 Villers-Guislain	X 19 a, b, c
Squaw Copse	62bSW1 Gricourt	M 36 b

Name	Map Sheet	Map Reference
Squeak Farm	28SE1 Wervicq	P 19 c 8.4
Squint Trench	51bSW1 Neuville Vitasse	M 20 c
Squirrel Trench	57cNE3 Hermies	K 2 b, d
St Acaire Wood	27NE1 Herzeele	D 30 a, b, c, d
St Accariushoek [W of Moorslede]	28NE1 Zonnebeke	E 8 d, 9 c
St Amé, Cité [miners' cottages]	36cSW1 Lens	M 22 b, 23 a
St Andrew's Avenue	57dSE4 Ovillers	W 24 b, c, d, X 19 a
St Andrew's Drive	28SW4 Ploegsteert	U 14 d, 15 c
St Aubert Farm	57bSW2 Clary	N 12 b 35.20
St Aubin Ditch [sunken road]	51bNW1 Roclincourt	A 15 d, 16 a, c
St Aubin Redoubt	51cNE2 Ecoivres / 4 Wagnonlieu	L 5 a, b, c, d
St Bruno Alley	66cNW1 Grugies	B 9 c
St Catherine Chapel	20SE2 Hooglede	R 11 b 45.65
St Christ Aerodrome [German, 1918]	62cSW4 St Christ	U 4 a, b
St Christophe Alley	62cSW3 Vermandovillers	T 2 d, 8 b, 9 a
St Cross Street	57dNE1 & 2 Fonquevillers	E 4 c, 10 a, b, d
St Die Alley	66cNW4 Berthenicourt	H 6 d
St Dunstans [farm & huts]	28NW4 Ypres	H 22 b 8.3
St Elie Avenue	36cNW3 Loos	G 5 d, 11 b
St Elie Trench	36cNW3 Loos	G 11 b
St Eloi [Bailleul suburb]	28SW3 Bailleul	S 20 b
St Eloi Craters	28SW2 Wytschaete	O 2 c, d
St Eloi Inn	27NE4 Abeele	K 29 c 6.8
St Etienne Trench	66cNW1 Grugies	B 19 c
St Firmin Alley	66cSW4 La Fère	T 22 c, d, 23 b, c, d, 24 a
St Firmin, Faubourg [ramparts trenches]	66cSW4 La Fère	U 19 a, c
St Floris [village]	36aSE1 St Venant	P 5 b, d, 6 a, b, c
St Genevieve Trench	57dNE3 & 4 Hébuterne	K 16 c
St George Alley	57cSW3 Longueval	S 10 c, d
St George's East & West Tunnels	36cNW3 Loos	G 12 c
St Germain Woods	62dSE [2 Proyart]	R 7 d, 8 c, 14 a
St Hélène [farm]	62bSW1 Gricourt	M 3 b, d
St Hélène [hamlet]	62bSW1 Gricourt	M 3 b, d
St Helen's Street	57dSE1 & 2 Beaumont	Q 4 c
St Hubertshoek [hamlet]	28NW3 Poperinghe	H 31 b, d, 32 a, c
St Jacques, Faubourg [Nesle]	66dNW4 Nesle	I 19 c, d
St James' Street	28NW2 St Julien / 28NW4 & NE3 Zillebeke	I 5 a, d
St James' Street	57dSE1 & 2 Beaumont	Q 16 b, 17 c
St James Street [Sept 1915]	36cNW1 La Bassée	A 9 c
St James' Street, & Keep	36cSW1 Lens	M 4 b
St James's Keep [Calonne]	36cSW1 Lens	M 9 a
St James's Road Keep [South Maroc]	36cSW1 Lens	M 9 a
St Jans Cappel [village]	27SE4 Meteren	R 35 b, 36 c, X 6 a
St Janshoek [farm / place name]	20SW4 Bixschoote	U 8 b 6.4
St Jan-ter-Biezen [hamlet]	27NE2 Proven	L 2 a
St Jean [village]	28NW2 St Julien	C 27 c, d, 28 c, I 3 a, b
St Jean Farm	27SE4 Meteren	Q 35 d 7.4
St Jean Farm	28NW2 St Julien	C 27 c 8.2
St Jean Post	28NW2 St Julien	C 27 d
St Jean Street	57dSE1 & 2 Beaumont	Q 23 b
St John Road [road]	36cSW4 Rouvroy	U 8 d, 9 c, 15 a, b, d
St Johns Cross [cross roads]	28NW1 Elverdinghe	A 23 a 3.1
St Johns Road [road]	36cSW1 Lens	M 18 c, d
St Joseph's Institute	28NE1 Zonnebeke	D 27 a 70.25

Name	Map Sheet	Map Reference
St Julien [village]	28NW2 St Julien	C 12 c, 17 b, 18 a
St Lawrence Camp	28NW3 Poperinghe	G 11 c
St Leger [village]	51bSW3 Boisleux / 57cNW2 Vaulx-Vraucourt	T 28, B 4
St Leger Reserve	57cNW2 Vaulx-Vraucourt	B 5 a
St Leger Wood	51bSW3 Boisleux / 57cNW2 Vaulx-Vraucourt	T 28 b, c, d, 29 a, c, B 4 a, b, d, 5 a
St Leonard, Faubourg [Nesle]	66dNW4 Nesle	H 24 b, d
St Louis Crater	36cSW1 Lens	N 20 c
St Maixent Trench	66cSW2 Vendeuil	O 3 b, 4 a
St Martin Alley	62bSW3 St Quentin	S 24 d
St Martin sur Cojeul [village]	51bSW1 Neuville Vitasse	N 33 a, b
St Martin Woods	62dSE [2 Proyart]	R 23, 28, 29
St Martin's Lane	36NW4 Bois Grenier	I 31 b
St Martin's Lane	57dNE1 & 2 Fonquevillers	E 27 d
St Martin's Trench	57cSW4 Combles	U 16 d, 17 c
St Michael's Statue [at road fork]	51bSW2 Vis-en-Artois	O 27 c 3.9
St Momens Street	57dSE4 Ovillers	X 19 a
St Nicholas [Boves]	62dSW [3 Boves]	N 8 a, c
St Nicholas, Faubourg [Nesle]	66dNW4 Nesle	I 13 c, d, 19 a
St Pancras Keep	36cSW1 Lens	M 2 b, 3 a, c
St Pancras Street	51bNW3 Arras	G 11 b, 12 a
St Pancras Tunnel	36cSW1 Lens	M 2 b
St Patrick [Trench; Sept 1915]	36cNW1 La Bassée	A 21 d
St Patrick's Avenue	57dSE1 & 2 Beaumont	Q 10 c
St Patrick's Avenue	62cNE2 Epéhy	F 4 c, d, 10 a
St Peter's Street	28NW4 & NE3 Zillebeke	I 24 d
St Pierre [Ypres, light rly locality 1917-18]	28NW4 Ypres	I 14 a
St Pierre Cut Off [light rly]	36cSW1 Lens	M 9 a
St Pierre Farm	62cNE1 Liéramont	D 15 c
St Pierre Vaast Wood	57cSW4 Combles / 62cNW2 Bouchavesnes	U 20, 21, 22, 26, 27, 28, C 2, 3, 4
St Pieter [hamlet]	28NE2 Moorslede	F 19 d
St Pol Alley	62bSW3 St Quentin	S 6 a, c, d
St Quentin Cabaret [Wulverghem]	28SW4 Ploegsteert	T 5 d 3.3
St Quentin Farm [Wulverghem]	28SW4 Ploegsteert	T 6 c 4.3
St Quentin Wood	62cSE4 [Attilly]	R 35, X 4, 5, 6, 10, 11, 12
St Quentin, Pont de [Wulverghem]	28SW4 Ploegsteert	T 5 d 75.37
St Ribert Farm	66eNW [4 Morisel]	I 21 d 6.8
St Riquier [village]	57eNW	A 34, 35, G 4, 5
St Rohart Factory	51bSW2 Vis-en-Artois	O 15 d 0.6
St Rohart Quarry	51bSW2 Vis-en-Artois	O 15 c 2.6
St Sauveur Tunnel	51bNW3 Arras	G 28, 29, 30
St Sauveur, Faubourg [Arras]	51bNW3 Arras	G 29 a, b, c, d, 30 c
St Servins Farm	51bSW2 Vis-en-Artois	O 24 d 8.7
St Sixte [hamlet]	28NW1 Elverdinghe	A 1 b, d, 2 a, c, 7 b
St Sixte [railway & light rly sidings]	28NW1 Elverdinghe	A 7 b, 8 a
St Sixte Junction [cross roads]	28NW1 Elverdinghe	A 2 a 6.7
St Sixte, Couvent des Trappistes	28NW1 Elverdinghe	A 1 d
St Vaast Dump	36SW3 Richebourg	M 32 d
St Vaast Post	36SW3 Richebourg	M 32 d 95.05
St Vaast Tramway	36SW3 Richebourg	M 32 d, 33 c, S 3 a, b, d, 4 c, 10 a
St Vincent Street	57dSE4 Ovillers	X 7 c, d
St Yves / St Yvon [hamlet]	28SW4 Ploegsteert	U 15 c
St Yves Avenue [road]	28SW4 Ploegsteert	U 15 c, d
St Yves Avenue [trench]	28SW4 Ploegsteert	U 15 c, d, 21 a
St Yves Post Office	28SW4 Ploegsteert	U 15 c 93.50

Name	Map Sheet	Map Reference
St Yves Trench [old Trenches 122 & 123]	28SW4 Ploegsteert	U 15 d, 21 b
St Yvon / St Yves [hamlet]	28SW4 Ploegsteert	U 15 c
Stab Trench	51bNW3 Arras	G 6 d
Stable Fort [Hill 63, E end]	28SW4 Ploegsteert	U 14 c 5.7
Stable, The [Post]	57cNE1 Quéant	D 24 a
Stables Retrenchment [Hooge]	28NW4 & NE3 Zillebeke	I 18 b
Stables, The [Eitel Fritz farm]	28NW2 St Julien	I 5 b 3.5
Staden - Zonnebeke Line	20SE3 Westroosebeke	V 16 a, c
Staden [town]	20SE1 Staden	P 18 a, b, c, d
Staenyzer Cabaret	28SW2 Wytschaete	O 20 c 15.80
Staff Copse	57dNE3 & 4 Hébuterne	K 22 d, 28 b
Staff Corner [road; Lovie Chateau]	27NE2 Proven	F 16
Staff Farm	20SE3 Westroosebeke	V 5 b 1.3
Staff House	20SE2 Hooglede	R 1 c 6.5
Staff Lane [road, Le Transloy]	57cSW2 Villers-au-Flos	N 30 d
Staffa Street	57dSE4 Ovillers	Q 36 d
Stafford [lt rly locality W of Langemarck 1917-18]	20SW4 Bixschoote	U 28 a
Stafford Alley	57cNE4 Marcoing	K 11 c, 17 a
Stafford Avenue	57dNE1 & 2 Fonquevillers	E 28 a
Stafford Corner [ENE of Festubert, May 1915]	36SW3 Richebourg	S 27 b
Stafford Crater	51bNW1 Roclincourt	A 4 d
Stafford House Trench	28NW4 & NE3 Zillebeke	I 29 c
Stafford Lane	36cNW3 Loos	G 10 d, 11 c
Stafford Lane	51bSW4 Bullecourt	U 13 d, 14 c
Stafford Lane [road]	51bNW2 Oppy / Fampoux	B 30 d, H 6 a, b, c, 11 b, d, 12 a, 17 b
Stafford Redoubt [La Bassée Road]	36cNW1 La Bassée	A 21 b, d
Stafford Reserve	57cSE2 Gonnelieu	Q 11 a, b
Stafford Road	36SW3 Richebourg / 36cNW1 La Bassée	S 27 c, A 3 a
Stafford Street	51bNW1 Roclincourt	A 4 c
Stafford Street	62dNE2 Méaulte	F 11 c, d
Stafford Support	57cSE2 Gonnelieu	Q 5 d, 11 b
Stafford Trench	28NW4 & NE3 Zillebeke	I 24 a, c
Stafford Trench	57cSE2 Gonnelieu	Q 5 d, 11 b
Stafford Trench [1918]	62dNE [3 Morlancourt]	K 20 a, c
Stafford Trench [Tranchées Ruault & Lère; FL]	36cSW1 Lens	M 20 b
Staffords Trench	57dNE1 & 2 Fonquevillers / 3 & 4 Hébuterne	K 6 b, c, d
Stag Alley	57cNE4 Marcoing	K 4 c, d, 10 a, b
Stag Trench	51bSW2 Vis-en-Artois	N 24 d, O 19 a
Stage House	28NE2 Moorslede	F 14 a 40.75
Stagger Farm	20SE2 Hooglede	R 4 d 8.3
Staines House	27SE2 Berthen	R 23 b 70.75
Stale Trench	51bNW3 Arras	G 6 c
Stall, The [Post]	57cNE1 Quéant	D 24 d
Stallion Farm	28NE2 Moorslede	E 29 a 75.75
Stamboul Trench [1918]	62dSW [4 Cachy]	U 5 b, d, 6 a
Stampe Trench	57cNE3 Hermies	K 20 c
Stampkot Trench	20SW4 Bixschoote	T 17 a, c, d
Stampkotmolen [windmill, Neuve Eglise]	28SW3 Bailleul	T 8 d 42.45
Stan Houses	28NE2 Moorslede	F 26 a 75.25
Stand Alley	66cSW2 Vendeuil	N 18 a, b, O 13 a
Standish Street	57dSE4 Ovillers	X 13 a, b
Stanhope Redoubt	51bSW4 Bullecourt	U 27 a
Stanley Avenue	62cNW1 Maricourt	A 10 c
Stanley Farm	28NE4 Dadizeele	K 28 b 0.8

Name	Map Sheet	Map Reference
Stanley Redoubt [house SW of Roupy]	66dNE [2 Roupy]	F 16 b
Stanley Street	57dSE4 Ovillers	X 1 b
Stanser's Farm	28NE4 Dadizeele	L 31 d 60.15
Stansfield / Stanifield Road [Sept 1915]	36cNW3 Loos	G 9 b, 10 a, b, 11 a
Stansfield Locality	36cNW3 Loos	G 11 a, b
Stanway Avenue	36NW4 Bois Grenier	I 31 b
Stanway Post	36NW4 Bois Grenier	I 31 a, b
Stanza Farm	27NE4 Abeele	L 20 d 2.9
Stanza Wood	27NE4 Abeele	L 19 b, d, 20 a, c
Star Alley	57dNE3 & 4 Hébuterne	K 18, 24, L 13
Star Corner	51bSW2 Vis-en-Artois	O 34 a 4.6
Star Fish Post	51cSE3 & 4 Ransart	R 31 d
Star Trench	51bNW3 Arras	G 6 d
Star Trench	57cNE4 Marcoing	K 28 c, 34 a, b
Star Trench	57cSW4 Combles	U 1 a, b
Star Trench	57dSW [4 Toutencourt]	U 29 b, 30 a, c
Star Wood	57dNE3 & 4 Hébuterne	K 24 b
Starboard House	28NW1 Elverdinghe	B 14 d 8.1
Stare Trench	51bNW3 Arras	G 6 c
Starfish Cross Roads	28SW1 Kemmel	M 17 d 2.2
Starfish Line	57cSW3 Longueval	M 34 a, b, c, d, 35 c, d
Starfish Trench	51bSW4 Bullecourt	U 23 d
Starfish, The	57cSW3 Longueval	M 35 c
Stark / Stars Trench	51bNW3 Arras	G 6 c
Starling Farm	28SW1 Kemmel	M 34 b 3.9
Starling Support [1918]	57dNE2 & 57cNW1 Courcelles	F 11 c
Starling Trench	51bSW2 Vis-en-Artois	N 30 a, c, d, O 25 c, d, 31 b, 32 a
Starling Wood	66cNW3 Essigny	H 9 a
Starry Wood	62cSW3 Vermandovillers	S 2 c, d, 8 a, b, c, d
Station [railway, S of Cairo House]	20SW4 Bixschoote	U 12 d 4.7
Station Alley	57dSE1 & 2 Beaumont	Q 12 a, c
Station Alley	66cNW1 Grugies / 3 Essigny	B 14, 15, 20, 25, 26, G 6, H 1
Station Avenue	36NW2 Armentières	C 9 c, d, 14 b, 15 a
Station Avenue [Ribécourt]	57cNE4 Marcoing	K 30 b, L 19 c, d, 25 a, c
Station Avenue West	57cNE4 Marcoing	K 30 d
Station Copse [South Chaulnes]	66dNW1 Punchy	A 17 a
Station Farm [Boesinghe]	28NW2 St Julien	B 12 c 8.7
Station House [1918]	28SW1 Kemmel	N 19 c 3.3
Station Inn [Caudescure]	36aNE3 Haverskerque	K 14 a 60.85
Station Redoubt	51bSW4 Bullecourt	U 26 d, 27 c
Station Redoubt [E of Grand Seraucourt]	66cNW1 Grugies / 3 Essigny	G 10, 11
Station Road [road]	57dSE2 Beaumont	Q 11 d, 12 c, 18 a, b
Station Road [trench]	36bSE4 Carency	X 15 a, b, 16 a, b
Station Trench	36cSW1 Lens	N 27 c
Station Trench	57dSE1 & 2 Beaumont	Q 12 c, d
Station Trench [1918]	51bSW3 Boisleux	S 24 b, T 19 a
Station Trench [Guillemont Station]	57cSW3 Longueval	S 24 d
Statuette Farm	20SW4 Bixschoote	T 24 d 9.2
Statuettes Avenue	20SW4 Bixschoote	T 24 d, 30 a, b
Staubwasser Weg	36cSW3 Vimy	S 22 c, d, 23 a, b, c
Stave Trench	62bNW1 Gouy	A 19 b
Ste. Geneviève Trench	57dNE3 & 4 Hébuterne	K 16 c
Steak Line / Lane [Beaumont Hamel]	57dSE1 & 2 Beaumont	Q 5 c, d
Stealth Farm	28NE2 Moorslede	F 1 a 3.4

Name	Map Sheet	Map Reference
Steam Mill	27SE4 Meteren	X 24 c 03.10
Steam Mill [Boesinghe, E of Canal]	28NW2 St Julien	B 6 d 3.2
Steam Mill [Paradis]	36aSE2 Lestrem	Q 18 c 4.4
Steel Back	36cSW3 Vimy	M 32 c
Steel Wood	66dNW1 Punchy	A 12 b
Steen Akker [hamlet]	27SE2 Berthen	R 2 b, 3 a
Steenstraat Avenue	20SW4 Bixschoote	T 17 c, d, 23 a
Steenstraat Work	20SW4 Bixschoote	T 17 d
Steentje Cabaret	28NW1 Elverdinghe	A 23 b 6.8
Steentje Mill [railway sidings & huts]	28NW1 Elverdinghe	A 23 a
Steentje Windmill	28NW1 Elverdinghe	A 23 b 9.8
Steenwerck [village]	36NW1 Steenwerck	A 17 a, b, c, d, 23 a, b
Steenwerck Railhead / Refilling Point	36NW1 Steenwerck	A 12 a, b
Steenwerck Station	36NW1 Steenwerck	A 12 a 3.3
Steep Alley	66cSW2 Vendeuil	O 15 c, d
Steep Alley [Lorette Spur]	36bSE4 Carency	X 5 d
Steignast Farm	28SW4 Ploegsteert	U 5 a 2.7
Stein Alley	66cNW1 Grugies	B 8 b
Stein Weg	28NW4 & NE3 Zillebeke	J 25 a
Stein Weg	57dNE1 & 2 Fonquevillers	E 28 b, 29 a, c
Steinlein Weg	51bNW1 Roclincourt	A 30 d, B 25 c
Stein's Farm	27SE4 Meteren	X 22 c 30.45
Stellar Cross [cross roads]	27SE4 Meteren	W 16 d 07.40
Stellite Junction [road jct]	28NE4 Dadizeele	K 12 b 4.1
Stellite O.P. [Fosse 11 Puits, 1917-18]	36cSW1 Lens	M 11 b 3.5
Stem Trench	51bNW3 Arras	G 6 c
Step Farm [1915]	36NW2 Armentières	C 17 b 2.4
Step Trench	57dNE4 & 57cNW3 Achiet	G 14 c, d, 19 b, 20 a
Step Wood	62bSW2 Fonsommes	O 35 a, b
Stephan's Walk	36SW3 Richebourg	S 11 c
Stephenson Avenue [Mesnil]	57dSE1 & 2 Beaumont	Q 28 c, d
Stern Farm	28NW1 Elverdinghe	B 21 b 4.6
Stettin Trench	62cNW4 Péronne	I 31 a, c
Stettin Trench [1918]	66eNW [2 Thennes]	C 16 c
Steven Trench [1918]	28NE3 Gheluvelt	J 20 d
Stevens Redoubt	62cSE4 [Attilly]	X 21 c, d
Stew Trench	51bNW3 Arras	G 6 c
Stew Trench [originally Sunken Road Trench]	57cSW3 Longueval	T 21 a, c, d
Stewart Street	28NW4 & NE3 Zillebeke	I 30 b
Sticky Trench [Hohenzollern]	36cNW1 La Bassée	G 4 b
Stifle Post	62bNW3 Bellicourt	G 31 b 6.2
Stiggins Avenue [1918]	57dSW [3 Talmas]	S 28 d, 29 a, c
Stink Inn	36aSE3 Gonnehem	W 8 d 2.6
Stink Post [Oder House / Odour Houses]	28NW2 St Julien	C 29 d
Stinking Farm	28SW4 Ploegsteert	U 7 a 5.7
Stinking Road [1917-18]	28SW4 Ploegsteert	U1 d, 2 c, 7 a, b
Stirling Castle	28NE3 Gheluvelt	J 13 d 6.3
Stirling Lane	28NW2 St Julien	C 19 d, 20 c
Stirling Track [1917-18]	28NW4 Ypres	I 24 b, c, d
Stirrup Lane [road]	51bSW2 Vis-en-Artois	O 4 c, d, 8 b, 9 b, c, d, 10 a
Stirrup Trench	51bSW2 Vis-en-Artois	O 9 c, 15 a
Stitch Farm	28NE2 Moorslede	F 27 a 2.8
Stitt Trench	36cSW1 Lens / 2 Harnes	N 22 a
Stoat Cottages	27NE2 Proven	E 29 c 2.8

Name	Map Sheet	Map Reference
Stock Trench	57cNE4 Marcoing	K 10 b
Stockhausen Weg	51bSW1 Neuville Vitasse	M 16 a, b, d
Stocking Farm	28NE2 Moorslede	E 18 a 60.75
Stocking Wood	51bNE4 Cantin	L 16 a
Stockport [lt rly locality W of Poelcappelle '17-18]	20SW4 Bixschoote	U 24 b, d
Stockweed Farm	20SE2 Hooglede	R 15 c 6.6
Stoic Farm	27SE4 Meteren	X 2 d 2.4
Stoke [lt rly locality NW of Pilckem 1917-18]	28NW2 St Julien	C 1 a
Stoke Hill [1918]	57dSW2 [Raincheval]	N 28, 29
Stoke Street	51bNW1 Roclincourt	A 4 c
Stoke Support	51bNW4 Fampoux	H 16 d, 17 a, c, 22 b
Stoke Trench	51bNW4 Fampoux	H 11 a, c, 17 a, b, d
Stokes Trench	51bNW4 Fampoux	I 26 d, 27 c, 32 b
Stollwerek [sic] Trench	66dNW1 Punchy	A 18 c, 23 b, c, d, 24 a
Stone Alley [Sept 1915]	36cNW3 Loos	G 12 a
Stone Farm	28NE3 Gheluvelt	J 28 b 15.50
Stone Lane	57cSE4 Villers-Guislain	X 22 d, 23 c
Stone Mill [Maretz]	57bSW4 Serain	U 12 a 20.45
Stone Post	57cNE4 Marcoing	K 10 a
Stone Street	28SW4 Ploegsteert	T 6 b 8.1
Stone Street	51bNW1 Roclincourt	A 4 c
Stone Street, & Tunnel	36cNW3 Loos	G 12 c, d, 18 a
Stone Trench	57cSE4 Villers-Guislain	X 23 c
Stonecross Corner	20SE2 Hooglede	Q 21 d 87.20
Stoneham Farm	20SE2 Hooglede	Q 28 d 35.70
Stonehaven Street	57dSE4 Ovillers	X 26 c
Stoney / Stony Trench	57dSE1 & 2 Beaumont	Q 24 b, d, R 19 a, c
Stoney Street	57cNE1 Quéant	D 8 a, b, c
Stoneygate Road	57dNE1 & 2 Fonquevillers	E 3 c, d, 4 a, b, c
Stony Mountain [Ger post, Rue d'Ouvert, June '15]	36cNW1 La Bassée	A 3 a / c / d
Stoomtuig [hamlet]	20SE2 Hooglede	R 8 c 60.75
Stop Copse [by Amiens Inner Defence Line]	62dSW [1 Longueau]	M 12 a
Stop Farm	28NE2 Moorslede	E 30 d 4.2
Storar Avenue	57cSE4 Villers-Guislain	X 15 b, 16 a
Store Farm	28SW2 Wytschaete	N 29 a
Store Trench	51bNW1 Roclincourt	A 4 c
Stork Support	51bSW2 Vis-en-Artois / 4 Bullecourt	O 31 b, c, d
Stork Support [1918]	57dNE2 & 57cNW1 Courcelles	F 11 b, d
Stork Trench	28SW2 Wytschaete	N 22 b
Stork Trench	36SW3 Richebourg	S 28 b
Stork Trench	51bSW2 Vis-en-Artois	O 31 b
Storknest Cross Roads	20SE2 Hooglede	Q 24 c 06.30
Stormy Loop	36SW3 Richebourg	S 28 a, b
Stormy Trench	57dSE2 & 57cSW1 Le Sars / SW4 Combles	N 21 a, b, d
Stoughton Farm	28NE4 Dadizeele	K 22 b 2.1
Stout Track (Duckboard) [1917-18]	28NE3 Gheluvelt	J 19 c, d, 20 c, d, 26 a, b
Stout Trench	57cSW3 Longueval	T 13 a, c, 19 a
Stout Trench [1918]	57dNE1 & 2 Fonquevillers	E 23, 24, 28, 29, K 4
Stout Wood	28NE3 Gheluvelt	J 20 d, 26 b
Stove Post	57cNE3 Hermies	K 3 d 5.0
Stove Wood	62dSE [3 Marcelcave]	V 23 b
Stowaway Fork [road jct]	28NE2 Moorslede	E 3 b 99.55
Straf Alley [Hohenzollern]	36cNW3 Loos	G 4 d, 5 c
Strafe House	36aSE4 Locon	W 4 b [approx]

Name	Map Sheet	Map Reference
Straffehem Railhead / Refilling Point	27NE2 Proven	F 2 c, d
Straffer's Nest	28SW4 Ploegsteert	U 14 c
Straggly Tree [trig; Filiform Tree/Arbre Filiforme]	62dNE2 Méaulte	F 26 a 05.05
Straight Trench	57cSW3 Longueval	T 8 d, 14 b, d
Straight, The	36cSW3 Vimy	M 32 c
Strand	36SW1 Aubers	M 12 d, 18 b
Strand [Delville Wood]	57cSW3 Longueval	S 12 c
Strand A	28NW2 St Julien	I 4 a, b
Strand B	28NW2 St Julien	C 29 c, I 5 a
Strand Cemetery	28SW4 Ploegsteert	U 20 b 8.2
Strand, The [Hooge, 1915]	28NW4 & NE3 Zillebeke	I 18 b, d
Strand, The [Ploegsteert Wood]	28SW4 Ploegsteert	U 19 c, d, 20 a, b, c, 21 a
Strand, The [road]	57cNE1 Quéant	D 20 b, d
Strangeways Reserve	51bSW4 Bullecourt	U 13 d, 19 b
Strap Trench	51bSW2 Vis-en-Artois	O 8 d
Strassburg Line	57dSE1 & 2 Beaumont	R 19 a
Strassburg Trench	36SW3 Richebourg	S 24 c, d, 30 a
Strassburg Trench	57dSE2 Beaumont	R 19 a
Strassburger Graben / Trench	51bNW3 Arras	G 6 c
Strathcona Walk	36cNW1 La Bassée	A 15 b, d
Stratigos Trench / Tranchée Stratigos	66cNW2 Itancourt	B 30 b, C 25 a, c, d
Stratton Lane [road / ride in Pacaut Wood]	36aSE1 St Venant / 3 Gonnehem	Q 33 a, c
Straw [Stack] Trench	28SW4 Ploegsteert	U 7 c 1.1
Straw Alley	36cNW3 Loos	G 18 b, 19 a, c
Straw Stack	28SW4 Ploegsteert	U 7 c 1.1
Straw Trench	36SW3 Richebourg	S 28 a, c
Straw Trench [1918]	20SW4 Bixschoote / 28NW2 St Julien	U 27 d, C 3 b
Stray Copse No.1	62cSE1 Bouvincourt	P 5 b
Stray Copse No.2	62cSE1 Bouvincourt	P 6 a
Stray Farm [Langemarck area]	28NW2 St Julien	C 3 c 2.7
Stray Farm Trench [1918]	28NW2 St Julien	C 3 a, c
Stray Reserve	51bSW4 Bullecourt	U 19 b, d
Stray Support, & Reserve	51bSW4 Bullecourt	U 13 c, d, 19 b
Strazeele [defended locality]	27SE4 Meteren	W 23 c, 28 b, 29 a, b
Strazeele [village]	27SE4 Meteren	W 28 b, 29 a
Strazeele Railhead / Refilling Point	36aNE2 Vieux Berquin	E 4 d, 5 c
Streaky Bacon Farm Post	36NW4 Bois Grenier	H 18 d
Strelitzer Weg	51bNW1 Roclincourt	A 24 c, d, 30 b
Strensall Road	28NW2 St Julien	C 19 c, d
Stretcher Lane	28SW4 Ploegsteert	N 35 d, 36 c
Stretford Street	62dNE2 Méaulte	F 11 d, 12 c
Stretton Lane [ride in wood]	36aSE1 St Venant / 3 Gonnehem	Q 33 a, c
Stretton Lane [road, Pacaut Wood]	36aSE1 St Venant / 2 Lestrem	Q 33 a, b, d
Strict Buildings	28NE2 Moorslede	E 30 b 9.8
String Houses	20SE3 Westroosebeke	V 13 d 4.6
String Trench	51bSW2 Vis-en-Artois	O 7 b, c, d, 14 b
String, The	51bSW1 Neuville Vitasse	N 1 a, c, 7 a
Strip Trench [Mametz Wood]	57dSE4 Ovillers	X 24 c, 30 a
Stripe Copse	51bSW2 Vis-en-Artois / SE1 Saudemont	O 24 d, P 19 c
Strong Farm	36cNW1 La Bassée	A 5 d 25.75
Strong Point	28NE1 Zonnebeke	D 17 a 6.7
Strong Point	28NE3 Gheluvelt	J 14 b
Strong Point	28NW4 & NE3 Zillebeke	I 20 b 7.5
Strong Point	28SW2 Wytschaete	O 16 c 0.8

Name	Map Sheet	Map Reference
Strong Point	36SW3 Richebourg	S 29 a 2.7
Strong Point	57cSW1 Gueudecourt	M 19 d 1.0
Strong Point	57cSW4 Combles	T 5 a 4.6
Strong Point	57dSE4 Ovillers	X 3 b 8.9
Strong Point [GFL, off Little Willie]	36cNW1 La Bassée	A 4 b
Strong Point [Meunier House]	20SE3 Westroosebeke	V 20 a 9.1
Stroo Farm [Strooiboomhoek]	28NE2 Moorslede	K 6 a 1.2
Strooiboomhoek	28NE2 Moorslede	K 4 b, d, 5 a, c
Stroom Trench	20SE3 Westroosebeke	V 25 a, c, d
Stroppe Farm	28NE1 Zonnebeke	D 1 d 3.2
Strypa Alley / Boyau de la Strypa	62cSW3 Vermandovillers	S 29 d, 30 a, c
Stuart Keep	36cNW3 Loos	G 10 b
Stuart Lane	28SW2 Wytschaete	N 12 b, d
Stuart Road	36cNW1 La Bassée	A 2 b, 3 a, c
Stuart Work	57dSE1 & 2 Beaumont	Q 5 d 6.6
Stud Alley	51bNW4 Fampoux	I 31 d
Student Cross Roads	28NE2 Moorslede	F 4 d 9.2
Stuff Redoubt [Feste Staufen]	57dSE1 & 2 Beaumont	R 21 c
Stuff Trench	57dSE1 & 2 Beaumont	R 20 a, b
Stump Alley	57dNE3 & 4 Hébuterne	K 11 d, 12 c
Stump Farm	28NE2 Moorslede	E 11 b 3.8
Stump Road [road]	57dSE1 & 2 Beaumont	R 15 a, c, 21 a
Stump Street	57dNE1 & 2 Fonquevillers	E 3 c
Stump Support	36SW3 Richebourg	S 16 b
Sturdee [light rly siding]	28NW2 St Julien	C 30 c
Sturgeon Avenue	57cNE3 Hermies	J 6 c, d, 11 b, d, 12 a, 17 b
Sturgeon Support	57cNE3 Hermies	J 6 d, 12 b
Sturmer Trench	70dNW4 St Gobain	H 24 a, b, c
Sturt Trench [Dead Cow Farm]	36NW4 Bois Grenier	I 20 b, d
Stuttgart Lane	57dNE3 & 4 Hébuterne	K 29 d
Stuttgart Trench	66cNW4 Berthenicourt	I 8 b
Stützpunkt I [N of Cité St Elie]	36cNW3 Loos	G 6 b
Stützpunkt II [S of Cité St Elie]	36cNW3 Loos	H 7 a
Stützpunkt III [S of Hulluch]	36cNW3 Loos	H 14 c, d
Stützpunkt IV [W of Bois des Dames]	36cNW3 Loos	H 20 d
Stützpunkt V [Bois de Quatorze]	36cNW3 Loos	H 27 a
Sty, The [Post]	57cNE1 Quéant	E 25 d
Stye Street [Sept 1915]	36cNW1 La Bassée	A 21 d
Styr Alley	62bSW3 St Quentin	S 30 b
Styx House	28NW4 Ypres	H 10 a 7.6
Styx Trench	57cSE1 Bertincourt	P 19 b, d
Subalton [sic] Hill	62bSW4 Homblières	U 3 b, 4 a
Subalton [sic] Wood	62bSW4 Homblières	O 33 d, 34 c
Subsidiary [Trench]	36NW2 Armentières	C 22, 28, I 3, 4
Subsidiary Line	28SW4 Ploegsteert	T 12 a, c, U 13 a, b, 14 a
Subterranean Passage [Powder Magazine]	66cSW2 Vendeuil	O 34 a
Suchard, Tranchée	70dSW [2 Coucy-le-Château]	N 17 b
Sucrerie Cemetery	36bSE4 & 36cSW3 Givenchy	X 11 d 4.8
Sucrerie Cemetery	36bSE4 & 36cSW3 Givenchy	X 11 a 1.8
Sucrerie Cemetery	57dNE3 & 4 Hébuterne	K 31 d 8.7
Sucrerie Post	57dNE1 & 2 Fonquevillers	E 28 c 40.65
Sucrerie Trench	62cSW3 Vermandovillers	T 7 d, 8 c, 13 b, 14 a
Sucrerie, Boyau de la [Sugar Factory]	62cSW1 Dompierre	M 9 b, d, 10 c
Sud [Exe] Trench	57dNE3 & 4 Hébuterne	K 4 d

Name	Map Sheet	Map Reference
Sud Alley	62cSW1 & 2 Belloy	N 5 d, a, b
Sud Graben	57dNE3 & 4 Hébuterne	K 4 d
Sud Trench	51bNW1 Roclincourt	A 24 c
Sud Weg	28NW4 & NE3 Zillebeke	J 19 a, c
Sudbury Trench	57dSE2 & 57cSW1 Le Sars	R 23 b, c, d
Suez Farm	20SW4 Bixschoote	U 11 b 7.7
Suez Trench	20SW4 Bixschoote	U 11 b, 12 a
Suffolk [strongpoint]	36NW3 Fleurbaix	G 12 c
Suffolk Avenue	36NW2 Armentières	C 3 b, 4 a
Suffolk Avenue	62dNE2 Méaulte	F 17 a
Suffolk Line	36aSE3 Gonnehem / 4 Locon	W 9 a, b
Suffolk Street	62dNE2 Méaulte	F 17 a
Suffolk Switch	36aSE3 Gonnehem / 4 Locon	W 9 a, b, d
Sufli, Tranchée de [500 yds NE of Lesboeufs]	57cSW4 Combles	N 34 d, 35 c
Sugar Drain [tributary of R. Lawes]	36aSE4 Locon	X 13 d, 19 b, 20 a, c
Sugar Factory	51bNW2 Oppy	B 16 a 5.5
Sugar Factory	51bNW2 Oppy	B 10 b 5.0
Sugar Factory	51bSW3 Boisleux	S 19 b 2.4
Sugar Factory	57cNE2 Bourlon	E 29 a 1.7
Sugar Factory	57cNW2 Vaulx-Vraucourt	B 24 b 8.2
Sugar Factory	57cSW2 Villers-au-Flos	N 23 d
Sugar Factory [Boiry-Ste. Rictrude]	51cSE4 Blaireville	X 27 a, c
Sugar Factory [Courcelette]	57dSE2 & 57cSW1 Le Sars	R 36 a
Sugar Factory Keep	51cSE & 51bSW Ficheux	R 28 a, b, d
Sugar Loaf / Sugarloaf salient	36SW1 Aubers	N 8 d
Sugar Mill	62bNW3 Bellicourt	H 8 central
Sugar Post	51bNW2 Oppy	B 10 d, 16 b
Sugar Post	62cNE2 Epéhy	L 6 a
Sugar Refinery	57cSW3 Longueval	S 18 c 9.1
Sugar Refinery	57cSW3 Longueval	S 18 d 2.2
Sugar Refinery	62bSW3 St Quentin	S 3 c
Sugar Refinery	62cNE4 Roisel	L 4 c 8.4
Sugar Refinery [La Basse Ville, Warneton]	28SW4 Ploegsteert	U 17 d 4.6
Sugar Trench	57dSE2 & 57cSW1 Le Sars	R 29 d, 30 c, 35 a, b, 36 a, M 25 d
Sugar Trench	62cNE2 Epéhy	L 6 a
Sugar Valley [1918]	51cSE4 Blaireville	X 23 c, d
Sugar Work	57cNW1 Gomiecourt	A 21 a
Suicide Bridge [across Bollaartbeek]	28SW2 Wytschaete	O 1 c 95.65
Suicide Corner [Kruisstraat]	28NW4 Ypres	I 13 c
Suicide Corner [La Polka, Kemmel]	28SW1 Kemmel	N 21 d 5.4
Suicide Corner [Menin Rd jct with Potijze rd]	28NW4 Ypres	I 8 d 55.35
Suicide Corner [near Beaucourt Station]	57dSE2 Beaumont	Q 18 b 5.9
Suicide Corner [NW of Ypres]	28NW4 Ypres	I 1 c 1.6
Suicide Corner [Pozières]	57dSE4 Ovillers	R 4
Suicide Corner [Vermelles]	36cNW3 Loos	G 13 d
Suicide Crossroads [Hellfire Corner]	28NW4 Ypres	I 10 c 95.20
Suicide Farm	27SE4 Meteren	W 24 a 40.65
Suicide Road [road]	28SW2 Wytschaete	N 29 a, b, 30 a
Sula Trench	66cSW2 Vendeuil	O 10 c, 15 b, 16 a
Sullivan Trench	36cSW1 Lens / 3 Vimy	N 32 b, d, 33 c, d, T 3 a
Sullivan Trench	57cSW4 Combles	U 14 b, d, 15 c
Sully Trench [near Sully Farm]	20SW2 Zwartegat	O 25 b
Sulphur Avenue	57cSW2 Villers-au-Flos	N 23 b, d, 24 a
Sulphur Avenue	57dSE4 Ovillers	X 3 a, b

Name	Map Sheet	Map Reference
Sultan Farm	28NE2 Moorslede	E 17 a 65.65
Summer House [house]	28NW2 St Julien	I 2 a
Summer House Post	57dSE1 & 2 Beaumont	Q 24 a 3.6
Summer Lane [trench]	57cNE4 Marcoing	K 10 b, d
Summer Reserve	57cNE1 Quéant	D 26 c, d
Summer Rill [stream]	51bSW4 Bullecourt	U 3 c, d
Summer Support	57cSW4 Combles	N 34 b, 35 c
Summer Trench	57cSW2 Villers-au-Flos	N 28 d
Summer Trench [1918]	51bNW1 Roclincourt	B 14 a, c
Summit Alley	57cSE1 Bertincourt	Q 3 a
Summit Lane	62cNW1 Maricourt	A 17 d
Summit Siding [light rly]	36bSE4 Carency	W 11 b
Summit Wood	57dSW [4 Toutencourt]	T 24 d, 30 a, b
Sump Farm	28SW3 Bailleul	M 31 d 5.7
Sun Alley	57cNE4 Marcoing	K 10 d
Sun Quarry	51bSW4 Bullecourt	O 33 c
Sun Trench	57cSW2 Villers-au-Flos	N 29 a, b, d, 30 c
Sun Trench [near Sun Quarry]	51bSW4 Bullecourt	O 33 c
Sunay Copse	62cSW4 St Christ	U 17 c
Sunbeam Cottage	27NE2 Proven	F 17 d 1.9
Sunday Avenue	51bNW1 Roclincourt / 3 Arras	G 5 b, c, d, 10 d, 11 a, b, 16 a, b
Sunken Alley	57cNE4 Marcoing	L 34 c
Sunken Avenue	28SW4 Ploegsteert	U 11 c, 16 b, 17 a
Sunken Copse	62cSE1 Bouvincourt	P 26 a, b
Sunken Farm	28SW4 Ploegsteert	U 11 c 7.0
Sunken Lane [road in west part of Le Barque]	57cSW1 Gueudecourt	M 12 b
Sunken Road	28SW2 Wytschaete	N 18 b
Sunken Road	51bNW4 Fampoux	H 11 c 7.5
Sunken Road	51bSE4 Marquion	X 8 d 8.1
Sunken Road	57cNW1 Gomiecourt	A 15 b
Sunken Road	57cSE2 Beaumont	R 20 c
Sunken Road	57dSE2 Beaumont	R 29 b 7.4
Sunken Road [E of Hébuterne]	57dNE3 & 4 Hébuterne	K 11 b, 12 c, 17 a, b, 18 a
Sunken Road [Hunter Street]	57dSE1 & 2 Beaumont	Q 4 d
Sunken Road [N from Fricourt]	57dSE4 Ovillers	X 27 b, d
Sunken Road [N of Thiepval Wood]	57dSE1 & 2 Beaumont	Q 24 d
Sunken Road [Railway Wood]	28NW4 & NE3 Zillebeke	I 11 b
Sunken Road [road, late 1915]	36SW3 Richebourg	M 35 d
Sunken Road [road]	36SW1 Aubers	M 29 c, 35 a, b
Sunken Road [S of Trones Wood]	57cSW3 Longueval & 62cNW1 Maricourt	S 29 d, 30 a, c
Sunken Road Post	57cSE2 Gonnelieu	Q 18 d
Sunken Road Trench	36SW1 Aubers	M 29 c, d, 35 b
Sunken Road Trench	51cSE3 & 4 Ransart	R 32 d
Sunken Road Trench	57dSE4 Ovillers	X 5 d, 11 a, b, c
Sunken Road Trench	62dNE2 Méaulte	F 9 b
Sunken Road Trench [Cuinchy sector]	36cNW1 La Bassée	A 27 b
Sunken Road Trench [Givenchy]	36cNW1 La Bassée	A 9 b
Sunken Road Trench [later Stew Trench]	57cSW3 Longueval	T 21 a, c, d
Sunken Road Trench [N from Fricourt]	57dSE4 Ovillers	X 27 b, d
Sunken Street [late 1915]	36SW1 Aubers	M 22 c, 28 a, b, d
Sunken Support	57cNE4 Marcoing / SE2 Gonnelieu	L 34 c, R 4 a
Sunken Trench	36cSW4 Rouvroy	T 29 d
Sunken Trench	57cNE4 Marcoing / SE2 Gonnelieu	L 34 c, R 4 a, c
Sunken Trench [1918]	51cSE4 Blaireville	X 20 d, 21 c

Name	Map Sheet	Map Reference
Sunny Copse	62cSW4 St. Christ	U 17 c
Sunray Trench	57cSW2 Villers-au-Flos	N 22 c, d
Sunset Trench [Puisieux-au-Mont]	57dNE3 & 4 Hébuterne	L 14 c, 19 b, 20 a, c
Sunshade Alley [S edge of Fricourt Wood]	62dNE2 Méaulte	F 4 a, b
Sunshine Alley [Fricourt]	62dNE2 Méaulte	F 4 a, b
Sunshine Corner [road jct]	28NE4 Dadizeele	L 19 b 8.9
Sunshine Trench	57cSW2 Villers-au-Flos	N 28 b
Sup Farm	20SE2 Hooglede	R 28 b 6.4
Super Cross Roads	28NE2 Moorslede	F 13 b 65.90
Supper Farms [1918]	28SW1 Kemmel	N 19 b 3.2
Support [Trench]	36SW2 Radinghem	N 4 d, 10 a, b
Support [Trench]	51bSW2 Vis-en-Artois	O 14 a
Support Avenue	62cNW1 Maricourt	A 9 b
Support Copse	62cNW1 Maricourt	A 24 a
Support Farm / London Support Farm, & trenches	36NW2 & NE1 Houplines	C 1 b
Support Farm [NNE of Vierstraat]	28SW2 Wytschaete	N 5 d 5.3
Support Line	27SE4 Meteren	X 13, 19
Support Line	51bNW3 Arras / SW1 Neuville Vitasse	G 30 a, c, M 4 a, b, c
Support Line	51cSE & 51bSW Ficheux	R 23 d, 29 b
Support Line [1918]	27SE4 Meteren	extensive
Support Line [High Wood]	57cSW3 Longueval	S 3 c, d, 9 a, b
Support Line [late 1915]	36SW1 Aubers	M 24 b, c, d
Support Point [Pont Fixe; Sept 1915]	36cNW1 La Bassée	A 14 a, c
Support Trench	28SW2 Wytschaete	N 12 b, c, d
Support Trench	36SW3 Richebourg	S 20 b 4.5
Support Trench	57cSE4 Villers-Guislain	X 25 b, 26 a
Support Trench	62dNE2 Méaulte	F 10 d, 16 b
Support Trench [Sept 1915]	36cNW1 La Bassée	A 21 d, 27 b
Surbiton Post [1918]	28NE3 Gheluvelt	J 13 b
Surbiton Track [1917-18]	28NE3 Gheluvelt	J 13 b, 14 a
Surbiton Villas [cluster of buildings]	28NE3 Gheluvelt	J 13 b 6.3
Surcouff Farm	20SW4 Bixschoote	U 4 a 4.3
Surcouff Wood	20SW4 Bixschoote	U 4 a, b
Surgeon Fork [road jct]	28NE2 Moorslede	F 17 c 5.5
Surin Trench / Tranchée du Surin	62cSW3 Vermandovillers	S 29 b, d
Surprise Trench	62cSW3 Vermandovillers	T 3 b, d
Surrey Camp	28NW3 Poperinghe	H 32 d
Surrey Crossing [level crossing]	20SE2 Hooglede	R 14 b 3.4
Surrey Farm	28NE3 Gheluvelt	J 20 c 1.2
Surrey HQ Farm	36NW2 Armentières	C 9 d
Surrey Lane	51bSW2 Vis-en-Artois	O 24 b
Surrey Lane [Br CT]	28SW4 Ploegsteert	T 6 a
Surrey Lane [Oct 1915]	36cNW3 Loos	G 17 d, 18 c
Surrey Ravine	57cSE2 Gonnelieu	R 13 b, 14 a
Surrey Road / Street [trench]	62dNE2 Méaulte	F 2 b, d
Surrey Road [road]	57cSE2 Gonnelieu	R 14 a, b, c
Survey Avenue [road; 5th FSC, Lovie Chateau]	27NE2 Proven	F 16 c, d, 22 a
Susan Farm	27NE2 Proven	E 16 d 1.6
Susan Wood	62dSE [1 Hamel]	Q 21 a, b, c, d
Susans Trench	36SW3 Richebourg	S 11 d
Susie Trench [1918]	28SW1 Kemmel / 3 Bailleul	M 32 b, d, 33 a
Sussex [strongpoint]	36NW3 Fleurbaix	H 1 d
Sussex Avenue	36NW2 Armentières	C 22 a, b
Sussex Avenue	51bSW2 Vis-en-Artois	N 29 c, d, 30 c, d

Name	Map Sheet	Map Reference
Sussex Avenue	62dNE2 Méaulte	F 8 b
Sussex Bridge [road over railway]	20SE2 Hooglede	R 2 b 15.35
Sussex Fort	57dNE3 & 4 Hébuterne	K 22 c
Sussex Lane	51bSW1 Neuville Vitasse	M 15 d, 21 b
Sussex Street [1918]	62dSW [2 Villers-Bretonneux]	O 24 c, d
Sussex Trench	36cNW1 La Bassée / 3 Loos	G 2 b, 3 a, c
Sussex Trench [Pozières]	57dSE4 Ovillers	X 5 d, 6 c
Sutherland Avenue	36SW1 Aubers	N 7 d, 13 b, 14 a
Sutherland Avenue	51bNW1 Roclincourt	A 20 b, 21 a, b, 22 a
Sutherland Avenue [Thiepval Wood]	57dSE1 & 2 Beaumont	Q 30 c, 36 a
Sutherland Trench [High Wood]	57cSW3 Longueval	S 3 d, 4 c
Sutton Farm	27SE2 Berthen	R 22 b 6.5
Suvla Lane / Trench	57dSE1 & 2 Beaumont	Q 12 b, R 7 a, b, 8 a
Suvla Wood [1918]	28SW1 Kemmel	M 10 c, d, 16 a, b
Suzanne [village]	62cNW3 Vaux	G 8, 9
Suzanne Avenue / Boyau de Suzanne	62cNW1 Maricourt / 3 Vaux	A 28 c, G 3 b, d, 4 a
Suzanne Landing Ground [German, 1918]	62cNW3 Vaux	G 9 b
Suzeu Trench	57cSE3 Sorel-le-Grand	V 20 a
Swab Farm	36NW1 Steenwerck	A 27 d 85.65
Swag Lane	62dNE2 Méaulte	F 10 d
Swagger Farm	28NE3 Gheluvelt	J 27 b 3.3
Swaine House	28NE4 Dadizeele	K 29 d 10.75
Swallow Farm	20SE2 Hooglede	R 2 b 5.1
Swallow Wood	66cNW3 Essigny / 4 Berthenicourt	H 9 d, 10 c
Swallows Trench	57cSE4 Villers-Guislain	X 29 b, d
Swan Chateau	28NW4 Ypres	I 19 c
Swan Chateau Wood	28NW4 Ypres	I 19 a, c
Swan Cross Roads	28NE2 Moorslede	E 22 d 5.6
Swan Lane	57cNE1 Quéant	D 19 b, 20 a
Swan Lane	57cSW1 Gueudecourt	M 24 c, d
Swan Trench	51bSW2 Vis-en-Artois	O 25 c, d
Swan Trench	51bSW2 Vis-en-Artois	O 3 c
Swan Trench	57dSE1 & 2 Beaumont	R 2 b, 3 a, b
Swan Trench [1918]	57dNE3 & 4 Hébuterne	K 11 d, 12 a, c
Swan Trench [1918]	57dSE3 [Bouzincourt]	W 21 c, 26 b, 27 a
Swan Work	62bNW3 Bellicourt	G 27 d 05.15
Swanage Farm	27SE2 Berthen	Q 12 b 3.9
Swank Farm	27NE1 Herzeele	E 25 d 8.6
Swanky Street	57dNE1 & 2 Fonquevillers	E 3 a, c, d
Swanley Junction [road jct]	28NE4 Dadizeele	L 24 c 2.9
Swansea [Post]	36NW3 Fleurbaix	G 26 c
Swansea Trench	57cSW3 Longueval	S 2 b, 3 c
Swanston Cross Roads	28NE4 Dadizeele	L 2 c 90.12
Swap Farm	36NW1 Steenwerck	A 18 d 9.7
Swartenbrouch [hamlet]	36aNE1 Morbecque	E 14 d, 20 a
Swatow Trench	28SW2 Wytschaete	N 17 b, d, 18 a
Swayne's Farm	28SW4 Ploegsteert	O 32 c 3.0
Sweat Farm	36NW1 Steenwerck	A 26 d 2.9
Swede Farm	20SE2 Hooglede	R 12 a 8.5
Sweep Cottage	28NE2 Moorslede	E 30 a 6.6
Swell Farm	28NE2 Moorslede	E 22 d 95.12
Swift Street [Hill 60]	28NW4 & NE3 Zillebeke	I 29 c
Swift Trench / Support	51bSW2 Vis-en-Artois	O 31 b
Swill Farm	36NW1 Steenwerck	G 2 a 05.86

Name	Map Sheet	Map Reference
Swilly Row [houses]	27NE2 Proven	F 1 d 40.65
Swinburne Trench / Loop	36cNW3 Loos	G 12 c
Swindleboom Camp	28NW4 Ypres	H 16 c, d
Swindon [railway locality, 1917]	28SW1 Kemmel	M 36 b
Swindon Camp	28SW3 Bailleul	S 19 d 1.8
Swindon Trench [1918]	57dNE1 & 2 Fonquevillers	E 11 c, d
Swipe Farm	20SE2 Hooglede	R 22 d 0.2
Swiss Cottage	62bNW4 Ramicourt	H 10 b 1.8
Swiss Cottage Depot Railhead / Refilling Point	20SW3 Oostvleteren	S 26 c
Swiss Farm	28NE2 Moorslede	E 28 c 75.95
Switch Elbow [Witch's Elbow]	57cSW3 Longueval	S 1 d
Switch Lane	51bSW1 Neuville Vitasse	M 28 c, d, 34 b
Switch Line / Trench [Foureaux-Riegel]	57dSE4 Ovillers / 57cSW3 Longueval	R 35, 36, X 6, M 32-3, S 1-6, T 1-9
Switch Line [April 1917]	51bSW1 Neuville Vitasse	N 7 b, d, 14 a
Switch Trench Cemetery	57cSW3 Longueval	S 6 d 9.6 to T 1 d 4.0
Swivel Copse [1918]	28SW1 Kemmel	M 14 d, 20 b
Swivel Cottage [1918]	28SW1 Kemmel	M 15 c 05.17
Swivel Cottages	36NW1 Steenwerck	A 25 b 8.1
Sword Copse	62cSE4 [Attilly]	R 34 d
Sword Lane [road]	51bSW2 Vis-en-Artois	N 6 a, b
Sword Wood	62cNW4 Péronne	H 30 a, b
Sword Wood	62cSE4 [Attilly]	R 34 b
Swynstael [farm & road jct]	27SE4 Meteren	X 24 c 15.10
Sycophantes Trench / Tranchée du Sycophantes	62cSW3 Vermandovillers	S 24 d, 30 a, b
Sydney Avenue	57cNW2 Vaulx-Vraucourt	C 4 d, 5 b, c, d, 9 d, 10 a, b, c
Sydney Cross	57cNW2 Vaulx-Vraucourt	C 5 c 5.7
Sydney End	57cNW2 Vaulx-Vraucourt	C 5 b
Sydney Sector [trenches] [1918]	62dSW [2 Villers-Bretonneux]	N 18, 24, 30, O 13, 19, 25
Sydney Street	57dSE4 Ovillers	R 34 d, 35 c
Sydney Street [1918]	57dSE3 [Bouzincourt]	V 24 d
Sydney Street [see also Sidney St]	57cNE1 Quéant	D 8 a, b, c
Sydney System [trenches] [1918]	62dSW [2 Villers-Bretonneux / 4 Cachy]	N 18, 24, 30, O 13, 19, 25, 31, U 1
Syke / Sykes Alley	57cSE1 Bertincourt	Q 3 a
Syme Sap	57cSE2 Gonnelieu	R 20 d 8.9
Symes Avenue	57cSE2 Gonnelieu	R 20 d
Syntaxe Trench	62cSW2 Barleux	O 31 a, b, d
Syria Trench / Tranchée du Syrie	66cNW2 Itancourt	B 5 a, c
Syria Trench [1918]	62dSW [4 Cachy] / SE [3 Marcelcave]	U 6 c, d, V 1 a, c
Syrup Trench	57cSW2 Villers-au-Flos	N 30 d, O 25 c
T 6 [trench, St Eloi]	28SW2 Wytschaete	O 2 b 35.50
T 7 [trench, St Eloi]	28SW2 Wytschaete	O 2 b 7.4
T Causeway	57cSW1 Gueudecourt	N 33 a
T Roads	28NW4 Ypres	I 9 a
T Trench	57cSW1 Gueudecourt	N 33 a
T Trench [N of Canal, Feb 1915]	28NW4 & NE3 Zillebeke	I 34
T Wood	57cNE4 Marcoing	K 28 b
T Work [1918]	66eNW [4 Morisel]	H 10 a, c
T.M. Trench [Trench Mortar]	62cNE2 Epéhy	F 18 a
Taaze Wood	20SE2 Hooglede	R 6 c
Tabby Trench	51bNW1 Roclincourt	A 4 d
Tabernacle, The [Ploegsteert Wood]	28SW4 Ploegsteert	U 21 b 0.2
Tabernaux, Cité des	36cNW3 Loos	H 9 b, 10 c
Table Wood	28NE1 Zonnebeke	D 24 c
Tabor Trench	36SW3 Richebourg	T 20 c, 26 a

Name	Map Sheet	Map Reference
Tackle Bridge [road over canal]	36aNE1 Morbecque	D 17 b 45.80
Tad Farm	28NW1 Elverdinghe	A 19 b 4.8
Tadpole Copse	57cNE1 Quéant	D 18 d
Tadpole Lane	57cNE1 Quéant	D 18 d
Tadpole Trench	51bNW1 Roclincourt	A 5 c, d
Tadpole, The [German front line, late 1915]	36SW2 Radinghem	N 10 b 7.4
Tadpole, The [German front line]	36SW2 Radinghem	N 11 a
Taff Post	57cSE2 Gonnelieu	Q 18 d
Taff Vale Avenue	57cSE2 Gonnelieu	R 7 d, 13 a, b
Taffin Farm	28SW2 Wytschaete	N 28 b 1.9
Taffy Farm	36NW1 Steenwerck	B 22 c 35.95
Taffy Trench / C.T.	57dSE2 Beaumont / 4 Ovillers	R 35 b, d
Tag Trench	51bNW1 Roclincourt	A 11 a
Tag Trench	51bNW3 Arras	G 12 a
Tagora / Tabora Trench	66cNW1 Grugies	B 2 a, b, d
Tail Trench	51bNW3 Arras	G 12 a
Tail Trench	57cSW3 Longueval	T 9 c, d, 15 a, b
Tail Trench	57dSE2 & 57cSW1 Le Sars	M 17 c
Tail, The	51bSW2 Vis-en-Artois	O 20 c
Tail, The [Snag - Butte de Warlencourt]	57dSE2 & 57cSW1 Le Sars	M 17 c
Tailings Mill	28NE2 Moorslede	F 3 d 97.57
Tailles Woods	62dNE [4 Bray-sur-Somme]	K 11, 12, 17, 18, 23, 24
Tailles, Bois des	62dNE [4 Bray-sur-Somme]	K 17 b
Tailloux Woods	62dSE [1 Hamel]	P 22 b, 23 a
Tailor Copse	57dSW [4 Toutencourt]	U 9 d
Tal Gobel	51bNW1 Roclincourt	G 6 a, b
Talana Farm	28NW2 St Julien	B 18 c 9.7
Talana Hill	62bSW1 Gricourt	N 7 d, 8 c, 13 b, 14 a
Talana Wood	62bSW1 Gricourt	N 7 d
Talbot Farm	28NW1 Elverdinghe	A 14 b 4.7
Talbot Trench [1918]	51bNW1 Roclincourt	B 19 d, 20 c, 26 a
Talk Trench	36SW3 Richebourg	T 20 a, c
Tall Alley [1918]	51bNW1 Roclincourt	B 25 c, d, G 6 b, d, H 1 a
Tally Farm	36NW1 Steenwerck	A 21 c 35.55
Tally-Ho Lane	57cNE3 Hermies	K 18 b, 19 a
Talmas [village]	57dSW3 [Talmas]	S 2, 3, 8, 9
Talus Boisé	62cNW1 Maricourt	A 9 a, c, 15 a
Talus Trench	62cSW3 Vermandovillers	T 8 c, d
Tamar Farms	27SE2 Berthen	Q 6 a 50.25
Tamarisk Trench	36cSW4 Rouvroy	T 30 b
Tambour du Clos	62dNE2 Méaulte	F 3 a
Tambour, The [British, Fricourt]	62dNE2 Méaulte	F 3 a, c
Tambour, The German [Fricourt]	62dNE2 Méaulte	F 3 c
Tamil Farm	28NE4 Dadizeele	L 34 b 4.9
Tammany Trench	36cSW3 Richebourg / 4 Sainghin	T 3 c, d, 4 c, 10 a, b
Tamworth [light rly locality E of Canal 1917-18]	28NW2 St Julien	C 7 c
Tamworth Trench	36cSW1 Lens	M 20 c
Tanchat / Tanchot / Tanchol / Tonchat, Boyau	36cSW3 Vimy	S 14 b, 15 a
Tandy Farm	36NW1 Steenwerck	B 20 a 3.5
Tangier Trench	62dNE2 Méaulte	F 2 b, d, 3 a, c
Tangle Alley	57cSW1 Gueudecourt	M 16 c, 22 a
Tangle House	36NW1 Steenwerck	A 26 b 30.85
Tangle North	57cSW3 Longueval	M 32 d
Tangle South	57cSW3 Longueval	M 32 c, d

Name	Map Sheet	Map Reference
Tangle Trench	57cSW3 Longueval	M 31 d, 32 c, S 2 a, b
Tangle, The [Le Sars]	57dSE2 & 57cSW1 Le Sars	M 22 a
Tango Buildings [1918]	28SW1 Kemmel	M 8 d 9.3
Tango Trench	51bNW1 Roclincourt	A 6 d, 12 b
Tango Trench	62cNW4 Péronne	I 32 d
Tank [derelict; strongpoint]	51bSW4 Bullecourt	U 30 a
Tank Alley	57dSE1 & 2 Beaumont	Q 6 d, 12 a, b
Tank Avenue	51bSW4 Bullecourt / 57cNW2 Vaulx-Vraucourt	U 28 b, d
Tank Farm	28NW4 Ypres	H 22 b
Tank Graveyard [astride Menin Road]	28NW4 & NE3 Zillebeke	J 13 a, b, c, d
Tank Row [ride, Nieppe Forest]	36aNE3 Haverskerque	K 14 a, c, 20 a, b
Tank Support	51bSW4 Bullecourt	U 22 d, 28 b
Tank Trench	51bSW4 Bullecourt	O 31 c
Tank Trench [1918]	57dNE3 & 4 Hébuterne	K 6 c
Tank Trench [1918]	66eNW [2 Thennes]	H 5 a, c
Tank Trench [E of Guémappe]	51bSW2 Vis-en-Artois	O 13 a, b
Tankard Farm	36aNE3 Haverskerque	K 9 b 55.50
Tanst Alley	36SW3 Richebourg	T 19 b
Tap Trench	51bNW3 Arras	G 12 a
Tape Street	57dSE1 & 2 Beaumont	R 33 c, d
Tape Trench	51bNW1 Roclincourt	A 11, 12
Tape Trench	51bSW2 Vis-en-Artois	O 8 a
Tapir Farm	27NE2 Proven	E 28 b 4.8
Tapir Wood	66eNW [2 Thennes]	B 6 a
Tapley House [1918]	28SW1 Kemmel	M 9 d 10.95
Tar Trench	51bNW3 Arras	G 12 a
Tara Hill	57dSE4 Ovillers	W 24 d, X 19 c
Tara Redoubt	57dSE4 Ovillers	W 24 d
Tara Valley	57dSE4 Ovillers	W 29, 30
Tarasque, Tranchée de la	62cSW3 & 4 Marchélepot	T 12 d, 16 a, b, c
Tara-Usna Line	57dSE4 Ovillers	W 18, 24, X 19
Tarbert Street	57dSE4 Ovillers	Q 36 d
Targauer Weg	36cSW1 Lens	M 27 b
Targelle Ravine	57cSE4 Villers-Guislain	X 15 c, d, 16 c, d
Targelle Road [road]	57cSE4 Villers-Guislain	X 17 c, d, 18 c, 23 a
Targelle Trench	57cSE4 Villers-Guislain	X 14 d
Targelle Valley	57cSE4 Villers-Guislain	X 22 a, b, 23 a
Targette, La [hamlet & crossroads]	57bNW3 Rumilly	H 14 d, 15 c
Targette, la [hamlet, W of Neuville St Vaast]	51bNW1 Roclincourt	A 2 c, 8 a
Tarrytown [hamlet]	62cSW4 St. Christ	U 17 d, 23 b
Tarsus Farm	28NE2 Moorslede	F 20 d 2.3
Tart Trench	51bNW1 Roclincourt	B 7 b
Tart Trench	51bNW3 Arras	G 12 a
Tartary Trench	66cNW1 Grugies	B 2 c, d, 8 b, 9 a
Tarvis Street	57dSE4 Ovillers	X 20 c
Tas / Tac de Bois [Pit Prop Corner]	36cSW1 Lens	M 21 a 1.9
Tas / Tac de Bois, Boyau de [Butterfly Walk]	36cSW1 Lens	M 14 d, 20 b
Task Trench	51bNW3 Arras	G 12 a
Tasmania Switch [1918]	62dSW [4 Cachy]	O 32 d, U 1 d, 2 a, b, c, 7 a
Tassche [place name]	20SE2 Hooglede	R 30 c
Tatler Trench	57cSW3 Longueval	T 1 c, d, 7 b
Tatoi Trench	62cNW1 Maricourt / 3 Vaux	H 2 b, d
Tatova [trench]	66cNW2 Itancourt	B 18 b, d, C 13 a

Name	Map Sheet	Map Reference
Tattenham Corner	28NW1 Elverdinghe	A 7 d
Tattenham Corner (The King's Horse Wins)	62bNE2 Méaulte [Fricourt-Becordel]	F 1 d 95.00
Tattenham Corner [Dead End]	28NW4 Ypres	I 2 c 1.5
Tattenham Corner [road jct; Lovie Chateau]	27NE2 Proven	F 16 c 9.8
Tattenham Corner [road jct]	12NW3 & 4 Middelkerke	H 34 d 3.4
Taube Farm / House	20SE3 Westroosebeke	V 7 a 7.0
Taunton [light rly locality]	28NW2 St Julien	B 30 b
Taupes, Tranchée des	70dSW [2 Coucy-le-Château]	O 9 a
Taupin Corner	57dNE3 & 4 Hébuterne	K 34 b
Taupin Trench	57dNE3 & 4 Hébuterne	K 32 b, d, 33 d
Taurus Trench / Tranchée du Taurus	66cNW2 Itancourt	B 12 a, b
Tausse Farm	28SE1 Wervicq	Q 26 b 7.4
Tauziolles, E. [Entonnoir=crater; BFL March '16]	36cSW1 Lens	M 20 c
Tavistock [light rly locality]	28NW1 Elverdinghe	H 1 b
Tavistock House [farm]	28NW1 Elverdinghe	H 1 b 6.1
Taw Trench	51bNW1 Roclincourt	B 26 c
Tawny Trench	51bNW1 Roclincourt	B 7 a, b
Tax Trench	51bNW1 Roclincourt	B 7 b
Tax Trench	51bNW3 Arras	G 12 a
Taxi Farm	36aNE3 Haverskerque	K 9 d 05.40
Taxi Switch	36aNE4 Merville	K 9 b, d, 10 a
Tay Lane	57cNW1 Gomiecourt	A 1 b
Tay Lane [1918]	51bSW3 Boisleux / 57cNW1 Gomiecourt	S 25 d, A 1 b
Tay Street	57dSE4 Ovillers	X 19 b
Taylor [light rly sidings, 1917-18]	28NW4 Ypres	I 9 d, 10 c
Taylors Farm	20SE2 Hooglede	R 21 c 5.1
Taza Alley [1918]	62dSW [4 Cachy]	U 7, 8, 14, 15, 21, 22
Tchad, Du [tranchée]	66cNW2 Itancourt	B 18 c, d
Tea Cup Corner	57dSE4 Ovillers	R 32 c 5.9
Tea Farm [Lindenhoek - Wulverghem]	28SW4 Ploegsteert	N 34 d 1.4 / 1.6
Tea House	36SW1 Aubers	N 13 a
Tea Lane	57cSW3 Longueval	S 6 c, 11 b, 12 a
Tea Post	62cNE2 Epéhy	F 26 a
Tea Pot Copse	57dSW [2 Raincheval]	O 6 a, c
Tea Support	57cSW3 Longueval	S 6 c, d, 12 b, T 7 a
Tea Trench	51bNW3 Arras	G 6 c, 12 a
Tea Trench	57cSW3 Longueval	S 11 b, 12 a
Tea Trench	57dSE2 & 57cSW1 Le Sars	R 9 d, 10 a, b, c
Teak Farm	27NE2 Proven	F 26 d 2.9
Teak Wood	27NE2 Proven	F 26 a, b
Teal Copse	62bSW1 Gricourt	N 15 a
Teale Trench	57cSW3 Longueval	S 30 a, b
Teall Cott	20SE3 Westroosebeke	V 30 b 1.5
Tear Trench	51bNW3 Arras	G 12 a
Tear Trench	57cSW3 Longueval	N 32 c
Ted Trench	51bNW1 Roclincourt	A 10 b, d
Teddie Gerrard Trench	36cSW3 Vimy	T 8 d, 9 c, 15 a, b, 16 a, c
Tee House	28NE3 Gheluvelt	J 28 d 1.9
Tee Trench	36cSW4 Rouvroy	T 30 c
Teem Trench	51bNW3 Arras	G 12 a, b
Tees Farm	27SE2 Berthen	Q 17 b 55.90
Tees Trench	51bNW3 Arras	H 7 a, b, 8 a
Tees Trench British Cemetery	51bNW3 Arras	H 7 a 3.6
Teetotal Corner	36SW3 Richebourg	S 15 a 2.5

Name	Map Sheet	Map Reference
Teisseyre [Ouvrage, NW of Fricourt, 1915]	62dNE2 Méaulte	F 2 b
Telegraph Hill	51bSW1 Neuville Vitasse	M 12 b, d, N 7 a, c
Telegraph Hill Switch Front Line [1918]	51bSW1 Neuville Vitasse	M 12, 15, 16, 17, 18, 21
Telegraph Hill Switch Support Line [1918]	51bSW1 Neuville Vitasse	M 12, 15, 16, 17
Telegraph Hill Trench	51bSW1 Neuville Vitasse	N 7 c, d, 13 b, d, 14 c, 20 a
Telegraph House	28NW2 St Julien	C 1 d 8.5
Telegraph Lane [trench]	51bSW1 Neuville Vitasse	M 6 a, c, d, 12 b
Telegraph Redoubt / Work	51bSW1 Neuville Vitasse	N 7 a
Telegraph Ridge	51bSW1 Neuville Vitasse	N 1, 2, 3, 7, 8, 9
Telegrapher Weg	51bNW1 Roclincourt	A 6 c, d
Telephone House	20SW4 Bixschoote	T 12 b 96.79
Telford Farm	28NE4 Dadizeele	L 1 d 1.4
Temar Farm	28NW1 Elverdinghe	B 3 c 5.1
Temesour Trench	62cNW2 Bouchavesnes	C 26 b, d
Temper Farm	28SW3 Bailleul	S 27 c 25.33
Tempest Trench	36cSW4 Rouvroy	T 23 b, 24 a
Temple Bar [farm]	36SW1 Aubers	M 12 c 40.45
Temple Bar Lane [road]	36SW1 Aubers	M 10 b, 11 a, b, d, 12 c
Temple Street	36cSW1 Lens	M 14 c, d
Temple Trench	57dNE1 & 2 Fonquevillers	K 3 a, b, c
Temple, Rue du [road in Calonne]	36cSW1 Lens	M 14 c, d
Temple, The	28SE3 Comines	V 20 d
Temple, The, & Temple Post	36NW4 Bois Grenier	H 36 a
Templeux Old Quarry	62cNE1 Liéramont	D 28 b, 29 a
Templeux Quarries [NE of Templeux-le-Guerard]	62cNE2 Epéhy	L 3 a, b
Templeux Switch	62cNE2 Epéhy	F 28 b, c, d, 29 a
Templeux Trench	62cNE1 Liéramont	D 22 c, 28 a, c
Templeux Wood	62cNE2 Epéhy	F 25 c
Templeux-la-Fosse [village]	62cNE1 Liéramont	D 28 d, 29 c, J 4 a, b, 5 a
Templeux-le-Guerard [village]	62cNE2 Epéhy / 4 Roisel	L 2 a, b, c, d
Ten Elms Camp	28NW1 Elverdinghe	A 25 d
Ten Tree Alley	57dNE3 & 4 Hébuterne	K 35, 36, L 31
Tenant Farm	28NE2 Moorslede	F 24 a 35.15
Tenbrielen [village]	28SE1 Wervicq	P 16 d, 17 c
Tench Alley	57cNE3 Hermies	K 7 a, c
Tench Post	57cNE3 Hermies	K 7 a
Tench Support	57cNE3 Hermies	K 7 c
Tender Farm	27NE2 Proven	F 27 b 7.2
Tenderloin / Tender Lane Street	57dSE1 & 2 Beaumont	Q 4 a
Tendon Farm	28NW3 Poperinghe	G 10 d 25.40
Tenet Farm	36aNE4 Merville	K 30 d 2.1
Tennis Farm	20SE4 Roulers	Q 34 d 1.2
Tennis Trench	57cSE4 Villers-Guislain	X 13 a
Tent Trench	51bNW1 Roclincourt	A 11 a
Tent Wood	20SE3 Westroosebeke	W 26 b, 27 a
Tenth Avenue	36cNW3 Loos	G 17 b, d, 23 b, c, d
Tenth Avenue	51bSW2 Vis-en-Artois / 4 Bullecourt	N 36 a, b, d, O 31 c
Tenth Avenue [1918]	57dNE1 & 2 Fonquevillers	F 13 a, b
Tenth Street	57cSW1 Gueudecourt	M 19 b, d
Teofani Crossing [road across rly]	28NE4 Dadizeele	L 14 a 7.7
Tepid Trench	51bNW1 Roclincourt	A 11 a
Termonde Trench	20SW3 Oostvleteren	T 10 a, c
Tern Farm	36aNE2 Vieux Berquin	E 17 b 35.40
Terra Nova Street	57dSE1 & 2 Beaumont	Q 16 b

Name	Map Sheet	Map Reference
Terrace Dump [light rly]	36bSE2 Boyeffles	R 15 c, d
Terrapin House	36aNE2 Vieux Berquin	F 3 a 90.35
Terre Neuve [hamlet]	62bSW4 Homblières	U 8 d
Terrier Alley	51bSW4 Bullecourt	U 17 c, d, 22 b, 23 a
Terrier Farm	20SE3 Westroosebeke	V 26 a 5.4
Terrière Wood	57bSW3 Honnecourt	S 10 c, d
Terrière, la [village]	57bSW3 Honnecourt	S 9 d, 10 c, 15 b, 16 a
Territorial Avenue / Territoriaux	51bNW1 Roclincourt	A 7, 8, 9, 10, 13
Terry Trench	51bNW1 Roclincourt	A 11 c
Test Wood	62cNW3 Vaux	H 7 a, c
Tetard Trench	12SW1 Nieuport	N 1 a
Tetleys Farm	28NE4 Dadizeele	K 18 c 25.55
Téton, P.C. [command post]	36cSW3 Vimy	S 2 d
Téton, Tranchée du [Allied front line Feb '16]	36cSW3 Vimy	S 2 d
Tetovo Alley	66cNW2 Itancourt	B 18 d
Teuton Trench	36SW3 Richebourg	T 13 d, 19 a, b
Teviot Farm	28SW3 Bailleul	S 25 b 3.8
Tewyn Farm	27SE4 Meteren	W 28 b 10.15
Texas Farm	36aNE1 Morbecque	D 9 d 9.8
Text Farm	28NE2 Moorslede	F 19 c 5.5
Text Trench	51bNW3 Arras	G 6 d, 12 b
Teychere Trench	62cSW3 Vermandovillers	T 9 a, b
Thalweg, Boyau du / Aberdeen Avenue	57dSE4 Ovillers	X 20 d, 26 a, b
Thames [farm & pillbox]	28NE1 Zonnebeke	D 22 b 3.5
Thames Alley	51bNW2 Oppy	B 29 c, d, 30, H 4
Thames Street [N of Canal, Bluff]	28NW4 & 28NE3 Zillebeke	I 34 c
Thames Wood	28NE1 Zonnebeke	D 22 b, d
Thames, Boyau	36cSW1 Lens	M 14 d
Thane Trench	51bNW1 Roclincourt	A 12 a, c
Thatch Barn	28NW4 & NE3 Zillebeke	I 10 b 97.73
Thatch Trench	51bNW1 Roclincourt	A 12 b
Thatched Cottage	28SW4 Ploegsteert	T 18 b
Thatched Cottage	28SW4 Ploegsteert	U 16 a 7.7
Thatched House	28NW2 St Julien	C 1 c 5.6
Thatched House	36NW2 Armentières	C 1 c
Thaw Trench	51bNW3 Arras	G 12 b
Thélus [village]	51bNW1 Roclincourt	A 11 b, 12 a, b
Thélus Redoubt	51bNW1 Roclincourt	G 5 b
Thélus Trench	51bNW1 Roclincourt	A 6 a, c
Thélus Wood	51bNW1 Roclincourt	A 6 d, 12 b
Thélus-Vimy-Lens Line	51bNW1 Roclincourt	A 6, 11, 12, 17, 23
Thennes [village]	66eNW [2 Thennes]	C 1 d, 2 c, 7 a, b, 8 a
Thennes Mill	66eNW [2 Thennes]	C 14 a 7.9
Théodore Trench / Tranchée Théodore	62cSW2 Barleux	O 19 b, c, 20 a
Theophile Farm	20SW3 Oostvleteren	T 8 c 6.2
Thermos Trench	51bNW1 Roclincourt	B 7 c, d
Thetis Alley	66dNW1 Punchy	A 16 c, d
Thevenard Alley	66cSW2 Vendeuil	O 25 c, d
Thézy-Glimont [village]	66eNW [4 Morisel]	H 4 b, c, d
Thézy-Glimont Halt [railway]	66eNW [4 Morisel]	H 5 c 3.2
Thick Oak Hedge	57dNE1 & 2 Fonquevillers	E 18 d, 24 b, F 13 a, c
Thick Trench	51bNW1 Roclincourt	A 10 d
Thicket, The [wood]	66dNW1 Punchy	B 14 a
Thiebault, Boyau	62cSW1 Dompierre	M 10 c

Name	Map Sheet	Map Reference
Thiennes Signal Pillar [trig]	66eNW [2 Thennes]	C 14 b 65.30
Thienshoek [hamlet & road jct]	27SE2 Berthen	R 35 b 3.3
Thiepval Avenue [road]	57dSE1 & 2 Beaumont	Q 36 b, c, d, R 25 c, d, 31 a
Thiepval Avenue [road]	57dSE1 & 2 Beaumont / 4 Ovillers	Q 36 c, d, R 25 c, 31 a
Thiepval Crucifix [East of Thiepval]	57dSE1 & 2 Beaumont	R 26 c 9.3
Thiepval Crucifix [North of Thiepval]	57dSE1 & 2 Beaumont	R 19 d 95.23
Thiepval Point North	57dSE1 & 2 Beaumont	R 25 a, c
Thiepval Point South	57dSE1 & 2 Beaumont	R 25 c
Thiepval Road [road]	57dSE1 & 2 Beaumont	Q 24 d, R 19 c, 25 a, b
Thiepval Valley	57dSE2 Beaumont	R 26 a, b, c, d
Thieves Trench	66cSW2 Vendeuil / 4 La Fère	O 34 b, d
Thilloy [village]	57cSW1 Gueudecourt	N 2 c, 8 a
Thin Trench	51bNW1 Roclincourt	A 10 d
Thin Trench	51bNW3 Arras	G 12 b
Thin Wood	62dSE [1 Hamel]	Q 13 d
Third Ave / Schwarzwald Graben [W of Pozières]	57dSE4 Ovillers	X 2 d, 3 b, c, 4 a
Third Parallel [Thiepval Wood]	57dSE1 & 2 Beaumont	R 19 c, 25 a
Third Street [German reserve line]	57dSE4 Ovillers	X 8 d, 14 b, 15 a
Third Trench [German]	36cSW3 Vimy	S 15 a, b, d, 16 c, 22 a
Thiriet Alley / Boyau / Trench	36cSW3 Vimy	S 8 b, d
Thistle / Whistle Alley [1918]	66eNW [2 Thennes]	B 28 b, d
Thistle Alley	57cSW3 Longueval	S 10 b, c, d
Thistle Camp	28NW3 Poperinghe	H 13 a
Thistle Dump	57cSW3 Longueval	S 10 c
Thistle Trench	57cSW4 Combles	N 34 c, T 4 b
Thistle Trench	62cNE2 Epéhy	F 16 b, c
Tholler Trench	62cSW2 Barleux	N 16 d, 17 c, 22 b
Thomas Street	36cNW3 Loos	G 35 d
Thomas, Boyau	36cSW1 Lens	M 14 d
Thomson Lines [huts]	28SW3 Bailleul	M 35 d
Thon Trench	66dNW3 Hattencourt / SW1 Roye	G 32 c, M 2 a
Thora Camp	27NE4 Abeele	L 7 d
Thorigny [village]	62bSW1 Gricourt	N 13 a, c
Thorn / Thorne Street / Lane	28NW4 & NE3 Zillebeke	I 34 a, b
Thorn Alley / Boyau de Thorn	66dNW3 Hattencourt / 66eNE4 Beaufort	G 31 b, 32 a, c, L 35 b, 36 a
Thorn Lane	62dNE2 Méaulte	F 4 c, 9 b, 10 a
Thorn Lane [road]	28NW4 & NE3 Zillebeke	I 28 c, 34 a, b
Thorn Post	51bSW2 Vis-en-Artois	O 14 c
Thorn Street	36NW4 Bois Grenier	I 20 b, d
Thorn Trench	62cSW2 Barleux	N 22 a, b
Thorner Graben	51bNW3 Arras	G 12 c, 18 a
Thornton Road [road]	28SW3 Bailleul	S 21 b, 22 a, b, 23 a
Thorp Farm	36NW1 Steenwerck	G 2 a 2.1
Thorpe Street	57dNE1 & 2 Fonquevillers	E 27 c, K 3 a
Thorpe Street West	57dNE1 & 2 Fonquevillers	K 3 a
Thorsby Street	57dSE4 Ovillers	X 7 a, b
Thourout Trench	20SW3 Oostvleteren	T 4 c, 10 a
Thouroux Farm	28SE1 Wervicq	P 9 d 8.4
Thouzellier Trench	62cNW1 Maricourt / 3 Vaux	H 2 b, c, d
Thrash Trench	51bNW1 Roclincourt	A 10 d
Thread Trench	51bNW1 Roclincourt	A 16 b
Threadneedle Street	28NW2 St Julien	C 21 d, 27 b
Three Apple Trees, The	62cSW3 Vermandovillers	S 22 c 1.1
Three Blobs [farm buildings]	28SW1 Kemmel	M 11 d 95.92

Name	Map Sheet	Map Reference
Three Copses Work [1918]	66eNW [4 Morisel]	H 36 c
Three Farm Trenches	20NW4 Dixmude	I 25 a, c
Three Farms	66dNW1 Punchy	B 14 c
Three Huns Farm [Ploegsteert Wood, St Yvon]	28SW4 Ploegsteert	U 15 d 13.04
Three Kings Junction [Trois-Rois, lt rly, 1917-18]	28NW4 Ypres	I 20 c 55.30
Three Savages / Trois Sauvages [farm]	62bSW1 Gricourt	M 23 d 55.85
Three Tree House [Le Pelerin]	28SW4 Ploegsteert	U 21 b 85.30
Three Trees	57dSE4 Ovillers	X 6 c 8.2
Three Trees Camp	36NW2 Armentières	B 4 d
Three Tubs Wood	62cNW4 Péronne / NE3 Buire	I 24 d, J 19 a, c
Threx Street	57cNE2 Bourlon	E 16 a, b, c
Throne Trench	51bNW1 Roclincourt	A 10 d, 16 b
Throstle Farm	28NW4 Ypres	H 16 c 5.9
Throttle Farm	36NW1 Steenwerck	A 28 a 80.55
Thrush Lane	51bSW2 Vis-en-Artois	O 31 b
Thrush Trench	28SW2 Wytschaete	N 17 a
Thrush Trench	51bNW1 Roclincourt	A 16 b
Thrush Valley	57cSE4 Villers-Guislain	X 20, 25, 26
Thud House	28SW3 Bailleul	S 16 a 2.3
Thud Trench	51bNW3 Arras	G 12 b
Thug Farm	28NE2 Moorslede	K 4 a 35.60
Thuin Trench	20SW1 Loo	N 7 c, 13 a
Thumb Trench	51bSW1 Neuville Vitasse	N 20 b
Thunder Cotts	36NW1 Steenwerck	B 28 a 35.85
Thunder Lane	57cSW1 Gueudecourt	N 21 b
Thunder Trench	57cSW4 Combles	T 5 c, d, 11 b, 12 a
Thunder Wood	28SW1 Kemmel	M 27 b, d
Thurles Dump	57dSE1 & 2 Beaumont	Q 9 d, 10 c
Thuro [sic] Sap [Truro Sap]	57cSE2 Gonnelieu	R 15 c
Thursday Avenue	51bNW1 Roclincourt / 3 Arras	A 28, 29, G 4
Thursday Trench	66dNW1 Punchy	A 10 d, 16 a, b
Thurso / Thuros [sic] Street [Thiepval Wood]	57dSE1 & 2 Beaumont	Q 24 d, 30 b
Tib Street	62dNE2 Méaulte	F 11 d
Tibbles [farm]	27NE2 Proven	F 17 d 8.2
Tiber [farm & pillbox]	28NE1 Zonnebeke	D 12 d 00.55
Tiber Wood	28NE1 Zonnebeke	D 12 c, d
Tibet Farm	27SE2 Berthen	R 33 a 15.25
Tich House	28NW1 Elverdinghe	G 5 a 45.05
Tick Copse	28NE2 Moorslede	F 9 c 10.55
Tick Lane [1918]	57dNE2 & 57cNW1 Courcelles	F 11 c
Tick Trench	36SW3 Richebourg	T 20 a
Tick Trench	51bNW1 Roclincourt	A 16 b
Tick Trench	51bNW3 Arras	G 12 a, b
Tick Trench	57cSW1 Gueudecourt	N 8 c, d
Ticker Copse	62cNW4 Péronne	H 24 c
Tickler Trench	36cSW4 Rouvroy	T 24 a
Ticlers Top [dugout, 1917-18]	28NE3 Gheluvelt	J 19 a 54.67
Tidsa / Tiosa Crater	36cSW3 Vimy	S 28 a
Tie Trench	51bNW1 Roclincourt	A 16 b
Tie Trench	51bNW3 Arras	G 12 b, H 7 a
Tiendenberg [hamlet, W of Westroosebeke]	20SE3 Westroosebeke	V 11 central
Tiffin Farm	27NE2 Proven	F 17 b 20.75
Tiffin Trench	51bNW1 Roclincourt	A 17 a
Tiflis House	36aNE2 Vieux Berquin	E 5 a 05.83

Name	Map Sheet	Map Reference
Tig Farms	36NW1 Steenwerck	B 26 b 65.90
Tiger Farm	36aNE2 Vieux Berquin	F 21 c 9.7
Tiger Lane	51bSW1 Neuville Vitasse	N 20 d, 21 c
Tiger Pop [Bécourt]	57dSE4 Ovillers	X 25, 26
Tiger Trench	51bSW2 Vis-en-Artois	N 24 b, d
Tiger Trench	51bSW4 Bullecourt	U 19 b, 20 a, c, 26 b, d
Tiger Trench	57cNE1 Quéant / 2 Bourlon	E 22 c, d, 27 b, 28 a
Tiger Trench	62cNE2 Epéhy / 62bNW1 Gouy	F 6 c, A 1 d
Tight Trench	62bSW3 St Quentin	S 6 b, d
Tigris Lane	51bSW1 Neuville Vitasse	N 15 b
Tigris Lane Cemetery	51bSW1 Neuville Vitasse	N 15 b 5.2
Tile Works [S of Homblières]	62bSW4 Homblières	U 26 a
Till Farm	27NE1 Herzeele	E 27 c 6.4
Till Support [Thilloy]	57cSW1 Gueudecourt	N 2 b, 3 a
Till Trench [Thilloy]	57cSW1 Gueudecourt	N 2, 3, 9, 16
Tilleloy North [keep, late 1915]	36SW1 Aubers	M 23 c 50.15
Tilleloy North Post	36SW1 Aubers	M 23 c
Tilleloy North Trench	36SW1 Aubers	M 22 b, d, 23 c, 29 a, b, d
Tilleloy South Post	36SW1 Aubers	M 28 b
Tilleloy South Trench	36SW1 Aubers	M 22 c, d, 28 b, 29 a, c, d
Tilleloy Street, North [late 1915]	36SW1 Aubers	M 22 d, 28 b, 29 a
Tilleloy Street, South [late 1915]	36SW1 Aubers	M 22 c, d, 28 b, 29 a
Tilleloy, le [hamlet]	36SW1 Aubers	N 7 c, d, 13 a, b
Tilleul [place name]	28NE4 Dadizeele	L 24 c
Tilleul de la Petite Munque [farm]	28SW4 Ploegsteert	T 24 a 8.1
Tilleul Farm	20SW4 Bixschoote	T 24 b 9.4
Tilleul Wood	20SW4 Bixschoote	T 24 b, d
Tilleul, la Ferme du	36NW2 & NE1 Houplines	C 2 c 6.3
Tilleuls Trench	62cSW3 Vermandovillers	S 6 d, T 1 c, d
Tilleuls Alley	62cSW3 Vermandovillers	S 13 d, 14 c
Tilleuls Trench	62cSW3 Vermandovillers	S 14 a, c
Tilleuls, les [hamlet, Vimy Ridge]	51bNW1 Roclincourt	A 5 c, d, 11 a, b
Tilleuls, Tr. des [practice trs. E of Courcelette]	57dSE2 & 57cSW1 Le Sars	M 20 c
Tilloy Chateau	51bNW3 Arras	H 31 d 1.3
Tilloy Farms	62bSW2 Fonsommes	N 30 b, d, O 25 a, c
Tilloy Lane	51bNW3 Arras	H 32 c, d, 33 c, d
Tilloy Quarry	51bNW3 Arras	H 31 d
Tilloy Trench [1918]	51bNW3 Arras	H 26 a, c, 32 a, c
Tilloy Wood	51bNW3 Arras	H 31 d
Tilloy-lez-Mafflaines [village]	51bNW3 Arras	H 31 a, b, c, d
Tilly Alley / Boyau de Tilly	66dNW1 Punchy	G 2 a, b, d
Tilt Trench	51bNW1 Roclincourt	A 16 b, 17 a
Tim Farms	36NW1 Steenwerck	A 25 d 2.6
Tim Trench	51bNW1 Roclincourt	A 16 b, d
Timber Street	57dNE3 & 4 Hébuterne	K 10 c, d
Timber Trench	57dNE3 & 4 Hébuterne	K 10 c
Time Farm [Tuimelaarehoek]	28NE2 Moorslede	E 18 d 3.6
Time Trench [Times]	57cSW3 Longueval	T 2 a, b, d
Timothy Trench	36SW3 Richebourg	N 32 c, T 2 a, b, 3 a, c
Tin Barn Avenue	36NW4 Bois Grenier / SW2 Radinghem	H 29, 35, N 5, 6
Tin Barn Tram	36NW4 Bois Grenier / SW2 Radinghem	H 28, 34, 35, N 5, 6
Tin Trench	51bNW3 Arras	G 6 d, 12 b
Tina Copse	62bSW4 Homblières	U 29 b, 30 a
Tinker Copse	57dSW [4 Toutencourt]	U 9 d

Name	Map Sheet	Map Reference
Tinkle Farm	28SW1 Kemmel	M 30 b 0.9
Tino Support	57cSE4 Villers-Guislain / 62bNW1 Gouy	X 30 c, A 1 b
Tino Trench	57cSE4 Villers-Guislain / 62cNE2 Epéhy	X 30 c, F 6 a
Tint Trench	51bNW1 Roclincourt	A 16 b
Tint Trench	51bNW3 Arras	G 12 b
Tinto Farm	36NW1 Steenwerck	G 3 a 25.95
Tiny Copse	28NE2 Moorslede	E 18 c 37.20
Tiny Farm	28SW2 Wytschaete	O 17 c 9.4
Tiny Trench	36cSW4 Rouvroy	T 24 d
Tiny Villa	28NW2 St Julien	B 28 b
Tip Farm	28NE2 Moorslede	F 5 a 9.4
Tip Work	57cSW1 Gueudecourt	N 2 b
Tip, The	57cSE2 Gonnelieu	Q 4 b
Tipperary Avenue	57dSE1 & 2 Beaumont	Q 8 d, 9 c, d
Tipperary Trench [1918]	62dSW [4 Cachy]	U 25 d, 26 a, b
Tippo Farm	27NE2 Proven	F 17 b 7.2
Tipsy Support	36SW3 Richebourg	T 8 d, 14 b, d
Tipsy Trench	36SW3 Richebourg	T 8 d, 14 b, d
Tipton Farm	36NW1 Steenwerck	G 3 a 85.95
Tipton Farm [1918]	28SW1 Kemmel	M 10 b 7.3
Tir Anglais, le [cottage or estaminet]	36aNE1 Morbecque	D 17 c 6.8
Tir Trench	57dNE3 & 4 Hébuterne	K 16 d
Tirailleurs Trench [1918]	62dSW [4 Cachy]	U 4 d, 10 a, b, c
Tired Alley	51bNW1 Roclincourt / 2 Oppy	B 4 c, d
Tired Locality	51bNW1 Roclincourt / 2 Oppy	B 4 c, d, 10 a, b
Tired Trench	51bNW1 Roclincourt	B 13 b, 14 a
Tirpitz Farm, Von	28NE1 Zonnebeke	D 7 b 3.7
Tirpitz Trench	36cNW1 La Bassée	G 5 a
Tirpitz Trench	62dNE2 Méaulte	F 10 b, d
Tirpitz Trench [1918]	62dSW [4 Cachy]	U 30 b
Tisza Trench	70dNW4 St Gobain	H 24 d, I 19 c, d
Tite Road [road]	28SW1 Kemmel / 3 Bailleul	N 27, 33
Tites Copse	51bSW2 Vis-en-Artois	O 8 a 90.15
Titgut / Tulgut Redoubt	36SW3 Richebourg	T 19 c
Tithebarn Street	57dSE4 Ovillers	X 1 a
Titmouse Wood	66cNW3 Essigny	H 3 d, 9 b
Tittle Copse	62dSE [3 Marcelcave]	V 13 a
Tivoli Wood	62cNW3 Vaux	G 21 a
To the Chateau Keep off the Grass [Ploeg. Wd]	28SW4 Ploegsteert	U 21 c 35.75
Toad Alley [1918]	62dSW [4 Cachy]	U 21 c, d, 22 c
Toad Copse	57dSW [4 Toutencourt]	U 29 c, d
Toad Support	36SW3 Richebourg	T 14 d, 20 b
Toad Trench	36SW3 Richebourg	T 14 c, d, 20 a
Toadley Farm	20SE2 Hooglede	R 19 b 1.2
Toads Alley	66cSW4 La Fère	U 10 d, 16 a, b
Toast Cottage	28NE2 Moorslede	E 12 d 9.9
Toast Trench	36cSW3 Vimy / 4 Rouvroy	T 10 d, 16 a, b, c, 21 b
Toast Trench	51bNW1 Roclincourt	B 13 a
Toast Trench	51bNW3 Arras	G 12 a
Tobacco Factory [Béthune]	36bNE2 Beuvry	E 17 b 90.85
Tobacco Trench	36cSW4 Rouvroy	T 24 d
Tobermoray Street	57dSE4 Ovillers	Q 36 d, W 6 b
Toc H / Talbot House [Poperinghe]	28NW3 Poperinghe	G 2 c 7.5
Tock Support	36SW3 Richebourg	T 25 a, b, c

Name	Map Sheet	Map Reference
Tock Trench	36SW3 Richebourg	T 25 a, b, c
Toe Trench	51bNW3 Arras	G 12 a
Toff Trench / Weg	51bNW1 Roclincourt	A 16 d
Toffee Trench [1918]	51bNW1 Roclincourt	A 16 b, d
Togoland Trench	62bSW3 St Quentin / 66cNW1 Grugies	T 26 c, B 2 a
Toine Post [Toine Wood]	62cNE2 Epéhy	F 28 b
Toine Trench [Toine Wood]	62cNE2 Epéhy	F 22 d, 28 b
Tok Trench	51bNW3 Arras	G 12 a
Tokio [farm]	28NE1 Zonnebeke	D 27 d, 28 c
Tokio Ridge [Spur]	28NE1 Zonnebeke	D 27 d, 28 c, d, J 4 a, b
Tokio Spur	28NE1 Zonnebeke	D 27 d, 28 c, d, J 4 a, b
Toledo Trench	36cSW3 Vimy / 4 Rouvroy	T 9 b, d, 10 c, d, 16 b
Toll Cross [cross roads]	36aNE3 Haverskerque	K 26 c 80.15
Tolmino Villas	28SE1 Wervicq	P 8 d 3.4
Tom Farm	27NE2 Proven	F 24 a 40.65
Tom Foy Trench	57dNE3 & 4 Hébuterne	K 34 d
Tom Trench	51bNW1 Roclincourt	A 10 b, d
Tomahawk Copse	62bSW1 Gricourt	M 30 c
Tomb Alley / Boyau d'Outre-Tombe	66dNW3 Hattencourt	G 7 d, 8 c
Tombe-Willot, la [farm]	36aSE4 Locon	R 31 c 83.05
Tombois Farm	20SE3 Westroosebeke	V 16 b 6.4
Tombois Farm	62cNE2 Epéhy	F 11 b 2.4
Tombois Road [road]	62cNE2 Epéhy	F 5 d, 6 a, c
Tombois Support	62bNW1 Gouy	A 1 d
Tombois Trench	62cNE2 Epéhy / 62bNW1 Gouy	F 6 c, A 1 d
Tombois Valley	62cNE2 Epéhy	F 5 b, d
Tombola Farm	20SE3 Westroosebeke	V 16 b 60.45
Tomlin Farm	28SW3 Bailleul	S 3 c or 9 a
Tommy Alley	51bNW1 Roclincourt / 2 Oppy	unlocated
Tommy Locality	51bNW1 Roclincourt / 2 Oppy	B 16 b
Tommy Post	51bNW2 Oppy	B 12 b
Tommy Trench	51bNW1 Roclincourt	B 13, 14, 15, 19
Tom's Cut	36cNW1 La Bassée	A 26 b
Tom's Cut	57dSE2 Beaumont / 4 Ovillers	R 34 b, c, d
Tom's Wood	20SW4 Bixschoote	U 1 d, 2 c, 8 b
Tonbridge Farm	20SE2 Hooglede	Q 34 b 5.1
Tonbridge Street	62dNE2 Méaulte	F 15 c
Tongue Trench	51bNW1 Roclincourt	A 18 b
Tongue Trench	57cSW1 Gueudecourt	N 2 b, c, d
Tonneau Farm [moated]	20SW4 Bixschoote	T 10 b 20.23
Tontine Cottage [1918]	28SW1 Kemmel	M 8 b 5.5
Took Street	57dNE3 & 4 Hébuterne	K 29 c
Took Way	36cNW3 Loos	G 36 c
Tool Cottage	36NW2 Armentières	C 16 a
Tool Farm	28SW2 Wytschaete	O 17 c 3.4
Tool Trench	51bSW2 Vis-en-Artois	O 8 b, c, d, 14 a
Toone Trench [E of Autreville]	70dNW [3 Sinceny]	G 17 b, c, d, 22 b, d, 23 a
Tooth House	20SE2 Hooglede	R 26 c 5.4
Top House	28NE3 Gheluvelt	J 32 c 2.9
Top Lane	62bNW1 Gouy	A 20 c, d, 21 c
Top Trench	51bNW3 Arras	G 12 c
Top Trench	62bNW1 Gouy	A 20 a
Top Trench [1918]	57dNE2 & 57cNW1 Courcelles	F 21 b, c, d, 22 a
Top Work	57cSW1 Gueudecourt	N 2 a, b

Name	Map Sheet	Map Reference
Toper Trench	36cSW4 Rouvroy	T 17 c, 22 b, 23 a
Topo Lane [trench]	62bNW1 Gouy	A 20 c, d, 21 a, b
Topping Farm	28NE2 Moorslede	F 26 c 9.1
Topsail Farm	28NW4 Ypres	H 10 b 4.6
Tor / Torr Top, & Tunnels	28NW4 & NE3 Zillebeke	I 24 d
Tor Copse	66dNW1 Punchy	A 18 a
Tor Line [lt rly sidings, Ploegsteert Wd, 1917-18]	28SW4 Ploegsteert	U 19 b 0.6
Tordoir Lock	57bSW1 Bantouzelle	M 4 d 7.2
Tordue, Tranchée	66cNW2 Itancourt	B 24 b, d, C 19 c
Tornado Trench	36SW3 Richebourg	T 25 b, 26 a
Toronto	28SW [Kemmel Defences]	N 26 c 8.8
Toronto [farm & pillboxes]	28NE1 Zonnebeke	D 14 a 7.4
Toronto [light rly junction]	28NW3 Poperinghe	G 11 b 3.5
Toronto Avenue	28SW4 Ploegsteert	U 15 a, c
Toronto Camp	28NW3 Poperinghe	G 18 a
Toronto Cemetery	28SW4 Ploegsteert	U 15 c 1.1
Toronto Dump	28SW1 Kemmel	N 26 a 8.8 or N 26 c 8.8
Toronto Farm	28NW3 Poperinghe	G 18 a 05.45
Toronto Road [road]	36cSW3 Vimy	T 2 b, 3 a, b, d, 9 b, d, 10 c
Toronto Street	36NW4 Bois Grenier	I 15 c, 21 a, b
Toronto Trench	36cSW3 Vimy	T 3 d
Toros Alley	62cNW4 Péronne	I 20 d, 26 b
Torpedo Trench	36SW3 Richebourg	T 20 a, b, 21 a
Torpor Copse [1918]	28SW1 Kemmel	M 23 a, b
Torquay Trench	36cSW4 Rouvroy	T 17 a
Torquil Farm [1918]	28SW1 Kemmel	M 3 d 6.6
Torr Trench	57dSE4 Ovillers	X 5 b
Torreken Cemetery	28SW2 Wytschaete	O 20 d 5.4
Torreken Corner	28SW2 Wytschaete	O 20 d
Torreken Farm	28SW2 Wytschaete	O 20 d 2.3
Torrens Trench, & Support [1918]	57dSE3 [Bouzincourt]	W 21 a
Torrid Farm	20SE2 Hooglede	Q 23 b 55.30
Torrid Trench	20SE2 Hooglede	Q 23 b
Tortelle Trench	62cNW4 Péronne	I 3 d, 4 c, 10 a, b
Tortillard Trench	62cSW3 Vermandovillers	T 13 b, 14 a, b
Tortoise Trench	36cSW4 Rouvroy	T 24 b, d
Tortoise, The	36cNW1 La Bassée	A 16 c
Torture Farm [1918]	28SW1 Kemmel	M 10 c 12.90
Tosh Alley	36cNW3 Loos	G 30 c, d, 36 a
Tosh Cemetery	36cNW3 Loos	G 30 c
Tosh Keep	36cNW3 Loos	G 36 a
Tot House	28NE2 Moorslede	E 18 b 25.92
Tot Trench	36cSW4 Rouvroy	T 17 d
Totnes Support	36cSW4 Rouvroy	T 10 c, d, 16 b
Totnes Trench	36cSW4 Rouvroy	T 10 d, 11 c, 17 a, b, d, 24 a
Tottenham Post	57cSE4 Villers-Guislain	W 30 c
Tottenham Road	36cSW3 Vimy	S 20 b, 21 a
Tottenham Subway	36cSW3 Vimy	S 21 a
Toucan Trench	28SW2 Wytschaete	N 16 d, 22 a, b
Toucan Trench [1918]	66eNW [2 Thennes]	B 6 a
Touffu Wood	66eNW [4 Morisel]	I 11 b, d, 12 a, c
Tough Trench	51bNW1 Roclincourt	A 11 b
Toulze, Tranchée	62cNW3 Vaux	G 29 a
Touquet Berthe Farm	28SW4 Ploegsteert	U 26 a 2.3

Name	Map Sheet	Map Reference
Touquet Parmentier [hamlet]	36NW1 Steenwerck	B 21 a, b
Touquet Parmentier Station	36NW1 Steenwerck	B 21 a 80.25
Touquet, le [hamlet]	36aNE3 Haverskerque	J 22 c
Tour, Tranchée de la [by tower]	62cSW1 & 2 Belloy	N 24 a, c
Touraine Alley	62cSW3 Vermandovillers	S 4 a, c
Tourbières [north of Annequin]	36bNE2 Beuvry	F 17 c, d
Tourelle Lane [trench]	20NW4 Dixmude	I 19 a, b
Touret Central Post, Le	36aSE4 Locon	X 16 central
Touret North Post, Le	36aSE4 Locon	X 10 b
Touret, le [hamlet]	36aSE4 Locon	X 16 c, d
Tourist Line [& slit trs A - F; Ploeg. Wd 1914-15]	28SW4 Ploegsteert	U 21 a, d
Tourists Peep, The [Ploegsteert Wood 1914-15]	28SW4 Ploegsteert	U 21 a
Tourists Peep, The [Ploegsteert Wood]	28SW4 Ploegsteert	U 21 b 02.10
Tournai Terrace / Trench	57dSE1 & 2 Beaumont	Q 4 a, b
Tournai Trench	57dNE3 & 4 Hébuterne	K 34 d
Tournant Farm	20SE3 Westroosebeke	V 28 b 4.1
Tourniquet, Tranchée du	66cNW2 Itancourt	B 5 c, 11 a, b
Tournoy Trench	62cNW2 Bouchavesnes / 4 Péronne	H 4 b, d
Tourriot Trench	62cNW4 Péronne	H 4 c
Tours, Tranchée de [ESE of Lesboeufs]	57cSW4 Combles	T 6 c, 12 a
Tourtereau	12SW1 Nieuport	N 14 d
Toutencourt St. Flank Left	57dSW [4 Toutencourt]	U 8 d, 9 c
Toutencourt Switch Reserve	57dSW [4 Toutencourt]	O 33 d, 34 c, U 2 d, 3 a,b,c, 8 b,d, 14 b
Toutencourt Switch Support	57dSW [4 Toutencourt]	U 3 b, c, d, 4 a, 8 b, d, 9 a
Toutencourt Switch Trench	57dSW [4 Toutencourt]	U 3 c, d, 4 a, c, 9 a, c, 15 a
Toutharp Trench [Toutencourt & Harponville]	57dSW [4 Toutencourt]	O 35 c, U 4 a, b, c, d
Touts Fork [road jct]	28NE2 Moorslede	E 6 b 00.35
Touvent / Toutvent Farm	57dNE3 & 4 Hébuterne	K 23 c
Tow House	28NE2 Moorslede	F 9 c 65.80
Tower [N of Villers-Carbonnel]	62cSW2 Barleux	N 24 c 05.12
Tower Bridge [pit winding towers, Loos villlage]	36cNW3 Loos	G 36 a
Tower Bridge [Ploegsteert Wood 1914-15]	28SW4 Ploegsteert	U 21 a
Tower Bridge [Ploegsteert Wood]	28SW4 Ploegsteert	U 21 a 5.1
Tower Hamlets	28NE3 Gheluvelt	J 21 c 2.5
Tower Hamlets Quadrilateral	28NE3 Gheluvelt	J 27 a
Tower House	20SW4 Bixschoote	T 30 a 6.9
Tower House [Monchy-au-Bois]	51cSE4 Blaireville	W 30 a
Tower Keep	36cNW3 Loos	G 9 d
Tower Mill	28SW2 Wytschaete	N 11 d
Tower Post	28NW2 St Julien	C 21 d 3.3
Tower Redoubt	51bSW4 Bullecourt	U 27 a, b
Tower Reserve Trench	36cNW1 La Bassée	A 21 c, d
Tower Siding [light rly, Vimy]	36cSW3 Vimy	S 18 c
Tower Street	36cNW3 Loos	G 5 c
Tower Support	51bSW4 Bullecourt	U 27 b, 28 a
Tower Trench	20SW4 Bixschoote	O 31 d, 32 c, d
Tower Trench	51bSW4 Bullecourt	U 28 c, 29 c, d
Tower Trench [Sept 1915]	36cNW1 La Bassée	A 21 b
Tower Trench [Tower Hamlets]	28NE3 Gheluvelt	J 21 c, d, 27 a
Tower, The	28NE3 Gheluvelt	J 14 d 9.4
Tower, The [Vermelles - Canal, July 1915]	36cNW1 La Bassée	A 27 b
Towers, The [Tower Bridge, Pylons, etc]	36cNW3 Loos	G 36 a
Town Defences	62cNW1 Maricourt	A 16, 22

Name	Map Sheet	Map Reference
Townsend Farm	28NE2 Moorslede	L 2 a 9.2
Towpath Alley	36cNW1 La Bassée	A 16 d, 17 c, d, 18 a, b, c
Towy Alley	51bNW2 Oppy / 4 Fampoux	H 2 - 5, B 26 - 30, C 25
Towy Post	51bNW2 Oppy	C 25 c
Towy Trench	51bNW3 Arras	H 3 a, b, 4 a, b
Toxin Farm	28NW3 Poperinghe	G 17 b 5.8
Toy Trench	51bNW3 Arras	G 12 d
Tracas Farm	20SE3 Westroosebeke	V 20 d 6.5
Track 5	28NE1 Zonnebeke	D 19 b, 20 a
Track 6	28NE1 Zonnebeke	D 8 d
Track A [military road / track 1917-18]	20SW4 Bixsch'te/SE3 Westroos'b'ke/ 28NW2 St J'l'n	U 18, 23, 24, 28, 29, V 13, C 3, 8
Track B [military road / track 1917-18]	20SW4 Bixsch'te/SE3 Westroos'b'ke/ 28NW2 St J'l'n	U 24, 28, 29, 30, V 19, C 4
Track Houses	28SE1 Wervicq	P 4 a 2.6
Traction Engine [in field]	28SW4 Ploegsteert	T 6 d 3.0
Trafalgar Square	36NW4 Bois Grenier	I 26 c
Trafalgar Square [road jct, Langemarck]	20SW4 Bixschoote	U 23 c 1.2
Trafalgar Square [trench junction]	62dNE2 Méaulte	F 9 d
Tragédie Trench	62cSW3 & 4 Marchélepot	T 7 a, b
Tragic Trench	36SW3 Richebourg	T 25 a, b, d
Tragique Farm	20SE3 Westroosebeke	V 13 c
Trail, The	51bSW2 Vis-en-Artois	O 20 c
Train Alley	36cNW1 La Bassée	A 28 a, b
Train Alley	62cNW1 Maricourt	A 3 c, d
Tralee Farm	28SE1 Wervicq	P 14 b central
Tralee Lines [camp]	28SW1 Kemmel	M 23 d
Trales / Tralee Crater	36cNW3 Loos	H 13 c 35.65
Tram Car Cot.	28NW2 St Julien	B 17 a 5.1
Tram Crossing Cemetery	57dSE4 Ovillers	X 4 c 4.0
Tram Farm	28NE3 Gheluvelt	J 27 d 7.1
Tram House	28SE1 Wervicq	P 13 d 8.3
Tram Street	36SW1 Aubers	M 29 b
Tram Support	36SW3 Richebourg	T 19 d, 20 a, c
Tram Trench	36SW3 Richebourg	T 19 b, c, d, 20 a
Tram Trench	51bNW3 Arras	G 12 d
Tram Trench [1918]	57dNE1 & 2 Fonquevillers / 3 & 4 Hébuterne	E 29, 30, K 4, 6
Tramline Avenue	36NW4 Bois Grenier	I 19 d, 26 a
Tramway Corner	36SW1 Aubers	N 26 d
Tramway Corner	57dSE4 Ovillers	X 9 b 7.7
Tramway Trench [Pozières, N of Bapaume Rd]	57dSE4 Ovillers	X 4
Tranchée de la Somme	70dSW [1 Folembray]	M 28 b
Tranchée de Péronne	70dSW [1 Folembray]	N 2 a
Tranchée Wood	62bSW1 Gricourt	N 8 b
Trancy Trench	36cSW3 Vimy	S 27 a
Tranquille Farm/Tranquille House/Tranquil House	20SW4 Bixschoote	U 12 d 85.50
Trans Continental [railway]	36cSW2 Harnes / 4 Rouvroy	N 28 c, d, 34 b, 35 a, c, d
Transit Dump [& railway sidings; Bailleul]	28SW3 Bailleul	S 27 a, b
Transloy Line [Allied, 1916-17]	57cSW2 Villers-au-Flos	N 28 d, 29 c, 35 a [approx]
Transport Corner [dugouts]	28NW4 & NE3 Zillebeke	I 35 a
Transport Farm	28NW4 & NE3 Zillebeke	I 21 a
Transvaal Trench	57cSE2 Gonnelieu	Q 10 a, c, d
Transversal Avenue	20SW3 Oostvleteren	T 15 b
Transversale No.1	62cSW1 Dompierre	M 10 d

Name	Map Sheet	Map Reference
Transversale No.2	62cSW1 Dompierre	M 10 b, d
Trap Farm	27NE1 Herzeele	E 7 b 99.36
Trap Trench	51bNW3 Arras	G 12 d
Trap Trench	57cSW1 Gueudecourt	N 1 d
Trapeze Wood	28NE2 Moorslede	F 14 d
Trapeze Wood	66eNW [4 Morisel]	I 12 d
Trappist Monastery [Mont des Cats?]	27SE2 Berthen	R 19 b 8.5
Trappistes Farm	27NE4 Abeele	K 17 b 1.3
Trash Trench	36SW3 Richebourg	T 25 c, d
Trash Trench	51bNW3 Arras	G 12 d
Trauer Wood	66dNW1 Punchy	A 5 b, 6 a
Traun Trench	51bNW3 Arras	G 12 a, b, d
Trautlein Weg	51bSW1 Neuville Vitasse	M 20 a, b, d
Travecy [Redoubt] [Hill N of village]	66cSW4 La Fère	U 1 a
Travecy Alley	66cSW3 Tergnier / 4 La Fère	N 36, T 4, 5, 6, 9, 10, O 31, U 1
Travel Trench	57cNE1 Quéant	D 25, 26, J 2, 3
Travers Farm	28SW3 Bailleul	S 26 c 25.37
Travers Road, & Keep	36cSW1 Lens	M 5 a
Travers Siding [light rly]	36cSW1 Lens	M 5 a
Traverse Trench	66dNW1 Punchy	B 8 b, 9 a, c, d, 10 a, c
Tray Trench	51bNW3 Arras	G 12 d
Treacle Trench	57cSW2 Villers-au-Flos	N 30 d, 36 b, O 31 a, b, c
Treble Post [NW of Loos]	36cNW3 Loos	G 29 c 9.3
Tree [lone, trig point]	51bNW1 Roclincourt	B 13 c 69.87
Tree Farm	27SE4 Meteren	X 10 c 2.3
Tree Farm	27SE4 Meteren	X 10 c 25.30
Tree Farm	28NE2 Moorslede	F 4 d 10.05
Tree Lane [trench]	51bSW1 Neuville Vitasse	N 19 a, b
Tree Trench	51bNW3 Arras	G 12 d
Tree Trench	51bNW4 Fampoux	I 33 c
Treize Alley [Boyau 13? Calonne]	36cSW1 Lens	M 9 a, b
Tremble Copse / Tremble, Bois du [Aspen Wood]	62cSW3 Vermandovillers	T 1 c
Trench 1 [Wulverghem, N of Douve, March 1915]	28SW4 Ploegsteert	U 8 a 4.6
Trench 100 [8/15, SE of Bécourt]	57dSE4 Ovillers / 62dNE2 Méaulte	X 26 d / F 2 b, 3 a
Trench 101 [1915, SE of Warnave Lodge]	28SW4 Ploegsteert	U 28 c
Trench 101 [8/15, SE of Bécourt]	57dSE4 Ovillers / 62dNE2 Méaulte	X 26 d, F 2 b, 3 a
Trench 102 [1915, SE of Warnave Lodge]	28SW4 Ploegsteert	U 28 c
Trench 102 [8/15, SE of Bécourt]	57dSE4 Ovillers	X 26 d
Trench 103 [1915, SE of Warnave Lodge]	28SW4 Ploegsteert	U 28 c
Trench 103 [8/15, SE of Bécourt]	57dSE4 Ovillers	X 26 d
Trench 104 [1915, E of Warnave Lodge]	28SW4 Ploegsteert	U 28 c
Trench 104 [8/15, SE of Bécourt]	57dSE4 Ovillers	X 26 b, d
Trench 105 [1915, NE of Warnave Lodge]	28SW4 Ploegsteert	U 28 c
Trench 105 [8/15, E of Bécourt]	57dSE4 Ovillers	X 26 b, d
Trench 106	57dSE4 Ovillers	X 26 a, b
Trench 106 [1915, S of Burnt Out Farm]	28SW4 Ploegsteert	U 28 a, c
Trench 107	57dSE4 Ovillers	X 26 a, b
Trench 107 [1915, S of Burnt Out Farm]	28SW4 Ploegsteert	U 28 a
Trench 108	57dSE4 Ovillers	X 26 b
Trench 108 [1915, Burnt Out Farm]	28SW4 Ploegsteert	U 28 a
Trench 109	57dSE4 Ovillers	X 26 b
Trench 109 [1915, N of Burnt Out Farm]	28SW4 Ploegsteert	U 28 a
Trench 10a [Wulverghem, March 1915]	28SW4 Ploegsteert	T 6 b 7.3
Trench 10b [Wulverghem, March 1915]	28SW4 Ploegsteert	T 6 b 3.7

Name	Map Sheet	Map Reference
Trench 11 [8/15, Moulin de Fargny]	62cNW1 Maricourt	A 29 b, d
Trench 110	57dSE4 Ovillers	X 26 b
Trench 110 [1915, N of Burnt Out Farm]	28SW4 Ploegsteert	U 28 a
Trench 111	57dSE4 Ovillers	X 20 c, d
Trench 111 [1915, E of Rutter Lodge]	28SW4 Ploegsteert	U 28 a
Trench 112	57dSE4 Ovillers	X 20 c
Trench 112 [1915, E of Rutter Lodge]	28SW4 Ploegsteert	U 28 a
Trench 113	57dSE4 Ovillers	X 20 c
Trench 113 [1915, E of Belchiers Cottages]	28SW4 Ploegsteert	U 22 c, 28 a
Trench 114	57dSE4 Ovillers	X 20 c
Trench 114 [1915, W of Picket House]	28SW4 Ploegsteert	U 21 d, 22 c
Trench 115	57dSE4 Ovillers	X 20 c
Trench 115 [1915, NW of Picket House]	28SW4 Ploegsteert	U 21 d
Trench 116	57dSE4 Ovillers	X 20 a
Trench 116 [1915, E of Hicks Houses]	28SW4 Ploegsteert	U 21 d
Trench 117	57dSE4 Ovillers	X 20 a
Trench 117 [1915, ENE of Palk Villa]	28SW4 Ploegsteert	U 21 d
Trench 118	57dSE4 Ovillers	X 20 a
Trench 118 [1915, N of Palk Villa]	28SW4 Ploegsteert	U 21 d
Trench 119	57dSE4 Ovillers	X 19 b
Trench 119 [1915, E of German House]	28SW4 Ploegsteert	U 21 b, d
Trench 11a [Wulverghem, March 1915]	28SW4 Ploegsteert	N 36 d 1.3
Trench 11b [Wulverghem, March 1915]	28SW4 Ploegsteert	N 36 d 0.5
Trench 12 [NW of Moulin de Fargny]	62cNW1 Maricourt	A 29 a, b
Trench 12 [Wulverghem, March 1915]	28SW4 Ploegsteert	N 36 c 9.8
Trench 120 [La Boisselle]	57dSE4 Ovillers	X 13 d, 19 b
Trench 120 [W of Elger House]	28SW4 Ploegsteert	U 21 b
Trench 121 [La Boisselle]	57dSE4 Ovillers	X 13 d
Trench 121 [NW of Elger House]	28SW4 Ploegsteert	U 21 b
Trench 122 [La Boisselle]	57dSE4 Ovillers	X 13 d
Trench 122 [W of Factory Farm]	28SW4 Ploegsteert	U 15 d
Trench 123	57dSE4 Ovillers	X 13 c
Trench 123 [E of St Yves / St Yvon]	28SW4 Ploegsteert	U 15 d
Trench 124	57dSE4 Ovillers	X 13 c
Trench 124 [NE of St Yves]	28SW4 Ploegsteert	U 15 b, d
Trench 125	57dSE4 Ovillers	X 13 a, c
Trench 125 [N of St Yves / St Yvon]	28SW4 Ploegsteert	U 15 a, b
Trench 126	57dSE4 Ovillers	X 13 a
Trench 126 [N of St Yves / St Yvon]	28SW4 Ploegsteert	U 15 a
Trench 127 [Anton's Farm]	28SW4 Ploegsteert	U 14 b, 15 a
Trench 128 [N of Prowse Point]	28SW4 Ploegsteert	U 14 b
Trench 129 [N of Prowse Point]	28SW4 Ploegsteert	U 14 b
Trench 13 [9/15, Maricourt sector]	62cNW1 Maricourt	A 23 / 29
Trench 13 [Wulverghem, March 1915]	28SW2 Wytschaete	N 36 a 7.2
Trench 130 [Seaforth Farm]	28SW4 Ploegsteert	U 8 d
Trench 131 [N of Seaforth Farm]	28SW4 Ploegsteert	U 8 c, d
Trench 132 [SW of Petite Douve Fm]	28SW4 Ploegsteert	U 8 c
Trench 133 [WSW of Petite Douve Fm]	28SW4 Ploegsteert	U 8 a
Trench 134 [W of Petite Douve Farm]	28SW4 Ploegsteert	U 8 a
Trench 135 [NW of Petite Douve Farm]	28SW4 Ploegsteert	U 8 a
Trench 136 [E of Gabion Farm]	28SW4 Ploegsteert	U 2 c
Trench 137 [NE of Gabion Farm]	28SW4 Ploegsteert	U 1 d
Trench 138 [N of Gabion Farm]	28SW4 Ploegsteert	U 1 d
Trench 139 [NW of Gabion Farm]	28SW4 Ploegsteert	U 1 d

Name	Map Sheet	Map Reference
Trench 14 [9/15, Maricourt sector]	62cNW1 Maricourt	A 23 / 29
Trench 14 [Wulverghem, March 1915]	28SW2 Wytschaete	N 36 a 3.3
Trench 140 [E of Boyle's Farm]	28SW4 Ploegsteert	U 1 b, d
Trench 141 [N of Boyle's Farm]	28SW4 Ploegsteert	U 1 a, b
Trench 142 [N of Boyle's Farm]	28SW4 Ploegsteert	U 1 a
Trench 15 [9/15, Maricourt sector]	62cNW1 Maricourt	A 23 / 29
Trench 15 [S of Canal, 3/15]	28SW2 Wytschaete	O 12 / 18
Trench 15 [Wulverghem, March 1915]	28SW2 Wytschaete	N 36 a 3.6
Trench 16 [9/15, Maricourt sector]	62cNW1 Maricourt	A 23 / 29
Trench 16 [S of Canal, 3/15]	28SW2 Wytschaete	O 12 / 18
Trench 17 [9/15, Maricourt sector]	62cNW1 Maricourt	A 23 / 29
Trench 17 [S of Canal, 3/15]	28SW2 Wytschaete	O 7
Trench 18 [9/15, Maricourt sector]	62cNW1 Maricourt	A 23 / 29
Trench 18 [S of Canal, 3/15]	28SW2 Wytschaete	O 7
Trench 19 [9/15, Maricourt sector]	62cNW1 Maricourt	A 23 / 29
Trench 19 [S of Canal, 3/15]	28SW2 Wytschaete	O 1 / 7
Trench 2 [Wulverghem, N of R Douve, March '15]	28SW4 Ploegsteert	U 2 c 15.30
Trench 20 [9/15, Maricourt sector]	62cNW1 Maricourt	A 23 / 29
Trench 20 [S of Canal, 3/15]	28SW2 Wytschaete	O 1 / 7
Trench 21 [9/15, Maricourt sector]	62cNW1 Maricourt	A 23 / 29
Trench 21 [S of Canal, 3/15]	28SW2 Wytschaete	O 2
Trench 22 [9/15, Maricourt sector]	62cNW1 Maricourt	A 23 / 29
Trench 22 [Calonne Sector]	36cSW1 Lens	M 9 a (area)
Trench 22 [S of Canal, 3/15]	28SW2 Wytschaete	O 2
Trench 23 [9/15, Maricourt sector]	62cNW1 Maricourt	A 23 / 29
Trench 23a [NW of Eikhof Farm]	28SW2 Wytschaete	O 3 c 3.7
Trench 23b [NW of Eikhof Farm]	28SW2 Wytschaete	O 3 c 5.8
Trench 24 [9/15, Maricourt sector]	62cNW1 Maricourt	A 23 / 29
Trench 24b [NW of Square Wood]	28SW2 Wytschaete	O 3 a 6.2
Trench 25 [9/15, Maricourt sector]	62cNW1 Maricourt	A 23 / 29
Trench 25 [NNE of Square Wood]	28SW2 Wytschaete	O 3 b 0.3
Trench 25A [Calonne Sector]	36cSW1 Lens	M 9 a area
Trench 26 [9/15, Maricourt sector]	62cNW1 Maricourt	A 23 / 29
Trench 26 [S edge of Triangular Wood]	28SW2 Wytschaete	O 3 b 40.25
Trench 27 [9/15, Maricourt sector]	62cNW1 Maricourt	A 23 / 29
Trench 27 [E end of Triangular Wood]	28SW2 Wytschaete	O 3 b 5.3
Trench 28 [9/15, Maricourt sector]	62cNW1 Maricourt	A 23 / 29
Trench 28 [S of Canal]	28SW2 Wytschaete	O 4 a 2.6
Trench 29 [9/15, Maricourt sector]	62cNW1 Maricourt	A 23 / 29
Trench 29 [9/15, Maricourt sector]	62cNW1 Maricourt	A 23 / 29
Trench 29 [NE end of The Bluff]	28NW4 & NE3 Zillebeke	I 34 c 6.2
Trench 3 [Wulverghem, N of Douve, March '15]	28SW4 Ploegsteert	U 2 c 05.40
Trench 30	51bNW1 Roclincourt	A 29 c, G 5 a, b
Trench 30 [9/15, Maricourt sector]	62cNW1 Maricourt	A 23 / 29
Trench 30a [The Bluff]	28NW4 & NE3 Zillebeke	I 34 c 7.3
Trench 30b [N of The Bluff]	28NW4 & NE3 Zillebeke	I 34 c 45.50
Trench 31 (New) [6/15, Bluff - Ravine]	28NW4 & NE3 Zillebeke	I 34 c
Trench 31 [9/15, Maricourt sector]	62cNW1 Maricourt	A 23 / 29
Trench 31 [Bluff - Ravine]	28NW4 & NE3 Zillebeke	I 34 c 4.7 to 8.5
Trench 32 [9/15, Maricourt sector]	62cNW1 Maricourt	A 23 / 29
Trench 32 [Bluff - Ravine]	28NW4 & NE3 Zillebeke	I 34 d 25.75
Trench 32a (New) [6/15, Bluff - Ravine]	28NW4 & NE3 Zillebeke	I 34 d
Trench 33 [9/15, Maricourt sector]	62cNW1 Maricourt	A 23 / 29
Trench 33 [The Ravine]	28NW4 & NE3 Zillebeke	I 34 b, d

Name	Map Sheet	Map Reference
Trench 34 [9/15, Maricourt sector]	62cNW1 Maricourt	A 15/16
Trench 34 [N of Ravine]	28NW4 & NE3 Zillebeke	I 34 b 5.3
Trench 35 [9/15, Carnoy sector]	62cNW1 Maricourt	A15/16
Trench 35 [N of Ravine]	28NW4 & NE3 Zillebeke	I 34 b 7.4
Trench 36 (New) [5/15, to Dump]	28NW4 & NE3 Zillebeke	I 34 b
Trench 36 [Carnoy]	62cNW1 Maricourt	A 15/16
Trench 36 [S of Dump]	28NW4 & NE3 Zillebeke	I 34 b 8.6
Trench 36 Reserve [SW of Dump]	28NW4 & NE3 Zillebeke	I 28 d, 34 b
Trench 37 [Carnoy]	62cNW1 Maricourt	A 7/8/9
Trench 37 [S of Railway Cutting]	28NW4 & NE3 Zillebeke	I 35 a 4.9
Trench 38 [Carnoy]	62cNW1 Maricourt	A 7/8/9
Trench 38 [Hill 60]	28NW4 & NE3 Zillebeke	I 29 c 6.2
Trench 38 CT [4/15, Hill 60]	28NW4 & NE3 Zillebeke	I 29 c
Trench 38a [4/15, Hill 60]	28NW4 & NE3 Zillebeke	I 29 c
Trench 39 [Carnoy]	62cNW1 Maricourt	A 7/8/9
Trench 39 [Hill 60]	28NW4 & NE3 Zillebeke	I 29 c 70.35
Trench 39 CT [4/15, Hill 60]	28NW4 & NE3 Zillebeke	I 29 c
Trench 39a [4/15, Hill 60]	28NW4 & NE3 Zillebeke	I 29 c
Trench 39a CT [4/15, Hill 60]	28NW4 & NE3 Zillebeke	I 29 c
Trench 4 [Wulverghem, N of Douve, March '15]	28SW4 Ploegsteert	U 1 d 7.6
Trench 40	51bNW1 Roclincourt / 3 Arras	G 4 b, 5 a, c
Trench 40 [Carnoy]	62cNW1 Maricourt	A 7/8/9
Trench 40 [Hill 60]	28NW4 & NE3 Zillebeke	I 29 c 90.33
Trench 41 [Carnoy]	62cNW1 Maricourt	A 7/8/9
Trench 41 [Hill 60]	28NW4 & NE3 Zillebeke	I 29 c 6.9
Trench 41 CT [4/15, Hill 60]	28NW4 & NE3 Zillebeke	I 29 c
Trench 42 [9/15, Carnoy sector]	62cNW1 Maricourt	A 7/8/9
Trench 42 [Hill 60]	28NW4 & NE3 Zillebeke	I 29 c 7.9
Trench 42 CT [4/15, Hill 60]	28NW4 & NE3 Zillebeke	I 29 c
Trench 42a [4/15, Hill 60]	28NW4 & NE3 Zillebeke	I 29 c
Trench 42a local reserve [4/15, Hill 60]	28NW4 & NE3 Zillebeke	I 29 c
Trench 43 [9/15, Carnoy sector]	62cNW1 Maricourt	A 7/8/9
Trench 43 [Zwarteleen]	28NW4 & NE3 Zillebeke	I 29 d 1.4
Trench 44 [9/15, Carnoy sector]	62cNW1 Maricourt	A 7/8/9
Trench 44 [Zwarteleen]	28NW4 & NE3 Zillebeke	I 29 d 3.3
Trench 45 [9/15, Carnoy sector]	62cNW1 Maricourt	A 7/8/9
Trench 45 [Zwarteleen Salient]	28NW4 & NE3 Zillebeke	I 29 d
Trench 46 [9/15, Carnoy sector]	62cNW1 Maricourt	A 7/8/9
Trench 46 [Zwarteleen]	28NW4 & NE3 Zillebeke	I 29 d 5.4
Trench 46S [5/15, Zwarteleen]	28NW4 & NE3 Zillebeke	I 29 d
Trench 47 [9/15, Carnoy sector]	62cNW1 Maricourt	A 7/8/9
Trench 47 [N of Zwarteleen salient]	28NW4 & NE3 Zillebeke	I 29 d 8.5
Trench 47S [5/15, joined to 47, Zwarteleen]	28NW4 & NE3 Zillebeke	I 29 d 8.5
Trench 48 [9/15, Carnoy sector]	62cNW1 Maricourt	A 7/8/9
Trench 48 N of Zwarteleen]	28NW4 & NE3 Zillebeke	I 29 d 9.6
Trench 49 [9/15, Carnoy sector]	62cNW1 Maricourt	A 7/8/9
Trench 49 [N of Zwarteleen]	28NW4 & NE3 Zillebeke	I 30 c 3.8
Trench 49S [6/15, N of Zwarteleen]	28NW4 & NE3 Zillebeke	I 30 c
Trench 5 [Wulverghem, March 1915]	28SW4 Ploegsteert	U 1 d 5.8
Trench 50	51bNW3 Arras	G 10 d, 11 c
Trench 50 [9/15, Maricourt sector]	62cNW1 Maricourt / 62dNE2 Méaulte	A 17 / 23
Trench 50 [NE of Zwarteleen]	28NW4 & NE3 Zillebeke	I 30 c 6.9
Trench 50S [6/15, N of Zwarteleen?]	28NW4 & NE3 Zillebeke	I 30 c
Trench 51 [6/15, N of Zwarteleen?]	28NW4 & NE3 Zillebeke	I 30 c

Name	Map Sheet	Map Reference
Trench 51 [9/15, Maricourt sector]	62cNW1 Maricourt	A 17 / 23
Trench 52 [9/15, Maricourt sector]	62cNW1 Maricourt	A 17 / 23
Trench 53 [9/15, Maricourt sector]	62cNW1 Maricourt	A 17 / 23
Trench 54 [9/15, Maricourt sector]	62cNW1 Maricourt	A 17 / 23
Trench 54 [nr Bois d'Etoile; Br, S of Somme, '15]	62cNW3 Vaux / 62cSW1 Becquincourt	G / M
Trench 55 [9/15, Maricourt sector]	62cNW1 Maricourt	A 17 / 23
Trench 56 [9/15, Maricourt sector]	62cNW1 Maricourt	A 17 / 23
Trench 56 [Observatory Ridge]	28NW4 & NE3 Zillebeke	I 24 d
Trench 56 [T56, Br tr S of Somme, 1915]	62cNW3 Vaux / 62cSW1 Becquincourt	G / M
Trench 57 [9/15, Maricourt sector]	62cNW1 Maricourt	A 17 / 23
Trench 57 [Observatory Ridge]	28NW4 & NE3 Zillebeke	I 24 d
Trench 57 [T57, Br tr S of Somme, 1915]	62cNW3 Vaux / 62cSW1 Becquincourt	G / M
Trench 58 [9/15, Maricourt sector]	62cNW1 Maricourt	A 17 / 23
Trench 59 [9/15, Maricourt sector]	62cNW1 Maricourt	A 17 / 23
Trench 6 [Wulverghem, March 1915]	28SW4 Ploegsteert	U 1 b 3.2
Trench 60 [8/15, S of Fricourt]	62dNE2 Méaulte	F
Trench 61 [8/15, S of Fricourt]	62dNE2 Méaulte	F
Trench 62 [8/15, S of Fricourt]	62dNE2 Méaulte	F
Trench 63 [8/15, S of Fricourt]	62dNE2 Méaulte	F
Trench 64 [8/15, S of Fricourt]	62dNE2 Méaulte	F 11 d
Trench 65 [8/15, S of Fricourt]	62dNE2 Méaulte	F
Trench 66 [8/15, S of Fricourt]	62dNE2 Méaulte	F 11 d
Trench 67 [8/15, S of Fricourt]	62dNE2 Méaulte	F
Trench 68 [8/15, S of Fricourt]	62dNE2 Méaulte	F 17 a
Trench 69 [8/15, S of Fricourt]	62dNE2 Méaulte	F 17 a
Trench 7 [Wulverghem, March 1915]	28SW4 Ploegsteert	U 1 a 8.3
Trench 70 [8/15, SE of Fricourt]	62dNE2 Méaulte	F 16 b
Trench 71 [8/15, SE of Fricourt]	62dNE2 Méaulte	F 16 b
Trench 72 [8/15, SE of Fricourt]	62dNE2 Méaulte	F 16 b
Trench 73 / 73 Street	62dNE2 Méaulte	F 10
Trench 74 [8/15, S of Fricourt]	62dNE2 Méaulte	F 10
Trench 75 [8/15, S of Fricourt]	62dNE2 Méaulte	F 10
Trench 76 [8/15, S of Fricourt]	62dNE2 Méaulte	F 10
Trench 77 [8/15, S of Fricourt]	62dNE2 Méaulte	F 10
Trench 78 [8/15, S of Fricourt]	62dNE2 Méaulte	F 10
Trench 79 [8/15, S of Fricourt]	62dNE2 Méaulte	F 10
Trench 8 [Wulverghem, March 1915]	28SW4 Ploegsteert	U 1 a 5.2
Trench 80 [8/15, S of Fricourt]	62dNE2 Méaulte	F 9 d
Trench 81 [D1 Sub-sector, 8/15, Fricourt]	62dNE2 Méaulte	F 10
Trench 81B [8/15, S of Fricourt]	62dNE2 Méaulte	F 10
Trench 82 [8/15, opposite Fricourt]	62dNE2 Méaulte	F 9, 10
Trench 82A [8/15, opposite Fricourt]	62dNE2 Méaulte	F 9, 10
Trench 83 [8/15, opposite Fricourt]	62dNE2 Méaulte	F 9, 10
Trench 84 [8/15, opposite Fricourt]	62dNE2 Méaulte	F 9, 10
Trench 85 [8/15, opposite Fricourt]	62dNE2 Méaulte	F 9, 10
Trench 86 [8/15, opposite Fricourt]	62dNE2 Méaulte	F 9, 10
Trench 87 [8/15, opposite Fricourt]	62dNE2 Méaulte	F 9
Trench 88 [8/15, opposite Fricourt]	62dNE2 Méaulte	F 9
Trench 89 [8/15, opposite Fricourt]	62dNE2 Méaulte	F 9
Trench 9 [Wulverghem, March 1915]	28SW4 Ploegsteert	U 1 a 1.1
Trench 90 [8/15, opposite Fricourt]	62dNE2 Méaulte	F 9
Trench 91 [8/15, SW of Tambour]	62dNE2 Méaulte	F 2 b, 3 a
Trench 92 [8/15, SW of Tambour]	62dNE2 Méaulte	F 2 b, 3 a
Trench 93 [8/15, SW of Tambour]	62dNE2 Méaulte	F 2 b, 3 a

Name	Map Sheet	Map Reference
Trench 94 [8/15, SW of Tambour]	62dNE2 Méaulte	F 2 b, 3 a
Trench 95 [8/15, Tambour]	62dNE2 Méaulte	F 2 b, 3 a
Trench 96 [8/15, Tambour]	62dNE2 Méaulte	F 2 b, 3 a
Trench 97 [8/15, Tambour]	62dNE2 Méaulte	F 2 b, 3 a
Trench 98 [8/15, Tambour]	62dNE2 Méaulte	F 2 b, 3 a
Trench 99 [8/15, NW of Tambour]	62dNE2 Méaulte	F 2 b, 3 a
Trench B [4/15, Hill 60]	28NW4 & NE3 Zillebeke	I 29 c
Trench C [4/15, Hill 60]	28NW4 & NE3 Zillebeke	I 29 c
Trench D [4/15, Hill 60]	28NW4 & NE3 Zillebeke	I 29 c
Trench Farm	28SW2 Wytschaete	O 16 d 6.1
Trench H [4/15, Hill 60]	28NW4 & NE3 Zillebeke	I 29 c
Trench Y [Observatory Ridge]	28NW4 & NE3 Zillebeke	I 23 d, 29 b
Trench Z [Observatory Ridge?]	28NW4 & NE3 Zillebeke	I 23 d, 29 b
Trent Depot [railway, light rly, huts]	28SW3 Bailleul	S 21 c, d, 22 c, 27 a, b, 28 a
Trent Junction [railway siding]	28SW3 Bailleul	S 21 a, c
Trent Trench	51bNW1 Roclincourt	G 6 a, b
Trent Trench / Support	51bNW4 Fampoux	H 5 a, c, d, 11 a
Trerrie [Tranchée, La Boisselle, 1915]	57dSE4 Ovillers	X 13 a
Trescault Alley	57cSE1 Bertincourt / 2 Gonnelieu	Q 15 b
Trescault Avenue	57cSE2 Gonnelieu	Q 9 d, 10 a, c
Trescault Support	57cSE2 Gonnelieu	Q 3 b, 4 a, c, d
Trescault Trench	57cSE2 Gonnelieu	Q 3 b, 4 a, b, c, d, 5 c
Tresckow Alley	66dNW3 Hattencourt	G 3 c, d, 9 b
Tress Trench	57cSW4 Combles	U 17 b, d
Trestle Farm	36NW1 Steenwerck	G 3 b 55.78
Treutlein Weg	51bSW1 Neuville Vitasse	M 20 b, d
Treves Trench [1918]	66eNW [2 Thennes]	C 26 b
Trial Farm	28NE2 Moorslede	F 17 b 45.83
Triangle	36NW2 Armentières	C 4 d
Triangle	57dSE4 Ovillers	X 15 d, 16 c
Triangle [Montauban]	57cSW3 Longueval	S 27 c
Triangle [Redoubt]	36cNW3 Loos	G 16 d 5.4
Triangle Alley	36cNW1 La Bassée	A 23 a, c
Triangle Cemetery	57cNE1 Quéant	E 8 c 2.6
Triangle Copse [Gomiecourt]	57cNW1 Gomiecourt	A 24 c
Triangle Crater [Hohenzollern]	36cNW3 Loos	G 4 d 7.7
Triangle Cuttings [railway]	36cSW4 Rouvroy	N 35 c, d, T 5 a, b
Triangle Dugouts [Triangular Bluff]	28SW2 Wytschaete	O 5 a
Triangle Farm	36NW2 Armentières	C 6 c
Triangle Farm [& pillbox]	28NW2 St Julien	C 6 c 7.1
Triangle Line	57cNE4 Marcoing	K 35 a, b, 36 a
Triangle Post	57cSW3 Longueval	S 27 b, 28 a
Triangle Post [N of Loos]	36cNW3 Loos	G 29 b 4.3
Triangle Trench	36cSW3 Vimy	S 14 d, 20 b
Triangle Trench	57dSE4 Ovillers	X 15 d
Triangle Trench	62bNW1 Gouy	A 19 d, 25 b, d
Triangle Trench	62bNW3 Bellicourt	G 7 d
Triangle Wood	51bSW2 Vis-en-Artois	O 21 b, d
Triangle Wood	57cNE4 Marcoing	K 29 c, 35 a
Triangle Wood	66dNW1 Punchy	A 17 b, d
Triangle, Méaulte	62dNE2 Méaulte	E 22 d 2.8
Triangle, The	28NW2 St Julien	C 6 c, d
Triangle, The	36aSE1 St Venant	Q 26 b
Triangle, The	57cSW3 Longueval	T 8 d

Name	Map Sheet	Map Reference
Triangle, The	62cNW1 Maricourt	A 7 b
Triangle, The [1,000 yards E of Beaumont Hamel]	57dSE1 & 2 Beaumont	Q 6 c, 12 a
Triangular Bluff, The	28SW2 Wytschaete	O 5 a
Triangular Fence [Sept 1915]	36cNW3 Loos	G 16 d 3.7
Triangular Orchard	57dNE4 & 57cNW3 Achiet	L 11 a 8.9
Triangular Wood	20SW4 Bixschoote	T 24 b, d
Triangular Wood	28SW2 Wytschaete	O 3 a, b
Triangular Wood	62cNW3 Vaux	G 35 c
Triangular Wood	66eNW [2 Thennes]	B 17 d, 18 c
Triangular Wood [Polygon Wood]	62cSW3 Vermandovillers / 66dNW1 Punchy	S 27 d, A 3 b, d, 4 a, c
Trichter Stellung	51bSW1 Neuville Vitasse	M 4 b, d, 5 a, c
Trick Farm	28NE2 Moorslede	F 14 a 9.5
Trident Alley	51bSW4 Bullecourt	U 15, 16, 21
Trieze [sic] Alley	36cSW1 Lens	M 9 a, b
Trifle Farm	36aNE4 Merville	K 22 c 5.3
Trig Avenue [road, 1918]	62dNE [3 Morlancourt]	K 14, 20
Trig Copse	51bNW4 Fampoux	I 36 b
Trig Post	57cSE2 Gonnelieu	Q 23 a
Trigger Alley	51bSW4 Bullecourt / SE3 Cagnicourt	U 12 b, c, d, V 7 a
Trigger Copse	51bSE3 Cagnicourt	V 7 a, c
Trigger Trench	62dNE2 Méaulte	F 30 c
Trigger Valley	62dNE2 Méaulte	F 30 c
Trigger Wood	62bNW3 Bellicourt	N 4 b
Trigger Wood	62dNE2 Méaulte	L 6 a
Trigger Wood Valley	62dNE2 Méaulte	F 30 c, L 6 a
Trim Trench	51bNW3 Arras	G 12 d
Trimble Farm	36NW1 Steenwerck	A 21 d 6.8
Tring [light rly locality W of Canal, 1917-18]	28NW2 St Julien	B 18 d
Trinity Farm	62cSW1 Dompierre	M 30 c, 36 a
Trinity Redoubt [300 yards from Trinket Redoubt]	62cNE4 Roisel	L 15
Trinket Alley	62bSW3 St Quentin	S 22 d, 23 c, 28 a, b, c
Trinket Redoubt [300 yards from Trinity Redoubt]	62cNE4 Roisel	L 15
Trio Farm	28SW2 Wytschaete	O 18 d 4.8
Trip Trench	51bNW3 Arras	G 12 d
Trip Trench	57cSW1 Gueudecourt	N 1 b
Tripe Trench	51bNW2 Oppy	H 5 a
Tripod Fork [road jct]	27NE2 Proven	E 22 b 7.2
Tripoli Trench	51bNW2 Oppy / 4 Fampoux	H 5 a, c, 11 a, b
Tripp's Farm	36aSE1 St Venant	P 18 a 1.4
Triscott House	28SW3 Bailleul	S 3 d 3.6
Tristan Trench	57cSW4 Combles	U 20 d, 21 c
Triumph Junction [road jct]	28NE4 Dadizeele	K 6 c 3.4
Triumph Trench	36cSW4 Rouvroy	T 24 c
Trocadero [cottage / estaminet]	36aNE1 Morbecque	D 9 a 75.80
Trois Amis, Au [Estaminet, Ploegsteert]	28SW4 Ploegsteert	U 25 c 75.65
Trois Arbres [farm]	36NW1 Steenwerck	B 13 b 2.7
Trois Arbres [level crossing]	36NW1 Steenwerck	B 13 b 2.5
Trois Pipes, les [hamlet]	36NW1 Steenwerck	B 3 b, d, 4 a, c
Trois Rois	28NW4 Ypres	I 20 c
Trois Rois [farm & place name]	28SW3 Bailleul	T 20 a, b
Trois Rois [farm]	36NW1 Steenwerck	B 15 b 7.7
Trois Rois Cabaret, Aux	28SW3 Bailleul	T 14 c
Trois Rois Camp	28SW3 Bailleul	T 20 c
Trois Rois Spur [light rly; near Shrapnel Corner]	28NW4 Ypres	I 20 a 6.3

Name	Map Sheet	Map Reference
Trois Rois, Aux	27NE2 Proven	E 22 d 7.6
Trois Sauvages / Three Savages [farm]	62bSW1 Gricourt	M 23 d 55.85
Trois Tilleuls Farm	28SW4 Ploegsteert	U 17 c 1.2
Trois Tours [railway sidings]	28NW1 Elverdinghe	B 27 b
Trois Tours, Château des	28NW2 St Julien	B 28 a 7.1
Trollope Trench	62bNW1 Gouy	A 19 d, 25 b
Trolly Trench	62bNW3 Bellicourt	G 4 d
Trombone Corner [road jct]	28NE4 Dadizeele	L 20 a 8.1
Tromeur Alley	66cSW2 Vendeuil	O 25 c, d, 26 c
Trompe Bridge [locality]	36aNE4 Merville	L 21 a 95.50
Trompe Cabaret, La	28SW3 Bailleul	T 9 d 35.05
Trompette, Tranchée de la [Trumpet]	62cSW3 & 4 Marchélepot	T 30 c, d
Tron, The	28SE3 Comines	V 7 b
Trônes Alley	57cSW3 Longueval	S 29 b, c, d
Trônes Wood	57cSW3 Longueval	S 23, 24, 29, 30
Trongate Street [Thiepval Wood]	57dSE1 & 2 Beaumont	R 25 c
Tronquoy [village]	57bSW2 Clary	O 6 b
Tronquoy Wood	62bSW1 Gricourt	N 9 b
Tronquoy, le [village]	62bSW1 Gricourt	N 2, 3, 8, 9
Tronville Switch [1918]	62dSW [2 Villers-Bretonneux]	N 18, 23, 24
Troon Farm	28SE1 Wervicq	P 2 b 9.7
Trooper Copse	28SW1 Kemmel	M 27 a, c
Trossacks, The	57dNE3 & 4 Hébuterne	K 22 d, 28 b
Trot House	28NE3 Gheluvelt	J 27 c 45.55
Trot Trench	51bNW3 Arras	G 12 d
Trou au Soldats, le [hamlet]	57bSE3 Busigny	V 7 b, 8 a, c, d
Trou Post	36SW1 Aubers	N 9 a
Trou, Le [hamlet / locality]	36SW1 Aubers	N 8 b, 9 a
Trouser Farm	28SW3 Bailleul	S 22 b 35.35
Trout Copse	62bSW2 Fonsommes	O 31 b
Trout Copse	62bSW3 St Quentin	M 32 c, S 2 a
Trout Farm	28SW2 Wytschaete	O 24 c 3.9
Trout Fork [road junction]	20SE2 Hooglede	R 12 c 60.98
Trout Post	57cNE3 Hermies	K 7 c 0.4
Trout Spur [light rly, 1918]	51bNW2 Oppy	B 29 d, H 5 b
Trout Trench	36cSW4 Rouvroy	T 24 d
Trout Trench	51bNW2 Oppy	B 29 d, H 5 b
Trout Trench	51bNW3 Arras	G 12 c
Trout Trench	51bSW1 Neuville Vitasse	M 6 c
Trout Trench [1918]	57dNE1 & 2 Fonquevillers / 3 & 4 Hébuterne	K 5 a, c
Trowel Alley	51bSW2 Vis-en-Artois	O 8 c, d
Troy [hamlet]	62cSW4 St. Christ	T 18 central
Troy Redoubt	36SW3 Richebourg	T 25 c
Troy Trench	51bNW4 Fampoux	H 11 b, d, 12 c
Truffe, Tranchée de la	66dNW2 Morchain	C 7 b, d, 8 a
Truie Farm / La Truie Ferme	28SW4 Ploegsteert	U 17 a 55.05
Truman Trench	51bNW1 Roclincourt	A 4 c
Trump Lane	51bSW1 Neuville Vitasse	N 14 c
Trumpet Cross Roads	28NE4 Dadizeele	L 14 d 70.75
Trumpette Trench	62cSW4 St. Christ	T 30 c, d
Trunk Farm	28SE1 Wervicq	P 19 a 6.7
Trunk Trench	51bNW4 Fampoux	I 33b, c, d
Trunk Trench	70dNW2 Servais	C 7 d, 8 a
Truro Sap	57cSE2 Gonnelieu	R 15 c

Name	Map Sheet	Map Reference
Truro Trench	36cSW3 Vimy	T 8 a
Truss Trench	51bNW3 Arras	G 12 c
Truth Trench	51bNW3 Arras	G 12 c, d
Truth Trench [Ginchy to Quadrilateral]	57cSW3 Longueval	T 14 c, d
Tsar, Boyau	62cSW1 Dompierre	M 4 d
Tub Communication [German CT]	28SW4 Ploegsteert	U 22 a
Tub Trench	51bNW3 Arras	G 12 c, d
Tub Trench [Tub Up]	36cSW4 Rouvroy	T 30 b, U 25 a
Tube Cross Roads	28SE1 Wervicq	P 8 a 30.85
Tube Lane	51bSW1 Neuville Vitasse	M 5 c
Tube Station Post	36SW3 Richebourg	S 21 b [S 21 a in 1915]
Tube Trench	51bNW3 Arras	G 12 c
Tubinger Stellung	57dNE3 & 4 Hébuterne	K 30 a, b, c
Tuchel / Tuchell Trench	62cNW4 Péronne / NE3 Buire	I 18 d, 24 b, J 19 a
Tuck Trench	51bNW3 Arras	G 12 c
Tuesday Avenue	51bNW1 Roclincourt / 3 Arras	G 5 a, b, c, 10 b
Tuffs / Toughs Farm	28SW4 Ploegsteert	U 27 b 7.4
Tuffs Bridge [1917-18]	20SW4 Bixschoote	U 27 b 9.5
Tuffs Farm [1917-18]	20SW4 Bixschoote	U 27 b 2.5
Tufnell Avenue	57cSE1 Bertincourt / 2 Gonnelieu	Q 3 b, d
Tug Copse	28NE2 Moorslede	F 9 a 1.2
Tug Cottage	28NE2 Moorslede	F 9 c 20.94
Tug Farm	28NE2 Moorslede	F 23 c 10.77
Tugela Farm	28NW2 St Julien	B 18 b 3.5
Tui Road	36NW4 Bois Grenier	I 31 a, b
Tuilerie [Zillebeke]	28NW4 Ypres	I 22 b 3.8
Tulip Copse	62bNW4 Ramicourt	H 24 a
Tulip Cotts	28NE1 Zonnebeke	D 20 b 1.5
Tulip Farm	20SE2 Hooglede	R 21 d 6.4
Tulip Trench	20SW3 Oostvleteren	T 9 b
Tulip Trench	36cSW4 Rouvroy	T 24 d
Tulloch Corner [road jct]	57dSE4 Ovillers	R 33 d 8.3
Tumbler Crossing [bridge / level crossing]	28NE2 Moorslede	F 14 b 52.65
Tummel Street	57dSE4 Ovillers	X 19 b
Tumulus [N of Pontru]	62bSW1 Gricourt	M 1 d 85.39
Tuning Fork Keep / Post	36bNE2 Beuvry	F 4 b 6.3
Tuning Fork Keep [near Gorre Wood]	36aSE4 Locon	X 29 d, 30 c
Tuning Fork Switch	36aSE4 Locon / 36bNE2 Beuvry	X 29 a, c, d, F 5 b, 6 a
Tuning Fork, The [road feature]	36bNE2 Beuvry	F 4 b, 5 a, b
Tunis House	27SE4 Meteren	W 12 d 60.12
Tunnel [Le Transloy]	57cSW2 Villers-au-Flos	N 30 c, d
Tunnel House [Hooge, 1915]	28NW4 & NE3 Zillebeke	I 18 b
Tunnel Junction [light rly, 1917-18]	28NW4 Ypres	I 21 c
Tunnel Support	51bSW4 Bullecourt	U 7 d, 8 c, 14 a
Tunnel Trench	51bSW4 Bullecourt	U 7, 14, 20
Tunnel, The [reverse slope of Mt Sorrel]	28NW4 & NE3 Zillebeke	I 30 a
Tunnel, The [The Bluff]	28SW2 Wytschaete	O 4 a
Tunnellers Walk [St Eloi 1917-18]	28SW2 Wytschaete	O 5 a, b
Tupman Avenue [1918]	57dSW [3 Talmas]	S 22 b, 23 a, c
Turbine House	36aNE1 Morbecque	D 27 a 65.10
Turbot Farm	28SE1 Wervicq	P 25 d 1.8
Turchin Trench	62cNE3 Buire	J 7 c, d, 13 a
Turck Farm	20SW3 Oostvleteren	T 7 d 9.2
Turco Camp	28NW2 St Julien	C 15 c 4.8

Name	Map Sheet	Map Reference
Turco Farm [French Fm / Engländerhof / Klokhof]	28NW2 St Julien	C 15 c 2.4
Turco Huts [1917-18]	28NW2 St Julien	C 14 d, 20 b
Turenne Alley	62bSW3 St Quentin	S 29 a
Turenne Crossing	20SE3 Westroosebeke	V 1 d 15.35
Turk Avenue	57cSW1 Gueudecourt	M 23 b, d, 24 c, 30 a
Turk Head [GFL, late 1915]	36SW2 Radinghem	N 5 d 45.20
Turk Lane	57cSW1 Gueudecourt / 3 Longueval	M 18, 23, 24, 30, 35, 36
Turk Street	57dSE2 Beaumont / 4 Ovillers	R 31 a, c, d
Turk Support	57cSW1 Gueudecourt	M 17 d, 18 c, 24 a
Turkey Alley	62bSW4 Homblières	T 23 c
Türknecke [strongpoint]	36SW2 Radinghem	N 16 b 2.7
Turko Trench / Graben	51bNW1 Roclincourt	A 5 b, d
Turks Alley	62bSW1 Gricourt	N 20 d
Turks Fork [road jct]	28NE2 Moorslede	E 17 a 85.50
Turks Valley	62bSW1 Gricourt	N 20 c, d, 21 c, d
Turmoil Cross [cross roads]	27NE2 Proven	F 11 d 45.75
Turn Table	36cNW1 La Bassée	A 11 a
Turnbull Farm	28NE4 Dadizeele	K 28 b 90.25
Turner Crater	57cSE4 Villers-Guislain	R 34 d 9.9
Turner Quarry	57cSE2 Gonnelieu / 4 Villers-Guislain	R 34 b, d
Turner Road	57cSE2 Gonnelieu	R 35 a, b, 36 a
Turnerstown Left, & Right	28SW2 Wytschaete	N 23 b
Turnham Corner [road jct]	27NE1 Herzeele	E 19 c 2.5
Turnip Alley	66cNW1 Grugies / 2 Itancourt	B 4 c, 10 a
Turnip Farm	28NW1 Elverdinghe	A 23 c 9.4
Turnip Field [St Yvon, Bairnsfather's]	28SW4 Ploegsteert	U 15 a
Turnip Lane [trench]	62bNW3 Bellicourt	G 7 d, 13 b
Turnstile Trench	66cNW2 Itancourt	B 11 b
Turntable Alley	36cNW1 La Bassée	A 17 c, 22 b, 23 a
Turo Farm, Elverdinghe	28NW1 Elverdinghe	B 15 a 6.5
Turpin Crossing [cross roads]	28SE1 Wervicq	P 23 b 03.10
Turpin Point	20SE1 Staden	P 18 c
Turtle Farm	20SE2 Hooglede	R 28 c 6.8
Turtle Farm	36aNE4 Merville	L 15 b 90.65
Turtle Trench	51bSW4 Bullecourt / SE3 Cagnicourt	U 18 d, V 19 a
Tusk Trench	51bNW3 Arras	G 12 c
Tusk Trench	51bNW4 Fampoux	I 33 a, b
Tuskar [sic] Farm [Tusker]	27NE2 Proven	F 9 a 40.85
Tweak House	27NE2 Proven	E 18 a 05.45
Tweed House	20SE3 Westroosebeke	V 25 d 8.6
Tweed Trench	51bNW1 Roclincourt	G 6 a, b
Tweezer Corner [road junction]	20SE2 Hooglede	R 33 b 3.5
Twelfth Avenue	36cSW4 Rouvroy	T 17 a, b, c
Twentieth Post	36NW3 Fleurbaix	H 14 a, c
Twenty Alley	36cNW1 La Bassée	A 22 c
Twenty Road [road]	57dSE2 & 57cSW1 Le Sars	M 19 d, 20 c, d, 21 c
Twenty Sixth Avenue	57dSE2 & 57cSW1 Le Sars	M 21 c, d, 26 a, b, 27 a
Twenty Street	51bNW3 Arras	G 36 a
Twenty Three Road	57dSE1 & 2 Beaumont	R 23 a
Twenty Two Avenue	57cSE4 Villers-Guislain	R 33 c, d, 34 c
Twenty Two Ravine	57cSE4 Villers-Guislain	R 33 c, d, 34 c
Twentyone Street	51bSW1 Neuville Vitasse	M 21 c
Twig Lane [trench]	51bSW1 Neuville Vitasse	N 19 b, 20 a
Twig Trench	51bNW3 Arras	G 12 c

Name	Map Sheet	Map Reference
Twin Copses	51bSW2 Vis-en-Artois	O 2 a, b
Twin Cots	36NW2 & NE1 Houplines	C 4 d 7.5
Twin Crater	62cSE2 Vermand	R 6 c 6.1
Twin Farms	36aSE3 Gonnehem	W 8 b 9.8
Twin Sap	36cNW1 La Bassée	A 27 b
Twin Trench	51bNW3 Arras	G 12 c
Twin Trench	51bSW2 Vis-en-Artois	O 2 a, b, d
Twine Farm	36NW1 Steenwerck	A 2 d 8.9
Twins Craters, The	36cSW3 Vimy	S 28 c
Twins, The	62cNW1 Maricourt	A 2 b
Twins, The	12SW1 Nieuport	M 22 b
Twins, The [strongpoint]	28SW2 Wytschaete	O 11 d, 12 c
Twinstead [farm]	20SE2 Hooglede	Q 18 d 3.0
Twist Trench	51bNW3 Arras	G 12 c
Twist Trench	66cNW2 Itancourt	C 19 c
Twisted Alley [road]	36cSW1 Lens	N 8 b, d, 14 b
Twisted Tree [Ruby Wood; trig point]	62bNW1 Gouy	G 2 a
Two Tree Farm	36SW1 Aubers	N 2 c 1.7
Tyhurst Quarry	57cSE4 Villers-Guislain	X 17 c
Tyndrum Street	57dSE4 Ovillers	Q 36 d
Tyne Alley	51bNW2 Oppy	B 23 a, d, 24 c
Tyne Alley, North	51bNW2 Oppy	B 23 b, d, 24 a
Tyne Cott	28NE1 Zonnebeke	D 17 a
Tyne Cott Cemetery [British]	28NE1 Zonnebeke	D 16 b 8.3
Tyne Cott Cemetery [German]	28NE1 Zonnebeke	D 17 a 6.2
Tyne Trench	57dSE4 Ovillers	X 2 d, 3 c
Typ Trench	51bNW3 Arras	G 12 c
Typhoon Corner [road jct]	28NE4 Dadizeele	L 31 b 90.75
Typhoon Trench	57cSW2 Villers-au-Flos	N 23 / 29
Tyre Trench	51bNW3 Arras	G 12 c
Tyro Farm [1918]	28SW1 Kemmel	M 36 a 9.2
U 23 Trench [St Eloi]	28SW2 Wytschaete	O 2
U 24 Trench [St Eloi]	28SW2 Wytschaete	O 2
U 25 Trench [St Eloi]	28SW2 Wytschaete	O 2
U 26 Trench [St Eloi]	28SW2 Wytschaete	O 2
U 27 Trench [St Eloi]	28SW2 Wytschaete	O 2
U 28 Trench [St Eloi]	28SW2 Wytschaete	O 2
U Works	62cNW1 Maricourt	A 21 a
Uber Alles Trench	62cNW4 Péronne	I 15 b, d, 21 a, b, c
Udine Trench / Tranchée Udine	66cNW2 Itancourt	B 11 a, b, 12 a
Uganda Copse	51bNW4 Fampoux	I 36 b
Uger Point [1918]	28SW4 Ploegsteert	U 21 b 7.8
Ugly Avenue	28SW4 Ploegsteert	U 11 c, d
Ugly Farm	28NE3 Gheluvelt	J 34 d 1.7
Ugly Lane	28SW4 Ploegsteert	O 31 c
Ugly Post	36NW2 Armentières	C 2 d 8.6
Ugly Reserve	28SW4 Ploegsteert	O 31 c
Ugly Support	28SW4 Ploegsteert	U 1 a
Ugly Switch	28SW4 Ploegsteert	N 36, T 6, U 1
Ugly Trench	28SW4 Ploegsteert	N 36, T 6, U 1
Ugly Wood	28NE3 Gheluvelt	J 34 a, c, d
Uhlan Alley	36cSW3 Vimy	S 14 a, b
Uhlan Avenue	28SW4 Ploegsteert	U 2 b
Uhlan Farm	28NW2 St Julien	C 29 b 5.5

Name	Map Sheet	Map Reference
Uhlan Keep [1918]	28NW2 St Julien	C 29 b 7.3
Uhlan Row	28SW4 Ploegsteert	U 2 a
Uhlan Street	28SW4 Ploegsteert	U 2 a
Uhlan Support	28SW4 Ploegsteert	U 2 a, c
Uhlan Trench	28SW4 Ploegsteert	U 2 a, c
Uhlan Trench	36cSW4 Rouvroy	U 20 b
Uhlans, Boyau des	36cSW3 Vimy	S 14 b
Uhlenfeld Graben	57dNE3 & 4 Hébuterne	K 12 b, L 7 a, c, d, 8 c
Ulcer Sap, & Reserve	28SW4 Ploegsteert	U 3 c
Ulcer Street	28SW4 Ploegsteert	U 2 d
Ulcer Support	28SW4 Ploegsteert	U 2 d
Ulcer Trench	28SW4 Ploegsteert	U 2 d
Ulm Farm	28NW2 St Julien	B 23 c
Ulm Trench	62cSW2 Barleux / 4 St. Christ	O 34 b, c, d
Ulm, Werk	51bNW1 Roclincourt	A 30 a, b, d
Ulna Avenue	28SW4 Ploegsteert	U 8 b, 9 a
Ulna Beak	28SW4 Ploegsteert	U 8 a, b
Ulna Support, & Switch	28SW4 Ploegsteert	U 8 b
Ulrica Trench, Sup, Sap, Row, Ave	28SW4 Ploegsteert	U 8 d, 9 c, d, 15 a
Ulrich Redoubt / Work	51bSW1 Neuville Vitasse	M 22 d, 23 c, 28 b, 29 a
Ulrich Weg	51bSW1 Neuville Vitasse	M 16 c, 22 b
Ulricker Graben	36cSW1 Lens	M 20 d, 21 c
Ulster Avenue	51bSW4 Bullecourt	U 10 a
Ulster Avenue [Thiepval Wood]	57dSE1 & 2 Beaumont	Q 30 c, 36 a
Ulster Camp	28SW3 Bailleul	M 35 c, S 5 a
Ulster House	28SW2 Wytschaete	O 27 a 1.1
Ulster Road [trench]	28SW2 Wytschaete	N 29 d, 35 b, 36 a, b
Ulster Trench	36cSW4 Rouvroy	U 19 b, c, d, 20 a, 25 a
Ulster Trench	51bSW4 Bullecourt	U 4 a, b, c
Ulster Trench, Supp, Res, Switch, Drive	28SW4 Ploegsteert	U 9 d, 10 a, 15 a, b
Ultimo Crater	28SW4 Ploegsteert	U 15 d 90.65
Ultimo Crater Post	28SW4 Ploegsteert	U 15 d, 16 a
Ultimo Lane [1918]	28SW4 Ploegsteert	U 17 a, c, d
Ultimo Tr, Sup, Res, Switch, Lane, Ave	28SW4 Ploegsteert	U 10 c, 15 b, d, 16 a, b, c
Ultra Trench, Support, & Lane	28SW4 Ploegsteert	U 15 d, 16 c, 21 b
Ulverstone Street	57dSE4 Ovillers	X 7 b
Umbo Drive, North & South	28SW4 Ploegsteert	U 22 a, b
Umbo Trench, Support, Row, Ave, Alley	28SW4 Ploegsteert	U 16 d, 21 b, 22 a, b
Umbria Street, North & South	28SW4 Ploegsteert	U 22 c
Umbria Trench, Support, Reserve	28SW4 Ploegsteert	U 22 a, c
Umgeni Trench [Brayelle Verb(indungs) Graben]	57dNE1 & 2 Fonquevillers	E 23 d
Umpire Avenue	28SW4 Ploegsteert	U 22 c, d, 28 a
Umpire Drive	28SW4 Ploegsteert	U 22 d, 23 c
Umpire Drive, North & South	28SW4 Ploegsteert	U 22 d, 23 a, c
Umpire Row	28SW4 Ploegsteert	U 22 c, d
Umpire Support	28SW4 Ploegsteert	U 22 b, d, 23 c
Umpire Switch	28SW4 Ploegsteert	U 17 c, d, 23 a
Umpire Trench, Alley	28SW4 Ploegsteert	U 22 c, 28 a, b, 29 a
Umpty Trench	36cSW4 Rouvroy	U 21 a
Umteen Farm	27NE2 Proven	F 27 c 50.75
Una Lane	51bSW4 Bullecourt	U 2 c, 3 a
Una Support	28SW4 Ploegsteert	U 22 d, 28 a, b, c, d
Una Trench, Res, St, Row, Av,	28SW4 Ploegsteert	U 28 a, b, c, d, 29 a
Unable Trench	28SW4 Ploegsteert	O 36 c, U 6 a, c

Name	Map Sheet	Map Reference
Unbearable Trench	28SW4 Ploegsteert	U 3 a, b
Unbent Trench	28SW4 Ploegsteert	U 6 c, 12 a, c
Uncanny Trench, & Support	28SW4 Ploegsteert	U 4 a
Uncertain Tr, Sup, Lane, Alley, Av, Row	28SW4 Ploegsteert	U 10 a, b, c, d, 11 a
Unchained Trench, & Avenue	28SW4 Ploegsteert	U 10 d, 16 b, 17 a, b
Uncivil Post	28SW4 Ploegsteert	U 15 c 3.9
Uncle Cuthbert Trench	51bNW2 Oppy	C 2 b, 3 a
Uncle Trench	36cSW4 Rouvroy	U 26 d
Uncle Trench, Support, Drive, Avenue	28SW4 Ploegsteert	U 16 d, 17 c, 23 a
Unclean Trench	28SW4 Ploegsteert	U 12 c, 18 a
Uncomfortable Crescent	28SW4 Ploegsteert	U 29 a, b
Uncommon Trench	28SW4 Ploegsteert	U 23 a, c
Uncouth Trench	36cSW4 Rouvroy	T 30 d, U 25 c
Uncovered Trench	28SW4 Ploegsteert	U 29 d, 30 c
Uncurl Support	28SW4 Ploegsteert	U 30 c
Uncurl Trench	28SW4 Ploegsteert	U 29 d, 30 a, c
Uncut Trench	28SW4 Ploegsteert	U 18 a, b, c, 24 a
Undated Trench	28SW4 Ploegsteert	U 5 c
Undaunted Trench	28SW4 Ploegsteert	U 11 b, 12 a
Under Trench	51bSW4 Bullecourt	U 3 a, b, d, 9 b, 10 a
Underhill Farm	28SW4 Ploegsteert	T 18 d 4.3
Undulating Support	28SW4 Ploegsteert	U 4 a, b, c, d
Undulating Trench	28SW4 Ploegsteert	U 4 a, b, c, d
Unending Trench	36cSW4 Rouvroy / 51bNW2 Oppy	U 26 c, d, 27 a, c, C 2 a
Uneven Support	28SW4 Ploegsteert	U 11 c, 17 a
Unfit Trench	36cSW4 Rouvroy	U 25 c, d
Ungarn Alley	62bSW4 Homblières	T 23 c
Ungodly Avenue	28SW4 Ploegsteert	U 4 c, d
Ungodly Trench	28SW4 Ploegsteert	U 4 c, d
Unicorn Avenue	51bSW4 Bullecourt	U 5 c, d, 10 b
Unicorn Trench	20SW4 Bixschoote	U 21 c
Unicorn Trench	36cSW4 Rouvroy	U 13 d, 19 b
Unicorn Trench	51bSW4 Bullecourt	U 4 b, d, 10 b
Uniform Trench	36cSW4 Rouvroy	U 13 d, 14 c, d, 15 a, 19 b
Union Street	28NW4 & NE3 Zillebeke	I 16 b, c, 17 a, b
Union Street	36cNW3 Loos	G 34 b
Union Street	57cSW3 Longueval	R 34 d
Union Street	57cSW4 Combles	N 34 c, d
Union Street [Thiepval Wood]	57dSE1 & 2 Beaumont	R 25 a
Union Trench	27SE4 Meteren	X 7 b, c, d, 13 a
Union Trench	51bSW2 Vis-en-Artois	O 34 b, 35 a
Union Trench	57dSE4 Ovillers	X 4 b, 5 a
Union Wood	62bSW2 Fonsommes / 4 Homblières	O 32 b, d, 33 a
Unique Trench	36cSW4 Rouvroy	U 20 d
Unit Trench	36cSW4 Rouvroy	U 20 c
Unity Farm	20SE2 Hooglede	R 13 d 85.05
Unknown Copse	28NE3 Gheluvelt	J 20 c
Unley Road [trench]	36NW4 Bois Grenier	I 9 d, 15 b
Unnamed Farm	62cNE2 Epéhy	L 6 a 2.1
Unnamed Keep, Travecy	66cSW4 La Fère	U 1 b, d
Unnamed Sap	28SW4 Ploegsteert	U 17 a
Unnamed Wood	28SW2 Wytschaete	N 18 d, O 13 c
Unseen Support	57cNE4 Marcoing	K 36 a, b, d
Unseen Trench	57cNE4 Marcoing	K 36 a, c, d

Name	Map Sheet	Map Reference
Untidy Trench	36cSW4 Rouvroy	U 26 c
Unusual Post [1918]	28SW4 Ploegsteert	U 8 d 3.1
Unwise Tower	28SW4 Ploegsteert	U 10 a 0.7
Up Trench	36cSW4 Rouvroy	U 25 a
Upnor Wood	62cNW3 Vaux	G 1 d, 7 b
Upper Bond Street	28NW4 & NE3 Zillebeke	I 18 c
Upper Cross [Monument]	62bSW3 St Quentin	S 10 d
Upper Cut [Sept 1915]	36cNW1 La Bassée	A 9 a
Upper Horwich Street	57dSE4 Ovillers	W 12, a, b, X 7 a
Upper Lovers Lane [Sept 1915]	36cNW1 La Bassée	A 15 d
Upper Lovers Walk [May 1915, Cuinchy]	36cNW1 La Bassée	A 15 d
Upper Oosthoek Farm	28NW4 Ypres	I 33 c 75.05
Upper Road	28NW2 St Julien	C 14 c
Upton Quarry	51bSW4 Bullecourt	O 35 c
Upton Trench	51bSW4 Bullecourt	O 35 c, U 5 a, b
Upton Trench [1918]	57dSE1 & 2 Beaumont	Q 29 c
Upton Wood	51bSW4 Bullecourt	O 35 c, d, U 5 a, b
Upton Wood Cemetery	51bSW4 Bullecourt	U 5 b 5.5
Ur Trench	57dNE1 & 2 Fonquevillers	E 24 c
Ural Trench	57dNE1 & 2 Fonquevillers	E 24 a, c
Uranus [German M.G. Post]	51bSW4 Bullecourt	U 14 b 25.65
Uranus Trench	62cSW3 Vermandovillers	S 9 c, 15 a
Uriah Street	57dNE3 & 4 Hébuterne	K 27 b
Uriah Trench	57dNE3 & 4 Hébuterne	K 28 c
Urn Farm	20SE2 Hooglede	R 14 d 95.68
Urvillers [village]	66cNW1 Grugies / 2 Itancourt	B 27, 28, H 3, 4
Urvillers, Bois d'	66cNW2 Itancourt / 4 Berthenicourt	H 6 a, b, c, d
Useful Lane	28SW4 Ploegsteert	U 10 b, 11 a
Useful Support	28SW4 Ploegsteert	U 10 b, 11 a
Usher Road	28SW2 Wytschaete	N 29 d, 35 b, 36 a
Usher Trench	51bSW4 Bullecourt	U 9 c, d, 10 c
Ushers Houses	28NE2 Moorslede	F 7 a 2.0
Usk Trench	57dNE1 & 2 Fonquevillers	E 23 d, 24 c
Uskub Trench	62cNW4 Péronne	I 2 d, 8 b
Uslar Trench	62cNW2 Bouchavesnes	C 28 c, I 4 a
Usna Hill	57dSE4 Ovillers	W 18 d, 24 b, X 13 c, 19 a
Usna Redoubt	57dSE4 Ovillers	W 18 d, 24 b
Usna Valley	57dSE4 Ovillers	W 23, 24
Usna-Tara Hill	57dSE4 Ovillers	W 18, 24, 30, X 13, 19, 25
Uvula Trench	28SW4 Ploegsteert	U 24 a, c
Uxbridge Road	57dSE1 & 2 Beaumont	Q 16 b, d
Uxe Farm	27SE4 Meteren	X 14 c 7.2
V.A.D. Avenue [1918]	57dNE3 & 4 Hébuterne	L 1 c, 7 a
V.C. Avenue	36SW1 Aubers	N 2 c, d, 8 b, 9 a
V.C. Corner	36SW1 Aubers	N 2 c 8.1
V.C. Road [road]	28SW2 Wytschaete	N 22 a, b, 23 a, b
Vacant Alley	57cSE2 Gonnelieu	R 16 d, 22 a, b
Vacant Trench	28SE3 Comines	V 15 a, b, d
Vacation Farm	20SE3 Westroosebeke	V 30 a 1.6
Vache, Boyau de la	62cNW3 Vaux	G 28 b
Vacher Farm	20SE3 Westroosebeke	V 26 d 8.3
Vaches Wood	36aNE1 Morbecque / 3 Haverskerque	J 5 b, c, d, 6 a, c, d, 11 b, 12 a
Vacillating Trench	28SE3 Comines	V 19 d, 20 c, 25 a, b
Vacquerie Support, la	57cSE2 Gonnelieu	R 16 a, c, d, 22 b

Name	Map Sheet	Map Reference
Vacquerie Trench, la	57cSE2 Gonnelieu	R 15 d
Vadencourt [village]	57dSW [4 Toutencourt]	U 21 d, 27 b
Vadencourt East [post]	62cSE2 Vermand	R 17 a
Vadencourt North [post]	62cSE2 Vermand	R 11 c
Vadencourt West [post]	62cSE2 Vermand	R 11 c
Vagabond Avenue	28SE3 Comines	V 19 a, c, d
Vagabond Trench	28SE3 Comines	V 13 b, 14 a, c
Vagrant / Vagrants Row	28SE3 Comines	V 19 a, b, 20 a
Vague Trench	28SE3 Comines	V 1 b
Vague Trench	66dNW1 Punchy	A 29 c
Vain Villa	20SE2 Hooglede	R 11 c 7.7
Vair [light rly locality, 1917-18]	28NW4 Ypres	I 31 c
Vaire Trench [1918]	62dSE [1 Hamel]	P 14 b, d
Vaire Wood	62dSE [1 Hamel]	P 14 b, d, 20 b
Val de-Maison, le [hamlet]	57dSW [1 Puchevillers]	M 36 a, b
Val Dion Support	57dSW [1 Puchevillers / 2 Raincheval]	N 3 b, 4 a, b
Val Dion Trench	57dSW [1 Puchevillers / 2 Raincheval]	N 4 b, c, d
Val Vion [Beauquesne]	57dSW [2 Raincheval]	N 4 central
Vale House	28NE1 Zonnebeke	D 7 b 99.82
Vale Street	62cNE2 Epéhy	F 12 c
Vale Trench	28NE1 Zonnebeke	D 7 b, 8 a
Vale, Rue [road in Calonne]	36cSW1 Lens	M 14 d
Valenciennes Alley	62cSW3 Vermandovillers	S 8 a
Valendu Trench	66cNW1 Grugies	A 4 b, d
Valentin Alley [1918]	66eNW [2 Thennes]	B 17 c, 22 b, 23 a
Valentine House	28NE4 Dadizeele	L 10 d 5.8
Valentine Trench	57dNE3 & 4 Hébuterne	K 23 a
Valerie Wood	62dSE [2 Proyart]	Q 28 a
Vallade Corner	57dNE3 & 4 Hébuterne	K 34 d
Vallade Trench	57dNE3 & 4 Hébuterne	K 34 a, b, d
Vallée Mulâtre, la	57bSE [4 Wassigny]	W 23 d, 24 c, 29 b
Vallée, Tranchée de la	70dSW [2 Coucy-le-Château]	O 2 a
Valley Avenue	57dNE1 & 2 Fonquevillers	K 3 a
Valley Copse	57cSE3 Sorel-le-Grand	V 9 a, b
Valley Cottages	28NW4 & NE3 Zillebeke	I 23 c, d
Valley Cross Roads	36cNW3 Loos	G 35 c
Valley of Death [between Fricourt Fm & Bazentin]	57cSW3 Long'val/57dSE4 Ovillers/ 62dNE2 Méaulte	S 14c, 19 b,d, 20a, X 28c, 29c,d, F 5b
Valley Posts	62cNE2 Epéhy	F 29 d, L 5 b
Valley Road	51bSW4 Bullecourt	U 8 c
Valley Support	51bSW4 Bullecourt	U 20 d
Valley Support	57cNE4 Marcoing	L 31 c, d
Valley Support	62cNW1 Maricourt	A 3 c
Valley Trench	51bSW4 Bullecourt	U 20 b, d, 21 c
Valley Trench	57cNE4 Marcoing	L 31 c, d
Valley Trench	57dNE1 & 2 Fonquevillers / 3 & 4 Hébuterne	K 2 a, b, d, 8 b
Valley Trench	57dSE4 Ovillers / 62dNE2 Méaulte	X 29 c, d, F 5 b
Valley Trench	62cNE2 Epéhy	L 5 b
Valley Trench	62cNW1 Maricourt	A 3 c, d, 9 a, b
Valley Trench [1918]	51cSE4 Blaireville	X 28 a, b, 29 a
Valley Trench [1918]	57dSE3 [Bouzincourt]	W 25 d
Valley Wood	51bNE3 Noyelle-sous-Bellonne	J 19 b, d, 20 a, c
Valley Wood	51cSE4 Blaireville	X 22 d, 23 c
Vallona Alley	66cNW2 Itancourt	B 24 b

Name	Map Sheet	Map Reference
Vallulart Wood	57cSE1 Bertincourt	P 26 d, 27 c, 32 b, 33 a, b
Valogne Trench	66cSW2 Vendeuil	O 13 a, c
Valour Farm	20SE3 Westroosebeke	V 29 d 8.6
Valse Trench	62cNW4 Péronne	I 32 d
Valuation Houses	20SE3 Westroosebeke	V 24 a 1.5
Valuet Trench	62cNW4 Péronne	I 32 d
Vamoose [railway locality, 1918]	28NE1 Zonnebeke	D 25 b, 26 a
Vamoose Siding	28NE1 Zonnebeke	D 26 a 0.6
Vamp Alley	36aSE3 Gonnehem	V 29 c, d
Vamp Trench	51bNW3 Arras	G 18 c
Vampir [farm]	28NE1 Zonnebeke	D 26 a 0.5
Vampir [locality, 1917-18]	28NE1 Zonnebeke	D 25 b, 26 a
Vampire [locality, 1917-18]	28SW2 Wytschaete	O 3 c, d
Vampire Farm	20NW4 Dixmude	I 24 c
Van Dyck Farm	20SE3 Westroosebeke	V 8 b 7.7
Van Exhem Farm	28NW1 Elverdinghe	B 7 b 9.8
Van Eycke Farm	20SW3 Oostvleteren	T 3 c 3.9
Van Horn	28SW2 Wytschaete	N 17 d, 18 c
Van Hove Farm	28SW2 Wytschaete	O 22 a 9.3
Van Isackere Farm	28NE1 Zonnebeke	D 21 a 2.6
Van Lane	62bNW1 Gouy	A 13 b
Van Meulen [farm & pillboxes]	28NE1 Zonnebeke	D 15 a 75.70
Van Trench	51bNW3 Arras	G 18 c
Van Tunnel	28SW2 Wytschaete	N 17 d, 23 b
Van Way	28SW2 Wytschaete	N 23 b, 24 a
Van Way	36cNW3 Loos	G 35 d
Vanackert / Vanaekert Farm	28NW2 St Julien	C 4 d 1.1
Vancouver [farm & pillbox]	28NW2 St Julien	C 6 d 2.3
Vancouver Avenue	28SW4 Ploegsteert	U 16 c, d, 21 b, 22 a
Vancouver Avenue	36NW2 Armentières	C 28 b
Vancouver Camp	28NW3 Poperinghe	H 14 a, c
Vancouver Farm	28NW3 Poperinghe	H 14 a 3.3
Vancouver Line [light rly]	36cSW3 Vimy	S 18 b, c, d, T 7 b, c, d, 8 a
Vancouver Railway [light rly]	28SW4 Ploegsteert	U 19 b, c, d, 20 a, b, 21 a
Vancouver Road [road]	36cSW3 Vimy / 4 Rouvroy / 51bNW1 Roclincourt	T 22 a, c, 28 a, c, B 3 b, 4 a
Vancouver Road British Cemetery	36cSW4 Rouvroy	T 28 a 4.6
Vancouver Street, & Avenue	28NW4 & NE3 Zillebeke	I 24 d
Vancouver Trench	57dSE2 Beaumont	R 18 c, 23 b, 24 a
Vandamme Farm	28SW2 Wytschaete	N 17 d 60.15
Vandamme Hill	28SW2 Wytschaete	N 18 c, 24 a
Vandenberghe Farm	28SW2 Wytschaete	N 18 c
Vandromme Farm	28NW1 Elverdinghe	A 17 b 2.8
Vane Alley	36aSE3 Gonnehem	V 30 b
Vanguard [1918]	28NE1 Zonnebeke	D 26 a
Vanguard Farm	20SE2 Hooglede	Q 16 c 6.4
Vanheule / Van Heule Farm	28NW2 St Julien	C 17 d 3.6
Vanilla Farm	27SE2 Berthen	R 35 a 3.5
Vanity Farm	28NE2 Moorslede	F 11 a
Vanity House	20SE3 Westroosebeke	V 29 c 5.6
Vannes, Boyau de	70dSW [4 Vauxaillon]	U 28 a
Vanzag Alley	36aSE3 Gonnehem	V 27 b, d
Vapeur Inn, La	20NW4 Dixmude	I 7 a 8.2
Vapeur Trench	20NW4 Dixmude	I 7 c

Name	Map Sheet	Map Reference
Vapour Farm	20SE3 Westroosebeke	V 29 c 2.7
Varax Trench	62bSW3 St Quentin / 66cNW1 Grugies	S 29 d, A 5 b
Vardar Alley	66cNW2 Itancourt	B 24 d
Vardar Trench	62cNW4 Péronne	I 7 c, d
Varlet Farm	20SE3 Westroosebeke	V 27 d 8.1
Varna Farm	28NW2 St Julien	C 4 a 5.1
Varna Trench	62cSW2 Barleux	O 2 c, 8 a
Varna Trench	66cSW2 Vendeuil	O 3 c, 8 b, 9 a
Varna, Tranchée de	62cSW1 & 2 Belloy	O 2 c, 7 d, 8 a, c
Varsity Farm	28NE2 Moorslede	F 11 a 00.05
Vase Avenue	51bNW1 Roclincourt	A 15 d, 20 b, 21 a
Vassal Farm	28SW3 Bailleul	S 10 d 4.6
Vasseau Lane / Boyau Vasseau	36cSW1 Lens	M 25 b, d
Vasset, Bois	62cSW3 & 4 Marchélepot	S 6 c, 12 a
Vat Alley	57cSW3 Longueval	T 13 a, b
Vat Cottages	20SE3 Westroosebeke	V 29 a 5.9
Vat Trench	51bNW3 Arras	G 18 c
Vatican Farm	28NE2 Moorslede	F 19 b 75.80
Vats, The	36NW2 Armentières	C 17 a
Vauban Avenue [trench board way]	28NW4 Ypres	H 30 c to H 36 b
Vauban Camp	28NW4 Ypres	H 30 c
Vauban Farm	20SW4 Bixschoote	T 29 b, 30 a
Vauban Trench	57dNE3 & 4 Hébuterne	K 22 a, b, d
Vauban, Par.	70dSW [2 Coucy-le-Château]	O 20 c
Vaucelle Alley	66cSW2 Vendeuil	O 9 d, 10 b, c, d, 11 a, 15 a, b
Vaucelles [hamlet]	57bSW1 Bantouzelle	M 15 d
Vaucelles Copse	57bSW1 Bantouzelle	M 21 b
Vaucelles Wood	57bSW1 Bantouzelle	M 21, 22, 27, 28, 34
Vaucour Trench [1918]	62dSW [4 Cachy]	U 21 c
Vaudeville Trench	28SE3 Comines	V 22 c, d
Vaudricourt [village]	36bNE [1 Labeuvrière] / 2 Beuvry	E 27 d, 28 c, K 3 b, 4 a
Vaudricourt Locality	36bNE [1] / 2 Beuvry / [3] / 4 Noeux-les-Mines	E 27, 28, K 3, 4, 9, 10
Vaughan's Redoubt [Contalmaison]	57dSE4 Ovillers	X 17 c
Vaulx Trench	57cNW2 Vaulx-Vraucourt	C 20, 21, 27-29, 35, 36
Vaulx Wood Switch	57cNW2 Vaulx-Vraucourt	C 22 c, d, 23 c, d, 27 b, 28 a
Vaulx, Bois de	57cNW2 Vaulx-Vraucourt	C 27 b, c, d
Vaulx-Vraucourt [village]	57cNW2 Vaulx-Vraucourt	C 25 d, 26 a, c, d
Vauthiers Trench [1918]	66cNW [2 Thennes / 4 Morisel]	H 4 a, b, c
Vautours Trench	57cSE3 Sorel-le-Grand	V 10 c, 16 a, c
Vaux [village]	62cNW3 Vaux	G 4 d, 10 b
Vaux Alley	57cSW4 Combles	U 22 d, 28 b, 29 a
Vaux Hangar [wood]	62cNW3 Vaux	G 4 d, 10 b
Vaux Post	57cSW3 Longueval	S 3 b
Vaux School	62cNW3 Vaux	G 10 d
Vaux Trench / Tranchée de Vaux	62cSW2 Barleux	N 29 d, 35 a, b
Vaux Wood	62cNW3 Vaux	G 4 c
Vaux Wood Trench	57cSW4 Combles	U 28 b, d, 29 a, c
Vaux, Bois des	57cSW4 Combles / 62cNW2 Bouchavesnes	U 29, 30, C 5, 6
Vaux-Andigny [village]	57bSE [3 Busigny]	W 19, 20
Vauxhall	36NW4 Bois Grenier	I 10 b
Vauxhall [light rly locality, 1917-18]	28NW4 Ypres	H 36 b
Vauxhall Camp	28SW3 Bailleul	S 18 d, 24 b
Vauxhall Farm	28SE1 Wervicq	P 32 b 5.6

Name	Map Sheet	Map Reference
Vauxhall Quarry	57bSW3 Honnecourt	T 25 a 8.5
Vauxhall Villa	28SW3 Bailleul	S 18 d 2.3
Veal Cottages	20SE3 Westroosebeke	V23 c 7.2
Veal Lane [1918]	57dNE2 & 57cNW1 Courcelles	F 9 c
Veal Trench	51bNW3 Arras	G 18 c
Veal Trench	57cSW3 Longueval	T 3 c, 9 a
Veau, le [farm]	36NW1 Steenwerck	B 14 a 65.25
Vee Bend [in road, & road junction]	20SW4 Bixschoote	U 11 d 10.63
Vega Farm	28NW1 Elverdinghe	A 24 a 9.9
Vegetable Farm	20SE3 Westroosebeke	V 29 d 8.3
Veguier Mill, le (Ruins)	62cNE4 Roisel	L 34 d
Vehicle Farm	28SE1 Wervicq	P 22 a 90.55
Veld Farm [Veldmolen]	28NE2 Moorslede	F 7 c 75.25
Velde Wood	28NE2 Moorslede	E 5 a, b
Veldhoek	28NE3 Gheluvelt	J 15 c
Veldhoek [place name]	20SW4 Bixschoote	U 4 d
Veldt [light rly locality, 1917-18]	28NW4 Ypres	I 31 a
Veldt Farm	20SE3 Westroosebeke	V 23 d 7.5
Velduden Trench [Veldhoek]	28NE3 Gheluvelt	J 15 d, 21 b
Veleurs Bridge	57bSW1 Bantouzelle	M 20 c 9.8
Velox [light rly locality, 1917-18]	28NW4 Ypres	I 32 b, 33 a
Velox Farm	20SE2 Hooglede	R 30 c 3.2
Velvet Copse	20SE3 Westroosebeke	V 18 c, d
Vendée Alley	66cNW1 Grugies	B 8 c, d
Vendette [locality, 1917-18]	28SW2 Wytschaete	O 9 a
Vendeuil Alley	66cSW2 Vendeuil / 4 La Fère	N 24, 29, 30, 34, 35, T 4
Vendeuil Fort	66cSW2 Vendeuil	N 18 c
Vendeuil Redoubt	66cSW2 Vendeuil	N 23 b, d, 24 a
Vendhuille Trench	62bNW1 Gouy	A 2 a
Vendin Alley	36cNW3 Loos	G 24 a, b
Vendin Lane	36cNW4 Pont-à-Vendin	H 23 c
Vendin Post	36cNW3 Loos	H 19 a 2.5
Vendin Road [road]	36cNW3 Loos	H 20 d, 21 c, d
Vengeance Farm	20NW4 Dixmude	I 14 b 6.6
Venise Trench	62cSW2 Barleux	N 24 b, O 19 a
Venise, Boyau	62cSW1 Dompierre	M 4 d
Venise, Tranchée de	62cSW1 & 2 Belloy	N 24 b, O 19 a
Venison Farm	20SE3 Westroosebeke	V 24 b 2.1
Venison Trench	20SE3 Westroosebeke	V 30 b
Venizelos Alley	66dNW1 Punchy	A 29 a, c, d, G 5 b, 6 a, b, d
Venn Alley	36aSE3 Gonnehem	V 30 a
Venter Tunnel	36cNW3 Loos	G 35 d
Venture Farm	20SE3 Westroosebeke	V 30 a 4.1
Venus Alley / Trench	57cSW2 Villers-au-Flos	N 10 c
Venus Cot.	28SW4 Ploegsteert	U 11 c 7.0
Venus Trench	62cSW3 Vermandovillers	S 14 a, c, d
Ver Wood Trench	62cNW1 Maricourt / 3 Vaux	H 3 a, c
Verbeek Farm	28NE3 Gheluvelt	J 14 b 95.53
Verbranden Road [road]	28NW4 & NE3 Zillebeke	I 28 a, b, d
Verbrandenmolen	28NW4 & NE3 Zillebeke	I 28 d 7.5
Verbrandenmolen Trench	28NW4 & NE3 Zillebeke	I 28 d, 29 c
Verbrandon [sic; light rly locality, 1917-18]	28NW4 Ypres	I 28 c, d
Vercingetorix Trench	57dNE3 & 4 Hébuterne	K 22 a, c, 28 a
Vercingetorix, Tranchée	70dSW [2 Coucy-le-Château]	O 13 d

Name	Map Sheet	Map Reference
Vercoe Trench	57dNE3 & 4 Hébuterne	K 16 a
Verdict Farm	28NE2 Moorslede	F 11 d 3.5
Verdrel Junction [light rly]	36bSE2 Boyeffles	Q 16 d
Verdun Alley	66cNW2 Itancourt	H 6 a, b
Verdun Trench	66cNW2 Itancourt	H 5 d
Verdun Trench	70dNW4 St Gobain	H 30 b, d
Verdun Trench [1918]	62dSW [4 Cachy]	T 18 d, 24 a, b, c
Verdun, Tranchée de	62cNW3 Vaux	G 29 c, 34 b
Vere Street	57dSE2 Beaumont	R 22 d, 28 b
Vergeld Farm	20SE2 Hooglede	Q 28 a 80.25
Vergelderhoek [hamlet]	20SE2 Hooglede	Q 28 a
Verger Farm	20SW4 Bixschoote	T 5 d 25.32
Verger Trench	62cSW3 Vermandovillers	S 13 d, 14 c, 20 a
Verger, Boyau de	51bNW1 Roclincourt	A 3 a
Verger, Redoute du	62cNW3 Vaux	G 33 b
Verger, Redoute Nord du	62cNW3 Vaux	G 27 d
Vergers Trench	20NW4 Dixmude	I 32 b, d, 33 a
Verguier, le [village]	62cNE4 Roisel	L 34 a, c
Verhaege Farm	28SW2 Wytschaete	O 22 b 8.1
Verhaest Farm	28SW2 Wytschaete	O 10 d 10.25
Veritas Farm	20SE2 Hooglede	R 1 d 9.3
Verity Crossing [level crossing]	36aNE2 Vieux Berquin	F 5 c 2.6
Verketst Farm	20SE2 Hooglede	R 9 a 9.6
Verlorenhoek	28NW2 St Julien	C 30 c 1.1
Vermand Alley [1918]	62dSE [4 Harbonnières]	X 6 c, 12 a
Vermandovillers [village]	62cSW3 & 4 Marchélepot	S 9, 10, 15, 16
Vermandovillers Alley	62cSW3 Vermandovillers	S 7 b, 8 a
Vermelles [town]	36cNW3 Loos	G 8 a, b, c, d
Vermelles Branch	36cNW3 Loos	G 20 c, 26 a
Vermelles Line	36cNW3 Loos	G 24 a, b [area of]
Vermouth Corner [road junction]	36aNE4 Merville	K 22 a 2.2
Vermouth Villa	28NW1 Elverdinghe	B 26 a 2.5
Vernaege Farm	28SW2 Wytschaete	O 22 b 8.1
Verne Road [road]	28SW2 Wytschaete	O 21 b, c, d
Vernon [Trench]	36cSW3 Vimy	S 28 a
Vernon Road [road]	36cSW4 Rouvroy	U 1 d, 2 c
Vernon Street	62cNW1 Maricourt	A 9 a
Vernon Trench	36bSE4 & 36cSW3 Givenchy	S 28 a
Verona [light rly locality, 1917-18]	28NW4 Ypres	H 36 b
Verquigneul [village]	36bNE4 Noeux-les-Mines	F 25 c, d, L 1 a
Verquin [village]	36bNE [1] / 2 Beuvry	E 28 d, 29 c, K 4 b, 5 a
Verquin, Cité de [miners' cottages]	36bNE4 Noeux-les-Mines	K 5 d, 6 c
Verret Ride [trench]	28NW4 & NE3 Zillebeke	I 29 a, c
Verrier Trench	62cNW4 Péronne	I 32 c, d
Verrier, le	36aNE2 Vieux Berquin	F 24 c
Verrier, le [hamlet]	36NW1 Steenwerck	A 19 d
Verse Cott.	20SE3 Westroosebeke	V 24 b 3.4
Versteque Post	12SW1 Nieuport	N 32 a
Vert Alley	36cNW1 La Bassée	A 17, 18, 24
Vert Bois / Greenwood / Green Wood Lane [rd]	36aSE4 Locon	Q 35 d, W 5 a, b, c, 10 b, 11 a
Vert Galand Aerodrome	57dSW [1 Puchevillers]	M 9 d
Vert Galand Farm	57dSW [1 Puchevillers]	M 9 d
Vert Galant Trench	70dNW4 St Gobain	I 33 b, d
Vert Halo	51bNW1 Roclincourt	A 4 c

Name	Map Sheet	Map Reference
Vert Support	36cNW1 La Bassée	A 18 b, d
Vert Trench	36cNW1 La Bassée	A 18 b, d, 24 b
Vert Work	51bSW2 Vis-en-Artois	O 3 d, 9 b
Vert, Boyau	51bNW3 Arras	G 29 b, 30 a
Vertbois Road [road]	36aNE3 Haverskerque	K 26 a, c
Vertbois, le [farm]	36aNE3 Haverskerque	K 26 a 6.8
Verte House	28NW2 St Julien	C 1 a 5.5
Verte Mill Pond	28NW2 St Julien	C 1 b 0.8
Verte Rue	36aNE2 Vieux Berquin	E 29 c
Vertical Cott.	20SE3 Westroosebeke	V 18 b 40.35
Very Trench [1918]	57dNE2 & 57cNW1 Courcelles	F 22 d
Vesco Farm	36NW1 Steenwerck	B 27 a 6.9
Vesée Post, La	36NW4 Bois Grenier	I 13 c, d, 19 a, b
Vesper Farm	28NW1 Elverdinghe	A 14 d 1.6
Vesta Alley [at le Tailly! cf. Vesta Tilley]	36aSE3 Gonnehem	V 19 b, 20 a
Vesta Tilley Trench	36cSW3 Vimy	T 9 d, 10 c, 15 b
Vesta Trench	62cNE1 Liéramont	D 3 c, d, 8 b, 9 a
Vestry House	20SE3 Westroosebeke	V 18 b 1.9
Vesuvius [light rly locality, 1917-18]	28SW2 Wytschaete	O 3 c
Vesuvius Crater [Cambrin]	36cNW1 La Bassée	A 21 d
Vesuvius Crater [Havrincourt]	57cNE3 Hermies	K 27 c 2.8
Vet [sic] Alley [Vat]	57cSW3 Longueval	T 13 a, b
Vétry Wood Trench	62cNE1 Liéramont	D 10 a, c, 16 a
Vex Trench	51bNW3 Arras	G 18 c
Vexiau Track [1917-18]	20SW4 Bixschoote	O 32 d, U 1 b, d, 2 a
Via Gellia	28SW2 Wytschaete	N 23 c, d, 24 c
Via Padova [ride, Nieppe Forest]	36aNE3 Haverskerque	J 13 c, d, 14 a, b, c
Via Roma [ride, Nieppe Forest]	36aNE3 Haverskerque	J 17 d, 18 b, c, d, K 13 a
Vibration Trench	57cSE3 Sorel-le-Grand	V 6 b, d
Vic Alley	36aSE3 Gonnehem	V 28 d, 29 a, c
Vic O.P [1917-18]	51bNW1 Roclincourt	B 7 b 8.5
Vic Way	28SW4 Ploegsteert	U 17 b, d
Vicars Cott.	20SE3 Westroosebeke	V 18 b 7.9
Vicar's Lane	28NW2 St Julien	C 20 b, 21 a
Vichy Trench	66cNW1 Grugies	B 7 c, 13 a
Vick Lane	62bNW1 Gouy	A 13 d
Victim Copse	27SE2 Berthen	R 23 b, 24 a
Victoire Trench, & Crater	51bNW1 Roclincourt	A 16 c
Victoria Camp	28SW1 Kemmel	M 17 b
Victoria Copse	51bNW4 Fampoux	I 28 d
Victoria Cross Roads	62bNW3 Bellicourt	G 33 a 25.70
Victoria Dump	36cSW3 Vimy	T 13 b 5.7
Victoria Dump [light rly]	36cSW3 Vimy	T 13 b
Victoria Farm	28NE1 Zonnebeke	D 7 b 6.1
Victoria House	28NE1 Zonnebeke	D 7 b 3.1
Victoria Road	36cSW3 Vimy	N 32 d
Victoria Station	36cNW3 Loos	G 20 d
Victoria Street	51bNW1 Roclincourt / 3 Arras	G 5 b, 6 c
Victoria Street	57dSE1 & 2 Beaumont	Q 17 c
Victoria Street Tunnel	28SW2 Wytschaete	O 2 a
Victoria Trench [later Bully Trench]	57cSW3 Longueval	T 15 c, 21 a
Victory Copse	62bSW4 Homblières	U 23 b
Victory Farm	20SW4 Bixschoote	U 2 c 5.7
Victory Lane [trench]	57cSE2 Gonnelieu	R 9 b

Name	Map Sheet	Map Reference
Victory Post	57dSE2 Beaumont	Q 12 c
Victory Post [1917-18]	20SW4 Bixschoote	U 2 c 9.4
Vieille Chapelle [village]	36aSE2 Lestrem	R 34 a
Vieille Chapelle Post	36aSE2 Lestrem	R 28 d
Vieilles Maisons	28NW2 St Julien	C 6 b 4.3
Vienna Redoubt	57cSW4 Combles	U 15 d
Vienna Road	57dNE1 & 2 Fonquevillers	E 9 c, 15 a, c, d
Vienna Trench	57cSW4 Combles	U 15 d, 16 c
Vienna Trench	66cNW1 Grugies	B 9 a, c, d
Vienne, Tranchée de la	70dSW [2 Coucy-le-Château]	O 33 a
Vier Crossing	20SE4 Roulers	W 28 c 30.85
Vierge, Boyau	62cNW3 Vaux	G 28 d, 29 c
Vierhouck [hamlet]	36aNE4 Merville	K 11 b, d, 12 a
Vierstraat Line	28SW1 Kemmel / 2 Wytschaete	N 11 c, 17 a
Vierstraat Switch	28SW2 Wytschaete	N 11 c, 17 a
Vieux Berquin [village]	36aNE2 Vieux Berquin	E 17 d, 23 b, 24 a, c
Vieux Berquin Railhead / Refilling Point	36aNE2 Vieux Berquin	E 18 d, F 13 a, b, c, d
Vieux Chien [farm]	28NE3 Gheluvelt	J 25 d 1.1
Vieux Corons, Boyau des [West Ham Lane]	36cSW1 Lens	M 8 c, d, 14 b, 15 a
View Alley	57cSE4 Villers-Guislain	R 34 d, 35 c, X 4 b
View Farm	28NW2 St Julien	C 21 c 9.7
View Lane	36NW2 Armentières	C 10 b
View Trench	51bNW3 Arras	G 18 c, d
View Trench	57dNE3 & 4 Hébuterne	K 33 c, d
Vigil Farm	20SE3 Westroosebeke	V 18 a 8.0
Vignette Wood	66eNW [2 Thennes]	C 18 b, d
Vigo Street	28NW4 & NE3 Zillebeke	I 24 d
Vigo Street	28SW2 Wytschaete	N 29 c, 35 a
Vigo Street	36cNW3 Loos	G 4 d, 5 c
Vigo Street	36SW1 Aubers	M 23 c, 28 c, 29 a
Vijfwegen [hamlet]	28NE4 Dadizeele	K 24 a
Vijfwegen [road jct]	28NE4 Dadizeele	K 24 a 45.45
Vijverhoek [light rly locality, 1917-18]	28NW4 Ypres	H 29 a
Vijverhoek [place name]	28NW4 Ypres	H 29 c
Vilain, Bois	36cSW4 Rouvroy	U 19 b
Vile Trench	28SE3 Comines	V 13 c
Villa Post	62cNE4 Roisel	L 12 c 20.75
Villa Seule Cabaret	28NW1 Elverdinghe	A 24 b 7.4
Villa Trench	57cSW3 Longueval	S 7 d, 13 b
Villa Wood	57dSE4 Ovillers	X 12 c
Village Alley [Warlencourt-Eaucourt]	57dSE2 & 57cSW1 Le Sars	M 10 b, d
Village Lane	57cSE2 Gonnelieu	R 22 a, b
Village Line	36bSE2 Boyeffles	R 12 c, 18 a
Village Line	36cNW1 La Bassée	A 26 b, d
Village Line	36SW3 Richebourg / 36cNW1 La Bassée / 3 Loos	S 20, 25, A 2 to 26, G 2 to 29
Village Line Switch	36cNW3 Loos	G 28 b, d, 29 a, 34 a, b
Village Support	57cSE2 Gonnelieu	Q 12 b
Village Trench	36cSW4 Rouvroy / 51bNW2 Oppy	U 25 d, C 1 b
Village Trench / Trenches [Givenchy, Feb 1915]	36cNW1 La Bassée	A 9 a, c
Village Trench [Fresnoy]	36cSW4 Rouvroy	U 25 a, c, d, C 1 b
Village Trench [Puisieux-au-Mont]	57dNE3 & 4 Hébuterne	L 14 c, 20 a, c, 26 a
Village Trench [Vis-en-Artois]	51bSW2 Vis-en-Artois	O 22 a, c, d
Village Wood	62cNW4 Péronne	I 25 a, c

Name	Map Sheet	Map Reference
Villain Alley	66cNW2 Itancourt	C 25 b
Villain Alley	66cNW4 Berthenicourt	H 24 b
Villain Trench	62bSW3 St Quentin	S 10 d, 11 a, c, 16 b
Villar Trench, de	66cNW1 Grugies	A12 b, B 7 a
Villbeau 1st Reserve [1918]	57dSW [1 Puchevillers]	N 8 c, 13 d, 14 a, c, 19 b
Villbeau 1st Support [1918]	57dSW [1 Puchevillers]	N 14 a, b, c, 20 a
Villbeau 2nd Reserve [1918]	57dSW [1 Puchevillers]	N 7 d, 8 c, 13 b, d
Villbeau 2nd Support [1918]	57dSW [1 Puchevillers]	N 14 a, c, 20 a
Villbeau Trench [1918]	57dSW [1 Puchevillers]	N 14 b, d, 20 b, d
Ville, Bois de la	51bNW1 Roclincourt	B 1 c, d, 7 b, 8 a
Villecourt [village]	66dNW2 Morchain	C 24 a, c
Villemay Trench	62bSW1 Gricourt	M 20 b
Villeret [village]	62cNE4 Roisel	L 11 d, 12 c, 17 b, 18 a
Villeret Lane [road]	62cNE4 Roisel / 62bNW3 Bellicourt	L 12 c, G 7 d
Villeret Lane [trench]	62cNE4 Roisel / 62bNW3 Bellicourt	L 12 c, G 7 d
Villeret Posts	62cNE4 Roisel	L 18 a, c
Villeret South [post]	62cNE4 Roisel	L 18 a 0.7
Villers Farm	28SE1 Wervicq	P 9 d 0.1
Villers Farm [Viller Outreaux]	57bSW3 Honnecourt	T 20 b 80.65
Villers Hill	57cSE4 Villers-Guislain	X 24, 8, 9, 14, 15
Villers Line [1918]	62dSW [2 Villers-Bretonneux]	O 24, 30 b, c, d, 36 a
Villers Outreaux [village]	57bSW3 Honnecourt / 4 Serain	T 9 a, b, c, d, 10 c, 14 b, d, 15 a, b, c, d
Villers Outreaux Ravine	57bSW4 Serain	T 4 c, d, 10 a, b, c, d, 16 a, b
Villers Ration Dump [light rly siding]	36bSE4 Carency	X 13 c, 19 a
Villers Street	57dNE3 & 4 Hébuterne	K 15 d, 22 a
Villers Switch [1918]	62dSW [2 Villers-Bretonneux]	O 27, 28, 29 a, b, 30 a, c
Villers System [1918]	62dSW [2 Villers-Bretonneux]	O 11, 17, 18, 24
Villers Trench	57cSE4 Villers-Guislain	X 2 a, c, d, 8 b, d
Villers-au-Flos [village]	57cSW2 Villers-au-Flos	O 7 b, c, d, 13 b
Villers-Bocage [village]	57dSW [3 Talmas] / 62dNW [1]	S 26, A 2
Villers-Bretonneux [village]	62dSW [2 Villers-Bretonneux]	O 28, 29, 30, 34, 35
Villers-Carbonnel [village]	62cSW2 Barleux	N 30 c, d, 36 a, b
Villers-Chatel [light rly siding]	36bSE3 [Mingoval]	W 19 b, d
Villeselve Aerodrome [German, 1918]	66dSE [4]	W 10 c
Villorba Camp [Nieppe Forest]	36aNE3 Haverskerque	J 15 c, d
Vim Trench	51bNW3 Arras	G 18 d
Vimy [light rly locality, 1917-18]	28NW4 Ypres	I 25 d
Vimy [village]	36cSW3 Vimy	S 24 d, 30 b, T 19 a, c, d, 25 a
Vimy Ridge	36cSW3 Vimy / 51bNW1 Roclincourt	extensive
Vince Street	28NW4 & NE3 Zillebeke	I 22 b, 23 a, b, 24 a, b
Vincent Street / Avenue	36cSW3 Vimy	S 14 d, 15 c, 20 b
Vinchy Lock	57bSW1 Bantouzelle	M 5 c 45.65
Vindictive Cross Roads	20SE3 Westroosebeke	V 30 d 3.7
Vindictive Trench	28SE3 Comines	V 28 a, b, c
Vine Avenue	51bSW2 Vis-en-Artois	N 4, 5, 6, O 7, 8
Vine Corner [trench junction]	28SW2 Wytschaete	N 35 a 85.75
Vine Cott.	20SE3 Westroosebeke	V 29 c 8.4
Vine Lane	51bSW2 Vis-en-Artois	N 12 b, O 7 a, b
Vine Street	36SW3 Richebourg	S 10 c
Vine Street [road; Lovie Chateau]	27NE2 Proven	F 16 d
Vinegar [locality, 1917-18]	28SW2 Wytschaete	O 3 b
Vinery [Potijze Chateau]	28NW2 St Julien	I 4 a 55.75
Vinke Buildings [De Vinke]	28NE2 Moorslede	F 6 c 0.6 to 3.4

Name	Map Sheet	Map Reference
Vintage Farm	36NW1 Steenwerck	A 22 b 9.6
Violaines Chateau	36cNW1 La Bassée	A 5 d 65.75
Violaines Trench	36cNW1 La Bassée	A 4 b, c, d, 5 a
Violet [light rly locality, 1917-18]	28NW4 Ypres	I 27 d, 28 c
Violet Farm	20SE2 Hooglede	R 2 d 8.7
Violet Lorraine [OP & possibly trench, Feb 1918]	51bNW1 Roclincourt	B 2 d 4.1
Violet Post	62cNE4 Roisel	L 12 c 40.35
Violet Trench	20SW3 Oostvleteren	T 3 c, 9 a
Violet Trench	36cNW1 La Bassée	A 4 b, d
Violin Farm	28NE4 Dadizeele	L 27 a 5.4
Viper Trench	51bNW4 Fampoux	H 34 c, d
Vipère, Bois	66eNE2 Vrély	F 28 b, 29 a
Vire Trench	66cSW2 Vendeuil	N 12 c, 18 a, c
Virgin Wood	62cNW3 Vaux	G 28 d, 34 b
Virginity Villa	28SW1 Kemmel	M 18 c 35.20
Virgo Cottage	28NW1 Elverdinghe	G 2 b 5.6
Virile Farm	20SE3 Westroosebeke	V 29 b 8.4
Virtue Farm	20SE3 Westroosebeke	V 30 a 0.1
Virtue Trench	28SW2 Wytschaete	O 2 d
Virus Villa	28SW3 Bailleul	S 22 a 60.25
Viry-Noureuil [trenches; front, support, reserve]	70dNW [1 Chauny]	A 4, 5, 10, 11, 16, 17
Vis Trench	51bSW2 Vis-en-Artois	O 17 a, c
Viscount Farm	28NE4 Dadizeele	L 27 d 60.35
Viscount Street	51bNW2 Oppy	B 24 a, b
Vis-en-Artois [village]	51bSW2 Vis-en-Artois	O 22 a, b, d, 23 a, c
Vis-en-Artois Switch	51bSW4 Bullecourt	U 6 a, b
Visit Trench	51bNW3 Arras	G 18 c
Vissec Avenue	51bNW1 Roclincourt	A 8, 9, 10, 13
Vissec Group [mine craters]	51bNW1 Roclincourt	A 10 c
Vistula Trench	51bNW1 Roclincourt	A 9 b
Vital Post	28SE3 Comines	V 4 c
Vitasse Lane [trench]	51bSW1 Neuville Vitasse	M 18 c, d, 24 b, N 19 a
Vitermont [NE of Englebelmer]	57dSE1 & 2 Beaumont	Q 19 b, 20 a
Vitermont Mill	57dSE1 & 2 Beaumont	Q 14 c 75.05
Vivier Mill	62dNE2 Méaulte	E 16 a 7.4
Vixen Trench	51bSE3 Cagnicourt	V 1 a, c, d
Vlamertinghe [village]	28NW3 Poperinghe	H 2 d, 3 c, 8 b, 9 a, b
Vlamertinghe Chateau [grounds]	28NW1 Elverdinghe	H 2 b, 3 a
Vlamertinghe Railhead / Refilling Point	28NW3 Poperinghe	H 9 b, 10 a
Vlamertinghe Switch [1918]	28NW3 Poperinghe	G 24, H 8, 13, 19
Vlampop Road, The	28NW3 Poperinghe / 4 Ypres	G 1 - 6, H 1, 2
Vlenvickhove [farm]	28SW1 Kemmel	M 13 b 6.0
Vocation Farm	20SE3 Westroosebeke	V 30 a 1.6
Vogel Trench	66dNW1 Punchy	A 28 d, 29 c
Vogue Farm	27NE4 Abeele	K 28 a 9.9
Vohitra Alley	66cNW4 Berthenicourt	I 8 c
Void Farm	20SE3 Westroosebeke	V 23 d 8.3
Void Trench	20SE3 Westroosebeke	V 23 d, 29 a, b, 30 a
Void Trench	51bNW3 Arras	G 18 c
Void Way	28SW4 Ploegsteert	U 17 c, d, 23 b
Voie Ferré/e Alley [by railway]	62cSW3 Vermandovillers	S 16 b, 17 a, b, 18 a, b, d
Volga Farm	28NE2 Moorslede	E 16 b 7.1
Volker Tunnel	51bNW1 Roclincourt	A 4, 5
Volley Farm	36aNE2 Vieux Berquin	E 28 a 5.8

Name	Map Sheet	Map Reference
Volnay House	28NW1 Elverdinghe	H 2 a 7.3
Volt Alley	36aSE3 Gonnehem	V 28 a, c
Volt Farm	20SE3 Westroosebeke	V 24 c1.7
Volt Trench	51bNW3 Arras	G 18 c
Volta Farm	27NE2 Proven	F 8 c 0.1
Voltigeur Farm	20SW4 Bixschoote	U 13 b
Voltigeurs Alley	70dNW4 St Gobain	H 30 d
Von Hügel Farm [formerly Von Kluck Farm]	28NW2 St Julien	C 23 d 1.5
Von Kluck Cots.	28NW2 St Julien	C 14 b 3.3
Von Kluck Farm [1915; later Von Hugel Farm]	28NW2 St Julien	C 23 d 1.5
Von Kluck Trench [1918]	66eNW [4 Morisel]	H 4 d, 10 a, b, c
Von Tirpitz Farm	28NE1 Zonnebeke	D 7 b 3.7
Von Werder House	28NW2 St Julien	C 10 b 2.5
Voormezeele [village]	28NW4 Ypres	I 31 c, d
Voormezeele Extension	28SW2 Wytschaete	O 1 d, 2 c
Voormezeele Junction [light rly, 1917-18]	28NW4 Ypres	I 31 a 7.3
Voormezeele Street	28SW2 Wytschaete	O 1 a, b, c
Voormezeele Switch	28NW4 & NE3 Zillebeke / SW2 Wytschaete	I 31 d, O 1 b, d
Vorststraat Cabaret, De	28SE1 Wervicq	P 9 b 95.85
Vosse Farm [Vossemolen]	28NE2 Moorslede	F 3 d 7.8
Vossemolen	28NE2 Moorslede	F 3 d, 4 c
Vote Trench	51bNW3 Arras	G 18 c
Vow Trench	20SE3 Westroosebeke	V 17 d
Vow Trench	51bNW3 Arras	G 18 c
Vox Alley	20SE3 Westroosebeke	V 24 c
Vox Farm	20SE3 Westroosebeke	V 30 a 05.75
Vox Support	20SE3 Westroosebeke	V 24 c, d
Vox Trench	20SE3 Westroosebeke	V 30 a
Vox Vrie [light rly sidings]	28NW1 Elverdinghe	A 9 d
Vox Vrie Farm	28NW1 Elverdinghe	A 15 b 2.4
Voyeau Alley	66cNW1 Grugies	B 8 c, d
Voyennes Aerodrome [German, 1918]	66dNE [3]	J 13 a
Vraignes Aerodrome [German, 1918]	62cSE1 Bouvincourt	Q 25 b, d, 26 a, c
Vraucourt [village]	57cNW2 Vaulx-Vraucourt	C 19 d, 25 b
Vraucourt Copse	57cNW2 Vaulx-Vraucourt	C 14 d, 15 c
Vraucourt Reserve	57cNW2 Vaulx-Vraucourt	C 13 c, d, 14 c
Vraucourt Switch	57cNW2 Vaulx-Vraucourt	C 15 d, 16 c, 20 b, 21 a, c
Vraucourt Trench	57cNW2 Vaulx-Vraucourt	B 24 b, C 13 d, 19 a, b, 20 a
Vrely Wood Trench	62cNE1 Liéramont	D 10 a, c, 16 c
Vroilandhoek	28SW2 Wytschaete	N 28 a 9.3
Vroilandhoek [farm]	28SW2 Wytschaete	N 28 a 7.3
Vulcain Trench	62cNE3 Buire	J 7 c, d, 13 a
Vulcain Trench	62cSW3 Vermandovillers	S 14 b, d
Vulcain Trench	66cNW4 Berthenicourt	I 8 c
Vulcan [German Pillbox]	51bSW4 Bullecourt	U 14 d 95.10
Vulcan [light rly locality, 1917-18]	28NW4 Ypres	I 33 d
Vulcan [lt rly locality NE of Pilckem 1917-18]	20SW4 Bixschoote	U 27 c
Vulcan Alley	51bSW4 Bullecourt	U 15 c, 20 b
Vulcan Alley	66cNW2 Itancourt	C 25 d
Vulcan Crossing	20SW4 Bixschoote	U 27 c 4.5
Vulture House	20SE3 Westroosebeke	V 24 b 6.6
Vulture Trench	66dNW1 Punchy	A 29 a, b, c
Vuttel Alley	66cNW4 Berthenicourt	H 12 d
W 48 [British front line, 1-7-16]	57dNE3 & 4 Hébuterne	K 10 d, 11 c

Name	Map Sheet	Map Reference
W 49 [British front line, 1-7-16]	57dNE3 & 4 Hébuterne	K 10 d
W 51 [British front line, 1-7-16]	57dNE3 & 4 Hébuterne	K 10 a, b, c, d
W Camp	27NE2 Proven / 28NW1 Elverdinghe	F 12 c, A 7 d
W. Redoubt	28SW2 Wytschaete	N 12 a
W. Yorks Alley	57cSW3 Longueval	S 10 d, 16 b
Waac Farm [1918]	27SE1 St Sylvestre	Q 7 c 8.6
WAAC Trench, & Support [1918]	57dNE3 & 4 Hébuterne	K 6 b, L 1 c
Waayenburg Railhead / Refilling Point	19SE4 [Beveren]	X 13 a, c
Wad Trench	51bNW3 Arras	G 18 a
Wad Trench	51bNW4 Fampoux	I 2 c
Wade Farm	28NE4 Dadizeele	L 32 c 2.9
Wade Lane [Thiepval Wood]	57dSE1 & 2 Beaumont	R 25 c
Wade Trench	51bNW3 Arras	G 18 a
Waenebeke [Elverdinghe, railway sidings]	28NW1 Elverdinghe	B 9 d, 15 a, b
Waes Trench	20SW1 Loo / 20SW3 Oostvleteren	N 33 a, c
Waft Trench	51bNW3 Arras	G 18 a
Wag Trench	51bNW3 Arras	G 18 a
Wag Trench	51bNW4 Fampoux	I 8 d
Waggon Road [road, Beaumont Hamel]	57dNE3 & 4 Hébuterne / 57dSE1 & 2 Beaumont	K 35 d, 36 c, Q 5 b, c, d
Wagner Trench	57cSW4 Combles	U 8 b, d
Wagon Farm	28NW2 St Julien	B 18 a 4.4
Wagram Avenue / Trench [later Nairn]	57dNE3 & 4 Hébuterne	K 21 c, d, 22 a, c, 23 a
Wagram Camp	57dNE3 & 4 Hébuterne	K 22 c
Wagram Cemetery	28NW2 St Julien	B 23 a 2.3
Wagram Farm	28NW2 St Julien	B 23 a
Wagtail Farm	20SE2 Hooglede	R 20 d 55.50
Waif Trench	51bNW3 Arras	G 18 a, c
Wail Trench	51bNW3 Arras	G 18 a
Wailly [village]	51cSE2 Beaumetz	R 16, 23
Wailly Keep	51cSE2 Beaumetz	R 23 a
Wailly Switch	51cSE2 Beaumetz	R 16 b, d
Wait Trench	51bNW2 Oppy	C 26 a, c, d
Wakatu Lines [camp]	28NW4 Ypres	H 29 b
Wake Trench	57dSE4 Ovillers	X 8 a, b
Wakefield Avenue	57cNW2 Vaulx-Vraucourt	C 17 b, 18 a
Wakefield Huts	28SW1 Kemmel	M 29 c 9.5
Wakefield Wood	28SW1 Kemmel	M 29 c, 35 a
Wakes Trench	57cSW3 Longueval	S 3 c, 8 b, 9 a
Wales Trench [Bernafay Wood]	57cSW3 Longueval	S 29 a, c
Walincourt - Audigny Line	57bSW2 Clary / 4 Serain	extensive
Walincourt [village]	57bSW2 Clary	N 24 a, b, c, d, 30 a, b
Walincourt Mill	57bSW2 Clary	N 36 b 4.5
Walincourt Wood	57bSW2 Clary	N 28 a, b, c, d
Walker Avenue	57dSE2 Beaumont	Q 5 b, 6 a
Walker Avenue	57dSE4 Ovillers	X 5 c, 11 a, b
Walker Camp	28NW3 Poperinghe	H 27 b
Walker Farm	28NW3 Poperinghe	H 27 b
Walker O.P. [1917-18]	36cSW3 Vimy	S 30 a 5.2
Walkman Trench	57dNE3 & 4 Hébuterne	K 23 b
Walkyries, P. des	36cSW3 Vimy	S 8 d, 14 b
Walkyries, Tranchée des	66dNW1 Punchy	A 27 b, d
Wall Avenue [Calonne]	36cSW1 Lens	M 9 a, b
Wall Farm	28SW2 Wytschaete	O 23 a 3.5

Name	Map Sheet	Map Reference
Wall of China [China Wall; Hooge]	28NW4 & NE3 Zillebeke	I 16 a, b, d, 17c
Wall Street [Mur de Calonne]	36cSW1 Lens	M 20 b
Wall Trench	51bNW2 Oppy	C 25 b, 26 a, c
Wall, The [Hooge, 1915]	28NW4 & NE3 Zillebeke	I 18 b, J 13 a
Wallaby Trench	57cNE2 Bourlon	E 28 b, d, 29 a
Wallace Post	36NW2 Armentières	C 14 b
Wallah Farm	28NE2 Moorslede	K 4 b 4.8
Wallangara [The Catacombs, Hill 63]	28SW4 Ploegsteert	T 18 d, U 13 c
Walled Garden [north Pozières]	57dSE4 Ovillers	X 4 b 10.65
Wallemolen	28NE1 Zonnebeke	D 3 b, 4 a
Wallsend Junction [light rly, St Jean]	28NW2 St Julien	C 27 d 5.3
Wally Support	28SW4 Ploegsteert	U 11 a, c
Walnut Trench	51bNW4 Fampoux	I 8 d, 9 c
Walnut Trench	57dNE3 & 4 Hébuterne	L 13 a, c, 19 a
Walpole Copse	28NE4 Dadizeele	K 29 a
Walrus Wood	62cNW3 Vaux	H 1 a
Walsh Support	57cNE3 Hermies	K 7 d, 8 a, c
Walsh Trench	57cNE3 Hermies	K 7 b, 8 a
Walter Camp	28NW3 Poperinghe	H 27 b
Walter Trench	57dNE3 & 4 Hébuterne	K 24 c, 29 b, d, 30 a
Waltney Street	57dSE4 Ovillers	X 7 b
Wam Farm	28SW2 Wytschaete	O 23 d 05.25
Wambaix [village]	57bNW3 Rumilly / 4 [Caudry]	H 15, 16
Wambaix Copse	57bNW3 Rumilly	H 3 d
Wancourt [village]	51bSW2 Vis-en-Artois	N 23 a, b
Wancourt Tower	51bSW2 Vis-en-Artois	N 24 d 14.00
Wancourt-Feuchy Line	51bSE2 Vis-en-Artois	extensive
Wandeling Cabaret, In de	28SW2 Wytschaete	N 6 a 2.5
Wandle Farm	36aNE4 Merville	L 22 c 6.9
Wangaratta [trench]	28NW4 & 28NE3 Zillebeke	I 29 c, d
Wangaratta Post	28NW4 & NE3 Zillebeke	I 29 c, d
Wangerie Avenue	36SW1 Aubers	M 17 b, 18 a, c, d
Wangerie Lane	36SW1 Aubers	M 11 c
Wangle Villa	36NW1 Steenwerck	A 20 a 60.95
Want Trench	51bNW2 Oppy	I 2 a
Waratah Camp	28NW3 Poperinghe	G 15 a, b, c
Waratah Corner	28NW3 Poperinghe	G 15 b 1.6
Waratah Farm	28NW3 Poperinghe	G 15 a 6.0
Warburg Camp	28NW3 Poperinghe	H 32 c, d
Ward Street [1918]	57dSE [3 Bouzincourt]	W 26 b, c, d
Ward Trench	51bNW4 Fampoux	I 9 a
Ward Walk & Tunnel	36cNW3 Loos	G 36 a
Warder Trench	66cNW2 Itancourt	C 27 c
Wardle Avenue	57dSW [3 Talmas]	S 28 a, c
Ware Road	36cNW1 La Bassée	A 9 a, c
Waring House	28NE4 Dadizeele	K 29 c 5.4
Warl 1st Support [1918] [Warlincourt-lez-Pas]	57dNE [1 Fonquevillers]	D 1 d, 7 a, b, c
Warl 2nd Support [1918] [Warlincourt-lez-Pas]	57dNE [1 Fonquevillers]	D 1 c, d, 7 a
Warl Trench [1918] [Warlincourt-lez-Pas]	57dNE [1 Fonquevillers]	D 7 b, c, d, 8 a
Warlencourt Alley	57cSW1 Gueudecourt	M 16 a, b
Warlencourt Road [road W of Le Barque]	57cSW1 Gueudecourt	M 11 a, b, 12 a, b
Warlencourt Trench	57cNW3 Bapaume / SW1 Gueudecourt	G 35 d, 36 c, d, M 3, 4, 5
Warlencourt-Eaucourt [village]	57cSW1 Gueudecourt	M 10 b, d, 11 a
Warlet Wood	66eNW [2 Thennes]	C 25 c, I 1 a, b

Name	Map Sheet	Map Reference
Warley Lodge	36NW2 & NE1 Houplines	C 3 d 05.85
Warlingham Crater [Givenchy]	36cNW1 La Bassée	A 10 c 0.1
Warm Farm	36NW1 Steenwerck	A 9 c 3.1
Warn Lane	28SW4 Ploegsteert	U 11 c, d
Warnave Avenue	28SW4 Ploegsteert	U 27 d
Warnave Lodge	28SW4 Ploegsteert	U 28 c 05.80
Warneton [village]	28SW4 Ploegsteert	U 12 b, c, d
Warneton Line	28SW2 Wytschaete / 4 Ploegsteert	O 24, 30, 36, U 6, 12, 18
Warp Farm	36NW1 Steenwerck	A 28 d 6.8
Warrego Trench [1918]	57dSE3 Bouzincourt / 62dNE1 [Dernancourt]	V 30 d, D 6 b
Warren Trench	57dSE2 & 57cSW1 Le Sars	R 23 c, d
Warren Trench	62cNW1 Maricourt	A 3 c
Warren Wood [1918]	28SW1 Kemmel	M 14 d, 20 b
Warren, The	62cNW1 Maricourt	A 3 c
Warren, The [Givenchy, N of Ducks Bill]	36cNW1 La Bassée	A 9 d
Warrington [lt rly locality NW of P'cappelle '17-18]	20SE3 Westroosebeke	V 13 a
Warrington Avenue / Street	28NW4 & NE3 Zillebeke	I 24 b
Warrington Road [plank road, 1917-18]	28NW4 Ypres	I 13 c,d, 14 c,d, 15 c,d, 16 c d, 20 a,b
Warrington Street	51bNW1 Roclincourt	A 4 c
Warrington Trench	28NW4 & NE3 Zillebeke	I 16 d
Warrior Street	57dNE3&4 Hébuterne	K 16 b, 17 a
Warry Copse	57cNW1 Gomiecourt	A 22 b 5.3
Warsaw [dump & light rly locality 1918]	28SW2 Wytschaete	N 24 c
Wart Farm	28SW3 Bailleul	S 16 d 85.35
Wart Trench	51bNW4 Fampoux	I 8 a, c
Wartburg Post	57cNE1 Quéant	E 7 d
Wartling Farm	20SE2 Hooglede	Q 5 d 6.1
Warts Walk [road; Officers Camp, Lovie Chateau]	27NE2 Proven	F 16 d, 22 b
Warwick [lt rly locality N of Pilckem 1917-18]	28NW2 St Julien	C 2 b
Warwick Arms	36aSE1 St Venant	P 35 b 1.1
Warwick Avenue	57dSE4 Ovillers	X 2 a, b
Warwick Bridge	36aSE1 St Venant	P 13 d 65.10
Warwick Cemetery	28SW4 Ploegsteert	U 14 d 89.85
Warwick Farm	28NW2 St Julien	C 29 c 6.3
Warwick Lane	28NW2 St Julien	C 29 c
Warwick Road [road]	36aNE4 Merville	K 15 d, 16 a, c
Warwick Trench	28NW2 St Julien	C 28 b, d, 29 c
Warwick Trench	57cSW3 Longueval	T 9 d, 15 b
Warwickshire Trench	57cSW4 Combles	T 5 c 9.9
Wash Trench	51bNW2 Oppy / 4 Fampoux	I 3 b, d
Wash Trench	51bNW3 Arras	G 18 a
Washington Farm	20SE3 Westroosebeke	V 6 c 45.20
Wasp Farm	28SW2 Wytschaete	O 23 b 5.5
Wasp Lane	57cNW1 Gomiecourt	A 1 b
Wasp Lane [trench]	57cNE1 Quéant	K 3 a
Wasp Trench	51bNW2 Oppy	C 21 d, 27 b
Wasp Trench	51bNW3 Arras	G 18 a
Wasp Trench, & Support [1918]	57dNE4 [Hébuterne / Achiet]	L 1 d, 2 c, d
Wassail House	36aNE1 Morbecque	D 21 a 60.65
Wasser Graben	51bNW1 Roclincourt	A 10 b, 11 a
Waste Trench	51bNW4 Fampoux	I 9 a, b
Waster Farm	36NW1 Steenwerck	A 13 d 65.55
Watch Alley	57cSW3 Longueval	S 7 a
Watchmaking Trench	62bSW2 Fonsommes / 4 Homblières	N 34 b, d

Name	Map Sheet	Map Reference
Wateau Road	57dSE1 & 2 Beaumont	Q 23 b
Water Boyau	36cNW1 La Bassée	G 3 b
Water Farm	36NW4 Bois Grenier	I 31 b
Water Farm [Waterdamhoek]	28NE2 Moorslede	E 28 b 0.9
Water Fort [German, late 1915]	36SW2 Radinghem	N 11 b 1.8
Water House	20SE3 Westroosebeke	V 13 b 1.8
Water Tank {Estaires]	36aNE4 Merville	L 29 b 4.6
Water Tower [Lens]	36cSW1 Lens	N 8 d 8.2
Water Tower [Vermelles]	36cNW3 Loos	G 8 d 99.35
Water Tower Keep [E of Vermelles]	36cNW3 Loos	G 8 d
Water Tower O.P. [Vermelles]	36cNW3 Loos	G 8 d 99.35
Waterdamhoek	28NE1 Zonnebeke / 2 Moorslede	E 21 c, d, 22 c, 27 b, 28 a
Waterdamhoek Cemetery [civilian]	28NE1 Zonnebeke	E 21 b 35.35
Waterend House	28NE1 Zonnebeke	V 13 b
Waterfields [farm]	28NE1 Zonnebeke	D 10 d
Waterlands [farm & place name]	36NW1 Steenwerck	B 27 a 1.2
Waterloo [farm & pillboxes]	28NE1 Zonnebeke	D 9 d 9.9
Waterloo Aid Post	28NE1 Zonnebeke	D 9 a 8.8
Waterloo Bridge	36aSE1 St Venant	Q 31 a 9.2
Waterloo Bridge	57dNE3 & 4 Hébuterne	K 33 b 6.8
Waterloo Camp	28SW3 Bailleul	S 18 c
Waterloo Canadian Cemetery	28NE1 Zonnebeke	D 9 d 9.9
Waterloo Road	36cNW1 La Bassée	A 14 b, 15 a, b, c
Waterloo Road	57dNE3 & 4 Hébuterne	K 33 b
Waterloo Road [road]	28SW3 Bailleul	S 18 c, d, 24 a, b, T 19 a, b, 20 a
Waterloo Street	51bNW3 Arras	G 5 d, 6 c
Waterlot Farm [Béhagnies]	57cNW1 Gomiecourt	H 1 b 8.2
Waterlot Farm [Longueval]	57cSW3 Longueval	S 18 c, d, 24 a, b
Water's Keep	36SW3 Richebourg	S 15 d 3.4
Waters Trench	57cSW3 Longueval	S 3 c, 9 a
Watery Wood [S of River Scarpe]	51bNW3 Arras	H 20 a, b
Watford [light rly locality & huts]	28NW1 Elverdinghe	B 21 b
Watling Crater	51bNW1 Roclincourt	A 4 a
Watling Street	28SW2 Wytschaete	N 17 a, b, d
Watling Street	51bNW1 Roclincourt	A 4 a
Watling Street	62dNE2 Méaulte	F 9 d, 10 c
Watling Street	36NW2 Armentières	C 4 c
Watling Street [CT, July 1915]	28SW2 Wytschaete	N 11 b, 12 a, c
Watling Street [road]	57dNE3 & 4 Hébuterne / 57dSE1 & 2 Beaumont	K 34 c, d, Q 4 b, d, 5 c
Watling Street [road]	62bNW3 Bellicourt	G 18 a
Watling Tram [trench tramway; Vierstraat]	28SW2 Wytschaete	N 17 a, b, c, d
Watney Cabaret	20SE3 Westroosebeke	V 3 c 8.3
Waton France [place name]	27NE4 Abeele	K 21 d, 22 c
Waton, le [farm & locality]	27SE4 Meteren	X 26 b 4.3
Watou [village]	27NE2 Proven	E 28 d, K 4 b, 5 a
Watou Depot Railhead / Refilling Point	27NE2 Proven	E 17 a, b, c, d, 23 a
Watou Line	27NE4 Abeele / SE2 Berthen	extensive
Watou Line [1918]	27SE2 Berthen	Q 5, 11, 17, 22, 23
Watson Street / Trench	57dNE3 & 4 Hébuterne	K 16 b, d, 17 a
Watson Trench	51bNW1 Roclincourt	A 26 b / d
Watsonville	28SW2 Wytschaete	N 17 d
Watt Trench	62bNW3 Bellicourt	G 27 c
Watter Weg	28NW4 & NE3 Zillebeke	J 19 c
Wattle Trench	57cSW1 Gueudecourt	N 19 c, d

Name	Map Sheet	Map Reference
Watts Farm	20SE3 Westroosebeke	W 20 c 65.25
Wave Trench	51bNW2 Oppy	C 27 c
Wave Trench	51bNW3 Arras	G 18 a
Wavy Trench	51bNW4 Fampoux	I 3 c
Wayfarer Cross Roads	28NE2 Moorslede	E 11 b 9.6
Weak Trench	51bNW2 Oppy / 4 Fampoux	I 2 b, d
Weal House	36NW1 Steenwerck	H 1 b 7.9
Weary Farm	28NW1 Elverdinghe	A 19 d 75.55
Weary Willows, The	36cSW3 Vimy	T 27 a
Weasel Farms	27NE2 Proven	F 8 d 4.4
Weasel Lane [trench]	57cNE1 Quéant	E 26 d
Weasel Trench	51bNW4 Fampoux	I 2 c
Weasel Wood	27NE2 Proven	F 8 d, 14 a, b
Weathercock Corner	36NW3 Fleurbaix	H 31 c 80.15
Web Lane	57cSW2 Villers-au-Flos	N 28 c
Web Street	57cSW2 Villers-au-Flos	N 28 c
Weber Trench	20SW2 Zwartegat	O 22 c, d
Weddell Avenue	57dSE4 Ovillers	X 3 c
Wedding Lane	57cSW1 Gueudecourt	N 7 b
Wedge Wood	28SW1 Kemmel	M 18 a, b, c
Wedge Wood	57cSW3 Longueval	T 26 c 1.3
Wedgewood Bank [slope]	28SW2 Wytschaete	N 18 b, d
Wednesday Avenue	51bNW1 Roclincourt / 3 Arras	A 29 c, G 4 d, 5 a, c, 10 b, c, d
Wee Cottage [Bellewaarde]	28NW4 & NE3 Zillebeke	I 12 c 85.40
Wee House [Trench]	36SW3 Richebourg	S 27 b, 28 a
Wee Trench	51bNW3 Arras	G 18 a
Wee Trench	51bSW1 Neuville Vitasse	M 16 c, d
Weed Lane [1918]	51bSW3 Boisleux	S 26 d
Weed Trench	51bNW3 Arras	G 12 c, 18 a
Weed Trench	51bNW4 Fampoux	I 8 b, 9 a, c,
Weedon [lt rly locality SW of Langemarck '17-18]	20SW4 Bixschoote	U 28 c
Weedon Post	62cNE2 Epéhy	F 1 a
Weevil Crossing [level crossing]	36aNE1 Morbecque	D 25 d 7.8
Weigel Trench	62cNW4 Péronne	I 31 d, 32 c
Weimar Trench [1918]	66eNW [2 Thennes]	C 9 c
Weissman Trench	51bNW3 Arras	G 6 d
Weka Lines	36NW2 Armentières	B 4 a
Weka Trench [1918]	57dNE4 [Hébuterne / Achiet]	L 7 d, 13 b, 14 a
Welbeck Grange	28NE3 Gheluvelt	J 32 a
Welbeck Grange	28NE3 Gheluvelt	J 32 a 1.5
Welch Alley	57dSE4 Ovillers / 57cSW3 Longueval	X 12 a, S 1 d, 7 b
Welch Trench	36cNW1 La Bassée	A 8 b
Welch Trench	36cSW1 Lens	M 4 c, d
Welch Trench [1918]	62dNE [1 Dernancourt]	D 24 b, d
Welcome Sap	57dNE3 & 4 Hébuterne	K 16 a 0.5
Welcome Street	57dNE3 & 4 Hébuterne	K 10 d, 11 c, 16 a, b
Welcome Street, New	57dNE3 & 4 Hébuterne	K 11 c
Welcome Trench	51bNW4 Fampoux	I 8 d
Well Alley [Oct 1915]	36cNW3 Loos	G 23 b, d
Well Avenue [road]	28SW4 Ploegsteert	U 7 b, c, d, 13 a
Well Avenue [trench]	28SW4 Ploegsteert	U 15 d
Well Cottage	28NW2 St Julien	C 22 d 95.53
Well Cross Roads	28NW4 Ypres	I 2 d 15.80
Well Farm [late 1915]	36SW2 Radinghem	N 6 d 05.95

Name	Map Sheet	Map Reference
Well Farm Fort [BFL]	36SW2 Radinghem	N 6 a, b
Well Farm Salient	36SW2 Radinghem	N 6 a, b
Well Lane	62dNE2 Méaulte	F 3 a, b
Well Lane Line [light rly]	28SW4 Ploegsteert	T 5 d, 11 b, 12 a
Wellbargain / Well-Bargain Farm	28NE4 Dadizeele	L 16 a 65.25
Wellcome Wood	62dNE [3 Morlancourt]	J 27 b
Weller Avenue	57dSW [3 Talmas]	S 27 a, b
Wellford Trench	51bNW4 Fampoux	H 30d, 36 b
Wellgate	28NW2 St Julien	C 7 c
Wellington [farm & pillboxes]	28NE1 Zonnebeke	D 2 b 3.2
Wellington Avenue	28SW4 Ploegsteert	O 34 b, d, 35 c, U 4 a
Wellington Avenue	36NW4 Bois Grenier	I 14 d, 20 b
Wellington Buildings	28NW3 Poperinghe	G 24 d 4.3
Wellington Crescent	28NW4 & NE3 Zillebeke	I 23 b
Wellington Junction [light rly]	28NW3 Poperinghe	G 24 d 55.25
Wellington Keep [SW of Philosophe]	36cNW3 Loos	G 25 b
Wellington Post	36aSE2 Lestrem	R 29 b
Wellington Redoubt	62dNE2 Méaulte	F 16 b
Wellington Road	36SW1 Aubers	M 25 b
Wellington Trench [new front line]	57dSE1 & 2 Beaumont	Q 10 c, d, 16 b, 17 a
Welsh Alley	57dSE4 Ovillers / 57cSW3 Longueval	X 12 a, S 2 a
Welsh Avenue	28SW2 Wytschaete	O 15 b, 16 c
Welsh Camp	28NW1 Elverdinghe	B 14 c, 20 a
Welsh Farm	28NW1 Elverdinghe	B 14 c 1.1
Welsh Farm	28NW2 St Julien	C 15 b 4.7
Welsh Ridge	57cSE2 Gonnelieu	R 9 b, c, d, 14 b, 15 a, b
Welsh Support	57cSE2 Gonnelieu	R 9 d, 15 a, b
Welsh Tree [E of Quinque Rue, NW of K3, 4/15]	36SW3 Richebourg / 36cNW1 La Bassée	S 26 d / A 2 b
Welsh Trench	36cNW3 Loos	G 34 a
Welsh Trench	57cSE2 Gonnelieu	R 8 d, 14 b
Welsh Trench [1918]	57dSE3 [Bouzincourt]	W 15 c, 21 a
Welyn Farm	36aNE4 Merville	L 12 a 6.0
Wendy Alley	62bSW3 St Quentin	T 8 a, b
Wenning Street	57dSE4 Ovillers	W 12 c, d, X 7 a, c
Werfer & Minen Copses [1918]	62dNE [3 Morlancourt]	K 26 c
Wervicq Switch	28NE3 Gheluvelt	J 35, 36
Weskit Cottage	28NW1 Elverdinghe	A 21 d 3.4
Wessex Avenue	36NW2 Armentières	C 22 c, d
West Avenue	62cNW1 Maricourt	A 9 c 9.9
West Copse	36cSW4 Rouvroy	U 27 a, b
West Cut	36cNW3 Loos	G 11 a
West Face [Hohenzollern Redoubt]	36cNW1 La Bassée / 3 Loos	G 4 d
West Farm	28NW4 & NE3 Zillebeke	I 10 b 8.2
West Fork Avenue	57cNE4 Marcoing	L 31 d, 32 a, b, c
West Ham Lane [Vieux Corons, Boyau des]	36cSW1 Lens	M 8 a, c, d, 14 b, 15 a
West Hazebrouck Line [1918]	27SE3 Borre	extensive
West Keep	62cNW1 Maricourt	A 15 d
West Lane [CT north of railway]	28NW4 & NE3 Zillebeke	I 9 d, 10 b, 11 a, b
West Lane [Railway Wood, S of rly]	28NW4 & NE3 Zillebeke	I 11 b
West Poperinghe Line [1918]	27NE2 Proven / 4 Abeele	extensive
West Poperinghe Line [1918]	28NW1 Elverdinghe	A 20, 21, 22, 25, 26
West Poperinghe Line [1918]	28SW1 Kemmel	extensive
West Princes[s] Street	36NW4 Bois Grenier	I 26 c
West Riding Trench	57dSE1 & 2 Beaumont	R 31 b, 32 c

Name	Map Sheet	Map Reference
West Skirt [Morval]	57cSW4 Combles	T 10 b, d
West Street	12SW1 Nieuport	M 6 d
West Street	28NW4 & NE3 Zillebeke	I 17 a, b, c
West Street [road, Le Transloy]	57cSW2 Villers-au-Flos	N 30 a, c
West Trench	57cNE3 Hermies	K 26 a
West Wood	20SE3 Westroosebeke	V 16 d, 17 c, 22 b
Westen Molen [locality & trenches]	27SE2 Berthen	R 12 a 7.5
Western Redoubt [Kemmel Defences 1918]	28SW2 Wytschaete	N 12 a 7.9
Western Trench [Pozières Trench]	57dSE4 Ovillers	X 4 a, c
Westhelsen [hamlet]	27SE2 Berthen	R 2 d 0.0
Westhoek	28NE3 Gheluvelt	J 7 b
Westhoek [hamlet]	28NE4 Dadizeele	K 17 a
Westhoek Post [1918]	28NE3 Gheluvelt	J 8 a, c
Westhoek Ridge	28NW4 & NE3 Zillebeke	J 1, 2, 7, 8
Westhoek Valley	28NE1 Zonnebeke / 3 Gheluvelt	J 1 c, d 7 a, b
Westhof Farm	28SW3 Bailleul	T 19 a 3.1
Westhof Road [road]	28SW3 Bailleul	S 24 b, d, 30 b, d, T 19 a
Westminster Avenue [St Yvon]	28SW4 Ploegsteert	U 15 c, d
Westminster Road [road]	36cSW1 Lens	N 27 b
Weston Avenue / Boyau Weston	62cNW1 Maricourt	A 15 b
Westonhoek [railway & light rly exchange sidings]	28NW1 Elverdinghe	A 28 c, G 3 b, 4 a
Westoutre [village]	28SW1 Kemmel	M 9 c, d, 15 a
Westoutre Line [1918]	28SW1 Kemmel	M 8 b, c, d, 9 a, 13 b, 14 a
Westphalia Trench	70dNW2 Servais	B 30 d, H 6 b
Westroosebeke [village]	20SE3 Westroosebeke	V 12 c, 18 a
Westwood House	20SE3 Westroosebeke	V 17 c 3.1
Westwood Trench	28SW4 Ploegsteert	U 15 a
Wet Pond	28SE1 Wervicq	P 1 b 6.6
Wet Trench	51bNW4 Fampoux	I 9 c
Wetherby Camp [& railway sidings]	28NW1 Elverdinghe	A 6 c, d
Wetsteen Inn	36NW1 Steenwerck	B 1 b
Wetzer Graben	51bNW1 Roclincourt	G 6 b
Wexford Farm	28SW1 Kemmel	M 16 d 15.70
Weymouth Avenue	62dNE2 Méaulte	F 15 b, d
Wez Macquart [village]	36NW4 Bois Grenier	I 16 d, 17 c, 22 b, 23 a
Whack Trench	51bNW2 Oppy	C 27 c, I 3 a
Whale Farm	28SW2 Wytschaete	O 30 d 45.05
Whale Trench	51bNW2 Oppy / 4 Fampoux	I 4 a, c, 10 a, d
Whale Trench	57dSE2 & 57cSW1 Le Sars	N 20 d
Whalley Street	57dSE4 Ovillers	X 13 a
What a Hope Cut [Hope Cut, June '16, Turco Fm]	28NW2 St Julien	C 15 c
Whatman Copse	28NE4 Dadizeele	K 28 b, c, d
Wheal Camp	28SW3 Bailleul	T 14 d
Wheat Pit	57cSW1 Gueudecourt	M 11
Wheat Support [1918]	51cSE4 Blaireville	X 29 d
Wheat Trench [Le Barque Switch]	57cSW1 Gueudecourt	M 11 c, d, 12 c, d, 17 a
Wheatley Corner [road jct]	28NE4 Dadizeele	K 30 d 05.85
Wheeze Farm	27NE2 Proven	E 16 d 9.3
Whine Trench	51bNW2 Oppy	C 26 b, d
Whip Cross Roads	51bNW4 Fampoux	I 2 c 3.5
Whip Trench	51bNW4 Fampoux	I 2 c, 8 a
Whippet Fork [road jct]	27NE2 Proven	L 4 b 7.2
Whirlwind Junction [road jct]	28NE4 Dadizeele	L 25 d 8.2
Whisk Farm	20SE3 Westroosebeke	W 19 d 1.9

Name	Map Sheet	Map Reference
Whisker Bridge [road over stream]	36NW1 Steenwerck	A 11 d3.8
Whiskey Corner	36SW3 Richebourg	S 8 b 5.5
Whiskey Farm	28NW4 Ypres	H 10 d 5.6
Whiskey Street	57dNE3 & 4 Hébuterne	K 10 c, d
Whiskey Street, New	57dNE3 & 4 Hébuterne	K 10 d, 11 c
Whiskey Trench	57dSE4 Ovillers	X 21 c, 27 a
Whisky Trench / Tranchée du Whisky	66dNW1 Punchy	A 26 d, 27 c, d, 28 a
Whisper Copse [1918]	28SW1 Kemmel	M 15 b, d
Whisper Trench	51bNW4 Fampoux	I 8 a
Whist House	36NW1 Steenwerck	A 20 c 9.3
Whistle Copse	62bNW3 Bellicourt	H 21 b
Whistle Trench	51bSW2 Vis-en-Artois	O 15 b
Whit Trench	51bNW4 Fampoux	I 2 c
Whitby Strong Point [1918]	57dNE1 & 2 Fonquevillers	E 30 b 5.5
Whitby Support	57cNW2 Vaulx-Vraucourt	C 12 c, 18 a
White Alley	70dNW2 Servais	C 19 d
White Cat, The	36SW3 Richebourg	S 6 c
White Chateau	28NW4 & NE3 Zillebeke	I 10 c
White Chateau	28SW1 Kemmel	M 28 c 9.7
White Chateau	28SW2 Wytschaete	O 4 d
White Chateau	51bNW3 Arras	G 34 d 6.7
White Chateau	62dSW [2 Villers-Bretonneux]	O 26 c 4.9
White Chateau Tunnel	28SW2 Wytschaete	O 4 d
White City	36NW4 Bois Grenier	H 36 b, I 31 a
White City Post	36NW4 Bois Grenier	H 36 b, I 31 a
White City, The [W of Beaumont Hamel]	57dSE1 & 2 Beaumont	Q 4 a, b
White Copse	66dNW3 Hattencourt	G 12 b, d
White Cottage	28NW2 St Julien	C 29 a 3.5
White Cottage [Ploegsteert]	28SW4 Ploegsteert	U 26 b 1.2
White Cottages [Ploegsteert]	28SW4 Ploegsteert	U 25 d 7.9
White Disc Railway Sign	36cNW3 Loos	G 9 a 1.5
White Ditch [sunken road]	51bNW1 Roclincourt	A 4 c, d, 10 a
White Estaminet [Le Pelerin]	28SW4 Ploegsteert	U 21 b 65.60
White Farm	36NW2 & NE1 Houplines	C 5 a 2.6
White Gates [farm, W end of Hill 63]	28SW4 Ploegsteert	T 18 a 12.85
White Harts Avenue	36cSW3 Vimy	S 15 c, d
White Hope Corner	28NW2 St Julien	B 10 d 6.6
White Horse Cellars [St Eloi]	28SW2 Wytschaete	O 2 b 05.35
White Horse Crater	36cNW1 La Bassée	A 9 b
White Horse Street	36NW4 Bois Grenier	I 16 c
White Horse Trench	57cSW3 Longueval	S 30 a, c
White House	20SW4 Bixschoote	U 24 c 5.1
White House	28NW4 Ypres	H 24 c 1.0
White House	36aSE4 Locon	W 30 a 8.9
White House	36NW2 & NE1 Houplines	C 4 d 1.4
White House	36SW2 Radinghem	O 1 a 9.4
White House	51bNW3 Arras	H 32 c
White House [Givenchy, April 1915]	36cNW1 La Bassée	A 2 / 8
White House British Cemetery	51bNW3 Arras	H 32 c 9.3
White Mill	20SW4 Bixschoote	U 24 c 1.1
White Mill Camp	28NW1 Elverdinghe	B 14 b, c, d, 15 c
White Mill, Elverdinghe	28NW1 Elverdinghe	B 14 d 6.5
White Mound [1915]	36cNW3 Loos	G 11 d 5.8
White Post	36NW2 Armentières	C 14 a

Name	Map Sheet	Map Reference
White Sap	28NW2 St Julien	C 29 a
White Spot Cottages	28SW4 Ploegsteert	U 3 b
White Spur [trench, 1918]	28NW4 Ypres	I 9 d
White Street	57cSW1 Gueudecourt	N 8 a
White Trench	28NW2 St Julien	C 13 a, b
White Trench	57dNE3 & 4 Hébuterne	K 29 d, 35 b, 36 a
White Trench [formerly Eagle Trench]	20SW4 Bixschoote	U 23 d, 29 b, 30 a
White Trench [S of Mametz Wood]	57dSE4 Ovillers / 57cSW3 Longueval	X 30 a, S 25 b, 26 a
Whitechapel [farm]	20SE3 Westroosebeke	V 15 c
Whitechapel [Sept 1915]	36cNW1 La Bassée	A 15 d
Whitechurch / Whitchurch St [Thiepval Wd]	57dSE1 & 2 Beaumont	Q 30 b, R 25 a
Whitehall	57dSE1 & 2 Beaumont	Q 17 a
Whitehall [light rly locality, 1917-18]	28SW2 Wytschaete	O 19 d
Whitehall [Sept 1915]	36cNW1 La Bassée	A 9 c
Whitehall [trench]	57cNE3 Hermies / 4 Marcoing	K 15 d
Whitehall Street [1918]	57dSE3 [Bouzincourt]	W 9 a
Whiteley's [farm buildings]	28NE2 Moorslede	F 8 a 95.25
Whitepole Junction [light rly, 1917-18]	28NW4 Ypres	I 1 c 20.45
Whites Farm	36aSE1 St Venant	Q 14 c 6.4
Whiting Copse	57dSW [3 Talmas]	T 2 a
Whiting Farm	36NW1 Steenwerck	A 8 b 35.05
Whiting Post	57cNE3 Hermies	J 5 c
Whitley Copse	20SE2 Hooglede	Q 11 b 5.9
Whitworth Junction [road jct]	28NE4 Dadizeele	L 2 c 20.65
Whiz Farm	28SW2 Wytschaete	O 17 d
Whizbang Avenue	57dNE1 & 2 Fonquevillers	E 22 d
Whizbang Corner [light rly, Lièvin]	36cSW1 Lens	M 22 d
Whizz Bang Corner [Lièvin]	36cSW1 Lens	M 22 d 4.5
Why Trench	51bNW4 Fampoux	I 3 c
Wibble Trench	51bNW2 Oppy	I 2 a, c
Wicart Farm / Ferme Wicart	28SW4 Ploegsteert	U 18 c 17.03
Wick [light railway locality, 1917]	28SW1 Kemmel	N 22 c
Wick Avenue & Group (Craters)	51bNW1 Roclincourt	A 16 c
Wick Salient	36SW1 Aubers	N 13 c, d
Wick Trench	51bNW2 Oppy	I 3 b
Wick Trench	51bNW3 Arras	G 18 c
Wick Walk	36cNW3 Loos	G 35 d
Wicked / Wicket Corner [Fricourt]	62dNE2 Méaulte	F 3 c
Wicker Trench	57dNE3 & 4 Hébuterne	K 34 b, 35 a
Wicket Buildings	28NE2 Moorslede	E 5 c 25.90
Wictes [farm]	36aNE3 Haverskerque	K 25 d 50.95
Wide Trench	51bNW2 Oppy	C 25 b
Widow Trench	51bNW2 Oppy	B 30 c, d, C 25 c
Widow's House	36NW2 & NE1 Houplines	C 9 d
Wieltje [village]	28NW2 St Julien	C 28 b
Wieltje Farm	28NW2 St Julien	C 28 a 4.5
Wieltje Keep	28NW2 St Julien	C 28 b
Wieltje Railhead / Refilling Point	28NW2 St Julien	C 22 d, 23 c, 28 b
Wieltje Subway	28NW2 St Julien	C 28 b
Wig Farm	20SE2 Hooglede	R 17 d 3.8
Wig Trench	51bNW4 Fampoux	I 8 c
Wigan [east strongpoint; Petit Moulin]	36NW1 Steenwerck	H 3 b 5.6
Wigan [lt rly locality E of Langemarck 1917-18]	20SW4 Bixschoote	U 24 c, 30 a
Wigan Lane	57dSE2 Beaumont	R 22 b, d

Name	Map Sheet	Map Reference
Wigan Way	62cNE2 Epéhy	F 18 c
Wight Crossing [level crossing]	20SE2 Hooglede	R 14 d 5.1
Wigton Farm	36NW1 Steenwerck	A 26 d 45.30
Wigwam Copse	27SE4 Meteren	R 33 c, X 3 a
Wijdendrift	20SW4 Bixschoote	U 21 a
Wijn House [Zwijnskot]	28NE2 Moorslede	F 29 a 63.90
Wijnberg [place name]	28NE4 Dadizeele	L 35 d
Wijnendaele [hamlet]	20SE2 Hooglede	R 14 c
Wijnendaele Station [railway]	20SE2 Hooglede	R 14 d 50.15
Wild Farm	28NE2 Moorslede	E 24 a 45.75
Wild Trench	51bNW3 Arras	G 18 b
Wilde Cottage	28NW2 St Julien	I 6 b 8.7
Wilde Wood	28NW2 St Julien	I 6 b
Wildwood How Spur [railway, 1917-18]	28NW4 Ypres	I 6 d
Wildy Camp	28SW3 Bailleul	T 8 c
Wilks Walk	36cSW3 Vimy	S 13 b, d
Will Trench	51bNW4 Fampoux	I 8 d
Willard Farm	28NE2 Moorslede	E 23 b 2.4
Willebeke Junction [light rly, 1918]	28NW4 Ypres	I 15 d
Willebeke Junction [light rly, 1918]	28SW1 Kemmel	N 15 b 2.5
Willerval [village]	51bNW1 Roclincourt	B 3 d, 4 c, 9 b
Willerval Chateau	51bNW1 Roclincourt	B 9 a 95.70
Willerval North [Post]	51bNW2 Oppy	B 4 a, b
Willerval South [Post]	51bNW1 Roclincourt / 2 Oppy	B 10 central
Willesden Camp B	28SW1 Kemmel	N 14 b, 15 a
Willesden Junction [rly locality, N of Kemmel vill.]	28SW1 Kemmel	N 9 c
Willesden Lines [huts]	28SW1 Kemmel	N 14 b 2.8
William Ravine	66eNW [2 Thennes]	C 26 d, 27 a, c
William Redan	57dSE1 & 2 Beaumont	Q 24 a
William Work [1918]	66eNW [4 Morisel]	H 17 c
Williams Avenue / Boyau Williams	62cNW1 Maricourt	A 16 a
Willie Support	51bNW2 Oppy	C 25 a, c, I 1 a
Willie Trench	51bNW2 Oppy	C 25 a, c, I 1 a, b
Willingdon Farm	20SE2 Hooglede	Q 4 c 1.9
Willis Avenue	57cSE2 Gonnelieu	R 33 b, 34 a
Willkind Trench	62cNW3 Vaux	H 21 a, c
Willot Lane [road, near La Tombe-Willot]]	36aSE4 Locon	Q 36 c, d, W 6 b, X 1 a, b
Willow Avenue	36NW4 Bois Grenier	I 20 b, d, 21 a, c
Willow Avenue [British trench]	62dNE2 Méaulte	F 2 d, 7 a, b, c, 8 a
Willow Avenue [Fricourt; track]	62dNE2 Méaulte	F 3 d, 4 b, c, d, 5 a
Willow Bridge [over stream]	36aNE3 Haverskerque	K 25 c 55.00
Willow Cemetery	28NW2 St Julien	C 20 b
Willow Cemetery	51cSE4 Blaireville	X 29 b
Willow Corner [1916]	36cNW1 La Bassée	A 2 b 5.4
Willow Dump	36cNW1 La Bassée	A 2 d
Willow Farm	20SE2 Hooglede	Q 18 a 50.85
Willow Lane [Fricourt]	62dNE2 Méaulte	F 3, 4
Willow Lane [Sept 1915]	36cNW1 La Bassée	A 14 d
Willow Lane North	36cNW1 La Bassée	A 14 d, 20 b, d
Willow Patch	57dSE4 Ovillers	X 27 a
Willow Patch "B"	57dNE1 & 2 Fonquevillers	E 14 b 40.15
Willow Patch "C"	57dNE1 & 2 Fonquevillers	E 14 d 60.85
Willow Road	36cNW1 La Bassée	A 2 b, c, d
Willow Road	51cSE4 Blaireville	X 29

Name	Map Sheet	Map Reference
Willow Road [road]	36aNE3 Haverskerque	K 25 c, d, 26 c
Willow Road [road]	36cNW1 La Bassée	A 2 b, c, d
Willow Road [trench]	36cNW1 La Bassée	A 2 a, b
Willow Stream / Willow Avenue Stream [Fricourt]	62dNE2 Méaulte	F 3 d, 4 b, c, d, 5 a
Willow Trench	51bNW4 Fampoux	I 8 b
Willow Trench	62bNW1 Gouy	A 7 d
Willow Trench	62dNE2 Méaulte	F 4 a, b, d
Willow Walk	28NW2 St Julien	C 15 c
Willow Walk	36NW2 Armentières	C 28 d, I 4 b
Willows Extension [light rly]	36cSW1 Lens	M 31 c, d, 32 c
Willows Street	51cSE3 & 4 Ransart	R 32 d, 33 c
Willows Support Line	36cNW1 La Bassée	A 20 d, 26 b
Willows, The	51bNW2 Oppy	B 10 d
Willows, The [trench]	28NW2 St Julien	C 20 b, 21 a
Wilson Farm	28NW2 St Julien	C 26 b 4.1
Wilson Farm Post	28NW2 St Julien	C 26 b 3.2
Wilson Street	36cSW3 Vimy	S 8 d, 9 c
Wilson Trench	51bNW1 Roclincourt	A 26 c
Wilson's House [OP, ruined house, Feb 1916]	36cNW1 La Bassée	A 20 d, 26 b [approx]
Wilson's Way	36cNW1 La Bassée	A 21 c, 27 a
Wilson's Way	36cSW3 Vimy	M 32 c
Wiltington / Withington Avenue	57dSE1 & 2 Beaumont	Q 15 c, d, 16 c
Wilts Street	57dSE1 & 2 Beaumont	R 31 c
Wiltshire Farm	28NW4 Ypres	H 35 c 35.10
Wiltshire Farm [light rly locality, 1917-18]	28NW4 Ypres	H 35 c
Wiltshire House	28SW2 Wytschaete	N 17 c 7.8
Wimbledon [buildings]	28NE1 Zonnebeke	D 15 a 1.8
Wimpole Street	36cNW1 La Bassée	A 20 d, 26 b
Winchester [keep, late 1915]	36SW1 Aubers	M 23 b, d
Winchester Farm [& pillboxes]	28NE1 Zonnebeke	D 2 a 5.4
Winchester House	51bNW1 Roclincourt	A 9 a
Winchester House [Ploegsteert Wood 1914-15]	28SW4 Ploegsteert	U 21 c 6.3
Winchester Post	36SW1 Aubers	M 23 a, c
Winchester Post Cemetery	36SW1 Aubers	M 23 a 3.3
Winchester Street / Road C.T.	36SW1 Aubers	M 23 a, c, d, 24 c
Winchester Street [late 1915]	36SW1 Aubers	M 23 c, d
Winchester Valley	57cSE1 Bertincourt	Q 19, 20, 21, 25, 26
Wind C.T., & Post [The Bluff]	28NW4 & NE3 Zillebeke	I 34 c
Wind Cotts	28SE1 Wervicq	P 2 d 4.5
Wind Trench	62bNW1 Gouy	A 25 b
Wind Trench	66cSW2 Vendeuil / 4 La Fère	O 29 c, 35 a, c, U 5 a
Wind Trench / Street	51bNW2 Oppy	C 27 a, b
Wind Trench / Street	51bNW3 Arras	G 18 b
Windlass Farm	20SE2 Hooglede	Q 16 d 15.15
Windmill [near Roeux]	51bNW4 Fampoux	I 14 b 88.95
Windmill [NW of Lesboeufs]	57cSW3 Longueval	N 33 d 65.48
Windmill British Cemetery	51bSW2 Vis-en-Artois	O 12 b 2.1
Windmill Cabaret	28NE1 Zonnebeke	D 21 a 95.10
Windmill Copse	51bNW4 Fampoux	I 8 d, 14 b
Windmill Farm [E of Adinfer]	51cSE4 Blaireville	X 23 a
Windmill Hill [Hill 40]	28NE1 Zonnebeke	D 21 d 3.8
Windmill Hill [Pozières]	57dSE2 & 57cSW1 Le Sars	R 35, X 5
Windmill Lane	57cSW1 Gueudecourt	N 31 b
Windmill Maze	51bNW2 Oppy	C 19 d

Name	Map Sheet	Map Reference
Windmill Mound	57cSW2 Villers-au-Flos	O 31 c
Windmill Reserve [1918]	51bSW4 Bullecourt	T 24 b, d, U 19 c, 25 a
Windmill Road [road]	36cNW3 Loos	G 36 a, b
Windmill Support	51bNW2 Oppy	C 19 b, d
Windmill Switch Front Line [1918]	51cSE4 Blaireville	X 17 c, 23 a, c, 29 a, b, d
Windmill Switch Support Line [1918]	51cSE4 Blaireville	X 22 d, 23 a, c, 28 b, 29 a, c, d
Windmill Trench	51bNW2 Oppy	C 13 c, 19 a
Windmill Trench [Longueval]	57cSW3 Longueval	S 17 a
Windmill, Fosse 2 de Azincourt	51bNE4 Cantin	L 12 a 5.6
Window Redoubt	36cNW3 Loos	G 5 c, d
Window, The [Hohenzoll. Rdt, Oct 1915]	36cNW3 Loos	G 5 c, d
Windsor Castle	36aSE1 St Venant	P 6 b 3.7
Windsor Castle Tram Line	28NW2 St Julien	C 13 a, c
Windsor Lane [1918]	57dSE1 & 2 Beaumont	Q 16 b
Windsor Road [road]	36cSW4 Rouvroy	T 11 b, 12 a, c, 18 a
Windward House	28NW4 Ypres	H 4 d 2.7
Windy Corner	36aSE1 St Venant	P 5 c 5.2
Windy Corner [Beaumont Hamel]	57dSE1 & 2 Beaumont	Q 4 c, 5 b
Windy Corner [Givenchy-lez-la-Bassée]	36cNW1 La Bassée	A 8 c 8.4
Windy Corner [Richebourg l'Avoué]	36SW3 Richebourg	S 9 a 55.85
Windy Corner [W end of Hermies]	57cNE3 Hermies	J 29 d 10.99
Windy Corner Switch [1918]	36bNE2 Beuvry / 36cNW1 La Bassée	F 5 b, 6 a, c, A 7 b, 8 a, c
Windy Cross Roads	28NE4 Dadizeele	L 19 d 4.7
Windy Post	36NW2 Armentières	C 2 d 9.1
Windy Post	36SW1 Aubers	N 1 a, b
Windy Reserve	57cSW2 Villers-au-Flos	N 34 a
Windy Trench	57cSW2 Villers-au-Flos / 4 Combles	N 34 a, c, d, T 4 a, b
Wine Alley	28NW4 Ypres	I 15 c
Wine Avenue	36NW4 Bois Grenier	I 14 b, 15 a, c, d
Wine Hill [hill]	28NW2 St Julien	C 18 c
Wine House	28NW2 St Julien	C 18 c 8.9
Wine Pond	28NW2 St Julien	C 18 c
Wine Street	28NW4 & NE3 Zillebeke	I 34 b, c, d
Wine Street	36NW4 Bois Grenier	I 15 c, d
Wine Trench	51bNW3 Arras	G 18 a, b
Wine Trench	51bNW4 Fampoux	I 3 d, 4 c, 9 a, b, c
Wing Corner [Fricourt]	62dNE2 Méaulte	F 9 a, b
Wing House	28NW4 & NE3 Zillebeke	I 18 a 15.50
Wing Trench	51bNW3 Arras	G 18 a, b
Wing Trench	57dNE3 & 4 Hébuterne	L 25 b, d, 26 c
Wingles Road [road]	36cNW3 Loos	H 9 c, d
Wings Way	36cNW3 Loos	G 11, 12, 17, 18
Wink Cottage	36NW1 Steenwerck	A 20 b 25.30
Wink Trench	51bNW3 Arras	G 18 b
Winkle Avenue [1918]	57dSW [3 Talmas]	S 22 c, 28 a
Winkle Trench	51bNW4 Fampoux	I 4 c, d, 10 b
Winkley Farm	20SE2 Hooglede	R 2 a 2.1
Winnezeele Line	27NE1 Herzeele / 3 Winnezeele	extensive
Winnipeg	28SW [Kemmel Defences]	N 26 a 8.9
Winnipeg [farm & pill boxes]	28NE1 Zonnebeke	D 7 c 3.7
Winnipeg Avenue	28SW4 Ploegsteert	U 7 b, c, d
Winnipeg Camp	28NW3 Poperinghe	H 19 b
Winnipeg Cross Roads	28NE1 Zonnebeke	D 7 c 02.75
Winnipeg Dump	28SW1 Kemmel	N 26 a 8.9

Name	Map Sheet	Map Reference
Winnipeg Farm	28NW3 Poperinghe	H 19 b 45.65
Winnipeg Road [road]	36cSW4 Rouvroy	T 11 a, c, 17 b, d, 23 b, d, 29 b, d
Winnipeg Street	28NW4 & NE3 Zillebeke	I 24 d, 30 b
Winnipeg Street	36NW4 Bois Grenier	I 21 a, b
Winnipeg Trench	36cSW4 Rouvroy	T 23 b, d
Winston Row	28SW3 Bailleul	S 10 c 3.2
Winter Reserve	57cNE1 Quéant	D 19 c, 25 a, b
Winter Reserve	57cSW4 Combles	N 34 d, 35 c
Winter Trench	28SW4 Ploegsteert	U 7 b
Winter Trench	51bNW2 Oppy / 4 Fampoux	C 27 b, d, I 4 a, c
Winter Trench [1918]	51bNW1 Roclincourt	B 13 b, 14 a
Wintern House	28NE4 Dadizeele	L 9 a 9.6
Winters Farm	20SE2 Hooglede	Q 18 a 5.2
Winters Nights Post	36NW3 Fleurbaix	H 31 d
Winton Cottage	28SW3 Bailleul	T 9 a 65.65
Winzig [pillboxes]	28NE1 Zonnebeke	D 8 a 35.90
Wipe Trench	51bNW3 Arras	G 18 a
Wippenhoek	27NE4 Abeele	L 28 c
Wippenhoek Line [1918]	27SE2 Berthen	Q 5, 6, R 1, 2, 3
Wippenhoek Railhead / Refilling Point	27NE4 Abeele	L 28 c, d, 29 c
Wire Road [trench]	57dSE1 & 2 Beaumont	Q 34 b, 35 a
Wireless [farm]	20SE3 Westroosebeke	V 28 d 98.98
Wirly Trench	51bSW1 Neuville Vitasse	M 18 b
Wirral Farm	28SW3 Bailleul	S 7 d 75.95
Wisbech Passage	36NW4 Bois Grenier	I 26 c
Wisdom Post	36NW2 Armentières	C 20 a
Wise Trench	51bNW3 Arras	G 18 b
Wise Way	36cNW3 Loos	G 12 c
Wish Trench	51bNW3 Arras	G 18 b
Wish Trench	51bNW4 Fampoux	I 1 b, d, 2 c
Wisp Trench	51bNW4 Fampoux	I 14 b
Wit Trench	51bNW2 Oppy / 4 Fampoux	I 1 b, 2 c
Wit Trench	51bNW3 Arras	G 12 d, 18 b
Witch/s Elbow / Sap [Switch Elbow]	57cSW3 Longueval	S 1 d
Withers Farm	28NE2 Moorslede	E 28 d 7.5
Withers Post	62bNW3 Bellicourt	G 31 b 4.8
Withuis Cabaret	28NW4 Ypres	I 19 c 92.15
Withy Trench	51bSW1 Neuville Vitasse	M 18 b
Witness House	28NE2 Moorslede	F 17 b 96.55
Witte Poort Farm	28NW4 & NE3 Zillebeke	I 11 d 3.6
Wittelsbacher Weg	51bNW1 Roclincourt	A 17, 22, 23, 24
Wizbang [sic] Post	36NW2 Armentières	C 2 d 8.3
Woad Farm	36aNE4 Merville	K 28 c 98.60
Wobble Trench	51bNW2 Oppy	C 26 c, I 2 a
Wobbly House	28NW3 Poperinghe	G 6 d 7.2
Woburn Abbey [Cuinchy]	36cNW1 La Bassée	A 20 b 5.7
Woburn Lines [huts]	28SW3 Bailleul	S 5 a
Woe Trench	51bNW2 Oppy	C 28 c, I 3 b, 4 a
Woemen / Woumen Trenches	20NW4 Dixmude	I 25 c, d, 26 a, 31 a, c
Woerth Trench [1918]	66eNW [2 Thennes]	C 15 a, c
Woesten [village]	28NW1 Elverdinghe	A 6 b, d, B 1 a, c
Woesten Windmill	28NW1 Elverdinghe	B 1 a 5.5
Wog Loop [road]	57cSE4 Villers-Guislain	X 17 c 1.2
Wohngraben [German FL]	36SW2 Radinghem	N 10 c, d

Name	Map Sheet	Map Reference
Woking Post	57cSE4 Villers-Guislain	X 3 d, 4 c
Wold Redoubt	57dSE4 Ovillers	X 15 b
Wolf Alley	51bSW4 Bullecourt	U 30 a
Wolf Camp, De	28SW3 Bailleul	T 3 c
Wolf Copse	28NE1 Zonnebeke	D 4 c
Wolf Farm	28NE1 Zonnebeke	D 4 c 3.8
Wolf Road [road]	28SW3 Bailleul / 4 Ploegsteert	N 33, 34, T 4, 5
Wolf Trench	57dNE3 & 4 Hébuterne	K 34 b, 35 a
Wolfe Road	36cNW1 La Bassée	A 9 d, 14 b, 15 a, b
Wolfhoek [farm & crossroads]	28SW1 Kemmel	M 26 c 45.40
Wolfs Chamber [La Chambre Loups] Wood	66cSW3 Tergnier / 4 La Fère	T 10 a
Wolfs Schlicht	51bNW1 Roclincourt	A 16 b
Wolgate	28NW2 St Julien	C 7 c 4.1
Wolsey House	28SW3 Bailleul	S 10 a 5.4
Wolverton [light rly locality E of Canal 1917-18]	28NW2 St Julien	B 6 c, d
Wolves Alley	66cSW2 Vendeuil	O 23 d, 24 c, 28 d, 29 a, b, c, 34 b
Wom Post [twin of Bat Post]	62cNE4 Roisel	L 30 c 15.00
Woman Street	57dNE3 & 4 Hébuterne	K 10 c, d
Won Copse	62bSW2 Fonsommes	O 35 a
Wonder Work [Wundt Werk]	57dSE1 & 2 Beaumont	R 31 b
Wonderboom Camp	28NW4 Ypres	H 16 a
Wonderland	20SE3 Westroosebeke	V 15 a
Wood 10	20SW4 Bixschoote	T 24 c
Wood 10	36bSE4 & 36cSW3 Givenchy	R 35 d, 36 c
Wood 109	66eNW [4 Morisel] / SW [2]	H 34 d, N 4 b
Wood 11	36bSE4 & 36cSW3 Givenchy	S 2 c
Wood 14 [Bois Quatorze]	20SW4 Bixschoote	T 30 b, c, d
Wood 15	20SW4 Bixschoote	T 30 d, U 25 c
Wood 15 Trench	20SW4 Bixschoote / 28NW2 St Julien	T 30 d, C 1 a
Wood 16	20SW4 Bixschoote	T 30 b, U 25 a
Wood 22	62cNW2 Bouchavesnes	B 22 a, b
Wood 37	20SW4 Bixschoote	U 19 d
Wood 4	36bSE4 & 36cSW3 Givenchy	R 35 b, d
Wood 9	36bSE4 & 36cSW3 Givenchy	R 36 c, M 31 d
Wood Alley	51bNW2 Oppy	B 24 c, C 19 a
Wood Alley	57dSE1 & 2 Beaumont	Q 29 a
Wood Alley, & Lane [both 1918]	51bSW4 Bullecourt	T 28 d, 29 c
Wood Avenue [1918, Hendecourt-lez-Ransart]	51cSE4 Blaireville	X 17 a, c, d
Wood Cemetery	28NW4 & NE3 Zillebeke	I 34 a 2.8
Wood Cemetery	51bNW3 Arras	H 31 c 2.8
Wood Dugouts	28NW4 & NE3 Zillebeke	I 34 c
Wood Farm	28NE3 Gheluvelt	J 31 d 5.2
Wood Farm	28NE3 Gheluvelt	J 3 d 5.4
Wood Farm	62cNE2 Epéhy	E 6 a, b
Wood Lane	36cSW3 Vimy	S 8 b
Wood Lane	57cSW3 Longueval	S 4 d, 10 b, 11 a, c
Wood Lane	57cSW4 Combles	U 22 c, 28 a, c
Wood Lane	62cNW2 Bouchavesnes	C 4 a, c
Wood Lane	51bSW2 Vis-en-Artois	O 17 b
Wood Place	57cSE1 Bertincourt	P 6 b
Wood Post	57dSE4 Ovillers	X 1 c
Wood Post	62cNE4 Roisel	L 22 c 7.8
Wood Post [Oppy Wood]	51bNW2 Oppy	B 18 b
Wood Road	57cSE4 Villers-Guislain	X 11 b

Name	Map Sheet	Map Reference
Wood Street	28NW4 & NE3 Zillebeke	I 34 a, c, d
Wood Street	57dNE3 & 4 Hébuterne	K 10 b, c, d
Wood Street / Boyau du Bois	62cNW1 Maricourt	A 29 a
Wood Support	57cSE2 Gonnelieu	R 2 b, 3 a
Wood Support [Oppy Wood]	51bNW2 Oppy	C 13 a, c
Wood Switch	57cNE4 Marcoing	K 29 a
Wood Trench	36SW3 Richebourg	S 6 c
Wood Trench	51bNW2 Oppy	B 18 b, d, 24 b
Wood Trench	51bNW4 Fampoux / SW2 Vis-en-Artois	I 33 c, O 3 a
Wood Trench	51bSW4 Bullecourt	O 31 c, d, U 1 b, 2 a
Wood Trench	57cSE2 Gonnelieu	R 2 b, d, 3 c
Wood Trench	57dSE4 Ovillers	X 23 d, 24 c
Wood Trench	62bNW1 Gouy	A 25 d, G 1 b
Wood Trench	62cNW1 Maricourt	A 23 d
Wood Trench [1918]	51cSE4 Blaireville / 57dNE2 [Fonquevillers]	X 26 d, 27 c, F 2 b
Wood Trench [Grand Priel Woods]	62cNE4 Roisel	L 22 a, c, d
Wood Trench [Railway Wood]	28NW4 & NE3 Zillebeke	I 11 b
Woodbine House	28NE4 Dadizeele	L 25 a 1.5
Woodcote [light rly locality, 1917-18]	28NW4 Ypres	I 25 b, 26 a
Woodcote Cemetery	28NW4 Ypres	I 26 b 4.8
Woodcote House	28NW4 Ypres	I 20 c 45.15
Wooden Mill [Buttes de Rouy]	70dNW [3 Sinceny]	H 1 d 70.85
Wood-king Farm	20SE2 Hooglede	R 15 a 3.0
Woodland [farm]	28NE1 Zonnebeke	D 4 b 9.9
Woodland Farm [1915]	28NW2 St Julien	C 17 c 5.4
Woodland Plantation	20SE3 Westroosebeke / 28NE1 Zonnebeke	V 28 d, 29 c, D 4 b, 5 a
Woodstock Road [road]	36cSW1 Lens	N 21 d, 27 b
Woodward Farm	20SE3 Westroosebeke	W 20 b 6.6
Woof Bridge [road over stream]	36NW1 Steenwerck	A 29 a 40.25
Woof Farms	36NW1 Steenwerck	A 29 a 2.3
Wookey Farm	36aNE4 Merville	K 34 c 9.2
Wool Trench	51bNW2 Oppy	I 2 a
Woolley Walk	28NW4 & NE3 Zillebeke	I 34 b
Worcester Bridge	36aSE1 St Venant	P 20 a 8.4
Worcester C.T. [to new front line]	57dSE1 & 2 Beaumont	Q 17 c
Worcester Lane [Sept 1915]	36cNW1 La Bassée	A 15 d
Worcester Street	57dSE1 & 2 Beaumont	R 31 c, d
Worcester Trench	57cSW3 Longueval	S 4 d, 10 b
Worcester Way	36SW1 Aubers / 3 Richebourg	M 34 a, c
Wordling Farm	20SE3 Westroosebeke	W 19 b 3.6
Work Farm	36NW1 Steenwerck	A 14 a 55.95
Work Trench	51bNW3 Arras	G 18 a
Works Trench	66cNW4 Berthenicourt	I 33 c
Worle Farm	36aNE4 Merville	L 21 b 50.35
Worley Avenue / Trench	57dNE3 & 4 Hébuterne	K 28 d, 29 c
Worm Alley	57cNE4 Marcoing	L 31 b, d, 32 a
Worm Trench	51bNW3 Arras	G 18 a, b
Worm Trench	51bNW4 Fampoux	I 9 c
Worm Trench	57cNE4 Marcoing	L 31 d
Wormlow Camp	28SW3 Bailleul	S 12 c
Worms Trench	62cNW4 Péronne	I 35 a, c, d
Wormwood Scrubs [copse]	62cNW3 Vaux	H 3 c
Wormwood Scrubs [railway locality 1917-18]	62cNW1 Maricourt / 3 Vaux	H 3 a, b, c, d
Worple [farm]	27SE4 Meteren	X 2 c 1.3

Name	Map Sheet	Map Reference
Worry House	36NW1 Steenwerck	A 8 d 60.55
Worry Trench	51bNW2 Oppy	C 26 c
Worthington Farm (Hospital)	28NE4 Dadizeele	K 17 c 95.40
Wortley Avenue	36cSW3 Vimy	S 19 b, d, 20 a, b, c
Worzel Farm	20SE2 Hooglede	R 5 a 8.8
Worzet [sic] Farm [Worzel Farm]	20SE2 Hooglede	R 5 a 8.8
Wotan Line [Drocourt-Quéant Line / Switch]	36cSE / 51bNW / 51bSE	extensive
Wounded Trench	36cSW1 Lens	M 19 b, d
Wrangle Avenue / Trench	57dNE3 & 4 Hébuterne	K 22 d, 23 a, b, c
Wrangle Farm	20SE3 Westroosebeke	W 19 c 1.5
Wrap Copse	20SE3 Westroosebeke	W 19 d, 25 b
Wrap Cott	20SE3 Westroosebeke	W 25 a 8.9
Wrath Copse	20SE3 Westroosebeke	W 25 b, d
Wrath Farm	20SE3 Westroosebeke	W 25 a 7.2
Wreck Farm	36NW1 Steenwerck	A 13 d 1.3
Wren Alley / Lane	51bSW2 Vis-en-Artois	O 31 b
Wren Copse	62bSW4 Homblières	U 5 b, 6 a
Wren Way	28SW2 Wytschaete	N 18 c, 24 a
Wretched Way	57dSE2 & 57cSW1 Le Sars	R 9 c, 14 b, 15 a
Wrexham Tunnel [Loos Crassier]	36cNW3 Loos	G 36 c
Wring House	20SE3 Westroosebeke	W 26 c 3.8
Wring Wood	20SE3 Westroosebeke	W 25 d, 26 c
Wrist Alley / Trench	51bNW4 Fampoux	I 25 c, d
Wrist Copse	20SE3 Westroosebeke	W 25 d
Written Farm	20SE3 Westroosebeke	W 20 c 5.0
Wry Trench	51bNW3 Arras	G 18 b
Wulfdam [place name]	28NE4 Dadizeele	L 5 c
Wulfdambeek [stream]	28NE4 Dadizeele	extensive
Wulverghem [village]	28SW4 Ploegsteert	T 5 a, c, d
Wulverghem Howitzer Spurs	28SW4 Ploegsteert	T 11 a, b, 12 a
Wulverghem Railhead / Refilling Point	28SW4 Ploegsteert	T 5 c, d, 11 a, b, 12 a
Wulverghem Switch	28SW4 Ploegsteert	T 4 b, 5 a, d
Wundt Werk [Wonder Work]	57dNE3 & 4 Hébuterne	L 32 b
Wurst Camp	28NE1 Zonnebeke	D 8 c 5.5
Wurst Farm	28NE1 Zonnebeke	D 7 d 7.9
Wurtemberg Trench	62cSW2 Barleux	N 28 b, d
Wurzburg Trench	62cSW2 Barleux / 4 St. Christ	O 29 d, 35 b, d, 36 c, U 5 b, d
Wurzel Street	57dNE3 & 4 Hébuterne	K 9 d, 10 c
Wurzel Trench	51bNW4 Fampoux	I 8 d, 9 c
Wurzel Valley	57cNW4 Beugny	H 6 a 3.5
Wyatt Track	28SW2 Wytschaete	O 33 b
Wyatts Lane	28NW2 St Julien	C 7 c 1.5
Wycliffe Trench	28SW2 Wytschaete	O 10 b, 11 a
Wye Farm	36NW4 Bois Grenier	H 35 b, 36 a
Wye Lane [The Harp]	51bSW1 Neuville Vitasse	N 1 c, d
Wye Trench	51bNW3 Arras	G 12 c, d, 18 a, H 13 a
Wye, The [The Dump]	28NW4 & NE3 Zillebeke	I 29 c
Wynd / Wynde Wynde Trench [N of Bluff]	28NW4 & NE3 Zillebeke	I 34 c
Wynd Angle [Bluff]	28NW4 & NE3 Zillebeke	I 34 c
Wynne Street [Thiepval Wood]	57dSE1 & 2 Beaumont	Q 24 c
Wytschaete [village]	28SW2 Wytschaete	O 19 b, d
Wytschaete Dump [German]	28SW2 Wytschaete	O 20 a 3.1
Wytschaete Valley	28SW2 Wytschaete	West of village
Wytschaete Wood [Godschalk Wood]	28SW2 Wytschaete	N 24 b, d, O 19 a, c

Name	Map Sheet	Map Reference
Wytschaete, Bois de [Wytschaete Wood]	28SW2 Wytschaete	N 24 b, d, O 19 a, c
X 1 [trench, 1916]	28NW4 & NE3 Zillebeke	I 10 b, d
X 2 [trench, 1916]	28NW4 & NE3 Zillebeke	I 4 d
X 3 [trench, 1916]	28NW2 St Julien / 28NW4 & NE3 Zillebeke	I 4 b, d
X Camp	28NW1 Elverdinghe	A 16 c 2.3
X Copse	62cNE2 Epéhy	F 16 b
X Copse Post	62cNE2 Epéhy	F 16 b
X Farm	36NW4 Bois Grenier	I 14 b 6.5
X Line	28NW2 St Julien	C 13 c, 19 b
X Line	28SW2 Wytschaete	O 16 a, 22 a, c
X Line [Potijze - Hell Fire Corner, 1916]	28NW2 St Julien / 28NW4 & NE3 Zillebeke	I 4 b, d, 10 b, d
X Track [1917-18]	28NE1 Zonnebeke	D 25 b, d,
X Track [1917-18]	28NW2 St Julien	C 22 a
X Trench [between Flers and Lesboeufs]	57cSW3 Longueval	T 2 b
X Trench [Square Wood]	28NW4 & NE3 Zillebeke	I 29 a, b
Y 47 [British front line, 1-7-16]	57dNE3 & 4 Hébuterne	K 10 a
Y 48 [British front line, 1-7-16]	57dNE3 & 4 Hébuterne	K 9 b
Y 49 [British front line, 1-7-16]	57dNE3 & 4 Hébuterne	K 9 b
Y 50 [British front line, 1-7-16]	57dNE3 & 4 Hébuterne	K 3 d
Y 6 - Y 11 [Y Wood, 1915]	28NW4 & NE3 Zillebeke	I 12 c, d
Y Copse	62cNE2 Epéhy	F 16 d
Y Copse Post	62cNE2 Epéhy	F 16 d
Y Corner [NE corner of Spoil Bank]	36cNW1 La Bassée	A 15 d
Y Lane	57cSW2 Villers-au-Flos	N 28 c
Y Ravine	57dSE1 & 2 Beaumont	Q 10 d, 11 c
Y Sap	57dSE4 Ovillers	X 13 d 5.5
Y Street	57dSE1 & 2 Beaumont	Q 10 a, b
Y Trench [between Flers and Lesboeufs]	57cSW3 Longueval	T 2 b
Y Trench [Observatory Ridge]	28NW4 & NE3 Zillebeke	I 23 d, 29 b
Y Wood	28NW4 & NE3 Zillebeke	I 11 d, 12 c
Y Wood	62cNW1 Maricourt	A 23 d
Y. & L. Trench [York & Lancaster?]	28NW2 St Julien	C 15 c
Y.L. Alley [York & Lancaster?]	57cSW3 Longueval	S 16 c, 22 a
Yacht Farm	20SE2 Hooglede	Q 18 a 3.3
Yak Post	62cNE2 Epéhy	F 10 d
Yakko Copse	62dNE [4 Bray-sur-Somme]	L 23 d
Yakko Wood	62cNW3 Vaux	G 32 d
Yale [light rly locality]	28NW3 Poperinghe	H 15 d 4.3
Yale Post	28SW4 Ploegsteert	U 17 d 35.95
Yam Farm	36aNE4 Merville	L 22 a 4.8
Yanco Farm	28SE1 Wervicq	P 31 a 5.2
Yank Post	28SW4 Ploegsteert	U 17 b 3.5
Yankee Street	57dNE3 & 4 Hébuterne	K 9 b, d, 10 a, c
Yankee Valley	57dNE4 & 57cNW3 Achiet	L 24 / G 19
Yard Farm	28NE2 Moorslede	F 23 c 9.7
Yarn [post]	28SW4 Ploegsteert	U 18 a 3.6
Yarra Avenue	57cSW1 Gueudecourt	M 24 c, d, 30 c, d, 36 a
Yarra Bank	57cSW1 Gueudecourt	M 24
Yarra Bend	57cSW1 Gueudecourt	M 24 b
Yarra Support	57cSW1 Gueudecourt	M 24 a, b
Yarra Trench [1918]	62dNE [1 Dernancourt]	E 2 c
Yatman Bridge [across Ancre]	57dSE4 Ovillers	Q 36 c
Yatton Farm	36aNE4 Merville	L 3 d 90.05
Yearling Farm	28NE2 Moorslede	E 23 c 35.65

Name	Map Sheet	Map Reference
Yellow Alley	70dNW2 Servais	C 19 d
Yellow Corner	20SE2 Hooglede	R 5 c 1.1
Yellow Cut [sunken road S of Le Barque]	57cSW1 Gueudecourt	N 7 c, 13 a
Yellow Road [road]	36cNW1 La Bassée	A 2 c, d
Yellow Street	57dNE3 & 4 Hébuterne	K 9 b, 10 a
Yeomanry Post	28NW4 & NE3 Zillebeke	I 17 d, 23 b
Yetta Houses	28NE1 Zonnebeke	D 3 d 4.7
Yew Support	57cSE4 Villers-Guislain	X 26 c
Yiddish Post	57dNE3 & 4 Hébuterne	K 9 b, 10 a
Yiddish Street	57dNE3 & 4 Hébuterne	K 9 b, 10 a
Yoho Trench [1918]	57dNE2 Essarts	E 30 d
Yoke Cottage	28NW3 Poperinghe	G 11 d 99.63
Yonge Street	28SW2 Wytschaete	N 23 c, 29 a
Yonge Street Dugouts	28SW2 Wytschaete	N 29 a 3.4 to 2.7
York & Lancs Redoubt	28NW4 & NE3 Zillebeke	I 36 b 6.8
York Alley	57cNW2 Vaulx-Vraucourt	C 18 a
York Alley	57cSW3 Longueval	S 18 c
York Avenue	36SW2 Radinghem	N 4 c, d, 10 b
York Camp	28NW3 Poperinghe	G 5 c, d
York Cross [cross roads]	28NW3 Poperinghe	G 5 d 0.2
York Farm	28NE1 Zonnebeke	D 2 a 1.6
York House	28SW2 Wytschaete	N 16 c 9.3
York Lane [road]	51bNW4 Fampoux	H 10 c,16 a, b, d, 17 c
York Post	36NW3 Fleurbaix	H 19 a, b
York Post	57cSE4 Villers-Guislain	X 9 d, 10 c
York Road	62cNW1 Maricourt	A 7 d
York Road [road]	28SW1 Kemmel / 2 Wytschaete	N 11 c, 16 b, c, d, 17 a, 22 a
York Road Line [light rly]	28SW2 Wytschaete	N 16 b, c, d, 17 a, 22 a
York Sap	36cSW3 Vimy	M 32 c
York Street	36cSW1 Lens	M 15 area
York Street	57dNE3 & 4 Hébuterne	K 9 b
York Street	62cNW1 Maricourt	A 8 c
York Street [1918]	62dSE [1 Hamel]	P 25 a, b
York Street [W of The Nab]	57dSE4 Ovillers	X 1 b, d
York Support	57cNW2 Vaulx-Vraucourt	C 18 a
York Trench	51bSW4 Bullecourt	U 1 b, c, d
York Trench	57cSW3 Longueval	S 16 c, d, 23 a, b
York Trench [Yorkshire Trench]	28NW2 St Julien	C 7 c, 13 a
York Way	28SW4 Ploegsteert	U 17 b
Yorker Houses	28NE2 Moorslede	E 4 d 8.7
Yorkshire Alley	57cNE3 Hermies	K 32 a, b
Yorkshire Alley	57cSW3 Longueval	M 32 d, S 2 b
Yorkshire Bank [Spoil Heap]	57cNE3 Hermies	K 32 a, b
Yorkshire Trench	28NW2 St Julien	C 7 c, 13 a
Yorkshire Trench [Beaucourt]	57dSE2 Beaumont	QR 1 c, d
Yorkshire Trench [Thiepval Wood]	57dSE1 & 2 Beaumont	Q 24 d, R 19 c, 25 a
Young Street	57dNE3 & 4 Hébuterne	K 9 b, 10 a
Youngster [light rly locality, 1917-18]	28NW4 Ypres	I 15 a
Yperlee Avenue	20SW3 Oostvleteren	T 3 d, 9 b
Ypres [city]	28NW4 Ypres	I 1, 2, 7, 8, 13, 14
Ypres Cross Roads	20SW4 Bixschoote	T 17 b 2.3
Ypres Defence Line	28NW4 Ypres	I 8 d, 9 a, c, 14 b, c, d
Ypres Street	57dSE1 & 2 Beaumont	Q 23 b
Yser Alley	66cNW2 Itancourt	B 29 a

Name	Map Sheet	Map Reference
Ytres [village]	57cSE1 Bertincourt	P 20 c, d, 26 a, b
Yukon Trench	51bNW1 Roclincourt / 2 Oppy	B 4 c
Yule Trench	57dNE3 & 4 Hébuterne	K 9 b
Yum-Yum Trench	28SW2 Wytschaete	N 18 a
Yussuf / Yussif Street	57dNE3 & 4 Hébuterne	K 3 d, 9 b
Yuz Street	57dNE3 & 4 Hébuterne	K 3 d
Yvetot Trench	66cNW4 Berthenicourt	H 30 a
Yvrench [village]	57eNW	B 3
Yvrencheux [village]	57eNW	B 2
Z Copse	62cNE2 Epéhy	F 17 c
Z Hedge [Front Line]	57dNE3 & 4 Hébuterne	K 4 c, 10 a
Z Orchard Post	36SW3 Richebourg	S 14 b 5.7
Z Road	57dNE1 & 2 Fonquevillers	E 28 b
Z Trench	51bNW2 Oppy	B 11 d, 12 c
Z Trench [between Flers and Lesboeufs]	57cSW3 Longueval	T 2 a, b, d
Z, Bois-en-	66eSE2 Guerbigny	R 10 b
Z, Little	57dNE1 & 2 Fonquevillers	E 23 c
Z, The	57dNE1 & 2 Fonquevillers	E 23 c
Z, Trench [Cuinchy Sector, Feb 1915]	36cNW1 La Bassée	A 15 d
Z.Z. Alley	57cSW3 Longueval	S 18 d, 24 b, T 19 a
Z.Z. Trench [E of Waterlot Farm]	57cSW3 Longueval	S 18 d, 24 b
Zag Buildings	28NE2 Moorslede	F 17 d 9.4
Zag Trench	62cSE2 Vermand	R 4 b
Zalost [Alley]	66cNW2 Itancourt	I 2 a
Zambuck Avenue / Street	57dNE3 & 4 Hébuterne	K 27 d, 28 c
Zambuck Post	28SW4 Ploegsteert	U 16 c
Zandvoorde [village]	28SE1 Wervicq	P 3 a, c
Zandvoorde Chateau	28SE1 Wervicq	P 4 a 38.50
Zandvoorde Switch	28NE3 Gheluvelt	J 34, 35, 36
Zareeba [thorn obstacle / hedge]	28SW4 Ploegsteert	U 3 b
Zareeba Road [road]	28SW4 Ploegsteert	U 3 b
Zealand Farm	28NW3 Poperinghe	G 16 a 05.33
Zealand Junction [light rly]	28NW3 Poperinghe	G 16 a
Zebra Lane [trench]	57cNE1 Quéant	E 27 b, c, d, K 3 a
Zebra Post	62cNE2 Epéhy	F 10 b
Zebra Trench / Trench [sic] du Zebre	66cNW2 Itancourt / 4 Berthenicourt	C 27 c, I 3 a, c
Zeebrugge Battery	5SW1 Zeebrugge	M 21 a
Zehner Weg / Zerner [sic] Alley	51bNW1 Roclincourt	B 19, 20, 25, 30
Zelobes [hamlet]	36aSE2 Lestrem	R 27 c
Zelobes Indian Cemetery	36aSE2 Lestrem	R 26 d 9.6
Zelobes Post	36aSE2 Lestrem	R 27 c
Zenith Trench	57cSW2 Villers-au-Flos	N 28 d, 34 b
Zenner Weg	51bNW1 Roclincourt	A 30 b, B 25 a
Zenobie Farm	20SW4 Bixschoote	N 35 c 15.53
Zephyr Trench	51bSW4 Bullecourt	U 28 c
Zephyrin Alley / Zéphyrin, Boyau	62cSW4 St. Christ	T 18 c, d, 24 b, U 19 a, b, d, 20 c, d
Zepp Copse [near Mazeppa Wood]	62bSW2 Fonsommes	N 24 d
Zeppelin Alley	36cNW1 La Bassée / 3 Loos	G 5 b, d
Zeppelin Battery	5SW1 Zeebrugge	M 20 c, d
Zero [post]	28SW4 Ploegsteert	U 17 b 9.6
Zero Avenue	57dSE4 Ovillers	X 3 b, c, d, 4 a
Zero Corner	28SW2 Wytschaete	O 13 d 2.8
Zero House	28SW2 Wytschaete	O 14 a 5.6
Zero Wood	28SW2 Wytschaete	O 14 a

Name	Map Sheet	Map Reference
Zerschossene Stellung	57cSW3 Longueval	S 6 c, d, 12 b
Zest Alley	66dNW1 Punchy	A 21 b, 22 a
Zeta [German Pillbox]	51bSW4 Bullecourt	U 8 a 4.3
Zeude, Tranchée [Liverpool Street]	36cSW1 Lens	M 15 c
Zevecoten [hamlet]	28NW3 Poperinghe	G 34 d, 35 c
Zevecoten Windmill	28SW1 Kemmel	M 5 a
Zevekoten	20SW4 Bixschoote	U 3 a
Zevekoten [hamlet / farm]	20SW4 Bixschoote	U 3 b 95.70
Ziegelei Graben / Trench	51bNW3 Arras	G 12 b
Ziegelei Weg	51bSW1 Neuville Vitasse	M 5 c
Ziel House	28NE3 Gheluvelt	J 7 a
Ziel House Dugout	28NE3 Gheluvelt	J 7 a 55.55
Zig Buildings	28NE2 Moorslede	F 17 a 2.1
Zig Zag Alley	36cNW1 La Bassée	A 4 d, 10 a, b
Zig Zag Trench	57cSW1 Gueudecourt	M 27 a, c
Zigomar Alley	62cSW1 Dompierre	M 30 b, N 25 a, b
Zigomar Trench	66cNW4 Berthenicourt	I 27 d
Zig-Zag [light rly siding]	36bSE2 Boyeffles	Q 16 d, 17 c
Zig-Zag Copse	28NE2 Moorslede	E 30 d 15.10
Zillebeke Bund [dugouts in embankment]	28NW4 & NE3 Zillebeke	I 15d, 21 b
Zillebeke Lake	28NW4 & NE3 Zillebeke	I 21 b
Zillebeke Lake Siding [railway, 1917-18]	28NW4 Ypres	I 20 b, 21 a
Zillebeke Street	28NW4 & NE3 Zillebeke	I 22 a to 24 b
Zillebeke Street Promenade	28NW4 & NE3 Zillebeke	I 21 b, 22 c, d
Zillebeke Switch	28NW4 & NE3 Zillebeke	I 23 c, 29 a, c
Zillebeke Switch, 2 & 3 Lines [May-June 1915]	28NW4 & NE3 Zillebeke	I 23 c, 29 a, c
Zillebeke Tuilerie [tile works]	28NW4 Ypres	I 22 b 3.8
Zillebeke Tunnel	28NW4 & NE3 Zillebeke	I 22 a 9.5
Zimmermann Alley	62cNW2 Bouchavesnes	C 27 d, 28 c
Zinc Farm	27NE2 Proven	E 23 c 95.50
Zinc Trench	62dNE2 Méaulte	F 9 b, 10 a
Zion Alley	51bNW4 Fampoux	H 11 d, 12 c, 17 b
Zip Track [1917-18]	28SW2 Wytschaete	O 28 d, 34 a, b
Zislin Alley	66dNW1 Punchy	A 16 b, d, 17 a
Zislin Wood, North	66dNW1 Punchy	A 17 a
Zislin Wood, South	66dNW1 Punchy	A 16 c
Zist Alley	66dNW1 Punchy	A 21 b, 22 a, b
Zittervadt [trench]	66cNW2 Itancourt	B 23 b, 24 a
Zitterwald Alley	66cNW2 Itancourt	B 18 c
Zitzewitz Graben	57dNE3 & 4 Hébuterne	K 12 b, L 1 c
Zivy [Redoubt]	51bNW1 Roclincourt	A 10 a
Zivy Crater	51bNW1 Roclincourt	A 10 b
Zivy Crater Group	51bNW1 Roclincourt	A 10 b
Zollern Graben	57dSE2 & 57cSW1 Le Sars	R 26 a, b, 27 a, b,28 a, b, 29 a, b
Zollern Redoubt	57dSE1 & 2 Beaumont	R 21 d, 27 b
Zollern Trench East [Zollern Graben]	57dSE2 & 57cSW1 Le Sars	R 27 b, 28 a, b, 29 a, b
Zollern Trench West [Zollern Graben]	57dSE1 & 2 Beaumont	R 26 a, b, 27 a
Zombor Trench	62cNW2 Bouchavesnes	C 26 c, I 2 a
Zommerbloom Cabaret	28NW1 Elverdinghe	B 8 c 8.5
Zon Cabaret, In De	20SW4 Bixschoote	T 22 d 2.9
Zonnebeke Chateau	28NE1 Zonnebeke	D 27 b 95.47
Zonnebeke Church	28NE1 Zonnebeke	D 28 a 10.77
Zonnebeke Redoubt	28NE1 Zonnebeke	D 26 d, J 2 b
Zonnebeke Track [1917-18]	28NE1 Zonnebeke / 3 Gheluvelt	D 26 c, d, J 1 b, c, d, 2 a

Name	Map Sheet	Map Reference
Zoo Trench	62bNW1 Gouy	A 19 d
Zoo Trench, The	51bSW1 Neuville Vitasse	N 20 d, 21 c, 27 a
Zoom Farm	27NE2 Proven	F 27 a 3.9
Zouave House	28NW2 St Julien	C 7 b 3.8
Zouave Siding [rly & light rly locality]	28NW2 St Julien	C 20 c, d
Zouave Track [past Zouave Villa & Siding]	28NW2 St Julien	C 20 d, 21 a, b, c, 25 b, d, 26 a
Zouave Track [past Zouave Wood]	28NW4 Ypres	I 17 d, 18 a, b, c, d
Zouave Trench	28NW4 & NE3 Zillebeke	I 18 c
Zouave Valley / Talus des Zouaves	36bSE4 & 36cSW3 Givenchy	S 14, 20, 21, 27
Zouave Villa [house]	28NW2 St Julien	C 20 c 65.10
Zouave Villa [railway locality]	28NW2 St Julien	C 26 a
Zouave Wood	28NW4 & NE3 Zillebeke	I 18 c, d
Zouaves Alley	66dNW1 Punchy	A 16 a, 17 c, d, 22 a, b
Zouaves Trench [1918]	62dSW [4 Cachy]	U 1 a, c, 7 a
Zuidhoek [farm]	28NE3 Gheluvelt	J 19 a 5.4
Zuidhoek [place name]	20SE2 Hooglede	R 28 a, b
Zuidhoek [place name]	28NE4 Dadizeele	K 18 c, d
Zuidhoek [place name]	28NE4 Dadizeele	L 3 d
Zulu Copse	62cNE4 Roisel	L 11 c, 17 a
Zulu Cross Roads	28NE2 Moorslede	E 17 c 35.07
Zust Trench	57dNE3 & 4 Hébuterne	K 16 a
Zwaanhoek	28NE3 Gheluvelt	J 12 c, d
Zwaanhof Farm, North & South	28NW2 St Julien	C 13 a, c
Zwartemolenhoek [place name]	28SW3 Bailleul	S 12 c
Zweier Graben	51bNW3 Arras	H 7 b, 8 a, b
Zwerg Cotts.	28NE1 Zonnebeke	D 24 b 75.40
Zwijnskot	28NE2 Moorslede	F 29 a
Zwischen Stellung	36cSW3 Vimy / 51bNW1 Roclincourt	S 28, 29, A 5 to 17
Zwischen Stellung	62cNW1 Maricourt	A 13, 19, 25
Zwolfer Trench	51bNW1 Roclincourt	A 11 c
Zwynland Brewery [Poperinghe]	27NE4 Abeele	L 12 c 1.4

If you enjoyed this, you may be interested in …

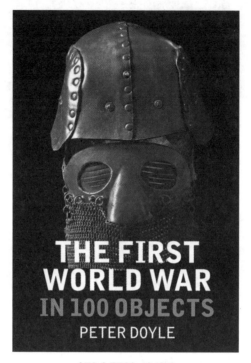

978 0 7509 6848 5

'A unique perspective on one of the most pivotal and volatile events of modern history' – Essential Book Reviews website